# THE MODERN LAW OF EVIDENCE

## Sixth Edition

### ADRIAN KEANE LLB

*of the Inner Temple, Barrister,*

*Professor of Law and Dean, Inns of Court School of Law,*

*City University, London*

OXFORD

UNIVERSITY PRESS

# OXFORD

### UNIVERSITY PRESS

Great Clarendon Street, Oxford OX2 6DP

Oxford University Press is a department of the University of Oxford.
It furthers the University's objective of excellence in research, scholarship,
and education by publishing worldwide in

Oxford New York

Auckland Cape Town Dar es Salaam Hong Kong Karachi
Kuala Lumpur Madrid Melbourne Mexico City Nairobi
New Delhi Shanghai Taipei Toronto

With offices in

Argentina Austria Brazil Chile Czech Republic France Greece
Guatemala Hungary Italy Japan Poland Portugal Singapore
South Korea Switzerland Thailand Turkey Ukraine Vietnam

Oxford is a registered trade mark of Oxford University Press
in the UK and in certain other countries

Published in the United States
by Oxford University Press Inc., New York

British Library Cataloguing in Publication Data

Data available

Library of Congress Cataloging in Publication Data

Data available

Typeset by RefineCatch Limited, Bungay, Suffolk
Printed in Great Britain
on acid-free paper by
Ashford Colour Press, Gosport, Hampshire
ISBN 0–40–697579–5   978–0–40–697579–9

3 5 7 9 10 8 6 4

# PREFACE TO THE SIXTH EDITION

The aim of this book remains as stated in the preface to the first edition: to explore the theory of the law of evidence and its practical application. Now, as then, I have borne in mind the needs of judges and practitioners, as well as students studying law at the undergraduate and vocational stages. I also continue to attempt to state the law in a way which is not only accurate, but also readable, placing the emphasis, wherever possible, on modern rather than moribund aspects of the subject.

Since the fifth edition of this work, there have been many major developments in the law of evidence. In consequence, a number of chapters have been completely re-written and many others have been substantially revised. Most of the work has been the direct result of the Criminal Justice Act 2003, which has brought about radical change to the rules on hearsay evidence and evidence of bad character, change largely premised on a welcome new confidence that fact-finders in criminal cases can be trusted to evaluate evidence correctly and to give it the weight it deserves. As to bad character, the provisions all but codify the law, abolishing the common law rules and replacing our old friend, if full of faults, section 1(3) of the Criminal Evidence Act 1898. However, the new rules are much more complex than section 1(3) of the 1898 Act and are likely to give rise to much new case law, in addition to *R v Hanson*, the first reported decision on the new provisions, in which the Court of Appeal has laid down important principles relating to evidence of propensity. The new hearsay provisions retain the hearsay rule, but expand the exceptions to it and create a new discretion to admit sufficiently reliable hearsay not covered by any of the other exceptions. The 2003 Act has also brought about other important changes, including those relating to live links in criminal cases, the admissibility of preparatory work on which an expert may base an opinion, confessions on which a co-accused wishes to rely, evidence by video-recording and the use of documents and transcripts of sound recordings to refresh memory.

The law of evidence in England and Wales has also continued to develop in response to arguments based on the Human Rights Act 1998, the European Convention on Human Rights, and the burgeoning jurisprudence of the European Court of Human Rights. These arguments have had a particular impact in relation to evidence obtained by illegal or unfair means, a subject which has been given its own chapter in this new edition. The arguments have also been directed at statutory provisions affecting the privilege against self-incrimination. There have been further challenges, in relation to the burden of proof, to statutory reverse onus provisions, on the basis that they are incompatible with Article 6(2) of the European Convention or, if not, should be read down so as to impose only an evidential burden on the accused. These have led to the important decisions of the House of Lords in *R v Johnstone* and *Attorney General's Reference (No 4 of 2002)*.

Other developments covered in this new edition include the Criminal Procedure

Rules 2005, which represent the first step towards the creation of a new consolidated and comprehensive criminal procedure code of the kind envisaged by Lord Justice Auld; new case law relating to the independence and reliability of expert witness; the decisions of the Court of Appeal and House of Lords in the various stages of the litigation in *Three Rivers District Council v Governor & Co of the Bank of England*, which have clarified, but not, alas, to the full extent desired, the scope of legal professional privilege, especially in the case in the case of corporate clients; and the growing categories of case in which there is a special need for caution, including cases in which reliance is placed on lip-reading evidence and cases of Sudden Infant Death Syndrome.

My thanks go to my new publishers, Oxford University Press, for their guidance and enthusiastic support; to loyal readers, including colleagues and students at the Inns of Court School of Law, for their helpful comments; and especially to my wife, Rosemary Samwell-Smith, LLB, LLM, Barrister, whose encouragement and understanding continue to know no bounds. The responsibility for errors and other imperfections remains entirely mine.

I have attempted to state the law as at 1 July 2005.

Adrian Keane
Hampstead, London
July 2005

# CONTENTS

*Preface to the Sixth Edition*                                              v

*Table of Statutes*                                                      xvii

*Table of Statutory Instruments*                                        xxix

*Table of Cases*                                                        xxxi

## 1 INTRODUCTION                                                          1

A    TRUTH AND THE FACT-FINDING PROCESS                          1

B    THE DEVELOPMENT OF THE LAW                                   2

## 2 PRELIMINARIES                                                         7

A    FACTS OPEN TO PROOF OR DISPROOF                              7

    1    Facts in issue                            7

    2    Relevant facts                            8

    3    Collateral facts                          9

B    THE VARIETIES OF EVIDENCE                                   10

    1    Testimony                                10

    2    Hearsay evidence                         10

    3    Documentary evidence                     11

    4    Real evidence                            12

    5    Circumstantial evidence                  13

C    RELEVANCE AND ADMISSIBILITY                                 21

    1    Relevance                                21

    2    The exclusionary rules                   27

    3    Multiple admissibility                   28

    4    Conditional admissibility                28

    5    The best evidence rule                   29

D    WEIGHT                                                      30

E    THE FUNCTIONS OF THE JUDGE AND JURY                         31

    1    Questions of law and fact                32

    2    The *voir dire*, or trial within a trial  36

    3    The sufficiency of evidence              39

    4    The summing-up                           42

F   JUDICIAL DISCRETION                                      45
    1   Inclusionary discretion                              45
    2   Exclusionary discretion                              46

G   PROOF OF BIRTH, DEATH, AGE, CONVICTIONS AND
    ACQUITTALS                                               52
    1   Birth and death                                      52
    2   Age                                                  53
    3   Convictions and acquittals                           53

3 EVIDENCE OBTAINED BY ILLEGAL OR UNFAIR
  MEANS                                                      55

A   LAW                                                      56
B   DISCRETION                                               58
    1   Civil cases                                          58
    2   Criminal cases                                       59

4 THE BURDEN AND STANDARD OF PROOF                           82

A   THE BURDEN OF PROOF                                      82
    1   The legal burden                                     83
    2   The evidential burden                                84
    3   The incidence of the legal burden                    86
    4   The incidence of the evidential burden               105
    5   The right to begin                                   108

B   THE STANARD OF PROOF                                     109
    1   The legal burden                                     109
    2   The evidential burden                                120

C   THE BURDEN AND STANDARD OF PROOF IN A TRIAL
    WITHIN A TRIAL                                           121

5 WITNESSES                                                  123

A   COMPETENCE AND COMPELLABILITY                            123
    1   The general rule                                     124
    2   The accused                                          125
    3   The spouse of an accused                             127
    4   Children and persons of unsound mind—criminal cases  133
    5   Children and persons of unsound mind—civil cases     137
    6   The sovereign and diplomats                          139
    7   Bankers                                              139

B   OATHS AND AFFIRMATIONS                                   139

| | | | |
|---|---|---|---|
| C | | LIVE LINKS | 141 |
| D | | THE TIME AT WHICH EVIDENCE SHOULD BE ADDUCED | 143 |
| E | | WITNESSES IN CIVIL CASES | 147 |
| | 1 | The witnesses to be called | 147 |
| | 2 | Witness statements | 148 |
| F | | WITNESSES IN CRIMINAL CASES | 150 |
| | 1 | The witnesses to be called | 151 |
| | 2 | The order of witnesses | 152 |
| | 3 | Evidence in chief by video-recording | 153 |
| | 4 | Special measures directions for vulnerable and intimidated witnesses | 155 |
| | 5 | Witness training and witness familiarization | 167 |

## 6 EXAMINATION-IN-CHIEF     169

| | | | |
|---|---|---|---|
| A | | LEADING QUESTIONS | 169 |
| B | | REFRESHING THE MEMORY | 170 |
| | 1 | Refreshing the memory in court | 171 |
| | 2 | Refreshing the memory out of court | 178 |
| C | | PREVIOUS CONSISTENT OR SELF-SERVING STATEMENTS | 180 |
| | 1 | The general rule | 180 |
| | 2 | The common-law exceptions | 182 |
| D | | UNFAVOURABLE AND HOSTILE WITNESSES | 193 |
| | 1 | The rule against a party impeaching the credit of his own witness | 193 |
| | 2 | Unfavourable witnesses | 194 |
| | 3 | Hostile witnesses | 194 |

## 7 CROSS-EXAMINATION AND RE-EXAMINATION     199

| | | | |
|---|---|---|---|
| A | | CROSS-EXAMINATION | 199 |
| | 1 | Liability to cross-examination | 199 |
| | 2 | Cross-examination by accused in person | 200 |
| | 3 | The permitted form of questioning in cross-examination | 202 |
| | 4 | The effect of a party's failure to cross-examine | 205 |
| | 5 | Cross-examination on documents | 206 |
| | 6 | Previous inconsistent statements | 207 |
| | 7 | Complainants in proceedings for sexual offences | 210 |
| | 8 | Finality of answers to collateral questions | 219 |
| B | | RE-EXAMINATION | 226 |

## 8 CORROBORATION AND CARE WARNINGS 228

A CORROBORATION REQUIRED BY STATUTE 229

  1 Speeding 231

  2 Perjury 231

  3 Treason 233

  4 Attempts 233

B CARE WARNINGS 233

  1 Accomplices testifying for the prosecution and complainants in sexual cases 233

  2 Other witnesses whose evidence may be tainted by an improper motive 240

  3 Children 243

  4 Matrimonial cases 244

  5 Claims against the estate of a deceased person 245

C CONFESSIONS BY THE METALLY HANDICAPPED 245

D IDENTIFICATION CASES 249

  1 Visual identification by the witnesses 249

  2 Visual identification by the jury 257

  3 Voice identification 257

E LIP-READING EVIDENCE 259

F SUDDEN INFANT DEATH SYNDROME 260

## 9 DOCUMENTARY AND REAL EVIDENCE 262

A DOCUMENTARY EVIDENCE 262

  1 Proof of contents 263

  2 Proof of due execution 272

B REAL EVIDENCE 275

  1 Material objects 275

  2 The appearance of persons and animals 276

  3 The demeanour of witnesses 276

  4 Lip-reading and facial mapping 277

  5 Documents 277

  6 Tape-recordings, films, and photographs 277

  7 Views and demonstrations 279

## 10 HEARSAY IN CRIMINAL CASES 281

A BACKGROUND AND RATIONALE 281

B ADMISSIBILITY OF HEARSAY UNDER THE CRIMINAL
JUSTICE ACT 2003 283
1 General 283
2 The meaning of hearsay in the Criminal Justice Act 2003 285
3 Cases where a witness is unavailable 300
4 Business and other documents 309
5 Admissibility in the interests of justice 313
6 Previous inconsistent statements of witnesses 316
7 Other previous statements of witnesses 317
8 Multiple hearsay 321
9 Other safeguards 323
10 Questions of proof 329
11 Evidence by video recording 331
12 Expert evidence: preparatory work 332
C EXPERT REPORTS 333
D WRITTEN STATEMENTS UNDER SECTION 9 OF THE
CRIMINAL JUSTICE ACT 1967 334
E DEPOSITIONS OF CHILDREN AND YOUNG PERSONS
UNDER SECTION 43 OF THE CHILDREN AND YOUNG
PERSONS ACT 1933 335

11 HEARSAY ADMISSIBLE BY STATUTE IN CIVIL
PROCEEDINGS 336
A THE BACKGROUND 336
B ADMISSIBILITY OF HEARSAY UNDER THE CIVIL EVIDENCE
ACT 1995 338
1 Abolition of the rule against hearsay 338
2 Conditions of admissibility 342
C SAFEGUARDS 344
1 The requirement to give advance notice 344
2 The power to call witnesses for cross-examination 347
3 Weighing hearsay evidence 348
4 Impeaching credibility 349
D PROOF OF STATEMENTS CONTAINED IN DOCUMENTS 350
1 Documents generally 350
2 Records of a business or public authority 351
E EVIDENCE FORMERLY ADMISSIBLE AT COMMON LAW 354
1 General 354
2 Informal admissions 354
F OGDEN TABLES 357

## 12 HEARSAY ADMISSIBLE AT COMMON LAW                    358

A    STATEMENTS IN PUBLIC DOCUMENTS                       359

   1    General                                         359

   2    Examples                                        360

   3    Conditions of admissibility                     360

B    WORKS OF REFERENCE                                   363

C    EVIDENCE OF AGE                                      364

D    EVIDENCE OF REPUTATION                               365

   1    Declarations as to pedigree                     366

   2    Declarations as to public and general rights    367

E    STATEMENTS FORMING PART OF THE *RES GESTAE*          368

   1    Statements by persons emotionally overpowered by an event    369

   2    Statements accompanying the maker's performance of an act    374

   3    Statements relating to a physical sensation or a mental state    376

## 13 CONFESSIONS                                         379

A    ADMISSIBILITY                                        379

   1    The background                                  379

   2    Confessions defined                             380

   3    The conditions of admissibility                 382

   4    Oppression                                      385

   5    Unreliability                                   389

   6    Section 105 of the Taxes Management Act 1970    396

B    THE DISCRETION TO EXCLUDE                            397

   1    Section 82(3) of the Police and Criminal Evidence Act 1984    397

   2    The caution                                     400

   3    Provisions governing procedural fairness        404

   4    Section 78(1) of the Police and Criminal Evidence Act 1984    409

C    THE *VOIR DIRE*                                      414

D    THE TRIAL                                            419

   1    Confessions implicating co-accused              421

   2    Editing                                         424

E    STATEMENTS MADE IN THE PRESENCE OF THE ACCUSED       424

F    FACTS DISCOVERED IN CONSEQUENCE OF INADMISSIBLE
     CONFESSIONS                                          428

## 14 STATUTORY INFERENCES FROM AN ACCUSED'S SILENCE OR CONDUCT 432

A    INFERENCES FROM SILENCE    432
1    The 'right to silence'    432
2    Failure to testify    434
3    Failure to mention facts when questioned or charged    441
4    Failure or refusal to account for objects, substances, marks etc    455

B    INFERENCES FROM REFUSAL TO CONSENT TO THE TAKING OF SAMPLES    458

C    INFERENCES FROM FAILURE TO PROVIDE ADVANCE DISCLOSURE OF THE DEFENCE CASE    460
1    Trials on indictment    460
2    Summary trials    464
3    Preparatory hearings    464

## 15 EVIDENCE OF CHARACTER: EVIDENCE OF CHARACTER IN CIVIL CASES 466

A    CHARACTER IN ISSUE OR RELEVANT TO A FACT IN ISSUE    466

B    EVIDENCE OF THE DISPOSITION OF THE PARTIES TOWARDS GOOD CONDUCT    467

C    EVIDENCE OF THE DISPOSITION OF THE PARTIES TOWARDS BAD CONDUCT    468

D    CHARACTER RELEVANT TO CREDIT    471

## 16 EVIDENCE OF CHARACTER: EVIDENCE OF THE GOOD CHARACTER OF THE ACCUSED 472

A    THE EVIDENCE ADMISSIBLE    472

B    THE DIRECTION TO THE JURY    473

C    THE MEANING OF 'GOOD CHARACTER'    475

## 17 EVIDENCE OF CHARACTER: EVIDENCE OF BAD CHARACTER IN CRIMINAL CASES 479

A    INTRODUCTORY    479
1    The background to the Criminal Justice Act 2003    479
2    Abolition of the common law rules    482
3    'Bad character' defined    482
4    The admissibility of evidence of bad character 'to do with' the facts of the offence or in connection with its investigation or prosecution    484

B   EVIDENCE OF THE BAD CHARACTER OF A PERSON OTHER
    THAN THE DEFENDANT                                                       484
    1    Section 100 of the Criminal Justice Act 2003                        484
    2    Threshold conditions for admissibility                             486
    3    The requirement of leave                                           488
    4    Discretion to exclude                                              489

C   EVIDENCE OF THE BAD CHARACTER OF THE DEFENDANT                          489
    1    Evidence admitted through inadvertence                             489
    2    The background to section 101 of the Criminal Justice Act 2003     490
    3    Section 101 of the Criminal Justice Act 2003                       491
    4    Section 101(1)(a)—evidence admitted by agreement of all the parties  494
    5    Section 101(1)(b)—evidence admitted by the defendant himself       494
    6    Section 101(1)(c)—important explanatory evidence                   495
    7    Section 101(1)(d)—prosecution evidence relevant to an important
         matter in issue between the defendant and the prosecution         498
    8    Section 101(1)(e)—evidence of substantial probative value in
         relation to an important issue between the defendant and a
         co-defendant                                                       524
    9    Section 101(1)(f)—prosecution evidence to correct a false
         impression given by the defendant                                  532
    10   Section 101(1)(g)—prosecution evidence where the defendant has
         made an attack on another person's character                      536
    11   Offences committed by defendant when a child                       544

D   GENERAL                                                                 544
    1    Assumption of truth in the assessment of relevance or probative value  544
    2    Stopping the case where evidence contaminated                      546
    3    Court's duty to give reasons for rulings                           547
    4    Rules of court                                                     548

E   OTHER PROVISIONS GOVERNING THE ADMISSIBILITY OF
    EVIDENCE OF BAD CHARACTER                                               548
    1    Section 27(3) of the Theft Act 1968                                549
    2    Section 1(2) of the Official Secrets Act 1911                      550
    3    Paragraph 6 of the Practice Direction (Criminal Proceedings:
         Consolidation)                                                     551

18 OPINION EVIDENCE                                                         552

A   EXPERT OPINION EVIDENCE                                                 553
    1    Matters calling for expertise                                      553
    2    Expert witnesses                                                   560

3     Restrictions on, and disclosure of, expert evidence in civil cases     572

4     The disclosure of expert evidence in criminal cases                     580

B     NON-EXPERT OPINION EVIDENCE                                             583

# 19 PUBLIC POLICY                                                            585

A     THE DEVELOPMENT OF THE MODERN LAW                                       586

1     Civil cases                                                             586

2     Criminal cases                                                          591

B     THE SCOPE OF EXCLUSION ON GROUNDS OF PUBLIC POLICY                      595

1     National security, diplomatic relations, and international comity       597

2     Information for the detection of crime                                  599

3     Judicial disclosures                                                    602

4     The proper functioning of the public service                           603

5     Confidential relationships                                             607

C     PROCEDURAL ISSUES                                                       615

1     Taking the objection                                                    615

2     Waiver and secondary evidence                                          616

3     Disclosure, production, and inspection                                  619

4     Partial disclosure                                                      621

# 20 PRIVILEGE                                                                623

A     THE PRIVILEGE AGAINST SELF-INCRIMINATION                               624

1     'Criminal charge, penalty, or forfeiture'                              627

2     'A tendency to expose'                                                  627

3     Spouses, strangers, and companies                                      629

4     Statutory provisions affecting the privilege                           629

5     Substituted protection                                                  636

B     LEGAL PROFESSIONAL PRIVILEGE                                           638

1     The protected material                                                  640

2     The subject matter of privilege: communications not facts              648

3     Pre-existing documents                                                  649

4     Exceptions to the privilege                                            650

5     Duration of the privilege                                              655

6     Secondary evidence                                                      656

7     Waiver                                                                  660

C     WITHOUT PREJUDICE NEGOTIATIONS                                         663

1     Settlement negotiations                                                 663

2     Matrimonial reconciliation cases                                        666

21 JUDGMENTS AS EVIDENCE OF THE FACTS UPON
WHICH THEY WERE BASED ..... 668

A CIVIL PROCEEDINGS ..... 669
1 Previous convictions ..... 670
2 Previous findings of adultery and paternity ..... 674
3 Previous acquittals ..... 675
4 Other previous findings ..... 676

B CRIMINAL PROCEEDINGS ..... 677
1 Previous convictions ..... 677
2 Previous acquittals ..... 683

22 PROOF OF FACTS WITHOUT EVIDENCE ..... 684

A PRESUMPTIONS ..... 684
1 Definitions and classification ..... 684
2 The presumption of marriage ..... 690
3 The presumption of legitimacy ..... 694
4 The presumption of death ..... 696
5 *Omnia praesumuntur rite esse acta* ..... 701
6 The presumption of sanity in testamentary cases ..... 702
7 *Res ipsa loquitur* ..... 703
8 Conflicting presumptions ..... 705

B JUDICIAL NOTICE ..... 706
1 Judicial notice without inquiry ..... 706
2 Judicial notice after inquiry ..... 708
3 Personal knowledge ..... 711

C FORMAL ADMISSIONS ..... 713
1 Civil cases ..... 714
2 Criminal cases ..... 714

*Index* ..... 717

# TABLE OF STATUTES

Abortion Act 1967 ... 607
Administration of Estates Act 1925—
   s 46(3) ... 699
Administration of Justice Act 1920—
   s 15 ... 35
Administration of Justice Act 1985—
   s 33 ... 639
Administration of Justice Act (Miscellaneous
     Provisions) 1934—
   s 2(2)(b) ... 581
Affiliation Proceedings Act 1957—
   s 4 ... 244

Bail (Amendment) Act 1993—
   s 1 ... 211
   s 99 ... 53
Bankers' Books Evidence Act 1879 ... 139, 264,
     270, 271, 341
   s 3 ... 270, 271
   ss 4, 5 ... 271
   s 7 ... 271
   s 9(1), (2) ... 270
Banking Act 1987 ... 399
   s 39(12A), (12B) ... 635
   s 41(10A), (10B) ... 635
   s 42(5A), (5B) ... 635
Bankruptcy Act 1986—
   s 352 ... 97, 98
   s 353(1) ... 97, 98
   s 357 ... 98
   s 357(1) ... 97, 98
Births and Deaths Registration Act 1953—
   s 34 ... 341, 359, 364
British Law Ascertainment Act 1859 ... 555
Building Societies Act 1986—
   s 57(5A), (5B) ... 635

Ceylon Evidence Ordinance 1895—
   s 116(1) ... 286
   s 116(2)(a) ... 286
Child Abduction Act 1984—
   ss 1, 2 ... 200
Child Support Act 1991 ... 342
Children Act 1989 ... 4, 651, 654, 656, 667
   s 8(2) ... 342
   s 92(2) ... 342
   s 96 ... 137, 341
   s 96(1) ... 137

s 96(2)(a), (b) ... 138, 342
s 96(7) ... 341
s 98 ... 633, 634
s 98(2) ... 634
s 105 ... 137
Children and Young Persons Act 1933—
   s 1 ... 164, 200
   s 34 (2), (3) ... 405
   s 38(1) ... 134, 243, 244
   s 42 ... 335
   s 43 ... 335
   s 50 ... 686, 687
Children and Young Persons Act 1969—
   s 16(1) ... 687
   s 16(2) ... 544
   s 16(3) ... 544
Civil Evidence Act 1968 ... 4, 336–39, 344, 352,
     669, 672
   s 6(1) ... 331, 351
   s 7(5) ... 350
   s 9 ... 354
   s 9(1), (2) ... 354
   s 11 ... 670, 672, 674, 675, 677, 684
   s 11(1) ... 670
   s 11(2) ... 672
   s 11(2)(a) ... 671, 672
   s 11(2)(b) ... 672
   s 11(4) ... 672
   s 11(5) ... 671
   s 12 ... 670, 672, 674–676, 684
   s 12(4) ... 672
   s 12(5) ... 674, 675
   s 13 ... 467, 670–73, 675
   s 13(1) ... 31, 687
   s 13(4) ... 672
   s 14(1) ... 627
   s 14(1)(a) ... 627
   s 14(1)(b) ... 629
   s 16(1)(a) ... 625
   s 16(1)(b) ... 623
   s 16(3) ... 623
   s 16(4) ... 694
   s 18(1) ... 670
Civil Evidence Act 1972 ... 4, 339, 579
   s 3(1) ... 569
   s 3(2) ... 177, 584
   s 3(3) ... 569, 584
   s 4 ... 555
   s 4(1) ... 561
   s 4(2)(a), (b) ... 555
   s 4(3) ... 555

s 4(5) . . . 555
Civil Evidence Act 1995 . . . 4, 53, 206, 263, 264,
    267, 279, 337, 338, 340–42, 344, 354–58,
    365, 366, 466, 672
s 1 . . . 177, 186, 197, 209, 338, 341–43
s 1(1) . . . 339, 355
s 1(2) . . . 339
s 1(2)(a) . . . 339
s 1(2)(b) . . . 356
s 1(3) . . . 341
s 1(4) . . . 341
s 2 . . . 341, 345, 365
s 2(1) . . . 346
s 2(1)(a) . . . 345, 346
s 2(4) . . . 346
s 2(4)(a) . . . 346
s 2(4)(b) . . . 346, 347
s 3 . . . 341, 347, 349, 355
s 4 . . . 341, 346, 348, 355, 365
s 4(2)(a), (b) . . . 348
s 4(2)(d) . . . 348, 349
s 4(2)(e) . . . 348, 349
s 4(2)(f) . . . 348
s 5 . . . 341
s 5(1) . . . 342, 343
s 5(2) . . . 349, 350
s 5(2)(a) . . . 350
s 5(2)(6) . . . 350
s 6 . . . 341, 343, 344
s 6(2) . . . 181, 186, 343, 349
s 6(2)(a) . . . 170, 193, 195, 343
s 6(2)(b) . . . 343
s 6(3) . . . 195, 197, 209, 343, 350
s 6(4) . . . 177, 186, 343
s 6(5) . . . 17, 197, 209, 350
s 7 . . . 358
s 7(1) . . . 265, 354
s 7(2) . . . 354, 358
s 7(2)(a) . . . 363
s 7(2)(b), (c) . . . 359, 360
s 7(3) . . . 358, 365
s 7(3)(a), (b) . . . 365
s 7(4) . . . 358
s 8 . . . 263, 264, 267, 331, 350, 351
s 8(1) . . . 351
s 8(1)(a) . . . 351
s 8(2) . . . 351
s 9 . . . 263, 264, 267, 352
s 9(1) . . . 263, 352
s 9(2) . . . 263
s 9(3) . . . 264
s 9(4) . . . 352
s 10 . . . 357
s 11 . . . 338, 341
s 13 . . . 263, 279, 339, 348, 351, 356
s 14 . . . 264
s 14(1) . . . 339
s 14(2), (3) . . . 264

Civil Evidence (Scotland) Act 1988 . . . 347
Civil Procedure Act 1997 . . . 4
    Sch 1, para 4 . . . 4
Civil Rights of Convicts Act 1828 . . . 124
Colonial Laws Validity Act 1865—
    s 6 . . . 555
Common Law Procedure (Amendment) Act
        1856—
    s 22 . . . 196
Companies Act 1948 . . . 360, 362
Companies Act 1967 . . . 676
Companies Act 1985 . . . 360, 630
    Part XIV . . . 634, 676
    s 434 . . . 630, 634
    s 434(5A), (5B) . . . 634
    s 436 . . . 389
    s 447(8A), (8B) . . . 635
Company Directors Disqualification Act 1986
        . . . 676
    s 7(3) . . . 646
    s 20(2)–(4) . . . 635
Consular Relations Act 1968 . . . 139
Consumer Credit Act 1974—
    s 137 . . . 105
    s 138 . . . 105
    s 171(7) . . . 105
Consumer Protection Act 1987—
    s 39 . . . 433
Contempt of Court Act 1981—
    s 8 . . . 45
    s 10 . . . 609–11
Copyright Act 1956—
    s 21 . . . 628
Copyright, Designs and Patents Act 1988—
    s 280 . . . 639
    s 284 . . . 639
County Courts Act 1984—
    s 63 . . . 553
    s 68 . . . 35
    s 134(2) . . . 707
Crime and Disorder Act 1998—
    s 1(1)(a) . . . 115
    s 2 . . . 469
    s 2(1)(a) . . . 114
    s 51 . . . 442, 581
    Sch 3, para 2 . . . 442
Crime (International Co-operation) Act 1990—
    s 7 . . . 310
Crime (International Co-operation) Act 2003
        . . . 142
Crimes Act 1958 (Australia)—
    s 400 . . . 129

Criminal Appeal Act 1968—
  s 2(1) . . . 44, 250
Criminal Appeal Act 1995—
  s 2(1) . . . 140
  s 9 . . . 141, 142
  s 11 . . . 141, 142
  s 13(1) . . . 140
  s 16(1) . . . 140
Criminal Attempts Act 1981—
  s 1 . . . 233
  s 2(2)(g) . . . 230, 233
  s 4(3) . . . 34
Criminal Damage Act 1971—
  s 1(3) . . . 436
  s 9 . . . 635
Criminal Evidence Act 1898 . . . 3, 124, 131, 483,
    494
  s 1 . . . 16, 22, 124, 126, 131, 433, 440, 472, 481,
    525
  s 1(b) . . . 433, 440
  s 1(1) . . . 126, 127
  s 1(2) . . . 126, 625, 626
  s 1(3) . . . 5, 480
  s 1(3)(ii) . . . 49, 528, 529, 533–35, 537, 538,
    540–42
  s 1(3)(iii) . . . 221, 529–31
  s 1(4) . . . 126
Criminal Evidence Act 1965 . . . 281, 352
  s 1 . . . 311
Criminal Evidence Act 1984—
  s 68 . . . 352
Criminal Evidence (Amendment) Act 1987—
  s 1 . . . 460
  s 2 . . . 460
Criminal Justice Act 1948—
  s 39 . . . 54
  s 83 . . . 53
Criminal Justice Act 1967—
  s 8 . . . 688
  s 9 . . . 5, 332, 334
  s 9(1) . . . 353
  s 9(2) . . . 334
  s 9(3) . . . 353
  s 9(4), (5) . . . 334, 353
  s 9(6) . . . 334
  s 10 . . . 8, 54, 109, 274, 555
  s 10(1) . . . 31
  s 11 . . . 5, 580, 582
Criminal Justice Act 1987 . . . 433
  s 2 . . . 634
  s 2(8) . . . 403, 634
  s 2(8AA) . . . 634
  s 2(13) . . . 403

s 4 . . . 581
s 7 . . . 433, 465
s 9 . . . 433, 465
s 10 . . . 433, 465
s 10(1) . . . 714
s 10(2)(b), (c) . . . 714
s 10(3), (4) . . . 714
Criminal Justice Act 1988 . . . 5, 53, 407
  s 23 . . . 121, 267, 282, 301, 305, 308, 309, 329
  s 23(a)–(c) . . . 302
  s 23(2)(b) . . . 303
  s 23(3) . . . 304
  s 24 . . . 267, 282, 305, 309, 329, 330
  s 24(1) . . . 330
  s 25 . . . 282, 308
  s 26 . . . 282, 308, 309
  s 26(i)–(iii) . . . 305
  s 27 . . . 263, 267, 282
  s 28 . . . 282
  s 30 . . . 267, 285
  s 30(1) . . . 333, 582
  s 30(2)–(5) . . . 333
  s 32 . . . 141, 302
  s 32(2)(a) . . . 130, 164
  s 32A . . . 139, 159
  s 33A(2A) . . . 133, 134
  s 32A(3)(c) . . . 159
  s 34(2) . . . 243
  s 77 . . . 636
  s 134 . . . 387
  s 139 . . . 96
  s 139(4) . . . 96
  s 139(5) . . . 96
  s 170(1) . . . 406
  Sch 13, para 6 . . . 310
Criminal Justice Act 1991 . . . 671
  s 53 . . . 581
  s 101(2) . . . 243
  Sch 13 . . . 243
Criminal Justice Act 2003 . . . 5, 193, 263, 264,
    279, 295, 296, 313, 340, 341, 368, 470, 479,
    481, 490
  s 32(3) . . . 142
  s 48(3), (5) . . . 32
  Part 8 (ss 51–56) . . . 142
  s 51(1)–(3) . . . 142
  s 51(4)(a), (b) . . . 142
  s 51(6), (7) . . . 142
  s 52(2) . . . 143
  s 52(5), (6) . . . 143
  s 54 . . . 143
  s 55 . . . 142
  s 56(2), (3) . . . 142
  s 56(4) . . . 142
  s 56(5)(a) . . . 142
  s 56(5)(b) . . . 143
  Part 11, Chapter 1 (ss 98–113) . . . 479, 480

s 98 ... 223, 482, 483, 519, 521
s 98(a) ... 484, 498, 512
s 98(b) ... 484, 488, 548
s 99 ... 204, 222, 223, 482
s 99(1) ... 480, 482, 484, 486
s 100 ... 204, 221, 223, 324, 470, 484, 485, 489,
       494, 537, 544, 547
s 100(1) ... 485
s 100(1)(a) ... 488
s 100(1)(b) ... 223, 486, 488, 496, 499
s 100(1)(c) ... 484, 488
s 100(1)(e) ... 499
s 100(2) ... 486, 488
s 100(2)(a) ... 486, 495
s 100(3) ... 487, 488
s 100(3)(a), (b) ... 487
s 100(3)(c) ... 487, 544
s 100(3)(d) ... 488, 544
s 100(4) ... 488, 489, 493
s 101 22.... 26, 126, 221, 436, 470, 483, 490,
       491, 494, 498, 512, 524, 539, 683
s 101(1) ... 492, 495, 544, 546
s 101(1)(a) ... 492–94, 521
s 101(1)(b) ... 492–95
s 101(1)(c) ... 492–96, 498, 546
s 101(1)(d) ... 492, 493, 498–502, 506, 512,
       513, 516, 519, 521–25, 535, 544, 546, 547
s 101(1)(e) ... 221, 492, 493, 524, 525, 528,
       529, 531, 544, 546
s 101(1)(f) ... 492–94, 532, 533, 535, 536, 544,
       546
s 101(1)(g) ... 49, 222, 492, 493, 495, 523, 524,
       536–41, 543, 546, 547
s 101(3) ... 489, 493, 494, 499, 501, 503, 512,
       524, 532, 539, 547
s 101(4) ... 501
s 102 ... 470, 492, 495
s 103 ... 470, 492, 499–502
s 103(1) ... 500, 519
s 103(1)(a) ... 500–2, 519, 524
s 103(1)(b) ... 522–24
s 103(2) ... 500–2, 504, 519
s 103(2)(a), (b) ... 501, 502
s 103(3) ... 501, 503
s 103(4)(a), (b) ... 502
s 103(5) ... 502
s 103(6) ... 499
s 104 ... 470, 492, 529
s 104(1) ... 529
s 104(2) ... 525
s 104(2)(b) ... 492
s 105 ... 470, 492, 532–34, 537, 538, 544
s 105(1)(a) ... 533
s 105(1)(b) ... 534
s 105(2) ... 535
s 105(2)(c), (d) ... 534
s 105(3) ... 535, 537
s 105(4) ... 533, 534

s 105(5) ... 533
s 105(6) ... 534
s 106 ... 470, 492, 536–38
s 106(1)(a) ... 537
s 106(1)(c) ... 537, 540, 543
s 106(2) ... 537, 538, 543
s 106(2)(a) ... 537
s 106(2)(b) ... 537
s 107 ... 546, 547
s 107(1) ... 546
s 107(1)(b)(ii) ... 547
s 107(3) ... 546
s 107(5)(a), (b) ... 547
s 108 ... 204, 221
s 108(2), (3) ... 544
s 109 ... 544, 545
s 109(2) ... 545
s 110 ... 547
s 111(1)–(4) ... 548
s 112(1) ... 482, 491, 492, 499, 501, 519, 522,
       525
s 112(2)(b) ... 492
s 112(3) ... 549
Part 11, Chapter 2 (ss 114–136) ... 282–84,
       312, 358, 494
s 114 ... 290, 291, 296, 301, 310, 312, 321
s 114(1) ... 283, 285, 287, 290, 313
s 114(1)(a), (b) ... 284
s 114(1)(c) ... 182, 284
s 114(1)(d) ... 171, 182, 284, 300, 313, 315,
       316, 327
s 114(1)(e) ... 315
s 114(2) ... 313, 315
s 114(2)(a)–(i) ... 327
s 114(3) ... 284, 285, 341
s 115(2) ... 263, 285, 296
s 115(3) ... 290–94, 296
s 115(3)(a), (b) ... 291, 291
s 116 ... 121, 300–2, 304, 312, 315, 321–23,
       326, 329, 359
s 116(1) ... 300, 301
s 116(1)(a) 301, 302.... 311
s 116(1)(b) ... 301, 302
s 116(1)(c) ... 301
s 116(2) ... 300, 303, 310, 329
s 116(2)(a)–(d) ... 302, 304, 312
s 116(2)(e) ... 302–5, 312, 329
s 116(3) ... 300, 304
s 116(4) ... 305, 327
s 116(4)(a)–(c) ... 305, 327
s 116(4)(d) ... 305, 308
s 116(5) ... 300, 304
s 117 ... 171, 174, 296, 309, 310, 321–24, 359
s 117(1) ... 311, 312
s 117(1)(a) ... 311
s 117(2) ... 312, 323
s 117(2)(a), (b) ... 311, 330
s 117(2)(c) ... 312

s 117(3) ... 311
s 117(4), (5) ... 312
s 117(5)(a) ... 329
s 117(5)(b) ... 312
s 117(6), (7) ... 312
s 118 ... 190, 283, 283, 330, 333, 358, 425
s 118(1) ... 9, 190, 193, 269, 358, 359, 365,
    374, 376, 423, 473, 482, 483, 568
s 118(1)(a) ... 363
s 118(1)(b), (c) ... 359
s 118(1)(d) ... 364
s 118(2) ... 284, 365
s 118(3) ... 365
s 118(4)(a) ... 369
s 118(4)(b) ... 374
s 118(4)(c) ... 376
s 119 ... 197, 321, 323
s 119(1) ... 209, 316, 317
s 119(1)(b) ... 322
s 119(2) ... 325
s 120 ... 173, 177, 317, 318, 321, 323
s 120(1) ... 173, 177, 187, 190
s 120(2) ... 187, 318
s 120(3) ... 177, 318
s 120(4) ... 173, 190, 319, 320, 322
s 120(5) ... 190, 319
s 120(6) ... 173, 319, 322
s 120(7) ... 182, 319, 320
s 120(7)(d)–(f) ... 320
s 120(8) ... 320
s 121 ... 321
s 121(1)(a), (b) ... 321
s 121(1)(c) ... 322, 327
s 122 ... 36, 173, 178
s 123(1), (2) ... 323
s 123(4) ... 323
s 124 ... 323, 324
s 124(2) ... 325
s 124(2)(a), (b) ... 324
s 124(2)(c) ... 308, 324, 325
s 124(3) ... 325
s 125 ... 229, 317, 326
s 125(3), (4) ... 326
s 126 ... 51, 283, 327
s 126(1) ... 327
s 126(1)(b) ... 327
s 126(2) ... 328, 494
s 127 ... 332, 333, 566
s 127(4) ... 332, 333
s 127(5) ... 332
s 128(1) ... 284, 384
s 128(2), (3) ... 284
s 129 ... 296
s 132 ... 329
s 133 ... 263, 264, 331
s 134(1) ... 263, 279, 283–85, 311, 331
s 136 ... 282
s 137 ... 153–55, 170, 331

s 137(1)(f) ... 155
s 137(2) ... 153
s 138(1) ... 154
s 138(2), (3) ... 155
s 138(4) ... 153
s 139 ... 171, 172, 174, 179
s 139(1) ... 171, 172, 174, 175
s 139(2) ... 171, 172
s 140 ... 174
s 331 ... 480, 679
Sch 36, para 79 ... 480
Sch 36, para 80(b) ... 480
Sch 36, para 85 ... 679
Criminal Justice and Public Order Act 1994 ... 5,
    230, 233, 433
s 32 ... 234–36, 243
s 32(1) ... 236
s 32(2) ... 243
s 33(1) ... 230
s 34 ... 95, 238, 289, 419, 425, 433, 441, 442,
    444–46, 450–52, 454, 456, 458
s 34(1) ... 443, 457
s 34(1)(a) ... 442, 443, 444
s 34(1)(b) ... 443, 444
s 34(2) ... 453, 454, 464
s 34(2)(b) ... 456
s 34(2)(c) ... 445
s 34(2A) ... 456, 457
s 34(3) ... 447
s 34(5) ... 455
s 35 ... 238, 255, 419, 425, 433, 434, 436, 453,
    454
s 35(1) ... 434, 435, 437
s 35(1)(b) ... 434
s 35(2) ... 434, 435
s 35(3) ... 434, 436, 454
s 35(4) ... 434, 436, 443
s 35(5) ... 434, 436
s 36 ... 238, 419, 425, 433, 454–58
s 36(1) ... 458
s 36(1)(a)(iv) ... 457
s 36(2) ... 454, 457, 458, 464
s 36(2)(b) ... 454
s 36(4), (5) ... 457
s 37 ... 238, 419, 425, 433, 454–58
s 37(1) ... 458
s 37(1)(b) ... 456
s 37(2) ... 454, 458, 464
s 37(2)(b) ... 454
s 38 ... 433
s 38(1) ... 455
s 38(2) ... 442, 456
s 38(2A) ... 442
s 38(3) ... 436, 438, 453, 454, 458
s 38(4) ... 454
s 38(6) ... 454, 458
s 51 ... 98
s 51(1) ... 98

s 51(1)(a)–(c) . . . 99
s 51(7) . . . 99
s 168(2) . . . 440
Sch 11 . . . 440
Criminal Law Act 1967—
  s 3(1) . . . 106
Criminal Law Act 1977—
  s 54 . . . 164
Criminal Procedure Act 1865—
  s 3 . . . 130, 195–97, 209, 316, 322, 343, 479,
    549
  s 4 . . . 197, 203, 206–9, 316, 343, 417
  s 5 . . . 197, 206–9, 316, 343
  s 6 . . . 221, 325, 479, 480
  s 7 . . . 273
  s 8 . . . 121, 273, 554
Criminal Procedure (Attendance of Witnesses)
    Act 1965 . . . 123
Criminal Procedure and Investigations Act
    1996—
  Part 1 (Ss 1–21) . . . 647
  s 3 . . . 460, 461, 464
  s 5 . . . 462, 580
  s 5(5) . . . 461
  s 5(9) . . . 461
  s 6 . . . 464
  s 6A . . . 461, 462
  s 6A(3) . . . 463
  s 6B . . . 462
  s 6B(1) . . . 462
  s 6B(3), (4) . . . 462
  s 6C . . . 462, 583
  s 6C(1) . . . 462
  s 6D . . . 583
  s 6E(2) . . . 462
  s 11 . . . 462, 463, 464
  s 11(3) . . . 464
  s 11(5) . . . 462, 464
  s 11(5)(b) . . . 464
  s 11(8)(a) . . . 464
  s 11(10) . . . 464
  s 11(12)(c) . . . 462
  s 11(12)(d), (e) . . . 463
  s 12 . . . 461
  ss 14, 15 . . . 591
  s 21(2) . . . 592
  s 29 . . . 464
  s 31 . . . 465
  s 31(4) . . . 465
  s 31(6) . . . 465
  s 31(8) . . . 465
  s 34 . . . 465
Criminal Procedure (Insanity) Act 1964 . . . 326
  s 4A(2) . . . 546
  s 6 . . . 87

Criminal Procedure (Insanity and Unfitness to
    Plead) Act 1991—
  s 1(1), (2) . . . 557, 560, 584
Crown Proceedings Act 1947—
  s 28 . . . 580, 615
Customs and Excise Management Act 1979—
  s 86 . . . 34

Data Protection Act 1984 . . . 652
Defamation Act 1952—
  s 7(3) . . . 34
Sched . . . 34
Diplomatic and Other Privileges Act 1971 . . .
  139
Diplomatic Privileges Act 1964 . . . 139
Divorce Reform Act 1969 . . . 118, 119
Documentary Evidence Act 1868—
  s 2 . . . 264
Documentary Evidence Act 1882—
  s 2 . . . 264, 270, 708

Employment Rights Act 1996—
  s 98 . . . 105
Environmental Protection Act 1990—
  s 71 . . . 633
  s 33(1)(a) . . . 89
European Communities Act 1972 . . . 627
  s 3(2) . . . 707
Evidence Act 1843 . . . 124
Evidence Act 1845—
  s 1 . . . 269
  s 2 . . . 707
  s 3 . . . 270, 708
Evidence Act 1851 . . . 124
  s 7 . . . 269
  s 14 . . . 269
Evidence Act 1938—
  ss 3, 4 . . . 274
Evidence (Amendment) Act 1853 . . . 124
Evidence (Colonial Statutes) Act 1907 . . . 555
  s 1 . . . 264, 555
Evidence (Foreign, Dominion and Colonial
    Documents) Act 1933 . . . 360
  s 1 . . . 53, 264, 354
Evidence (Further Amendment) Act 1869 . . .
  124
Extradition Act 1989—
  Sch1, para 12 . . . 54

Factories Act 1961—
  s 29(1) . . . 90
  s 155(1) . . . 90

Family Law Reform Act 1969—
s 4 . . . 245
s 20 . . . 15, 16, 245
s 23 . . . 15, 16
s 23(1) . . . 17
s 26 . . . 117, 119, 692, 696
Family Law Reform Act 1987—
s 17 . . . 245
s 26 . . . 685
s 29 . . . 674
Fatal Accidents Act 1846 . . . 86
Finance Act 1942—
s 34 . . . 396
Financial Services Act 1986—
s 105(5A), (5B) . . . 635
s 177(6A), (6B) . . . 635
s 189 . . . 221
Financial Services and Markets Act 2000—
Part 4 . . . 270
Firearms Act 1968—
s 5(1)(b) . . . 34
s 21 . . . 548
Foreign Law Ascertainment Act 1861 . . . 555
Forestry Act 1967—
s 17 . . . 102
Fox's Libel Act 1792 . . . 34

Health and Safety at Work Act 1974 . . . 101
s 40 . . . 101
Highways Act 1980—
s 32 . . . 364, 367
s 140(1) . . . 89
s 161(1) . . . 89
Homicide Act 1957—
s 2(2) . . . 85, 88
s 4 . . . 98, 558
s 4(2) . . . 98
Hong Kong Evidence Ordinance—
s 13 . . . 417
Human Rights Act 1998 . . . 3, 74, 87, 88, 93–95, 342
s 3 . . . 94, 101, 216, 217
s 3(1) . . . 380
Indecency with Children Act 1960 . . . 164
Indian Evidence Act (I of 1872)—
s 148 . . . 204
Inheritance (Family Provision) Act 1938 . . . 692
Insolvency Act 1986 . . . 632
s 235 . . . 633
s 354 . . . 633
s 354(3) . . . 633
s 433(2)–(4) . . . 635

Insurance Companies Act 1982—
s 43A(6), (7) . . . 635
s 44(5A), (5B) . . . 635
Interception of Communications Act 1985—
s 9 . . . 57
International Organisations Act 1968 . . . 139
Interpretation Act 1978—
s 3 . . . 270, 708
s 22 . . . 708
Sch 3, para 2 . . . 708
Intestates' Estates Act 1952—
s 1(4) . . . 699
Irish Criminal Evidence Act 1984—
ss 18, 19 . . . 455

Landlord and Tenant Act 1954 . . . 566
Larceny Act . . . 1916
s 1(1) . . . 33
s 43(1) . . . 50, 550
Law of Property Act 1925—
s 184 . . . 699
Legal Aid Act 1974—
ss 22, 23 . . . 654
Legal Aid Act 1988—
ss 38, 39 . . . 653
Licensing Act 1964—
s 160(1)(a) . . . 90
Limitation Act 1980—
s 33 . . . 656
Local Government Act 1972–
s 238 . . . 269
Local Government (Miscellaneous Provisions) Act 1982—
s 75 . . . 89
Sch 3, para 6 . . . 89
Sch 3, para 20(1)(a) . . . 89

Magistrates' Courts Act 1952—
s 81 . . . 88–90
Magistrates' Courts Act 1980—
s 97 . . . 123
s 101 . . . 88–91
Maintenance Orders Act 1950—
s 22(2) . . . 708
Marriage Act 1949—
s 65(3) . . . 341, 359
Matrimonial Causes Act 1965—
s 43(1) . . . 694
Matrimonial Causes Act 1973 . . . 118
s 19(1), (3) . . . 700
s 48(1) . . . 694

Mental Health Act 1983 ... 162
Merchant Shipping Act 1970—
　s 75 ... 53
Misuse of Drugs Act 1971 ... 108
　s 5 91.... 96
　s 5(3) ... 34, 94
　s 28 ... 94–96
　s 28(2), (3) ... 91

Northern Ireland (Emergency Provisions) Act
　　1978 ... 418
　s 8(2) ... 387

Oaths Act 1978—
　s 1(1), (2) ... 140
　s 1(3) ... 140
　s 3 ... 140
　s 4(2) ... 141
　s 5(1) ... 140
　s 5(2) ... 140, 141
　s 5(3) ... 140
Oaths and Evidence (Overseas Authorities and
　　Countries) Act 1963—
　s 3 ... 354
Obscene Publications Act 1959—
　s 4 ... 554
Offences Against the Person Act 1861 ... 335
　s 16 ... 89
　s 57 ... 92, 700
Offences Against the State Act 1939—
　s 21 ... 631
　s 52 ... 631
Official Secrets Act 1911—
　s 1 ... 399
　s 1(1) ... 550
　s 1(2) ... 549, 550, 683

Partnership Act 1890—
　s 5 ... 357
Perjury Act 1911—
　s 1 ... 141, 142
　s 1(1) ... 36
　s 1(6) ... 36
　s 2 ... 635
　s 5 ... 635
　s 13 ... 232
　s 14 ... 54
Police Act 1964—
　s 64 ... 248
Police and Criminal Evidence Act 1984 ... 5, 17,
　　63, 69, 80, 127, 131, 132, 189, 379, 386,
　　399, 400, 404, 419, 454, 580, 669
　s 8 ... 649, 650

s 9 ... 649, 650, 654
s 9(2) ... 649
s 10 ... 638, 649, 654
s 10(1)(c) ... 648, 649
s 10(2) ... 649, 653, 654
s 14(2) ... 649, 650
s 15 ... 404
s 18(8) ... 68
s 28(1)–(3) ... 404
s 29 ... 404
s 34(1), (2) ... 404
s 37 ... 411
s 37(2) ... 404
s 37(7) ... 444
s 37(7)(b) ... 404
s 38(1) ... 404
s 39(1) ... 404
s 40(1) ... 404
s 41 ... 404
s 41(2) ... 406
ss 42, 43 ... 404
s 46(1), (2) ... 404
s 56 ... 405, 406
s 56(1) ... 405
s 56(2)(a), (b) ... 406
s 56(3), (4) ... 406
s 56(5) ... 407
s 56(5)(a) ... 76
s 56(6), (7) ... 407
s 56(8) ... 40, 407
s 57 ... 405
s 58 ... 66, 69, 188, 394, 405, 406, 410, 411,
　　441
s 58(4) ... 396
s 58(5) ... 406
s 58(6)(a), (b) ... 406
s 58(7) ... 406
s 58(8)–(10) ... 407
s 61 ... 15, 460
s 62 ... 458, 459
s 62(4) ... 458
s 62(10) ... 17, 238, 459
s 63 ... 459, 460
s 64 ... 67
s 64(3B) ... 67
s 65 ... 15, 458, 459
s 66 ... 190
s 67(9) ... 63, 399, 443
s 62(10) ... 432
s 67(11) ... 385, 419
s 68 ... 282, 312
s 68(2) ... 303
s 68(2)(a)(ii) ... 303, 329
s 69 ... 282
s 70 ... 282
s 71 ... 263, 267, 282
s 72 ... 282
s 73 ... 397, 550, 683

s 73(4) . . . 54

s 74 . . . 52, 285, 397, 422, 502, 677, 678, 680, 681, 684, 685

s 74(1) . . . 679, 682, 683

s 74(2) . . . 679, 682

s 74(3) . . . 501, 682, 683

s 74(4)(a), (b) . . . 678

s 75 . . . 397, 501, 502, 681

s 75(1)–(4) . . . 678

s 76 . . . 246, 248, 284, 288, 382, 384, 385, 396, 397, 415, 420, 425, 429

s 76(1) . . . 382, 383, 397, 417

s 76(2) . . . 36, 38, 39, 121, 383, 385, 386, 397, 400, 414, 415, 417, 420, 421, 425

s 76(2)(a) . . . 385, 386

s 76(2)(b) . . . 246, 386, 388–95, 398, 570

s 76(3) . . . 385, 414

s 76(4) . . . 429, 431

s 76(5) . . . 430

s 76(8) . . . 386, 387

s 76A . . . 314, 384, 425

s 76A(2) . . . 384, 385, 425

s 76A(3) . . . 385

s 76A(4) . . . 429, 431

s 76A(5), (6) . . . 430

s 76A(7) . . . 386

s 77 . . . 246–48, 384, 395, 397, 398

s 77(1) . . . 246, 247

s 77(1)(a) . . . 247

s 77(1)(b) . . . 248

s 77(3) . . . 247, 248

s 78 . . . 38, 39, 52, 59, 60, 62, 63, 65, 66, 69, 75, 76, 78–81, 149, 148, 253, 258, 300, 309, 327, 328, 373, 389, 394, 397, 403, 409, 410, 413–15, 418–20, 429, 454, 489, 493, 494, 593, 657, 680–82

s 78(1) . . . 51, 52, 62–65, 75–77, 130, 246, 397, 409

s 78(3) . . . 64

s 79 . . . 153, 397

s 80 . . . 124, 129, 397

s 80(A) . . . 17

s 80(1) . . . 128

s 80(2) . . . 131

s 80(2A)–(4A) . . . 129

s 80(2A) . . . 129, 132

s 80(2A)(a) . . . 132

s 80(2A)(b) . . . 130

s 80(3) . . . 129, 132

s 80(4) . . . 131, 132

s 80(5) . . . 132, 133

s 80(6) . . . 129

s 80(7) . . . 130

s 80(9) . . . 623, 694

s 81 . . . 397

s 82 . . . 284, 397

s 82(1) . . . 380–82, 417, 424, 429, 678, 679

s 82(3) . . . 52, 246, 248, 397, 420, 424

s 107(1) . . . 407

s 116(1) . . . 406

s 116(6), (7) . . . 406

s 118 . . . 15

Part IX . . . 606

Sch 5 . . . 406

Sch 7 . . . 623

Codes of Practice . . . 63–65, 75, 80, 190, 191, 383, 385, 394, 395, 399, 400, 404, 409, 444, 454

Code A . . . 63, 399

Code B . . . 63, 67, 68, 399

   para 3 . . . 404

   para 6.4 . . . 404

Code C . . . 63, 68–70, 79, 80, 396, 397, 399, 400, 402, 406, 407, 410–13

   para 1.7(b) . . . 248

   note 1B . . . 396

   para 3.1 . . . 410, 412

   para 3.2 . . . 410, 412

   para 3.5 . . . 410

   para 3.21 . . . 404

   para 5 . . . 405

   para 6 . . . 405

   para 6.12 . . . 405

   para 6.12A . . . 405

   para 6.13 . . . 405

   para 10 . . . 396, 400

   para 10D . . . 443

   para 10.1 . . . 400, 402, 403, 411, 412

   para 10.2 . . . 412

   para 10.3 . . . 404

   para 10.4 . . . 401, 402

   para 10.5 . . . 401, 443

   para 10.7 . . . 401, 443

   para 10.8 . . . 401, 403, 412

   para 11.1 . . . 396, 412

   para 11.1A . . . 406, 411

   para 11.2 . . . 412

   para 11.4 . . . 443

   para 11.5 . . . 412

   para 11.6 . . . 443

   para 11.7 . . . 396, 412

   para 11.10 . . . 412

   para 11.11 . . . 396

   para 11.13 . . . 412

   para 11.15 . . . 68, 248, 396, 410, 412

   para 11.17 . . . 410

   para 11.18 . . . 248, 410

   para 11.19 . . . 410

para 11.20 . . . 410

para 16 . . . 400

para 16.1 . . . 401, 443

para 16.2 . . . 401, 403

para 16.5 . . . 396, 403

annex B . . . 407

    para A1 . . . 407

    para A1 . . . 407

annex D . . . 402

    para 2 . . . 402

annex E . . . 248

Code D . . . 63, 70–72, 249, 253, 257, 258, 399

    para 1.2 . . . 257

    para 3.3 . . . 191

    para 3.11 . . . 71

    para 3.12 . . . 70, 71

    para 3.12(ii) . . . 192

    para 3.23 . . . 71

    para 3.28 . . . 191

    para 6.3 . . . 459

    note 6D . . . 459

    para 18 . . . 257

    annex B . . . 257

    annex E . . . 191

Code E . . . 63, 122, 263, 399

Code F . . . 399

Police (Property) Act 1897 . . . 671

Prevention of Corruption Act 1906 . . . 615

Prevention of Crime Act 1953—

    s 1(1) . . . 686

Protection of Children Act 1978 . . . 130, 164, 200, 335

Protection from Eviction Act 1977—

    s 1(2) . . . 98

Public Bodies Corrupt Practices Act 1889 . . . 615

    s 5 . . . 33, 34

Public Records Act 1958—

    s 9 . . . 269

Regulation of Investigatory Powers Act 2000—

    s 17 . . . 57, 599

Rehabilitation of Offenders Act 1974 . . . 551

    s 4(1) . . . 221, 222

    s 4(1)(a) . . . 551

    s 5(1), (2) . . . 551

    s 6 . . . 222

    s 7(2)(a) . . . 551

    s 7(3) . . . 221, 551

Road Safety Act 1967—

    s 2(2)(b) . . . 287

Road Traffic Act 1972 . . . 298, 702

    s 10(2) . . . 687

    s 10(3)(a) . . . 299

Road Traffic Act 1988 . . . 401, 702

    s 5(2) . . . 99, 100

    s 7 . . . 192, 406

    s 103 . . . 548

    s 172 . . . 383, 631

    s 172(2)(a) . . . 630

    s 172(3) . . . 630

Road Traffic Offenders Act 1988—

    s 15 . . . 96

    s 15(2), (3) . . . 687

    s 16(1)(a) . . . 299

    s 31(1) . . . 54

    s 44(1) . . . 54

Road Traffic Regulation Act 1984—

    s 89(2) . . . 231, 583

Sale of Food and Drugs Act 1875 . . . 712

Sex Discrimination Act 1975—

    s 63A . . . 105

Sexual Offences Act 1956 . . . 164, 230

    s 39(1) . . . 131

Sexual Offences Act 1967 . . . 164

Sexual Offences Act 1985—

    s 1(1) . . . 712

Sexual Offences Act 2003 . . . 130, 335

    Part 1 . . . 130, 200, 211

    s 75 . . . 106, 214

    s 76 . . . 214, 687

    s 77 . . . 214

Sexual Offences (Amendment) Act 1976—

    s 2 . . . 210, 214

Solicitors Act 1974—

    s 18 . . . 341, 701

Stamp Act 1891—

    s 14 . . . 275

State Immunity Act 1978 . . . 139

Statute Law (Repeals) Act 1981 . . . 124

Supreme Court Act 1981—

    s 33 . . . 623

    s 33(2) . . . 656

    s 34 . . . 623

    s 50 . . . 553

    s 69(5) . . . 35

    s 72 . . . 626, 636

    s 72(3), (5) . . . 636

Supreme Court of Judicature Act 1875 . . . 4

    s 1(3) . . . 4

Taxes Management Act 1970—

    s 6 . . . 604

    s 20 . . . 631, 701

s 98(1) . . . 631
s 105 . . . 396, 397, 429
s 105(1) . . . 396
Sch1 . . . 604

Terrorism Act 2000 . . . 401, 632
s 11(1) . . . 100
s 11(2) . . . 100, 101
s 11(2)(b) . . . 100
s 117 . . . 101
s 118 . . . 101
s 118(2) . . . 106
Sch 14, para 6 . . . 401

Theft Act 1968 . . . 635–37
s 1(1) . . . 33
s 22(1) . . . 33, 688
s 27(3) . . . 50, 549, 550
s 27(3)(a) . . . 549
s 27(3)(b) . . . 550, 683
s 30(3) . . . 131
s 31 . . . 635, 637
s 31(1) . . . 635

Torts (Interference with Goods) Act 1977—
s 3(3) . . . 610

Trade Marks Act 1994—
s 92 . . . 101
s 92(5) . . . 96, 97

Treason Act 1795—
s 1 . . . 233

Video Recordings Act 1984—
s 11(1) . . . 77

Wills Act 1837—
s 21 . . . 275

Wireless Telegraphy Act 1949 . . . 116

Youth Justice and Criminal Evidence Act 1999
. . . 5, 128, 131, 133
ss 16–33 . . . 155
s 16 . . . 162, 164
s 16(1) . . . 161
s 16(1)(a) . . . 162, 164, 165
s 16(2) . . . 161
s 16(3)–(5) . . . 162
s 17 . . . 164
s 17(1) . . . 161, 162
s 17(2) . . . 162
s 17(4) . . . 162
s 18(1) . . . 156
s 19 . . . 135, 159, 161, 305
s 19(2) . . . 163, 164
s 19(3) . . . 163
s 20(1), (2) . . . 163
s 20(5) . . . 163
s 21 . . . 163–65, 314
s 22 . . . 165

s 23 . . . 156
s 23(1), (2) . . . 156
s 24 . . . 134, 142, 156, 163, 164
s 24(3) . . . 157
s 25 . . . 157
s 25(3), (4) . . . 157
s 26 . . . 157
s 27 . . . 135, 139, 146, 158–61, 163–66, 200
s 27(1) . . . 157
s 27(2) . . . 157, 159, 164
s 27(3) . . . 157
s 27(4)–(9) . . . 158
s 27(11) . . . 158
s 28 . . . 160, 163, 165, 166
s 28(1) . . . 159, 160
s 28(2) . . . 160
s 28(4)–(6) . . . 160
s 29 . . . 160
s 29(2), (3) . . . 160
s 30 . . . 161
s 31(1)–(4) . . . 166
s 31(8) . . . 166
s 32 . . . 166
s 34 . . . 200, 201
s 35 . . . 200, 201, 452
s 35(2) . . . 201
s 35(3)(a)–(d) . . . 164, 165, 200, 201
s 35(5) . . . 200
s 36 . . . 200, 201
s 36(1), (2) . . . 201
s 36(2)(a) . . . 201
s 36(3) . . . 201
s 36(4)(a), (b) . . . 201
s 37 . . . 200
s 37(4) . . . 201
s 38 . . . 200
s 38(1)–(3) . . . 201
s 38(4) . . . 201, 536
s 38(5) . . . 201
s 39 . . . 200, 201
s 41 . . . 204, 209, 581, 211, 212, 214–16, 218–20, 479, 485, 488, 489, 549
s 41(1) . . . 211, 212
s 41(2) . . . 212
s 41(2)(b) . . . 213, 218
s 41(3) . . . 212
s 41(3)(a) . . . 213, 214
s 41(3)(b) . . . 214, 215, 218
s 41(3)(c) . . . 214–17
s 41(3)(c)(i) . . . 211
s 41(4) . . . 212, 218
s 41(5) . . . 212, 218
s 41(5)(a) . . . 211
s 41(6) . . . 212, 219
s 41(7), (8) . . . 212
s 42 . . . 209, 479
s 42(1) . . . 215
s 42(1)(a) . . . 212

s 42(1)(b) . . . 211, 215
s 42(1)(c) . . . 211, 218
s 42(1)(d) . . . 211
s 42(2), (3) . . . 211
s 43 . . . 209, 479
s 43(1), (2) . . . 219
s 53 . . . 125, 323
s 53(1) . . . 124, 126–28, 131–33, 472
s 53(2) . . . 133
s 53(3) . . . 126, 128, 133, 134, 136, 314
s 53(4) . . . 128, 133
s 53(5) . . . 125, 128
s 54 . . . 134
s 54(1) . . . 134
s 54(2) . . . 121
s 54(3) . . . 135, 159
s 54(4)–(6) . . . 135

s 55(1) . . . 135
s 55(2) . . . 135, 136, 140
s 55(2)(b) . . . 136
s 55 (3) . . . 136
s 55(5)–(8) . . . 136
s 56(1) . . . 136
s 56(2) . . . 134, 136
s 56(3), (4) . . . 136
s 56(5) . . . 139
s 57 . . . 136
s 62 . . . 157, 162, 211

United States Federal Rules of Evidence 1975 . . .
     39
Rule 104(a) . . . 39
Rule 104(c) . . . 37
Rule 702 . . . 563

# TABLE OF STATUTORY INSTRUMENTS

Abortion Regulations 1968 (SI 1968/390) . . . 607

Civil Procedure Rules 1998 (SI 1998/3132) . . . 4,
    46, 147, 268, 573, 579
  Part 1 . . . 578
  r 1.1 . . . 47
  r 1.1(1) . . . 47, 202
  r 1.1(2) . . . 47, 48
  r 1.2 . . . 47, 202, 470
  r 1.4 . . . 470
  r 2.1 . . . 470
  r 14.1(1) . . . 714
  r 14.1(2) . . . 714
  r 14.1(5) . . . 714
  r 14.4–14.7 . . . 714
  r 16.4(1) . . . 8
  r 16.5(1) . . . 8
  r 16.5(1)(c) . . . 714
  r 16.5(3) . . . 8
  r 16.5(4) . . . 8
  r 16.5(5) . . . 8, 714
  r 18.1 . . . 623, 714
  Part 19 . . . 676
  Part 20 . . . 676
  r 22.1(6) . . . 148
  r 22.3 . . . 149
  r 26.5(3) . . . 714
  r 27.2 . . . 345
  r 27.2(1) . . . 46, 148
  r 27.2(1)(e) . . . 572
  r 27.4 . . . 148
  r 27.8 . . . 1
  r 27.8(4) . . . 139
  r 28.2 . . . 148, 580
  r 28.3 . . . 148, 580
  r 29.2 . . . 148, 580
  r 29.4 . . . 580
  Part 31 . . . 274, 279, 585
  r 31.4 . . . 263, 279
  r 31.6 . . . 619
  r 31.12 . . . 619
  r 31.17 . . . 270
  r 31.19 . . . 615
  r 31.19(6) . . . 615
  r 31.20 . . . 657, 659
  Part 32 . . . 149, 222
  r 32 . . . 647
  r 32.1 . . . 46, 148, 169, 347
  r 32.1(1) . . . 47, 147
  r 32.1(2) . . . 46–48, 58, 147
  r 32.1(3) . . . 48, 202
  r 32.2 . . . 169
  r 32.3 . . . 10, 141
  r 32.4 . . . 150

  r 32.4(1) . . . 148, 646
  r 32.4(2), (3) . . . 148
  r 32.4(3)(a) . . . 149
  r 32.5 . . . 149, 170
  r 32.5(2) . . . 149, 343, 647
  r 32.5(3) . . . 149, 150
  r 32.5(3)(a) . . . 647
  r 32.5(4) . . . 149
  r 32.5(5) . . . 647
  r 32.5(5)(b) . . . 348
  r 32.8 . . . 148
  r 32.9 . . . 150, 194
  r 32.10 . . . 149, 150, 646
  r 32.11 . . . 647
  r 32.14 . . . 148
  r 32.18 . . . 714
  r 32.19(1) . . . 274, 279
  Part 33 . . . 345
  r 33.2 . . . 345, 346
  r 33.3 . . . 345, 346
  r 33.4 . . . 347
  r 33.6(2)–(4) . . . 353
  r 33.6(8) . . . 353
  r 33.7 . . . 555
  r 34.2 . . . 123, 268, 270
  r 34.3–34.6 . . . 123
  r 34.13 . . . 272
  Part 35 . . . 572
  r 35 . . . 552, 562, 647
  r 35.1 . . . 572, 574
  r 35.3 . . . 572
  r 35.4 . . . 572, 573
  r 35.5 . . . 573
  r 35.6 . . . 576, 579
  r 35.6(2) . . . 577
  r 35.7 . . . 572–76
  r 35.8 . . . 572, 575
  r 35.9 . . . 575
  r 35.10(1), (2) . . . 577
  r 35.10(3) . . . 577, 578, 647
  r 35.10(4) . . . 577–79, 647
  r 35.11 . . . 579, 647
  r 35.12 . . . 578
  r 35.13 . . . 339, 579, 647
  r 35.14 . . . 580
  r 35.15 . . . 553
  Part 36 . . . 666
  r 36.20 . . . 666

County Court Rules 1981 (SI 1981/1687) . . . 4

Criminal Evidence (NI) Order 1988 (SI 1988/
    1987) (NI 120) . . . 439, 441
  art 4 . . . 439

Criminal Justice Act 2003 (Categories of
        Offences) Order 2004 (SI 2004/3346) . . .
        502
Criminal Procedure and Investigations Act 1996
        (Defence Disclosure Time Limits)
        Regulations 1997 (SI 1997/684)—
    reg 2 . . .  461
Criminal Procedure Rules 2005 (SI 2005/384) . . .
        6, 150, 333

    r 2 . . .  6
    r 3(3) . . .  6, 150
    r 3.9 . . .  150
    r 3.10 . . .  150
    r 24 . . .  333, 433, 580
    r 24.1 . . .  581, 582
    r 24.1(1) . . .  582
    r 24.2 . . .  581
    r 24.3 . . .  582
    r 34 . . .  329
    r 35 . . .  548
Crown Court (Criminal Procedure and
        Investigations Act 1996) (Disclosure)
        **Rules 1997 (SI 1997/698) . . . 593**
Crown Court (Special Measures Directions
        and Directions Prohibiting
        Cross-Examination) Rules 2002
        (SI 2002/1688) . . .  163

Disciplinary Tribunals Regulations 1993—
    reg 10 . . .  109

Employment Tribunals (Constitution etc)
        Regulations 2001 (SI 2001/1171)—
    reg 11(1) . . .  1

Family Proceedings Rules 1991—
    r 10.14 . . .  359

Magistrates' Courts (Criminal Procedure and
        Investigations Act 19961996)
        (Disclosure) Rules 1997 (SI 1997/703)
        . . . 593
Merchant Shipping (Returns of Births and
        Deaths) Regulations . . .  1979
    (SI 1979/1577) . . .  53
Misuse of Drugs Regulations 1973
        (SI 1973/797) . . .  91

National Police Records (Recordable Offences)
        Regulations 1985 (SI 1985/1941) . . .  459

Rehabilitation of Offenders Act (Exceptions)
        Order 1975 (SI 1975/1023)—
    Sch 3 . . .  221
Rules of the Supreme Court 1965 (SI 1965/1779)
        . . . 4

    Ord 24, r 8 . . .  268, 608
    Ord 38, r 2A . . .  647

**European Materials**
European Convention of Human Rights . . .  3,
        63, 76, 78
    Art 3 . . .  120, 386
    Art 6 . . .  75, 78, 79, 81, 88, 89, 96, 98, 100, 101,
        141, 161, 166, 300, 307–9, 313, 322, 328,
        446, 448, 452, 591, 593, 594, 630–33, 662
    Art 6(1) . . .  78, 342, 420, 593, 631
    Art 6(2) . . .  87, 93–95, 97
    Art 6(3) . . .  309
    Art 6(3)(c) . . .  69
    Art 8 . . .  58, 77, 78, 651, 662
    Art 10 . . .  609, 610, 612
    Art 10(2) . . .  614

# TABLE OF CASES

## A

A (minors), Re [1992] 1 All ER 153, [1991]
1 WLR 1026, 89 LGR 796, [1992] 1 FLR 439,
[1992] Fam Law 98, 8 BMLR 89, sub nom Re C
and L [1991] FCR 351; affd sub nom C,
Re [1992] 1 FCR 57, CA . . . 595

Ablitt v Mills & Reeve (a firm) (1995) Times,
25 October . . . 658

Abrath v North Eastern Rly Co (1883) 11 QBD
440, 47 JP 692, 52 LJQB 620, 15 Cox CC 354,
32 WR 50, 49 LT 618, CA; on appeal 11 App
Cas 247, 50 JP 659, 55 LJQB 457, [1886–90]
All ER Rep 179, 55 LT 63, 2 TLR 416,
HL . . . 103

Adamson v Waveney District Council [1997]
2 All ER 898, 161 JP 787 . . . 551

Adelaide Chemical and Fertilizer Co Ltd v Carlyle
(1940) 64 CLR 514 . . . 368

Admiral Management Services Ltd v Para-Protect
Europe Ltd [2002] 1 WLR 272, ChD562

Aegis Blaze, The [1986] 1 Lloyd's Rep 203,
130 Sol Jo 15, CA . . . 656

Agassiz v London Tramway Co (1872)
21 WR 199, 27 LT 492 . . . 25

Ahmed v Brumfitt (1967) 112 Sol Jo 32,
CA . . . 181

Ainsworth v Wilding [1900] 2 Ch 315, 69 LJ Ch
695, 48 WR 539, 44 Sol Jo 529 . . . 641

Air Canada v Secretary of State for Trade [1983]
2 AC 394, [1983] 2 WLR 494, 126 Sol Jo 709,
sub nom Air Canada v Secretary of State for
Trade (No 2) [1983] 1 All ER 161, CA; affd
[1983] 2 AC 394, [1983] 1 All ER 910, sub nom
Air Canada v Secretary of State for Trade
[1983] 2 WLR 494, 127 Sol Jo 205, HL . . . 590,
603, 619–21

Ajami v Comptroller of Customs [1954] 1 WLR
1405, 98 Sol Jo 803, PC . . . 561

Ajodha v The State [1982] AC 204, [1981] 2 All
ER 193, [1981] 3 WLR 1, 73 Cr App Rep 129,
125 Sol Jo 305, PC . . . 36, 122, 414, 415, 421

Ajum Goolam Hossen & Co v Union Marine
Insurance Co [1901] AC 362, 70 LJPC 34,
9 Asp MLC 167, 84 LT 366, 17 TLR 376,
PC . . . 689

Aldersey, Re, Gibson v Hall [1905] 2 Ch 181,
74 L7 Ch 548, [1904–7] All ER Rep 644,
92 LT 826 . . . 699

Alderson v Clay (1816) 1 Stark 405 . . . 266, 355

Alexander v Arts Council of Wales [2001] 4 All
ER 205, CA . . . 42

Alexander v Rayson [1936] 1 KB 169, 105 LJKB
148, [1935] All ER Rep 185, 80 Sol Jo 15, 154
LT 205, 52 TLR 131, CA . . . 441

Al Fayed v Metropolitan Police Commissioner
[2002] EWCA Civ 780 . . . 659

Alfred Crompton Amusement Machines Ltd v
Customs and Excise Commissioners [1974]
AC 405 . . . 605, 607, 618, 619, 638

Ali (Mohammed Fazor) v Secretary of State for
the Home Department [1988] Imm AR 274,
CA . . . 116

Alivon v Furnival (1834) 1 Cr M & R 277, 3 Dowl
202, 3 LJ Ex 241, 4 Tyr 751, [1824–34] All ER
Rep 705 . . . 269

Allen v UK (2002) 36 EHRR 143 . . . 81, 632

Alli v Alli [1965] 3 All ER 480, 130 JP 6, 109 Sol Jo
629 . . . 244

Alves v DPP [1992] 4 All ER 787, HL . . . 197

AM & S Europe Ltd v EC Commission [1983]
QB 878 . . . 638

Amore v R [1994] 1 WLR 547, 99 Cr App Rep
279, 138 Sol Jo LB 78, PC . . . 252

Anderson v Bank of British Columbia (1876)
2 Ch D 644, 45 LJ Ch 449, 3 Char Pr Cas 212,
24 WR 624, [1874–80] All ER Rep 396, 35 LT
76, CA . . . 644

Anderson v Morice (1875) LR 10 CP 609, 44
LJCP 341, 3 Asp MLC 31, 24 WR 30, 33 LT 355,
Ex Ch; affd 1 App Cas 713, 46 LJQB 11, 3 Asp
MLC 290, 25 WR 14, 35 LT 566, HL . . . 689

Anderson v R [1972] AC 100, [1971] 3 All ER
768, [1971] 3 WLR 718, 115 Sol Jo 791,
PC . . . 276, 571

Anderson v Weston (1840) 6 Bing NC 296,
9 LJCP 194, 4 Jur 105, 8 Scott 583 . . . 275

Anderson v Whalley (1852) 3 Car & Kir 54,
19 LTOS 365 . . . 174

An Inquiry Under the Company Securities
(Insider Dealing) Act 1985, Re [1988] 1 All ER
203, HL . . . 611, 614

Ankin v London and North Eastern Rly Co
[1930] 1 KB 527, 99 LJKB 293, [1929] All ER
Rep 65, 74 Sol Jo 26, 142 LT 368, 46 TLR 172,
CA . . . 603

Anthony v Anthony (1919) 35 TLR 559 . . . 603

Aquarius Financial Enterprises Inc v Certain
Underwriters at Lloyd's (2001) NLJ
694 . . . 148

Arab Monetary Fund v Hashim [1989] 3 All ER
466, [1989] 1 WLR 565, 133 Sol Jo 749, [1989]
26 LS Gaz R 35 . . . 627

Arab Monetary Fund v Hashim (No 2) [1990]
    1 All ER 673 . . . 627, 671

Armory v Delamirie (1722) 1 Stra 505, 93 ER 664,
    [1558–1774] All ER Rep 121 . . . 276

Armstrong v First York Ltd (2005) The Times,
    19 Jan . . . 571

Arthurton v R [2004] 2 Cr App R 559, PC . . . 473

Ashburton (Lord) v Pape [1913] 2 Ch 469,
    82 LJ Ch 527, [1911–13] All ER Rep 708,
    57 Sol Jo 644, 109 LT 381, 29 TLR 623,
    CA . . . 213, 215, 223, 224, 657, 658, 660

Ashworth Hospital Authority v MGN Ltd [2001]
    1 WLR 515 . . . 610, 612, 614

Asiatic Petroleum Co Ltd v Anglo Persian Oil Co
    Ltd [1916] 1 KB 822, 85 LJKB 1075, [1916–17]
    All ER Rep 637, 60 Sol Jo 417, 114 LT 645,
    32 TLR 367, CA . . . 587

Associated Provincial Picture Houses Ltd v
    Wednesbury Corpn [1948] 1 KB 223, [1947]
    2 All ER 680, 45 LGR 635, 112 JP 55, [1948]
    LJR 190, 92 Sol Jo 26, 177 LT 641, 63 TLR 623,
    CA . . . 65, 237, 435

Atlan v UK [2002] 34 EHRR 833 . . . 593

A-G v Bowman (1791) 2 Bos & P 532n . . . 468

A-G v Good (1825) M'Cle & Yo 286 . . . 289

A-G v Hitchcock (1847) 11 JP 904, 2 New Pract
    Cas 321, 16 LJ Ex 259, 1 Exch 91, 11 Jur 478,
    9 LTOS 270 . . . 25, 219, 220, 223

A-G v Lundin (1982) 75 Cr App Rep 90, [1982]
    Crim LR 296, DC . . . 609

A-G v Mulholland [1963] 2 QB 477, [1963]
    1 All ER 767, [1963] 2 WLR 658, 107 Sol Jo
    154, CA . . . 609

A-G v Radloff (1854) 10 Exch 84 . . . 468

A-G v Theakstone (1820) 8 Price 89 . . . 360

A-G of Hong Kong v Yip Kai-foon [1988]
    AC 642, [1988] 1 All ER 153, [1988] 2 WLR
    326, 86 Cr App Rep 368, 132 Sol Jo 264, [1988]
    3 LS Gaz R 33, PC . . . 688

A-G's Reference (No 3 of 1979) (1979) 69 Cr App
    Rep 411, [1979] Crim LR 786, 123 Sol Jo 704,
    CA . . . 175

A-G's Reference (No 3 of 1999) [2001] 1 All ER
    577, HL . . . 67

A-G's Reference (No 2 of 2000) [2001] 1 Cr App
    R 503 . . . 40

A-G's Reference (No 7 of 2000) [2001] 2 Cr App
    R 286, CA . . . 632

A-G's Reference (No 2 of 2002) [2003] 1 Cr App
    R 321 . . . 278

A-G's Reference (No 1 of 2003) [2003] 2 Cr App
    R 453, CA . . . 373

A-G's Reference (No 4 of 2002) [2005] 1 All ER
    237 . . . 93, 98, 99

A-G's Reference (No 1 of 2004) [2004] 1 WLR
    2111 . . . 97, 99

A-G (Rudely) v Kenny (1960) 94 ILTR
    185 . . . 584

Augustien v Challis (1847) 2 New Pract Cas 486,
    17 LJ Ex 73, 1 Exch 279, 10 LTOS 115 . . . 266

Aveson v Lord Kinnaird (1805) 6 East 188,
    sub nom Avison v Lord Kinnaird 2 Smith KB
    286 . . . 376

Axon v Axon (1937) 59 CLR 395,
    HC of A . . . 692, 700


B

B (A Minor) v DPP [2000] 2 AC 428 . . . . . . 571

B v Auckland District Law Society [2003]
    2 AC 736, PC . . . 650, 651, 660

B v B [1992] 1 FCR 223, [1991] 2 FLR 487, [1991]
    Fam Law 518 . . . 595

B v Chief Constable of Avon and Somerset
    Constabulary [2001] 1 WLR 340, DC . . . 114

Bains v DPP [1992] Crim LR 795 . . . 137

Baker v Rabetts (1954) 118 JPN 303 . . . 137

Balabel v Air India [1988] Ch 317, [1988]
    2 All ER 246, [1988] 2 WLR 1036, 132 Sol Jo
    699, [1988] NLJR 85, CA . . . 394, 642, 643

Baldwin and Francis Ltd v Patents Appeal
    Tribunal [1959] AC 663, [1959] 2 All ER 433,
    [1959] 2 WLR 826, [1959] RPC 221, 103 Sol Jo
    451, HL . . . 708

Balfour v Foreign and Commonwealth Office
    [1994] 2 All ER 588, [1994] 1 WLR 681, [1994]
    ICR 277, CA . . . 587, 597, 621

Banbury Peerage Case (1811) 1 Sim & St 153,
    [1803–13] All ER Rep 171 . . . 694

Bank of England v Riley [1992] Ch 475, [1992]
    1 All ER 769, [1992] 2 WLR 840, CA . . . 630

Bank of England v Vagliano Bros [1891] AC 107,
    55 JP 676, 60 LJQB 145, 39 WR 657, [1891–4]
    All ER Rep 93, 64 LT 353, 7 TLR 333, HL . . .
    387

Bankers' Books Evidence Act 1879, Re, R v Bono
    (1913) 29 TLR 635, DC . . . 272

Banque Keyser Ullmann SA v Skandia (UK)
    Insurance Co Ltd [1986] 1 Lloyd's Rep 336,
    CA . . . 653, 654

Barclays Bank plc v Eustice [1995] 4 All ER 511,
    [1995] 1 WLR 1238, [1995] 2 BCLC 630,
    [1995] BCC 978, [1995] NLJR 1503, CA . . .
    652

Barford v Barford and McLeod [1918] P 140, 87
    LJP 68, 62 Sol Jo 439, 118 LT 820, 34 TLR 306
    . . . 561

Barings plc, Re [1998] 1 All ER 673, Ch D . . . 646

Barings plc v Coopers and Lybrand [2001] EWCA Civ 1163 . . . 21

Barings plc, Re. See Secretary of State for Trade and Industry v Baker

Barker v Wilson [1980] 2 All ER 81, [1980] 1 WLR 884, 70 Cr App Rep 283, 144 JP 425, [1980] Crim LR 373, 124 Sol Jo 326 . . . 271

Barking and Dagenham London Borough Council v O [1993] Fam 295, [1993] 4 All ER 59, [1993] 3 WLR 493, [1993] 2 FLR 651, [1993] Fam Law 670, sub nom Re B (minors) [1993] 2 FCR 241 . . . 654

Barkway v South Wales Transport Co Ltd [1949] 1 KB 54, [1948] 2 All ER 460, [1948] LJR 1921, 92 Sol Jo 528, 64 TLR 462, CA; revsd [1950] AC 185, [1950] 1 All ER 392, 114 JP 172, 94 Sol Jo 128, 66 (pt 1) TLR 597, HL . . . 29, 704

Barlow Clowes Gilt Managers Ltd, Re [1992] Ch 208, [1991] 4 All ER 385, [1992] 2 WLR 36, [1991] BCLC 750, [1991] BCC 608 . . . 607

Barnes v Chief Constable of Durham [1997] 2 Cr App Rep 505 . . . 192

Baron de Bode's Case (1845) 8 QB 208 . . . 561

Barrett v Long (1851) 3 HL Cas 395, 18 LTOS 145, HL . . . 469

Bastable v Bastable and Sanders [1968] 3 All ER 701, [1968] 1 WLR 1684, 112 Sol Jo 542, CA . . . 118, 691

Bastin v Carew (1824) Ry & M 127 . . . 186

Bater v Bater [1951] P 35, [1950] 2 All ER 458, 48 LGR 466, 114 JP 416, 94 Sol Jo 533, 66 (pt 2) TLR 589, CA . . . 110, 115, 117, 118

Battie-Wrightson, Re, Cecil v Battie-Wrightson [1920] 2 Ch 330, 89 LJ Ch 550, [1920] All ER Rep 597, 64 Sol Jo 585, 124 LT 84, 36 TLR 693 . . . 265

Bayer v Clarkson Puckle Overseas Ltd [1989] NLJR 256 . . . 147, 566

Beare v Garrod (1915) 85 LJKB 717, 113 LT 673, 8 BWCC 474, CA . . . 203

Beatson v Skene (1860) 5 H & N 838, 29 LJ Ex 430, 6 Jur NS 780, 8 WR 544, 2 LT 378 . . . 597

Beazer (C H) (Commercial and Industrial) Ltd v R M Smith Ltd (1984) 3 Const LJ 196 . . . 658

Beck v Ministry of Defence [2004] PIQR 1 . . . 579

Beckford v R (1993) 97 Cr App Rep 409, [1993] Crim LR 944, PC . . . 251, 253

Beckles v UK [2001] 31 EHRR 1 . . . 451

Beckwith v Sydebotham (1807) 1 Camp 116 . . . 565

Beech v Jones (1848) 5 CB 696 . . . 175

Beer v W H Clench (1930) Ltd [1936] 1 All ER 449, 34 LGR 187, 100 JP 191, 24 Ry & Can Tr Cas 118, 30 Cox CC 364, 80 Sol Jo 266, 154 LT 428, 52 TLR 300, DC . . . 357

Benedetto v R [2003] 1 WLR 1545, PC . . . 241

Benham Ltd v Kythira Investments Ltd [2003] EWCA Civ 1794 . . . 41

Bennett v Metropolitan Police Commissioner [1995] 2 All ER 1, [1995] 1 WLR 488 . . . 617

Beresford v St Albans Justices (1905) 69 JP 520, 22 TLR 1, DC . . . 16

Berger v Raymond & Son Ltd [1984] 1 WLR 625, 128 Sol Jo 223 . . . 469

Berkeley Peerage Case (1811) 4 Camp 401, [1803–13] All ER Rep 201, HL: . . . 366, 367

Bermudez v Chief Constable of Avon and Somerset [1988] Crim LR 452 . . . 330

Berry Trade Ltd v Moussavi [2003] EWCA Civ 715, [2003] All ER (D) 315 (May), CA . . . 665

Berryman v Wise (1791) 4 Term Rep 366 . . . 701

Bessela v Stern (1877) 2 CPD 265, 42 JP 197, 46 LJCP 467, 25 WR 561, 37 LT 88, CA . . . 355

Bhimji v Chatwani (No 3) [1992] 4 All ER 912, sub nom Bhimji v Chatwani (No 2) [1992] 1 WLR 1158, sub nom Chatwani v Bhimji (No 2) [1992] BCLC 387 . . . 627

BHP Billiton Petroleum Ltd v Dalmine SpA [2003] BLR 271, CA . . . 103

Bird v Keep [1918] 2 KB 692, 87 LJKB 1199, 62 Sol Jo 666, 118 LT 633, 34 TLR 513, 11 BWCC 133, CA . . . 361, 677

Bishopsgate Investment Management Ltd (in provisional liquidation) v Maxwell [1993] Ch 1, [1992] 2 All ER 856, [1992] 2 WLR 991, [1992] BCLC 475, [1992] BCC 222, [1992] 18 LS Gaz R 35, 136 Sol Jo LB 69, CA . . . 601, 626

Black & Decker Inc v Flymo Ltd (1991) 3 All ER 158, [1991] 1 WLR 753, [1991] FSR 93 . . . 647

Blake v DPP (1992) 97 Cr App Rep 169, [1993] Crim LR 283, [1992] 44 LS Gaz R 34 . . . 601

Blunt v Park Lane Hotel Ltd [1942] 2 KB 253, [1942] 2 All ER 187, 111 LJKB 706, 167 LT 359, 58 TLR 356, CA . . . 214, 239, 625

Blyth v Blyth and Pugh [1966] AC 643, [1966] 1 All ER 524, [1966] 2 WLR 634, 110 Sol Jo 148, HL . . . :117, 118, 691

BNP Paribas v Mezzotero UKEAT/0218/04/RN . . . 664, 666

Bolsom (Sidney) Investment Trust Ltd v E Karmios & Co (London) Ltd [1956] 1 QB 529, [1956] 1 All ER 536, [1956] 2 WLR 625, 100 Sol Jo 169, 167 Estates Gazette 179, CA . . . 613

Bowen v Norman [1938] 1 KB 689, [1938] 2 All ER 776, 36 LGR 192, 102 JP 123, 107 LJKB 273,

30 Cox CC 674, 82 Sol Jo 77, 158 LT 257,
54 TLR 342 . . . 695

Bowker v Williamson (1889) 5 TLR 382 . . . 275

Bowman v Hodgson (1867) LR 1 P & D 362,
31 JP 678, 36 LJP & M 124, 16 LT 392 . . . 274

Bow Spring (Owners) v Manzanillo II (Owners)
[2004] All ER 899, CA . . . 553

Boyle v Wiseman (1855) 24 LJ Ex 284, 11 Exch
360, 1 Jur NS 894, 3 WR 577, 3 CLR 1071,
25 LTOS 203 . . . 266

Bradley v Ricardo (1831) 8 Bing 57, 1 LJCP 36,
1 Moo & S 133 . . . 194

Bradshaw, Re, Blandy v Willis [1938] 4 All ER
143, 82 Sol Jo 909 . . . 694

Bradshaw v Bradshaw [1956] P 274n, [1955]
3 WLR 965n, 99 Sol Jo 890 . . . 697

Brady (Inspector of Taxes) v Group Lotus Car
Companies plc [1987] 3 All ER 1050, [1987]
STC 635, 60 TC 359, [1987] LS Gaz R 2536,
CA . . . 84

Brailey v Rhodesia Consolidated Ltd [1910]
2 Ch 95, 79 LJ Ch 494, 17 Mans 222,
54 Sol Jo 475, 102 LT 805 . . . 561

Bramblevale Ltd, Re [1970] Ch 128, [1969]
3 All ER 1062, [1969] 3 WLR 699, [1971]
3 WLR 821n, 113 Sol Jo 775, CA . . . 114

Brandao v Barnett (1846) 12 CB&Fin 787 . . . 710

Bratty v A-G for Northern Ireland [1963] AC 386,
[1961] 3 All ER 523, [1961] 3 WLR 965, 46 Cr
App Rep 1, 105 Sol Jo 865, HL . . . 106–8, 120,
689

Breadalbane Case, Campbell v Campbell (1867)
LR 1 Sc & Div 182, 39 Sc Jur 576, 5 M 115,
HL . . . 693, 694

Brenan and Galen's Case (1847) 10 QB 492,
2 Cox CC 193, 11 Jur 775, sub nom R v Brenan
and Gallan 11 JP 727, 16 LJQB 289· sub nom
Re Brennan and Gillon 9 LTOS 147 . . . 708

Brennan v UK [2002] Crim LR 217 . . . 69

Brewster v Sewell (1820) 3 B & Ald 296 . . . 9, 36,
268

Briamore Manufacturing Ltd (in liquidation),
Re [1986] 3 All ER 132, [1986] 1 WLR 1429,
130 Sol Jo 924, [1987] L5 Gaz R 36, [1986] NLJ
Rep 642 . . . 658

Brierley v Brierley and Williams [1918] P 257,
87 LJP 153, 62 Sol Jo 704, 119 LT 343,
34 TLR 458 . . . 361

Brighty v Pearson [1938] 4 All ER 127, 36 LGR
664, 102 JP 522, 31 Cox CC 177, 82 Sol Jo 910,
159 LT 619, DC . . . 231

Briginshaw v Briginshaw (1938)
60 CLR 336 . . . 117

Brinks Ltd v Abu-Saleh (No 2) [1995] 4 All ER 74,
[1995] 1 WLR 1478 . . . 672

Briscoe v Briscoe [1968] P 501, [1966] 1 All ER
465, [1966] 2 WLR 205, 130 JP 124, 109 Sol Jo
996 . . . 147

Bristol Corpn v Cox (1884) 26 Ch D 678,
53 LJ Ch 1144, 33 WR 255, 50 LT 719 . . . 640

Bristow v Sequeville (1850) 3 Car & Kir 64,
19 LJ Ex 289, 5 Exch 275, 14 Jur 674 . . . 561

British Coal Corpn v Dennis Rye Ltd (No 2)
[1988] 3 All ER 816, [1988] 1 WLR 1113,
132 Sol Jo 1430, CA . . . 660

British Railways Board v Herrington [1972]
AC 877, [1972] 1 Ail ER 749, [1972] 2 WLR
537, 116 Sol Jo 178, 223 Estates Gazette 939,
HL . . . 16

British Steel Corpn v Granada Television Ltd
[1981] AC 1096, [1981] 1 All ER 417, [1980]
3 WLR 774; on appeal [1981] AC 1096, 1121,
[1981] 1 All ER 417, 435, [1980] 3 WLR 774,
797, 124 Sol Jo 376, CA; affd [1981] AC 1096,
1144, [1981] 1 All ER 417, 452, [1980] 3 WLR
774, 818, 124 Sol Jo 812, HL . . . 608, 628, 629

British Thomson-Houston Co v British Insulated
and Helsby Cables Ltd [1924] 2 Ch 160, 93 LJ
Ch 467, 41 RPC 345, [1924] All ER Rep 446,
68 Sol Jo 560, 131 LT 688, 40 TLR 581, CA;
affd 42 RPC 180, 41 TLR 259, HL . . . 357

Brizzalari v R (2004) The Times, 3 Mar, [2004]
EWCA Crim 310 . . . 450

Broome v Broome (Edmundson cited) [1955]
P 190, [1955] 1 All ER 201, [1955] 2 WLR 401,
99 Sol Jo 114 . . . 586, 603

Brown v Foster (1857) 21 JP 214, 1 H & N 736,
26 LJ Ex 249, 3 Jur NS 245, 5 WR 292,
28 LTOS 274 . . . 648

Brown v Matthews [1990] Ch 662, [1990]
2 All ER 155, [1990] 2 WLR 879, sub nom B v
M [1990] FCR 581, [1990] 2 FLR 46, [1990]
Fam Law 346, [1990] 13 LS Gaz R 44,
CA . . . 595

Brown v Stott [2001] 2 WLR 817, PC . . . 630, 631

Brown (Christopher) Ltd v Genossenschaft
Osterreichischer Waldbesitzer
Holzwirtschaftsbertriebe Registrierte GmbH
[1954] 1 QB 8, [1953] 2 All ER 1039, [1953]
3 WLR 689, [1953] 2 Lloyd's Rep 373,
97 Sol Jo 744 . . . 701

Browne v Dunn (1893) 6 R 67, HL . . . 205

Bruce v Garden (1869) 5 Ch App 32, 39 LJ
Ch 334, 18 WR 384, 22 LT 595 . . . 355

Brutus v Cozens [1973] AC 854, [1972] 2 All ER
1297, [1972] 3 WLR 521, 56 Cr App Rep 799,
136 JP 636, 116 Sol Jo 647, HL . . . 33, 34

Bryce v Bryce [1933] P 83, 102 LJP 1, [1932]
All ER Rep 788, 77 Sol Jo 49, 148 LT 351,
49 TLR 177 . . . 375

Buckingham v Daily News Ltd [1956] 2 QB 534, [1956] 2 All ER 904, [1956] 3 WLR 375, 100 Sol Jo 528, CA . . . 30, 279, 280

Buckley v Law Society (No 2) [1984] 3 All ER 313, [1984] 1 WLR 1101, 128 Sol Jo 565, [1984] LS Gaz R 3017 . . . 596

Bullard v R [1957] AC 635, [1961] 3 All ER 470n, [1957] 3 WLR 656, 42 Cr App Rep 1, 121 JP 576, 101 Sol Jo 797, PC . . . 40, 82, 106

Bulley's Settlement, Re [1886] WN 80 . . . 364

Bullivant v A-G for Victoria [1901] AC 196, 70 LJKB 645, 50 WR 1, [1900–3] All ER Rep 812, 84 LT 737, 17 TLR 457, HL . . . 639

Bullock v Bullock [1960] 2 All ER 307, [1960] 1 WLR 975, 104 Sol Jo 685 . . . 698

Bumper Development Corpn Ltd v Metropolitan Police Commissioner (Union of India, claimants) [1991] 4 All ER 638, [1991] 1 WLR 1362, 135 Sol Jo 382, CA . . . 555

Burmah Oil Co Ltd v Bank of England [1980] AC 1090, [1979] 3 All ER 700, [1979] 3 WLR 722, 123 Sol Jo 786, HL . . . 588, 589, 603, 615, 619–21

Burns v Edman [1970] 2 QB 541, [1970] 1 All ER 886, [1970] 2 WLR 1005, [1970] 1 Lloyd's Rep 137, 114 Sol Jo 356 . . . 707

Burr v Ware RDC [1939] 2 All ER 688, CA . . . 357

Burrough v Martin (1809) 2 Camp 112 . . . 174

Burton v Gilbert [1984] RTR 162, 147 JP 441 . . . 231

Butler v Board of Trade [1971] Ch 680, [1970] 3 All ER 593, [1970] 3 WLR 822, 114 Sol Jo 604 . . . 651, 660

Butler v Mountgarret (1859) 7 HL Cas 633, HL . . . 366

Buttes Gas and Oil Co v Hammer (No 3) [1981] QB 223, [1980] 3 All ER 475, [1980] 3 WLR 668, 124 Sol Jo 630, CA; revsd [1982] AC 888, [1981] 3 All ER 616, [1981] 3 WLR 787, 125 Sol Jo 776, HL . . . 598, 641, 645, 646

Byrne v Boadle (1863) 2 H & C 722, 33 LJ Ex 13, 10 Jur NS 1107, 3 New Rep 162, 12 WR 279, 159 ER 299, 9 LT 450, [1861–73] All ER Rep Ext 1528 . . . 703

C

C (a minor) (care proceedings: disclosure), Re [1997] 2 WLR 322, CA . . . 634

C v C and C [1972] 3 All ER 577, [1972] 1 WLR 1335, 136 JP 775, 116 Sol Jo 663 . . . 276

C v DPP [1996] AC 1, [1995] 2 All ER 43, [1995] 2 WLR 383, [1995] RTR 261, [1995] 2 Cr App Rep 166, [1995] 1 FLR 933, [1995] Fam Law 400, 159 JP 269, [1995] Crim LR 801, [1995] NLJR 416, HL . . . 4

Calcraft v Guest [1898] 1 QB 759, 67 LJQB 505, 46 WR 420, [1895–9] All ER Rep 346, 42 Sol Jo 343, 78 LT 283, CA . . . 56, 655, 656, 659

Calderbank v Calderbank [1976] Fam 93, [1975] 3 All ER 333, [1975] 3 WLR 586, [1976] Fam Law 93, 119 Sol Jo 490, CA . . . 240, 664, 666

Calenti v North Middlesex NHS Trust (2001) LTL 10 Apr, QBD . . . 573

Callis v Gunn [1964] 1 QB 495, [1963] 3 All ER 677, [1963] 3 WLR 931, 48 Cr App Rep 36, 128 JP 41, 107 Sol Jo 831, DC . . . 59, 379

Calvert v Flower (1836) 7 C & P 386 . . . 206

Camelot Group plc v Centaur Communications Ltd [1999] QB 124, [1998] 1 All ER 251, [1998] 2 WLR 379, [1998] IRLR 80, [1997] 43 LS Gaz R 30, [1997] NLJR 1618, 142 Sol Jo LB 19, [1998] EMLR 1, CA . . . 612

Campbell v DPP [2003] All ER (D) 212 . . . 69

Campbell v Tameside Metropolitan Borough Council [1982] QB 1065, [1982] 2 All ER 791, [1982] 3 WLR 74, 80 LGR 700, 126 Sol Jo 361, CA . . . 219, 229, 590, 617

Campbell v Wallsend Slipway and Engineering Co Ltd [1978] ICR 1015, [1977] Crim LR 351, 121 Sol Jo 334 . . . 702

Campbell and Cosans v United Kingdom (1982) 4 EHRR 293, ECtHR . . . 387

Canada and Dominion Sugar Co Ltd v Canadian National (West Indies) Steamships Ltd [1947] AC 46, [1947] LJR 385, 62 TLR 666, PC . . . 594, 613

Carlson v Townsend [2001] 3 All ER 663, CA . . . 576

Carl Zeiss Stiftung v Rayner and Keeler Ltd (No 2) [1967] 1 AC 853, [1966] 2 All ER 536, [1966] 3 WLR 125, [1967] RPC 497, 110 Sol Jo 425, HL . . . 710

CAS (Nominees) Ltd v Nottingham Forest plc [2001] 1 All ER 954, Ch D . . . 641

Castle v Cross [1985] 1 All ER 87, [1984] 1 WLR 1372, [1985] RTR 62, [1984] Crim LR 682, 128 Sol Jo 855 . . . 297, 299, 690

Catherina Maria, The (1866) LR 1 A & E 53, 12 Jur NS 380 . . . 360

Cecil v Battie-Wrightson [1920] Ch 330 . . . 265

Central London Property Trust Ltd v High Trees House Ltd [1947] KB 130, [1956] 1 All ER 256n, [1947] LJR 77, 175 LT 332, 62 TLR 557 . . . 614

Chalkey v United Kingdom [2003] Crim LR 51 . . . 78

Chambers v DPP [1995] Crim LR 896, CA . . . 34

Chambers v Mississippi 410 US 295 (1973),
US SC . . . 315

Chandler v Church [1987] NLJ Rep 451 . . . 653

Chandrasekera (alias Alisandiri) v R [1937]
AC 220, [1936] 3 All ER 865, 106 LJPC 30,
30 Cox CC 546, 80 Sol Jo 1012, 156 LT 204,
53 TLR 137, PC . . . 286, 294

Chan Kau (alias Chan Kai) v R [1955] AC 206,
[1955] 1 All ER 266, [1955] 2 WLR 192,
99 Sol Jo 72, PC . . . 106

Chan Wei-Keung v R [1967] 2 AC 160, [1967]
2 WLR 552, 51 Cr App Rep 257, 111 Sol Jo 73,
sub nom Chan Wai-Keung v R [1967] 1 All ER
948, PC . . . 242, 419

Chapman v Kirke [1948] 2 KB 450, [1948]
2 All ER 556, 46 LGR 507, 112 JP 399, [1949]
LJR 255, 92 Sol Jo 558, 64 TLR 519, DC . . . 707

Chapman v Walton (1833) 10 Bing 57, 2 LJCP
210, 3 Moo & S 389, [1824–34]
All ER Rep 384 . . . 20

Chappell v DPP (1988) 89 Cr App Rep 82 . . . 15

Chappell (Fred) Ltd v National Car Parks Ltd
(1987) Times, 22 May . . . 105

Chapronière v Mason (1905) 21 TLR 633,
CA . . . 703

Chard v Chard (otherwise Northcott) [1956]
P 259, [1955] 3 All ER 721, [1955] 3 WLR 954,
99 Sol Jo 890 . . . 26, 684, 688, 696, 697

Chatterton v Secretary of State for India in
Council [1895] 2 QB 189, 59 JP 596, 64 LJQB
676, 14 R 504, [1895–9] All ER Rep 1035,
72 LT 858, 11 TLR 462, CA . . . 597, 616

Cheddar Valley Engineering Ltd v Chaddlewood
Homes Ltd [1992] 4 All ER 942, [1992]
1 WLR 820, [1992] 27 LS Gaz R 35 . . . 664

Chief Constable of Avon and Somerset
Constabulary v Jest [1986] RTR 372, [1986]

Crim LR 62 . . . 41

Chief Constable of Greater Manchester v
McNally [2002] 2 Cr App R 617, CA . . . 602

Chipchase v Chipchase [1939] P 391, [1939]
3 All ER 895, 108 LJP 154, 83 Sol Jo 798,
55 TLR 1067 . . . 697, 699

Chocoladefabriken Lindt and Sprungli AG v
Nestlé Co Ltd [1978] RPC 287 . . . 664

Clark (H) (Doncaster) Ltd v Wilkinson [1965]
Ch 694, [1965] 1 All ER 934, [1965] 2 WLR
751, 109 Sol Jo 110, CA . . . 714

Clarke v Clarke (1879) 5 LR Ir 47 . . . 274, 277

Clarke v Saffery (1824) Ry & M 126 . . . 196

Cleveland County Council v F [1995] 2 All ER
236, [1995] 1 WLR 785, [1995] 3 FCR 174,
[1995] 1 FLR 797, [1995] Fam Law 473 . . . 595,
634

Clifford v Clifford [1961] 3 All ER 231, [1961]
1 WLR 1274, 105 Sol Jo 709 . . . 222

Clingham v Kensington and Chelsea London
Borough Council (2001) The Times, 20 Feb,
DC . . . 342

Closmadeuc v Carrel (1856) 18 CB 36,
25 LJCP 216, 2 Jur NS 474, 4 WR 547,
27 LTOS 135 . . . 275

Clough v Tameside and Glossop Health Authority
[1998] 2 All ER 971, [1998] 1 WLR 1478,
[1998] 3 FCR 133 . . . 660

Cobra Golf Inc v Rata [1998] Ch 109, [1997]
2 All ER 150, [1997] 2 WLR 629 . . . 627

Coldman v Hill [1919] 1 KB 443, 88 LJKB 491,
[1918–19] All ER Rep 434, 63 Sol Jo 166, 120
LT 412, 35 TLR 146, CA . . . 104

Collier v Nokes (1849) 2 Car & Kir 1012, 15 LTOS
189 . . . 709

Collier v Simpson (1831) 5 C & P 73 . . . 567

Collins v Carnegie (1834) 1 Ad & E1695,
3 LJKB 196, 3 Nev & MKB 703 . . . 360

Collinson v Mabbott (1984) Times, 10 October
. . . 231

Colvilles Ltd v Devine [1969] 2 All ER 53, [1969]
1 WLR 475, 113 Sol Jo 287, 1969 SC (HL) 67,
1969 SLT 154, HL . . . 704

Comfort Hotels Ltd v Wembley Stadium Ltd
(Sillon, third party) [1988] 3 All ER 53, [1988]
1 WLR 872, 132 Sol Jo 967, [1988] 26 LS Gaz R
43 . . . 647

Commonwealth v Cleary (1898)
172 Mass 175 . . . 201

Comptroller of Customs v Western Lectric Co
Ltd [1966] AC 367, [1965] 3 All ER 599, [1965]
3 WLR 1229, 109 Sol Jo 188, PC . . . 356

Computer Machinery Co Ltd v Drescher [1983]
3 All ER 153, [1983] 1 WLR 1379,
127 Sol Jo 823, [1984] LS Gaz R 123 . . . 666

Concha v Concha (1886) 11 App Cas 541, 56 LJ
Ch 257, 35 WR 477, 55 LT 522, HL . . . 602

Condron v United Kingdom (2001) 31 EHRR 1,
ECHR . . . 436, 448, 452, 454, 458

Conerney v Jacklin [1985] Crim LR 234,
129 Sol Jo 285, CA . . . 606

Conlon v Conlons Ltd [1952] 2 All ER 462,
[1952] WN 403, 96 Sol Jo 547, [1952] 2 TLR
343, CA . . . 655

Constantine (Joseph) Steamship Line Ltd v
Imperial Smelting Corpn Ltd, The Kingswood
[1942] AC 154, [1941] 2 All ER 165, 110 LJKB
433, 46 Com Cas 258, 165 LT 27, 57 TLR 485,
70 L1 L Rep 1, HL . . . 104

Conway v Hotten [1976] 2 All ER 213, 63 Cr App
Rep 11, 140 JP 355, DC . . . 403

Conway v Rimmer [1968] AC 910, [1968] 1 All
ER 874, [1968] 2 WLR 998, 112 Sol Jo 191,
HL . . . 587, 595, 598, 603, 619–21

Cook v DPP [2001] Crim LR 321, DC . . . 145

Cooke v Tanswell (1818) 8 Taunt 450, 2 Moore
CP 513 . . . 274

Coombs (TC) & Co (a firm) v IRC. See R v IRC,
ex p TC Coombs & Co

Cooper v Rowlands [1971] RTR 291, [1972]
Crim LR 53 . . . 702

Cope v Cope (1833) 5 C & P 604, 1 Mood &
R 269 . . . 695

Corfield v Hodgson [1966] 2 All ER 205, [1966]
1 WLR 590, 130 JP 271, 110 Sol Jo 170,
DC . . . 238

Corke v Corke and Cook (or Cooke) [1958] P 93,
[1958] 1 All ER 224, [1958] 2 WLR 110, 102
Sol Jo 68, CA . . . 181

Cornwell v Myskow [1987] 2 All ER 504, [1987]
1 WLR 630, 131 Sol Jo 476, [1987] LS Gaz R
1243, CA . . . 467

Cosgrave v Pattison [2001] CPLR 177,
ChD . . . 576

Coulson v Disborough [1894] 2 QB 316,
58 JP 784, 9 R 390, 42 WR 449, 38 Sol Jo 416,
70 LT 617, 10 TLR 429, CA . . . 200

Council of Civil Service Unions v Minister for the
Civil Service [1985] AC 374, [1984] 3 All ER
935, [1984] 3 WLR 1174, [1985] ICR 14, 128
Sol Jo 837, [1985] LS Gaz R 437, sub nom
R v Secretary of State for Foreign and
Commonwealth Affairs, ex p Council of Civil
Service Unions [1985] IRLR 28, HL . . . 598

Countess of Shelburne v Earl of Inchiquin (1784)
1 Bro CC 338 . . . 119

Coventry Newspapers Ltd, ex p [1993] QB 278,
[1993] 1 All ER 86, [1992] 3 WLR 916, sub
nom R v Bromell [1992] 35 LS Gaz R 32,
[1992] NLJR 1232, 136 Sol Jo LB 254,
CA . . . 606

Crease v Barren (1835) 1 Cr M & R 919,
4 LJ Ex 297, 5 Tyr 458, [1835–42] All ER
Rep 30 . . . 367

Credland v Knowler (1951) 35 Cr App Rep 48,
DC . . . 238

Crescent Farm (Sidcup) Sports Ltd v Sterling
Offices Ltd [1972] Ch 553, [1971] 3 All ER
1192, [1972] 2 WLR 91, 116 Sol Jo 59 . . . 652,
655

Crest Homes plc v Marks [1987] AC 829, [1987]
2 All ER 1074, [1987] 3 WLR 293, [1988] RPC
21, 131 Sol Jo 1003, [1987] LS Gaz R 2362,
[1987] NLJ Rep 662, HL . . . 627

Crippen's Estate, Re [1911] P 108, 80 LJP 47,
[1911–13] All ER Rep 207, 55 Sol Jo 273,
104 LT 224, 27 TLR 258 . . . 669

Crosdale v R [1995] 2 All ER 500, [1995] 1 WLR
864, [1995] 24 LS Gaz R 38, [1995] NLJR 594,
PC . . . 40

Crossland v DPP [1988] 3 All ER 712, [1988] RTR
417, 153 JP 63, [1988] Crim LR 756 . . . 231

Cummins, Re, Cummins v Thompson [1972]
Ch 62, [1971] 3 All ER 782, [1971] 3 WLR 580,
115 Sol Jo 567, CA . . . 245

Curtiss v Curtis (1905) 21 TLR 676 . . . 244

Customglass Boats Ltd v Salthouse Bros Ltd
[1976] RPC 589, [1976] 1 NZLR 36 . . . 377

Customs and Excise Commissioners v Harz
[1967] 1 AC 760, [1967] 1 All ER 177, [1967]
2 WLR 297, 51 Cr App Rep 123, 131 JP 146,
111 Sol Jo 15, HL . . . 379, 380

Cutts v Head [1984] Ch 290, [1984] 1 All ER 597,
[1984] 2 WLR 349, 128 Sol Jo 117, [1984]
LS Gaz R 509, CA . . . 379, 380

**D**

D (infants), Re [1970] 1 All ER 1088, [1970]
1 WLR 599, 68 LGR 183, 134 JP 387,
114 Sol Jo 188, CA . . . 595

D (a minor), Re [1986] 2 FLR 189, [1986]
Fam Law 263 . . . 302, 252

D (minors), Re [1993] Fam 231, [1993] 2 All ER
693, [1993] 2 WLR 721, [1993] 1 FCR 877,
[1993] 1 FLR 932, [1993] Fam Law 410, [1993]
NLJR 438, CA . . . 667

D v National Society for the Prevention of
Cruelty to Children [1978] AC 171, [1976]
2 All ER 993, [1976] 3 WLR 124, 120 Sol Jo
422, CA; revsd [1978] AC 171, [1977] 1 All ER
589, [1977] 2 WLR 201, 121 Sol Jo 119,
HL . . . 46, 596, 601, 605–7, 660, 666

Daintrey, Re, ex p Holt [1893] 2 QB 116,
62 LJQB 511, 10 Morr 158, 5 R 414, 41 WR
590, [1891–4] All ER Rep 209, 37 Sol Jo 480,
69 LT 257, 9 TLR 452, DC . . . 665

Dale v Smith [1967] 2 All ER 1133, [1967]
1 WLR 700, 131 JP 378, 111 Sol Jo 330,
DC . . . 459

Daley v R [1994] AC 117, [1993] 4 All ER 86,
[1993] 3 WLR 666, 98 Cr App Rep 447, [1994]
Crim LR 931, [1993] NLJR 1331, 137 Sol Jo LB
210, PC . . . 255, 326

Daniel v Wilkin (1852) 21 LJ Ex 236,
7 Exch 429 . . . 361

Daniels v Walker [2001] 1 WLR 1382, CA . . . 575

Daubert v Merrell Dow Pharmaceuticals 509 US
579 (1993) . . . 563

Davey v Harrow Corpn [1958] 1 QB 60, [1957]
2 All ER 305, [1957] 2 WLR 941, 101 Sol Jo
405, CA . . . 710

Davie v Edinburgh Magistrates 1953 SC 34,
1953 SLT 54 . . . 567, 570, 571

Davies v DPP [1954] AC 378, [1954] 1 All ER 507,
[1954] 2 WLR 343, 38 Cr App Rep 11,
118 JP 222, 98 Sol Jo 161, HL . . . 233, 234

Davies v Fortior Ltd [1952] 1 All ER 1359n,
96 Sol Jo 376 . . . 369

Davies v Lowndes (1843) 12 LJ Ex 506, 6 Man &
G 471, 7 Scott NR 141, Ex Ch . . . 366

Dawson v McKenzie (1908) 45 SLR 473,
15 SLT 951 . . . 238

Dawson v R (1961) 106 CLR l, HC of A . . . 112

Day v Grant [1987] QB 972, [1987] 3 All ER 678,
[1987] 3 WLR 537n, [1985] RTR 299, [1985]
LS Gaz R 1091, CA . . . 605

DB Deniz Nakliyati TAS v Yugopetrol [1992]
1 All ER 205, [1992] 1 WLR 437, CA . . . 271

Dean v Dean [1987] FCR 96, [1987] 1 FLR 517,
[i987] Fam Law 200, CA . . . 114

De Beéche v South American Stores (Gath and
Chaves) Ltd and Chilian Stores (Gath and
Chaves) Ltd [1935] AC 148, 104 LJKB 101,
40 Com Cas 157, [1934] All ER Rep 284, 152
LT 309, 51 TLR 189, HL . . . 561

Dellow's Will Trusts, Re, Lloyds Bank Ltd v
Institute of Cancer Research [1964] 1 All ER
771, [1964] 1 WLR 451, 108 Sol Jo 156 . . . 110,
116

Den Norske Bank ASA v Antonatos [1999]
QB 271; [1998] 3 All ER 74, [1998] 3 WLR 711,
CA . . . 628

Dennis v A J White & Co [1916] 2 KB 1,
85 LJKB 862, 9 BWCC 250, 60 Sol Jo 385, 114
LT 579, CA; revsd [1917] AC 479, 86 LJKB
1074; 10 BWCC 280, 61 Sol Jo 558, 116 LT 774,
33 TLR 434, HL . . . 707

Deokinanan v R [1969] 1 AC 20, [1968] 2 All ER
346, [1968] 3 WLR 83, 52 Cr App Rep 241,
112 Sol Jo 333, 11 WIR 482, PC . . . 379

Derby & Co Ltd v Weldon (No 7) [1990] 3 All ER
161; [990] 1 WLR 1156 . . . 640, 652

Derby & Co Ltd v Weldon (No 8) [1990] 3 All ER
762, [1991] 1 WLR 73; varied [1990] 3 All ER
762, [1991] 1 WLR 73, 135 Sol Jo 84,
CA . . . 659

Derby & Co Ltd v Weldon (No 10) [1991] 2 All
ER 908, [1991] 1 WLR 660 . . . 224, 661, 662

De Thoren v A-G (1876) 1 App Cas 686, 3 R 28,
HL . . . 691

Devala Provident Gold Mining Co, Re (1883)
22 Ch D 593, 52 L7 Ch 434, 31 WR 425, 48 LT
259, [1881–5] All ER Rep Ext 1568 . . . 357

Deybel's Case (1821) 4 B & Ald 243, [1814–23]
All ER Rep 752 . . . 709

Dickinson v Rushmeer (2002) 152 NLJ 58 . . . 640

Digby v Essex County Council (1993)
15 BMLR 34, [1994] PIQR P 53, CA . . . 244

Dillon v R [1982] AC 484, [1982] 1 All ER 1017,
[1982] 2 WLR 538, 74 Cr App Rep 274, [1982]
Crim LR 438, 126 Sol Jo 117, PC . . . 24, 702

Dingwall v J Wharton (Shipping) Ltd [1961]
2 Lloyd's Rep 213, HL . . . 108

DPP v A and BC Chewing Gum Ltd [1968] 1 QB
159, [1967] 2 All ER 504, [1967] 3 WLR 493,
131 JP 373, 111 Sol Jo 331 . . . 556, 569, 570

DPP (Jamaica) v Bailey [1995] 1 Cr App Rep 257,
[1995] Crim LR 313, PC . . . 106

DPP v Billington [1988] 1 All ER 435, sub nom
Corywright v East [1988] 1 WLR 535,
87 Cr App Rep 68, 152 7P 1, [1987]
Crim LR 772, 132 Sol Jo 498, [1988] 10 LS Gaz
R 45 . . . 406

DPP v Blake [1989] 1 WLR 432, 89 Cr App Rep
179, 153 JP 425, 133 Sol Jo 483 361

DPP v Boardman [1975] AC 421, [1974] 3 WLR
673, 118 Sol Jo 809, sub nom Boardman v
DPP [1974] 3 All ER 887, 60 Cr App Rep 165,
139 JP 52, HL . . . 505, 507, 509, 510, 515, 516,
520, 545

DPP v D (a juvenile) [1992] RTR 246, 94 Cr App
Rep 185 . . . 406

DPP v Evans [2003] Crim LR 338, DC . . . 69

DPP v Hester [1973] AC 296, [1972] 3 All ER
1056, [1972] 3 WLR 910, 57 Cr App Rep 212,
137 JP 45, 116 Sol Jo 966, HL . . . 228, 230

DPP v Humphrys [1977] AC 1, [1976] 2 All ER
497, [1976] 2 WLR 857, [1976] RTR 339,
63 Cr App Rep 95, 140 JP 386, [1977] Crim LR
421, 120 Sol Jo 420, HL . . . 595, 603, 610, 611

DPP v Hynde [1998] 1 All ER 649, [1998] 1 WLR
1222, [1998] 1 Cr App Rep 288, 161 JP 671,
[1998] Crim LR 72 . . . 707

DPP v Jordan [1977] AC 699, [1976] 3 All ER
775, [1976] 3 WLR 887, 64 Cr App Rep 33,
141 JP 13, 120 Sol Jo 817, HL . . . 554, 556

DPP v Kavanagh [2005] NLJ 69- . . . 434

DPP v Kilbourne [1973] AC 729, [1973] 1 All ER
440, [1973] 2 WLR 254, 57 Cr App Rep 381,
137 JP 193, 117 Sol Jo 144, HL . . . 13, 22 230

DPP v M [1998] QB 913, [1997] 2 All ER 749,
[1998] 2 WLR 604, [1997] 2 Cr App Rep 70,
[1997] 2 FLR 804, [1998] Fam Law 11,
161 JP 491 . . . 134

DPP v McGladrigan [1991] RTR 297, 155 JP 785,
[1991] Crim LR 851 . . . 66

DPP v Morgan [1976] AC 182, [1975] 2 All ER
347, [1975] 2 WLR 913, 61 Cr App Rep 136,
139 JP 476, 119 Sol Jo 319, HL . . . 83

DPP v P [1991] 2 AC 447, [1991] 3 WLR 161, 93 Cr App Rep 267, 156 JP 125, 135 Sol Jo LB 69, sub nom R v P [1991] 3 All ER 337, [1992] Crim LR 41, HL . . . 470, 506, 508, 510–12, 516

DPP v Ping Lin [1976] AC 574, [1975] 3 All ER 175, [1975] 3 WLR 419, 62 Cr App Rep 14, 139 JP 651, 119 Sol Jo 627, HL . . . 379, 392

DPP v Rous [1992] RTR 246, 94 Cr App Rep 185 . . . 406

DPP v Smith [1961] AC 290, [1960] 3 All ER 161, [1960] 3 WLR 546, 44 Cr App Rep 261, 124 JP 473, 104 Sol Jo 683, HL . . . 687

DPP v Stonehouse [1978] AC 55, [1977] 2 All ER 909, [1977] 3 WLR 143, 65 Cr App Rep 192, 141 JP 473, [1977] Crim LR 544, 121 Sol Jo 491, HL . . . 34, 44, 45

DPP v Wilson [1991] RTR 284, 156 JP 916, [1991] Crim LR 441 . . . 61

DPP v Wynne (2001) The Independent, 19 Feb, DC . . . 571

Dixons Stores Group Ltd v Thames Television plc [1993] 1 All ER 349 . . . 664

Doe d Arundel (Lord) v Fowler (1850) 14 QB 700, 14 JP 114, 19 LJQB 151, 14 Jur 179, 14 LTOS 417 . . . 274

Doe d Banning v Griffin (1812) 15 East 293 . . . 366

Doe d Bowley v Barnes (1846) 8 QB 1037, 1 New Pract Cas 401, 15 LJQB 293, 10 Jur 520, 7 LTOS 139 . . . 701

Doe d Church and Phillips v Perkins (1790) 3 Term Rep 749 . . . 175

Doe d Devine v Wilson (1855) 10 Moo PCC 502, PC . . . 115

Doe d France v Andrews (1850) 15 QB 756 . . . 361, 698

Doe d Gilbert v Ross (1840) 8 Dowl 389, 10 LJ Ex 201, 4 Jur 321, 7 M & W 102 . . . 267

Doe d Jenkins v Davies (1847) 10 QB 314, 16 LJQB 218, 11 Jur 607 . . . 37, 367

Doe d Mudd v Suckermore (1837) 5 Ad & E1703, 7 LJQB 33, 2 Nev & PKB 16, Will Woll & Dav 405 . . . 272, 554, 583

Doe d Strode v Seaton (1834) 2 Ad & El 171, 4 LJKB 13, 4 Nev & MKB 81 . . . 360

Doe d Tatum v Catomore (1851) 16 QB 745, sub nom Doe d Tatham v Cattamore 15 JP 673, 20 LJQB 364, 15 Jur 728, 17 LTOS 74 . . . 275

Doe d Tilman v Tarver (1824) Ry & M 141 . . . 367Doe d Warren v Bray (1828) 8 B & C 813, 7 LJOSKB 161, 2 Man & Ry MC 66, 3 Man & Ry KB 428 . . . 362

Doe d West v Davis (1806) 7 East 363 . . . 265

Doland (George) Ltd v Blackburn, Robson, Coates & Co (a firm) [1972] 3 All ER 959, [1972] 1 WLR 1338, 116 Sol Jo 713 . . . 661, 662

Dost Aly Khan's Goods, Re (1880) 6 PD 6, 49 LJP 78, 29 WR 80 . . . 561

Douglas v Hello! Ltd [2003] EWCA Civ 322 . . . 348

Dowling v Dowling (1860) 10 ICLR 236 . . . 29

Dowsett v UK [2003] Crim LR 890 . . . 591

Drinkwater v Porter (1835) 7 C & P 181, NP . . . 367

Driscoll v R (1977) 137 CLR 517, 51 ALJR 731, HC of A . . . 197

Dubai Aluminium Co Ltd v A1 Alawi [1999] 1 All ER 703, [1999] 1 WLR 1964, [1999] 1 Lloyd's Rep 478 . . . 652

Dubai Bank Ltd v Galadari [1990] Ch 98, [1989] 3 All ER 769, [1989] 3 WLR 1044, [1990] BCLC 90, [1989] NLJR 1301, CA . . . 644

Dubai Bank Ltd v Galadari (No 7) [1992] 1 All ER 658, [1992] 1 WLR 106 . . . 644, 649

Duchess Di Sora v Phillipps (1863) 10 HL Cas 624 . . . 555

Duff Development Co Ltd v Kelantan Government [1924] AC 797, 93 LJ Ch 343, [1924] All ER Rep 1, 68 Sol Jo 559, 131 LT 676, 40 TLR 566, HL . . . 708, 710

Duke of Beaufort v John Aird & Co (1904) 20 TLR 602 . . . 360

Duke of Beaufort v Smith (1849) 4 Exch 450 . . . 360

Duke of Wellington, Re (Glentanar v Wellington) [1947] Ch 506 . . . 35, 561

Duncan, Re, Garfield v Fay [1968] P 306, [1968] 2 All ER 395, [1968] 2 WLR 1479, 112 Sol Jo 254 . . . 638

Duncan v Cammell Laird & Co Ltd [1942] AC 624, [1942] 1 All ER 587, 111 LJKB 406, 86 Sol Jo 287, 166 LT 366, 58 TLR 242, HL . . . 586–88, 597, 616, 618, 620

Dunlop Slazenger International Ltd v Joe Bloggs Sports Ltd [2003] EWCA Civ 901 . . . 661

Dunn v Snowden (1862) 2 Drew & Sm 201, 32 LJ Ch 104, 11 WR 160, 7 LT 558 . . . 698

Dwyer v Collins (1852) 21 LJ Ex 225, 7 Exch 639, 16 Jur 569 . . . 268, 648

E

Ealing London Borough v Woolworths ple [1995] Crim LR 58, DC . . . 77

Earl v Hector Whaling Ltd [1961] 1 Lloyd's Rep 459, 105 Sol Jo 321, CA . . . 119

Earl of Dunraven v Llewellyn (1850) 15 QB 791 . . . 367

Easson v London and North Eastern Rly Co
    [1944] KB 421, [1944] 2 All ER 425, 113 LJKB
    449, 88 Sol Jo 143, 170 LT 234, 60 TLR 280,
    CA . . . 703

East London Rly Co v River Thames
    Conservators (1904) 68 JP 302, 90 LT 347, 20
    TLR 378 . . . 364

Edwards v Brookes (Milk) Ltd [1963] 3 All ER 62,
    [1963] 1 WLR 795, 61 LGR 430, 127 JP 497,
    107 Sol Jo 477 . . . 39, 364

Edwards and Osakwe v DPP [1992] Crim LR 576
    . . . 373

Edwards v UK (2003) 15 BHRC 189 . . . 593, 594

EG Music v SF Distributors [1978] FSR
    121 . . . 469

Ellis v Home Office [1953] 2 QB 135, [1953]
    2 All ER 149, [1953] 3 WLR 105, 97 Sol Jo 436,
    CA . . . 586, 603

Ellor v Selfridge & Co Ltd (1930) 74 Sol Jo 140, 46
    TLR 236 . . . 703

Engelke v Musmann [1928] AC 433, 97 LJKB 789,
    [1928] All ER Rep 18, 139 LT 586, 44 TLR 731,
    HL . . . 710

English and American Insurance Co Ltd v
    Herbert Smith & Co [1988] FSR 232, [1987]
    NLJ Rep 148 . . . 658

English Exporters (London) Ltd v Eldonwall Ltd
    [1973] Ch 415, [1973] 1 All ER 726, [1973]
    2 WLR 435, 25 P & CR 379, 117 Sol Jo 224,
    [1972] RVR 612, 225 Estates Gazette 255 . . .
    10, 566

Enoch and Zaretzky, Bock & Co's Arbitration,
    Re [1910] 1 KB 327, 79 LJKB 363, [1908–10]
    All ER Rep 625, 101 LT 801, CA . . . 147

Environment Agency v ME Foley Contractors Ltd
    [2002] 1 WLR 1754, DC . . . 89

Environmental Defence Society Inc v South
    Pacific Aluminium Ltd (No 2) [1981] 1 NZLR
    153 . . . 590

ES v Chesterfield & North Derbyshire Royal
    Hospital NHS Trust (2003) EWCA Civ 1284
    . . . 574

Essex County Council v R [1994] Fam 167n,
    [1994] 2 WLR 407n, [1993] 2 FLR 826, [1993]
    Fam Law 670, sub nom Re R (a minor)
    (disclosure of privileged material) [1993]
    4 All ER 702, [1994] 1 FCR 225 . . . 654

Esso Petroleum Co Ltd v Southport Corpn
    [1956] AC 218, [1955] 3 All ER 864, [1956]
    2 WLR 81, 54 LGR 91, [1955] 2 Lloyd's Rep
    655, 120 JP 54, 100 Sol Jo 32, HL . . . 8

Ettenfield v Ettenfield [1940] P 96, [1940] 1 All
    ER 293, 109 LJP 41, 84 Sol Jo 59, 162 LT 172, 56
    TLR 315, CA . . . 696

Evans v Chief Constable of Surrey [1988] QB 588,
    [1988] 3 WLR 127, 132 Sol Jo 898, [1988]

28 LS Gaz R 45, sub nom Evans v Chief
    Constable of Surrey Constabulary
    (A-G intervening) [1989] 2 All ER 594 . . . 604,
    619

Evans v Getting (1834) 6 C & P 586 . . . 364, 711

Everingham v Roundell (1838) 2 Mood & R
    138 . . . 267

Ewer v Ambrose (1825) 3 B & C 746, 3 LJOSKB
    115, 5 Dow & Ry KB 629 . . . 194, 196

F

F (an infant) v Chief Constable of Kent [1982]
    Crim LR 682 . . . 37

F (Minors) [1989] Fam 18, CA . . . 595

F v Child Support Agency [1999] 2 FLR 244,
    QBD . . . 695

F v F [1968] P 506, [1968] 1 All ER 242, [1968]
    2 WLR 190, 112 Sol Jo 214 . . . 117

F v R [1994] 4 ll ER 260, CA . . . 124

Fagernes, The [1927] P 311, 96 LJP 183,
    17 Asp MLC 326, 71 Sol Jo 634, 138 LT 30,
    43 TLR 746, CA . . . 710

Fairfield-Mabey Ltd v Shell UK Ltd
    (Metallurgical Testing Services (Scotland) Ltd,
    third party) [1989] 1 All ER 576, 45 BLR 113
    . . . 206, 661

Fairman v Fairman [1949] P 341, [1949] 1 All ER
    938, 47 LGR 455, 113 JP 275, [1949] LJR 1073,
    93 Sol Jo 321, 65 TLR 320 . . . 233, 244

Fallon v Calvert [1960] 2 QB 201, [1960] 1 All ER
    281, [1960] 2 WLR 346, 104 Sol Jo 106,
    CA . . . 147

Family Housing Association (Manchester) Ltd v
    Michael Hyde and Partners (a firm) [1993]
    2 All ER 567, [1993] 1 WLR 354, [1993]
    2 EGLR 239, CA . . . 664

Farrell v Secretary of State for Defence [1980]
    1 All ER 166, [1980] 1 WLR 172, 70 Cr App
    Rep 224, 124 Sol Jo 133, HL . . . 8

Faulder v Silk (1811) 3 Camp 126 . . . 360, 677

Fayed v Al-Tajir [1988] QB 712, [1987] 2 All ER
    396, [1987] 3 WLR 102, 131 Sol Jo 744, [1987]
    LS Gaz R 1055, CA . . . 598, 604

Fazil-Alizadeh v Nikbin (1993) The Times,
    19 Mar, CA . . . 665

Fennell v Jerome Property Maintenance Ltd
    (1986) Times, 26 November . . . 180

Ferguson v R [1979] 1 All ER 877, [1979]
    1 WLR 94, 122 Sol Jo 696, PC . . . 112, 113

Field v Leeds City Council [2001]
    CPLR 129 . . . 562

Fitzwalter Peerage (1844) 10 C1 & Fin 193, 946,
    HL . . . 273

Flack v Baldry [1988] 1 All ER 673, [1988] 1 WLR
    393, 87 Cr App Rep 130, 152 JP 418, [1988]

Crim LR 610, 132 Sol Jo 334, [1988] 12 LS Gaz R 39, [1988] NLJR 63, HL . . . 34

Flanagan v Fahy [1918] 2 IR 361 . . . 186

Fleet v Murton (1871) LR 7 QB 126, 41 LJQB 49, 20 WR 97, 26 LT 181 . . . 20

Fletcher, Re, Reading v Fletcher [1917] 1 Ch 339, 86 LJ Ch 317, 61 Sol Jo 267, 116 LT 460, [1916–17] All ER Rep Ext 1257, CA . . . 377

Folkes v Chadd (1782) 3 Doug KB 157 . . . 25, 561

Forbes v Samuel [1913] 3 KB 706, 82 LJKB 1135, 109 LT 599, 29 TLR 544 . . . 265

Forster v Friedland [1992] CA Transcript 1052 . . . 665

Fowke v Berington [1914] 2 Ch 308, 83 LJ Ch 820, 878, 58 Sol Jo 379, 610, 111 LT 440 . . . 364

Fox v Chief Constable of Gwent [1985] 3 All ER 392 . . . 61

Fox v General Medical Council [1960] 3 All ER 225, [1960] 1 WLR 1017, 124 JP 467, 104 Sol Jo 725, PC . . . 186

Foxley v UK (2000) 8 BHRC 751 . . . 651

Francis & Francis (a firm) v Central Criminal Court. See R v Central Criminal Court, ex p Francis

Fred Chappell Ltd v National Car Parks Ltd (1987) The Times, 22 May, QBD . . . 105

Freemantle v R [1994] 3 All ER 225, [1994] 1 WLR 1437, [1994] Crim LR 930, [1994] 37 LS Gaz R 49, 138 Sol Jo LB 174, PC . . . 249

Frye v US 293 F 1013 (1923) . . . 563

Fryer v Gathercole (1849) 18 LJ Ex 389, 4 Exch 262, 13 Jur 542, 13 LTOS 285 . . . 583

Fryer v Pearson and Another (2000) Times, 4 April, CA . . . 28, 30, 703

Fuld's Estate (No 3), Re, Hartley v Fuld [1968] P 675, [1965] 3 All ER 776, [1966] 2 WLR 717, 110 Sol Jo 133 . . . 119, 555

Fuller v Strum (2000) The Times, 14 Feb . . . 571

Funke v France (1993) 60 EHRR 297 . . . 630

G

G (a minor) (social worker: disclosure), Re [1996] 2 All ER 65, [1996] 1 WLR 1407, [1996] 1 FLR 276; [1996] Fam Law 143, [1995] 44 LS Gaz R 30, [1996] NLJR 85, [1995] TLR 588, 140 Sol Jo LB 10, sub nom G (a minor) (care proceedings: disclosure), Re [1996] 3 FCR 77, CA . . . 595, 634

G (minors), Re [1990] 2 All ER 633, [1990] 2 FLR 347, [1991] Fam Law 64, sub nom Re R and G (minors) [1990] FCR 495 . . . 124

G v DPP [1998] QB 919, [1997] 2 All ER 755, [1998] 2 WLR 609, [1997] 2 Cr App Rep 78, [1997] 2 FLR 810, [1998] Fam Law 12, 161 JP 498 . . . 133, 159, 559

G (A) v G (T) [1970] 2 QB 643, [1970] 3 All ER 546, [1970] 3 WLR 132, 135 JP 13, sub nom G v G 114 Sol Jo 493, CA . . . 357

Galler v Galler [1954] P 252, [1954] 1 All ER 536, [1954] 2 WLR 395, 118 JP 216, 98 Sol Jo 176, CA . . . 117, 233, 244

Gamlen Chemical Co (UK) Ltd v Rochem Ltd [1980] 1 All ER 1049, [1980] 1 WLR 614, 123 Sol Jo 838, CA . . . 652

Garcin v Amerindo Investment Advisors Ltd [1991] 4 All ER 655, [1991] 1 WLR 1140 . . . 138

Garner v DPP [1990] RTR 208, 90 Cr App Rep 178, 154 JP 277, [1989] Crim LR 583 . . . 299

Garton v Hunter (Valuation Officer) [1969] 2 QB 37, [1969] 1 All ER 451, [1969] 2 WLR 86, 67 LGR 229, [1969] RA 11, 14 RRC 136, 133 JP 162, 112 Sol Jo 924, 208 Estates Gazette 1087, CA . . . 293

Garvin v Domus Publishing Ltd [1989] Ch 335, [1989] 2 All ER 344, [1988] 3 WLR 344, 132 Sol Jo 1091, [1988] 33 LS Gaz R 44 . . . 627

Gaskin v Liverpool City Council [1980] 1 WLR 1549, 79 LGR 21, 124 Sol Jo 498, CA . . . 595

Gatland v Metropolitan Police Commissioner [1968] 2 QB 279, [1968] 2 All ER 100, [1968] 2 WLR 1263, 66 LGR 519, 132 JP 323, 112 Sol Jo 336, DC . . . 89

Gatty and Gatty v A-G [1951] P 444, 95 Sol Jo 610, [1951] 2 TLR 599 . . . 692

Geest plc v Lansiquot [2002] 1 WLR 3111, PC . . . 103

General Accident Fire and Life Assurance Corpn Ltd v Tanter, The Zephyr [1984] 1 All ER 35, [1984] 1 WLR 100, [1984] 1 Lloyd's Rep 58, 91n, 127 Sol Jo 733; revsd [1995] 2 Lloyd's Rep 529, CA . . . 661, 662

George v Davies [1911] 2 KB 445, 80 LJKB 924, [1911–13] All ER Rep 914, 55 Sol Jo 481, 104 LT 648, 27 TLR 415 . . . 710

Getty (Sarah C) Trust, Re, Getty v Getty [1985] QB 956, [1985] 2 All ER 809, [1985] 3 WLR 302, 129 Sol Jo 523 . . . 640

Gibbins v Skinner [1951] 2 KB 379, [1951] 1 TLR 1159, sub nom Boyd-Gibbins v Skinner [1951] 1 All ER 1049, 49 LGR 713, 115 JP 360, DC . . . 702

Gilbey v Great Western Rly Co (1910) 3 BWCC 135, 102 LT 202, CA . . . 376

Ginesi v Ginesi [1948] P 179, [1948] 1 All ER 373, 46 LGR 124, 112 JP 194, [1948] LJR 892, 92 Sol Jo 140, 64 TLR 167, CA . . . 116, 118

Glasgow Corpn v Central Land Board [1956] JPL 442, 1956 SC (HL) 1, 1956 SLT 41 . . . 587

Glendarroch, The [1894] P 226, 63 LJP 89, 7 Asp
MLC 420, 6 R 686, [1891–4] All ER Rep 484, 38
Sol Jo 362, 70 LT 344, 10 TLR 269, CA . . . 105

Glinski v McIver [1962] AC 726, [1962] 1 All ER
696, [1962] 2 WLR 832, 106 Sol Jo 261,
HL . . . 299

Gnitrow Ltd v Cape plc [2000] 1 WLR 2327,
CA . . . 663

Goddard v Nationwide Building Society [1987]
QB 670, [1986] 3 All ER 264, [1986] 3 WLR
734, 130 Sol Jo 803, [1986] LS Gaz R 3592,
[1986] NLJ Rep 775, CA . . . 657–60

Goldman v Hesper [1988] 1 WLR 1238,
CA . . . 662

Gollins v Gollins [1964] AC 644, [1963] 2 All ER
966, [1963] 3 WLR 176; 107 Sol Jo 532,
HL . . . 56, 688

Goodridge v Chief Constable of Hampshire
Constabulary [1999] 1 All ER 896, [1999]
1 WLR 1558 . . . 621, 639

Goodright d Stevens v Moss (1777)
2 Cowp 591 . . . 366

Goodwin v United Kingdom (1996) 22 EHRR
123, ECtHR . . . 612, 613

Goody v Odhams Press Ltd [1967] 1 QB 333,
[1966] 3 All ER 369, [1966] 3 WLR 460, 110
Sol Jo 793, CA . . . 467, 673

Goold v Evans & Co [1951] 2 TLR 1189,
CA . . . 280

Gordon v Gordon [1903] P 141, 72 LJP 33,
[1904–7] All ER Rep 702, 89 LT 73 . . . 695

Gorman v Hand-in-Hand Insurance Co (1877)
IR 11 . . . CL 224 . . . 105

Gough v Chief Constable of the Derbyshire
Constabulary [2002] QB 1213, CA . . . 115

Grant v Southwestern and County Properties Ltd
[1975] Ch 185, [1974] 2 All ER 465, [1974]
3 WLR 221, 118 Sol Jo 548 . . . 641

Great Atlantic Insurance Co v Home Insurance
Co [1981] 2 All ER 485, [1981] 1 WLR 529,
[1981] 2 Lloyd's Rep 138, 125 Sol Jo 203,
CA . . . 661

Great Future International Ltd v Sealand Housing
Corporation (2002) LTL 25 July . . . 47, 626

Greaves v Greenwood (1877) 2 Ex D 289, 46
LJQB 252, 25 WR 639, 36 LT 1, CA . . . 698

Greek Case (1969) 12 YB 1, EComHR . . . 387

Green v R (1971) 126 CLR 28 . . . 112

Greenough v Eccles (1859) 5 CBNS 786,
28 LJCP 160, 5 Jur NS 766, 7 WR 341,
33 LTOS 91 . . . 196

Greenough v Gaskell (1833) 1 My & K 98,
Coop temp Brough 96, [1824–34] All ER Rep
767 . . . 649

Greenwood v Fitts (1961) 29 DLR (2d) 260,
BC CA . . . 665

Gregory v Tavernor (1833) 6 C & P 280, 2 Nev &
MMC 175 . . . 176

Grinsted v Hadrill [1953] 1 All ER 1188, [1953]
1 WLR 696, 97 Sol Jo 351, CA . . . 42

Grobbelaar v Sun Newspapers Ltd (1999)
The Times, 12 Aug . . . 47

Grosvenor Hotel, London (No 2), Re [1965] Ch
1210, [1964] 3 All ER 354, [1964] 3 WLR 992,
108 Sol Jo 674, CA . . . 587

Guinness Peat Properties Ltd v Fitzroy Robinson
Partnership (a firm) [1987] 2 All ER 716,
[1987] 1 WLR 1027, 131 Sol Jo 807, [1987]
LS Gaz R 1882, [1987] NLJ Rep 452,
38 BLR 57, CA . . . 641, 645, 646, 657

Gull v Scarborough [1987] RTR 261n . . . 61

Gumbley v Cunningham [1989] AC 281, [1989]
1 All ER 5, [1989] 2 WLR 1, [1989] RTR 49, 88
Cr App Rep 273, 154 JP 686, 133 Sol Jo 84,
[1989] 4 LS Gaz R 43, HL . . . 553

GUR Corpn v Trust Bank of Africa Ltd [1987]
QB 599, [1986] 3 All ER 449, [1986] 3 WLR
583, [1986] 2 Lloyd's Rep 451, 130 Sol Jo 748,
[1986] LS Gaz R 2659, [1986] NLJ Rep 895,
CA . . . 710

H

H (minors) (sexual abuse: standard of proof),
Re [1996] AC 563, [1996] 1 All ER 1, [1996]
2 WLR 8, [1996] 1 FCR 509, [1996] 1 FLR 80,
[1996] Fam Law 74, 140 Sol Jo LB 24,
HL . . . 119

H v Schering Chemicals Ltd [1983] 1 All ER 849,
[1983] 1 WLR 143, 127 Sol Jo 88 . . . 352, 567

Haines v Guthrie (1884) 13 QBD 818, 48 JP 756,
53 LJQB 521, 33 WR 99, 51 LT 645, CA . . . 247,
366

Hajigeorgiou v Vasiliou [2005] EWCA Civ 236
. . . 579

Halawa v Federation Against Copyright Theft
[1995] 1 Cr App Rep 21, 159 JP 816, [1995]
Crim LR 409 . . . 38, 39

Hales v Kerr [1908] 2 KB 601, 77 LJKB 870,
99 LT 364, 24 TLR 779 . . . 23, 468

Halford v UK (1997) 24 EHRR 523 . . . 58

Hall v R [1971] 1 All ER 322, [1971] 1 WLR 298,
55 Cr App Rep 108, 135 JP 141, 115 Sol Jo 172,
16 WIR 276, PC . . . 426, 427, 432

Hamilton v Naviede [1995] 2 AC 75, [1994] 3 All
ER 814, [1994] 3 WLR 656, [1994] 2 BCLC
738, [1994] BCC 641, [1994] NLJR 1203,
HL . . . 604

Handmade Films (Productions) Ltd v Express
Newspapers [1986] FSR 463 . . . 610, 611

Hargreaves (Joseph) Ltd, Re [1900] 1 Ch 347, 4 TC 173, 69 LJ Ch 183, 7 Mans 354, 48 WR 241, 44 Sol Jo 210, 82 LT 132, 16 TLR 155, CA . . . 603

Hammond v Wilkinson [2001] Crim LR 323 . . . 145

Harmony Shipping Co SA v Saudi Europe Line Ltd [1979] 3 All ER 177, [1979] 1 WLR 1380, [1980] 1 Lloyd's Rep 44, 123 Sol Jo 690, CA . . . 123, 561

Harris v DPP [1952] AC 694, [1952] 1 All ER 1044, 36 Cr App Rep 39, 116 JP 248, 96 Sol Jo 312, [1952] 1 TLR 1075, HL . . . 505, 514

Harrison v Turner (1847) 10 QB 482, 16 LJQB 295, 11 Jur 817 . . . 356

Hart v Lancashire and Yorkshire Rly Co (1869) 21 LT 261 . . . 23

Harvey v R [1901] AC 601, 70 LJPC 107, 84 LT 849, 17 TLR 601, PC . . . 677

Hatton v Cooper [2001] RTR 544, CA . . . 468

Hawick Jersey International Ltd v Caplan (1988) Times, 11 March . . . 665

Haw Tua Tau v Public Prosecutor [1982] AC 136, [1981] 3 All ER 14, [1981] 3 WLR 395, 125 Sol Jo 497, PC . . . 440

Haynes v Doman [1899] 2 Ch 13, 68 LJ Ch 419, 43 Sol Jo 553, 80 LT 569, 15 TLR 354, CA . . . 569

Heaney and McGuinness v Ireland [2001] Crim LR 481, ECHR . . . 631, 633

Heath, Re, Stacey v Bird [1945] Ch 417, 115 LJ Ch 120, 89 Sol Jo 358, 173 LT 326, 61 TLR 554 . . . 695

Heath v Deane [1905] 2 Ch 86, 74 LJ Ch 466, 92 LT 643, 21 TLR 404 . . . 361

Heather (Inspector of Taxes) v P-E Consulting Group Ltd [1973] Ch 189, [1972] 2 All ER 107, [1972] 2 WLR 918, 48 TC 293, 50 ATC 461, [1971] TR 465, 116 Sol Jo 125, L (TC) 2436; affd [1973] Ch 189, [1973] 1 All ER 8, [1972] 3 WLR 833, 48 TC 293, 51 ATC 255, [1972] TR 237, 116 Sol Jo 824, L(TC) 2466, CA . . . 710

Hehir v Metropolitan Police Commissioner [1982] 2 All ER 335, [1982] 1 WLR 715, 126 Sol Jo 330, CA . . . 617, 618

Hellenic Mutual War Risks Association (Bermuda) Ltd and General Contractors Importing and Services Enterprises v Harrison, The Sagheera [1997] 1 Lloyd's Rep 160 . . . 642

Helliwell v Piggott-Sims [1980] FSR 582 . . . 58

Henderson v Henry E Jenkins & Sons and Evans [1970] AC 282, [1969] 3 All ER 756, [1969] 3 WLR 732, [1970] RTR 70, [1969] 2 Lloyd's Rep 603, 113 Sol Jo 856, HL . . . 704

Hennessy v Wright (1888) 21 QBD 509, 53 JP 52, 57 LJQB 530, 59 LT 323, 4 TLR 597 . . . 597

Herniman v Smith [1938] AC 305, [1938] 1 All ER 1, 107 LJKB 225, 82 Sol Jo 192, HL . . . 35

Hetherington v Hetherington (1887) 12 PD 112, 51 JP 294, 56 LJP 78, 36 WR 12, [1886–90] All ER Rep 170, 57 LT 533 . . . 696

Hickman v Berens [1895] 2 Ch 638, 64 LJ Ch 785, 12 R 602, 73 LT 323, CA . . . 139

Hickman v Peacey [1945] AC 304, [1945] 2 All ER 215, 114 LJ Ch 225, 89 Sol Jo 339, 173 LT 89, 61 TLR 489, HL . . . 699

Highgrade Traders Ltd, Re [1984] BCLC 151, CA . . . 645, 646

Hill v Clifford [1907] 2 Ch 236, 76 LJ Ch 627, 97 LT 266, 23 TLR 601, CA; on appeal [1908] AC 12, 77 LJ Ch 91, 52 Sol Jo 92, 98 LT 64, 24 TLR 112; HL . . . 360, 677

Hill v Hill [1959] 1 All ER 281, [1959] 1 WLR 127, 103 Sol Jo 111, PC . . . 690, 691

Hill v Manchester and Salford Water Works Co (1833) 5 B & Ad 866, 3 LJKB 19, 2 Nev & MKB 573 . . . 361

Hinds v London Transport Executive [1979] RTR 103, CA . . . 561

Hinds v Sparks [1964] Crim LR 717 . . . 673

Hitchins v Eardley (1871) LR 2 P & D 248, 40 LJP & M 70, 25 LT 163 . . . 37

HIV Haemophiliac Litigation, Re [1990] NJLR 1349 . . . 590

Hobbs v CT Tinling & Co Ltd [1929] 2 KB 1, 98 LJKB 421, [1929] All ER Rep 33, 73 Sol Jo 220, 141 LT 121, 45 TLR 328, CA . . . 204, 467, 485

Hocking v Ahlquist Bros Ltd [1944] KB 120, [1943] 2 All ER 722, 42 LGR 7, 107 JP 217, 113 LJKB 65, 170 LT 3, 60 TLR 60, DC . . . 29, 276

Hoe v Bentinck (1820) 2 Brod&Bing 130 . . . 597

Holcombe v Hewson (1810) 2 Camp 391 . . . 23

Hollingham v Head (1858) 4 CBNS 388, 27 LJCP 241, 4 Jur NS 379, 6 WR 442, sub nom Hothingham v Head 31 LTOS 85 . . . 23, 25

Hollington v F Hewthorn & Co Ltd [1943] KB 587, [1943] 2 All ER 35, 112 LJKB 463, 87 Sol Jo 247, 169 LT 21, 59 TLR 321, CA . . . 4, 552, 669–71, 673–77, 683

Home v Bentinck (1820) 2 Brod & Bing 130, 4 Moore CP 563, 8 Price 225, 1 State Tr NS App 1348, Ex Ch . . . 532

Homes v Newman [1931] 2 Ch 112, 100 LJ Ch 281, [1931] All ER Rep 85, 145 LT 140 . . . 368, 375

Hornal v Neuberger Products Ltd [1957] 1 QB
247, [1956] 3 All ER 970, [1956] 3 WLR 1034,
100 Sol Jo 915, CA . . . 22, 23, 110, 115, 116,
118, 689

Hoskyn v Metropolitan Police Commissioner
[1979] AC 474, [1978] 2 All ER 136, [1978]
2 WLR 695, 67 Cr App Rep 88, HL . . . 128, 129

Howe v Malkin (1878) 27 WR 340, 40 LT 196,
DC . . . 375

Howglen Ltd, Re [2001] 1 All ER 376,
Ch D . . . 270

Hui Chi-ming v R [1992] 1 AC 34, [1991] 3 All
ER 897, [1991] 3 WLR 495, 94 Cr App Rep 236,
PC . . . 23, 419, 683

Hunter v Chief Constable of Lancashire Police
Force [1980] QB 283, [1980] 2 All ER 227,
[1980] 2 WLR 689, 144 JP 291, 124 Sol Jo 83,
CA; affd sub nom Hunter v Chief Constable of
West Midlands Police [1982] AC 529, [1981]
3 All ER 727, [1981] 3 WLR 906, 125 Sol Jo
829, HL . . . 672

Hunter v Chief Constable of West Midlands
Police [1982] AC 529, [1981] 3 All ER 727,
[1981] 3 WLR 906, 125 Sol Jo 829, HL . . . 676

Hurst v Evans [1917] 1 KB 352, 86 LJKB 305,
[1916–17] All ER Rep 975, 116 LT 252, 33 TLR
96 . . . 105, 115

Huth v Huth [1915] 3 KB 32, 84 LJKB 1307,
[1914–15] All ER Rep 242, 113 LT 145, 31 TLR
350, CA . . . 707


I

IBM Corporation v Phoenix International
(Computers) Ltd [1995] 1 All ER 413,
Ch D . . . 638, 659

IBM United Kingdom Ltd v Prima Data
International Ltd [1994] 4 All ER 748, [1994]
1 WLR 719 . . . 626

Ibrahim v R [1914] AC 599, 83 LJPC 185, 24 Cox
CC 174, [1914–15] All ER Rep 874, 111 LT 20,
30 TLR 383, PC . . . 379

Ingram v Percival [1969] 1 QB 548, [1968] 3 All
ER 657, [1968] 3 WLR 663, 133 JP 1, 112 Sol Jo
722, DC . . . 712

Ireland v United Kingdom (1978) 2 EHRR 25,
ECtHR . . . 397

Irish Society v Bishop of Derry (1846) 12 Cl &
Fin 641, HL . . . 359, 360, 363, 677

Isaacs (M) & Sons Ltd v Cook [1925] 2 KB 391,
94 LJKB 886, 69 Sol Jo 810, 134 LT 286, 41 TLR
647 . . . 597

Issais v Marine Insurance Co Ltd (1923) 15 Ll L
Rep 186, CA . . . 115

Istel (AT & T) Ltd v Tully [1993] AC 45, [1992]
3 All ER 523, [1992] 3 WLR 344, [1992] 32 LS

Gaz R 37, [1992] NLJR 1089, 136 Sol Jo LB
227, HL . . . 625, 636, 637

ISTIL Group Inc v Zahoor [2003] 2 All ER 252,
Ch D . . . 657

Italia Express, The. See Ventouris v Mountain and
(No 2), The Italia Express

ITC Film Distributors v Video Exchange Ltd
[1982] Ch 431, [1982] 2 All ER 241, [1982]
3 WLR 125, [1982] Crim LR 237, 125 Sol Jo
863 . . . 56, 659


J

Jackson, Re, Jackson v Ward [1907] 2 Ch 354,
76 LJ Ch 553 . . . 698

Jackson v Marley Davenport Ltd (2004)
The Times, 7 Oct . . . 579

Jaggers v Binnings (1815) 1 Stark 64 . . . 357

James v R (1970) 55 Cr App Rep 299, 16 WIR 272,
PC . . . 239

James v South Glamorgan County Council
(1994) 99 Cr App Rep 321 . . . 145

Jamieson v Jamieson [1952] AC 525, [1952] 1 All
ER 875, 116 JP 226, [1952] 1 TLR 833, 1952 SC
(HL) 44, 1952 SLT 257, HL . . . 688

Jasiewicz v Jasiewicz [1962] 3 All ER 1017, [1962]
1 WLR 1426, 106 Sol Jo 882 . . . 555

Jayasena v R [1970] AC 618, [1970] 1 All ER 219,
[1970] 2 WLR 448, 114 Sol Jo 56, PC . . . 84,
120

JB v Switzerland [2001] Crim LR 748,
ECHR . . . 632

JC v CC [2001] EWCA Civ 1625 . . . 343

Jeffrey v Black [1978] QB 490, [1978] 1 All ER
555, [1977] 3 WLR 895, 66 Cr App Rep 81,
142 JP 122, [1977] Crim LR 555, 121 Sol Jo
662, DC . . . 57, 59

Jenion, Re, Jenion v Wynne [1952] Ch 454, [1952]
1 All ER 1228, 96 Sol Jo 360, [1952] 2 TLR 17,
CA . . . 695

John v Humphreys [1955] 1 All ER 793, [1955]
1 WLR 325, 53 LGR 321, 119 JP 309, 99 Sol Jo
222, DC . . . 90

Johnson v Lawson (1824) 2 Bing 86, 2 LJOSCP
136, 9 Moore CP 183 . . . 366

Johnson v Lindsay (1889) 53 JP 599, 5 TLR 454,
DC; affd 23 QBD 508, CA; revsd [1891] AC
371, 55 JP 644, 61 LJQB 90, 40 WR 405, 65 LT
97, 7 TLR 715, HL . . . 357

Jones v DPP [1962] AC 635, [1962] 1 All ER 569,
[1962] 2 WLR 575, 46 Cr App Rep 129, 126 JP
216, 106 Sol Jo 192, HL . . . 61, 64, 542, 625

Jones v GD Searle & Co Ltd [1978] 3 All ER 654,
[1979] 1 WLR 101, 122 Sol Jo 435, CA . . . 655

Jones v Godrich (1845) 5 Moo PCC 16, 9 Jur 313,
3 Notes of Cases 487, PC . . . 648

Jones v Great Central Rly Co [1910] AC 4, 79 LJKB 191, 53 Sol Jo 428, 100 LT 710, HL . . . 645

Jones v Great Western Rly Co (1930) 36 Com Cas 136, 144 LT 194, 47 TLR 39, HL . . . 86

Jones v Greater Manchester Police Authority [2001] EWHC Admin 189, [2002] ACD 4, DC . . . 469

Jones v Metcalfe [1967] 3 All ER 205, [1967] 1 WLR 1286, 131 JP 494, 111 Sol Jo 563, DC . . . 100, 242

Jones v Owens (1870) 34 JP 759 . . . 57

Jones v University of Warwick [2003] 3 All ER 760, CA . . . 58

Joseph v Joseph [1915] P 122, 78 JP 520, 84 LJP 104, 112 LT 170 . . . 244

Joseph Hargreaves, Re [1900] 1 Ch 347 . . . 603

Joy v Federation Against Copyright Theft Ltd [1993] Crim LR 588 . . . 399

Joy v Phillips, Mills & Co Ltd [1916] 1 KB 849, 85 LJKB 770, 9 BWCC 242, 114 LT 577, CA . . . 23, 469

Judd v Minster of Pensions and National Insurance [1966] 2 QB 580, [1965] 3 All ER 642, [1966] 2 WLR 218, 109 Sol Jo 815 . . . 114

K

K (minors), Re [1988] Fam 1, [1988] 1 All ER 214, [1987] 3 WLR 1233, [1988] 1 FLR 435, [1988] Fam Law 166, 152 JP 185, 131 Sol Jo 1697, [1987] LS Gaz R 3501 . . . 124

K (minors), Re [1994] 3 All ER 230, [1994] 2 FCR 805, [1994] 1 FLR 377, [1994] Fam Law 247, sub nom Kent County Council v K [1994] 1 WLR 912 . . . 595, 634

Kajala v Noble (1982) 75 Cr App Rep 149, CA . . . 29, 262, 278

Kanapathipillai v Parpathy [1956] AC 580, [1956] 3 WLR 584, 100 Sol Jo 618, PC . . . 695

Karamat v R [1956] AC 256, [1956] 1 All ER 415, [1956] 2 WLR 412, 40 Cr App Rep 13, 120 JP 136, 100 Sol Jo 109, PC . . . 280

Karia v Director of Public Prosecutions (2002) 166 JP 753 . . . 192

Karuma, Son of Kaniu v R [1955] AC 197, PC . . . 57, 59

Kaslefsky v Kaslefsky [1951] P 38, [1950] 2 All ER 398, 48 LGR 520, 114 JP 404, 94 Sol Jo 519, 66 (pt 2) TLR 616, CA . . . 688

Keane v Mount Vernon Colliery Co Ltd [1933] AC 309, 102 LJPC 97, 77 Sol Jo 157, 149 LT 73, 49 TLR 306, 26 BWCC 245, HL . . . 712

Kelly v Purvis [1983] QB 663, [1983] 1 All ER 525, [1983] 2 WLR 299, 76 Cr App Rep 165, 147 JP 135, [1983] Crim LR 185, 127 Sol Jo 52 . . . 290

Kelly Communications Ltd v DPP [2003] Crim LR 479, CA . . . 690

Kennedy v DPP [2003] Crim Lr 120, DC . . . 69

Kennedy v HM Advocate 1944 JC 171, 1945 SLT 111, 1944 SN 40 . . . 106

Khan v Khan [1982] 2 All ER 60, [1982] 1 WLR 513, 126 Sol Jo 187, CA . . . 628, 636

Khan v United Kingdom (2000) Times, 23 May, ECtHR . . . 78, 81

Khawaja v Secretary of State for the Home Department [1984] AC 74, [1983] 1 All ER 765, [1983] 2 WLR 321, [1982] Imm AR 139, 127 Sol Jo 137, HL . . . 110, 116

Kilby v R (1973) 129 CLR 460, 47 ALJR 369, HC of A . . . 186

Kilgour v Owen (1889) 88 LT Jo 7 . . . 268

Kinch v Walcott [1929] AC 482, 98 LJPC 129, [1929] All ER Rep 720, 141 LT 102, PC . . . 601

King v R [1969] 1 AC 304, [1968] 2 All ER 610, [1968] 3 WLR 391, 52 Cr App Rep 353, 112 Sol Jo 419, 12 WIR 268, PC . . . 59, 429

Kingshott v Associated Kent Newspapers Ltd [1991] 1 QB 88, [1991] 2 All ER 99, [1990] 3 WLR 675, CA . . . 34

Kingswood, The. See Constantine (Joseph) Steamship Line Ltd v Imperial Smelting Corpn Ltd, The Kingswood

Kirby v Hickson (1850) 14 JP 370, 1 LM & P 364, Cox M & H 309, 14 Jur 625, Rob L & W 372, 15 LTOS 138 . . . 709

Kirkup v DPP [2004] Crim LR 230, SC . . . 69

Kite, The [1933] P 154, 102 LJP 101, 18 Asp MLC 413, [1933] All ER Rep 234, 149 LT 498, 49 TLR 525, 46 Ll L Rep 83 . . . 29, 703

Knight v David [1971] 3 All ER 1066, [1971] 1 WLR 1671, 115 Sol Jo 740 . . . 352

Knowles v Knowles [1962] P 161, [1962] 1 All ER 659, [1962] 2 WLR 742, 105 Sol Jo 1011 . . . 695

Konigsberg (a bankrupt), Re, ex p Trustee v Konigsberg [1989] 3 All ER 289, [1989] 1 WLR 1257, [1990] Fam Law 94, 133 Sol Jo 1337, [1989] NLJR 1302 . . . 641

Koscot AG, Re [1972] 3 All ER 829 . . . 352

Koscot Interplanetary (UK) Ltd, Re, Re Koscot AG [1972] 3 All ER 829 . . . 352

Kuruma, Son of Kaniu v R [1955] AC 197, [1955] 1 All ER 236, [1955] 2 WLR 223, 119 JP 157, 99 Sol Jo 73, PC . . . 154, 159, 162, 429

Kuwait Airways Corporation v Iraqui Airways Co [2005] EWCA 286 . . . 653

L

L (a minor) (police investigation: privilege),
Re [1997] AC 16, [1996] 2 All ER 78, [1996]
2 WLR 395, 160 LG Rev 417, [1996] 2 FCR 145,
[1996] 1 FLR 731, [1996] Fam Law 400, [1996]
15 LS Gaz R 30, [1996] NLJR 441, 140 Sol Jo
LB 116, HL . . . 223, 643

L, Re [1997] 1 AC 16, HL . . . 655

Lafone v Griffin (1909) 25 TLR 308 . . . 266

Lal Chand Marwari v Mahant Ramrup Gir (1925)
42 TLR 159, PC . . . 698, 699

Lam Chi-ming v R [1991] 2 AC 212, [1991] 3 All
ER 172, [1991] 2 WLR 1082, 93 Cr App Rep
358, [1991] Crim LR 914, 135 Sol Jo 445,
PC . . . 430

Land Securities plc v Westminster City Council
[1993] 1 WLR 286 . . . 676

Lanford v General Medical Council [1990] 1 AC
13, [1989] 2 All ER 921, [1989] 3 WLR 665,
4 BMLR 71, [1989] 29 LS Gaz R 46, PC . . . 508

Lang v Lang [1955] AC 402, [1954] 3 All ER 571,
[1954] 3 WLR 762, 119 JP 368, 98 Sol Jo 803,
PC . . . 688

Langham v Wellingborough School Governors
and Fryer (1932) 30 LGR 276, 96 JP 236, 101
LJKB 513, 147 LT 91, CA . . . 703

La Roche v Armstrong [1922] 1 KB 485, 91 LJKB
342, [1922] All ER Rep 311, 66 Sol Jo 351,
126 LT 699, 38 TLR 347 . . . 663

Lask v Gloucester Area Health Authority (1985)
2 PN 96, CA . . . 644

Lau Pak Ngam v R [1966] Crim LR 443 . . . 178

Lauderdale Peerage (1885) 10 App Cas 692,
HL . . . 690

Lawrence v Chester Chronicle (1986) Times,
8 February, CA . . . 110

Lee v South West Thames Regional Health
Authority [1985] 2 All ER 385, [1985] 1 WLR
845, 128 Sol Jo 333, [1985] LS Gaz R 2015,
[1985] NLJ Rep 438, CA . . . 656

Leeds City Council v Azam and Fazi [1989] RTR
66, 153 JP 157 . . . 89

Leeds City Council v Hussain [2002] EWHC 1145
(Admin) (2002) The Times, 8 July . . . 339

Legge v Edmonds (1855) 20 JP 19, 25 LJ Ch 125,
4 WR 71, 26 LTOS 117 . . . 694

Lego Systems A/S v Lego M Lemelstrich [1983]
FSR 155 . . . 554

Levene v Roxhan [1970] 3 All ER 683, [1970]
1 WLR 1322, 114 Sol Jo 721, CA . . . 673

Levison v Patent Steam Carpet Cleaning Co Ltd
[1978] QB 69, [1977] 3 All ER 498, [1977]
3 WLR 90, 121 Sol Jo 406, CA . . . 104

Levy v Assicurazioni Generali [1940] AC 791,
[1940] 3 All ER 427, 84 Sol Jo 633, 56 TLR 851,
67 LI L Rep 174, PC . . . 105

Lidderdale, Re (1912) 57 Sol Jo 3 . . . 697

Lilley v Pettit [1946] KB 401, sub nom Pettit v
Lilley [1946] 1 All ER 593, 44 LGR 171, 110 JP
218, 115 LJKB 385, 90 Sol Jo 380, 175 LT 119,
62 TLR 359, DC . . . 363

Lillicrap v Nalder & Son (a firm) [1993] 1 All ER
724, [1993] 1 WLR 94, [1992] NLJR 1449,
CA . . . 662

Line v Taylor (1862) 3 F & F 731 . . . 276

Li Shu-ling v R [1989] AC 270, [1988] 3 All ER
138, [1988] 3 WLR 671, 88 Cr App Rep 82,
132 Sol Jo 1268, PC . . . 30, 382

Liverpool Roman Catholic Diocese Trustees Inc. v
Goldberg (No 3) [2001] 1 WLR 2337,
ChD . . . 562

Lloyd v Mostyn (1842) 2 Dowl NS 476, 12 LJ Ex 1,
6 Jur 974, 10 M & W 478 . . . 56

Lobban v R [1995] 2 All ER 602, [1995] 1 WLR
877, [1995] 2 Cr App Rep 573, [1995] Crim LR
881, [1995] 21 LS Gaz R 37, [1995] NLJR 688,
139 Sol Jo LB 140, PC . . . 50, 383, 421, 494

Lockheed-Arabia Corpn v Owen [1993] QB 806,
[1993] 3 All ER 641, [1993] 3 WLR 468, [1993]
26 LS Gaz R 37, [1993] NLJR 654, CA . . . 273

London and County Securities Ltd v Nicholson
[1980] 3 All ER 861, [1980] 1 WLR 948, 124
Sol Jo 544 . . . 605

London General Omnibus Co Ltd v Lavell [1901]
1 Ch 135, 70 LJ Ch 17, 18 RPC 74, 83 LT 453,
17 TLR 61, CA . . . 279

Lonrho Ltd v Shell Petroleum Co Ltd [1981] 2 All
ER 456, [1980] 1 WLR 627, 124 Sol Jo 412, 130
NLJ 605, HL . . . 604, 607

Lonrho plc v Fayed (No 4) [1994] 1 All ER 870;
on appeal [1994] QB 775, [1994] 1 All ER 870,
[1994] 2 WLR 209, 66 TC 220, CA . . . 604, 607

Lonsdale v Heaton (1830) 1 You 58 . . . 367

Lord Talbot de Malahide v Cusack (1864)
17 ICLR 213 . . . 173

Loughans v Odhams Press Ltd [1963] 1 QB 299,
[1962] 1 All ER 404, [1962] 2 WLR 692, 106
Sol Jo 262, CA . . . 673, 675

Lowery v R [1974] AC 85, [1973] 3 All ER 662,
[1973] 3 WLR 235, 58 Cr App Rep 35,
117 Sol Jo 583, PC . . . 527, 528, 559, 560

Luca v Italy [2003] 36 EHRR 46 . . . 309

Lucas v Barking, Havering and Redbridge
Hospitals NHS Trust [2003] 4 All ER 720,
CA . . . 578

Lucas v Williams & Sons [1892] 2 QB 113, 61
LJQB 595, 66 LT 706, 8 TLR 575, CA . . . 583

Lui-Mei Lin v R [1989] AC 288, [1989] 1 All ER 359, [1989] 2 WLR 175, 88 Cr App Rep 296, [1989] Crim LR 364, PC . . . 203

Lustre Hosiery Ltd v York (1936) 54 CLR 134, HC of A . . . 356

Lyell v Kennedy (1889) 14 App Cas 437, 59 LJQB 268, 38 WR 353, 62 LT 77, HL . . . 360

Lyell v Kennedy (No 3) (1884) 27 Ch D 1, 53 LJ Ch 937, [1881–5] All ER Rep 814, 50 LT 730, CA . . . 644, 649

**M**

M (a minor) (disclosure of material), Re (1990) 88 LGR 841, [1990] FCR 485, [1990] 2 FLR 36, [1990] Fam Law 259, CA . . . 595

M (a minor) (No 2), Re [1995] 1 FCR 417, [1994] 1 FLR 59, [1994] Fam Law 374, CA . . . 101

M and R (minors) (sexual abuse: video evidence), Re [1996] 4 All ER 239, sub nom Re M and R (minors) (expert opinion: evidence) [1996] 2 FCR 617, sub nom Re M and R (child abuse: evidence) [1996] 2 FLR 195, [1996] Fam Law 541, CA . . . 20, 181

McCarthy v Ship Melita (Owners) (1923) 16 BWCC 222, 130 LT 445, CA . . . 364

M'Cormick v Garnett (1854) 5 De GM & G 278, 23 LJ Ch 777, 2 Eq Rep 536, 18 Jur 412, 2 WR 408, 23 LTOS 136 . . . 555

MacDarmaid v A-G [1950] P 218, [1950] 1 All ER 497, 94 Sol Jo 211, 66 (pt 1) TLR 543 . . . 688

MacDonnell v Evans (1852) 16 JP 88, 3 Car & Kir 51, 11 CB 930, 21 LJCP 141, 16 Jur 103, 18 LTOS 241 . . . 265

McDowell v Hirschheld Lipson & Rumney and Smith [1992] 2 FLR 126, [1992] Fam Law 430 . . . 665

McGrath v Field [1987] RTR 349, [1987] Crim LR 275 . . . 63

McGreevy v DPP [1972] NI 125, [1973] 1 All ER 503, [1973] 1 WLR 276, 57 Cr App Rep 424, 137 JP 315, 117 Sol Jo 164, HL . . . 13, 113

McIlkenny v Chief Constable of West Midlands [1980] QB 283, [1980] 2 All ER 227, [1980] 2 WLR 689, 144 JP 291, 124 Sol Jo 83, CA; affd sub nom Hunter v Chief Constable of West Midlands Police [1982] AC 529, [1981] 3 All ER 727, [1981] 3 WLR 906, 125 Sol Jo 829, HL . . . 672, 676

MacKinnon v Donaldson Lufkin and Jenrette Securities Corpn [1986] Ch 482, [1986] 1 All ER 653, [1986] 2 WLR 453, 130 Sol Jo 224 . . . 272

McPhilemy v Times Newspapers Ltd [1999] 3 All ER 775, CA . . . 47

McQuaker v Goddard [1940] 1 KB 687, [1940) 1 All ER 471, 109 LJKB 673, 84 Sol Jo 203, 162 LT 232, 56 TLR 409, CA . . . 709

McTaggart v McTaggart [1949] P 94, [1948] 2 All ER 754, 46 LGR 527, [1949] LJR 82, 92 Sol Jo 617, 64 TLR 558, CA . . . 666

McVeigh v Beattie [1988] Fam 69, [1988] 2 All ER 500, [1988] 2 WLR 992, [1988] FCR 516, [1988] 2 FLR 67, [1988] Fam Law 290, 132 Sol Jo 125 . . . 17

Mahadervan v Mahadervan [1964] P 233, [1962] 3 All ER 1108, [1963] 2 WLR 271, 106 Sol Jo 533 . . . 119, 691

Mahon v Osborne [1939] 2 KB 14, [1939] 1 All ER 535, 108 LJKB 567, 83 Sol Jo 134, 160 LT 329, CA . . . 684

Makanjuola v Metropolitan Police Commissioner [1992] 3 All ER 617, [1989] NL7R 468, CA . . . 616, 617

Makin v A-G for New South Wales [1894] AC 57, 58 JP 148, 63 LJPC 41, 17 Cox CC 704, 6 R 373, [1891–4] All ER Rep 24, 69 LT 778, 10 TLR 155, PC . . . 506

Manchester Brewery Co v Coombs [1901] 2 Ch 608, 70 LJ Ch 814, 82 LT 347, 16 TLR 299 . . . 294, 340

Mancini v DPP [1942] AC 1, [1941] 3 All ER 272, 28 Cr App Rep 65, 111 LJKB 84, 165 LT 353, 58 TLR 25, HL . . . 40, 106, 112

Manda, Re [1993] Fam 183, [1993] 1 All ER 733, [1993] 2 WLR 161, [1993] 1 FLR 205, [1993] Fam Law 217, [1992] 39 LS Gaz R 33, [1992] NLJR 1233, 136 Sol Jo LB 253, CA . . . 595

Marchioness of Blandford v Dowager Duchess of Marlborough (1743) 2 Atk 542 . . . 364

Marcq v Christie Manson and Woods Ltd [2002] 4 All ER 1005, QBD . . . 104

Marks v Beyfus (1890) 25 QBD 494, 55 JP 182, 59 LJQB 479, 17 Cox CC 196, 38 WR 705, 63 LT 733, 6 TLR 406, CA . . . 599

Mash v Darley [1914] 1 KB 1, 78 JP 4, 83 LJKB 78, 23 Cox CC 661, 58 Sol Jo 49, 109 LT 873, 30 TLR 5, DC; affd [1914] 3 KB 1226, 79 JP 33, 83 LJKB 1740, 24 Cox CC 414, 58 Sol Jo 652, 111 LT 744, 30 TLR 585, [1914–15] All ER Rep Ext 1522, CA . . . 672, 673

Matthews, Re, ex p Powell (1875) 1 Ch D 501, 45 LJ Bcy 100, 24 WR 378, 34 LT 224, CA . . . 710

Matthews v Morris [1981] Crim LR 495 . . . 145

Matto v Crown Court at Wolverhampton (or DPP) [1987] RTR 337, [1987] Crim LR 641 . . . 52, 64, 66, 409

Mattouk v Massad [1943] AC 588, [1943] 2 All ER 517, PC . . . 233

Maturin v A-G [1938] 2 All ER 214, 82 Sol Jo 275, 54 TLR 627 . . . 695

Maugham v Hubbard (1828) 8 B & C 14, 6 LJOSKB 229, 2 Man & Ry KB 5 . . . 172, 173

Mawaz Khan v R and Amanat Khan [1967] 1 AC 454, [1967] 1 All ER 80, [1966] 3 WLR 1275, 110 Sol Jo 869, PC . . . 289

Mawdsley v Chief Constable of the Cheshire Constabulary [2004] 1 WLR 1035 . . . 383, 631

Maxwell v DPP [1935] AC 309, 32 LGR 335, 24 Cr App Rep 152, 98 JP 387, 103 LJKB 501, 30 Cox CC 160, [1934] All ER Rep 168, 151 LT 477, 50 TLR 499, HL . . . 60, 62, 483, 535

Maxwell v Pressdram Ltd [1987] 1 All ER 656, [1987] 1 WLR 298, 131 Sol Jo 327, [1987] LS Gaz R 1148, CA . . . 611

Mears v R [1993] 1 WLR 818, 97 Cr App Rep 239, [1993] Crim LR 885, 137 Sol Jo LB 133, PC . . . 44

Meath (Bishop) v Marquis of Winchester (1836) 3 Bing NC 183, 10 Bli NS 330, 4 CI & Fin 445, 3 Scott 561, HL . . . 274

Mechanical and General Inventions Co Ltd and Lehwess v Austin and Austin Motor Co Ltd [1935] AC 346, 104 LJKB 403, [1935] All ER Rep 22, 153 LT 153, HL . . . 48, 202

Medway v Doublelock Ltd [1978] 1 All ER 1261, [1978] 1 WLR 710, 122 Sol Jo 248 . . . 596

Memory Corpn plc v Sidhu [2000] 1 All ER 434, [2000] 2 WLR 1106, [2000] 04 LS Gaz R 33, 144 Sol Jo LB 51 . . . 626

Mercer v Chief Constable of the Lancashire Constabulary [1991] 2 All ER 504, [1991] 1 WLR 367, CA . . . 149

Mercer v Denne [1905] 2 Ch 538, 3 LGR 1293, 70 JP 65, 74 LJ Ch 723, 54 WR 303, [1904–7] All ER Rep, 93 LT 412, 21 TLR 760, CA . . . 363, 367

Mercer v Whall (or Wall) (1845) 5 QB 447, 1 New Pract Cas 246, 14 LJQB 267, 9 Jur 576, 5 LTOS 304 . . . 108

Merricks v Nott-Bower [1965] 1 QB 57, [1964] 1 All ER 717, [1964] 2 WLR 702, 128 JP 267, 108 Sol Jo 116, CA . . . 587

Metropolitan Asylum District Managers v Hill (Appeal No 1) (1882) 47 JP 148, 47 LT 29, HL . . . 25

Metropolitan Police Commissioner v Caldwell [1982] AC 341, [1981] 2 WLR 509, sub nom R v Caldwell [1981] 1 All ER 961, 73 Cr App Rep 13, 145 JP 211, 125 Sol Jo 239, HL . . . 34

Metropolitan Police Commissionerr v Locker [1993] 3 All ER 584, [1993] ICR 440, [1993] IRLR 319, [1993] NLJR 543, EAT . . . 607

Metropolitan Rly Co v Wright (1886) 11 App Cas 152, 55 LJQB 401, 34 WR 746, [1886–90] All ER Rep 391, 54 LT 658, 2 TLR 553, HL . . . 228

Michael, The. See Piermay Shipping Co SA and Brandy s Ltd v Chester, The Michael

Middleton v Rowlett [1954] 2 All ER 277, [1954] 1 WLR 831, 52 LGR 334, 118 JP 362, 98 Sol Jo 373 . . . 145

Mighell v Sultan of Johore [1894] 1 QB 149, 58 JP 244, 63 LJQB 593, 9 R 447, [1891–4] All ER Rep 1019, 70 LT 64, 10 TLR 115, CA . . . 710

Millard v DPP [1990] RTR 201, 91 Cr App Rep 108, 154 JP 626, [1990] Crim LR 601 . . . 687

Miller v Margaret Cawley [2002] All ER (D) 452 . . . 42, 114

Miller v Minister of Pensions [1947] 2 All ER 372, [1948] LJR 203, 91 Sol Jo 484, 177 LT 536, 63 TLR 474 . . . 110, 114, 696

Mills v Oddy (1834) 6 C & P 728 . . . 268

Mills v R [1995] 3 All ER 865, [1995] 1 WLR 511, [1995] Crim LR 884, Sol Jo LB 84, PC . . . 252

Minet v Morgan (1873) 8 Ch App 361, 42 LJ Ch 627, 21 WR 467, 28 LT 573 . . . 655

Minter v Priest [1930] AC 558, 99 LJKB 391, [1930] All ER Rep 431, 74 Sol Jo 200, 143 LT 57, 46 TLR 301, HL . . . 240, 640

Miranda v Arizona (1975) 384 US 436, US Sup Ct . . . 381

M'Naghten's Case (1843) 10 CI&Fin 200, HL . . . 87, 689

Mitchell v R [1998] AC 695, [i998] 2 WLR 839, [1998] 2 Cr App Rep 35, PC . . . 416

Mole v Mole [1951] P 21, [1950] 2 All ER 328, 48 LGR 439, 94 Sol Jo 518, 66 (pt 2) TLR 129, CA . . . 666, 667

Monckton v Tarr (1930) 23 BWCC 504, CA . . . 692, 693, 705

Monroe v Twisleton (1802) Peake Add Cas 219 . . . 124

Mood Music Publishing Co Ltd v De Wolfe Publishing Ltd [1976] Ch 119, [1976] 1 All ER 763, [1976] 2 WLR 451, 119 Sol Jo 809, CA . . . 241, 469

Moor v Moor [1954] 2 All ER 458, [1954] 1 WLR 927, 98 Sol Jo 438, CA . . . 169

Moorhouse v Lord (1863) 10 HL Cas 272, 32 LJ Ch 295, 9 Jur NS 677, 1 New Rep 555, 11 WR 637, 8 LT 212 . . . 119

Moriarty v London Chatham and Dover Rly Co (1870) LR 5 QB 314, 34 JP 692, 39 LJQB 109, 18 WR 625, 22 LT 163 . . . 355

Morris v Beardmore [1981] AC 446, [1980] 2 All ER 753, [1980] 3 WLR 283, [1980] RTR 321, 71 Cr App Rep 256, 144 JP 331, 124 Sol Jo 512, HL . . . 48, 60

Morris v Davies (1837) 5 Cl & Fin 163, 1 Jur 911, [1835–42] All ER Rep 270, HL . . . 691, 695, 696

Morris v Miller (1767) Bull NP 27b, 4 Burr 2057, 1 Wm B1632, 96 ER 366 . . . 693

Morris v Stratford-on-Avon RDC [1973] 3 All ER 263, [1973] 1 WLR 1059, 117 Sol Jo 601, CA . . . 244

Morrow, Geach and Thomas v DPP [1994] Crim LR 58 . . . 607

Mortimer v M'Callan (1840) 9 LJ Ex 73, 4 Jur 172, 6 M & W 58 . . . 269

Morton v Morton, Daly and McNaught [1937] P 151, [1937] 2 All ER 470, 106 LJP 100, 81 Sol Jo 359, 157 LT 46, 53 TLR 659 . . . 357

Moseley v Davies (1822) 11 Price 162 . . . 367

Mullan v Birmingham City Council (1999) Times, 29 July . . . 42

Mullen v Hackney London Borough Council [1997] 2 All ER 906, [1997] 1 WLR 1103, 29 HLR 592, CA . . . 709, 713

Muller v Linsley & Mortimer (a firm) [1995] 03 LS Gaz R 38, 139 Sol Jo LB 43, [1996] PNLR 74, CA . . . 663

Mullin, Re [1993] Crim LR 390 . . . 54

Multi Guarantee Co Ltd v Cavalier Insurance Co Ltd (1986) Times, 24 June . . . 605, 618

Munro, Brice & Co v War Risks Association [1918] 2 KB 78, 88 LJKB 509, 14 Asp MLC 312, [1916–17] All ER Rep 981n, 118 LT 708, 34 TLR 331; revsd [1920] 3 KB 94, 89 LJKB 1009, 15 Asp MLC 45, 25 Com Cas 112, 123 LT 562, 36 TLR 241, 2 Ll L Rep 2, CA . . . 105

Murdoch v Taylor [1965] AC 574, [1965] 1 All ER 406, [1965] 2 WLR 425, 49 Cr App Rep 119, 129 JP 208, 109 Sol Jo 130, HL . . . 52–54, 529

Murray v DPP [1994] 1 WLR 1, 97 Cr App Rep 151, 99 Cr App Rep 396, HL . . . 438–40

Murray v United Kingdom (1996) 22 EHRR 29, ECtHR . . . 58, 135, 235, 440, 452

Mutch v Allen [2001] CPLR 200, CA . . . 577

Mutual Life Insurance Co v Hillman 145 US 285 (1892) . . . 378

Myatt v Myatt and Parker [1962] 2 All ER 247, [1962] 1 WLR 570, 106 Sol Jo 246 . . . 357

Myers v DPP [1965] AC 1001, [1964] 3 WLR 145, sub nom R v Myers [1964] 1 All ER 877, 108 Sol Jo 221, CCA; affd sub nom Myers v DPP [1965] AC 1001, [1964] 2 All ER 881, [1964] 3 WLR 145, 48 Cr App Rep 348, 128 JP 481, 108 Sol Jo 519, HL . . . 299, 315

N

National Justice Cia Naviera SA v Prudential Assurance Co Ltd (The Ikarian Reefer) [1993] 2 Lloyd's Rep 68 . . . 562

Nederlandse Reassurantie Groep Holding NV v Bacon & Woodrow (a firm) [1995] 1 All ER 976, [1995] 2 Lloyd's Rep 77 . . . 642, 662

Neill v North Antrim Magistrates' Court [1992] 4 All ER 846, [1992] 1 WLR 1220, 97 Cr App Rep 121, 158 JP 197, [1993] Crim LR 945, [1993] 9 LS Gaz R 44, HL . . . 330, 377

Neilson v Harford (1841) 1 Web Pat Cas 295, 11 LJ Ex 20, 8 M & W 806 . . . 34

Neilson v Laugharne [1981] QB 736, [1981] 1 All ER 829, [1981] 2 WLR 537, 125 Sol Jo 202, CA . . . 606, 617, 620, 644

Nelson (Earl) v Lord Bridport (1845) 8 Beav 527, 10 Jur 871, [1843–60] All ER Rep 1032, 8 LTOS 18 . . . 555

Nevill v Fine Arts and General Insurance Co [1897] AC 68, 61 JP 500, 66 LJQB 195, [1895–9] All ER Rep 164, 75 LT 606, 13 TLR 97, HL . . . 34

New Brunswick Rly Co v British and French Trust Corpn Ltd [1939] AC l, [1938] 4 All ER 747, 108 LJKB 115, 44 Com Cas 82, 83 Sol Jo 132, 160 LT 137, 55 TLR 260, HL . . . 598, 601

Ng Chun Pui v Lee Chuen Tat [1988] RTR 298, 132 Sol Jo 1244, PC . . . 704

Nicholas v Penny [1950] 2 KB 466, 94 Sol Jo 437, 66 (pt 1) TLR 1122, sub nom Penny v Nicholas [1950] 2 All ER 89, 48 LGR 535, 114 7P 335, DC : . . . 231, 690

Nicholls v Parker (1805) 14 East 331n . . . 367

Niemietz v Germany (1992) 16 EHRR 97 . . . 58

Nimmo v Alexander Cowan & Sons Ltd [1968] AC 107, [1967] 3 All ER 187, [1967] 3 WLR 1169, 111 Sol Jo 668, 1967 SC (HI,) 79, 1967 SLT 277 . . . 89, 92

Nisbett, ex p (1844) 8 JP 823, 8 Jur 1071, 4 LTOS 120, sub nom R v Nesbitt 2 Dow & L 529, sub nom Re Nesbitt 14 LJMC 30, 1 New Sess Cas 366 . . . 708

Nixon v United States 418 US 683 (1974) . . . 590

Noble v Kennoway (1780) 2 Doug KB 510, [1775–1802] All ER Rep 439 . . . 20

Nominal Defendant v Clement (1960) 104 CLR 476, HC of A . . . 186

North Yorkshire Trading Standards Department v Williams (1994) 159 JP 383, DC . . . 192

Norwich Pharmacal Co v Customs and Excise Commissioners [1974] AC 133, [1972] 3 All ER 813, [1972] 3 WLR 870, [1972] RPC 743, 116 Sol Jo 823, CA; revsd [1974] AC 133, [1973] 2 All ER 943, [1973] 3 WLR 164, [1973] FSR 365, [1974] RPC 101, 117 Sol Jo 567, HL . . . 605, 608, 611, 623

Nottingham City Council v Amin [2000] 2 All ER 946, [2000] 1 WLR 1071, [2000] RTR 122,

[2000] 1 Cr App Rep 426, [2000]
Crim LR 174 . . . 73

Nye v Niblett [1918] 1 KB 23, 16 LGR 57,
82 JP 57, 87 LJKB 590, 26 Cox CC 113,
[1916–17] All ER Rep 520 . . . 707


O

O, Re [1991] 2 QB 520, [1991] 1 All ER 330,
[1991] 2 WLR 475, [1990] NLJR 1755,
CA . . . 636, 637

O, (Thomas), Re [1992] 4 All ER 814, CA . . . 637

Oakes v Uzzell [1932] P 19, 100 LJP 99, 75 Sol Jo
543, 146 LT 95, 47 TLR 573 . . . 274

O'Brien v Chief Constable of South Wales [2005]
UKHL 26 . . . 469

O'Connell v Adams [1973] Crim LR 313 . . . 206

O'Connor v Marjoribanks (1842) 11 LJCP 267,
6 Jur 509, 4 Man & G 435, 5 Scott NR
394 . . . 124

Official Solicitor to the Supreme Court v
K [1965] AC 201, [1963] 3 All ER 191, [1963]
3 WLR 408, 107 Sol Jo 616, HL . . . 338

Omichund v Barker (1745) 2 Eq Cas Abr 397,
Willes 538, sub nom Omychund v Barker 1 Atk
21, sub nom Ormichund v Barker 1 Wils
84 . . . 29, 124

O'Rourke v Darbishire [1920] AC 581, 89 LJ Ch
162, [1920] All ER Rep 1, 64 Sol Jo 322,
123 LT 68, 36 TLR 350, HL . . . 652

Osborne (or Osborn) v Chocqueel [1896] 2 QB
109, 65 LJQB 534, 44 WR 575, 40 Sol Jo 532, 74
LT 786, 12 TLR 437 . . . 469

Ovens's Goods, Re (1892) 29 LR Ir 451 . . . 274

Overbury, Re, Sheppard v Matthews [1955] Ch
122, [1954] 3 All ER 308, [1954] 3 WLR 644, 98
Sol Jo 768 . . . 695

Overseas Programming Co Ltd v
Cinematographische Commerz-Anstalt and
Iduna Film GmbH (1984) Times,
16 May . . . 627, 630

Owen v Chesters [1985] RTR 191, 149 JP 295,
[1985] Crim LR 156, 128 Sol Jo 856 . . . 299

Owen v Edwards (1983) 77 Cr App Rep 191, 147
JP 245, [1983] Crim LR 800 . . . 178, 180

Owner v Bee Hive Spinning Co Ltd [1914] 1 KB
105, 12 LGR 421, 78 JP 15, 83 LJKB 282, 23 Cox
CC 626, 109 LT 800, 30 TLR 21, DC . . . 269

Oxford Poor Rate Case, Re. See R v Vice-
Chancellor of Oxford University

Oxfordshire County Council v M [1994] Fam
151, [1994] 2 All ER 269, [1994] 2 WLR 343,
[1994] 1 FCR 753, [1994] 1 FLR 175,
CA . . . 654, 655

Oxfordshire County Council v P [1995] Fam 161,
[1995] 2 All ER 225, [1995] 2 WLR 543, [1995]
2 FCR 212, [1995] 1 FLR 552, [1995] Fam Law
294 . . . 595, 634

Oxley v Penwarden [2001] Lloyd's Rep 347,
CA . . . 574


P

P, Re [1989] Crim LR 897, CA . . . 203

Packer v Clayton (1932) 31 LGR 98, 97 JP 14,
DC . . . 675

Palastanga v Solman [1962] Crim LR 334, 106 Sol
Jo 176 . . . 145

Palermo, The (1883) 9 PD 6, 53 LJP 6, 5 Asp MLC
165, 32 WR 403, 49 LT 551, CA . . . 644

Palmer v R [1971] AC 814, [1971] 1 All ER 1077,
[1971] 2 WLR 831, 55 Cr App Rep 223, 243n,
115 Sol Jo 264, 16 WIR 499, 511, PC . . . 106

Pamplin v Express Newspapers Ltd (No 2) [1988]
1 All ER 282, [1988] 1 WLR 116n, 129 Sol Jo
190, CA . . . 467

Parks v Clout [2003] EWCA Civ 1030 . . . 116

Parkes v R [1976] 3 All ER 380, [1976] 1 WLR
1251, 64 Cr App Rep 25, 140 JP 634, 120 Sol Jo
720, PC . . . 238, 427, 455

Parkin v Moon (1836) 7 C & P 408 . . . 169, 202

Parkinson v Parkinson [1939] P 346, [1939]
3 All ER 108, 83 Sol Jo 642, 161 LT 251,
55 TLR 860 . . . 700

Parry v Boyle [1987] RTR 282, 83 Cr App Rep
310, [1986] Crim LR 551 . . . 280

Parry v News Group Newspapers Ltd [1990]
NLJR 1719, CA . . . 641

Parry's Estate, Re, Parry v Fraser [1977] 1 All ER
309, [1977] 1 WLR 93n, 121 Sol Jo 70 . . . 108

Partington v Partington and Atkinson [1925]
P 34, 94 LJP 49, 69 Sol Jo 294, 132 LT 495, 41
TLR 174 . . . 669

Patel v Comptroller of Customs [1966] AC 356,
[1965] 3 All ER 593, [1965] 3 WLR 1222, 109
Sol Jo 832 . . . 86

Paterson v DPP [1990] RTR 329, [1990] Crim LR
651 . . . 334

Paul v DPP (1989) 90 Cr App Rep 173, [1989]
Crim LR 660, sub nom Paul v Luton Justices,
ex p Crown Prosecution Service 153 JP
512 . . . 712

Payne v Harrison [1961] 2 QB 403, [1961] 2 All
ER 873, [1961] 3 WLR 309, 105 Sol Jo 528,
CA . . . 42

Peach v Metropolitan Police Commissioner
[1986] QB 1064, [1986] 2 All ER 129, [1986]
2 WLR 1080, 130 Sol Jo 448, [1986] LS Gaz R
1725, CA . . . 606

Pearce v Foster (1885) 15 QBD 114, 50 JP 4, 54 LJQB 432, 33 WR 919, 52 LT 886, 1 TLR 502, CA . . . 655

Peatling, Re [1969] VR 214 . . . 700, 706

Peet v Mid Kent Healthcare Trust [2002] 1 WLR 210, CA . . . 574, 575, 577

Peete, Re, Peete v Crompton [1952] 2 All ER 599, [1952] WN 406, 96 Sol Jo 561, [1952] 2 TLR 383 . . . 688, 692, 693

Percy v DPP [1995] 3 All ER 124, [1995] 1 WLR 1382, 159 JP 337, [1995] Crim LR 714, [1995] 09 LS Gaz R 38 . . . 114

Perkins v Vaughan (1842) 12 LJCP 38, 6 Jur 1114, 4 Man & G 988, 5 Scott NR 881 . . . 340

Perry v Gibson (1834) 1 Ad & E148, 3 LJKB 158, 3 Nev & MKB 462 . . . 139

Perry v United Kingdom [2003] Crim LR 281 . . . 78

PG and JH v United Kingdom [2002] Crim LR 308 . . . 78

Phené's Trusts, Re (1870) 5 Ch App 139, 39 LJ Ch 316, 18 WR 303, [1861–73] All ER Rep 514, 22 LT 111, CA . . . 698

Phoenix Marine Inc v China Ocean Shipping Co [1999] 1 Lloyd's Rep 682, QBD . . . 556

Piche v R [1971] SCR 23, 11 DLR (3d) 709 . . . 381

Pickup v Thames and Mersey Marine Insurance Co Ltd (1878) 3 QBD 594, 47 LJQB 749, 4 Asp MLC 43, 26 WR 689, 39 LT 341, CA . . . 689

Piermay Shipping Co SA and Brandys Ltd v Chester, The Michael [1979] 1 Lloyd's Rep 55; affd [1979] 2 Lloyd's Rep 1, CA . . . 116

Piers v Piers (1849) 2 HL Cas 331, 13 Jur 569, 9 ER 1118, [1843–60] All ER Rep 159, 13 LTOS 41 . . . 119, 690, 691

Piggott v Sims [1973] RTR 15, [1972] Crim LR 595, DC . . . 145

Pim v Curell (1840) 6 M & W 234 . . . 367

Pizzey v Ford Motor Co [1993] 17 LS Gaz R 46, [1994] PIQR P 15, CA . . . 659

Plant v Taylor (1861) 7 H & N 211, 31 LJ Ex 289, 8 Jur NS 140, 5 LT 318 . . . 367

Plato Films Ltd v Speidel [1961] AC 1090, [1961] 1 All ER 876, [1961] 2 WLR 470, 105 Sol Jo 230, HL . . . 467

Polanski v Conde Nast Publications Ltd [2005] 1 All ER 945, HL . . . 141, 347

Police v Anderon [1972] NZLR 233 . . . 121

Pontifex v Jolly (1839) 9 C & P 202 . . . 108

Popek v National Westminster Bank plc [2002] EWCA Civ 42 . . . 577

Post Office v Estuary Radio Ltd [1968] 2 QB 740; [1967] 3 All ER 663, [1967] 1 WLR 1396, [1967] 2 Lloyd's Rep 299, 111 Sol Jo 636, CA . . . 116

Post Office Counters v Mahida [2003] EWCA Civ 1583 . . . 30, 267

Poulett Peerage [1903] AC 395, 72 LJKB 924, 19 TLR 644, HL . . . 695

Pozzi v Eli Lilley & Co (1986) Times, 3 December . . . 661

Practice Direction (Criminal Proceedings: Consolidation) [2002] 1 WLR 2870 . . . . . . 32, 37, 41, 122, 124, 151, 157, 221, 263, 277, 334, 399, 415, 424, 435, 549, 551, 714, 715

Practice Direction (Submission of No Case) [1962] 1 All ER 448, sub nom Practice Direction [1962] 1 WLR 227, 106 Sol Jo 133, DC . . . 41

Preston-Jones v Preston-Jones [1951] AC 391, [1951] 1 All ER 124, 49 LGR 417, 95 Sol Jo 13, [1951] 1 TLR 8, HL . . . 117, 118, 707

Price v Earl of Torrington (1703) 2 Ld Raym 873, 1 Salk 285, Holt KB 300 . . . 277

Price v Humphries [1958] 2 QB 353, [1958] 2 All ER 725, [1958] 3 WLR 304, 122 JP 423, 102 Sol Jo 583, DC . . . 145

Price v Manning (1889) 42 Ch D 372, 58 LJ Ch 649, 37 WR 785, 61 LT 537, CA . . . 195

Prince v Samo (1838) 7 Ad & El 627, 7 LJQB 123, 2 Jur 323, 3 Nev & PKB 139, 1 Will Woll & H 132 . . . 227

Pringle v R [2003] All ER (D) 236 (Jan) . . . 241

Proulx, Re [2001] 1 All ER 57, DC . . . 76, 391

Prudential Assurance Co v Edmonds (1877) 2 App Cas 487, HL . . . 26, 697

Prudential Assurance Co Ltd v Prudential Insurance Co of America [2002] EWHC 2809, Ch D . . . 664

PS v Germany (2000) EHRR CD 301 . . . 309

Q

Queen Caroline's Case (1820) 2 Brod & Bing 284, 1 State Tr NS App 1348 . . . 208, 227

R

R (Crown Prosecution Service) v Bolton Magistrates' Court [2004] 1 WLR 835, DC . . . 628

R (D) v Camberwell Green Youth Court [2005] 1 All ER 999, HL . . . 161, 165

R (DPP) v Acton Youth Court [2001] 1 WLR 1828 . . . 595

R (Grundy & Co Excavations Ltd) v Halton Division Magistrates' Court (2003) 167 JP 387, DC . . . 88, 102

R (Hallinan) v Middlesex Guildhall Crown Court [2005] All ER (D) 242 (Nov) . . . 654

R (Hillman) v Richmond Magistrates' Court [2003] All ER (D) 455 (Oct) . . . 201

R (Howe) v South Durham Magistrates' Court [2004] Crim LR 963, DC . . . 648

R (McCann) v Crown Court of Manchester [2003] 1 AC 787, HL . . . 115

R (Minors), Re [1991] 2 All ER 193, CA . . . 124

R (MJ) (an infant) [1975] 2 All ER 749 . . . 595

R (Morgan Grenfell) v Special Commissioners of Income Tax [2003] 1 AC 563, HL . . . 650, 651

R (N) v Dr M [2003] 1 WLR 562, CA . . . 120

R (on the application of the Crown Prosecution Service Harrow) v Brentford Youth Court [2004] Crim LR 159, DC . . . 158

R, Re (a minor) [1993] 4 All ER 702 . . . 654

R (S) v Waltham Forest Youth Court [2004] 2 Ce App R 335, SC . . . 142, 161, 166, 200

R (Thompson) v Chief Constable of the Northumberland Constabulary [2001] 1 WLR 1342, CA . . . 405

R v A (No. 2) [2002] 1 AC 45 . . . 210, 214–17

R v Abadom [1983] 1 All ER 364, [1983] 1 WLR 126, 76 Cr App Rep 48, [1983] Crim LR 254, 126 Sol Jo 562, [1982] LS Gaz R 1412, CA . . . 333, 568

R v Abbott [1955] 2 QB 497, [1955] 2 All ER 899, [1955] 3 WLR 369, 39 Cr App Rep 141, 119 JP 526, 99 Sol Jo 544, CCA . . . 40

R v Abraham (1848) 2 Car & Kir 550, 3 Cox CC 430 . . . 190

R v Abramovitch (1914) 11 Cr App Rep 45, 79 JP 184, 84 LJKB 396, 24 Cox CC 591, [1914–15] All ER Rep 204, 59 Sol Jo 288, 112 LT 480, 31 TLR 88, CCA . . . 688

R v Absolam (1988) 88 Cr App Rep 332, [1988] Crim LR 748, CA . . . 70

R v Ackinclose [1996] Crim LR 774, CA . . . 435

R v Acott [1997] 1 All ER 706, [1997] 1 WLR 306, [1997] 2 Cr App Rep 94, 161 JP 368, [1997] Crim LR 514, [1997] 10 LS Gaz R 31, [1997] NLJR 290, 141 Sol Jo LB 65, HL . . . 107

R v Acton Justices, ex p McMullen (1990) 92 Cr App Rep 98, 154 JP . . . 304, 330

R v Adair [1990] Crim LR 571, CA . . . 529

R v Adams [1980] QB 575, [1980] 1 All ER 473, [1980] 3 WLR 275, 70 Cr App Rep 149, [1980] Crim LR 53, 124 Sol Jo 527, CA . . . 60, 62

R v Adams [1993] Crim LR 525, CA . . . 33

R v Adams [1996] 2 Cr App Rep 467, CA . . . 554

R v Adams [1997] Crim LR 292, CA . . . 591

R v Agar [1990] 2 All ER 442, 90 Cr App Rep 318, 154 JP 89, [1990] Crim LR 183, [1989] NLJR 116, CA . . . 600

R v Agricultural Land Tribunal (South Western Province), ex p Benney [1955] 2 QB 140, [1955] 2 All ER 129, [1955] 2 WLR 872, 53 LGR 281, 99 Sol Jo 275, CA . . . 364

R v Ahmed (1984) 80 Cr App Rep 295, 6 Cr App Rep (S) 391, [1985] Crim LR 250 . . . 109

R v Aitken (1991) 94 Cr App Rep 85, CA . . . 145

R v Akaidere [1990] Crim LR 808, CA . . . 255, 256

R v Akram [1995] Crim LR 50, CA . . . 24

R v All Saints, Worcester Inhabitants (1817) 6 M & S 194 . . . 629

R v Alladice (1988) 87 Cr App Rep 380, [1988] Crim LR 608, [1988] NLJR 141, CA . . . 69, 394, 407–9, 411, 441

R v Allan [1969] 1 All ER 91, [1969] 1 WLR 33, 133 JP 87, 112 Sol Jo 861, CA . . . 112, 113

R v Allen [1996] Crim LR 426, CA . . . 191, 252

R v Allen (No 2) [2001] 4 All ER 768 . . . 429, 631

R v Allerton [1979] Crim LR 725 . . . 386

R v Ameer and Lucas [1977] Crim LR 104, CA . . . 59

R v Ananthanarayanan [1994] 2 All ER 847, [1994] 1 WLR 788, 98 Cr App Rep 1, 157 JP 1081, [1994] Crim LR 675, CA . . . 76, 545

R v Anderson (1929) 21 Cr App Rep 178, 29 Cox CC 102, 142 LT 580, CCA . . . 208

R v Anderson [1972] 1 QB 304, [1971] 3 All ER 1152, [1971] 3 WLR 939, 56 Cr App Rep 115, 136 JP 97, 115 Sol Jo 847, CA . . . 556

R v Anderson [1988] QB 678, [1988] 2 All ER 549, [1988] 2 WLR 1017, 87 Cr App Rep 349, [1988] Crim LR 297, 132 Sol Jo 460, [1988] 16 LS Gaz R 41, CA . . . 61, 481, 512, 513, 626

R v Anderson [1991] Crim LR 361, CA . . . 108

R v Anderson [1993] Crim LR 447, CA . . . 63, 411

R v Andover Justices, ex p Rhodes [1980] Crim LR 644, DC . . . 271

R v Andrews [1987] AC 281, [1987] 1 All ER 513, [1987] 2 WLR 413, 84 Cr App Rep 382, 151 JP 548, [1987] Crim LR 487, 131 Sol Jo 223, [1987] LS Gaz R 901, [1987] NLJ Rep 147, HL . . . 370–74

R v Andrews (1993) 15 Cr App Rep (S) 88, [1993] Crim LR 590, CA . . . 251

R v Angeli [1978] 3 All ER 950, [1979] 1 WLR 26, 68 Cr App Rep 32, 143 JP 89, 122 Sol Jo 591, CA . . . 121

R v Antill [2002] All ER (D) 176 (sep) . . . 27

R v Antrim County Justices [1895] 2 IR 603 . . . 712

R v Apicella (1985) 82 Cr App Rep 295, [1986] Crim LR 238, CA . . . 61

R v Argent [1997] 2 Cr App Rep 27, 161 JP 190,
    [1997] Crim LR 346, CA . . . 88, 90, 91, 100,
    446, 449, 452, 453, 620

R v Arif (1993) Times, 17 June, CA . . . 176

R v Armstrong [1995] Crim LR 831, CA . . . 152

R v Arnold [2005] Crim LR 56, CA . . . 304, 309

R v Asghar [1995] 1 Cr App Rep 223, [1994]
    Crim LR 941, CA . . . 242

R v Ashford Justices, ex p Hilden [1993] QB 555,
    [1993] 2 WLR 529, 96 Cr App Rep 92, 156 JP
    869, [1992] Crim LR 879, sub nom R v Ashford
    Magistrates' Court, ex p Hilden [1993]
    2 All ER 154 . . . 330

R v Asif (1985) 82 Cr App Rep 123, [1985]
    Crim LR 679, CA . . . 497

R v Askew [1981] Crim LR 398, CA . . . 209

R v Aspinall [1999] 2 Cr App Rep 115, [1999]
    Crim LR 741, 49 BMLR 82, CA . . . 68

R v Ataou [1988] QB 798, [1988] 2 All ER 321,
    [1988] 2 WLR 1147, 87 Cr App Rep 210, 152 JP
    201, [1988] Crim LR 461, 132 Sol Jo 537,
    [1988] 6 LS Gaz R 36, CA . . . 251, 650

R v Attard (1958) 43 Cr App Rep 90 . . . 286

R v Attfield [1961] 3 All ER 243, [1961]
    1 WLR 1135, 45 Cr App Rep 309, 125 JP 581,
    105 Sol Jo 633, CCA . . . 43

R v Audley [1907] 1 KB 383, 71 JP 101, 76 LJKB
    270, 21 Cox CC 374, 51 Sol Jo 146, 96 LT 160,
    23 TLR 211, [1904–7] All ER Rep Ext 1180,
    CCR . . . 92

R v Aves [1950] 2 All ER 330, 48 LGR 495, 34 Cr
    App Rep 159, 114 JP 402, 94 Sol Jo 475,
    sub nom Practice Note 66 (pt 2) TLR 156,
    CCA . . . 688

R v Aziz [1996] AC 41, [1995] 3 All ER 149,
    [1995] 3 WLR 53, [1995] 2 Cr App Rep 478,
    159 JP 669, [1995] Crim LR 897, [1995] 28 LS
    Gaz R 41, [1995] NLJR 921, 139 Sol Jo LB 158,
    HL . . . 189, 380, 475–77

R v B [1996] Crim LR 499, CA . . . 146

R v B [1997] Crim LR 220, CA . . . 182

R v B (C) [2004] 2 Cr App R 570, CA . . . 526

R v B (MT) [2000] Crim LR 181, CA . . . 237, 445

R v Badjan (1966) 50 Cr App Rep 141, 110 Sol Jo
    146, CCA . . . 43

R v Bagshaw [1984] 1 All ER 971, [1984] 1 WLR
    477, 78 Cr App Rep 163, [1984] Crim LR 233,
    128 Sol Jo 64, [1984] LS Gaz R 510, CA . . . 243

R v Bailey (1977) 66 Cr App Rep 31n,
    CCA . . . 571

R v Bailey [1993] 3 All ER 513, 97 Cr App Rep
    365, [1993] Crim LR 681, CA . . . 77, 403

R v Bailey [1995] 2 Cr App Rep 262, [1995]
    Crim LR 723, CA . . . 243, 246–48

R v Bailey [2001] All ER (D) 185 (Mar) . . . 174

R v Baldwin (1925) 18 Cr App Rep 175, 89 JP 116,
    28 Cox CC 17, [1925] All ER Rep 402, 69 Sol Jo
    429, 133 LT 191, CCA . . . 202

R v Baldwin [1986] Crim LR 681, CA . . . 196

R v Ball (1910) 5 Cr App Rep 238, 80 LJKB 89,
    22 Cox CC 364, 104 LT 47, CCA; on appeal
    [1911] AC 47, 75 JP 180, 103 LT 738, sub nom
    DPP v Ball (No 2) 6 Cr App Rep 31, 80 LJKB
    691, 22 Cox CC 366, [1908–10] All ER Rep
    111, 55 Sol Jo 139, HL . . . 14, 496, 506

R v Balmforth [1992] Crim LR 825, CA . . . 152

R v Bansal [1999] Crim LR 484, CA . . . 453

R v Barber (1844) 8 JP 644, 1 Car & Kir 434;
    sub nom R v Richards, Barber; Fletcher and
    Dorey 1 Cox CC 62; 3 LTOS 142 . . . 199

R v Barbery (1975) 62 Cr App Rep 248;
    CA . . . 188

R v Barker [1941] 2 KB 381, [194i] 3 All ER 33, 38
    Cr App Rep 52, 110 LJKB 680, 85 Sol Jo 405,
    166 LT 39, 57 TLR 626, CCA . . . 396, 429

R v Barking and Dagenham Justices, ex p DPP
    (1994) 159 JP 373, [1995] Crim LR 953 . . . 41

R v Barner-Rasmussen [1996] Crim LR 497,
    CA . . . 513

R v Barnes [1994] Crim LR 691, CA . . . 211, 253

R v Barnes [1995] 2 Cr App Rep 491, [1996] Crim
    LR 39, [1995] 30 LS Gaz R 33, CA . . . 518

R v Barnett [2002] Crim App R 168, CA . . . 19

R v Barratt [2000] Crim LR 847, CA . . . 543

R v Barratt and Sheehan [1996] Crim LR 495,
    CA. . . . 135, 138

R v Barrington [1981] 1 All ER 1132, [1981]
    1 WLR 419, 72 Cr App Rep 280, [1981] Crim
    LR 174, 125 Sol Jo 218, CA . . . 509, 510

R v Barry (1991) 95 Cr App Rep 384, CA . . . 391,
    396

R v Barsoum [1994] Crim LR 194, CA . . . 18, 543

R v Barton [1972] 2 All ER 1192, [1973] 1 WLR
    115, 136 JP 614, 117 Sol Jo 72 . . . 251, 650

R v Barton (1986) 85 Cr App Rep 5, [1987] Crim
    LR 399, 131 Sol Jo 74, [1987] LS Gaz R 574,
    CA . . . 214

R v Bashir and Manzur [1969] 3 All ER 692,
    [1969] 1 WLR 1303, 54 Cr App Rep 1,
    133 JP 687, 113 Sol Jo 703 . . . 207

R v Baskerville [1916] 2 KB 658, 12 Cr App Rep
    81, 80 JP 446, 86 LJKB 28, 25 Cox CC 524,
    [1916–17] All ER Rep 38, 60 Sol Jo 696, 115 LT
    453, CCA . . . 229

R v Bass [1953] 1 QB 680, [1953] 1 All ER 1064,
    [1953] 2 WLR 825, 37 Cr App Rep 51,
    117 JP 246, 97 Sol Jo 282, CCA . . . 176

R v Bath (1990) 154 JP 849, [1990] Crim LR 716,
CA . . . 250

R v Bathurst [1968] 2 QB 99, [1968] 1 All ER
1175, [1968] 2 WLR 1092, 52 Cr App Rep 251,
112 Sol Jo 272, CA . . . 433, 439

R v Batt (1994) 158 JP 883, [1994] Crim LR 592,
CA . . . 26

R v Batt [1995] Crim LR 240, CA . . . 306

R v Bayliss (1993) 98 Cr App Rep 235, 157 JP
1062, [1994] Crim LR 687, CA . . . 399

R v Beales [1991] Crim LR 118 . . . 388

R v Bean [1991] Crim LR 843, CA . . . 603

R v Beard [1998] Crim LR 585, CA . . . 225

R v Beattie (1989) 89 Cr App Rep 302, CA . . . 18,
209

R v Beck [1982] 1 All ER 807, [1982] 1 WLR 461,
74 Cr App Rep 221, 146 JP 225, [1982] Crim
LR 586, 126 Sol Jo 134, CA . . . 242

R v Beckett (1913) 8 Cr App Rep 204, 29 TLR 332,
CCA . . . 583, 584

R v Beckford (1991) 94 Cr App Rep 43, [1991]
Crim LR 918, CA . . . 203, 383

R v Beckles [1999] Crim LR 148, CA . . . 251

R v Beckles [2005] 1 All ER 705, CA . . . 450, 452

R v Beckwith [1981] Crim LR 646 . . . 40

R v Bedford (1990) 93 Cr App Rep 113,
CA . . . 504, 516, 545

R v Bedi and Bedi (1991) 95 Cr App Rep 21,
[1992] Crim LR 299, CA . . . 110

R v Bedingfield (1879) 14 Cox CC 341 . . . 369,
370

R v Beezley (1830) 4 C & P 220 . . . 226

R v Beggs (1989) 90 Cr App Rep 430, [1989] Crim
LR 898, CA . . . 514

R v Bellamy (1985) 82 Cr App Rep 222, [1986]
Crim LR 54, CA . . . 138, 140

R v Bellis [1966] 1 WLR 234 . . . 364

R v Belmarsh Magistrates' Court, ex p Gilligan
[1998] 1 Cr App Rep 14; affd sub nom Gilligan,
Re [2000] 1 All ER 113, [1999] 46 LS Gaz R 37,
143 Sol Jo LB 281, sub nom R v Governor of
Belmarsh Prison, ex p Gilligan [1999] 3 WLR
1244, HL . . . 39, 339

R v Benjamin (1913) 8 Cr App Rep 146,
CCA . . . 186

R v Bennett (1978) 68 Cr App Rep 168,
CA . . . 108

R v Bennett (1988) 153 JP 317, [1988] Crim LR
686, CA . . . 681

R v Bennett [1995] Crim LR 877, CA . . . 43

R v Bentley (1991) 99 Cr App Rep 342,
CA . . . 253

R v Bentley (deceased) [2001] 1 Cr App R 307,
CA . . . 43

R v Bentum (1989) 153 JP 538, CA . . . 570

R v Bernadotti (1869) 11 Cox CC 316 . . .

R v Berriman (1854) 6 Cox CC 388 . . . 430

R v Berry (1986) 83 Cr App Rep 7, 8 Cr App Rep
(S) 303, [1986] Crim LR 394, CA . . . 14, 496

R v Berry [1998] Crim LR 487, CA . . . 40

R v Betterley and Betterley [1994] Crim LR 764,
CA . . . 680

R v Betts [2001] 2 Cr App R 257, CA . . . 446, 450,
452

R v Bevan (1993) 98 Cr App Rep 354,
157 JP 1121, CA . . . 127

R v Beveridge (1987) 85 Cr App Rep 255, [1987]
Crim LR 401, CA . . . 62, 190, 255

R v Beycan [1990] Crim LR 185, CA . . . 411

R v Binham [1991] Crim LR 774 . . . 289

R v Birchall [1999] Crim LR 311, CA . . . 249, 438

R v Bircham [1972] Crim LR 430, CA . . . 205

R v Birks [2003] 2 Cr App R 122, CA . . . 184, 185,
320

R v Birtles (1911) 6 Cr App Rep 177, 75 JP 288, 27
TLR 402, CCA . . . 693

R v Bishop [1975] QB 274, [1974] 2 All ER 1206,
[1974] 3 WLR 308, 59 Cr App Rep 246,
138 JP 654, 118 Sol Jo 515, CA . . . 248

R v Black (1922) 16 Cr App Rep 118,
CCA . . . 376, 426

R v Black [1995] Crim LR 640, CA . . . 76, 81, 518

R v Blake [1991] Crim LR 119 . . . 394, 413

R v Blake [1993] Crim LR 133, CA . . . 421

R v Blake and Tye (1844) 6 QB 126, 8 JP 596,
13 LJMC 131, 8 Jur 666 . . . 423

R v Bland (1987) 151 JP 857, [1988] Crim LR 41,
CA . . . 40

R v Blastland [1986] AC 41, [1985] 2 All ER 1095,
[1985] 3 WLR 345, 81 Cr App Rep 266, [1985]
Crim LR 727, 129 Sol Jo 557, [1985] LS Gaz R
2331, [1985] NLJ Rep 780, HL . . . 24, 282, 288,
315, 330

R v Bleakley [1993] Crim LR 203, CA . . . 191

R v Bliss (1837) 7 Ad & El 550, 7 LJQB 4, 1 Jur
959, 2 Nev & PKB 464, Will Woll & Dav 624,
[1835–42] All ER Rep 372 . . . 367, 375

R v Bloom [1962] 2 QB 245, [1961] 3 All ER 88,
[1961] 3 WLR 611, 45 Cr App Rep 179, 125 JP
565, 105 Sol Jo 590, CCA . . . 29

R v Boal [1965] 1 QB 402, [1964] 3 All ER 269,
[1964] 3 WLR 593, 128 JP 573, 108 Sol Jo 694,
48 Cr App Rep 342, CCA . . . 127, 131

R v Bond [1906] 2 KB 389, 70 JP 424, 75 LJKB 693, 21 Cox CC 252, 54 WR 586, [1904–7] All ER Rep 24, 50 Sol Jo 542, 95 LT 296, 22 TLR 633, CCR . . . 496

R v Bone [1968] 2 All ER 644, [1968] 1 WLR 983, 52 Cr App Rep 546, 132 JP 420, 112 Sol Jo 480, CA . . . 106

R v Bonnick (1977) 66 Cr App Rep 266, 121 Sol Jo 791, CA . . . 106

R v Bonnor [1957] VLR 227 . . . 701

R v Botmeh [2002] 1 WLR 531, CA . . . 593

R v Bottrill, ex p Kuechenmeister [1947] KB 41, [1946] 2 All ER 434, 175 LT 232, 62 TLR 570, sub nom R v Kuechenmeister, ex p Bottrill 115 LJKB 500, CA . . . 710

R v Bournemouth Justices, ex p Grey [1987] 1 FLR 36, [1986] Fam Law 337, 150 JP 392 . . . 596

R v Bowden [1993] Crim LR 379, 380, CA . . . 253

R v Bowden [1999] 4 All ER 43, [1999] 1 WLR 823, [1999] 2 Cr App Rep 176, 163 JP 337, 143 Sol Jo LB 73, CA . . . 134, 136, 147, 149, 449

R v Bowditch [1991] Crim LR 831, CA . . . 43

R v Bower [1994] Crim LR 281, CA . . . 591

R v Bowers (1998) 163 JP 33, [1998] Crim LR 817, CA . . . 445, 453

R v Bowles [1992] Crim LR 726, CA . . . 145

R v Boyes (1861) 25 JP 789, 1 B & S 311, 30 LJQB 301, 9 Cox CC 32, 7 Jur NS 1158, 9 WR 690, [1861–73] All ER Rep 172, 5 LT 147 . . . 627

R v Boyson [1991] Crim LR 274, CA . . . 474, 679, 680

R v Bracewell (1978) 68 Cr App Rep 44, CA . . . 527, 528, 560

R v Brackenbury [1965] 1 All ER 960, [1965] 1 WLR 1475n, 49 Cr App Rep 189, 129 JP 292 . . . 403

R v Bradford Justices, ex p Wilkinson [1990] 2 All ER 833, [1990] 1 WLR 692, [1990] RTR 59, 91 Cr App Rep 390, 154 JP 225, [1990] Crim LR 267, [1990] 12 LS Gaz R 39 . . . 123

R v Bradley (1979) 70 Cr App Rep 200, 2 Cr App Rep (S) 12, [1980] Crim LR 173, CA . . . 549

R v Bradshaw (1985) 82 Cr App Rep 79, [1985] Crim LR 733, CA . . . 567, 568

R v Brady [2004] 3 All ER 520, CA . . . 633

R v Brasier (1779) 1 East PC 443, 1 Leach 199, CCR . . . 137

R v Bray (1988) 88 Cr App Rep 354, 153 JP 1 l, [1988] Crim LR 829, CA . . . 303

R v Breslin (1984) 80 Cr App Rep 226, CA . . . 254

R v Briley [1991] Crim LR 444, CA . . . 43

R v Brine [1992] Crim LR 122, CA . . . 52, 66

R v Britton [1987] 2 All ER 412, [1987] 1 WLR 539, 85 Cr App Rep 14, 151 JP 473, [1987] Crim LR 490, 131 Sol Jo 536, [1987] LS Gaz R 1238, CA . . . 172, 176

R v Britzman [1983] 1 All ER 369, [1983] 1 WLR 350, 76 Cr App Rep 134, 147 JP 531, [1983] Crim LR 106, 127 Sol Jo 187, 133 NLJ 132, CA . . . 51, 529, 538

R v Bromley Magistrates' Court, ex p Smith [1995] 4 All ER 146, [1995] 1 WLR 944, [1995] 2 Cr App Rep 285, 159 JP 251, [1995] Crim LR 248, [1995] 02 LS Gaz R 36 . . . 595

R v Brooks (1990) 92 Cr App Rep 36, CA . . . 511

R v Brophy [1982] AC 476, [1981] 2 All ER 705, [1981] 3 WLR 103, 73 Cr App Rep 287, 145 JP 423, [1981] Crim LR 831, 125 Sol Jo 479, HL . . . 417, 418

R v Brower [1995] Crim LR 746, CA . . . 43

R v Brown (1987) 87 Cr App Rep 52, [1987] Crim LR 239, CA . . . 383, 601

R v Brown (1990) 92 Cr App Rep 106, [1990] Crim LR 863, CA . . . 399

R v Brown [1991] Crim LR 368, CA . . . 256, 286

R v Brown [1997] Crim LR 502, CA . . . 519

R v Brown [1998] 2 Cr App R 364, CA . . . 200

R v Brown [2002] 1 Cr App R 46, CA . . . 41

R v Brown [2004] Crim LR 1034, CA . . . 167

R v Brown (Winston) [1994] 1 WLR 1599, [1995] 1 Cr App Rep 191, [1994] 31 LS Gaz R 36, 138 Sol Jo LB 146, CA; affd [1998] AC 367, [1997] 3 All ER 769, [1997] 3 WLR 447, [1998] 1 Cr App Rep 66, 161 JP 625, [1998] Crim LR 60, [1997] 33 LS Gaz R 28, [1997] NLJR 1149, HL . . . 591

R v Brown and Brown [1997] 1 Cr App Rep 112, CA . . . 151

R v Browne (1943) 29 Cr App Rep 106, CCA . . . 146

R v Browning (1991) 94 Cr App Rep 109, CA . . . 251

R v Browning [1995] Crim LR 227, CA . . . 556

R v Bruce [1975] 3 All ER 277, [1975] 1 WLR 1252, 61 Cr App Rep 123, 139 JP 832, 119 Sol Jo 459, CA . . . 530

R v Bryce [1992] 4 All ER 567, 95 Cr App Rep 320, [1992] Crim LR 728, [1992] NLJR 1161, CA . . . 75, 80, 412

R v Buckingham (1994) 99 Cr App Rep 303, Crim LR 283, CA . . . 680

R v Buckley (1873) 13 Cox CC 293 . . . 15, 377

R v Burge and Pegg [1996] 1 Cr App Rep 163, CA . . . 18–20, 92, 171, 175

R v Burgess (1956) 40 Cr App Rep 144, CCA . . . 234

R v Burgess [1968] 2 QB 112, [1968] 2 All ER 54n, [1968] 2 WLR 1209, 52 Cr App Rep 258, 132 JP 314, 112 Sol Jo 272, CA . . .  419

R v Burgess [1991] 2 QB 92, [1991] 2 All ER 769, [1991] 2 WLR 1206, 93 Cr App Rep 41, [1991] Crim LR 548, 135 Sol Jo 477, [1991] 19 LS Gaz R 31, [1991] NLJR 527, CA . . .  107

R v Burgess and McLean [1995] Crim LR 425, CA . . .  106

R v Burke (1858) 8 Cox CC 44 . . .  220, 325

R v Burke (1985) 82 Cr App Rep 156, [1985] Crim LR 660, CA . . .  540

R v Burke and Kelly (1847) 2 Cox CC 295 . . .  190

R v Burnett and Lee [1973] Crim LR 748 . . .  59

R v Burns (1973) 58 Cr App Rep 364, CA . . .  107

R v Burrows [2000] Crim LR 48, CA . . .  240

R v Busby (1981) 75 Cr App Rep 79, [1982] Crim LR 232, CA . . .  224

R v Butler (1986) 84 Cr App Rep 12, 150 JP 458, CA . . .  509, 510

R v Butler (Diana) [1999] Crim LR 835, CA . . .  476, 497

R v Butterwasser [1948] 1 KB 4, [1947] 2 All ER 415, 45 LGR 570, 32 Cr App Rep 81, 111 JP 527, 91 Sol Jo 586, 63 TLR 463, CCA . . .  536

R v Button [2005] EWCA Crim 516 . . .  78

R v Buzalek and Schiffer [1991] Crim LR 115, CA . . .  477

R v Byrne [1960] 2 QB 396, [1960] 3 All ER 1, [1960] 3 WLR 440, 44 Cr App Rep 246, 104 Sol Jo 645, CCA . . .  557

R v Byrne [2002] 2 Cr App R 311 . . .  24

R v Byrne and Trump [1987] Crim LR 689, CA . . .  191

R v C (2003) unreported, 25 Nov, CA . . .  511

R v Cadette [1995] Crim LR 229, CA . . .  79, 80

R v Cain [1994] 2 All ER 398, [1994] 1 WLR 1449, 99 Cr App Rep 208, 15 Cr App Rep (S) 448, CA . . .  475

R v Cairns [2003] 1 Cr App R 38, CA . . .  461

R v Caldwell (1993) 99 Cr App Rep 73, [1993] Crim LR 862, CA . . .  254

R v Callan (1993) 98 Cr App Rep 467, 158 JP 33, [1994] Crim LR 198, CA . . .  314, 383

R v Callender [1998] Crim LR 337, CA . . .  368, 377

R v Cambridge [1994] 2 All ER 760, [1994] 1 WLR 971, 99 Cr App Rep 142, 158 JP 799, [1994] Crim LR 690, [1994] 12 LS Gaz R 37, [1994] NLJR 267, CA . . .  106

R v Camelleri [1922] 2 KB 122, 16 Cr App Rep 162, 86 JP 135, 91 LJKB 671, 27 Cox CC 246, 66 Sol Jo 667, 127 LT 228, CCA . . .  183

R v Cameron [1973] Crim LR 520, CA . . .  106

R v Campbell (1984) unreported, 20 Dec, CA . . .  496

R v Campbell (1986) 84 Cr App Rep 255, [1987] Crim LR 257, CA . . .  88

R v Campbell [1994] Crim LR 357, CA . . .  191

R v Campbell [1995] 1 Cr App Rep 522, [1995] Crim LR 157, CA . . .  247

R v Campbell and Williams [1993] Crim LR 448, CA . . .  383, 527

R v Camplin [1978] AC 705, [1978] 2 WLR 679, 67 Cr App Rep 14, 142 JP 320, 122 Sol Jo 280, sub nom DPP v Camplin [1978] 2 All ER 168, HL . . .  559

R v Canale [1990] 2 All ER 187, 91 Cr App Rep 1, 154 JP 286, [1990] Crim LR 329, CA . . .  65, 66, 70, 413

R v Cannan [1998] Crim LR 284, CA . . .  205

R v Cannings [2004] 1 All ER 725 . . .  260, 261, 552, 554, 564, 565

R v Canny (1945) 30 Cr App Rep 143, 89 Sol Jo 213, CCA . . .  31

R v Cape [1996] 1 Cr App Rep 191, CA . . .  251

R v Carass [2002] 1 WLR 1714 . . .  98

R v Carnall [1995] Crim LR 944, CA . . .  372, 374

R v Carr-Briant [1943] KB 607, [1943] 2 All ER 156, 41 LGR 183, 29 Cr App Rep 76, 107 JP 167, 112 LJKB 581, 169 LT 175, 59 TLR 300, CCA . . .  108, 113, 120, 682

R v Carrington [1990] Crim LR 330, CA . . .  497

R v Carrington (1993) 99 Cr App Rep 376, [1994] Crim LR 438, CA . . .  312

R v Carroll (1993) 99 Cr App Rep 381, [1993] Crim LR 613, CA . . .  232

R v Cartwright (1914) 10 Cr App Rep 219, CCA . . .  192

R v Cascoe [1970] 2 All ER 833, 54 Cr App Rep 401, 134 JP 603, CA . . .  106

R v Case [1991] Crim LR 192, CA . . .  303, 330

R v Cash [1985] QB 801, [1985] 2 All ER 128, [1985] 2 WLR 735, 80 Cr App Rep 314, [1985] Crim LR 311, 129 Sol Jo 268, [1985] LS Gaz R 1330, CA . . .  688

R v Castillo [1996] 1 Cr App Rep 438, [1996] Crim LR 193, 140 Sol Jo LB 12, CA . . .  303, 330

R v Castle [1989] Crim LR 567, CA . . .  256, 680

R v Castleton (1909) 3 Cr App Rep 74, CCA . . .  15

R v Causley [1999] Crim LR 572, CA . . .  243

R v Central Criminal Court, ex p Francis & Francis (a firm) [1989] AC 346, [1988] 3 WLR 989, 88 Cr App Rep 213, [1989] Crim LR 444, 132 Sol Jo 1592, [1989] 1 LS Gaz R 37, [1988]

NLJR 316, sub nom Francis & Francis (a firm) v Central Criminal Court [1988] 3 All ER 775, HL . . . 215, 638, 653

R v Chalkley and Jeffries [1998] QB 848, [1998] 2 All ER 155, [1998] 3 WLR 146, [1998] 2 Cr App Rep 79, [1999] Crim LR 214, [1998] 05 LS Gaz R 29, 142 Sol Jo LB 40, CA . . . 65, 75

R v Challenger [1994] Crim LR 202, CA . . . 478

R v Chance [1988] QB 932, [1988] 3 All ER 225, [1988] 3 WLR 661, 87 Cr App Rep 398, 132 Sol Jo 1215, [1988] NLJR 249, CA . . . 234, 239

R v Chandler [1976] 3 All ER 105, [1976] 1 WLR 585, 63 Cr App Rep 1, 140 JP 582, 120 Sol Jo 96, CA . . . 238, 427

R v Chandor [1959] 1 QB 545, [1959] 1 All ER 702, [1959] 2 WLR 522, 43 Cr App Rep 74, 123 JP 131, 123 JP 194, 103 Sol Jo 314, CCA . . . 515

R v Chan-Fook [1994] 2 All ER 552, [1994] 1 WLR 689, 99 Cr App Rep 147, [1994] Crim LR 432, CA . . . 557

R v Chapman (1838) 8 C & P 558 . . . 151

R v Chapman [1969] 2 QB 436, [1969] 2 All ER 321, [1969] 2 WLR 1004, 53 Cr App Rep 336, 133 JP 405, 113 Sol Jo 229, CA . . . 287

R v Chapman [1989] Crim LR 60, CA . . . 473

R v Chapman [1991] Crim LR 44, CA . . . 681, 682

R v Chard (1971) 56 Cr App Rep 268, CA . . . 558

R v Charles [1977] AC 177, 68 Cr App Rep 334n, [1977] Crim LR 615, HL . . . 35, 230

R v Chauhan (1981) 73 Cr App Rep 232 . . . 239

R v Cheema [1994] 1 All ER 639, [1994] 1 WLR 147, 98 Cr App Rep 195, [1994] Crim LR 206, [1993] 40 LS Gaz R 41, [1993] NLJR 1439, 137 Sol Jo LB 231, CA . . . 240, 338

R v Cheltenham Justices, ex p Secretary of State for Trade [1977] 1 All ER 460, [1977] 1 WLR 95, 141 JP 175, 121 Sol Jo 70 . . . 605

R v Cheng (1976) 63 Cr App Rep 20, [1976] Crim LR 379, 120 Sol Jo 198, CA . . . 175

R v Chenia [2004] 1 All ER 543, CA . . . 258, 450–53

R v Chief Constable of Avon and Somerset Constabulary, ex p Robinson [1989] 2 All ER 15, [1989] 1 WLR 793, 90 Cr App Rep 27, [1989] Crim LR 440, 133 Sol Jo 264, [1989] 9 LS Gaz R 41 . . . 405

R v Chief Constable of South Wales, ex p Merrick [1994] 2 All ER 560, [1994] 1 WLR 663, [1994] Crim LR 852 . . . 405

R v Chief Constable of West Midlands Police, ex p Wiley [1995] 1 AC 274, [1994] 3 All ER 420, [1994] 3 WLR 433, 159 LG Rev 181, [1995] 1 Cr App Rep 342, [1994] 40 LS Gaz R 35,

[1994] NLJR 1008, 138 Sol Jo LB 156, HL . . . 616, 618, 619, 622

R v Chisnell [1992] Crim LR 507, CA . . . 175

R v Christie [1914] AC 545, [1914–15] All ER Rep 63, sub nom DPP v Christie 10 Cr App Rep 141, 78 JP 321, 83 LJKB 1097, 24 Cox CC 249, 58 Sol Jo 515, 111 LT 220, 30 TLR 471, HL . . . 29, 48, 50, 183, 190, 368, 375, 425, 426, 428

R v Christou [1992] QB 979, [1992] 4 All ER 559, [1992] 3 WLR 228, 95 Cr App Rep 264, [1992] Crim LR 729, [1992] 26 LS Gaz R 29, [1992] NLJR 823, 136 Sol Jo LB 182, CA . . . 65, 66, 75, 79, 403

R v Chung (1990) 92 Cr App Rep 314, [1991] Crim LR 622, CA . . . 396

R v Churchill [1993] Crim LR 285, CA . . . 329

R v Clancy [1997] Crim LR 290, CA . . . 220

R v Clapham (1829) 4 C & P 29 . . . 361

R v Clare [1995] 2 Cr App Rep 333, 159 JP 412, [1995] Crim LR 947, [1995] 17 LS Gaz R 47, CA . . . 278, 556

R v Clark [1955] 2 QB 469, [1955] 3 All ER 29, [1955] 3 WLR 313, 39 Cr App Rep 120, 119 JP 531, 99 Sol Jo 527, CCA . . . 538

R v Clark [2003] EWCA Crim 1020 . . . 583

R v Clarke (1977) 67 Cr App Rep 398, CA . . . 511

R v Clarke [1989] Crim LR 892, CA . . . 409

R v Clarke [1995] 2 Cr App Rep 425, CA . . . 278, 279, 514, 553

R v Cleal [1942] 1 All ER 203, 28 Cr App Rep 95, CCA . . . 243

R v Cleary (1963) 48 Cr App Rep 116, 108 Sol Jo 77, CCA . . . 390

R v Cleghorn [1967] 2 QB 584, [1967] 1 All ER 996, [1967] 2 WLR 1421, 51 Cr App Rep 291, 131 JP 320, 111 Sol Jo 175, CA . . . 151

R v Cliburn (1898) 62 JP 232 . . . 200

R v Clifton [1986] Crim LR 399, CA . . . 249

R v Clowes [1992] 3 All ER 440, 95 Cr App Rep 440, [1992] BCLC 1158 . . . 591, 607, 621

R v Cobden (1862) 3 F & F 833 . . . 512

R v Cochrane [1993] Crim LR 48, CA . . . 296

R v Cole (1941) 39 LGR 262, 28 Cr App Rep 43, 105 JP 279, 165 LT 125, CCA . . . 415

R v Cole [1990] 2 All ER 108, [1990] 1 WLR 866, 90 Cr App Rep 478, 154 JP 692, [1990] Crim LR 333, 134 Sol Jo 908, [1990] 13 LS Gaz R 42, CA . . . 305–8

R v Coleman (1987) Times, 21 November, CA . . . 151

R v Coles [1995] 1 Cr App Rep 157, CA . . . 558

R v Coll (1889) 25 LR Ir 522 . . . 181

R v Collier [1965] 3 All ER 136, [1965] 1 WLR 1470, 49 Cr App Rep 344, 129 JP 531, 109 Sol Jo 593, CCA . . . 403

R v Collins (1960) 44 Cr App Rep 170, CCA . . . 267

R v Collins [2003] 2 Cr App R 199, CA . . . 427

R v Colman [2004] EWCA Crim 3252, [2004] All ER (D) 345 (Dec) . . . 683

R v Coltress (1978) 68 Cr App Rep 193, CA . . .

R v Compton [2002] All ER (D) 149 (Dec), [2002] EWCA Crim 2835 . . . 450, 457

R v Condron and Condron [1997] 1 WLR 827, [1997] 1 Cr App Rep 185, 161 JP 1, [1997] Crim LR 215, CA . . . 447–49, 454

R v Connolly and McCartney (5 June 1992, unreported) . . . 449

R v Constantinou (1989) 91 Cr App Rep 74, 153 JP 619, [1989] Crim LR 571, CA . . . 251, 279, 287

R v Conti (1973) 58 Cr App Rep 387, CA . . . 127

R v Conway (1990) 91 Cr App Rep 143, [1990] Crim LR 402, CA . . . 133

R v Conway [1994] Crim LR 838, CA . . . 413

R v Cook [1987] QB 417, [1987] 1 All ER 1049, [1987] 2 WLR 775, 84 Cr App Rep 369, [1987] Crim LR 402, 131 Sol Jo 21, [1987] LS Gaz R 339, CA . . . 279, 287

R v Cooke (1986) 84 Cr App Rep 286, CA . . . 24, 419, 683

R v Cooke [1995] 1 Cr App Rep 318, CA . . . 67, 106

R v Cooper [1969] 1 QB 267, [1969] 1 All ER 32, [1968] 3 WLR 1225, 53 Cr App Rep 82, 112 Sol Jo 904, CA . . . 228, 314

R v Cooper (1985) 82 Cr App Rep 74, [1985] Crim LR 592, CA . . . 203

R v Cooper and Schaub [1994] Crim LR 531, CA . . . 156

R v Corelli [2001] Crim LR 913, CA . . . 203, 221

R v Corrie and Watson (1904) 68 JP 294, 20 TLR 365, CCR . . . 439

R v Coshall [1995] 12 LS Gaz R 34, CA . . . 159

R v Cottrill [1997] Crim LR 56, CA . . . 657

R v Coughlan (1976) 63 Cr App Rep 33, [1976] Crim LR 631, CA . . . 490

R v Coulson [1997] Crim LR 886, CA . . . 714

R v Court (1960) 44 Cr App Rep 242, CCA . . . 15

R v Courtnell [1990] Crim LR 115, CA . . . 251, 254

R v Courtney [1995] Crim LR 63, CA . . . 412, 529, 538

R v Cousins [1982] QB 526, [1982] 2 All ER 115, [1982] 2 WLR 621, 74 Cr App Rep 363, 146 JP 264, [1982] Crim LR 444, 126 Sol Jo 154, CA . . . 89, 92

R v Couzens and Frankel (1992) 14 Cr App Rep (S) 33, [1992] Crim LR 822, CA . . . 16

R v Cowan, Gayle and Ricardi [1996] QB 373, [1995] 4 All ER 939, [1995] 3 WLR 818, [1996] 1 Cr App Rep 1, 160 JP 165, [1996] Crim LR 409, [1995] 38 LS Gaz R 26, [1995] NLJR 1611, 139 Sol Jo LB 215, CA . . . 369, 392, 435–40

R v Cowell [1940] 2 KB 49, [1940] 2 All ER 599, 38 LGR 273, 27 Cr App Rep 191, 104 JP 237, 109 LJKB 667, 84 Sol Jo 334, 163 LT 158, 56 TLR 629, CCA . . . 126

R v Cox [1898] 1 QB 179, 67 LJQB 293, 18 Cox CC 672, [1895–9] All ER Rep 1285, 42 501 Jo 135, 77 LT 534, 14 TLR 122, CCR . . . 583

R v Cox [1991] Crim LR 276, CA . . . 246, 391

R v Cox (1992) 96 Cr App Rep 464, 157 JP 785, [1993] Crim LR 382, CA . . . 412

R v Cox [1995] 2 Cr App Rep 513, [1995] Crim LR 741, [1995] 15 LS Gaz R 40, 139 Sol Jo LB 86, CA . . . 107

R v Cox and Railton (1884) 14 QBD 153, 49 JP 374, 54 LJMC 41, 15 Cox CC 611, 33 WR 396, [1881–5] All ER Rep 68, 52 LT 25, 1 TLR 181, CCR . . . 396, 651, 654

R v Crabtree, McCann, and Foley [1992] Crim LR 65, CA . . . 191, 254

R v Cramp (1880) 14 Cox CC 390; affd 5 QBD 307, 44 JP 411, 39 LJMC 44, 14 Cox CC 401, 28 WR 701, 42 LT 442 . . . 238

R v Crampton (1990) 92 Cr App Rep 369, [1991] Crim LR 277, CA . . . 390, 391–93

R v Crawford (Charisse) [1997] 1 WLR 1329, [1998] 1 Cr App Rep 338, 161 JP 681, [1997] 30 LS Gaz R 27, 141 Sol Jo LB 129, CA . . . 53, 529, 531

R v Crees [1996] Crim LR 830, CA . . . 146

R v Cresswell (1876) 1 QBD 446, 40 JP 536, 45 LJMC 77, 13 Cox CC 126, 24 WR 281, 33 LT 760, CCR . . . 701

R v Cross (1990) 91 Cr App Rep 115, [1991] BCLC 125, [1990] BCC 237, CA . . . 203

R v Crown Court at Inner London Sessions, ex p Baines & Baines (a firm) [1988] QB 579, [1987] 3 All ER 1025, [1988] 2 WLR 549, 87 Cr App Rep 111, [1988] Crim LR 50, 132 Sol Jo 418, [1987] NLJ Rep 945 . . . 394, 642

R v Crown Court at Manchester, ex p Rogers [1999] 4 All ER 35, [1999] 1 WLR 832, [1999] 2 Cr App Rep 267, [1999] Crim LR 743 . . . 641

R v Crown Court at Northampton, ex p DPP (1991) 93 Cr App Rep 376 . . . 654

R v Crown Court at Snaresbrook, ex p DPP [1988] QB 532, [1988] 1 All ER 315, [1987]

3 WLR 1054, 86 Cr App Rep 227, 131 Sol Jo 1487, [1987] LS Gaz R 3335 . . . 653

R v Crown Court at Southampton, ex p J and P [1993] Crim LR 962 . . . 650

R v Crown Prosecution Service, ex p Warby (1993) 158 JP 190, [1994] Crim LR 281 . . . 528

R v Crush [1978] Crim LR 357 . . . 709

R v Cruttenden [1991] 2 QB 66, [1991] 3 All ER 242, [1991] 2 WLR 921, 93 Cr App Rep 119, 155 JP 798, [1991] Crim LR 537, CA . . . 132

R v Cullinane [1984] Crim LR 420, CA . . . 230

R v Cummings [1948] 1 All ER 551, 92 Sol Jo 284, CCA . . . 184, 320

R v Cunningham [1989] Crim LR 435, CA . . . 312

R v Curgerwen (1865) LR 1 CCR 1, 29 JP 820, 35 LJMC 58, 10 Cox CC 152, 11 Jur NS 984, 14 WR 55, 13 LT 383, [1861–73] All ER Rep Ext 1368 . . . 92, 701

R v Curry [1983] Crim LR 737, CA . . . 253

R v Curry [1988] Crim LR 527, CA . . . 52, 681

R v Curtin [1996] Crim LR 831, CA . . . 43

R v D (1995) Times, 15 November, CA . . . 134

R v D [2002] 2 Cr App R 601, CA . . . 308

R v Dadson (1983) 77 Cr App Rep 91, 147 JP 509, [1983] Crim LR 540, 127 Sol Jo 306, CA . . . 271

R v Daley (1987) 87 Cr App Rep 52, [1988] Crim LR 239, CA . . . 383, 601

R v Daley [2002] 2 Cr App R 201, CA . . . 452

R v Dallagher [2003] 1 Cr App R 195, CA . . . 553, 563

R v Dalloz (1908) 1 Cr App Rep 258, CCA . . . 16

R v Daniel [1998] 2 Cr App Rep 373, 162 JP 578, [1998] Crim LR 818, CA . . . 134

R v Darby [1989] Crim LR 817, CA . . . 194

R v Da Silva [1990] 1 All ER 29, [1990] 1 WLR 31, 90 Cr App Rep 233, 153 JP 636, [1990] Crim LR 192, CA . . . 179

R v Dat [1998] Crim LR 488, CA . . . 194

R v David R [1999] Crim LR 909, CA . . . 220

R v Davies [1962] 3 All ER 97, [1962] 1 WLR 1111, 46 Cr App Rep 292, 126 JP 455, 106 Sol Jo 393, C-MAC . . . 584

R v Davies [1992] 2 All ER 183, [1992] 1 WLR 380, 95 Cr App Rep 1, CA 385

R v Davies [2002] EWCA Crim 2949, CA . . . 101, 124

R v Davis [1975] 1 All ER 233, [1975] 1 WLR 345, 60 Cr App Rep 157, 139 JP 143, 119 Sol Jo 82, CA . . . 530

R v Davis (1975) 62 Cr App Rep 194, CA . . . 146

R v Davis [1979] Crim LR 167 . . . 398

R v Davis [1990] Crim LR 860, CA . . . 414, 417

R v Davis (1992) 95 Cr App Rep 81, [1992] Crim LR 650, [1992] NLJR 160, CA . . . 419, 421, 601

R v Davis, Johnson and Rowe [1993] 2 All ER 643, [1993] 1 WLR 613, 97 Cr App Rep 110, [1993] 10 LS Gaz R 35, [1993] NLJR 330, 137 Sol Jo LB 19, CA . . . 593

R v Davis [1998] Crim LR 659, CA . . . 289

R v Davison-Jenkins [1997] Crim LR 816, CA . . . 386, 542

R v Day [1940] 1 All ER 402, 38 LGR 155, 27 Cr App Rep 168, 104 JP 181, 31 Cox CC 391, 162 LT 407, CCA . . . 144

R v Daye [1908] 2 KB 333, 72 JP 269, 77 LJKB 659, 21 Cox CC 659, 99 LT 165 226 . . . 262

R v Deakin [1994] 4 All ER 769, [1995] 1 Cr App Rep 471, [1994] 21 LS Gaz R 41, [1994] NLJR 707, CA . . . 37

R v Deenik [1992] Crim LR 578, CA . . . 63, 79, 583

R v Dehar [1969] NZLR 763, NZCA . . . 18

R v Delaney (1988) 88 Cr App Rep 338, 153 JP 103, [1989] Crim LR 139, CA . . . 56, 395

R v Dempster [2001] Crim LR 567, CA . . . 540

R v Dennison (1989) 91 Cr App Rep 43, 154 JP 177, [1990] Crim LR 190, CA . . . 412

R v De Oliveira [1997] Crim LR 600, CA . . . 200

R v Derby Magistrates' Court, ex p B [1996] AC 487, [1995] 4 All ER 526, [1995] 3 WLR 681, [1996] 1 Cr App Rep 385, [1996] 1 FLR 513, [1996] Fam Law 210, 159 JP 785, [1996] Crim LR 190, [1995] NLJR 1575, 139 Sol Jo LB 219, HL . . . 207, 639, 650, 651

R v Derodra [2000] 1 Cr App Rep 41, [1999] Crim LR 978, CA . . . 312

R v Dervish [2002] 2 Cr App R 105, CA . . . 444

R v De Silva [2003] 2 Cr App R 74, CA . . . 412

R v Devonport and Pirano [1996] 1 Cr App Rep 221, [1996] Crim LR 255, CA . . . 122, 423

R v Dhillon [1997] 2 Cr App Rep 104, [1997] Crim LR 286, [1997] Crim LR 295, CA . . . 106

R v Dillon [1984] RTR 270, 85 Cr App Rep 29n, 149 JP 182, [1984] Crim LR 100, CA . . . 176, 177

R v DPP, ex p Kebeline [1999] 4 All ER 801, [1999] 3 WLR 175, [2000] 1 Cr App Rep 275, [1999] Crim LR 994; revsd [1999] 4 All ER 801, [1999] 3 WLR 972, [2000] 1 Cr App Rep 275, [1999] 43 LS Gaz R 32, HL . . . 103

R v DPP, ex p Warby. See R v Crown Prosecution Service, ex p Warby

R v Director of Serious Fraud Office, ex p Smith [1993] AC 1, [1992] 3 WLR 66, 95 Cr App Rep 191, [1992] 27 LS Gaz R 34, [1992] NLJR 895, 136 Sol Jo LB 182, sub nom Smith v Director of Serious Fraud Office [1992] 3 All ER 456, [1992] BCLC 879, HL . . . 399

R v Dix (1981) 74 Cr App Rep 306, [1982] Crim LR 302, CA . . . 557

R v Docherty [1999] 1 Cr App Rep 274, CA . . . 490

R v Dodd (1981) 74 Cr App Rep 50, CA . . . 386

R v Dodson [1984] 1 WLR 971, 79 Cr App Rep 220, [1984] Crim LR 489, 128 Sol Jo 364, [1984] LS Gaz R 1677, CA . . . 257, 278, 287

R v Doheny and Adams [1997] 1 Cr App Rep 369, CA . . . 554

R v Dolan [2003] 1 Cr App R 281, CA . . . 497

R v Doldur [2000] Crim LR 178, [1999] 47 LS Gaz R 29, 144 Sol Jo LB 5, CA . . . 252, 452

R v Donaldson (1976) 64 Cr App Rep 59 . . . 188

R v Donat (1985) 82 Cr App Rep 173, CA . . . 29, 423

R v Donoghue (1987) 86 Cr App Rep 267, [1988] Crim LR 60, CA . . . 42, 43

R v Donohoe [1963] SRNSW 38 . . . 121

R v Donovan [1934] 2 KB 498, 32 LGR 439, 25 Cr App Rep 1, 98 JP 409, 103 LJKB 683, 30 Cox CC 187, [1934] All ER Rep 207, 78 Sol Jo 601, 152 LT 46, 50 TLR 566, CCA . . . 87

R v Doolan [1988] Crim LR 747, CA . . . 391, 396

R v Doolin (1882) 1 Jebb CC 123, IR . . . 199

R v Doosti (1985) 82 Cr App Rep 181, [1985] Crim LR 665, CA . . . 419, 683

R v Doran (1972) 56 Cr App Rep 429, 116 Sol Jo 238, CA . . . 143

R v Dossi (1918) 13 Cr App Rep 158, 87 LJKB 1024, 34 TLR 498, CCA . . . 237

R v Douglass [1989] RTR 271, 89 Cr App Rep 264, [1989] Crim LR 569, CA . . . 528

R v Dowley [1983] Crim LR 168, CA . . . 237

R v Downey [1995] 1 Cr App Rep 547, [1995] Crim LR 414, CA . . . 258, 518

R v Dragic [1996] 2 Cr App Rep 232, 160 JP 771, [1996] Crim LR 580, CA . . . 306

R v Drake [1996] Crim LR 109, CA . . . 20

R v Drummond (1784) 1 Leach 337 . . . 96

R v Ducsharm [1956] 1 DLR 732, [1955] OR 824, 113 CCC l, 22 CR 129, [1955] OWN 817 . . . 512

R v Dudley [2004] All ER (D) 374 (Nov) . . . 553

R v Duffy [1999] QB 919, [1998] 3 WLR 1060, [1999] 1 Cr App Rep 307, [1998] Crim LR 650, [1998] 20 LS Gaz R 33, 142 Sol Jo LB 149, CA . . . 307

R v Dunbar [1958] 1 QB 1, [1957] 2 All ER 737, [1957] 3 WLR 330, 41 Cr App Rep 182, 121 JP 506, 101 Sol Jo 594, CCA . . . 114

R v Duncan (1981) 73 Cr App Rep 359, [1981] Crim LR 560, CA . . . 188, 189, 475

R v Duncan (1992) Times, 24 July, CA . . . 257

R v Dunford (1990) 91 Cr App Rep 150, [1991] Crim LR 370, [1990] NLJR 517, CA . . . 69, 410, 411

R v Dunkley [1927] 1 KB 323, 19 Cr App Rep 78, 90 JP 75, 96 LJKB 15, 28 Cox CC 143, [1926] All ER Rep 187, 134 LT 632, CCA . . . 538

R v Dunn (1990) 91 Cr App Rep 237, [1990] Crim LR 572, [1990] NLJR 592, CA . . . 145, 146, 412

R v Dunphy (1993) 98 Cr App Rep 393, CA . . . 64, 159, 400

R v Durbin [1995] 2 Cr App Rep 84, CA . . . 476, 477

R v Dures [1997] 2 Cr App Rep 247, [1997] Crim LR 673, CA . . . 65

R v Dwyer [1925] 2 KB 799, 18 Cr App Rep 145, 89 JP 27, 95 LJKB 109, 27 Cox CC 697, [1924] All ER Rep 272, 132 LT 351, 41 TLR 186, CCA . . . 191

R v E [2005] Crim LR 227, CA . . . 211, 212

R v Eades [1972] Crim LR 99 . . . 224

R v Early [2003] 1 Cr APP R 288, CA . . . 592

R v Edwards [1975] QB 27, [1974] 2 All ER 1085, [1974] 3 WLR 285, 59 Cr App Rep 213, 138 JP 621, 118 Sol Jo 582, CA . . . 90, 700

R v Edwards [1987] 1 All ER 1 . . . 88, 91, 92

R v Edwards [1991] 2 All ER 266, [1991] 1 WLR 207, 93 Cr App Rep 48, [1991] Crim LR 372, CA . . . 220, 224, 419, 485, 683

R v Edwards [1997] Crim LR 348, CA . . . 81

R v Edwards [1998] Crim LR 207, CA . . . 27

R v Edwards [2001] EWCA Crim 2185 . . . 568

R v Eleftheriou [1993] Crim LR 947, CA . . . 174

R v Elleray [2003] 2 Cr App R 165, CA . . . 413

R v El-Hannachi [1998] 2 Cr App Rep 226, [1998] Crim LR 881, CA . . . 438

R v Ellis (1826) 6 B & C 145, 5 LJOSMC 25, 4 Dow & Ry MC 268 . . . 498

R v Elworthy (1867) LR 1 CCR 103, 32 JP 54, 37 LJMC 3, 10 Cox CC 579, 16 WR 207, 17 LT 293, CCR . . . 266

R v Ely Justices, ex p Burgess (1992) 157 JP 484, [1992] Crim LR 888, [1992] 34 LS Gaz R 34, 136 Sol Jo LB 244 . . . 280

R v Emmerson (1990) 92 Cr App Rep 284, [1991] Crim LR 194, CA . . . 122, 146, 278, 388

R v Ensor [1989] 2 All ER 586, [1989] 1 WLR 497, 89 Cr App Rep 139, [1989] Crim LR 562, 133 Sol Jo 483, [1989] 15 LS Gaz R 36, [1989] NLJR 575, CA . . . 239

R v Epping and Ongar Justices, ex p Manby [1986] Crim LR 555 . . . 38

R v Evans [1965] 2 QB 295, [1964] 3 All ER 401, [1964] 3 WLR 1173, 48 Cr App Rep 314, 129 JP 7, CCA . . . 243

R v Evans (1991) 156 JP 539, [1992] Crim LR 125, CA . . . 222

R v Evans-Jones (1923) 17 Cr App Rep 121, 87 JP 115, 67 Sol Jo 707, 39 TLR 458, CCA . . . 107

R v Everett [1988] Crim LR 826, CA . . . 394

R v Everett [1995] Crim LR 76, CA . . . 44

R v Ewens [1967] 1 QB 322, [1966] 2 All ER 470, [1966] 2 WLR 1372, 50 Cr App Rep 171, 110 Sol Jo 483, CCA . . . 90

R v Ewing [1983] QB 1039, [1983] 2 All ER 645, [1983] 3 WLR 1, 77 Cr App Rep 47, [1983] Crim LR 472, 127 Sol Jo 390, CA . . . 121, 122, 273

R v Exall (1866)4F&F922 . . . 13

R v Fairfax [1995] Crim LR 949, CA . . . 304, 306, 330

R v Fallon [1993] Crim LR 591, CA . . . 230

R v Fannon (1922) 22 SRNSW 427 . . . 191

R v Farnham Justices, ex p Gibson [1991] RTR 309, 155 JP 792, [1991] Crim LR 642 . . . 127

R v Farr (1998) 163 JP 193, [1999] Crim LR 506, CA . . . 44

R v Fedrick [1990] Crim LR 403, CA . . . 680

R v Feely [1973] QB 530, [1973] 1 All ER 341, [1973] 2 WLR 201, 57 Cr App Rep 312, 137 JP 157, [1973] Crim LR 193, 117 Sol Jo 54, CA . . . 33

R v Feest [1987] Crim LR 766, CA . . . 329

R v Fenlon (1980) 71 Cr App Rep 307, [1980] Crim LR 573, 124 Sol Jo 478, CA . . . 176, 177, 265

R v Fergus (1993) 98 Cr App Rep 313, 158 JP 49, CA . . . 108, 192, 252, 255

R v Ferguson [1925] 2 KB 799, 18 Cr App Rep 145, 89 JP 27, 95 LJKB 109, 27 Cox CC 697, [1924] All ER Rep 272, 132 LT 351, 41 TLR 186, CCA . . . 191

R v Field, etc Justices, ex p White (1895) 64 LJMC 158, 11 TLR 240, DC . . . 712

R v Findlay [1992] Crim LR 372, CA . . . 411, 412

R v Finley [1993] Crim LR 50, CA . . . 71

R v Fitton [2001] All ER (D) 28 (Feb), [2001] EWCA Crim 215, CA . . . 474

R v Fitzpatrick [1999] Crim LR 832, CA . . . 571

R v Flack [1969] 2 All ER 784, [1969] 1 WLR 937, 53 Cr App Rep 166, 133 JP 445, 113 Sol Jo 33, CA . . . 515

R v Flemming (1987) 86 Cr App Rep 32, [1987] Crim LR 690, 131 Sol Jo 972, [1987] LS Gaz R 2272, CA . . . 62, 255, 414

R v Flicker [1995] Crim LR 493, CA . . . 28

R v Flynn (1957) 42 Cr App Rep 15, CCA . . . 146

R v Foote [1964] Crim LR 405, CCA . . . 106

R v Forbes [1992] Crim LR 593, CA . . . 255

R v Forbes [2001] 1 AC 473 . . . 72

R v Forsyth [1997] 2 Cr App Rep 299, [1997] Crim LR 581, CA . . . 142

R v Foster (1834) 6 C & P 325 . . . 369

R v Foster [1975] RTR 553, [1974] Crim LR 544, CA . . . 432

R v Foster [1985] QB 115, [1984] 2 All ER 679, [1984] 3 WLR 401, 79 Cr App Rep 61, 148 JP 747, [1984] Crim LR 423, 128 Sol Jo 531, [1984] LS Gaz R 1677, CA . . . 671, 679

R v Foster [1987] Crim LR 821, CC . . . 412

R v Foster [1995] Crim LR 333, CA . . . 156

R v Fotheringham [1975] Crim LR 710, 119 Sol Jo 613, CA . . . 175

R v Foulder, Foulkes and Johns [1973] Crim LR 45 . . . 59

R v Fowden and White [1982] Crim LR 588, CA . . . 254, 278, 298

R v Fowkes (1856) Times, 8 March . . . 192, 369

R v Fowler (1987) 86 Cr App Rep 219, [1987] Crim LR 769, CA . . . 550

R v Fox [1986] AC 281, [1985] 1 WLR 1126, [1985] RTR 337, 82 Cr App Rep 105, 150 JP 97, [1986] Crim LR 59, 129 Sol Jo 757, [1985] NLJ Rep 1058, sub nom Fox v Chief Constable of Gwent [1985] 3 All ER 392, HL . . . 61

R v Foxley [1995] 2 Cr App Rep 523, 16 Cr App Rep (S) 879, CA . . . 39, 311, 330, 331

R v Francis (1874) LR 2 CCR 128, 38 JP 469, 43 LJMC 97, 12 Cox CC 612, 22 WR 663, 30 LT 503, [1874–80] All ER Rep Ext 2028, CCR . . . 29, 30, 276

R v Francis [1991] 1 All ER 225, [1990] 1 WLR 1264, 91 Cr App Rep 271, 154 JP 358, [1990] Crim LR 431, 134 Sol Jo 860, [1990] 26 LS Gaz R 38, CA . . . 145

R v Francis [1992] Crim LR 372, CA . . . 411, 412

R v Franklin [1989] Crim LR 499, CA . . . 239

R v Fraser (1956) 40 Cr App Rep 160, CCA . . . 195

R v French and Gowhar (1993) 97 Cr App Rep 421 . . . 303, 306

R v Friend [1997] 2 All ER 1011, [1997] 1 WLR
    1433, [1997] 2 Cr App Rep 231, [1997] Crim
    LR 817, CA . . . 370, 434, 435
R v Frost (1839) 9 C & P 129, 162, 2 Mood CC
    140, 4 State Tr NS 85, 386, 1 Town St Tr 1,
    [1835–42] All ER Rep 106, Gurney's Rep 749,
    CCR . . . 144
R v Fulcher [1995] 2 Cr App Rep 251, [1995]
    Crim LR 883, CA . . . 497
R v Fulling [1987] QB 426, [1987] 2 All ER 65,
    [1987] 2 WLR 923, 85 Cr App Rep 136, 151 JP
    485, [1987] Crim LR 492, 131 Sol Jo 408,
    [1987] LS Gaz R 980, CA; affd [1987] 1 WLR
    1196, HL . . . 387–89, 395
R v Funderburk [1990] 2 All ER 482, [1990]
    1 WLR 587, 90 Cr App Rep 466, [1990] Crim
    LR 405, 134 Sol Jo 578, [1990] 17 LS Gaz R 31,
    CA . . . 203, 207, 220, 221, 224
R v G [2004] 2 Cr App R 638, CA . . . 561
R v Galbraith [1981] 2 All ER 1060, [1981] 1
    WLR 1039, 73 Cr App Rep 124, 144 JP 406,
    [1981] Crim LR 648, 125 Sol Jo 442, CA . . . 40,
    42, 245, 326, 523
R v Gale [1994] Crim LR 208, CA . . . 44
R v Gall (1990) 90 Cr App Rep 64, [1989] Crim
    LR 745, CA . . . 71, 190
R v Gallagher [1974] 3 All ER 118, [1974] 1 WLR
    1204, 59 Cr App Rep 239, 138 JP 663, 118 Sol
    Jo 680, CA . . . 16, 44
R v Gandfield (1846) 2 Cox CC 43 . . . 377
R v Garbett (1847) 13 JP 602, 2 Car & Kir 474,
    1 Den 236, 2 Cox CC 448, 9 LTOS 51, Ex
    Ch . . . 240, 430, 630
R v Gardiner [1994] Crim LR 455, CA . . . 87
R v Garrod [1997] Crim LR 445, CA . . . 189, 475
R v Garth [1949] 1 All ER 773, 47 LGR 527,
    33 Cr App Rep 100, 113 JP 222, 93 Sol Jo 321,
    CCA . . . 688
R v Gayle [1994] Crim LR 679, CA . . . 59
R v Gayle [1999] Crim LR 502, CA . . . 443
R v Gaynor [1988] Crim LR 242 . . . 190
R v Geering (1849) 18 LJMC 215, 8 Cox CC 450n
    . . . 507
R v Gent [1990] 1 All ER 364, 89 Cr App Rep 247,
    CA . . . 44
R v Genus and Britton [1996] Crim LR 502,
    CA . . . 20
R v George [2003] Crim LR 441, CA . . . 250
R v Giannetto [1997] 1 Cr App Rep 1, [1996]
    Crim LR 722, 140 Sol Jo LB 167, CA . . . 496
R v Gibson (1887) 18 QBD 537, 51 JP 742, 56
    LJMC 49, 16 Cox CC 181, 35 WR 411, 56 LT
    367, 3 TLR 442, CCR . . . 286, 375
R v Gibson (1991) 93 Cr App Rep 9, 135 Sol Jo
    574, CA . . . 474

R v Gibson [1993] Crim LR 453, CA . . . 207
R v Gilbert (1977) 66 Cr App Rep 237, [1978]
    Crim LR 216, CA . . . 432
R v Gilder [1997] Crim LR 668, CA . . . 146
R v Gilfoyle [2001] 2 Cr App R 57, CA . . . 288,
    563
R v Gill [1963] 2 All ER 688, [1963] 1 WLR 841,
    47 Cr App Rep 166, 127 JP 429, 107 Sol Jo 417,
    CCA . . . 106
R v Gill [1994] 1 All ER 898, 98 Cr App Rep 437,
    158 JP 165, [1994] Crim LR 53, [1993] 37 LS
    Gaz R 49, [1993] NLJR 1568, 137 Sol Jo LB
    235, CA . . . 75–77, 140, 141
R v Gill [2001] 1 Cr App R 150, CA . . . 451
R v Gill [2004] 1 WLR 49, CA . . . 68, 397, 399
R v Gillard and Barnett (1990) 92 Cr App Rep 61,
    155 JP 352, [1991] Crim LR 280, CA . . . 413
R v Gillespie (1967) 51 Cr App Rep 172,
    111 Sol Jo 92, CA . . . 203
R v Glaves [1993] Crim LR 685, CA . . . 413
R v Gloster (1888) 16 Cox CC 471 . . . 376
R v Glover [1991] Crim LR 48, CA . . . 374
R v Gokal [1997] 2 Cr App Rep 266, CA . . . 98,
    120 , 307
R v Goldenberg (1988) 88 Cr App Rep 285,
    152 JP 557, [1988] Crim LR 678, CA . . . 391,
    392
R v Golder [1960] 3 All ER 457, [1960] 1 WLR
    1169, 45 Cr App Rep 5, 124 JP 505, 104 Sol Jo
    893, CCA . . . 197
R v Golder [1987] QB 920, [1987] 3 All ER 231,
    [1987] 3 WLR 327, 85 Cr App Rep 304, 151 JP
    761, [1987] Crim LR 627, 131 Sol Jo 1002,
    [1987] LS Gaz R 2004, CA . . . 25, 52, 679–81
R v Golizadeh [1995] Crim LR 232, CA . . . 566
R v Gonzales de Arango [1992] Crim LR 180,
    CA . . . 303
R v Goodway [1993] 4 All ER 894, 98 Cr App Rep
    11, [1993] Crim LR 948, [1993] 37 LS Gaz R
    50, [1993] NLJR 1151, 137 Sol Jo LB 203, CA
    . . . 17–19, 197, 464
R v Gordon (1789) 1 East PC 315, 1 Leach 515,
    CCR . . . 701
R v Gordon (1987) 92 Cr App Rep 50n, 9 Cr App
    Rep (S) 343, CA . . . 44
R v Gordon [1995] 2 Cr App Rep 61, [1995] Crim
    LR 142, CA . . . 26, 554
R v Gordon [2002] All ER (D) 99 (Feb),
    CA . . . 179
R v Goss [2005] Crim LR 61, CA . . . 475
R v Gough [2002] Cr App R 121, CA . . . 435
R v Gould (1840) 9 C & P 364 . . . 430

R v Governor of Brixton Prison, ex p Levin [1997] AC 741, [1997] 3 All ER 289, [1997] 3 WLR 117, [1998] 1 Cr App Rep 22, [1997] Crim LR 891, [1997] 30 LS Gaz R 28, [1997] NLJR 990, 141 Sol Jo LB 148, HL . . . 298

R v Governor of Brixton Prison, ex p Osman [1992] 1 All ER 108, [1991] 1 WLR 281, 93 Cr App Rep 202, [1991] Crim LR 533 . . . 423, 591, 599, 618, 621, 652, 656

R v Governor of Pentonville Prison, ex p Alves [1993] AC 284, [1992] 3 WLR 844, 97 Cr App Rep 161, [1993] Crim LR 956, [1992] LS Gaz R 34, [1992] NLJR 1539, sub nom Alves v DPP [1992] 4 All ER 787, 158 JP 229, HL . . . 197

R v Governor of Pentonville Prison, ex p Chinoy [1992] 1 All ER 317 . . . 76

R v Governor of Pentonville Prison, ex p Voets [1986] 2 All ER 630, [1986] 1 WLR 470, 130 Sol Jo 245, [1986] LS Gaz R 1058 . . . 191

R v Gowan [1982] Crim LR 821, CA . . . 386, 394

R v Gowland-Wynn [2002] 1 Cr App R 569 . . . 451

R v Grafton [1993] QB 101, [1992] 4 All ER 609, [1992] 3 WLR 532, 96 Cr App Rep 156, 156 JP 857, [1992] Crim LR 826, [1992] 21 LS Gaz R 27, 136 Sol Jo LB 113, CA . . . 151

R v Grafton [1995] Crim LR 61, CA . . . 332

R v Graham [1973] Crim LR 628 . . . 175

R v Graham [1994] Crim LR 212, CA . . . 252

R v Grannell (1989) 90 Cr App Rep 149, CA . . . 65, 70, 190

R v Grant (1865) 4 F & F 322 . . . 14

R v Grant [1960] Crim LR 424 . . . 87

R v Grant [1996] 1 Cr App Rep 73, CA . . . 27

R v Grant [1996] 2 Cr App Rep 272, CA . . . 518

R v Gray (1973) 58 Cr App Rep 177, CA . . . 113

R v Gray [1995] 2 Cr App Rep 100, [1995] Crim LR 45, [1994] 39 LS Gaz R 38, 138 Sol Jo LB 199, CA . . . 423

R v Gray [2004] 2 Cr App R 498, CA . . . 474, 476

R v Gray and Evans [1998] Crim LR 570, CA . . . 203

R v Greenwood [2005] Crim LR 59, CA . . . 25

R v Greer [1994] Crim LR 745, CA . . . 23

R v Greer [1998] Crim LR 572, CA . . . 39, 306, 330

R v Gregory [1993] Crim LR 623, CA . . . 43

R v Gregory and Mott [1995] Crim LR 507, CA . . . 307

R v Gregson [2003] 2 Cr App R 34, CA . . . 288

R v Griffin (1809) Russ & Ry 151, CCR . . . 430

R v Griffiths [1998] Crim LR 567, CA . . . 27

R v Grimer [1982] Crim LR 674, 126 Sol Jo 641, CA . . . 278

R v Grimes [1994] Crim LR 213, CA . . . 601

R v Groark [1999] Crim LR 669, CA . . . . . . 106

R v Grossman (1981) 73 Cr App Rep 302, [1981] Crim LR 396, CA . . . 271, 272

R v Grossman [1985] QB 819, [1985] 2 All ER 705, [1985] 2 WLR 1001, 81 Cr App Rep 9, [1985] Crim LR 317, 129 Sol Jo 299, [1985] LS Gaz R 1409, CA . . . 556

R v Groves [1998] Crim LR 200, CA . . . 513

R v Guildhall Magistrates' Court, ex p Primlaks Holdings Co (Panama) Inc [1990] 1 QB 261, [1989] 2 WLR 841, 89 Cr App Rep 215, [1989] Crim LR 448, 133 Sol Jo 628 . . . 649

R v Gummerson [1999] Crim LR 680, CA . . . 258, 680

R v Gunewardene [1951] 2 KB 600, [1951] 2 All ER 290, 49 LGR 594, 35 Cr App Rep 80, 115 JP 415, 95 Sol Jo 548, [1951] 2 TLR 315, CCA . . . 28, 225, 421

R v Guney [1998] 2 Cr App Rep 242, [1999] Crim LR 485, [1998] 15 LS Gaz R 30, 142 Sol Jo LB 99, CA . . . 27

R v Gunning (1994) 98 Cr App Rep 303n, CA . . . 169

R v Gurney [1976] Crim LR 567, CA . . . 280

R v Gurney [1994] Crim LR 116, CA . . . 511

R v H [1987] Crim LR 47 . . . 80

R v H (or Henri) (1989) 90 Cr App Rep 440, [1990] Crim LR 51, CA . . . 23, 419

R v H [1992] Crim LR 516 . . . 180, 400

R v H [1994] Crim LR 205, CA . . . 476

R v H [1995] 2 AC 596, [1995] 2 All ER 865, [1995] 2 WLR 737, [1995] 2 Cr App Rep 437, 159 JP 469, [1995] Crim LR 717, [1995] 24 LS Gaz R 39, [1995] NLJR 853, HL . . . 510, 545–47

R v H [2001] Crim LR 815 . . . 304

R v H [2003] EWCA Crim 1208 . . . 161

R v H [2004] 2 2 AC 134 . . . 591, 594, 595

R v Haas (1962) 35 DLR (2d) 172, BC, CA . . . 15

R v Hacker [1995] 1 All ER 45, [1994] 1 WLR 1659, [1995] RTR 1, [1995] 1 Cr App Rep 332, 159 JP 62, [1995] Crim LR 321, [1995] 06 LS Gaz R 37, [1994] NLJR 1625, 138 Sol Jo LB 241, HL . . . 550

R v Hagan (1873) 12 Cox CC 357 . . . 377

R v Halford (1978) 67 Cr App Rep 318, CA . . . 144

R v Hall [1952] 1 KB 302, [1952] 1 All ER 66, 35 Cr App Rep 167, 116 JP 43, [1951] 2 TLR 1264, CCA . . . 428

R v Hall [1983] 1 All ER 369, [1983] 1 WLR 350, 76 Cr App Rep 134, 147 JP 531, [1983] Crim

LR 106, 127 Sol Jo 187, 133 NLJ 132, CA . . .  51, 529, 539

R v Hall (1987) Times, 15 July, CA . . .  558

R v Hall [1993] Crim LR 527, CA . . .  680

R v Hallett [1986] Crim LR 462 . . .  599

R v Halpin [1975] QB 907, [1975] 2 All ER 1124, [1975] 3 WLR 260, 61 Cr App Rep 97, 119 Sol Jo 541, CA . . .  360, 362

R v Halpin [1996] Crim LR 112, CA . . .  27

R v Hamand (1985) 82 Cr App Rep 65, [1985] Crim LR 375, [1985] LS Gaz R 1561, CA . . .  189

R v Hamid (1979) 69 Cr App Rep 324 . . .  229, 232

R v Hammer [1923] 2 KB 786, 17 Cr App Rep 142, 87 JP 194, 92 LJKB 1045, 27 Cox CC 458, 68 Sol Jo 120, 129 LT 479, 39 TLR 670, CCA . . .  35

R v Hammond [1941] 3 All ER 318, 40 LGR 1, 28 Cr App Rep 84, 106 JP 35, 86 Sol Jo 78, 166 LT 135, CCA . . .  37, 415, 416

R v Hampshire [1996] QB 1, [1995] 2 All ER 1019, [1995] 3 WLR 260, [1995] 2 Cr App Rep 319, CA . . .  133–35, 159

R v Handbridge [1993] Crim LR 287, CA . . .  475

R v Hanson [2005] All ER (D) 380 (Mar), CA . . .  491, 502, 524, 538

R v Hanton (1985) Times, 14 February, CA . . .  242

R v Harborne Inhabitants (1835) 2 Ad & E 1540, 4 LJMC 49, 1 Har & W 36, 2 Nev & MMC 517, 4 Nev & MKB 341 . . .  688

R v Harden [1963] 1 QB 8, [1962] 1 All ER 286, [1962] 2 WLR 553, 46 Cr App Rep 90, 126 JP 130, 106 Sol Jo 264, CCA . . .  273, 554

R v Hardy (1794) 1 East PC 60, 99, 24 State Tr 199, 414, 753, 755, 1065 . . .  599

R v Haringey Justices, ex p DPP [1996] QB 351, [1996] 1 All ER 828, [1996] 2 WLR 114, [1996] 2 Cr App Rep 119, 160 JP 326, [1996] Crim LR 327 . . .  151

R v Harman (1984) 148 JP 289, [1985] Crim LR 326, CA . . .  172

R v Harris (1927) 20 Cr App Rep 144, CCA . . .  197

R v Harris [1972] 2 All ER 699, [1972] 1 WLR 651, 56 Cr App Rep 450, 136 JP 538, 116 Sol Jo 313 . . .  37, 122, 278

R v Harris (1986) 84 Cr App Rep 75, CA . . .  31

R v Harris [1986] Crim LR 123, CA . . .  33, 44

R v Harris [2001] Crim LR 227, CA . . .  682

R v Harron [1996] 2 Cr App Rep 457, [1996] Crim LR 581, CA . . .  19, 20

R v Harry (1987) 86 Cr App Rep 105, [1987] Crim LR 325, CA . . .  292

R v Hart (1932) 23 Cr App Rep 202, CCA . . .  205

R v Hart (1957) 42 Cr App Rep 47, CCA . . .  207

R v Hartley [2003] All ER (D) 208 (Oct), CA . . .  183

R v Harvey [1988] Crim LR 241 . . .  391, 395

R v Harwood [1989] Crim LR 285, CA . . .  62

R v Haslam (1925) 19 Cr App Rep 59, 28 Cox CC 105, 134 LT 158, CCA . . .  191

R v Hassan [1970] 1 QB 423, [1970] 1 All ER 745, [1970] 2 WLR 82, 54 Cr App Rep 56, 134 JP 266, 113 Sol Jo 997, CA . . .  669, 677

R v Hassan [1995] Crim LR 404, CA . . .  420

R v Hatton (1976) 64 Cr App Rep 88, CA . . .  530

R v Hay (1983) 77 Cr App Rep 70, 148 JP 138, [1983] Crim LR 390, CA . . .  24, 419, 683

R v Hayes [1977] 2 All ER 288, [1977] 1 WLR 234, 64 Cr App Rep 194, 141 JP 349, 120 Sol Jo 855, CA . . .  137, 138

R v Hayes [2004] All ER (D) 315, CA . . .  663

R v Hayter [2005] 2 All ER 209, HL . . .  422

R v Hearne (4 May 2000, unreported), CA . . .  451

R v Heath [1994] 13 LS Gaz R 34, CA . . .  476

R v Heaton [1993] Crim LR 593, CA . . .  388

R v Hedges (1909) 3 Cr App Rep 262, CCA . . .  185

R v Hegarty [1994] Crim LR 353, CA . . .  557

R v Helliwell [1995] Crim LR 79, CA . . .  108

R v Hendrick [1992] Crim LR 427, CA . . .  530, 682

R v Hendry (1988) 88 Cr App Rep 187, 153 JP 166, [1987] Crim LR 766, CA . . .  414

R v Hennessey (1978) 68 Cr App Rep 419, CA . . .  599

R v Henry [1990] Crim LR 574 . . .  432

R v Hepworth and Fearnley [1955] 2 QB 600, [1955] 2 All ER 918, [1955] 3 WLR 331, 39 Cr App Rep 152, 119 JP 516, 99 Sol Jo 544, CCA . . .  111–13, 688

R v Herron [1967] 1 QB 107, [1966] 2 All ER 26, [1966] 3 WLR 374, 50 Cr App Rep 132, 130 JP 266, 110 Sol Jo 544, CCA . . .  50

R v Herron (1975) 62 Cr App Rep 118, 120 Sol Jo 28, CA . . .  505

R v Herrox (5 October 1993, unreported), CA . . .  476

R v Hersey [1998] Crim LR 281, CA . . .  257–59

R v Hertfordshire County Council, ex p Green Environmental Industries [2000] 1 All ER 773, [2000] 2 WLR 373, [2000] 09 LS Gaz R 42,

[2000] NLJR 277, [2000] EGCS 27, HL . . . 630, 633

R v Hetherington [1972] Crim LR 703, CA . . . 380

R v Hewitt (1991) 95 Cr App Rep 81, [1992] Crim LR 650, [1992] NLJR 160, CA . . . 601

R v Hickin [1996] Crim LR 584, CA . . . 71

R v Hickmet [1996] Crim LR 588, CA . . . 476

R v Hill (1851) 15 JP 387, 2 Den 254, T & M 582, 20 LJMC 222, 5 Cox CC 259, 15 Jur 470, 4 New Sess Cas 613 . . . 138

R v Hill (1992) 96 Cr App Rep 456, CA . . . 584

R v Hill [1996] Crim LR 419, CA . . . 19

R v Hillier and Farrar (1992) 97 Cr App Rep 349, 157 JP 906, CA . . . 43, 680

R v Hills (1987) 86 Cr App Rep 26, [1987] Crim LR 567, 131 Sol Jo 537, [1987] LS Gaz R 1328, CA . . . 239

R v Hilton [1972] 1 QB 421, [1971] 3 All ER 541, [1971] 3 WLR 625, 55 Cr App Rep 466, 135 JP 590, 115 Sol Jo 565, CA . . . 126, 199

R v Hinds and Butler [1979] Crim LR 111 . . . 211

R v Hoare [2005] 1 Cr App R 355, CA . . . 442, 450

R v Hobson [1998] 1 Cr App Rep 31, CA . . . 553

R v Hodge, Hodge's Case (1838) 2 Lew CC 227 . . . 113

R v Hodges and Walker [2003] 2 Cr App R 247, CA . . . 561, 568, 570

R v Hodgson, Beckett v Ramsdale (1885) 31 Ch D 177, CA . . . 245

R v Hogan [1997] Crim LR 349, CA . . . 146, 312

R v Holden (1838) 8 C & P 606 . . . 151

R v Holmes [1953] 2 All ER 324, [1953] 1 WLR 686, 37 Cr App Rep 61, 117 JP 346, 97 Sol Jo 355, CCA . . . 570

R v Holt (1793) 2 Leach 593, 22 State Tr 1189, 5 Term Rep 436 . . . 360

R v Holy Trinity (Inhabitants) (1827) 7 B & C 611, 6 LJOSMC 24, 1 Man & Ry MC 146, 1 Man & Ry KB 444 . . . 266

R v Honeyghon [1999] Crim LR 221, CA . . . 194

R v Hookway [1999] Crim LR 750, CA . . . 570

R v Hopper [1915] 2 KB 431, 11 Cr App Rep 136, 79 JP 335, 84 LJKB 1371, 25 Cox CC 34, [1914–15] All ER Rep 914, 59 Sol Jo 478, 113 LT 381, 31 TLR 360, CCA . . . 106

R v Horley [1999] Crim LR 488, CA . . . 146

R v Horn (1912) 7 Cr App Rep 200, 76 JP 270, 28 TLR 336, CCA . . . 87

R v Horne [1990] Crim LR 188, CA . . . 427

R v Horne [1994] Crim LR 584, CA . . . 293, 557

R v Horry [1949] NZLR 791 . . . 509

R v Horseferry Road Magistrates' Court, ex p Bennett (No 2) [1994] 1 All ER 289, 99 Cr App Rep 123, [1994] Crim LR 370 . . . 592, 604, 616

R v Horwood [1970] 1 QB 133, [1969] 3 All ER 1156, [1969] 3 WLR 964, 53 Cr App Rep 619, 134 JP 23, 113 Sol Jo 895, CA . . . 521

R v Houlden (1993) 99 Cr App Rep 244, CA . . . 474

R v Howden-Simpson [1991] Crim LR 49, CA . . . 412

R v Howe [1982] 1 NZLR 618 . . . 556

R v Howe [1987] AC 417, [1987] 1 All ER 771, [1987] 2 WLR 568, 85 Cr App Rep 32, 151 JP 265, [1987] Crim LR 480, 131 Sol Jo 258, [1987] LS Gaz R 900, [1987] NLJ Rep 197, HL . . . 107

R v Howell [2005] 1 Cr App R 1, CA . . . 447, 450

R v Hoyte [1994] Crim LR 215, CA . . . 68, 402

R v Huckerby [2004] EWCA Crim 3251 . . . 559

R v Hudson (1980) 72 Cr App Rep 163, [1981] Crim LR 107, CA . . . 387

R v Hudson [1994] Crim LR 920, CA . . . 24, 683

R v Humphreys and Tully [1993] Crim LR 288, CA . . . 682

R v Hundal [2004] 2 Cr App R 307, CA . . . 632

R v Hunjan (1978) 68 Cr App Rep 99, CA . . . 249

R v Hunt (1820) 3 B & Ald 566, 1 State Tr NS 171, [1814–23] All ER Rep 456, CCR . . . 269

R v Hunt [1987] AC 352, [1987] 1 All ER 1, [1986] 3 WLR 1115, 84 Cr App Rep 163, [1987] Crim LR 263, 130 Sol Jo 984, [1987] LS Gaz R 417, [1986] NLJ Rep 1183, HL . . . 88, 90–3

R v Hunt [1992] Crim LR 582, CA . . . 402

R v Hunt (1994) 16 Cr App Rep (S) 87, [1994] STC 819, 68 TC 132, [1994] Crim LR 747, CA . . . 681

R v Hunter [1969] Crim LR 262, 113 Sol Jo 161, CA . . . 17

R v Hunter [1985] 2 All ER 173, [1985] 1 WLR 613, 81 Cr App Rep 40, [1985] Crim LR 309, 129 Sol Jo 268, [1985] LS Gaz R 1330, CA . . . 280

R v Hurst [1995] 1 Cr App Rep 82, CA . . . 305, 557

R v Hutchinson (1985) 82 Cr App Rep 51, [1985] Crim LR 730, 129 Sol Jo 700, CA . . . 144

R v Hutton (1988) Times, 27 October, CA . . . 188

R v Ilyas and Knight [1996] Crim LR 810, CA . . . 331, 423

R v Imran and Hussain [1997] Crim LR 754, CA . . . 146

R v Inch (1989) 91 Cr App Rep 51, C-MAC . . . 561

R v Inder (1977) 67 Cr App Rep 143, CA . . . 511

R v Ioannou [1999] Crim LR 586, CA . . . 443

R v IRC, ex p TC Coombs & Co [1991] 2 AC 283, [1991] 2 WLR 682, [1991] STC 97, 64 TC 124, sub nom TC Coombs & Co (a firm) v IRC [1991] 3 All ER 623, HL . . . 701

R v Irish [1995] Crim LR 145, CA . . . 220, 221

R v Iroegbu (1988) Times, 2 August, CA . . . 44

R v Isequilla [1975] 1 All ER 77, [1975] 1 WLR 716, 60 Cr App Rep 52, 139 JP 129, 118 Sol Jo 736, CA . . . 363 R v Islam [1999] 1 Cr App Rep 22, 162 JP 391, [1998] Crim LR 575, [1998] 17 LS Gaz R 29, 142 Sol Jo LB 123, CA . . . 398

R v Ismail (1990) 92 Cr App Rep 92, CA . . . 389, 394

R v Jacks [1991] Crim LR 611, CA . . . 582

R v Jackson [1996] 2 Cr App Rep 420, [1996] Crim LR 732, CA . . . 145, 566

R v Jackson [2000] Crim LR 377, CA . . . 592

R v James [1996] 2 Cr App Rep 38, 160 JP 9, [1995] Crim LR 812, CA . . . 364

R v James [1996] Crim LR 650, CA . . . 402

R v Jameson (1896) Stephen's Digest of the Law of Evidence (10th edn) p 48 . . . 364

R v Jefferson [1994] 1 All ER 270, 99 Cr App Rep 13, 158 JP 76, [1993] Crim LR 880, CA . . . 396

R v Jeffries [1997] Crim LR 819, CA . . . 570

R v Jeffries [1998] 2 All ER 155, [1998] 2 Cr App Rep 79, [1999] Crim LR 214, [1998] 05 LS Gaz R 29, 142 Sol Jo LB 40, CA . . . 51

R v Jelen (1989) 90 Cr App Rep 456, CA . . . 80

R v Jenkins (1869) LR 1 CCR 187, 33 JP 452, 38 LJMC 82, 11 Cox CC 250, 17 WR 621, 20 LT 372, CCR . . . 121

R v Jenkins (1923) 17 Cr App Rep 121, 87 JP 115, 67 Sol Jo 707, 39 TLR 458, CCA . . . 108

R v Jenkins (1945) 44 LGR 42, 31 Cr App Rep 1, 110 JP 86, 114 LJKB 425, 89 Sol Jo 458, 173 LT 311, CCA . . . 49

R v Jenkins [2003] Crim LR 107, CA . . . 423

R v Jennings and Miles [1995] Crim LR 810, CA . . . 39, 329, 330

R v Jiminez-Paez (1993) 98 Cr App.Rep 239, [1993] Crim LR 596, CA . . . 302

R v John [1973] Crim LR 113, CA . . . 192

R v Johnson (1847) 2 Car & Kir 354 . . . 376

R v Johnson [1961] 3 All ER 969, [1961] 1 WLR 1478, 46 Cr App Rep 55, 126 JP 40, 105 Sol Jo 1108, CCA . . . 108

R v Johnson [1989] 1 All ER 121, [1988] 1 WLR 1377, 88 Cr App Rep 131, [1988] Crim LR 831, 132 Sol Jo 1430, CA . . . 106, 600

R v Johnson [1994] Crim LR 376, CA . . . 43

R v Johnson [1995] 2 Cr App Rep 41, CA . . . 517

R v Johnson [1995] Crim LR 242, CA . . . 108

R v Johnson [1996] Crim LR 504, CA . . . 71

R v Johnson (2005) The Times, 3 May, CA . . . 443

R v Johnstone [2003] 1 WLR 1736, HL . . . 97–99

R v Jones (1883) 11 QBD 118, 47 JP 535, 52 LJMC 96, 15 Cox CC 284, 31 WR 800, 48 LT 768, CCR . . . 701

R v Jones (1909) 3 Cr App Rep 67, 74 JP 30, 26 TLR 59, CCA . . . 529

R v Jones (1923) 17 Cr App Rep 117, 87 JP 147, 67 Sol Jo 751, 39 TLR 457; CCA . . . 538

R v Jones [1969] 3 All ER 1559, [1970] 1 WLR 16, [1970] RTR 35, 54 Cr App Rep 63, 134 JP 124, 113 Sol Jo 962, CA . . . 708

R v Jones [1970] 1 WLR 16, CA . . . 711

R v Jones [1978] 2 All ER 718, [1978] 1 WLR 195, 66 Cr App Rep 246; 142 JP 453, 122 Sol Jo 94, CA . . . 352

R v Jones [1997] 2 Cr App Rep 119, CA . . . 423

R v Jones [2004] 1 Cr App R 60, CA . . . 240, 241

R v Jones (Terence) [1992] Crim LR 365, CA . . . 71, 256

R v Joseph [1993] Crim LR 206, CA . . . 412

R v JP [1999] Crim LR 401, CA . . . 301

R v Juett [1981] Crim LR 113, CA . . . 40

R v Justice of the Peace for Peterborough, ex p Hicks [1978] 1 All ER 225, [1977] 1 WLR 1371, 142 JP 103, [1977] Crim LR 621, 121 Sol Jo 605 . . . 649

R v K (DT) (1993) 97 Cr App Rep 342, [1993] 2 FLR 181, [1993] Fam Law 515, [1993] Crim LR 281, 13 BMLR 104, [1993] 1 LS Gaz R 44, 136 Sol Jo LB 328, CA . . . 607

R v Kabariti (1990) 92 Cr App Rep 362, CA . . . 476

R v Kachikwu (1968) 52 Cr App Rep 538, 112 Sol Jo 460, CA . . . 106

R v Kai-Whitewind (2005) The Times, 11 May, CA . . . 565

R v Kalia (1974) 60 Cr App Rep 200, [1975] Crim LR 181, CA . . . 202

R v Kane (1977) 65 Cr App Rep 270, CA . . . 143, 144, 249

R v Katz (1989) 90 Cr App Rep 456, CA . . . 80

R v Kay (1887) 16 Cox CC 292 . . . 686, 691

R v Keane [1994] 2 All ER 478, [1994] 1 WLR 746, 99 Cr App Rep 1, [1995] Crim LR 225, 138 Sol Jo LB 76, CA . . . 249, 591, 593, 599

R v Kearley [1992] 2 AC 228, [1992] 2 All ER 345, [1992] 2 WLR 656, 95 Cr App Rep 88, [1992]

Crim LR 797, [1992] 21 LS Gaz R 28, [1992] NLJR 599, 136 Sol Jo LB 130, HL . . . 24, 281, 290, 291, 295

R v Kearns [2003] 1 Cr App R 111, CA . . . 631–33

R v Keast [1998] Crim LR 748, CA . . . 25

R v Keenan [1990] 2 QB 54, [1989] 3 All ER 598, [1989] 3 WLR 1193, 90 Cr App Rep 1, 154 JP 67, [1989] Crim LR 720, 134 Sol Jo 114, [1990] 1 LS Gaz R 30, CA . . . 62, 64, 65, 69, 409, 411

R v Kelly (1985) Times, 27 July, CA . . . 123

R v Kelsey [1982] RTR 135, 74 Cr App Rep 213, [1982] Crim LR 435, 126 Sol Jo 97, CA . . .

R v Kemble [1990] 3 All ER 116, [1990] 1 WLR 1111, 91 Cr App Rep 178, 154 JP 593, [1990] Crim LR 719, [1990] 27 LS Gaz R 40, CA . . . 140

R v Kempster [1989] 1 WLR 1125, 90 Cr App Rep 14, [1989] Crim LR 747, CA679, 680, 682

R v Kennedy [1992] Crim LR 37, CA . . . 52, 528

R v Kennedy [1994] Crim LR 50, CA . . . 306

R v Kenny [1992] Crim LR 800, CA . . . 419

R v Kenny [1994] Crim LR 284, CA . . . 391

R v Kerawalla [1991] Crim LR 451, CA . . . 405

R v Khan (1981) 73 Cr App R 190, CA . . . 137

R v Khan (1987) 84 Cr App R 44, CA . . . 129

R v Khan [1993] Crim LR 54, CA . . . 68

R v Khan [1995] Crim LR 78, CA . . . 195

R v Khan [2003] 3 Crim LR 428, CA . . . 195, 198

R v Khan (Sultan) [1997] AC 558, [1996] 3 All ER 289, [1996] 3 WLR 162, [1996] Crim LR 733, [1996] 28 LS Gaz R 29, [1996] NLJR 1024, 140 Sol Jo LB 166, sub nom R v Khan [1996] 2 Cr App Rep 440, HL . . . 57, 61, 68, 71

R v Kidd [1995] Crim LR 406, CA . . . 81, 513

R v King (1914) 10 Cr App Rep 117, 24 Cox CC 223, [1914–15] All ER Rep 621, 111 LT 80, 30 TLR 476, CCA . . . 234, 242

R v King [1967] 2 QB 338, [1967] 1 All ER 379, [1967] 2 WLR 612, 51 Cr App Rep 46, 110 Sol Jo 965, CA . . . 520, 521

R v King [1983] 1 All ER 929, [1983] 1 WLR 411, 77 Cr App Rep 1, 147 JP 65, [1983] Crim LR 326, 127 Sol Jo 88, CA . . . 240, 649

R v King's Lynn Magistrates' Court, ex p M (or Moore) [1988] FCR 436, [1988] 2 FLR 79, [1988] Fam Law 393 . . . 695

R v Kinghorn [1908] 2 KB 949, 72 JP 478, 78 LJKB 33, 21 Cox CC 727, 99 LT 794, 25 TLR 219, DC . . . 271

R v Kinglake (1870) 11 Cox CC 499, 18 WR 805, 22 LT 335 . . . 624

R v Kinsella (1993) unreported, Dec, Belfast CC . . . 450

R v Kirk [1999] 4 All ER 698, [2000] 1 WLR 567, [2000] 1 Cr App Rep 400, CA . . . 411

R v Kirkpatrick [1998] Crim LR 63, CA . . . 53, 531

R v Kiszko (1978) 68 Cr App Rep 62, CA . . . 571

R v Knight (1946) 31 Cr App Rep 52, CCA . . . 424

R v Knight [1966] 1 All ER 647, [1966] 1 WLR 230, 50 Cr App Rep 122, 130 JP 187, 110 Sol Jo 71, CCA . . . 239

R v Knight [2004] 1 WLR 340, CA . . . 444, 450

R v Knott [1973] Crim LR 36, CA . . . 550

R v Knowlden and Knowlden (1983) 77 Cr App Rep 94, CA . . . 240

R v Knutton (1992) 97 Cr App Rep 115, [1993] Crim LR 208, CA . . . 527

R v Konscol [1993] Crim LR 950, CA . . . 69

R v Koon Cheung Tang [1995] Crim LR 813, CA . . . 270

R v Kritz [1950] 1 KB 82, [1949] 2 All ER 406, 48 LGR 88, 33 Cr App Rep 169, 113 JP 449, [1949] LJR 1535, 93 Sol Jo 648, 65 TLR 505, CCA . . . 112, 113

R v Kromer [2002] All ER (D) 420 (May), CA . . . 107

R v L [1999] Crim LR 489, CA . . . 244, 388

R v Ladlow [1989] Crim LR 219 . . . 190

R v Laidman and Agnew [1992] Crim LR 428, CA . . . 511

R v Lake (1976) 64 Cr App Rep 172, CA . . . 421

R v Lamb (1980) 71 Cr App Rep 198, CA . . . 191

R v Lambert [2002] 2 AC 545, HL . . . 93, 94–96, 99, 101, 102

R v Lambert, Ali and Jordan [2001] 32 WLR 211, CA . . . 88

R v Lamont [1989] Crim LR 813, CA . . . 247, 248

R v Land [1999] QB 65, [1998] 1 All ER 403, [1998] 3 WLR 322, [1998] 1 Cr App Rep 301, [1998] 1 FLR 438, [1998] Fam Law 133, [1998] Crim LR 70, [1997] 42 LS Gaz

R 32, CA . . . 556

R v Landon [1995] Crim LR 338, CA . . . 19

R v Lanfear [1968] 2 QB 77, [1968] 1 All ER 683, [1968] 2 WLR 623, 52 Cr App Rep 176, 132 JP 193, 112 Sol Jo 132, CA . . . 571

R v Langford [1990] Crim LR 653 . . . 600

R v Lang-Hall (1989) Times, 24 March, CA . . . 43

R v Langiert [1991] Crim LR 777, CA . . . 70

R v Langley [2001] Crim LR 651, CA . . . 415

R v Langton (1876) 2 QBD 296, 41 JP 134, 46 LJMC 136, 13 Cox CC 345, 35 LT 527, CCR . . . 174, 701

R v La Rose [2003] All ER (D) 24 (May), [2003] EWCA Crim 1471 . . . 453

R v Lasseur [1991] Crim LR 53, CA . . . 541

R v Latif [1996] 1 All ER 353, [1996] 1 WLR 104, [1996] 2 Cr App Rep 92, [1996] Crim LR 414, [1996] 05 LS Gaz R 30, [1996] NLJR 121, 140 Sol Jo LB 39, HL . . . 73, 76

R v Law (1996) The Times, 15 Aug . . . 591

R v Lawal [1994] Crim LR 746, CA . . . 290

R v Lawless (1993) 98 Cr App Rep 342, [1993] Crim LR 974, CA . . . 199, 384

R v Lawrence [1995] Crim LR 815, CA . . . 221

R v Lawrence [2002] Crim LR 584, CA . . . 593

R v Law-Thompson [1997] Crim LR 674, CA . . . 68

R v Leatham (1861) 25 JP 468, 3 E & E 658, 30 LJQB 205, 8 Cox CC 498, 7 Jur NS 674, 9 WR 334, 3 LT 777, [1861–73] All ER Rep Ext 1646 . . . 57

R v Leckey [1944] KB 80, [1943] 2 All ER 665, 29 Cr App Rep 128, 113 LJKB 98, 87 Sol Jo 447, 170 LT 198, 60 TLR 50, CCA . . . 432

R v Lee [1953] OR 34, 104 CCC 400, 15 CR 397, [1953] OWN 15 . . . 121

R v Lee (1973) 60 Cr App Rep 150, CA . . . 60

R v Lee [1996] 2 Cr App Rep 266, 160 JP 462, [1996] Crim LR 412, CA . . . 111, 135

R v Lee [1996] Crim LR 825, CA . . . 130, 164, 519, 682

R v Leeds Magistrates' Court, ex p Dumbleton [1993] Crim LR 866 . . . 649, 654

R v Lesley [1996] 1 Cr App Rep (S) 39, [1995] Crim LR 946, CA . . . 19, 20

R v Levy (1966) 50 Cr App Rep 238, [1966] Crim LR 381, 110 Sol Jo 565, CCA . . . 144, 538

R v Lewes Justices, ex p Secretary of State for the Home Department [1972] 1 QB 232, [1971] 2 All ER 1126, [1971] 2 WLR 1466, 135 JP 442, 115 Sol Jo 306; on appeal sub nom Rogers v Secretary of State for the Home Department [1973] AC 388, [1972] 2 All ER 1057, [1972] 3 WLR 279, 136 JP 574, 116 Sol Jo 696, HL . . . 604, 616, 618

R v Lewis (1973) 57 Cr App Rep 860, 117 Sol Jo 696, CA . . . 432

R v Lewis (1982) 76 Cr App Rep 33, 147 JP 493, CA . . . 515

R v Lewis [1989] Crim LR 61, CA . . . 715

R v Lewis [1996] Crim LR 260, CA . . . 248

R v Lillyman [1896] 2 QB 167, 60 JP 536, 65 LJMC 195, 18 Cox CC 346, 44 WR 654, [1895–9] All ER Rep 586, 40 501 Jo 584, 74 LT 730, 12 TLR 473, CCR . . . 183

R v Lin, Hung and Tsui [1995] Crim LR 817, CA . . . 80

R v List [1965] 3 All ER 710, [1966] 1 WLR 9, 50 Cr App Rep 81, 130 JP 30, 110 Sol Jo 12 . . . 49, 50, 550

R v Liverpool Juvenile Court, ex p R [1988] QB 1, [1987] 2 All ER 668, [1987] 3 WLR 224, 86 Cr App Rep 1, 151 JP 516, [1987] Crim LR 572, 131 Sol Jo 972, [1987] LS Gaz R 2045 . . . 38, 414, 415, 420

R v Llanfaethly Inhabitants (1853) 18 JP 8, 2 E & B 940, 23 LJMC 33, 17 Jur 1123, 2 WR 61, 2 CLR 230, 22 LTOS 117 . . . 268

R v Lloyd [2000] 2 Cr App R 355, CA . . . 474

R v Loan (1977) 66 Cr App Rep 252, [1978] Crim LR 94, CA . . . 370, 371

R v Lobell [1957] 1 QB 547, [1957] 1 All ER 734, [1957] 2 WLR 524, 41 Cr App Rep 100, 121 JP 282, 101 Sol Jo 268, CCA . . . 106

R v Lockley [1995] 2 Cr App Rep 554, [1996] Crim LR 113, CA . . . 308, 312

R v Longman [1988] 1 WLR 619, 88 Cr App Rep 148, [1988] Crim LR 534, 132 Sol Jo 790, [1988] 15 LS Gaz R 35, CA . . . 404

R v Loosely; Attorney-General's Reference (No 3 of 2000) [2001] 1 WLR 2060 . . . 60, 72

R v Lovell [1990] Crim LR 111, CA . . . 242

R v Lovelock [1997] Crim LR 821, CA . . . 205

R v Loveridge [2001] 2 Cr ASpp R 591, CA . . . 78

R v Lucas [1981] QB 720, [1981] 2 All ER 1008, [1981] 3 WLR 120, 73 Cr App Rep 159, 145 JP 471, [1981] Crim LR 624, 125 Sol Jo 426, CA . . . 18, 237, 237, 444

R v Lucas [1991] Crim LR 844, CA . . . 603

R v Lucas [1995] Crim LR 400, CA . . . 27

R v Luffe (1807) 8 East 193, [1803–13] All ER Rep 726 . . . 707

R v Lumley (1869) LR 1 CCR 196, 33 JP 597, 38 LJMC 86, 11 Cox CC 274, 17 WR 685, 20 LT 454 . . . 688, 700

R v Lunnon (1988) 88 Cr App Rep 71, [1988] Crim LR 456, CA . . . 52, 681

R v Lunt (1986) 85 Cr App Rep 241, [1987] Crim LR 405, CA . . . 505, 514

R v Lupien (1970) 9 DLR (3d) 1 . . . 558

R v Luttrell [2004] 2 Cr App R 520, CA . . . 259, 277, 554, 564

R v Luvaglio (1968) 53 Cr App R 1, CA . . . 112

R v Lydon (1987) 85 Cr App Rep 221, [1987] Crim LR 407, CA . . . 293

R v M (evidence: replaying video) [1996] 2 Cr App Rep 56, 140 Sol Jo LB 37, CA . . . 146

R v M (KJ) [2003] 2 Cr App R 322, CA . . . 309, 328

R v M (T) [2000] 1 WLR 421, CA . . . 497

R v MacKenney [2004] 2 Cr App R 32, CA . . . 225, 560

R v McAndrew-Bingham [1999] 1 WLR 1897, [1999] 2 Cr App Rep 293, [1999] Crim LR 830, 143 Sol Jo LB 38, CA . . . 130, 164

R v McCallion (1986) 86 Cr App Rep 7, CA . . . 199

R v McCarthy [1996] Crim LR 818, CA . . . 67

R v McCay [1991] 1 All ER 232, [1990] 1 WLR 645, 91 Cr App Rep 84, 154 JP 621, [1990] Crim LR 338, 134 Sol Jo 606, [1990] 19 LS Gaz R 39, CA . . . 375

R v McCleary [1994] Crim LR 121, CA . . . 189

R v McDonald [1991] Crim LR 122, CA . . . 59, 414

R v McDowell [1984] Crim LR 486, CA . . . 151

R v McEvilly (1973) 60 Cr App Rep 150, CA . . . 60

R v McEvoy [1997] Crim LR 887, CA . . . 71

R v McGarry [1998] 3 All ER 805, [1999] 1 WLR 1500, [1999] 1 Cr App Rep 377, [1999] Crim LR 316, 142 Sol Jo LB 239, CA . . . 453

R v McGee and Cassidy (1979) 70 Cr App Rep 247, [1980] Crim LR 172, CA . . . 442, 444, 445

R v McGillivray (1992) 97 Cr App Rep 232, 157 JP 943, CA . . . 302

R v McGovern (1990) 92 Cr App Rep 228, [1991] Crim LR 124, CA . . . 393, 394

R v McGranaghan [1995] 1 Cr App Rep 559n, CA . . . 518

R v McGrath and Casey (1983) 5 Cr App Rep (S) 460 . . . 109

R v McGuinness [1999] Crim LR 318, CA . . . 19, 443

R v McInnes (1989) 90 Cr App Rep 99, [1989] Crim LR 889, CA . . . 230, 256

R v McIntosh [1992] Crim LR 651, CA . . . 293

R v McIvor [1987] Crim LR 409 . . . 142, 406, 407

R v McKay [1967] NZLR 139, NZCA . . . 180, 181

R v McKenna (1956) 40 Cr App Rep 65, CCA . . . 145, 146

R v McKenzie (Practice Note) [1993] 1 WLR 453, 96 Cr App Rep 98, [1992] 34 LS Gaz R 34, [1992] NLJR 1162, 136 Sol Jo LB 260, CA . . . 245

R v Maclean [1993] Crim LR 687, CA . . . 79, 80

R v McLeod [1994] 3 All ER 254, [1994] 1 WLR 1500, [1995] 1 Cr App Rep 591, [1995] Crim LR 54, [1994] NLJR 531, CA . . . 387, 531, 541

R v McLernon [1992] NIJB 41 . . . 439, 445

R v McManus [2002] 1 Arch News 2, [2001] EWCA Crim 2455 . . . 439

R v McNab [2002] Crim LR 129, CA . . . 69

R v McNamara [1996] Crim LR 750, CA . . . 257

R v McNamara [1998] Crim LR 278, CA . . . 40

R v McNaughton (1843) 1 Car & Kir 130n, 1 Town St Tr 314, 4 St Tr NS 847, sub nom M'Naghten's Case 10 Cl & Fin 200, [1843–60] All ER Rep 229, sub nom Insane Criminals 8 Scott NR 595, HL . . . 87, 689

R v McQuiston [1998] 1 Cr App Rep 139, [1998] Crim LR 69, CA . . . 146

R v McVey [1988] Crim LR 127 . . . 43

R v Madden [1986] Crim LR 804, CA . . . 289

R v Maggs [1990] RTR 129, 91 Cr App Rep 243, [1990] Crim LR 654, 134 Sol Jo 933, [1990] 12 LS Gaz R 39, CA . . . 147

R v Maginnis [1987] AC 303, [1987] 1 All ER 907, [1987] 2 WLR 765, 85 Cr App Rep 127, 151 JP 537, [1987] Crim LR 564, 131 Sol Jo 357, [1987] LS Gaz R 1141, [1987] NLJ Rep 244, HL . . . 34

R v Maguire [1992] QB 936, [1992] 2 All ER 433, [1992] 2 WLR 767, 94 Cr App Rep 133, CA . . . 582

R v Mahmood and Manzur [1997] 1 Cr App Rep 414, [1997] Crim LR 447, CA . . . 680

R v Makanjuola [1995] 3 All ER 730, [1995] 1 WLR 1348, [1995] 2 Cr App Rep 469, 159 JP 701, [1996] Crim LR 44, [1995] 22 LS Gaz R 40, [1995] NLJR 959, CA . . . 236, 237, 239, 240, 243, 244

R v Makin and Wife (1893) 14 LRNSW 1 . . . 481

R v Malik [2000] Crim LR 197, CA . . . 27

R v Mallinson [1977] Crim LR 161, CA . . . 384

R v Malloy [1997] 2 Cr App Rep 283, CA . . . 639

R v Maloney [1994] Crim LR 525, CA . . . 303

R v Manji [1990] Crim LR 512, CA . . . 62, 77

R v Mann (1972) 56 Cr App Rep 750, CA . . . 194, 432

R v Manning (1923) 17 Cr App Rep 85, CCA . . . 522

R v Mansfield [1978] 1 All ER 134, [1977] 1 WLR 1102, 65 Cr App Rep 276, 121 Sol Jo 709, CA . . . 505

R v Mansfield Inhabitants (1841) 1 QB 444, 5 JP 420, 10 LJMC 97, 1 Gal & Dav 7, 5 Jur 505 . . . 695

R v Maqsud Ali [1966] 1 QB 688, [1965] 2 All ER 464, [1965] 3 WLR 229, 49 Cr App Rep 230, 129 JP 396, 109 Sol Jo 331, CCA . . . 277, 298

R v Marcus (2004) The Times, 3 Dec, CA . . . 71

R v Marlborough Street Magistrates' Court
Metropolitan Stipendiary Magistrate, ex p
Simpson (1980) 70 Cr App Rep 291, [1980]
Crim LR 305, DC . . . 271

R v Marlow, Tiley and Lloyd [1997] Crim LR 457,
CA . . . 680

R v Marriner [2002] All ER (D) 120 (Dec) . . . 78

R v Marsh [1994] Crim LR 52, CA . . . 534, 535

R v Martin (1872) LR 1 CCR 378, 36 JP 549, 41
LJMC 113, 12 Cox CC 204, 20 WR 1016,
26 LT 778, CCR . . . 280

R v Martin [1996] Crim LR 589, CA . . . 304

R v Martin [2004] 2 Cr App R 354, CA . . . 218

R v Martin and Nicholls [1994] Crim LR 218,
CA . . . 62, 71

R v Martin and White [1998] 2 Cr App Rep 385,
CA . . . 637

R v Martinez-Tobon [1994] 2 All ER 90, [1994]
1 WLR 388, 98 Cr App Rep 375, 158 JP 559,
[1994] Crim LR 359, 138 Sol Jo LB 6, [1994]
Crim LR 359, CA . . . 439

R v Marylebone Magistrates' Court, ex p Gatting
and Emburey (1990) 154 JP 549, [1990] Crim
LR 578 . . . 123

R v Masih [1986] Crim LR 395, CA . . . 558

R v Mason (1911) 7 Cr App Rep 67, 76 JP 184, 28
TLR 120, CCA . . . 566, 570

R v Mason [1987] 3 All ER 481, [1988] 1 WLR
139, 86 Cr App Rep 349, 151 JP 747, [1987]
Crim LR 757, 131 Sol Jo 973, [1987] LS Gaz R
2118, CA . . . 63, 65, 66, 79, 409

R v Matheson [1958] 2 All ER 87, [1958] 1 WLR
474, 42 Cr App Rep 145, 102 Sol Jo 309,
CCA . . . 85, 571

R v Mathias [1989] Crim LR 64; revsd [1989]
NLJR 1417, CA . . . 132, 421

R v Mattey and Queeley [1995] 2 Cr App Rep 409,
[1995] Crim LR 308, [1994] 41 LS Gaz R 41,
138 Sol Jo LB 208, CA . . . 121, 330

R v Matthews (1989) 91 Cr App Rep 43,
154 JP 177, [1990] Crim LR 190, CA . . . 412

R v Matthews [2004] QB 690, CA . . . 96

R v Mattison [1990] Crim LR 117, [1989]
NLJR 1417, CA . . . 52, 680

R v Maw [1994] Crim LR 841, CA . . . 195, 197,
198

R v May (1952) 36 Cr App Rep 91, CCA . . . 380,
398

R v Mead (1824) 2 B & C 605, 4 Dow & Ry KB
120 . . . 283

R v Mealey (1974) 60 Cr App Rep 59, [1975]
Crim LR 154, CA . . . 60

R v Meany (1867) 10 Cox CC 506, IR 1 CL 500,
CCR . . . 423

R v Mehrban [2002] 1 Cr App R 561, CA . . . 140

R v Menard [1995] 1 Cr App Rep 306, CA . . . 412

R v Mendy (1976) 64 Cr App Rep 4, CA . . . 9,
222, 223

R v Menga and Marshalleck [1998] Crim LR 58,
CA . . . 600

R v Meredith (1943) 29 Cr App Rep 40 . . . 126

R v Mertens [2005] Crim LR 301, CA . . . 526

R v Miah [1997] 2 Cr App Rep 12, [1997] Crim
LR 351, CA . . . 474

R v Miao (2003) The Times, 26 Nov, CA . . . 107

R v Middleton [2001] Crim LR 251 . . . 18

R v Milford [2001] Crim LR 330, CA . . . 451, 452

R v Millard [1987] Crim LR 196 . . . 415

R v Miller [1952] 2 All ER 667, 36 Cr App Rep
169, 116 JP 533 . . . 527, 528

R v Miller [1986] 3 All ER 119, [1986] 1 WLR
1191, 83 Cr App Rep 192, [1986] Crim LR 548,
130 Sol Jo 612, [1986] LS Gaz R 1995,
CA . . . 368, 388, 398

R v Miller [1997] 2 Cr App Rep 178, 161 JP 158,
[1997] Crim LR 217, CA . . . 338, 443

R v Miller [1998] Crim LR 209, CA . . . 65

R v Milliken (1969) 53 Cr App Rep 330,
CA . . . 144

R v Mills [1962] 3 All ER 298, [1962] 1 WLR
1152, 46 Cr App Rep 336, 126 JP 506, 106 Sol
Jo 593, CCA . . . 174, 175

R v Mills [1992] Crim LR 802, CA . . . 475

R v Minors [1989] 2 All ER 208, [1989] 1 WLR
441, 89 Cr App Rep 102, [1989] Crim LR 360,
133 Sol Jo 420, [1989] 19 LS Gaz R 39, CA . . .
329

R v Mir, Ahmed and Dalil [1989] Crim LR 894,
CA . . . 530

R v Mitchell (1892) 17 Cox CC 503 . . . 238, 427

R v Mitchell [2005] All ER (D) 182 (Mar) . . . 553

R v Moghal (1977) 65 Cr App Rep 56, CA . . . 377

R v Mokrecovas [2002] 1 Cr App R 226, CA . . .
214R v Moloney [1985] AC 905, [1985] 1 All
ER 1025, [1985] 2 WLR 648, 81 Cr App Rep 93,
149 JP 369, [1985] Crim LR 378, 129 Sol Jo
220, [1985] LS Gaz R 1637, [1985] NLJ Rep
315, HL . . . 688

R v Momodou [2005] 2 All ER 571, CA . . . 167

R v Montague [1999] Crim LR 148, CA . . . 251

R v Montgomery [1996] Crim LR 507, CA . . . 63

R v Moon [2004] All ER (D) 167 (Nov),
CA . . . 72

R v Moore (1992) 14 Cr App Rep (S) 273, [1992]
Crim LR 882, CA . . . 307

R v Morgan (1875) 14 Cox CC 337 . . . 284

R v Morgan [1993] Crim LR 56, CA . . . 464

R v Morgan [1993] Crim LR 870, CA . . . 41

R v Morley [1994] Crim LR 919, CA . . . 76

R v Morris (1959) 43 Cr App Rep 206, CCA . . . 441

R v Morris (1969) 54 Cr App Rep 69, [1970] Crim LR 172, 113 Sol Jo 997, CA . . . 521

R v Morris [1994] Crim LR 596, CA . . . 33

R v Morris [1995] 2 Cr App Rep 69, CA . . . 26

R v Morris [1998] 1 Cr App Rep 386, [1997] 43 LS Gaz R 29, 141 Sol Jo LB 231, CA . . . 146, 557

R v Morrison (1911) 6 Cr App Rep 159, 75 JP 272, 22 Cox CC 214, CCA . . . 152

R v Morse [1991] Crim LR 195 . . . 396

R v Moshaid [1998] Crim LR 420, CA . . . 89, 158, 445

R v Moss (1990) 91 Cr App Rep 371, [1990] NLJR 665, CA . . . 190, 246, 248, 395

R v Mountford [1999] Crim LR 575, CA . . . 127, 136, 451

R v Muir (1983) 79 Cr App Rep 153, [1984] Crim LR 101, [1983] LS Gaz R 3077, CA . . . 295, 300, 315

R v Mukadi [2004] Crim LR 373, CA . . . 215

R v Mullen [1992] Crim LR 735, CA . . . 517, 518

R v Mullin [1993] Crim LR 390, DC . . . 54

R v Mullins (1848) 12 JP 776, 3 Cox CC 526 . . . 234

R v Muncaster [1999] Crim LR 409, CA . . . 240

R v Munnery (1990) 94 Cr App Rep 164, CA . . . 145

R v Murphy [1965] NI 138, C-MAC . . . 59

R v Murphy [1980] QB 434, [1980] 2 All ER 325, [1980] 2 WLR 743, [1980] RTR 145, 71 Cr App Rep 33, [1980] Crim LR 309, 124 Sol Jo 189, CA . . . 561

R v Murray [1951] 1 KB 391, [1950] 2 All ER 925, 49 LGR 90, 34 Cr App Rep 203, 114 JP 609, 94 Sol Jo 726, 66 (pt 2) TLR 1007, CCA . . . 419

R v Murray [1995] RTR 239, [1994] Crim LR 927, CA . . . 472

R v Murray [1997] 2 Cr App Rep 136, [1997] Crim LR 506, CA . . . 423

R v Muscot (1713) 10 Mod Rep 192 . . . 231

R v Mushtaq [2005] UKHL 25 . . . 419

R v Mussell [1995] Crim LR 887, CA . . . 108, 253

R v Mustafa (1976) 65 Cr App Rep 26 . . . 522

R v Mutch [1973] 1 All ER 178, 57 Cr App Rep 196, 137 JP 127, CA . . . 439

R v Myers [1998] AC 124, [1997] 4 All ER 314, [1997] 3 WLR 552, [1998] 1 Cr App Rep 153, 161 JP 645, [1997] Crim LR 888, [1997] 35 LS Gaz R 33, [1997] NLJR 1237, 141 Sol Jo LB 211, HL . . . 203, 383, 416, 527

R v N (1992) 95 Cr App Rep 256, [1992] 21 LS Gaz R 28, 136 Sol Jo LB 136, CA . . . 136

R v N [1998] Crim LR 886, CA . . . 159

R v NK [1999] Crim LR 980, CA . . . 183

R v Nagah (1990) 92 Cr App Rep 344, 155 JP 229, [1991] Crim LR 55, CA . . . 63

R v Nagrecha [1997] 2 Cr App Rep 401, [1998] Crim LR 65, CA . . . 208, 220

R v Nagy [1990] Crim LR 187, CA . . . 256

R v Napper (1995) 161 JP 16, [1996] Crim LR 591, CA . . . 57, 437

R v Nash [2005] Crim LR 232, CA . . . 252

R v Nathaniel [1995] 2 Cr App Rep 565, CA . . . 67

R v Naudeer [1984] 3 All ER 1036, 80 Cr App Rep 9, [1984] Crim LR 501, CA . . . 17

R v Nazeer [1998] Crim LR 750, CA . . . 264

R v Neale (1977) 65 Cr App Rep 304, CA . . . 527

R v Neale [1998] Crim LR 737, CA . . . 208, 220

R v Neil [1994] Crim LR 441, CA . . . 413

R v Nelson (1978) 68 Cr App Rep 12 . . . 538

R v Nelson [1992] Crim LR 653, CA . . . 198

R v Nelson [1998] 2 Cr App Rep 399, [1998] Crim LR 814, CA . . . 68, 413

R v Nethercott [2002] 2 Cr App R 117, CA . . . 22

R v Newell [1989] Crim LR 906, CA . . . 106

R v Newport [1998] Crim LR 581, CA . . . 370

R v Newsome (1980) 71 Cr App Rep 325, CA . . . 188

R v Newton (1912) 7 Cr App Rep 214, 28 TLR 362, CCA . . . 603

R v Nicholas [1995] Crim LR 942, CA . . . 26

R v Nickolson [1999] Crim LR 61, CA . . . 445

R v Nightingale [1977] Crim LR 744 . . . 527

R v Norfolk Stipendiary Magistrate, ex p Taylor (1997) 161 JP 773, [1998] Crim LR 276 . . . 528

R v Northam (1967) 52 Cr App Rep 97, 111 Sol Jo 965, CA . . . 390

R v Norton [1910] 2 KB 496, 5 Cr App Rep 65, 74 JP 375, 79 LJKB 756, [1908–10] All ER Rep 309, 54 Sol Jo 602, 102 LT 426, 26 TLR 550, CCA . . . 425, 426, 432, 455

R v Nottingham Justices, ex p Lynn (1984) 79 Cr App Rep 238, [1984] Crim LR 554 . . . 272

R v Nowaz (alias Karim) [1976] 3 All ER 5, [1976] 1 WLR 830, 63 Cr App Rep 178, 140 JP 512, 120 Sol Jo 402, CA . . . 268

R v Nugent [1977] 3 All ER 662, [1977] 1 WLR 789, 65 Cr App Rep 40, 141 JP 702, 121 Sol Jo 286 . . . 152

R v Nye (1977) 66 Cr App Rep 252, [1978] Crim LR 94, CA . . . 370, 371

R v Nye (1982) 75 Cr App Rep 247, CA . . . 476

R v Oakley [1979] RTR 417, 70 Cr App Rep 7, CA . . . 561

R v Oakwell [1978] 1 All ER 1223, [1978] 1 WLR 32, 66 Cr App Rep 174, 142 JP 259, 122 Sol Jo 30, CA . . . 250, 253

R v O'Boyle (1990) 92 Cr App Rep 202, [1991] Crim LR 67, 134 Sol Jo 1076, CA . . . 203

R v O'Brien [1982] Crim LR 746 . . . 560

R v O'Connor (1986) 85 Cr App Rep 298, [1987] Crim LR 260, CA . . . 681

R v Odeyemi [1999] Crim LR 828, CA . . . 444

R v O'Doherty [2003] 1 Cr App R 77, CA (NI) . . . 258, 564

R v O'Donnell (1917) 12 Cr App Rep 219, CCA . . . 31

R v Ofori (No 2) (1993) 99 Cr App Rep 223, CA . . . 555, 708

R v O' Hadhmaill [1996] Crim LR 509, CA . . . 144

R v Okafor [1994] 3 All ER 741, 99 Cr App Rep 97, [1994] Crim LR 221, [1993] 43 LS Gaz R 47, 137 Sol Jo LB 244, CA . . . 412

R v Okorodu [1982] Crim LR 747 . . . 95, 100

R v Okusanya [1995] Crim LR 941, CA . . . 26

R v O'Leary (1988) 87 Cr App Rep 387, 153 JP 69, [1988] Crim LR 827, CA . . . 52, 65, 409

R v O'Leary [2002] EWCA Crim 2055, CA . . . 251

R v Oliphant [1992] Crim LR 40, CA . . . 411

R v Olisa [1990] Crim LR 721, CA . . . 352

R v Oliva [1965] 3 All ER 116, [1965] 1 WLR 1028, 49 Cr App Rep 298, 129 JP 500, 109 Sol Jo 453, CCA . . . 152, 197

R v Oliver [1944] KB 68, [1943] 2 All ER 800, 42 LGR 37, 29 Cr App Rep 137, 108 JP 30, 113 LJKB 119, 170 LT 110, 60 TLR 82, CCA . . . 90

R v Oliver, Hartrey and Baldwin [2003] 2 Cr App R (S) 151 . . . 412

R v O'Loughlin [1988] 3 All ER 431, 85 Cr App Rep 157, [1987] Crim LR 632 . . . 63

R v Olumegbon [2004] All ER (D) 60 (Aug) . . . 194

R v O'Neill [1969] Crim LR 260, CA . . . 207

R v Oni [1992] Crim LR 183, CA . . . 403

R v Ormerod (1987) 90 Cr App Rep 91, CA . . . 134, 185

R v Orton (1873) Stephen's Digest of the Law of Evidence (10th edn) p 48 . . . 364

R v Osborne [1905] 1 KB 551, 69 JP 189, 74 LJKB 311, 53 WR 494, 92 LT 393, 21 TLR 288, [1904–7] All ER Rep 54, CCR . . . 183, 184

R v Osbourne (or Osborne) [1973] QB 678, [1973] 1 All ER 649, [1973] 2 WLR 209, 57 Cr App Rep 297, 137 JP 287, 117 Sol Jo 123, CA . . . 190, 300, 402

R v Oscar [1991] Crim LR 778, CA . . . 71

R v O'Shea [1993] Crim LR 951, CA . . . 476

R v O'Sullivan [1969] 2 All ER 237, [1969] 1 WLR 497, 53 Cr App Rep 274, 133 JP 338, 113 Sol Jo 161, CA . . . 273

R v Owen [1952] 2 QB 362, [1952] 1 All ER 1040, 36 Cr App Rep 16, 116 JP 244, 96 Sol Jo 281, [1952] 1 TLR 1220, CCA . . . 146

R v Owen (1985) 83 Cr App Rep 100, CA . . . 539

R v Oxfordshire County Council [1992] Fam 150, [1992] 3 All ER 660, [1992] 3 WLR 88, sub nom Oxfordshire County Council v R [1992] 1 FLR 648, [1992] Fam Law 338 . . . 342

R v Oyesiku (1971) 56 Cr App Rep 240, 136 JP 246, CA . . . 186, 227

R v P [1991] 3 All ER 337, HL . . . 470, 506, 508, 510–12, 516

R v P [2002] 1 AC 146 . . . 79

R v P (GR) [1998] Crim LR 663, CA . . . 181, 207

R v Pall (1991) 156 JP 424, [1992] Crim LR 126, CA . . . 68

R v Palmer (1914) 10 Cr App Rep 77, CCA . . . 191

R v Palmer (1993) 99 Cr App Rep 83, 158 JP 138, [1994] Crim LR 122, CA . . . 125

R v Palmer (1998) 193 CLR 1 (Aus High Ct) . . . 204

R v Paris (1992) 97 Cr App Rep 99, [1994] Crim LR 361, CA . . . 388, 389

R v Park (1993) 99 Cr App Rep 270, CA . . . 380, 412, 425

R v Parker [1995] Crim LR 233, CA . . . 386, 388

R v Parris (1988) 89 Cr App Rep 68, [1989] Crim LR 214, CA . . . 64, 69, 408, 410

R v Patel [1951] 2 All ER 29, 49 LGR 589, 35 Cr App Rep 62, 115 JP 367, 95 Sol Jo 354, [1951] 1 TLR 1018, CCA . . . 25

R v Patel [1981] 3 All ER 94, 73 Cr App Rep 117, 146 JP 29, CA . . . 295, 315, 353

R v Patel [1992] Crim LR 739, (1992) 97 Cr App Rep 294, [1993] Crim LR 291, CA . . . 143, 305, 306, 308

R v Pattemore [1994] Crim LR 836, CA . . . 76

R v Pattinson [1996] 1 Cr App Rep 51, CA . . . 253, 384

R v Paul [1920] 2 KB 183, 14 Cr App Rep 155, 84 JP 144, 89 LJKB 801, 26 Cox CC 619, [1920] All ER Rep 535, 64 Sol Jo 447, 123 LT 336, 36 TLR 418, CCA . . . 126

R v Payne [1950] 1 All ER 102, 48 LGR 187, 34 Cr App Rep 43, 114 JP 68, 94 Sol Jo 116, 66 (pt 1) TLR 53, CCA . . . 125

R v Payne [1963] 1 All ER 848, [1963] 1 WLR 637, 47 Cr App Rep 122, 127 JP 230, 107 Sol Jo 97, CCA . . . 60, 79

R v Peach [1990] 2 All ER 966, [1990] 1 WLR 976, 91 Cr App Rep 279, [1990] Crim LR 741, [1990] 26 LS Gaz R 39, CA . . . 232

R v Peach [1995] 2 Cr App Rep 333, 159 JP 412, [1995] Crim LR 947, [1995] 17 LS Gaz R 47, CA . . . 278, 556

R v Peacock [1998] Crim LR 681, CA . . . 20

R v Pearce (1979) 69 Cr App Rep 365, [1979] Crim LR 658, CA . . . 187, 188, 424

R v Pearce [2002] 1 WLR 1553, CA . . . 129

R v Pemberton (1993) 99 Cr App Rep 228, CA . . . 257

R v Penny (1991) 94 Cr App Rep 345, [1992] Crim LR 184, CA . . . 64, 222

R v Perman [1996] 1 Cr App Rep 24, [1995] Crim LR 736, CA . . . 240

R v Perry [1984] Crim LR 680 . . . 550

R v Pestano [1981] Crim LR 397, CA . . . 197

R v Petcherini (1855) 7 Cox CC 79 . . . 377

R v Petkar [2004] 1 Cr App R 270, CA . . . 241, 452

R v Peters [1995] 2 Cr App Rep 77, [1995] Crim LR 722, CA . . . 513

R v Pettigrew (1980) 71 Cr App Rep 39, [1980] Crim LR 239, CA . . . 297

R v Pettman (2 May 1985, unreported), CA . . . 375, 486, 496

R v Phillips (1936) 35 LGR 36, 26 Cr App Rep 17, 101 JP 117, 30 Cox CC 536, 156 LT 80, CCA . . . 220, 223

R v Phillips [2003] 2 Cr App R 528, CA . . . 14, 496, 497

R v Phillipson (1989) 91 Cr App Rep 226, [1990] Crim LR 407, CA . . . 144

R v Pieterson [1995] 1 WLR 293, [1995] 2 Cr App Rep 11, [1995] Crim LR 402, [1995] 02 LS Gaz R 36, 138 Sol Jo LB 228, CA . . . 15

R v Pigram [1995] Crim LR 808, CA . . . 679

R v Pilcher (1974) 60 Cr App Rep 1, [1974] Crim LR 613, CA . . . 143

R v Pipe (1966) 51 Cr App Rep 17, 110 Sol Jo 829, CA . . . 125

R v Pitt [1983] QB 25, [1982] 3 All ER 63, [1982] 3 WLR 359, 75 Cr App Rep 254, 12 Fam Law 152, [1982] Crim LR 513, 126 Sol Jo 447, [1982] LS Gaz R 953, CA . . . 130, 629

R v Pitts (1912) 8 Cr App Rep 126, CCA . . . 234

R v Podola [1960] 1 QB 325, [1959] 3 All ER 418, [1959] 3 WLR 718, 43 Cr App Rep 220, 103 Sol Jo 856, CCA . . . 88

R v Pointer [1997] Crim LR 676, CA . . . 443

R v Polin [1991] Crim LR 293, CA . . . 189

R v Pommell [1995] 2 Cr App Rep 607, [1995] 27 LS Gaz R 32, [1995] NLTR 960n, CA . . . 85

R v Pook (1871) 13 Cox CC 172n . . . 377

R v Porritt [1961] 3 All ER 463, [1961] 1 WLR 1372, 45 Cr App Rep 348, 125 JP 605, 105 Sol Jo 991, CCA . . . 43

R v Potter (15 September 1977, unreported), CA . . . 125

R v Pountney [1989] Crim LR 216, 222, CA . . . 239

R v Powell [1986] 1 All ER 193, [1985] 1 WLR 1364, 82 Cr App Rep 165, [1986] Crim LR 175, 129 Sol Jo 869, CA . . . 51, 195, 541, 542

R v Power [1919] 1 KB 572, 14 Cr App Rep 17, 83 JP 124, 88 LJKB 593, 26 Cox CC 399, 120 LT 577, 35 TLR 283, CCA . . . 40

R v Prager [1972] 1 All ER 1114, [1972] 1 WLR 260, 56 Cr App Rep 151, 136 JP 287, 116 Sol Jo 158, CA . . . 379, 380, 385, 386, 398

R v Prater [1960] 2 QB 464, [1960] 1 All ER 298, [1960] 2 WLR 343, 44 Cr App Rep 83, 124 JP 176, 104 Sol Jo 109, CCA . . . 240

R v Price [1991] Crim LR 707, CA . . . 307

R v Price [2005] Crim LR 304, CA . . . 526

R v Priestley (1965) 50 Cr App Rep 183, 51 Cr App Rep ln, [1966] Crim LR 507, 116 NLJ 948, CCA . . . 386

R v Pryce [1991] Crim LR 379, CA . . . 244

R v Pullen [1991] Crim LR 457, CA . . . 106

R v Purcell [1992] Crim LR 806, CA . . . 402

R v Putland and Sorrell [1946] 1 All ER 85, 44 LGR 73, 31 Cr App Rep 27, 110 JP 115, 62 TLR 117, sub nom R v Sorrell and Putland 90 Sol Jo 116, 174 LT 148, CCA . . . 92

R v Qadir [1998] Crim LR 828, CA . . . 253

R v Quinn [1962] 2 QB 245, [1961] 3 All ER 88, [1961] 3 WLR 611, 45 Cr App Rep 279, 125 JP 565, 105 Sol Jo 590, CCA . . . 29

R v Quinn [1990] Crim LR 581, CA . . . 52, 64, 66, 69, 71

R v Quinn [1995] 1 Cr App Rep 480, [1995] Crim LR 56, 138 Sol Jo LB 77, CA . . . 253

R v R [1994] 4 All ER 260, [1994] 1 WLR 758, [1994] 13 LS Gaz R 34, 138 Sol Jo LB 54, CA . . . 29, 253

R v R [1994] 4 All ER 260, CA . . . 648

R v R [2003] All ER (D) 346 (Oct) . . . 217

R v Radak [1999] 1 Cr App Rep 187, [1999] Crim LR 223, CA . . . 302, 307

R v Rajakuruna [1991] Crim LR 458, CA . . . 70

R v Rampling [1987] Crim LR 823, CA . . . 122, 277

R v Ramsden [1991] Crim LR 295, CA . . . 253

R v Rance (1975) 62 Cr App Rep 118, 120 Sol Jo 28, CA . . . 505

R v Randall [2004] 1 All ER 466 . . . 22, 525–28, 560

R v Rankine [1986] QB 861, [1986] 2 All ER 566, [1986] 2 WLR 1075, 83 Cr App Rep 18, [1986] Crim LR 464, 130 Sol Jo 315, [1986] LS Gaz R 1225, CA . . . 599, 600, 601

R v Raphaie [1996] Crim LR S 12, CA . . . 62, 68, 493

R v Rappolt (1911) 6 Cr App Rep 156, CCA . . . 538

R v Rasini (1986) Times, 20 March, CA . . . 550

R v Raviraj (1986) 85 Cr App Rep 93, CA . . . 432

R v Rawlings [1995] 1 All ER 580, [1995] 1 WLR 178, [1995] 2 Cr App Rep 222, [1995] Crim LR 335, [1995] 02 LS Gaz R 36, [1994] NLJR 1626, 138 Sol Jo LB 223, CA . . . 146

R v Reading [1966] 1 All ER 521n, [1966] 1 WLR 836, 50 Cr App Rep 98, 130 JP 160, 110 Sol Jo 368, CCA . . . 521, 522

R v Rearden (1864) 4 F & F 76 . . . 498, 512

R v Redgrave (1981) 74 Cr App Rep 10, CA . . . 473

R v Redguard [1991] Crim LR 213, CA . . . 219

R v Redpath (1962) 46 Cr App Rep 319, 106 Sol Jo 412, CCA . . . 239

R v Reeves (1979) 68 Cr App Rep 331, [1979] Crim LR 459, CA . . . 35

R v Regan (1887) 16 Cox CC 203 . . . 265

R v Reid [1989] Crim LR 719, CA . . . 531

R v Reilly [1994] Crim LR 279, CA . . . 600

R v Rennie [1982] 1 All ER 385, [1982] 1 WLR 64, 74 Cr App Rep 207, 146 JP 170, 125 Sol Jo 860, CA . . . 386, 392

R v Reynolds [1950] 1 KB 606, [1950] 1 All ER 335, 48 LGR 239, 34 Cr App Rep 60, 114 JP 155, 94 Sol Jo 165, 66 (pt 1) TLR 333, CCA . . . 37

R v Reynolds [1989] Crim LR 220, CA . . . 558

R v Riaz (1991) 94 Cr App Rep 339, 156 JP 721, CA . . . 122, 146

R v Rice [1963] 1 QB 857, [1963] 1 All ER 832, [1963] 2 WLR 585, 47 Cr App Rep 79, 127 JP 232, 107 Sol Jo 117, CCA . . . 143, 203, 277, 286, 293, 294

R v Richards (1844) 1 Cox CC 62 . . . 199

R v Richards [1997] Crim LR 499, CA . . . 27

R v Richardson (1967) 51 Cr App Rep 381 . . . 127

R v Richardson [1969] 1 QB 299, [1968] 2 All ER 761, [1968] 3 WLR 15, 52 Cr App Rep 317, 132 JP 371, 112 Sol Jo 353, CA . . . 331

R v Richardson [1971] 2 QB 484, [1971] 2 All ER 773, [1971] 2 WLR 889, 55 Cr App Rep 244, 135 JP 371, 115 Sol Jo 263, CA . . . 174, 178

R v Richardson (1993) 98 Cr App Rep 174, CA . . . 151

R v Rider (1986) 83 Cr App Rep 207, [1986] Crim LR 626, CA . . . 232

R v Riley (1866) 4 F & F 964 . . . 209

R v Riley (1887) 18 QBD 481, 56 LJMC 52, 16 Cox CC 191, 35 WR 382, 56 LT 371, CCR . . . 210, 214

R v Rimmer [1972] 1 All ER 604, [1972] 1 WLR 268, 56 Cr App Rep 196, 136 JP 242, 116 Sol Jo 158, CA . . . 380

R v Rimmer and Beech [1983] Crim LR 250, CA . . . 560

R v Rizwan Mawji (2003) LTL 16/10/2003, CA . . . 287

R v Roads [1967] 2 QB 108, [1967] 2 All ER 84, [1967] 2 WLR 1014, 51 Cr App Rep 297, 131 JP 324, 111 Sol Jo 212, CA . . . 603

R v Robb (1991) 93 Cr App Rep 161, [1991] Crim LR 539, 135 Sol Jo 312, CA . . . 554, 564, 570, 583

R v Roberts (1878) 42 JP 630, 14 Cox CC 101, 38 LT 690 . . . 701

R v Roberts [1942] 1 All ER 187, 28 Cr App Rep 102, 86 Sol Jo 98, 58 TLR 138, CCA . . . 180, 181

R v Roberts [1997] 1 Cr App R 217, CA . . . 80

R v Roberts (1998) 162 JP 691, [1998] Crim LR 682, CA . . . 287

R v Roberts [2000] Crim LR 183, CA . . . 258

R v Robertson [1968] 3 All ER 557, [1968] 1 WLR 1767, 52 Cr App Rep 690, 133 JP 5, 112 Sol Jo 799, CA . . . 88

R v Robertson [1987] QB 920, [1987] 3 All ER 231, [1987] 3 WLR 327, 85 Cr App Rep 304, 151 JP 761, [1987] Crim LR 627, 131 Sol Jo 1002, [1987] LS Gaz R 2044, CA . . . 25, 52, 679–81

R v Robinson [1994] 3 All ER 346, 98 Cr App Rep 370, [1994] Crim LR 356, 18 BMLR 152, [1993] 45 LS Gaz R 40, [1993] NLJR 1643, 137 Sol Jo LB 272, CA . . . 225, 559, 560

R v Robinson [1996] Crim LR 417, CA . . . 20

R v Robinson [2001] Crim LR 478, CA . . . 534

R v Roble [1997] Crim LR 449, CA . . . 449

R v Robson [1972] 2 All ER 699, [1972] 1 WLR 651, 56 Cr App Rep 450, 136 JP 538, 116 Sol Jo 313 . . . 37, 122, 278

R v Rogers [1993] Crim LR 386, CA . . . 171

R v Rogers [1995] 1 Cr App Rep 374, CA . . . 275–77

R v Rogers and Tarran [1971] Crim LR 413 . . . 421

R v Romeo [2004] 1 Cr App R 417, CA . . . 239

R v Roncoli [1998] Crim LR 584, CA . . . 199

R v Rose [1998] 2 Cr App Rep 399, [1998] Crim LR 814, CA . . . 68, 413

R v Rossiter [1994] 2 All ER 752, 95 Cr App Rep 326, [1992] NLJR 824, CA . . . 106

R v Rothwell (1994) 99 Cr App Rep 388, CA . . . 285

R v Rouse [1904] 1 KB 184, 3 Cr App Rep 64, 68 JP 14, 73 LJKB 60, 20 Cox CC 592, 52 WR 236, 48 Sol Jo 85, 89 LT 677, 20 TLR 68, [1900–3] All ER Rep Ext 1054, CCR . . . 538

R v Rowson [1986] QB 174, [1985] 2 All ER 539, [1985] 3 WLR 99, 80 Cr App Rep 218, [1985] Crim LR 307, 129 Sol Jo 447, [1985] LS Gaz R 1330, CA . . . 203, 416

R v Rowton (1865) 29 JP 149, Le & Ca 520, 34 LJMC 57, 10 Cox CC 25, 11 Jur NS 325, 5 New Rep 428, 13 WR 436, [1861–73] All ER Rep 549, 11 LT 745, CCR . . . 472, 473

R v Roy [1992] Crim LR 185, CA . . . 511

R v Royce-Bentley [1974] 2 All ER 347, [1974] 1 WLR 535, 59 Cr App Rep 51, 138 JP 479, 118 Sol Jo 258, CA . . . 234

R v Rubin [1995] Crim LR 332, CA . . . 518

R v Rudd (1948) 32 Cr App Rep 138, 92 Sol Jo 206, 64 TLR 240, CCA . . . 126, 421

R v Ruiz [1995] Crim LR 151, CA . . . 517

R v Russell-Jones [1995] 3 All ER 239, [1995] 1 Cr App Rep 538, [1995] Crim LR 832, CA . . . 151

R v Rutherford [1998] Crim LR 490, CA . . . 330

R v Ryan [1990] Crim LR 50, CA . . . 256

R v Ryan [1992] Crim LR 187, CA . . . 67, 71, 220

R v Ryder [1994] 2 All ER 859, 98 Cr App Rep 242, 157 JP 1095, [1993] Crim LR 601, CA . . . 251

R v S [1993] Crim LR 293, CA . . . 518

R v S [2003] 1 Cr App R 602, CA . . . 96, 97, 101

R v S [2004] 3 All ER 689, CA . . . 184, 185

R v St Louis and Fitzroy Case (1984) 79 Cr App Rep 53, CA . . . 538

R v Salisbury (1831) 5 C & P 155 . . . 512

R v Samms, Elliot and Bartley [1991] Crim LR 197 . . . 66, 71

R v Samuel (1956) 40 Cr App Rep 8, CCA . . . 533, 535

R v Samuel [1988] QB 615, [1988] 2 All ER 135, [1988] 2 WLR 920, 87 Cr App Rep 232, 152 JP 253, [1988] Crim LR 299, 132 Sol Jo 623, [1988] 14 LS Gaz R 45, CA . . . 52, 65, 69, 405, 407, 408, 410

R v Samuel [1992] Crim LR 189, CA . . . 307

R v Sanders (1991) 93 Cr App Rep 245, [1991] Crim LR 781, CA . . . 571

R v Sanderson [1953] 1 All ER 485, [1953] 1 WLR 392, 37 Cr App Rep 32, 117 JP 173, 97 Sol Jo 136, CCA . . . 146

R v Sandhu [1997] Crim LR 288, [1996] NPC 179, [1997] JPL 853, CA . . . 24

R v Sang [1980] AC 402, [1979] 2 All ER 46, [1979] 2 WLR 439, 68 Cr App Rep 240, 143 JP 352, 123 Sol Jo 232, CA; affd [1980] AC 402, [1979] 2 All ER 1222, [1979] 3 WLR 263, 69 Cr App Rep 282, 143 JP 606, 123 Sol Jo 552, HL . . . 48, 49, 57, 59–61, 63, 380, 397

R v Sanghera [2001] 1 Cr App R 299 . . . 67

R v Sansom [1991] 2 QB 130, [1991] 2 All ER 145, [1991] 2 WLR 366, 92 Cr App Rep 115, [1991] Crim LR 126, 134 Sol Jo 1300, [1990] 41 LS Gaz R 35, CA . . . 144

R v Sanusi [1992] Crim LR 43, CA . . . 399, 411

R v Sappleton (1989) 89 Cr App Rep 273, [1989] Crim LR 653, CA . . . 147

R v Sargent [1993] Crim LR 713, CA . . . 43, 240

R v Sargent [2003] 1 AC 347, HL . . . 79

R v Sartori, Gavin and Phillips [1961] Crim LR 397 . . . 121

R v Sat-Bhambra (1988) 88 Cr App Rep 55, 152 JP 365, [1988] Crim LR 453, 132 Sol Jo 896, [1988] 12 LS Gaz R 39, CA . . . 380, 395, 398, 415, 420

R v Saunders [1899] 1 QB 490, 63 JP 150, 68 LJQB 296, 43 Sol Jo 245, 80 LT 28, 15 TLR 186, CCR . . . 286, 289

R v Saunders [1995] 2 Cr App Rep 313, CA . . . 147

R v Saunders [1996] 1 Cr App Rep 463, [1996] Crim LR 420, [1995] 45 LS Gaz R 31, 140 Sol Jo LB 22, CA . . . 18

R v Sawoniuk [2002] 2 Cr App R 220, CA . . . 497

R v Sayles [1999] Crim LR 221, CA . . . 194

R v Scarrott [1978] QB 1016, [1978] 1 All ER 672, [1977] 3 WLR 629, 65 Cr App Rep 125, 142 JP 198, 121 Sol Jo 558, CA . . . 230, 508, 509

R v Schama (1914) 11 Cr App Rep 45, 79 JP 184, 84 LJKB 396, 24 Cox CC 591, [1914–15] All ER Rep 204, 59 Sol Jo 288, 112 LT 480, 31 TLR 88, CCA . . . 688

R v Schofield (1917) 12 Cr App Rep 191, CCA . . . 384

R v Schreiber and Schreiber [1988] Crim LR 112, CA . . . 311

R v Scott (1856) 20 JP 435, Dears & B 47, 25 LJMC 128, 7 Cox CC 164, 2 Jur NS 1096, 4 WR 777, 169 ER 909, 27 LTOS 254, CCR . . . 629

R v Scott (1984) 79 Cr App Rep 49, 148 JP 731, [1984] Crim LR 235, [1984] LS Gaz R 586, CA . . . 144

R v Scott [1991] Crim LR 56, CA . . . 412

R v Scott [1994] Crim LR 947, CA . . . 23

R v Scott [1996] Crim LR 652, CA . . . 27

R v Scranage [2001] All ER (D) 195 (Apr), [2001] EWCA Crim 1171, CA . . . 474

R v Seaboyer [1991] 2 SCR 577 (Sup Ct of Can) . . . 210

R v Sealby [1965] 1 All ER 701 . . . 286, 361, 362

R v Seaman (1978) 67 Cr App Rep 234, CA . . . 505, 509

R v Sed [2005] 1 Cr App R 55, CA . . . 134

R v Seelig [1991] 4 All ER 429, [1991] BCLC 869, [1991] BCC 569, sub nom R v Seelig, R v Spens [1992] 1 WLR 148, 94 Cr App Rep 17, [1991] NLJR 638, CA . . . 399, 443

R v Sekhon (1986) 85 Cr App Rep 19, [1987] Crim LR 693, 131 Sol Jo 356, [1987] LS Gaz R 736, CA . . . 173, 174, 176

R v Senat (1968) 52 Cr App Rep 282, [1968] Crim LR 269, 112 Sol Jo 252, CA . . . 277

R v Setz-Dempsey and Richardson (1994) 98 Cr App Rep 23, [1994] Crim LR 123, CA . . . 302, 306

R v Shannon [2001] 1 WLR 51, CA . . . 75

R v Sharp [1988] 1 All ER 65, [1988] 1 WLR 7, 86 Cr App Rep 274, 152 JP 164, [1988] Crim LR 303, 132 Sol Jo 21, [1988] 7 LS Gaz R 38, [1988] 6 LS Gaz R 34, [1988] NLJR 6, HL . . . 189, 281, 380, 475

R v Sharp [1994] QB 261, [1993] 3 All ER 225, [1994] 2 WLR 84, [1993] NLJR 510, CA . . . 199

R v Shaw (1888) 16 Cox CC 503 . . . 223

R v Shaw [2002] All ER (D) 79 (dec), CA . . . 179

R v Shaw [2003] Crim LR 278 . . . 497

R v Shellard (1840) 9 C & P 277, 4 State Tr NS App 1386 . . . 423

R v Shepherd (1991) 93 Cr App Rep 139, CA; affd [1993] AC 380, [1993] 1 All ER 225, [1992] 2 WLR 102, 96 Cr App Rep 345, 157 JP 145, [1993] Crim LR 295, [1993] 4 LS Gaz R 38, [1993] NLJR 127, 137 Sol Jo LB 12, HL . . . 298

R v Shepherd (1980) 71 Cr App Rep 120, [1980] Crim LR 428, 124 Sol Jo 290, CA . . . 482, 631

R v Shepherd [1995] Crim LR 153, CA . . . 478

R v Sheridan (1974) 60 Cr App Rep 59, [1975] Crim LR 154, CA . . . 60

R v Shone (1982) 76 Cr App Rep 72, CA . . . 295, 353

R v Shore (1988) 89 Cr App Rep 32, CA . . . 515

R v Sidhu (1993) 98 Cr App Rep 59, [1993] Crim LR 773, CA . . . 497

R v Silcott and Others [1987] Crim LR 765 . . . 421, 558, 570

R v Silverlock [1894] 2 QB 766, 58 JP 788, 63 LJMC 233, 18 Cox CC 104, 10 R 431, 43 WR 14, 38 Sol Jo 664, 72 LT 298, 10 TLR 623, CCR . . . 273, 561

R v Simmonds [1969] 1 QB 685, [1967] 3 All ER 399n, [1967] 3 WLR 367, 51 Cr App Rep 316, 131 JP 341, 111 Sol Jo 274, CA . . . 172, 174

R v Simmonds [1996] Crim LR 816, CA . . . 139

R v Simmons [1987] Crim LR 630, CA . . . 234

R v Simms [1995] Crim LR 304, CA . . . 27

R v Simons (1834) 6 C & P 540, 2 Nev & MMC 598 . . . 355

R v Simpson (1967) 51 Cr App Rep 172, 111 Sol Jo 92, CA . . . 203

R v Simpson [1983] 3 All ER 789, [1983] 1 WLR 1494, 78 Cr App Rep 115, 148 JP 33, [1984] Crim LR 39, 127 Sol Jo 748, CA . . . 707

R v Simpson (1993) 99 Cr App Rep 48, CA . . . 511

R v Sims [1946] KB 531, [1946] 1 All ER 697, 31 Cr App Rep 158, [1947] LJR 160, 90 Sol Jo 381, 175 LT 72, 62 TLR 431, CCA . . . 8, 515

R v Sin (1968) 52 Cr App Rep 282, CA . . . 277

R v Singleton [1995] 1 Cr App Rep 431, [1995] Crim LR 236, CA . . . 650

R v Skinner (1993) 99 Cr App Rep 212, 158 JP 931, [1994] Crim LR 676, 137 Sol Jo LB 277, CA . . . 176, 179

R v Skinner, Pick, Skinner and Mercer [1995] Crim LR 805, CA . . . 680

R v Skirving [1985] QB 819, [1985] 2 All ER 705, [1985] 2 WLR 1001, 81 Cr App Rep 9, [1985] Crim LR 317, 129 Sol Jo 299, [1985] LS Gaz R 1409, CA . . . 556

R v Slaney (1832) 5 C & P 213 . . . 628

R v Slater [1995] 1 Cr App Rep 584, [1995] Crim LR 244, CA . . . 251

R v Slowcombe [1991] Crim LR 198 . . . 600

R v Smails [1987] AC 128, [1986] 2 All ER 928, [1986] 3 WLR 348, 83 Cr App Rep 277, 151 JP 177, 130 Sol Jo 572, [1986] NLJ Rep 733, HL . . . 243

R v Smith (1915) 11 Cr App Rep 229, 80 JP 31, 84 LJKB 2153, 25 Cox CC 271, [1914–15] All ER Rep 262, 59 Sol Jo 704, 114 LT 239, 31 TLR 617, CCA . . . 506–8

R v Smith [1959] 2 QB 35, [1959] 2 All ER 193, [1959] 2 WLR 623, 43 Cr App Rep 121, 123 JP 295, 103 Sol Jo 353, C-MAC . . . 390

R v Smith [1968] 2 All ER 115, [1968] 1 WLR 636, 52 Cr App Rep 224, 132 JP 312, 112 Sol Jo 231, CA . . . 152, 153

R v Smith [1979] 3 All ER 605, [1979] 1 WLR 1445, 69 Cr App Rep 378, [1979] Crim LR 592, 123 Sol Jo 602, CA . . . 557, 570

R v Smith [1994] 1 WLR 1396, 99 Cr App Rep 233, CA . . . 399

R v Smith [1998] 2 Cr App Rep 1, CA . . . 593

R v Smith [2003] EWCA Crim 927 . . . 560

R v Smith (Brian) [1995] Crim LR 658, CA . . . 77

R v Smith (Eric) [1987] Crim LR 579 . . . 406, 407

R v Smith (Ivory) [1995] Crim LR 940, CA . . . 26

R v Smith (Percy) [1976] Crim LR 511, CA . . . 287

R v Smith (Robert William) (1985) 81 Cr App Rep 286, [1985] Crim LR 590, CA . . . 432

R v Smith and Doe (1986) 85 Cr App Rep 197, [1987] Crim LR 267, CA 38 . . . 255

R v Smurthwaite [1994] 1 All ER 898, 98 Cr App Rep 437, 158 JP 165, [1994] Crim LR 53, [1993] 37 LS Gaz R 49, [1993] NLJR 1568, 137 Sol Jo LB 235, CA . . . 75–77, 140, 141

R v Somers [1963] 3 All ER 808, [1963] 1 WLR 1306, 61 LGR 598, 48 Cr App Rep 11, 128 JP 20, 107 Sol Jo 813, CCA . . . 561

R v South Ribble Magistrates, ex p Cochrane [1996] 2 Cr App Rep 544, 160 JP 517, [1996] Crim LR 741 . . . 179

R v South Worcestershire Magistrates, ex p Lilley [1995] 4 All ER 186, [1995] 1 WLR 1595, [1996] 1 Cr App Rep 420, 159 JP 598, [1995] Crim LR 954, [1995] 13 LS Gaz R 31 . . . 595

R v Sparks [1991] Crim LR 128, CA . . . 70, 412

R v Spencer [1987] AC 128, [1986] 2 All ER 928, [1986] 3 WLR 348, 83 Cr App Rep 277, 151 JP 177, 130 Sol Jo 572, [1986] NLJ Rep 733, HL . . . 243

R v Spens [1991] 4 All ER 421, [1991] 1 WLR 624, 93 Cr App Rep 194, CA . . . 33

R v Spiby (1990) 9l Cr App Rep 186, [1991] Crim LR 199, CA . . . 298

R v Spinks [1982] 1 All ER 587, 74 Cr App Rep 263, CA . . . 669, 677

R v Stafford [1968] 3 All ER 752n, 53 Cr App Rep 1, 133 JP 34, CA . . . 112

R v Stamford [1972] 2 QB 391, [1972] 2 All ER 427, [1972] 2 WLR 1055, 56 Cr App Rep 398, 136 JP 522, 116 Sol Jo 313, CA . . . 556

R v Stannard [1965] 2 QB 1, [1964] 1 All ER 34, [1964] 2 WLR 461, 48 Cr App Rep 81, 128 JP 224, CCA . . . 240

R v Stanton (2004) The Times, 28 Apr . . . 150

R v Steadman [1999] Crim LR 680, CA . . . 258, 680

R v Steane [1947] KB 997, [1947] 1 All ER 813, 45 LGR 484, 32 Cr App Rep 61, 111 JP 337, [1947] LJR 969, 91 Sol Jo 279, 177 LT 122, 63 TLR 403, CCA . . . 687

R v Stenning [1965] 3 All ER 136, [1965] 1 WLR 1470, 49 Cr App Rep 344, 129 JP 531, 109 Sol Jo 593, CCA . . . 403

R v Stephens (2002) The Times, 27 June, CA . . . 113

R v Stevenson [1971] 1 All ER 678, [1971] 1 WLR 1, 55 Cr App Rep 171, 135 JP 174, 115 Sol Jo 11 . . . 37, 122, 278

R v Stewart (1972) 56 Cr App Rep 272 . . . 398

R v Stewart (1986) 83 Cr App Rep 327, CA . . . 234

R v Stewart (1989) 89 Cr App Rep 273, [1989] Crim LR 653, CA . . . 147

R v Stewart [1995] Crim LR 500, CA . . . 67

R v Stewart [1999] Crim LR 746, CA . . . 681

R v Stipendiary Magistrate for Norfolk, ex p Taylor [1998] Crim LR 276, DC . . . 595

R v Stockwell (1993) 97 Cr App Rep 260, CA . . . 553, 570, 571

R v Stone [2005] All ER (D) 191 (Jan), CA . . . 242

R v Storey (1968) 52 Cr App Rep 334, 112 Sol Jo 417, CA . . . 187

R v Straffen [1952] 2 QB 911, [1952] 2 All ER 657, 36 Cr App Rep 132, 116 JP 536, 96 Sol Jo 749, [1952] 2 TLR 589, CCA . . . 505, 506, 517

R v Stretton (1986) 86 Cr App Rep 7, CA . . . 199

R v Stripp (1978) 69 Cr App Rep 318, CA . . . 106

R v Strudwick (1993) 99 Cr App Rep 326, CA . . . 17, 557

R v Sullivan (1887) 16 Cox CC 347 . . . 384

R v Sullivan [1923] 1 KB 47, 16 Cr App Rep 121, 86 JP 167, 91 LJKB 927, 27 Cox CC 187, [1922] All ER Rep 431, 126 LT 643, CCA . . . 146

R v Sullivan [1971] 1 QB 253, [1970] 2 All ER 681, [1970] 3 WLR 210, 54 Cr App Rep 389, 134 JP 583, 114 Sol Jo 664, CA . . . 582

R v Sullivan [1978] 2 All ER 718, [1978] 1 WLR 195, 66 Cr App Rep 246, 142 JP 453, 122 Sol Jo 94, CA . . . 352

R v Sullivan (2003) The Times, 18 Mar . . . 528

R v Summers [1952] 1 All ER 1059, 36 Cr App Rep 14, 116 JP 240, 96 Sol Jo 281, [1952] 1 TLR 1164, CCA . . . 112, 113

R v Surgenor [1940] 2 All ER 249, 38 LGR 179, 27 Cr App Rep 175, 104 JP 213, 31 Cox CC 389, 84 Sol Jo 344, 163 LT 182, CCA . . . 137

R v Sutton (1816) 4 M & S 532 . . . 360

R v Sutton (1969) 53 Cr App Rep 504, 113 Sol Jo 605, CA . . . 490

R v Sutton (1991) 94 Cr App Rep 70, CA . . . 172

R v Suurmeijer [1991] Crim LR 773, CA . . . 40

R v Sweet-Escott (1971) 55 Cr App Rep 316 . . . 204, 205, 208, 222

R v Sweeting and Thomas [1999] Crim LR 75, CA . . . 308

R v Sykes [1997] Crim LR 752, CA . . . 15

R v Symonds (1924) 18 Cr App Rep 100, CCA . . . 127

R v T [1998] 2 NZLR 257 (NZ Ct of App) . . . 204

R v T [2002] 1 WLR 632, CA . . . 211

R v T [2004] 2 Cr App R 32, CA . . . 216

R v Tagg [2002] 1 Cr App R 22, CA . . . 584

R v Tanner (1977) 66 Cr App Rep 56, 142 JP 209, CA . . . 538

R v Tattenhove [1996] 1 Cr App Rep 408, [1996] 2 Cr App Rep (S) 91, CA . . . 593

R v Taylor (1923) 17 Cr App Rep 109, 87 JP 104, CCA . . . 522, 593

R v Taylor 1961 (3) SA 614 . . . 374

R v Taylor [1991] Crim LR 541, CA . . . 404

R v Taylor [1993] Crim LR 223, CA . . . 433

R v Taylor [1994] Crim LR 680, CA . . . 18

R v Taylor [1998] Crim LR 822, CA . . . 18

R v Taylor [1999] Crim LR 77, CA . . . 437, 449

R v Taylor, Weaver and Donovan (1928) 21 Cr App Rep 20, CA . . . 13

R v Teasdale [1993] 4 All ER 290, 99 Cr App Rep 80, [1993] NLJR 1404, CA . . . 477

R v Thomas (1982) 77 Cr App Rep 63, CA . . . 87

R v Thomas [1985] Crim LR 445, CA . . . 198, 230

R v Thomas [1986] Crim LR 682 . . . 278

R v Thomas [1994] Crim LR 745, CA . . . 178, 192, 314

R v Thomas (Sharon) [1995] Crim LR 314, CA . . . 106

R v Thompson [1893] 2 QB 12, 57 JP 312, 62 LJMC 93, 17 Cox CC 641, 5 R 392, 41 WR 525, [1891–4] All ER Rep 376, 37 Sol Jo 457, 69 LT 22, 9 TLR 435, CCR . . . 121, 379, 384

R v Thompson (1946) 31 Cr App Rep 52, CCA . . . 424

R v Thompson [1962] 1 All ER 65, 46 Cr App Rep 72, 126 JP 55, CCA . . . 603

R v Thompson (1976) 64 Cr App Rep 96, CA . . . 195, 196

R v Thompson [1984] 3 All ER 565, [1984] 1 WLR 962, 79 Cr App Rep 191, [1984] Crim LR 427, 128 Sol Jo 447, [1984] LS Gaz R 1438, CA . . . 44

R v Thompson [1995] 2 Cr App Rep 589, [1995] Crim LR 821, CA . . . 51R v Thompson [1999] Crim LR 747, CA . . . 306

R v Thomson [1912] 3 KB 19, 7 Cr App Rep 276, 76 JP 431, 81 LJKB 892, 23 Cox CC 187, 107 LT 464, 28 TLR 478, CCA . . . 203, 281, 377

R v Thornton [1995] 1 Cr App Rep 578, 158 JP 1155, CA . . . 251

R v Threlfall (1914) 10 Cr App Rep 112, 24 Cox CC 230, 111 LT 168, CCA . . . 232

R v Tibbs [2002] 2 Cr App R 309, CA . . . 464

R v Tilley [1961] 3 All ER 406, [1961] 1 WLR 1309, 45 Cr App Rep 360, 125 JP 611, 105 Sol Jo 685, CCA . . . 273, 276

R v Tillman [1962] Crim LR 261, CCA . . . 43

R v Timson [1993] Crim LR 58, CA . . . 476

R v Tiplady (1995) 159 JP 548, [1995] Crim LR 651, CA . . . 71

R v Tirado (1974) 59 Cr App Rep 80, CA . . . 352

R v Tobin [2003] Crim LR 408, CA . . . 226

R v Tolson (1864) 4 F & F 103 . . . 583

R v Tompkins (1977) 67 Cr App Rep 181, sub nom R v Tomkins [1978] Crim LR 290, CA . . . 56, 657

R v Toner (1991) 93 Cr App Rep 382, CA . . . 558

R v Tonge (1993) 157 JP 1137, [1993] Crim LR 876, CA . . . 122, 146

R v Tooke (1989) 90 Cr App Rep 417, 154 JP 318, [1990] Crim LR 263, CA . . . 188, 377

R v Tovey [1979] RTR 220, 69 Cr App Rep 115, CA . . . 423

R v Tower Bridge Magistrates' Court, ex p Lawlor (1990) 92 Cr App Rep 98, 154 JP 901 . . . 304, 330

R v Tragen [1956] Crim LR 332 . . . 35, 230

R v Treacy [1944] 2 All ER 229, 30 Cr App Rep 93, 88 Sol Jo 367, 60 TLR 544, CCA . . . 202, 203, 416

R v Tregear [1967] 2 QB 574, [1967] 1 All ER 989, [1967] 2 WLR 1414, 51 Cr App Rep 280, 131 JP 314, 111 Sol Jo 175, CA . . . 151, 200

R v Trew [1996] 2 Cr App Rep 138, [1996] Crim LR 441, CA . . . 250

R v Tricoglus (1976) 65 Cr App Rep 16, CA . . . 510

R v Trump [1980] RTR 274, 70 Cr App Rep 300, [1980] Crim LR 379, 124 Sol Jo 85, CA . . . 61

R v Tucker [1994] Crim LR 683, CA . . . 18

R v Tudor (18 July 1988, unreported) . . . 511

R v Turnbull [1977] QB 224, [1976] 3 All ER 549, [1976] 3 WLR 445, 63 Cr App Rep 132, 140 JP 648, 120 Sol Jo 486, CA . . . 40, 192, 249–53, 256–58, 299

R v Turnbull (1985) 80 Cr App Rep 104, [1984] Crim LR 620, CA . . . 371

R v Turner (1816) 5 M & S 206, [1814–23] All ER Rep 713 . . . 90

R v Turner (1832) 1 Lew CC 119, 1 Mood CC 347 . . . 677

R v Turner [1910] 1 KB 346, 3 Cr App Rep 103, 74 JP 81, 79 LJKB 176, 22 Cox CC 310, 54 Sol Jo 164, 102 LT 367, 26 TLR 112, CCA . . . 356

R v Turner (1975) 61 Cr App Rep 67, 119 Sol Jo 422, 575, CA . . .

R v Turner [1975] QB 834, [1975] 1 All ER 70, [1975] 2 WLR 56, 60 Cr App Rep 80, 139 JP 136, 118 Sol Jo 848, CA . . . 24, 125, 258, 299, 314, 527, 556, 559, 560, 566

R v Turner [1991] Crim LR 57 . . . 680

R v Turner [1995] 3 All ER 432, [1995] 1 WLR 264, [1995] 2 Cr App Rep 94, CA . . . 593, 600

R v Turner [2004] 1 All ER 1025, CA . . . 444

R v Turpin [1990] Crim LR 514, CA . . . 680

R v Twaites (1990) 92 Cr App Rep 106, [1990] Crim LR 863, CA . . . 399

R v Tyagi (1986) Times, 21 July, CA . . . 172

R v Tyler (1992) 96 Cr App Rep 332, 157 JP 272, [1993] Crim LR 60, CA . . . 252, 253

R v Tyndale [1999] Crim LR 320, CA . . . 186

R v Tyrer (1988) Times, 13 October, CA . . . 489

R v Tyrer (1989) 90 Cr App Rep 446, CA . . . 392, 416

R v Tyson [1985] Crim LR 48, CA . . . 249, 250

R v Udenze [2001] EWCA Crim 1381 . . . 570

R v Uljee [1982] 1 NZLR 561, NZCA . . . 660

R v Umanski [1961] VLR 242 . . . 693

R v Umoh (1986) 84 Cr App Rep 138, [1987] Crim LR 258, CA . . . 607

R v Underwood [1999] Crim LR 227, CA . . . 497

R v Uxbridge Justices, ex p Sofaer (1986) 85 Cr App Rep 367 . . . 276

R v Vaillencourt [1993] Crim LR 311, CA . . . 600

R v Valentine [1996] 2 Cr App Rep 213, CA . . . 185, 320

R v Van Vreden (1973) 57 Cr App Rep 818, CA . . . 294

R v Varley (1914) 10 Cr App Rep 125, CCA . . . 191

R v Varley [1982] 2 All ER 519, 75 Cr App Rep 242, 126 Sol Jo 242, CA . . . 530, 531

R v Venn [2003] All ER (D) 207 (Feb) . . . 25, 516

R v Verelst (1813) 3 Camp 432 . . . 701

R v Vernon [1962] Crim LR 35 . . . 233

R v Vibert (21 October 1974, unreported) . . . 194

R v Vice-Chancellor of Oxford University (1857) 21 JP 644, 5 WR 872, 29 LTOS 343, sub nom Re Oxford Poor Rate Case 8 E & B 184, 27 LJMC 33, 3 Jur NS 1249 . . . 707

R v Vickers [1972] Crim LR 101, CA . . . 542

R v Vincent, Frost and Edwards (1840) 9 C & P 275, 4 State Tr NS App 1366 . . . 377

R v Viola [1982] 3 All ER 73, [1982] 1 WLR 1138, 75 Cr App Rep 125, [1982] Crim LR 515, 126 Sol Jo 536, CA . . . 211

R v Virgo (1978) 67 Cr App Rep 323, [1978] Crim LR 557, CA . . . 173

R v Virtue [1973] QB 678, [1973] 1 All ER 649, [1973] 2 WLR 209, 57 Cr App Rep 297, 137 JP 287, 117 Sol Jo 123, CA . . . 190, 300, 402

R v Voisin [1918] 1 KB 531, 13 Cr App Rep 89, 82 JP 96, 87 LJKB 574, 26 Cox CC 224, [1918–19] All ER Rep 491, 62 Sol Jo 423, 118 LT 654, 34 TLR 263, CCA . . . 15, 430

R v Voke (1823) Russ & Ry 531, CCR . . . 512

R v Voss (1989) 91 Cr App Rep 43, 154 JP 177, [1990] Crim LR 190, CA . . . 412

R v Vye [1993] 3 All ER 241, [1993] 1 WLR 471, 97 Cr App Rep 134, [1993] 14 LS Gaz R 42, [1993] NLJR 400, CA . . . 473–75, 477

R v W [1994] 2 All ER 872, [1994] 1 WLR 800, 99 Cr App Rep 185, [1994] Crim LR 586, CA . . . 545

R v W (John) [1998] 2 Cr App Rep 289, CA . . . 516, 517

R v Wahab [2003] 1 CR App R 15 . . . 391, 393

R v Wainwright (1875) 13 Cox CC 171 . . . 15, 377

R v Wainwright (1925) 19 Cr App Rep 52, CCA . . . 191

R v Walch [1993] Crim LR 714, CA . . . 107

R v Walker [1998] Crim LR 211, CA . . . 394, 560

R v Waller [1910] 1 KB 364, 3 Cr App Rep 213, 74 JP 81, 79 LJKB 184, 22 Cox CC 319, 54 Sol Jo 164, 102 LT 400, 26 TLR 142, CCA . . . 145

R v Wallett [1968] 2 QB 367, [1968] 2 All ER 296, [1968] 2 WLR 1199, 52 Cr App Rep 271, 132 JP 318, 112 Sol Jo 232, CA . . . 688

R v Wallwork (1958) 42 Cr App Rep 153, 122 JP 299, CCA . . . 134, 195

R v Walsh (1989) 91 Cr App Rep 161, [1989] Crim LR 822, CA . . . 67, 69, 409, 410

R v Walters [1979] RTR 220, 69 Cr App Rep 115, CA . . . 423

R v Wang [2005] 1 All ER 782, HL . . . 44

R v Wannell (1922) 17 Cr App Rep 53, 87 JP 48, CCA . . . 183

R v Ward [1993] 2 All ER 577, [1993] 1 WLR 619, 96 Cr App Rep 1, [1993] Crim LR 312, [1992] 27 LS Gaz R 34, [1992] NLJR 859, 136 Sol Jo LB 191, CA . . . 560, 582, 591, 592

R v Ward (1993) 98 Cr App Rep 337, CA . . . 412

R v Ward, Andrews and Bradley [2001] Crim LR 316 . . . 64, 383

R v Warickshall (1783) 1 Leach 263 . . . 428

R v Warner (1992) 96 Cr App Rep 324, CA . . . 682

R v Warren (1956) 40 Cr App Rep 160, CCA . . . 195

R v Warwickshall (1783) 1 Leach 263 . . . 428, 430

R v Waters [1989] Crim LR 62, CA . . . 395

R v Waters (1997) 161 JP 249, [1997] Crim LR 823, [1997] 09 LS Gaz R 33, 141 Sol Jo LB 58, CA . . . 330

R v Watford Magistrates' Court, ex p Lenman [1993] Crim LR 388 . . . 156

R v Watson (1834) 6 C & P 653 . . . 146

R v Watts [1983] 3 All ER 101, 77 Cr App Rep 126, 148 JP 156, CA . . . 543

R v Wayte (1982) 76 Cr App Rep 110, CA . . . 267, 268

R v Weaver [1968] 1 QB 353, [1967] 1 All ER 277, [1967] 2 WLR 1244, 51 Cr App Rep 77, 131 JP 173, 111 Sol Jo 174, CA . . . 364, 424, 490

R v Webber (Martin) [1987] Crim LR 412, CA . . . 230

R v Webber [2004] 1 WLR 404 . . . 445, 446, 453

R v Weeder (1980) 71 Cr App Rep 228, CA . . . 254

R v Weekes (1982) 74 Cr App Rep 161, CA . . . 125

R v Weekes [1988] Crim LR 244, CA . . . 181

R v Weekes (1993) 97 Cr App Rep 222, [1993] Crim LR 211, CA . . . 392, 412

R v Weerdesteyn [1995] 1 Cr App Rep 405, [1995] Crim LR 239, CA . . . 412

R v Weightman (1990) 92 Cr App Rep 291, [1991] Crim LR 204, CA . . . 560

R v Welch [1992] Crim LR 368, CA . . . 432

R v Weller [1994] Crim LR 856, CA . . . 16, 17

R v Wellingborough Magistrates' Court, ex p François (1994) 158 JP 813 . . . 151

R v Wellington [1991] Crim LR 543, CA . . . 554

R v Wellington [1993] Crim LR 616, CA . . . 107

R v Welstead [1996] 1 Cr App Rep 59, [1996] Crim LR 48, CA . . . 159

R v West [1996] 2 Cr App Rep 374, CA . . . 517

R v West London Coroner, ex p Gray [1988] QB 467, [1987] 2 All ER 129, [1987] 2 WLR 1020, 151 JP 209, 131 Sol Jo 593, [1987] LS Gaz R 1571 . . . 109

R v Westlake [1979] Crim LR 652 . . . 386

R v Westwell [1976] 2 All ER 812, 62 Cr App Rep 251, 140 JP 456, 120 Sol Jo 283, CA . . . 180

R v Wheeler [1917] 1 KB 283, 12 Cr App Rep 159, 81 JP 75, 86 LJKB 40, 25 Cox CC 603, [1916–17] All ER Rep 1111, 61 Sol Jo 100, 116 LT 161, 33 TLR 21, CCA . . . 126

R v Wheeler [1995] Crim LR 312, CA . . . 542

R v Wheeler [2001] Crim LR 745, CA . . . 461

R v Whitaker (1976) 63 Cr App Rep 193, CA . . . 240

R v White (1922) 17 Cr App Rep 59 . . . 197

R v White [1991] Crim LR 779, CA . . . 412

R v White [2004] All ER (D) 103 (Mar) . . . 217, 219

R v Whitehead (1848) 3 Car & Kir 202 . . . 23

R v Whitehead [1929] 1 KB 99, 27 LGR l, 21 Cr App Rep 23, 92 JP 197, 98 LJKB 67, 28 Cox CC 547, [1928] All ER Rep 186, 139 LT 640, CCA . . . 230, 239

R v Whitton [1998] Crim LR 492, CA . . . 17

R v Wholesale Travel Group (1991) 3 SCR 154 . . . 101, 102

R v Wilbourne (1917) 12 Cr App Rep 280 . . . 184, 320

R v Wilkins [1975] 2 All ER 734, 60 Cr App Rep 300, 139 JP 543, CA . . . 550

R v Williams [1984] 1 WLR 971, 79 Cr App Rep 220, [1984] Crim LR 489, 128 Sol Jo 364, [1984] LS Gaz R 1677, CA . . . 257, 278, 287

R v Williams (1986) 84 Cr App Rep 299, [1987] Crim LR 198, CA . . . 14, 496

R v Williams [1990] Crim LR 409, CA . . . 14

R v Williams [1992] 2 All ER 183, [1992] 1 WLR 380, 95 Cr App Rep 1, CA . . . 421

R v Williams (1994) 99 Cr App Rep 163, [1994] 2 LS Gaz R 41, CA . . . 43

R v Williams [2002] All ER (D) 200 (Oct) . . . 423

R v Willis [1960] 1 All ER 331, [1960] 1 WLR 55, 44 Cr App Rep 32, 124 JP 111, 103 Sol Jo 1029, CCA . . . 289

R v Willis (29 January 1979, unreported), CA . . . 513

R v Willis [2004] All ER (D) 287 (Dec) . . . 657

R v Willoughby (1988) 88 Cr App Rep 91, [1988] Crim LR 301, CA . . . 256

R v Willshire (1881) 6 QBD 366, 45 JP 375,
50 LJMC 57, 14 Cox CC 541, 29 WR 473,
44 LT 222, CCR . . . 686, 706

R v Wilmot (1988) 89 Cr App Rep 341, CA . . . 16,
514

R v Wilson (1957) 41 Cr App Rep 226,
CCA . . . 146

R v Wilson [1991] Crim LR 838, CA . . . 202

R v Windass (1988) 89 Cr App Rep 258,
CA . . . 203

R v Winn-Pope [1996] Crim LR 521, CA . . . 44

R v Withecombe [1969] 1 All ER 157, [1969]
1 WLR 84, 133 JP 123, CA . . . 702

R v Witts and Witts [1991] Crim LR 562,
CA . . . 152, 242

R v Wolverhampton Coroner, ex p McCurbin
[1990] 2 All ER 759, [1990] 1 WLR 719,
155 JP 33, CA . . . 109

R v Wong [1986] Crim LR 683 . . . 195, 226

R v Wood (1982) 76 Cr App Rep 23, [1982] Crim
LR 667, CA . . . 278, 297

R v Wood [1987] 1 WLR 779, 85 Cr App Rep 287,
[1987] Crim LR 414, 131 Sol Jo 840, [1987] LS
Gaz R 1055, CA . . . 549

R v Wood [1990] Crim LR 264, CA . . . 558

R v Wood [1994] Crim LR 222, CA . . . 413

R v Wood and Fitzsimmons [1998] Crim LR 213,
CA . . . 329, 330

R v Woodcock (1789) 1 Leach 500 . . . 89

R v Woodcock [1963] Crim LR 273 . . . 175

R v Woods (25 October 1977, unreported),
CA . . . 125

R v Wright (1821) Russ & Ry 456, CCR . . . 570

R v Wright (1866) 4 F & F 967 . . . 209

R v Wright (1910) 5 Cr App Rep 131,
CCA . . . 538

R v Wright (1934) 25 Cr App Rep 35,
78 Sol Jo 879, CCA . . . 580

R v Wright (1987) 90 Cr App Rep 91, CA . . . 134,
185

R v Wright [1993] Crim LR 607, CA . . . 147

R v Wright [1994] Crim LR 55, CA . . . 26, 68

R v Wright [2000] Crim LR 851, CA . . . 483

R v Wyatt [1990] Crim LR 343 . . . 199

R v X Y and Z (2000) Times, 23 May, CA . . . 156

R v Y [1992] Crim LR 436, CA . . . 419, 683

R v Y [1995] Crim LR 155, CA . . . 202

R v Yacoob (1981) 72 Cr App R 313, CA . . . 129

R v Yalman [1998] 2 Cr App Rep 269, [1998]
Crim LR 569, CA . . . 513

R v Yap Chuan Ching (1976) 63 Cr App Rep 7,
CA . . . 111, 707

R v Young (1976) 63 Cr App Rep 33, CA . . . 490

R v Yousry (1914) 11 Cr App Rep 13, 78 JP 521,
84 LJKB 1272, 24 Cox CC 523, 112 LT 311, 31
TLR 27, CCA . . . 203

R v Yusef [2003] 2 Cr App R 488, CA . . . 123

R v Z [1990] 2 QB 355, [1990] 2 All ER 971,
[1990] 3 WLR 113, 91 Cr App Rep 203, [1991]
Fam Law 137, CA . . . 134

R v Z [2003] 1 WLR 1489, CA, [2002] 2 AC 483,
HL . . . 379–81, 483, 504

R v Zaveckas [1970] 1 All ER 413, [1970] 1 WLR
516, 54 Cr App Rep 202, 134 JP 247,
114 Sol Jo 31, CA . . . 390

R v Zoppola-Barraza [1994] Crim LR 833,
CA . . . 477

Railways Commissioner v Murphy (1967)
41 ALJR 77, HC of A . . . 280

Rall v Hume [2001] 3 All ER 248 . . . 48, 279

Ramsay v Watson (1961) 108 CLR 642,
35 ALJR 301 . . . 566

Rank Film Distributors Ltd v Video Information
Centre (a firm) [1982] AC 380, [1980] 2 All ER
273, [1980] 3 WLR 487, [1980] FSR 242,
124 Sol Jo 757, CA; affd [1982] AC 380, [1981]
2 All ER 76, [1981] 2 WLR 668, [1981] FSR
363, 125 Sol Jo 290, HL . . . 626–28, 636

Ras Behari Lal v R (1933) 102 LJPC 144, 30 Cox
CC 17, [1933] All ER Rep 723, 77 Sol Jo 571,
150 LT 3, 50 TLR 1, PC . . . 603, 671

Ratten v R [1972] AC 378, [1971] 3 All ER 801,
[1971] 3 WLR 930, 56 Cr App Rep 18, 136 JP
27, 115 Sol Jo 890, PC . . . 288, 369–71, 374

Rawlinson v Miller (1875) 1 Ch D 52,
46 LJ Ch 252 . . . 698

Rawson v Haigh (1824) 2 Bing 99, 2 LJOSCP 130,
9 Moore CP 217 . . . 374, 375

Read v Bishop of Lincoln [1892] AC 644,
56 JP 725, 62 LJPC 1, [1891–4] All ER Rep 227,
67 LT 128, 8 TLR 763 . . . 364, 711

Reckitt & Colman Products Ltd v Borden Inc
(No 2) [1987] FSR 407 . . . 554

Redpath v Redpath and Milligan [1950] 1 All ER
600, 48 LGR 334, 114 JP 199, 94 Sol Jo 193,
CA . . . 104

Reed Executive plc v Reed Business Information
Ltd [2004] 4 All ER 942, CA . . . 666

Reid v R [1990] 1 AC 363, [1993] 4 All ER 95n,
[1989] 3 WLR 771, 90 Cr App Rep 121, [1990]
Crim LR 113, PC . . . 249, 252, 253

Rejfek v McElroy (1965) 112 CLR 517,
39 ALJR 177, HC of A . . . 118

Renworth Ltd v Stephansen [1996] 3 All ER 244,
CA . . . 636

Reynolds, Re, ex p Reynolds (1882) 20 Ch D 294,
46 JP 533, 51 LJ Ch 756, 15 Cox CC 108,
30 WR 651, [1881–5] All ER Rep 997,
46 LT 508, CA . . . 629

Reynolds v Llanelly Associated Tinplate Co Ltd
[1948] 1 All ER 140, 40 BWCC 240, CA . . . 712

Reynolds v Metropolitan Police Commissioner
[1985] QB 881, [1984] 3 All ER 649, [1985]
2 WLR 93, 80 Cr App Rep 125, [1984] Crim LR
688, 128 Sol Jo 736, [1984] LS Gaz R 2856,
CA . . . 35, 103

Reza v General Medical Council [1991] 2 AC 182,
[1991] 2 All ER 796, [1991] 2 WLR 939,
135 Sol Jo 383, 6 BMLR 125, PC . . . 520

Rhodes, Re, Rhodes v Rhodes (1887)
36 Ch D 586, 56 LJ Ch 825, 57 LT . . . 699

Rice v Connolly [1966] 2 QB 414, [1966]
2 All ER 649, [1966] 3 WLR 17, 130 JP 322,
110 Sol Jo 371, DC . . . 432

Rice v Howard (1886) 16 QBD 681, 55 LJQB 311,
34 WR 532, 2 TLR 457, DC . . . 195

Rich v Pierpont (1862) 3 F & F 35 . . . 569

Richards v Morgan (1863) 28 JP 55, 4 B & S 641,
33 LJQB 114, 10 Jur NS 559, 3 New Rep 198,
12 WR 162, 9 LT 662 . . . 357

Rickards and Rickards v Kerrier District Council
(1987) 151 JP 625 . . . 85

Ridgeway v The Queen (1995) 184 CLR 19 . . . 72

Rio Tinto Zinc Corpn v Westinghouse Electric
Corpn [1978] AC 547, [1978] 1 All ER 434,
[1978] 2 WLR 81, 122 Sol Jo 23, HL . . . 627–29

Robers v Secretary of State for the Home
Department. See R v Lewes Justices, ex p
Secretary of State for the Home Department

Roberts v DPP [1994] Crim LR 926 . . . 293

Robinson v South Australia State (No 2) [1931]
AC 704, 100 LJPC 183, [1931] All ER Rep 333,
73 Sol Jo 458, 145 LT 408, 47 TLR 454,
PC . . . 586

Robson v Kemp (1802) 4 Esp 233 . . . 377

Rogers v Home Secretary [1973] AC 388 . . . 585,
588, 595, 604

Rogers v Wood (1831) 2 B & Ad 245 . . . 367

Rose v R [1995] Crim LR 939, PC . . . 252

Rosher, Re, Rosher v Rosher (1884) 26 Ch D 801,
53 LJ Ch 722, 32 WR 821, 51 LT 785 . . . 660

Rouch v Great Western Rly Co (1841) 1 QB 51,
2 Ry & Can Cas 505, 4 Per & Dav 686, sub nom
Roach v Great Western Rly Co 10 LJQB 89,
5 Jur 821 . . . 374, 710

Rover International Ltd v Cannon Films Sales Ltd
(No 2) [1987] 3 All ER 986, [1987] 1 WLR
1597, 3 BCC 369, 131 Sol Jo 1591, [1987]

LS Gaz R 3658; revsd (1988) Financial Times,
10 June, CA . . . 339

Rowe and Davis v United Kingdom [2000] Crim
LR 584, ECtHR . . . 591, 593

Rowland v Bock [2002] 4 All ER 370,
QBD . . . 141

Rowley v London and North Western Rly Co
(1873) LR 8 Exch 221, 42 LJ Ex 153,
21 WR 869, [1861–73] All ER Rep 823,
29 LT 180 . . . 364

Royal Brompton Hospital NHS Trust v
Hammond [2001] BLR 297, CA . . . 114

Rumping v DPP [1964] AC 814, [1962]
3 WLR 763, sub nom R v Rumping [1962]
2 All ER 233, 106 Sol Jo 330, CCA; affd sub
nom Rumping v DPP [1964] AC 814, [1962]
3 All ER 256, [1962] 3 WLR 763, 46 Cr App
Rep 398, 106 Sol Jo 668, HL . . . 355, 656

Rush v Smith (1834) 1 Cr M & R 94, 2 Dowl 687,
3 LJ Ex 355, 4 Tyr 675 . . . 199

Rush & Tompkins Ltd v Greater London Council
[1989] AC 1280, [1988] 3 All ER 737, [1988]
3 WLR 939, 22 Con LR 114, 132 Sol Jo 1592,
[1988] NLJR 315, 43 BLR 1, HL . . . 240, 663

Russell v A-G [1949] P 391, [1949] LJR 1247,
93 Sol Jo 406, 65 TLR 369 . . . 690. 691

Ryan and French v DPP (1994) 158 JP 485,
[1994] Crim LR 457, CA . . . 688

S

S (a child) (adoption: psychological evidence)
[2004] EWCA Civ 1029 . . . 559

S v S [1972] AC 24, [1970] 3 All ER 107, [1970]
3 WLR 366, 114 Sol Jo 635, HL . . . 27

SCF Finance Co Ltd v Masri (No 3) [1987] QB
1028, [1987] 1 All ER 194, [1987] 2 WLR 81,
131 Sol Jo 22, [1987] LS Gaz R 37, CA . . . 696

S County Council v B [2000] 2 FLR 161 . . . 655

Sagheera, The. See Hellenic Mutual War Risks
Association (Bermuda) Ltd and General
Contractors Importing and Services
Enterprises v Harrison, The Sagheera

Saifi, Re [2001] 4 All ER 168, DC . . . 62, 63

Salabiaku v France (1988) 13 EHRR 379,
ECtHR . . . 93

Salsbury v Woodland [1970] 1 QB 324, [1969]
3 All ER 863, [1969] 3 WLR 29, 113 Sol Jo 327,
CA . . . 280

Sambasivam v Malaya Federation Public
Prosecutor [1950] AC 458, 66 (pt 2) TLR 254,
PC . . . 419, 683

Sandilands, Re (1871) LR 6 CP 411, sub nom Re
Mayer 40 LJCP 201, 19 WR 641,
24 LT 273 . . . 275

Sankey v Whitlam (1978) 142 CLR 1,
21 ALR 505 . . . 590

Sastry Velaider Aronegary v Sembecutty Vaigalie (1881) 6 App Cas 364, 50 LJPC 28, 44 LT 895, PC . . . 693, 694

Sattin v National Union Bank (1978) 122 Sol Jo 367, CA . . . 23, 469

Saunders v Punch Ltd (t/a Liberty Publishing) [1998] 1 All ER 234, [1998] 1 WLR 986, [1998] EMLR 18 . . . 614

Saunders v United Kingdom (1996) 23 EHRR 313, [1998] 1 BCLC 363, [1997] BCC 872, ECtHR . . . 380, 381, 630, 632, 633

Savage v Chief Constable of the Hampshire Constabulary [1997] 2 All ER 631, CA . . . 602

Savings and Investment Bank Ltd v Fincken [2004] 1 All ER 1125, CA . . . 665

Savings and Investment Bank Ltd v Gasco Investments (Netherlands) BV [1984] 1 All ER 296, [1984] 1 WLR 271, [1984] BCLC 179, 128 Sol Jo 115, [1984] LS Gaz R 657 . . . 352, 676

Savings and Investment Bank Ltd v Gasco Investments (Netherlands) BV (No 2) [1988] Ch 422, [1988] 1 All ER 975, [1988] 2 WLR 1212, 132 Sol Jo 790, [1987] NLJ Rep 1088, CA . . . 339

Saxby v Fulton [1909] 2 KB 208, 78 LJKB 781, [1908–10] All ER Rep 857, 53 Sol Jo 397, 101 LT 179, 25 TLR 446, CA . . . 708

Scappaticci v A-G [1955] P 47, [1955] 1 All ER 193n, [1955] 2 WLR 409, 99 Sol Jo 114 . . . 375

Schering Corporation v Cipla Ltd (2004) The Times, 10 Nov, Ch D . . . 665

Schneider v Leigh [1955] 2 QB 195, [1955] 2 All ER 173, [1955] 2 WLR 904, 99 Sol Jo 276, CA . . . 656

Schultz v R [1982] WAR 171 . . . 558

Science Research Council v Nassé [1979] QB 144, [1978] 3 All ER 1196, [1978] 3 WLR 754, [1978] ICR 1124, [1978] IRLR 352, 122 Sol Jo 593, CA; affd [1980] AC 1028, [1979] 3 All ER 673, [1979] 3 WLR 762, [i979] ICR 921, [1979] IRLR 465, 123 Sol Jo 768, HL . . . 585, 588, 605, 608, 617, 622

Scott v Baker [1969] 1 QB 659, [1968] 2 All ER 993, [1968] 3 WLR 796, 52 Cr App Rep 566, 132 JP 422, 112 Sol Jo 425 . . . 702

Scott v London and St Katherine Docks Co (1865) 3 H & C 596, 34 LJ Ex 220, 11 Jur NS 204, 5 New Rep 420, 13 WR 410, 159 ER 665, [1861–73] All ER Rep 246, 13 LT 148, Ex Ch . . . 28, 703

Scott v Martin [1987] 2 All ER 813, [1987] 1 WLR 841, 55 P & CR 171, 131 Sol Jo 887, [1987] LS Gaz R 2194, 2535, CA . . . 83

Scott v R [1989] AC 1242, [1989] 2 All ER 305, [1989] 2 WLR 924, 89 Cr App Rep 153, [1989]

Crim LR 820, 133 Sol Jo 421, PC . . . 249, 250, 306

Scott v Sampson (1882) 8 QBD 491, 46 JP 408, 51 LJQB 380, 30 WR 541, [1881–5] All ER Rep 628, 46 LT 412, DC . . . 467

Secretary of State for Defence v Guardian Newspapers Ltd [1985] AC 339, [1984] 3 All ER 601, [1984] 3 WLR 986, 128 Sol Jo 751, [1984] LS Gaz R 3426, HL . . . 610–12, 709

Secretary of State for Trade and Industry v Baker [1998] Ch 356, [1998] 2 WLR 667, [1998] BCC 888, sub nom Barings plc, Re, Secretary of State for Trade and Industry v Baker [1998] 1 All ER 673, [1998] 1 BCLC 16 . . . 646

Secretary of State for Trade and Industry v Bairstow [2003] 3 WLR 841, CA . . . 676

Selvey v DPP [1970] AC 304, [1968] 2 All ER 497, [1968] 2 WLR 1494, 52 Cr App Rep 443, 132 JP 430, 112 Sol Jo 461, HL . . . 48, 49, 51, 538, 540–42

Senat v Senat [1965] P 172, [1965] 2 All ER 505, [1965] 2 WLR 981 . . . 176

Serio v Serio (1983) 4 FLR 756; 13 Fam Law 255, CA . . . 117, 119

Settebello Ltd v Banco Totta and Acores [1985] 2 All ER 1025, [1985] 1 WLR 1050, [1986] ECC 11, [1985] 2 Lloyd's Rep 448, 129 Sol Jo 683, [1985] LS Gaz R 2658, CA . . . 598

Seyfang v GD Searle & Co [1973] QB 148, [1973] 1 All ER 290, [1973] 2 WLR 17, 117 Sol Jo 16 . . . 567

Shand v R [1996] 1 All ER 511, [1996] 1 WLR 67, [1996] 2 Cr App Rep 204, 140 Sol Jo LB 24, PC . . . 251, 254

Shannon v UK [2005] Crim LR 133, ECHR . . . 75

Sharp v Loddington Ironstone Co Ltd (1924) 17 BWCC 171, 132 LT 229, CA . . . 203

Shedden v A-G (1860) 30 LJPM & A 217, 6 Jur NS 1163, 2 Sw & Tr 170, 9 WR 285, 3 LT 592; affd sub nom Shedder v Patrick and A-G LR 1 Sc & Div 470, HL . . . 366

Shenton v Tyler [1939] Ch 620, [1939] 1 All ER 827, 108 LJ Ch 256, 83 Sol Jo 194, 160 LT 314, 55 TLR 522, CA . . . 124

Shephard, Re, George v Thyer [1904] 1 Ch 456, 73 LJ Ch 401, [1904–7] All ER Rep 186, 90 LT 249 . . . 693

Sherrard v Jacob [1965] NI 151, NICA . . . 584

Shrewsbury Peerage Case (1858) 7 HL Cas 1, 11 ER 1 . . . 366

Shrewsbury (Warden and Combrethren of Crafts of Mercers, Ironmongers and Goldsmiths) v Hart (1823) 1 C & P 113 . . . 360

Simaan General Contracting Co v Pilkington Glass Ltd [1987] 1 All ER 345, [1987] 1 WLR 516, 131 Sol Jo 297, [1987] LS Gaz R 819, [1986] NLJ Rep 824, 3 Const LJ 300, CA . . . 664

Simba-Tola v Elizabeth Fry Hospital [2001] EWCA Civ 1371 . . . 608

Slatterie v Pooley (1840) 10 LJ Ex 8, H & W 18, 4 Jur 1038, 6 M & W 664 . . . 265

Slattery v Mance [1962] 1 QB 676, [1962] 1 All ER 525, [1962] 2 WLR 569, [1962] 1 Lloyd's Rep 60, 106 Sol Jo 113 . . . 115

Slingsby v A-G (1916) 33 TLR 120, HL . . . 276

Smith v Blandy (1825) Ry & M 257 . . . 356

Smith v Smith (1836) 3 Bing NC 29, 7 C & P 401, 5 LJCP 305, 2 Hodg 130, 3 Scott 352 . . . 357

Smiths Group plc v Weiss [2002] EWHC 582, Ch D . . . 664

Sociedade National de Combustiveis de Angola UEE v Lundqvist [1991] 2 QB 310, [1990] 3 All ER 283, [1991] 2 WLR 280, CA . . . 626, 628, 629, 635

Society of Lloyd's v Jaffray (2000) The Times, 3 Aug, QBD . . . 147

Sodastream Ltd v Thorn Cascade Co Ltd [1982] Com LR 64, [1982] RPC 459, CA . . . 554

Sodeman v R [1936] 2 All ER 1138, 80 Sol Jo 532, 55 CLR 192, PC . . . 114

Solicitor, a, Re [1991] NLJR 1447 . . . 109

Solway, The (1885) 10 PD 137, 54 LJP 83, 5 Asp MLC 482, 34 WR 232, 53 LT 680 . . . 357

Somatra Ltd v Sinclair Roche and Temperley [2000] 1 WLR 2453 . . . 664

South Coast Shipping Co Ltd v Havant Borough Council [2003] 3 All ER 779, Ch D . . . 662

South Shropshire District Council v Amos [1987] 1 All ER 340, [1986] 1 WLR 1271, 130 Sol Jo 803, [1986] 2 EGLR 194, [1986] LS Gaz R 3513, [1986] NLJ Rep 800, [1986] RVR 235, 280 Estates Gazette 635, CA . . . 665

South Staffordshire Tramways Co v Ebbsmith [1895] 2 QB 669, 65 LJQB 96, 44 WR 97, 40 Sol Jo 49, 73 LT 454, 12 TLR 32, CA . . . 271

Southwark Water Co v Quick (1878) 3 QBD 315, 47 LJQB 258, 26 WR 341, CA . . . 644

Soward v Leggatt (1836) 7 C & P 613 . . . 103

Sparks v R [1964] AC 964, [1964] 1 All ER 727, [1964] 2 WLR 566, 108 Sol Jo 154, PC . . . 46, 314

Spigelman v Hocken (1933) 77 Sol Jo 852, 150 LT 256, 50 TLR 87 . . . 586

Spivack v Spivack (1930) 28 LGR 188, [1930] WN 46, 94 JP 91, 99 LJP 52, 29 Cox CC 91, [1930] All ER Rep 133, 74 Sol Jo 155, 142 LT 492, 46 TLR 243 . . . 691

Springsteen v Flute International Ltd [2001] EMLR 654, CA . . . 29, 266

Statue of Liberty, The, Sapporo Maru M/S (Owners) v Steam Tanker Statue of Liberty (Owners) [1968] 2 All ER 195, [1968] 1 WLR 739, [1968] 1 Lloyd's Rep 429, 112 Sol Jo 380 . . . 278, 297

Stainer v Diotwisch (Burgesses) (1695) 12 Mod Rep 85, sub nom Stainer v Droitwich (Burgesses) 1 Salk 281, sub nom Steyner v Droitwich (Burgesses) Holt KB 290, Skin 623 . . . 364

Stevens v Gullis (Pile, third party) [2000] 1 All ER 527, [1999] BLR 394, [1999] 44 EG 143, CA . . . 578

Stevens (formerly Ludlow) v Simons [1988] CLY 1161, CA . . . 571

Stirland v DPP [1944] AC 315, [1944] 2 All ER 13, 42 LGR 263, 30 Cr App Rep 40, 109 JP 1, 113 LJKB 394, 88 Sol Jo 255, 171 LT 78, 60 TLR 461, HL . . . 483

Stockdale v Hansard (1839) 9 Ad & El 1, 3 State Tr NS 723, 8 LJQB 294, 3 Jur 905, 2 Per & Dav 1 . . . 709

Stollery, Re, Weir v Treasury Solicitor [1926] Ch 284, 24 LGR 173, 90 JP 90, 95 LJ Ch 259, [1926] All ER Rep 67, 70 Sol Jo 385, 134 LT 430, 42 TLR 253, CA . . . 361

Stoney v Eastbourne RDC [1927] 1 Ch 367, 24 LGR 333, 90 JP 173, 95 LJ Ch 312, 70 Sol Jo 690, 135 LT 281, CA . . . 367

Stowe v Querner (1870) LR 5 Exch 155, 39 LJ Ex 60, 3 Mar LC 341, 18 WR 466, 22 LT 29 . . . 37

Stroud v Stroud [1963] 3 All ER 539, [1963] 1 WLR 1080, 107 Sol Jo 273 . . . 176, 206

Stupple v Royal Insurance Co Ltd [1971] 1 QB 50, [1970] 1 All ER 390, [1970] 2 WLR 124, [1969] 2 Lloyd's Rep 570, 113 Sol Jo 817; affd [1971] 1 QB 50, [1970] 3 All ER 230, [1970] 3 WLR 217, [1970] 2 Lloyd's Rep 127, 114 Sol Jo 551, CA . . . 671

Sturla v Freccia (1880) 5 App Cas 623, 44 JP 812, 50 LJ Ch 86, 29 WR 217, [1874 80] All ER Rep 657, 43 LT 209, HL . . . 360, 361, 363

Subramaniam v Public Prosecutor [1956] 1 WLR 965, 100 Sol Jo 566, PC . . . 289

Sugden v Lord St Leonards (1876) 1 PD 154, 45 LJP 49, 2 Char Pr Cas 160, 24 WR 479, 860, [1874–80] All ER Rep 21, 34 LT 369, 372, CA . . . 377

Sumitomo Corporation v Credit Lyonnais Rouse Ltd [2002] 1 WLR 479, CA . . . 644

Summers v Moseley (1834) 2 Cr & M 477, 1 Cr M & R 96n, 3 LJ Ex 128, 4 Tyr 158 . . . 199

Sumner and Leivesley v John Brown & Co (1909) 25 TLR 745 . . . 194

Sutton v Sadler (1857) 3 CBNS 87, 26 LJCP 284, 3 Jur NS 1150, 5 WR 880, 30 LTOS 65 . . . 86, 702

Sutton v Sutton [1969] 3 All ER 1348, [1970] 1 WLR 183, 113 Sol Jo 426 . . . 668, 675

T

Talbot v Von Boris [1911] 1 KB 854, 80 LJKB 661, 55 Sol Jo 290, 104 LT 524, 27 TLR 266, CA . . . 106

Tameshwar v R [1957] AC 476, [1957] 2 All ER 683, [1957] 3 WLR 157, 41 Cr App Rep 161, 121 JP 477, 101 Sol Jo 532, PC . . . 280

Taplin, Re, Watson v Tate [1937] 3 All ER 105, 81 Sol Jo 526 . . . 693, 694

Tate Access Floors Inc v Boswell [1991] Ch 512, [1990] 3 All ER 303, [1991] 2 WLR 304, 134 Sol Jo 1227, [1990] 42 LS Gaz R 35, [1990] NLJR 963 . . . 626, 629, 635

Tate & Lyle International Ltd v Government Trading Corpn [1984] LS Gaz R 3341, CA . . . 660

Taylor, Re, Taylor v Taylor [1961] 1 All ER 55, [1961] 1 WLR 9, 105 Sol Jo 37, CA . . . 691–94, 705

Taylor v Anderton (Police Complaints Authority intervening) [1995] 2 All ER 420, [1995] 1 WLR 447, [1995] 11 LS Gaz R 37, CA . . . 603, 606, 619

Taylor v Chief Constable of Cheshire [1987] 1 All ER 225, [1986] 1 WLR 1479, 84 Cr App Rep 191, 151 JP 103, [1987] Crim LR 119, 130 Sol Jo 953, [1987] LS Gaz R 412 . . . 257, 278, 298

Taylor v Taylor (Taylor intervening, Holmes cited) [1970] 2 All ER 609, [1970] 1 WLR 1148, 114 Sol Jo 415, CA . . . 352, 671

Taylor's Central Garages (Exeter) Ltd v Roper [1951] WN 383, 115 JP 445, sub nom Roper v Taylor's Central Garages (Exeter) Ltd [1951] 2 TLR 284 . . . 710

Teixeira de Castro v Portugal (1998) 28 EHRR 101, [1998] Crim LR 751, [1998] HRCD 8, 4 BHRC 533, ECtHR . . . 75

Teper v R [1952] AC 480, [1952] 2 All ER 447, 116 JP 502, 96 Sol Jo 493, [1952] 2 TLR 162, PC . . . 13, 292

T (H) v T (E) [1971] 1 All ER 590, sub nom T (HH) v T (E) [1971] 1 WLR 429, 115 Sol Jo 186 . . . 696

Theodoropoulas v Theodoropoulas [1964] P 311, [1963] 2 All ER 772, [1963] 3 WLR 354, 107 Sol Jo 632 . . . 666, 667

Thomas v David (1836) 7 C & P 350 . . . 222

Thomas v Jenkins (1837) 1 JP 211, 6 Ad & E1525, 6 LJKB 163, 1 Jur 261, 1 Nev & PKB 587, Will Woll & Dav 265 . . . 367

Thomas v Metropolitan Police Commissioner [1997] QB 813, [1997] 1 All ER 747, [1997] 2 WLR 593, CA . . . 221, 551

Thompson v R [1918] AC 221, sub nom Thompson v DPP 13 Cr App Rep 61, 82 JP 145, 87 LJKB 478, 26 Cox CC 189, [1918] 19 All ER Rep 521, 62 Sol Jo 266, 118 LT 418, 34 TLR 204, HL . . . 76, 83, 516, 519–22

Thompson v Thompson [1957] P 19, [1957] 1 All ER 161, [1957] 2 WLR 138, 101 Sol Jo 87, CA . . . 700

Thompson v Trevanion (1693) Holt KB 286, Skin 402 . . . 369

Thompson Newspapers Ltd v Director of Investigations & Research (1990) 54 CCC 417 (Sup Ct of Can) . . . 632

Thorpe v Chief Constable of Greater Manchester Police [1989] 2 All ER 827, [1989] 1 WLR 665, 87 LGR 537, 133 Sol Jo 750, [1989] NLJR 467, CA . . . 469, 671

Thrasyvoulos Ioannou v Papa Christoforos Demetriou [1952] AC 84, [1952] 1 All ER 179, [1951] 2 TLR 1177, PC . . . 361, 363

Three Rivers District Council v Govenor and Company of the Bank of England [2003] EWCA Civ 474, CA . . . 640

Three Rivers District Council v Govenor and Company of the Bank of England (No 3) [2003] 2 AC 1, HL . . . 677

Three Rivers District Council v Govenor and Company of the Bank of England (No 5) [2004] 3 All ER 168, CA . . . 639

Three Rivers District Council v Govenor and Company of the Bank of England (No 6) [2004] UKHL 43 . . . 642

Thurtell v Beaumont (1823) 1 Bing 339, 2 LJOSCP 4 . . . 115

Tingle Jacobs & Co v Kennedy [1964] 1 All ER 888n, [1964] 1 WLR 638n, 108 Sol Jo 196, CA . . . 690

Tobi v Nicholas [1988] RTR 343, 86 Cr App Rep 323, [1987] Crim LR 774 . . . 373, 715

Tomlin v Standard Telephones and Cables Ltd [1969] 3 All ER 201, [1969] 1 WLR 1378, [1969] 1 Lloyd's Rep 309, 113 Sol Jo 641, CA . . . 665

Toohey v Metropolitan Police Commissioner [1965] AC 595, [1965] 1 All ER 506, [1965] 2 WLR 439, 49 Cr App Rep 148, 129 JP 181, 109 Sol Jo 130, HL . . . 9, 224, 225, 325, 560

Topham v M'Gregor (1844) 1 Car & Kir 320 . . . 175

Trelawney v Coleman (1817) 1 B & Ald 90, 2
Stark 191, 106 ER 33 . . . 377

Triplex Safety Glass Co Ltd v Lancegaye Safety
Glass (1934) Ltd [1939] 2 KB 395, [1939]
2 All ER 613, 108 LJKB 762, 83 Sol Jo 415,
160 LT 595, 55 TLR 726, CA . . . 628

Tripodi v R (1961) 104 CLR 1, [1961] ALR 780,
HC of A . . . 121, 423

Truman (Frank) Export Ltd v Metropolitan
Police Commissioner [1977] QB 952, [1977]
3 All ER 431, [1977] 3 WLR 257, 64 Cr App
Rep 248, 141 JP 609, [1977] Crim LR 476,
121 Sol Jo 512 . . . 649

TSB Bank plc v Robert Irving and Burns Colonia
Baltica Insurance (third party) [2000] 2 All ER
826, [1999] Lloyd's Rep IR 528, CA . . . 641

TSB Scotland plc v James Mills (Montrose) Ltd
(in receivership) 1992 SLT 519 . . . 347

Tumahole Bereng v R [1949] AC 253, [1949] LJR
1603, PC . . . 238

Turner v Underwood [1948] 2 KB 284, [1948]
1 All ER 859, 46 LGR 357, 112 JP 272, [1949]
LJR 680, 92 Sol Jo 378 . . . 424

Tweney v Tweney [1946] P 180, [1946] 1 All ER
564, 115 LJP 60, 174 LT 335, TLR 266 . . . 692

Twyman v Knowles (1853) 13 CB 222, 22 LJCP
143, 17 Jur 238, sub nom Ingram v
Knowles 20 LTOS 208 . . . 266

U

U (A Child) (Serious Injury: Standard of Proof),
In Re (2004) The Times, 27 May, CA . . . 119,
261

Unilever plc v Procter & Gamble Co [2001]
1 All ER 783, CA . . . 663, 665

Union Carbide Corpn v Naturin Ltd [1987]
FSR 538, CA . . . 671

Universal City Studios Inc v Hubbard [1984]
Ch 225, [1984] 1 All ER 661, [1984] 2 WLR
492, [1984] RPC 43, 128 Sol Jo 246, CA . . . 636

Urquhart v Butterheld (1887) 37 Ch D 357, 57 LJ
Ch 521, 36 WR 376, 385n, 57 LT 780,
4 TLR 161, CA . . . 714

USA v Philip Morris Inc [2004] All ER (D) 448
(Mar), [2004] EWCA Civ 330, CA . . . 643

V

Vander Donckt v Thellusson (1849) 8 CB 812, 19
LJCP 12, 14 LTOS 253 . . . 561

Vel v Chief Constable of North Wales (or Owen)
(1987) 151 JP 510, [1987] Crim LR 496 . . . 38

Ventouris v Mountain, The Italia Express [1991]
3 All ER 472, [1991] 1 WLR 607, [1991] 1
Lloyd's Rep 441, [1991] NLJR 236, CA . . . 639,
644

Ventouris v Mountain (No 2), The Italia Express
[1992] 3 All ER 414, [1992] 1 WLR 887, [1992]
2 Lloyd's Rep 216, CA . . . 331, 336

Vernon v Bosely (No. 1) [1997] 3 All ER 414,
CA . . . 351

Versailles Trade Finance Ltd v Clough [2001]
All ER (D) 209, (2001) The Times, 1 Nov,
CA . . . 626

Vetrovec v R [1982] 1 SCR 811, 136 DLR (3d)
89 . . . 235

Vowles v Young (1806) 13 Ves 140 . . . 366

W

W (a minor), Re (1992) Times, 22 May,
CA . . . 687

W (Children) (Care Proceedings: Disclosure),
Re [2004] 1 All ER 787, Fam . . . 602

W (minors) (social worker: disclosure), Re [1998]
2 All ER 801, [1999] 1 WLR 205, [1998]
2 FCR 405, [1998] 2 FLR 135, [1998]
Fam Law 387, 142 Sol Jo LB 132, CA . . . 595

W, Re [2001] 4 All ER 88, CA . . . 84

W v K [1988] 1 FLR 86, [1988] Fam Law 64,
151 JP 589 . . . 119, 696

Wagstaff v Wilson (1832) 4 B & Ad 339, 1 Nev &
MKB 4 . . . 357

Wakeford v Bishop of Lincoln [1921] 1 AC 813,
90 LJPC 174, 65 Sol Jo 532, 125 LT 513,
PC . . . 273

Wakelin v London and South Western Rly Co
(1886) 12 App Cas 41, 51 JP 404, 56 LJQB 229,
35 WR 141, 55 LT 709, 3 TLR 233, [1886–90]
All ER Rep Ext 1655, HL . . . 86

Waldridge v Kennison (1794) 1 Esp 143 . . . 665

Walker v Wilsher (1889) 23 QBD 335, 54 JP 213,
58 LJQB 501, 37 WR 723, 5 TLR 649,
CA . . . 663–65

Walsh v Holst & Co Ltd [1958] 3 All ER 33,
[1958] 1 WLR 800, 102 Sol Jo 545, CA . . . 704

Walters, Re [1987] Crim LR 577 . . . 406, 408

Walters v R [1969] 2 AC 26, [1969] 2 WLR 60,
113 Sol Jo 14, 13 WIR 354, PC . . . 111–13

Walton v R [1978] AC 788, [1978] 1 All ER 542,
[1977] 3 WLR 902, 66 Cr App Rep 25, [1977]
Crim LR 747, 121 Sol Jo 728, PC . . . 571

Ward v Tesco Stores Ltd [1976] 1 All ER 219,
[1976] 1 WLR 810, [1976] IRLR 92, 120 Sol Jo
555, CA . . . 703, 704

Wardlaw v Farrar [2003] 4 All ER 1358,
CA . . . 580

Warren v Warren [1997] QB 488, [1996] 4 All ER
664, [1996] 3 WLR 1129, [1997] 1 FCR 237,
[1996] 2 FLR 777, [1996] Fam Law 720, CA
. . . 603

Waterhouse v Barker [1924] 2 KB 759, 93 LJKB
    897, [1924] All ER Rep 777, 69 Sol Jo 51,
    132 LT 15, 40 TLR 805, CA . . . 272

Waters v Sunday Pictorial Newspapers Ltd [1961]
    2 All ER 758, [1961] 1 WLR 967, 105 Sol Jo
    492, CA . . . 467

Watkins, Re, Watkins v Watkins [1953]
    2 All ER 1113, [1953] 1 WLR 1323, 97 Sol Jo
    762 . . . 697

Watkinson, Re (1952) ALR 361, [1952]
    VLR 123 . . . 700

Watson v Cammell Laird & Co (Shipbuilders and
    Engineers) Ltd [1959] 2 All ER 757, [1959]
    1 WLR 702, [1959] 2 Lloyd's Rep 175, 103 Sol
    Jo 470, CA . . . 644

Watson v Chief Constable of Cleveland Police
    [2001] All ER (D) 193 (Oct) . . . 48, 222

Watson v DPP [2003] All ER (D) 132, (Jun),
    DC . . . 412

Watson v England (1844) 14 Sim 29,
    2 LTOS 455 . . . 697

Waugh v British Railways Board [1980] AC 521,
    [1979] 2 All ER 1169, [1979] 3 WLR 150,
    [1979] IRLR 364, 123 Sol Jo 506, HL . . . 639,
    644, 656

Webster v James Chapman & Co (a firm) [1989]
    3 All ER 939 . . . 658, 659

Wednesbury Corpn v Ministry of Housing and
    Local Government [1965] 1 All ER 186, [1965]
    1 WLR 261, 63 LGR 51, 129 JP 123, 108 Sol Jo
    1012, CA . . . 491, 587

Wellington (Duke), Re, Glentanar v Wellington
    [1947] Ch 506, [1947] 2 All ER 854, [1947] LJR
    1451, 91 Sol Jo 369, 63 TLR 295; affd [1948]
    Ch 118, [1947] 2 All ER 854, [1949] LJR 612,
    92 Sol Jo 11, 64 TLR 54, CA . . . 35, 561

Wendo v R (1963) 109 CLR 559 . . . 121

Wentworth v Lloyd (1864) 10 HL Cas 589, 33 LJ
    Ch 688, 10 Jur NS 961, 10 LT 767, HL . . . 624

Westbrook's Trusts, Re [1873] WN 167 . . . 699

Western v DPP [1997] 1 Cr App Rep 474 . . . 189

Westminster City Council v Croyalgrange Ltd
    [1986] 2 All ER 353, [1986] 1 WLR 674, 84
    LGR 801, 83 Cr App Rep 155, 150 JP 449,
    [1986] Crim LR 693, 130 Sol Jo 409, [1986] LS
    Gaz R 2089, [1986] NLJ Rep 491, HL . . . 89

Wetherall v Harrison [1976] QB 773, [1976] 1 All
    ER 241, [1976] 2 WLR 168, [1976] RTR 125,
    140 JP 143, 119 Sol Jo 848, DC . . . 711

Wharam v Routledge (1805) 5 Esp 235 . . . 176

White v R [1999] 1 AC 210, [1998] 3 WLR 992,
    [1999] 1 Cr App Rep 153, 142 Sol Jo LB 260,
    PC . . . 182, 183, 185

White v Taylor [1969] 1 Ch 150, [1967]
    3 All ER 349, [1967] 3 WLR 1246,
    111 Sol Jo 585 . . . 361,—63, 367

Whitehead v Scott (1830) 1 Mood & R 2 . . . 266

Whitehouse v Jordan [1981] 1 WLR 246,
    HL . . . 562

Whitley v DPP [2003] All ER (D) 212 . . . 69

Wiedemann v Walpole [1891] 2 QB 534, 60 LJQB
    762, 40 WR 114, 7 TLR 722, CA . . . 355

Wilkinson v DPP [2003] All ER (D) 294
    (Feb) . . . 206

Williams v DPP [1993] 3 All ER 365, [1994]
    RTR 61, 98 Cr App Rep 209, [1993]
    Crim LR 775 . . . 74, 77

Williams v East India Co (1802) 3 East 192 . . . 29,
    689

Williams v Home Office [1981] 1 All ER
    1151 . . . 590, 603

Williams v Innes (1808) 1 Camp 364 . . . 357

Williams v Summerfield [1972] 2 QB 512, [1972]
    2 All ER 1334, [1972] 3 WLR 131, 56 Cr App
    Rep 597, 136 JP 616, 116 Sol Jo 413, DC . . . 272

Williams v Williams [1964] AC 698, [1963] 2 All
    ER 994, [1963] 3 WLR 215, 107 Sol Jo 533, HL
    . . . 688

Williams v Williams [1988] QB 161, [1987] 3 All
    ER 257, [1987] 3 WLR 790, [1988] 1 FLR 455,
    [1988] Fam Law 204, 131 Sol Jo 1214, [1987]
    LS Gaz R 2455, CA . . . 270

Willis v Bernard (1832) 8 Bing 376, 5 C & P 342,
    1 LJCP 118, 1 Moo & S 584, 131 ER 439 . . . 28,
    377

Willmett v Harmer (1839) 8 C & P 695 . . . 115

Willyams v Scottish Widows' Fund Life
    Assurance Society (1888) 52 JP 471, 4 TLR 489
    . . . 697

Wilton & Co v Phillips (1903) 19 TLR 390 . . .
    361, 364

Wing v Angrave (1860) 8 HL Cas 183, 30 LJ Ch 65
    . . . 699

Wong Kam-Ming v R [1980] AC 247, [1979] 1 All
    ER 939, [1979] 2 WLR 81, 69 Cr App Rep 47,
    [1979] Crim LR 168, 123 Sol Jo 47, PC . . .
    416–18

Wood v Braddick (1808) 1 Taunt 104 . . . 357

Wood v Mackinson (1840) 2 Mood &
    R 273 . . . 200

Woodhouse v Hall (1980) 72 Cr App Rep 39,
    [1980] Crim LR 645, DC . . . 89

Woodhouse & Co Ltd v Woodhouse (1914)
    30 TLR 599 . . . 641

Woods v Duncan [1946] AC 401, [1946] 1 All ER
    420n, [1947] LJR 120, 174 LT 286, 62 TLR 283,
    HL . . . 704

Woolf v Woolf [1931] P 134, 100 LJP 73, [1931]
All ER Rep 196, 145 LT 36, 47 TLR 277,
CA . . . 15

Woolmington v DPP [1935] AC 462, 25 Cr App
Rep 72, 104 LJKB 433, 30 Cox CC 234, [1935]
All ER Rep l, 79 Sol Jo 401, 153 LT 232, 51 TLR
446, HL . . . 91, 112, 687, 689

Woolway v Rowe (1834) 1 Ad & El 114, 3 LJKB
121, 3 Nev & MKB 849 . . . 357

Worley v Bentley [1976] 2 All ER 449, 62 Cr App
Rep 239 . . . 179

Wright v Doe d Tatham (1837) 7 Ad & El 313,
7 LJ Ex 340, Ex Ch; affd 14 Bing NC 489, 7 LJ
Ex 363, 2 Jur 461, sub nom Wright v
Tatham 5 CL & Fin 670, 6 Scott 58, HL . . . 292,
294, 340, 584

Wright v Wright (1948) 77 CLR 191 . . . 118

X

X (minors), Re [1992] Fam 124, [1992] 2 All ER
595, [1992] 2 WLR 784, sub nom Re X, Y and Z
[1991] FCR 954, [1992] 1 FLR 84, [1991] Fam
Law 318, [1991] NLJR 708 . . . 595

X v Y [1988] 2 All ER 648, [1988] RPC 379,
3 BMLR 1, [1987] NLJ Rep 1062 . . . 615

X Ltd v Morgan-Grampian (Publishers) Ltd
[1991] 1 AC 1, [1990] 2 All ER 1, [1990]
2 WLR 1000, 134 Sol Jo 546, [1990] 17 LS Gaz
R 28, [1990] NLJR 553, HL . . . 612

Y

Y v DPP [1991] Crim LR 917 . . . 389,
413

Yianni v Yianni [1966] 1 All ER 231n, [1966]
1 WLR 120, 110 Sol Jo 111 . . . 147

Young v HM Advocate 1932 SLR 466, 1932
JC 63 . . . 126

Young v Rank [1950] 2 KB 510, [1950] 2 All ER
166, 94 Sol Jo 437, 66 (pt 2) TLR 231, 84 Ll L
Rep 26 . . . 42

Z

Zephyr, The. *See* General Accident Fire and
Life Assurance Corpn Ltd v Tanter,
The Zephyr

# 1

# INTRODUCTION

Evidence is information by which facts tend to be proved, and the law of evidence is that body of law and discretion regulating the means by which facts may be proved in both courts of law and tribunals and arbitrations in which the strict rules of evidence apply.[1] It is adjectival rather than substantive law and overlaps with procedural law.

At the risk of over-simplification, the broad governing principle underlying the English law of evidence can be stated in no more than nine words: all relevant evidence is admissible, subject to the exceptions.

## A  TRUTH AND THE FACT-FINDING PROCESS

In most litigation the parties will dispute the facts. In an ideal world, perhaps, the court inquiring into those facts would take account of all evidence which is relevant to the dispute, that is all evidence that logically goes to prove or disprove the existence of those facts and would thereby get to the truth of the matter.[2] In the real world, however, a variety of factors operate to restrict the evidence taken into account. First, there are practical constraints inherent in the fact-finding process and common to all legal systems: considerations of time and cost and the need for finality to litigation.[3] Secondly, under the English adversary system of trial, whatever its undoubted merits, the court itself cannot undertake a search for relevant evidence but must reach its decision solely on the basis of such evidence as is presented by the parties. Thirdly, there is the law of evidence itself, much of which comprises rules which exclude relevant evidence for a variety of different reasons. For example, evidence may be insufficiently relevant or of only minimal probative force; it may give rise to a multiplicity of essentially subsidiary issues, which could distract the court from the main issue; it may be insufficiently reliable or too unreliable; its potential for prejudice to the party

---

[1] The strict rules of evidence do not apply, for example, to civil claims which have been allocated to the small claims track (see CPR r 27.8) or at hearings before employment tribunals (see r 11(1), Employment Tribunals (Constitution etc) Regulations 2001, SI 2001/1171.

[2] In support of the view that trials should be a search for the truth, see the Government's White Paper, 'Justice for All', Cm 563 (2002) at 32 and Lord Justice Auld's 'Review of the Criminal Courts of England and Wales', HMSO, 2001, para 154, ch 10.

[3] See generally Morgan *Introduction to the American Law Institute Model Code of Evidence* (1942) 3–4.

against whom it is introduced may be out of all proportion to its probative value on behalf of the party introducing it; its disclosure may be injurious to the national interest; and so on. Thus the court may aspire to the ascertainment of the truth, but at the end of the day it must come to a decision and settle the dispute even if the evidence introduced is inadequate or inconclusive.

The risk that the court will not get to the truth of the matter is heightened by virtue of the fact that litigation is, of course, a human endeavour and therefore will, in one way or another, provide scope for differences of opinion, error, deceit and lies. Thus judges, who are called upon to decide what evidence is relevant and to be taken into account, may take different views about whether one fact is relevant to prove or disprove another. As to the parties to litigation, they are hardly impartial and may well be more concerned with winning their case than in assisting to establish the truth. As to the fact-finders, they are most likely to use inferential reasoning to supplement the evidence in the case and fill the gaps in it, which may involve the creation of non-existent facts.[4] Finally, there are the witnesses who, if not telling the truth, will either be lying or mistaken. As to mistakes, there is obvious scope for error, not only in their observation of events, but also in their memory of it and in their recounting of those events in court. There is also the risk that witnesses may give truthful but unreliable evidence of facts which have been created by parties involved in the legal process, a classic example being evidence of a false confession produced during the interrogation of a suspect.[5]

## B  THE DEVELOPMENT OF THE LAW

The largely exclusionary ethos of the modern law of evidence reflects its common law history. Many of the rules evolved at a time when the tribunal of fact comprised either jurors or lay justices to whom the judges adopted a paternalistic and protective attitude, excluding relevant evidence such as hearsay evidence, evidence of character, and the opinion evidence of non-experts on the basis that lay persons might overvalue its weight and importance, or even treat it as conclusive. A typical example is evidence of the accused's previous convictions or of his disposition towards wrongdoing which to an extent remains inadmissible because of fears that it might influence jurors disproportionately against the accused and distract their attention from other evidence tending to prove his guilt or innocence. Distrust of the jury probably had little to do with the origin of the rule against hearsay evidence, but much to do with the delay in the growth of exceptions to that rule. Historically, the judges also suffered from an ingrained fear of the deliberate concoction or manufacture of evidence by the parties

---

[4]  See generally Pennington and Hastie, 'The story model for juror decision making' in R Hastie (ed) *Inside the Juror* (Cambridge 1993).

[5]  See M McConville, A Sanders, and R Leng, *The Case for the Prosecution* (London 1991).

to litigation and their witnesses. This accounted for the general ban on statements made out of court by a witness and consistent with his present testimony (the rule against previous consistent or self-serving statements). In large measure, it also explained why an out-of-court statement, even if it could be shown to be of virtually indisputable reliability, was generally excluded as evidence of the truth of its contents under the rule against hearsay. The dread of manufactured evidence went much further than the exclusion of specific kinds of evidence: it also meant that whole classes of persons were treated as incompetent to give evidence at all. For example, the incompetence of persons with a pecuniary or proprietary interest in the outcome of the proceedings, including the parties themselves in civil cases, was not fully abolished until the mid-nineteenth century, and it was not until the Criminal Evidence Act 1898 that the accused and his spouse were entitled, in all criminal cases, to give evidence on oath. Another factor which contributed to the largely exclusionary nature of the law of evidence in criminal proceedings stemmed from an understandable desire, at a time when the dice were unfairly loaded against the accused, to offer some judicial protection against injustice. Trials were often conducted with indecent haste, accused persons enjoyed far less legal representation and convictions could be questioned only on narrow legal grounds.[6]

In civil cases, nowadays, trial is usually by a judge sitting alone who is perfectly capable, by virtue of his training, qualifications, and experience, of attaching no more weight to an item of evidence than the circumstances properly allow. In criminal cases, the scales can no longer be said to be unfairly loaded against the accused, especially since the coming into force of the Human Rights Act 1988. No doubt, it remains necessary to prevent some material being placed before juries on the grounds of irretrievable prejudice against the accused, but the quality of juries and lay magistrates has greatly improved and it is questionable whether they are incapable, given clear and proper judicial direction, of properly evaluating the weight and reliability of some relevant evidence which continues to be excluded, such as evidence of the previous consistent statements of witnesses.

Over the years, there has been much statutory reform, sometimes significant, including in particular the enactments designed to bring domestic law into line with the European Convention of Human Rights. Statutory reform has done much to reduce the number of restrictions on the admissibility of relevant evidence, to rationalize and clarify the law, to enhance the discretionary powers of the judge, and to remove some of the more anomalous and unnecessary discrepancies between the rules in civil and criminal cases. Reform, however, has been piecemeal, sporadic, slow and usually limited to one specific area of the law, with little or no consideration of the impact of change on other related areas of the subject. The current law of evidence, therefore, may be likened to a machine which has been constructed on common law principles by judicial engineers, but which is subject to periodic alteration by

---

[6] See generally Criminal Law Revision Committee, 11th Report, *Evidence (General)*, Cmnd 4991, paras 21 et seq.

parliamentary mechanics, who variously remove or re-design parts or bolt on new parts. The judges oil and maintain the machine, and continually seek to refine, modify and develop it to meet the continually changing needs it is designed to serve. But there are constraints and limitations. Developments can only occur in relation to the specific issues brought before the judges by litigants, some of which are slow to surface.[7] Moreover, in relation to the issues that do surface, the basic framework of the law may be so unprincipled or out of line with contemporary needs or moral and social values that the judges, bound by *stare decisis* or saddled with antiquated legislation, can only act on a 'make do and mend' basis and put out a call for parliamentary assistance.[8] Whether the call is answered, however, is something of a lottery, with the odds improving if the proposals are based on, or supported by, the recommendations of a law reform agency. Some proposals, however, are simply unacceptable to the government of the day or too dull to win votes, being technical or relating to the quality rather than the content of the law.

Speaking generally, statutory reform has done much to improve the civil rules. In consequence of a review of the law of evidence in civil cases, the Law Reform Committee recommended a variety of changes, including those now embodied in the Civil Evidence Acts of 1968 and 1972, relating to judgments as evidence of the facts on which they were based,[9] privilege,[10] and opinion and expert evidence.[11] More recently, the Children Act 1989 made provision for children to give unsworn evidence in civil cases and the Civil Evidence Act 1995, an almost verbatim copy of the draft Bill of the Law Commission,[12] has, subject to safeguards, swept away the hearsay rule in civil proceedings. As a result of Lord Woolf's review of the procedural rules in the civil courts,[13] the Civil Procedure Act 1997 made provision for the creation of the Civil Procedure Rules (and supplementary Practice Directions), a unified set of rules to be followed in the civil division of the Court of Appeal, the High Court and county courts. The Act makes clear that the rules may modify the rules of evidence.[14] The rules which have been created, and which replace the former Rules of the Supreme Court and County Court Rules, constitute the most radical reform of the ethos and procedure of civil litigation since the Supreme Court of Judicature Act 1875. The jury is still out on whether they render the civil justice system as a whole more accessible, fair and efficient,[15] but concerning the law of evidence, they have done much to simplify and rationalize the relevant procedural rules.

---

[7] For example, it was only in the early 1990s that the courts were first asked to give detailed consideration to the applicability, in criminal proceedings, of the general doctrine of public interest immunity.

[8] In recent times, for example, there have been repeated judicial requests for reform of the privilege against self-incrimination. See also the comments in *C v DPP* [1995] 2 All ER 43, HL, concerning the presumption of *doli incapax*, subsequently abolished by statute.

[9] *The Rule in Hollington v Hewthorn & Co Ltd* (Cmnd 3391) (1967).

[10] *Privilege in Civil Proceedings* (Cmnd 3472) (1967).

[11] *Evidence of Opinion and Expert Evidence* (Cmnd 4489) (1970).

[12] See *The Hearsay Rule in Civil Proceedings* (Cm 2321) (1993).

[13] Access to Justice, Final Report (HMSO, 1996).      [14] See Sch 1, para 4 to the Act.

[15] See s 1(3) of the Act.

Parliament has also rationalized and improved many of the criminal rules. A major review of the law was undertaken by the Criminal Law Revision Committee, virtually all of its recommendations being contained in its eleventh report.[16] Published in 1972, it aroused considerable controversy, mainly but not exclusively because of the proposed restriction of the so-called 'right of silence' enjoyed by suspects when interrogated by the police. For the next decade it did little more than collect dust on the parliamentary shelf. However, many of the recommendations contained in the report were, in substance, embodied in the Police and Criminal Evidence Act 1984. Those that still remain relate to the proof of previous convictions and acquittals, the admissibility of previous convictions as evidence of the facts on which they were based, the admissibility of confessions, and the competence and compellability of the accused's spouse. The proposed restriction on the 'right of silence' was eventually given statutory force by the Criminal Justice and Public Order Act 1994. The combined effect of the Criminal Justice Act 1988 and the Criminal Justice and Public Order Act 1994 has been to rationalize the law relating to corroboration and corroboration warnings.[17] Further major changes were introduced by the Youth Justice and Criminal Evidence Act 1999, which has improved the rules governing the competence of children to give evidence in criminal proceedings and made provision for Special Measures Directions in the case of vulnerable and intimidated witnesses, for the protection of witnesses from cross-examination by the accused in person, and for the protection of complainants in proceedings for sexual offences.

The Criminal Justice Act 2003 has brought about radical change in relation to hearsay evidence and evidence of bad character. The provisions are premised on a welcome new confidence that fact-finders can be trusted to evaluate evidence correctly, reflecting the view in Lord Justice Auld's 'Review of the Criminal Courts of England and Wales' that 'the English law of criminal evidence should, in general, move away from technical rules of inadmissibility to trusting judicial and lay fact finders to give relevant evidence the weight it deserves'.[18] As to bad character, the Government's approach has also been informed by the Law Commission Report 'Evidence of Bad Character in Criminal Proceedings'.[19] The provisions all but codify the law, abolishing the common law rules and replacing section 1(3) of the Criminal Evidence Act 1898, an ill-considered provision which should have been replaced many years ago. The new scheme, however, is complex, in parts less than transparent, and likely to give rise to much case law. As to the hearsay provisions, which are based on the proposals of the Law Commission Report 'Evidence in Criminal Proceedings: Hearsay and Related Topics',[20] they retain the hearsay rule but expand the exceptions to it and create a 'safety valve' discretion to admit sufficiently reliable hearsay not covered by any of the exceptions.

---

[16] *Evidence (General)* (Cmnd 4991) (1972). See also the 9th Report (Cmnd 3145) (1966): the recommendations are embodied in ss 9–11 of the Criminal Justice Act 1967.

[17] See also Law Commission Report No 202 (Cmnd 1620).     [18] Para 78.

[19] Law Com No 273, Cm 5257 (2001).     [20] Law Com No 245, Cm 3670 (1997).

The Criminal Procedure Rules 2005[21] represent the first steps towards the creation of a new consolidated and comprehensive criminal procedure code of the kind recommended by Lord Justice Auld in the 'Review of the Criminal Courts of England and Wales'. Although the rules merely consolidate and adopt all the pre-existing rules of court, rule 1.1 sets out a new overriding objective of the code that criminal cases be dealt with justly. Under rule 3.2 the court must further the overriding objective by actively managing the case, which includes ensuring that evidence, whether disputed or not, is presented in the shortest and clearest way; and under rule 3.3 each party must (a) actively assist the court in fulfilling its duty under rule 3.2, without or if necessary with a direction and (b) apply for a direction if needed to further the overriding objective

'It would be unfortunate', it has been said, 'if the law of evidence was allowed to develop in a way which was not in accordance with the common sense of ordinary folk',[22] not least, one might add, because it has to be used and understood not only by professional judges, but also by part-time judges, lay magistrates, jurors and, increasingly, the police. Recent developments give some cause for cautious optimism. Looking at the law of evidence overall, however, there are strong grounds for believing that fairness, coherence, clarity and accessibility will only come, not from common law development coupled with piecemeal statutory intervention, but from codification.

[21] SI 2005/384.     [22] Per Lawton LJ in *R v Chandler* [1976] 1 WLR 585 at 590, CA.

# 2

# PRELIMINARIES

## A  FACTS OPEN TO PROOF OR DISPROOF

The facts which are open to proof or disproof in English courts of law are facts in issue, relevant facts and collateral facts.

### 1  FACTS IN ISSUE

A fact in issue is sometimes referred to as a 'principal fact' or '*factum probandum*'. The facts in issue in any given case are those facts which the claimant (or the prosecutor) must prove in order to succeed in his claim (prosecution) together with those facts which the defendant (or the accused) must prove in order to succeed in his defence. The nature and number of facts in issue in a case is determined not by the law of evidence, but partly by reference to the substantive law and partly by reference to what the parties allege, admit and deny. For example, in an action for damages for breach of contract in which the defendant simply denies the facts on which the claimant relies for his claim, the facts in issue will be those facts which, if proved, will establish the formation of a binding contract between the parties, breach of contract by the defendant and consequential loss and damage suffered by the claimant. However, if the defendant, in his defence, pleads discharge by agreement, admitting that the contract was made but denying the breach and loss alleged by the claimant, then the facts in issue will then be those which, if proved, will establish breach by the defendant and consequential loss and damage suffered by the claimant together with those facts which, if proved, will establish that the parties discharged the contract by agreement. Another possibility is that the defendant admits the contract and its breach and makes no counterclaim. The only facts in issue will then be those which, if proved, will establish consequential loss and damage and the amount of damages to which the claimant claims he is entitled. There are many other possibilities. In civil proceedings, the facts in issue are usually identifiable by reference to the statement of case, its very purpose being to set out the factual (and legal) issues on which the parties agree and disagree so that they and the court know in advance exactly what matters are left in dispute and what facts, therefore, have to be proved or disproved at the trial.[1] Under CPR rule 16.4(1):

Particulars of claim must include—
   (a) a concise statement of the facts on which the claimant relies; . . .

Under rule 16.5(1):

In his defence, the defendant must state—
   (a) which of the allegations in the particulars of claim he denies;
   (b) which allegations he is unable to admit or deny, but which he requires the claimant to prove; and
   (c) which allegations he admits.

As a general rule, a defendant who fails to deal with an allegation shall be taken to admit it.[2]

In criminal cases in which the accused pleads not guilty, the facts in issue are all those facts which the prosecution must prove in order to succeed, including the identity of the accused, the commission by him of the actus reus and the existence of any necessary knowledge or intent on his part,[3] together with any further facts that the accused must prove in order to establish any defence other than a simple denial of the prosecution case. However, under section 10 of the Criminal Justice Act 1967, any fact of which oral evidence may be given in any criminal proceedings may be admitted for the purpose of those proceedings by or on behalf of either the prosecution or defence and an admission made by any party of any such fact shall be 'conclusive' evidence of the fact admitted. In other words, a fact which is formally admitted under the section is not open to contradictory proof and in effect ceases to be a fact in issue: the court must find the fact to have been proved.[4]

## 2  RELEVANT FACTS

A relevant fact, sometimes called a 'fact relevant to the issue', an 'evidentiary fact' or '*factum probans*', is a fact from which the existence or non-existence of a fact in issue may be inferred. If the only facts which were open to proof or disproof were facts in issue, many claims and defences would fail. If, for example, the fact in issue is whether a man shot his wife, obviously an eye-witness to the incident may be called to give evidence that he saw the shooting. However, in many cases a statement by a witness

---

[1] See *Esso Petroleum Co Ltd v Southport Corpn* [1956] AC 218 at 241, HL; *Farrell v Secretary of State for Defence* [1980] 1 WLR 172, HL.

[2] CPR r 16.5(5). Under r 16.5(3), a defendant who fails to deal with an allegation but sets out in his defence the nature of his case in relation to the issue to which that allegation is relevant, shall be taken to require that allegation to be proved. Under r 16.5(4), where the claim includes a money claim, a defendant shall be taken to require that any allegation relating to the amount of money claimed to be proved unless he expressly admits the allegation.

[3] Per Lord Goddard CJ in *R v Sims* [1946] KB 531 at 539.

[4] See further under Ch 22, C **Formal admissions**.

that he perceived a fact in issue with one of his senses, which is described as 'direct evidence', is quite simply unavailable. Very often the only available evidence is that which can establish some other fact or facts relevant to the fact in issue, for example the evidence of a gunsmith that on the day before the shooting the man bought a gun from him, the evidence of a policeman that after the shooting he found that gun buried in the garden of the man's house and the evidence of a forensic expert that the gun bore the man's fingerprints. Evidence of relevant facts is described as 'circumstantial evidence', some further examples of which are given later in this chapter. Where a party to proceedings seeks to establish a relevant fact the existence of which is denied by his opponent, the relevant fact may also be said to be a 'fact in issue'.

## 3 COLLATERAL FACTS

Collateral facts, sometimes referred to as 'subordinate facts', are of three kinds: (i) facts affecting the competence of a witness; (ii) facts affecting the credibility of a witness; and (iii) facts, sometimes called 'preliminary facts', which must be proved as a condition precedent to the admissibility of certain items of evidence tendered to prove a fact in issue or a relevant fact. As to the first, an example would be that a potential witness suffers from a mental handicap rendering him incompetent to testify. An example of a collateral fact of the second kind would be that a witness, who testifies to the effect that he saw a certain event at a distance of 50 yards, suffers from an eye complaint which prevents him from seeing anything at a distance greater than 20 yards. Such a witness may be cross-examined about his eye complaint and, if he denies its existence, evidence in rebuttal may be given by an oculist.[5] Similarly, a witness may be cross-examined about his bias or partiality towards one of the parties to the proceedings and again, if he denies it, evidence may be called to contradict his denial.[6] A collateral fact of the third kind may be illustrated by reference to an exception to the rule against hearsay: in criminal proceedings a statement made by a participant in or observer of an event is admissible as evidence of the truth of its contents, by way of exception to the rule against hearsay, *on proof that* it was made by a person so emotionally overpowered by the event that the possibility of concoction or distortion can be disregarded.[7] Another illustration is an exception to the general rule that a party seeking to rely upon the contents of a document must adduce the original: a copy is admissible as evidence of the contents *on proof that* the original has been destroyed or cannot be found after due search.[8]

Where a party to proceedings seeks to establish a collateral fact the existence of which is denied by his opponent, the collateral fact may also be said to be a 'fact in

---

[5] See per Lord Pearce in *Toohey v Metropolitan Police Comr* [1965] AC 595 at 608, HL (see Ch 7).
[6] See per Geoffrey Lane LJ in *R v Mendy* (1976) 64 Cr App R 4, CA at 6 (see Ch 7).
[7] See Ch 10 and s 118(1) of the Criminal Justice Act 2003.
[8] *Brewster v Sewell* (1820) 3 B & Ald 296 (see Ch 9).

issue'. The existence or non-existence of a preliminary fact in issue is, as we shall see, decided by the judge, not the jury, as part of his general function to rule on all questions concerning the admissibility of evidence.

# B  THE VARIETIES OF EVIDENCE

The evidence by which facts may be proved or disproved in court is known as 'judicial evidence'. Judicial evidence takes only three *forms*, namely oral evidence, documentary evidence and things. Judicial evidence, however, is open to classification not only in terms of the form in which it may be presented in court but also in terms of its substantive content, the purpose for which it is presented and the rules by which its admissibility is determined. Thus, any given item of judicial evidence may attract more than one of the labels by which the varieties of evidence have been classified. The principal labels are 'testimony', 'hearsay evidence', 'documentary evidence', 'real evidence' and 'circumstantial evidence'.

## 1  TESTIMONY

Testimony is the oral statement of a witness made on oath in open court[9] and offered as evidence of the truth of that which is asserted. 'Direct testimony' is a term used to describe a witness's statement that he perceived a fact in issue, relevant fact or collateral fact with one of his five senses. In other words, it is testimony relating to facts of which the witness has or claims to have personal or first-hand knowledge.[10] Direct testimony, or 'direct evidence' as it is sometimes called, is a term commonly used in contrast with 'hearsay evidence'. The term is also used in contrast with 'circumstantial evidence'.

## 2  HEARSAY EVIDENCE

In common parlance, hearsay is used to describe statements, often gossip, that one hears but does not know to be true. In the law of evidence, the word is used in a broader technical sense. The common law concept of hearsay may be defined as any statement, other than one made by a witness in the course of giving his evidence in

---

[9] In criminal proceedings, some witnesses may give their evidence by live television link; video recordings of interviews of some witnesses may be admitted as their evidence in chief; and recordings of cross-examination and re-examination may also be admitted: see Ch 5. In civil proceedings, the court may allow a witness to give evidence through a video link or by other means (eg by telephone): see CPR r 32.3.

[10] An appropriately qualified expert may give oral evidence of opinion, as opposed to fact, on a matter calling for the expertise which he possesses and, what is more, may do so even though substantial contributions to the formation of his opinion have been made by matters of which he has no personal or first-hand knowledge: see per Megarry J in *English Exporters (London) Ltd v Eldonwall Ltd* [1973] Ch 415 at 423. A statement of opinion may also be made by a non-expert witness, but only as a way of conveying *facts* personally perceived: see generally Ch 18.

the proceedings in question, by any person, whether it was made on oath or unsworn and whether it was made orally, in writing or by signs and gestures, which is offered as evidence of the truth of its contents. If the statement is tendered for any purpose other than that of proving the truth of its contents, for example to prove simply that the statement was made or to prove the state of mind of the maker of the statement, it is not hearsay but 'original evidence'. Provided that it is relevant to a fact in issue, original evidence is admissible. At common law, hearsay could only be received in evidence exceptionally. Under the modern law, in civil cases the rule has been abrogated; in criminal cases there are a variety of statutory exceptions; and in both civil and criminal cases a number of common law exceptions have been preserved and given statutory force.

The meaning of 'hearsay' and 'original evidence' and the distinction between them is perhaps best understood by way of examples. Suppose a fact in issue in criminal proceedings is whether a man, H, shot his wife, W. X was an eye-witness to the shooting and later said to Y: 'H shot W'. Y repeated X's statement to Z. If X is called as a witness to the proceedings he may, of course, give direct testimony of the shooting. It is something of which he has personal or first-hand knowledge, something he perceived with his own eyes. However, X may not narrate to the court the statement that he made to Y in order to prove that H shot W unless his statement comes within one of the exceptions to the rule against hearsay. The statement was made other than in the course of giving evidence in the proceedings in question and would be tendered in order to prove that H shot W (the truth of its contents). For the same reasons neither Y nor Z, if called, could recount X's out-of-court statement unless, again, it comes within one of the exceptions to the rule against hearsay. Now suppose a fact in issue in criminal proceedings is whether D is physically capable of speech. D is charged with obtaining property by deception. The prosecution allege that he dishonestly obtained money from a charity by pretending that he was incapable of speech. D, leaving the offices of the charity, held a conversation with E. E, if called as a witness for the prosecution, may give evidence of what D said, not to prove the truth of anything that D said, but simply to prove that D's statements were made, that D could speak. D's out-of-court statements are received as original evidence.

These are simple examples of difficult concepts. The meaning of hearsay evidence and the distinction between hearsay and original evidence give rise to difficult legal problems which are explored fully in Chapter 10. The numerous common law and statutory exceptions to the rule against hearsay comprise the largest topic in this work. They are considered in Chapters 10–13.

## 3 DOCUMENTARY EVIDENCE

Documentary evidence usually consists of a document or a copy of a document, produced for inspection by the court. However, in some cases the evidence may be presented electronically, by a simultaneous display to all parties via courtroom monitors, thereby ensuring that all involved are looking at the same item of evidence at the same time.[11]

A document, for the purposes of the law of evidence, has no single definition. The meaning of the word varies according to the nature of the proceedings and the particular context in question. Suffice it to say, for present purposes, that in certain circumstances the word is defined to include not only documents in writing, but also maps, plans, graphs, drawings, photographs, discs, tapes, video-tapes, films, and negatives.[12] Documents may be produced to show their contents, their existence or their physical appearance. The contents of a document may be received as evidence of their truth, by way of exception to the hearsay rule, or for some other purpose, for example to identify the document or to show what its author thought or believed. It is convenient to regard the contents of documents as a separate category of judicial evidence because although, like oral statements, they are subject to the general rules of evidence on admissibility, their reception in evidence is also subject to two additional requirements. One of these relates to the proof of their contents.[13] The matter is explored fully in Chapter 9. It is mentioned here merely in order to explain the distinction, mainly of importance in connection with documents, between 'primary evidence', which may be regarded as the best available evidence, and 'secondary evidence', that is evidence which by its nature suggests that better evidence may be available. As a general rule, a party seeking to rely on the contents of a document must adduce primary evidence of those contents, which is usually the original of the document in question, as opposed to secondary evidence of those contents, for example a copy of the document, a copy of a copy of the document or oral evidence of the contents.[14] Where a document is produced to show the bare fact of its existence or its physical appearance, for example the substance of which it is made or the condition which it is in, it constitutes a variety of 'real evidence'.

## 4  REAL EVIDENCE

Real evidence usually takes the form of some material object produced for inspection in order that the court may draw an inference from its own observation as to the existence, condition or value of the object in question. Although real evidence may be extremely valuable as a means of proof, little if any weight attaches to such evidence in the absence of some accompanying testimony identifying the object in question and explaining its connection with, or significance in relation to, the facts in issue or relevant to the issue. In addition to material objects, including documents, examples of real evidence also include the physical appearance of persons and animals, the

---

[11] See *A Guide to the Electronic Presentation of Evidence (EPE) at Trial*, <http://www.courtservice.gov.uk/notices/eps_trial.htm>.

[12] See further Ch 9.

[13] The other concerns proof of the fact that the document was properly executed.

[14] The distinction between primary and secondary evidence is also of importance in relation to the proof of facts contained in a document to which a privilege attaches: see Ch 20.

demeanour of witnesses, the intonation of voices on a tape recording, views, that is inspections out of court, of the *locus in quo* or of some object which it is impossible or highly inconvenient to bring to court, and, possibly, out-of-court demonstrations or re-enactments of acts or events into which the court is enquiring. Real evidence is considered in greater detail in Chapter 9.

## 5 CIRCUMSTANTIAL EVIDENCE

### (a) General

Circumstantial evidence has already been defined as evidence of relevant facts (facts from which the existence or non-existence of a fact in issue may be inferred) and contrasted with 'direct evidence', a term which is used to mean testimony relating to facts in issue of which a witness has or claims to have personal or first-hand knowledge. Circumstantial evidence may take the form of oral or documentary evidence (including admissible hearsay) or real evidence.

'It is no derogation of evidence to say that it is circumstantial.'[15] Its importance lies in its potential for proving a variety of different relevant facts all of which point to the same conclusion, as when it is sought to establish that an accused committed murder by evidence of his preparation, motive and opportunity for its commission, together with evidence of the discovery of a weapon, capable of having caused the injuries sustained by the victim, buried in the accused's back garden and bearing his fingerprints. Circumstantial evidence, it has been said, 'works by cumulatively, in geometrical progression, eliminating other possibilities'[16] and has been likened to a rope comprised of several cords:

One strand of the cord might be insufficient to sustain the weight, but three stranded together may be quite of sufficient strength. Thus it may be in circumstantial evidence—there may be a combination of circumstances, no one of which would raise a reasonable conviction or more than a mere suspicion; but the three taken together may create a conclusion of guilt with as much certainty as human affairs can require or admit of.[17]

In criminal proceedings in which the Crown's case is based on circumstantial evidence, there is no rule of law requiring the judge to direct the jury to acquit unless they are sure that the facts proved are not only consistent with guilt but also inconsistent with any other reasonable conclusion.[18] However, as Lord Normand observed in *Teper v R:*[19]

Circumstantial evidence may sometimes be conclusive, but it must always be narrowly examined, if only because evidence of this kind may be fabricated to cast suspicion on another. Joseph commanded the steward of his house, 'put my cup, the silver cup in the

---

[15] *R v Taylor, Weaver and Donovan* (1928) 21 Cr App R 20, CA.
[16] Per Lord Simon in *DPP v Kilbourne* [1973] AC 729 at 758, HL.
[17] Per Pollock CB in *R v Exall* (1866) 4 F & F 922 at 929.
[18] *McGreevy v DPP* [1973] 1 WLR 276, HL.      [19] [1952] AC 480 at 489, PC.

sack's mouth of the youngest', and when the cup was found there Benjamin's brethren too hastily assumed that he must have stolen it.[20] It is also necessary before drawing the inference of the accused's guilt from circumstantial evidence to be sure that there are no other co-existing circumstances which would weaken or destroy the inference . . .

## (b) Examples

The circumstances in which a fact may be said to be relevant to a fact in issue, in the sense that the existence of the former gives rise to an inference as to the existence or non-existence of the latter, are many and various. Certain types of circumstantial evidence arise so frequently that they have been referred to as 'presumptions of fact' or 'provisional presumptions' such as the presumptions of intention, guilty knowledge, continuance of life, and seaworthiness, all of which are more conveniently considered in Chapter 22. Another type of circumstantial evidence is evidence of facts which are so closely associated in time, place and circumstances with some transaction which is in issue that they can be said to form a part of that transaction. Such facts, referred to as facts forming part of the *res gestae*, are more conveniently explored in Chapter 12: the *res gestae* doctrine is mainly concerned with the admissibility of statements of fact as evidence of the truth of their contents by way of common law exception to the hearsay rule and has been described, not unfairly, in terms of a 'collection of fact situations . . . so confusing in its scope as almost to demand that a reader cease thinking before he go mad'![21] The following examples of circumstantial evidence are more typical and pose less danger to mental health.

*(i) Motive.* Evidence of facts which supply a motive for a particular person to do a particular act is often received to show that it is more probable that he performed that act. Such evidence is admissible notwithstanding that the motive is irrational.[22]

Surely in an ordinary prosecution for murder you can prove previous acts or words of the accused to show that he entertained feelings of enmity towards the deceased, and this is evidence not merely of the malicious mind with which he killed the deceased, but of the fact that he killed him . . . it is more probable that men are killed by those that have some motive for killing them than by those who have not.[23]

Conversely, evidence of absence of motive may be relevant to show the relative unlikelihood of a particular person having performed a particular act.[24]

*(ii) Plans and preparatory acts.* Facts which tend to suggest that a person made plans or other preparations for the performance of a particular act are relevant to the question of whether he subsequently performed that act. Thus evidence may be given

---

[20] See Genesis, 44: 2.    [21] Wright, 20 Can B R 714 at 716.

[22] *R v Phillips* [2003] 2 Cr App R 528, CA at [30], disapproving *R v Berry* (1986) 83 Cr App R 7, insofar as it suggests otherwise.

[23] Per Lord Atkinson in *R v Ball* [1911] AC 47, HL at 68; affirmed in *R v Williams* (1986) 84 Cr App Rep 299, CA. Any doubt that may have been cast upon this classic statement in *R v Berry*, ibid, should be disregarded: *R v Phillips* [2003] 2 Cr App R 528, CA at [26].

[24] See *R v Grant* (1865) 4 F&F 322.

of the purchase by an alleged murderer of poison, or as the case may be, of a gun or dagger. On the question of whether a person's declaration of intention to do a certain act is relevant to prove its performance by him, the authorities conflict.[25]

*(iii) Capacity.* Evidence of a person's mental or physical capacity or incapacity to do a particular act has an obvious relevance to the question of whether he in fact performed it.

*(iv) Opportunity.* Circumstantial evidence of opportunity or lack of opportunity is evidence of the fact that a person was present or absent at the time and place of some act allegedly performed by him, for example evidence, to establish adultery in divorce proceedings, that a couple occupied the same hotel bedroom for two nights[26] or evidence, to establish innocence in criminal proceedings, of an alibi.

*(v) Identity.* Circumstantial evidence of identity often takes the form of expert testimony that the fingerprints of the accused[27] or samples taken from his body match those discovered on or taken from some material object at the scene of the crime or the victim of the offence in question.[28] It can also take the form of evidence that a tracking dog tracked the accused by scent from the scene of the crime.[29] Identity may also be established by evidence that both the accused and the criminal share the same name, the same physical idiosyncrasy, for example left-handedness, the same style of handwriting or the same particular manner of expression in speech or writing.[30] In civil proceedings, evidence as to the paternity of a person may be given by expert medical evidence of blood tests showing that a man is or is not excluded from being the father of that person.[31]

*(vi) Continuance.* The fact that a certain act or event was taking place at one point in time may justify the inference that it was also taking place at some prior or subsequent

---

[25] See *R v Buckley* (1873) 13 Cox CC 293, *R v Wainwright* (1875) 13 Cox CC 171 etc (see Ch 12).

[26] *Woolf v Woolf* [1931] P 134, CA.

[27] *R v Castleton* (1909) 3 Cr App Rep 74; cf *R v Court* (1960) 44 Cr App R 242, CCA.

[28] It is for the prosecution to prove formally that the *sample* fingerprints were taken from the accused and evidence, by him, that he cannot explain, or does not know, how 'his' fingerprints were found on the material object does not amount to an admission that the fingerprints were his: *Chappell v DPP* (1988) 89 Cr App R 82. The police have the power to take fingerprints, including palm prints, of a person without his consent. The circumstances in which this may be done include (i) where he is detained at a police station, if he is detained in consequence of his arrest for a recordable offence or he has been charged with, or informed that he will be reported for, such an offence; and (ii) where he has been convicted of a recordable offence, given a caution in respect of a recordable offence which he has admitted or has been warned or reprimanded for a recordable offence: ss 61, 65, and 118 of the Police and Criminal Evidence Act 1984.

[29] See *R v Haas* (1962) 35 DLR (2d) 172 (Court of Appeal of British Columbia). Evidence of tracking by a dog is admissible provided that (i) there is detailed evidence establishing the reliability of the dog by reason of its training and experience and (ii) the jury are directed to consider the evidence carefully and with circumspection, since the dog may not always be reliable and cannot be cross-examined: *R v Pieterson* [1995] 2 Cr App R 11, CA. See also *R v Sykes* [1997] Crim LR 752, CA.

[30] See, eg, *R v Voisin* [1918] 1 KB 531: 'Bloody Belgian' written as 'Bladie Belgiam'.

[31] In any civil proceedings in which the paternity of any person falls to be determined, the court may direct the taking of blood samples from that person, the mother of that person and any party alleged to be the father of that person: s 20 of the Family Law Reform Act 1969. Section 20 is restricted to blood tests. Section 23 of

point in time. Thus evidence of the speed at which someone was driving at a particular point in time may be given to show the speed at which he was likely to have been driving a few moments earlier[32] or later.[33]

*(vii) Failure to give evidence or call witnesses.* In civil cases, one party's failure to give evidence or call witnesses may justify the court in drawing all reasonable inferences from the evidence which has been given by his opponent as to what the facts are which the first party chose to withhold.[34]

The inferences that may be drawn, in criminal cases, from the accused's election not to give evidence, call for a more detailed analysis. The subject is covered in Chapter 14. Concerning the accused's failure to call a witness (other than his or her spouse), in appropriate cases the judge may comment adversely on the fact that the witness was not called, but should exercise the same degree of care as when commenting on the failure of the accused himself to give evidence and in particular should avoid the suggestion that the failure is something of importance when there may be a valid reason for not calling the witness.[35] Whether a comment is justified and, if so, the terms in which it should be cast, are matters dependent upon the facts of the particular case. In *R v Khan*[36] the Court of Appeal gave the following guidance. (1) A universal requirement to direct the jury not to speculate would be unfair. On the other hand, to give no direction could invite speculation and work injustice; and to comment adversely might work injustice, since there might be a good reason but one which it would be unfair to disclose to the jury. Moreover, there might be an issue between the prosecution and defence as to whether a witness was available. There was no simple answer and much depended upon the judge's sense of fairness. (2) The dangers of making adverse comments, and failing to warn the jury not to speculate, are the paramount considerations. (3) On the other hand, now that a defendant's failure to disclose his case in advance can be the subject of comment, the case for permitting comment on an absent witness may be stronger. (4) If the judge comments on a failure to call a witness, a reference to the burden of proof may be appropriate. (5) A judge who is proposing to make a comment should first invite submissions from counsel in the absence of the jury.

Concerning the failure of the spouse of an accused to testify, comment by the *prosecution* was prohibited by proviso (b) to section 1 of the Criminal Evidence Act 1898. The Criminal Law Revision Committee proposed the lifting of this prohibition,[37]

---

the Family Law Reform Act 1987, amending s 20, makes provision for the taking of 'bodily samples', defined as samples of bodily fluid or tissue taken for the purpose of scientific tests (which could include eg DNA genetic fingerprint tests).

[32] *R v Dalloz* (1908) 1 Cr App R 258.

[33] *Beresford v St Albans Justices* (1905) 22 TLR 1. See also the presumption of continuance of life, Ch 22.

[34] See per Lord Diplock in *British Railways Board v Herrington* [1972] AC 877 at 930.

[35] Per Megaw LJ in *R v Gallagher* [1974] 1 WLR 1204, CA. See also *R v Wilmot* (1988) 89 Cr App R 341 at 352, CA and *R v Couzens* [1992] Crim LR 822, CA; and cf *R v Weller* [1994] Crim LR 856.

[36] [2001] Crim LR 673, CA.    [37] Para 154 (Cmnd 4991) (1972).

a proposal rejected by Parliament. Re-enacting the relevant parts of the proviso, section 80(A) of the Police and Criminal Evidence Act 1984 provides that:

The failure of the wife or husband of a person charged in any proceedings to give evidence in the proceedings shall not be made the subject of any comment by the prosecution.

Under proviso (b), it was held that where counsel for the prosecution does make an adverse comment on the failure of the accused to call his spouse to give evidence on his behalf, it is the duty of the trial judge, depending upon the circumstances of each case, to remedy that breach in his summing up, especially when the accused is a man of good character and this is central to his defence.[38] It may be assumed that a breach of section 80(A) should be remedied in the same way.

Section 80(A) applies only to the prosecution. In appropriate circumstances, therefore, the *judge* may comment on the failure of the spouse of the accused to testify. However, if the judge, in the exercise of his discretion, does decide to make a comment, he must, save in exceptional circumstances, do so with a great deal of circumspection.[39] The same degree of circumspection would also seem to be required in the case of comment on failure to call cohabitees, who are not covered by section 80(A).[40]

A breach of section 80(A) is unlikely to result in a successful appeal if the judge, in summing up, makes appropriate and suitable comments on the failure of the spouse to testify: the error made by counsel is subsumed in the summing-up.[41]

*(viii) Failure to provide evidence.* Under section 23(1) of the Family Law Reform Act 1969, if, in any civil proceedings in which the paternity of any person falls to be determined, the court directs a party to undergo a blood test and that party fails to obey the direction, the court may draw such inferences as appear proper in the circumstances.[42] Similarly, section 62(10) of the Police and Criminal Evidence Act 1984 provides that where an accused has refused without good cause the taking from him of an intimate body sample the court, in determining whether there is a case to answer, and the court or jury, in determining whether he is guilty of the offence charged, 'may draw such inferences from the refusal as appear proper'. Section 62 is considered further in Chapter 14, together with the inferences that may be drawn, pursuant to statute, from an accused's silence or conduct.

*(ix) Lies.* Lies told by an accused, on their own, do not prove that a person is guilty of any crime.[43] However such lies may indicate a consciousness of guilt and in appropriate circumstances may be relied upon by the prosecution as evidence supportive of guilt, as in *R v Goodway*[44] in which the accused's lies to the police as to his whereabouts at the time of the offence were used in support of the identification evidence

---

[38] *R v Naudeer* [1984] 3 All ER 1036, CA. See also *R v Dickman* (1910) 5 Cr App R 135 and *R v Hunter* [1969] Crim LR 262, CA.

[39] Per Purchas LJ in *R v Naudeer* [1984] 3 All ER 1036 at 1039, CA.

[40] See *R v Weller* [1994] Crim LR 856, CA.     [41] See *R v Whitton* [1998] Crim LR 492, CA.

[42] See *McVeigh v Beattie* [1988] 2 All ER 500.       [43] *R v Strudwick* (1993) 99 Cr App R 326, CA at 331.

[44] [1993] 4 All ER 894, CA.

adduced by the prosecution. It was held that whenever a lie told by an accused is relied on by the Crown, or may be used by the jury to support evidence of guilt, as opposed merely to reflecting on his credibility (and not only when it is relied on as corroboration or as support for identification evidence), a direction should be given to the jury that: (1) the lie must be deliberate and must relate to a material issue; (2) they must be satisfied that there was no innocent motive for the lie, reminding them that people sometimes lie, for example, in an attempt to bolster up a just cause, or out of shame or a wish to conceal disgraceful behaviour; and in cases where the lie is relied upon as corroboration,[45] (3) the lie must be established by evidence other than that of the witness who is to be corroborated.[46] It was also said, however, that such a direction need not be given where it is otiose, as indicated in *R v Dehar*,[47] ie where the rejection of the explanation by the accused almost necessarily leaves the jury with no choice but to convict as a matter of logic. An example is *R v Barsoum*,[48] where the lie related to the presence of another person, M, at the scene of the crime and if M was present, B was entitled to be acquitted, but if M was an invention it automatically followed that B must be guilty.[49] Where a direction is given, it should also make the point that the lie must be admitted or proved beyond reasonable doubt.[50]

The topic has spawned much case law and in *R v Middleton*[51] it was held, *per curiam*, that when the question arises whether a direction should be given, it will usually be more useful to analyse the question in the context of the individual case by examining the principles to be derived from the authorities rather than by trawling through hosts of cases. The court emphasized that the point of the direction is to avoid the risk of the forbidden reasoning that lies necessarily demonstrate guilt: where there is no risk that the jury may follow this prohibited line of reasoning, a direction is unnecessary. It was also said that, generally, a direction is unlikely to be appropriate in relation to lies told by an accused in evidence because that situation is covered by the general directions on burden and standard of proof.

In *R v Burge*[52] it was held that a *Goodway* direction, which is often referred to as a *Lucas* direction,[53] is usually required in only four situations, which may overlap:

1.   Where the defence relies on an alibi.

2.   Where the judge suggests that the jury should look for support or corroboration

---

[45] See Ch 8.

[46] Applied in *R v Taylor* [1994] Crim LR 680, CA. See also *R v Taylor* [1998] Crim LR 822, CA. If a lie is relied on merely to attack credibility, a direction may be appropriate in exceptional circumstances, as when the lie figures largely in the case and the jury may think that the accused must be guilty because he lied: *R v Tucker* [1994] Crim LR 683, CA.

[47] [1969] NZLR 763, NZCA.        [48] [1994] Crim LR 194, CA.

[49] Cf *R v Wood* [1995] Crim LR, CA, where the accused may have been influenced by panic or confusion and therefore guilt was not the only possible explanation for the lies he told. But see also *R v Saunders* [1996] 1 Cr App R 463, CA at 518–19, where it was held that a direction was not required, the accused having explained his lies on the basis that he was confused and under pressure, and the judge having dealt with that explanation fairly in his summing up.

[50] *R v Burge* [1996] 1 Cr App R 163, CA.        [51] [2001] Crim LR 251.        [52] Ibid.

[53] See *R v Lucas* [1981] QB 720, CA.

of one piece of evidence from other evidence in the case, and amongst that other evidence draws attention to lies told or allegedly told by the accused.

3.  Where the prosecution seeks to show that something said in or out of court in relation to a separate and distinct issue was a lie and to rely on that lie as evidence of guilt, ie to use it, in effect, as an implied admission of guilt.

4.  Where, although the prosecution has not adopted the approach described in (3), the judge reasonably envisages that there is a real danger that the jury may do so.[54]

The Court of Appeal stressed that the direction is not required in run-of-the-mill cases in which the defence case is contradicted by the evidence of the prosecution witnesses in such a way as to make it necessary for the prosecution to say that the accused's account is untrue. Similarly, in *R v Hill*[55] it was said that a direction is not required simply because the jury reject the evidence of an accused about a central issue in the case, since that situation is covered by the general direction that the judge will give on burden and standard of proof. *R v Landon*[56] is to similar effect. In that case Hobhouse LJ emphasized that a direction should be given where lies told by the accused are relied upon by the Crown, or may be relied upon by the jury, as *additional* evidence of guilt, and not where there is no distinction between the issue of guilt and the issue of lies.[57]

Concerning the first situation identified in *R v Burge*, the Judicial Studies Board specimen direction relating to evidence called in support of an alibi concludes with the warning:

even if you conclude that the alibi is false, that does not itself entitle you to convict the defendant. The prosecution must still make you sure of his guilt. An alibi is sometimes invented to bolster a genuine defence.

In *R v Lesley*[58] it was held that this version of the *Goodway* direction should be given routinely, although whether a failure to do so renders a conviction unsafe depends on the facts of the case and the strength of the evidence. The accused in that case had served an alibi notice but did not call the person named in it and did not give evidence himself. The prosecution inferentially invited the jury to conclude that the alibi was

---

[54] However, the Court of Appeal is unlikely to be persuaded that there was such a danger if defence counsel did not ask the trial judge to consider giving an appropriate direction: *R v Burge* [1996] 1 Cr App R 163 at 174. The failure of defence counsel to raise the matter at trial may also be taken into account in cases in which both the third and the fourth situations arise, and may lead the Court of Appeal to conclude that the absence of a direction did not make the conviction unsafe: *R v McGuinness* [1999] Crim LR 318, CA.

[55] [1996] Crim LR 419, CA. See also *R v Harron* [1996] 2 Cr App R 457, CA, below.

[56] [1995] Crim LR 338, CA.

[57] Nor is a direction likely to be required in the numerous cases of handling in which the accused denies knowledge or belief that the goods were stolen, including those in which the accused has given different and inconsistent versions as to how he came by the goods and the prosecution assert that the evidence is a lie: *R v Barnett* [2002] Crim App R 168, CA.

[58] [1996] 1 Cr App R(S) 39, CA.

false and therefore evidence of guilt. Having regard to some weaknesses in the evidence given by the chief prosecution witness, it was held that failure to give the standard direction rendered the verdict unsafe.[59] *R v Lesley* was distinguished in *R v Harron,*[60] in which it was held that the judge had not erred in failing to give the standard direction because the central issue in the case was whether the prosecution witnesses were lying (rather than mistaken) or the accused was: lies had not played a part in the way the prosecution had put their case and were not a matter which the jury might have taken into account separate from their determination of the main issue of who was telling the truth. In these circumstances, it would only have confused the jury to have directed them that, if they accepted the evidence of the prosecution witnesses as to the presence of the accused, and therefore rejected the accused's evidence to the contrary, his evidence might have been falsified to bolster a genuine defence.

R v Genus[61] furnishes an example of the third situation identified in *R v Burge*. The accused claimed to have been acting under duress. The prosecution case was that the accused had told lies to the police, and in their evidence, on collateral issues, ie issues not directly relevant to the question of duress, by reason of which the jury should disbelieve their evidence of duress. It was held that the case cried out for a *Goodway* direction. In *R v Robinson*[62] the accused was charged with possession of drugs with intent to supply. In his summing up the judge gave considerable prominence to the issue whether the accused, in his evidence, had lied about when he had first complained to the police that they had planted the drugs on him. It was held that the issue whether the allegation of planting was a late invention was a separate issue, not a central one, and fell clearly within the fourth situation identified in *R v Burge*. The jury should have been directed on the possibility that the accused had lied to bolster a potentially weak defence.

*(x) Standards of comparison.* In cases where it is necessary to decide whether a person's conduct meets some objective standard of behaviour, evidence of what other persons would do in the same circumstances is admissible as a standard of comparison. Thus, in *Chapman v Walton,*[63] where it was alleged that a broker was negligent in failing to vary the terms upon which certain goods were insured on receiving ambiguous information concerning their destination, evidence from other brokers as to what they would have done in such circumstances was admitted for the purpose of deciding whether the broker had exercised a reasonable degree of care, skill and judgment in the performance of his duties. Similarly, where the issue concerns the existence of a practice in a trade carried out in a particular location, evidence may be admissible of the existence or non-existence of that practice in a similar trade located elsewhere. In *Noble v Kennoway,*[64] for example, the issue being whether underwriters were entitled to repudiate liability on an insurance of a ship's cargo on the grounds

---

[59] Cf *R v Drake* [1996] Crim LR 109, CA, and see also *R v Peacock* [1998] Crim LR 681, CA.
[60] [1996] 2 Cr App R 457, CA.      [61] [1996] Crim LR 502, CA.      [62] [1996] Crim LR 417, CA.
[63] (1833) 10 Bing 57.        [64] (1780) 2 Doug KB 510. See also *Fleet v Murton* (1871) LR 7 QB 126.

that its discharge in Labrador had been unreasonably delayed, it was held that evidence of a practice of delaying the discharge of cargo in the Newfoundland trade was admissible to show the likely existence of a similar practice in the Labrador trade.

# C RELEVANCE AND ADMISSIBILITY

Such evidence as a court will receive for the purpose of determining the existence or non-existence of facts in issue is referred to as admissible evidence. The admissibility of evidence is a matter of law for the judge. The most important feature of the English law of evidence is that all evidence which is sufficiently relevant to prove or disprove a fact in issue and which is not excluded by the judge, either by reason of an exclusionary rule of evidence or in the exercise of his discretion, is admissible.[65] It will be convenient, therefore (i) to consider the meaning of relevance and (ii) to examine, in outline, some of the exclusionary rules of evidence to which the bulk of the remainder of this book is devoted. Reference will then be made to the principles of multiple and conditional admissibility and an evidentiary ghost of marginal contemporary significance known as 'the best evidence rule'.

## 1 RELEVANCE

The classic definition of relevance is contained in Article 1 of Stephen's *Digest of the Law of Evidence*,[66] according to which the word means that—

any two facts to which it is applied are so related to each other that according to the common course of events one either taken by itself or in connection with other facts proves or renders probable the past, present or future existence or non-existence of the other.

Stephen also suggests that relevance may be tested by the use of a syllogism,[67] a form of reasoning in which a conclusion is drawn from two given or assumed propositions, a major premise, a generalization, and a minor premise, which in the context under discussion is a proposition of fact the relevance of which is being tested. For example, to test the relevance of motive on a charge of murder, which has already been considered under the heading of 'Circumstantial evidence', the major premise is the generalization that those who had a motive to kill a person are more likely to have done so than those who had no such motive; the minor premise is that the accused had a motive to kill the person; and the conclusion is that the accused is more likely

---

[65] However, there is no principle that a judge cannot read or hear material that is actually or potentially inadmissible, especially if he is judge of both law and fact: see *Barings plc v Coopers and Lybrand* [2001] EWCA Civ 1163, [2001] CPLR 451, where it was held that to read background documentation in preparation for a long and complex case involved no danger of the judge being so influenced by the material that he would not decide the case on the basis of the admissible evidence.

[66] 12th edn.       [67] *General View of the Criminal Law* (1st edn) 236.

to have killed the person than those without a motive for killing him. As Cross and Tapper point out, care may have to be taken in selecting the appropriate major premise.[68] Indeed, the validity of this form of reasoning depends entirely upon the validity of the major premise, which has to be formulated having regard to common sense and general experience. This accords with the requirement in Stephen's definition of relevance that it be determined 'according to the common course of events'.

As Stephen's definition also makes clear, a fact may be relevant to the past, present or future existence of another fact. *R v Nethercott* [69] provides an example of relevance to the past existence of a fact. N's defence was that he had acted under duress as a result of threats by his co-accused G and gave evidence that he feared for his own safety having regard to the way in which G had acted on previous occasions. It was held that evidence of the fact that three months later G had stabbed N with a knife was also relevant because it made it more likely that N, at the time of the offence, had genuinely feared for his safety.

As one commentator has pointed out,[70] Stephen's definition of relevance appears to set the standard too high in that it requires a relevant fact to 'prove or render probable' the fact requiring proof. In contrast, under the simpler working definition of Lord Simon of Glaisdale in *DPP v Kilbourne*,[71] the relevant fact need only make the matter requiring proof more (or less) probable:

Evidence is relevant if it is logically probative or disprobative of some matter which requires proof. I do not pause to analyse what is involved in 'logical probativeness' except to note that the term does not of itself express the element of experience which is so significant of its operation in law, and possibly elsewhere. It is sufficient to say, even at the risk of etymological tautology, that relevant (i.e. logically probative or disprobative) evidence is evidence which makes the matter which requires proof more or less probable.[72]

In *R v Randall* [73] Lord Steyn cited and applied the statement appearing in the fifth edition of this book that 'relevance is a question of degree determined, for the most part, by common sense and experience'. R and G were tried together on a charge of murder. Each raised a cut-throat defence, each blaming the other for the infliction of the fatal injuries. Both therefore lost the protection of section 1 of the Criminal Evidence Act 1898[74] and were asked questions about their previous convictions and bad character. R had relatively minor convictions for driving offences and disorderly behaviour. G had a bad record, including convictions for burglary, the most recent being for burglary committed by a gang in which G had been armed with a screwdriver. G also admitted in cross-examination that at the date of the killing he was on the run from the police, having been involved in a robbery committed by a gang, all

---

[68] *Cross and Tapper on Evidence* (9th edn Butterworths London, 1999) 56.
[69] [2002] 2 Cr App R 117, CA.
[70] IH Dennis, *The Law of Evidence* (2nd edn Sweet & Maxwell London, 2002) 54–5.
[71] [1973] AC 729 at 756, HL.
[72] Concerning the role of probability theory in legal proceedings, see Sir R Eggleston, *Evidence, Proof and Probability* (2nd edn 1983).
[73] [2004] 1 All ER 467 at 474.          [74] See now s 101 of the Criminal Justice Act 2003.

the robbers having been armed with knives. The House of Lords held that in the particular circumstances of the case the evidence of G's propensity to use and threaten violence was relevant not only in relation to the truthfulness of his evidence, but also because the imbalance between that history and the antecedent history of R tended to show that the version of events put forward by R was more probable than that put forward by G.

Other examples of evidence sufficiently relevant to prove or disprove a fact in issue have already been given under the rubric of circumstantial evidence which, it will be recalled, is a term used to refer to evidence of *relevant* facts. Consideration may now be given to some examples of evidence which has been excluded on the grounds of irrelevance or insufficient relevance. *Holcombe v Hewson*[75] concerned an alleged breach of covenant by the defendant, a publican, to buy his beer from the plaintiff, a brewer. The plaintiff, in order to rebut the defence that he had previously supplied bad beer, intended to call publicans to give evidence that he had supplied them with good beer. Excluding this evidence, Lord Ellenborough said:

We cannot here enquire into the quality of different beer furnished to different persons. The plaintiff might deal well with one, and not with the others. Let him call some of those who frequented the defendant's house, and there drank the beer which he sent in; or let him give any other evidence of the quality of his beer . . .

In *Hollingham v Head*[76] the defendant, in order to defeat an action for the price of goods sold and delivered, sought to establish that the contract was made on certain special terms by evidence that the plaintiff had entered into contracts with other customers on similar terms. The evidence was held to be inadmissible on the grounds that it would have afforded no reasonable inference as to the terms of the contract in dispute.[77] On a charge of manslaughter against a doctor, expert evidence may be adduced as to the doctor's skill as shown by his treatment of the case under investigation, but evidence of his skilful treatment of other patients on other occasions must be excluded.[78] Evidence that after an accident the defendants to a negligence action altered and improved their practice has no relevance to the question whether the accident was caused by their negligence: 'Because the world gets wiser as it gets older, it was not therefore foolish before.'[79]

In *Hui Chi-ming v R*[80] it was held that where two criminal trials arise out of the same transaction, evidence of the outcome of the first will generally be inadmissible

---

[75] (1810) 2 Camp 391, KB.  [76] (1858) 27 LJCP 241.

[77] Evidence of 'similar facts' is not invariably excluded, however: see, eg, *Hales v Kerr* [1908] 2 KB 601, DC; *Joy v Phillips, Mills & Co Ltd* [1916] 1 KB 849, CA; and *Sattin v National Union Bank* (1978) 122 Sol Jo 367, CA, all considered in Ch 15.

[78] *R v Whitehead* (1848) 3 Car & Kir 202.

[79] Per Bramwell B in *Hart v Lancashire & Yorkshire Rly Co* (1869) 21 LT 261.

[80] [1991] 3 All ER 897, PC. See also, concerning the admissibility, at a retrial, of the first jury's acquittal on some counts and failure to agree on others, *R v H* (1989) 90 Cr App R 440, CA; *R v Greer* [1994] Crim LR 745, CA; *R v Scott* [1994] Crim LR 947, CA; and, generally, A L-T Choo 'The Notion of Relevance' [1993] Crim LR 114.

at the second because the verdict in the first, reached by a different jury, whether on the same or different evidence, will be irrelevant, amounting to nothing more than evidence of the opinion of that jury; some exceptional feature is needed before it will be considered relevant.[81] Evidence of an acquittal at the first trial based on a ruling by the trial judge that there was insufficient evidence for the case to go to the jury, would also appear to be generally inadmissible.[82]

In *R v Sandhu*[83] it was held that, insofar as an offence of strict liability involves no proof of *mens rea*, evidence of motive, intention or knowledge on the part of the accused is inadmissible because irrelevant to the issue of his guilt and merely prejudicial to him.[84]

Another, but controversial, example of irrelevance is to be found in the decision of the House of Lords in *R v Blastland*.[85] The appellant B was charged with the buggery and murder of a boy. At the trial B admitted that he had met the boy and engaged in homosexual activity with him but said that when he saw another man nearby, who might have witnessed what he had done, he panicked and ran away. B gave a description of the other man which corresponded closely to M and alleged that M must have committed the offences charged. At the trial there were formal admissions[86] by the prosecution. Some related to M's movements on the evening in question and others showed that M had been investigated by the police after the murder and had been known to engage in homosexual activities in the past with adults but not children. The defence sought leave to call a number of witnesses to elicit from them that, before the victim's body had been found, M had made statements to them that a boy had been murdered. The trial judge held this evidence to be inadmissible. B was convicted on both counts. Before the House of Lords the appellant submitted that, although the statements made by M were inadmissible hearsay if tendered for the truth of any fact stated, they were admissible, as original evidence, if tendered to prove the state of mind of their maker, ie to show M's knowledge of the murder before the body had been found.[87] Lord Bridge, giving the judgment of the House, held that original evidence of this kind is only admissible if the state of mind in question 'is either itself directly in issue at the trial or is of direct and immediate relevance to an issue which arises at the trial'. The issue at the trial was whether B had committed the crimes and what was relevant to that issue was not the fact of M's knowledge but how he had come by it; since he might have done so in a number of different ways, there was no

---

[81] See, eg, *R v Hay* (1983) 77 Cr App R 70, CA and *R v Cooke* (1986) 84 Cr App R 286, CA, Ch 13. As to the relevance and admissibility of previous convictions as evidence of the facts on which they were based, see Ch 21.

[82] *R v Hudson* [1994] Crim LR 920, CA.      [83] [1997] Crim LR 288, CA.

[84] See also, applying *R v Sandhu*, *R v Byrne* [2002] 2 Cr App R 311.

[85] [1985] 2 All ER 1095, HL, applied in *R v Williams* [1998] Crim LR 494, CA. See also *R v Kearley* [1992] 2 All ER 345, HL, Ch 10; and *R v Akram* [1995] Crim LR 50, CA.

[86] See above, under *Facts in issue*. There were also a number of *informal* admissions, M having successively made and withdrawn admissions of his own guilt of the offences in question, but these were properly rejected by the trial judge as inadmissible hearsay: see *R v Turner* (1975) 61 Cr App R 67, CA.

[87] See above under **B The varieties of evidence, 2 Hearsay evidence**.

rational basis on which the jury could be invited to draw an inference as to the source of that knowledge or conclude that he rather than B was the offender. The evidence, therefore, had been properly rejected. The flaw in this reasoning, it is submitted, is the unwarranted introduction of the requirement that the evidence be 'of direct and immediate relevance'. The evidence was no less relevant than the evidence relating to M's movements which was thought to have been properly admitted, albeit that neither item, by itself, could show that M, rather than B, was the offender.[88]

R v Keast[89] is another surprising decision on relevance and, it is submitted, one which is in need of review. In that case it was held that unless there is some concrete basis for regarding long-term demeanour and state of mind of an alleged victim of sexual abuse as confirming or disproving the occurrence of such abuse, it cannot assist a jury bringing their common sense to bear on who is telling the truth.[90]

There are occasions when the effect of evidence, albeit technically admissible, is likely to be so slight that it is wiser not to adduce it, particularly if, in a criminal trial, there is any danger that its admission will have an adverse effect on the fairness of the proceedings.[91] Evidence of marginal relevance may also be excluded on the grounds that it would lead to a multiplicity of subsidiary issues which, in addition to distracting the court from the main issue,[92] might involve the court in a protracted investigation[93] or a difficult and doubtful controversy of precisely the same kind as that which the court has to determine.[94] In *Agassiz v London Tramway Co*[95] the plaintiff, a passenger in an omnibus, claimed damages for serious personal injuries arising out of a collision allegedly caused by the driver's negligence. The action was dismissed for want of evidence as to how the accident had happened. After the accident, the conductor, in reply to the suggestion of another passenger that the driver's conduct should be reported, said: 'Sir, he has been reported, for he has been off the points five or six times today; he is a new driver.' Kelly CB held that this evidence was properly excluded, since it neither related to the conduct of the driver at the relevant time nor explained the actual cause of the collision, but merely gave rise to a multiplicity of side issues.

On charges of possession of drugs with intent to supply, there is a difficult distinction

---

[88] See also *R v Greenwood* [2005] Crim LR 59, CA, where it was held that an accused charged with murder is entitled to seek to establish that a third party had a motive to murder the victim.

[89] [1998] Crim LR 748, CA.

[90] See also, applying *R v Keast*, *R v Venn* [2003] All ER (D) 207 (Feb), [2003] EWCA Crim 236; and cf *R v Townsend* (2003) LTL 23 Oct.

[91] Per Lord Lane CJ in *R v Robertson; R v Golder* [1987] 3 All ER 231 at 237, CA in relation to the admissibility of evidence under s 74 of the Police and Criminal Evidence Act 1984. See also *R v Williams* [1990] Crim LR 409, CA.

[92] See per Byrne J in *R v Patel* [1951] 2 All ER 29 at 30.

[93] See per Rolfe B in *A-G v Hitchcock* (1847) 1 Exch 91 at 105 and per Willes J in *Hollingham v Head* (1858) 27 LJCP 241 at 242: 'litigants are mortal . . .'

[94] Per Lord Watson in *Metropolitan Asylum District Managers v Hill* (1882) 47 LT 29, HL, where a majority of the House was of the opinion, without deciding the point, that in considering the effect of a smallpox hospital on the health of local residents, evidence of the effect of similar hospitals in other localities on their residents would be admissible. See also *Folkes v Chadd* (1782) 3 Doug KB 157.

[95] (1872) 21 WR 199.

to be drawn between evidence which is relevant to the intention to supply the drug found, and evidence which, although of some relevance to that issue, is unduly prejudicial because it relates to past dealing or dealing generally.[96] In *R v Batt*,[97] a charge of possession of cannabis resin with intent to supply, the Court of Appeal did not question the admissibility in evidence of B's possession of weights and scales (on which there were traces of cannabis resin), but held that evidence of the discovery of £150 in an ornamental kettle in her house was inadmissible because it had nothing to do with intent to supply in future the drugs found, but had a highly prejudicial effect as 'a hallmark of a propensity to supply generally, or a hallmark of the fact that there had been a past supply, or that the money will be used in future to obtain cannabis for future supply'.

However, it seems that *Batt* has not laid down any general principle that evidence of possession of money is never admissible on a charge of possession with intent to supply, and on one view the decision in that case turned upon the fact that the trial judge had failed to direct the jury as to how they could properly use the evidence of the possession of money.[98] In *R v Wright*[99] it was held that drug traders needed to keep by them large sums of cash and therefore evidence of the discovery of £16,000 could have given rise to an inference of dealing and tended to prove that the drugs found were for supply. This approach was followed in *R v Gordon*,[100] where it was held that although evidence as to past deposits in and withdrawals from savings accounts was irrelevant, because it could only found an inference of past drug dealing, evidence of the discovery of £4,200 in G's home was admissible ('cash for the acquisition of stock for present active drug dealing must be relevant to a count of possession with intent to supply'), subject to an appropriate direction on any possible innocent explanations for the presence of the cash.[101] The jury should be directed that they should regard the finding of the money as relevant only if they reject any innocent explanation for it put forward by the accused, but that if they conclude that the money indicates not merely past dealing, but an ongoing dealing in drugs, they may take into account the finding of it, together with the drugs, in considering whether intent to supply has been

[96] The principles to be derived from the cases in the ensuing text are unaffected, it is submitted, by s 101 of the Criminal Justice Act 2003: see generally Ch 17.

[97] [1994] Crim LR 592, CA.

[98] See *R v Morris* [1995] 2 Cr App R 69, CA, and *R v Nicholas* [1995] Crim LR 942, CA. Alternatively, it should be regarded as a case confined to its own facts, remembering that £150 was too small, and its hiding place too unremarkable, to be the hallmark of present and active drug dealing: *R v Okusanya* [1995] Crim LR 941, CA.

[99] [1994] Crim LR 55, CA.

[100] [1995] 2 Cr App R 61, CA. See also *R v Morris* [1995] 2 Cr App R 69, CA.

[101] Concerning the accounts, cf *R v Okusanya* [1995] Crim LR 941, CA: evidence of money in three accounts was admissible to rebut O's explanation for having £8,800 in his possession (that, as a Nigerian, it was not his custom to put money in banks). But see also *R v Smith (Ivor)* [1995] Crim LR 940, CA: evidence that £9,000 had been deposited in S's account in recent months, of which £2,100 was unexplained by various legitimate transactions, was admissible (subject to an appropriate direction).

proved.[102] The jury should also be directed not to treat such evidence as evidence of propensity, ie not to pursue the line of reasoning that, by reason of past dealing, the accused is likely to be guilty of the offence charged.[103]

At one stage it was thought that where possession of drugs is in issue, evidence of possession of money or drugs paraphernalia can never be relevant to that issue.[104] However, in *R v Guney*[105] the Court of Appeal, declining to follow the earlier authorities, held that although evidence of possession of a large sum of cash or enjoyment of a wealthy lifestyle does not, on its own, prove possession, there are numerous sets of circumstances in which it may be relevant to that issue, not least to the issue of knowledge as an ingredient of possession. The issue in that case was whether the accused was knowingly in possession of some 5 kilos of heroin or whether it had been 'planted', and the defence conceded that if possession were to be proved, then it would be open to the jury to infer intent to supply. It was held that, in all the circumstances, evidence of the finding of nearly £25,000 in cash in the wardrobe of the accused's bedroom, in close proximity to the drugs, was relevant to the issue of possession.[106]

## 2 THE EXCLUSIONARY RULES

Evidence must be sufficiently relevant to be admissible, but sufficiently relevant evidence is only admissible insofar as it is not excluded by any rule of the law of evidence (or by the exercise of judicial discretion). The consequence, of course, is that some relevant evidence is excluded. Thus although statutes make provision for the admissibility of various categories of hearsay, ie out-of-court assertions admitted as evidence of the matters stated, not *all* relevant hearsay is admissible.[107] Relevant evidence, including highly relevant evidence, may also be withheld as a matter of public policy on the grounds that its production and disclosure would jeopardize national security or would be injurious to some other national interest.[108] The opinion evidence of a non-expert is generally regarded as being insufficiently relevant to a subject not calling for any particular expertise but, whatever its degree of relevance, it is generally excluded on the basis that the tribunal of fact might be tempted simply to accept the opinion proffered rather than draw its own inferences from the facts of the case.[109] These and other exclusionary rules make up much of the law of evidence and are considered throughout this book.

---

[102] *R v Grant* [1996] 1 Cr App Rep 73, CA; cf *R v Antill* [2002] All ER (D) 176 (Sep), [2002] EWCA Crim 2114. However, the judge is not tied to this or any other particular form of words: *R v Malik* [2000] Crim LR 197, CA.

[103] See *R v Simms* [1995] Crim LR 304, CA, and *R v Lucas* [1995] Crim LR 400, CA.

[104] See *R v Halpin* [1996] Crim LR 112, CA and *R v Richards* [1997] Crim LR 499, CA.

[105] [1998] 2 Cr App R 242.

[106] Applied in *R v Griffiths* [1998] Crim LR 567, CA. See also *R v Edwards* [1998] Crim LR 207, CA and *R v Scott* [1996] Crim LR 652, CA.

[107] See generally Chs 10–13.      [108] See Ch 19.      [109] See Ch 18.

## 3 MULTIPLE ADMISSIBILITY

Where evidence is admissible for one purpose, but inadmissible for another, it remains admissible in law for the first purpose (although it may be excluded by the exercise of judicial discretion). For example, an out-of-court statement may be inadmissible for the purpose of proving the truth of its contents, being inadmissible hearsay, but admissible, as original evidence, for the purpose of proving that the statement was made. The principle has been described, somewhat misleadingly, as one of 'multiple admissibility'.[110] Where it applies, the judge is often required to warn the jury of the limited purpose for which the evidence has been admitted.[111] The risk that the jury may misunderstand or ignore such a warning is felt to be more than outweighed by the greater mischief that would be occasioned if the evidence were to be excluded altogether.[112]

## 4 CONDITIONAL ADMISSIBILITY

An item of evidence, viewed in isolation, may appear to be irrelevant and therefore inadmissible. Taken together with, or seen in the light of, some other item of evidence, its relevance may become apparent. Evidence, however, can only be given at a trial in piecemeal fashion, by degrees, and it may be difficult to adduce the second item of evidence before the first. In order to overcome this difficulty, the first item of evidence may be admitted conditionally or *de bene esse*. If, viewed in the light of evidence subsequently adduced, it becomes relevant, it may be taken into account. If, notwithstanding the evidence subsequently adduced, it remains irrelevant, it must be disregarded. The operation of the principle may be illustrated by reference to the admissibility of accusations made in the presence of the accused, the relevance of which may depend on evidence, subsequently adduced, of the accused's reaction to them. An accusation made in the presence of the accused upon an occasion on which he might reasonably be expected to make some observation, explanation or denial is, in certain circumstances, admissible in evidence against him, provided that a foundation for its admission is laid by proof of facts from which, in the opinion of the judge, a jury might reasonably draw the inference that the accused, by his answer, whether given by word, conduct or silence, acknowledged the truth of the accusation made. The accusation may be admitted in evidence, however, even where the evidential

---

[110] Wigmore *A Treatise on the Anglo-American System of Evidence* (3rd edn 1940) I, para 13.

[111] For example, where a confession, admissible as evidence of the truth of its contents by way of exception to the hearsay rule, implicates both its maker and a co-accused, the trial judge is duty bound to impress upon the jury that it can be used only against its maker and not against the co-accused: *R v Gunewardene* [1951] 2 KB 600, CCA (see Ch 13). Similarly, where a statement containing an admissible confession also contains inadmissible material which cannot be edited out without prejudice to the sense of the confession, the jury should be directed to ignore the inadmissible material: *R v Flicker* [1995] Crim LR 493, CA, where the court appears to doubt, wrongly it is submitted, the existence of a discretionary power to exclude the whole statement.

[112] See per Tindall CJ in *Willis v Bernard* (1832) 8 Bing 376 at 383.

foundation has not been laid, provided that, if evidence is *not* subsequently adduced from which it can be inferred that the accused did acknowledge the truth of the accusation made, the judge directs the jury to disregard the accusation altogether.[113]

## 5  THE BEST EVIDENCE RULE

The so-called best evidence rule, at one time thought to be a fundamental principle of the law of evidence, is now applied so rarely as to be virtually extinct. In 1745, Lord Hardwicke said: 'the judges and sages of the law have laid it down that there is but one general rule of evidence, the best that the nature of the case will allow.' That statement was made in the case of *Omychund v Barker*,[114] where it was held that depositions of witnesses of the Gentoo religion were admissible in evidence notwithstanding that they did not accept the authority of the Gospel, and on one view the rule to which Lord Hardwicke referred may be regarded as having been of an inclusionary nature, allowing for the admissibility of the best evidence available that a party to litigation could produce. The rule, however, was rarely used in this way and as an inclusionary doctrine of general application certainly finds no place in the modern law of evidence. The authorities show that the rule was treated as being of an exclusionary nature, preventing the admissibility of evidence where better was available.[115] Even as an exclusionary principle, however, the rule is now virtually defunct. The rule that a party seeking to rely upon the contents of a document must adduce primary evidence of the contents, secondary evidence being admissible only exceptionally,[116] is sometimes said to be the only remaining instance of the best evidence rule,[117] notwithstanding that it pre-dates the best evidence rule, but in *Springsteen v Flute International Ltd*[118] it was held, in this context, that it could be said with confidence that the best evidence rule, long on its deathbed, had finally expired. Prior to that decision, the rule did make a rare appearance in *R v Quinn and R v Bloom*.[119] The accused, two club proprietors, were charged with keeping a disorderly house. The charge arose out of certain allegedly indecent striptease acts performed at their clubs. One of the accused sought to put in evidence a film made three months after the events complained of and showing what the performers actually did, together with

---

[113] Per Lords Atkinson and Reading in *R v Christie* [1914] AC 545, HL at 554 and 565 respectively. For another example, see *R v Donat* (1985) 82 Cr App R 173, CA.

[114] (1745) 1 Atk 21 at 49.

[115] See, eg, *Chenie v Watson* (1797) Peake Add Cas 123, where oral evidence relating to the condition of a material object was excluded on the grounds that the object itself ought to have been produced for inspection by the court; and *Williams v East India Co* (1802) 3 East 192, where circumstantial evidence was excluded because direct evidence was available. Both cases have, on the point in question, been reversed: as to the former, see now *R v Francis* (1874) LR 2 CCR 128 and *Hocking v Ahlquist Bros Ltd* [1944] KB 120 (which are considered in Ch 9); as to the latter, see now *Dowling v Dowling* (1860) 10 ICLR 236.

[116] See Ch 9.

[117] See, eg, per Lord Denning MR in *Garton v Hunter* [1969] 2 QB 37 at 44, CA and per Ackner LJ in *Kajala v Noble* (1982) 75 Cr App R 149, CA at 152.

[118] [2001] EMLR 654, CA.        [119] [1962] 2 QB 245.

evidence that the performances shown in the film were identical with those in question. The Court of Criminal Appeal held that this evidence had been properly excluded. Ashworth J, giving the judgment of the court, said:

> it was admitted that some of the movements in the film (for instance, that of a snake used in one scene) could not be said with any certainty to be the same movements as were made at the material time . . . this objection goes not only to weight, as was argued, but to admissibility: it is not the best evidence.[120]

Although out-of-court demonstrations and re-enactments are admissible as a variety of real evidence,[121] the court held that a reconstruction made privately for the purpose of constituting evidence at a trial is inadmissible.[122]

As an exclusionary principle, the best evidence rule may be of no more than marginal contemporary significance, but where a party fails to make use of the best evidence available and relies upon inferior evidence, the absence of the best evidence or the party's failure to account for its absence may always be the subject of adverse judicial comment. The inferior evidence may be slighted or ignored on the grounds that it lacks weight.[123] For example, in *Post Office Counters Ltd v Mahida*,[124] a debt action, it was held that the claimant company, which relied upon secondary evidence of documents submitted to them by the defendant, having itself destroyed the originals, had failed to prove the debts in question.

# D  WEIGHT

The weight of evidence is its cogency or probative worth in relation to the facts in issue. The assessment of the weight of evidence is in large measure a matter of common sense and experience, dependent upon a wide variety of factors such as: (i) the extent to which it is supported or contradicted by other evidence adduced; (ii) in the case of direct testimony, the demeanour, plausibility, and credibility of the witness and all the circumstances in which he claims to have perceived a fact in issue; and (iii) in the case of hearsay, all the circumstances from which any inference can reasonably be drawn as to the accuracy or otherwise of the out-of-court statement including, for example, whether the statement was made contemporaneously with the occurrence or existence of the facts stated and whether its maker had any incentive to conceal or

---

[120] Cf *R v Thomas* [1986] Crim LR 682, a case of reckless driving in which a video recording of the route taken by the accused was admitted to remove the need for maps and still photographs and to convey a more accurate picture of the roads in question.

[121] See, eg, *Buckingham v Daily News Ltd* [1956] 2 QB 534, CA: a demonstration of the way in which a worker cleaned the blades of a rotary press in a printing house.

[122] Cf *Li Shu-ling v R* [1988] 3 All ER 138, PC: a video recording of a re-enactment of the crime by the accused may be admitted in evidence as a confession (see Ch 13).

[123] See per Lord Coleridge CJ in *R v Francis* (1874) LR 2 CCR 128.

[124] [2003] EWCA Civ 1583, (2003) *The Times* 31 Oct 2003.

misrepresent the facts.[125] Weight, like relevance, is a question of degree: at one extreme, an item of evidence may be of minimal probative value in relation to the facts in issue; at the other extreme, it may be virtually conclusive of them. Where the evidence adduced by a party in relation to a fact in issue is, even if uncontradicted, so weak that it could not reasonably justify a finding in his favour, it is described as 'insufficient evidence'. Where the evidence adduced by a party is so weighty that it could reasonably justify a finding in his favour, it is described as 'prima facie evidence'. Somewhat confusingly, however, this term is also used to describe evidence adduced by a party which is, in the absence of contradictory evidence, so weighty that it does justify a finding in his favour. 'Conclusive evidence' might be thought to denote the weightiest possible evidence. In fact, the term refers to evidence which, irrespective of its weight, concludes the fact in issue: the fact ceases to be in issue and is not even open to contradictory proof because the court must find the fact to have been proved.[126]

The issue of the weight to be attached to an item of evidence is related to, but distinct from, the issue of its admissibility. The weight of evidence is a question of fact, its admissibility a question of law. Thus, in a jury trial, the judge decides whether an item of evidence is relevant and admissible and, if the evidence is admitted, the jury decides what weight, if any, to attach to it. It does not follow from this, however, that the weight of evidence is solely the concern of the tribunal of fact. For a variety of different purposes, the judge must also form a view as to the weight of evidence. In determining admissibility, he must consider whether evidence is sufficiently relevant and this will depend, to some extent, on his assessment of its weight. In examining the evidence adduced to establish preliminary facts, which, it will be recalled, must be proved as a condition precedent to the admissibility of certain items of evidence, the weight of the evidence should be taken into account. As we shall see, a judge should withdraw an issue from the tribunal of fact where a party has adduced 'insufficient evidence' in support of that issue. As we shall also see, the judge has a discretion to exclude certain items of evidence and for these purposes also may have regard to, inter alia, the weight of the evidence in question. Last, and by no means least, in his summing-up the judge is entitled to comment upon the cogency of the evidence admitted, provided that he does not usurp the jury's function as the tribunal of fact.[127]

## E THE FUNCTIONS OF THE JUDGE AND JURY

The division of functions between judge and jury, which dates from a time when jury trial was the norm in both civil and criminal proceedings, has left a deep impression

---

[125] See s 4 of the Civil Evidence Act 1995 (Ch 11).

[126] See, eg, s 10(1) of the Criminal Justice Act 1967 (Ch 22) and s 13(1) of the Civil Evidence Act 1968 (see Ch 21).

[127] *R v O'Donnell* (1917) 12 Cr App R 219; *R v Canny* (1945) 30 Cr App R 143.

on the modern law of evidence, even as it now applies in cases tried without a jury. It will be convenient to explore the division and the extent to which the judge controls the jury under the headings of: (i) questions of law and fact; (ii) the *voir dire* (or trial within a trial); (iii) the sufficiency of evidence; and (iv) the summing-up.

## 1  QUESTIONS OF LAW AND FACT

The resolution of disputes in courts of law gives rise to questions of fact, or questions of law, and often both. In jury trials the general rule is that questions of law are decided by the judge and questions of fact by the jury. This is not as straightforward a division as it may appear at first blush, because some questions of 'fact' for the jury, for example the issue of dishonesty in theft and related offences, may be considered to be as much questions of law as of fact, and some questions of 'law' for the judge, for example the existence or non-existence of preliminary facts, are essentially questions of fact.[128]

Questions of law for the judge include those relating to the substantive law, the competence of a person to give evidence as a witness, the admissibility of evidence, the withdrawal of an issue from the jury and the way in which he should direct the jury on both the substantive law and the evidence adduced. Questions of fact for the jury include those relating to the credibility of the witnesses called, the weight to be attached to the evidence adduced and ultimately, of course, the existence or non-existence of the facts in issue. In trials on indictment without a jury, ie complex fraud cases and trials where there is a real danger of jury tampering, the judge decides all questions of both law and fact and, if the accused is convicted, must give a judgment which states the reasons for the conviction.[129] In the case of a trial by lay justices, the bench decides all questions of both law and fact, but on questions of law, including the law of evidence, questions of mixed law and fact and matters of practice and procedure, should give heed to the advice of its clerk or legal adviser.[130] Theoretically in the same position, district judges (magistrates' courts) tend to decide questions of law as well as fact. In civil cases tried by a judge sitting alone, the judge decides all questions of both law and fact.

Although questions of fact are generally decided by the jury, the judicial function includes the investigation of preliminary facts (for the purpose of determining the admissibility of evidence), the assessment of the sufficiency of evidence (for the purpose of deciding whether to withdraw an issue from the jury) and the evaluation of evidence adduced (for the purpose of commenting upon the matter to the jury in summing up). Each of these matters is considered separately below. Additionally, there is a variety of special cases in which questions of fact are also capable of being

---

[128] See generally Glanville Williams, *Law and Fact* [1976] Crim LR 472 and Allen and Pardo, *Facts in Law and Facts of Law* (2003) 7 E&P 153.

[129] Section 48(3) and (5) of the Criminal Justice Act 2003.

[130] For the duties of the clerk or legal adviser, see para 55, *Practice Direction (Criminal Proceedings: Consolidation)* [2002] 1 WLR 2870.

questions of law or are treated as being questions of law or for some other reason fall to be decided, wholly or in part, by the judge. They include the following.

## (a) The construction of ordinary words

The modern authorities are in a state of disarray on the important question whether, in criminal cases, the construction of ordinary statutory words is a question for the tribunal of fact. The leading authority on the point, *Brutus v Cozens*,[131] expressly supports an affirmative answer. The appellant, during the annual tennis tournament at Wimbledon, had gone on to No 2 Court while a match was in progress, blown a whistle and thrown leaflets around. He was charged with using insulting behaviour whereby a breach of the peace was likely to be occasioned under section 5 of the Public Order Act 1986. The magistrates dismissed the information on the grounds that the appellant's behaviour was not insulting. On a case stated, the question was whether, on the facts found, the decision was correct in law. This assumed that the meaning of the word 'insulting' in section 5 was a matter of law. Allowing the appellant's appeal against the decision of the Divisional Court, the House of Lords rejected this assumption. Lord Reid said:[132]

The meaning of an ordinary word of the English language is not a question of law. The proper construction of a statute is a question of law.[133] If the context shows that a word is used in an unusual sense the court will determine in other words what that unusual sense is. But here there is in my opinion no question of the word 'insulting' being used in any unusual sense. It appears to me . . . to be intended to have its ordinary meaning. It is for the tribunal which decides the case to consider, not as law but as fact, whether in the whole circumstances the words of the statute do or do not as a matter of ordinary usage of the English language cover or apply to the facts which have been proved. If it is alleged that the tribunal has reached a wrong decision then there can be a question of law but only of a limited character. The question would normally be whether their decision was unreasonable in the sense that no tribunal acquainted with the ordinary use of language could reasonably reach that decision.

Applying this dictum in *R v Feely*,[134] an appeal from a trial by judge and jury, Lawton LJ held that whereas the word 'fraudulently' which was used in section 1(1) of the Larceny Act 1916 had acquired a special meaning as a result of case law, the word 'dishonestly' as used in section 1(1) of the Theft Act 1968 was an ordinary word in common use. Accordingly, it was a question of fact for the jury and required no direction by the judge as to its meaning.[135]

---

[131] [1973] AC 854.       [132] [1973] AC 854 at 861.

[133] See also *R v Spens* [1991] 4 All ER 421, CA: it is for the judge to construe binding agreements between parties, and all forms of parliamentary and local government legislation, including codes which sufficiently resemble legislation as to require such construction, eg the City Code on Takeovers and Mergers; and cf *R v Adams* [1993] Crim LR 525, CA, and *R v Morris* [1994] Crim LR 596, CA.

[134] [1973] QB 530, CA.

[135] See also *R v Harris* (1986) 84 Cr App R 75, CA: the words 'knowledge or belief' are words of ordinary usage and therefore, in most cases of handling stolen goods contrary to s 22(1) of the Theft Act 1968, all that

In *DPP v Stonehouse*[136] the question whether acts are sufficiently proximate to the intended complete offence to rank as an attempt, was treated as a question of fact. This was justified by Lord Diplock on the grounds that the concept of proximity is a question of degree on which the opinion of reasonable men may differ and as to which the legal training and experience of a judge does not make his opinion more likely to be correct than that of a non-lawyer.[137]

Lord Reid's dictum, however, although never expressly disowned, has largely been ignored. As one commentator has observed, the number of cases when *Cozens v Brutus* ought to have been cited but was not 'are as the sands of the sea'.[138] This disregard extends to the House of Lords itself. In *Metropolitan Police Comr v Caldwell*,[139] for example, 'recklessly' was held to be an ordinary word, but given a legal definition. A similar approach has been taken in relation to the word 'supply' in section 5(3) of the Misuse of Drugs Act 1971[140] and the word 'discharge' in section 5(1)(b) of the Firearms Act 1968.[141] The need for such legal definition of ordinary words stems from the potential diversity of interpretation by jurors, and indeed judges, and the concomitant risk of inconsistent verdicts, and for these reasons, it is submitted, Lord Reid's dictum should continue to be ignored until it is expressly repudiated.

In civil cases tried with a jury, there is old authority to support the view that the meaning of ordinary words is a question of construction for the judge.[142]

## (b) Defamation

As a result of Fox's Libel Act 1792—which provides that, in criminal prosecutions for libel, it is for the jury, having been directed by the judge on the law, to give a general verdict of guilty or not guilty upon the whole matter put in issue—there has developed a rule whereby the judge decides whether the writing in question is capable of the defamatory meaning alleged by the prosecution and, if satisfied that this is the case, the jury, construing the writing, then decides whether it does, in fact, constitute a criminal libel. This division of functions between judge and jury also applies in civil proceedings for libel.[143]

---

need be said to a jury is to ask whether the prosecution has established receipt, knowing or believing that the goods were stolen; *R v Jones* [1987] 2 All ER 692, CA: whether a person is 'armed' while being concerned in the illegal importation of cannabis contrary to s 86 of the Customs and Excise Management Act 1979; and *Chambers v DPP* [1995] Crim LR 896, DC: 'disorderly behaviour' contrary to s 5 of the Public Order Act 1986.

136 [1978] AC 55, HL.        137 [1978] AC 55 at 69. See now s 4(3) of the Criminal Attempts Act 1981.
138 D W Elliott '*Brutus v Cozens*; Decline & Fall' [1989] Crim LR 323 at 324.
139 [1982] AC 341, HL.        140 *R v Maginnis* [1987] AC 303, HL.
141 *Flack v Baldry* [1988] 1 All ER 673, HL.
142 Per Parke B in *Neilson v Harford* (1841) 8 M&W 806 at 823.
143 *Nevill v Fine Arts & General Insurance Co Ltd* [1897] AC 68, HL. Where a defendant claims qualified privilege for a report as a fair and accurate report of the proceedings of an inquiry within the Schedule to the Defamation Act 1952, the issues of fairness and accuracy are questions of fact for the jury, as are questions of public concern and public benefit under s 7(3) of the Act: *Kingshott v Associated Kent Newspapers Ltd* [1991] 2 All ER 99, CA.

### (c)  Corroboration

In the now rare cases in which a conviction cannot be based on uncorroborated evidence, it is for the judge to direct the jury as to what evidence is capable, in law, of amounting to corroboration and for the jury to decide whether that evidence does, in fact, constitute corroboration.[144]

### (d)  Foreign law

In the courts of England and Wales, questions of foreign law, that is questions relating to the law of any jurisdiction other than England and Wales, are issues of fact to be decided, on the evidence adduced, by the judge. Section 15 of the Administration of Justice Act 1920 provides that:

Where for the purposes of disposing of any action or other matter which is being tried by a judge with a jury in any court in England or Wales it is necessary to ascertain the law of any other country which is applicable to the facts of the case, any question as to the effect of the evidence given with respect to that law shall, instead of being submitted to the jury, be decided by the judge alone.

This provision applies to criminal proceedings only,[145] but has been re-enacted, in relation to High Court proceedings and County Court proceedings, by section 69(5) of the Supreme Court Act 1981 and section 68 of the County Courts Act 1984 respectively. Foreign law is usually proved by the evidence of an appropriately qualified expert, who may refer to foreign statutes and decisions, or by the production of a report of a previous decision by an English court of superior status on the point of foreign law in question.[146] Where necessary, the judge must determine the point by deciding between the conflicting opinion evidence of the expert witnesses.[147]

### (e)  Questions of reasonableness

What is reasonable is a question of fact and therefore normally decided by the jury. In some civil cases, however, it must be decided by the judge on the basis of facts which, if not agreed, have been ascertained by the jury.

In an action for malicious prosecution, for example, it is the function of the jury to ascertain the facts, if disputed, which operated on the mind of the prosecutor, and the function of the judge, on the basis of the facts thus ascertained, to decide whether the prosecutor did or did not have reasonable and probable cause for commencing the prosecution in question.[148]

---

[144] *R v Tragen* [1956] Crim LR 332; *R v Charles* (1976) 68 Cr App R 334n, HL; *R v Reeves* (1979) 68 Cr App R 331, CA. See generally Ch 8.

[145] *R v Hammer* [1923] 2 KB 786, CCA.

[146] See Ch 18. For the circumstances in which judicial notice may be taken of points of foreign law, see Ch 22.

[147] See, eg, *Re Duke of Wellington, Glentanar v Wellington* [1947] Ch 506.

[148] *Herniman v Smith* [1938] AC 305, HL, applied, in relation to the tort of procuring the grant of a search warrant falsely, maliciously and *without reasonable and probable cause*, in *Reynolds v Metropolitan Police Comr* (1984) 80 Cr App R 125, CA.

## (f) Perjury

The offence of perjury is committed where a person lawfully sworn as a witness or interpreter in a judicial proceeding wilfully makes a statement *material* in that proceeding which he knows to be false or does not believe to be true.[149] Section 1(6) of the Perjury Act 1911 provides that 'the question whether a statement on which perjury is assigned was material is a question of law to be determined by the court of trial'.

## (g) Autrefois acquit and convict

An accused charged with an offence which is the same as an offence in respect of which he has previously been acquitted or convicted or an offence in respect of which he could on some previous indictment have been lawfully convicted, may tender a special plea in bar of *autrefois acquit* or *convict* in order to quash the indictment. Where such a plea is tendered, it is for the judge to decide the issue, without empanelling a jury.[150]

## 2  THE *VOIR DIRE*, OR TRIAL WITHIN A TRIAL

Preliminary facts, as we have seen, must be proved as a condition precedent to the admissibility of certain items of evidence. For example, where the prosecution proposes to adduce evidence of a confession made by the accused and the defence object to its admissibility on the grounds that it was or may have been obtained by oppression of the accused or in consequence of something said or done which was likely, in the circumstances, to render unreliable any confession which might be made by him in consequence thereof, the court shall not allow the confession to be admitted except in so far as the prosecution proves to the court that the confession was not obtained by such means.[151] Proof of due search for the original of a lost document, on the contents of which a party seeks to rely, is a condition precedent to the admissibility of a copy of that document.[152] Similarly, it may become necessary to show that a person is competent to give evidence as a witness or that a witness is privileged from answering a particular question. Questions of this kind are matters of law for the judge. The preliminary facts may be agreed or assumed, but where they are in dispute it is for the judge to hear evidence and adjudicate upon them.[153] The witnesses give their

---

[149]  Perjury Act 1911, s 1(1).        [150]  Criminal Justice Act 1988, s 122.

[151]  Police and Criminal Evidence Act 1984, s 76(2) (see Ch 13). However, if the prosecution relies on oral statements and the defence case is that they were never made, or the prosecution relies on written statements and the defence case is that they are forgeries, no question of admissibility arises; whether or not the statements were made is a question of fact for the jury: *Ajodha v The State* [1981] 2 All ER 193, PC at 201–2, applied in *R v Flemming* (1987) 86 Cr App R 32, CA.

[152]  *Brewster v Sewell* (1820) 3 B & Ald 296 (see Ch 8).

[153]  However, where the preliminary facts are identical with the facts in issue, the condition precedent is held to be established if the judge is satisfied that there is *sufficient evidence* of it to go before the jury. For example, if a party seeks to adduce a tape-recording in evidence, the question of whether it is genuine and original being ultimately for the determination of the jury, the judge need satisfy himself by no more than prima facie evidence that the tape is genuine and original and therefore competent to be considered by the

evidence on a special form of oath known as a *voir dire*. The hearing before the judge is called a hearing on the *voir dire* or a 'trial within a trial'.

In the Crown Court, questions of admissibility, including those involving the hearing of evidence on the *voir dire*, are usually determined in the absence of the jury because of the impossibility of deciding such questions without some reference either to the disputed evidence, which in the event may be ruled inadmissible, or to other material prejudicial to the accused. Thus where the prosecution proposes to adduce a certain item of evidence and counsel for the defence intends to make a submission that it is inadmissible, the normal practice is for defence counsel to inform the prosecution of his intention at the Plea and Directions Hearing[154] or immediately before the trial commences so that the evidence is not referred to in the presence of the jury, whether in the prosecution opening speech or otherwise. The prosecution will adduce their evidence in the normal way but at that point in time when the evidence would otherwise be admitted, counsel will intimate to the judge that a point of law has arisen which falls to be decided in the absence of the jury and the jury will be told to retire.[155] Whether or not the jury, on returning to court, hears the disputed evidence depends, of course, on the judge's ruling on its admissibility. In *R v Reynolds*[156] Lord Goddard CJ was of the opinion that the determination of preliminary facts in the absence of the jury is confined to exceptional cases, such as those relating to the admissibility of a confession, where it is almost impossible to prevent some reference to the terms of the confession.[157] However, the modern practice is to ask the jury to retire whenever there is a risk of them being exposed to material which might be ruled inadmissible or which, in any event, would be likely to prejudice the accused.[158] The modern position, therefore, is probably accurately reflected in rule 104(c) of the United States Federal Rules, which provides that hearings on the admissibility of confessions shall always be conducted in the absence of the jury and that hearings on other matters shall be so conducted when the interests of justice require.

In *F (an infant) v Chief Constable of Kent*[159] Lord Lane CJ observed that since the function of the *voir dire* is to allow the arbiter of law to decide a legal point in the

---

jury: *R v Robson, R v Harris* [1972] 1 WLR 651; cf *R v Stevenson* [1971] 1 WLR 1. See Ch 4, under *The burden and standard of proof in a trial within a trial*. See also *Stowe v Querner* (1870) LR 5 Exch 155, where one party sought to admit secondary evidence of the contents of an insurance policy, the other party denying that the policy had ever existed; and per Lord Penzance in *Hitchins v Eardley* (1871) LR 2 P&D 248. However, it has been said that where one of the disputed preliminary facts happens to be identical to one of the facts in issue to be decided by the jury, the judge must nonetheless reach a definite decision on the preliminary fact in question: see per Lord Denman CJ in *Doe d Jenkins v Davies* (1847) 10 QB 314.

[154] See para 41.13 (j) *Practice Direction (Criminal Proceedings: Consolidation)* [2002] 1 WLR 2870.

[155] Occasionally it is necessary to determine admissibility immediately after the jury has been empanelled, eg, where the evidence of a confession is so crucial to the prosecution case that, without reference to it, their case cannot even be opened: see *R v Hammond* [1941] 3 All ER 318.

[156] [1950] 1 KB 606.     [157] See further Ch 13, under C **The** *voir dire*.

[158] See *R v Deakin* [1994] 4 All ER 769, CA.     [159] [1982] Crim LR 682, DC.

absence of the arbiter of fact, in proceedings before magistrates, where the justices are judges of both fact and law, there can be no question of a trial within a trial. In that case, it was held that once the question of the admissibility of a confession has been decided as a separate issue, the magistrates having heard evidence on the preliminary facts and having ruled in favour of admissibility, it is unnecessary for the evidence about the confession to be repeated later in the trial proper. Lord Lane CJ also held that it was impossible to lay down any general rule as to when a question of admissibility should be taken in a summary trial or as to when the magistrates should announce their decision on it, every case being different. This flexible approach was reiterated in *R v Epping and Ongar Justices, ex p Manby*,[160] where the accused contested the admissibility of certain documentary evidence tendered by the prosecution and sought leave to have the question resolved as a preliminary issue. The magistrates refused and admitted the evidence as providing a prima facie case for the accused to deal with later, if he saw fit. The Divisional Court held that the justices had not erred: within statutory constraints, they should determine their own procedure.

Section 78 of the Police and Criminal Evidence Act 1984, whereby a criminal court has a discretion to exclude evidence on which the prosecution proposes to rely on the grounds that it would have an adverse effect on the fairness of the proceedings,[161] is not a statutory constraint for these purposes and accordingly does not entitle an accused to have an issue of admissibility settled as a preliminary issue in a trial within a trial.[162]

In *Halawa v Federation Against Copyright Theft*[163] it was held that the duty of a magistrate, on an application under section 78, is either to deal with it when it arises or to leave the decision until the end of the hearing, the objective being to secure that the trial is fair and just to both sides. Thus, in some cases there will be a trial within a trial in which the accused is given the opportunity to exclude the evidence before he is required to give evidence on the main issues (because, if denied that opportunity, his right to remain silent on the main issues is impaired); but in most cases the better course will be for the whole of the prosecution case to be heard, including the disputed evidence, before any trial within a trial is held (because under section 78 regard should be had to 'all the circumstances', and fairness to the prosecution requires that the whole of its case, in this regard, be before the court). In order to decide, the court may ask the accused the extent of the issues to be addressed by his evidence in the trial within a trial—a trial within a trial might be appropriate if the issues are limited, but not if it is likely to be protracted, raising issues which will have to be re-examined in the trial proper.

In contrast, section 76(2) of the 1984 Act[164] is a statutory constraint and an exception to the generally flexible approach. In *R v Liverpool Juvenile Court, ex p R*[165] the Divisional Court held that if, in a summary trial, the accused, before the close of the

---

[160] [1986] Crim LR 555, DC.        [161] See further below.
[162] *Vel v Owen* [1987] Crim LR 496, DC.        [163] [1995] 1 Cr App R 21, DC.
[164] See above.        [165] [1987] 2 All ER 668, DC.

prosecution case, represents to the court that a confession was or may have been obtained by the methods set out in section 76(2), the magistrates are required to hold a trial within a trial, in which the accused is entitled to give evidence relating to the issue of admissibility, and are also required to make their ruling on admissibility before or at the end of the prosecution case.[166] In such a case, an alternative contention based on section 78 would also be examined at the same trial within a trial, at the same time.[167]

Somewhat surprisingly, given the importance of the matter, there is little authority on the question whether the tribunal of law, whether judge or magistrates, in deciding what evidence is admissible for the purpose of proving or disproving disputed preliminary facts, is bound by the rules of evidence which apply at the trial proper,[168] including those relating to oaths and affirmations.[169] Under the United States Federal Rules[170] the judge is only bound by those rules of evidence which concern privilege.

## 3 THE SUFFICIENCY OF EVIDENCE

The obligation on a party to adduce sufficient evidence on a fact in issue to justify a finding on that fact in his favour, is referred to as 'the evidential burden'.[171] A party discharges an evidential burden borne by him by adducing sufficient evidence for the issue in question to be submitted to the jury (tribunal of fact). Whether there is sufficient evidence is a question of law for the judge. If the party has adduced enough evidence to justify, *as a possibility*, a favourable finding by the jury, the judge leaves it to them to decide whether or not the issue has been proved; if the evidence is insufficient, the judge withdraws the issue from the jury, whatever their view of the matter, directing them either to return a finding on that issue in favour of the other party or, in appropriate circumstances, to return a verdict on the whole case in favour of the other party. For example, in criminal proceedings, the evidential burden in relation to most common law defences is borne by the accused. If the accused, on a charge of murder, fails to adduce sufficient evidence of, say, provocation, the judge will withdraw that issue from the jury, directing them that it must be taken as proved against

---

[166] A trial within a trial will only take place before the close of the prosecution case if a representation is made pursuant to s 76(2). If no such representation is made, the accused may raise the question of the admissibility or weight of the confession at any subsequent stage of the trial. However, at this later stage in the proceedings, although the court retains an inherent jurisdiction to exclude the confession, as well as the power to exclude by virtue of s 78, it is not required to embark on a trial within a trial: see per Russell LJ at 672–3.

[167] *Halawa v Federation Against Copyright Theft* [1995] 1 Cr App R 21, per Ralph Gibson LJ at 33.

[168] In the case of statutory exceptions to the hearsay rule, it has been held that preliminary facts call for proof by admissible evidence: see per Lord Mustill, obiter, in *Neill v North Antrim Magistrates' Court* [1992] 4 All ER 846, HL, at 854, applied in *R v Belmarsh Magistrates' Court, ex p Gilligan* [1998] 1 Cr App R 14, DC and *R v Wood and Fitzsimmons* [1998] Crim LR 213, CA. But cf *R v Foxley* [1995] 2 Cr App R 523, CA. See also *Edwards v Brookes (Milk) Ltd* [1963] 1 WLR 795, QBD.

[169] See *R v Greer* [1998] Crim LR 572, CA, and contrast *R v Jennings* [1995] Crim LR 810, CA.

[170] Rule 104(a). [171] The meaning of this term is considered fully in Ch 4.

the accused.[172] The prosecution normally bears the evidential burden in relation to all those facts essential to the Crown case. If the prosecution fails to adduce sufficient evidence in relation to an essential element of the offence, they not only fail on that issue, but also in the whole case and the judge will direct the jury to acquit.

In criminal cases tried with a jury, the judge has no power to prevent the prosecution from calling evidence and to direct the jury to acquit on the basis that he thinks that a conviction is unlikely, because that would be to trespass on the right of the Crown Prosecution Service to present its case and the right of the jury to form its own view of the evidence and to express it in its verdict.[173] However, after the prosecution has adduced all its evidence and closed its case, the defence may make a submission of no case to answer.[174] If there is no evidence that the alleged crime has been committed by the accused, no evidence of an essential ingredient of that offence or no corroborative evidence where corroboration is required as a matter of law, the submission will be upheld. Likewise, if the judge comes to the conclusion that the Crown's evidence, taken at its highest, is such that a jury properly directed could not properly convict on it, it is his duty to stop the case.[175] However, where the Crown's evidence is such that its strength or weakness depends on the view to be taken of a witness's reliability, or other matters which are, generally speaking, within the jury's province, and where on one view of the facts there is evidence on which a jury could properly conclude that the accused is guilty, the submission will fail; the accused should call his evidence in the usual way and the matter should go before the jury.[176] Cases in which the evidence is purely circumstantial are not in a special category; the judge should not withdraw

---

[172] *Mancini v DPP* [1942] AC 1, HL. But see also *Bullard v R* [1957] AC 635, PC (see Ch 4).

[173] *Attorney-General's Reference (No 2 of 2000)* [2001] 1 Cr App R 503.

[174] The submission should be made in the absence of the jury and, if the trial proceeds thereafter, should not be referred to by the judge in his summing up: see *R v Smith and Doe* (1986) 85 Cr App R 197, CA, and, in the case of visual identification evidence, *R v Akaidere* [1990] Crim LR 808, CA (see Ch 8). See also *Crosdale v R* [1995] 2 All ER 500, PC: if the judge rejects the submission, the jury need know nothing about the decision—no explanation is required; and if the judge rules in favour of the submission on some charges but not on others, all the jury need be told is that the decision was taken for legal reasons—any further explanation will risk potential prejudice.

[175] See, eg, *R v Bland* (1987) 151 JP 857, CA, where the only evidence that the accused had assisted a man in the commission of an offence was that she was living with him at a time when he possessed and dealt in drugs. It was held that knowledge could be inferred from the circumstances, but assistance, though passive, required more than knowledge; there should have been some evidence to prove the further element of encouragement or control. Cf *R v Suurmeijer* [1991] Crim LR 773, CA; *R v McNamara* [1998] Crim LR 278, CA; and *R v Berry* [1998] Crim LR 487, CA.

[176] See generally per Lord Lane CJ in *R v Galbraith* [1981] 1 WLR 1039, CA; cf *R v Beckwith* [1981] Crim LR 646. The Royal Commission on Criminal Justice recommended replacement of the rule in *R v Galbraith* by a new power for the judge to withdraw from the jury an issue or the whole case if he considers the evidence too weak or demonstrably unsafe or unsatisfactory: see para 42, ch 4, *Report of the Royal Commission on Criminal Justice*, Cm 2263 (1993). For the correct approach in cases where the issue is mistaken identity, see *R v Turnbull* [1977] QB 224, CA and *Daley v R* [1993] 4 All ER 86, PC (Ch 8). Where a judge improperly rejects a defence submission of no case to answer, a conviction may be set aside on appeal on the grounds that he made a wrong decision on a question of law. As to the position on appeal in cases where, subsequent to the improper rejection of the submission, evidence was given entitling the jury to convict, see *R v Power* [1919] 1 KB 572; and contrast *R v Abbott* [1955] 2 QB 497 and *R v Juett* [1981] Crim LR 113, CA.

the case from the jury simply because the proved facts do not exclude every reasonable inference besides that of guilt, for that would be to usurp the jury's task.[177]

The judge also has a power to withdraw a case from the jury at any time after the close of the prosecution case, even as late as the end of the defence case, and whether or not a submission of no case to answer has been made at the end of the prosecution case. This is a power to be very sparingly exercised and only if the judge is satisfied that no jury properly directed could safely convict.[178]

In criminal cases tried by magistrates, the position is not entirely clear. The test, contained in a *Practice Direction*, used to be that a submission of no case may be properly made and upheld (1) when there has been no evidence to prove an essential ingredient of the offence alleged[179] or (2) when the evidence adduced by the prosecution has been so discredited as a result of cross-examination or is so manifestly unreliable that no reasonable tribunal could safely convict on it.[180] This *Practice Direction* was revoked[181] but not replaced. There can be no doubt that the first limb of the *Practice Direction* remains good law. As to the second limb, it is submitted that it should continue to apply, on the basis that the magistrates are the tribunal of fact as well as law. Thus although it has been said that questions of credibility, except in the clearest of cases, should not normally be taken into account by justices on a submission of no case,[182] if magistrates conclude that the prosecution evidence has been so discredited or is so manifestly unreliable that they cannot safely convict on it in any event, there can be no point in allowing the case to continue.

In civil cases tried by a judge sitting alone, the rule used to be that a defendant could submit that there was no case to answer at the close of the claimant's case, but in most cases the judge could only rule on the submission if the defendant elected not to call evidence.[183] However, in *Benham Ltd v Kythira Investments Ltd*[184] the Court of Appeal, after reviewing the authorities, held that there were two disadvantages of entertaining a submission of no case to answer. First, it interrupted the trial and required the judge to make up his mind as to the facts on the basis of one side's evidence only, applying the lower test of a prima facie case, with the result that, if he rejected the submission, he had to make up his mind afresh in the light of further evidence and on the application of a different test. Secondly, if the judge acceded to a submission of no case, his judgment might be reversed on appeal, with all the expense

---

[177] *R v Morgan* [1993] Crim LR 870, CA.     [178] *R v Brown* [2002] 1 Cr App R 46, CA.

[179] See, eg, *Chief Constable of Avon and Somerset Constabulary v Jest* [1986] RTR 372, DC: magistrates were entitled to dismiss charges of taking a conveyance without consent and driving whilst uninsured, where the evidence against the accused was his denial of ever having been in the type of car concerned together with evidence that his left thumbprint was found on the rear view mirror of the car in question; proof was needed that the accused had not only been in the car but also that he had taken it for his own use and used it.

[180] *Practice Direction (Submission of No Case)* [1962] 1 WLR 227.

[181] *Practice Direction (Criminal Proceedings: Consolidation)* [2002] 1 WLR 2870.

[182] *R v Barking and Dagenham Justices, ex p DPP* (1995) 159 JP 373, DC, in which it was held that the prosecutor should be given the opportunity to reply to the submission or, where the magistrates are minded to dismiss the case of their own motion, to address the court.

[183] *Alexander v Rayson* [1936] 1 KB 169 at 178, CA.     [184] [2003] EWCA Civ 1794.

and inconvenience of resuming or retrying the action. The court concluded that rarely, if ever, should a judge trying a civil action without a jury entertain a submission of no case, although it conceded that 'conceivably', as Mance LJ had suggested in *Miller v Margaret Cawley*,[185] there may be some flaw of fact or law of such a nature as to make it entirely obvious that the claimant's case must fail, and the determination at that stage may save significant costs. The decision, it is submitted, is unnecessarily inflexible, especially in the light of the wide powers of case management under the Civil Procedure Rules, which should enable a court to consider a submission with or without putting the defendant to his election. In some cases, albeit rare, there will be grounds for contending that the claimant has no reasonable prospect of success whether or not the defendant gives evidence, as when the judge forms the view that the claimant is not a reliable witness of fact and that the position will not change even if the defendant calls evidence.[186]

In civil cases tried with a jury, the judge has a discretion whether to rule on a submission of no case to answer without requiring the defendant to elect to call no evidence[187] and a submission may also be made, after all the evidence has been adduced, that there is insufficient evidence to go before the jury.[188] The test would appear to be the same test as is used in criminal jury trials,[189] namely whether the evidence, taken at its highest, is such that a jury properly directed could not properly reach a necessary factual conclusion.[190]

## 4 THE SUMMING-UP

At a trial on indictment, after the conclusion of all the evidence and closing speeches by counsel, the judge must sum up the case to the jury. In addition to directing them on the substantive law and reminding them of the evidence that has been given, the judge must also explain a number of evidential points.[191] Many directions will reflect or be based upon the specimen directions of the Judicial Studies Board.[192] The judge should begin with a direction as to which party bears the obligation to prove what facts and the standard of proof required to be met before they are entitled to conclude

---

[185] [2002] All ER (D) 452.

[186] See *Mullan v Birmingham City Council* (1999) *The Times*, 29 July QBD.

[187] *Young v Rank* [1950] 2 KB 510.

[188] *Grinsted v Hadrill* [1953] 1 WLR 696, CA. In civil cases, with or without a jury, if the judge rejects a submission of no case to answer, albeit improperly, and the defendant subsequently adduces evidence and is found liable, the Court of Appeal may consider all of the evidence adduced, including that of the defendant: *Payne v Harrison* [1961] 2 QB 403, CA.

[189] See *R v Galbraith* [1981] 1 WLR 1039, CA, above.

[190] See *Alexander v Arts Council of Wales* [2001] 4 All ER 205, CA per May LJ at [37].

[191] It would be helpful if prosecuting counsel made a check list of the directions on the law which they considered the trial judge ought to give and drew the attention of the judge to any failure on his part to give an essential direction before the jury retired: per Watkins LJ in *R v Donoghue* (1987) 86 Cr App R 267, CA.

[192] See <http://www.jsboard.co.uk>.

that those facts have been proved.[193] He should remind the jury of the evidence adduced by the prosecution and defence[194] and refer to any defence which that evidence discloses,[195] even if it has not been relied upon by defence counsel.[196] He should also explain, where necessary, that the onus of disproving certain defences, such as provocation and self-defence, rests on the prosecution. Depending on the nature of the case and the evidence called, it may be necessary: (i) to give a warning on or to explain the requirement for corroboration, indicating the meaning of that word and pointing out the evidence capable in law of amounting to corroboration; (ii) to direct on any relevant presumptions of law, making it clear, where necessary, that if the jury are satisfied that certain matters are proved, they *must* find that other matters are proved; (iii) to warn of the special need for caution, where the case against the accused depends wholly or substantially on the correctness of one or more identifications, before convicting in reliance on the correctness of the identification or identifications; and (iv) to explain that certain items of evidence can only be used for certain restricted purposes, for example that a confession made by an accused implicating both himself and a co-accused is evidence only against the accused and not the co-accused. On all these and other such matters the judge is duty bound to direct the jury.

The judge is entitled to comment on the plausibility and credibility of the witnesses and the weight of the evidence. He may do so in strong or emphatic terms provided that he also makes it clear that, apart from whatever he says about the law, the jury are in no way bound by any view of his own about the evidence which he may have

---

[193] See *R v McVey* [1988] Crim LR 127. See also, as to burden of proof, *R v Donoghue* (1987) 86 Cr App R 267, and as to standard of proof, *R v Edwards* (1983) 77 Cr App R 5 and *R v Bentley (Deceased)* [2001] 1 Cr App R 307, CA. Where the prosecution case depends solely on the identification of a single witness, it is particularly important to give a general clear and simple direction on burden and standard: *R v Lang-Hall* (1989) *The Times*, 24 Mar CA. In cases involving injuries to a very small child, any temptation on the part of the jury to succumb to emotion should be countered by a very clear direction on the burden of proof: *R v Bowditch* [1991] Crim LR 831, CA.

[194] *R v Tillman* [1962] Crim LR 261. See also *R v Gregory* [1993] Crim LR 623, CA, and cf *R v Sargent* [1993] Crim LR 713, CA. It may be that, in a straightforward case, failure to sum up on the facts is not necessarily a fatal defect (*R v Attfield* (1961) 45 Cr App R 309), but in the majority of cases it is clearly desirable that the judge should do so: *R v Brower* [1995] Crim LR 746, CA.

[195] *R v Badjan* (1966) 50 Cr App R 141. The judge is under no duty to build up a defence for an accused who has elected not to testify, but need only remind the jury of any relevant matter contained in pre-trial statements and interviews with the police and the assistance, if any, provided by the Crown's witnesses: *R v Hillier* (1992) 97 Cr App R 349, CA. See also *R v Curtin* [1996] Crim LR 831, CA. If the accused has said nothing in police interviews and adduces no evidence to refute, qualify or explain the case against him, the judge is under no duty to remind the jury of the defence case: *R v Briley* [1991] Crim LR 444, CA.

[196] *R v Porritt* (1961) 45 Cr App R 348. See also *R v Bennett* [1995] Crim LR 877, CA. The duty only arises, however, if there is a reasonable possibility of the jury finding in favour of the defence, and not where the matter is merely fanciful and speculative: *R v Johnson* [1994] Crim LR 376, CA. See also *R v Williams* (1994) 99 Cr App R 163, CA: although in most cases the judge will be guided, in reminding the jury of the facts, by the way the case has been put by the prosecution and defence, if they present the jury with an incomplete picture of the range of options open to them, the judge may be under a duty to direct the jury on a version of the facts advanced by neither side.

appeared to express.[197] The specimen direction of the Judicial Studies Board concerning comments by the judge on the evidence includes the following passage: 'If I mention or emphasize evidence that you regard as unimportant, disregard that evidence. If I do not mention evidence that you regard as important, follow your own view and take that evidence into account.' Such a direction is best given at the start of the summing up, especially if the judge is minded to express strong views on the evidence.[198]

The judge should never give an express indication of his own disbelief in relation to the evidence of a witness, especially the evidence of an accused, even in a case in which the evidence warrants incredulity;[199] and on certain matters, such as the accused's failure to call a particular witness,[200] the judge is restricted in the comments that he may properly make. Although it is clear that if a judge is satisfied that there is no evidence before the jury which could justify them in convicting the accused and that it would be perverse for them to do so, it is his duty to direct them to acquit, there is no converse rule; if he is satisfied on the evidence that the jury would not be justified in acquitting the accused and that it would be perverse of them to do so, he has no power to direct them to convict, because the jury alone have the right to decide that the accused is guilty. In *DPP v Stonehouse*,[201] from which this principle derives, the trial judge had directed the jury that if they were satisfied that the accused had falsely staged his death by drowning, dishonestly intending that claims should be made and money obtained by his wife under policies on his life with insurance companies, that would constitute the offence of attempting to obtain property by deception. This amounted to a withdrawal from the jury of the question of fact of whether the accused's conduct was sufficiently proximate to the complete offence. A majority of the House of Lords held that this was a misdirection, being of the opinion that even where a reasonable jury properly directed on the law must on the facts reach a guilty verdict, the trial judge should still leave issues of fact to the jury. However, since no reasonable jury could have had the slightest doubt that the facts proved did establish the attempt charged, it was further held that no miscarriage of justice could have resulted from the direction. The proviso to section 2(1) of the Criminal Appeal Act 1968 was applied and the conviction affirmed.[202] In *R v Wang*[203] the House of

---

[197] It is undesirable for judges to make comments which place police witnesses in any special category or which may lead a jury to think that there will be adverse consequences for police officers if a verdict of not guilty is returned: *R v Harris* [1986] Crim LR 123, CA. Nor should the prosecution suggest that an acquittal will ruin a prosecution witness: *R v Gale* [1994] Crim LR 208, CA. If the witness refers in his evidence to the consequences of his evidence being disbelieved, the judge should direct the jury that their verdict should not be influenced by such a consideration: *R v Gale*. See also *Mears v R* (1993) 97 Cr App R 239, PC, where the comments were unduly weighted against the accused.

[198] See *R v Everett* [1995] Crim LR 76, CA.

[199] *R v Iroegbu* (1988) *The Times*, 2 Aug CA ('it is obvious to everyone, in this court, is it not, that I think [the accused] is lying . . .'). See also *R v Winn-Pope* [1996] Crim LR 521, CA and *R v Farr* [1999] Crim LR 506, CA.

[200] *R v Gallagher* [1974] 1 WLR 1204, CA.     [201] [1978] AC 55, HL.

[202] See also per Lloyd LJ in *R v Gent* [1990] 1 All ER 364, CA at 367 and cf per May LJ in *R v Thompson* [1984] 3 All ER 565, CA at 571, approved in *R v Gordon* (1987) 92 Cr App R 50n, CA.

[203] [2005] 1 All ER 782, HL.

Lords has confirmed that there are no circumstances in which a judge is entitled to direct a jury to convict and that no distinction is to be drawn between cases in which a burden lies on the defence and those in which the burden lies solely on the Crown, because that distinction is inconsistent with the rationale of the majority in *DPP v Stonehouse*, which is that no matter how inescapable a judge may consider a conclusion to be, in the sense that any other conclusion would be perverse, it remains his duty to leave the decision to the jury and not to dictate what the verdict should be.

Many of the rules governing the way in which a judge should sum up rest on largely uninvestigated assumptions about the way in which jurors analyse and evaluate evidence. Section 8 of the Contempt of Court Act 1981 operates to prevent research involving real juries and therefore research within the jurisdiction has been confined to simulated and shadow juries, who obviously do meet real parties and are not responsible for making real decisions. However, the research, together with research projects undertaken elsewhere with real jurors has shed much light on the extent to which jurors understand, recall and apply directions on such matters as the standard of proof and the use to which character evidence may be put. It also indicates the need for clearer guidance for juries at the start of the trial, for the use of simpler language, and for greater use of written material in what remains a predominantly oral process.[204]

# F  JUDICIAL DISCRETION

If all evidence was either legally admissible or legally inadmissible, the law of evidence would be more certain. The price of such increased certainty, however, would be a rigidity that would do nothing to promote the integrity of the judicial process because it would sometimes occasion injustice by the exclusion of highly relevant evidence or the admission of evidence that would be unduly prejudicial or unfair to one of the parties. This can be avoided if the judge, over and above his general duty to rule on the admissibility of evidence as a matter of law, has a discretionary power to admit legally inadmissible evidence and to exclude legally admissible evidence. The former, inclusionary discretion, is virtually non-existent in English law. The latter, exclusionary discretion may be exercised in civil cases in favour of either party and in criminal cases in favour of the accused. It will be convenient to consider each separately.

## 1  INCLUSIONARY DISCRETION

Despite the absence of express authority on the point, it seems clear that at common law, in both civil and criminal cases, a judge has no discretionary power to admit

---

[204] See W Young *Summing-up to Juries in Criminal Cases—What Jury Research says about Current Rules and Practice* [2003] Crim LR 665, which refers to much of the relevant literature.

legally inadmissible evidence. In *Sparks v R*[205] the accused, a white man aged 27, was convicted of indecently assaulting a girl. At the trial, the judge held that evidence by the girl's mother to the effect that shortly after the assault her daughter had said 'it was a coloured boy' was inadmissible. The child gave no evidence at the trial. The Privy Council held that the evidence had been properly excluded as hearsay evidence which came within no recognized exception to the rule against hearsay in criminal cases.[206] It seems clear that Lord Morris, who delivered the opinion of the Privy Council, was operating on the assumption that where evidence is inadmissible as a matter of law, there is no inclusionary discretion:[207]

It was said that it was manifestly unjust to be left throughout the whole trial with the impression that the child could not give any clue to the identity of her assailant. The cause of justice is, however, best served by adherence to rules which have long been recognized and settled.

## 2 EXCLUSIONARY DISCRETION

### (a) Civil cases

Prior to the introduction of the Civil Procedure Rules, a judge in a civil case had no discretionary power to exclude evidence that would otherwise be admissible as a matter of law. There was an exception, arguably, in the case of information given and received under the seal of confidence. On one view, the judge had a wide discretion to permit a witness, whether or not a party to the proceedings, to refuse to disclose information where disclosure would be a breach of some ethical or social value and non-disclosure would be unlikely to result in serious injustice in the case in which it was claimed.[208] In *D v National Society for the Prevention of Cruelty to Children*[209] Lords Hailsham and Kilbrandon were of the opinion that such a discretionary power did exist, but Lords Simon and Edmund-Davies disagreed. Lord Simon was of the view that although the judge could exercise a considerable 'moral authority' on the course of a trial, by which he could either seek to persuade counsel not to ask the question or gently guide the witness to overcome his reluctance to answer it, when 'it comes to the forensic crunch . . . it must be law not discretion which is in command'.[210]

   CPR rule 32.1(2) has introduced a general exclusionary discretion in civil cases.[211] Rule 32.1 provides as follows:

   (1) The court may control the evidence by giving directions as to—
      (a)  the issues on which it requires evidence;
      (b)  the nature of the evidence which it requires to decide those issues; and
      (c)  the way in which the evidence is to be placed before the court.

---

[205] [1964] AC 964, PC.        [206] The appeal was allowed on different grounds.
[207] [1964] AC 964 at 978. See also per Lord Reid in *Myers v DPP* [1965] AC 1001 at 1024.
[208] 16th Report of the Law Reform Committee, *Privilege in Civil Proceedings* (Cmnd 3472) (1967), para 1.
[209] [1978] AC 171.        [210] [1978] AC 171 at 239.
[211] Including claims allocated to the small claims track: CPR r 27.2(1).

(2) The court may use its power under this rule to exclude evidence that would otherwise be admissible.

(3) The court may limit cross-examination.

When the court decides to exercise its power to exclude evidence under rule 32.1(2), as when exercising any other power given to it by the rules, it must seek to give effect to the 'overriding objective',[212] which is to enable the court 'to deal with cases justly'.[213] Rule 1.1(2) provides as follows:

(2) Dealing with a case justly includes, so far as is practicable—
    (a) ensuring that the parties are on an equal footing;
    (b) saving expense;
    (c) dealing with the case in ways which are proportionate—
        (i)   to the amount of money involved;
        (ii) to the importance of the case;
        (iii) to the complexity of the issues; and
        (iv) to the financial position of each party;
    (d) ensuring that it is dealt with expeditiously and fairly; and
    (e) allotting to it an appropriate share of the court's resources, while taking into account the need to allot resources to other cases.

Rule 32.1(1) invests the court with extraordinarily wide powers, whereby it can override the views of the parties as to which issues call for evidence, the nature of the evidence appropriate to decide the issues, and the way in which the evidence should be given, eg in documentary form rather than orally.

Rule 32.1(2) also confers extremely wide powers: subject to rule 1.1, there are no express limitations as to the extent of the power or the manner of its exercise.[214] However, as we have seen, civil courts already have the common law power to exclude evidence of marginal relevance,[215] and although in theory rule 32.1(2) allows the court to exclude evidence even if plainly relevant, it has been said that the more relevant the evidence is, the more reluctant the court is likely to be to exercise its discretion to exclude and that the power to exclude under rule 32.1(2) should be exercised with great circumspection.[216] Nonetheless rule 32.1(2) can be used to exclude peripheral material which is not essential to the just determination of the real issues between the parties[217] and, in appropriate circumstances, evidence that has been obtained illegally or improperly.[218] It can also be used, it is submitted, to restrict the number of witnesses and exclude superfluous evidence.

At common law the judge has a discretion to prevent any questions in cross-examination which in his opinion are unnecessary, improper or oppressive. Cross-examination, it has been held, should be conducted with restraint and a

---

[212] CPR r 1.2.     [213] CPR r 1.1(1).

[214] *Grobbelaar v Sun Newspapers Ltd* (1999) *The Times*, 12 Aug 1999.

[215] See above, under **C Relevance**.

[216] *Great Future International Ltd v Sealand Housing Corporation* (2002) LTL 25 July.

[217] See *McPhilemy v Times Newspapers Ltd* [1999] 3 All ER 775, CA.

[218] See Ch 3 under **B Discretion, Civil cases**.

measure of courtesy and consideration to the witness.[219] Rule 32.1(3) supplements the common law powers of the judge and may be used to impose limits on the time permitted for cross-examination.[220] It may also be used to limit cross-examination about a witness's previous convictions. Thus although a witness may be asked about his convictions even where the offence is not one of dishonesty, in order to attack his credit,[221] rule 32.1(3) gives the judge a discretion as to which previous convictions can be put. However, where sitting with a jury, he should be more hesitant to exercise the discretion because it is for the jury to decide what weight to give to such matters in relation to a witness's credibility.[222]

Because circumstances vary infinitely, it is submitted that it would be undesirable for the courts to go beyond the wording of rule 1.1(2) with a view to providing additional guidance as to the way in which the discretion under rule 32.1(2) and (3) should be exercised. It is further submitted that exercise of the discretionary powers should only be impugned on appeal if perverse in the *Wednesbury* sense,[223] ie where the court makes a decision which no reasonable tribunal could have reached.

## (b) Criminal cases

That a judge in a criminal trial has a discretion to exclude legally admissible evidence tendered by the prosecution has been accepted for some time[224] and was confirmed by the House of Lords in *R v Sang*.[225] The House was of the unanimous albeit obiter view[226] that the judge, as a part of his inherent power and overriding duty in every case to ensure that the accused receives a fair trial, always has a discretion to refuse to admit legally admissible evidence if, in his opinion, its prejudicial effect on the minds of the jury outweighs its true probative value.[227] Exercise of the discretion is a subjective matter,[228] each case turning on its own facts and circumstances.[229] The judge must balance on the one hand the prejudicial effect of the evidence against the accused on the minds of the jury and on the other its weight and value having regard to the purpose for which it is adduced. Where the former is out of all proportion to the latter, the judge should exclude it. In one sense, of course, all relevant evidence adduced by

---

[219] See *Mechanical and General Inventions Co Ltd v Austin* [1935] AC 346 at 360 and generally Ch 7 under A3 **The permitted form of questioning in cross-examination.**

[220] *Rall v Hume* [2001] 3 All ER 248.

[221] See Ch 7 under **A3 The permitted form of questioning in cross-examination.**

[222] *Watson v Chief Constable of Cleveland Police* [2001] All ER (D) 193 (Oct), [2001] EWCA Civ 1547.

[223] *Associated Provincial Picture Houses Ltd v Wednesbury Corpn* [1948] 1 KB 223, CA.

[224] See, eg, *R v Christie* [1914] AC 545, HL.          [225] [1980] AC 402.

[226] A view affirmed by Lord Roskill in *Morris v Beardmore* [1981] AC 446, HL at 469.

[227] This 'fair trial' discretion may be exercised not only in the case of evidence the prejudicial effect of which outweighs its probative value, but also in the case of evidence obtained from the accused, after the commission of the offence charged, by improper or unfair means: see per Lords Diplock, Fraser, and Scarman at 436, 450, and 456 respectively. See Ch 3.

[228] Per Lord Fraser at 450.

[229] Per Lord Scarman at 456. See also per Lord Guest in *Selvey v DPP* [1970] AC 304 at 352: 'If it is suggested that the exercise of this discretion may be whimsical and depend on the individual idiosyncrasies of the judge, this is inevitable where it is a question of discretion.'

the prosecution is prejudicial to the accused and the greater its probative value, the greater its prejudicial effect. In some cases, however, there will be a serious risk that the jury will attach undue weight to an item of evidence which is, in reality, of dubious reliability or of no more than trifling or minimal probative value, and in these circumstances the judge should exclude. In the words of Roskill J in *R v List*:[230]

A trial judge always has an overriding duty in every case to secure a fair trial, and if in any particular case he comes to the conclusion that, even though certain evidence is strictly admissible, yet its prejudicial effect once admitted is such as to make it virtually impossible for a dispassionate view of the crucial facts of the case to be thereafter taken by the jury, then the trial judge, in my judgment, should exclude that evidence.

The case law on the basis of which the House of Lords in *R v Sang* came to its conclusion shows the discretion operating in a number of different sets of circumstances in relation to particular kinds of evidence. Their Lordships, however, were of the firm view that the cases were no more than examples of the exercise of a single discretion of general application and not of several specific or limited discretions.[231] Moreover, it was recognized that the existing cases were not the only ones in which the discretion could be exercised. Lord Salmon said:[232]

I recognize that there may have been no categories of cases, other than those to which I have referred, in which technically admissible evidence proffered by the Crown has been rejected by the court on the ground that it would make the trial unfair. I cannot, however, accept that a judge's undoubted duty to ensure that the accused has a fair trial is confined to such cases. In my opinion the category of such cases is not and never can be closed except by statute.

There has been much scope for exercise of the discretion in relation to otherwise admissible evidence of the accused's bad character. For example, where the accused became liable to cross-examination about his previous convictions and bad character under section 1(3)(ii) of the Criminal Evidence Act 1898, ie where the nature or conduct of the defence was such as to involve imputations on the character of the prosecutor or witnesses for the prosecution (see now section 101(1)(g) of the Criminal Justice Act 2003), the judge could exercise his discretion to disallow it.

He may feel that even though the position is established in law, still the putting of such questions as to the character of the accused person may be fraught with results which immeasurably outweigh the result of questions put by the defence and which make a fair trial of the accused person almost impossible. On the other hand, in the ordinary and normal case he may feel that if the credit of the prosecutor or his witnesses has been attacked, it is only fair that the jury should have before them material on which they can form their judgment whether the accused person is any more worthy to be believed than those he has attacked.[233]

---

230 [1966] 1 WLR 9 at 12.    231 Per Lords Scarman and Fraser at 452 and 447 respectively.
232 At 445. See also per Lord Dilhorne at 438.
233 Per Singleton J in *R v Jenkins* (1945) 31 Cr App Rep 1 at 15, approved in *Selvey v DPP* [1970] AC 304, HL, where it was held that there is no general rule that the discretion should be exercised in favour of the

A judge can also exercise his discretion to exclude evidence otherwise admissible under section 27(3) of the Theft Act 1968. Under that subsection, where a person is charged with handling stolen goods and evidence is given of his possession of the goods, evidence that he has within the five years preceding the date of the offence charged been convicted of theft or handling stolen goods is admissible to prove that he knew or believed the goods to be stolen. The trial judge has a discretion to disallow the admission of such evidence, albeit strictly admissible, if, on the facts of the particular case, there is a risk of injustice. This may occur, for example, where possession is in issue in the case and it will be difficult, therefore, for the jury to appreciate that the evidence is relevant not to that issue but only to the issue of guilty knowledge.[234]

The discretion can also be used to exclude an out-of-court accusation directed at the accused which is admissible in evidence against him because by his conduct or demeanour it is possible to infer that he accepted, in whole or in part, the truth of the accusation made. Again, in these circumstances, the judge may exercise his discretion to exclude where the prejudicial effect of the evidence in the minds of the jury is out of all proportion to its true evidential value.[235]

Having considered some specific examples, it remains to note two matters of general importance relating to the exercise of the discretion now under discussion. First, the discretion may only be exercised to exclude evidence on which the prosecution, as opposed to any co-accused, proposes to rely. There is no discretion to exclude, at the request of one co-accused, evidence tendered by another. This principle, and the description of it appearing in the third edition of this work, were approved by the Privy Council in *Lobban v R*.[236] In that case L and R were charged with three murders. R, under caution, made a 'mixed' statement, ie a statement which contained admissions as well as an exculpatory explanation. An integral part of the exculpatory explanation implicated L by name. The prosecution tendered R's statement for the truth of its contents against R—it was no evidence against L. Counsel for L submitted that the trial judge should have exercised his discretion to edit R's statement so as to exclude the parts which implicated L on the basis that the prejudice to L by allowing the whole statement to be admitted outweighed the relevance of the disputed material to the defence of R. The Privy Council held that no such discretion existed—counsel's submission, if accepted, would result in a serious derogation of an accused's liberty to defend himself by such legitimate means as he thinks it wise to employ. It was held that the discretionary power applies only to evidence on which the prosecution proposes to rely. Although R's statement was *tendered* by the prosecution, the disputed material supported R's defence and the prosecution were not entitled to rely on it as evidence against L. Thus, although a trial judge has a discretion to exclude or edit

---

accused where the imputations on the character of the witnesses for the prosecution are a necessary part of the accused's defence.

[234] *R v List* [1966] 1 WLR 9, Assizes, a decision under s 43(1) of the Larceny Act 1916, which was repealed by the Theft Act 1968 but re-enacted, with some modification, in s 27(3). The decision was approved in *R v Herron* [1967] 1 QB 107, CCA. See further Ch 17.

[235] See per Lord Moulton in *R v Christie* [1914] AC 545, HL at 559.     [236] [1995] 2 All ER 602, PC.

evidence tendered by the prosecution which is wholly inculpatory and probative of the case against one co-accused on the ground that it is unduly prejudicial against another co-accused, there is no discretion to exclude the exculpatory part of a 'mixed' statement on which one co-accused wishes to rely on the grounds that it implicates another. One remedy to the latter situation is to order separate trials, but if that is not done then the interests of the implicated co-accused must be protected by the most explicit direction by the judge to the effect that the statement of the one co-accused is not evidence against the other.[237]

The second matter to note is that because exercise of the discretion is, as we have seen, a subjective matter, each case turning on its own peculiar facts, it is difficult to appeal successfully against a judge's decision not to exclude. Thus although an appellate court will interfere with exercise of the discretion if there is no material on which the trial judge could properly have arrived at his decision, or where he has erred in principle,[238] it is not enough that the appellate court thinks that it would have exercised the discretion differently. However, the appellate courts have from time to time set out guidelines for exercise of the discretion in relation to various types of evidence.[239] This assists judges. It also assists defence counsel in advising and deciding tactics, to predict whether the discretion will be exercised.

The discretionary common law power to exclude evidence on the basis that its prejudicial effect outweighs its probative value has now been supplemented by section 78(1) of the Police and Criminal Evidence Act 1984, which provides that:

the court may refuse to allow evidence on which the prosecution proposes to rely to be given if it appears to the court that, having regard to all the circumstances, including the circumstances in which the evidence was obtained, the admission of the evidence would have such an adverse effect on the fairness of the proceedings that the court ought not to admit it.[240]

Section 78(1) is generally regarded as conferring a discretionary power, although strictly speaking it does not involve an exercise of discretion because if a court decides that admission of the evidence in question would have such an adverse effect on the fairness of the proceedings that it ought not to admit it, it cannot logically exercise a discretion to admit it, despite the permissive opening words of the subsection ('may refuse').[241]

---

[237] But see also *R v Thompson* [1995] 2 Cr App R 589, CA: without a discretion to exclude evidence which is relevant and therefore admissible in relation to an accused but inadmissible and prejudicial in relation to a co-accused, the only safeguard is the cumbersome device of separate trials. The court observed that this seemed undesirable and that it might be preferable to allow a discretion where the prejudice is substantial and the evidence is of only limited benefit to the accused.

[238] See per Viscount Dilhorne in *Selvey v DPP* [1970] AC 304, HL at 342 and per Lord Lane CJ in *R v Powell* [1986] 1 All ER 193, CA at 197.

[239] See, eg, per Lawton LJ in *R v Britzman; R v Hall* [1983] 1 All ER 369, CA at 373–4.

[240] Section 78(1) is of general application. Statute may also empower a criminal court to exclude, in the exercise of its discretion, specific varieties of otherwise admissible evidence. See, in the case of hearsay, s 126, Criminal Justice Act 2003, Ch 10.

[241] See per Auld LJ in *R v Chalkley and Jeffries* [1998] 2 All ER 155, CA at 178.

A simple example of the application of section 78(1) is *R v O'Connor*.[242] B and C were jointly charged in one count with having conspired to obtain property by deception. B pleaded guilty and C not guilty. The evidence of B's conviction was then admitted at the trial of C under section 74 of the Police and Criminal Evidence Act 1984 to prove that B had committed the offence charged.[243] The Court of Appeal held that the conviction should have been excluded under section 78 because evidence of B's admission of the offence charged might have led the jury to infer that C in his turn must have conspired with B.[244]

Section 78(1) operates without prejudice to the discretionary common law power to exclude. Section 82(3) of the 1984 Act provides that 'Nothing in this Part of this Act shall prejudice any power of a court to exclude evidence (whether from preventing questions from being put or otherwise) at its discretion'. The terms of section 78(1) are clearly wide enough to apply to items of prosecution evidence already subject to the common law discretion[245]—and the weighing of probative value against prejudicial effect can be an important factor in exercising the discretion under section 78(1)[246]—but section 78(1) is not confined to such cases.

Section 78(1) directs the court, when considering exercise of the discretion, to have regard to all the circumstances, 'including the circumstances in which the evidence was obtained'. Thus, although it is clear that section 78(1) can be applied by a court in the absence of any illegality or impropriety,[247] the chief importance of the subsection lies in its potential for the exclusion of evidence illegally or improperly obtained. That topic is considered in Chapter 3.

# G  PROOF OF BIRTH, DEATH, AGE, CONVICTIONS AND ACQUITTALS

## 1  BIRTH AND DEATH

The normal and easiest way of proving a person's birth or death is by (a) producing to the court a certified copy of an entry in the register of births (deaths),[248] which is

---

[242] (1986) 85 Cr App R 298, CA. See also *R v Curry* [1988] Crim LR 527, CA; *R v Kempster* (1989) 90 Cr App R 14, CA; and *R v Mattison* [1990] Crim LR 117, CA (see Ch 21).

[243] See Ch 21.

[244] Cf *R v Lunnon* [1988] Crim LR 456, CA, and see also *R v Robertson; R v Golder* [1987] 3 All ER 231, CA (see Ch 21).

[245] See *Matto v Crown Court at Wolverhampton* [1987] RTR 337, DC, per Woolf LJ at 346: '[s 78] certainly does not reduce the discretion of the court to exclude unfair evidence which existed at common law. Indeed, in my view in any case where the evidence could properly be excluded at common law, it can certainly be excluded under s 78.'

[246] Per Lord Lane CJ in *R v Quinn* [1990] Crim LR 581, CA.

[247] *R v Samuel* [1988] QB 615, CA; *R v O'Leary* (1988) 87 Cr App R 387, CA at 391; *R v Brine* [1992] Crim LR 122, CA.

[248] See s 34 of the Births and Deaths Registration Act 1953.

admissible under an exception to the hearsay rule[249] and admissible, therefore, as evidence of the truth of its contents; *and* (b) adducing some evidence to identify the person whose birth (death) is in question with the person named in the birth (death) certificate.[250] Proof of birth or death may also be effected by the testimony of someone present at the time of birth (death), by hearsay statements admissible under either the Civil Evidence Act 1995 or the Criminal Justice Act 2003[251] or, in proceedings in which a question of pedigree is directly in issue, by a declaration as to pedigree made by a deceased blood relation or spouse of a blood relation.[252] A person's death may also be proved in reliance on the presumption of death, which is considered in Chapter 22, or by the testimony of someone who saw the corpse and was capable of identifying it as that of the person whose death is in question.

## 2  AGE

The date of a person's birth being contained in his or her birth certificate, the normal way of proving a person's age is by (a) producing to the court a certified copy of an entry in the register of births, which, as we have seen, is admissible as evidence of the truth of its contents; *and* (b) adducing some evidence identifying the person whose age is in question with the person named in the birth certificate. A person's age may also be proved by the testimony of someone present at the time of his or her birth, by inference from his or her appearance,[253] by hearsay statements admissible by statute and by declarations as to pedigree.

## 3  CONVICTIONS AND ACQUITTALS

Section 73 of the Police and Criminal Evidence Act 1984, which superseded a variety of outdated statutory provisions, is a modernized provision for the proof of convictions and acquittals by means of a certificate signed by an appropriate court officer together with evidence identifying the person whose conviction (acquittal) is in question with the person named in the certificate. It provides as follows:

> (1)  Where in any proceedings[254] the fact that a person has in the United Kingdom been convicted or acquitted of an offence otherwise than by a Service court is admissible in evidence, it may be proved by producing a certificate of conviction or, as the case may be, of acquittal relating to that offence, and proving that the person named in the

---

[249] See generally Chs 10–12.

[250] See also s 1 of the Evidence (Foreign, Dominion and Colonial Documents) Act 1933 whereby an Order in Council may be made providing for the proof by authorized copy of extracts from properly kept public registers kept under the authority of the law of the country in question and recognized by the courts of that country as authentic records. Concerning births (deaths) on board ship, see the Merchant Shipping (Returns of Births and Deaths) Regulations, 1979, made under s 75 of the Merchant Shipping Act 1970.

[251] See Chs 10 and 11.        [252] See Ch 12.

[253] See, eg, s 99 of the Children and Young Persons Act 1933 and s 80(3) of the Criminal Justice Act 1948.

[254] 'Proceedings' means criminal proceedings including proceedings before a court-martial or Courts-Martial Appeal Court.

certificate as having been convicted or acquitted of the offence is the person whose conviction or acquittal of the offence is to be proved.

(2) For the purposes of this section a certificate of conviction or of acquittal—

    (a) shall, as regards a conviction or acquittal on indictment, consist of a certificate, signed by the proper officer of the court where the conviction or acquittal took place, giving the substance and effect (omitting the formal parts) of the indictment and of the conviction or acquittal; and

    (b) shall, as regards a conviction or acquittal on a summary trial, consist of a copy of the conviction or of the dismissal of the information, signed by the proper officer of the court where the conviction or acquittal took place or by the proper officer of the court, if any, to which a memorandum of the conviction or acquittal was sent;

and a document purporting to be a duly signed certificate of conviction or acquittal under this section shall be taken to be such a certificate unless the contrary is proved.

(3) In subsection (2) above 'proper officer' means—

    (a) in relation to a magistrates' court in England and Wales, the designated officer for the court; and

    (b) in relation to any other court, the clerk of the court, his deputy or any other person having custody of the court record.

The section contains a saving for 'any other authorised manner of proving a conviction or acquittal'.[255] This could be proof by the testimony of someone present in court at the relevant time, by a formal admission under section 10 of the Criminal Justice Act 1967[256] or by means of fingerprints, including palm-prints, under section 39 of the Criminal Justice Act 1948.[257]

For the purposes of extradition proceedings, proof of the fact of a conviction overseas may be effected by the production of a properly certified copy of the court record.[258]

---

[255] Section 73(4).    [256] See Ch 22.

[257] Section 39 provides for proof of a conviction in criminal proceedings by a certificate signed by or on behalf of the Commissioner of Police of the Metropolis, containing particulars of the conviction taken from criminal records kept by him, together with certificates showing that the fingerprints of the person convicted and those of the person against whom it is sought to prove the conviction are the fingerprints of one and the same person. See also s 14 of the Perjury Act 1911 (proof by certificate of a former trial on indictment at which the perjury was allegedly committed) and ss 31(1) and 44(1) of the Road Traffic Offenders Act 1988 (endorsements on a driving licence of the particulars of a conviction or disqualification may be produced as prima facie evidence of the matters endorsed).

[258] See Extradition Act 1989, Sch 1, para 12 and *Re Mullin* [1993] Crim LR 390, DC.

# 3

# EVIDENCE OBTAINED BY ILLEGAL OR UNFAIR MEANS

This chapter concerns the circumstances in which relevant evidence can be excluded, as a matter of law or discretion, on the grounds that it was obtained illegally, improperly or unfairly. It also considers a related matter, the circumstances in which criminal proceedings should be stayed as an abuse of the court's process on the grounds of entrapment.

Evidence may be obtained illegally, for example by a crime, tort, or breach of contract or in contravention of statutory or other provisions governing the powers and duties of the police or others involved in investigating crime. Evidence may also be obtained improperly or unfairly, for example by trickery, deception, bribes, threats, or inducements. At one extreme, the view could be taken that evidence which is relevant and otherwise admissible should not be excluded because of the means by which it was obtained, whether illegal, improper, or unfair; to exclude it would, in some cases, result in injustice including the acquittal of the guilty. On this view, all evidence which is necessary to enable justice to be done would be admitted; and those responsible for the illegality or impropriety could be variously prosecuted (in the case of crime), sued (in the case of actionable wrongs) or disciplined (in the case of conduct amounting to breach of some statutory, professional, or other code of conduct). The view at the other extreme would be that illegally or improperly obtained evidence should always be excluded; to admit it might encourage the obtaining of evidence by such means. On this view, all such evidence would be excluded, even if this would sometimes result in injustice, including the guilty going free, in order that those responsible for the illegality or impropriety are in future compelled to respect, and deterred from invading, the civil liberties of the citizen.

The modern law of evidence in this country represents a compromise between these two extreme views. Thus although, generally speaking, it reflects the first view in relation to admissibility *as a matter of law*, it also empowers the trial judge to exclude *as a matter of discretion*. However, the rationale of discretionary exclusion has yet to be fully articulated or developed. Thus although in criminal cases it has been held that the discretion is not to be exercised in order to discipline the police, the fact that the police acted *mala fide* can be taken into account, presumably because part of the rationale for exclusion, albeit rarely expressed, is promotion of the integrity of the criminal process. Equally, there is no doubt that in many cases the discretion has been exercised in order to protect the important rights of the suspect and exclude evidence which, if admitted, would result in unfairness in the proceedings, as when the police fail to make a contemporaneous note of an interview, thereby depriving the court of evidence of what was said or of what induced the accused to confess.[1] However, it is not altogether clear what rights will rank as 'important' for these purposes. Nor is it clear what factors should be taken into account when, despite obvious illegality or impropriety, whether deliberate or innocent, it has had no effect on the quality or reliability of the evidence which it is sought to exclude.[2]

# A   LAW

Subject to exceptions, the rules of English *law* make no provision for the exclusion of relevant evidence on the grounds that it was obtained illegally or improperly. One exception concerns privileged documents. Although there is a general rule allowing secondary evidence of privileged documents to be adduced, even though obtained illegally or improperly,[3] where one party to litigation obtains by a trick documents belonging to the other party and brought into court by him, he will not be permitted to adduce copies of those documents because, it has been held, the public interest in the ascertainment of truth in litigation is outweighed by the public interest that litigants should be able to bring their documents into court without fear that they may be filched by their opponents.[4] A second exception relates to confessions in criminal proceedings.[5] If it is represented to the court that a confession made by the accused was or may have been obtained by oppression or in consequence of anything said or done which was likely, in the circumstances, to render unreliable any confession which might be made by the accused in consequence thereof, the confession shall

---

[1]  See per Lord Lane CJ in *R v Delaney* (1988) 88 Cr App R 338 at 341–2, CA.

[2]  For an interesting analysis of the question whether to admit illegally obtained evidence and the short-comings of the exclusionary principle, see AAS Zuckerman *The Principles of Criminal Evidence* (Oxford 1989) ch 16. See also P Mirfield *Silence, Confessions and Improperly Obtained Evidence* (Oxford 1997).

[3]  In *Lloyd v Mostyn* (1842) 10 M&W 478, Parke B said: 'Where an attorney intrusted confidentially with a document communicates the contents, or suffers another to take a copy, surely the secondary evidence so obtained may be produced. Suppose the instrument were even stolen, and a correct copy taken, would it not be reasonable to admit it?' This dictum was applied by Lindley MR in *Calcraft v Guest* [1898] 1 QB 759 at 764, CA. Note, however, that where a party has not yet used the material as secondary evidence, the mere fact that he intends to do so is no answer to a claim against him, by the person in whom the privilege is vested, for delivery up of the copies or to restrain him from disclosure or use of any information contained therein: see per May LJ in *Goddard v Nationwide Building Society* [1987] QB 670, CA.

[4]  *ITC Film Distributors v Video Exchange Ltd* [1982] Ch 431. Warner J also held that to obtain documents in such circumstances was probably a contempt of court which the court should not countenance by admit-ting the documents in evidence. Cf *R v Tompkins* (1977) 67 Cr App R 181, CA, where there was no impropriety, and see generally Ch 20.

[5]  See Ch 13.

be excluded unless the prosecution proves to the court that the confession was not obtained by such means.[6]

Subject to the exceptions, the law is accurately represented by the following words of Crompton J in *R v Leatham*:[7] 'It matters not how you get it; if you steal it even, it would be admissible in evidence.' Thus evidence remains admissible in law if obtained by the use of *agent provocateurs*,[8] or by invasion of privacy,[9] or by the unlawful search of persons or premises.

In *Jones v Owens*[10] a constable, in unlawfully searching the accused, found a number of young salmon. The evidence was admitted on a subsequent charge of unlawful fishing on the grounds that to exclude evidence obtained by illegal means 'would be a dangerous obstacle to the administration of justice'. In *Kuruma, Son of Kaniu v R*[11] the accused was charged with the unlawful possession of ammunition which had been found in his pocket by officers who were of insufficiently senior rank to have carried out the search. Evidence of the search was admitted and the accused was convicted. His appeal to the Privy Council was dismissed. Lord Goddard CJ, of the opinion that where evidence is relevant and admissible the court is not concerned with how it was obtained, said: 'While this proposition may not have been stated in so many words in any English case, there are decisions which support it, and in their Lordships' opinion it is plainly right in principle.' The proposition was readily accepted by the Divisional Court in *Jeffrey v Black*.[12] The accused, who was charged with unlawful possession of cannabis, was originally arrested for stealing a sandwich. Police officers, without the accused's consent and without a search warrant, then searched his home and found the cannabis which formed the subject matter of the charge. The magistrates excluded evidence of the finding of the cannabis on the grounds that it had been obtained as a result of an illegal search and dismissed the charge. Allowing an appeal by way of case stated, Lord Widgery CJ said:[13]

I have not the least doubt that an irregularity in obtaining evidence does not render the evidence inadmissible. Whether or not the evidence is admissible depends on whether or not it is relevant to the issues in respect of which it is called.

---

[6] Police and Criminal Evidence Act 1984, s 76(2). See also s 17 of the Regulation of Investigatory Powers Act 2000, which appears to contain a third exception. Section 17, like its statutory precursor s 9 of the Interception of Communications Act 1985, renders inadmissible evidence which tends to suggest the commission of an offence of intentional interception, at any place in the United Kingdom, of any communication in the course of its transmission by means of a public postal service or by means of a public telecommunication system. A detailed consideration of the 2000 Act is beyond the scope of this work.

[7] (1861) 8 Cox CC 498 at 501.        [8] *R v Sang* [1980] AC 402, HL.

[9] *R v Khan (Sultan)* [1997] AC 558, HL.        [10] (1870) 34 JP 759.        [11] [1955] AC 197, PC.

[12] [1978] QB 490.        [13] [1978] QB 490 at 497.

# B  DISCRETION

## 1  CIVIL CASES

Prior to the introduction of the Civil Procedure Rules, such authority as there was suggested that in civil proceedings there was no discretion to exclude evidence obtained illegally or improperly. In *Helliwell v Piggott-Sims*[14] Lord Denning MR, assuming certain evidence to have been obtained unlawfully, said:

so far as civil cases are concerned, it seems to me that the judge has no discretion. The evidence is relevant and admissible. The judge cannot refuse it on the ground that it may have been unlawfully obtained . . .

As we have seen, under CPR rule 32.1(2) the court may now exclude evidence that would otherwise be admissible, and in deciding whether to do so must seek to give effect to the overriding objective of enabling the court to deal with cases justly.[15] It is submitted that, in appropriate circumstances, therefore, the court may exercise the discretionary power to exclude evidence which, although relevant, has been obtained illegally or improperly. In *Jones v University of Warwick*,[16] a claim for damages for personal injuries, the defendant was allowed to introduce a video of the claimant obtained by trespass and in breach of Article 8 of the European Convention on Human Rights (the right of respect for private and family life). Inquiry agents acting for the defendant's insurers had gained access to the claimant's home by deception and had filmed her without her knowledge. It was held that the court should consider two conflicting public interests, on the one hand the achieving of justice in the particular case and on the other, considering the effect of its decision upon litigation generally, the risk that if the improper conduct goes uncensored, improper practices of the type in question will be encouraged. The weight to be attached to each public interest will vary according to the circumstances. The significance of the evidence will differ as will the gravity of the breach of Article 8, and the decision will depend on all the circumstances. In the case before it, the Court of Appeal held that the conduct of the insurers was not so outrageous that the defence should be struck out and that it would be artificial and undesirable to exclude the evidence, which would involve the instruction of fresh medical experts from whom relevant evidence would have to be concealed. However, it was also held that the conduct of the insurers was improper and unjustified and that the trial judge should take it into account when deciding the appropriate order for costs.[17]

---

[14] [1980] FSR 582.      [15] See Ch 2 under **F2 Exclusionary discretion.**
[16] [2003] 3 All ER 760, CA.
[17] See also *Niemietz v Germany* (1992) 16 EHRR 97 and *Halford v UK* (1997) 24 EHRR 523.

## 2 CRIMINAL CASES

### (a) The background

That a judge, in criminal proceedings, has a discretionary power to exclude otherwise admissible evidence on the grounds that it was obtained improperly or unfairly was, until recently, only clearly established in relation to evidence of admissions and confessions. The power to exclude, as a matter of discretion, an otherwise admissible admission or confession is a large and complex topic which is considered separately in Chapter 13. Admissions and confessions apart, there was also an unbroken series of dicta from a variety of impressive sources to suggest that in criminal proceedings the trial judge also has a general discretion to exclude evidence tendered by the prosecution which has been obtained oppressively, improperly or unfairly[18] or as a result of the activities of an *agent provocateur*.[19] However, despite these weighty dicta, this discretion was rarely exercised. A very rare reported example is *R v Payne*[20] where the accused, charged with drunken driving, agreed to a medical examination to see if he was suffering from any illness or disability on the understanding that the doctor would not examine him to assess his fitness to drive. At the trial the doctor gave evidence of the accused's unfitness to drive and the Court of Criminal Appeal quashed the conviction on the grounds that the trial judge should have exercised his discretion to exclude the doctor's evidence. In *R v Sang*[21] Lords Diplock, Fraser, and Scarman regarded the decision as based on the maxim *nemo tenetur se ipsum prodere* ('no man is to be compelled to incriminate himself') and analogous, therefore, to cases in which an accused is unfairly induced to confess to, or make a damaging admission in respect of, an offence.[22]

In *R v Sang* the House of Lords held that the judicial discretion to exclude admissible evidence does not extend to excluding evidence of a crime on the grounds that it was instigated by an *agent provocateur*, because if it did it would amount to a procedural device whereby the judge could avoid the substantive law under which it is

---

[18] See per Lord Goddard CJ in *Kuruma, Son of Kaniu v R* [1955] AC 197, PC at 203–4 (evidence obtained 'by a trick'); per Lord Parker CJ in *Callis v Gunn* [1964] 1 QB 495, DC at 505 (evidence obtained 'oppressively, by false representations, by a trick, by threats, by bribes, anything of that sort'); and per Lord Widgery CJ in *Jeffrey v Black* [1978] QB 490, DC at 497–8 (exceptional cases where 'not only have the police officers entered without authority, but they have been guilty of trickery, or they have misled someone, or they have been oppressive, or they have been unfair, or in other respects they have behaved in a manner which is morally reprehensible'). See also per Lord Hodson in *King v R* [1969] 1 AC 304, PC at 319.

[19] See per Lord McDermott CJ in *R v Murphy* [1965] NI 138, C-MAC, a case decided before the rejection of entrapment as a defence. See also *R v Foulder, Foulkes and Johns* [1973] Crim LR 45; *R v Burnett and Lee* [1973] Crim LR 748; and *R v Ameer and Lucas* [1977] Crim LR 104, CA.

[20] [1963] 1 WLR 637.     [21] [1980] AC 402.

[22] At 435, 449 and 455 respectively. Cf *R v McDonald* [1991] Crim LR 122, CA, a decision under s 78 of the Police and Criminal Evidence Act 1984: it is not unfair for a psychiatrist to give evidence of an admission made by the accused on a non-medical issue in the course of a psychiatric examination. *R v McDonald* was followed in *R v Gayle* [1994] Crim LR 679, CA and, in the case of confessions to probation officers, *R v Elleray* [2003] 2 Cr App R 165, CA.

clearly established that there is no defence of entrapment.[23] The primary importance of *R v Sang*, however, is the obiter answer given to the certified point of law of general importance, namely 'Does a trial judge have a discretion to refuse to allow evidence, being evidence other than evidence of an admission, to be given in any circumstances in which such evidence is relevant and of more than minimal probative value?' On that wider issue, the House was of the unanimous opinion that: (i) a trial judge always has a discretion to exclude prosecution evidence where its prejudicial effect outweighs its probative value;[24] but (ii) since the court is not concerned with how evidence sought to be adduced by the prosecution has been obtained, but with how it is used by the prosecution at the trial, a judge has no discretion to refuse to admit admissible evidence on the grounds that it was obtained by improper or unfair means except in the case of admissions, confessions and evidence obtained from the accused after the commission of the offence. Although, as noted above, the judgment in this respect was obiter, Lord Roskill declared later that it would be a retrograde step to enlarge the narrow limits of, or to engraft an exception on, the discretion to exclude as defined in *R v Sang*.[25] Unfortunately, however, the scope of the discretion defined, despite their Lordships' apparent unanimity, is far from clear, particularly insofar as it extends to 'evidence obtained from the accused after the commission of the offence'. For Lord Diplock, that phrase seems to refer to evidence tantamount to a self-incriminating admission obtained from the accused by means which would justify a judge in excluding an actual confession which had the like self-incriminating effect[26] and there is no discretion to exclude evidence discovered as the result of an illegal search.[27] For Lord Salmon, the decision whether to exclude being dependent upon the 'infinitely variable' facts and circumstances of each particular case, the category of cases in which evidence could be rejected on the grounds that it would make a trial unfair was not closed and never could be closed except by statute.[28] Lord Fraser appears to have understood the phrase as referring to evidence and documents obtained from an accused or from premises occupied by him, but also said that their Lordships' decision would leave judges with a discretion to be exercised in accordance with their individual views of what is unfair, oppressive or morally reprehensible.[29] For Lord Scarman, it referred exclusively to the obtaining of evidence from the *accused*.[30]

The subsequent case law has done little to clarify the meaning of the phrase 'evidence obtained from the accused after the commission of the offence' but has put a major gloss on *R v Sang* to the effect that the discretion should not be exercised if those who

---

[23] See *R v McEvilly*; *R v Lee* (1973) 60 Cr App R 150, CA; *R v Mealey*; *R v Sheridan* (1974) 60 Cr App Rep 59, CA. As to the discretion to exclude, however, see now *R v Looseley* [2001] 1 WLR 2060, considered under s 78 of the Police and Criminal Evidence Act 1984, below.

[24] See Ch 2 under **F Judicial discretion**.          [25] *Morris v Beardmore* [1981] AC 446, HL at 469.

[26] See also *R v Payne* [1963] 1 WLR 637, CCA, above.

[27] [1980] AC 402 at 436. See also *R v Adams* [1980] QB 575, CA, below.

[28] [1980] AC 402 at 445. See also per Lord Fraser at 450.          [29] [1980] AC 402 at 450.

[30] ibid at 456.

obtained such evidence unlawfully did so on the basis of a bona fide mistake as to their powers. In *R v Trump*[31] the Court of Appeal, while acknowledging that the phrase was not fully considered by the House, treated it as referring to cases analogous to improperly obtained admissions. The accused was convicted of driving while unfit through drink. Following an unlawful arrest, a specimen of blood was obtained without the accused's consent within the meaning of section 7 of the Road Traffic Act 1972. It was held that although the giving of blood by the accused was very close to an oral admission by him that he had drunk to excess, and was therefore subject to the discretion, the judge would have erred if he had excluded the evidence because, although the sample was given as a result of a threat, the police officer in question was acting in good faith and the evidence could not undermine the fairness of the trial. On a similar charge in *Fox v Chief Constable of Gwent*[32] the House of Lords held that evidence of a breath specimen obtained by officers acting in good faith and in accordance with the statutory procedure was not inadmissible merely because the accused had been unlawfully arrested. Lord Fraser said:[33]

Of course, if the appellant had been lured to the police station by some trick or deception, or if the police officers had behaved oppressively towards the appellant, the justices' jurisdiction to exclude otherwise admissible evidence recognized in *R v Sang* might have come into play. But there is nothing of that sort suggested here. The police officers did no more than make a bona fide mistake as to their powers.[34]

In *R v Khan (Sultan)*[35] it was held that evidence of an incriminating conversation obtained by means of a secret electronic surveillance device did not fall within the category of admissions, confessions and other evidence obtained from the accused after the commission of the offence, on the basis that the accused had not been 'induced' to make the recorded admissions.

In *R v Apicella*[36] the accused was convicted on three counts of rape. Each of the victims had contracted an unusual strain of gonorrhoea. The accused, whilst held on remand, was suspected by the prison doctor to be suffering from gonorrhoea. The doctor, for solely therapeutic reasons, called in a consultant who took a sample of body fluid in order to enable diagnosis. The consultant assumed that the accused was consenting. In fact, he submitted because he had been told by a prison officer that he had no choice. The sample showed that the accused was suffering from the same strain of gonorrhoea as the victims, and the prosecution called evidence to that effect. The Court of Appeal flatly rejected a submission that the evidence was the physical equivalent of an oral confession.[37] It was held that use of the

---

[31] (1979) 70 Cr App R 300, CA at 302.   [32] [1985] 3 All ER 392, HL.   [33] Ibid at 397.
[34] Applied in *Gull v Scarborough* [1987] RTR 261n. See also *DPP v Wilson* [1991] RTR 284.
[35] [1997] AC 558, HL.   [36] (1985) 82 Cr App R 295, CA.
[37] No reference was made to *R v Trump* (1979) 70 Cr App R 300, above.

evidence was not unfair and the judge correct in the exercise of his discretion not to exclude it.[38]

## (b) Section 78 of the Police and Criminal Evidence Act 1984

Section 78 of the Police and Criminal Evidence Act 1984 provides as follows:

(1) In any proceedings the court may refuse to allow evidence on which the prosecution proposes to rely to be given if it appears to the court that, having regard to all the circumstances, including the circumstances in which the evidence was obtained, the admission of the evidence would have such an adverse effect on the fairness of the proceedings that the court ought not to admit it.

(2) Nothing in this section shall prejudice any rule of law requiring a court to exclude evidence.

The effect of section 78(2) is that if an item of evidence is inadmissible by virtue of any of the exclusionary rules of evidence, it *must* be excluded. As to the discretionary power to exclude under section 78(1), the question of exclusion may be raised by any accused against whom the evidence is to be used. Section 78(1) confers a power in terms wide enough for its exercise on the court's own motion.[39] However, if the accused is represented by an apparently competent advocate, who does not raise the issue, perhaps for tactical reasons, the judge is under no duty to exercise the discretion of his own motion, even in the case of a flagrant abuse of police power, although he may make a pertinent enquiry of the advocate in the jury's absence.[40] Section 78(1) refers to evidence on which the prosecution *proposes* to rely. Thus, in *R v Harwood*[41] it was doubted whether section 78(1) empowers a judge to exclude evidence, after it has been adduced, in the absence of any submission to exclude before it was adduced. At trials on indictment, if there is a dispute as to the circumstances in which the evidence was obtained, it would seem to be necessary to hold a trial within a trial.[42] Thus if the accused disputes that he was cautioned, it is the duty of the judge to hold a *voir dire* and make a finding on the issue.[43] However, concerning the admissibility of identification evidence, it has been held that although there may be rare occasions when it will be desirable to hold a *voir dire*, in general the judge should decide on the basis of the depositions, statements and submissions of counsel.[44] It is not clear under section

---

[38] See also *R v Adams* [1980] QB 575, CA, where it was held that a judge should not exercise the discretion to exclude as evidence articles obtained by means of an unlawful entry, search and seizure: 'There is no material suggesting that the error of the police as to the continuing validity of the warrant . . . was oppressive in the sense that the adjective is used in *R v Sang*.' According to Lord Diplock in *R v Sang*, evidence discovered as the result of an illegal search is not even subject to the discretion to exclude.

[39] *Re Saifi* [2001] 4 All ER 168, DC at [52].          [40] *R v Raphaie* [1996] Crim LR 812, CA.

[41] [1989] Crim LR 285, CA.

[42] Concerning proceedings before magistrates, see Ch 2 under E **The functions of the judge and jury.**

[43] *R v Manji* [1990] Crim LR 512, CA.

[44] *R v Beveridge* [1987] Crim LR 401, CA (identification parade evidence); and *R v Martin and Nicholls* [1994] Crim LR 218, CA (evidence of informal identification). Cf *R v Flemming* (1987) 86 Cr App R 32, CA. Concerning confessions, see also *R v Keenan* [1989] 3 All ER 598, CA (Ch 13).

78(1) where the burden of proof lies.[45] If there is a dispute as to the circumstances in which the evidence was obtained, in principle, it is submitted, there should be an evidential burden on the accused, ie an obligation to adduce sufficient evidence of the relevant facts to justify a finding on those facts in his favour, on the discharge of which there should be a legal burden on the prosecution to disprove those facts beyond reasonable doubt.[46] However, it was said in *Re Saifi*,[47] albeit in the context of extradition proceedings, that the words of section 78 provide no support for such a contention, and that the absence from section 78 of words suggesting that facts are to be established or proved to any particular standard is deliberate, leaving the matter open and untrammeled by rigid evidential considerations.

Concerning the scope of section 78(1), it applies to *any* evidence on which the prosecution proposes to rely, whether tendered by the prosecution or (presumably) a co-accused. Thus it may be used to attempt to exclude, inter alia, the following types of otherwise admissible evidence: evidence of the accused's previous convictions or bad character; hearsay evidence, including depositions and documentary records[48] and admissions and confessions;[49] evidence of opinion, including identification evidence;[50] and evidence of an intoximeter reading.[51] Insofar as the subsection may be used to exclude evidence obtained by improper or unfair means, it is *not* confined, as is the common law power described in *R v Sang*, to admissions, confessions and evidence obtained from the accused after the commission of the offence—it extends to any evidence on which the prosecution proposes to rely, whenever it was obtained and whether it was obtained from the accused, his premises or any other source.[52]

In deciding whether or not to exercise the discretion, section 78(1) directs the court to have regard to all the circumstances, including those in which the evidence was obtained. In particular, the court may be invited to take into account any illegality, impropriety or unfairness by means of which the evidence was obtained, including conduct in breach of the European Convention on Human Rights, or any abuse by the police of their powers under the Police and Criminal Evidence Act 1984, and the Codes of Practice issued pursuant to that Act relating to stop and search (Code A), the search of premises and the seizure of property (Code B), detention, treatment and questioning (Code C), identification (Code D), and tape recording of interviews (Code E).[53] When considering breaches of an earlier Code, the provisions of the

---

[45] Acknowledged, *per curiam*, in *R v Anderson* [1993] Crim LR 447, CA.   [46] See generally Ch 4.

[47] [2001] 4 All ER 168, DC at [50]–[61].   [48] *R v O'Loughlin* [1988] 3 All ER 431, CCC.

[49] *R v Mason* [1987] 3 All ER 481, CA.

[50] *R v Nagah* (1990) 92 Cr App R 344, CA. See also *R v Deenik* [1992] Crim LR 578, CA (voice identification).

[51] *McGrath v Field* [1987] RTR 349, DC.

[52] Contrast, *sed quaere*, the dictum of Watkins LJ in *R v Mason* [1987] 3 All ER 481 at 484: 's 78 . . . does no more than restate the power which judges had at common law before the 1984 Act was passed.'

[53] Even where the evidence in question was obtained by someone other than a police officer (or a person charged with the duty of investigating offences or charging offenders—see s 67(9) of the 1984 Act, Ch 13), the principles underlying Code C may be of assistance in considering the discretion to exclude under s 78(1): *R v Smith* (1994) 99 Cr App R 233, CA. The Cleveland guidelines, contained in the report of Butler-Sloss LJ on

current version may well be relevant to the question of unfairness under section 78, because they reflect current thinking as to what is fair.[54] The discretion can only be exercised, however, if in all the circumstances admission of the evidence would have an adverse effect on the fairness of the 'proceedings'. The first use of the word 'proceedings' in section 78(1) suggests that it means 'court proceedings'. Section 78(3), since repealed, which referred to 'proceedings *before* a magistrates' court' supports such an interpretation. However, it is possible that use of the phrase 'fairness of the proceedings' was designed to encompass not just fairness at the trial, which of course in some cases will be affected by abuse of pre-trial process, but also the fairness of the investigative process itself.

Trial judges, as we have seen, already have a duty to ensure that the accused receives a fair trial, in the exercise of which they may exclude any evidence the prejudicial effect of which outweighs its probative value. Section 78(1), however, goes beyond this. Thus although the fact that evidence was obtained improperly or unfairly will not by itself automatically have such an adverse effect on the fairness of the proceedings that the court should not admit it, it is implicit in the wording of the sub-section that the circumstances in which the evidence was obtained *may* have such an adverse effect.[55]

In *R v Quinn*[56] Lord Lane CJ said:

The function of the judge is therefore *to protect the fairness of the proceedings*, and normally proceedings are fair if a jury hears *all* relevant evidence which either side wishes to place before it, but proceedings may become unfair if, for example, one side is allowed to adduce relevant evidence which, for one reason or another, the other side cannot properly challenge or meet, or where there has been an abuse of process, eg because evidence has been obtained in deliberate breach of procedures laid down in an official code of practice.

It is, of course, impossible to catalogue, precisely or at all, the kinds of impropriety which will be treated as having an adverse effect on the fairness of the proceedings. A breach of the 1984 Act or of the Codes does not mean that any statement made by an accused after such breach will necessarily be excluded—every case has to be determined on its own particular facts.[57] Equally, the fact that evidence has been obtained by conduct which may be typified as 'oppressive' will not automatically result in

the Inquiry into Child Abuse in Cleveland, set out what is considered to be the best practice when children are interviewed in connection with sexual abuse. Unlike the Codes of Practice, the guidelines are not given any effect by statute. However, they should be regarded as expert advice as to what will normally be the best practice to adopt in seeking to ensure that a child's evidence is reliable. If they are not observed, there are grounds for a judge or jury to consider with particular care whether the child is reliable. Much the same, it is submitted, can be said of *Achieving Best Evidence in Criminal Proceedings: Guidance for Vulnerable or Intimidated Witnesses, Including Children* ('*The Memorandum*'), published by the Home Office: see, *R v Dunphy* (1993) 98 Cr App R 393, CA, a decision on the precursor to the current Memorandum. See also C Keenan et al '*Interviewing Allegedly Abused Children*' [1999] Crim LR 863.

54  *R v Ward* (1993) 98 Cr App R 337, CA at 340.
55  Per Woolf LJ in *Matto v Crown Court at Wolverhampton* [1987] RTR 337.
56  [1990] Crim LR 581, CA.
57  Per Lord Lane CJ in *R v Parris* (1988) 89 Cr App R 68, CA at 72. See also per Hodgson J in *R v Keenan* [1990] 2 QB 54 at 69.

exclusion, because oppressive conduct, depending on its degree and actual or possible effect, may or may not affect the fairness of admitting particular evidence.[58]

A judge's exercise of his discretion under the subsection can be impugned if it is perverse according to *Wednesbury* principles,[59] ie a decision to which no reasonable trial judge could have come, in which case the Court of Appeal will exercise its own discretion.[60] The Court of Appeal will also interfere if the trial judge exercised his discretion on a wrong basis, eg by adverting to an out-of-date version of a relevant Code of Practice.[61] Circumstances vary infinitely, and for this reason it has been said that it is undesirable to attempt any general guidance on the way in which the discretion should be exercised,[62] but some such guidance is available from the reported decisions.

They show, with a reasonable degree of clarity, that the purpose of section 78(1) is not disciplinary, but protective, and that although deliberate or wilful misconduct on the part of the police may render exclusion more likely, the determinative factor is the extent to which the suspect has been denied the right of a fair trial by reason of breaches of the provisions governing procedural fairness from the time of being stopped or questioned through to the time of trial.

## (c) The disciplinary principle

The *effect* of excluding relevant evidence which has been obtained improperly or unfairly may be to discourage the police from obtaining evidence in such a way, but a decision to exclude under section 78(1) should not be taken *in order to* discipline or punish the police.[63] The Court of Appeal may well deplore police ignorance of the provisions of the Codes[64] and lament deliberate, cynical and flagrant breaches of such provisions,[65] but as Lord Lane CJ said in *R v Delaney*:[66] 'It is no part of the duty of the court to rule a statement inadmissible simply in order to punish the police for failure to observe the Codes of Practice.' Similarly, in *R v Chalkley and Jeffries*,[67] in which it was held that a determination under section 78 is distinct from the exercise of discretion in determining to stay criminal proceedings as an abuse of process (which, according to the circumstances, may involve balancing the countervailing interests of prosecuting a criminal and discouraging abuse of power), Auld LJ stressed that the critical test under section 78 is whether any impropriety affects the fairness of the proceedings: the court cannot exclude evidence under section 78 simply as a mark of

[58]  *R v Chalkley and Jeffries* [1998] 2 All ER 155, CA at 177–8.

[59]  *Associated Provincial Picture Houses Ltd v Wednesbury Corpn* [1948] 1 KB 223.

[60]  *R v O'Leary* (1988) 87 Cr App R 387 at 391, CA; *R v Christou* [1992] QB 979, CA; *R v Dures* [1997] 2 Cr App R 247, CA; and *R v Khan* [1997] Crim LR 508, CA. See also Tucker J, *per curiam*, in *R v Grannell* (1989) 90 Cr App R 149, CA: the citation of decisions of judges or recorders of the Crown Court, not being High Court judges, is of no assistance to the Court of Appeal in deciding whether a judge has exercised his discretion properly.

[61]  See *R v Miller* [1998] Crim LR 209, CA.          [62]  Per Hodgson J in *R v Samuel* [1988] QB 615, CA.

[63]  See per Watkins LJ in *R v Mason* [1987] 3 All ER 481 at 484, CA.

[64]  See per Hodgson J in *R v Keenan* [1989] 3 All ER 598 at 601, CA.

[65]  See per Lord Lane CJ in *R v Canale* [1990] 2 All ER 187, CA at 190 and 192.

[66]  (1988) 88 Cr App R 338 at 341, CA.          [67]  [1998] 2 All ER 155, CA.

its disapproval of the way in which it was obtained.[68] This view, it is submitted, clearly accords with the wording of section 78. Nonetheless in some of the authorities great stress has been placed on whether the police acted *mala fide*, *deliberately* flouting the law or *wilfully* abusing their powers, and evidence of such conduct has been allowed to tip the scales in favour of the accused. In some cases this can be justified on the basis that although the impropriety does not affect the reliability of the evidence, it does involve the breach of important rights. An example is *Matto v Crown Court at Wolverhampton*.[69] In that case the accused was convicted of driving with excess alcohol. Police officers, when requesting a specimen of breath on the accused's property, had realized that they were acting illegally. The specimen was positive. The accused was arrested and later provided another positive specimen of breath at the police station. Allowing the appeal, it was held that the officers, having acted *mala fide* and oppressively, the circumstances were such that if the Crown Court had directed itself properly it could have exercised its discretion to exclude the evidence under section 78. In other cases it is possible to justify the reliance upon deliberate misconduct on the basis that it is that misconduct itself which has rendered the evidence unreliable. For example, in *R v Mason*[70] where a confession had been made after the police had practised a deceit on the accused and his solicitor by alleging that they had fingerprint evidence which they did not in fact have, it was held that the trial judge should have excluded the confession under section 78.[71]

### (d)  The protective principle

*(i)  General.* The governing principle is protective, ie to protect the suspect from serious breaches of the important provisions set out in the 1984 Act, the Codes and elsewhere, governing procedural fairness on arrest, search, detention etc. It is clear that the discretion may be exercised on this basis whether the breaches in question were wilful or merely ignorant. Thus in *R v Alladice*,[72] a case of improper denial of the right of access to a solicitor under section 58 of the 1984 Act, it was held that if the police had acted in bad faith, the court would have had little difficulty in ruling any confession inadmissible, but that if they had acted in good faith, it was still necessary to decide whether admission of the evidence would adversely affect the fairness of the proceedings to such an extent that the confession should be excluded. Similarly, in *R v Walsh*[73] Saville J, referring to breaches of section 58 or the provisions of the Code, said:

---

[68] [1998] 2 All ER 155 at 178–80.          [69] [1987] RTR 337.

[70] [1987] 3 All ER 481, CA (see Ch 13).

[71] See also *R v Alladice* (1988) 87 Cr App R 380, CA, and *R v Canale* [1990] Crim LR 329, CA, below; and cf *R v Christou* [1992] QB 979, CA.

[72] (1988) 87 Cr App R 380, CA.

[73] (1989) 91 Cr App R 161 at 163, CA. See also *R v Quinn* [1990] Crim LR 581, CA, below, *DPP v McGladrigan* [1991] Crim LR 851, DC, *R v Samms* [1991] Crim LR 197 and *R v Brine* [1992] Crim LR 122, CA.

although bad faith may make substantial or significant that which might not otherwise be so, the contrary does not follow. Breaches which are themselves significant and substantial are not rendered otherwise by the good faith of the officers concerned.

This does not mean, however, that in every case of a significant or substantial breach the evidence in question will be excluded—the task of the court is not merely to consider whether there will be an adverse effect on the fairness of the proceedings, but such an adverse effect that justice requires the evidence to be excluded.[74] This is the most likely explanation for the *obiter dicta* in *R v Cooke*,[75] a rape case, that where a sample of hair is not taken in accordance with the relevant statutory provisions but obtained by an assault, and is then used to prepare a DNA profile implicating the accused, the evidence will be admitted on the basis that the means used to obtain the evidence have done nothing to cast doubt on its reliability and strength. This approach has been buttressed by the obiter comments of Lord Hutton in *Attorney-General's Reference (No 3 of 1999)*,[76] another rape case in which there was no question as to the reliability of the DNA evidence the admissibility of which was in dispute. Lord Hutton was of the view that in a case of the kind in question, involving the commission of a very grave crime, in exercise of the section 78 discretion the interests of the victim and the public must be considered, as well as the interests of the accused.

The reasoning in *R v Cooke* and *Attorney-General's Reference (No 3 of 1999)*, it is submitted, is preferable to the approach taken in *R v Nathaniel*.[77] In that case a DNA profile taken from the appellant's blood in relation to charges of raping A and B, of which he was acquitted, was not destroyed in accordance with section 64 of the 1984 Act, but formed the main prosecution evidence on a charge of raping C. It was held that the evidence should have been excluded. The accused was misled, in consenting to give the blood sample, by statements and promises which were not honoured. He was told that it was required for the purposes of the case involving A and B; that it would be destroyed if he was prosecuted in relation to A and B and acquitted; and that if he refused without good cause to give the sample, the jury, in any proceedings against him for the rape of A and B, could draw inferences from his refusal.[78]

The reasoning in *R v Cooke* also serves to explain the admission in evidence of the fruits of an improper search, as in *R v Stewart*,[79] where, following an entry involving a number of breaches of Code B, the accused was found in possession of apparatus to divert the gas and electricity supplies so as to bypass the meters. The outcome was the same in *R v Sanghera*[80] where, a search having been conducted in breach of the Code without written consent, there was no issue as to the reliability of the evidence as to what had been discovered. However, it should be otherwise if the means used to obtain the evidence could have affected its quality, for example a case in which the

---

[74] *R v Walsh* (1989) 91 Cr App R 161 at 163, CA and *R v Ryan* [1992] Crim LR 187, CA.
[75] [1995] 1 Cr App R 318, CA.    [76] [2001] 1 All ER 577, HL at 590.
[77] [1995] 2 Cr App R 565, CA.    [78] See now s 64(3B) of the 1984 Act.
[79] [1995] Crim LR 500, CA. See also *R v McCarthy* [1996] Crim LR 818, CA.
[80] [2001] 1 Cr App R 299, CA.

accused, following a search of his premises during which he was improperly kept out of the way, claims that the property found was 'planted'.[81] Equally, although officers are entitled to delay taking a suspect to a police station in order that a search may be conducted with his assistance, if they abuse that entitlement to ask questions, beyond those necessary to the search, on matters which properly ought to be asked under the rules of Code C applying at a police station, the answers may be excluded on the grounds of unfairness.[82]

It is clear that the outcome depends upon the precise facts. In *R v Pall*[83] it was said that the absence of a caution was bound to be significant in most circumstances, and in *R v Nelson and Rose*[84] it was held that a failure to caution should have led to the exclusion of the whole of an interview. However, in *R v Hoyte*[85] a confession was admitted, despite a failure to caution, on the basis that the police had acted in good faith and in the particular circumstances there could have been no unfairness. Similarly in *R v Gill*[86] it was held that lies told during an Inland Revenue investigation of tax fraud were admissible, despite a failure to caution. Clarke LJ said that the principal purpose of the caution was to ensure, so far as possible, that interviewees do not make admissions unless they wish to do so and are aware of the consequences, and not to prevent interviewees from telling lies. Although lies may be excluded where there has been a failure to caution, each case depends on its own facts. On the facts, the Revenue had not acted in bad faith and the appellants were aware that criminal proceedings were in prospect and must have known that they were not obliged to answer the questions.[87] In *R v Aspinal*[88] the accused, a schizophrenic, was interviewed, about 13 hours after his arrest, without an 'appropriate adult', in breach of what is now paragraph 11.15 of Code C, and without a solicitor. It was held that an accused of this kind may not be able to judge for himself what is in his best interests, which may put him at a considerable disadvantage, not least because the record of the interview may not seem unreliable to a jury. However, in appropriate circumstances the confession of a mentally disordered accused may be properly admitted notwithstanding that it was made in breach of paragraph 11.15.[89]

Another good example, in this regard, relates to the right to legal advice in section 58 of the 1984 Act, which has been judicially described as 'one of the most important

---

[81] But see *R v Wright* [1994] Crim LR 55, CA, where evidence of a search was admitted notwithstanding that a record of it had not been made in W's custody record (contrary to s 18(8) of the 1984 Act) and there were said to have been breaches of Code B in that no communication was made with W, he was not present at the search and no proper list had been made of the property. Noting that there had been no deliberate breach of the Code, it was held that the judge had taken into account the breach of s 18(8) and the other matters could not have placed W at any disadvantage. See also *R v Khan* [1997] Crim LR 508, CA.

[82] *R v Khan* [1993] Crim LR 54, CA, applied in *R v Raphaie* [1996] Crim LR 812, CA.

[83] (1991) 156 JP 424, CA.     [84] [1998] 2 Cr App R 399, CA.     [85] [1994] Crim LR 215, CA.

[86] [2004] 1 WLR 49, CA.

[87] See also *R v Senior* [2004] 3 All ER 9, CA: questioning by customs officers to establish ownership of a suspicious baggage, prior to administering a caution, will not necessarily require the evidence to be excluded.

[88] [1999] Crim LR 741, CA.     [89] See *R v Law-Thompson* [1997] Crim LR 674, CA

and fundamental rights of a citizen'.[90] It has been held that significant and substantial breaches of that section (or the provisions of Code C) will, prima facie, have an adverse effect on the fairness of the proceedings.[91] Breach of the section, however, is no guarantee of the exclusion of any statement made thereafter. In *R v Alladice*, for example, it was held that if the trial judge had considered section 78, he would not have been obliged to exclude the confession, because the circumstances showed that the accused was well able to cope with the interviews, understood the cautions that he had been given, at times exercising his right to silence, and was aware of his rights, so that, had the solicitor been present, his advice would have added nothing to the knowledge of his rights which the accused already had.[92] In *R v Parris*,[93] on the other hand, another case involving breach of section 58, it was held that evidence of a confession should have been excluded because, had a solicitor been present, the accused would probably have accepted his advice to remain silent. Furthermore, the solicitor could have given evidence on whether the police had fabricated the confession; alternatively, his presence would have discouraged any such fabrication.[94]

In *R v Konscol*[95] the trial judge admitted evidence of an interview with K, containing lies, conducted by a Belgian customs officer. There was no dispute that K had said what was recorded, and that the interview was conducted fairly according to Belgian law, but K was neither cautioned nor advised that he could have a lawyer present. The Court of Appeal dismissed the appeal and declined to lay down guidelines as to when a court should admit a statement made overseas according to rules which did not coincide with the provisions of the Police and Criminal Evidence Act 1984.[96]

In *R v Keenan*[97] records of an interview with the accused were compiled in plain breach of Code C: the record was not made during the course of the interview; the reason for not completing it at that time was not recorded in the officer's pocket book; and the accused was not given the opportunity to read it and to sign it as correct or to indicate the respects in which he considered it inaccurate. The accused's defence, unknown to the trial judge at the time when the submission on admissibility was made, was that the interview had been fabricated. The judge, ruling that any unfairness

---

[90] Per Hodgson J in *R v Samuel* [1988] 2 All ER 135, CA. See also *Brennan v UK* [2002] Crim LR 217, ECHR: the right to consult with a lawyer *in private* is part of the basic requirements of a fair trial and follows from Art 6(3)(c) of the European Convention on Human Rights.

[91] Per Saville J in *R v Walsh* (1989) 91 Cr App R 161 at 163, CA. However, in the case of drink-driving offences the public interest requires that the obtaining of specimens should not be delayed to any significant extent to enable a suspect to take legal advice: *Kennedy v DPP* [2003] Crim LR 120, DC. See also *Campbell v DPP* [2003] Crim LR 118, DC, *Kirkup v DPP* [2004] Crim LR 230, DC and *Whitley v DPP* [2003] All ER (D) 212, [2003] EWHC 2512 (Admin). Similarly, in the case of juveniles, there is no reason to delay the obtaining of specimens in order for an 'appropriate adult' to be present: *DPP v Evans* [2003] Crim LR 338, DC.

[92] See also, to similar effect, *R v Dunford* (1990) 91 Cr App R 150, CA.

[93] (1988) 89 Cr App R 68, CA. See also *R v Walsh* (1989) 91 Cr App R 161.

[94] This argument could have been, but was not, employed in *R v Alladice* (1988) 87 Cr App R 380, CA, where fabrication was also alleged.

[95] [1993] Crim LR 950.

[96] See also *R v Quinn* [1990] Crim LR 581, CA and *R v McNab* [2002] Crim LR 129, CA.

[97] [1989] 3 All ER 598, CA.

to the accused could be cured by the accused going into the witness box and giving his version of the interview, admitted the evidence. On appeal, it was held that the relevant provisions of Code C are designed to make it difficult for detained persons to make unfounded allegations against the police which might otherwise appear credible and to provide safeguards against the police inaccurately recording or inventing the words used in questioning a detained person. Where there have been significant and substantial breaches of the 'verballing' provisions, evidence so obtained should be excluded, because if the other evidence in the case is strong, then it may make no difference to the eventual result if the evidence in question is excluded, and if the other evidence is weak or non-existent, that is just the situation where the protection of the rules is most needed. It was wrong to assume that any unfairness could be cured by the accused going into the witness box: if he intended not to testify if the evidence was excluded, then its admission unfairly robbed him of his right to remain silent; if the defence case was to be (as it turned out to be) that the evidence was concocted, then its admission forced the accused to give evidence and also, by attacking the police, to put his character in issue; and if the defence was to be that the interview was inaccurately recorded, it placed the accused at a substantial disadvantage because he had been given no contemporaneous opportunity to correct any inaccuracies. For these reasons, the conviction was quashed.

In *R v Canale*[98] the way in which records of two interviews with the accused were obtained involved breaches very similar to those which occurred in *R v Keenan*. In this case, however, at two subsequent and contemporaneously recorded interviews, the accused repeated admissions allegedly made in the first two interviews. On the *voir dire* and in evidence the accused admitted that he had made the admissions but said that they were untrue and that the police had induced him to make them by a trick. The Court of Appeal held that by reason of the flagrant and cynical breaches of the Code, the judge was deprived of the very evidence which would have enabled him to reach a more certain conclusion on the question of admissibility and, had he ruled in favour of admission, the jury would have been deprived of the evidence necessary to decide the truth of the accused's denial of the offence. The initial breaches affected the whole series of alleged admissions, all of which should have been excluded.[99]

Many of the reported decisions have involved breaches of Code D (identification). Under paragraph 3.12 of Code D, whenever (i) a witness has identified or purported to identify a suspect or (ii) there is a witness available who expresses an ability to identify the suspect, or there is a reasonable chance of the witness being able to do so, and the suspect disputes the identification, an identification procedure shall be held, ie a video identification, an identification parade or a group identification. The exception is where an identification procedure is not practicable or it would serve no

---

[98] [1990] 2 All ER 187, CA.

[99] See also *R v Absolam* (1988) 88 Cr App R 332, CA, and *R v Sparks* [1991] Crim LR 128, CA; and cf *R v Langiert* [1991] Crim LR 777, CA (failure to record the reason for not making a contemporaneous record), and *R v Rajakuruna* [1991] Crim LR 458, CA (failure to inform a person not under arrest that he is not obliged to remain with the officer).

useful purpose, for example when it is not disputed that the suspect is already well known to the witness.[100] Breach of paragraph 3.12 will not necessarily result in the exclusion of the other evidence of identification, of which there may be an abundance.[101] The critical issue is the impact of the breach on the fairness of the trial.[102] Thus in *R v Samms*,[103] where it was not shown that it was impracticable to hold a parade (or group identification),[104] it was held that it would be unfair to admit the evidence of identification of the suspect by confrontation because the confrontation that occurred partook of the dangers sought to be prevented by a parade (or group identification).[105] It will also be unfair to make use of identification evidence obtained by a video identification procedure which used images of persons bearing an insufficient resemblance to the accused.[106] On the other hand, in *R v Grannell*[107] it was held that no unfairness arose from the failure, in breach of what is now para 3.17 of the Code, to explain to the suspect prior to an identification procedure, such matters as the purpose of the identification and the procedures for holding it; and in *R v Ryan*[108] it was held that a clear breach of what is now para 3.11 of the Code—an officer involved with the investigation of the case took part in the identification procedures—had caused no prejudice to the accused.

Where a breach of Code D has been established but the judge has rejected an application to exclude the evidence in question, he should explain to the jury that there has been a breach and how it has arisen and invite them to consider the possible effects of the breach. For example, in the case of an improper failure to hold an identification parade, the jury should ordinarily be told that a parade enables a suspect to put the reliability of the identification to the test, that he has lost the benefit of that safeguard and that they should take account of that fact in their assessment of the

---

[100] For the issues that arise where a suspect admits his presence at the scene of the offence, but denies committing the offence, see Andy Roberts 'Questions of "Who was there?" and "Who did what?": The Application of Code D in Cases of Dispute as to Participation but not Presence' [2003] Crim LR 709.

[101] See *R v McEvoy* [1997] Crim LR 887, CA, a decision under an earlier version of para 3.12.

[102] This remains the case where the identification is not strictly governed by Code D at all (see *R v Hickin* [1996] Crim LR 584, CA) or where the evidence of identification has come into existence abroad as a result of arrangements made by a foreign police force (see *R v Quinn* [1990] Crim LR 581, CA).

[103] [1991] Crim LR 197, CC.

[104] See also *R v Johnson* [1996] Crim LR 504, CA (confrontation by video).

[105] See now para 3.23, Code D. See also *R v Martin and Nicholls* [1994] Crim LR 218, CA (evidence of informal identification by young witnesses a very long time after the offence and in unsatisfactory conditions outside the court while the accused and witnesses were awaiting allocation of the case to a court). Cf *R v Tiplady* [1995] Crim LR 651, CA (a group identification in the foyer of a magistrates' court where T had been bailed to attend). It was held that the venue was not inappropriate and *Martin and Nicholls* was distinguished on the basis that whereas in that case there were striking limitations on the choice open to the identifying witnesses (the accused wore 'funky dreads') in *Tiplady* at any one time between 20 and 30 people had been present, most of them in T's age group. Cf also *R v Quinn* [1990] Crim LR 581, CA: evidence of an informal identification as a result of a chance meeting would be admissible. See also *R v Oscar* [1991] Crim LR 778, CA, and *R v Rogers* [1993] Crim LR 386, CA.

[106] See *R v Marcus* [2005] Crim LR 384, CA.    [107] (1989) 90 Cr App R 149, CA.

[108] [1992] Crim LR 187, CA. See also *R v Jones (Terence)* [1992] Crim LR 365, CA, and *R v Khan* [1997] Crim LR 584, CA; and cf *R v Gall* (1989) 90 Cr App R 64, CA, and *R v Finley* [1993] Crim LR 50, CA.

whole case, giving it such weight as they think fair. However failure to direct the jury about a breach of Code D will not necessarily infringe an accused's right to a fair trial or render a conviction unsafe.[109]

*(ii) Entrapment and undercover operations.* R v Looseley and *Attorney-General's Reference (No 3 of 2000)*[110] are the leading authorities on the circumstances in which criminal proceedings should be stayed, or evidence excluded, on the grounds of entrapment.[111] Hearing both appeals together, the House of Lords held as follows.

(1) Entrapment is not a substantive defence, but where an accused can show entrapment the court may stay the proceedings as an abuse of the court's process or it may exclude evidence under section 78.

(2) As a matter of principle, a stay of the proceedings rather than exclusion of evidence should normally be regarded as the appropriate response. A prosecution founded on entrapment would be an abuse of the court's process. Police conduct which brings about state-created crime is unacceptable and improper and to prosecute in such circumstances would be an affront to the public conscience.

(3) In deciding whether conduct amounts to state-created crime, the existence or absence of a predisposition on the part of the accused to commit the crime is not the criterion by which the acceptability of police conduct is to be decided, because it does not make acceptable what would otherwise be unacceptable conduct on the part of the police or negative misuse of state power.[112]

(4) A useful guide is to consider whether the police did no more than present the accused with an unexceptional opportunity to commit a crime. The yardstick for these purposes is, in general, whether the police conduct preceding the commission of the offence was no more than might have been expected from others in the circumstances. 'The State can justify the use of entrapment techniques to induce the commission of an offence only when the inducement is consistent with the ordinary temptations and stratagems that are likely to be encountered in the course of criminal activity . . . But once the State goes beyond the ordinary, it is likely to increase the incidence of crime by artificial means.'[113] Of its nature, the technique of providing an opportunity to commit a crime is intrusive. The greater the degree of intrusiveness, the closer will the courts scrutinize the reason for using it.

(5) Usually, a most important factor, but not necessarily decisive, will be whether an officer can be said to have caused the commission of the offence, rather than

---

[109] See *R v Forbes* [2001] 2 WLR 1, HL.     [110] [2001] 1 WLR 2060, HL.

[111] See A Ashworth, 'Redrawing the Boundaries of Entrapment' [2002] Crim LR 161.

[112] Cf *R v Moon* [2004] All ER (D) 167 (Nov), CA, where the absence of predisposition on the part of M to deal with or supply heroin was regarded as a critical factor in concluding that a test purchase by an undercover officer, who claimed that she was suffering from heroin withdrawal symptoms, was an abuse of process.

[113] Per McHugh J in *Ridgeway v The Queen* (1995) 184 CLR 19 at 92.

merely providing an opportunity for the accused to commit it with an officer rather than in secrecy with someone else. A good example of the latter situation is furnished by *Nottingham City Council v Amin*[114] where a taxi driver who was not licensed to ply for hire in a particular district, and was flagged down by plain clothes officers in that district, took them to their stated destination. Lord Bingham CJ said:[115] 'it has been regarded as unobjectionable if a law enforcement officer gives a defendant an opportunity to break the law, of which the defendant freely takes advantage, in circumstances where it appears that the defendant would have behaved in the same way if the opportunity had been offered by anyone else', by which he meant, in that case, that the officers behaved like ordinary members of the public in flagging the taxi down. They did not, for example, wave £50 notes or pretend to be in distress. The test of whether a police officer acted like an ordinary member of the public works well and is likely to be decisive in many cases of regulatory offences committed with ordinary members of the public, such as selling liquor without a licence, but ordinary members of the public do not become involved in large scale drug dealing, conspiracy to rob or hiring assassins. The appropriate standards of behaviour in such cases are more problematic; and even in the case of offences committed with ordinary members of the public, other factors may require a purely causal test to be modified.

(6) The causal question cannot be answered by a mechanical application of a distinction between 'active' and 'passive' conduct on the part of the undercover policeman. For example, drug dealers can be expected to show some wariness about dealing with a stranger and therefore some protective colour in dress or manner as well as a certain degree of persistence may be necessary. Equally, undercover officers who infiltrate conspiracies to murder, rob or commit terrorist offences could hardly remain concealed unless they showed some enthusiasm for the enterprise. A good deal of active behaviour may therefore be acceptable without crossing the boundary between causing the offence to be committed and providing an opportunity for the accused to commit it.

(7) Ultimately the overall consideration is always whether the conduct of the police was so seriously improper as to bring the administration of justice into disrepute. Other formulations substantially to the same effect are: a prosecution which would affront the public conscience[116] or conviction and punishment which would be deeply offensive to ordinary notions of fairness.[117] In applying these formulations, the court has regard to all the circumstances of the case. One cannot isolate any single factor or devise any formula that will always produce the correct answer. There are a cluster of relevant factors but

---

[114] [2000] 1 WLR 1071, DC.        [115] At 1076–7.

[116] Per Lord Steyn in *R v Latif* [1996] 1 WLR 104, HL at 112.

[117] Per Lord Bingham in *Nottingham City Council v Amin* [2000] 1 WLR 1071, DC at 1076.

their relevant weight and importance depends on the particular facts of the case. The following are of particular relevance.

(a) The nature of the offence. The use of proactive techniques is more appropriate in the case of some offences, for example dealing in unlawful substances, offences with no immediate victim, such as bribery, offences which victims are reluctant to report and conspiracies. The secrecy and difficulty of detection, and the manner in which the criminal activity is carried on, are relevant considerations. However the fact that the offence is a serious one is not in itself a sufficient ground for the police to ignore the provisions of the Undercover Operations Code of Practice (issued jointly by all UK police authorities and HM Customs and Excise in response to the Human Rights Act 1998) or for the courts to condone their actions by allowing the prosecution to proceed.

(b) The reason for the particular police operation and supervision. As to the former, the police must act in good faith. Having reasonable grounds for suspicion is one way good faith may be established, but having grounds for suspicion of a particular individual is not always essential. The police may, in the course of a bona fide investigation into suspected criminality, provide an opportunity for the commission of an offence which is taken by someone to whom no suspicion previously attached, as in *Williams v DPP*.[118] This can happen when a human or inanimate decoy is used in the course of the detection of crime which has been prevalent in a particular place. Sometimes random testing may be the only way of policing a particular trading activity. As to supervision, to allow officers or controlled informers to undertake entrapment activities unsupervised carries great danger, not only that they will try to improve their performances in court, but of oppression, extortion and corruption. The need for reasonable suspicion and proper supervision are both stressed in the Undercover Operations Code of Practice.

(c) The nature and extent of police participation in the crime. The greater the inducement held out by the police, and the more forceful or persistent their overtures, the more readily may a court conclude that they overstepped the boundary. In assessing the weight to be attached to the police inducement, regard is to be had to the accused's circumstances, including his vulnerability. It will not normally be regarded as objectionable for the police to behave as would an ordinary customer of a trade, whether lawful or unlawful, being carried on by the accused.

(d) The accused's criminal record. This is unlikely to be relevant unless it can be linked to other factors grounding reasonable suspicion that he is engaged in criminal activity.

---

[118] [1993] 3 All ER 365. See below.

(8) A decision on whether to stay the proceedings is distinct from a decision on the fairness of admitting evidence.[119] Different tests are applicable to these two decisions. If an application under section 78 is in substance a belated application for a stay, it should be treated as such and decided according to the principles appropriate to the grant of a stay. If the court is not satisfied that a stay should be granted, the question under section 78 is not whether the proceedings should have been brought but, as Potter LJ held in *R v Shannon*:[120]

> It is whether the fairness of the proceedings will be adversely affected by admitting the evidence of the agent provocateur or evidence which is available as the result of his action or activities. So, for instance, if there is good reason to question the credibility of evidence given by an agent provocateur, or which casts doubt on the reliability of other evidence procured by or resulting from his actions, and that question is not susceptible of being properly or fairly resolved in the course of the proceedings from available, admissible and 'untainted' evidence, then the judge may readily conclude that such evidence should be excluded.

(9) Neither section 78 nor the power to stay proceedings has been modified by Article 6 of the European Convention on Human Rights and the jurisprudence of the European Court of Human Rights. There is no appreciable difference between the requirements of Article 6, or the Strasbourg jurisprudence on Article 6, and the English law. Nor is there anything in *Teixeira de Castro v Portugal*[121] which suggests any difference from the current English approach to entrapment.

In *R v Smurthwaite and Gill*[122] the Court of Appeal considered the application of section 78(1) to evidence obtained as a result of police undercover operations. It was held that the relevant factors *include*:

1. whether the undercover officer was acting as an *agent provocateur*, ie enticing the accused to commit an offence he would not otherwise have committed;

2. the nature of any entrapment;

3. whether the evidence consists of admissions to a completed offence or relates to the actual commission of an offence;

4. how active or passive the officer's role was in obtaining the evidence;

5. whether there is an unassailable record of what occurred or whether it is strongly corroborated; and

6. whether the officer abused his role to ask questions which ought properly to have been asked as a police officer and in accordance with the Codes.[123]

---

[119] Citing *R v Chalkley* [1998] 2 Cr App R 79, CA at 105.      [120] [2001] 1 WLR 51, CA at 68.

[121] (1998) 28 EHRR 101. See further below.      [122] [1994] 1 All ER 898.

[123] The same factors also apply in the case of evidence obtained by undercover journalists acting on their own initiative and not on police instructions: *R v Shannon* [2001] 1 WLR 51, CA and *Shannon v UK* [2005] Crim LR 133, ECHR. As to the sixth factor, see also *R v Christou* [1992] QB 979, CA, and *R v Bryce* [1992] 4 All ER 567, CA, both below.

Both *Smurthwaite* and *Gill* were trials for soliciting to murder. In each case the person solicited was an undercover police officer posing as a contract killer and the prosecution case depended upon secret tape recordings of meetings held between the undercover officer and the accused. In S's case, the Court of Appeal was not persuaded that the officer was an *agent provocateur*. There was an element of entrapment and a trick. However, the tapes recorded not admissions about some previous offence but the actual offence being committed; they showed that S made the running and that the officer had taken a minimal role in the planning and had used no persuasion towards S; they were an accurate and unchallenged record; and the officer had not abused his role to ask questions which ought properly to have been asked as a police officer. In these circumstances, the judge's decision not to exclude the evidence was upheld. The outcome was the same in G's case: the facts were very similar and although the first meeting between G and the officer was not recorded and there was a stark conflict of evidence as to what was said at that meeting, the existence of a total record was only one factor, and both the contents of the subsequent taped conversations and statements made by G in her formal police interviews supported the officer's account of the first meeting.[124]

*R v Governor of Pentonville Prison, ex p Chinoy*[125] concerned the setting up of a bank account to facilitate the laundering of money alleged to be the proceeds of drug trafficking. The Divisional Court held that the fact of entrapment was one of the circumstances which should be taken into account when carrying out the balancing exercise under section 78(1), but concluded that the circumstances did not require the exclusion of the evidence. It was held that the detection and proof of certain types of criminal activity may necessitate the employment of underhand and even unlawful means. On the facts, although the evidence was obtained by means which were criminal in France and, according to French law, in breach of the European Convention on Human Rights, there was no breach of English law and the means employed by the undercover agents were appropriate to the situation they were investigating and did not require the exclusion of the evidence they obtained. In *R v Latif*[126] S was convicted of being knowingly concerned in the importation of drugs which had been brought into the country by an undercover customs officer. Although S had been lured into England by the deceit of an informer, and both he and the undercover officer had possibly committed the offence of possessing heroin in Pakistan, the House of Lords upheld the judge's refusal to either stay the proceedings or exclude the informer's evidence under section 78.[127]

An application under section 78 will not succeed where a police officer gives an accused an opportunity to break the law, of which the accused freely takes advantage, in circumstances in which the accused would have behaved in the same way if the opportunity had been offered by anyone else. An example is *DPP v Marshall*,[128] where,

---

[124] Cf *Re Proulx* [2001] 1 All ER 57, DC.     [125] [1992] 1 All ER 317.     [126] [1996] 1 WLR 104.
[127] See also *R v Pattemore* [1994] Crim LR 836, CA, and *R v Morley* [1994] Crim LR 919, CA.
[128] [1988] 3 All ER 683, DC.

on a charge of selling alcohol without a licence, evidence was received of purchases made by plain clothes officers. The same approach was adopted in *Ealing London Borough v Woolworths plc*,[129] in which it was held that, on a charge under section 11(1) of the Video Recordings Act 1984, justices were in error in excluding evidence that a boy aged 11, acting under instructions of officers of the Trading Standards Department, had entered the store and purchased an 18-category video film. In *Williams v DPP*,[130] the trick, based on the expectation that someone might act dishonestly, was to leave in a busy street an insecure van containing an apparently valuable load, a stratagem which, it was held, left the accused free whether to succumb or not.

It seems that the police cannot circumvent section 78(1) by using, as *agents provocateurs*, informants who will not be called as witnesses. Thus if an informant, C, acting on police instructions rather than on his own initiative, incites or entraps an accused, D, into committing an offence (the supply of drugs, say) and D is then approached by E, an undercover police officer, in whose presence the offence is committed (D supplies E with drugs), this may form the basis of a submission to exclude E's evidence under section 78(1) notwithstanding that E, by reference to the relevant factors as set out in *Smurthwaite and Gill*, behaved throughout with perfect propriety.[131]

*(iii) Undercover operations after commission of an offence.* Whether section 78(1) operates to exclude evidence obtained by undercover operations or other forms of trickery *after* commission of the offence, as in the case of other types of evidence, often turns on the reliability or otherwise of the evidence to be adduced, as much as the extent to which the accused has been deprived of his important procedural rights, each case turning on its own facts.

Many of the cases have involved covert recording or filming. In *R v Bailey*[132] two co-accused, having exercised their right to silence when interviewed, were charged and placed in the same bugged cell by officers who, in order to lull them into a false sense of security, pretended that they had been forced to put them in the same cell by an uncooperative custody officer. Evidence of incriminating conversations obtained by this subterfuge was held to be admissible. In *R v Khan (Sultan)*[133] the House of Lords held that the fact that evidence has been obtained in circumstances which amount to a breach of Article 8 of the European Convention on Human Rights (the right to respect for private life, home and correspondence) may be relevant to exercise of the section 78 power, but the significance of the breach turns on its effect on the fairness of the proceedings. In that case the police had made a recording of an incriminating conversation relating to the importation of heroin, by means of an electronic surveillance device attached to a house without the knowledge or consent of the owner or occupier. On these facts, it was held that the judge had been entitled to conclude that the circumstances in which the evidence had been obtained, even if they constituted a breach of Article 8, were not such as to require exclusion of the evidence. The

---

[129] [1995] Crim LR 58, DC.    [130] [1993] 3 All ER 365, DC.
[131] See *R v Smith (Brian)* [1995] Crim LR 658, CA, and cf *R v Mann* [1995] Crim LR 647, CA.
[132] [1993] 3 All ER 513, CA.    [133] [1997] AC 558.

European Court of Human Rights subsequently held that although the recording was obtained in breach of Article 8, its use at the trial did not conflict with the right to a fair hearing under Article 6, because there was no risk of the recording being unreliable, the accused had the opportunity to challenge its admissibility, and if its admission would have given rise to substantive unfairness, the domestic court could have excluded it under section 78.[134] The European Court of Human Rights has reached similar conclusions in relation to evidence obtained in breach of Article 8 by the unlawful installation of a listening device in the accused's home[135] and, in *PG and JH v United Kingdom*,[136] by the unlawful use of covert listening devices in police cells.[137] In *PG and JH v United Kingdom*, where the recordings did not contain any incriminating statements, but were used at trial as a control to identify the voices of the accused on other tapes, it was held that they could be regarded as akin to blood, hair or other physical or objective specimens used in forensic analysis and to which the privilege against self-incrimination does not apply. In that case the European Court also reiterated that:

Whilst Article 6 guarantees the right to a fair hearing, it does not lay down any rules on the admissibility of evidence as such, which is therefore primarily a matter for regulation under national law. . . . It is not the role of the court to determine, as a matter of principle whether particular types of evidence, for example unlawfully obtained evidence—may be admissible or, indeed, whether the applicant was guilty or not. The question which must be answered is whether the proceedings as a whole, including the way in which the evidence was obtained, were fair.[138]

The European Court has followed the same approach in relation to covert filming. In *Perry v United Kingdom*,[139] the applicant having failed to attend identification parades, the police, infringing official guidelines, filmed him covertly for the purposes of a video identification of which neither he nor his solicitor were aware. It was held that the application was manifestly ill-founded on the grounds that the use of evidence obtained without a proper legal basis or through unlawful means will not generally contravene Article 6(1) so long as proper procedural safeguards are in place and the source of the material is not tainted.[140]

---

[134] *Khan v United Kingdom* (2001) 31 EHRR 1016.

[135] *Chalkley v United Kingdom* [2003] Crim LR 51.        [136] [2002] Crim LR 308.

[137] See also *R v Mason* [2002] 2 Cr App R 628, CA; and *R v Button* [2005] Crim LR 571, where the 'startling proposition' that the court is bound to exclude any evidence obtained in breach of Art 8 because otherwise it would be acting unlawfully was rejected on the basis that any breach of Art 8 is subsumed by the Art 6 duty to ensure a fair trial.

[138] For a fuller examination of approaches to exclusion of evidence obtained in breach of Art 8, see D Ormerod, 'ECHR and the Exclusion of Evidence: Trial Remedies for Article 8 Breaches' [2003] Crim LR 61. See also R Mahoney 'Abolition of New Zealand's Prima Facie Exclusionary Rule' [2003] Crim LR 607.

[139] [2003] Crim LR 281.

[140] See also *R v Loveridge* [2001] 2 Cr App R 591, CA, where the accused were covertly filmed in court, which was both unlawful and in breach of Art 8, to enable comparison with pictures of the crime as recorded on a CCTV film; and *R v Marriner* [2002] All ER (D) 120 (Dec), [2002] EWCA Crim 2855, where the accused were covertly recorded on video and tape by undercover journalists.

In *R v P*[141] it was argued that although telephone intercept evidence was properly obtained in accordance with the Convention and the law of a country overseas, its use in an English trial was contrary to Article 6 and the policy of the English law. Rejecting this argument, the House of Lords held that the fair use of intercept evidence at a trial is not a breach of Article 6, even if it was unlawfully obtained, the criterion of fairness in Article 6 is the criterion to be applied by the judge under section 78, and there is no principle of exclusion of intercept evidence independently of the statutory provisions.[142] The House has also held that where intercept evidence is inadmissible pursuant to statutory provisions, there is no rule prohibiting the use of the intercepts at police interviews and, subject to section 78, such use will not render the interview evidence inadmissible, although the interview transcript will need to be edited to remove any direct or indirect references to the intercept.[143]

In *R v Christou*[144] the police set up a shop staffed by two undercover police officers who purported to be willing to buy stolen jewellery. Transactions in the shop were recorded, the object being to recover stolen property and obtain evidence against thieves or receivers. The accused, charged as a result of the operation, unsuccessfully sought to exclude all the evidence obtained thereby. It was argued that the evidence was obtained by a trick designed to deprive visitors to the shop of their privilege against self-incrimination and that a caution should have been administered. The Court of Appeal, distinguishing *R v Payne* and *R v Mason*,[145] held that the accused had voluntarily applied themselves to the trick (in the sense that what they did in the shop was exactly what they intended to do) and this had resulted in no unfairness.[146] Concerning the alleged breach of Code C, the court acknowledged that the officers had grounds to suspect the accused of an offence, but held that the Code was not intended to apply in the present context. The Code was intended to protect suspects who are vulnerable to abuse or pressure from officers or who may believe themselves to be so. Where a suspect, even if not in detention, is being questioned by an officer, acting as such, for the purpose of obtaining evidence, the officer and the suspect are not on equal terms: the officer is perceived to be in a position of authority and the suspect may be intimidated or undermined. On the facts, however, the accused were not questioned by officers acting as such, conversation was on equal terms, and there was no question of pressure or intimidation.

In *Christou* the court held that it *would* be wrong for the police to adopt an undercover pose or disguise to enable them to ask questions about an offence uninhibited by the Code and with the effect of circumventing it, and it would then be open to a judge to exclude under section 78. On the facts, however, the questions and comments of the officers were, for the most part, simply those necessary to conduct

---

[141] [2002] 1 AC 46.          [142] See now the Regulation of Investigatory Powers Act 2000.

[143] *R v Sargent* [2003] 1 AC 347, HL.          [144] [1992] QB 979, CA.

[145] [1963] 1 All ER 848 and [1987] 3 All ER 481.

[146] Similar reasoning was applied in *R v Maclean* [1993] Crim LR 687, CA, and *R v Cadette* [1995] Crim LR 229, CA, both below. See also *R v Deenik* [1992] Crim LR 578, CA (police evidence of voice identification, D not having been warned that an officer was listening).

the bartering and to maintain their cover, and not questions about the offence. Thus, although officers had asked questions about the origin of the goods, they had formed a part of their undercover pose as receivers: receivers need such information to prevent them from re-selling goods in the area from which they were stolen. The position was the same in *R v Lin*,[147] where an undercover officer, introduced to the accused not for the purpose of obtaining evidence about a past offence involving a stolen Inland Revenue cheque, but to discover the plans of the accused in relation to an ongoing conspiracy to handle stolen cheques, held a conversation about the Inland Revenue cheque as a necessary part of establishing his credentials as a 'criminal'.

In *R v Bryce*,[148] on the other hand, in which an undercover officer, posing as a potential buyer of a car, asked B how recently the car had been stolen, it was held that evidence of the answers should have been excluded. The questions were not necessary to the maintenance of the undercover pose. They went directly to the issue of guilty knowledge, they were hotly disputed, and there had been no caution and no contemporary record.

In a number of cases the trickery, or subterfuge, has involved the use of an accomplice. An example is *R v Jelen; R v Katz*.[149] In that case D and J were charged with conspiracy. On arrest, D made admissions and implicated J. The police, who until then had no knowledge of J's involvement, took the view that they would have to caution J if they were to question him but that they had insufficient evidence to arrest and charge him. They asked D to hold a recorded conversation with J, without J knowing that it was being recorded. D then held such a conversation, during which D lied to J, telling him that he had said nothing to the police, and J made certain remarks from which his guilt could have been inferred. It was submitted that evidence of the recording should be excluded because of D's lie, the confidential nature of the conversation, and the fact that by using D in this way, the police had avoided complying with Code C. The Court of Appeal held that, although there was an element of entrapment, it could see no reason to disagree with the judge's decision not to exclude.[150] In *R v Cadette*[151] B, arrested as a suspected drugs courier, was asked by customs officers to telephone C, in accordance with an arrangement previously made between B and C, but to pretend that she had not been arrested and to try to persuade C to come to the airport. Evidence of their conversation, which was recorded, was held to have been properly admitted. The court observed that, in practical terms, there comes a point when officers move from following up available lines of inquiry to obtain evidence against others involved to a stage where they seek in effect to deprive a suspect of the protection afforded by the 1984 Act and the Codes, but held that the officers had not crossed the line. The provisions of the 1984 Act did not apply; there was a reliable

---

[147] [1995] Crim LR 817, CA.     [148] [1992] 4 All ER 567, CA.     [149] (1989) 90 Cr App R 456, CA.

[150] See also *R v Roberts* [1997] 1 Cr App R 217, CA and *R v Maclean* [1993] Crim LR 687, CA; and cf *R v H* [1987] Crim LR 47, CC, where recorded telephone conversations, instigated by the complainant with the connivance of the police, were excluded under s 78 on the basis that the conversations were a trap, the complainant having told the accused that she was *not* recording the conversations.

[151] [1995] Crim LR 229, CA.

record of the conversation; and the ruse, of itself, did not give rise to unfairness for the purposes of section 78.[152]

The line was crossed, however, in *Allan v United Kingdom*.[153] A, suspected of murder, was interviewed by officers on several occasions but, acting on legal advice, consistently refused to answer questions. H, an experienced informer, who had undergone coaching by police informers, was fitted with recording devices and placed in A's cell for the specific purpose of questioning him to obtain information about the murder. At the trial H gave evidence, which proved to be decisive, that A had admitted his presence at the scene of the murder, but this conversation had not been recorded on tape. A was convicted. The European Court of Human Rights was satisfied that using statements obtained in a manner which effectively undermines a suspect's right to make a meaningful choice whether to speak to the authorities or to remain silent infringes procedural rights inherent in Article 6. The court acknowledged that whether the right to silence is undermined to such an extent as to invoke Article 6 will depend upon the circumstances of the case, but, distinguishing *Khan v United Kingdom*, was satisfied that evidence of the conversation had been obtained without sufficient regard to fair trial guarantees:

the admissions allegedly made by the applicant to H ... were not spontaneous and unprompted statements volunteered by the applicant, but were induced by the persistent questioning of H who, at the instance of the police, channeled their conversations into discussions of the murder in circumstances which can be regarded as the functional equivalent of interrogation, without any of the safeguards which would attach to a formal police interview, including the attendance of a solicitor and the issuing of the usual caution.[154]

---

[152] See also *R v Edwards* [1997] Crim LR 348, CA.     [153] (2002) 36 EHRR 143.     [154] At para 52.

# 4

# THE BURDEN AND STANDARD OF PROOF

## A  THE BURDEN OF PROOF

Standing alone, the expression 'burden of proof' is self-explanatory: it is the obligation to prove. There are two principal kinds of burden, the legal burden and the evidential burden. The legal burden is a burden of proof. However, as we shall see, it is confusing and misleading to speak of the evidential burden as a burden of proof, first because when borne by a defendant it may be discharged by evidence other than the evidence adduced by the defence and therefore may not in substance be a burden at all,[1] and secondly because it can be discharged by the production of evidence that falls short of proof.[2]

The content of the first half of this chapter is largely concerned with the rules governing which party bears the legal and evidential burdens on which facts in issue. The practical importance of these rules is fourfold. They can, of course, determine the eventual outcome of the proceedings. Additionally they determine which party has the right to begin adducing evidence in court; in what circumstances a defendant, at the end of the case for the prosecution, or claimant, may make a successful submission of no case to answer; and how the trial judge should direct the jury. However, easy as it is to outline the nature and importance of this subject, detailed analysis is made difficult by problems of classification and terminology. First, it is not entirely clear from the authorities precisely how many types of burden, in law, there are, and what each signifies. Secondly, judges, when speaking of 'the burden', all too often fail to specify which type of burden—legal, evidential, or other—they have in contemplation. A final and unnecessarily complicating factor is that even in those cases where the burdens in question are specified and distinguished, different judges frequently employ different labels to refer to the same burden. It will be convenient, then, to begin by defining and distinguishing the legal, evidential and other burdens before considering in detail which burden is borne by each of the parties on the various facts in issue in any given case.

---

[1]  See *Bullard v R* [1957] AC 635, PC, below, and per Pill LJ in *L v DPP* [2003] QB 137, DC at [23].

[2]  Per Lord Devlin in *Jayasena v R* [1970] AC 618, PC at 624.

## 1 THE LEGAL BURDEN

This burden has been referred to as 'the burden of proof' or 'probative burden'[3] and as 'the ultimate burden'. Another label, 'the burden of proof on the pleadings',[4] is used to show that this burden is sometimes indicated by the pleadings. Two further phrases, 'the risk of non-persuasion'[5] and 'the persuasive burden', are used to show that a party bearing the burden on a particular fact in issue will lose on that issue if he fails to discharge the burden. Most of these labels are, to some extent, misleading, and in the ensuing text this burden will be referred to simply as 'the legal burden'.

The legal burden may be defined as the obligation imposed on a party by a rule of law to prove a fact in issue. Whether a party has discharged this burden and proved a fact in issue is decided only once, by the tribunal of fact, at the end of the case when both parties have called all their evidence. The standard of proof required to discharge the legal burden depends upon whether the proceedings are criminal or civil. In the former the standard required of the prosecution is proof 'beyond reasonable doubt', in the latter the standard required is proof 'on the balance of probabilities'. A party who fails to discharge a legal burden borne by him to the required standard of proof will lose on the issue in question.

The legal burden relates to particular facts in issue.[6] Most cases, of course, involve more than one issue and the legal burden of proof in relation to these issues may be distributed between the parties to the action. We shall see, for example, that in a criminal case where insanity is raised by way of defence, the legal burden in relation to that issue is borne by the defendant, whereas the prosecution may well bear the legal burden on all the other facts in issue. In civil proceedings, an example would be a negligence action in which the defendant alleges contributory negligence: the claimant bears the legal burden on the issue of negligence, the defendant on contributory negligence. The obligation on a party to prove a fact in issue may oblige that party to negative or disprove a particular fact. In criminal proceedings, for example, the prosecution bears the legal burden of proving lack of consent on a charge of rape.

Which party bears the legal burden of proof in relation to any given fact in issue is determined by the rules of substantive law discussed below. Judges sometimes refer to the 'shifting' of a burden of proof from one party to his opponent. The phrase is apt to mislead. The only sense in which the legal burden may be said to shift is on the operation of a rebuttable presumption of law. Rebuttable presumptions of law are considered in detail in Chapter 22, but it is convenient, at this stage, briefly to consider their operation. Where such a presumption applies, once a primary fact is proved or admitted, in the absence of further evidence another fact must be presumed. The quantity and quality of evidence required to rebut the presumed fact is determined by

---

[3] See *DPP v Morgan* [1976] AC 182, HL.    [4] Phipson *Law of Evidence* (14th edn London, 1990).

[5] Wigmore *A Treatise on the Anglo-American System of Evidence* (3rd edn Boston 1940) ch IX, paras 248–9.

[6] A question of construction is a question of *law* in respect of which no burden lies on either side; but if a party relies on surrounding circumstances as an aid to construction, then the onus is on him to prove them: see per Nourse LJ, construing a conveyance in *Scott v Martin* [1987] 2 All ER 813, CA at 817.

the substantive law in relation to the presumption in question. The party relying on the presumption bears the burden of proving the primary fact. Once he has adduced sufficient evidence on that fact, in the case of a 'persuasive' presumption his adversary will bear the legal burden of disproving the presumed fact. The burden may be said to have shifted. However, when judges refer to a shifting of the burden in circumstances other than on the operation of rebuttable presumptions of law, they mean that the burden may, at any given moment in the course of the trial, *appear* to have been satisfied by the party on whom it lies by virtue of the evidence adduced by that party. Insofar as this places a burden on that party's opponent, the opponent bears a 'tactical' burden. The legal burden has not shifted because, as noted above, whether the legal burden has been discharged by a party is only determined once and that is at the end of the trial when *all* the evidence has been adduced.[7] The tactical burden is discussed more fully in contrast with the evidential burden.

## 2  THE EVIDENTIAL BURDEN

This burden is also referred to as 'the burden of adducing evidence' and 'the duty of passing the judge'. It may be defined as the obligation on a party to adduce sufficient evidence of a fact to justify a finding on that fact in favour of the party so obliged. In other words, it obliges a party to adduce sufficient evidence for the issue to go before the tribunal of fact. It is confusing and misleading, therefore, to call the evidential burden a burden of *proof*: it can be discharged by the production of evidence that falls short of proof.[8] Whether a party has discharged the burden is decided only once in the course of a trial, and by the judge as opposed to the tribunal of fact. The burden is discharged when there is sufficient evidence to justify, as a possibility, a favourable finding by the tribunal of fact. Thus in a criminal trial in which the prosecution bears the evidential burden on a particular issue, it must adduce sufficient evidence to prevent the judge from withdrawing that issue from the jury. If the prosecution discharges the evidential burden, it does not necessarily mean that it will succeed on the issue in question. The accused will not necessarily lose on that issue, even if he adduces no evidence in rebuttal, although if he takes that course that is a clear risk he runs. If the prosecution also bears the legal burden on the same issue, and fails to discharge the evidential burden, it necessarily fails on that issue since the judge refuses to let the issue go before the jury. However, it does not follow that a discharge of the

---

[7] 'Where there is only one issue in the case and the burden of proof rests on one party, it seems to me wrong to say that the burden of proof shifts after one witness has been called and given evidence which, if believed, would discharge that burden. Courts do not make up their minds on an issue when they have heard only part of the evidence. Surely one can say, if one wishes, "Well, the plaintiff is doing quite well. I wonder if there is going to be any evidence from the defendants?" But to say that the burden of proof has shifted seems to me to be wrong. One should make up one's mind on that issue having heard all the evidence on it . . .': per Sir Christopher Staughton in *Re W* [2001] 4 All ER 88, CA at 93–4. See also per Mustill LJ in *Brady (Inspector of Taxes) v Group Lotus Car Companies plc* [1987] 3 All ER 1050, CA at 1059.

[8] Per Lord Devlin in *Jayasena v R* [1970] AC 618 PC at 624.

evidential burden necessarily results in a discharge of the legal burden; the issue in question goes before the jury, who may or may not find in favour of the prosecution on that issue.

Like the legal burden, the evidential burden relates to particular facts in issue. The evidential burden in relation to the various issues in a given case may be distributed between the parties to the action. Normally, a party bearing the legal burden in relation to a particular fact at the commencement of the proceedings also bears an evidential burden in relation to the same fact. However, this is not invariably so. Thus although, as we shall see, the prosecution bears the legal burden of negativing most common law and certain statutory defences (including the defences of provocation, self-defence, duress, and non-insane automatism), such a defence will not be put before the jury unless the accused has discharged the evidential burden in that regard. Equally, and further to complicate matters, the evidential burden borne by the accused in these circumstances may be discharged by *any* evidence in the case, whether given by the accused, a co-accused or the prosecution, and in this sense the so-called evidential burden is not a burden on the accused at all.[9] If the evidential burden is discharged, whether by defence or prosecution evidence, the prosecution will then bear the legal burden of disproving the defence in question, but if there is no evidence to support the defence, then the judge is entitled to withdraw it from the jury.[10]

As in the case of the legal burden, judges sometimes refer to the 'shifting' of the evidential burden. The evidential burden may sensibly be said to shift on the operation of a rebuttable presumption of law of the 'evidential' variety.[11] However, the phrase has also been employed in other circumstances. Where a party discharges an evidential burden borne by him in relation to a particular fact, his adversary will be under an obligation, referred to as the provisional or tactical burden, to adduce counter-evidence in order to convince the tribunal of fact in his favour. If he chooses not to adduce such counter-evidence, he runs the risk of a finding on that issue in favour of the other party. It is in these circumstances, also, that judges refer to a shifting of the evidential burden.[12] This conjures up a vision of the trial as a ball-game, with the evidential burden as the ball, which is continuously bounced to and fro between the contenders. This is misleading because although examination followed

---

[9] Per Pill LJ in *L v DPP* [2003] QB 137, DC at [23].

[10] *R v Pommell* [1995] 2 Cr App R 607, CA, where it was also held that although normally a judge will not have to decide whether to leave a particular defence to the jury until the conclusion of the evidence, in rare cases where the nature of the evidence to be called is clear, it may be appropriate, in order to save time and costs, for the judge to indicate at an early stage what his ruling is likely to be.

[11] Where a party relying on an 'evidential' presumption has adduced sufficient evidence on the primary or basic fact, his adversary will bear an evidential burden to adduce some evidence to rebut the presumed fact. See further Ch 22.

[12] See, eg, per Lord Goddard CJ in *R v Matheson* [1958] 1 WLR 474, CCA at 478, where a conviction of murder was reduced to one of manslaughter. The legal burden of proving diminished responsibility is borne by the accused: Homicide Act 1957, s 2(2). The accused's evidence of diminished responsibility was said to have shifted the burden onto the prosecution, who had adduced no medical evidence in rebuttal. See also *Rickards and Rickards v Kerrier District Council* (1987) 151 JP 625, DC.

by cross-examination of witnesses often results in swings of fortune for and then against a party, normally in a trial, whether civil or criminal, one party first adduces all of his evidence before his adversary then adduces his. But there is a more important sense in which the phrase misleads. The evidential burden only needs to be considered by the court on two occasions, first at the beginning of a trial, to determine which party starts, and secondly when, during the trial, the judge determines whether sufficient evidence has been adduced to leave an issue before the tribunal of fact. If the judge decides at the latter stage that insufficient evidence has been adduced, the issue will be withdrawn from the tribunal of fact and further consideration of the evidential burden is irrelevant. But further consideration of the evidential burden is equally irrelevant when the judge allows the issue to go before the tribunal of fact. It is certainly possible to say, at this stage, that the evidential burden has shifted to the opponent and that he, by adducing counter-evidence, may cause the evidential burden to shift back to the first party, and so on, but such observations are of no legal significance. So far as the court is concerned, the evidential burden requires no further consideration; the only burden remaining at this stage is the legal burden.[13]

## 3  THE INCIDENCE OF THE LEGAL BURDEN

Which party bears the legal burden is determined by the rules of substantive law set out in the precedents and statutes. Speaking generally, the determination of where the legal burden falls is a matter of common sense. If certain facts are essential to the claim of, for example, the claimant in civil proceedings or the prosecution in criminal proceedings, that party must prove them. A useful starting-point—although, as we shall see, a far from reliable guide—is the maxim 'he who asserts must prove' (*ei incumbit probatio qui dicit, non qui negat*). In *Wakelin v London and South Western Rly Co*[14] a widow brought an action in negligence under the Fatal Accidents Act 1846. The only available evidence was that her husband had been found dead near a level crossing at the side of a railway line. Lord Halsbury LC held that the widow bore the burden of proving that her husband's death had been caused by the defendants' negligence; if she could not discharge that burden, she failed. Even assuming that the husband had been knocked down by a train while on the crossing, the evidence adduced was as capable of leading to the conclusion that the husband had been negligent as it was of showing the defendants' negligence and, accordingly, the defendants' negligence was not proved.[15] A detailed examination of the incidence of the legal burden of proof requires that criminal and civil cases be considered separately.

### (a)  Criminal cases

Speaking generally, the legal burden of proving any fact essential to the prosecution case rests upon the prosecution and remains with the prosecution throughout the trial.

---

[13] See *Sutton v Sadler* (1857) 3 CBNS 87 (see Ch 22).    [14] (1886) 12 App Cas 41, HL.
[15] Cf *Jones v Great Western Rly Co* (1930) 144 LT 194, HL.

Negative as well as positive allegations may be essential to the case for the prosecution. Thus the prosecution bears the legal burden of proving absence of consent on a charge of rape or assault.[16] Generally, therefore, the accused bears no legal burden in respect of the essential ingredients of an offence, whether they be positive or negative and whether or not he denies any or all of them. In *Woolmington v DPP*[17] the accused, charged with the murder of his wife, gave evidence that he had shot her accidentally. The trial judge directed the jury that once it was proved that the accused had shot his wife, he bore the burden of disproving malice aforethought. The House of Lords held this to be a misdirection and Lord Sankey LC said, in a now famous passage:[18]

Throughout the web of the English criminal law one golden thread is always to be seen, that it is the duty of the prosecution to prove the prisoner's guilt subject to what I have already said as to the defence of insanity and subject also to any statutory exception . . . No matter what the charge or where the trial, the principle that the prosecution must prove the guilt of the prisoner is part of the common law of England and no attempt to whittle it down can be entertained . . . It is not the law of England to say, as was said in the summing up in the present case: 'if the Crown satisfy you that this woman died at the prisoner's hands then he has to show that there are circumstances to be found in the evidence which has been given from the witness-box in this case which alleviate the crime so that it is only manslaughter or which excuse the homicide altogether by showing it was a pure accident . . .'

The rule enunciated by Lord Sankey is subject to three categories of exception: where the accused raises the defence of insanity, where a statute expressly places the legal burden on the defence, and where a statute impliedly places the legal burden on the defence. The statutory exceptions are often referred to as reverse onus provisions. Since the coming into force of the Human Rights Act 1998, any such provision is open to challenge on the basis of its incompatibility with the presumption of innocence guaranteed by Article 6(2) of the European Convention of Human Rights. This aspect of the topic receives separate treatment, below.

*(i) Insanity.* Where an accused raises insanity as a defence, he bears the legal burden of proving it.[19] Where an accused is charged with murder and raises the issue of *either* insanity *or* diminished responsibility, the prosecution, pursuant to section 6 of the Criminal Procedure (Insanity) Act 1964, is allowed to adduce evidence to prove the other of those issues. In this event, the prosecution bears the legal burden of proving the other issue on which they have adduced evidence.[20] If an accused is alleged to be under a disability rendering him unfit to plead and stand trial, the issue may be raised, under section 4 of the 1964 Act, by either the prosecution or defence. If the issue is

---

[16] *R v Horn* (1912) 7 Cr App R 200; *R v Donovan* [1934] 2 KB 498. But see also ss 75 and 76 of the Sexual Offences Act 2003.

[17] [1935] AC 462, HL.     [18] [1935] AC 462 at 481–2.

[19] *M'Naghten's Case* (1843) 10 Cl&Fin 200, HL.

[20] The standard to be met by the prosecution in these circumstances is proof beyond reasonable doubt: *R v Grant* [1960] Crim LR 424.

raised by the prosecution, they must prove it and satisfy the jury beyond reasonable doubt;[21] if the issue is raised by the defence, they must prove it, but only on a balance of probabilities, the lower standard of proof.[22]

*(ii) Express statutory exceptions.* A number of statutes expressly place on the accused the legal burden of proving specified issues. The legal burden of proof in relation to all issues other than those so specified remains on the prosecution. For example, section 2(2) of the Homicide Act 1957 places upon the accused the legal burden of establishing the statutory defence of diminished responsibility on a charge of murder.[23] Section 2(2) does not contravene Article 6 of the European Convention of Human Rights.[24] Other examples are considered below under the heading of 'Reverse onus provisions and the Human Rights Act 1998'.

*(iii) Implied statutory exceptions.* Section 101 of the Magistrates' Courts Act 1980, formerly section 81 of the Magistrates' Courts Act 1952, provides as follows:

Where the defendant to an information or complaint relies for his defence on any exception, exemption, proviso, excuse or qualification, whether or not it accompanies the description of the offence or matter of complaint in the enactment creating the offence or on which the complaint is founded, the burden of proving the exception, exemption, proviso, excuse or qualification shall be on him; and this notwithstanding that the information or complaint contains an allegation negativing the exception, exemption, proviso, excuse or qualification.

This section applies to summary trials but at common law similar principles applied to trials on indictment and it was held by the Court of Appeal in *R v Edwards*,[25] and confirmed by the House of Lords in *R v Hunt*,[26] that the section sets out the common law rule in statutory form. If this were not so, then in the case of an offence triable either way, the incidence of the burden of proof could vary—but for no good reason—according to whether the accused is tried summarily or on indictment.

Implied statutory exceptions within section 101 of the 1980 Act are capable of derogating from Article 6 of the European Convention;[27] and the cases, in the ensuing text, in which, by virtue of section 101 or the common law principles on which it is based, particular statutory provisions have been construed to impose a legal burden on the accused, must now be read subject to the Human Rights Act 1998 and the cases

---

[21] *R v Robertson* [1968] 1 WLR 1767, CA.     [22] *R v Podola* [1960] 1 QB 325, CCA.

[23] Section 2(2) not only dictates which party shoulders the burden of proof once the issue is raised, but also leaves it to the defence to decide whether the issue should be raised at all; if, therefore, the defence does not raise the issue but there is evidence of diminished responsibility, the trial judge is not bound to direct the jury to consider the matter but, at most, should in the absence of the jury draw the matter to the attention of the defence so that they may decide whether they wish the issue to be considered by the jury: per Lord Lane CJ, obiter, in *R v Campbell* (1986) 84 Cr App R 255, CA.

[24] See *R v Lambert; R v Ali; and R v Jordan* [2001] 2 WLR 211 (CA).     [25] [1975] QB 27.

[26] [1987] 1 All ER 1.

[27] See per Clarke LJ in *R (Grundy & Co Excavations Ltd) v Halton Division Magistrates' Court* (2003) 167 JP 387, DC at [61].

in which reverse onus provisions have been challenged on the basis of incompatibility with Article 6.[28]

Section 101 applies to statutory provisions which define a criminal offence and use words such as 'unless', 'provided that', 'except' or 'other than', to set out an exception, proviso, etc which amounts to a defence. The definition of an offence, and the exception or proviso to it, are not always readily distinguishable. However, before considering the kind of statute capable of giving rise to difficulty, two reasonably straightforward examples of the kind of provision to which section 101 applies may be given: (i) the offence of driving a vehicle on a road without being the holder of a current driving licence;[29] and (ii) section 161(1) of the Highways Act 1980, which provides that if a person, without lawful authority or excuse, deposits anything whatsoever on a highway in consequence of which a user of the highway is injured or endangered, that person shall be guilty of an offence. In *Gatland v Metropolitan Police Comr*[30] Lord Parker CJ held that although it was for the prosecution to prove that a thing had been deposited on the highway and that in consequence thereof a user of the highway had been injured or endangered, it was for the accused to raise and prove lawful authority or excuse pursuant to section 81 of the Magistrates' Courts Act 1952.[31] In *Westminster City Council v Croyalgrange Ltd*,[32] by contrast, no reliance could be placed on what is now section 101 of the 1980 Act. A company which had let premises to a person who used them as a sex establishment without a licence was charged under Schedule 3, paragraph 20(1)(a), of the Local Government (Miscellaneous Provisions) Act 1982, whereby a person who knowingly causes or permits the use of premises contrary to Schedule 3, paragraph 6, commits an offence. Paragraph 6 provides that no persons shall use any premises as a sex establishment except under and in accordance with a licence. The House of Lords held that section 101 was inapplicable because the exception in question qualified the prohibition created by paragraph 6 and not the offence created by paragraph 20(1)(a). The prosecution bore the burden of proving, inter alia, that the directors of the company knew that no licence had been obtained by the tenant.[33]

*Nimmo v Alexander Cowan & Sons Ltd*[34] was another case giving rise to some difficulty. This was a Scottish case brought by an injured workman under section

[28] See below.

[29] See also *Leeds City Council v Azam* (1988) 153 JP 157, DC: it is for the accused to prove that he is *exempted* from the need for a licence for the operation of a private hire vehicle under s 75 of the Local Government (Miscellaneous Provisions) Act 1976.

[30] [1968] 2 QB 279, a decision under s 140(1) of the Highways Act 1959, re-enacted in s 161(1) of the 1980 Act.

[31] Cf Offences Against the Person Act 1861, s 16: a person who without lawful excuse makes to another a threat, intending that the other would fear it would be carried out, to kill that other or a third person shall be guilty of an offence. In *R v Cousins* [1982] QB 526, CA, it was held that on a charge under s 16, the onus is on the prosecution to prove absence of lawful excuse for making the threat.

[32] (1986) 83 Cr App R 155, HL.

[33] See also, construing s 33(1)(a) of the Environmental Protection Act 1990, *Environment Agency v M E Foley Contractors Ltd* [2002] 1 WLR 1754, DC.

[34] [1968] AC 107.

29(1) of the Factories Act 1961, which provides that 'every place at which any person has at any time to work . . . shall, so far as is reasonably practicable, be made and kept safe for any person working therein'. The workman alleged that his place of work was not kept safe but did not aver that it was reasonably practicable to make it safe. Section 155(1) of the 1961 Act makes a breach of section 29(1) a summary offence and although the case in question was a civil one, the House of Lords referred to the Scottish equivalent of section 81 of the Magistrates' Courts Act 1952 and Lord Pearson made it clear that the incidence of the burden of proof would be the same whether the proceedings were civil or criminal.[35] The House held, Lords Reid and Wilberforce dissenting, that there was no burden on the plaintiff employee to prove that it was reasonably practicable to keep the premises safe; the defendant employers bore the burden of proving that it was *not* reasonably practicable to keep the premises safe. In reaching this decision, the majority was of the opinion that where, on the face of the statute, it is unclear on whom the burden should lie, a court, in order to determine Parliament's intention, may go beyond the mere form of the enactment and look to other, policy, considerations such as the mischief at which the Act was aimed and the ease or difficulty that the respective parties would encounter in discharging the burden. Given that the defendant was better able to discharge the legal burden than the plaintiff, the construction of the majority, it is submitted, best achieved the object of the enactment in question, namely to provide a safe place of work.

On its wording, section 101 applies to summary trials. Concerning trials on indictment, the leading authorities are *R v Edwards*[36] and *R v Hunt*.[37] In *R v Edwards* the accused was convicted on indictment of selling intoxicating liquor without holding a justices' licence authorizing such sale contrary to section 160(1)(a) of the Licensing Act 1964. Edwards appealed, one of his grounds being that the prosecution had not called any evidence to prove that he did not hold a licence. It was submitted, on his behalf, that at common law the burden of proving an exception, exemption, proviso, excuse, or qualification fell on the defence only when the facts constituting it were peculiarly within the defendant's own knowledge and that in the instant case they were not.[38] The clerk to the licensing justices for any district is statutorily bound to keep a register of local licences and accordingly the police had access to a public source of knowledge. The Court of Appeal held that the legal burden of proving that the accused was the holder of a justices' licence rested on the defence and not the prosecution. After an extensive review of the authorities, Lawton LJ continued:[39]

---

[35] [1968] AC 107 at 134. Although Lord Reid dissented, his opinion on this point was the same (at 115).

[36] [1975] QB 27, CA.          [37] [1987] 1 All ER 1, HL.

[38] In *R v Turner* (1816) 5 M&S 206 at 211 it was said that 'if a negative averment be made by one party which is peculiarly within the knowledge of the other, the party within whose knowledge it lies, and who asserts the affirmative, is to prove it and not he who asserts the negative'. *R v Turner* was followed in a number of cases: see, eg, *R v Oliver* [1944] KB 68 (dealing in sugar without a licence) and *John v Humphreys* [1955] 1 All ER 793 (driving without a licence). Under the cases following *R v Turner* and prior to *R v Edwards* it became increasingly clear that the legal, as opposed to evidential, burden was being placed on the accused: see, eg, *R v Ewens* [1967] 1 QB 322, CCA (possessing drugs without a prescription).

[39] [1975] QB 27 at 39–40.

In our judgment this line of authority establishes that over the centuries the common law, as a result of experience and the need to ensure that justice is done both to the community and to the defendants, has evolved an exception to the fundamental rule of our common law that the prosecution must prove every element of the offence charged. This exception, like so much else in the common law, was hammered out on the anvil of pleading. It is limited to offences arising under enactments which prohibit the doing of an act save in specified circumstances or by persons of specified classes or with specified qualifications or with the licence or permission of specified authorities. Whenever the prosecution seeks to rely on this exception, the court must construe the enactment under which the charge is laid. If the true construction is that the enactment prohibits the doing of acts, subject to provisos, exemptions and the like, then the prosecution can rely upon the exception.

In our judgment its application does not depend upon either the fact, or the presumption, that the defendant has peculiar knowledge enabling him to prove the positive of any negative averment.

In *R v Hunt*[40] the accused was charged with the unlawful possession of morphine contrary to section 5 of the Misuse of Drugs Act 1971. Under the Misuse of Drugs Regulations 1973, it is provided that section 5 shall not have effect in relation to, inter alia, any preparation of morphine containing not more than 0.2 per cent of morphine. At the trial the defence submitted that there was no case to answer because the prosecution had adduced no evidence as to the proportion of morphine in the powder which had been found in Hunt's possession. The judge ruled against the submission. Hunt changed his plea to guilty. The appeal to the Court of Appeal was dismissed. In support of his further appeal to the House of Lords the accused raised two arguments: (i) *R v Edwards* was wrongly decided; and (ii) on the true construction of the provisions in question, the prosecution bore the burden of proving that the facts fell outside the 'exception' contained in the 1973 Regulations. The prosecution submitted that *R v Edwards* did apply and that the burden was on the accused to show that the facts fell within the 'exception'.

The House of Lords allowed the appeal. The reasoning was as follows.

1. When, in *Woolmington v DPP*,[41] Lord Sankey used the phrase 'any statutory exception', he was not referring *only* to statutory exceptions in which Parliament has placed the burden of proof on the accused expressly. A statute can place the legal burden of proof on an accused either expressly or by implication, ie on its true construction.[42]

2. Where a statute places the legal burden on the accused by implication, that burden is on the accused whether the case be tried summarily or on indictment; section 101 of the Magistrates' Court Act 1980 reflects and applies to summary trials the rule relating to the incidence of the burden of proof evolved by judges on trials on indictment.

---

[40] [1987] 1 All ER 1, HL.    [41] [1935] AC 462, HL.
[42] See per Lords Griffiths and Ackner [1987] 1 All ER 1 at 6–7 and 15 respectively.

3.  *R v Edwards* was decided correctly subject to one qualification: on occasions, albeit rarely, a statute will be construed as imposing the legal burden on the accused although it is outside the ambit of the formula given by Lawton LJ. The present case did not come within the formula, which was 'limited to offences arising under enactments which prohibit the doing of an act save in specified circumstances or by persons of specified classes or with specified qualifications or with the licence or permission of specified authorities'. The formula, although 'a helpful approach'[43] and 'an excellent guide to construction',[44] was not intended to be and is not exclusive in its effect.

4.  In the final analysis, each case must turn on the construction of the particular legislation. If the linguistic construction of a statute does not clearly indicate on whom the burden should lie, the court, in construing it, is not confined to the form of wording of the provision but, as in *Nimmo v Alexander Cowan & Sons Ltd*,[45] may have regard to matters of policy including practical consider-ations and in particular the ease or otherwise that the respective parties would encounter if required to discharge the burden.[46] Parliament, however, can never lightly be taken to have imposed the duty on an accused to prove his innocence in a criminal case and the courts should be very slow to draw any such inference from the language of a statute.[47]

5.  Policy, in the present case, pointed to the legal burden being on the prosecu-tion. This would not be an undue burden because in most cases the substance in question would have been analysed before a prosecution was brought and therefore there would be no difficulty in producing evidence to show that it did contain a certain percentage of morphine. If the burden was on the accused, however, he would have real practical difficulties because the substance is usu-ally seized by the police and he has no statutory entitlement to a proportion of it. Moreover, the substance may already have been analysed by the police and destroyed in the process.

6.  The question of construction being one of obviously real difficulty and

---

[43] Per Lord Ackner at 19.     [44] Per Lord Griffiths at 11.     [45] [1968] AC 107.

[46] On this basis it is now possible to explain cases formerly difficult to reconcile with *R v Edwards* such as *R v Putland and Sorrell* [1946] 1 All ER 85, CCA, where the charge being the acquisition of rationed goods without surrendering clothing coupons, it was held that the burden was on the prosecution to prove that the goods were bought without such surrender. In *R v Hunt* Lord Griffiths said that it would be a matter of the utmost difficulty for a defendant to establish that he had given the appropriate number of coupons for the goods in question. See also *R v Cousins* [1982] QB 526, CA, above, and *R v Curgerwen* (1865) LR 1 CCR 1, which concerned the construction of s 57 of the Offences against the Person Act 1861. After defining bigamy, the section contains a proviso against its extension 'to any second marriage contracted elsewhere than in England and Ireland by any other than a subject of Her Majesty, or to any person marrying a second time whose husband or wife shall have been continually absent from such person for the space of seven years then last past, and shall not have been known by such person to be living within that time'. In *R v Curgerwen* it was held that the prosecution bear the legal burden of proving that the accused knew the first spouse to be living. Cf *R v Audley* [1907] 1 KB 383: it is for the accused to prove that he is not a subject of Her Majesty.

[47] Per Lord Griffiths [1987] 1 All ER 1 at 11.

offences involving the misuse of hard drugs being among the most serious of offences, any ambiguity should be resolved in favour of the accused. For these reasons, therefore, the appeal was allowed.

In its 11th report, the Criminal Law Revision Committee was strongly of the opinion that both on principle and for the sake of clarity and convenience in practice, burdens on the defence should be evidential only.[48] In *R v Hunt*, Lord Griffiths thought that such a fundamental change was a matter for Parliament and not a decision for the House of Lords.[49]

*(iv) Reverse onus provisions and the Human Rights Act 1998.* Since the coming into force of the Human Rights Act 1998, any reverse onus provision is open to challenge on the basis of its incompatibility with Article 6(2) of the European Convention of Human Rights, under which 'Everyone charged with a criminal offence shall be presumed innocent until proved guilty according to law.' Clearly, a reverse onus provision will not inevitably give rise to a finding of incompatibility,[50] but if a provision does unjustifiably infringe Article 6(2), the further issue will arise whether it should be read down, in accordance with the obligation under section 3 of the 1998 Act, so as to impose an evidential and not a legal burden on the accused.

The underlying rationale of the presumption of innocence in both domestic law and in the Convention, is that it is repugnant to ordinary notions of fairness for a prosecutor to accuse an accused of a crime and for the accused then to be required to disprove the accusation on pain of conviction and punishment if he fails to do so.[51] Under domestic law, as will be apparent from the foregoing text, Parliament does not regard the presumption as an absolute or unqualified right. Equally, the Article 6(2) right is neither absolute nor unqualified. In reaching a decision on the question of incompatibility, the test is whether the modification or limitation of the Article 6(2) right pursues a legitimate aim and whether it satisfies the principle of proportionality: a balance has to be struck between the general interest of the community and the protection of the fundamental rights of the individual.[52] In *Attorney General's Reference (No 4 of 2002)*[53] Lord Bingham considered the scope of the presumption under the Convention. After an extensive review of the jurisprudence of the European Court, including the leading authority of *Salabiaku v France*,[54] his Lordship summarized the relevant principles to be derived from the Strasbourg case law.

The overriding concern is that a trial should be fair, and the presumption of innocence is a fundamental right directed to that end. The Convention does not outlaw presumptions of fact or law[55] but requires that these should be kept within reasonable limits and should not be arbitrary. It is open to states to define the constituent elements of a criminal offence,

---

[48] Subject to two minor exceptions: see Cmnd 4991, paras 140–1.     [49] [1987] 1 All ER 1 at 12.

[50] Per Lord Hope in *R v Lambert* [2002] 2 AC 545, HL, at [87].

[51] Per Lord Bingham in *Attorney General's Reference (No 4 of 2002)* [2005] 1 All ER 237 at [9].

[52] Per Lord Hope in *R v Lambert* [2002] 2 AC 545 at [88].     [53] [2005] 1 All ER 237, HL at [21].

[54] (1988) 13 EHRR 379, ECHR.     [55] See Ch 22.

excluding the requirement of mens rea. But the substance and effect of any presumption adverse to a defendant must be examined, and must be reasonable. Relevant to any judgment on reasonableness or proportionality will be the opportunity given to the defendant to rebut the presumption, maintenance of the rights of the defence, flexibility in application of the presumption, retention by the court of a power to assess the evidence, the importance of what is at stake and the difficulty which a prosecutor may face in the absence of a presumption. Security concerns do not absolve member states from their duty to observe basic standards of fairness. The justifiability of any infringement of the presumption of innocence cannot be resolved by any rule of thumb, but on examination of all the facts and circumstances of the particular provision as applied in the particular case.

In *R v Lambert*,[56] L, found in possession of a duffle bag containing two kilograms of cocaine, was charged with, and convicted of, possession of cocaine with intent to supply, contrary to section 5(3) of the Misuse of Drugs Act 1971. L had relied upon section 28 of the 1971 Act, asserting that he did not believe or suspect or have reason to suspect that the bag contained cocaine or any controlled drug. The trial judge had directed the jury that in order to establish possession of a controlled drug, the Crown merely had to prove that L had the bag in his possession and that in fact it contained a controlled drug, and that thereafter the burden was on L to bring himself within section 28 and 'to prove', on a balance of probabilities, that he did not know that the bag contained a controlled drug. The House of Lords held, by majority, that since the trial had taken place before the coming into force of the 1998 Act, L was not entitled to rely on an alleged breach of his rights under the European Convention. However, the House was of the view (Lord Hutton dissenting) that section 28 is not compatible with Article 6(2) and, under section 3 of the 1988 Act, may be read as imposing no more than an evidential burden on the accused.

Lord Steyn approached the question of compatibility by applying a three-stage test: (i) whether there has been a legislative interference with the presumption in Article 6(2); (ii) if so, whether there is an objective justification for such interference; and (iii) if so, whether the interference is proportionate, ie no greater than is necessary. As to the first stage, it was held that, taking account of the fact that under section 28 an accused will be denying moral blameworthiness and that the maximum penalty for the offence is life imprisonment, knowledge of the existence and control of the contents of the container is the gravamen of the offence, and therefore section 28 derogates from the presumption of innocence. Lord Steyn also reached this conclusion on broader grounds. His Lordship noted that the distinction between constituent elements of the crime and defensive issues will sometimes be unprincipled and arbitrary: a true constituent element may not be within the definition of the crime but cast as a defensive issue and conversely a definition of the crime may be so formulated as to include all possible defences within it. It is necessary, therefore, to concentrate not on technicalities and niceties of language, but on matters of substance. A defence may be so closely linked with mens rea and moral blameworthiness that it will derogate from

---

[56] [2002] 2 AC 545, HL.

the presumption of innocence to place the burden of proving that defence on the accused. In the case before the House, the issues under section 28, even if regarded as a pure defence, bore directly on the moral blameworthiness of the accused and therefore derogated from the presumption of innocence.

As to the second stage, Lord Steyn was satisfied that there is an objective justification for the legislative interference with the presumption of innocence, namely that sophisticated drug smugglers, dealers and couriers typically secrete drugs in some container, thereby enabling the person in possession of the container to say that he was unaware of the contents. Such a defence is commonplace and poses real difficulties for the police and prosecuting authorities.

As to the third stage, it was held that the burden is on the state to show that the legislative means adopted were no greater than necessary. The principle of proportionality required the House to consider whether there was a pressing necessity to impose a legal rather than an evidential burden. The burden of showing that only a reverse legal burden can overcome the difficulties of the prosecution in drugs cases is a heavy one. In a case of possession of controlled drugs with intent to supply, although the prosecution must establish that controlled drugs were in the possession of the accused and that he knew that the package contained something, under section 28 the accused must prove on a balance of probabilities that he did not know that the package contained controlled drugs. If the jury is not satisfied of this on a balance of probabilities, or considers that the accused's version is as likely to be true as not, they must convict him. Thus a guilty verdict may be returned in respect of an offence punishable by life imprisonment even though the jury may consider that it is reasonably possible that the accused has been duped. It was held that section 28 was a disproportionate reaction to perceived difficulties facing the prosecution in drugs cases. A new realism had significantly reduced the scope of the problems faced by the prosecution. First, possession of the container presumptively suggests, in the absence of exculpatory evidence, that the possessor knew of its contents. Secondly, section 34 of the Criminal Justice and Public Order Act 1994, enabling a judge to comment on an accused's failure to mention facts when questioned or charged, has strengthened the position of the prosecution.[57] Thirdly, where a 'mixed statement', ie an out-of-court statement made by the accused which is partly inculpatory and partly exculpatory, is introduced in evidence, and the accused elects not to testify, the judge may point out to the jury that the incriminating parts are likely to be true whereas the excuses do not have the same weight, and may also comment on the election of the accused not to testify.[58] For these reasons, Lord Steyn concluded that section 28 was incompatible with Article 6(2). However, it was further held that under section 3 of the Human Rights Act 1998, where section 28(2) and (3) require the accused to 'prove' the matters specified, the word can be read to mean 'give sufficient evidence', thereby placing only an evidential burden on the accused.

*R v Lambert* was distinguished in *L v DPP*,[59] which involved a charge of being in

---

[57] See Ch 14.     [58] See *R v Duncan* (1981) 73 Cr App R 359, Ch 6.     [59] [2003] QB 137, DC.

possession of a lock-knife in a public place contrary to section 139 of the Criminal Justice Act 1988, in relation to section 139(4), which provides that it shall be a defence for an accused to prove that he had good reason or lawful authority for having the knife with him in a public place. It was held that, striking a fair balance, section 139(4) does not conflict with Article 6 of the Convention.[60] Six reasons were given. (1) Unlike section 28 of the Misuse of Drugs Act 1971, under section 139 it is for the prosecution to prove that the accused knowingly had the offending article in his possession. (2) There is a strong public interest in bladed articles not being carried in public without good reason. Parliament is entitled, without infringing the Convention, to deter the carrying of bladed or sharply pointed articles in public to the extent of placing the burden of proving a good reason on the carrier. (3) The accused is proving something within his own knowledge. (4) The accused is entitled under Article 6 to expect the court to scrutinize the evidence with a view to deciding if a good reason exists, whether he gives evidence or not. (5) Although there will be cases in which the tribunal of fact may attach significance to where the burden of proof rests, in the great majority of cases it needs to make a value judgment as to whether, upon all the evidence, the reason is a good one, without the decision depending on whether it has to be proved that there is a good reason. (6) In striking the balance, some, albeit limited, weight should be given to the much more restricted power of sentence for an offence under section 139 than for an offence under section 5 of the Misuse of Drugs Act 1971.

*R v Lambert* was also distinguished in *R v Drummond*[61] in relation to the so-called 'hip flask' defence in section 15 of the Road Traffic Offenders Act 1988, under which it is for the accused to prove that he consumed alcohol after the offence but before providing a specimen. It was held that driving while over the limit and causing death by driving while over the limit are both social evils which Parliament sought to minimize by the legislation and that the legislative interference with the presumption of innocence was not only justified, but no greater than was necessary. Four reasons were given. (1) Conviction follows after a scientific test which is intended to be as exact as possible. (2) In most cases the test is exact or, to the extent that it is less than exact, the inexactness works in favour of the accused. (3) It is the accused himself who, by drinking after the event, defeats the aim of the legislature by doing something which makes the scientific test potentially unreliable. In many, perhaps most cases, the accused will have taken the alcohol after the event for the precise purpose of defeating the scientific test. (4) The relevant scientific evidence to set against the result ascertained from the specimen of breath or blood, including the amount which the accused drank after the offence, is all within the knowledge or means of access of the accused.

In *R v S*[62] the Court of Appeal considered section 92(5) of the Trade Marks Act 1994, which provides that it is a defence for a person charged with the unauthorized use of a registered trade mark to show that he believed on reasonable grounds that the

---

[60] See also *R v Mathews* [2004] QB 690, CA: the court, agreeing with and adopting the reasoning in *L v DPP*, held that neither s 139(4) nor s 139(5) of the 1988 Act was incompatible with Art 6.

[61] [2002] 2 Cr App R 352, CA.　　　[62] [2003] 1 Cr App R 602, CA.

use of the sign was not an infringement of the registered trade mark. It was held that section 92(5) imposed a legal burden on the accused and was compatible with Article 6(2). The same issue arose, but did not call for decision, in *R v Johnstone*,[63] in which the House of Lords, approving *R v S*, was of the same, albeit obiter, view. Lord Nicholls, in a speech endorsed by Lords Hope, Hutton and Rodger, said:[64]

for a reverse burden of proof to be acceptable there must be a compelling reason why it is fair and reasonable to deny the accused person the protection normally guaranteed to everyone by the presumption of innocence . . . A sound starting point is to remember that if an accused is required to prove a fact on the balance of probability to avoid conviction, this permits a conviction in spite of the fact-finding tribunal having a reasonable doubt as to the guilt of the accused . . . This consequence of a reverse burden of proof should colour one's approach when evaluating the reasons why it is said that, in the absence of a persuasive burden on the accused, the public interest will be prejudiced to an extent which justifies placing a persuasive burden on the accused. The more serious the punishment which may flow from conviction, the more compelling must be the reasons. The extent and nature of the factual matters required to be proved by the accused, and their importance relative to the matters required to be proved by the prosecution, have to be taken into account. So also does the extent to which the burden on the accused relates to facts which, if they exist, are readily provable by him as matters within his own knowledge or to which he already has access. In evaluating these factors the court's role is one of review. Parliament, not the court, is charged with the primary responsibility for deciding, as a matter of policy, what should be the constituent elements of a criminal offence . . . The court will reach a different conclusion from the legislature only when it is apparent the legislature has attached insufficient import-ance to the fundamental right of an individual to be presumed innocent until proved guilty.

As to section 92(5), Lord Nicholls had regard to the fact that counterfeiting is a serious contemporary problem with adverse economic effects on genuine trade and adverse effects on consumers in terms of quality of goods and, sometimes, on the health or safety of consumers. His Lordship also noted that the section 92(5) defence relates to facts within the accused's own knowledge. Two other factors were said to constitute compelling reasons why section 92(5) should place a legal burden on the accused. First, those who trade in brand products are aware of the need to be on guard against counterfeit goods. Secondly, by and large it is to be expected that those who supply traders with counterfeit goods, if traceable at all by outside investigators, are unlikely to be cooperative, so if the prosecution are required to prove that traders acted dis-honestly, fewer investigations will be undertaken and there will be fewer prosecutions.

In *Attorney General's Reference (No 1 of 2004)*[65] a five-judge Court of Appeal heard five conjoined appeals. The first two appeals concerned sections 352, 353(1), and 357(1) of the Bankruptcy Act 1986. Under section 353(1), a bankrupt is guilty of an offence if he does not inform the official receiver of a disposal of a property comprised in his estate. Under section 357(1), a bankrupt is guilty of an offence if he makes, or in the five years before the start of the bankruptcy made, any gift or transfer

---

[63] [2003] 1 WLR 1736, HL.      [64] At [49]–[51].      [65] [2004] 1 WLR 2111, CA.

of, or any charge on, his property. Under section 352, a person is not guilty of an offence under either section 353(1) or 357(1) if he proves that, at the time of the conduct constituting the offence, he had no intent to defraud or to conceal the state of his affairs. It was held that section 352, as it applies to section 353(1), does not breach Article 6. The reasons given to justify this reverse burden included the fact that concealment or disposal of assets to the disadvantage of creditors can be done alone and in private and whether there has been fraud will often be known only to the individuals in question.[66] It was also held, however, that section 352, as it applies to section 357(1), does breach Article 6 and should be read down so as to impose only an evidential burden. The reason given for this conclusion was the very wide ambit of section 357. For example, it can apply to disposals made long before the commencement of bankruptcy and possibly at a time when there was no indication of insolvency and the prosecution does not have to prove that the bankrupt was aware of the possibility of his insolvency and does not have to establish anything unusual or irregular in relation to the gift or disposition.

The third appeal related to section 1(2) of the Protection from Eviction Act 1977, whereby a person is guilty of an offence if he unlawfully deprives the residential occupier of any premises of his occupation or the premises 'unless he proves that he believed, and had reasonable cause to believe, that the residential occupier had ceased to reside in the premises'. Three reasons were given to justify this reverse burden: that the essence of the offence is unlawful deprivation of occupation, the defence only being available to the accused who can bring himself within a narrow exception; the circumstances relied upon by the accused are peculiarly within his own knowledge; the public interest in deterring landlords from ejecting tenants unlawfully.

The fourth appeal concerned section 4 of the Homicide Act 1957. Under section 4(1), it is manslaughter and not murder for a person acting in pursuance of a suicide pact between himself and another to kill the other. Under section 4(2), 'Where it is shown that a person charged with the murder of another killed the other, it shall be for the defence to prove that the person charged was acting in pursuance of a suicide pact between him and the other.' This reverse burden was justified on the basis that it provides protection for society from murder disguised as a suicide pact killing and that, although the mandatory death penalty for murder is the harshest the court can impose, the defence only arises once the prosecution has proved murder and the facts necessary to establish the defence lie within the accused's knowledge.

The fifth appeal concerned section 51 of the Criminal Justice and Public Order Act 1994. Under section 51(1):

A person commits an offence if
   (a) he does an act which intimidates, or is intended to intimidate another person;
   (b) he does the act knowing or believing that the victim is assisting in the investigation of

---

[66] The court was of the view that the decision in *R v Carass* [2002] 1 WLR 1714, should be treated as impliedly overruled by *R v Johnstone*, a view endorsed by the House of Lords in *Attorney General's Reference (No 4 of 2002)* [2005] 1 All ER 237 at [32].

an offence or is a witness or potential witness or a juror or a potential juror in proceedings for an offence; and

(c) he does it intending thereby to cause the investigation or the course of justice to be obstructed, perverted or interfered with.

Under section 51(7), if the matters in section 51(1)(a) and (b) are proved, the accused shall be presumed to have done the act with the intention required by section 51(1)(c) unless the contrary is proved. This reverse burden was justified on the basis that although it related to an ingredient of the offence rather than a special defence, witness and jury intimidation, which continues to increase, is a very serious threat to the proper administration of criminal justice, and in balancing the potential detriment to the accused against the mischief which Parliament is seeking to eradicate, the balance comes down firmly in favour of the prosecution.

In *Attorney General's Reference (No 1 of 2004)*, Lord Woolf CJ, giving the judgment of the court, noted the significant difference in emphasis between the approaches of Lord Steyn in *R v Lambert* and Lord Nicholls in *R v Johnstone*, and noted in particular the likelihood that 'few provisions will be left as imposing a legal burden on Lord Steyn's approach'.[67] It was held that until clarification of a further decision of the House of Lords, lower courts, if in doubt as to the outcome of a challenge to a reverse burden, should follow the approach of Lord Nicholls. With a view to further assisting the lower courts, Lord Woolf also set out 'General Guidance' in the form of ten general principles. However, in *Attorney General's Reference (No 4 of 2002)*,[68] the House of Lords held that both *R v Lambert* and *R v Johnstone*, unless or until revised or supplemented, should be regarded as the primary domestic authorities on reverse burdens; that nothing said in *R v Johnstone* suggested an intention to depart from or modify *R v Lambert*, which should not be treated as superseded or implicitly over-ruled; and that the differences in emphasis were explicable by the difference in the subject matter of the two cases. The House also expressly declined to endorse Lord Woolf's 'General Guidance', save to the extent that it was in accordance with the opinions of the House in *R v Lambert* and *R v Johnstone*.[69] Lord Bingham said that the task of the court is never to decide whether a reverse burden should be imposed on a defendant, but always to assess whether a burden enacted by Parliament unjustifiably infringes the presumption of innocence, and questioned Lord Woolf's assumption that Parliament would not have made an exception without good reason. Such an assumption, it was held, may lead the court to give too much weight to the enactment under review and too little to the presumption of innocence and the obligation imposed on it by section 3.

In *Attorney General's Reference (No 4 of 2002)*, the House heard two conjoined appeals. The first concerned section 5(2) of the Road Traffic Act 1988, whereby it is a defence for a person charged with an offence of being in charge of a motor vehicle on

---

[67] At [38].     [68] [2003] 3 WLR 1153, HL.

[69] See per Lord Bingham at [30] and [32]. Lords Steyn and Phillips agreed with the speech of Lord Bingham and Lords Rodger and Carswell appear to endorse these parts of Lord Bingham's speech.

a road or other public place after consuming excess alcohol, to prove that at the time
he is alleged to have committed the offence, the circumstances were such that there
was no likelihood of his driving the vehicle whilst the proportion of alcohol in his
breath, blood or urine remained likely to exceed the prescribed limit. It was held that
even on the assumption that section 5(2) infringes the presumption of innocence, it
was directed to the legitimate object of preventing death, injury and damage caused
by unfit drivers and met the tests of acceptability identified in the Strasbourg jurisprudence. It was not objectionable to criminalize conduct in these circumstances
without requiring the prosecutor to prove criminal intent. The accused has a full
opportunity to show that there was no likelihood of his driving, a matter so closely
conditioned by his own knowledge at the time as to make it much more appropriate
for him to prove the absence of a likelihood of his driving on the balance of probabilities than for the prosecutor to prove such a likelihood beyond reasonable doubt.
The imposition of a legal burden did not go beyond what was necessary. Counsel had
submitted that all burdens on the defence should be evidential only. It was held that
such a fundamental change was not mandated by Strasbourg authority and remained
a matter for Parliament and not the House of Lords.

The second appeal concerned section 11(1) and (2) of the Terrorism Act 2000,
which are in the following terms.

(1) A person commits an offence if he belongs or professes to belong to a proscribed
organisation.
(2) It is a defence for a person charged with an offence under subsection (1) to prove—
(a) that the organisation was not proscribed on the last (or only) occasion on which
he became a member or began to profess to be a member, and
(b) that he has not taken part in the activities of the organisation at any time while it
was proscribed.

The House of Lords was of the unanimous opinion that the ingredients of the offence
are set out fully in section 11(1) and that section 11(2) adds no further ingredient to
section 11(1). The House also held, by majority, that section 11(2) was incompatible
with Article 6 and should be read and given effect as imposing on the accused an
evidential burden only. Six reasons were given for the conclusion of incompatibility
with Article 6. (1) The extraordinary breadth of section 11(1) and the uncertain scope
of the word 'profess' are such that some of those liable to be convicted and punished
under section 11(1) may be guilty of no conduct which could reasonably be regarded
as blameworthy or such as should properly attract criminal sanctions. As to the
breadth of section 11(1), for example, it covers a person who joined an organization
when it was not a terrorist organization or when, if it was, he did not know that it was.
It also covers a person who joined an organization when it was not proscribed or, if it
was, did not know that it was. There would be a clear breach of the presumption of
innocence and a real risk of unfair conviction if such persons could exonerate themselves only by establishing the defence provided and it is the clear duty of the courts to
protect defendants against such a risk. (2) As to section 11(2)(b), it may be all but

impossible for an accused to show that he had not taken part in the activities of the organization. Terrorist organizations do not generate minutes or records on which he could rely and although he could assert his non-participation, his evidence might well be discounted as unreliable. (3) If section 11(2) imposes a legal burden and the accused fails to prove the matters specified, there is no room for the exercise of discretion—the court must convict him. (4) The penalty for the offence, imprisonment for up to ten years, is severe. (5) Security considerations carry weight, but they do not absolve member states from their duty to ensure that basic standards of fairness are observed. (6) Little significance can be attached to the requirement in section 117 that the Director of Public Prosecutions gives his consent to a prosecution because Article 6 is concerned with the procedure relating to the trial of a criminal case and not the decision to prosecute. As to the reading down of section 11(2), there could be no doubt that Parliament intended section 11(2) to impose a legal burden on the accused because section 118 of the Act lists a number of sections which are to be understood as imposing an evidential burden only and section 11(2) is not among those listed. For the majority, however, section 11(2) should be treated as if section 118 applied to it on the basis that although that was not the intention of Parliament when enacting the 2000 Act, it was the intention of Parliament when enacting section 3 of the Human Rights Act 1998.

According to the authorities, the imposition of a legal burden on the accused is likely to be more acceptable in the case of offences which are concerned to regulate the conduct of particular conduct in the public interest and which are not regarded as 'truly criminal'. In R v Lambert,[70] Lord Clyde said:

The requirement to have a licence in order to carry on certain types of activity is an obvious example. The promotion of health and safety and the avoidance of pollution are among the purposes to be served by such controls. These kinds of cases may propely be seen as not truly criminal. Many may be relatively trivial and only involve a monetary penalty. Many may carry with them no real social disgrace or infamy.

This dictum was applied in R v S,[71] in respect of an offence of unauthorized use of a trade mark contrary to section 92 of the Trade Marks Act 1994. The court noted that, although the offence is potentially serious and carries a maximum sentence of ten years' imprisonment, most cases are brought in the magistrates' court and, in the case of conviction, the majority result in a fine. R v Davies[72] concerned section 40 of the Health and Safety at Work Act 1974, which requires the accused to prove that 'it was not reasonably practicable to do more than was in fact done' to satisfy his health and safety duties. It was held that section 40 is not incompatible with the Convention, but justified, necessary and proportionate. In reaching this conclusion, the court relied upon the regulatory nature of the 1974 Act and the 'convincing and extremely helpful' analysis of Cory J in the Canadian Supreme Court in R v Wholesale Travel Group.[73]

---

[70] [2002] 2 AC 545, HL at [154].       [71] [2003] 1 Cr App R 602, CA at [48].
[72] [2002] EWCA Crim 2949, CA.       [73] (1991) 3 SCR 154.

Cory J expressed the rationale for the distinction between truly criminal and regulatory offences as follows.

Regulatory legislation involves the shift of emphasis from the protection of individual interests and the deterrence and punishment of acts involving moral fault to the protection of public and societal interests. While criminal offences are usually designed to condemn and punish past, inherently wrongful conduct, regulatory measures are generally directed to the prevention of future harm through the enforcement of minimum standards of conduct and care.

It follows that regulatory offences and crimes embody different concepts of fault. Since regulatory offences are directed primarily not to conduct itself but to the consequences of conduct, conviction of a regulatory offence may be thought to import a significantly lesser degree of culpability than conviction of a true crime. The concept of fault in regulatory offences is based upon a reasonable care standard and, as such, does not imply moral blameworthiness in the same manner as criminal fault. Conviction for breach of a regulatory offence suggests nothing more than that the defendant has failed to meet a prescribed standard of care.

Justifying the distinction by what he called the licensing argument and the vulnerability justification, he continued:

while in the criminal context the essential question to be determined is whether the accused has made the choice to act in the manner alleged in the indictment, the regulated defendant is by virtue of the licensing argument, assumed to have made the choice to engage in the regulated activity. Those who choose to participate in regulated activities have in doing so placed themselves in a responsible relationship to the public generally and must accept the consequences of that responsibility . . . Regulatory legislation . . . plays a legitimate and vital role in protecting those who are most vulnerable and least able to protect themselves.

In *R (Grundy & Co Excavations Ltd) v Halton Division Magistrates' Court*,[74] it was held that the offence of tree felling without a licence contrary to section 17 of the Forestry Act 1967 was a case of the kind which Lord Clyde had in mind in *R v Lambert* and which Cory J had in mind in *R v Wholesale Travel Group*: it was a classic regulatory offence, designed to protect the nation's trees, involving only a monetary penalty and carrying no real social disgrace or infamy and no real moral stigma or obloquy.

To some, including the author of this work, it remains repugnant in principle that jurors or magistrates should be under a legal duty to convict if left in doubt as to whether the accused has established his defence, or are of the view that his version of events is as likely to be true as not. In some cases, as we have seen, the courts will rule that the reverse onus provision in question is incompatible with Article 6 and can be read down so as to impose only an evidential burden. However, Parliament has decided not to legislate that all burdens borne by the accused should be evidential only. In the last edition of this work, reference was made to the views of one distinguished commentator who pointed out that if Parliament did not intervene and

---

[74] (2003) 167 JP 387.

therefore the question of compatibility fell to be determined in respect of each reverse onus provision, there would be a long period of uncertainty and much expensive and wasteful litigation, with inconsistent results, because courts would have differing views.[75] That prediction is proving to be all too accurate, and the scale of the problem remains vast because some 40 per cent of the offences triable in the Crown Court impose a legal burden on the accused to prove at least one element of the offence or statutory defence.[76]

## (b) Civil cases

The general rule, in civil cases, is that he who asserts must prove. Certain issues are 'essential' to the case of a party to civil proceedings in the sense that they must be proved by him if he is to succeed in the action. The legal burden of proof will generally lie on the party asserting the affirmative of such an issue. For example, in an action for negligence, the claimant bears the legal burden of proving duty of care, breach of such duty and loss suffered in consequence. The legal burden of proving a defence which goes beyond a simple denial of the claimant's assertions, such as *volenti non fit injuria* or contributory negligence, lies on the defendant. The burden of proving a failure to mitigate is also borne by the defendant.[77] Similarly, the legal burden of proving a contract, its breach and consequential loss lies on the claimant; and the legal burden of proving a defence which goes beyond a simple denial of the claimant's assertions, such as discharge by agreement or by frustration, lies on the defendant.

In *BHP Billiton Petroleum Ltd v Dalmine SpA*[78] it was held that, although in most civil proceedings the statements of case are likely to be a good guide to the incidence of the legal burden of proof, they cannot be definitive, because a party cannot, by poor pleading, take upon himself a burden which the law does not impose on him, or free himself from a burden which the law does impose on him. Thus a party cannot escape a legal burden borne by him on a particular issue essential to his case by drafting his claim or defence, in relation to the issue, by way of a negative allegation. In *Soward v Leggatt*[79] the plaintiff, a landlord, alleged that his tenant 'did not repair' a certain house. The defendant replied that he 'did well and sufficiently repair' the house. Lord Abinger CB, observing that the plaintiff might have pleaded that the defendant 'let the house become dilapidated', held that it was not the form of the issue which required consideration, but its substance and effect. Accordingly, it was for the plaintiff to prove the defendant's breach of covenant.

In *Abrath v North Eastern Rly Co*,[80] an action for malicious prosecution, the Court

---

[75] See Professor Sir John Smith's commentary on *R v DPP, ex p Kebilene* [1999] Crim LR 994.

[76] See Andrew Ashworth and Meredith Blake 'The Presumption of Innocence in English Criminal Law' [1996] Crim LR 306.

[77] *Geest plc v Lansiquot* [2002] 1 WLR 3111, PC, disapproving *Selvanayagam v University of the West Indies* [1983] 1 WLR 585, PC.

[78] [2003] BLR 271, CA at [28].      [79] (1836) 7 C&P 613.

[80] (1883) 11 QBD 440, CA. The case was affirmed on appeal ((1886) 11 App Cas 247, HL) and applied in *Reynolds v Metropolitan Police Comr* (1984) 80 Cr App R 125, CA (procuring the grant of a search warrant falsely, maliciously, and *without reasonable and probable cause*).

of Appeal held that the burden was on the plaintiff to prove not only that the defendant instituted proceedings against him, but also that he did so without reasonable and probable cause. It had been argued that the burden of showing reasonable and probable cause fell on the defendant, but Bowen LJ held that the assertion of a negative being an essential part of the plaintiff's case, the burden of proof rested on the plaintiff. However, Bowen LJ's reasoning begs the question as to when an assertion, be it positive or negative, is to be treated as an essential part of a party's case. The incidence of the legal burden of proof in civil cases can often be discovered from the precedents concerned with the issue of substantive law in question. In the absence of such a precedent, however, the courts are prepared to decide not on the basis of any general principles but more as a matter of policy given the particular rule of substantive law in question.[81] In *Joseph Constantine Steamship Line Ltd v Imperial Smelting Corpn Ltd*[82] a ship on charter was destroyed by an explosion the cause of which was unclear. The charterers claimed damages from the owners for failure to load. The owners' defence was frustration. The charterers argued that the owners could not rely upon frustration unless they proved that the explosion was not caused by fault on their part. The owners replied that they could rely upon the defence of frustration unless the charterers showed that the explosion was caused by their fault, that is fault on the part of the owners. The House of Lords held that in order to defeat the defence of frustration, the burden of proof was upon the charterers to prove fault on the part of the owners. Accordingly, the cause of the explosion being unclear, the appeal of the owners was allowed. It is possible to justify this outcome on the basis that it is more difficult to prove absence of fault than it is to prove fault. This justification, however, should not be regarded as an inflexible *rule*: in bailment cases, for example, the bailor having proved bailment, the bailee has the onus of proving that the goods were lost or damaged without fault on his part.[83] Similarly, in an action for conversion, the burden is on the bailee to prove that he dealt with the goods in good faith and without notice.[84] Thus the cases have been decided as a matter of policy on their own merits.[85]

In civil, as in criminal cases, the incidence of the legal burden of proof may be determined by statute. For example, whereas it is for the former employee claiming unfair dismissal to prove that he was dismissed, it is for the employer to show the reason for the dismissal and that it constitutes one of the grounds set out in the statute

---

[81] See Stone (1944) 60 LQR 262.        [82] [1942] AC 154, HL.

[83] *Coldman v Hill* [1919] 1 KB 443, CA; cf *Levison v Patent Steam Carpet Cleaning Ltd* [1978] QB 69, CA.

[84] *Marcq v Christie Manson and Woods Ltd* [2002] 4 All ER 1005, QBD.

[85] In some civil cases exposition of the law is rendered difficult by a judicial failure to make clear which burden, legal or evidential, is in contemplation. One example is where rape is pleaded as a defence to adultery. It is unclear whether the legal burden is on the petitioner to prove that the intercourse was consensual or on the defendant to prove that it was non-consensual. In *Redpath v Redpath and Milligan* [1950] 1 All ER 600, CA the judgment of Bucknill LJ suggests the former, that of Vaisey J the latter, although neither distinguished between the legal and evidential burden.

on which a dismissal is capable of being fair. If the employer fails to show such a reason, the dismissal is automatically unfair.[86] Equally, the parties themselves may expressly agree upon the incidence of the burden of proof.[87] The parties may do this, for example, in the case of written contracts, but in the absence of express agreement the matter becomes one of construction for the court. In *Munro, Brice & Co v War Risks Association*[88] an insurance policy covered a ship subject to an exemption in respect of loss by capture or in consequence of hostilities. The ship in question had disappeared for reasons unknown and a claim was made. The question for the court was whether the plaintiffs had to prove that the ship was not lost by reason of enemy action. The court found for the plaintiff on the basis that the defendants bore the burden of proving that the facts fell within the exception and this they had clearly failed to do.[89] However, where a claimant in these circumstances relies upon a proviso to an exemption clause, the burden of proving that the facts fall within the proviso may well be on him. In *The Glendarroch*[90] the plaintiffs brought an action in negligence for non-delivery of goods, the goods in question having been lost when the boat carrying them sank. Under the bill of lading, there was a clause exempting the defendants in respect of loss or damage caused by perils of the sea provided that the defendants were not negligent. It was held that the plaintiffs bore the burden of proving the contract and non-delivery; that if the defendants relied upon the exemption clause, it was for them to prove that the facts fell within it, ie that loss was caused by a peril of the sea; but that if the plaintiffs then relied upon the proviso to the exemption clause, it was for them to prove that the facts fell within the proviso, ie that loss was caused by the negligence of the defendants.

## 4 THE INCIDENCE OF THE EVIDENTIAL BURDEN

As a general rule in both civil and criminal proceedings, a party bearing the legal burden on a particular issue will also bear the evidential burden on that issue. This rule has given rise to little difficulty or case law in civil proceedings. As in criminal cases, the incidence of the evidential burden in civil cases may be affected by the operation of a presumption, a matter considered in detail in Chapter 22.[91] In criminal

---

[86] See Employment Rights Act 1996, s 98. A further example is the Consumer Credit Act 1974, s 171(7): if a debtor alleges that a credit bargain is extortionate (within the meaning of ss 137 and 138), it is for the creditor to prove to the contrary. See also s 63A of the Sex Discrimination Act 1975.

[87] See, eg, *Levy v Assicurazioni Generali* [1940] AC 791, PC and *Fred Chappell Ltd v National Car Parks Ltd* (1987) *The Times*, 22 May, QBD.

[88] [1918] 2 KB 78.

[89] Cf *Hurst v Evans* [1917] 1 KB 352, where the plaintiff made a claim under an insurance policy covering loss of jewellery subject to an exception in the case of theft by the plaintiff's servants. The court held that the plaintiff bore the burden of proving that the exemption clause did not apply ie that loss was not caused by the theft of his servants. See also *Gorman v Hand-in-Hand Insurance Co* (1877) IR 11 CL 224.

[90] [1894] P 226, CA.

[91] See, eg, s 30(2) of the Bills of Exchange Act 1882: 'Every holder of a bill is prima facie deemed to be a holder in due course; but if in an action on a bill it is admitted or proved that the acceptance, issue, or

cases, where, as we have seen, the prosecution generally bears the legal burden of proving those facts essential to the Crown case, the prosecution normally also bears the evidential burden in relation to those facts. Similarly, where the defence bears the legal burden of proving insanity (as required at common law) or some other issue (pursuant to an express or implied statutory exception), the defence also bears the evidential burden on such issues.

In the case of most common law defences, the evidential burden is on the defence and, once discharged, the legal burden of disproving the defence is then on the prosecution.[92] However, the evidential burden may be discharged by *any* evidence in the case, whether adduced or elicited by the defence, a co-accused or the prosecution;[93] and where there is sufficiently cogent evidence of such a defence, then the judge must leave it to the jury, even if it has not been mentioned by the defence[94] or has been expressly disclaimed by them[95] (or they have conveyed to the judge their opinion that he should not leave it to the jury)[96] and notwithstanding that it may be inconsistent with the accused's defence.[97] The above principles apply to the common law defences of provocation,[98] self-defence,[99] duress,[100] non-insane automatism,[101] and drunkenness.[102]

subsequent negotiation of the bill is affected with fraud, duress, or force and fear, or illegality, the burden of proof is shifted, unless and until the holder proves that subsequent to the alleged fraud or illegality, value has in good faith been given for the bill.' The effect of this provision is that if a party sues on a bill of exchange he only bears the evidential burden on the issue whether he gave value for the bill in good faith if the defendant has adduced prima facie evidence that the acceptance, issue etc of the bill is affected with fraud, duress etc. See *Talbot v Von Boris* [1911] 1 KB 854 at 866, CA.

[92] This is also the case in relation to a variety of statutory defences. See, eg, s 3(1) of the Criminal Law Act 1967 (reasonable force in the prevention of crime etc) and *R v Cameron* [1973] Crim LR 520, CA and *R v Khan* [1995] Crim LR 78, CA. See also s 75 of the Sexual Offences Act 2003 and s 118(2) of the Terrorism Act 2000.

[93] *Bullard v R* [1957] AC 635, PC.

[94] *Palmer v R* [1971] AC 814, PC at 823. See also *R v Hopper* [1915] 2 KB 431; *R v Cascoe* [1970] 2 All ER 833, CA; *R v Bonnick* (1977) 66 Cr App R 266, CA; *R v Johnson* [1989] 2 All ER 839, CA; and *DPP (Jamaica) v Bailey* [1995] 1 Cr App R 257, PC.

[95] *R v Kachikwu* (1968) 52 Cr App R 538, CA at 543.

[96] *R v Burgess and McLean* [1995] Crim LR 425, CA and *R v Dhillon* [1997] 2 Cr App R 104, CA. But see also *R v Groark* [1999] Crim LR 669, CA, below.

[97] See *R v Newell* [1989] Crim LR 906 and generally Sean Doran 'Alternative Defences: the "invisible burden" on the trial judge' [1991] Crim LR 878.

[98] *Mancini v DPP* [1942] AC 1, HL and *R v Cascoe* [1970] 2 All ER 83, CA. See also *R v Rossiter* [1994] 2 All ER 752, CA and *R v Cambridge* [1994] 2 All ER 760, CA.

[99] *R v Lobell* [1957] 1 QB 547, CCA. See also *Chan Kau v R* [1955] AC 206, PC.

[100] *R v Gill* [1963] 1 WLR 841, CCA. See also *R v Bone* [1968] 1 WLR 983, CA.

[101] *Bratty v A-G for Northern Ireland* [1963] AC 386, HL. See also *R v Stripp* (1978) 69 Cr App R 318, CA at 321 and *R v Pullen* [1991] Crim LR 457, CA. The situation is different in the case of insanity, because that defence places a burden of proof on the accused, although in rare and exceptional cases the judge may of his own volition raise the issue and leave it to the jury: see *R v Thomas (Sharon)* [1995] Crim LR 314, CA.

[102] See *Kennedy v HM Advocate* 1944 JC 171 and *R v Foote* [1964] Crim LR 405. However, in *R v Groark* [1999] Crim LR 669, CA, it was held that if, in a case of wounding with intent, there is evidence of drunkenness which might give rise to the issue whether the accused had the specific intent, but the defence is that the accused knew what was happening and acted in self-defence, if the defence object to a direction on drunkenness in relation to intent, such a direction need not be given.

In relation to the defence of provocation, it has been held that the judge is required to leave the defence to the jury only if there is some evidence, from whatever source, suggestive of the reasonable possibility that the accused might have lost his self-control due to provoking words or conduct. If there is no such evidence, but merely the speculative possibility of an act of provocation, the issue does not arise and suggestions in cross-examination cannot by themselves raise the issue.[103] Equally, a judge is under no duty to put before the jury strained and implausible inferences to create a defence of provocation for which there is no true basis.[104] In *R v Cox*[105] it was held that where there is evidence of provocation and the defence do not rely upon it at trial, it is most unsatisfactory that the judge's failure to direct the jury on it can then found an appeal against conviction, and therefore if it appears to counsel for either side that there is evidence of provocation, it is their duty to point it out to the judge before he sums up. It is submitted that this duty should not be confined to cases of provocation, but should be extended to the other common law and statutory defences in respect of which the accused bears the evidential but not the legal burden.

Where the defence of non-insane automatism is raised by an accused, the judge must decide two questions before it can be left to the jury: whether there is a proper evidential foundation for it and whether the evidence shows the case to be one of insane or non-insane automatism. If the judge rules it to be a case of insanity, the jury must then decide whether the accused is guilty or not guilty by reason of insanity.[106] It was held by the Court of Appeal in *R v Burns*[107] that where the issues of both insanity and non-insane automatism arise in the same case, the judge should direct the jury that while the accused bears the legal burden of proving insanity, he bears only the evidential burden in relation to non-insane automatism.

The law relating to the above defences is reasonably well settled and clear. It is less clear, however, whether the defence bears the evidential burden in relation to a defence which amounts to nothing more than a denial of the prosecution case and therefore raises no new issue. On one view, an accused should not bear an evidential burden in relation to a defence of, say, alibi or accident, because the onus is already on the prosecution to prove, in the one case, that the accused was present at the scene of the crime and, in the other, that he had the requisite mens rea.[108] There are *obiter dicta*, however, to the effect that the evidential burden, in the case of both of these

---

[103] *R v Acott* [1977] 1 WLR 306, HL. See also *R v Kromer* [2002] All ER (D) 420 (May), CA and *R v Miao* (2003) *The Times*, 26 Nov 2003, CA.

[104] *R v Walch* [1993] Crim LR 714, CA. See also *R v Wellington* [1993] Crim LR 616, CA.

[105] [1995] 2 Cr App R 513, CA.  [106] *R v Burgess* (1991) 93 Cr App R 41, CA.

[107] (1973) 58 Cr App R 364; cf *Bratty v A-G for Northern Ireland* [1963] AC 386 at 402–3.

[108] See Professor Glanville Williams (1977) 127 NLJ at 157–8 and generally per Lord Hailsham LC in *R v Howe* [1987] 1 All ER 771, HL at 781 et seq.

defences, is on the accused.[109] Moreover, in *R v Bennett*[110] it was held that the accused bore the evidential burden in relation to impossibility on a charge of conspiracy to contravene the provisions of the Misuse of Drugs Act 1971[111] and in *Bratty v A-G for Northern Ireland*, as we have seen, the accused was held to bear the evidential burden on non-insane automatism.

Where the evidential burden alone, in relation to a particular defence, is borne by the accused, the judge, if he decides that insufficient evidence has been adduced on the matter, will direct the jury that the issue must be taken as proved against the accused. If the defence has adduced sufficient evidence, the judge will direct the jury that the prosecution bears the legal burden of negativing the defence in question and must satisfy them beyond reasonable doubt on the matter. However, where the legal burden is borne by the accused, the jury should be directed that it is for the defence to satisfy them on a balance of probabilities and that if they are not so satisfied the issue must be taken as proved against the accused.[112] Accordingly, the judge may direct the jury that if they cannot decide on the evidence whether the defence case is more probable than not, they should find against the accused.

## 5 THE RIGHT TO BEGIN

The right to begin adducing evidence is determined by the incidence of the evidential burden. As a general rule, the claimant has the right to begin adducing evidence in civil proceedings and the prosecution in criminal proceedings. In civil cases, the claimant has the right to adduce his evidence first unless the defendant bears the evidential burden on every issue.[113] In *Mercer v Whall*[114] an attorney's clerk brought an action for unliquidated damages for wrongful dismissal. The defendant admitted the dismissal but pleaded justification on the basis of the plaintiff's misconduct. It was held that the plaintiff was entitled to begin because he bore the evidential burden in relation to damages. The defendant would have had the right to begin if the claim had been for a liquidated sum because the only fact in issue would then have been the question of misconduct on which the defendant bore the evidential burden. In criminal cases

---

[109] *R v Johnson* [1961] 3 All ER 969, CCA (alibi); *Bratty v A-G for Northern Ireland* [1963] AC 386, HL per Lord Kilmuir LC at 405 (accident). There is no dispute, however, that if the defence do adduce evidence in support of an alibi, the prosecution bear the legal burden of disproof (*R v Helliwell* [1995] Crim LR 79, CA and *R v Fergus* (1993) 98 Cr App R 313, CA) and ideally the judge should give a specific direction on the burden of proof in relation to the alibi (*R v Anderson* [1991] Crim LR 361, CA and *R v Johnson* [1995] Crim LR 242, CA). See also *R v Mussell* [1995] Crim LR 887, CA: a specific direction is needed if the nature of the alibi is that the accused was at a specific place elsewhere, raising the question why he did not call witnesses in support, but not if the evidence amounts to little more than a denial that he committed the crime.

[110] (1978) 68 Cr App R 168, CA.

[111] However, it was further held that if the prosecution has in its possession evidence which might show that at the time when the agreement was made the carrying out of the agreement would have been impossible, it is the duty of the prosecution either to call the evidence or to make it available to the defence.

[112] See *R v Evans-Jones, R v Jenkins* (1923) 87 JP 115 and *R v Carr-Briant* [1943] KB 607.

[113] See *Pontifex v Jolly* (1839) 9 C & P 202 and *Re Parry's Estate, Parry v Fraser* [1977] 1 All ER 309.

[114] (1845) 14 LJ QB 267.

where there is a plea of not guilty, the prosecution will normally have the right to adduce their evidence first. The reason appears to be that they will almost always bear an evidential burden on at least one issue. However, this may not be the case where the accused has made formal admissions pursuant to section 10 of the Criminal Justice Act 1967 or agreed to a statement of facts admitted in evidence pursuant to section 9 of the same Act. Where the accused pleads *autrefois acquit* or *convict* and there is a dispute of fact requiring evidence, the accused has the right to begin.

## B  THE STANDARD OF PROOF

### 1  THE LEGAL BURDEN

Whether a party to civil or criminal proceedings has discharged a legal burden borne by him in relation to a particular issue is, as we have seen, decided by the tribunal of fact at the end of the case. To discharge the burden and succeed on that issue the evidence adduced by that party must, in the opinion of the tribunal of fact, be more cogent or convincing than that adduced by his opponent. How much more cogent or convincing the evidence is required to be is determined by rules of law relating to the standard of proof. The standard of proof required to discharge a legal burden depends upon whether the proceedings are criminal or civil, the standard being higher in the former than in the latter. In criminal proceedings, the standard required of the prosecution before the jury can find the accused guilty is proof beyond reasonable doubt.[115] In civil proceedings, the standard of proof required to be met by either party seeking to discharge a legal burden is proof on a balance of probabilities.

The notion of a third and intermediate standard of proof lying between the standards required in criminal and civil cases has not found favour in the courts.[116] However, although in the remainder of this chapter reference will only be made to the two standards of proof, as if each refers to a precise or fixed degree of probability, it should be stressed that in civil cases, at any rate, the degree of cogency required of evidence can vary from case to case according to the seriousness of the allegations made and the potential consequences of the decision for the parties to the proceedings.[117] 'The more

---

[115] The same standard has to be met: (i) by a judge determining the facts for the purpose of sentence, the accused having pleaded guilty and having put forward a version of the facts which differs significantly from the prosecution's version (*R v McGrath and Casey* (1983) 5 Cr App R (S) 460 and *R v Ahmed* (1984) 6 Cr App R (S) 391); (ii) by a jury in a coroner's court considering a verdict of unlawful killing or suicide (*R v West London Coroner, ex p Gray* [1987] 2 All ER 129, DC and *R v Wolverhampton Coroner, ex p McCurbin* [1990] 2 All ER 759, CA); and (iii) by a Solicitor's Disciplinary Tribunal investigating what is tantamount to a criminal offence: *Re a Solicitor* [1991] NLJR 1447, DC. See also reg 10 of the Disciplinary Tribunals Regulations 1993, Annexe N, Code of Conduct of the Bar of England and Wales.

[116] See, eg, per Lord Tucker in *Dingwall v J Wharton (Shipping) Ltd* [1961] 2 Lloyd's Rep 213 at 216, HL.

[117] For a conceptual framework for understanding the civil standard of proof, see Mike Redmayne 'Standards of Proof in Civil Litigation' (1999) MLR vol 62, 167.

serious the allegation the more cogent is the evidence required to overcome the unlikelihood of what is alleged and thus to prove it.'[118] As Morris LJ remarked in *Hornal v Neuberger Products Ltd*,[119] 'the very elements of gravity become a part of the whole range of circumstances which have to be weighed in the scale when deciding as to the balance of probabilities'. The point is sometimes made by reference to degrees of proof within the same standard. Thus, Denning LJ in *Bater v Bater*[120] said:

a higher standard of proof is required in criminal cases than in civil cases. But this is subject to the qualification that there is no absolute standard in either case. In criminal cases the charge must be proved beyond reasonable doubt, but there may be degrees of proof within that standard ... so also in civil cases the case must be proved by a preponderance of probability, but there may be degrees of probability within that standard.

The matter has, as we shall see, given rise to some difficulty in civil proceedings.

## (a) Criminal cases

The rules prescribing the standard of proof are a matter of law for the judge. Whether the evidence adduced meets the standard is a question for the jury as tribunal of fact. In criminal trials, therefore, the judge must direct the jury on the standard of proof that the prosecution is required to meet.[121] In *Miller v Minister of Pensions*[122] Denning J described the standard of proof required to be met in a criminal case, before an accused person may be found guilty, in the following terms:

It need not reach certainty, but it must carry a high degree of probability. Proof beyond a reasonable doubt does not mean proof beyond the shadow of a doubt. The law would fail to protect the community if it admitted fanciful possibilities to deflect the course of justice. If the evidence is so strong against a man as to leave only a remote possibility in his favour, which can be dismissed with the sentence 'of course it is possible but not in the least probable' the case is proved beyond reasonable doubt, but nothing short of that will suffice.

Given the enormous difficulty of defining degrees of probability clearly as well as precisely, Denning J's dictum might fairly be regarded as a model. It does not follow, however, that it should be recited to the jury either verbatim or as a matter of course: as we shall see, definitions and explanations are generally to be avoided and there is no requirment to use any formula or particular form of words.

---

[118] Per Ungoed-Thomas J in *Re Dellow's Will Trusts* [1964] 1 WLR 451, Ch D.

[119] [1957] 1 QB 247, CA at 266. These words of Morris LJ were approved and adopted by the House of Lords in *Khawaja v Secretary of State for the Home Department* [1983] 1 All ER 765 in relation to the detention pending deportation of persons alleged to be illegal immigrants: see per Lord Scarman at 783–4. See also *Lawrence v Chester Chronicle* (1986) *The Times*, 8 Feb, CA: in defamation actions, it is not generally necessary for the judge to direct the jury as to the flexibility of the civil standard of proof according to the seriousness of the alleged defamatory statement; in most cases it is a matter for the jury's common sense.

[120] [1951] P 35 at 36, CA.

[121] See Ch 2 under **E4 The summing-up.**

[122] [1947] 2 All ER 372 at 373–4.

*(i) Definitions and explanations.* In *R v Yap Chuan Ching*[123] the judge in his summing-up had directed the jury that it was for the prosecution to prove the charges so that they were sure that they had been made out, or to prove them beyond a reasonable doubt. The judge explained that these were two different ways of saying the same thing. After retirement the jury came back into court and the judge understood the foreman to ask for a further direction on the standard of proof. The judge repeated the test of proof beyond a reasonable doubt and continued:

A reasonable doubt ... is a doubt to which you can give a reason as opposed to a mere fanciful sort of speculation such as 'Well, nothing in this world is certain, nothing in this world can be proved' ... It is sometimes said the sort of matter which might influence you if you were to consider some business matter. A matter, for example, of a mortgage concerning your house, or something of that nature.

Four minutes later the jury returned to court and found the defendant guilty on one count by a majority of eleven to one. The Court of Appeal thought that the judge's direction on the standard of proof in his summing-up could not have been clearer or more accurate. However, taking judicial notice of the fact that one of the popular forms of television entertainment is reconstructed trials which have a striking degree of realism, and observing that most jurors currently know something about burden and standard before they even get into the jury box, the Court of Appeal concluded that in most cases judges should not attempt any gloss upon the meaning of 'sure' or 'reasonable doubt'. The court held that judicial comments of that kind usually create difficulties and are more likely to confuse than help. 'We point out and emphasize ... that if judges stopped trying to define that which is almost impossible to define there would be fewer appeals.'[124] However, it was acknowledged that in exceptional cases the jury does require help. The case in question was such a case and, so far as his additional direction was concerned, the judge was right in what he did. The appeal was accordingly dismissed.[125]

In fact, as we shall see, judges often define and explain the burden to the jury, and in *Walters v R*[126] the Privy Council observed that it has been for many years a common practice of judges to expand the bare expression 'reasonable doubt' by use of analogies. The Privy Council did not appear to regard the matter as exceptional but took the view that it was a matter of discretion for the judge to choose the most appropriate set of words to enable the particular jury in question to understand that they must not return a verdict against a defendant unless sure of his guilt.

*(ii) Formulae.* On the basis that definitions and explanations are generally regarded as undesirable, it would not be unreasonable to expect a requirement that judges use a particular form of words when referring to the standard of proof. In fact, the authorities have been consistently opposed to such a course. 'It has been said a good many

---

[123] (1976) 63 Cr App R 7, CA.     [124] (1976) 63 Cr App R 7 at 11.
[125] See also per Goddard CJ in *R v Hepworth and Fearnley* [1955] 2 QB 600, CCA at 603.
[126] [1969] 2 AC 26.

times that it is not a matter of some precise formula or particular form of words being used.'[127] However, in *Ferguson v R*[128] Lord Scarman observed that 'though the law requires no particular formula, judges are wise, as a general rule, to adopt one'. The particular formulae that judges are wise to adopt are, as we shall see, 'sure of the defendant's guilt' and 'satisfied beyond reasonable doubt'. This is, of course, tanta-mount to a requirement of that which is being proscribed, a certain form of words. The point is well illustrated by *R v Kritz*,[129] where the trial judge had directed the jury that they must be 'reasonably satisfied' and did not use the words 'satisfied beyond reasonable doubt'. On appeal, Lord Goddard CJ held that the accuracy of a summing up did not depend on the use of a particular form of words and continued:[130]

It is not the particular formula that matters: it is the effect of the summing up. If the jury are made to understand that they have to be satisfied and must not return a verdict against a defendant unless they feel sure, and that the onus is all the time on the prosecution and not the defence, then whether the judge uses one form of language or another is neither here nor there . . .[131]

*(iii) Proper and improper directions.* The most reliable guidance as to how a judge should properly direct a jury is discovered by contrasting those directions which, on appeal, have been approved and disapproved. 'The time honoured formula is that the jury must be satisfied beyond reasonable doubt.'[132] Although in *R v Summers*[133] Lord Goddard objected to the use of this phrase, three years later in *R v Hepworth and Fearnley*[134] he approved of it, explaining that his earlier objection was based on the difficulties of explaining to a jury what a reasonable doubt is. To explain to a jury that it is not a fanciful doubt offers no real guidance and to tell them that it is such a doubt as to cause them to hesitate in their own affairs does not convey any particular standard; one jury member might say he would hesitate over something whereas another might say that that would not cause him to hesitate at all.[135] In *R v Stafford, R v Luvaglio*[136] Edmund Davies LJ said:

We do not . . . agree with the trial judge when, directing the jury upon the standard of proof he told them to 'Remember that a reasonable doubt is one for which you could give reasons if you were asked', and we dislike such a description or definition.[137]

---

[127] Per Fenton Atkinson LJ in *R v Allan* [1969] 1 All ER 91, CCA at 92.

[128] [1979] 1 WLR 94, PC.     [129] [1950] 1 KB 82, CCA.     [130] [1950] 1 KB 82 at 89–90.

[131] Cited with approval by the Privy Council in *Walters v R* [1969] 2 AC 26.

[132] Per Lord Scarman in *Ferguson v R* [1979] 1 WLR 94, PC. The phrase has been approved by the House of Lords in *Woolmington v DPP* [1935] AC 462 and *Mancini v DPP* [1942] AC 1.

[133] (1952) 36 Cr App R 14 at 15.     [134] [1955] 2 QB 600, CCA.

[135] [1955] 2 QB 600 at 603. Cf Lord Diplock in *Walters v R* [1969] 2 AC 26, PC: it is otiose to describe 'doubt' as subjective; it is the duty of each individual juror to make up his mind and inevitably, because of differences of temperament or experience, some jurors will take more convincing than others.

[136] (1968) 53 Cr App R 1 at 2, CA.

[137] Cf per Barwick CJ in *Green v R* (1971) 126 CLR 28 at 32–3: 'Jurymen themselves set the standard of what is reasonable in the circumstances . . . A reasonable doubt which a jury may entertain is not to be confined to a "rational doubt" or a "doubt founded on reason".'

In *R v Gray*[138] the trial judge defined a reasonable doubt as 'a doubt based upon good reason and not a fanciful doubt' and as 'the sort of doubt which might affect you in the conduct of your everyday affairs'. The Court of Appeal held that if the judge had referred to the sort of doubt which may affect the mind of a person in the conduct of important affairs, there could have been no criticism, but a reference to 'everyday affairs' might have suggested to the jury too low a standard of proof. In *Walters v R*[139] the Privy Council upheld the direction of the trial judge that 'a reasonable doubt is that quality and kind of doubt which, when you are dealing with matters of importance in your own affairs, you allow to influence you one way or the other'. In *R v Hodge*,[140] a murder case where the prosecution evidence was entirely circumstantial, the jurors were directed by Alderson B that before returning a verdict of guilty they should be satisfied that the evidence was consistent with the guilt of the accused and inconsistent with any other rational conclusion than the defendant's guilt. However, the House of Lords in *McGreevy v DPP*[141] held that there is no rule requiring a special or additional direction where the evidence against the defendant is wholly or partially circumstantial; it suffices to direct the jury that the prosecution has the burden of proving the defendant's guilt beyond reasonable doubt.

Another classic formulation of the criminal standard of proof is to direct the jury that in order to return a guilty verdict they must 'be sure' or 'satisfied so that they feel sure'.[142] In *R v Hepworth and Fearnley*[143] Lord Goddard CJ held that it is a proper direction to say, 'You, the jury, must be completely satisfied', or better still, 'You must feel sure of the prisoner's guilt.' In that case the appeal was allowed because the judge had merely directed the jury that they must be 'satisfied'. To direct the jury to be 'satisfied' without any indication of the degree of satisfaction required is an inadequate direction.[144] However, it is sufficient to direct the jury to be satisfied so that they are sure of guilt, and it is not helpful to seek to draw a distinction between being sure of guilt and being certain of guilt.[145] In *Ferguson v R*[146] the two classic formulations were combined and Lord Scarman held that: 'It is generally sufficient and safe to direct a jury that they must be satisfied beyond reasonable doubt so that they feel sure of the defendant's guilt.'

*(iv) Where the accused bears the legal burden.* In criminal cases, the legal burden is, as we have seen, generally borne by the prosecution. Where the legal burden on a particular issue is borne by the accused, it is discharged by the defence satisfying the jury on a balance of probabilities. In *R v Carr-Briant*[147] Humphreys J said:[148]

---

[138] (1973) 58 Cr App R 177.　　[139] [1969] 2 AC 26, PC.　　[140] (1838) 2 Lew CC 227.

[141] [1973] 1 WLR 276, HL.

[142] See per Lord Goddard CJ in *R v Kritz* [1950] 1 KB 82, CCA at 89–90 (approved by the Privy Council in *Walters v R* [1969] 2 AC 26 and in *R v Summers* (1952) 36 Cr App R 14, CCA at 15).

[143] [1955] 2 QB 600 at 603, CCA.

[144] See also per Fenton Atkinson LJ in *R v Allan* [1969] 1 All ER 91, CCA.

[145] *R v Stephens* (2002) *The Times* 27 June 2002, CA　　[146] [1979] 1 WLR 94 at 99, PC.

[147] [1943] KB 607, CCA.　　[148] [1943] KB 607 at 612.

In any case where, either by statute or at common law, some matter is presumed against an accused person 'unless the contrary is proved', the jury should be directed that it is for them to decide whether the contrary is proved, that the burden of proof required is less than that required at the hands of the prosecution in proving the case beyond a reasonable doubt, and that the burden may be discharged by evidence satisfying the jury of the probability of that which the accused is called upon to establish.

Similarly, where the defence bears the legal burden of proving insanity[149] or diminished responsibility,[150] the burden is discharged by satisfying the jury on a balance of probabilities.

### (b) Civil cases

In civil trials, the standard of proof required to be met by either party seeking to discharge the legal burden of proof is on a balance of probabilities.[151] The same standard should also be used in reaching a decision on a submission of no case to answer when the defendant has elected not to adduce any evidence.[152] In *Miller v Minister of Pensions*[153] Denning J described as well settled the degree of cogency required to discharge the legal burden in a civil case. He continued:[154]

It must carry a reasonable degree of probability, but not so high as is required in a criminal case. If the evidence is such that the tribunal can say: 'we think it more probable than not', the burden is discharged, but if the probabilities are equal it is not.

To the general rule on the standard of proof in civil proceedings are a number of clearly defined exceptions. First, the appropriate standard in committal proceedings for civil contempt of court is the criminal standard, proof beyond reasonable doubt.[155] Second, the criminal standard may also be required in civil proceedings pursuant to statute.[156] Third, it has been held that an exacting civil standard of proof, which for all practical purposes is indistinguishable from the criminal standard of proof, applies to the following civil proceedings: applications for sex offender orders (in relation to the condition, set out in section 2(1)(a) of the Crime and Disorder Act 1998, that the person against whom the order is sought is a 'sex offender');[157] applications for football banning orders under section 14B of the Football Spectators Act

---

[149] *Sodeman v R* [1936] 2 All ER 1138 at 1140, PC.        [150] *R v Dunbar* [1958] 1 QB 1.

[151] The same standard is not necessarily appropriate for interim applications. For example, an application for summary judgment is decided not by application of the normal standard of proof but by application of the test whether the respondent has a case with a real prospect of success: *Royal Brompton Hospital NHS Trust v Hammond* [2001] BLR 297, CA.

[152] *Miller v Cawley* (2002) *The Times* 6 Sept 2002, CA.        [153] [1947] 2 All ER 372.

[154] [1947] 2 All ER 372 at 374.

[155] *Re Bramblevale Ltd* [1970] Ch 128, CA; *Dean v Dean* [1987] 1 FLR 517, CA. Proceedings to bind over for breach of the peace are probably criminal proceedings, but even if properly classified as civil proceedings, call for proof to the criminal standard, because failure to comply with an order to enter into a recognisance may result in imprisonment: *Percy v DPP* [1995] 3 All ER 124, DC.

[156] See *Judd v Minister of Pensions and National Insurance* [1966] 2 QB 580.

[157] *B v Chief Constable of Avon and Somerset Constabulary* [2001] 1 WLR 340, DC.

1989;[158] and applications for anti-social behaviour orders (in relation to the condition, set out in section 1(1)(a) of the Crime and Disorder Act 1998, that the person against whom the order is sought has acted 'in an anti-social manner').[159] As to the last case, it has been held that magistrates, to make their task more straightforward, should always apply the *criminal* standard.[160]

As previously noted, the civil standard of proof is not an absolute or fixed standard but can vary according to the seriousness of the allegations being made and the consequences of the decision for the parties to the proceedings. This topic is explored by reference to (i) allegations of crime in civil proceedings (ii) matrimonial causes and (iii) a miscellany of different cases.

*(i) Allegations of crime in civil proceedings.* Prior to the decision of the Court of Appeal in *Hornal v Neuberger Products Ltd*,[161] it was unclear, on the authorities, what standard of proof was appropriate in civil cases in which a party made an allegation of criminal conduct. One line of authorities supported the view that the standard was as high as that required of the prosecution in a criminal case.[162] Other authorities took the view that the appropriate standard was the normal civil standard on a balance of probabilities.[163] In *Hornal v Neuberger Products Ltd* the plaintiff claimed damages for breach of warranty or alternatively for fraud. The defendant company had sold a lathe to the plaintiff. The plaintiff alleged that one of the company directors had represented that the lathe had been 'Soag reconditioned'. If the director did so represent, there was clearly a fraudulent misrepresentation because he knew that the machine had not been reconditioned. The question became whether the representation had been made or not. Dismissing the claim for damages for breach of warranty on the grounds that the parties did not intend the director's statement to have contractual effect, the trial judge said that he was satisfied on a balance of probabilities, but not beyond reasonable doubt, that the statement was made and accordingly awarded damages for fraud. On appeal, the Court of Appeal held that on an allegation of a crime in civil proceedings the standard of proof is on a balance of probabilities.

One of the reasons for the decision was put clearly by Denning LJ:[164] 'I think it would bring the law into contempt if a judge were to say on the issue of warranty he finds the statement was made, and that on the issue of fraud he finds it was not made.' In support of his conclusion that the civil standard applied, his Lordship referred to the views which he had expressed in *Bater v Bater*[165] where he said—

---

[158] *Gough v Chief Constable of the Derbyshire Constabulary* [2002] QB 1213, CA.

[159] *R (McCann) v Crown Court at Manchester* [2003] 1 AC 787, HL.          [160] Ibid.

[161] [1957] 1 QB 247.

[162] See, eg, *Thurtell v Beaumont* (1823) 1 Bing 339; *Issais v Marine Insurance Co Ltd* (1923) 15 Ll L Rep 186, CA (allegations of arson on the part of the assured in an action on an insurance policy); and *Willmett v Harmer* (1839) 8 C&P 695 (an allegation of bigamy in a libel suit).

[163] See *Doe d Devine v Wilson* (1855) 10 Moo PCC 502, PC (an allegation of forgery in an action based on a deed); *Hurst v Evans* [1917] 1 KB 352, KBD (an allegation of theft on the part of the servant of the assured in an action on an insurance policy); and *Slattery v Mance* [1962] 1 QB 676 (an allegation of arson on the part of the assured in an action on an insurance policy).

[164] [1957] 1 QB 247 at 258.          [165] [1951] P 35 at 37, CA.

in civil cases the case must be proved by a preponderance of probability, but there may be degrees of probability within that standard. The degree depends on the subject-matter. A civil court, when considering a charge of fraud, will naturally require for itself a higher degree of probability than that which it would require when asking if negligence is established. It does not adopt so high a degree as a criminal court, even when it is considering a charge of a criminal nature; but still it does require a degree of probability which is commensurate with the occasion.

To talk of degrees of probability within the same standard is, it is submitted, a contradiction in terms. A standard of proof being defined by the degree of probability it requires, if there are different degrees of probability, there are as many different standards. Morris LJ, although in support of the same conclusion that the civil standard applied, adopted a different approach:[166]

The phrase 'balance of probabilities' is often employed as a convenient phrase to express the basis upon which civil issues are decided. It may well be that no clear-cut logical reconciliation can be formulated in regard to the authorities on these topics. But perhaps they illustrate that 'the life of the law is not logic but experience' . . . In some civil cases the issues may involve questions of reputation which can transcend in importance even questions of personal liberty. Good name in man or woman is 'the immediate jewel of their souls' . . . Though no court and no jury would give less careful attention to issues lacking gravity than to those marked by it, the very elements of gravity become a part of the whole range of circumstances which have to be weighed in the scale when deciding as to the balance of probabilities.

Against the background of conflicting authorities preceding it, *Hornal v Neuberger Products Ltd* would appear to have settled this area of the law in favour of the normal civil standard. It was applied in *Re Dellow's Will Trusts*,[167] civil proceedings in which the issue was whether a wife feloniously killed her husband. As Ungoed-Thomas J pertinently observed: 'There can hardly be a graver issue than that.' It was also applied in *Post Office v Estuary Radio Ltd*,[168] where an allegation of a criminal offence under the Wireless Telegraphy Act 1949 was made on an application for an injunction under the same Act.[169]

*(ii) Matrimonial causes.* The authorities remain in conflict as to the standard of proof appropriate to matrimonial causes, earlier decisions requiring the criminal standard of beyond reasonable doubt, more recent cases favouring the ordinary civil standard on a balance of probabilities. In *Ginesi v Ginesi*,[170] where it was held that adultery must be proved to the criminal standard, the Court of Appeal relied upon the fact that

---

[166] [1957] 1 QB 247 at 266.     [167] [1964] 1 WLR 451, Ch D.     [168] [1967] 1 WLR 1396, CA.

[169] See also *Piermay Shipping Co SA and Brandt's Ltd v Chester, The Michael* [1979] 1 Lloyd's Rep 55 (an allegation of deliberately scuttling a ship); *Khawaja v Secretary of State for the Home Department* [1983] 1 All ER 765, HL (detention pending deportation of persons alleged to be illegal immigrants), distinguished in *Ali v Secretary of State for the Home Department* [1988] ImmAR 274, CA; and *Parks v Clout* [2003] EWCA Civ 1030 (an allegation of obtaining letters of administration by fraud).

[170] [1948] P 179, CA.

adultery was regarded by the ecclesiastical courts as a quasi-criminal offence.[171] In *Bater v Bater*[172] the Court of Appeal upheld the direction of the judge, on a petition for divorce on the ground of cruelty, that the petitioner was required to prove the case beyond reasonable doubt. Bucknill LJ, with Somervell LJ agreeing, stressed the importance of divorce proceedings to the parties and to the state.[173] Denning LJ held, as we have seen, that there is no absolute standard in either civil or criminal cases, the degree of probability in civil cases depending on the subject matter in question. On that basis, he agreed that the use of the phrase 'reasonable doubt' by the trial judge was not a misdirection but thought that if the trial judge had said that the case had to be proved with the same strictness as a crime is proved in a criminal court, that would have amounted to a misdirection. Reasons similar to those of Bucknill LJ in *Bater v Bater* were used some months later in support of the criminal standard in *Preston-Jones v Preston-Jones*.[174] A husband petitioned for divorce on the ground of adultery and proved that his wife had given birth to a normal child 360 days after the last opportunity he could have had for intercourse with her. The House of Lords upheld the trial judge's decision that adultery had been proved beyond reasonable doubt, Lord MacDermott stressing the gravity and public importance of the issues involved: 'The jurisdiction in divorce involves the status of the parties and the public interest requires that the marriage bond shall not be set aside lightly or without strict inquiry.'[175] Because the result of a finding of adultery would have been in effect to render the child illegitimate, the decision in this case may be regarded as little more than an application of the law, as it then stood,[176] that the presumption of legitimacy could only be rebutted by proof beyond reasonable doubt.[177] In *F v F*[178] the husband petitioned for divorce on the ground of adultery alleging that the child to which his wife subsequently gave birth was not his. Rees J, relying upon *Preston-Jones v Preston-Jones*, held that because a finding of adultery would inevitably have the effect of bastardizing the child, the husband could only succeed in establishing adultery if he met the standard of beyond reasonable doubt.

When the question of the appropriate standard in matrimonial causes next fell to be considered by the House of Lords, in *Blyth v Blyth*,[179] the tide had begun to turn. A husband petitioning for divorce on the ground of adultery sought to negative the presumption of condonation which arose from his sexual intercourse with his wife on a date subsequent to the adultery. The question arose as to the standard of proof required to negative condonation. The dissenting minority, consisting of Lords Morris and Morton, held that proof was required beyond reasonable doubt, but the

---

[171] Contrast *Briginshaw v Briginshaw* (1938) 60 CLR 336, a decision of the High Court of Australia favouring proof to the civil standard.

[172] [1951] P 35, CA.

[173] [1951] P 35 at 36. Reference was made to stigma, loss of maintenance, and the loss of custody of children.

[174] [1951] AC 391.      [175] See also *Galler v Galler* [1954] P 252.

[176] See now Family Law Reform Act 1969, s 26, but see also *Serio v Serio* (1983) 13 Fam Law 255, CA, below.

[177] See particularly the speech of Lord Simonds.      [178] [1968] P 506.      [179] [1966] AC 643.

majority of the House, comprising Lords Pearson, Denning and Pearce held that proof was required on a balance of probabilities. Lord Pearson was of the view that the requirement of proof beyond reasonable doubt was confined to the grounds of divorce and did not extend to the bars to divorce. Lord Denning, however, held that both the grounds for and the bars to divorce may be proved on a preponderance of probability. His Lordship disapproved *Ginesi v Ginesi*, preferring *Wright v Wright*,[180] a decision of the High Court of Australia in the same year, in which it was held that adultery required proof to the civil standard, and relied upon his own dicta in *Bater v Bater* and the decision in *Hornal v Neuberger Products Ltd*. Lord Pearce also drew the distinction made by Lord Pearson between the grounds for and the bars to divorce, but nevertheless expressed his agreement with Lord Denning's views on *Ginesi v Ginesi* and *Wright v Wright*, and, in this connection, did not find *Preston-Jones v Preston-Jones* in conflict. Referring to that decision, his Lordship said:[181] 'The real question was whether, on the assumption that proof beyond reasonable doubt was needed to establish adultery, such proof had been forthcoming on the evidence under review.'

In the light of the various dicta in *Preston-Jones v Preston-Jones* and *Blyth v Blyth*, it was not surprising to find the Court of Appeal in the ensuing case of *Bastable v Bastable and Sanders*[182] openly expressing the difficulties of determining what standard of proof should be applied in relation to proof of adultery.[183] Willmer LJ, with Winn LJ in agreement, being of the view that in both of the cases none of their Lordships' dicta in this respect was strictly necessary for the decisions in question, but should be regarded as obiter, adopted the dicta of Denning LJ in *Bater v Bater*, which were approved by the Court of Appeal in *Hornal v Neuberger Products Ltd*, to the effect that the court requires a degree of probability proportionate to the subject matter. On that basis, and satisfied that the commission of adultery is a serious matrimonial offence, Wilmer LJ held that a high standard of proof is required.[184]

*Bastable v Bastable*, it is submitted, is a decision which fully accords with the spirit of the then un-enacted Divorce Reform Act 1969,[185] which abolished the old grounds for divorce, largely based on the concept of the matrimonial offence, replacing them with one ground, that the marriage has irretrievably broken down. The fact that the ecclesiastical courts regarded adultery as a quasi-criminal offence is, under the present philosophy of divorce law, not a convincing reason for the application of the criminal standard of proof, especially now that the civil standard of proof is held to be

---

180 (1948) 77 CLR 191.      181 [1966] AC 643 at 673.      182 [1968] 1 WLR 1684.

183 See per Willmer LJ [1968] WLR 1684 at 1685.

184 The third member of the Court of Appeal, Edmund Davies LJ agreed with the majority on the outcome of the case but was satisfied that Lord Denning's observations in *Blyth v Blyth* on the standard appropriate to a matrimonial offence, as opposed to the issue of condonation, were obiter. Referring to the proposition that 'In proportion as the offence is grave, so ought the proof to be clear' Edmund Davies LJ said (at 1691–2): 'I take leave to doubt that such a distinction could effectively be made by a jury, or indeed by many judges and lawyers. I should have thought, with respect, that an offence is either proved or is not proved, in accordance with the standard (civil or criminal) appropriate to the case under consideration.' See also *Rejfek v McElroy* (1965) 112 CLR 517 at 521–2, HC of A, which Edmund Davies LJ cited with approval.

185 See now the Matrimonial Causes Act 1973.

appropriate in civil cases in which allegations of crime are made. The matter may be one of statutory construction; under the current legislation irretrievable breakdown may be established if the petitioner 'satisfies' the court of one of five facts. The same word 'satisfied' was used in the legislation prior to the Divorce Reform Act 1969 under which the decisions set out above were decided. However, it seems most unlikely that the criminal standard will in the future be re-imposed by way of statutory construction or because of the importance of divorce to the parties and to the state.

*(iii) Miscellaneous.* On various different issues arising in civil cases it has been suggested either (a) that the appropriate standard is higher than the ordinary civil standard (sometimes as high as the criminal standard) or, in any event, (b) that the more improbable the event being alleged, the stronger the evidence required to prove it (on a balance of probabilities). The following examples may be given.

(1) A party desiring to prove an intention to change domicile must do so 'clearly and unequivocally'.[186]

(2) There is a strong common law presumption that a marriage ceremony celebrated between persons who intended it to constitute a valid marriage is formally valid. Evidence in rebuttal is required to be 'strong, distinct, and satisfactory'[187] or 'evidence which satisfied beyond reasonable doubt that there was no valid marriage'.[188]

(3) A party claiming rectification is required to prove his case by 'strong irrefragable evidence'.[189]

(4) In cases involving the care of children, the standard is the ordinary civil standard, but the more serious or improbable an allegation of abuse, the stronger the evidence required to prove both the abuse[190] and the identity of the abuser.[191]

(5) The standard required to make a finding of paternity is a heavy one, commensurate with the gravity of the issue, and although not as heavy as in criminal proceedings, more than the ordinary civil standard of balance of probabilities.[192]

---

[186] *Moorhouse v Lord* (1863) 10 HL Cas 272 at 236. See also *Fuld's Estate (No 3)* [1968] P 675 at 685.

[187] *Piers v Piers* (1849) 2 HL Cas 331 at 389.      [188] *Mahadervan v Mahadervan* [1964] P 233 at 246.

[189] *Countess of Shelburne v Earl of Inchiquin* (1784) 1 Bro CC 338 at 341. See also *Earl v Hector Whaling Ltd* [1961] 1 Lloyd's Rep 459, CA.

[190] See *Re H (minors) (sexual abuse: standard of proof)* [1996] AC 563, HL and *In re U (a Child) (Serious Injury: Standard of Proof)* (2004) *The Times* 27 May 2004, CA. See also V Smith 'Sexual Abuse: Standard of Proof' [1994] Fam Law 626 and J Spencer 'Evidence in child abuse cases—too high a price for too high a standard?' (1994) 6 JCL 160.

[191] *Re G (A Child) (Non-accidental Injury: Standard of Proof)* [2001] 1 FCR 97, CA.

[192] *W v K* [1988] Fam Law 64. See also *Serio v Serio* (1983) 13 Fam Law 255, divorce proceedings in which the paternity of the wife's son was in dispute. The Court of Appeal held that notwithstanding s 26 of the Family Law Reform Act 1969, the standard on an issue of paternity is slightly higher than the balance of probabilities.

(6) For a court to approve medical treatment for an incompetent mentally ill patient without infringing Article 3 of the European Convention on Human Rights, it must be 'convincingly shown' that the proposed treatment is medically necessary, a standard that may be met notwithstanding that there is a responsible body of opinion against the proposed treatment.[193]

## 2 THE EVIDENTIAL BURDEN

Whether a party to civil or criminal proceedings has discharged an evidential burden borne by him in relation to a particular issue is, as we have seen, decided by the judge as opposed to the tribunal of fact. This may account for the dearth of authority on the standard required to discharge the evidential burden. In criminal cases, the standard required to discharge the evidential burden depends upon whether it is borne by the prosecution or defence. We have seen that in criminal trials either party bearing an evidential burden must adduce sufficient evidence to prevent the judge from withdrawing the issue in question from the jury, and this is done when there is sufficient evidence to justify as a possibility a favourable finding by the tribunal of fact. Where the evidential burden is borne by the prosecution, it is discharged by the adduction of 'such evidence as, if believed and if left uncontradicted and unexplained, could be accepted by the jury as proof'.[194] This means that the prosecution must adduce sufficient evidence to justify as a possibility a finding by the tribunal of fact that the legal burden on the same issue has been discharged, discharge of the legal burden, of course, requiring proof beyond reasonable doubt. However, where the evidential burden is borne by the accused, it is discharged by the adduction of such evidence as 'might leave a jury in reasonable doubt'.[195] This standard applies only where the defence bears the evidential but not the legal burden on a particular issue, as when the defence is one of provocation, self-defence or duress. Where the defence bears both the legal and evidential burden in relation to an issue, as when the defence is one of insanity or diminished responsibility, the evidential burden is discharged by the adduction of such evidence as *might* satisfy the jury of the probability of that which the accused is called upon to establish.[196] In civil cases, whichever party bears the evidential burden on a particular issue, it is discharged by the adduction of sufficient evidence to justify as a possibility a finding by the tribunal of fact that the legal burden on the same issue has been discharged, discharge of the legal burden, of course, requiring proof on a balance of probabilities.

---

[193] *R(N) v Dr M* [2003] 1 WLR 562, CA.
[194] Per Lord Devlin in *Jayasena v R* [1970] AC 618 at 624.
[195] Per Lord Morris in *Bratty v A-G for Northern Ireland* [1963] AC 386 at 419, HL.
[196] See per Humphreys J in *R v Carr-Briant* [1943] KB 607 at 612.

## C THE BURDEN AND STANDARD OF PROOF IN A TRIAL WITHIN A TRIAL

Preliminary facts are those facts which must be proved as a condition precedent to the admissibility of certain items of evidence. It is for the judge alone, if necessary in a trial within a trial, to determine whether preliminary facts have been proved. The burden of proving such facts is borne by the party who alleges their existence and who seeks to admit the evidence in question.[197] On the question whether a witness is competent to give evidence in criminal proceedings, it is for the party calling the witness to satisfy the court on a balance of probabilities that the witness is competent.[198] Where the prosecution bears the burden of proving preliminary facts, the standard of proof required to discharge the burden is proof beyond reasonable doubt.[199] It would seem to follow that where the burden under discussion is borne by the defendant in criminal proceedings, or by either party to civil proceedings, the appropriate standard is proof on a balance of probabilities.[200] In *R v Ewing*[201] the Court of Appeal considered what standard of proof was appropriate to the question whether samples of handwriting, allegedly written by the accused, were 'genuine' for the purposes of section 8 of the Criminal Procedure Act 1865. That section provides as follows:

Comparison of a disputed writing with any writing proved to the satisfaction of the judge to be genuine shall be permitted to be made by witnesses; and such writings, and the evidence of witnesses respecting the same, may be submitted to the court and jury as evidence of the genuineness or otherwise of the writing in dispute.

In the earlier decision of *R v Angeli*,[202] the Court of Appeal, on the basis that the 1865 Act applied to the criminal courts a provision which had already been in operation in the civil courts, held that the standard of proof under the section, whether applied in criminal or civil proceedings, was the civil one, on the balance of probabilities. In *R v Ewing* the Court of Appeal, unable to agree with this reasoning, and of the view that *R v Angeli* was decided per incuriam, held that, since section 8 did not deal with the standard of proof required to satisfy the judge, the matter was governed by the common law. O'Connor LJ said:[203] 'It follows that when the section is applied in civil cases, the civil standard of proof is used, and when it is applied in criminal cases, the criminal standard should be used.'

---

[197] See, at common law, *R v Jenkins* (1869) LR 1 CCR 187 (a dying declaration) and *R v Thompson* [1893] 2 QB 12 (a confession). As to the former, see now s 116 of the Criminal Justice Act 2003. As to the latter, see now s 76(2) of the Police and Criminal Evidence Act 1984.

[198] Youth Justice and Criminal Evidence Act 1999, s 54(2).

[199] See *R v Sartori* [1961] Crim LR 397 in relation to confessions, *R v Jenkins* (1869) LR 1 CCR 187 in relation to dying declarations, and generally *R v Ewing* [1983] 2 All ER 645. By contrast, in Australia, New Zealand and Canada, the civil standard has been held to apply: see *Wendo v R* (1963) 109 CLR 559; *R v Donohoe* [1963] SRNSW 38; *Police v Anderson* [1972] NZLR 233; and *R v Lee* (1953) 104 CCC 400.

[200] See, in the case of a defence application under s 23 of the Criminal Justice Act 1988, *R v Mattey and Queeley* [1995] 2 Cr App R 409, CA.

[201] [1983] 2 All ER 645.     [202] [1978] 3 All ER 950.     [203] [1983] 2 All ER 645 at 1047.

There are cases similar to, but quite distinct from, those discussed above in which the judge, before allowing particular issues to go before the jury, must be satisfied of certain matters by prima facie evidence. For example, if the prosecution seeks to admit a confession allegedly made by the accused, the defence case being that the confession never was made, the judge must be satisfied by prima facie evidence that the accused did make the confession.[204] Likewise, if the prosecution seeks to adduce a tape recording in evidence, the judge must be satisfied that the prosecution has made out a prima facie case of originality and genuineness by evidence which defines and describes the provenance and history of the recording up to the moment of its production in court.[205] In *R v Robson, R v Harris*[206] it was held that in these circumstances the judge is required to be satisfied to the civil standard, on a balance of probabilities, because application of the higher standard of proof, beyond reasonable doubt, would amount to a usurpation by the judge of the function of the jury. If the judge satisfies himself that the evidence is competent to be considered by the jury and should not be withdrawn from them, the very same issues of originality and genuineness may then fall to be considered by them. The standard of proof is then proof beyond reasonable doubt. It has been convincingly argued, however, that a better approach, also involving no usurpation of the function of the jury, would be for the judge to decide the issue in exactly the same way as he is required to decide whether an evidential burden has been discharged.[207] In other words, the judge should not be required to be satisfied on a balance of probabilities; the test should be whether the party seeking to put the evidence before the jury has adduced sufficient evidence on the facts in issue to justify, as a possibility, a finding by the jury on those facts in that party's favour.

---

[204] See further, *Ajodha v The State* [1981] 2 All ER 193, PC (see Ch 13).

[205] In *R v Rampling* [1987] Crim LR 823, CA the Court of Appeal gave the following general guidance upon the use in trials of tape recordings and transcripts of police interviews: (i) the tape can be produced and proved by the interviewing officer or any other officer present when it was taken; (ii) the officer should have listened to the tape before the trial so that he can, if required, deal with any objections to its authenticity or accuracy; (iii) as to authenticity, he can, if required, prove who spoke the recorded words; (iv) as to accuracy, he can deal with any challenge, eg that the recording has been falsified by addition or omission; (v) the transcript of the recording can be produced by the officer who, before the trial, should have checked it against the recording for accuracy; the tape recording is the evidence in the case and can be made an exhibit; the transcript, not in itself evidence, may be used as a convenience to the jury; (vi) use of the transcript is an administrative matter to be decided in his discretion by the trial judge; in many cases the accused will agree to its use and will not require the tape to be played at all, in which case the transcript will be read out by the officer who produced it; however, the accused is entitled, if he so wishes, to have any part of the tape played to the jury; (vii) if any part of the tape is played, it is for the judge to decide whether the jury should have the transcript, in order to follow the tape, and have it with them when they retire; the use of the transcript is within the judge's discretion and not dependent on the consent of the parties; a transcript is usually of very considerable value to the jury but each case has to be decided on its own facts. See also *R v Emmerson* (1990) 92 Cr App R 284, CA; *R v Riaz* (1991) 94 Cr App R 339, CA; and *R v Tonge* [1993] Crim LR 876, CA (all in Ch 5); the Code of Practice on Tape Recording of Interviews with Suspects, Code E; para 43 of *Practice Direction (Criminal Proceedings: Consolidation)* [2002] 1 WLR 2870; and John Baldwin and Julie Bedward 'Summarising Tape Recordings of Police Interviews' [1991] Crim LR 671.

[206] [1972] 1 WLR 651; cf *R v Stevenson* [1971] 1 WLR 1.

[207] *Cross & Tapper on Evidence* (9th edn London 1999) at 170.

# 5

# WITNESSES

This chapter concerns the competence and compellability of witnesses, oaths and affirmations, live television links, the time at which evidence should be adduced, additional rules relating to witnesses in civil cases (the rule as to the witnesses to be called and witness statements) and additional rules relating to witnesses in criminal cases (the rules as to the witnesses to be called, the order of witnesses, evidence in chief by video-recording, special measures directions for vulnerable and intimidated witnesses and witness training and familiarization).

## A COMPETENCE AND COMPELLABILITY

A witness is said to be competent if he may be called to give evidence and compellable if, being competent, he may be compelled by the court to do so.[1] A compellable witness who chooses to ignore a witness summons is in contempt of court and faces the penalty of imprisonment.[2] The same applies in the case of a compellable witness who attends court but refuses to testify, although such a witness may be entitled, on grounds of public policy or privilege, to refuse to answer some or all of the questions put to him.[3]

No party has any property in the evidence of a witness. Even if there is a contract between a party and a witness under which the latter binds himself not to give evidence to the court on a matter on which the judge can compel him to give evidence, it is contrary to public policy and unenforceable. Thus an expert witness is compellable if, having inadvertently advised both parties, he is loath to appear on behalf of one of them.[4] However, once a witness in criminal proceedings has given evidence for the prosecution, he cannot be called to give evidence for the defence;[5]

---

[1] In civil cases a witness summons may be issued by the court requiring a person to attend court to give evidence: see CPR r 34.2–34.6. In trials on indictment, the attendance of witnesses reluctant to attend may be secured by means of a witness summons: see Criminal Procedure (Attendance of Witnesses) Act 1965. For the position in magistrates' courts, see s 97 of the Magistrates' Courts Act 1980, *R v Bradford Justices, ex p Wilkinson* [1990] 2 All ER 833, DC; and *R v Marylebone Justices, ex p Gatting and Emburey* [1990] Crim LR 578, DC.

[2] See *R v Yusuf* [2003] 2 Cr App R 488, CA.     [3] See Chs 19 and 20.

[4] *Harmony Shipping Co SA v Saudi Europe Line Ltd* [1979] 1 WLR 1380, CA

[5] *R v Kelly* (1985) *The Times*, 27 July, CA.

and an expert witness may not be called by one party if his opinion is based on privileged information, such as communications with the other party, and cannot be divorced from it.[6]

## 1 THE GENERAL RULE

At common law, the law of competence and compellability is governed by a general rule with two limbs. The first limb is that anyone is a competent witness in any proceedings. This part of the general rule has now been put on a statutory footing in criminal cases. Section 53(1) of the Youth Justice and Criminal Evidence Act 1999 provides that: 'At every stage in criminal proceedings all persons are (whatever their age) competent to give evidence.' The second limb of the general rule is that all competent witnesses are compellable.

There used to be many categories of exception to the first limb of the general rule, but these were whittled down, over the centuries, by piecemeal judicial and statutory reform: see, in the case of non-Christians and atheists, *Omychund v Barker*[7] and the Evidence Further Amendment Act 1869; in the case of those with criminal convictions or with a personal pecuniary or proprietary interest in the outcome of the proceedings, the Civil Rights of Convicts Act 1828 and the Evidence Act 1843; in the case of the parties to civil proceedings and their spouses, the Evidence Act 1851, the Evidence Amendment Act 1853 and the Evidence Further Amendment Act 1869;[8] in the case of the accused as a witness for the defence, section 1 of the Criminal Evidence Act 1898;[9] and in the case of the spouse of the accused, section 80 of the Police and Criminal Evidence Act 1984, whereby the spouse became competent as a witness for the accused, a co-accused or, except where jointly charged with the accused, the prosecution. The only remaining exceptions to the first limb of the general rule relate to the accused as a witness for the prosecution, children and persons of defective intellect. The only remaining exceptions to the second limb of the general rule relate to the accused, his or her spouse, heads of sovereign states, diplomats, and, in certain circumstances, bankers.[10]

---

[6] *R v Davies* (2002) 166 JP 243, CA. See also *R v R* [1994] 4 All ER 260, CA, Ch 20.

[7] (1745) 1 Atk 21.

[8] In *Monroe v Twisleton* (1802) Peake Add Cas 219, followed in *O'Connor v Marjoribanks* (1842) 4 Man&G 435, it was held that a former spouse of a party to civil proceedings is incompetent following the termination of his or her marriage insofar as his or her evidence relates to events which occurred during the marriage. Reversal of the decision is long overdue, although arguably it could be ignored on the basis that the words 'husbands' and 'wives' in the Evidence Amendment Act 1853, by which the spouses were rendered competent and compellable, should be taken to cover former husbands and wives, but cf *Shenton v Tyler* [1939] Ch 620, CA.

[9] And the Statute Law (Repeals) Act 1981.

[10] The leave of the wardship court is not required to call a ward to give evidence at a criminal trial: *Re K (minors)* [1988] 1 All ER 214, Fam D; and *Re R (minors)* [1991] 2 All ER 193, CA. Concerning interviews with wards by the prosecution or police, see *Practice Direction (Criminal Proceedings: Consolidation)* [2002] 1 WLR 2870, para 5; and *Re R, Re G (minors)* [1990] 2 All ER 633, Fam D. As to interviews with wards by those representing the accused, see *Re R (minors)* [1991] 2 All ER 193, CA.

## 2  THE ACCUSED

### (a)  For the prosecution

Under section 53 of the Youth Justice and Criminal Evidence Act 1999, the accused, whether charged solely or jointly, is incompetent as a witness for the prosecution. Section 53 provides as follows:

(1)  At every stage in criminal proceedings all persons are (whatever their age) competent to give evidence.

(2)  Subsection (1) has effect subject to subsections (3) and (4).

(3)  A person is not competent to give evidence in criminal proceedings if it appears to the court that he is not a person who is able to—
(a)  understand questions put to him as a witness, and
(b)  give answers to them which can be understood.

(4)  A person charged in criminal proceedings is not competent to give evidence in the proceedings for the prosecution (whether he is the only person, or is one of two or more persons, charged in the proceedings).

(5)  In subsection (4) the reference to a person charged in criminal proceedings does not include a person who is not, or is no longer, liable to be convicted of any offence in the proceedings (whether as a result of pleading guilty or for any other reason).

Thus if the prosecution wish to call a co-accused to give evidence for them, they may only do so if, in effect, he has ceased to be a co-accused. This may happen, as section 53(5) indicates, as a result of pleading guilty.[11] It may also happen in three other ways: the co-accused may be acquitted, for example where no evidence is offered against him or he makes a successful submission of no case to answer at the close of the prosecution case; an application to sever the indictment may succeed so that he is not tried with the other accused; or the Attorney-General may enter a *nolle prosequi*, thereby putting an end to the proceedings against him. In any of these circumstances a former co-accused becomes both a competent and compellable witness for the prosecution.[12] Where a co-accused has pleaded guilty and proposes to give evidence for the prosecution, as a general rule he should be sentenced after the trial of the other accused.[13] However, the rule would appear to be one of practice only and the matter remains within the discretion of the judge. The same may be said of the rule in *R v Pipe*[14] that an accomplice who is not an accused in the proceedings in question but against whom proceedings are pending should only be called by the prosecution if they have undertaken to discontinue the proceedings against him.[15]

---

[11] If there are separate committal proceedings for two accomplices and one is committed and pleads guilty, the Crown may call him, even before he has been sentenced, to give evidence at the committal proceedings in respect of the other: *R v Palmer* (1993) 99 Cr App R 83, CA.

[12] If he is an accomplice, a care warning may be called for (see Ch 8).

[13] Per Boreham J in *R v Weekes* (1982) 74 Cr App R 161 at 166, CA. Contrast *R v Payne* [1950] 1 All ER 102, CCA. See also *R v Woods* (25 Oct 1977, unreported), CA and *R v Potter* (15 Sept 1977, unreported), CA.

[14] (1966) 51 Cr App R 17, CA.        [15] *R v Turner* (1975) 61 Cr App R 67, CA.

### (b) For himself

The accused is a competent but not compellable witness for the defence in all criminal proceedings. As to competence, the authority is now to be found in section 53(1) of the Youth Justice and Criminal Evidence Act 1999, whereby, as we have seen, subject to section 53(3), 'At every stage in criminal proceedings all persons are (whatever their age) competent to give evidence.' As to compellability, section 1(1) of the Criminal Evidence Act 1898[16] provides that: 'A person charged in criminal proceedings shall not be called as a witness in the proceedings except upon his own application.'

The phrase, in section 53(1), 'at every stage in criminal proceedings', is most likely to be construed in the same way as was the phrase 'at every stage of the proceedings' in the original unamended version of section 1 of the 1898 Act, so as to allow the accused to give evidence on the *voir dire*[17] and, after conviction, in mitigation of sentence,[18] as well as during the trial proper. If the accused elects to give evidence, he may of course be cross-examined by the prosecution and, even if he has not given evidence against a co-accused, by counsel for any co-accused.[19] Indeed, having elected to give evidence, then subject to section 1(2) and (4) of the 1898 Act, and section 101 of the Criminal Justice Act 2003, which are described in outline below, he will be treated like any other witness and his evidence will be evidence for all the purposes of the case. Thus the evidence of an accused in his own defence may be used against a co-accused whether such evidence was given in chief[20] or elicited in cross-examination. In *R v Paul*[21] an accused had confined his evidence in chief to an admission of his own guilt. A cross-examination of him, which had elicited evidence undermining the defence of a co-accused, was held by the Court of Criminal Appeal to have been properly permitted.[22]

Section 1(2) of the 1898 Act removes from the accused who testifies the privilege against self-incrimination in respect of any offence with which he is charged. It provides that 'Subject to section 101 of the Criminal Justice Act 2003 (admissibility of evidence of defendant's bad character), a person charged in criminal proceedings who is called as a witness in the proceedings may be asked any question in cross-examination notwithstanding that it would tend to criminate him as to any offence with which he is charged in the proceedings.'[23] Section 101 of the Criminal Justice Act 2003 sets out the only circumstances in which evidence of the bad character of the accused is admissible.[24] Section 1(4) of the 1898 Act provides that 'every person charged in criminal proceedings who is called as a witness in the proceedings shall,

---

[16] As amended by the Youth Justice and Criminal Evidence Act 1999.

[17] *R v Cowell* [1940] 2 KB 49.         [18] *R v Wheeler* [1917] 1 KB 283.

[19] *R v Hilton* [1972] 1 QB 421, CA.

[20] See *R v Rudd* (1948) 32 Cr App R 138; cf *R v Meredith* (1943) 29 Cr App R 40.

[21] [1920] 2 KB 183.

[22] But see *Young v HM Advocate* 1932 JC 63, where the view was expressed that in these circumstances the judge should exercise his discretion to prevent such cross-examination.

[23] See also Ch 20 under **A The privilege against self-incrimination.**

[24] See further Ch 17 under C **Evidence of the bad character of the defendant.**

unless otherwise ordered by the court, give his evidence from the witness box or other place from which the other witnesses give their evidence'. The court may 'order otherwise' if the accused is too infirm to walk to the witness box or too violent to be controlled there.[25] Subject to exceptional circumstances of this kind, the proviso does not confer a discretion to direct where evidence should be given from, and it is improper to offer the accused a choice as to whether he wishes to give his evidence from the dock or witness box.[26] If an accused elects not to give evidence, it should be the invariable practice of counsel to record the decision and to cause the accused to sign the record, giving a clear indication that he has by his own will decided not to testify bearing in mind the advice, if any, given to him by his counsel.[27]

### (c) For a co-accused

It will be clear from section 53(1) of the 1999 Act and section 1(1) of the 1898 Act that an accused is a competent but not compellable witness for a co-accused. A person who has ceased to be an accused is both competent and compellable for a co-accused. This may happen where he has pleaded guilty,[28] where he has been acquitted (for example where no evidence has been offered against him or he has made a successful submission of no case to answer at the close of the prosecution case),[29] or where an application to sever the indictment has succeeded so that he is not tried with the other accused.[30]

## 3 THE SPOUSE OF AN ACCUSED

### (a) For the prosecution

Prior to the Police and Criminal Evidence Act 1984, the spouse of the accused was generally incompetent as a witness for the prosecution. There were a number of common law and statutory exceptions, but in almost all of these cases the spouse, although competent, was not compellable for the prosecution. In its 11th Report, the Criminal Law Revision Committee considered to what extent the spouse of the accused should be competent and compellable for the prosecution. The problem was seen as a question of balancing the desirability that all available and relevant evidence should be before the court against (i) the objection on social grounds to disturbing marital harmony; and (ii) the harshness of compelling one spouse to give evidence against the other. The Committee felt that the older objections based on the theoretical unity of the spouses, the interest of the accused's spouse in the outcome of the proceedings and the likelihood of a spouse being biased in favour of the accused, were of no contemporary value.[31] Concerning competence, the Committee concluded that

[25] *R v Symonds* (1924) 18 Cr App R 100 at 101.
[26] *R v Farnham Justices, ex p Gibson* [1991] Crim LR 642, DC.
[27] *R v Bevan* (1993) 98 Cr App R 354, CA.    [28] *R v Boal* [1965] 1 QB 402 at 414.
[29] *R v Conti* (1973) 58 Cr App R 387, CA.    [30] *R v Richardson* (1967) 51 Cr App R 381.
[31] Para 147 (Cmnd 4991) (1972).

the wife should be competent for the prosecution in all cases: 'If she is willing to give evidence, we think that the law would be showing excessive concern for the preservation of marital harmony if it were to say that she must not do so.'[32] This view was given effect by section 80(1) of the Police and Criminal Evidence Act 1984. Section 80(1) was repealed by the Youth Justice and Criminal Evidence Act 1999: the spouse of an accused is now competent to give evidence for the prosecution under section 53(1) of the 1999 Act whereby, as we have seen, subject to section 53(3), in criminal proceedings all persons are competent to give evidence. As we have also seen, section 53(1) is also subject to section 53(4), whereby a person charged in criminal proceedings is not competent to give evidence in the proceedings for the prosecution, whether he is the only person, or one of two or more, charged in the proceedings. Thus if a husband and wife are co-accused, whether charged jointly with the same offence or charged with different offences, neither is competent to give evidence for the prosecution. As section 53(5) indicates, the spouse may only become competent for the prosecution if he or she ceases to be a co-accused. This may happen if the spouse pleads guilty or is acquitted (because no evidence is offered against the spouse or the spouse makes a successful submission of no case to answer), or if one of the spouses makes a successful application to sever the indictment.

Concerning compellability, the Criminal Law Revision Committee was in favour of maintaining the common law rule, as it then stood, of compellability in the case of offences involving personal violence by the accused against his or her spouse. The reasons included the public interest in the punishment of those committing crimes of violence and the fact that compellability would make it easier for the accused's spouse to counter the effect of possible intimidation by the accused and persuade him or her to give evidence.[33] It was also proposed to make the spouse compellable in the case of offences of a violent or sexual nature against children under the age of 16 belonging to the same household as the accused. Among the reasons given by the Committee were: (i) the seriousness of some of these cases; (ii) the reluctance to testify of a wife in fear of her husband; (iii) the difficulties of proving such offences, especially in cases in which the child is unable to testify; and (iv) the fact that in some cases the spouse, although not prosecuted, is a party to or at least acquiesces in the offence committed.[34] Subsequent to the Committee's Report and prior to the 1984 Act, in a decision which came as a surprise to most lawyers, a majority of the House of Lords in *Hoskyn v Metropolitan Police Comr*[35] held that where an accused is charged with an offence of violence against his or her spouse, that spouse is competent but *not compellable* for the prosecution. The majority of their Lordships were reluctant to compel a wife to testify against her husband on a charge of violence, however trivial, and regardless of the consequences to herself, her family, and her marriage. Lord Edmund Davies, the sole dissentient, regarded as extremely unlikely prosecutions based on trivial violence and was of the opinion that cases of serious physical violence by one spouse against the other were too grave to depend upon the willingness of the injured spouse to testify

---

[32] Para 148.        [33] Para 149.        [34] Para 150.        [35] [1979] AC 474.

and 'ought not to be regarded as having no importance extending beyond the domestic hearth'. Against this background of differing and strongly held opinion, Parliament, effectively reversing the majority view in *Hoskyn v Metropolitan Police Comr*, not only adopted but extended the proposals of the Criminal Law Revision Committee.[36] Section 80(2A)–(4A) of the Police and Criminal Evidence Act 1984 provide as follows:

(2A)  In any proceedings the wife or husband of a person charged in the proceedings shall, subject to subsection (4) below, be compellable—
   (a)  to give evidence on behalf of any other person charged in the proceedings but only in respect of any specified offence with which that other person is charged; or
   (b)  to give evidence for the prosecution but only in respect of any specified offence with which any person is charged in the proceedings.

(3)   In relation to the wife or husband of a person charged in any proceedings, an offence is a specified offence for the purposes of subsection (2A) above if—
   (a)  it involves an assault on, or injury or a threat of injury to, the wife or husband or a person who was at the material time under the age of 16;[37]
   (b)  it is a sexual offence alleged to have been committed in respect of a person who was at the material time under that age; or
   (c)  it consists of attempting or conspiring to commit, or of aiding, abetting, counselling, procuring or inciting the commission of, an offence falling within paragraph (a) or (b) above.

(4)   No person who is charged in any proceedings shall be compellable by virtue of subsection (2) or (2A) above to give evidence in the proceedings.

(4A)  References in this section to a person charged in any proceedings do not include a person who is not, or is no longer, liable to be convicted of any offence in the proceedings (whether as a result of pleading guilty or for any other reason).

The subsections apply 'in any proceedings', a phrase which encompasses criminal proceedings brought by one spouse against the other. Thus in the unlikely event of such proceedings being pursued by a spouse who declines to give evidence, then he or she may nonetheless be compellable in accordance with section 80(2A) and (3).

It is submitted that the words 'wife' and 'husband' refer to a married person whose marriage, wherever it was celebrated, would be recognized by English law.[38] In *R v Pearce*,[39] it was held, construing section 80 prior to its amendment by the Youth Justice and Criminal Evidence Act 1999, that the phrase 'wife or husband of the accused' does not cover the cohabitee of an accused and that the proper respect for private and family life envisaged by Article 8 of the European Convention on

---

[36] An alternative solution is to make the wife compellable in all cases subject only to exemption at the discretion of the trial judge: see s 400 of the Crimes Act 1958, Australian State of Victoria.

[37] Where the age of any person at any time is material for the purposes of s 80(3), his age at the material time shall 'be deemed to be or to have been that which appears to the court to be or to have been his age at that time': s 80(6).

[38] See, at common law, *R v Khan* (1987) 84 Cr App R 44, CA and *R v Yacoob* (1981) 72 Cr App R 313, CA.

[39] [2002] 1 WLR 1553, CA.

Human Rights does not require that such a person should not be a compellable witness.

The meaning of the phrase 'involves an assault on, or injury or a threat of injury to' is unclear. A purposive approach, having regard to some of the reasons advanced by the Criminal Law Revision Committee in favour of their recommendations, might support a broad construction so as to cover not only cases in which an assault, injury or threat of injury is required to be proved by virtue of the way in which the offence in question is defined, but also cases in which that is not so, but nonetheless evidence is adduced to show that the offence did in fact involve an assault, injury or threat of injury.[40] The issue could arise, for example, in a case of reckless driving in which the evidence discloses that the spouse, or person under 16 years of age, sustained injuries as a passenger in the car driven by the accused. Similar reasoning could be used to conclude that 'threat of injury' does not relate to the state of mind of the accused, but means risk of injury.[41] In subsection 3(b) 'sexual offence' means an offence under the Protection of Children Act 1978 or Part 1 of the Sexual Offences Act 2003.[42]

Where the accused is charged with two or more offences in respect of only one of which the spouse is compellable, it seems from the wording of subsection (2A)(b) that the spouse is compellable to give evidence for the prosecution on the one offence, but not the other or others, even where such a distinction is artificial because the evidence is relevant to the other or others. Let us suppose, for example, that in the course of a neighbourhood dispute that develops into a fracas, A assaults both B and B's 15-year-old son. It seems that A's wife would only be compellable to give evidence in relation to the assault on B's son, but her evidence would be likely to be relevant to both offences charged. Presumably, in such a case, A could apply for separate trials for each of the offences, or might apply to exclude the evidence of his wife relying upon section 78(1) of the 1984 Act or the common law discretion to exclude in order to ensure a fair trial. It may be doubted, however, that either application would have much prospect of success.[43]

An accused's spouse who is called as a competent but not compellable witness for the prosecution but proves adverse for the purposes of section 3 of the Criminal Procedure Act 1865,[44] may be treated as a hostile witness in the normal way. This was established prior to the 1984 Act in *R v Pitt*,[45] an authority which may be assumed to remain good law. The Court of Appeal held that the choice of a wife whether or not to give evidence, being a competent but not compellable witness for the prosecution, is not lost because she makes a witness statement or gives evidence at the committal proceedings. She retains the right of refusal up to the point when she takes the oath in the witness box, and waiver of her right of refusal is effective only if made with full

---

[40] Cf *R v McAndrew-Bingham* [1999] Crim LR 830, CA, a decision under s 32(2)(a) of the Criminal Justice Act 1988.

[41] Cf *R v Lee* [1996] 2 Cr App R 266, CA, another decision under s 32(2)(a) of the 1988 Act.

[42] Section 80(7).

[43] See Peter Creighton 'Spouse Competence and Compellability' [1990] Crim LR 34.         [44] See Ch 6.

[45] [1982] 3 All ER 63.

knowledge of her right to refuse. However, if she knowingly waives her right of refusal, she becomes an ordinary witness and, having started her evidence, must complete it, unable to retreat behind the barrier of non-compellability. Accordingly, if the nature of her evidence warrants it, an application may be made to treat her as a hostile witness. For these reasons, the Court of Appeal thought it desirable that the judge should explain to the wife, in the absence of the jury and before she takes the oath, that she has the right to give evidence but that if she chooses to do so she may be treated like any other witness. In appropriate circumstances the Court of Appeal may upset a verdict if it feels that injustice may have occurred because a wife gave evidence without appreciating that she had a right to refuse to do so.

## (b) For the accused

Prior to the 1984 Act, the accused's spouse was competent but not compellable as a witness for the accused.[46] The Criminal Law Revision Committee had no doubt that the accused's spouse should be made competent and compellable for the accused in all cases,[47] a recommendation implemented by the 1984 Act. The wife or husband of an accused is now competent to give evidence on behalf of the accused under section 53(1) of the 1999 Act, and this remains the case even if the wife or husband is also charged in the same proceedings. As to compellability, section 80(2) provides as follows:

> (2)   In any proceedings the wife or husband of a person charged in the proceedings shall, subject to subsection (4) below, be compellable to give evidence on behalf of that person.

The only exception to section 80(2) is in cases in which the spouses are both charged in the same proceedings.[48]

## (c) For a co-accused

Under the Criminal Evidence Act 1898, the accused's spouse was, with the consent of the accused, competent but not compellable as a witness for any other person jointly charged with the accused.[49] The Criminal Law Revision Committee recommended that the spouse of an accused should be competent to give evidence on behalf of any co-accused whether or not the accused consents. This proposal was given effect by section 80(1) of the 1984 Act, which was repealed by the Youth Justice and Criminal Evidence Act 1999. The wife or husband of an accused is now competent to give evidence on behalf of any person jointly charged with the accused by virtue of section 53(1) of the 1999 Act, and this is the case even if the wife or husband is also charged in the same proceedings.

---

[46]  See s 1 of the Criminal Evidence Act 1898; *R v Boal* [1965] 1 QB 402 at 416; s 30(3) of the Theft Act 1968; and s 39(1) of the Sexual Offences Act 1956.

[47]  Para 153.        [48]  Section 80(4), above.

[49]  Section 1 and proviso (c) thereto. In certain circumstances a spouse was competent for a co-accused without the consent of the accused.

The more difficult question related to compellability on behalf of a co-accused. The interests of justice would seem to require that the co-accused should be able to compel the spouse if he or she is able to give relevant evidence in his defence. On the other hand, if the spouse is compelled to testify in such circumstances, the prosecution, in cross-examination of the spouse, may well elicit evidence incriminating the accused, a result which is inconsistent with the general rule that the prosecution may not compel a spouse to testify for them. Given these competing interests of the accused and the co-accused, the Committee proposed that the spouse should be compellable on behalf of a co-accused in any case where he or she would be compellable on behalf of the prosecution.[50] The substance of these proposals has been enacted in section 80(2A) and (3) of the 1984 Act, which provide that in any proceedings the spouse of the accused shall be compellable to give evidence on behalf of any other person charged in the proceedings, but only in respect of any specified offence with which that other person is charged.[51] The only exception is in cases in which the spouse is both charged in the same proceedings.[52] Where co-accused A and B are charged with two or more offences in respect of only one of which the spouse of B is compellable to give evidence on behalf of A, then it seems from the wording of section 80(2A)(a) that the spouse of B is compellable to give evidence on behalf of A on that offence even if that evidence is also relevant to the other offence(s).

### (d) Former spouses

Fortunately, it is no longer necessary to consider the anomalous and complicated state of the law, prior to the Police and Criminal Evidence Act 1984, on the competence and compellability of former spouses in criminal proceedings. In criminal proceedings, a former spouse of an accused is competent under section 53(1) of the Youth Justice and Criminal Evidence Act 1999. Such a person is also compellable. Section 80(5) of the Police and Criminal Evidence Act 1984 provides that:

In any proceedings a person who has been but is no longer married to the accused shall be compellable to give evidence as if that person and the accused had never been married.

The effect of these two sections is to render former spouses, after their marriage has been dissolved, both competent and compellable to give evidence for either the defence or prosecution, whether the evidence relates to events which occurred before, during, or after the terminated marriage.[53] In section 80(5) of the 1984 Act the phrase 'in any proceedings' means any proceedings which took place after section 80(5) came into effect on 1 January 1986, and therefore an ex-spouse is competent and compellable to give evidence in such proceedings about any relevant matter whether it took place before or after that date.[54] The phrase 'is no longer married' is apt to apply where the spouses have been divorced and where their marriage, being voidable, has been annulled. If there is evidence to show that a marriage was void *ab initio*, a legally

---

[50] Para 155.      [51] The offences are set out in s 80(3), above.      [52] Section 80(4), above.
[53] See *R v Mathias* [1989] Crim LR 64, CC.      [54] *R v Cruttenden* [1991] 3 All ER 242, CA.

valid marriage never having existed, the parties to such a union are, in accordance with the general rules, both competent and compellable throughout. Spouses who are judicially separated, although often treated in law as the equivalent of divorced spouses, cannot be said to be 'no longer married' for the purposes of section 80(5). Likewise, the subsection has no application to spouses who are not cohabiting, whether without any arrangement or agreement, or pursuant to a separation agreement, non-cohabitation order or informal arrangement. The Criminal Law Revision Committee considered whether to provide that judicially separated or non-cohabiting spouses should be treated for the purposes of competence and compellability as if they were unmarried. It is difficult to disagree with their conclusions against such a provision:[55]

if there is little prospect that they will become reconciled, the spouse in question is likely to be willing to give evidence; and if there is a prospect of reconciliation, it may be better to avoid the risk of spoiling this prospect by compelling the spouse to give evidence when he or she would not have been compellable in the ordinary case.

## 4 CHILDREN AND PERSONS OF UNSOUND MIND—CRIMINAL CASES

Between 1991 and 1999 various statutory attempts were made to improve the law governing the competence of children to give sworn and unsworn evidence in criminal proceedings. The current provisions, which are in the Youth Justice and Criminal Evidence Act 1999, reflect the constructive judicial and academic criticism of those earlier legislative efforts. The new provisions are of general application. The competence of all witnesses to give evidence in criminal proceedings is governed by section 53(1)–(3) of the Youth Justice and Criminal Evidence Act 1999, which provide as follows:

(1) At every stage in criminal proceedings all persons are (whatever their age) competent to give evidence.

(2) Subsection (1) has effect subject to subsections (3) and (4).[56]

(3) A person is not competent to give evidence in criminal proceedings if it appears to the court that he is not a person who is able to—
    (a) understand questions put to him as a witness, and
    (b) give answers to them which can be understood.

Concerning the test in section 53(3), it is submitted that there is no need to decide whether the witness knows the difference between the truth and a lie, or the importance of speaking the truth.[57] Equally, however, it is submitted that a person should be treated as unable to understand questions put to him as a witness, and unable to give answers to them which can be understood, if he is unable to distinguish truth from

---

[55] Para 156.    [56] As to s 53(4), see under 2 **The accused**, above.

[57] Cf *G v DPP* [1997] 2 All ER 755 (approving Auld J, obiter, in *R v Hampshire* [1995] 3 WLR 260 at 268, CA), a decision under s 33A(2A) of the Criminal Justice Act 1988, whereby a child's evidence was to be received unless it appeared to the court that the child was 'incapable of giving intelligible testimony'.

fiction or fact from fantasy.[58] In the case of young children, obviously, the younger the child the more likely it is that he will be incapable of satisfying the test in section 53(3), and care clearly needs to be taken if the question of competence arises. However, it is submitted that a court cannot properly conclude that a child is incapable of satisfying the test on the basis of age alone: as we shall see, under section 56(2) it is mandatory for a child who is competent but not permitted to be sworn for the purpose of giving evidence on oath, to give evidence unsworn.[59] This submission reflects the views of Lord Lane CJ in *R v Z*,[60] disapproving *R v Wallwork*.[61] In the latter case, Lord Goddard CJ said that it was most undesirable to call a child as young as five years old, a dictum approved in *R v Wright, R v Ormerod*.[62] However, in *R v Z* Lord Lane CJ was of the opinion that the decision in *R v Wallwork* had been overtaken by events. Part of Lord Goddard's concern related to the presence of the child in court, a problem largely cured by the introduction of video links.[63] Furthermore, the repeal of the proviso to section 38(1) of the Children and Young Persons Act 1933, whereby an accused was not liable to be convicted on the uncorroborated unsworn evidence of a child, indicated 'a change of attitude by Parliament, reflecting in its turn a change of attitude by the public in general to the acceptability of the evidence of young children'.

In *R v Sed*,[64] which concerned the competence of an 81-year-old woman who suffered from Alzheimer's disease, it was said that, depending on the length and nature of the questioning and the complexity of the subject matter, section 53 may not always require 100 per cent, or near 100 per cent, mutual understanding between the questioner and the questioned and that the judge should also make allowance for the fact that the witness's performance and command of detail may vary according to the importance to him of the subject matter, how recent it was, and any strong feelings that it may have engendered.

The question whether a witness is competent to give evidence in criminal proceedings may be raised either by a party to the proceedings or by the court of its own motion, but either way must be determined by the court in accordance with section 54 of the 1999 Act.[65] It is clear from this that a judge is only bound to investigate a witness's competence if he has, or is given, any reason to doubt it.[66] Under section 54(2), the burden is on the party calling the witness to satisfy the court, on a balance of probabilities, that the witness is competent. In determining whether the witness is competent, the court must treat the witness as having the benefit of any special

---

[58] Cf *R v D* (1995) *The Times*, 15 Nov, CA.

[59] Cf *DPP v M* [1997] 2 All ER 749, DC, a decision under s 33A(2A) of the Criminal Justice Act 1988.

[60] [1990] 2 All ER 971, CA at 974.       [61] (1958) 42 Cr App R 153.

[62] (1987) 90 Cr App R 91, CA.

[63] See s 24 of the Youth Justice and Criminal Evidence Act 1999, and now, other 'special measures directions', below.

[64] [2005] 1 Cr App R 55, CA at [45].       [65] Section 54(1).

[66] Where this is not the case, the judge may find it appropriate to remind a child, in the presence of the accused and jury, of the importance of telling the truth, by saying, eg: 'Tell us all you can remember of what happened. Don't make anything up or leave anything out. This is very important.' See per Auld J in *R v Hampshire* [1995] 2 All ER 1019, CA at 1029.

measures directions under section 19 of the 1999 Act[67] which the court has given or proposes to give in relation to the witness.[68] Under section 54(4), any proceedings for the determination of the question shall take place in the absence of the jury (if there is one); under section 54(5), expert evidence may be received on the question (which is always likely to be required in the case of the mentally handicapped);[69] and under section 54(6), any questioning of the witness, where the court considers that necessary, shall be conducted by the court in the presence of the parties.

The questioning of children under section 54(6), it is submitted, is best conducted in the spirit suggested in *R v Hampshire*:[70] it should be a matter of the judge's perception of the child's understanding demonstrated in the course of ordinary discourse. It is submitted that there is also much to be said in favour of two other propositions that derive from that case: (1) the question of competence should be dealt with at the earliest possible moment, not as an act of purported 'ratification' after the evidence has been given; and (2) where there is video-recorded evidence,[71] the judge's pre-trial view of the recording, if the interview has been properly conducted, should normally enable him to form a view as to the child's competence, but if it has left him in doubt, he should conduct an investigation.[72]

A witness who is competent to give evidence in criminal proceedings may be sworn for the purpose of giving his evidence on oath, or may give his evidence unsworn. Section 55(1)–(4) of the 1999 Act provide as follows:

(1) Any question whether a witness in criminal proceedings may be sworn for the purpose of giving evidence on oath, whether raised—
   (a) by a party to the proceedings, or
   (b) by the court of its own motion,
   shall be determined by the court in accordance with this section.

(2) The witness may not be sworn for that purpose unless—
   (a) he has attained the age of 14, and
   (b) he has a sufficient appreciation of the solemnity of the occasion and of the particular responsibility to tell the truth which is involved in taking an oath.

(3) The witness shall, if he is able to give intelligible testimony, be presumed to have a sufficient appreciation of those matters if no evidence tending to show the contrary is adduced (by any party).

(4) If any such evidence is adduced, it is for the party seeking to have the witness sworn to satisfy the court that, on a balance of probabilities, the witness has attained the age

---

[67] See under **F Witnesses in criminal cases,** below.    [68] Section 54(3).

[69] In *R v Barratt and Sheehan* [1996] Crim LR 495, CA it was held that the proper course is to adduce expert medical evidence so that it is not normally necessary to call the witness said to suffer from mental illness.

[70] [1995] 2 All ER 1019, CA.

[71] See s 27 of the Youth Justice and Criminal Evidence Act 1999, under **F Witnesses in criminal cases,** below.

[72] Para 3.10 of the *Memorandum of Good Practice on Video Recorded Interviews with Child Witnesses for Criminal Proceedings* (1992) advises that, at the start of the interview, the interviewer should impress upon the child the importance of speaking the truth.

of 14 and has a sufficient appreciation of the matters mentioned in subsection (2)(b).

For the purposes of section 55(3), a person is able to give intelligible testimony if he is able to (a) understand questions put to him as a witness, and (b) give answers to them which can be understood.[73] This test is the same as that for testing competence in section 53(3). Thus a witness aged 14 or over who is competent as a witness must be presumed to satisfy the test set out in section 55(2)(b), provided that there is no evidence tending to show the contrary. Under section 55(5), any proceedings for the determination of the question whether a witness may be sworn for the purpose of giving his evidence on oath shall take place in the absence of the jury (if there is one); under section 55(6), expert evidence may be received on the question; and, under section 55(7), any questioning of the witness, where the court considers that necessary, shall be conducted by the court in the presence of the parties.

Section 56 (1)–(4) of the 1999 Act provide as follows:

(1) Subsections (2) and (3) apply to a person (of any age) who—
   (a) is competent to give evidence in criminal proceedings, but
   (b) (by virtue of s 55(2)) is not permitted to be sworn for the purpose of giving evidence on oath in such proceedings.
(2) The evidence in criminal proceedings of a person to whom this subsection applies shall be given unsworn.
(3) A deposition of unsworn evidence given by a person to whom this subsection applies may be taken for the purpose of criminal proceedings as if that evidence had been given on oath.
(4) A court in criminal proceedings shall accordingly receive in evidence any evidence given unsworn in pursuance of subsection (2) or (3).

Under the mandatory terms of section 56(2), therefore, the evidence of any child under the age of 14 who is competent to testify must be given unsworn; and the same applies to anyone who has attained that age and is competent to testify if (a) evidence is adduced that he does not have a sufficient appreciation of the solemnity of the occasion and of the particular responsibility to tell the truth which is involved in taking an oath, and (b) the party seeking to have him sworn fails to satisfy the court, on a balance of probabilities, that he has such an appreciation.

It is an offence for a person giving unsworn evidence in pursuance of section 56(2) and (3) wilfully to give false evidence in such circumstances that, had the evidence been given on oath, he would have been guilty of perjury;[74] but the mere fact that a child under the age of 10 cannot be prosecuted is not a reason to prevent him from giving unsworn evidence.[75]

---

[73] Section 55(8).    [74] Section 57 of the 1999 Act.    [75] See *R v N* (1992) 95 Cr App R 256, CA.

## 5 CHILDREN AND PERSONS OF UNSOUND MIND—CIVIL CASES

### (a) Children

In civil cases, until fairly recently, a child who did not understand the nature of an oath was incompetent to testify and could not be called as a witness.[76] Section 96 of the Children Act 1989 now provides that:

(1) Subsection (2) applies where a child who is called as a witness in any civil proceedings does not, in the opinion of the court, understand the nature of an oath.

(2) The child's evidence may be heard by the court if, in its opinion—
   (a) he understands that it is his duty to speak the truth; and
   (b) he has sufficient understanding to justify his evidence being heard.

A child, for these purposes, is a person under the age of 18.[77] In deciding, under section 96(1), whether or not a child understands the nature of an oath, it is submitted that the court should be guided by the common law authorities which governed in criminal as well as civil cases prior to parliamentary intervention. The issue is for the court to decide and the judge should put preliminary questions in order to form an opinion.[78] Whether a child warrants such examination is a matter of discretion for the judge. There is no fixed age above which a child should be treated as competent and below which a child should be examined. In *R v Khan*,[79] however, it was held that although much depends on the type of child before the court, in the experience of all three members of the court, as a general working rule, inquiry is necessary in the case of a child under the age of 14. Originally, the competence of children to give sworn evidence depended on 'the sense and reason they entertain of the danger and impiety of falsehood'.[80] On this basis, judges would ask questions designed to discover whether the child was aware of the divine sanction of the oath, such as 'Do you have religious instruction at school?' and 'Do you know what I mean by God?' It was questioning of this kind that led the Court of Appeal in *R v Hayes*[81] to adopt a secular approach. Acknowledging that in the present state of society the divine sanction of the oath is probably not generally recognized amongst the adult population, it was held that the important consideration is:[82]

whether the child has a sufficient appreciation of the solemnity of the occasion and the added responsibility to tell the truth, which is involved in taking an oath, over and above the duty to tell the truth which is an ordinary duty of normal social conduct.

The court, in *R v Hayes*, also appears to have accepted a concession made by counsel for the defence that 'the watershed dividing children who are normally considered old enough to take the oath and children normally considered too young to take the oath, probably falls between the ages of eight and ten'.

---

[76] *Baker v Rabetts* (1954) 118 JPN 303.    [77] Section 105.
[78] *R v Surgenor* (1940) 27 Cr App R 175.
[79] (1981) 73 Cr App R 190, CA. But see also *Bains v DPP* [1992] Crim LR 795, DC.
[80] *R v Brasier* (1779) 1 Leach 199.    [81] [1977] 1 WLR 234.    [82] [1977] 1 WLR 234 at 237.

If, in civil proceedings, a child fails on the secular test in *R v Hayes*, his or her evidence may be given unsworn if, in the opinion of the court, the conditions in section 96(2)(a) and (b) are satisfied. It would appear that 'the duty to speak the truth' under section 96(2)(a) should be taken to mean the duty to tell the truth which is an ordinary duty of normal social conduct.

### (b) Persons of unsound mind

In civil proceedings, in deciding on the competence of a person of unsound mind, it is submitted that the courts should be guided by the common law authorities which governed in criminal as well as civil cases prior to parliamentary intervention. In *R v Hill*[83] a patient of a lunatic asylum, labouring under a delusion that he had a number of spirits about him which were continually talking to him, but with a clear understanding of the obligation of the oath, was held competent to give evidence for the Crown on a charge of manslaughter.[84] Three principles were established in the case:

1. If in the opinion of the judge a proposed witness, by reason of defective intellect, does not understand the nature and sanction of an oath, he is incompetent to testify.

2. A person of defective intellect who does understand the nature of an oath may give evidence and it will be left to the jury to attach such weight to his testimony as they see fit.

3. If his evidence is so tainted with insanity as to be unworthy of credit, the jury may properly disregard it.

Since *R v Hill* there has been one important development: the test to be applied by the judge should be the secular one adopted in *R v Hayes*. In *R v Bellamy*[85] it was held that the trial judge had, in the case of a woman aged 33 with a mental age of 10, unnecessarily embarked upon an inquiry into the extent of her belief in and knowledge of God; the proper test of the competence of a mentally handicapped person is whether that person has a sufficient appreciation of the seriousness of the occasion and a realization that taking the oath involves something more than the duty to tell the truth in ordinary day-to-day life. Resolution of the question calls for appropriate expert medical evidence: it will not normally be necessary to call the witness said to be suffering from mental illness.[86]

A witness unable to understand the nature of the oath, his intellect being temporarily impaired by reason of drink or drugs, may become competent after an adjournment of suitable length.

---

[83] (1851) 2 Den 254.

[84] Lord Campbell CJ was doubtless sobered by his observation that any rule to the contrary would have excluded the evidence of Socrates 'for he believed that he had a spirit always prompting him'.

[85] (1985) 82 Cr App R 222, CA.          [86] *R v Barratt and Sheehan* [1996] Crim LR 495, CA.

## 6 THE SOVEREIGN AND DIPLOMATS

The Sovereign and heads of other sovereign states are competent but not compellable to give evidence. A number of statutes provide for varying degrees of immunity from compellability in the case of diplomats, consular officials, and certain officers of prescribed international organizations.[87]

## 7 BANKERS

We shall see in Chapter 9 that, pursuant to the Bankers' Books Evidence Act 1879, copies of entries in bankers' books are, subject to certain safeguards, admissible as evidence of their contents. To protect bank personnel from the unnecessary inconvenience of either providing the originals of such books or appearing as witnesses, section 6 of the Act provides that:

A banker or official of a bank shall not, in any legal proceedings to which the bank is not a party, be compellable to produce any banker's book the contents of which can be proved under this Act, or to appear as a witness to prove the matters, transactions, and accounts therein recorded, unless by order of a judge made for special cause.

# B OATHS AND AFFIRMATIONS

Sworn evidence is evidence given by a witness who has either taken an oath or made an affirmation. The general rule in both civil and criminal proceedings is that the evidence of any witness should be sworn. In civil claims which have been allocated to the small claims track, the court need not take evidence on oath.[88] The exceptions in the case of certain children and those of unsound mind have already been considered. There are two other minor exceptions at common law. A witness called only to produce a document may give unsworn evidence provided that the identity of the document is either not disputed or can be established by another witness.[89] Counsel acting for one of two parties who have reached a compromise may give unsworn evidence of its terms.[90] Where a video-recording of an interview with a child is admitted in evidence, and the child is at that stage aged 14 or over, the oath should be administered before the start of the cross-examination.[91] However, under section 56(5) of the Youth Justice and Criminal Evidence Act 1999, where a witness who is competent to give evidence in criminal proceedings has given evidence in such

---

[87] See the Diplomatic Privileges Act 1964; Consular Relations Act 1968; International Organisations Act 1968; Diplomatic and other Privileges Act 1971; and State Immunity Act 1978.

[88] CPR r 27.8(4).  [89] *Perry v Gibson* (1834) 1 Ad & El 48.

[90] *Hickman v Berens* [1895] 2 Ch 638, CA.

[91] *R v Simmonds* [1996] Crim LR 816, CA, a decision under s 32A of the Criminal Justice Act 1988. See now s 27 of the Youth Justice and Criminal Evidence Act 1999, below.

proceedings unsworn, no conviction, verdict or finding in those proceedings shall be taken to be unsafe, for the purposes of the grounds of appeal set out in sections 2(1), 13(1), or 16(1) of the Criminal Appeal Act 1968, by reason only that the witness was in fact a person falling within section 55(2) of the 1999 Act[92] and accordingly should have given his evidence on oath.

The modern law of oaths and affirmations is governed by the Oaths Act 1978. Section 1(1) provides for the manner of administration of the oath in the case of Christians and Jews. Unless a person about to take the oath in this form and manner objects thereto, or is physically incapable of so taking the oath, it will be administered without inquiry on the part of the judge.[93] It is therefore incumbent on those of other religious beliefs or those who wish to affirm, to object to the taking of such an oath.[94] In the case of those of other religious beliefs, section 1(3) provides that the oath shall be administered 'in any lawful manner'. Such witnesses usually take the oath upon such holy book as is appropriate to their religious belief. Section 3 of the Act expressly permits a witness to be sworn with uplifted hand in the form and manner in which an oath is usually administered in Scotland. Whether an oath is administered in a 'lawful manner' under section 1(3) does not depend on the intricacies of the particular religion which is adhered to by the witness but on whether the oath is one which appears to the court to be binding on the conscience of the witness and, if so, whether it is an oath which the witness himself considers to be binding on his conscience. Both conditions were satisfied in *R v Kemble*,[95] in which a Muslim had taken the oath using the New Testament, whereas under the strict tenets of Islam, no oath taken by a Muslim is valid unless taken on a copy of the Koran in Arabic.

Any person who objects to the taking of an oath shall be permitted instead, the choice being his, to make a solemn affirmation.[96] An affirmation is of the same force and effect as an oath,[97] and if there is a real risk that the jury will attach less weight to the evidence of a witness of a particular faith because he has affirmed, rather than taken the oath on the relevant holy book, then the judge has a discretion to allow the witness to be questioned, in a sensitive manner, as to why he did not take the oath on the particular holy book.[98]

Occasionally, a court may find itself unequipped to administer an oath in the manner appropriate to a person's particular religious belief. Accordingly, it is provided that a person may be permitted, and indeed required, to affirm where 'it is not reasonably practicable without inconvenience or delay to administer an oath in the manner appropriate to his religious belief'.[99]

---

[92] See under **A5 Children and persons of unsound mind—civil cases**, above.          [93] Section 1(2).

[94] For the arguments against the continued use of religious oaths, see the eleventh report of the Criminal Law Revision Committee, *Evidence (General)* (Cmnd 4991) (1972), paras 279–81 and Lord Justice Auld's *Review of the Criminal Courts of England and Wales*, HMSO (2001) 598–600.

[95] [1990] 3 All ER 116, CA.          [96] Section 5(1). See *R v Bellamy* (1985) 82 Cr App R 222, CA.

[97] Section 5(4).

[98] See *R v Mehrban* [2002] 1 Cr App R 561, CA, where one of the accused, a Muslim, had affirmed because 'unclean', not having been able to wash himself in the appropriate way before swearing.

[99] Section 5(2) and (3).

A person who has taken a duly administered oath could with relative ease subsequently allege that it was of no binding effect because at the time of taking it he had no religious belief. Section 4(2) avoids this possibility by providing that the fact that a person had, at the time of taking the oath, no religious belief 'shall not for any purpose affect the validity of the oath'.

A witness who, having taken an oath or made an affirmation, wilfully makes a statement material to the proceedings in question which he knows to be false or does not believe to be true, commits perjury and may be prosecuted accordingly.[100]

## C LIVE LINKS

In civil proceedings, CPR rule 32.3 provides that the court may allow a witness to give evidence 'through a video link or by other means'.[101] No defined limit or set of circumstances should be placed upon discretionary exercise of this power to permit video link evidence, which is not confined to cases of 'pressing need', as when a witness is too ill to attend in person. Relevant factors include whether failure to attend is an abuse or contemptuous or designed to obtain a collateral advantage, as well as considerations of cost, time and inconvenience. The court should also have regard to Article 6 of the European Convention on Human Rights and the need to see that the parties are on an equal footing.[102] In *Polanski v Condé Nast Publications Ltd*[103] the House of Lords held, by a majority, that although special cases may arise, as a general rule a claimant's unwillingness to come to the UK because he is a fugitive from justice is a valid reason, and can be a sufficient reason, for making a video conferencing order, because such a person, despite his status, is entitled to invoke the assistance of the court and its procedures in protection of his civil rights. Since such a person can bring or defend proceedings without bringing the administration of justice into disrepute, it was difficult to see why it should be brought into disrepute by his making use of a procedural facility flowing from a technological development readily available to all litigants.

In criminal cases, there are three sets of rules governing the use that may be made of live links. First, section 32 of the Criminal Justice Act 1988, which provides that, in trials on indictment[104] or proceedings in youth courts,[105] a person other than the accused who is outside the United Kingdom may, with the leave of the court, give

---

[100] See s 1 of the Perjury Act 1911 and s 5(4) of the Oaths Act 1978, above.

[101] See also CPR PD 32, Annex 3, Videoconferencing Guidance.

[102] *Rowland v Bock* [2002] 4 All ER 370, QBD.     [103] [2005] 1 All ER 945, HL.

[104] Or an appeal to the Court of Appeal (Criminal Division) or the hearing of a reference of a case to the Court of Appeal under s 9 of the Criminal Appeal Act 1995.

[105] Or appeals to the Crown Court arising out of such proceedings or hearings of references under s 11 of the Criminal Appeal Act 1995 so arising.

evidence through a live television link.[106] Secondly, under section 24 of the Youth Justice and Criminal Evidence Act 1999, a special measures direction may provide for a child or other vulnerable witness to give evidence by a live television link. Section 24 is considered, together with other special measures directions, separately, below. Thirdly, under Part 8 of the Criminal Justice Act 2003 (sections 51–6) general provision is made for the use of live links in criminal cases.[107] There is no common law power to permit evidence to be given by live link—the statutory regime provides exclusively for the circumstances in which live link evidence may be used in the course of a criminal trial and is incompatible with any parallel common law jurisdiction.[108]

Part 8 of the 2003 Act, which now falls to be considered in more detail, has been introduced without any indication as to the relationship between its general provisions and the provisions in the 1999 Act, except to state that Part 8 is without prejudice to 'any power of a court . . . to give directions . . . in relation to any witness'.[109] Under section 51(1)–(3) of the 2003 Act, a court may, on the application of a party, or of its own motion, direct that a witness, other than the accused, give evidence through a live link in the following criminal proceedings: a summary trial, an appeal to the Crown Court arising out of such a trial, a trial on indictment, and an appeal to the criminal division of the Court of Appeal.[110] A 'live link' means a live television link or other arrangement by which a witness, while at a place in the United Kingdom which is outside the building where the proceedings are being held, is able both to see and hear a person at the place where the proceedings are being held and to be seen and heard by the accused, the judge, the justices, and the jury (if there is one), the legal representatives and any interpreter or other person appointed by the court to assist the witness.[111] Rules of court may make provision as to the procedure to be followed in connection with an application for a direction to give evidence through a live link and as to the arrangements or safeguards to be put in place in connection with the operation of the link.[112] Under section 51(4)(a), a direction may not be given unless the court is satisfied that it is in the interests of the efficient or effective administration of justice.[113] Under section 51(6), in deciding whether to give a direction, the court must consider all the circumstances. Section 51(7) provides that:

---

[106] A statement made on oath by such a witness shall be treated for the purposes of s 1 of the Perjury Act 1911 as having been made in the proceedings in which it is given in evidence: s 32(3). However, it is not a condition of admissibility that the witness is in a country from which he can be extradited to stand trial for perjury: *R v Forsyth* [1997] 2 Cr App R 299, CA.

[107] See also the Crime (International Cooperation) Act 2003.

[108] *R(S) v Waltham Forest Youth Court* [2004] 2 Cr App R 335, DC at [86]–[89].

[109] Section 56(5)(a) of the Criminal Justice Act 2003.

[110] Also the hearing of a reference under s 9 or s 11 of the Criminal Appeal Act 1995, a hearing before a magistrates' court or the Crown Court which is held after the accused has entered a plea of guilty, and a hearing before the Court of Appeal under s 80 of the 2003 Act (application for retrial following acquittal): s 51 (2).

[111] Section 56(2) and (3). For these purposes, the extent (if any) to which a person is unable to see or hear by reason of any impairment of eyesight or hearing is to be disregarded: s 56(4).

[112] Section 55.

[113] Also the Secretary of State must have notified the court that suitable facilities for receiving evidence through a live link are available in the area: s 51(4)(b).

(7) Those circumstances include in particular—
    (a) the availability of the witness,
    (b) the need for the witness to attend in person,
    (c) the importance of the witness's evidence to the proceedings,
    (d) the views of the witness,
    (e) the suitability of the facilities at the place where the witness would give evidence through a live link,
    (f) whether a direction might tend to inhibit any party to the proceedings from effectively testing the witness's evidence.

If the court refuses an application for a direction, it must state its reasons in open court and, if it is a magistrates' court, must cause them to be entered in the register of its proceedings.

Where a direction has been given, the witness may not give evidence otherwise than through the link,[114] and therefore will also be subject to cross-examination and any re-examination through the link, but the court may rescind a direction if there has been a material change of circumstances since the direction was given.[115] Where the evidence is given through a live link, the court retains the power to exclude evidence at its discretion (whether by preventing questions from being put or otherwise),[116] and the judge may give the jury such direction as he thinks necessary to ensure that the jury gives the same weight to the evidence as if it had been given by the witness in the courtroom.[117]

# D  THE TIME AT WHICH EVIDENCE SHOULD BE ADDUCED

In both civil and criminal proceedings, as a general rule of practice rather than law, a party should adduce all the evidence on which he intends to rely before the close of his case.[118] If, in a criminal case, evidence becomes available to the prosecution for the first time *after* the close of its case, the question of its admissibility should be referred to and decided by the judge.[119] The evidence may be admitted, even if not strictly of a rebutting character, but the court should take care, in the exercise of its discretion, in case injustice is done to the accused, and should consider whether to grant the defence an adjournment.[120] Similarly, in a civil case, the claimant, after the close of the trial but before the judgment has been handed down, may introduce in

---

[114] Section 52(2).        [115] Section 52(5) and (6).        [116] Section 56(5)(b).
[117] Section 54.
[118] *R v Rice* (1963) 47 Cr App R 79, CCA.        [119] *R v Kane* (1977) 65 Cr App R 270, CA.
[120] *R v Doran* (1972) 56 Cr App R 429, CA and *R v Patel* [1992] Crim LR 739, CA; cf *R v Pilcher* (1974) 60 Cr App R 1, CA.

evidence a document which ought to have been disclosed by the defendant and which the claimant could not have obtained by other means.[121]

Although, in criminal cases, the general rule applies not only to the adducing of evidence, but also to matters to be put in cross-examination of an accused,[122] it is confined to evidence probative of his guilt, rather than evidence going only to his credit.[123] If evidence capable of forming part of the affirmative case for the prosecution case did not form part of the evidence on which the accused was committed for trial, the practice is to give notice of the additional evidence to the defence before it is tendered.[124] The fact that the accused might then trim his evidence is not a reason for withholding the material until he gives evidence, because an accused needs to know in advance the case against him if he is to have a proper opportunity of answering that case to the best of his ability. He is also entitled to such knowledge when deciding whether to testify. It is better in the interests of justice that an accused is not induced, by thinking it is safe to do so, to exaggerate, embroider or lie. To do so might be to ambush the accused.[125]

To the general rule of practice there are two exceptions and a 'wider discretion' to be exercised outside the two exceptions sparingly. As to the first exception, evidence is allowed in rebuttal of matters arising *ex improviso*, which no human ingenuity could have foreseen.[126] Under this exception, it is for the judge, in his discretion, to determine whether the relevance of the evidence could *reasonably* have been anticipated.[127] If the prosecution can reasonably foresee that the evidence is relevant to their case, it must be adduced as a part of that case and not to remedy defects in that case after it has been closed.[128] In *R v Milliken*,[129] the accused, when giving evidence, for the first time accused officers of a conspiracy to fabricate evidence. Evidence in rebuttal was allowed, because it only became relevant when the accused gave evidence. Equally, the prosecution may rely on this exception where the evidence in question was not, at the outset, *clearly* relevant, but only marginally, minimally or doubtfully relevant[130] or constituted fanciful and unreal statements such as allegations which were obviously ridiculous and untrue.[131]

Under the second exception, the judge has a discretion to admit evidence which has not been adduced by reason of inadvertence or oversight. Although this exception is

---

[121] *Stocznia Gdanska SA v Latvian Shipping Co* (2000) LTL 19/10/2000, QBD.

[122] *R v Kane* (1977) 65 Cr App R 270, CA.       [123] *R v Halford* (1978) 67 Cr App R 318, CA.

[124] *R v Kane* (1977) 65 Cr App R 270, CA.

[125] *R v Phillipson* (1989) 91 Cr App R 226, CA. See also *R v Sansom* [1991] 2 QB 130, CA.

[126] *R v Frost* (1839) 4 State Tr NS 85. The exception may be used by the prosecution to adduce evidence in rebuttal of not only defence *evidence*, but also matters unsupported by evidence but arising by implication from the defence closing speech: *R v O'Hadhmaill* [1996] Crim LR 509, CA.

[127] *R v Scott* (1984) 79 Cr App R 49, CA.       [128] *R v Day* (1940) 27 Cr App R 168.

[129] (1969) 53 Cr App R 330, CA.       [130] *R v Levy* (1966) 50 Cr App R 198.

[131] *R v Hutchinson* (1985) 82 Cr App R 51, CA.

usually said to apply only in the case of evidence of a formal or uncontentious nature,[132] the cases show that the evidence may relate to a matter of substance.[133]

In *R v Francis*[134] the prosecution established where a man was standing at a group identification, but failed to call evidence that the man in that position was the accused. After the close of their case, the prosecution were allowed to adduce such evidence. It was held that although the failure was not a mere technicality, but an essential if minor link in the chain of identification evidence, the discretion of the judge to admit evidence after the close of the prosecution case is not confined to the two well-established exceptions: there is a wider discretion, but it should only be exercised outside the two exceptions on the rarest of occasions. In *R v Munnery*[135] it was held that this last proposition could be expanded to include the words 'especially when the evidence is tendered after the case for the defendant has begun'. An example of evidence being admitted even at this late stage is *James v South Glamorgan County Council*.[136] In that case, in which the defence had not made a submission of no case to answer, the prosecution, after the accused had given his evidence-in-chief, were allowed to re-open their case to call their main witness, whose evidence was important, if not essential to their case, the witness having arrived late by reason of transport difficulties and genuine confusion about the location of the court house. *Jolly v DPP*,[137] a decision relating to a summary trial, also supports a wider discretionary approach to admissibility. It was held that it was 'beyond argument' that there was a general discretion to permit the prosecution to call evidence after the close of their case, which, in a magistrates' court, extended up to the time when the bench retired. The court would look carefully at the interests of justice overall and in particular the risk of prejudice to the accused, as when the defence would have been conducted differently had the evidence been adduced as part of the prosecution case. Thus the discretion would be exercised sparingly, but it was doubted whether it assisted to speak in terms of 'exceptional circumstances'.[138]

In appropriate circumstances, rather than have the prosecution re-open its case, a judge may, in the interests of justice, admit evidence himself. In *R v Bowles*[139] it was held that a judge was justified in calling certain evidence to provide an answer to a question raised by the jury during the defence case: the defence had not closed their case, and the evidence, which was non-controversial and did not contradict that of the accused, helped the jury resolve an issue on the basis of known facts, rather than

---

[132] For example, failure to prove that leave of the Director of Public Prosecutions to bring proceedings has been obtained (*R v Waller* [1910] 1 KB 364, CCA, applied in *Price v Humphries* [1958] 2 All ER 725, DC) or failure to prove a statutory instrument by production of a Stationery Office copy (*Palastanga v Solman* [1962] Crim LR 334 and *Hammond v Wilkinson* [2001] Crim LR 323). See also *R v McKenna* (1956) 40 Cr App R 65.

[133] See, eg, *Piggott v Sims* [1973] RTR 15 (an analyst's certificate); *Matthews v Morris* [1981] Crim LR 495 (a statement by the owner of the property allegedly stolen); and *Middleton v Rowlett* [1954] 1 WLR 831 (evidence of identification).

[134] [1991] 1 All ER 225, CA.     [135] (1990) 94 Cr App R 164, CA.

[136] (1994) 99 Cr App R 321, DC. See also (applying *R v Francis*) *R v Jackson* [1996] 2 Cr App R 420, CA.

[137] [2000] Crim LR 471, DC.     [138] See also *Cook v DPP* [2001] Crim LR 321, DC.

[139] [1992] Crim LR 726, CA. See also *R v Aitken* (1991) 94 Cr App R 85, CA.

speculation. In the exercise of his discretion, the judge may also recall or permit the recall of a witness at any stage in the proceedings before the end of his summing-up.[140] However, when the jury or justices have retired to consider their verdict on the conclusion of the summing-up, no further evidence may be admitted, whether by the calling or re-calling of witnesses,[141] and the jury must not be given any additional matter or material to assist them,[142] whether given at their own request, or in error.[143]

When the jury retire, an exhibit may be taken into the jury room for inspection. Where a silent film or video has been shown in court and the jury, after retirement, ask to see it again, they may do so, but it is better that they do so in open court.[144] Concerning tapes, if nothing turns on tone of voice, it will usually suffice for the jury to have a transcript, much of which should be summarized, but where tone of voice is all-important, then, subject to editing out inadmissible material, the jury should have the original tape.[145] If the tape is not played during the trial, the jury may listen to it after retirement, but if there is a risk that they may hear inadmissible material, the tape should be played in open court.[146] If the prosecution do not rely on parts of a tape, the jury may only hear it as edited.[147] However, if the tape, of which there is an agreed transcript, has already been played in court and does not contain inadmissible material, the judge has a discretion to permit the jury to play it in their retiring room.[148] In the case of a video-recording used as a child's evidence pursuant to section 27 of the Youth Justice and Criminal Evidence Act 1999, if the jury, after they have retired, wish to be reminded of *what* the witness said, the judge should remind them from the transcript or his own notes; but if they wish to be reminded of how the words were spoken, the judge may in his discretion allow the video, or relevant part, to be replayed, provided that the replay takes place in court.[149] Either way, the judge should warn the jury that by reason of hearing the evidence again they should guard against the risk of giving it disproportionate weight and bear well in mind the other evidence in the case, and the judge should remind the jury, from his notes, of the cross-examination and re-examination of the complainant.[150] Video-recordings

---

[140] *R v Sullivan* [1923] 1 KB 47; *R v McKenna* (1956) 40 Cr App R 65. The witness may be cross-examined on new evidence given: *R v Watson* (1834) 6 C&P 653.

[141] *R v Browne* (1943) 29 Cr App R 106; *R v Owen* (1952) 36 Cr App R 16; *R v Wilson* (1957) 41 Cr App R 226. In *R v Flynn* (1957) 42 Cr App R 15, evidence in rebuttal was called immediately before the summing-up; contrast *R v Sanderson* (1953) 37 Cr App R 32, where fresh evidence was called after the summing-up. The Criminal Law Revision Committee proposed that evidence be allowed to be given at any time prior to verdict: see 11th Report (Cmnd 499), paras 213–16.

[142] *R v Davis* (1975) 62 Cr App R 194. See also *R v Crees* [1996] Crim LR 830, CA, where the jury were improperly given a ruler which they wished to use as if it were a knife, for the purposes of a re-enactment.

[143] See *R v Gilder* [1997] Crim LR 668, CA.          [144] *R v Imran* [1997] Crim LR 754, CA.

[145] *R v Emmerson* (1990) 92 Cr App R 284, CA.          [146] *R v Riaz* (1991) 94 Cr App R 339, CA.

[147] See *R v Hagan* [1997] 1 Cr App R 464, CA.          [148] *R v Tonge* [1993] Crim LR 876, CA.

[149] In normal circumstances it is inappropriate for the video to be replayed unless there has been a specific request to that effect from the jury: *R v M* [1996] 2 Cr App R 56, CA.

[150] See, in the case of a reminder from the transcript, *R v McQuiston* [1998] 1 Cr App R 139, CA and *R v Morris* [1998] Crim LR 416, CA; and see, in the case of a replay, *R v Rawlings* [1995] 1 All ER 580, CA, applied in *R v M* [1996] 2 Cr App R 56, CA and *R v B* [1996] Crim LR 499, CA. The principles, however, do not lay down an inflexible practice to be followed to the letter in every case: *R v Horley* [1999] Crim LR 488, CA. For

introduced to show inconsistency on the part of a witness may also be replayed to remind the jury of how the words were spoken, subject to a proper warning that they are not evidence in the case.[151]

A jury request for equipment, such as weighing scales, to enable them to carry out unsupervised scientific experiments with exhibits, should not be met.[152]

# E  WITNESSES IN CIVIL CASES

## 1  THE WITNESSES TO BE CALLED

Prior to the Civil Procedure Rules, a party to civil proceedings was under no obligation to call particular witnesses, could call such witnesses to support his case as he saw fit, and could call them in the order of his choice.[153] As to the judge, he had no right to call witnesses against the will of the parties,[154] except in cases of civil contempt,[155] but did have the power to recall a witness called by a party.[156] CPR rule 32.1(1) now provides that the court may control the evidence by giving directions as to the nature of the evidence which it requires to decide the issues on which it requires evidence, and the way in which the evidence is to be placed before the court; and under rule 32.1(2) the court may use its power under the rule to exclude evidence that would otherwise be admissible. In exercising these powers, the judge must seek to give effect to the 'overriding objective' of the Civil Procedure Rules, which is to enable the court 'to deal with cases justly'.[157] It seems that CPR rule 32.1(1) does not empower the court to dictate to a litigant what evidence he should tender. Thus a party who has disclosed a witness statement in accordance with pre-trial directions cannot be ordered by the court to call the witness, although he should notify the other parties of his decision and whether he proposes to put the statement in as hearsay.[158] In appropriate circumstances, however, the judge may take the view that, in order to give effect to the overriding objective, he should give directions under CPR rule 32.1(1) as to the order in which witnesses should give their evidence, and as to those witnesses

---

example, it is unnecessary to remind the jury of the cross-examination if the judge dealt with it in detail in his summing up and the jury have declined an offer of further assistance in that regard: *R v Saunders* [1995] 2 Cr App R 313, CA.

[151] *R v Atkinson* [1995] Crim LR 490, CA.

[152] *R v Stewart, R v Sappleton* (1989) 89 Cr App R 273, CA; cf *R v Wright* [1993] Crim LR 607, CA. A magnifying glass, a ruler or a tape-measure do not normally raise the possibility of such an experiment: *R v Maggs* (1990) 91 Cr App R 243, CA.

[153] *Briscoe v Briscoe* [1966] 1 All ER 465; but cf *Bayer v Clarkson Puckle Overseas Ltd* [1989] NLJR 256.

[154] *Re Enoch and Zaretzky, Bock & Co's Arbitration* [1910] 1 KB 327, CA, where an arbitrator was held to be in the same position.

[155] *Yianni v Yianni* [1966] 1 WLR 120.          [156] *Fallon v Calvert* [1960] 2 QB 201, CA.

[157] See further Ch 2 under **F2 Exclusionary discretion**.

[158] *Society of Lloyd's v Jaffray* (2000) *The Times*, 3 Aug 2000 (QBD).

who are not required to decide the issues and whose evidence, therefore, although admissible, should not be heard.

## 2 WITNESS STATEMENTS

The rules for the exchange of witness statements in civil cases have been designed to promote the fair disposal of proceedings and to save costs: they identify the real issues, encourage the parties to make appropriate admissions of fact, promote fair settlements, remove the element of surprise as to the witnesses each party intends to call and give to the cross-examining party the advantage of knowing in advance what each witness will say in his examination-in-chief.

A witness statement is a written statement signed by a person which contains the evidence which that person would be allowed to give orally.[159] Under CPR rule 32.4(2), the court will order a party to serve on the other parties any witness statement of the oral evidence which the party serving the statement intends to rely on in relation to any issues of fact to be decided at the trial; and under rule 32.4(3) the court may give directions as to the order in which the statements are to be served.[160] The court will give directions for the service of witness statements when it allocates a case to the fast track[161] or multi-track.[162] Normally, the court will direct the simultaneous exchange of statements,[163] but sequential exchange may be appropriate where one party will not know fully or precisely the case he has to answer until he has had sight of his opponent's witness statements. If a party fails to serve witness statements, any other party may apply for an order to enforce compliance or for a sanction to be imposed,[164] and, ultimately, the court has the power to strike out the claim or defence.[165]

A witness statement should be dated.[166] It must, if practicable, be in the intended witness's own words and should be expressed in the first person.[167] It must also indicate which of the statements in it are made from the witness's own knowledge and which are matters of information or belief.[168] The statement is the equivalent of the oral evidence which the witness would, if called, give in evidence, and must include a statement of truth by the intended witness, ie a signed statement that he believes the facts in it are true.[169] If it is not verified by a statement of truth, then the court may

---

[159] CPR r 32.4(1). The statement, therefore, should not contain material which is irrelevant or otherwise inadmissible.

[160] Although CPR Pt 32 (except r 32.1) does not apply to claims which have been allocated to the small claims track (r 27.2(1)), in the case of many such claims directions for the exchange of witness statements will be given nonetheless: see r 27.4 and PD 27.

[161] Rule 28.2, r 28.3 and PD 28.          [162] Rule 29.2 and PD 29.

[163] PD 28, para 3.9 and PD 29, para 4.10.          [164] See PD 28, para 5.1 and PD 29, para 7.1.

[165] See r 3.4.          [166] Rule 32.8 and PD 32, para 17.2.          [167] Ibid para 18.1.

[168] Ibid para 18.2.

[169] PD 32, para 20.1 and CPR r 22.1(6). Proceedings for contempt of court may be brought against a person making a false statement in a document verified by a statement of truth without an honest belief in its truth: CPR r 32.14. In *Aquarius Financial Enterprises Inc v Certain Underwriters at Lloyd's* (2001) NLJ 694, QBD, where there was evidence that a witness statement had been obtained by bullying, inducements and

direct that it shall not be admissible as evidence.[170] Equally, if it does not comply with CPR Part 32 or Practice Direction 32 in relation to its form, the court may refuse to admit it as evidence.[171]

CPR rule 32.5 provides as follows:

(1) If—
    (a) a party has served a witness statement; and
    (b) he wishes to rely at trial on the evidence of the witness who made the statement, he must call the witness to give oral evidence unless the court orders otherwise or he puts the statement in as hearsay evidence.

(2) Where a witness is called to give evidence under paragraph (1), his witness statement shall stand as his evidence in chief unless the court orders otherwise.

(3) A witness giving oral evidence at trial may with the permission of the court—
    (a) amplify his witness statement;
    (b) give evidence in relation to new matters which have arisen since the witness statement was served on the other parties.

(4) The court will give permission under paragraph (3) only if it considers that there is good reason not to confine the evidence of the witness to the contents of his witness statement.

(5) If a party who has served a witness statement does not—
    (a) call the witness to give evidence at trial; or
    (b) put the witness statement in as hearsay evidence,
any other party may put the witness statement in as hearsay evidence.

As to rule 32.5(2), it is likely that the court, in deciding whether to order that the statement should not stand as the witness's evidence-in-chief, will have regard to such matters as the extent to which his evidence is likely to be controversial and to go to the heart of the dispute, and the extent to which his credibility will be in issue.[172] As to rule 32.5(4), the pertinent factors would seem to be the relevance of the evidence to the issues, any prejudice likely to be caused to the party against whom the evidence is to be used and, in the case of rule 32.5(3)a, the reason why the witness statement did not include the additional material.

Under rule 32.9, provision is made for a party who is unable to obtain a witness statement to apply for permission to serve a witness summary instead. Rule 32.9 covers cases where a party knows the name and address of a particular witness, but the witness is reluctant or unwilling to give evidence or, having indicated his willingness to give evidence, changes his mind. A typical example is the employee who is loath

---

threats, it was held that it was part of the duty of solicitors to ensure, so far as lay within their power, that statements are taken either by themselves or, if that is not practicable, by somebody who can be relied upon to exercise the same standard as should apply when statements are taken by solicitors.

[170] Rule 22.3.      [171] PD 32, para 25.1.

[172] See *Mercer v Chief Constable of the Lancashire Constabulary* [1991] 2 All ER 504, CA, a decision under an earlier version of the rules.

to give evidence, on behalf of an ex-employee, against his employer.[173] Rule 32.9 provides as follows:

(1) A party who—
   (a) is required to serve a witness statement for use at trial; but
   (b) is unable to obtain one,
   may apply, without notice, for permission to serve a witness summary instead.

(2) A witness summary is a summary of—
   (a) the evidence, if known, which would otherwise be included in a witness statement; or
   (b) if the evidence is not known, the matters about which the party serving the witness summary proposes to question the witness.

(3) Unless the court orders otherwise, a witness summary must include the name and address of the intended witness.

(4) Unless the court orders otherwise, a witness summary must be served within the period in which a witness statement would have had to be served.

(5) Where a party serves a witness summary, so far as practicable, rules 32.4 (requirement to serve witness statements for use at trial), 32.5(3) (amplifying witness statements), and 32.8 (form of witness statement) shall apply to the summary.

Under rule 32.10, if a witness statement or witness summary is not served in respect of an intended witness within the time specified by the court, then the witness may not be called to give oral evidence unless the court gives permission. In deciding whether to give permission, the relevant factors would appear to be the length of delay, whether there is a good reason for failure to serve the statement or it is a result of incompetence on the part of the legal advisers, the relevance of the evidence, including the risk of injustice to the party seeking to call the witness if permission is not given, and any prejudice likely to be caused to his opponent if permission is given.

## F  WITNESSES IN CRIMINAL CASES

Under rule 3.3 of the Criminal Procedure Rules 2005,[174] each party to criminal proceedings must (a) actively assist the court in fulfilling the court's duty to further the overriding objective (that criminal cases be dealt with justly) by actively managing the case, without or if necessary with a direction and (b) apply for a direction if needed to further the overriding objective. Under rule 3.9, which applies to the parties' preparation for trial, each party, in fulfilling his duty under rule 3.3, must, inter alia, take every reasonable step to make sure his witnesses will attend when they are needed; and under rule 3.10, in order to manage the trial, the court may require a party to

---

[173] See further Ch 6 under **D Unfavourable and hostile witnesses.**        [174] SI 2005/384.

identify (a) which witnesses he intends to give oral evidence (b) the order in which he intends those witnesses to give their evidence (c) whether he requires an order compelling the attendance of a witness and (d) what arrangements, if any, he proposes to facilitate the giving of evidence by a witness.[175]

## 1 THE WITNESSES TO BE CALLED

In criminal proceedings, the choice as to which witnesses are called rests primarily with the parties. A trial judge also has the right to call a witness not called by either the prosecution or defence, and without the consent of either party if, in his opinion, this course is necessary in the interests of justice.[176] Justices have the same right in summary proceedings.[177] This right may be exercised by the judge even after the close of the case for the defence, but only where a matter has arisen *ex improviso*.[178] The prosecution is under an obligation to call certain witnesses and to have others available at court to be called by the defence. In the case of trials on indictment, the principles were set out in *R v Russell-Jones*:[179]

1. Generally speaking the prosecution must bring to court all the witnesses 'named on the back of the indictment', a phrase reflecting the old practice, nowadays meaning those whose statements have been served as witnesses on whom the prosecution intend to rely, if the defence want those witnesses to attend.[180]

2. The prosecution have a discretion to call, or to tender for cross-examination by the defence, any witness it requires to attend, but the discretion is not unfettered.

3. The discretion must be exercised in the interests of justice so as to promote a fair trial.

---

[175] He may also be required to identify (e) what arrangements, if any, he proposes to facilitate the participation of any other person, including the accused (f) what written evidence he intends to introduce (g) what other material, if any, he intends to make available to the court in the presentation of the case (h) whether he intends to raise any point of law that could affect the conduct of the trial and (i) what timetable he proposes and expects to follow.

[176] *R v Chapman* (1838) 8 C&P 558 and *R v Holden* (1838) 8 C&P 606; cf *R v McDowell* [1984] Crim LR 486, CA. The power should rarely be exercised: *R v Grafton* (1993) 96 Cr App R 156, CA. If it is, an adjournment may be necessary to enable one of the parties to call evidence in rebuttal: see *R v Coleman* (1987) *The Times*, 21 Nov CA.

[177] *R v Wellingborough Magistrates' Court, ex p François* (1994) 158 JP 813 and *R v Haringey Justices, ex p DPP* [1996] 2 Cr App R 119, DC.

[178] See *R v Cleghorn* [1967] 2 QB 584, CA; cf *R v Tregear* [1967] 2 QB 574, CA.

[179] [1995] 3 All ER 239, CA. See also *R v Brown and Brown* [1997] 1 Cr App R 112, CA. Similar principles apply to summary proceedings: see *R v Haringey Justices, ex p DPP* [1996] 2 Cr App R 119, DC.

[180] If, at the plea and directions hearing, the defence indicate that they do not require particular witnesses to attend the trial, clearly those witnesses need not be called: see *Practice Direction (Criminal Proceedings: Consolidation)* [2002] 1 WLR 2870, para 41. Nor are the prosecution under any duty to call the makers of statements which have never formed part of the prosecution case because inconsistent with it and which have been served on the defence as unused material: *R v Richardson* (1993) 98 Cr App R 174, CA.

4.    The prosecution should normally call or offer to call all the witnesses who can give direct evidence of the primary facts of the case, even if there are inconsistencies between one witness and another, unless for good reason, in any instance, the prosecutor regards the witness's evidence as unworthy of belief.[181] In *R v Oliva*,[182] for example, it was held that the prosecution were not obliged to call the victim of an offence who gave evidence at the committal proceedings first implicating and then exonerating the accused. The witness had proved himself unworthy of belief and, if called by the prosecution, would have confused the jury.[183] However, if the prosecution are of the view that part of a witness's evidence is capable of belief, even though they do not rely on other parts of his evidence, they are entitled to exercise their discretion to call him, since it would be contrary to the interests of justice to deprive the jury of that part of his evidence which could be of assistance to them.[184]

5.    It is for the prosecution to decide which witnesses can give direct evidence of the primary facts.

6.    The prosecutor is also the primary judge of whether or not a witness to the material events is unworthy of belief.

7.    A prosecutor properly exercising his discretion will not be obliged to proffer a witness merely in order to give the defence material with which to attack the credit of other witnesses on whom the Crown relies.

## 2  THE ORDER OF WITNESSES

Although in criminal proceedings the parties are generally free to call their witnesses in the order of their choice, at common law the defence was required to call the accused before any of his witnesses: 'He ought to give his evidence before he has heard the evidence and cross-examination of any witness he is going to call.'[185] In *R v Smith*[186] the Court of Appeal approved this rule, subject to 'rare exceptions such as when a formal witness, or a witness about whom there is no controversy, is interposed before the accused person with the consent of the court in the special circumstances then prevailing'. The Criminal Law Revision Committee favoured retention of the rule but was of the opinion that the court should be given a discretion, wider than that stated in

---

[181]  Reading out the material parts of the statement of a witness may discharge the duty on the prosecution: see *R v Armstrong* [1995] Crim LR 831, CA.

[182]  [1965] 1 WLR 1028. Cf *R v Witts and Witts* [1991] Crim LR 562, CA.

[183]  In *R v Nugent* [1977] 3 All ER 662 it was held that the prosecution were not obliged to call eight alibi witnesses. Their names had been supplied by the defence and were contained in an alibi notice served on the prosecution after committal, and their statements were tendered by the prosecution in committal proceedings. Their evidence was not essential to the narrative of the prosecution case and might have confused the jury as to the nature of that case. The case is, apparently, an illustration of the *R v Oliva* principle, rather than a qualification to it conferring a wider discretion on the prosecution: *R v Balmforth* [1992] Crim LR 825, CA.

[184]  *R v Cairns* [2003] 1 Cr App R 662, CA.

[185]  Per Lord Alverstone CJ in *R v Morrison* (1911) 6 Cr App R 159 at 165.

[186]  (1968) 52 Cr App R 224.

*R v Smith*, to call other witnesses before the accused.[187] Section 79 of the Police and Criminal Evidence Act 1984, implementing this recommendation, provides that:

If at the trial of any person for an offence—
    (a) the defence intends to call two or more witnesses to the facts of the case; and
    (b) those witnesses include the accused,
the accused shall be called before the other witness or witnesses unless the court in its discretion otherwise directs.


## 3 EVIDENCE IN CHIEF BY VIDEO-RECORDING

In his 'Review of the Criminal Courts of England and Wales'[188] Lord Justice Auld recommended that, further to the use of video-recorded evidence in chief for vulnerable witnesses,[189] video-recorded evidence should also be admissible for the witnesses of all serious crimes. The government, in adopting this proposal, recognized the two key advantages of allowing the video recording to replace the witness's evidence in chief, the fact that the witness's recollection of the events in question is likely to have been better at the time of the recording, and the reduction in levels of stress when giving evidence on oath. The danger that the witness may, in the recording, make statements elicited in answer to leading questions, was not thought to be serious given that it would be 'completely evident' whether the witness had been led. Under section 137 of the Criminal Justice Act 2003, therefore (i) where a prosecution witness, or a defence witness other than the accused, is called in proceedings for an offence triable only on indictment, or for an offence triable either way prescribed in an order made by the Secretary of State; (ii) he claims to have witnessed the offence or part of it, or other closely connected events; and (iii) a video-recording of his account of events has been made at a time when the events were fresh in his memory, the court may direct that the recording be admitted as his evidence in chief.[190] Such a direction may only be given, however, if it appears to the court that his recollection of events is likely to have been significantly better at the time of the recording than it will be when he gives oral evidence and it is in the interests of justice for the recording to be admitted, having regard in particular to certain prescribed matters, such as factors that might affect the reliability of what the witness said. Under section 137(2), which effectively side-steps the hearsay rule, the statements in the recorded account are not treated as out-of-court statements admissible as evidence of the matters stated, but shall be treated as if made by the witness in his evidence if, or to the extent that, in his oral evidence he asserts the truth of them. Section 137 provides as follows:

---

[187] 11th Report (Cmnd 4991), para 107. The Committee gave as an example a witness who is to speak of some event which occurred before the events about which the accused is to give evidence.

[188] HMSO, 2001, at 555.        [189] See below.

[190] The court may not make a direction unless the Secretary of State has notified the court that arrangements can be made, in the area in which it appears to the court that the proceedings will take place, for implementing directions under s 137: s 138(4).

(1) This section applies where—
    (a) a person is called as a witness in proceedings for an offence triable only on indictment, or for a prescribed offence triable either way,
    (b) the person claims to have witnessed (whether visually or in any other way)—
        (i)  events alleged by the prosecution to include conduct constituting the offence or part of the offence, or
        (ii) events closely connected with such events,
    (c) he has previously given an account of the events in question (whether in response to questions asked or otherwise),
    (d) the account was given at a time when those events were fresh in the person's memory (or would have been, assuming the truth of the claim mentioned in paragraph (b)),
    (e) a video recording was made of the account,
    (f)  the court has made a direction that the recording should be admitted as evidence in chief of the witness, and the direction has not been rescinded, and
    (g) the recording is played in the proceedings in accordance with the direction.

(2) If, or to the extent that, the witness in his oral evidence in the proceedings asserts the truth of the statements made by him in the recorded account, they shall be treated as if made by him in that evidence.

(3) A direction under subsection (1)(f)—
    (a) may not be made in relation to a recorded account given by the defendant;
    (b) may be made only if it appears to the court that—
        (i)  the witness's recollection of the events in question is likely to have been significantly better when he gave the recorded account than it will be when he gives oral evidence in the proceedings, and
        (ii) it is in the interests of justice for the recording to be admitted, having regard in particular to the matters mentioned in subsection (4).

(4) Those matters are—
    (a) the interval between the time of the events in question and the time when the recorded account was made;
    (b) any other factors that might affect the reliability of what the witness said in that account;
    (c) the quality of the recording;
    (d) any views of the witness as to whether his evidence in chief should be given orally or by means of the recording.

(5) For the purposes of subsection (2) it does not matter if the statements in the recorded account were not made on oath.

(6) In this section 'prescribed' means of a description specified in an order made by the Secretary of State.

Nothing in section 137 affects the admissibility of any video recording which would be admissible apart from the section.[191]

Under section 138(1) of the 2003 Act, the witness may not, in his evidence-in-chief,

---

[191] Section 138(5).

give oral evidence about any matter which, in the opinion of the court, has been dealt with adequately in the recording. Section 138(2) makes clear that section 137 applies to a part of a recording as it applies to the whole of a recording, but under section 138(3), in deciding whether parts of a recording should be excluded, the court should consider whether those parts carry a risk of prejudice to the accused and, if so, whether it is in the interests of justice nonetheless that the whole, or substantially the whole, of the recording be shown. Section 138(1), (2), and (3) provide as follows.

(1) Where a video recording is admitted under section 137, the witness may not give evidence in chief otherwise than by means of the recording as to any matter which, in the opinion of the court, has been dealt with adequately in the recorded account.

(2) The reference in subsection (1)(f) of section 137 to the admission of a recording includes a reference to the admission of part of the recording; and references in that section and this one to the video recording or to the witness's recorded account shall, where appropriate, be read accordingly.

(3) In considering whether any part of a recording should not be admitted under section 137, the court must consider—
    (a) whether admitting that part would carry a risk of prejudice to the defendant, and
    (b) if so, whether the interests of justice nevertheless require it to be admitted in view of the desirability of showing the whole, or substantially the whole, of the recorded interview.

## 4  SPECIAL MEASURES DIRECTIONS FOR VULNERABLE AND INTIMIDATED WITNESSES

Sections 16–33 of the Youth Justice and Criminal Evidence Act 1999 introduce a range of 'special measures' which were proposed in *Speaking Up for Justice* (Home Office, 1998) and are designed to minimize the ordeal and trauma experienced by certain types of vulnerable and intimidated witnesses when giving evidence in criminal cases.[192] The provisions introduce sensible modifications to orthodox trial procedures to meet the real needs of children and other vulnerable witnesses. Unfortunately, however, the new statutory scheme is needlessly complex (in parts almost impenetrable), unduly inflexible and, in the case of children, makes a crude distinction between sexual offences and offences of physical violence.

The judge may give a direction providing for the following special measures to apply to evidence given by vulnerable and intimidated witnesses:

---

[192] See also *Report of the Advisory Group on Video-Recorded Evidence* (Home Office, 1989) (the 'Pigot Report'), Law Commission Consultation Paper No 130, *Mentally Incapacitated and Other Vulnerable Adults: Public Law Protection*, and generally Professor Di Birch 'A Better Deal for Vulnerable Witnesses?' [2000] Crim LR 223 and Laura Hoyano 'Variations on a Theme by Pigot: Special Measures Directions for Child Witnesses' [2000] Crim LR 250 and 'Striking a Balance between the Rights of Defendants and Vulnerable Witnesses: Will Special Measures Directions Contravene Guarantees of a Fair Trial?' [2001] Crim LR 948.

1. screening the witness;

2. giving evidence by live link;

3. giving evidence in private;

4. the removal of wigs and gowns;

5. admitting a video-recording of an interview of the witness as the evidence-in-chief of the witness;

6. video recording the cross-examination and re-examination of the witness and admitting such a recording as the evidence of the witness under cross-examination and on re-examination;[192a]

7. the examination of the witness through an intermediary, and

8. the provision of appropriate aids to communication with the witness.

Special measures are only available to 'eligible witnesses', namely (i) witnesses eligible for assistance on grounds of age or incapacity, for whom all the above special measures are available, and (ii) witnesses eligible for assistance on grounds of fear or distress about testifying, for whom all but the last two of the above special measures are available.[193] It will be convenient to consider in more detail the nature of the special measures available and the types of witness eligible for assistance before turning to consider the circumstances in which a special measures direction may or must be given.

## (a) Special measures directions

*(i) Screens.* Under section 23(1) of the 1999 Act, a special measures direction may provide for the witness while giving evidence or being sworn in court to be prevented by means of a screen or other arrangement from seeing the accused. However, the screen must not prevent the witness from being able to see, and to be seen by, the judge or justices, the jury (if there is one), legal representatives acting in the case, and any interpreter or other person appointed to assist the witness.[194]

*(ii) Live link.* Under section 24, a special measures direction may provide for the witness to give evidence by a live television link or other arrangement whereby the witness, while absent from the courtroom, is able to see and hear a person there and to be seen and heard by the judge or justices, the jury (if there is one), the legal representatives in the case, and any interpreter or other person appointed to assist the witness. Where a direction has been given providing for the witness to give evidence by live

---

[192a] This special measure (see s 28) is unlikely to be introduced.

[193] See s 18(1).

[194] Section 23(2). See also, prior to the enactment of s 23, Home Office Circular 61/1990, *Use of Screens in Magistrates' Courts*; and *R v X, Y and Z* (1989) 91 Cr App R 36, CA; *R v Watford Magistrates' Court, ex p Lenman* [1993] Crim LR 388, DC; *R v Cooper and Schaub* [1994] Crim LR 531, CA; and *R v Foster* [1995] Crim LR 333, CA.

link, the court may later give permission for the witness to give evidence in some other way, if it appears to be in the interests of justice to do so.[195]

*(iii) Evidence in private.* Under section 25, a special measures direction may provide for the exclusion from the court, during the giving of the witness's evidence, of persons of any description specified in the direction other than the accused, legal representatives acting in the case, or any interpreter or other person appointed to assist the witness.[196] However, such a direction may only be given where the proceedings relate to a sexual offence[197] or it appears to the court that there are reasonable grounds for believing that any person other than the accused has sought, or will seek, to intimidate the witness in connection with testifying in the proceedings.[198]

*(iv) Removal of wigs and gowns.* Under section 26, provision may be made for the wearing of wigs and gowns to be dispensed with during the giving of the witness's evidence.

*(v) Video-recorded evidence-in-chief.* Sections 27(1)–(3) provide as follows:

   (1) A special measures direction may provide for a video recording of an interview of the witness to be admitted as evidence in chief of the witness.

   (2) A special measures direction may, however, not provide for a video recording, or part of such a recording, to be admitted under this section if the court is of the opinion, having regard to all the circumstances of the case, that in the interests of justice the recording, or that part of it, should not be so admitted.

   (3) In considering, for the purposes of subsection (2) whether any part of a recording should not be admitted under this section, the court must consider whether any prejudice to the accused which might result from that part being so admitted is outweighed by the desirability of showing the whole, or substantially the whole, of the recorded interview.

Subsection (2) allows the court to direct that any part of the recording be excluded, in which case the party admitting the video must then edit it accordingly.[199] The effect of section 27(3) is not to extend the common law rules as to the admissibility of evidence so as to lead to the admission of otherwise inadmissible evidence, for example inadmissible evidence of bad character. Such evidence will normally be edited out. Section 27(3) is designed to cover unusual cases in which the evidence of the witness cannot be given in a way that is coherent and understandable to the listener without

---

[195] Sections 24(3).

[196] Where the persons specified are representatives of the media, the direction shall be expressed not to apply to one named person nominated by one or more news gathering or reporting organizations: s 25(3).

[197] 'Sexual offence' is defined in s 62 of the 1999 Act as any offence under Part 1 of the Sexual Offences Act 2003.

[198] Section 25(4).

[199] See *Practice Direction (Criminal Proceedings: Consolidation)* [2002] 1 WLR 2870, para 40, which also governs the procedure for production and proof of the recording.

the inclusion of the inadmissible material.[200] In such cases, it is submitted, the judge will need to give a direction to the jury—which, in the circumstances, is likely to be difficult for them to comprehend—that the offending material is not evidence of the matters stated.

Where a recording (or part of it) is admitted, then: (a) the witness must be called by the party tendering it in evidence, unless either (i) a special measures direction provides for the witness's evidence on cross-examination to be given otherwise than by testimony in court or (ii) the parties in the proceedings have agreed that there is no need for the witness to be available for cross-examination; and (b) the witness may not give evidence-in-chief otherwise than by means of the recording (or part of it) (i) as to any matter which in the opinion of the court has been dealt with adequately in the witness's recorded testimony (or part of it), or (ii) without the permission of the court, as to any other matter which, in the opinion of the court, is dealt with in that testimony (or part of it).[201] The court may give such permission if it appears to the court to be in the interests of justice to do so either (a) on an application by a party to the proceedings, if there has been a material change of circumstances since the time when the direction was given (or, if a previous application has been made, the time when the application or last application was made) or (b) of its own motion.[202] Where a special measures direction provides for a recording (or part of it) to be admitted under section 27, the court may nevertheless subsequently make a direction to the contrary if it appears to the court that (i) the witness will not be available for cross-examination (whether conducted in the ordinary way or in accordance with a special measures direction) and the parties have not agreed that there is no need for the witness to be so available, or (ii) any rules of court requiring disclosure of the circumstances in which the recording (or part of it) was made have not been complied with to the satisfaction of the court.[203] Nothing in section 27 affects the admissibility of any video-recording which would be admissible apart from the section.[204]

Video-recorded interviews with child witnesses should be conducted in accordance with the guidance given in 'Achieving Best Evidence in Criminal Proceedings: Guidance for Vulnerable or Intimidated Witnesses, Including Children' ('The Memorandum'),[205] a non-statutory code published by the Home Office, which deals with such matters as leading questions, previous statements and the bad character of the accused. The guidance should be regarded as expert advice as to what will normally be the best practice to adopt in seeking to ensure that a child's evidence is reliable, and if it is not observed there are grounds for a judge or jury to consider with particular care

---

[200] *R (on the application of the Crown Prosecution Service Harrow) v Brentford Youth Court* [2004] Crim LR 159 (DC).

[201] Section 27(5) and (6).

[202] Section 27(7) and (8). The court may, in giving permission, direct that the evidence in question be given by the witness by means of a live link: s 27(9).

[203] Section 27(4) and (6).       [204] Section 27(11).

[205] Available at <http://www.homeoffice.gov.uk>.

whether the child is reliable.[206] In *G v DPP*[207] consideration was given to the question whether failure to comply with an earlier version of the Memorandum goes to the weight of the video evidence or should lead to its exclusion under section 32A(3)(c) of the Criminal Justice Act 1988, the statutory precursor to section 27(2) of the 1999 Act. It was held that although it is of great importance that the Memorandum be followed, and that failure to do so may well result in exclusion, whether such failure should lead to exclusion will not necessarily be a question that can be answered by simply considering the nature and extent of the breaches. Regard should also be had to the extent to which passages in the evidence affected by the breaches are supported by other passages not so affected, and also the extent to which the other evidence in the case corroborates the video evidence.

In order to reach a decision under section 27(2), the judge, in most—if not all—cases, must watch the video-recording. In the case of interviews with some child witnesses, the court will need to decide upon the competence of the child.[208] If, on viewing the recording, he considers that the child is incompetent to give evidence, the evidence should not be admitted; but if he concludes that the child is competent, there is no need to investigate the child's competence again at the trial before the playing of the recording. Nonetheless, he still has the power to exclude the evidence if, in the course of it, he forms the view that the child is, after all, incompetent.[209]

In a decision under section 32A of the Criminal Justice Act 1988, the statutory precursor to section 27, it was held that where a video-recording has been admitted and there is a transcript, the jury may be provided with copies, on three conditions: (i) the transcript must be likely to assist them in following the evidence, as when a child suffers from a speech disorder or poor articulation; (ii) the judge must make it clear that the transcript has been provided only for that limited purpose and that they should concentrate primarily on the oral evidence; and (iii) the judge should give them such directions as would be likely to be effective safeguards against the risk of disproportionate weight being given to the transcript.[210] It has also been held, however, that unless the defence consents, the jury should not normally be permitted to retire with the transcript.[211]

*(vi) Video-recorded cross-examination or re-examination.* Under section 28(1), where a special measures direction provides for a video-recording to be admitted as evidence-in-chief of the witness under section 27, the direction may also provide for any cross-examination and any re-examination of the witness to be recorded by means of a video-recording and for such a recording, so far as it relates to any such cross-examination or re-examination, to be admitted as evidence of the witness under

---

[206] *R v Dunphy* (1993) 98 Cr App R 393 at 395, CA, a decision under an earlier version of the Memorandum.

[207] [1997] 2 All ER 755, DC.

[208] In deciding, the court shall treat the witness as having the benefit of any directions under s 19 which the court has given, or proposes to give, in relation to the witness: s 54(3) of the 1999 Act.

[209] See *R v Hampshire* [1995] 2 All ER 1019, CA, a decision under s 32A of the Criminal Justice Act 1988.

[210] *R v Welstead* [1996] 1 Cr App R 59, CA.

[211] *R v Coshall* [1995] 12 LS Gaz R 34, CA. See also *R v N* [1998] Crim LR 886, CA.

cross-examination or re-examination. Under section 28(2), such a recording must be made in the presence of such persons as rules of court or the direction may provide, and in the absence of the accused, but in circumstances in which (a) the judge or justices (or both) and legal representatives acting in the proceedings are able to see and hear the examination of the witness and to communicate with those in whose presence the recording is being made, and (b) the accused is able to see and hear any such examination and to communicate with any legal representative acting for him.[212] Where a special measures direction provides for a recording to be admitted under section 28, the court may nevertheless subsequently make a direction to the contrary if any requirement of section 28(2) or rules of court or the direction itself has not been complied with to the satisfaction of the court.[213] Where in pursuance of section 28(1) a recording has been made, the witness may not be subsequently cross-examined or re-examined in respect of any evidence given by the witness (whether or not in any recording admissible under section 27 or section 28) unless the court gives a further special measures direction,[214] but such a further direction may only be given if it appears to the court (a) that the proposed cross-examination is sought by a party to the proceedings as a result of that party having become aware, since the time when the original recording was made, of a matter which that party could not with reasonable diligence have ascertained by then, or (b) that for any other reason it is in the interests of justice to give the further direction.[215]

*(vii) Examination of witness through intermediary.* Under section 29, a special measures direction may provide for any examination of the witness (however and wherever conducted) to be conducted through an interpreter or other intermediary approved by the court. The function of the intermediary is to communicate to the witness questions put to the witness, to communicate to the person asking such questions the answers given by the witness in reply, and to explain such questions or answers so far as necessary to enable them to be understood.[216] Any examination under section 29 must take place in the presence of such persons as rules of court or the direction may provide, but in circumstances in which (a) the judge or justices (or both) and legal representatives acting in the proceedings are able to see and hear the examination of the witness and to communicate with the intermediary, and (b) the jury, if there is one, are able to see and hear the examination of the witness (except in the case of a video-recorded examination).[217] A special measures direction may provide for a recording of an interview, conducted through an intermediary, to be admitted under

---

[212] Section 28 has no application in relation to any cross-examination of the witness by the accused in person: s 28(7).

[213] Section 28(4).      [214] Section 28(5).      [215] Section 28(6).

[216] Section 29(2). As to the extent to which s 29 will assist eligible witnesses to give their best evidence or promote more empathic communication during cross-examination, see L Ellison 'The Mosaic Art?: cross-examination and the vulnerable witness' (2001) 21 LS 353 and 'Cross-examination and the Intermediary: Bridging the Language Divide?' [2002] Crim LR 114.

[217] Section 29(3).

section 27, provided that the intermediary has been approved by the court before the direction is given.[218]

*(viii) Aids to communication.* Under section 30, a special measures direction may provide for the witness, while giving evidence (whether in court or otherwise), to be provided with such device as the court considers appropriate with a view to enabling questions or answers to be communicated to or by the witness despite any disability or disorder or other impairment which the witness has or suffers from.

### (b) The witnesses eligible for assistance

There is no power to make a special measures direction, pursuant to the statutory provisions, in relation to the evidence of an accused.[219] In *R(S) v Waltham Forest Youth Court*[220] it was held that it was Parliament's clear intention to exclude the accused from the provisions and that the statute, in this respect, is not incompatible with Article 6 of the European Convention of Human Rights, since it does not derogate from the powers and safeguards already in place under the provisions of domestic law.[221] The provisions were designed not to restrict the rights of the accused but to augment the protection available for other witnesses, and in any event there remains an obligation to ensure a fair trial and, in particular, to see that an accused does not suffer injustice through inequality of arms. It was also held that since Parliament had sought to provide exclusively for the circumstances in which live link might be used in a criminal trial, there was no inherent power to allow an accused to give evidence by live link, but this was doubted by the House of Lords in *R(D) v Camberwell Green Youth Court*.[222] In that case it was held that the court had wide and flexible inherent powers to ensure that the accused is not at a substantial disadvantage compared with the prosecution and receives a fair trial, including a fair opportunity of giving the best evidence he can.[223] Baroness Hale acknowledged that there were obvious difficulties about admitting a video-recorded interview with the accused as his evidence in chief, but was of the view that in exceptional circumstances special measures designed to shield a vulnerable or intimidated witness can apply in the case of the accused, giving as a possible example the use of live link by a younger child accused too scared to give evidence in the presence of her co-accused.

*(i) Witnesses eligible for assistance on grounds of age or incapacity.* Sections 16(1) and (2) of the 1999 Act provide as follows:

> (1) ... a witness in criminal proceedings (other than the accused) is eligible for assistance by virtue of this section—
> > (a) if under the age of 17 at the time of the hearing; or

---

[218] Section 29(6).     [219] See ss 16(1) and 17(1), below.     [220] [2004] 2 Cr App R 335, DC.
[221] See s 19.     [222] [2005] 1 All ER 999, HL.
[223] For example, the court can allow an accused with learning and communication difficulties to have the equivalent of an interpreter to assist with communication, and his written statement can be read to the jury so that they know what he wants to say: see *R v H* [2003] EWCA Crim 1208, [2003] All ER (D) 436 (Mar).

(b) if the court considers that the quality of the evidence given by the witness is likely to be diminished by reason of any circumstances falling within subsection (2).

(2) The circumstances falling within this subsection are—
    (a) that the witness—
        (i) suffers from mental disorder within the meaning of the Mental Health Act 1983; or
        (ii) otherwise has a significant impairment of intelligence and social functioning;
    (b) that the witness has a physical disability or is suffering from a physical disorder.

In section 16(1)(a), 'the time of the hearing', in relation to a witness, means the time when it falls to the court to decide whether to make a special measures direction.[224] In deciding whether a witness has a physical disability or is suffering from a physical disorder, the court must consider any views expressed by the witness.[225] References to the quality of a witness's evidence, in section 16 and in other sections relating to special measures directions, are to its quality in terms of completeness, coherence and accuracy; and for this purpose 'coherence' refers to a witness's ability in giving evidence to give answers which address the questions put to the witness and can be understood both individually and collectively.[226]

*(ii) Witnesses eligible for assistance on grounds of fear or distress about testifying.* Under section 17(1) of the Act, a witness other than the accused is eligible for assistance if the court is satisfied that the quality of evidence given by the witness is likely to be diminished by reason of fear or distress on the part of the witness in connection with testifying in the proceedings. In deciding whether a witness falls within section 17(1), the court must take into account, in particular: (a) the nature and alleged circumstances of the offence to which the proceedings relate; (b) the age of the witness; (c) such of the following matters as appear to the court to be relevant, namely (i) the social and cultural background and ethnic origins of the witness, (ii) the domestic and employment circumstances of the witness and (iii) any religious beliefs or political opinions of the witness; and (d) any behaviour towards the witness on the part of the accused, members of the family or associates of the accused, or any other person who is likely to be an accused or a witness in the proceedings.[227] In deciding, the court must also consider any views expressed by the witness.[228] A complainant in respect of a sexual offence[229] who is a witness in proceedings relating to that offence, or to that offence and any other offences, is automatically eligible for assistance unless he or she has informed the court of his or her wish not to be so eligible.[230]

There is no obvious or compelling reason for excluding the accused from eligibility for assistance under either section 16 or section 17.

---

[224] Section 16(3).    [225] Section 16(4).    [226] Section 16(5).    [227] Section 17(2).
[228] Section 17(3).
[229] A 'sexual offence' is defined in s 62 of the 1999 Act as any offence under Part 1 of the Sexual Offences Act 2003.
[230] Section 17(4).

## (c) The circumstances in which special measures directions are given

*(i) General.* A party to the proceedings may make an application for the court to give a special measures direction or the court of its own motion may raise the issue whether such a direction should be given.[231] Section 19(2) provides as follows:

> (2) Where the court decides that the witness is eligible for assistance by virtue of section 16 or 17, the court must then—
>
> (a) determine whether any of the special measures available in relation to the witness (or any combination of them), would, in its opinion, be likely to improve the quality of evidence given by the witness; and
>
> (b) if so—
>
> > (i) determine which of those measures (or combination of them) would, in its opinion, be likely to maximise so far as practicable the quality of such evidence; and
> >
> > (ii) give a direction under this section providing for the measure or measures so determined to apply to evidence given by the witness.

In deciding whether any special measure or measures would or would not be likely to improve, or to maximize so far as practicable, the quality of evidence given by the witness, the court must consider all the circumstances of the case, including in particular any views expressed by the witness and whether the measure or measures might tend to inhibit such evidence being effectively tested by a party to the proceedings.[232] Under section 20(1), as a general rule a special measures direction has binding effect from the time it is made until the proceedings for the purposes of which it is made are either determined or abandoned in relation to the accused or (if there is more than one) in relation to each of them. The court may discharge or vary a special measures direction if it appears to the court to be in the interests of justice to do so.[233] The court must state in open court its reasons for giving or varying, or refusing an application for, a special measures direction.[234]

*(ii) Child witnesses.* Section 21 of the 1999 Act makes special provision in the case of child witnesses. In the case of witnesses under the age of 17, in effect it creates a presumption in favour of a special measures direction in accordance with section 27 (video-recorded evidence to be admitted as evidence-in-chief) and, in the case of any evidence given by such witnesses which is not given by means of a video-recording, in accordance with section 24 (evidence by live link). Section 21 also provides that in the case of child witnesses under the age of 17 'in need of special protection' (because the offence to which the proceedings relate is one of a number of specified offences), if a special measures direction is made in accordance with section 27, then it must also provide for the special measure available under section 28 (video-recorded cross-examination or re-examination). Section 21 provides as follows:

---

[231] Section 19(1). Applications must be made in writing in the form prescribed in the Crown Court (Special Measures Directions and Directions Prohibiting Cross-examination) Rules 2002, SI 2002/1688.

[232] Section 19(3).     [233] Section 20(2).     [234] Section 20(5).

(1) For the purposes of this section—

  (a) a witness in criminal proceedings is a 'child witness' if he is an eligible witness by reason of section 16(1)(a) (whether or not he is an eligible witness by reason of any other provision of sections 16 or 17);

  (b) a child is 'in need of special protection' if the offence (or any other offences) to which the proceedings relate is—

    (i) an offence falling within section 35(3)(a) (sexual offences etc),[235] or

    (ii) an offence falling within section 35(3)(b), (c) or (d) (kidnapping, assaults etc);[236] and

  (c) a 'relevant recording', in relation to a child witness, is a video recording of an interview of the witness made with a view to its admission as evidence in chief of the witness.

(2) Where the court, in making a determination for the purposes of section 19(2), determines that a witness in criminal proceedings is a child witness, the court must—

  (a) first have regard to subsections (3) to (7) below; and

  (b) then have regard to section 19(2);

  and for the purposes of section 19(2), as it then applies to the witness, any special measures required to be applied in relation to him by virtue of this section shall be treated as if they were measures determined by the court, pursuant to section 19(2)(a) and (b)(i), to be ones that (whether on their own or with any other special measures) would be likely to maximise, so far as practicable, the quality of his evidence.

(3) The primary rule in the case of a child witness is that the court must give a special measures direction in relation to the witness which complies with the following requirements—

  (a) it must provide for any relevant recording to be admitted under section 27 (video recorded evidence in chief); and

  (b) it must provide for any evidence given by the witness in the proceedings which is not given by means of a video recording (whether in chief or otherwise) to be given by means of a live link in accordance with section 24.

(4) The primary rule is subject to the following limitations—

  (a) ...

  (b) the requirement contained in subsection (3)(a) ... has effect subject to subsection 27(2); and

---

[235] Any offence under the Protection of Children Act 1978 or Part 1 of the Sexual Offences Act 2003.

[236] Kidnapping, false imprisonment or an offence under s 1 or s 2 of the Child Abduction Act 1984, any offence under s 1 of the Children and Young Persons Act 1933 and any offence (other than the foregoing offences and those listed in n 235 above) 'which involves an assault on, or injury or a threat of injury to, any person'. This phrase was also used in s 32(2)(a) of the Criminal Justice Act 1988, which the current provisions have replaced. In *R v McAndrew-Bingham* [1999] Crim LR 830, CA, a decision under that subsection, it was held that the phrase should be given a broad purposive interpretation to protect children who were likely to be traumatized by confrontation with the accused, so as to cover offences which may, but do not necessarily, involve an assault, injury or threat of injury. See also *R v Lee* [1996] 2 Cr App R 266, CA, another decision under s 32(2)(a), in which 'threat of injury' was held not to relate to the state of mind of the accused, but was taken to mean risk of injury.

(c) the rule does not apply to the extent that the court is satisfied that compliance with it would not be likely to maximise the quality of the witness's evidence so far as practicable (whether because the application to that evidence of one or more other special measures available in relation to the witness would have the result or for any other reason).

(5) However, subsection (4)(c) does not apply in relation to a child witness in need of special protection.

(6) Where a child witness is in need of special protection by virtue of subsection (1)(b)(i), any special measures direction given by the court which complies with the requirement contained in subsection (3)(a) must in addition provide for the special measure available under s 28 (video-recorded cross-examination or re-examination) to apply in relation to—

(a) any cross-examination of the witness otherwise than by the accused in person, and

(b) any subsequent re-examination.

(7) The requirement contained in subsection (6) has effect subject to the following limitations—

(a) ...

(b) it does not apply if the witness has informed the court that he does not want that special measure to apply in relation to him.

(8) Where a special measures direction is given in relation to a child witness who is an eligible witness by reason only of section 16(1)(a), then—

(a) subject to subsection (9) below, and

(b) except where the witness has already begun to give evidence in the proceedings,

the direction shall cease to have effect at the time when the witness attains the age of 17.

(9) Where a special measures direction is given in relation to a child witness who is an eligible witness by reason only of section 16(1)(a) and

(a) the direction provides—

(i) for any relevant recording to be admitted under section 27 as evidence in chief of the witness, or

(ii) for the special measure available under section 28 to apply in relation to the witness, and

(b) if it provides for that special measure to so apply, the witness is still under the age of 17 when the video recording is made for the purposes of section 28,

then, so far as it provides as mentioned in paragraph (a)(i) or (ii) above, the direction shall continue to have effect in accordance with section 20(1) even though the witness subsequently attains that age.[237]

In *R(D) v Camberwell Green Youth Court*[238] the House of Lords held that section

---

[237] See also s 22, which extends the provisions of s 21 to witnesses who were over the age of 17 at the time of the hearing, but who were under that age when a relevant recording was made, if the offence to which the proceedings relate is an offence falling within s 35(3)(a)–(d).

[238] [2005] 1 All ER 999, HL.

21(5) is compliant with Article 6 of the European Convention on Human Rights insofar as it prevents individualized consideration of the necessity for a special measures direction at the stage at which the direction is made and that there is nothing in the special measures provisions inconsistent with the principles set out by the European Court of Human Rights in *Kostovski v Netherlands*.[239] All the evidence is produced at the trial in the presence of the accused, some of it in pre-recorded form and some of it by contemporaneous television transmission. The accused can see and hear it all and has every opportunity to challenge and question the witnesses against him at the trial itself. A face to face confrontation is missing, but the Convention does not guarantee a right to such a confrontation. The court also has the opportunity to scrutinize the video-recorded interview at the outset and exclude all or part of it. Furthermore, at the trial it has the fallback of allowing the witness to give evidence in the court room or to expand upon the video-recording if the interests of justice require this.

### (d) The status of video-recorded evidence etc

Section 31(1)–(4) of the 1999 Act provide as follows:

(1) Subsections (2) to (4) apply to a statement[240] made by a witness in criminal proceedings which, in accordance with a special measures direction, is not made by the witness in direct oral testimony in court but forms part of the witness's evidence in those proceedings.[241]

(2) The statement shall be treated as if made by the witness in direct oral testimony in court; and accordingly—
    (a) it is admissible evidence of any fact of which such testimony from the witness would be admissible;
    (b) it is not capable of corroborating any other evidence given by the witness.

(3) Subsection (2) applies to a statement admitted under sections 27 or 28 which is not made by the witness on oath even though it would have been required to be made on oath if made by the witness in direct oral testimony in court.

(4) In estimating the weight (if any) to be attached to the statement, the court must have regard to all the circumstances from which an inference can reasonably be drawn (as to the accuracy of the statement or otherwise).

Section 32 of the 1999 Act provides that where, on a trial on indictment with a jury, evidence has been given in accordance with a special measures direction, the judge must give the jury such warning (if any) as the judge considers necessary to ensure that the fact that the direction was given in relation to the witness does not prejudice

---

[239] (1990) 12 EHRR 434 at pp 447–8.

[240] 'Statement' includes any representation of fact, whether made in words or otherwise: s 31(8).

[241] Ie statements given in evidence by live television link or recorded in a video-recording admitted as evidence: see *R(S) v Waltham Forest Youth Court* [2004] 2 Cr App R 335 at [76].

the accused. In the case of the use of screens, for example, it may suffice to say that they must not allow their use by witnesses to prejudice them in any way against the accused.[242]

## 5 WITNESS TRAINING AND WITNESS FAMILIARIZATION

The Court of Appeal in *R v Momodou*[243] has made it clear that in criminal proceedings, witness training or coaching is prohibited, but witness familiarization is permitted. The following reasons were given for the ban on training or coaching. It reduces the possibility that one witness may tailor his evidence in the light of what anyone else has said. Even if the training takes place one-to-one with someone completely remote from the facts of the case, the witness may come, even unconsciously, to appreciate which aspects of his evidence are not quite consistent with what others are saying or not quite what is required of him. An honest witness may alter the emphasis of his evidence. A dishonest witness will very rapidly calculate how his evidence may be 'improved'. Where a witness is jointly trained with other witnesses to the same events, the dangers dramatically increase: recollections change, memories are contaminated and witnesses bring their respective accounts into what they believe to be better alignment with others. They may even collude deliberately.

The ban on witness training or coaching, however, does not preclude pre-trial arrangements, usually in the form of a visit to the court, to familiarize witnesses with the court layout, the likely sequence of events, and a balanced appraisal of the different responsibilities of the various participants. Such arrangements are welcomed because witnesses should not be disadvantaged by ignorance of the process nor, when they come to give evidence, be taken by surprise at the way it works. None of this involves discussions about proposed evidence. Equally, the ban does not prohibit the out-of-court training of expert and similar witnesses in, for example, the technique of giving comprehensive evidence of a specialist kind to a jury, both in examination-in-chief and in cross-examination, and developing the ability to resist the inevitable pressure of going further in evidence than matters covered by the witness's specific expertise. However, such training should not be arranged in the context of, nor be related to, any forthcoming trial.

It was also held in *R v Momoudou* that where arrangements are to be made for familiarization in the case of prosecution witnesses by outside agencies, the Crown Prosecution Service should be informed in advance and the proposals should be reduced into writing so that they can be amended if they breach the permitted limits. If the defence engages in the process, it is wise to seek counsel's advice in advance, and in any event the trial judge and the Crown Prosecution Service should be informed of any familiarization process organized using outside agencies. The familiarization process itself should normally be supervised or conducted by a solicitor or barrister,

---

[242] See *R v Brown* [2004] Crim LR 1034, CA.
[243] [2005] 2 All ER 571, CA.

but no one involved should have any personal knowledge of the matters in issue, none of the material should bear any similarity whatever to the issues in the trial, nothing in it should play on or trigger the witness's recollection of events, and if discussion of the trial begins, it must be stopped. Records should be maintained of all those present and the identity of those responsible for the process. All documents used in the process should be retained and handed to the Crown Prosecution Service or, in the case of defence witnesses, should be produced to the court.

# 6

# EXAMINATION-IN-CHIEF

The general rule, in both civil and criminal trials, is that any fact which needs to be proved by the evidence of witnesses is to be proved by their oral evidence, given in public.[1] The questioning of witnesses, which generally falls into three stages known as examination-in-chief, cross-examination, and re-examination, is central to the English adversary system of justice. The first stage, examination-in-chief, is the questioning of a witness by the party calling him. In examination-in-chief the party calling a witness, or counsel on his behalf, will seek to elicit evidence which supports his version of the facts in issue.[2] This chapter concerns the rules governing the manner in which this may be done. They are considered under the headings of 'Leading questions', 'Refreshing the memory', 'Previous consistent or self-serving statements', and 'Unfavourable and hostile witnesses.'

## A  LEADING QUESTIONS

A party calling a witness and seeking to elicit evidence supporting his case often faces a witness who, although favourable, is not particularly forthcoming. The party calling him may be sorely tempted to put words into the witness's mouth and thereby explain what he wants him to say. In examination-in-chief, however, the general rule is that a witness may not be asked leading questions.[3] Evidence elicited by leading questions is not inadmissible but the weight to be attached to it may be reduced.[4] Leading questions are usually those so framed as to suggest the answer sought. Thus it would be a leading question if counsel for the prosecution, seeking to establish an assault, were to ask the victim, 'Did X hit you in the face with his fist?' The proper course would be to

---

[1] However, in civil cases this is subject to any provision to the contrary, whether in the Civil Procedure Rules or elsewhere, or to any order of the court: CPR r 32.2. A civil court, in exercise of its power under r 32.1 to control evidence, may direct that in order to decide a particular issue, it only requires evidence in written form.

[2] Excessive questioning of a witness by the judge may improperly interfere with the opportunity which counsel should be given to present the witness's evidence in the most impressive way he or she can devise: see *R v Gunning* (1994) 98 Cr App R 303n, CA.

[3] Leading questions may be put in cross-examination: *Parkin v Moon* (1836) 7 C&P 408.

[4] *Moor v Moor* [1954] 1 WLR 927, CA.

ask, 'Did X do anything to you?' and, if the witness then gives evidence of having been hit, to ask the questions 'Where did X hit you?' and 'How did X hit you?' Questions are also leading if so framed as to assume the existence of facts yet to be established. If evidence has yet to be given of the assault, it would be improper, for example, to ask, 'What were you doing immediately before X hit you?' The examples given are reasonably straightforward, but in practice the avoidance of leading questions often requires considerable skill and experience. An over-strict adherence to the rule against leading questions would render examination-in-chief extremely difficult. The question 'Did X do anything to you?', even if it does not suggest that X hit the witness, suggests that X did something, whereas in fact he might have been asleep at the relevant time. 'And what happened next?' is a solution often resorted to. However, the judge, and counsel for the other side, will not always demand strict adherence to the rule, and for good reason: ' "leading" is a relative, not an absolute term.'[5]

To the general prohibition on leading questions there are frequently recurring exceptions. A witness may be asked leading questions on formal and introductory matters, such as his name, address and occupation. Leading questions are also permissible on facts which are not in dispute, and counsel for the other side may well indicate, in the case of any witness, those matters on which he has no objection to such questions being put. Leading questions may also be put to a witness called by a party who has been granted leave to treat him as hostile.[6]

# B  REFRESHING THE MEMORY

Witnesses often experience difficulty in recollecting the events to which their evidence relates, especially when the events took place a long time ago. In consequence, common law rules have evolved to allow a witness to refresh his memory from a document made or verified by him at an earlier time. The common law rules have been supplemented and, in part, superseded by, statutory provisions. However, the scope for use of the memory-refreshing rules has diminished by reason of the growth in the categories of admissible hearsay and the introduction of rules permitting a witness statement or a video-recorded account to stand as a witness's evidence-in-chief. Thus in civil proceedings a witness statement will normally stand as a witness's evidence-in-chief, unless the court orders otherwise,[7] and the previous documentary statement of a witness is admissible with the leave of the court as evidence of any facts contained in it pursuant to section 6(2)(a) of the Civil Evidence Act 1995.[8] In criminal proceedings, section 137 of the Criminal Justice Act 2003 provides that, in the case of offences triable only on indictment and other serious offences, a video-recording of an

---

[5] Best, *Law of Evidence* (12th edn London 1922) 562.     [6] See below.
[7] See CPR r 32.5, Ch 5.     [8] See Ch 11.

account, given by a witness to the offence, may stand as his evidence in chief, provided that it was given at a time when the events were fresh in his memory, his recollection of the events is likely to have been significantly better at that time, and it is in the interests of justice to do so.[9] Furthermore, in criminal proceedings a previous statement made by a witness with personal knowledge of the matters dealt with, and contained in a document created or received by a person in the course of, inter alia, a trade, business or profession, may be admitted as evidence of any facts contained in it, under section 117 of the Criminal Justice Act 2003; and under section 114(1)(d) of that Act, the court also has a discretionary power to admit a hearsay statement in the interests of justice.[10]

## 1  REFRESHING THE MEMORY IN COURT

### (a)  The rules

At common law, a witness in either civil or criminal proceedings, in the course of giving his evidence, may refer to a document, such as a diary, log-book or account-book, in order to refresh his memory. The conditions are that the document (i) was made or verified by him either contemporaneously with the events in question or so shortly thereafter that the facts were still fresh in his memory (ii) is, in prescribed cases, the original and (iii) is produced for inspection by either the court or the opposite party.

In criminal proceedings, this common-law rule has not been repealed, but has in effect been replaced, and relaxed, by section 139(1) of the Criminal Justice Act 2003. Section 139(1) substitutes for the requirement of contemporaneity, or that the facts were still fresh in the memory, two different conditions. The first is that the witness testifies that the document records his recollection at the time when he made it. The second is that his recollection is likely to have been significantly better at that time than at the time of his oral evidence. The common-law rule has also been sup-plemented by section 139(2), which provides for the refreshing of memory from a transcript of a sound recording, a provision designed to avoid the practical difficulties that would otherwise be encountered in refreshing the memory from the sound recording itself. Section 139 is in the following terms.

(1) A person giving oral evidence in criminal proceedings about any matter may, at any stage in the course of doing so, refresh his memory of it from a document made or verified by him at an earlier time if—
   (a) he states in his oral evidence that the document records his recollection of the matter at that earlier time, and
   (b) his recollection of the matter is likely to have been significantly better at that time than it is at the time of his oral evidence.

(2) Where—

---

[9] See Ch 5.      [10] See Ch 10.

(a) a person giving oral evidence in criminal proceedings about any matter has previously given an oral account, of which a sound recording was made, and he states in that evidence that the account represented his recollection of the matter at that time,

(b) his recollection of the matter is likely to have been significantly better at the time of the previous account than it is at the time of his oral evidence, and

(c) a transcript has been made of the sound recording,

he may at any stage in the course of giving his evidence, refresh his memory of the matter from that transcript.

An application for a witness to refresh his memory will normally be made by the party calling the witness, but it is a proper function of the judge, where the interests of justice so demand, to suggest that a witness, including in a criminal case, a witness for the prosecution, refresh his memory.[11] Both section 139(1) and (2) refer to 'a person giving oral evidence', ie any person giving oral evidence, and therefore apply, as does the common law rule, to any witness, including the accused.[12] Both subsections also permit the witness to refresh his memory 'at any stage' in the course of giving his evidence. Thus, as at common law, although a witness will normally refresh his memory in examination-in-chief, there is nothing wrong in principle in allowing him to do so during re-examination.[13]

## (b)  Present recollection revived and past recollection recorded

The common law rule on refreshing memory applies in the case of both 'present recollection revived' and 'past recollection recorded'.[14] 'Present recollection revived' is a phrase used to describe the genuine refreshing of memory on sight of the document. In the case of 'present recollection revived', both at common law and under section 139, it is the oral testimony of the witness whose memory has been refreshed, and not the document, which constitutes the evidence in the case. 'Past recollection recorded' refers to the situation in which the witness, although he has no current recollection of the events, his memory being a perfect blank, is prepared to testify as to the accuracy of the contents of the document. Thus in *Maugham v Hubbard*[15] a witness, called to prove that he had received a sum of money, looked at an unstamped acknowledgment signed by himself and thereupon gave evidence that he had no doubt that he had received the money although he had no recollection of having done so. It was held that the witness's oral evidence sufficed to establish receipt of the money, the written acknowledgment not being evidence in the case because it was unstamped.[16] It has

---

[11] *R v Tyagi* (1986) *The Times*, 21 July, CA.      [12] See *R v Britton* [1987] 2 All ER 412, CA.

[13] *R v Harman* (1984) 148 JP 289, CA and *R v Sutton* (1991) 94 Cr App R 70, CA.

[14] See J H Wigmore *Evidence in Trials at Common Law*, vol 3 (rev J H Chadbourn) (Boston Mass 1970) ch 28.

[15] (1828) 8 B&C 14.

[16] See also *R v Simmonds* (1967) 51 Cr App R 316, where it was argued that customs officers were not entitled to read from their notes of interviews with the accused. The Court of Appeal held that the practice was 'long established and not open to objection'.

always been inaccurate to describe the witness in such a case as having 'refreshed his memory'.[17] The term is equally inapposite in the case of the police officer who, with no recollection of the relevant events, simply reads from his notes.[18] However at common law, cases of 'past recollection recorded' are treated in the same way as cases of 'present recollection recorded' in that the oral evidence of the witness, and not the document, constitutes the evidence in the case.[19] The view that, in principle, it would be better to regard such out-of-court documentary statements as a variety of admissible hearsay,[20] has now been adopted in criminal proceedings. Under section 120 of the Criminal Justice Act 2003, in criminal proceedings, a previous statement of a witness, which may be a statement made orally or a statement made in a document, is admissible as evidence of any matter stated, provided that the witness testifies that to the best of his belief he made the statement and it states the truth, and that he does not remember the matters and cannot reasonably be expected to do so. Section 120(1), (4) and (6) of the 2003 Act provide as follows:

(1) This section applies where a person (the witness) is called to give evidence in criminal proceedings.

(4) A previous statement by the witness is admissible as evidence of any matter stated of which oral evidence by him would be admissible, if—
(a) any of the following three conditions is satisfied, and
(b) while giving evidence the witness indicates that to the best of his belief he made the statement, and to the best of his belief it states the truth.

(6) The second condition is that the statement was made by the witness when the matters stated were fresh in his memory but he does not remember them, and cannot reasonably be expected to remember them, well enough to give oral evidence of them in the proceedings.

Section 120(4) only applies in the case of a statement *made* by the witness, and has no application, therefore, in the case of a statement *verified* by him.

If, on a trial before a judge and jury, a statement made in a document is admitted in evidence under section 120, and the document or a copy of it is produced as an exhibit, the exhibit must not accompany the jury when they retire to consider their verdict unless the court considers it appropriate or all the parties to the proceedings agree that it should accompany the jury.[21]

---

[17] See per Hayes J in *Lord Talbot de Malahide v Cusack* (1864) 17 ICLR 213 at 220.

[18] The view has been expressed that in nine cases out of ten the witness's memory is not at all refreshed: see per Hayes J (1864) 171 ICLR 213 at 220.

[19] See *Maugham v Hubbard* (1828) 8 B&C 14, but see also *R v Sekhon* (1987) 85 Cr App R 19 and *R v Virgo* (1978) 67 Cr App R 323, both considered below.

[20] See, eg, the 5th edition of this book at 144.     [21] Section 122 of the Criminal Justice Act 2003.

## (b) The conditions

*(i) A document.* At common law a document includes a tape recording,[22] but in criminal proceedings, for the purposes of section 139(1) of the Criminal Justice Act 2003, it means anything in which information of any description is recorded, but not including any recordings of sounds or moving images.[23]

*(ii) Made or verified.* Both at common law and under section 139(1) of the 2003 Act, a witness may refresh his memory either from a document made by himself or by another, provided that, if made by another, the witness verified the document, ie checked the contents of the document, while the events were still fresh in his memory, and satisfied himself as to their accuracy.[24] For example, in *Anderson v Whalley*[25] it was held that entries in a ship's log-book made by the mate and verified by the captain about a week later could be used to refresh the memory of the latter. It is submitted that under section 139(1), as at common law, verification can be either visual or aural. In *R v Kelsey*,[26] H, a witness called for the prosecution, was allowed to refresh his memory as to the registration number of a car from a note which he had dictated to a police officer. The officer had read his note back aloud and H had confirmed that it was correct. Although H had seen the officer making the note, he had not read it himself. The officer gave evidence that the note used in court was the one that the witness saw him make. The Court of Appeal held that verification could be either visual or aural, the important matter being that the witness satisfies himself, while the matters are fresh in his mind, (i) that a record has been made and (ii) that it is accurate. However, where a witness dictates a note to another, hears it read back and confirms its accuracy without reading it himself, another witness must be called to prove that the note used in court is the one that was dictated and read back. The officer in the instant case having given evidence to that effect, Kelsey's appeal was dismissed.[27]

*(iii) Contemporaneity.* At common law, but not under section 139 of the 2003 Act, the document, whether made or verified by the witness, 'must have been written either at the time of the transaction or so shortly afterwards that the facts were fresh in his memory'.[28] Commenting on this definition, the Court of Appeal has observed that it provides 'a measure of elasticity and should not be taken to confine witnesses to an over-short period'.[29] In *R v Simmonds*[30] customs officers who had conducted interviews

---

[22] *R v Bailey* [2001] All ER (D) 185 (Mar), [2001] EWCA Crim 733.        [23] Section 140.

[24] See *Burrough v Martin* (1809) 2 Camp 112 and *R v Langton* (1876) 2 QBD 296.

[25] (1852) 3 Car&Kir 54. See also *R v Sekhon* (1986) 85 Cr App R 19, CA and cf *R v Eleftheriou* [1993] Crim LR 947, CA.

[26] (1981) 74 Cr App R 213.

[27] Contrast *R v Mills* [1962] 1 WLR 1152 at 1156, per Winn J, obiter. The officer's note, in *R v Kelsey*, would now be admissible as evidence of the matters stated under s 117 of the 2003 Act (business and other documents): see Ch 10.

[28] See *Phipson on Evidence* (11th edn London 1970) p 634, para 1528.

[29] *R v Richardson* [1971] 2 QB 484.        [30] (1967) 51 Cr App R 316.

with the accused did not make any notes of what was said at the time, but made up their notes at the first available opportunity, on returning to their offices. The Court of Appeal, in no doubt that the condition of contemporaneity had been satisfied, held the matter to be one of fact and degree. Thus although literal contemporaneity is not necessary, the permitted gap between the date of the statement and that of the events to which it relates cannot be fixed with precision. The precedents are therefore of very limited value.[31]

*(iv) Originals and copies.* There is no requirement, either at common law or under section 139(1) of the 2003 Act, that the memory-refreshing document be the first or only document made or verified by the witness recording his recollection of the matters in question. A witness, therefore, may refresh his memory from a document which is based on original notes or a tape-recording made by him. In *A-G's Reference (No 3 of 1979)*[32] the Court of Appeal held that a police officer could refresh his memory from notes compiled, at a time when the facts were still fresh in his memory, from earlier brief jottings of an interview. In *R v Cheng*[33] the Court of Appeal held that a police officer was entitled to rely on a statement which was a partial but not exact copy of earlier notes from which it was prepared (and which were not available at the trial) on the grounds that the statement 'substantially' reproduced the notes. Similarly, in *R v Mills*[34] a police officer, who had heard and made a tape-recording of a conversation between two accused, was allowed to refer to his notes written up with the assistance of that tape-recording, which was not itself put in evidence. A witness may also refresh his memory from a copy of his original document, provided that the court is satisfied that the copy is accurate or substantially reproduces the contents of the original. Thus, in *Topham v McGregor*[35] the author of an article written some fourteen years earlier was allowed to refresh his memory from a copy of the newspaper in which it had appeared, evidence being given of the destruction of the original and the accuracy of the copy. More recently, in *R v Chisnell*[36] an officer was allowed to use a statement made nine months after an interview and compiled on the basis of a contemporaneous note, the court being satisfied that the note, which had been lost, had been accurately transcribed into the statement. However, in cases of 'past recollection recorded' in which the original has *not* been lost or destroyed, then there is old authority that the original document must be used.[37]

*(ii) Production of the document.* A document used to refresh memory in court must be produced for inspection by the opposite party who may wish to cross-examine the witness on its contents.[38] At the request of the opposite party, the document may also be shown to the jury, if this is necessary to their determination of a point in issue in

---

[31] *R v Woodcock* [1963] Crim LR 273 (3-month gap treated as too long); *R v Graham* [1973] Crim LR 628 (one-month gap regarded as doubtful); *R v Fotheringham* [1975] Crim LR 710, CA (21-day gap accepted).
[32] (1979) 69 Cr App R 411.    [33] (1976) 63 Cr App R 20.    [34] [1962] 1 WLR 1152, CCA.
[35] (1844) 1 Car&Kir 320.    [36] [1992] Crim LR 507, CA.
[37] *Doe d Church and Phillips v Perkins* (1790) 3 Term Rep 749.    [38] *Beech v Jones* (1848) 5 CB 696.

the case. In *R v Bass*[39] the only evidence against the appellant was a confession allegedly made to two police officers. They read identical accounts of the interview with the appellant but denied that they had been prepared in collaboration. The trial judge refused a defence application that the jury be allowed to examine the notebooks. The Court of Criminal Appeal, allowing the appeal, held that the jury, by an inspection of the notebooks, might have been assisted in their evaluation of the credibility and accuracy of the officers.[40] Similarly, in cases in which the witness's evidence is long and involved, it may be convenient for the jury to use the document as an *aide memoire* as to that evidence, but care should be exercised in adopting this course in cases where the evidence is bitterly contested, because of the danger that the jury will improperly regard the document as constituting evidence in the case.[41]

## (c)  Cross-examination on the document

In the majority of cases, the fact that there is cross-examination on the basis of a document used to refresh memory in court will neither entitle the jury to inspect the document nor make it evidence in the case.[42] Cross-examining counsel may inspect the document without thereby making it evidence[43] and may cross-examine on it without thereby making it evidence provided that his cross-examination goes no further than the parts which were used by the witness to refresh his memory. However, cross-examination on new matters deriving from other parts of the document not used by the witness to refresh his memory entitles the party calling the witness to put the document in evidence and to let the tribunal of fact see the document upon which such cross-examination is based.[44] Two other situations have been identified in which the document may be admitted in evidence.[45] First, where the nature of the cross-examination involves a suggestion that the witness has subsequently fabricated his evidence, which will usually involve the allegation that the record is concocted, the document is then admissible to rebut this suggestion and, if the document assists as to this, to show whether or not it has the appearance of being a contemporaneous

---

[39] [1953] 1 QB 680; cf *R v Fenlon* (1980) 71 Cr App R 307, CA.

[40] The court also made it clear that it is not improper for two or more police officers to refresh their memories from notes in the making of which they have collaborated. However, as a general rule discussions between witnesses as to the evidence they will give should not take place: *R v Skinner* (1993) 99 Cr App R 212, CA. If they have taken place, each case should be dealt with on its own facts. If the discussion may have led to fabrication, it may be unsafe to leave any of the evidence to the jury. In other cases it may suffice to direct the jury on the implications of such conduct in relation to the reliability of the evidence. See *R v Arif* (1993) *The Times*, 17 June, CA.

[41] Per Woolf LJ in *R v Sekhon* (1986) 85 Cr App R 19 at 23, CA: the document may also be put before the jury where it is difficult for them to follow the *cross-examination* of the witness who has refreshed his memory without having the document before them. But cf *R v Dillon* (1983) 85 Cr App R 29n, CA.

[42] Per Woolf LJ in *R v Sekhon* (1986) 85 Cr App R 19 at 22, CA.

[43] A party calling for and inspecting a document in the possession of the other party which has *not* been used to refresh a witness's memory must put it in evidence if called upon so to do. See *Wharam v Routledge* (1805) 5 Esp 235 and *Stroud v Stroud* [1963] 1 WLR 1080 (see Ch 7).

[44] *Gregory v Tavernor* (1833) 6 C&P 280; *Senat v Senat* [1965] P 172 per Sir Jocelyn Simon P at 177; *R v Britton* [1987] 2 All ER 412, CA.

[45] *R v Sekhon* (1986) 85 Cr App R 19 at 22–3, CA.

record which has not subsequently been altered.[46] Secondly, where the document is inconsistent with the evidence, the document is then admissible as evidence of this inconsistency.

Where, as a result of cross-examination, a memory-refreshing document is admitted in evidence in civil proceedings, it is admitted as evidence of any matter stated. Under section 1 of the Civil Evidence Act 1995, in civil proceedings evidence shall not be excluded on the ground that it is hearsay. Section 6(4) and (5) of the 1995 Act provide as follows:

(4) Nothing in this Act affects any of the rules of law as to the circumstances in which, where a person called as a witness in civil proceedings is cross-examined on a document used by him to refresh his memory, that document may be made evidence in the proceedings.

(5) Nothing in this section shall be construed as preventing a statement of any description referred to above from being admissible by virtue of s 1 as evidence of the matters stated.

Although section 6(5) refers to 'a statement of any description referred to above' and section 6(4) makes no reference to a 'statement' as such, it seems reasonably clear that the parliamentary intention was to perpetuate the rule formerly stated with clarity in section 3(2) of the Civil Evidence Act 1968, ie that where a memory-refreshing document is made evidence in civil proceedings, any statement made in the document is admissible as evidence of any matter stated therein.

Where, as a result of cross-examination, a memory-refreshing document *made* by a witness is admitted in evidence in criminal proceedings, it is admitted as evidence of any matter stated. Section 120(1) and (3) of the Criminal Justice Act 2003 provide as follows:

(1) This section applies where a person (the witness) is called to give evidence in criminal proceedings.

(3) A statement made by the witness in a document—
   (a) which is used by him to refresh his memory while giving evidence,
   (b) on which he is cross-examined, and
   (c) which as a consequence is received in evidence in the proceedings,
   is admissible as evidence of any matter stated of which oral evidence by him would be admissible.

Section 120 does not apply in the case of a statement *verified* by a witness which, as a result of cross-examination, is admitted in evidence. In criminal proceedings, therefore, such a statement is not admitted as evidence of any of the matters stated in it, but as evidence of the witness's consistency or inconsistency, going only to his credit.

If, on a trial before a judge and jury, a statement made in a document is admitted in evidence under section 120, and the document or a copy of it is produced as an

---

[46] Cf *R v Fenlon* (1980) 71 Cr App R 307, CA and *R v Dillon* (1983) 85 Cr App R 29n, CA.

exhibit, the exhibit must not accompany the jury when they retire to consider their verdict unless the court considers it appropriate or all the parties to the proceedings agree that it should accompany the jury.[47]

## 2  REFRESHING THE MEMORY OUT OF COURT

It is a common practice, in both civil and criminal proceedings, for witnesses, before going into the witness box, to look at and refresh their memories from their own previous statements. Such a statement may have been made by a witness for some personal reason, may constitute a 'proof of evidence' made at the request of the solicitor for the party calling him or, in the case of a prosecution witness, may be a signed statement which he made to the police.[48] Whatever form it takes, however, it would appear that the conditions on which a witness may refresh his memory while giving evidence do not apply to the witness who refreshes his memory outside the witness box.[49] In *R v Richardson*[50] the accused was convicted of burglary offences which had been committed some 18 months earlier. Before the trial, four prosecution witnesses were shown the statements which they had made to the police. Those statements were not contemporaneous for the purposes of the common-law rule on refreshing memory in court and the accused argued, on appeal, that the evidence of the four witnesses was, in the circumstances, inadmissible. Dismissing the appeal, and noting the unenforceability of any rule prohibiting witnesses from refreshing their memory out of court, the Court of Appeal approved the following two observations of the Supreme Court of Hong Kong in *Lau Pak Ngam v R*:[51]

1.  Testimony in the witness box becomes more a test of memory than of truthfulness if witnesses are deprived of the opportunity of checking their recollection beforehand by reference to statements or notes made at a time closer to the events in question.

2.  Refusal of access to statements would tend to create difficulties for honest witnesses but be likely to do little to hamper dishonest witnesses.

However, it was also observed in *R v Richardson* that it would obviously be wrong for several witnesses to be handed statements in circumstances enabling one to compare with another what each had said. Equally, as a general rule, discussions between witnesses, particularly just before going into court to give evidence, should not take place, and statements or proofs should not be read to witnesses in each other's

---

[47]  Section 122 of the Criminal Justice Act 2003.

[48]  A circular issued in April 1969, with the approval of the Lord Chief Justice and the judges of the Queen's Bench Division, recognized that prosecution witnesses are normally entitled, if they so request, to copies of any statements taken from them by the police.

[49]  Yet see *R v Thomas* [1994] Crim LR 745, CA, where, for reasons that are not disclosed, it was held to be undesirable for a child aged 8 to be shown her signed police statement. See also *Owen v Edwards* (1983) 77 Cr App R 191, DC, below.

[50]  [1971] 2 QB 484.        [51]  [1966] Crim LR 443.

presence.[52] It is incumbent on prosecuting authorities and judges to ensure that witnesses are informed that they should not discuss cases in which they are involved.[53]

In *R v Da Silva*[54] it was held that it is open to the judge, in the exercise of his discretion and in the interests of justice, to permit a witness who has begun to give his evidence, to withdraw and refresh his memory from a statement made near to the time of the events in question, even if not 'contemporaneous', provided he is satisfied that: (i) the witness indicates that he cannot now recall the details of the events because of the lapse of time; (ii) he made a statement much nearer the time of the event,[55] the contents of which represented his recollection at the time he made it; (iii) he has not read the statement before giving evidence; and (iv) he wishes to read the statement before he continues to give evidence. It does not matter whether the witness withdraws from the witness box to read his statement or reads it in the witness box, but if the former course is adopted, no communication must be had with the witness other than to see that he can read the statement in peace. If either course is adopted, the statement must be removed from him when he continues to give his evidence and he should not be permitted to refer to it again. However, in criminal proceedings, the witness may be permitted to make further use of the document to refresh his memory in the witness box, provided that the conditions of section 139 of the Criminal Justice Act 2003 are met.[56]

In *R v South Ribble Magistrates' Court, ex p Cochrane*[57] it was held that *R v Da Silva* does not lay down as a matter of law that all four conditions to which it refers must be satisfied, because the court has a 'real discretion', ie a choice free of binding criteria, whether to permit a witness to refresh his memory from a non-contemporaneous statement. In that case it was held that a witness who had read his statement before giving evidence, but who had not taken it in properly, and therefore did not satisfy condition (iii), had been properly permitted to refresh his memory. The discretion is a broad fact-sensitive discretion to be exercised in the interests of fairness and justice.[58]

The fact that a witness has refreshed his memory out of court and before entering the witness box may be relevant to the weight which can properly be attached to his evidence, so that in a criminal case injustice may be caused to the accused if the matter is not brought to the attention of the jury. For this reason, the Court of Appeal in *R v Westwell*[59] held that the prosecution, if aware that statements have been seen by their witnesses, should inform the defence. Informing the defence, however, is 'desirable but not essential' and 'if for any reason this is not done, the omission cannot of

---

[52] *R v Skinner* (1993) 99 Cr App R 212, CA at 216.     [53] *R v Shaw* [2002] All ER (D) 79 (Dec), CA.

[54] [1990] 1 All ER 29, CA.

[55] On the facts of the case, the statement was made one month after the events to which it related.

[56] See above.     [57] [1996] 2 Cr App R 544, DC.

[58] *R v Gordon* [2002] All ER (D) 99 (Feb), CA, where a witness who was dyslexic and unable to read the statement himself, adopted it after it had been read out to him by counsel in the absence of the jury.

[59] [1976] 2 All ER 812. See also *Worley v Bentley* [1976] 2 All ER 449.

itself be a ground for acquittal'.[60] *R v Westwell* left undecided the question whether a
party may call for, inspect, and cross-examine on a document which a witness called
by the opposite party has used to refresh his memory outside court but has not used
while giving evidence. The issue arose in *Owen v Edwards*.[61] A policeman, outside the
court room and before giving evidence for the prosecution, refreshed his memory
from a notebook which he did not use in the witness box. The Divisional Court held
that defence counsel was entitled not only to inspect the notebook but also to cross-
examine the witness upon relevant matters contained in it. It was further held that
although defence counsel may cross-examine upon the material in the notebook from
which the witness has refreshed his memory without the notebook being made evidence in the case, if he cross-examines on material in the notebook which has not
been referred to by the witness, he runs the risk of the notebook being put in evidence. McNeill J said: 'the rules which apply to refreshing memory in the witness box
should be the same as those which apply if memory has been refreshed outside the
door of the court.'[62] As we have seen, in civil cases, the document will be admitted as
evidence of the matters stated. The same applies in criminal cases, but only in the case
of statements made, as opposed to verified, by the witness. The weight to be attached
to the documentary evidence will obviously vary according to the precise circumstances, but a note made a long time after the events in question, may be viewed by the
tribunal of fact with considerable caution, if not suspicion.

# C  PREVIOUS CONSISTENT OR SELF-SERVING STATEMENTS

## 1  THE GENERAL RULE

There is a general common-law rule that a witness may not be asked in examination-
in-chief about former oral or written statements made by him and consistent with his
evidence in the proceedings. Evidence of the earlier statement may not be given either
by the witness who made it or by any other witness. The reason usually given for the
rule is the danger of manufactured evidence.[63] A resourceful witness, minded to
deceive the court, could with ease deliberately repeat his version of the facts to a
number of people prior to trial with a view to showing consistency with the story he
tells in the witness box, thereby bolstering his credibility.[64]

---

[60] See also, *sed quaere, R v H* [1992] Crim LR 516: child victims of sexual offences should only refresh their
memory out of court with the *consent* of the defence.

[61] (1983) 77 Cr App R 191.        [62] (1983) 77 Cr App R 191 at 195.

[63] See, eg, per Humphreys J in *R v Roberts* [1942] 1 All ER 187 at 191.

[64] But see *Fennell v Jerome Property Maintenance Ltd* (1986) *The Times*, 26 Nov QBD: as a matter of
principle, evidence produced by the administration of some mechanical, chemical or hypnotic truth test on a
witness is inadmissible to show the veracity (or otherwise) of that witness. See also *R v McKay* [1967] NZLR

The rule also applies to re-examination. Thus the credibility of a witness may not be bolstered by evidence of a previous consistent statement merely because his testimony has been impeached in cross-examination.[65] This remains the case 'even if the impeachment takes the form of showing a contradiction or inconsistency between the evidence given at the trial and something said by the witness on a former occasion'.[66] However, the court does have a residual discretion to permit re-examination to show consistency by reference to a previous statement to ensure that the jury is not positively misled by the cross-examination as to the existence of some fact or the terms of an earlier statement.[67]

The rule is distinct from the common law rule against hearsay, whereby an out-of-court statement is inadmissible as evidence of the facts stated. A previous consistent or self-serving statement of a witness is excluded as evidence of his consistency. The distinction may be illustrated by the following two cases. In *Corke v Corke and Cook*[68] a husband petitioned for divorce on the ground of adultery. Late one night he had accused his wife of having recently committed adultery with a lodger. The Court of Appeal held that the wife, who denied adultery, had been improperly permitted to give evidence that some 10 minutes after the husband's accusation she had telephoned her doctor and asked him to examine herself and the lodger with a view to showing that there had been no recent sexual intercourse. In *R v Roberts*[69] the accused was convicted of the murder of a girl by shooting her. His defence was that the gun went off accidentally while he was trying to make up a quarrel with the girl. Evidence that two days after the event the accused had told his father that his defence would be accident was held by the Court of Criminal Appeal to have been properly excluded. In both of these cases the evidence in question was hearsay and inadmissible as evidence of the facts stated, that is to show in the one case that there was no sexual intercourse and in the other that the gun went off accidentally. But it was also inadmissible, by reason of the rule against previous consistent statements, to bolster the credibility of the witnesses in question by demonstrating their consistency.

Where a previous statement of a witness is admitted as hearsay, ie as evidence of the matters stated, it will also be received as evidence of consistency. Thus a decision such as *Corke v Corke and Cook* might be decided differently today, because in civil proceedings the previous statements of a witness may be admitted, with the leave of the court, both as evidence of the matters stated, and also, therefore, as evidence of consistency, under section 6(2) of the Civil Evidence Act 1995. The admissibility of such statements is considered in Chapter 11. Similarly, if a previous statement of a witness is admitted in criminal proceedings as evidence of the matters stated, under section

139, NZCA: a psychiatrist is not permitted to give evidence of statements made by the accused while under the influence of a truth drug and consistent with his (the accused's) evidence.

[65] *R v Coll* (1889) 25 LR Ir 522.

[66] Per Holmes J (1889) 25 LR Ir 522 at 541. See also *R v Weekes* [1988] Crim LR 244, CA; *R v Beattie* (1989) 89 Cr App R 302 per Lord Lane CJ at 306–7; and *R v P (GR)* [1998] Crim LR 663, CA. Contrast, *sed quaere*, *Ahmed v Brumfitt* (1967) 112 Sol Jo 32, CA.

[67] *R v Ali* [2004] 1 Cr App R 501, CA.      [68] [1958] P 93.      [69] [1942] 1 All ER 187.

114(1)(c) of the Criminal Justice Act 2003, ie where all parties agree to it being admissible, or under section 114(1)(d) of that Act, ie where the court is satisfied that it is in the interests of justice for it to be admissible, then it will also be received as evidence of consistency.

To the rule against previous consistent statements, there are a number of common-law exceptions, The statutory categories of admissible hearsay now embrace almost all of the varieties of statement admissible by way of the common-law exceptions to the rule against previous consistent statements, in some cases expanding their scope. Such justification as there is for separate treatment of the common-law exceptions stems from the fact that (a) the overlap is not total (wholly exculpatory statements made on accusation, for example, are not admissible as evidence of the matters asserted) (b) Parliament has elected not to repeal any of the common law exceptions and (c) in some cases (statements admissible to rebut allegations of recent fabrication and statements in documents used to refresh the memory and received in evidence), Parliament, rather than give the common-law exception a statutory formulation, has chosen to identify it as a category of hearsay by simply referring to the circumstances in which the statement may be admitted at common law.

## 2 THE COMMON-LAW EXCEPTIONS

### (a) Complaints in sexual cases

If, in cases of rape and other sexual offences, the complainant made a voluntary complaint shortly after the alleged offence, the person to whom the complaint was made may give evidence of the particulars of that complaint in order to show the consistency of that conduct with the complainant's evidence and, in cases in which consent is in issue, to negative consent. Section 120(7) of the Criminal Justice Act 2003 has extended the principle to cover a previous statement by a person against whom *any* offence has been committed, provided that it is an offence to which the proceedings relate, that the statement consists of a complaint about conduct which would, if proved, constitute the offence, and the complainant, in giving evidence, indicates that to the best of his belief, he made the statement and it states the truth. A statement received under section 120(7) is admissible as evidence of the matters stated and, provided that the evidence is given by the person to whom the complaint was made,[70] also goes to the consistency of the witness. Section 120(7), which is considered in Chapter 10, is much wider than the common-law exception. The common-law exception, therefore, is likely to be invoked only rarely and falls to be considered in outline only.

The common-law exception applies to written, as well as oral, complaints, and even extends to a written note given to a friend by mistake.[71] Where the exception applies, it is essential to direct the jury that the complaint is not evidence of the facts

---

[70] See *White v R* [1999] 1 Cr App R 153, PC.        [71] *R v B* [1997] Crim LR 220, CA.

complained of, and cannot be independent confirmation of the complainant's evidence since it does not come from a source independent of her, but may assist in assessing her veracity.[72]

In *White v R*[73] it was held that if the person to whom the complaint was made does not give evidence, the complainant's own evidence that she made a complaint cannot assist in either proving her consistency or negativing consent because, without independent confirmation, her own evidence that she complained takes the jury nowhere in deciding whether she is worthy of belief. In that case, Lord Hoffmann held that although it does not follow that evidence that the complainant spoke to someone after the incident is inadmissible, the complainant should not be allowed to say that she had told people 'what had happened', because the jury will be bound to infer that she had made statements in terms substantially the same as her evidence. It was said that it is important not to infringe the spirit of the rule against previous consistent statements by conveying indirectly to the jury that the complainant has given a previous account of the incident, in similar terms, with a view to inviting them to infer that her credibility is supported by the fact of the complaint. It was also held that where evidence is given of the bare fact that the complainant spoke to someone after the incident, it is incumbent on the judge to give the jury clear instructions that they are not entitled to treat the evidence as confirming the complainant's credibility.

*(i) Rape and other sexual offences.* The common-law exception applies only in the case of complaints of rape and other sexual offences, but is not restricted to sexual offences where absence of consent is among the facts in issue.[74] Nor is the exception confined to sexual offences against females. Although in *R v Christie*[75] the House of Lords refused to consider the application of the exception to the complaint of a boy, in *R v Camelleri*[76] the Court of Criminal Appeal held that a boy's complaint of an offence of gross indecency committed against him was admissible under the exception.

*(ii) The fact and the particulars of the complaint.* There is a two-stage test for the jury to follow, first to decide whether the recent complaint was in fact made and, if so, secondly to decide whether it is consistent with the complainant's evidence.[77] In *R v Lillyman*,[78] it was held that the person to whom the complaint had been made could give detailed evidence as to what the complainant had said. To limit evidence to the bare fact that the complaint was made would be to leave to the witness to whom the statement was made determination of the question whether a complaint really was made and thereby prevent the jurors from judging for themselves whether the complaint in question was consistent with the complainant's evidence.

---

[72]  *R v Islam* [1999] 1 Cr App R 22, CA, applied in *R v NK* [1999] Crim LR 980, CA.
[73]  [1999] 1 Cr App R 153, PC.         [74]  *R v Osborne* [1905] 1 KB 551, CCR.         [75]  [1914] AC 545.
[76]  [1922] 2 KB 122. See also *R v Wannell* (1922) 17 Cr App R 53.
[77]  *R v Hartley* [2003] All ER (D) 208 (Oct), CA.          [78]  [1896] 2 QB 167.

Consistency is a question of degree. In *R v S*[79] it was held that evidence of a recent complaint will be admissible where it is sufficiently consistent that it can, depending on the view of the evidence taken by the jury, support or enhance the credibility of the complainant. Whether the complaint is sufficiently consistent must depend on the facts. It is not necessary that the complaint discloses the ingredients of the offence, but it is usually necessary that it discloses evidence of material and relevant unlawful sexual conduct on the part of the accused which can support the complainant's credibility. Thus it is not usually necessary that the complaint describes the full extent of the unlawful sexual conduct alleged by the complainant in the witness box, provided that it is capable of supporting the credibility of the complainant's evidence. Differences may be accounted for by a variety of matters, including for example the complainant's reluctance to disclose the full extent of the conduct at the time of the complaint, but it is for the jury to assess such matters.

*(iii) Voluntariness.* It is a condition of the admissibility of a complaint in a sexual case that it should have been made voluntarily, and not in reply to questions of a suggestive, leading or intimidating character. The nature of this requirement was explained in the clearest of terms by Ridley J in *R v Osborne*:[80]

the mere fact that the statement is made in answer to a question in such cases is not of itself sufficient to make it inadmissible as a complaint. Questions of a suggestive or leading character will, indeed, have that effect . . . but a question such as this, put by the mother or other person, 'What is the matter?' or 'Why are you crying?' will not do so. These are natural questions which a person in charge will be likely to put. On the other hand, if she were asked, 'Did so-and-so (naming the prisoner) assault you?' 'Did he do this and that to you?' then the result would be different . . . In each case the decision on the character of the question put, as well as other circumstances, such as the relationship of the questioner to the complainant, must be left to the discretion of the presiding judge. If the circumstances indicate that but for the questioning there probably would have been no voluntary complaint, the answer is inadmissible. If the question merely anticipates a statement which the complainant was about to make, it is not rendered inadmissible by the fact that the questioner happens to speak first . . .

On the facts of the case, the complaint, which had been made in reply to the questions 'Why are you going home? Why did you not wait until we came back?', was held to be admissible.

*(iv) The time of complaint.* A complaint is only admissible in evidence under the exception 'when it is made at the first opportunity after the offence which reasonably offers itself'.[81] In every case, the court must also be satisfied that the complaint was 'recent'.[82] Whether a complaint was made as soon as was reasonably practicable after

---

[79] [2004] 3 All ER 689, CA.            [80] [1905] 1 KB 551 at 556.

[81] Per Ridley J [1905] 1 KB 551 at 561. See also *R v Cummings* [1948] 1 All ER 551, CCA. However, the fact that the complaint was not the first to be made is not, per se, sufficient to exclude it: *R v Wilbourne* (1917) 12 Cr App R 280.

[82] *R v Birks* [2003] 2 Cr App R 122, CA.

the occurrence of the offence is a question of fact and degree to be decided by the judge in each case.[83] The answer will depend on the circumstances, including the character of the complainant and the relationship between the complainant and the person to whom she might have complained but did not do so. Victims often need time before they can bring themselves to tell what has happened, and whereas some will find it impossible to complain to anyone other than a parent or member of their family, others may feel it impossible to tell their parents or members of their family.[84] As to 'recency', in R v Birks[85] it was held, albeit reluctantly, that a complaint made at the earliest two months after the alleged offences, was inadmissible, notwithstanding that the complaint was made spontaneously, the alleged offences began when the accused was only 5 or 6 years old, and the accused had allegedly threatened her by saying that if she told her mother she would be put in a home.

(v) Admissibility to show consistency. At common law, the complaint is not evidence of the facts complained of and may be used only as evidence of the consistency of the complaint with the testimony of the complainant and, in cases where consent is in issue, as evidence inconsistent with consent. Thus if the terms of the complaint are not ostensibly consistent with the terms of the complainant's testimony, the introduction of the complaint has no purpose.[86] Likewise, in cases where the complainant does not testify, there being no evidence with which the complaint may be consistent, the particulars of the complaint are inadmissible. Thus in R v Wallwork,[87] where the accused was charged with incest with his daughter, aged five, who went into the witness box but was unable to give evidence, it was that the child's grandmother had been improperly allowed to give evidence of particulars of a complaint made to her by the child because there was no evidence given by the child with which it could be consistent. On the same reasoning, evidence of the mere fact of the complaint should also have been excluded, but Lord Goddard CJ said: 'there would have been no objection to the grandmother saying: "The little girl made a complaint to me." ' It is submitted that such evidence, inadmissible as evidence of the facts complained of, and clearly incapable of showing consistency, should be excluded.[88]

Where evidence of a complaint is admitted but it is, in part, inconsistent with the evidence given by the complainant in the witness box, the judge should make clear to the jury the extent and significance of the inconsistency, drawing to their attention any reason given for the inconsistency and telling them that it is for them to take all these matters into account in deciding whether the complainant is telling the truth.[89]

(vi) Admissibility to negative consent. In cases where consent is in issue, evidence of a complaint is admissible as evidence inconsistent with such consent. Australian

---

[83] A complaint made one week after the offence was admitted in R v Hedges (1909) 3 Cr App R 262.
[84] R v Valentine [1996] 2 Cr App R 213, CA.          [85] [2003] 2 Cr App R 122, CA.
[86] R v Wright and R v Ormerod (1987) 90 Cr App R 91, CA.          [87] (1958) 42 Cr App R 153, CCA.
[88] See Cross (1958) 74 LQR 352. See also per Lord Hoffmann in White v R [1999] 1 Cr App R 153 at 160.
[89] R v S [2004] 3 All ER 689, CA.

authority suggests that the complaint is received as evidence relevant to the credibility of the victim who, in testifying, denies consent.[90]

### (b) Statements admissible to rebut allegations of recent fabrication

If, in cross-examination, it is suggested to a witness that his account of some incident or set of facts is a recent invention or fabrication, evidence of prior statements made by him to the same effect is admissible to support his credit.[91] Such prior statements will normally be put to the witness in re-examination. In *R v Oyesiku*[92] the accused was convicted of assaulting a police officer. In cross-examination, it was put to the accused's wife, who had given evidence that the police officer was the aggressor, that her evidence had been recently fabricated. The Court of Appeal held that the trial judge had improperly refused to admit evidence of a previous statement consistent with her testimony and made by her to a solicitor after her husband's arrest but before she had seen him. Karminski LJ, giving the judgment of the court, accepted as a correct statement of the law the judgment of Dixon CJ in *Nominal Defendant v Clement*,[93] from which the following propositions derive. The exception is brought into play where it is suggested in cross-examination that the witness's account 'is a late invention or has been recently reconstructed, even though not with conscious dishonesty'. The prior statement is admissible 'if it was made by the witness contemporaneously with the event or at a time sufficiently early to be inconsistent with the suggestion that his account is a late invention or reconstruction'. The judge, in determining whether the exception has been brought into play, should exercise care to assure himself of the following three matters: (i) 'that the account given by the witness in his testimony is attacked on the ground of recent invention or reconstruction or that a foundation for such an attack has been laid'; (ii) 'that the contents of the statement are in fact to the like effect as his account given in his evidence'; and (iii) 'that having regard to the time and circumstances in which it was made, it (the statement) rationally tends to answer the attack'.

In both civil and criminal proceedings, the previous consistent statement is now admissible both to negative the suggestion of invention or reconstruction and thereby confirm the witness's credit, and as evidence of the matters stated. Under section 1 of the Civil Evidence Act 1995, in civil proceedings evidence shall not be excluded on the ground that it is hearsay. Section 6(2) and (5) of the 1995 Act provide as follows:

> (2) A party who has called or intends to call a person as a witness in civil proceedings may not in those proceedings adduce evidence of a previous statement made by that person, except—. . .
>
> (b) for the purposes of rebutting a suggestion that his evidence has been fabricated.

---

[90] *Kilby v R* (1973) 129 CLR 460, HC of A.

[91] Evidence of a complaint in a sexual case may be admissible on this basis notwithstanding that it was not made at the first reasonably practicable opportunity (see above): *R v Tyndale* [1999] Crim LR 320, CA.

[92] (1971) 56 Cr App R 240. See also *R v Benjamin* (1913) 8 Cr App R 146; *Flanagan v Fahy* [1918] 2 IR 361; and *Fox v General Medical Council* [1960] 1 WLR 1017.

[93] (1961) 104 CLR 476, HC of A. The extracts given in the text are at 479.

(5) Nothing in this section shall be construed as preventing a statement of any description referred to above from being admissible by virtue of section 1 as evidence of the matters stated.

In criminal proceedings, section 120(1) and (2) of the Criminal Justice Act 2003 provide as follows:

(1) This section applies where a person (the witness) is called to give evidence in criminal proceedings.

(2) If a previous statement by the witness is admitted as evidence to rebut a suggestion that his oral evidence has been fabricated, that statement is admissible as evidence of any matter stated of which oral evidence by the witness would be admissible.

## (c) Statements made on accusation

Provided that the conditions of admissibility are satisfied, and subject to the exclusionary discretion of the court, an admission made by an accused is admissible, by way of exception to the general rule against hearsay, as evidence of the facts contained in it.[94] There is also, however, a well-established practice on the part of the prosecution, which has been approved by the Court of Appeal,[95] 'to admit in evidence all unwritten and most written statements made by an accused person to the police whether they contain admissions or whether they contain denials of guilt'. If such statements are wholly exculpatory, they are not admitted as evidence of the facts stated. In *R v Storey*,[96] the police having found a large quantity of cannabis in the accused's flat, she explained that it belonged to a man who had brought it there against her will. The Court of Appeal upheld the judge's rejection of a submission of no case to answer, at the close of the prosecution case, on the ground that the accused's statement was not evidence of the facts contained in it. The statement was admissible 'because of its vital relevance as showing the reaction of the accused when first taxed with the incriminating facts'.[97] It does not follow from these words, however, that the only statements admissible as evidence of reaction are those which the accused made on the first encounter with his accusers. In *R v Pearce*[98] the Court of Appeal decided that statements subsequently made are also admissible, although 'the longer the time that has elapsed after the first encounter the less the weight which will be attached to the denial', a matter on which the judge may direct the jury. Thus, in that case it was held that a judge had improperly excluded self-serving statements made by the accused to the police after his arrest, which took place two days after he was first taxed by his employer's security officer with incriminating facts relating to handling stolen goods. However, this principle cannot be relied upon to admit a statement which adds nothing to evidence of reaction which has already been

---

[94] See Ch 13.   [95] *R v Pearce* (1979) 69 Cr App R 365 at 368 and 370.
[96] (1968) 52 Cr App R 334.   [97] Per Widgery LJ at 337.   [98] (1979) 69 Cr App R 365 at 369.

admitted. In *R v Tooke*[99] the accused made an exculpatory statement shortly after the time of the offence. Some 40 minutes later, he went to the police station and made a spontaneous exculpatory witness statement. The first statement was admitted, but the defence were not permitted to cross-examine a constable to prove the statement made at the station. The fact that it was a witness statement and not a statement in answer to a charge made no difference, because the same test applied. It was inadmissible because it added nothing to the evidence of reaction already before the jury.

Impromptu exculpatory statements made on accusation are admissible as evidence of consistency in the case of an accused who testifies. However, in a case where the accused gives no evidence, there is no duty on the judge to remind the jury of voluntary statements made by the accused to the police exonerating himself.[100] Moreover, the accused will not be permitted to take unfair advantage of the rule:

Although in practice most statements are given in evidence even when they are largely self-serving, there may be a rare occasion when an accused produces a carefully prepared written statement to the police, with a view to it being made a part of the prosecution evidence. The trial judge would probably exclude such a statement as inadmissible.[101]

A careful distinction needs to be drawn between a purely exculpatory statement and a 'mixed' statement, that is a statement containing both inculpatory and exculpatory parts, such as 'I killed X. If I had not done so, X would certainly have killed me there and then.'[102] When the prosecution admits in evidence a statement relied upon as an admission, the whole statement, including qualifications, explanations, and other exculpatory parts of it favourable to the accused, becomes admissible. Any other course would be unfair and misleading.[103] The jury must decide whether the statement viewed as a whole constitutes an admission. As to the question whether the judge should then direct the jury (a) that the statement is not evidence of the facts contained in it except insofar as it constitutes an admission (the 'purist' approach), or (b) that the whole statement is evidence of the truth of the facts it contains (the 'common sense' approach), in *R v Duncan*[104] the Court of Appeal came down firmly in favour of the latter approach. The appellant, who elected not to testify, was convicted of murder. He had made a statement in which he admitted that he killed a woman but suggested that he must have lost his temper when she teased him. The trial judge held that insofar as his statements were self-serving, they were not evidence of the facts contained in them. Rejecting this reasoning as erroneous, Lord Lane CJ, in a

---

[99]  (1989) 90 Cr App R 417, CA.

[100]  *R v Barbery* (1975) 62 Cr App R 248, CA. Contrast *R v Donaldson* (1976) 64 Cr App R 59 at 69.

[101]  *R v Pearce* (1979) 69 Cr App R 365 at 370. See, eg, *R v Newsome* (1980) 71 Cr App R 325, CA, in which a self-serving statement, dictated by the accused to the police after consultation with and in the presence of his solicitor, was held to be inadmissible. Such a statement remains inadmissible notwithstanding that access to the solicitor is delayed by the police in exercise of their right to do so under s 58 of the Police and Criminal Evidence Act, 1984: *R v Hutton* (1988) *The Times*, 27 Oct, CA.

[102]  See per Lord Lane CJ in *R v Duncan* (1981) 73 Cr App R 359 at 364, CA.

[103]  *R v Pearce* (1979) 69 Cr App R 365 at 369–70.         [104]  (1981) 73 Cr App R 359.

dictum which has subsequently been applied by the Court of Appeal (*R v Hamand*[105]) and unanimously endorsed by the House of Lords (*R v Sharp*[106]), said:[107]

Where a 'mixed' statement is under consideration by the jury in a case where the defendant has not given evidence, it seems to us that the simplest, and, therefore, the method most likely to produce a just result, is for the jury to be told that the whole statement, both the incriminating parts and the excuses or explanations, must be considered by them in deciding where the truth lies. It is, to say the least, not helpful to try to explain to the jury that the exculpatory parts of the statement are something less than evidence of the facts they state. Equally, where appropriate, as it usually will be, the judge may, and should, point out that the incriminatory parts are likely to be true (otherwise why say them?) whereas the excuses do not have the same weight.[108]

The principle established in *R v Duncan* applies whether the 'mixed' statement is a written statement or a record of questions and answers at an interview.[109] In the case of a suspect who asserts his innocence, his answers in interview will almost always contain *some* admissions of relevant fact, but statements will only be treated as 'mixed' for the purposes of the principle if they contain an admission of fact which is 'significant' in relation to an issue in the case, ie capable of adding some degree of weight to the prosecution case on an issue which is relevant to guilt.[110] However, there is no requirement that any act admitted be unlawful per se.[111]

It remains unclear whether the principle applies if the statement is not relied on by the prosecution. On one view, the self-serving parts of the statement are only admissible for their truth if the prosecution elect to rely on the statement as containing an admission.[112] However, it is submitted that there are compelling reasons against any such additional requirement. As Butterfield J pointed out in *Western v DPP*,[113] whether a statement is mixed or not should not depend on the accident of what other evidence is available to the prosecution; and in cases in which the statement is *not* relied on by the prosecution, the view advanced would mean reviving the unintelligible direction, repudiated in *R v Duncan*, to the effect that although the admission is evidence of the facts stated, the self-serving parts of the statement are only evidence of reaction.[114]

---

[105] (1985) 82 Cr App R 65, CA.     [106] [1988] 1 All ER 65. See also *R v Aziz* [1995] 3 All ER 149, HL.

[107] (1981) 73 Cr App R 359 at 365. The appeal was dismissed, however, because on the facts nothing in the statements amounted to a claim of provocation.

[108] Cf cl 2(4) of the draft Bill attached to the 11th Report of the Criminal Law Revision Committee (Cmnd 4991). It provides that confessions are admissible as evidence of any fact stated therein 'including any fact or matter favourable to the accused: Provided that . . . the court shall not be required to treat an issue as having been raised . . . by reason only of evidence favourable to the accused which is admissible by virtue of this subsection.' The provisions of the Police and Criminal Evidence Act 1984 governing the admissibility of confessions contain no equivalent to cl 2(4).

[109] *R v Polin* [1991] Crim LR 293, CA.     [110] *R v Garrod* [1997] Crim LR 445, CA.

[111] *R v McCleary* [1994] Crim LR 121, CA.

[112] See per Lord Steyn in *R v Aziz* [1995] 3 All ER 149, HL at 155.

[113] [1997] 1 Cr App R 474, DC at 484–5.

[114] See generally Di Birch 'The Sharp End of the Wedge: Use of Mixed Statements by the Defence' [1997] Crim LR 416.

The common-law rule relating to the admissibility of mixed statements as evidence of the matters stated is among the common law rules preserved by section 118 of the Criminal Justice Act 2003.[115]

### (d)  Statements made on discovery of incriminating articles

In cases of handling and theft, if it is shown that the accused was found in possession of recently stolen goods, but failed to give a credible innocent explanation, the jury *may* infer guilty knowledge or belief and return a finding of guilt.[116] Any explanation which is given by the accused is admissible, if the accused testifies to the same effect, as evidence of consistency.[117]

### (e)  Previous identification

Where, in criminal proceedings, a witness gives evidence identifying the accused as the person who committed the offence charged, evidence of a previous identification of the accused by that witness may be given, either by the witness himself or by any other person who witnessed the previous identification,[118] for example a police officer who conducted a formal identification procedure such as a video identification or an identification parade, as evidence of consistency.[119] Section 120(5) of the Criminal Justice Act 2003, when read in conjunction with section 120(1) and (4) of the 2003 Act, has extended the principle to cover a previous statement of a witness which identifies *or describes* a person, *object or place*, provided that the witness, while giving evidence, indicates that to the best of his belief, he made the statement and it states the truth. A statement received under section 120(5) is admitted as evidence of any matter stated, and will also be evidence of the witness's consistency. Section 120(5) is considered in Chapter 10. The text which follows relates to the common-law principle.

In *R v Christie*[120] the accused was convicted of indecent assault on a boy. The boy gave unsworn evidence in which he described the assault, and identified the accused, but made no reference to any previous identification. The House of Lords, by a majority of five to two, held that both the boy's mother and a constable had been properly allowed to give evidence that shortly after the alleged act they saw the boy

---

[115]  Section 118(1) 5.

[116]  See Ch 22 under A1(c)(ii) **The presumption of guilty knowledge.**

[117]  See *R v Abraham* (1848) 3 Cox CC 430. For further authorities and discussion, see RN Gooderson 'Previous Consistent Statements' (1968) CLJ 64 at 70–3.

[118]  For the difficulties which arise where the witness fails to identify the accused in court, having previously identified him outside court, see *R v Osbourne* and *R v Virtue* [1973] QB 678 and *R v Burke and Kelly* (1847) 2 Cox CC 295 (see Ch 10).

[119]  The detailed rules governing the proper conduct of formal identification procedures, which are contained in the Code of Practice issued by the Home Secretary pursuant to s 66 of the Police and Criminal Evidence Act, 1984, are beyond the scope of this book. Failure on the part of the police to observe the provisions may be taken into account by the court when deciding whether to exclude identification evidence and by the jury when assessing the weight of such evidence. See *R v Beveridge* [1987] Crim LR 401, CA; *R v Gaynor* [1988] Crim LR 242, CC; *R v Ladlow* [1989] Crim LR 219, CC; *R v Gall* (1990) 90 Cr App R 64, CA; and *R v Grannell* (1989) 90 Cr App R 149, CA (see Ch 3).

[120]  [1914] AC 545.

approach the accused, touch his sleeve and identify him by saying, 'That is the man'. Evidence of the previous identification was admissible as evidence of the witness's consistency, 'to show that the witness was able to identify at the time' and 'to exclude the idea that the identification of the prisoner in the dock was an afterthought or mistake'.[121] Evidence that a witness previously identified the accused from a photograph is also admissible for these purposes provided that the photograph does not come from police files or, if it does, cannot be identified as such.[122] Thus, evidence of identification from a photograph which forms part of an album of police photographs[123] or which shows the accused wearing prison clothes[124] should be excluded, unless the jury have been or will be made aware of the accused's record for some other good reason.[125] The accused should not be prejudiced by the jury being informed or allowed to suspect that he has previous convictions.[126]

The admissibility of evidence of previous identification of the accused has been justified on the ground that:

In cases where there has been a considerable lapse of time between the offence and the trial, and where there might be a danger of the witness's recollection of the prisoner's features having become dimmed, no doubt it strengthens the value of the evidence if it can be shown that in the meantime, soon after the commission of the offence, the witness saw and recognized the prisoner.[127]

The evidence of a witness who identifies the accused as the person who committed the offence charged is, in the absence of a previous identification, treated with considerable suspicion. There is the obvious danger stemming from delay. There is also the real risk of prejudice, because a witness, asked if he sees the person who committed the offence in court, might all too readily point to the person standing in the dock, overriding any doubts in his mind, especially in cases where he gave a description to

---

[121] Per Viscount Haldane LC [1914] AC 545 at 551.

[122] Such a photograph may also be used to show that between commission of the offence and arrest, the accused had strikingly changed his appearance and thereby thwarted an attempt by the identifying witness to pick him out of an identification parade: *R v Byrne and Trump* [1987] Crim LR 689, CA.

[123] *R v Wainwright* (1925) 19 Cr App R 52, CCA.

[124] *R v Dwyer* and *R v Ferguson* [1925] 2 KB 799, CCA. See also *R v Varley* (1914) 10 Cr App R 125.

[125] See, eg, *R v Allen* [1996] Crim LR 426, CA.

[126] However, the nature or conduct of the defence may justify the admission of such evidence: see *R v Lamb* (1980) 71 Cr App R 198, CA and *R v Bleakley* [1993] Crim LR 203, CA; and cf *R v Campbell* [1994] Crim LR 357, CA. See also *R v Governor of Pentonville Prison, ex p Voets* [1986] 2 All ER 630, QBD: such photographs are admissible in law and their exclusion discretionary. The police should not show photographs, including that of a suspect, to potential witnesses where the suspect is already under arrest: *R v Haslam* (1925) 19 Cr App R 59. Such witnesses should not be shown photographs of an accused whom they will be asked to identify in court: *R v Dwyer* and *R v Ferguson* [1925] 2 KB 799. However, the police, if in doubt as to the identity of a criminal, may show photographs to potential witnesses in order to discover who the offender is: *R v Palmer* (1914) 10 Cr App R 77. See also *R v Crabtree* [1992] Crim LR 65, CA: it is permissible for officers to identify the accused from photographs taken as part of a surveillance operation and shown to them before the offence was committed. As to the rules to be observed when a witness is shown photographs for identification purposes, see paras 3.3 and 3.28 of, and Annex E to, Code D, the Code of Practice on Identification issued pursuant to s 66 of the Police and Criminal Evidence Act 1984.

[127] Per Ferguson J in *R v Fannon* (1922) 22 SRNSW 427 at 430.

the police, by the thought: 'Surely the police would not have brought the wrong person to court?' For these reasons, it is undesirable to invite a witness to make a 'dock identification', that is to identify the accused for the first time in court,[128] and the usual practice, in cases where there has been a prior out-of-court identification, is to elicit evidence on this *before* asking a question such as, 'Is that person in court today?'[129]

Although it has been held that it would be wrong to apply one approach to dock identifications for minor offences and another for more serious offences,[130] it seems that the usual practice in a magistrates' court is now different from that in the Crown Court, in the case of driving offences at least. In *Barnes v Chief Constable of Durham*,[131] B was convicted of failing to provide a specimen contrary to section 7 of the Road Traffic Act 1988. There was no indication by the defence at any time after B was charged that identity was in issue, and no formal identification procedure was requested. At the trial, B was identified in the dock by an officer who had last seen him some 33 months earlier. The Divisional Court held that on the facts it had not been unfair to allow the dock identification. It was said that dock identifications were customary in magistrates' courts, in relation to driving offences at least, and that if, in every case where the defendant did not distinctly admit driving there had to be a formal identification procedure, the whole process of justice in a magistrates' court would be severely impaired. This approach was followed in *Karia v DPP*,[132] a case of speeding and failing to produce insurance and other documents, where the court rejected a submission that *Barnes v Chief Constable of Durham* could be distinguished on the basis that in that case the defendant had been arrested and interviewed, whereas Karia was summonsed and had had no opportunity to explain that he was not the driver.

## (f)  Statements admissible as part of the *res gestae*

The common-law principle of *res gestae*, which is considered in Chapter 12, renders admissible all those events and statements which may be said to constitute a part of a transaction which is in issue. For example, in *R v Fowkes*[133] the accused, charged with murder, was commonly known, in the circumstances somewhat unfortunately it may be thought, as 'the butcher'. The son of the deceased gave evidence that he was sitting

---

[128]  *R v Cartwright* (1914) 10 Cr App R 219.

[129]  A dock identification is justified if the suspect has refused to take part in a formal identification procedure (*R v John* [1973] Crim LR 113, CA) or if the identifying witness claims to recognize the suspect as a person he already knows well (see para 3.12(ii) of Code D). However, a formal identification procedure is necessary where the witness has seen the suspect only once, or on a few occasions, before: *R v Fergus* [1992] Crim LR 363. Where a dock identification is made but not solicited by the prosecution, it is insufficient for the judge merely to direct the jury that such an identification is abnormal and unfair—they should probably be told to disregard it altogether: see *R v Thomas* [1994] Crim LR 128, CA. For the guidelines adopted by the courts to lessen the dangers of mistaken identification in criminal cases, see *R v Turnbull* [1977] QB 224, CA (see Ch 8).

[130]  See *North Yorkshire Trading Standards Dept v Williams* (1994) 159 JP 383, DC.

[131]  [1997] 2 Cr App R 505, DC.        [132]  (2002) 166 JP 753.        [133]  (1856) *The Times*, 8 Mar, Assizes.

in a room with his father and a police officer, that a face appeared at the window through which a shot was fired, and that he thought the face was that of the accused. Both the son and the police officer, who had not seen the face, were allowed to give evidence that the son, on seeing the face, had shouted, 'There's Butcher'. A statement forming part of the *res gestae* is admissible at common law as evidence of the matters stated and also as evidence of consistency insofar as it confirms testimony given by the witness to the same effect. In criminal proceedings the common-law rules in this regard have been preserved by the Criminal Justice Act 2003.[134] In civil proceedings, a previous statement forming part of the *res gestae* may only be adduced with the leave of the court.[135]

### (g) Statements in documents used to refresh the memory and received in evidence

As we have seen earlier in this chapter, where a party, or counsel on his behalf, cross-examines a witness on a document used by him to refresh his memory, and goes beyond the parts relied upon by the witness, the document may be recceived in evidence. As we have also seen, in civil proceedings, statements in the document are admitted as evidence of the matters stated; and the same applies in criminal proceedings, provided that the statement was made, as opposed to verified, by the witness. Where such statements are received in evidence, they may also go to the consistency of the witness.

# D UNFAVOURABLE AND HOSTILE WITNESSES

## 1 THE RULE AGAINST A PARTY IMPEACHING THE CREDIT OF HIS OWN WITNESS

A party seeking to elicit evidence in support of his version of the facts in issue may call a witness who fails to come up to proof or who gives evidence in support of the other party's version of the facts in issue. A party thus disappointed, in order to remedy the situation, may understandably wish to change course and attack the credibility of the witness. The general rule at common law, however, is that a party is not permitted to impeach the credit of a witness he calls: the party may neither question the witness about, nor call evidence concerning, his bad character, convictions, prior inconsistent statements or bias. In short, if the witness gives adverse evidence, the party may not turn round and cross-examine him as if he were a witness for the opposite party: 'It would be repugnant to principle, and likely to lead to abuse, to enable a party, having called a witness on the basis that he is at least in general going to tell the truth, to question him or call other evidence designed to show that he is a liar.'[136]

---

[134] Section 118(1) 4.    [135] See s 6(2)(a) of the Civil Evidence Act 1995 (see Ch 11).
[136] 11th Report, Criminal Law Revision Committee (Cmnd 4991), para 162.

## 2 UNFAVOURABLE WITNESSES

An unfavourable witness may be defined as a witness who, although he displays no hostile animus to the party calling him, fails to come up to proof or gives evidence unfavourable to the case of that party. At common law a party is not permitted to impeach the credit of an unfavourable witness by any of the means outlined in the preceding paragraph but may call other witnesses to give evidence of those matters in relation to which the unfavourable witness failed to come up to proof. Thus in *Ewer v Ambrose*,[137] the defendant having called a witness to prove a partnership and the witness having testified to the contrary, it was held that while the defendant could not adduce general evidence to show that the witness was not to be believed on his oath, he was entitled to contradict him by calling other witnesses. If the rule were otherwise, undue importance would attach to the order in which witnesses are called. As Littledale J observed, 'if a party had four witnesses upon whom he relied to prove his case, it would be very hard that, by calling first the one who happened to disprove it, he should be deprived of the testimony of the other three'.

## 3 HOSTILE WITNESSES

A hostile witness may be defined as a witness who, in the opinion of the judge, shows no desire to tell the truth at the instance of the party calling him, to whom he displays a hostile animus.[138] In a civil case, it seems that a party may call a person even if he has shown signs that he is likely to be a hostile witness by refusing to make a statement.[139] Similarly, in a criminal case, the prosecution may call a person who has shown such signs, for example by retracting a statement, or making a second statement, prior to the trial,[140] but it appears that in cases in which the person refuses to assist the prosecution or court, or claims to be no longer able to remember anything, the judge has a discretion to hold a *voir dire* in order to decide whether to prevent him from being called at all.[141] However, although the question whether a witness is hostile is for the judge alone, the evidence and demeanour of the potentially hostile witness should usually be tested in the presence of the jury.[142] It is only in very exceptional cases that a *voir dire* should be held to decide whether or not a witness who has yet to be called might prove to be hostile.[143] Equally, once a witness has started to give his evidence, a *voir dire* before a decision on whether to treat him as hostile is only appropriate in

---

[137] (1825) 3 B&C 746. See also *Bradley v Ricardo* (1831) 8 Bing 57; cf Hamilton J in *Sumner and Leivesley v John Brown & Co* (1909) 25 TLR 745.

[138] See Stephen *Digest of the Law of Evidence* (12th edn London 1948) Art 147.

[139] See CPR r 32.9 (whereby a party unable to obtain a witness statement may seek permission to serve a witness summary instead) (see Ch 4).

[140] See *R v Mann* (1972) 56 Cr App R 750, CA; *R v Vibert* (21 Oct 1974, unreported), CA; and *R v Dat* [1998] Crim LR 488, CA.

[141] *R v Honeyghon and Sayles* [1999] Crim LR 221, CA. See also *R v Dat* [1998] Crim LR 488.

[142] *R v Darby* [1989] Crim LR 817, CA. Cf *R v Jones* [1998] Crim LR 579, CA.

[143] *R v Olumegbon* [2004] All ER (D) 60 (Aug).

exceptional circumstances, because the jury may see the witness apparently giving evidence in one frame of mind and then see a complete turn-around after events which have taken place in their absence.[144]

At common law a judge may allow cross-examination of a hostile witness by the party calling him.[145] An application to treat a witness as hostile may be made at any time during the witness's evidence, even at the late stage of re-examination.[146] The judge has a discretion whether to grant leave to cross-examine and his decision will seldom be challenged successfully on appeal.[147] In deciding whether a witness is not merely unfavourable but should be treated as hostile, the judge may take into account the attitude and demeanour displayed by the witness, his willingness to cooperate, and the extent to which any prior statement made by him is inconsistent with his testimony. If a hostile witness gives evidence contrary to an earlier statement, or fails to give the evidence expected, the party calling him and the trial judge should first consider inviting him to refresh his memory from material which it is legitimate to use for that purpose, and should not immediately proceed to treat him as hostile, unless he displays such an excessive degree of hostility that that is the only appropriate course.[148] In *R v Fraser* and *R v Warren*[149] Lord Goddard CJ went so far as to state, and it is perhaps best regarded as an over-statement, that if the prosecution have in their possession a previous statement 'in flat contradiction' of the witness's testimony, they are *entitled* to cross-examine and should apply for leave to do so. Be that as it may, if a witness is treated as hostile, the party calling him may ask leading questions[150] but may neither cross-examine him on his previous misconduct or convictions, nor adduce evidence to show that he is not to be believed on oath. At common law, it was doubtful whether the party could prove prior statements made by the witness and inconsistent with his testimony, a matter which is now governed by section 3 of the Criminal Procedure Act 1865.[151] Section 3 provides that:

A party producing a witness shall not be allowed to impeach his credit by general evidence of bad character, but he may, in case the witness shall, in the opinion of the judge, prove adverse, contradict him by other evidence, or, by leave of the judge, prove that he has made at other times a statement inconsistent with his present testimony; but before such last mentioned proof can be given the circumstances of the supposed statement, sufficient to

---

[144] *R v Khan* [2003] Crim LR 428, CA.

[145] It appears that the party calling the witness retains the right to *re-examine* him on any new matters arising out of cross-examination by the other party to the action: *R v Wong* [1986] Crim LR 683, Crown Court.

[146] *R v Powell* [1985] Crim LR 592, CA.

[147] *Rice v Howard* (1886) 16 QBD 681 and *Price v Manning* (1889) 42 Ch D 372, CA.

[148] *R v Maw* [1994] Crim LR 841, CA.     [149] (1956) 40 Cr App R 160, CCA.

[150] *R v Thompson* (1976) 64 Cr App R 96, CA.

[151] Section 3 applies to both civil and criminal proceedings. In civil proceedings the prior statement of any witness may with the leave of the court be admitted as evidence of the facts contained in it: see s 6(2)(a) of the Civil Evidence Act 1995 (see Ch 11). The evidential status of a prior inconsistent statement of a hostile witness in civil proceedings is governed by s 6(3) of the same Act: see below.

designate the particular occasion, must be mentioned to the witness, and he must be asked whether or not he has made such statement.

Section 3 was not drafted with felicity.[152] In *Greenough v Eccles*[153] it was held that the word 'adverse' in the section means 'hostile' and not 'unfavourable'. Bearing this in mind, the section may be analysed in terms of three rules governing a party's entitlement to discredit his own witness. The first is that he is not entitled to impeach the witness's credit by general evidence of his bad character. In other words, he may neither cross-examine the witness on his previous misconduct or convictions nor adduce evidence of a general nature to show that the witness is not to be believed on oath. This rule applies to both unfavourable and hostile witnesses and amounts to no more than a statutory re-statement of the common law. The second rule, that the party may contradict the witness by other evidence, applies under the statute only to hostile witnesses. The section suggests that this rule does not apply to unfavourable witnesses, but in *Greenough v Eccles*, Williams and Willes JJ held that the section has not affected the rule at common law that a party may contradict an unfavourable witness by calling other witnesses.[154] The third rule, that the party may prove that the witness made at other times a statement inconsistent with his present testimony, applies only in the case of hostile witnesses.[155] In this connection, it remains to note that section 3 has not removed the common-law right of the judge, in his discretion, to allow cross-examination when a witness proves hostile. In *R v Thompson*[156] the accused was convicted of indecent assault and incest. His daughter, who had given a statement to the police implicating him, was called into the witness box but stood mute of malice, refusing to give evidence. The judge gave leave to treat her as a hostile witness, and she was then asked leading questions and her former statement was put to her. On appeal, it was argued that since the girl had given no 'testimony', the case did not fall within section 3. Dismissing the appeal, Lord Parker CJ held it unnecessary to decide whether section 3 applied, since there was authority at common law for what the judge had done.[157]

If a hostile witness, on being cross-examined on a previous inconsistent statement,

---

[152] 'Section 3 of the 1865 Act certainly requires thorough revision': 11th Report, Criminal Law Revision Committee (Cmnd 4991), para 161. See also cl 11 of the draft Bill.

[153] (1859) 5 CBNS 786, a decision on the construction of s 22 of the Common Law Procedure (Amendment) Act 1856, which was repealed but re-enacted by s 3 of the 1865 Act.

[154] See *Ewer v Ambrose* (1825) 3 B&C 746. The Criminal Law Revision Committee was of the opinion that there is no need to make statutory provision for a party to be allowed to call evidence to contradict an unfavourable witness because this is allowed by common law: see 11th Report (Cmnd 4991), para 163. The attempt to deal with the matter in s 3 was 'the great blunder in the drawing of it': per Cockburn CJ in *Greenough v Eccles* (1859) 5 CBNS 786 at 806.

[155] Acceptance by the witness that he made some parts of the statement and signed it may constitute proof for these purposes: see *R v Baldwin* [1986] Crim LR 681, CA.

[156] (1976) 64 Cr App R 96, CA.

[157] Reliance was placed upon *Clarke v Saffery* (1824) Ry&M 126 and *Bastin v Carew* (1824) Ry&M 127. It remains unclear whether if, in circumstances such as those in *R v Thompson*, the witness denies making the previous statement, it can be proved at common law.

adopts and confirms the contents (or part of them), then what he says becomes part of his evidence and, subject to the assessment of his credibility by the tribunal of fact, it is capable of being accepted.[158] However, even if the witness does not admit the truth of the previous statement, it is admitted in both civil and criminal proceedings as evidence of the matters stated. Under section 1 of the Civil Evidence Act 1995, in civil proceedings evidence shall not be excluded on the ground that it is hearsay. Section 6(3) and (5) of the 1995 Act provide as follows:

(3) Where in the case of civil proceedings sections 3, 4 or 5 of the Criminal Procedure Act 1865 applies, which make provision as to—
(a) how far a witness may be discredited by the party producing him, . . .
this Act does not authorise the adducing of evidence of a previous inconsistent or contradictory statement otherwise than in accordance with those sections.

(5) Nothing in this section shall be construed as preventing a statement of any description referred to above from being admissible by virtue of section 1 as evidence of the matters stated.

As to criminal proceedings, section 119 of the Criminal Justice Act 2003 provides as follows:

(1) If in criminal proceedings a person gives oral evidence and—
(a) he admits making a previous inconsistent statement, or
(b) a previous inconsistent statement made by him is proved by virtue of section 3, 4 or 5 of the Criminal Procedure Act 1865 (c. 18),
the statement is admissible as evidence of any matter stated of which oral evidence by him would be admissible.

In *R v Golder*[159] Lord Parker CJ said: 'When a witness is shown to have made previous statements inconsistent with the evidence given by that witness at the trial, the jury should . . . be directed that the evidence given at the trial should be regarded as unreliable.' The statement has since been cited with approval[160] but it may be doubted whether it was ever intended to be regarded as a rigid formula or precise form of words to be recited to juries in every case. It has since been said that it is not always necessary or appropriate, as an inflexible rule, to direct the jury that the evidence of the witness should be treated as unreliable.[161] In some cases the evidence given by the witness may be regarded as reliable notwithstanding his prior inconsistent statement—for example when the witness is able to give a convincing explanation of the inconsistency. It is submitted that the strength of the direction on the weight to be attached to the witness's evidence should vary according to the particular circumstances of the case in

---

[158] *R v Maw* [1994] Crim LR 841, CA.

[159] [1960] 1 WLR 1169 at 1172–3. See also *R v White* (1922) 17 Cr App R 59 and *R v Harris* (1927) 20 Cr App R 144.

[160] See *R v Oliva* [1965] 1 WLR 1028 at 1036–7.

[161] *Driscoll v R* (1977) 137 CLR 517, HC of A, a view supported by *R v Pestano* [1981] Crim LR 397, CA; *Alves v DPP* [1992] 4 All ER 787, HL; and *R v Goodway* [1993] 4 All ER 894 at 899, CA.

question. *R v Thomas*[162] is a case in point. The accused was convicted of the murder of his 6-month-old son. The accused's sister, who had made a number of admissions to the police that she had handled the child roughly, was called for the defence, went back on these admissions, was treated as a hostile witness and then admitted violence to the child. The trial judge in effect directed the jury to disregard her evidence. The Court of Appeal, substituting a verdict of manslaughter, held that since the sister's evidence was to the benefit of the accused, the judge should have invited the jury to consider whether it cast doubt upon the prosecution case and should have pointed out that she would have every motive for denying violence but very few for admitting it.[163] However, it is necessary for the jury to consider whether a hostile witness should be treated as creditworthy at all. The judge should give a clear warning about the dangers of a witness who has contradicted himself. It is insufficient to tell the jury to approach the evidence with great caution and reservation. It is only if the jury consider that they can give any credence to the witness, that they may then go on to consider which parts of his evidence, if any, they accept.[164]

[162]  [1985] Crim LR 445, CA.
[163]  See also *R v Nelson* [1992] Crim LR 653, CA and *R v Khan* [2003] Crim LR 428, CA.
[164]  *R v Maw* [1994] Crim LR 841, CA.

# 7

# CROSS-EXAMINATION AND RE-EXAMINATION

## A CROSS-EXAMINATION

Cross-examination is the questioning of a witness, immediately after his examination-in-chief, by the opponent of the party calling him or by any other party to the proceedings.[1] Thus if an accused elects to testify, he will be open to cross-examination not only by the prosecution but also by a co-accused; and the co-accused is entitled to cross-examine him whether he has given evidence unfavourable to the co-accused or has merely given evidence in his own defence.[2]

## 1 LIABILITY TO CROSS-EXAMINATION

All witnesses are liable to be cross-examined. If a witness dies before cross-examination, his evidence-in-chief is admissible, though little weight may attach to it.[3] If a witness, during cross-examination, becomes incapable through illness of giving further evidence, the judge may allow the trial to continue on the basis of the evidence already given, subject to an appropriate direction to the jury to acquit if they feel that the truncated cross-examination prevented them from judging fairly the witness's credibility.[4]

To the general rule that all witnesses are liable to cross-examination, there are three minor exceptions in the case of: (i) a witness who is not sworn, being called merely to produce a document;[5] (ii) a witness called by mistake, because he is unable to speak as to the matters supposed to be within his knowledge, where the mistake is discovered

---

[1] Concerning the extent to which the judge may intervene, see *R v Sharp* [1993] 3 All ER 225, CA and *R v Roncoli* [1998] Crim LR 584, CA. The order of cross-examination where two or more accused are jointly indicted and separately represented by counsel is the order in which the names of the accused appear on the indictment: *R v Barber* (1844) 1 Car&Kir 434; *R v Richards* (1844) 1 Cox CC 62.

[2] *R v Hilton* [1972] 1 QB 421, CA.      [3] *R v Doolin* (1882) 1 Jebb CC 123, IR.

[4] *R v Stretton* and *R v McCallion* (1986) 86 Cr App R 7, CA. See also *R v Wyatt* [1990] Crim LR 343. However, if the only direct evidence on one important part of the prosecution case is given by a witness who, at the end of his examination-in-chief, is unable to give further evidence, it is at least doubtful whether any direction to the jury, however strongly expressed, can overcome the powerful prejudice of his evidence going wholly untested by cross-examination: see *R v Lawless* (1993) 98 Cr App R 342, CA.

[5] *Summers v Moseley* (1834) 2 Cr&M 477. Nor may such a witness be cross-examined if he was sworn unnecessarily: *Rush v Smith* (1834) 1 Cr M&R 94.

before the examination-in-chief has begun but after the witness has been sworn;[6] and (iii) a witness called by the judge, in which case neither party is entitled to cross-examine him without the leave of the judge, although such leave should be given if the evidence is adverse to either party.[7]

## 2  CROSS-EXAMINATION BY ACCUSED IN PERSON

Cross-examination may be conducted by a legal representative or by a party in person. In criminal cases, as a general rule, an unrepresented accused is entitled to cross-examine in person any witness called by the prosecution. However, there are common-law restrictions on this rule, as well as statutory exceptions to it. As to the former, the judge is not obliged to give an unrepresented accused his head to ask whatever questions, at whatever length, he wishes;[8] and although he should not descend into the arena on behalf of the accused, it is generally desirable for the judge to ask such questions as he sees fit to test the reliability and accuracy of the witness.[9] Sections 34–39 of the Youth Justice and Criminal Evidence Act 1999 protect three categories of witness from cross-examination by an accused in person. Under section 34, no person charged with a sexual offence[10] may cross-examine in person the complainant, either in connection with the offence, or in connection with any other offence (of whatever nature) with which that person is charged in the proceedings. Under section 35, no person charged with one of a number of specified offences[11] may cross-examine in person a 'protected witness', either in connection with the offence, or in connection with any other offence (of whatever nature) with which that person is charged in the proceedings. A 'protected witness' is a witness[12] who (a) is the complainant or is alleged to have been a witness to the commission of the offence and (b) either is a child or falls to be cross-examined after giving evidence-in-chief (i) by means of a video recording made for the purposes of section 27 of the 1999 Act (video-recorded

---

[6] However, if counsel seeks to withdraw a witness who can give relevant evidence because he might also reveal other inconvenient matters, the witness is liable to cross-examination: *Wood v Mackinson* (1840) 2 Mood&R 273.

[7] *Coulson v Disborough* [1894] 2 QB 316, CA; *R v Cliburn* (1898) 62 JP 232. See also *R v Tregear* [1967] 2 QB 574 at 580, CA.

[8] *R v Brown* [1998] 2 Cr App R 364, CA.          [9] *R v De Oliveira* [1997] Crim LR 600, CA.

[10] A 'sexual offence' is defined in s 62 as any offence under Part 1 of the Sexual Offences Act 2003.

[11] The offences are any offence under the Protection of Children Act 1978 or Part 1 of the Sexual Offences Act 2003 (s 35(3)(a)); and kidnapping, false imprisonment or an offence under s 1 or s 2 of the Child Abduction Act 1984, any offence under s 1 of the Children and Young Persons Act 1933, and any offence (not already listed) which involves an assault on, or injury or a threat of injury to, any person (s 35(3)(b), (c) and (d)).

[12] A 'witness' includes a witness who is charged with an offence in the proceedings: s 35(5). Thus an accused may not cross-examine in person a 'protected witness' who is a co-accused: *R(S) v Waltham Forest Youth Court* [2004] 2 Cr App R 335 at [27].

evidence admitted as evidence-in-chief)[13] at a time when the witness was a child or (ii) in any other way at any such time.[14]

Section 36 gives the court a general power, in a case where neither section 34 nor section 35 operates, to give a direction prohibiting the accused from cross-examining a witness in person.[15] An application for such a direction may be made by the prosecutor or the court may raise the issue of its own motion.[16] Under section 36(2), such a direction may be given if it appears to the court (a) 'that the quality of evidence[17] given by the witness on cross-examination—(i) is likely to be diminished if the cross-examination . . . is conducted by the accused in person, and (ii) would be likely to be improved if a direction were given . . .' and (b) it would not be contrary to the interests of justice. In deciding whether section 36(2)(a) applies, the court must have regard to various matters, including any views expressed by the witness, the nature of the questions likely to be asked, the accused's behaviour during the proceedings, any relationship (of any nature) between the witness and the accused, and any special measures direction[18] which the court has given or proposes to give in relation to the witness.[19] The accused should be given the opportunity to make representations in relation to these matters.[20] The court must state in open court its reasons for giving or refusing an application for a direction under section 36.[21]

Where an accused is prevented from cross-examining a witness in person under section 34, section 35, or section 36, the court must invite the accused to arrange for a legal representative to act for him for the purpose of the cross-examination, and if the invitation is not taken up, must consider whether it is necessary in the interests of justice for the witness to be cross-examined by a legal representative appointed to represent the interests of the accused.[22] If the court decides that it is necessary to do so, it will choose and appoint the representative, who will not be responsible to the accused.[23] In a trial on indictment with a jury in which an accused is prevented from cross-examining a witness in person under section 34, section 35, or section 36, the judge must give the jury such warning (if any) as is considered necessary to ensure that the accused is not prejudiced by any inferences that might be drawn from the fact that such cross-examination has been prevented or the fact that the cross-examination was carried out by a court-appointed legal representative.[24]

---

[13] See Ch 5.

[14] Section 35(2). Child means, where the offence falls within s 35(3)(a), a person under the age of 17; or, where the offence falls within s 35(3)(b), (c) or (d), a person under the age of 14. See n 11, above.

[15] A 'witness', for these purposes, does not include any other person who is charged with an offence in the proceedings: s 36(4)(a).

[16] Section 36(1).

[17] 'The quality of evidence' is to be construed in accordance with s 16(5) (s 36(4)(b)): see Ch 5 under F4 **Special measures directions for vulnerable and intimidated witnesses.**

[18] See Ch 5.        [19] Section 36(3).

[20] *R (Hillman) v Richmond Magistrates' Court* [2003] All ER (D) 455 (Oct), [2003] EWHC 2580 (Admin).

[21] Section 37(4).        [22] Section 38(1)–(4).        [23] Section 38(4) and (5).        [24] Section 39.

## 3  THE PERMITTED FORM OF QUESTIONING IN CROSS-EXAMINATION

The permitted form of questioning in cross-examination is most conveniently considered by reference to the objects of cross-examination. These are twofold. The cross-examiner will seek (i) to elicit evidence which supports his version of the facts in issue and (ii) to cast doubt upon the witness's evidence. Before giving further consideration to these objects of cross-examination, it will be useful to consider two general matters. First, it may be noted that a witness under cross-examination may be asked leading questions, even if he appears to be more favourable to the cross-examiner than to the party who called him, and whether the questions are directed to either the first or second of the two objects of cross-examination.[25] Secondly, it may be noted that all cross-examination is subject to an important general constraint which applies whether the questions to be put to the witness go to the matters in issue or to credit only. This is the discretion of the judge to prevent any questions which in his opinion are unnecessary, improper or oppressive. Cross-examination, a powerful weapon entrusted to counsel, should be conducted with restraint and with a measure of courtesy and consideration to the witness.[26] Thus counsel will be restrained from embarking on lengthy cross-examination on matters that are not really in issue[27] and from framing his questions in such a way as to invite argument rather than elicit evidence on the facts in issue.[28] In civil proceedings, CPR rule 32.1(3) bluntly provides that: 'The court may limit cross-examination.' When exercising this power, the judge must seek to give effect to the 'overriding objective',[29] which is to enable the court 'to deal with cases justly'.[30]

### (a)  Cross-examination as to matters in issue

The questions of the cross-examiner are not restricted to matters proved in examination-in-chief but may relate to any fact in issue or relevant to a fact in issue. This does not mean that evidence which is otherwise inadmissible can become admissible by being put to a witness in cross-examination: the ordinary rules relating to the inadmissibility of certain types of evidence operate to prevent such evidence from being elicited in cross-examination as well as in examination-in-chief. Thus in *R v Treacy*[31] the accused, charged with murder, was held by the Court of Criminal Appeal

---

[25]  *Parkin v Moon* (1836) 7 C&P 408.

[26]  See per Sankey LC in *Mechanical & General Inventions Co Ltd v Austin* [1935] AC 346 at 360, HL. See also the Code of Conduct of the Bar of England and Wales at paras 610 and 708; paras 5.10 and 5.11, Annexe F, General Standards; and paras 11.1 and 13.5, Annexe F, Standards applicable to Criminal Cases.

[27]  *R v Kalia* [1975] Crim LR 181, CA and *Mechanical & General Inventions Co Ltd v Austin* [1935] AC 346 at 359, HL.

[28]  See per Lord Hewart CJ in *R v Baldwin* (1925) 18 Cr App R 175. Thus counsel should not put to a witness what somebody else has said or is expected to say (at 178–9). Nor should the judge put such questions: *R v Wilson* [1991] Crim LR 838, CA.

[29]  CPR r 1.2.          [30]  CPR r 1.1(1). See further Ch 2 under **F2 Exclusionary discretion (a) Civil cases.**

[31]  [1944] 2 All ER 229.

to have been improperly cross-examined upon certain inadmissible confessions made on arrest and inconsistent with his testimony.[32] Similarly, a party is unable to admit an inadmissible hearsay statement contained in a document by handing it to a witness under cross-examination and requiring him to read it aloud. Counsel may, of course, properly produce the document to the witness and ask him if he accepts the contents as true,[33] and, if the witness does, the contents of the document become evidence in the case. However, if the witness does not accept the contents as true, it would be improper for counsel to request the witness to read aloud from the document, the contents of which remain inadmissible hearsay evidence.[34]

The principle laid down in *R v Treacy* that a person solely accused cannot be cross-examined by the *prosecution* in such a way as to reveal that he made a confession which has been ruled inadmissible, also obtains in favour of any co-accused of the maker of such a confession.[35] However, where an accused has made a confession statement which has been ruled inadmissible but which is relevant to the defence of a co-accused, then if the accused gives evidence which is inconsistent with his statement, he may be cross-examined on it by the *co-accused*, provided that the judge directs the jury not to treat it as evidence of its maker's guilt.[36]

### (b) Cross-examination as to credit

Concerning the second object of cross-examination, at common law there is a wide variety of ways in which the cross-examining party may seek to cast doubt upon the witness's evidence-in-chief and to show that the witness ought not to be believed on his oath. He may cross-examine him about omissions or inconsistencies in previous statements, if the omission or inconsistency will affect his likely standing with the tribunal of fact;[37] he may question him about his means of knowledge of the facts to which he has testified; he may challenge the quality of his memory and his powers of

[32] See also *R v Thomson* [1912] 3 KB 19 (inadmissible oral hearsay); *Re P* [1989] Crim LR 897, CA (a complaint in a sexual case inadmissible because not 'recent'); *R v Windass* (1988) 89 Cr App R 258 (inadmissible documentary hearsay); and *R v Gray* [1998] Crim LR 570, CA (an interview with a co-accused inadmissible as against the accused). In civil proceedings, see *Beare v Garrod* (1915) 85 LJKB 717, CA and *Sharp v Loddington Ironstone Co Ltd* (1924) 132 LT 229, CA.

[33] He should not, however, describe the nature or contents of the document to the court: see *R v Yousry* (1914) 11 Cr App R 13, CCA.

[34] *R v Gillespie* and *R v Simpson* (1967) 51 Cr App R 172, CA, applied in *R v Cooper* (1985) 82 Cr App R 74, CA; and *R v Cross* (1990) 91 Cr App R 115, CA.

[35] Per Winn J in *R v Rice* [1963] 1 QB 857 at 868–9.

[36] *R v Rowson* [1985] 2 All ER 539, CA, followed in *Lui-Mei Lin v R* [1989] AC 288, PC and *R v Corelli* [2001] Crim LR 913, CA. See also *R v O'Boyle* (1990) 92 Cr App R 202, CA. The co-accused may also cross-examine prosecution witnesses on the confession if to do so will affect the cogency of the prosecution evidence against him: *R v Beckford* (1991) 94 Cr App R 43, CA. See also *R v Myers* [1997] 4 All ER 314, HL (see Ch 13).

[37] He may do so even if evidence of the making of the statement would not be allowed because it is not 'relative to the subject matter of the indictment or proceeding' for the purposes of s 4 of the Criminal Procedure Act 1865: *R v Funderburk* [1990] 2 All ER 482, CA. Section 4 of the 1865 Act is considered below. But see also Juliet Cohen 'Errors of Recall and Credibility: Can omissions and discrepancies in successive statements reasonably be said to undermine credibility of testimony?' (2001) Med Leg J vol 69, pt 1, 25–34.

perception; he may ask him about his unreliability by reason of any physical or mental disability; and he may ask him to explain any omissions, mistakes, or inconsistencies in his evidence insofar as they militate against his veracity or plausibility. As to omissions, for example, where an accused is charged with a sexual offence and asserts fabrication on the part of the complainant, he may be cross-examined as to what facts are known to him that might explain why the complainant would make a false accusation against him.[38]

The cross-examining party may also ask questions about the witness's bad character and previous misconduct, including questions about previous convictions and questions with a view to showing his prejudice or bias. However, section 99 of the Criminal Justice Act 2003 abolishes the common law rules governing the admissibility of evidence of 'bad character' in criminal proceedings and the intention appears to be to abolish not only the rules as to the introduction of such evidence, but also the rules governing cross-examination about bad character. The effect is that in criminal cases such cross-examination is only permitted if it comes within one of a number of specified categories of admissibility set out in section 100 (non-defendant's bad character) or section 101 (defendant's bad character). Evidence of bad character, for the purposes of these provisions, is evidence of, or of a disposition towards, misconduct, other than evidence which 'has to do' with the alleged facts of the offence charged or evidence of misconduct in connection with the investigation or prosecution of that offence. Section 108 of the 2003 Act imposes an additional restriction in relation to offences committed by the accused when a child. Finally, under section 41 of the Youth Justice and Criminal Evidence Act 1999, in the case of sexual offences, except with the leave of the court, no question may be asked in cross-examination about any sexual behaviour of the complainant. The restrictions in the Criminal Justice Act 2003 are considered in Chapter 17. The restriction in section 41 of the Youth Justice and Criminal Evidence Act 1999 is considered below.

*Hobbs v Tinling*[39] and *R v Sweet-Escott*[40] set out the general principles, now applicable in civil proceedings only, as to the propriety of cross-examining a witness on his bad character. In *Hobbs v Tinling* Sankey LJ held that the court, in the exercise of its discretion to disallow questions as to credit in cross-examination, should have regard to the following considerations:[41]

1. Such questions are proper if they are of such a nature that the truth of the imputation conveyed by them would seriously affect the opinion of the court as to the credibility of the witness on the matter to which he testifies.

2. Such questions are improper if the imputation which they convey relates to matters so remote in time, or of such a character, that the truth of the

---

[38] *R v Brook* [2003] EWCA Crim 951, preferring *R v T* [1998] 2 NZLR 257 (New Zealand Court of Appeal) to *R v Palmer* (1998) 193 CLR 1 (Australian High Court).
[39] [1929] 2 KB 1 at 51, CA.          [40] (1971) 55 Cr App R 316, Assizes.
[41] The principles derive from s 148 of the Indian Evidence Act (I of 1872).

imputation would not affect, or would affect in a slight degree, the opinion of the court as to the credibility of the witness on the matter to which he testifies.

3. Such questions are improper if there is a great disproportion between the importance of the imputation made against the witness's character and the importance of his evidence.

In *R v Sweet-Escott* Lawton J posed the question: 'How far back is it permissible for advocates when cross-examining as to credit to delve into a man's past and to drag up such dirt as they can find there?' It was held that:

Since the purpose of cross-examination as to credit is to show that the witness ought not to be believed on oath, the matters about which he is questioned must relate to his likely standing after cross-examination with the tribunal which is trying him or listening to his evidence.[42]

## 4 THE EFFECT OF A PARTY'S FAILURE TO CROSS-EXAMINE

A party may decide that there is no need to cross-examine at all, especially if the witness in question has proved to be unfavourable or even hostile to the party calling him. A party's failure to cross-examine, however, has important consequences. It amounts to a tacit acceptance of the witness's evidence-in-chief. A party who has failed to cross-examine a witness upon a particular matter in respect of which it is proposed to contradict his evidence-in-chief or impeach his credit by calling other witnesses, will not be permitted to invite the jury or tribunal of fact to disbelieve the witness's evidence on that matter.[43] A cross-examiner who wishes to suggest to the jury that the witness is not speaking the truth on a particular matter must lay a proper foundation by putting that matter to the witness so that he has an opportunity of giving any explanation which is open to him. Thus in *Browne v Dunn*,[44] a libel action in which certain witnesses were not cross-examined on a particular matter, it was held by the House of Lords improper subsequently to invite the jury to disbelieve them. The rule, however, is not absolute or inflexible. Thus if it is proposed to invite the jury to disbelieve a witness on a matter, it is not always necessary to put to him explicitly that he is lying, provided that the overall tenor of the cross-examination is designed to show that his account is incapable of belief.[45] In other cases, as was acknowledged in *Browne v Dunn*, the story told by a witness may be so incredible that the matter upon which he is to be impeached is manifest, and in such circumstances it is unnecessary to waste time in putting questions to him upon it. The most effective

[42] (1971) 55 Cr App R 316 at 320.

[43] Evidence to contradict a witness which was not put to the witness in cross-examination, may still be admitted, provided that the witness is recalled and cross-examination of him re-opened in order to put the new evidence to him: *R v Cannan* [1998] Crim LR 284, CA.

[44] (1893) 6 R 67. See also *R v Hart* (1932) 23 Cr App R 202, CCA; *R v Bircham* [1972] Crim LR 430, CA; and *R v Fenlon* (1980) 71 Cr App R 307, CA.

[45] *R v Lovelock* [1997] Crim LR 821, CA.

cross-examination in such a situation would be, in the words of Lord Morris, 'to ask him to leave the box'. The rule has also been held to be unsuitable in the case of proceedings in magistrates' courts.[46]

## 5  CROSS-EXAMINATION ON DOCUMENTS

In civil proceedings, where a witness is called to give evidence at trial, he may be cross-examined on his witness statement,[47] whether or not the statement or any part of it was referred to during his evidence-in-chief.[48] Cross-examining counsel may also put to an opposing witness a statement taken on behalf of the cross-examiner's own client, but may not, it seems, cross-examine a witness called by an opposing party by reference to a statement of another witness who may or may not be called in the future by that opposing party or by someone other than the party on whose behalf the cross-examination is being conducted.[49]

The law relating to the cross-examination of a witness upon a previous statement made by him relative to the subject matter of the indictment or proceeding and inconsistent with his testimony, the proof of such a statement, and the evidential use to which it may be put, is governed by sections 4 and 5 of the Criminal Procedure Act 1865, which are considered later in this chapter. The common law and statutory rules on the cross-examination of a witness upon a document used by him to refresh his memory, the circumstances in which such a document may be put in evidence and the evidential effect of so doing, are considered in Chapter 6.

So far as other documents are concerned, there is an obscure common law rule that, where a party calls for and inspects a document in the possession of another party, that other party may require him to put it in evidence. This rule was applied in *Stroud v Stroud*.[50] A doctor was called as a witness on behalf of a wife petitioning for divorce on the ground of cruelty. Counsel for the husband, in the course of cross-examining the doctor, called for and read certain medical reports made by other doctors and in the possession of the witness. It was held that, as a result of this conduct, the wife could require that the reports be put in evidence. It is submitted that the rule in *Stroud v Stroud* is obsolete in civil proceedings, given the combined effect of the modern law on disclosure and the provisions of the Civil Evidence Act 1995, and should be abolished. Although Wrangham J clearly envisaged that the rule might apply to criminal proceedings, this would appear never to have happened. The Criminal Law Revision Committee recommended abolition of the rule in criminal proceedings on the grounds that (i) it may be impossible, or difficult to find out who supplied the information contained in the document, or what his authority was for

---

[46] *O'Connell v Adams* [1973] Crim LR 313, DC. See also *Wilkinson v DPP* [2003] All ER (D) 294 (Feb), [2003] EWHC 865 (Admin).

[47] See Ch 5.          [48] CPR r 32.11.

[49] *Fairfield-Mabey Ltd v Shell UK Ltd* [1989] 1 All ER 576, QBD, a decision on an earlier version of the rules.

[50] [1963] 3 All ER 539, relying on *Calvert v Flower* (1836) 7 C&P 386.

doing so and (ii) the information may have come from someone incompetent to give evidence to the same effect as the information.[51] For these reasons, and given the general obscurity of the rule, it is submitted that in criminal proceedings, also, it should be abolished.

## 6 PREVIOUS INCONSISTENT STATEMENTS

If it is put to a witness, in cross-examination, that he has made a previous oral or written statement inconsistent with his testimony, and the witness admits that he has made such a statement, no further proof of the making of the statement is needed or permitted.[52] However, if the witness denies making the statement, or does not distinctly admit that he made it, and the statement is 'relative to the subject matter of the indictment', then it may be proved against him. The proof of such a statement in both civil and criminal proceedings is governed by sections 4 and 5 of the Criminal Procedure Act 1865. Section 5 applies only to written statements, whereas section 4 applies to both oral and written statements.[53] Section 4 provides that:

If a witness, upon cross-examination as to a former statement made by him relative to the subject matter of the indictment or proceeding, and inconsistent with his present testimony, does not distinctly admit that he has made such a statement, proof may be given that he did in fact make it; but before such proof can be given, the circumstances of the supposed statement, sufficient to designate the particular occasion, must be mentioned to the witness, and he must be asked whether or not he has made such statement.

This section assumes, correctly, the existence of a common-law right to cross-examine a witness about a former inconsistent statement. It is not confined to previous statements made on oath.[54] The section refers to a witness who 'does not distinctly admit' his previous statement and accordingly applies not only to a witness who clearly denies the statement but also to a witness who, neither denying nor admitting the statement, is equivocal, asserts that he has no recollection of it, or refuses to answer.

Whether a statement is 'relative to the subject matter of the indictment or proceeding' is a matter within the discretion of the judge.[55] In *R v Funderburk*[56] F was charged with counts of sexual intercourse with a girl of 13. She gave evidence of a number of acts of intercourse with F, and her evidence of the first act clearly described the loss of her virginity. The defence claimed that she was lying and in order to explain how a girl of her age, if lying, could have given such detailed and varied accounts of the acts of intercourse, wished to show that she was sexually experienced and had either transposed to F experiences with others or fantasized about experiences with F. They wished (a) to put to her that she had told a Miss P that, before the first incident

---

[51] See para 223 and cl 29 of the draft Bill (Cmnd 4991).          [52] *R v P (GR)* [1998] Crim LR 663, CA.

[53] *R v Derby Magistrates' Court, ex p B* [1995] 4 All ER 526, HL, per Lord Taylor CJ at 533.

[54] *R v Hart* (1957) 42 Cr App R 47, CCA; *R v O'Neill* [1969] Crim LR 260, CA.

[55] See per Veale J in *R v Bashir and Manzur* [1969] 1 WLR 1303 at 1306.

[56] [1990] 2 All ER 482, CA. Cf, *sed quaere, R v Gibson* [1993] Crim LR 453, CA.

complained of, she had had sexual intercourse with two men, and (b) if she denied making this previous inconsistent statement, to call P to prove the conversation. As to (a), it was held that the proper test for cross-examination as to credit was not the test set out in the 1865 Act, but that suggested by Lawton LJ in *R v Sweet-Escott*,[57] and that the cross-examination should have been allowed because the jury might then have wished to reappraise the girl's evidence about the loss of her virginity. As to (b), it was held that the conversation, if denied, could have been proved, because the previous statement did not merely go to credit but was also 'relative to the subject matter of the indictment': where the disputed issue is a sexual one between two persons in private, the difference between questions going to credit and questions going to the issue is reduced to vanishing-point.[58]

Unlike section 4, section 5 applies only to previous written statements and constitutes a considerable departure from, and improvement on, the rules at common law.[59] It provides that:

A witness may be cross-examined as to previous statements made by him in writing or reduced into writing relative to the subject-matter of the indictment or proceeding, without such writing being shown to him; but if it is intended to contradict such witness by the writing, his attention must, before such contradictory proof can be given, be called to those parts of the writing which are to be used for the purpose of so contradicting him; provided always, that it shall be competent for the judge, at any time during the trial, to require the production of the writing for his inspection, and he may thereupon make such use of it for the purposes of the trial as he may think fit.

A witness under cross-examination is often taken by surprise when, without being shown a previous written statement made by him, he is asked by counsel whether he has ever said something inconsistent with his present testimony. Section 5 expressly permits the cross-examination of a witness about a previous statement contained in a document without that document being shown to him, but because the judge, pursuant to section 5, may require production of the document and make such use of it as he may think fit, the cross-examining party must have the document with him even if he does not intend to contradict the witness with it.[60]

If that party wishes to contradict the witness, he should, without reading the contents of the document aloud, hand it to the witness, direct his attention to the relevant part of its contents, ask him to read that part of the document to himself and then inquire whether he still wishes to stand by the evidence which he has given. If the witness adopts the previous statement, it becomes part of his evidence, which has therefore changed, and to that extent his credibility will have been impeached. If the witness adheres to his original evidence, there is no obligation on the cross-examining party to put the document in evidence, a course which he may well wish to avoid if the discrepancy is minor or the document, taken as a whole, tends to confirm rather than

---

[57] (1971) 55 Cr App R 316, above.

[58] See also *R v Nagrecha* [1997] 2 Cr App R 401, CA; and cf *R v Neale* [1998] Crim LR 737, CA.

[59] See *Queen Caroline's Case* (1820) 2 Brod&Bing 284.          [60] *R v Anderson* (1929) 21 Cr App R 178.

contradict the witness.[61] The cross-examining party, therefore, may simply accept the answer given and move on to some other matter. However, if the cross-examining party does wish to contradict the witness, he must then prove the document and put it in evidence.[62] Reading aloud the relevant parts of the previous statement, the cross-examining party will put it to the witness that the truth of the matter is contained in the earlier statement as opposed to his evidence. Once the document has been put in evidence, the tribunal of fact may inspect it in its entirety, looking at those passages, if any, which are consistent, as well as those which are inconsistent with the evidence given by the witness. However, although the *whole* document may be put before the jury, because under section 5 the judge may 'make such use of it for the purposes of the trial as he may think fit', he has a discretion to permit the jury to see only those parts on which the cross-examination was based, and not other parts relating to other unconnected matters.[63]

Where a prior inconsistent statement has been put in evidence under section 4 or section 5 of the 1865 Act, in both civil and criminal proceedings it is admitted not merely as evidence of inconsistency going to credit, but also as evidence of the matters stated. Under section 1 of the Civil Evidence Act 1995, in civil proceedings evidence shall not be excluded on the ground that it is hearsay. Section 6(3) and (5) of the 1995 Act provide as follows:

(3) Where in the case of civil proceedings section . . . 4 or 5 of the Criminal Procedure Act 1865 applies, which make provision as to— . . .
(b) the proof of contradictory statements made by a witness, and
(c) cross-examination as to previous statements made in writing,
this Act does not authorise the adducing of evidence of a previous inconsistent or contradictory statement otherwise than in accordance with those sections.

(5) Nothing in this section shall be construed as preventing a statement of any description referred to above from being admissible by virtue of s 1 as evidence of the matters stated.

As to criminal proceedings, section 119(1) of the Criminal Justice Act 2003, which is considered further in Chapter 10, provides as follows:

(1) If in criminal proceedings, a person gives oral evidence and—
(a) he admits making a previous inconsistent statement, or
(b) a previous inconsistent statement made by him is proved by virtue of section 3, 4 or 5 of the Criminal Procedure Act 1865,
the statement is admissible as evidence of any matter stated of which oral evidence by him would be admissible.

---

[61] For an example of a case where the admission of a prior inconsistent statement must have been, at best, a mixed blessing, see *R v Askew* [1981] Crim LR 398, CA, where defence counsel cross-examined the victim of an alleged rape on a statement made to the police in which she had incriminated the appellant. But see *R v Beattie* (1989) 89 Cr App R 302, CA, below.

[62] Per Channell B in *R v Riley* (1866) 4 F&F 964; *R v Wright* (1866) 4 F&F 967.

[63] *R v Beattie* (1989) 89 Cr App R 302, CA.

In both civil and criminal cases, therefore, the tribunal of fact will have to decide whether the truth is to be found in what the witness said on oath, in what he said in the previous statement but denied on oath, or is to be found elsewhere because neither version can be accepted as the truth of the matter.

## 7 COMPLAINANTS IN PROCEEDINGS FOR SEXUAL OFFENCES

In cases of rape and other sexual offences, whether, and to what extent, evidence may be adduced, or the complainant cross-examined, about her or his sexual experience with the accused or any other person, is now governed by sections 41–43 of the Youth Justice and Criminal Evidence Act 1999. These provisions, which restrict the use that the accused can make of evidence of the complainant's sexual history, reflect a recognition that it is bad for society if victims of sexual crimes do not complain, for fear that they will be harassed unfairly at trial by questions about their previous sexual experiences, because in consequence the guilty may escape justice. However, the intention underlying the provisions is also to counter what in the Canadian jurisprudence has been described as the twin myths that unchaste women are more likely to consent to intercourse and in any event are less worthy of belief.[64] Lord Steyn, in the leading case of *R v A (No 2)*, said:[65]

Such generalized, stereotyped and unfounded prejudices ought to have no place in our legal system. But even in the very recent past such defensive strategies were habitually employed. It resulted in an absurdly low conviction rate in rape cases. It also inflicted unacceptable humiliation on complainants in rape cases.

Prior to the coming into force of the provisions of the 1999 Act, a distinction was drawn between previous sexual experiences with the accused and with other men. Thus at common law, in prosecutions for rape, evidence of previous voluntary acts of sexual intercourse with the accused was admissible, on the grounds that such evidence rendered it more likely that the complainant consented on the occasion under investigation,[66] but under section 2 of the Sexual Offences (Amendment) Act 1976, now repealed, no evidence and no question in cross-examination could be adduced or asked about any sexual experience of the complainant with a person other than the accused unless the judge was satisfied that it would be unfair to the accused to refuse to allow the evidence to be adduced or the question to be asked. No such distinction exists under the 1999 Act, but a number of new and difficult distinctions have been introduced. The new provisions, together with the case law which they have generated, have given rise to lively academic debate.[67]

---

[64] See per McLachlin J in *R v Seaboyer* [1991] 2 SCR 577 (Supreme Court of Canada) at 604 and per Lords Steyn and Hutton in *R v A (No 2)* [2002] 1 AC 45 at [27] and [147] respectively.

[65] Ibid at [27].          [66] *R v Riley* (1887) 18 QBD 481, CCR.

[67] See Neil Kibble 'The Sexual History Provisions: Charting a course between inflexible legislative rules and wholly untrammelled judicial discretion?' [2000] Crim LR 274 and 'Judicial Perspectives on the Operation of s 41 and the Relevance and Admissibility of Prior Sexual History Evidence: Four Scenarios' [2005]

## (a) The restriction

Section 41(1) of the Youth Justice and Criminal Evidence Act 1999 provides as follows:

(1) If at a trial a person is charged with a sexual offence, then, except with the leave of the court—
(a) no evidence may be adduced, and
(b) no question may be asked in cross-examination,
by or on behalf of any accused at the trial, about any sexual behaviour of the complainant.

Section 41 applies to a number of other proceedings, as it applies to a trial, including any hearing held, between conviction and sentencing, for the purposes of deciding matters relevant to the court's decision as to how the accused is to be dealt with, and the hearing of an appeal; and references in section 41 to a person charged with an offence accordingly include a person convicted of an offence.[68] Under section 62, a 'sexual offence', for the purposes of section 41, means any offence under Part 1 of the Sexual Offences Act 2003.[69] 'Sexual behaviour' is defined in section 42(1)(c), which provides as follows:

(c) 'sexual behaviour' means any sexual behaviour or other sexual experience, whether or not involving any accused or other person, but excluding (except in s 41(3)(c)(i) and (5)(a)) anything alleged to have taken place as part of the event which is the subject matter of the charge against the accused;

Such a definition, it is submitted, covers not only physical advances of a sexual nature, but also verbal advances.[70] The definition also covers sexual behaviour or sexual experience even if it does not involve any other person. Leave would be required, for example, to introduce evidence of the possession of a vibrator, which could be relevant as evidence of the possible cause of the ruptured state of a complainant's hymen.[71] Whether behaviour or experience is 'sexual' cannot depend upon the perception of the complainant, because that would result in many vulnerable people, including children and those with learning difficulties, losing the protection of section 41.[72]

In *R v T*[73] it was held that normally, questions or evidence about the complainant's past false statements about sexual assaults, or about a failure to complain about the assault which is the subject matter of the charge at the time when she complained

---

Crim LR 190; Jennifer Temkin 'Sexual History Evidence—Beware the Backlash' [2003] Crim LR 217; Di Birch 'Rethinking Sexual History Evidence: Proposals for Fairer Trials' [2002] Crim LR 531 and 'Untangling Sexual History Evidence: A Rejoinder to Professor Temkin' [2003] Crim LR 370; and Mike Redmayne 'Myths, relationships and coincidences: The new problems of sexual history' (2003) 7 E&P 75.

[68] Section 42(3).        [69] See also s 42(1)(d) and (2).

[70] See *R v Hinds* [1979] Crim LR 111 and *R v Viola* [1982] 1 WLR 1138, CA, both decided under the 1976 Act.

[71] Cf *R v Barnes* [1994] Crim LR 691, CA.

[72] *R v E* [2005] Crim LR 227, CA.        [73] [2002] 1 WLR 632, CA.

about sexual assaults by others, are not 'about' any sexual behaviour of the complainant, because they relate not to her sexual behaviour but to her past statements or her past failure to complain, and the purpose of the 1999 Act was not to exclude such evidence. However, it was also held, *per curiam*, that if the defence wish to put questions about previous false complaints, they should seek a ruling from the judge that section 41 does not exclude them. It would be improper to put such questions as a device to smuggle in evidence about the complainant's past sexual behaviour. Moreover, in any such case the defence must have a proper evidential basis for asserting that the previous statement was both made and untrue. Without such a basis, the questions are not about lies but about sexual behaviour within the meaning of section 41(1).[74]

### (b) When the restriction may be lifted

Under section 41(2) of the 1999 Act, the court may not give leave in relation to any evidence or question unless satisfied (a) that the evidence or question is of the kind specified in section 41(3) or (5) and (b) a refusal of leave might render unsafe a conclusion of the jury or court on any 'relevant issues in the case', ie any issue falling to be proved by the prosecution or defence in the trial of the accused.[75] Subsection (3) covers evidence or questions relating to a relevant issue in the case and draws an important distinction between cases in which that issue is not an 'issue of consent' and cases in which it is. An 'issue of consent', for these purposes, means any issue whether the complainant in fact consented to the conduct constituting the offence with which the accused is charged (and accordingly does not include any issue as to the belief of the accused that the complainant so consented).[76] Subsection (5) covers evidence or questions to rebut or explain evidence adduced by the prosecution about any sexual behaviour of the complainant.

Section 41(2) to (8) provide as follows:

(2) The court may give leave in relation to any evidence or question only on an application made by or on behalf of an accused, and may not give such leave unless it is satisfied—
(a) that subsection (3) or (5) applies; and
(b) that a refusal of leave might have the result of rendering unsafe a conclusion of the jury or (as the case may be) the court on any relevant issue in the case.

(3) This subsection applies if the evidence or question relates to a relevant issue in the case and either—
(a) that issue is not an issue of consent; or
(b) it is an issue of consent and the sexual behaviour of the complainant to which the evidence or question relates is alleged to have taken place at or about the same time as the event which is the subject matter of the charge against the accused; or
(c) it is an issue of consent and the sexual behaviour of the complainant to which the evidence or question relates is alleged to have been, in any respect, so similar—

---

[74] Applied in *R v E* [2005] Crim LR 227, CA.     [75] Section 42(1)(a).     [76] Section 42(1)(b).

>    (i) to any sexual behaviour of the complainant which (according to evidence adduced or to be adduced by or on behalf of the accused) took place as part of the event which is the subject matter of the charge against the accused, or
>    (ii) to any other sexual behaviour of the complainant which (according to such evidence) took place at or about the same time as that event,
> that the similarity cannot reasonably be explained as a coincidence.

(4) For the purposes of subsection (3) no evidence or question shall be regarded as relating to a relevant issue in the case if it appears to the court to be reasonable to assume that the purpose (or main purpose) for which it would be adduced or asked is to establish or elicit material for impugning the credibility of the complainant as a witness.

(5) This subsection applies if the evidence or question—
> (a) relates to any evidence adduced by the prosecution about any sexual behaviour of the complainant; and
> (b) in the opinion of the court, would go no further than is necessary to enable the evidence adduced by the prosecution to be rebutted or explained by or on behalf of the accused.

(6) For the purposes of subsections (3) and (5) the evidence or question must relate to a specific instance (or specific instances) of alleged sexual behaviour on the part of the complainant (and accordingly nothing in those subsections is capable of applying in relation to the evidence or question to the extent that it does not so relate).

(7) Where this section applies in relation to a trial by virtue of the fact that one or more of a number of persons charged in the proceedings is or are charged with a sexual offence—
> (a) it shall cease to apply in relation to the trial if the prosecutor decides not to proceed with the case against that person or those persons in respect of that charge; but
> (b) it shall not cease to do so in the event of that person or those persons pleading guilty to, or being convicted of, that charge.

(8) Nothing in this section authorizes any evidence to be adduced or any question to be asked which cannot be adduced or asked apart from this section.

Before leave can be granted, the test in section 41(2)(b) must always be met. It would seem that 'a refusal of leave might have the result of rendering unsafe a conclusion of the jury . . . on any relevant issue' (which typically, in a rape case, will be the issue of consent or mistaken belief in consent), where to disallow the evidence or question would prevent the jury (or court) from hearing (taking into account) something which might cause them to change their minds on that issue. This hurdle, therefore, is not particularly high: the court need only be satisfied that a refusal of leave *might* have the consequence specified, not that such a consequence is probable or even likely.

The last point is of particular significance where section 41(3)(a) applies, ie where the evidence or question relates to a relevant issue in the case other than whether the complainant in fact consented, because in such cases section 41(2)(b) is the *only* condition to be met. The following examples may be given of issues falling within section 41(3)(a): (i) the defence of reasonable belief in consent; (ii) that the complainant was biased against the accused or had a motive to fabricate the evidence; (iii) that there is an alternative explanation for the physical conditions on which the Crown relies to establish that intercourse took place; and (iv) especially in the case of young complainants, that the detail of their account must have come from some other sexual activity before or after the event which provides an explanation for their knowledge of that activity.[77] As to (i), in *R v Barton*[78] it was stressed that, when considering the effect of the complainant's past sexual behaviour on the accused's belief in consent, whereas evidence of his belief that the complainant was consenting to intercourse is relevant, evidence of his belief that the complainant would consent if advances were made is irrelevant. *R v Barton* was a decision under section 2 of the 1976 Act relating to a defence of *mistaken* belief in consent, but it is submitted that the distinction remains valid for the purposes of a decision under section 41 of the 1999 Act relating to a defence of *reasonable* belief in consent under the Sexual Offences Act 2003.

In *R v Mokrecovas*,[79] a case of rape in which the defence was consent, the issue was whether it was open to the defence under section 41(3)(a) to cross-examine the complainant about an allegation that she had had consensual sexual intercourse with the accused's brother on two occasions in the 12 hours before the alleged rape. It was submitted that the cross-examination did not go to the issue of consent but to the separate issue of the complainant's motive for lying to her father when she first complained of rape. The foundations for the allegation of this motive were that the rape had occurred when the complainant had stayed away from home without the permission of her parents, that she had drunk to excess, and that she had stayed in the flat of the two brothers and her parents may well have thought that she had been guilty of sexual behaviour of which they would disapprove. It was held that cross-examination about sexual intercourse with the accused's brother would add nothing to these foundations for the allegation.

Subsections (3)(b) and (c) were designed to reverse the decision in *R v Riley*:[80] in a rape case, leave will not be granted in relation to evidence or questions about sexual behaviour of the complainant simply because the behaviour in question is previous voluntary sexual intercourse with the accused. In many cases, however, the jury will be likely to infer such behaviour by virtue of the other evidence in the case, as when evidence is introduced that the accused and the complainant are married or have cohabited for a period of time, and in this situation, it is submitted, the judge, rather than simply ignore the likelihood of such an inference being drawn, should direct the jury that any such inference can have no bearing on the issues to be decided.

To come within section 41(3)(b), the evidence or question must relate to sexual behaviour alleged to have taken place at or about the same time as the event which is the subject matter of the charge, other than anything alleged to have taken place as

---

[77] See per Lord Hope in *R v A (No 2)* [2002] 1 AC 45 at [79]. As to (i), Lord Hope referred to the defence of 'honest' belief in consent, but see now ss 1(1)(c) and 75–77 of the Sexual Offences Act 2003.

[78] (1986) 85 Cr App R 5.        [79] [2002] 1 Cr App R 226, CA.        [80] (1887) 18 QBD 481, above.

part of that event.[81] The distinction between sexual behaviour which took place at the same time as the event, and sexual behaviour which took place as part of the event, is not readily apparent. The meaning of 'the event which is the subject matter of the charge' is also unclear, but seems designed to embrace more than 'the conduct constituting the offence'.[82] The phrase 'at or about the same time as the event', although it provides a degree of elasticity, is a narrow temporal restriction and prima facie prohibits questions both as to a continuous period of cohabitation or sexual activity, and as to individual events more than a very limited period before or after the 'event', generally no more than 24 hours before or after the offence.[83] Section 41(3)(b) could cover behaviour such as any sexual advances made by the complainant towards the accused or other men shortly before or after 'the event' and other behaviour relevant to the issue of consent. An example would be an allegation that the complainant invited the accused to have sexual intercourse with her earlier in the evening.[84]

*R v Mukadi*[85] was a rape case in which the issue was consent. The complainant said that she went to the accused's flat to get to know him better and see if they might become friends and that although she did not want to go beyond kissing, she had reluctantly agreed to allow him to perform oral sex on her before intercourse took place. At trial, the judge refused leave to cross-examine her about an incident earlier in the day when she had got into a large expensive car driven by a man who was a good deal older than her and had later exchanged telephone numbers with him. On appeal, it was held that if this behaviour on the part of the complainant was not sexual behaviour, then section 41 did not apply, but in any event the cross-examination should have been allowed, because if the jury had heard about her earlier behaviour they could properly have inferred that when she got into the car she anticipated that some form of sexual activity would follow, which would have been relevant when assessing her evidence that when she went to the accused's flat she merely intended getting to know him with a view to becoming friends, and as a consequence it could have influenced their conclusions on the crucial issue of consent.

Subsection (3)(c) covers the sexual behaviour of the complainant with the accused (or another man) on another occasion, provided that it is sufficiently similar in nature to her behaviour during, or shortly before or after, the event which is the subject matter of the charge. It was included in the Act in response to the *Romeo and Juliet* scenario advanced by Baroness Mallalieu.[86] She envisaged a complainant in a rape case who says that the accused climbed up onto her balcony and into her bedroom, but who, on occasions both before and after the alleged rape—but not 'at or about the same time as the event' under section 41(3)(b)—invited men to re-enact the *Romeo and Juliet* balcony scene prior to consensual sexual intercourse. An example, provided

---

[81] Section 42(1)(c).    [82] A phrase also used in s 42(1): see s 42(1)(b).

[83] *R v A (No 2)* [2002] 1 AC 45, per Lords Slynn, Steyn and Hope at [9], [40] and [82] respectively. But see also per Lord Clyde at [132], who was of the view that it is undesirable to prescribe any test in terms of days or hours, while accepting that it may be difficult to extend the period to 'several days'.

[84] Ibid, per Lord Steyn at [40].    [85] [2004] Crim LR 373, CA.

[86] House of Lords Committee Stage, Hansard, 1 Feb 1999, col 45.

by Lord Steyn in *R v A (No 2)*,[87] would be, in a rape case in which the accused says that after consensual intercourse the complainant tried to blackmail him by alleging rape, evidence of a previous occasion when she similarly tried to blackmail him.[88] Such evidence is introduced under section 41(3)(c) not so much to show that history has been repeated as to indicate a state of mind on the part of the complainant which is potentially highly relevant to her state of mind on the occasion in question.[89] A comparison can be made between the wording of section 41(3)(c) and the concept of similar fact evidence as formulated by Lord Salmon in *DPP v Boardman*:[90] 'The similarity would have to be so unique or striking that common sense makes it inexplicable on the basis of coincidence.' However, as Lord Clyde said in *R v A (No 2)*[91] the phrase 'striking similarity' is not used in section 41(3)(c)—the standard is something short of a striking similarity. Elaborating on this, Lord Clyde said:[92]

It is only a similarity that is required, not an identity. Moreover the words 'in any respect' deserve to be stressed. On one view any single factor of similarity might suffice to attract the application of the provision, provided that it is not a matter of coincidence. That the behaviour was with the same person, the defendant, must be at least a relevant consideration. But if the identity of the defendant was alone sufficient as the non-coincidental factor that would seem to open the way in almost every case for a complete inquiry into the whole of the complainant's sexual behaviour with the defendant at least in the recent past, and that can hardly have been the intention of the provision. What must be found is a similarity in some other or additional respect. Further the similarity must be such as cannot reasonably be explained as coincidence. To my mind that does not necessitate that the similarity has to be in some rare or bizarre conduct.

However, in *R v A (No 2)* the House of Lords also recognized that as a matter of common sense a prior sexual relationship between the accused and the complainant may, depending on the circumstances, be relevant to the issue of consent, as a species of prospectant evidence which, although it cannot prove consent on the occasion in question, may throw light on the complainant's state of mind.[93] Recognizing further that section 41 is therefore prima facie capable of preventing an accused from putting forward relevant evidence which may be critical to his defence, whether one of consent or belief in consent, the House was of the unanimous view that it is possible under section 3 of the Human Rights Act 1998 to read section 41 of the 1999 Act, and in particular section 41(3)(c), as subject to the implied provision that evidence or questioning which is required to ensure a fair trial under Article 6 of the European Convention on Human Rights should not be treated as inadmissible. The result is that sometimes logically relevant evidence of sexual experience between a complainant

---

[87] [2002] 1 AC 45 at [42].

[88] See also *R v T* [2004] 2 Cr App R 32, CA, where the alleged rape took place in a climbing frame in a park and there was evidence that three to four weeks earlier the accused and the complainant had had consensual intercourse in the same climbing frame and had adopted the same positions (both standing and the complainant facing away from the accused).

[89] Per Lord Clyde in *R v A (No 2)* at [133].      [90] [1975] AC 421, HL at p. 462.

[91] [2002] 1 AC 45 at [133].      [92] Ibid at [135].      [93] See, eg, per Lord Steyn at [31].

and an accused may be admitted under section 41(3)(c). Lord Steyn said:[94] 'section 3 of the 1998 Act requires the court to subordinate the niceties of the language of section 41(3)(c) of the 1999 Act, and in particular the touchstone of coincidence, to broader considerations of relevance judged by logical and commonsense criteria of time and circumstances.' Members of the House were agreed as to the effect of its decision, namely that:

under s 41(3)(c) of the 1999 Act, construed where necessary by applying the interpretative obligation under s 3 of the 1998 Act, and due regard always being paid to the importance of seeking to protect the complainant from indignity and from humiliating questions, the test of admissibility is whether the evidence (and questioning in relation to it) is nevertheless so relevant to the issue of consent that to exclude it would endanger the fairness of the trial under art 6 of the Convention. If this test is satisfied, the evidence should not be excluded.[95]

Thus where there has been a recent close and affectionate relationship between the complainant and the accused, it is probable that the evidence will be relevant and admissible, not to prove consent, but to show the complainant's specific mindset towards the accused, namely her affection for him. But where, as in *R v A (No 2)* itself, there have only been some isolated acts of intercourse, even if fairly recently, without the background of an affectionate relationship, it is probable that the evidence will not be relevant. It is not possible to state with precision where the line is to be drawn—it will depend on the facts of the individual case as assessed by the trial judge.[96] *R v A (No 2)* was applied in *R v R*[97] where it was held that permission should have been given to the defence to cross-examine the complainant about both a previous consensual sexual relationship with the accused and consensual sexual intercourse with the accused occurring some 11 months after the alleged offence.

It is very much more difficult to show relevance to the issue of consent in the case of evidence of the complainant's sexual behaviour with men other than the accused than in the case of evidence of sexual behaviour with the accused himself.[98] In *R v White*,[99] W denied rape and said that the complainant had asked him for money which he had refused to give her, and that after consensual intercourse he had woken up to find her with his wallet. It was held that the judge had properly refused an application to cross-examine the complainant on her previous and ongoing activities as a prostitute. A prostitute was as entitled as any other person to say 'no' to sex and the fact that the complainant was a prostitute did not mean that she was more ready than any other to say 'yes'. The bare fact that the complainant was a prostitute was therefore irrelevant to the issue of consent. There had to be something about the specific circumstances that satisfied the test in section 41(3)(c). *R v A (No 2)*, it was held, could be distinguished, since it did not concern the introduction of evidence of sexual behaviour with men other than the accused, and it would take a very special

---

[94] At [45].    [95] Per Lord Steyn at [46].    [96] Per Lord Hutton at [152].
[97] [2003] All ER (D) 346 (Oct), [2003] EWCA Crim 2754.
[98] See per Lord Clyde at [125]–[127].    [99] [2004] All ER (D) 103 (Mar).

case to admit such evidence in circumstances where it could not be admitted by an ordinary reading of section 41.

Section 41(4) only applies where 'the purpose' or the 'main purpose' for adducing the evidence or asking the question is to impugn the credibility of the complainant. In *R v Martin*[100] a case of indecent assault involving enforced oral sex, M alleged that the complainant had fabricated her evidence because he had rejected her advances. It was held that the defence should have been allowed to question her about his allegation that two days earlier she had not merely pestered him for sex, but had performed an act of oral sex upon him, after which he had rejected her. It was held that although one purpose of the questioning was to impugn the credibility of the complainant, it also went to the accused's credibility and strengthened the defence case of fabrication, because the jury might have interpreted a rejection after the performance of oral sex as more hurtful than rejection after mere verbal advances.

Section 41(4), construed literally, would mean that where the purpose or main purpose of adducing evidence or asking a question about any sexual behaviour of the complainant is to impugn her credibility, the evidence or question cannot be regarded as relating to a relevant issue in the case, even where it plainly does relate to such an issue and where to refuse leave to adduce the evidence or ask the question, might have the result, to use the words of section 41(2)(b), 'of rendering unsafe a conclusion of the jury . . . on any relevant issue in the case'. Such a construction, however, would in very large measure seem to defeat the purposes of section 41(3)(b) and (c), because when the issue is consent and the sexual behaviour of the complainant is relevant to that issue, in many if not most cases it will satisfy the test in section 41(2)(b) on the basis that the jury will hear something which will cause them to change their minds about the complainant's evidence in relation to the issue of consent, which all too often, of course, will be to impugn the credibility of the complainant. For these reasons, it is submitted, section 41(4) should be taken to mean that no evidence or question shall be regarded as relating to a relevant issue if the purpose (or main purpose) is to suggest nothing more than that the complainant, by reason of her sexual behaviour, ought not to be believed on oath.

Subsection (5) concerns evidence, or a question, in rebuttal or explanation of prosecution evidence about *any* sexual behaviour of the complainant, including anything alleged to have taken place as part of the event which is the subject matter of the charge.[101] Thus, where, in a rape case, the complainant gives evidence that she has only ever enjoyed sexual relations with her husband or lover (X), evidence or questions might be permitted about previous acts of intercourse with the accused (Y) or some other man (Z). The subsection only allows the defence to rebut *evidence* adduced by the prosecution about the sexual behaviour of the complainant, and not,

---

[100] [2004] 2 Cr App R 354, CA.          [101] See s 42(1)(c).

it seems, inferences about her sexual behaviour that may reasonably be drawn from evidence adduced by the prosecution.[102]

Section 41(6) would rule out, for example, evidence or questions revealing the complainant to be, for example, a prostitute or of a promiscuous nature. Nor will the requirements of section 41(6) be met, in the case of a prostitute, by the information contained in a list of previous convictions for prostitution.[103] However, in some cases, of course, evidence or questions relating to specific instances may well allow the jury to infer that the complainant was a prostitute or promiscuous, as would happen, for example, if evidence were to be introduced that the accused had on a number of previous occasions agreed to sleep with men for money.

### (c) The procedure on applications under section 41

An application for leave under section 41 shall be heard in private and in the absence of the complainant.[104] After the court has reached its decision, it must state in open court, but in the absence of the jury (if there is one), its reasons for giving or refusing leave and, if it gives leave, the extent to which evidence may be adduced or questions asked in pursuance of the leave.[105]

## 8  FINALITY OF ANSWERS TO COLLATERAL QUESTIONS

### (a) The rule

A party eliciting from a witness under cross-examination evidence unfavourable to his case, may understandably seek to adduce evidence in rebuttal. To allow that party to adduce such evidence without restriction, however, would lead to a multiplicity of issues, some of which might be of minimal relevance to the facts in issue in the case, and thereby prolong the trial unnecessarily. As a general rule, therefore, the answers given by a witness under cross-examination to questions concerning collateral matters, that is matters which are irrelevant to the issues in the proceedings, must be treated as final. Finality for these purposes does not mean that the tribunal of fact is obliged to accept the answers as true, but simply that the cross-examining party is not permitted to call further evidence with a view to contradicting the witness.

Whether a question is collateral is not always easy to decide. According to the often cited test formulated by Pollock CB in *A-G v Hitchcock*,[106] if the witness's answer is a matter on which the cross-examining party would be allowed to introduce evidence-in-chief, because of its connection with the issues in the case, then the matter is not

---

[102]  Cf *R v Redguard* [1991] Crim LR 213, CA, a decision under the 1976 Act. R was charged with raping the complainant in her flat. His defence was consent. The complainant having given evidence that she would only allow her boyfriend to stay at her flat, the defence were entitled to cross-examine her about a consensual sexual encounter with a man who had stayed at her flat two weeks after the alleged rape.

[103]  *R v White* [2004] All ER (D) 103 (Mar).        [104]  Section 43(1).

[105]  Section 43(2). A magistrates' court must also cause such matters to be entered in the register of its proceedings: s 43(2).

[106]  (1847) 1 Exch 91 at 99.

collateral and may be rebutted.[107] Relevance, however, is a question of degree, the answer to which may turn on whether the matter which the cross-examining party seeks to prove is a single fact which is easy of proof or a broad issue which will require the jury to embark on a difficult and complex task.[108] Questions which go merely to the credit of the witness are clearly collateral. However, where the disputed issue is a sexual one between two persons in private, the difference between questions going to credit and questions going to the issue is reduced to vanishing-point because sexual intercourse, whether or not consensual, most often takes place in private and leaves few visible traces of having occurred, so that the evidence is often effectively limited to that of the parties, and much is likely to depend upon the balance of credibility between them.[109] This principle, however, is not confined to cases involving sexual intercourse.[110]

Whether cross-examination goes merely to credit or can be said to be relevant to the issue in the proceedings is clearly a question of some difficulty. The nicety of the distinction is apparent in the authorities, some of which are difficult to reconcile. In *R v Burke*[111] an Irish witness who gave evidence through an interpreter and was cross-examined about his knowledge of English, denied that he was able to speak the language. The witness's ability to speak English being irrelevant to any matter directly in issue in the proceedings, it was held that evidence in rebuttal was inadmissible. In *A-G v Hitchcock*[112] a maltster was charged with the use of a cistern in breach of certain statutory requirements. A prosecution witness, who gave evidence that the cistern had been used, was asked in cross-examination whether he had not said to one Cook that the Excise officers offered him £20 to give evidence that the cistern had been used. The witness denied this allegation and it was held that counsel for the defence was not permitted to call Cook to give evidence in rebuttal of what the witness had said. Pollock CB said:[113]

it is totally irrelevant to the matter in issue, that some person should have thought fit to offer a bribe to the witness to give an untrue account of a transaction, and it is of no importance whatever, if that bribe was not accepted.

Some of the criminal authorities as to the application of the rule, such as *R v Edwards*,[114] must be treated with caution insofar as they involved questioning the

---

[107] The test seems to be circular, but its utility may lie in the fact that the answer is an instinctive one, based on the sense of fair play of the prosecutor and the court rather than any philosophic or analytic process: per Henry J in *R v Funderburk* [1990] 2 All ER 482 at 491, CA. But see also per Evans LJ in *R v Neale* [1998] Crim LR 737, CA: the decision is ultimately a matter of common sense and logic.

[108] *R v S* [1992] Crim LR 307, CA.

[109] Per Henry J in *R v Funderburk* [1990] 2 All ER 482 at 491, citing *Cross on Evidence* (6th edn London 1985) 295.

[110] See *R v Nagrecha* [1997] 2 Cr App R 401, CA, a case of indecent assault, and *R v David R* [1999] Crim LR 909, CA; but see also s 41 of the Youth Justice and Evidence Act 1999.

[111] (1858) 8 Cox CC 44.          [112] (1847) 1 Exch 91; cf *R v Phillips* (1936) 26 Cr App R 17, CCA, below.

[113] (1847) 1 Exch 91 at 101.

[114] [1991] 2 All ER 266 at 274, CA. See also *R v Clancy* [1997] Crim LR 290, CA and *R v Irish* [1995] Crim LR 145.

witness about his previous misconduct or disposition towards such misconduct. As previously noted, in criminal proceedings, the asking of questions about a witness's bad character is governed by sections 100 and 101 of the Criminal Justice Act 2003, which are considered in Chapter 17.

## (b) The exceptions

To the general rule on the finality of answers to collateral questions there are three exceptions, although it may be that the categories of exception are not closed.[115]

*(i) Previous convictions.* Under section 6 of the Criminal Procedure Act 1865:

If, upon a witness being lawfully questioned as to whether he has been convicted of any felony or misdemeanour, he either denies or does not admit the fact, or refuses to answer, it shall be lawful for the cross-examining party to prove such conviction.[116]

Section 6 applies to both civil and criminal proceedings. In criminal proceedings, a witness will only be 'lawfully questioned' as to his previous convictions where the questions are lawful having regard to the relevant provisions of the Criminal Justice Act 2003, namely section 100 in the case of the previous convictions of a non-defendant and section 101 in the case of the previous convictions of the defendant. These provisions are considered in Chapter 17. In civil proceedings, cross-examination of any witness about 'spent' convictions is prohibited by section 4(1) of the Rehabilitation of Offenders Act 1974,[117] unless the judge is satisfied that it is not possible for justice to be done except by admitting the convictions.[118] This section does not apply in criminal proceedings, but under a *Practice Direction* issued by the Lord Chief Justice in 1975 no reference should be made to a spent conviction if that can be 'reasonably avoided'.[119] However, according to *R v Corelli*,[120] the *Practice Direction* does not operate to remove an unfettered statutory entitlement of a co-accused to cross-examine another co-accused on his previous convictions.[121] Subject to *R v Corelli*, the effect of the *Practice Direction* is to give the judge a wide discretion with the exercise of which the Court of Appeal will be loath to interfere. Thus in *R v Lawrence*,[122] where the trial judge refused the defence permission to question the

---

[115] *R v Funderburk* [1990] 2 All ER 482, per Henry J at 492, CA.

[116] However, if the witness accepts the conviction but claims his innocence, the cross-examining party may be prevented from adducing evidence in rebuttal: see *R v Irish* [1995] Crim LR 145, CA.

[117] Exceptions to the applicability of s 4(1) are to be found in Sch 3 to the Rehabilitation of Offenders Act (Exceptions) Order 1975 (SI 1975/1023) and in s 189 of the Financial Services Act 1986.

[118] Section 7(3). Evidence of the conviction may be admitted under s 7(3) not only if relevant to an issue in the case, but also if relevant merely to the credit of the witness, but the judge should weigh its relevance and its prejudicial effect and only admit it if satisfied that otherwise the parties would not have a fair trial or the witness's credit could not be fairly assessed: *Thomas v Metropolitan Police Comr* [1997] 1 All ER 747, CA.

[119] See now *Practice Direction (Criminal Proceedings: Consolidation)* [2002] 1 WLR 2870, para 6. See also s 108 of the Criminal Justice Act 2003 (Ch 17).

[120] [2001] Crim LR 913, CA.

[121] The statutory entitlement in the case arose under s 1(3)(iii) of the Criminal Evidence Act 1898. See now s 101(1)(e) of the Criminal Justice Act 2003 (Ch 17).

[122] [1995] Crim LR 815, CA.

victim of a wounding in detail on his twenty previous spent convictions, most of which were for offences of dishonesty, but did allow questions on four more recent offences, the Court of Appeal held that although it might have exercised the discretion differently and permitted cross-examination on one of the spent convictions, which involved perverting the course of justice, the judge had not erred in principle. In *R v Evans*,[123] on the other hand, a case of wounding with intent, the defence being self-defence, it was held that the judge should have allowed cross-examination of the victim on her previous but spent convictions for dishonesty and violence because, evidentially speaking, there was a head-on collision between the accused and the victim.

There is authority to suggest that, in civil proceedings, subject to section 4(1) of the Rehabilitation of Offenders Act 1974, section 6 permits a witness to be cross-examined about his convictions irrespective of their relevance to his credibility or the issues in the case. In *Clifford v Clifford*[124] Cairns J, although not referring expressly to section 6, said:

It has never, I think, been doubted that a conviction for any offence could be put to a witness by way of cross-examination as to credit, even though the offence was not one of dishonesty.

In that case, a divorce suit, it was held that a wife charged with cruelty could be cross-examined about her adultery with a view to discrediting her as a witness. It seems clear, however, that cross-examination about a witness's previous convictions is subject to the general power of the judge to restrain unnecessary, irrelevant, or unduly oppressive questions in cross-examination.[125] In civil proceedings, a judge may use the general exclusionary discretion under CPR rule 32[126] to limit cross-examination on previous convictions to the convictions of offences of dishonesty, although where sitting with a jury should be more hesitant in exercising the discretion.[127] It remains to mention that, in criminal proceedings, section 101(1)(g) of the Criminal Justice Act 2003 operates as a powerful disincentive to the use of section 6 by defence counsel in cross-examination of prosecution witnesses. We shall see in Chapter 17 that, under section 101(1)(g), the accused, by making an attack on another person's character, thereby renders admissible evidence of his own bad character.

*(ii) Bias.* 'It has always been permissible to call evidence to contradict a witness's denial of bias or partiality towards one of the parties and to show that he is prejudicial so far as the case being tried is concerned.'[128] Thus where a female servant of the claimant is called as his witness and denies in cross-examination that she is his kept mistress, the defendant may call evidence to contradict her.[129] Under s 99 of the Criminal Justice Act 2003, this common law principle has been abolished in criminal

---

[123] [1992] Crim LR 125, CA.        [124] [1961] 1 WLR 1274 at 1276.
[125] See, eg, per Lawton J in *R v Sweet-Escott* (1971) 55 Cr App R 316, above.        [126] See Ch 2.
[127] *Watson v Chief Constable of Cleveland Police* [2001] All ER (D) 193 (Oct), [2001] EWCA Civ 1547.
[128] Per Geoffrey Lane LJ in *R v Mendy* (1976) 64 Cr App R 4, CA at 6.
[129] *Thomas v David* (1836) 7 C&P 350.

proceedings to the extent that it allows the introduction of evidence of the witness's bad character, ie evidence of, or of a disposition towards, misconduct on his part. However, much evidence of bias is likely to remain admissible at common law, because outside the statutory definition of evidence of bad character in section 98 of the 2003 Act, which excludes 'evidence of, or of a disposition towards misconduct . . . which has to do with the alleged facts of the offence with which the defendant is charged, or is evidence of misconduct in connection with the investigation or prosecution of that offence'. Alternatively, to the extent that the evidence is not admissible on that basis, it is likely to be admitted under section 100(1)(b) of the 2003 Act, ie as evidence of the bad character of a person other than the defendant which has substantial probative in relation to a matter which is in issue in the proceedings and of substantial importance in the context of the case as a whole.[130] Thus the *outcome* in each of the following examples of the common law doctrine is likely to remain the same.

In *R v Shaw*[131] it was held that the accused may call evidence to contradict a prosecution witness who, in cross-examination, denies having threatened to be revenged on the accused following a quarrel with him. A more recent example is provided by *R v Mendy*,[132] where in the course of a trial for assault, and while a detective was giving evidence, a man in the public gallery was observed to be taking notes. The man was seen to leave the court and hold a conversation, apparently concerning the detective's evidence, with the accused's husband, who, as a prospective witness, had been kept out of court in accordance with the normal practice. The husband subsequently gave evidence and under cross-examination denied that he had spoken to the man in question. The Court of Appeal held that the trial judge had properly allowed evidence to be given in rebuttal. The jury were entitled to know that, in order to deceive them and help the accused, the witness was prepared to cheat.

The line dividing questions put to a witness in cross-examination concerning facts tending to show prejudice or bias, and those concerning collateral facts on which the witness's answers must be treated as final, is often a very fine one. Although in *A-G v Hitchcock*,[133] as we have seen, it was held that the witness's denial of an alleged statement by him that he had been *offered* a bribe, being a collateral matter, could not be contradicted, the court acknowledged that where a witness denies *acceptance* of a bribe to testify, a matter tending to show his partiality, evidence in rebuttal is admissible. *R v Phillip*[134] also falls to be contrasted with the actual decision in *A-G v Hitchcock*. The accused was charged with incest. His defence was that the principal prosecution witnesses, his two daughters, had been 'schooled' by their mother into giving false evidence. In cross-examination, the girls denied that their testimony was no more than a repetition of what their mother had told them to say. The girls also denied that on separate occasions each of them had admitted to another person that their evidence in previous criminal proceedings against their father for indecent

---

[130] Sections 99 and 100 of the 2003 Act are considered in Ch 17.      [131] (1888) 16 Cox CC 503.
[132] (1976) 64 Cr App R 4.      [133] (1847) 1 Exch 91.      [134] (1936) 26 Cr App R 17.

assault had been false. The trial judge refused to allow defence counsel to call two women to whom these admissions were alleged to have been made. The Court of Criminal Appeal, quashing the conviction, held that this evidence was admissible on the grounds that the questions were directed not to the credibility of the two girls but went to the very foundation of the accused's defence.

In *R v Busby*[135] police officers were cross-examined on the basis that they had made up statements attributed to the accused and indicative of his guilt, and had threatened W, a potential witness for the defence, to stop him giving evidence. The allegations were denied. The trial judge ruled that W, who was subsequently called for the defence, could not give evidence that he had been threatened by the officers, because this would go solely to their credit. The Court of Appeal, allowing the appeal against conviction, held that the judge had erred: W's evidence was relevant to an issue which had to be tried, in that if true it showed that the police were prepared to go to improper lengths in order to secure a conviction, and this would have supported the accused's case that the statements attributed to him had been fabricated. In *R v Funderburk*[136] *R v Busby* was treated as having created a new exception to the rule against finality, but in *R v Edwards*[137] it was held that the facts came within the exception of bias and that if the case could not be explained on that basis, it was inconsistent with the general rule itself.

*(iii) Evidence of physical or mental disability affecting reliability.* The credibility of a witness may be impeached by expert medical evidence which shows that he suffers from some physical or mental disability that affects the reliability of his evidence.

If a witness purported to give evidence of something which he believed that he had seen at a distance of 50 yards, it must surely be possible to call the evidence of an oculist to the effect that the witness could not possibly see anything at a greater distance than 20 yards, or the evidence of a surgeon who had removed a cataract from which the witness was suffering at the material time and which would have prevented him from seeing what he thought he saw. So, too, must it be allowable to call medical evidence of mental illness which makes a witness incapable of giving reliable evidence, whether through the existence of delusions or otherwise.

These examples were given by Lord Pearce in *Toohey v Metropolitan Police Comr.*[138] Toohey was convicted with others of an assault with intent to rob. The defence was that the alleged victim had been drinking and that while they were trying to help him by taking him home, he became hysterical and accused them of the offence charged. The trial judge held that, although a doctor called for the defence could give evidence that when he examined the victim he was hysterical and smelt of alcohol, he could not give evidence that in his opinion drink could exacerbate hysteria and that the alleged victim was more prone to hysteria than a normal person. The Court of Criminal Appeal dismissed the appeal, but the House of Lords, quashing the convictions, held

---

[135] (1981) 75 Cr App R, CA.          [136] [1990] 2 All ER 482, CA at 486.
[137] [1991] 2 All ER 266, CA at 274.
[138] [1965] AC 595 at 608. See also *R v Eades* [1972] Crim LR 99, Assizes.

that the doctor's evidence had been improperly excluded.[139] Lord Pearce, in a speech with which the other members of the House concurred, held that the evidence was admissible not only because of its relevance to the facts in issue, regardless of whether or not it affected the credibility of the alleged victim as a witness, but also to show that the evidence of the alleged victim was unreliable.

Medical evidence is admissible to show that a witness suffers from some disease or defect or abnormality of mind that affects the reliability of his evidence. Such evidence is not confined to a general opinion of the unreliability of the witness but may give all the matters necessary to show, not only the foundation of and reasons for the diagnosis, but also the extent to which the credibility of the witness is affected.[140]

Expert opinion evidence is admissible in relation to matters requiring special knowledge or expertise, not matters within the ordinary experience and knowledge of the tribunal of fact. Thus expert medical evidence on the reliability of a witness will only be admissible if the disability from which the witness suffers is a proper subject of such evidence. As Lord Pearce observed in *Toohey v Metropolitan Police Comr*:[141]

Human evidence ... is subject to many cross-currents such as partiality, prejudice, self-interest and above all, imagination and inaccuracy. Those are matters with which the jury, helped by cross-examination and common sense, must do their best. But when a witness through physical (in which I include mental) disease or abnormality is not capable of giving a true or reliable account to the jury, it must surely be allowable for medical science to reveal this vital hidden fact to them.

In *R v MacKenney*[142] the accused were convicted of murder. At their trial, they had alleged that the chief prosecution witness had fabricated his evidence and wished to call a psychologist by whom the witness had refused to be examined. The psychologist had watched the witness give his evidence and as a result had formed the opinion that he was a psychopath who was likely to be lying and whose mental state was such that his demeanour and behaviour when giving evidence would not convey the usual indications to the jury as to when he was lying. The evidence of the psychologist was ruled inadmissible. The convictions were upheld on appeal. On referral to the Court of Appeal by the Criminal Cases Review Commission, there was fresh evidence from a psychiatrist. He, too, had not examined the witness. His opinion was very similar to that of the psychologist who had attended the trial. It was held that the evidence of the psychologist would today be admissible and that the absence of an examination by the expert went to the weight to be attached to his opinion, not its admissibility. Deciding the reference on the fresh evidence, the conviction was quashed.

In *R v Robinson*[143] it was held that although a party, A, cannot call a witness of fact, W, and then, without more, call a psychologist or psychiatrist to give reasons why the

---

[139] The Court of Criminal Appeal was bound by the case of *R v Gunewardene* [1951] 2 KB 600, which the House of Lords overruled.

[140] [1965] AC 595 at 609.     [141] [1965] AC 595 at 608.     [142] [2004] 2 Cr App R 32, CA.

[143] [1994] 3 All ER 346, CA. See also *R v Beard* [1998] Crim LR 585, CA.

jury should regard W as reliable, if the other party, B, proposes to call an expert to say that W should be regarded as unreliable due to some mental abnormality outside the jury's experience, then A may call an expert in rebuttal or even, anticipating B's expert, as part of his own case. Where B does not call an expert, but puts a case in cross-examination that W is unreliable by reason of mental abnormality, this may also be open to rebuttal by expert evidence, although much may depend on the nature of the abnormality and of the cross-examination. If such expert evidence is admitted, it must be restricted to the specific challenge, and should not extend to 'oath-helping'. Thus on the facts of that case, since B had not called evidence impugning W's reliability and had not put a specific case in cross-examination that W was peculiarly suggestible or liable to fantasize as a result of her mental impairment, expert evidence to suggest the opposite was inadmissible.

The rule against 'oath-helping', however, will not necessarily prevent a non-expert from giving evidence as to the good character of a witness from which his likely reliability may be inferred. In *R v Tobin*,[144] a case of indecent assault on a girl, the defence claimed that the sexual activity had been initiated by the girl. The accused gave evidence that he was a married man with no previous convictions for sexual offences and called five character witnesses. The girl's mother was allowed to give evidence that she had never had problems with her daughter, who had done well at school, got on well with her siblings, was very polite and quiet, and had been brought up to respect people. It was held that the evidence did go to boost the claimant's credibility, but since full evidence had been given about the accused's character, the court's sense of fair play was not offended by admission of the evidence as to the complainant's character.

# B  RE-EXAMINATION

A witness who has been cross-examined may be re-examined by the party who called him.[145] The object of re-examination is, in broad terms, to repair such damage as has been done by the cross-examining party insofar as he has elicited evidence from the witness supporting his version of the facts in issue and cast doubt upon the witness's evidence-in-chief.

The cardinal rule of re-examination is that it must be confined to such matters as arose out of the cross-examination.[146] Thus although the witness may be asked to clarify or explain any matters, including evidence of new facts, which arose in

---

[144] [2003] Crim LR 408, CA.

[145] Even a hostile witness, apparently, may be re-examined by the party who called him (on any new matters which arose out of cross-examination by the other party to the action): *R v Wong* [1986] Crim LR 683 (Crown Court).

[146] The rule applies in the case of a witness whose name was 'on the back of the indictment' and who was called by the prosecution merely to allow the defence to cross-examine him: *R v Beezley* (1830) 4 C&P 220.

cross-examination, questions on other matters may only be asked with the leave of the judge. In *Prince v Samo*[147] Lord Denman CJ held that where a witness under cross-examination has given evidence of part of a conversation, evidence may not be given in re-examination about everything that was said in that conversation, but only about so much of it as is in some way connected with the evidence given in cross-examination. For example, the witness may be re-examined about things said which qualify or explain the statement on which he was cross-examined, but not about things said on other distinct and unrelated matters.

Evidence which was not admissible in examination-in-chief may become admissible in re-examination as a result of the nature of the cross-examination. Thus although in criminal proceedings an earlier statement of a witness which is consistent with his testimony on a particular matter is generally inadmissible in chief, it will become admissible in re-examination if, in cross-examination, it is suggested to him that his evidence on that matter is a recent fabrication.[148] It remains to note that leading questions may be asked in re-examination to the same limited extent as in examination-in-chief.

---

[147] (1838) 7 Ad&El 627. See also *Queen Caroline's Case* (1820) 2 Brod&Bing 284.
[148] See, eg, *R v Oyesiku* (1971) 56 Cr App R 240, CA (see Ch 6).

# 8

# CORROBORATION AND CARE WARNINGS

'Any risk of the conviction of an innocent person is lessened if conviction is based upon the testimony of more than one acceptable witness.'[1] In civil, as well as criminal cases, it would not be unreasonable to expect a general rule requiring a party who seeks to prove certain facts by the testimony of a single witness, to adduce additional independent evidence, by way of confirmation or support, so that the tribunal of fact is double-sure before it makes a particular finding, or gives judgment, in that party's favour. Although this is the case in most civil law jurisdictions, there is no general rule to this effect in English law. Thus in a criminal trial, provided that the jury is satisfied beyond all reasonable doubt of the guilt of the accused, a conviction may be based on the testimony of a single prosecution witness who swears that he saw the accused commit the crime in question, and this remains the case even if part or all of his evidence is contradicted by the testimony of one or more witnesses called by the defence.[2] A party is, of course, free to adduce evidence which corroborates or supports the other evidence that he has tendered,[3] and to the extent that this would strengthen an otherwise weak case, as a matter of common sense he would be well advised to do so. As a general rule, however, there is (a) no requirement that evidence be corroborated and (b) no requirement that the tribunal of fact be warned of the danger of acting on uncorroborated evidence.

This chapter is concerned with the exceptions to the general rule. There are three categories of exception. The first is where corroboration (probably in a technical sense) is required as a matter of law. In cases falling within this category, the ambit of which is clearly defined, comprising as it does four cases governed by statute (speeding, perjury, treason and attempts to commit such offences), a conviction cannot be based on uncorroborated evidence and, if it is, will be reversed on appeal. Thus in the absence of such corroboration, the judge should direct an acquittal. Depending on the statute in question, the corroboration may be required to take a particular form, such

---

[1] Per Lord Morris in *DPP v Hester* [1973] AC 296, HL at 315.

[2] However, a conviction in such circumstances may be set aside where it is unsafe: see *R v Cooper* [1969] 1 QB 267 at 271, CA. In civil cases, a new trial may be ordered where the verdict of the jury is against the weight of the evidence: see per Lord Selborne in *Metropolitan Rly Co v Wright* (1886) 11 App Cas 152, HL at 153.

[3] Subject to the inherent power of the court to prevent, for reasons of cost and time, the admission of superfluous evidence.

as the evidence of another witness, or may be permitted to take any form, whether testimony, real evidence or documentary evidence.

In the second category, which comprises a miscellany of different cases, neither corroboration in a technical sense nor supportive evidence is required as a matter of law, but in appropriate circumstances the tribunal of fact should be warned to exercise caution before acting on the evidence of certain types of witness, if unsupported. The witnesses in question include: (i) accomplices giving evidence for the prosecution; (ii) complainants in sexual cases; (iii) other witnesses whose evidence may be tainted by an improper motive; and (iv) children. Whether a warning is given at all is a matter of judicial discretion dependent on the circumstances of the case, and therefore failure to give a warning will not necessarily furnish a good ground of appeal. Where a warning is given, the strength of the warning and the extent to which the judge should elaborate upon it, for example by referring to the potentially supportive material, also depends upon the particular circumstances of the case.

The third category comprises five cases in which corroboration in a technical sense is not required as a matter of law, and there is no obligation to warn the tribunal of fact of the danger of acting on the evidence in question *simply* by reason of the fact that it is uncorroborated or unsupported, but there is a special need for caution which has led to requirements analogous to, but distinct from, those relating to the first two categories. The five cases are confessions by mentally handicapped persons, identification evidence, lip-reading evidence, cases of Sudden Infant Death Syndrome (colloquially 'cot deaths'), and unconvincing hearsay. The last of these cases is governed by section 125 of the Criminal Justice Act 2003, which requires a judge to direct an acquittal or discharge the jury if satisfied that the case against the accused is based wholly or partly on a hearsay statement and the evidence provided by the statement is so unconvincing that the accused's conviction would be unsafe. It is convenient to consider section 125 in Chapter 10, 'Hearsay in criminal cases'.[4]

# A CORROBORATION REQUIRED BY STATUTE

At common law a trial judge was required as a matter of law to warn the jury of the danger of acting on certain types of evidence if uncorroborated. Corroboration, for these purposes, bore a technical meaning. Corroboration, where required by statute, probably bears the same technical meaning. This appears to have been the view of Lord Reading CJ in *R v Baskerville*.[5] Moreover, corroboration in the technical sense *is* required in the case of the statutory provision relating to perjury;[6] and although, as we shall see, neither the perjury provision nor the provisions relating to speeding and

---

[4] See Ch 10 under **B9 Other safeguards (c) Stopping the case where the evidence is unconvincing.**
[5] [1916] 2 KB 658 at 667.
[6] See para 3.9, Law Commission Working Paper No 115 (1990), citing *R v Hamid* (1979) 69 Cr App R 324.

treason expressly require 'corroboration', section 2(2)(g) of the Criminal Attempts Act 1981 has been drafted on the assumption that that is exactly what they require. It is necessary to consider first, therefore, the meaning of corroboration in the technical sense.

To be capable of amounting to corroboration in the technical sense, evidence must be (i) relevant, (ii) admissible, (iii) credible, (iv) independent and (v) evidence which implicates the accused in the way that the specific statute requires. The first two requirements[7] apply to evidence generally and need no further explanation in the present context. As to the third requirement: 'Corroboration can only be afforded . . . by a witness who is otherwise to be believed. If a witness's testimony falls of its own inanition, the question of his . . . being capable of giving corroboration does not arise.'[8] Under the fourth requirement, independence, the evidence must emanate from a source other than the witness who is to be corroborated.[9] The fifth requirement, implication, is best explored by reference to the statutory provisions themselves. Before turning to them, it remains to note the respective functions of the judge and jury.[10] Where a judge does give a direction to the jury on corroboration, he must explain what it is. No particular form of words is necessary and there is no need even to use the word 'corroboration' provided that the requirements of credibility, independence and implication are made clear.[11] The judge should also indicate what evidence is (and is not) capable of being corroboration.[12] Having directed the jury as to what evidence is capable in law of amounting to corroboration, the judge should explain that it falls to them, as the tribunal of fact, to decide whether the evidence does in fact constitute corroboration.[13]

Corroboration is now required by statute only in the four cases already mentioned. The requirement of corroboration in the case of procuration offences was abrogated by the Criminal Justice and Public Order Act 1994.[14]

[7] See per Scarman LJ in *R v Scarrott* [1978] QB 1016, CA at 1021.

[8] Per Lord Hailsham in *DPP v Kilbourne* [1973] AC 729 at 746. See also per Lord Morris in *DPP v Hester* [1973] AC 296 at 315 ('Corroborative evidence will only fill its role if it itself is completely credible') and *R v Thomas* (1985) 81 Cr App R 331, CA.

[9] See, eg, *R v Whitehead* [1929] 1 KB 99, CCA.

[10] It is submitted that the authorities that follow, which mainly related to common law corroboration requirements, also apply where corroboration is required by statute.

[11] See *R v Fallon* [1993] Crim LR 591, CA.

[12] *R v Charles* (1976) 68 Cr App R 334n; *R v Cullinane* [1984] Crim LR 420, CA; and *R v Webber* [1987] Crim LR 412, CA. If the judge fails to do so, this is unlikely to result in a successful appeal if there was in fact ample corroboration and the Court of Appeal is in no doubt that if a proper direction had been given, the jury would still have convicted: see *R v McInnes* (1989) 90 Cr App R 99, CA.

[13] *R v Tragen* [1956] Crim LR 332; *R v McInnes* (1989) 90 Cr App R 99, CA.

[14] Section 33(1), repealing the relevant provisions of the Sexual Offences Act 1956, which required corroboration in the case of procuring a woman to have unlawful sexual intercourse, administering drugs to obtain or facilitate sexual intercourse, causing prostitution and procuring girls under 21 years of age.

## 1 SPEEDING

The opinion evidence of non-experts is generally inadmissible.[15] One of the exceptions to this rule is opinion evidence relating to speed. Section 89(2) of the Road Traffic Regulation Act 1984, in recognition of the danger of such evidence being inaccurate, provides that a person charged with an offence of driving a motor vehicle on a road at an excessive speed 'shall not be liable to be convicted solely on the evidence of one witness to the effect that in the opinion of the witness the person prosecuted was driving the vehicle at a speed exceeding a specified limit'. The opinion evidence of two or more people that a vehicle was exceeding the speed limit is sufficient to justify a conviction under this provision provided that their evidence relates to the speed of the vehicle at the same place and time.[16] The provision only applies to evidence of mere opinion and not to evidence of fact. Thus in *Nicholas v Penny*[17] it was held that magistrates could convict on the evidence of a police officer who had checked a vehicle's speed from the speedometer of his own car which was driven at an even distance behind the defendant's car. Speedometers and other similar devices[18] will be presumed, in the absence of evidence to the contrary, to have been working properly at the material time.

In *Crossland v DPP*[19] Bingham LJ said: 'It is plain . . . that the subsection is intended to prevent the conviction of a defendant on evidence given by a single witness of his unsupported visual impression of a defendant's speed.' An expert in accident reconstruction testified that he had inspected the scene of a road traffic accident, including skid marks and damage to the defendant's car, carried out speed and braking tests on the car, and calculated that its speed had been not less than 41 mph. It was held that this was not just the opinion evidence of one witness: the expert had also described the objectively determined phenomena on which his opinion was based.

## 2 PERJURY

The rationale for the requirement of corroboration in relation to offences of perjury is not entirely clear. Historically, perjury was first punished in the Star Chamber, which usually required a second witness. Prior to the statutory provisions, the requirement at common law was held to be justified 'else there is only oath against oath'.[20] This argument did not seem strong to the Criminal Law Revision Committee 'as there may be more than oath against oath when the falsity of the accused's evidence is corroborated although not by a second witness'. Furthermore, 'there are many cases where corroboration is not required but the decision depends on the choice between two pieces of sworn evidence'. However, a majority of the Committee felt that to make a

---

[15] See Ch 18.    [16] *Brighty v Pearson* [1938] 4 All ER 127.
[17] [1950] 2 KB 466.
[18] See *Collinson v Mabbott* (1984) *The Times*, 10 Oct, DC (corroboration by radar gun); and *Burton v Gilbert* [1984] RTR 162, DC (corroboration by radar speed meter).
[19] [1988] 3 All ER 712 at 714.    [20] *R v Muscot* (1713) 10 Mod Rep 192.

prosecution for perjury too easy might discourage persons from giving evidence and create the danger of a successful party to litigation, his evidence having been preferred, seeking to have his adversary, or his adversary's witnesses, prosecuted for perjury.[21]

Section 13 of the Perjury Act 1911 provides that:

A person shall not be liable to be convicted of any offence against this Act, or of any other offence declared by any other Act to be perjury or subornation of perjury, or to be punishable as perjury or subornation of perjury, solely upon the evidence of one witness as to the falsity of any statement alleged to be false.

The judge is therefore required to direct the jury that, before a conviction of perjury can be recorded, there must be evidence before them, which they accept, of more than one witness, ie either evidence of at least one other witness or some other supporting evidence, by way of confession or otherwise, which supplements that of a single witness.[22]

The section requires corroboration not only in relation to the offence of perjury in judicial proceedings, but also in relation to the many other offences under the Perjury Act of making false statements, on oath, in statutory declarations or otherwise, but not in judicial proceedings.[23] The corroboration need relate only to the *falsity* of the statement in question. Thus, if the accused admits that the statement was untrue, the prosecution need call no evidence to prove this fact and section 13 does not apply.[24] Nor does the section apply to certain allegations of perjury contrary to section 1(1) of the 1911 Act, which provides that if any person lawfully sworn as a witness wilfully makes a statement material in the proceedings which he knows to be false *or does not believe to be true*, he shall be guilty of an offence. It is clear, from the words italicized, that proof of falsity is not a prerequisite to a conviction. Thus in those cases, albeit rare, in which the prosecution elects to proceed on the basis that the truth or falsehood of the statement forms no part of their case, section 13 does not apply.[25] Where section 13 does apply, it will be satisfied if two witnesses testify to having heard the accused admit the falsity of the statement *on the same occasion*.[26] The section, however, does not require the corroboration to take the form of a second witness or indeed any other particular form.[27]

---

[21]  Paras 178 and 190, 11th Report (Cmnd 4991).

[22]  See *R v Hamid* (1979) 69 Cr App R 324, CA and *R v Carroll* (1993) 99 Cr App R 381, CA. Failure to direct the jury in accordance with s 13 may afford grounds for a successful appeal: see *R v Rider* (1986) 83 Cr App R 207, CA.

[23]  The Criminal Law Revision Committee and the Law Commission (para 45, Published Working Paper No 33, *Perjury and Kindred Offences*) saw no need to preserve the latter requirement.

[24]  *R v Rider* (1986) 83 Cr App R 207, CA.       [25]  Ibid.

[26]  *R v Peach* [1990] 2 All ER 966, CA.

[27]  See *R v Threlfall* (1914) 10 Cr App R 112: a letter suborning another to commit perjury in relation to the same matter in respect of which the false statement was made may constitute corroboration.

## 3 TREASON

Section 1 of the Treason Act 1795 requires corroboration in the form of evidence given by a second witness. It provides that a person charged with the offence of treason by compassing the death or restraint of the Queen or her heirs shall not be convicted except on 'the oaths of two lawful and credible witnesses'. The Criminal Law Revision Committee recommended the repeal of this provision.[28]

## 4 ATTEMPTS

Under section 2(2)(g) of the Criminal Attempts Act 1981, any provision whereby a person may not be convicted on the uncorroborated evidence of one witness (including any provision requiring the evidence of not less than two credible witnesses) shall have effect with respect to an offence under section 1 of the Act of attempting to commit an offence as it has effect with respect to the offence attempted.

# B CARE WARNINGS

## 1 ACCOMPLICES TESTIFYING FOR THE PROSECUTION AND COMPLAINANTS IN SEXUAL CASES

### (a) The background

Prior to the Criminal Justice and Public Order Act 1994, there existed at common law a category of exception to the general rule under which, although corroboration (in the technical sense) was not required as a matter of law, the tribunal of fact had to be warned, as a matter of law, of the danger of acting on evidence if not corroborated (in the technical sense). This obligatory warning was required in respect of the evidence of (a) accomplices testifying on behalf of the prosecution[29] and (b) complainants in sexual cases.[30] As to the former, accomplices were defined as: (i) parties to the offence in question; (ii) handlers of stolen goods, in the case of thieves from whom they receive, on the trial of the latter for theft; and (iii) parties to another offence committed by the accused in respect of which evidence is admitted under the similar fact evidence doctrine.[31] Whether a particular witness was an accomplice was a question

---

[28] Para 195, 11th Report (Cmnd 4991).

[29] But see *Galler v Galler* [1954] P 252: in divorce proceedings 'an adulterer who gives evidence of his own adultery is in the same position as an accomplice in a criminal case'. See also *Fairman v Fairman* [1949] P 341.

[30] The need for such a warning was not confined to criminal proceedings. In *Mattouk v Massad* [1943] AC 588, a civil suit, the Privy Council was of the opinion that to accept the uncorroborated evidence of a girl aged 15 in charging a man with sexual intercourse was very dangerous and required great caution.

[31] *Davies v DPP* [1954] AC 378, HL. An accomplice, for these purposes, also included a thief from whom a handler has received goods, on the trial of the latter for receiving (*R v Vernon* [1962] Crim LR 35) but

usually answered by the witness himself, by confessing to participation, by pleading guilty to it or by being convicted of it. If not answered by the witness himself, the question whether he was in fact an accomplice was for the jury (provided that there was evidence on which a reasonable jury could have concluded that the witness was an accomplice).[32] As to complainants in sexual cases, the warning was required in respect of the victims, whether male or female,[33] of sexual offences.[34]

There were only two exceptions to the requirement that a warning be given. A warning was not required where an accomplice gave evidence, on behalf of the prosecution, which was mainly favourable to the accused and more harm would have been done to the accused by giving the warning than by not giving it.[35] Nor was a warning required in sexual cases in which identification was in issue, but not the commission of the offence itself.[36] Subject to these exceptions, failure to give the warning furnished a good ground of appeal. The warning to be given to the jury became known as the 'full' warning, which comprised four parts:

1.  The warning itself, ie that it was dangerous to convict on the uncorroborated evidence of the 'suspect' witness but that if they, the jury, were satisfied of the truth of such evidence, they might none the less convict.

2.  An explanation of the meaning of corroboration in the technical sense.

3.  An indication of what evidence was (and was not) capable in law of amounting to corroboration.

4.  An explanation that it fell to the jury, as the tribunal of fact, to decide whether that evidence did in fact constitute corroboration.

By reason of section 32 of the Criminal Justice and Public Order Act 1994, full warnings are no longer required. In order to understand the effect of section 32, it is important to consider first both the justification for the rules requiring a full warning and the reasons for their abolition. The justification given for the requirement of a warning in the case of an accomplice giving evidence for the prosecution was that such a witness may have a purpose of his own to serve: he may give false evidence against the accused out of spite, to exaggerate or even invent the accused's role in the crime, or with a view to minimizing the extent of his own culpability. Concerning sexual offences (as in procuration cases), the requirement of a warning stemmed from an assumption that such a charge is easy to make but difficult to refute. There is also

---

not an *agent provocateur* (*R v Mullins* (1848) 3 Cox CC 526), a child victim of a sexual offence (*R v Pitts* (1912) 8 Cr App R 126) or a woman upon whose immoral earnings the accused was charged with having lived (per Lord Reading CJ in *R v King* (1914) 10 Cr App R 117, CCA) unless, on the facts, there was evidence of aiding and abetting the accused, eg evidence of collecting money on behalf of the accused from other prostitutes (as in *R v Stewart* (1986) 83 Cr App R 327, CA).

[32]  *Davies v DPP* [1954] AC 378.          [33]  *R v Burgess* (1956) 40 Cr App R 144, CCA.

[34]  The rule did not apply to other kinds of offence, even if their commission was allegedly accompanied by some form of sexual activity on the part of the accused: *R v Simmons* [1987] Crim LR 630, CA.

[35]  See *R v Royce-Bentley* [1974] 1 WLR 535, CA.          [36]  See *R v Chance* [1988] 3 All ER 225, CA.

'the danger that the complainant may have made a false accusation owing to sexual neurosis, jealousy, fantasy, spite or a girl's refusal to admit that she consented to an act of which she is now ashamed'.[37] Such a danger may be hidden, yet the nature of the evidence may well make jurors sympathetic to the complainant and so prejudice them against the accused.

The reasons in favour of the abolition of mandatory corroboration warnings were compelling.[38] The first and most serious objection was that the rules applied irrespective of the circumstances of the particular case and the credibility of the particular witness. Thus on the facts it may have been obvious that there was no danger of the 'suspect' witness giving false evidence (eg a case of indecent assault on an elderly person), yet the judge still had to give the warning. Secondly, since many sexual offences are committed in circumstances in which corroboration is difficult if not impossible to obtain, the requirement was capable of resulting in the acquittal of the guilty. In cases involving the sexual abuse of children, the mandatory warning simply compounded the difficulty of securing a conviction.[39] Thirdly, the full warning had become extremely complex, not least because of the technical rules on what constituted corroboration, and this often led to successful appeals. Fourthly, there was an element of self-contradiction in directing jurors that it was 'dangerous' to convict on uncorroborated evidence and then proceeding to direct them that they could nonetheless do so. Finally, there was some evidence to suggest that where a warning was given, far from operating as a safeguard for the accused, the jury were more likely to convict.[40]

### (b) Section 32 of the Criminal Justice and Public Order Act 1994

Section 32 of the Criminal Justice and Public Order Act 1994 provides as follows:

(1) Any requirement whereby at a trial on indictment it is obligatory for the court to give the jury a warning about convicting the accused on the uncorroborated evidence of a person merely because that person is—
(a) an alleged accomplice of the accused, or
(b) where the offence charged is a sexual offence, the person in respect of whom it is alleged to have been committed,
is hereby abrogated.

. . .

(3) Any requirement that—
(a) is applicable at the summary trial of a person for an offence, and
(b) corresponds to the requirement mentioned in subsection (1) above . . .
is hereby abrogated.

---

[37] Para 186, 11th Report, Criminal Law Revision Committee (Cmnd 4991).

[38] See generally paras 183–6, 11th Report, Criminal Law Revision Committee (Cmnd 4991); Law Commission Working Paper No 115 (1990); Law Commission Report No 202 (Cm 1620) (1991); and Ch 8, Royal Commission on Criminal Justice (Cm 2263) (1993).

[39] See para 5.17, *Report of the Advisory Group on Video Evidence* (Home Office, 1989).

[40] See paras 2.9 and 2.18, Law Commission Working Paper No 115 and *Vetrovec v R* (1982) 136 DLR (3d) 89 at 95.

Thus in cases involving the evidence of an alleged accomplice or of a complainant in a sexual case, section 32 has simply abrogated any requirement whereby it was *obligatory* for the tribunal of fact to be given a full warning—the judge still has a discretion to give some form of warning whenever he considers it necessary to do so. The leading authority on section 32 is *R v Makanjuola*,[41] in which Lord Taylor CJ summarized the relevant principles as follows:[42]

1. Section 32(1) abrogates the requirement to give a corroboration direction in respect of an alleged accomplice or a complainant of a sexual offence simply because a witness falls into one of those categories.

2. It is a matter for the judge's discretion what, if any, warning he considers appropriate in respect of such a witness, as indeed in respect of any other witness in whatever type of case. Whether he chooses to give a warning and in what terms will depend on the circumstances of the case, the issues raised and the content and quality of the witness's evidence.

3. In some cases, it may be appropriate for the judge to warn the jury to exercise caution before acting upon the unsupported evidence of a witness. This will not be so simply because the witness is a complainant of a sexual offence nor will it necessarily be so because a witness is alleged to be an accomplice. There will need to be an evidential basis for suggesting that the evidence of the witness may be unreliable. An evidential basis does not include mere suggestions by cross-examining counsel.

4. If any question arises as to whether the judge should give a special warning in respect of a witness, it is desirable that the question be resolved by discussion with counsel in the absence of the jury before final speeches. (The judge will often consider that no special warning is required at all. Where, however, the witness has been shown to be unreliable, he or she may consider it necessary to urge caution. In a more extreme case, if the witness is shown to have lied, to have made previous false complaints, or to bear the defendant some grudge, a stronger warning may be thought appropriate and the judge may suggest it would be wise to look for some supporting material before acting on the impugned witness's evidence. We stress that these observations are merely illustrative of some, not all, of the factors which judges may take into account in measuring where a witness stands in the scale of reliability and what response they should make at that level in their directions to the jury.)[43]

5. Where the judge does decide to give some warning in respect of a witness, it will be appropriate to do so as part of the judge's review of the evidence and his comments as to how the jury should evaluate it rather than a set-piece legal direction.

6. Where some warning is required, it will be for the judge to decide the strength and terms of the warning. It does not have to be invested with the whole florid regime of the old corroboration rules.

7. It follows that we emphatically disagree with the tentative submission [that if a judge does give a warning, he should give a full warning and should tell the jury what corroboration is in the technical sense and identify the evidence capable of being

---

[41] [1995] 3 All ER 730, CA.    [42] [1995] 3 All ER 730 at 733.
[43] The bracketed material is set out in an earlier part of the judgment (at 732).

corroborative]. Attempts to re-impose the straitjacket of the old corroboration rules are strongly to be deprecated.

8. Finally, this court will be disinclined to interfere with a judge's exercise of his discretion save in a case where that exercise is unreasonable in the *Wednesbury* sense.[44]

## (c) 'Supporting material'

Following *R v Makanjuola*, if there is an evidential basis for suggesting that the witness may be unreliable, and the trial judge therefore decides to direct the jury that it would be wise to look for some 'supporting material', the judge is no longer required to identify for the jury what evidence is and is not capable of being corroboration in the technical sense. However, once such a direction is given, it has been held that it is then incumbent on the judge to identify any 'independent supporting evidence'.[45] It seems reasonably clear that such evidence may be furnished by the accused himself, as when evidence is given of an out-of-court confession or the accused makes a damaging admission in the course of giving his evidence.[46] It seems equally clear that it may be furnished by (i) the accused's lies, whether told in or out of court, (ii) his silence, (iii) his refusal to consent to the taking of samples, or (iv) his misconduct. It will be convenient to consider, briefly, these examples before turning to some items of evidence which, arguably, cannot constitute 'supporting material'.

Lies by the accused may amount to 'supporting material' depending on the nature of the lie and the nature of the other evidence in the case. It is submitted that the criteria for determining whether a lie constitutes 'supporting material' are the same as those previously employed for determining whether a lie amounted to corroboration in the technical sense. Those criteria, applicable to lies whether told in or out of court, were established in *R v Lucas*:[47]

To be capable of amounting to corroboration the lie ... must first of all be deliberate.[48] Secondly it must relate to a material issue. Thirdly the motive for the lie must be a realisation of guilt and a fear of the truth. The jury should in appropriate cases be reminded that people sometimes lie, for example, in an attempt to bolster up a just cause, or out of shame or out of a wish to conceal disgraceful behaviour from their family. Fourthly the statement must clearly be shown to be a lie by evidence other than that of the [witness] who is to be corroborated, that is to say by admission or by evidence from an independent witness.

Thus where an accused, charged with a sexual offence, tells the police that on the evening in question he did not leave his house, but subsequently admits that this statement was false, his lie may be used to support the evidence of the victim that the

---

[44] See *Associated Provincial Picture Houses Ltd v Wednesbury Corpn* [1948] 1 KB 223. This is a heavy burden for an appellant to discharge: see *R v R* [1996] Crim LR 815, CA.

[45] *R v B (MT)* [2000] Crim LR 181, CA.

[46] See *R v Dossi* (1918) 13 Cr App Rep 158, CCA: on a charge of indecently assaulting a girl, an admission by the accused, in court, that he had innocently fondled her, is some corroboration of her evidence.

[47] [1981] QB 720, CA at 724.

[48] A lie being an *intentional* false statement, the meaning of the first requirement is obscure.

offence had taken place near to the accused's home,[49] because 'a false statement . . . may give to a proved opportunity a different complexion from what it would have borne had no such false statement been made'.[50] *R v Lucas* itself concerned the fourth criterion. The appeal was allowed because the jury had been invited to prefer the evidence of an accomplice to that of the accused and then to use their disbelief of the accused as corroboration of the accomplice. The direction was erroneous because the 'lie' told by the accused was not shown to be a lie by evidence other than that of the accomplice who was to be corroborated.[51]

Where a person is accused of a crime, by a person speaking to him on even terms, in circumstances such that it would be natural for him to reply, evidence of his silence may be admitted, at common law, to show that he admits the truth of the charge made[52] and may constitute 'supporting material'.[53] Such material, it is submitted, may also be derived from inferences properly drawn from (i) the accused's failure to mention facts when questioned by a constable or on being charged with an offence, (ii) his silence at trial, (iii) his failure or refusal to account for objects, substances, marks or presence at a particular place,[54] or (iv) his refusal to consent to the taking of 'intimate samples'.[55] Supporting material may also take the form of evidence of the accused's misconduct on some other occasion admitted under the similar fact evidence doctrine as evidence relevant to the question of guilt on the charge before the court.[56]

Whether a given item of evidence is capable of amounting to 'supporting material' is not always as easy as the above examples might suggest. For example, in a case of rape in which the complainant is shown to have made previous false complaints and a warning is properly given, should any of the following items be treated as 'supporting material', and in any event, how should the judge direct the jury in their regard: (i) a recent complaint admitted under the exception to the rule against previous consistent statements; (ii) evidence of the distressed condition of the complainant; and (iii) medical evidence showing that someone had had intercourse with the complainant at a time consistent with her evidence? There are compelling reasons to suggest that each of these items, by itself, should not be treated as 'supporting material' and the judge should direct the jury accordingly. As to a recent complaint, the trial judge should, at the least, explain to the jury that the evidence emanates from the

---

[49] See *Credland v Knowler* (1951) 35 Cr App R 48, DC. For an example of a lie told in court, see *Corfield v Hodgson* [1966] 2 All ER 205.

[50] Per Lord Dunedin in *Dawson v McKenzie* (1908) 45 SLR 473.

[51] See also per Lord MacDermott in *Tumahole Bereng v R* [1949] AC 253 at 270.

[52] See *R v Mitchell* (1892) 17 Cox CC 503; *R v Chandler* [1976] 3 All ER 105, CA; *Parkes v R* [1976] 1 WLR 1251; and generally Ch 13.

[53] See *R v Cramp* (1880) 14 Cox CC 390, a decision on corroboration in the technical sense.

[54] See Criminal Justice and Public Order Act 1994, ss 34–37 (Ch 14).

[55] See *R v (Robert William) Smith* (1985) 81 Cr App R 286, CA and Police and Criminal Evidence Act 1984, s 62(10) (Ch 14).

[56] See Ch 17.

complainant herself.[57] As to evidence of distress, the same point could be made, but such a direction would be inappropriate if, for example, the distress was witnessed shortly after the offence, the complainant was unaware that she was being observed and there is nothing to suggest that she put on an act and simulated distress.[58] However, in appropriate cases the jury should now be alerted to the very real risk that distress may have been feigned.[59] Concerning medical evidence of intercourse, the trial judge might sensibly direct the jury that it does not, by itself, show that intercourse took place without consent or that the accused was a party to it.[60] It is to be hoped that commonsensical guidance and helpful directions of this kind will not be regarded as 'attempts to re-impose the straitjacket of the old corroboration rules'. It would be a pity if the baby of common sense were to be thrown out with the corroboration bath water.

## (d) Sexual cases in which identification is in issue

There is nothing to suggest that the principles established in *R v Makanjuola* should not apply to sexual cases in which identification is in issue. If the identity of the offender is in issue, but the fact that someone committed the offence is not in issue, either because formally admitted by the accused or, if not formally admitted, because there has been no suggestion by the defence that there is any doubt as to the commission of the offence, it will normally suffice to direct the jury, in accordance with *R v Turnbull*,[61] about the need for caution before convicting on identification evidence; a further warning about the complainant's evidence as to the *offence* is only required where there is an evidential basis for suggesting that her evidence in that regard is unreliable.[62]

---

[57] Such evidence was not corroboration in the technical sense because not independent of the witness requiring to be corroborated: see *R v Whitehead* [1929] 1 KB 99, CCA.

[58] Evidence of distress *could* amount to corroboration in the technical sense, but juries had to be warned that except in special circumstances little weight should be given to it: see per Lord Parker CJ in *R v Knight* [1966] 1 WLR 230 at 233. For examples, see *R v Redpath* (1962) 46 Cr App R 319, CCA; *R v Chauhan* (1981) 73 Cr App R 232, CA; and *R v Dowley* [1983] Crim LR 168, CA.

[59] *R v Romeo* [2004] 1 Cr App R 417, CA.

[60] For these reasons, such evidence was not corroboration in the technical sense: *James v R* (1970) 55 Cr App R 299, PC. However, if there was *also* evidence that the accused alone had been with the complainant at the relevant time, and evidence that her underclothing was torn and that she had injuries to her private parts, the combined effect of all the evidence was capable of amounting to corroboration: see per Lord Lane CJ in *R v Hills* (1987) 86 Cr App R 26, CA at 31. In a case in which the only issue is consent, it would seem that evidence of injuries is, by itself, capable of supporting the complainant's assertion of lack of consent. However, where two or more accused are charged with successive acts of rape, the question whether the material can support the complainant's case against more than one of them will turn on the particular circumstances of the case: see *R v Pountney* [1989] Crim LR 216, CA and *R v Franklin* [1989] Crim LR 499, CA, decisions on corroboration in the technical sense. See also *R v Ensor* [1989] 1 WLR 497, CA.

[61] [1977] QB 224, CA (see below).

[62] Cf *R v Chance* [1988] 3 All ER 225, CA, a decision on corroboration in the technical sense.

## 2 OTHER WITNESSES WHOSE EVIDENCE MAY BE TAINTED BY AN IMPROPER MOTIVE

There are a number of common-law authorities to the effect that the jury should be warned to exercise caution before acting on the evidence of a witness who may have a purpose of his own to serve. These authorities are considered in the paragraphs that follow. Some of the authorities preceding *R v Makanjuola* suggested that in some circumstances, at any rate, the warning was obligatory. It is now clear, from the decision in *R v Muncaster*,[63] that all such authorities need to be looked at afresh in the light of *R v Makanjuola*. It was held that the guidance in *R v Makanjuola* must be read as applying generally to all cases in which a witness may be suspect because he falls into a certain category.

An accomplice who is a co-accused may incriminate another co-accused when giving evidence in his own defence. Because, in these circumstances, an accomplice may be regarded as having some purpose of his own to serve, it has been held that it is desirable, but only as a matter of practice, to warn the jury of the danger of acting on his unsupported evidence, and that every case must be looked at in the light of its own facts.[64] In *R v Cheema*,[65] following a full review of the authorities, Lord Taylor CJ said:

although a warning in suitable terms as to the danger of a co-defendant having an axe to grind is desirable, there is no rule of law or practice requiring a full corroboration direction . . . what is required when one defendant implicates another in evidence is simply to warn the jury of what may very often be obvious—namely that the defendant witness may have a purpose of his own to serve.[66]

Following *R v Makanjuola*, it is clear that whether a warning is given, and if so, its strength, remain matters of judicial discretion dependent on the circumstances of the case.[67] In *R v Jones*[68] it was held that in the case of cut-throat defences, including mirror-image cut-throat defences, a warning should normally be considered and given and, if given, should at least warn the jury to examine the evidence of each accused with care because each has or may have an interest of his own to serve.[69] There is a particular need for some such warning where, as in *R v Jones* itself, one of the accused has refused to answer questions in interview and is therefore able, if he wishes, to tailor his defence to the facts in evidence. It was further held that, subject to

---

[63]  [1999] Crim LR 409, CA.

[64]  *R v Prater* [1960] 2 QB 464, CCA at 466. See also *R v Knowlden* (1983) 77 Cr App R 94, CA; *R v Stannard* [1964] 1 All ER 34 at 40, per Winn J; and *R v Whitaker* (1976) 63 Cr App R 193, CA at 197, per Lord Widgery. However, if the evidence incriminates the accused in one material respect but otherwise exonerates him, there is no need for a warning (which could operate to the *disadvantage* of the accused): see *R v Perman* [1995] Crim LR 736, CA.

[65]  [1994] 1 All ER 639, CA at 647–9.

[66]  See also *R v Sargent* [1993] Crim LR 713, CA: the defendant witness may well have a 'row of his own to hoe'.

[67]  *R v Muncaster* [1999] Crim LR 409, CA.          [68]  [2004] 1 Cr App R 60, CA.

[69]  Contrast *R v Burrows* [2000] Crim LR 48, CA, where, according to *R v Jones*, the court was heavily influenced by the particular facts.

what justice demands on the particular facts of each case, in many or most cases a judge might consider four points to put to the jury: (1) to consider the case for and against each accused separately; (2) to decide the case on all the evidence, including the evidence of each co-accused; (3) when considering the evidence of each co-accused, to bear in mind that he may have an interest to serve or 'an axe to grind'; and (4) to assess the evidence of co-defendants in the same way as the evidence of any other witness in the case. *R v Jones* was followed in *R v Petkar*,[70] where Rix LJ, giving the judgment of the court, nonetheless voiced two concerns. The first was that the warning serves to devalue the evidence of both co-accused in the eyes of the jury. The second was that point (3) in the recommended direction in *R v Jones* does not appear to lie easily with point (4). As to the latter, it was suggested that a distinction should be drawn between evidence in a co-accused's own defence, which should be treated like that of any other witness, and evidence which incriminates the other co-accused. It was acknowledged, however, that such a distinction is sometimes impossible, as in *R v Petkar* itself, where P's co-accused, by giving evidence in his own defence that he was acting under the duress of P, directly incriminated P. In *R v Petkar* the trial judge failed to give a warning of any kind, but the failure was regarded as venial because it would have been obvious to the jury that each man was trying to save his own skin by landing the other in it.

There are no special conditions of admissibility for cell confessions, and no requirement that they be corroborated.[71] However, in *Pringle v R*[72] it was held that a judge must always be alert to the possibility that the evidence of one prisoner against another is tainted by an improper motive, especially where a prisoner who has yet to face trial gives evidence that the other prisoner has confessed to the crime for which he is being held in custody. The indications that the evidence may be tainted by an improper motive must be found in the evidence—described as 'not an exacting test'—and the surrounding circumstances may justify the inference that his evidence is so tainted. Where such indications are present, the judge should draw the jury's attention to them and to their significance and then advise the jury to be cautious before accepting the evidence. This approach was followed in *Benedetto v R*,[73] where the Privy Council observed that the prisoners giving the evidence will almost always have strong reasons of self-interest for seeking to ingratiate themselves with those who may be in a position to reward them for volunteering the evidence, and that the accused is always at a disadvantage because he has none of the usual protections against the inaccurate recording or invention of words when interviewed by the police, and if the informer has a bad character, it may be difficult for him to obtain all the information needed to expose it fully. It does not follow from this, however, that every case involving a cell confession requires the detailed direction discussed in

---

[70] [2004] 1 Cr App R 270, CA.

[71] For an analysis of the issues, see Jeremy Dein, 'Non Tape Recorded Cell Confession Evidence—On Trial' [2002] Crim LR 630.

[72] [2003] All ER (D) 236 (Jan), 2003 UKPC 9.     [73] [2003] 1 WLR 1545, PC.

*Pringle v R* and *Benedetto v R*. In *R v Stone*[74] it was held that cell confession cases will prompt the most careful consideration by the trial judge, but that consideration is not trammelled by fixed roles and the trial judge is best placed to decide the strength of any warning and the necessary extent of any accompanying analysis. The summing-up should be tailored by the trial judge to the circumstances of the particular case.

In *R v Beck*[75] it was argued that an accomplice warning should be given in cases where a witness has a substantial interest of his own for giving false evidence even though there is no material to suggest any involvement by the witness in the crime. Although rejecting the argument, Ackner LJ said that the court did not wish to detract from 'the obligation on a judge to advise a jury to proceed with caution where there is material to suggest that a witness's evidence may be tainted by an improper motive', continuing, 'and the strength of that advice must vary according to the facts of the case'.[76] Thus a warning may be given where there is evidence to suggest that a witness is acting out of spite or malevolence, has a financial or other personal interest in the outcome of the proceedings, or is otherwise biased or partial.[77] Where a witness, awaiting sentence, gives evidence for the prosecution in another case in circumstances in which he knows that at the very least by doing so he stands a chance of having his sentence reduced, it has been held that the potential fallibility of his evidence should be put squarely before the jury.[78] In *R v Asghar*[79] a group of men became involved in a fight in which someone was fatally stabbed. A was charged with murder. Three others from the group pleaded guilty to affray and gave evidence for the prosecution against A. It was held that the judge should have exercised his discretion to direct the jury on the danger of convicting A on the evidence of the other three without some independent supporting evidence because: (i) the defence case was that the three had put their heads together with others to fabricate a story incriminating A in order to protect one of their number; (ii) this suggested motive for their alleged lies was directly linked with the murder charge and did not arise from some unconnected cause; and (iii) the three were not on trial with A and not at risk, their position being akin to those of accomplices in the strict sense.[80] Similarly, a judge may be justified in warning the jury of the danger of acting on the unsupported evidence of a woman upon whose immoral earnings the accused is charged with having lived, even if she is not an accomplice.[81] The spouse of an accomplice may give evidence to support his or

---

[74] [2005] Crim LR 569, CA.　　　[75] [1982] 1 WLR 461, CA.

[76] [1982] 1 WLR 461 at 469. See also *R v Witts and Witts* [1991] Crim LR 562, CA.

[77] A warning is unnecessary, however, if it would do more harm than good, as when it is obvious to the jury, from the circumstances of the case, that a witness is suspect: *R v Lovell* [1990] Crim LR 111, CA.

[78] *Chan Wai-Keung v R* [1995] 2 All ER 438, PC.　　　[79] [1995] 1 Cr App R 223, CA.

[80] Although the final reason is no longer compelling (see s 32 of the Criminal Justice and Public Order Act 1994, above), it is submitted that in such a case the need for some form of warning remains.

[81] See per Lord Reading CJ in *R v King* (1914) 10 Cr App R 117; and cf *R v Hanton* (1985) *The Times*, 14 Feb, CA.

her evidence, but there may be good reason for the evidence of the spouse to be treated with caution.[82]

*R v Spencer, R v Smails*[83] may be regarded as a further example. In that case, nursing staff at a secure hospital were charged with ill-treating patients convicted of crimes and suffering from mental disorders. The prosecution case consisted of the evidence of patients who were characterized as being mentally unbalanced, of bad character, anti-authoritarian and prone to lie or exaggerate and who could have had old scores to settle. The House of Lords held that where the only evidence for the prosecution is that of a witness who, by reason of his particular mental condition and criminal connection, fulfils criteria analogous to those which (formerly) justified a full corroboration warning (accomplices testifying for the prosecution and complainants in sexual cases), the judge should warn the jury that it is dangerous to convict on his uncorroborated evidence, but such a warning need not amount to the full warning.[84] Thus while it may often be convenient to use the words 'danger' or 'dangerous', the use of such words is not essential to an adequate warning, so long as the jury is made fully aware of the dangers of convicting on such evidence, and the extent to which the judge should refer to the corroborative material, if any exists, depends on the facts of each case.[85] It may be doubted whether 'corroborative material', for these purposes, was ever intended to mean corroboration in the strict sense; and it is submitted that, notwithstanding the analogy drawn with cases which (formerly) justified a full corroboration warning (which, in the light of section 32 of the 1994 Act, would suggest that a warning is no longer obligatory), a warning of the kind indicated in *R v Spencer, R v Smails* should still be given in respect of witnesses sharing the same unfortunate characteristics as the witnesses in that case. Following *R v Makanjuola*, however, it is clear that where a warning is given, its terms will depend on the precise circumstances of the particular case.[86]

## 3 CHILDREN

Under the proviso to section 38(1) of the Children and Young Persons Act 1933, where the unsworn evidence of a child was given on behalf of the prosecution, the accused was not liable to be convicted unless that evidence was corroborated by some other material evidence implicating him; and at common law, the sworn evidence of a child required a corroboration warning as a matter of law.[87] Section 38(1) has been repealed[88] and section 34(2) of the Criminal Justice Act 1988[89] provides that: 'Any requirement whereby at a trial on indictment it is obligatory for the court to give the

---

[82] *R v Evans* [1965] 2 QB 295.        [83] [1986] 2 All ER 928, HL.

[84] Overruling, in this respect, *R v Bagshaw* [1984] 1 All ER 971, CA.

[85] See also, concerning confessions made by the mentally handicapped, *R v Bailey* [1995] Crim LR 723, CA and Police and Criminal Evidence Act 1984, s 77, below.

[86] See *R v Causley* [1999] Crim LR 572, CA.        [87] See, eg, *R v Cleal* [1942] 1 All ER 203, CCA.

[88] Criminal Justice Act 1991, s 101(2) and Sch 13.

[89] As amended by Criminal Justice and Public Order Act 1994, s 32(2).

jury a warning about convicting the accused on the uncorroborated evidence of a child is abrogated.' The rationale underlying the proviso to section 38(1) and the common-law rule was the danger that the evidence of a child, especially if unsworn, but even if sworn, may be unreliable by reason of childish imagination, suggestibility, or fallibility of memory. These dangers remain, and although in *R v Pryce*[90] it was held that a direction to treat the evidence of a 6-year-old girl with caution was not required, because this would amount to a re-introduction of the abrogated rule, it is clear, following *R v Makanjuola*, that judges do retain a discretionary power to give such a direction, but whether such a direction should be given, and if so, its precise terms, are matters dependent on the circumstances of the case.[91] In the case of children, the relevant factors include the age and intelligence of the child, whether the evidence is given on oath and, if the evidence is unsworn, how well the child in question understands the duty of speaking the truth. In *R v Pryce* itself, the Court of Appeal thought that it was sufficient for the trial judge to have told the jury to take into account the fact that the witness was a child. In other cases, a stronger direction will be called for.

## 4  MATRIMONIAL CASES

Where a matrimonial 'offence' is alleged, whether in proceedings in the High Court or in a summary court, the gravity of the consequences of proof of such an allegation and the risk of a miscarriage of justice in acting on the uncorroborated evidence of a spouse have led the courts to acknowledge the desirability of corroboration. Corroboration is sought as a matter of practice rather than as a matter of law. Thus the court may act on the uncorroborated evidence of a spouse if in no doubt where the truth lies.[92] However, in cases where sexual misconduct is alleged, or the evidence of adultery is that of a willing participant,[93] the appellate court will intervene unless the trial court expressly warned itself of the danger of acting on uncorroborated evidence. In other types of case, the absence of an express indication that the desirability of corroboration was in mind will not of itself cause an appellate court to intervene.[94] These clear principles were enunciated by Sir Jocelyn Simon P in *Alli v Alli*.[95] It remains to be seen whether, in the light of recent changes to the analogous rules of evidence applicable in criminal proceedings, these principles remain good law or, as seems more likely, fall to be re-stated in terms of the need, in appropriate circumstances, to exercise caution before acting on the evidence in question, if unsupported.

Section 4 of the Affiliation Proceedings Act 1957 provides that in affiliation proceedings the court shall not adjudge the defendant to be the putative father of the child, in a case where evidence is given by the mother, unless her evidence is

---

[90] [1991] Crim LR 379, CA.      [91] See *R v L* [1999] Crim LR 489, CA.
[92] See *Curtis v Curtis* (1905) 21 TLR 676.
[93] See *Galler v Galler* [1954] P 252, CA and *Fairman v Fairman* [1949] P 341.
[94] See *Joseph v Joseph* [1915] P 122.      [95] [1965] 3 All ER 480.

corroborated in some material particular. Under section 17 of the Family Law Reform Act 1987, the 1957 Act shall cease to have effect. Despite the abolition of affiliation proceedings, the question of paternity will, of course, continue to arise in family and other proceedings. What corroboration requirement, if any, remains? The justification for the corroboration requirement in section 4, which was the comparative ease with which a false allegation as to paternity could be made, and the difficulty of rebutting it, is no longer entirely convincing. Section 20 of the Family Law Reform Act 1969 provides that, in any civil proceedings in which the parentage of any person falls to be determined, the court may direct the taking of blood samples of that person, the mother of that person and any party alleged to be the father of that person. Presumably, although there is no longer any requirement for corroboration, or even a warning, it is likely that the courts will be aware of the need for caution, if only in those cases in which, no direction having been given under section 20, the mother adduces no material in support of her allegation.

## 5  CLAIMS AGAINST THE ESTATE OF A DECEASED PERSON

Where a claim is advanced by a person against the estate of a deceased person, it is natural to look for corroboration in support of the claimant's evidence, but there is no rule of law which prevents the court from acting on the claimant's uncorroborated evidence, if it is convincing.[96]

# C  CONFESSIONS BY THE
# MENTALLY HANDICAPPED

In *R v MacKenzie*[97] Lord Taylor CJ, applying the guidance given in *R v Galbraith*[98] to cases involving confessions by the mentally handicapped, held that where (i) the prosecution case depends wholly on confessions, (ii) the defendant suffers from a significant degree of mental handicap and (iii) the confessions are unconvincing to a point where a jury properly directed could not properly convict on them, then the judge, assuming he has not excluded the confessions earlier, should withdraw the case from the jury. It was held that confessions may be unconvincing, for example, because they lack the incriminating details to be expected of a guilty and willing confessor, because they are inconsistent with other evidence, or because they are otherwise inherently improbable. In a case which is not withdrawn from the jury, the fact that the confession was made by a mentally handicapped person may be taken into account by the judge not only for the purpose of deciding whether it should be

---

[96]  *Re Hodgson, Beckett v Ramsdale* (1885) 31 Ch D 177, CA; *Re Cummins* [1972] Ch 62, CA.
[97]  [1993] 1 WLR 453, CA.        [98]  [1981] 2 All ER 1060 (Ch 2).

excluded as a matter of law (under section 76 of the Police and Criminal Evidence Act 1984), but also in deciding whether to exercise his discretion to exclude (under section 82(3) or section 78(1) of that Act).[99] Thus in *R v Moss*[100] it was held that confessions made by an accused on the borderline of mental handicap, in the absence of a solicitor or any other independent person, in the course of nine interviews held over nine days, should have been excluded under section 76(2)(b).

Where, notwithstanding the above possibilities, the confession of a mentally handicapped person is admitted in evidence, section 77 of the Police and Criminal Evidence Act 1984 imposes on the court a duty, in certain circumstances, to warn the tribunal of fact of the dangers of convicting such a person in reliance on his confession. It provides that:

(1) Without prejudice to the general duty of the court at a trial on indictment with a jury to direct the jury on any matter on which it appears to the court appropriate to do so, where at such a trial—

(a) the case against the accused depends wholly or substantially on a confession by him; and

(b) the court is satisfied—

(i) that he is mentally handicapped; and

(ii) that the confession was not made in the presence of an independent person, the court shall warn the jury that there is a special need for caution before convicting the accused in reliance on the confession, and shall explain that the need arises because of the circumstances mentioned in paragraphs (a) and (b) above.

(2) In any case where at the summary trial of a person for an offence it appears to the court that a warning under subsection (1) above would be required if the trial were on indictment with a jury, the court shall treat the case as one in which there is a special need for caution before convicting the accused on his confession.

(2A) In any case where at the trial on indictment without a jury of a person for an offence it appears to the court that a warning under subsection (1) above would be required if the trial were with a jury, the court shall treat the case as one in which there is a special need for caution before convicting the accused on his confession.

Concerning the 'general duty' referred to in section 77(1), in *R v Bailey*[101] it was held that in cases where the accused is significantly mentally handicapped and the prosecution would not have a case in the absence of the accused's confessions, the judge should give a full and proper statement of the accused's case against the confessions being accepted by the jury as true and accurate, which should include not only the points made on the accused's behalf, but also any points which appear to the judge to be appropriate. The matters which in *that* case should have been put before the jury[102]

---

[99] See generally Ch 13.

[100] (1990) 91 Cr App R 371, CA. See also *R v Cox* [1991] Crim LR 276, CA and *R v Wood* [1994] Crim LR 222, CA.

[101] [1995] Crim LR 723, CA.

[102] The court held that nothing in its judgment was to be taken as of general application.

included: (i) that the experience of the courts has shown that people with significant mental handicap do make false confessions for a variety of reasons; (ii) the various possible reasons for the accused having made false confessions; and (iii) that without the confessions, there was no case against the accused.

Concerning section 77(1)(a), the word 'substantially' should not be given a restricted meaning: section 77 is not confined to cases where either the whole or 'most of the case' depends on the confession.[103] In deciding whether a case depends 'substantially' on the confession, the test to be applied is whether the case for the Crown is substantially less strong without the confession, a test which may not be satisfied if there is other prosecution evidence such as identification evidence and evidence of another confession which was made in the presence of an independent adult.[104]

Although para (a) of section 77(1), unlike para (b), does not expressly state that it is for the court to be satisfied of the circumstances mentioned therein, it seems clear that the need for a direction to the jury can only arise where the *judge* is satisfied as to the circumstances mentioned in paragraph (a) as well as paragraph (b),[105] since the judge, when a warning is given, must explain that the need for caution arises because of the circumstances mentioned in both paragraphs. Accordingly, the judge should not direct the jury that a special need for caution *may* arise if *they* are satisfied of the circumstances mentioned in the paragraphs, but that there is a special need for caution which has arisen because the case against the accused *does* depend wholly or substantially on a confession, the accused is mentally handicapped and the confession *was not* made in the presence of an independent person.

In *R v Campbell*[106] it was held that, as to the 'warning', the judge does not have to follow any specific form of words, but would be wise to use the phrase 'special need for caution', and as to the 'explanation', the judge should explain that persons who are mentally disordered or mentally handicapped may, without wishing to do so, provide information which is unreliable, misleading or self-incriminating. The explanation should be tailored to the particular evidence in the case, for example evidence that the accused is particularly suggestible or prone to acquiesce, comply or give in to pressure. The judge should then explain that the function of the appropriate adult is designed to minimize the risk of the accused giving unreliable information by seeing that the interview is conducted properly and fairly and facilitating, if need be, communication between the police and the suspect.

A person is mentally handicapped if 'he is in a state of arrested or incomplete development of mind which includes significant impairment of intelligence and social functioning'.[107] An 'independent person' is defined negatively as not including a

---

[103] *R v Bailey* [1995] Crim LR 723, CA.     [104] See *R v Campbell* [1995] 1 Cr App R 522, CA.

[105] However, concerning para (b), see also, *sed quaere*, *R v Lamont* [1989] Crim LR 813, CA: the trial judge should have directed the jury to exercise the caution called for if *they* accepted the evidence of mental handicap.

[106] [1995] 1 Cr App R 522, CA.

[107] Section 77(3).

police officer or a person employed for, or engaged on, 'police purposes'[108] and could include, for example, a relative or friend of the accused or his solicitor.[109] Should a dispute arise on the issue whether the accused is mentally handicapped (or whether his confession was made in the presence of an independent person) evidence, if necessary expert medical evidence, may be adduced to enable the judge to come to a decision. In these circumstances, the section is silent as to the incidence of the burden of proof. Presumably, the onus is on the defence to prove the circumstances mentioned in section 77(1)(b) on a balance of probabilities, rather than on the prosecution to prove their non-existence beyond reasonable doubt.

The number of cases in which a section 77 warning will be required is likely to be very small. The possibilities of withdrawing the case from the jury or excluding the confession under sections 76, 78, or 82(3) have already been mentioned. It should also be noted that, under Code C, a person who is mentally handicapped must not be interviewed in the absence of an 'appropriate adult' (a concept which in large measure overlaps with that of an 'independent person' for the purposes of section 77)[110] unless an officer of the rank of superintendent or above considers that delay would be likely (a) to lead to interference with or harm to evidence or interference with or physical harm to other people, (b) to lead to the alerting of other people suspected of having committed an offence but not yet arrested for it, or (c) to hinder the recovery of property obtained in consequence of the commission of an offence.[111] Thus it seems that section 77 is confined to cases in which the confession was made either in an interview conducted in breach of the Code or in an 'urgent interview'.[112] In the rare cases in which section 77 does apply, however, failure to warn the jury as required is grounds for a successful appeal. In *R v Lamont*,[113] a case of attempted murder, the trial judge failed to warn the jury notwithstanding that the only evidence of intent was a confession made, in the absence of an independent person, by a mentally subnormal accused. Quashing the conviction, it was held that the direction under section 77 was not a matter of prudence, but an essential part of a fair summing-up.

---

[108] Section 77(3). 'Police purposes' has the meaning assigned to it by s 64 of the Police Act 1964, which defines such purposes as including 'the purposes of special constables appointed for that area, of police cadets undergoing training with a view to becoming members of the police force maintained for that area and of civilians employed for the purposes of that force or of any such special constables or cadets'.

[109] Although the definition of an 'independent person' suggests that s 77 only applies in the case of questioning by police officers, in *R v Bailey* [1995] Crim LR 723, CA it was held that a s 77 warning should have been given in respect of a confession made to a member of the public.

[110] It is defined to include, inter alia, a relative, guardian or other person responsible for his care or custody: see para 1.7(b), Code C. See also *R v Lewis* [1996] Crim LR 260, CA.

[111] Paras 11.15 and 11.18 and Annex E, Code C.

[112] See per Taylor LJ in *R v Moss* (1990) 91 Cr App R 371, CA at 377.     [113] [1989] Crim LR 813, CA.

# D IDENTIFICATION CASES

## 1 VISUAL IDENTIFICATION BY WITNESSES

In *R v Turnbull*[114] Lord Widgery CJ, giving the judgment of the Court of Appeal, laid down important guidelines relating to evidence of allegedly mistaken visual identification of the accused.[115] Mistaken identification of the accused, especially in cases of visual identification, may be regarded as the greatest cause of wrong convictions.[116] The guidelines in *R v Turnbull* were designed to lessen this danger. The Court of Appeal attempted to follow the recommendations in the Report of the Committee on Evidence of Identification in Criminal Cases chaired by Lord Devlin.[117] The Committee had recommended the enactment of a general rule precluding a conviction in any case in which the prosecution relies wholly or mainly on evidence of visual identification by one or more witnesses, but the guidelines fall considerably short of the Committee's proposals.

Failure to follow the guidelines is likely to result in a conviction being quashed if, on all the evidence, the verdict is unsafe.[118] It will be otherwise, however, if the Court of Appeal is convinced that had the jury been directed correctly, they would nevertheless have come to the same conclusion.[119] Privy Council authority is to the same effect. Thus although it has been said that a significant failure to follow the guidelines *will* cause a conviction to be quashed because it will have resulted in a substantial miscarriage of justice,[120] it has also been said that in 'exceptional circumstances' a conviction based on uncorroborated identification evidence may be sustained in the absence of a *Turnbull* direction.[121] In *Freemantle v R*[122] the trial judge failed to give such a direction. The identification, which was by way of recognition evidence, was of exceptionally good quality: both identification witnesses had more than a fleeting glance of the accused and one of them said to the accused that he recognized him, to which the accused had replied in a way which appeared to acknowledge that he had been correctly identified. The Board was of the opinion that 'exceptional circumstances' include the fact that the evidence of identification is of exceptionally good quality and

---

[114] [1977] QB 224.

[115] Identification of the voice of the accused, which the defence alleges to be mistaken, is considered separately, below. Other aspects of identification evidence are considered elsewhere: the exclusion of such evidence, if obtained in breach of Code D, under s 78 of the Police and Criminal Evidence Act 1984 (Ch 3); the admissibility of evidence of previous identification, and dock identifications (Ch 6); identification by samples (Ch 14); identification by photographs, films, photofits and sketches (Ch 9); and expert evidence on identification by voice (Ch 18).

[116] See para 196, 11th Report, Criminal Law Revision Committee (Cmnd 4991).

[117] Cmnd 338 (1976).

[118] *R v Kane* (1977) 65 Cr App R 247, CA. See also *R v Tyson* [1985] Crim LR 48, CA.

[119] *R v Hunjan* (1978) 68 Cr App R 99, CA, where the conviction was in fact quashed; and cf *R v Clifton* [1986] Crim LR 399, CA, where the prosecution case was exceptionally strong.

[120] Per Lord Ackner in *Reid v R* (1989) 90 Cr App R 121 at 130, PC.

[121] Per Lord Griffiths in *Scott v R* [1989] 2 All ER 305 at 314–15, PC.     [122] [1994] 3 All ER 225, PC.

accordingly held that application of a proviso similar in its terms to section 2(1) of the Criminal Appeal Act 1968 was justified.

It is advisable, in every case in which a *Turnbull* direction may be required, for there to be a discussion between the judge and counsel, prior to the closing speeches and the summing-up, as to how identification issues will be addressed.[123]

The *Turnbull* guidelines are extensive. It will be convenient to consider separately seven extracts from the judgment of the Court of Appeal, together with subsequent developments in relation to each.

### (a) The special need for caution

First, whenever the case against an accused depends wholly or substantially on the correctness of one or more identifications of the accused which the defence alleges to be mistaken, the judge should warn the jury of the special need for caution before convicting the accused in reliance on the correctness of the identification or identifications. In addition he should instruct them as to the reason for the need for such a warning and should make some reference to the possibility that a mistaken witness can be a convincing one and that a number of such witnesses can all be mistaken. Provided that this is done in clear terms, the judge need not use any particular form of words.

Although Lord Widgery CJ himself said that *Turnbull*'s case 'is intended primarily to deal with the ghastly risk run in cases of fleeting encounters ...',[124] the warning should be given even if the opportunities for observation were good and the identifying witness is convinced that he has correctly identified the accused.[125] A warning must also be given notwithstanding that the identifying witness has picked out the accused at a formal identification procedure such as an identification parade.[126] It is of the utmost importance to give a warning where the sole evidence of identification is contained in the deposition of a deceased witness and the identification may have been based on a fleeting glance.[127]

Where identification is in issue and there is strong prosecution evidence that the accused was with some other person at the relevant time, then the evidence identifying that other, unless unchallenged by the defence, should normally be the subject of a *Turnbull* direction.[128] Although a *Turnbull* direction as such is not required in relation to the identification of a car, the judge should draw the jury's attention to the opportunity which the witness had to identify the car and to his apparent ability or inability to distinguish between the makes and characteristics of cars and should

---

[123] *R v Stanton* (2004) *The Times*, 28 Apr, [2004] EWCA Crim 490.

[124] *R v Oakwell* (1978) 66 Cr App R 174 at 178.    [125] *R v Tyson* [1985] Crim LR 48, CA.

[126] Per Lord Griffiths in *Scott v R* [1989] 2 All ER 305 at 314, PC. Where the witness picks out a volunteer, there is no obligation to give a 'reverse *Turnbull* direction', ie that the witness may be honest but mistaken in identifying the volunteer, because the purpose of the *Turnbull* direction is to lessen the danger of a wrongful conviction, not a wrongful acquittal: see *R v Trew* [1996] Crim LR 441, CA. For the special issues that arise where there has been a qualified identification, see *R v George* [2003] Crim LR 282, CA and Andrew Roberts, 'The perils and possibilities of qualified identification: *R v George*' (2003) 7 E&P 130.

[127] *Scott v R* [1989] 2 All ER 305 at 314–15.    [128] *R v Bath* [1990] Crim LR 716, CA.

direct them to decide how far the witness is genuinely recollecting what he saw and how far his mind has invented or absorbed information from somewhere else.[129]

According to *R v Slater*,[130] where there is no issue as to the presence of the accused at or near the scene of the offence, but the issue is as to what he was doing, whether a *Turnbull* direction is necessary will depend on the circumstances of the case. It was held that it will be necessary where, on the evidence, the possibility exists that the identifying witness may have mistaken one person for another, for example because of similarities in face, build or clothing between two or more people present,[131] but where there is no possibility of such a mistake, there is no need to give a *Turnbull* direction. On the facts, the accused was six foot six inches tall and there was no evidence to suggest that anyone else present was remotely similar in height. It was therefore held that there was no basis for any mistake: the issue in the case was not identification, but what the accused did, and accordingly a *Turnbull* direction was not required. The court observed that in some cases, where presence is admitted but conduct disputed, it would be contrary to common sense to require a *Turnbull* direction, as when a black man and a white man are present and the complainant says that it was the white man.[132]

It has also been said that a full direction is not required if none of the identifying witnesses purports to identify the accused, their evidence merely serving to provide a description which is not inconsistent with the appearance of the accused and forming only one part, albeit a very important part, of all the evidence, because such a case does not depend wholly or substantially upon the correctness of their evidence.[133] In *R v Constantinou*,[134] where none of the witnesses purported to identify the accused but merely gave descriptions which might have been consistent with his appearance, and a photofit was admitted which also might have been consistent with his appearance, it was held that no *Turnbull* warning was required in respect of the photofit. This decision, it is submitted, is in need of review.

In a case where identification is in issue but the defence is that the identifying witness is lying, rather than mistaken, a *Turnbull* direction is not required. In *R v Courtnell*[135] the defence was one of alibi and it was alleged that the purported identification, by someone who had known the accused for a week, was a fabrication. It was held that the trial judge had properly withdrawn the issue of mistaken identity from the jury: the sole issue was the veracity of the identifying witness and therefore a *Turnbull* direction would only have confused the jury.[136]

---

129  *R v Browning* (1991) 94 Cr App R 109, CA.    130  [1995] 1 Cr App R 584, CA.

131  See, eg, *R v Thornton* [1995] 1 Cr App R 578, CA, where the appellant and others were similarly dressed.

132  See also *R v Conibeer* [2002] EWCA Crim 2059 and cf *R v O'Leary* [2002] EWCA Crim 2055, CA.

133  *R v Browning* (1991) 94 Cr App R 109. Cf *R v Andrews* [1993] Crim LR 590, CA.

134  (1989) 91 Cr App R 74, CA.    135  [1990] Crim LR 115, CA.

136  See also, applying *R v Courtnell*, *R v Cape* [1996] 1 Cr App R 191, CA; *R v Beckles and Montague* [1999] Crim LR 148, CA; and *R v Ryder* [1994] 2 All ER 859, CA, a case of recognition in which a failure to give a *Turnbull* direction was excused on the grounds that the defence was not one of mistaken identity, but that the identifying witness had deliberately falsified her evidence through animosity. Contrast *Beckford v R* (1993) 97 Cr App R 409, PC, applied in *Shand v R* [1996] 1 All ER 511, PC, below.

As to the terms of the direction, *R v Turnbull* is not a statute and does not require an incantation of a formula or set form of words: provided that the judge complies with the sense and spirit of the guidance given, he has a broad discretion to express himself in his own way.[137] Thus as to the reason for the warning, failure to use the word 'convincing' ('a mistaken witness can be a convincing one') need not be fatal to the summing up.[138] However, it is insufficient merely to say that 'even an honest witness may be mistaken': the judge should explain that evidence of visual identification is a category of evidence which experience has shown to be particularly vulnerable to error, in particular by honest and impressive witnesses, and that this has been known to result in wrong convictions.[139] There is a requirement to make clear that the need for special caution is rooted in the court's actual experience of miscarriages of justice.[140]

## (b)  The circumstances of the identification and specific weaknesses in the identification evidence

Secondly, the judge should direct the jury to examine closely the circumstances in which the identification by each witness came to be made. How long did the witness have the accused under observation? At what distance? In what light? Was the observation impeded in any way, as for example by passing traffic or a press of people? Had the witness ever seen the accused before? How often? If only occasionally, had he any special reason for remembering the accused? How long a time elapsed between the original observation and the subsequent identification to the police? Was there any material discrepancy between the description of the accused given to the police by the witness when first seen by them and his actual appearance? If in any case the prosecution have reason to believe that there is such a material discrepancy, they should supply the accused or his legal advisers with particulars of the description the police were first given. In all cases, if the accused asks to be given particulars of such descriptions, the prosecution should supply them. Finally, he should remind the jury of any specific weaknesses which had appeared in the identification evidence.

Simply paying lip service to the guidelines, without reference to the particular circumstances relevant to the accuracy of the identification will not suffice.[141] Nor is it sufficient for the judge simply to invite the jury to take into account what counsel for the defence has said about 'specific weaknesses': the judge must fairly and properly summarize for the jury any such weaknesses which can arguably be said to have been exposed in the evidence.[142] However, provided that the judge does identify all the

---

[137] Per Lord Steyn in *Mills v R* [1995] 3 All ER 865, PC at 872.

[138] See *Rose v R* [1995] Crim LR 939, PC.

[139] Per Lord Ackner in *Reid v R* (1989) 90 Cr App R 121 at 134–5.

[140] *R v Nash* [2005] Crim LR 232, CA. However, it has also been held that failure to refer to past miscarriages of justice is not fatal: *R v Tyler* [1993] Crim LR 60, CA. Indeed, in jurisdictions in which there is no history of well-publicized miscarriages of justice, eg Jamaica, such a reference would be unnecessary and unhelpful: *Amore v R* (1994) 99 Cr App R 279, PC.

[141] *R v Graham* [1994] Crim LR 212, CA, applied in *R v Allen* [1995] Crim LR 643, CA, where the trial judge took no steps to remove the possible prejudice resulting from an improper refusal to hold an identification parade. Cf *R v Doldur* [2000] Crim LR 178, CA.

[142] *R v Fergus* (1993) 98 Cr App R 313, CA.

specific weaknesses, there is no obligation to do so in a particular way, for example by bringing them together and listing them, rather than by dealing with them in context when reviewing the evidence in the case.[143] Equally, in the case of minor discrepancies between what the identifying witnesses have said, it is a matter for the judge's discretion whether simply to refer to them in his review of the evidence, or to categorize them specifically as potential weaknesses.[144]

The same rules apply to police officers as to other identifying witnesses, but sometimes an officer, because an officer, pays particular attention to the identity of a person, even in a fleeting glance type case, and the judge should then specifically direct the jury as to the likelihood of the officer being correct, when a 'mere casual observer' might not be, because an officer has a greater appreciation of the importance of identification, is trained, and is less likely to be affected by the excitement of the situation.[145]

Where evidence of a formal identification procedure at which the accused was identified is central to the prosecution case but the judge, notwithstanding breaches of Code D, properly decides not to exercise his discretion under section 78 of the Police and Criminal Evidence Act 1984 to exclude it, then in his summing-up he should make specific references to the breaches and leave it to the jury to consider what their approach should be in the light of them.[146]

### (c) Recognition

Recognition may be more reliable than identification of a stranger; but even when the witness is purporting to recognize someone whom he knows, the jury should be reminded that mistakes in recognition of close relatives and friends are sometimes made.

Many people experience seeing someone in the street whom they know, only to discover that they are wrong. The expression 'I could have sworn it was you' indicates the sort of warning which a judge should give, because that is exactly what a witness does—he swears that it was the person he thinks it was. In the field of recognition, there are degrees of danger, but perhaps less where the parties have known each other for many years or where there is no doubt that the person identified was at the scene at the time. Even here, it is at least advisable to alert the jury to the possibility of honest mistake and to the dangers, and the reasons why such dangers exist.[147] In *Beckford v R*[148] the Privy Council held as follows. (1) A general warning on *Turnbull*

---

[143] *R v Mussell* [1995] Crim LR 887, CA; *R v Barnes* [1995] 2 Cr App R 491, CA; and *R v Qadir* [1998] Crim LR 828, CA. Cf *R v Pattinson* [1996] 1 Cr App R 51, CA.

[144] *R v Barnes* [1995] 2 Cr App R 491 at 500, CA.

[145] *R v Ramsden* [1991] Crim LR 295, CA; *R v Tyler* [1993] Crim LR 60, CA. Cf per Lord Ackner in *Reid v R* (1989) 90 Cr App R 121 at 137: 'experience has undoubtedly shown that police identification can be just as unreliable [as that of an ordinary member of the public].'

[146] *R v Quinn* [1995] 1 Cr App R 480, CA

[147] *R v Bentley* (1991) 99 Cr App R 342, CA; *R v Bowden* [1993] Crim LR 379, CA. Cf *R v Curry* [1983] Crim LR 737 and *R v Oakwell* (1978) 66 Cr App R 174, CA.

[148] (1993) 97 Cr App R 409, PC.

lines *must* normally be given in recognition cases and failure to do so will nearly always *by itself* suffice to invalidate a conviction substantially based on identification evidence. (2) Such a warning should be given even if the sole or main thrust of the defence is directed to the issue of the identifying witness's credibility, ie whether his evidence is true or false as distinct from accurate or mistaken. The first question for the jury is whether the witness is honest, and if the answer to that question is Yes, the next question is whether he could be mistaken. (3) This 'strong general rule' is subject to only very rare exceptions:

If, for example, the witness's identification evidence is that the accused was his workmate whom he has known for 20 years and that he was conversing with him for half an hour face to face in the same room and the witness is sane and sober, then, if credibility is the issue, it will be the only issue.[149]

Police officers may give recognition evidence, including recognition evidence based on a viewing of a video tape of the crime recorded by a security camera, notwithstanding that the jury may then infer that the accused has previously been in trouble with the police, because the fact of the officers' knowledge is of critical significance to the quality of the identification, and to exclude the evidence would unfairly advantage those with criminal records.[150]

### (d) Identification evidence of good quality

When the quality [of the identification evidence] is good, as for example when the identification is made after a long period of observation, or in satisfactory conditions by a relative, a neighbour, a close friend, a workmate and the like, the jury can safely be left to assess the value of the identifying evidence even though there is not other evidence to support it: provided always, however, that an adequate warning has been given about the special need for caution.

Where the quality of the identification evidence is such that the jury can be safely left to assess its value, even though there is no other evidence to support it, then the judge is fully entitled, if so minded, to direct the jury that an identification by one witness can constitute support for the identification by another, *provided* that he warns them in clear terms that even a number of honest witnesses can all be mistaken.[151]

---

[149] (1993) 97 Cr App R 409 at 415, applied in *Shand v R* [1996] 1 All ER 511, PC. Contrast *R v Courtnell* [1990] Crim LR 115, CA and *R v Ryder* [1994] 2 All ER 859, CA, both above.

[150] See *R v Crabtree* [1992] Crim LR 65, CA and *R v Caldwell* (1993) 99 Cr App R 73, CA; and cf *R v Fowden and White* [1982] Crim LR 588, CA. The defence then face difficulties in challenging the extent of the officers' knowledge of the accused. In *R v Caldwell* the Court of Appeal thought the difficulty was 'manageable', approving the sensitive ruling of the trial judge that the officers should not refer to any convictions or criminal associations of the accused, their families, etc.

[151] Per Lord Lane CJ in *R v Weeder* (1980) 71 Cr App R 228, CA at 231. In *R v Breslin* (1984) 80 Cr App R 226, CA it was held that this direction (and warning) should be given in all identification cases to which it applies.

### (e) Identification evidence of poor quality

When, in the judgment of the trial judge, the quality of the identifying evidence is poor, as for example when it depends solely on a fleeting glance or on a longer observation made in difficult conditions, the situation is very different. The judge should then withdraw the case from the jury and direct an acquittal unless there is other evidence which goes to support the correctness of the identification. This may be corroboration in the sense that lawyers use that word; but it need not be so if its effect is to make the jury sure that there has been no mistaken identification.

Under this guideline, a case is withdrawn from the jury not because the judge considers that the witness is lying, but because the evidence, even if taken to be honest, has a base which is so slender that it is unreliable and therefore insufficient to found a conviction. The jury is protected from acting upon the type of evidence which, even if believed, experience has shown to be a possible source of injustice.[152]

Even in the absence of a submission, the judge is under a duty to invite submissions when, in his view, the identification evidence is poor and unsupported.[153] Moreover, *R v Turnbull* plainly contemplates that the position must be assessed not only at the end of the prosecution case, but also at the close of the defence case.[154] In exceptional cases, a ruling can be made even before the close of the prosecution case, on the depositions, but apparently in any event a *voir dire* should not be held.[155] A judge should not direct a jury that he would have withdrawn the case from them on a submission of no case to answer, had he thought that there was insufficient identification evidence, because the jury may mistakenly take this to mean that the evidence is sufficiently strong for them to convict.[156]

### (f) Supporting evidence

The trial judge should identify to the jury the evidence which he adjudges is capable of supporting the evidence of identification. If there is any evidence or circumstances which the jury might think was supporting when it did not have this quality, the judge should say so. A jury, for example, might think that support could be found in the fact that the accused had not given evidence before them. An accused's absence from the witness box cannot provide evidence of anything and the judge should tell the jury so.[157] But he would be entitled to tell them that, when assessing the quality of the identification evidence, they could take into consideration the fact that it was uncontradicted by any evidence coming from the accused himself.

---

[152] Per Lord Mustill in *Daley v R* [1993] 4 All ER 86 at 94, PC.

[153] *R v Fergus* (1993) 98 Cr App R 313, CA.        [154] Ibid, citing *R v Turnbull* [1977] QB 224 at 228–9.

[155] See *R v Flemming* (1987) 86 Cr App R 32, CA and cf *R v Beveridge* [1987] Crim LR 401, CA.

[156] *R v Smith and Doe* (1986) 85 Cr App R 197, CA. See also *R v Akaidere* [1990] Crim LR 808, CA: a judge should not direct the jury that the identification evidence is so poor that he would have stopped the case if it had stood alone.

[157] Failure to give such a direction will found a successful appeal. This remains the case, where the failure may have led the jury to believe that the accused's absence from the witness box was supportive, even if the quality of the identification evidence was good and there was evidence supportive of it: *R v Forbes* [1992] Crim LR 593, CA. But see now Criminal Justice and Public Order Act 1994, s 35 (Ch 14).

It is essential for the judge to make clear to the jury that although he has adjudged that certain evidence is capable of supporting the evidence of identification, it is for them to decide, if they accept it, whether it does in fact support the evidence of identification.[158] The support may be provided by evidence of the accused's association with other suspects who have been identified[159] or by evidence that the identifying witness correctly identified another suspect seen with the accused at the relevant time.[160] In a case of purported recognition in circumstances such that, had it been a case of identification by a stranger, the quality of the evidence would have been poor, the fact that it was a recognition may itself form part of the evidence in support.[161]

In *R v Willoughby*[162] it was held that the physical appearance of an accused, however singular, and however closely it corresponds with the evidence of a witness describing the criminal, cannot amount without more to corroboration of that evidence because it does not establish the reliability of the witness's evidence that the criminal had such an appearance. However, in *R v McInnes*,[163] a case concerning corroboration in the strict sense, in which the victim of a kidnapping gave a detailed description of the inside of the criminal's car, a description which fitted the inside of the accused's car, it was held that the victim's detailed *knowledge* of the inside of the car was independent corroboration on the issue of identification as surely as if she had left a piece of her clothing in the car, or a fingerprint. *R v Willoughby* was distinguished on the basis that in that case there was nothing to confirm the evidence of the identifying witness that her assailant had a spot on his face—it was even in issue whether the accused had a spot at the time of the offence.

### (g) False alibis

Care should be taken by the judge when directing the jury about the support for an identification which may be derived from the fact that they have rejected an alibi. False alibis may be put forward for many reasons: an accused, for example, who has only his own truthful evidence to rely on may stupidly fabricate an alibi and get lying witnesses to support it out of fear that his own evidence will not be enough. Further, alibi witnesses can make genuine mistakes about dates and occasions like any other witnesses can. Only when the jury is satisfied that the sole reason for the fabrication was to deceive them and there is no other explanation for its being put forward can fabrication provide any support for identification evidence. The jury should be reminded that proving the accused has told lies about where he was at the material time does not by itself prove that he was where the identifying witness says he was.

---

[158] *R v Akaidere* [1990] Crim LR 808, CA.          [159] *R v Penny* (1991) 94 Cr App R 345, CA.

[160] *R v Castle* [1989] Crim LR 567, CA and *R v Jones (Terence)* [1992] Crim LR 365, CA. See also *R v Brown* [1991] Crim LR 368, CA.

[161] *R v Turnbull* [1977] QB 224. See also *R v Ryan* [1990] Crim LR 50, CA: it is rare for the court to feel concern about the rightness of a conviction based on evidence of recognition.

[162] (1988) 88 Cr App R 91, CA.

[163] (1989) 90 Cr App R 99, CA. See also *R v Nagy* [1990] Crim LR 187, CA.

Such a direction should be given even if the prosecution has not relied on the collapse of the alibi as part of the material supporting its case.[164]

## 2 VISUAL IDENTIFICATION BY THE JURY

In a case in which the jurors themselves are asked to 'identify' the accused, whom they have seen in court, from a photograph or video recording of the offender committing the offence, they should be warned of the risk of mistaken identity and of the need to exercise particular care in any identification which they make. One factor which they must take into account is whether the appearance of the accused has changed since the visual recording was made, but a full *Turnbull* direction is inappropriate because the process of identifying a person from a photograph is a commonplace and every-day event and some things are obvious from the photograph itself. For example, the jury does not need to be told that the photograph is of good quality or poor, nor whether the person is shown in close-up or was distant from the camera, or was alone or part of a crowd.[165] However, an accused who has elected not to testify is under no obligation to meet a jury request that he stand up and turn around, in order that they may be given a better view of him.[166]

## 3 VOICE IDENTIFICATION

Unlike visual identification, in the case of aural or voice identification, little judicial thought has been given to the danger of mistakes being made or to the safeguards necessary to lessen the danger. Moreover Code D all but ignores the subject and simply states that the Code does not preclude the police from making use of aural identification procedures, such as a 'voice identification parade', where they judge that appropriate.[167] In *R v Hersey*[168] two men wearing balaclava helmets robbed a shop, a robbery lasting some 15 minutes and involving considerable speech on the part of the robbers. The shopkeeper recognized the voice of one of them as a long-standing customer. A voice identification parade was held at which eleven volunteers and the accused, H, read a passage of text from a previous unrelated interview with H. On a *voir dire* an expert gave evidence that twelve voices was too many, that almost all of them were of a pitch higher than that of H, and only H had read the passage in a way which made sense. He also gave evidence of the effect of stress on pitch. The trial

---

[164] See *R v Duncan* (1992) *The Times*, 24 July, CA and *R v Pemberton* (1993) 99 Cr App R 228, CA.

[165] *R v Blenkinsop* [1995] 1 Cr App R 7, CA, approving *R v Downey* [1995] 1 Cr App R 547, CA. Cf *R v Dodson and Williams* (1984) 79 Cr App R 220, CA; and see also *Taylor v Chief Constable of Cheshire* [1987] 1 All ER 225, DC (Ch 10). Research, however, shows that there are difficulties and dangers: see Bruce, 'Fleeting Images of Shade' (1998) *The Psychologist* 331 and Henderson et al 'Matching the Faces of Robbers Captured on Video' (2001) 15 Applied Cognitive Psychology 445.

[166] *R v McNamara* [1996] Crim LR 750, CA.

[167] Para 1.2. See also para 18, Annex B, which deals with the situation in which a witness at a visual identification parade wishes to hear any parade member speak.

[168] [1998] Crim LR 281, CA.

judge decided not to exclude the identification evidence under section 78 of the Police and Criminal Evidence Act 1984, and ruled that the evidence of the expert was not admissible before the jury. The Court of Appeal held that evidence of the parade had been properly admitted and that the jurors did not require the assistance of the expert, who had dealt with matters which were within their own experience and competence.[169] It was also held that the judge should give the jury a direction based on the guidelines in *Turnbull*, but tailored for the purposes of voice identification or recognition: it was vital that the judge spell out the risk of mistaken identification and the reasons why a witness may be mistaken, point out that a truthful witness may yet be mistaken, and deal with the strengths and weaknesses in the identification evidence.

The Court of Appeal has since acknowledged, in *R v Roberts*,[170] that according to the expert research that has been done, voice identification is more difficult than visual identification, especially in the case of a stranger, and therefore should attract an even more stringent warning than that given in the case of visual identification. It is also clear that where a tape-recording, including a covert tape-recording, of a voice alleged to be that of the accused is admitted in evidence, the opinion evidence of an expert in phonetics is admissible on the question whether the voice matches that of the accused. Indeed, in appropriate cases, without such expert assistance the jury should not be asked to compare what they hear on a recording with either what they hear on another recording or the voice of the accused when giving evidence.[171]

Further guidance is clearly needed on aural dock identifications which, it is submitted, are no less dangerous than visual dock identifications.[172] Further detailed guidance is also required on the dangers of mistaken voice identification, and on the relevant factors to be taken into account by a judge in assessing the quality of voice identification so that he may properly decide (i) whether it is of such poor quality that he should withdraw the case from the jury and, if not, (ii) how he may adequately warn the jury about the special need for caution. Such factors are likely to include, for example, distinctive vocal features, duration of speech, and the effect of stress or of an attempt to disguise a voice.[173]

As to the pre-trial procedure, it has been made clear since *R v Hersey* that there is no duty to hold a voice identification parade under Code D, which relates only to visual identification, and that the matter is properly dealt with by a suitably adapted *Turnbull* warning.[174] However, it is submitted that there is an obvious need for a pre-trial procedure and not one crudely modelled on the procedures used for parades in the case of visual identification, because that would be to duck important issues of the

---

[169] See *R v Turner* [1975] QB 834, CA, Ch 18.        [170] [2000] Crim LR 183, CA.

[171] *R v Chenia* [2004] 1 All ER 543, CA at [106] and [107]. See also *R v O'Doherty* [2003] 1 Cr App R 77, Ch 18.

[172] See Ch 6 under **C Previous consistent or self-serving statements, 2(e) Previous identification**.

[173] See generally R Bull and B Clifford *Earwitness Testimony* ch 13; A Heaton-Armstrong, E Shepherd, and D Wolchover (eds) *Analysing Witness Testimony* (London 1999).

[174] *R v Gummerson and Steadman* [1999] Crim LR 680, CA.

kind raised by the expert in *R v Hersey*, for example questions relating to the number of voices that should be heard, the nature of the text that should be used, and the method by which the police should select those whose voices, so far as possible, resemble that of the accused.[175]

# E LIP-READING EVIDENCE

An expert lip-reader who has viewed a video or CCTV recording of a person talking, may give expert opinion evidence as to what was said, notwithstanding that such evidence is always, to some extent, unreliable, because not all words can be identified by vision alone, single syllabus words with little context are very difficult to interpret, and even when the words are presented in clearly spoken sentences, the best lip readers can only achieve up to 80 per cent correctness. In *R v Luttrell*[176] the Court of Appeal considered two issues: when such evidence should be excluded; and, where such evidence is admitted, the nature of the special warning that the judge must give to the jury. As to the former, Rose LJ said:[177]

The decision in each case is likely to be highly fact sensitive. For example, a video may be of such poor quality or the view of the speaker's face so poor that no reliable interpretation is possible. There may also be cases where the interpreting witness is not sufficiently skilled. A judge may properly take into account: whether consistency with extrinsic facts confirms or inconsistency casts doubt on the reliability of an interpretation; whether information provided to the lip reader might have coloured the reading; and whether the probative effect of the evidence depends on the interpretation of a single word or phrase or on the whole thrust of the conversation. In the light of such considerations, (which are not intended to be exhaustive) a judge may well rule on the *voir dire* that any lip-reading evidence proffered should not be admitted before the jury.

The court was in no doubt that where the evidence is admitted, it requires a warning from the judge as to its limitations and the concomitant risk of error, not least because the expert may fall significantly short of complete accuracy. Rose LJ said:[178]

As with any 'special warning', its precise terms will be fact-dependent, but in most, if not all cases, the judge should spell out to the jury the risk of mistakes as to the words that the lip reader believes were spoken; the reasons why the witness may be mistaken; and the way in which a convincing, authoritative and truthful witness may yet be a mistaken witness. Furthermore, the judge should deal with the particular strengths and weaknesses of the material in the instant case, carefully setting out the evidence, together with the criticisms that can properly be made of it because of other evidence. The jury should be reminded that

---

[175] For an analysis of the dangers of using voice identification and recognition evidence and possible safeguards for its use both before and at the trial, see David Ormerod 'Sounds Familiar?—Voice Identification Evidence' [2001] Crim LR 595.

[176] [2004] 2 Cr App R 520, CA.       [177] At [38].       [178] At [44].

the quality of the evidence will be affected by such matters as the lighting at the scene, the angle of the view in relation to those speaking, the distances involved, whether anything interfered with the observation, familiarity on the part of the lip-reader with the language spoken, the extent of the use of single syllable words, any awareness on the part of the expert witness of the context of the speech and whether the probative value of the evidence depends on isolated words or phrases or the general impact of long passages of conversation.

However, the court was also of the view that there was no reason in principle why lip-reading evidence adduced by the prosecution should not establish a prima facie case, although in reaching this conclusion the court may have been influenced by its own— and, it is submitted, questionable—observation that it is highly unlikely that lip reading evidence will ever stand alone.

## F SUDDEN INFANT DEATH SYNDROME

Infant deaths are attributed to Sudden Infant Death Syndrome (SIDS), known colloquially as 'cot deaths', where the immediate cause of death is apnoea, loss of breath or cessation of breathing occurring naturally, the underlying cause or causes being as yet unknown. Infant deaths cannot be attributed to SIDS, therefore, if they are clinically explicable or consequent on demonstrable trauma.

In *R v Cannings*[179] the appellant had been convicted of the murder of two of her four children, J who had died six weeks after his birth and M who had died eighteen weeks after his birth. Her eldest child, G, had died thirteen weeks after her birth. The Crown's case, for which there was no direct evidence, was that the accused had smothered all three of the children and that the deaths of J and M formed part of an overall 'pattern'. Their case depended on expert evidence that the conclusion of smothering could be drawn from the extreme rarity of three separate infant deaths in the same family. The appellant's case was that the deaths were attributable to SIDS and at the appeal she relied on fresh expert evidence to the effect that infant deaths occurring in the same family can and do occur naturally, even when unexplained. Allowing the appeal, it was held that where three infant deaths have occurred in the same family, each apparently unexplained, and for each of which there is no evidence extraneous to the expert evidence that harm was or must have been inflicted—for example, indications or admissions of violence or a pattern of ill-treatment—the proper approach is start with the fact that three unexplained deaths in the same family are indeed rare, but to proceed on the basis that if there is nothing to explain them, in our current state of knowledge they remain unexplained and, despite the known fact that some parents do smother their infant children, possible natural deaths. Whether there are one, two or even three deaths, the exclusion of currently known natural causes of infant death does not establish that the death or deaths resulted from the

---

[179] [2004] 1 All ER 725, CA.

deliberate infliction of harm. If, on examination of all the evidence, every possible cause has been excluded, the cause remains unknown. It was further held that, for the time being, where a full investigation into two or more sudden unexplained infant deaths in the same family is followed by a serious disagreement between reputable experts about the cause of death, and a body of such expert opinion concludes that natural causes, whether explained or not, cannot be excluded as a reasonable (and not a fanciful) possibility, a prosecution for murder should not be started or continued unless there is additional cogent evidence, extraneous to the expert evidence tending to support the conclusion that one of the infants was deliberately harmed, such as indications or admissions of violence or a pattern of ill-treatment.

The impact of the decision in *R v Cannings* in care proceedings was considered in *In re U (a Child) (Serious Injury: Standard of Proof)*.[180] It was held that although *R v Cannings* had provided a useful warning to judges in care proceedings against ill-considered conclusions or conclusions resting on insufficient evidence, a local authority should not refrain from proceedings or discontinue proceedings in any case where there is a substantial disagreement among the medical experts. However, there were considerations emphasized by the judgment in *R v Cannings* that were of direct application in care proceedings: (i) the cause of an injury or episode that cannot be explained scientifically remains equivocal; (ii) recurrence is not of itself probative; (iii) particular caution is necessary where medical experts disagree, with one opinion declining to exclude a reasonable possibility of natural cause; (iv) the court has to be on its guard against the over-dogmatic expert, an expert whose reputation or amour propre is at stake or one who has developed a scientific prejudice; and (v) it should never be forgotten that today's medical certainty may be discarded by the next generation of experts or that scientific research will throw light into corners that are, at present, dark.

[180] (2004) *The Times* 27 May 2004, CA.

# 9

# DOCUMENTARY AND REAL EVIDENCE

## A DOCUMENTARY EVIDENCE

Statements contained in documents, like oral statements, are subject to the general rules of evidence on admissibility which are considered elsewhere in this book.[1] This chapter concerns two additional requirements relating to the proof of documents on the contents of which a party seeks to rely. The first relates to proof of the contents, the essential question being whether the party relying on the document must produce primary evidence, for example the original, as opposed to secondary evidence, for example a copy of the original. The second relates to proof of the fact that the document was properly executed.[2]

In *R v Daye*[3] Darling J defined a document in the following terms:

any written thing capable of being evidence is properly described as a document and . . . it is immaterial on what the writing may be inscribed. It might be inscribed on paper, as is the common case now; but the common case once was that it was not on paper, but on parchment; and long before that it was on stone, marble, on clay, and it might be, and often was, on metal.

Nowadays, it would be reasonable to assume that the word bears a somewhat wider meaning. Today's equivalent of paper is often a disc, tape or film and conveys information by symbols, diagrams and pictures as well as by words and numbers. It is clear from the modern authorities, however, that the definition of a document varies according to the nature of the proceedings and the particular context in question. Concerning proof of a document in criminal proceedings, the word has been narrowly defined. In *Kajala v Noble*[4] the accused was convicted of using threatening behaviour likely to occasion a breach of the peace. A prosecution witness who was familiar with the accused gave evidence that he had recognized him on a BBC news programme concerning the incident. The BBC's policy was not to allow originals of

---

[1] Principal among these, in criminal cases, is the rule against hearsay. The admissibility of documentary statements as evidence of the truth of the facts contained in them is considered in Chs 10–12.

[2] A third issue, relating to the admissibility of extrinsic evidence for the purpose of explaining, contradicting, varying or adding to the terms of a document, is beyond the scope of the present work: see Cross *Evidence* (10th edn London 2004) 724–9.

[3] [1908] 2 KB 333 at 340.      [4] (1982) 75 Cr App R 149, CA.

their films to leave the premises and therefore a video cassette recording of the incident, which the court was satisfied was an authentic copy of the original, was admitted in evidence. On the question whether the original film should have been produced in court, Ackner LJ, referring to the rule that if an original document is available in a party's hands, that party must produce it and cannot give secondary evidence by producing a copy, concluded: 'the old rule is limited and confined to written documents in the strict sense of the term, and has no relevance to tapes or films.'[5]

In civil proceedings, by contrast, 'document', for the purposes of the rules on the disclosure and inspection of documents, means 'anything in which information of any description is recorded',[6] a definition wide enough to cover not only documents in writing, but also maps, plans, graphs, drawings, discs, audio-tapes, sound-tracks, photographs, negatives, video-tapes, and films. The same definition is used in relation to documents, including computer-produced documents, containing hearsay statements admissible under the Civil Evidence Act 1995 or the Criminal Justice Act 2003.[7]

## 1 PROOF OF CONTENTS

Proof of the contents of a document on which a party seeks to rely is now largely governed, in criminal cases, by section 133 of the Criminal Justice Act 2003 and section 71 of the Police and Criminal Evidence Act 1984, and in civil cases by sections 8 and 9 of the Civil Evidence Act 1995.[8] Section 133 of the 2003 Act provides that:

Where a statement in a document is admissible as evidence in criminal proceedings, the statement may be proved by producing either—

(a) the document, or

(b) (whether or not the document exists) a copy of the document or of the material part of it,

authenticated in whatever way the court may approve.[9]

Under section 71 of the Police and Criminal Evidence Act 1984, in any criminal proceedings the contents of a document may (whether or not the document is still in existence) be proved by the production of an enlargement of a microfilm copy of that document or the material part of it, authenticated in such manner as the court may approve.

Section 8 of the Civil Evidence Act 1995 is cast in terms similar to those of section 133 of the Criminal Justice Act 2003. Under section 9(1) and (2) of the 1995 Act, a

---

[5] (1982) 75 Cr App R 149 at 152. As an authority on the *proof of contents* in a criminal case, this decision should now be read subject to s 133 of the Criminal Justice Act 2003, below.

[6] CPR r 31.4.     [7] Civil Evidence Act 1995, s 13 and Criminal Justice Act 2003, s 134(1).

[8] In the case of tape recordings and transcripts of police interviews sought to be introduced in criminal proceedings, s 133 of the 2003 Act must be read in conjunction with the Code of Practice on Tape Recording of Interviews with Suspects (Code E) and para 43, *Practice Direction (Criminal Proceedings: Consolidation)* [2002] 1 WLR 2870.

[9] For the meaning of the words 'statement', 'document' and 'copy', see s 115(2) and s 134(1) of the 2003 Act, Ch 10.

document which is certified as forming part of the records of a business or public authority may be received in evidence in civil proceedings without further proof; and under section 9(3) of that Act, the *absence* of an entry in the records of a business or public authority may be proved by the affidavit of an officer of the business or authority.[10]

Section 133 of the 2003 Act and section 8 of the 1995 Act appear to be of general application, ie to apply to *any* statement contained in a document, and thus not confined to hearsay statements in documents admissible under the Criminal Justice Act 2003 or the Civil Evidence Act 1995. Likewise, section 9 of the 1995 Act appears to apply to *any* document forming part of the records of a business or public authority and not merely documents containing hearsay statements admissible under the 1995 Act. On this reading, these provisions have reversed completely the general rule at common law that a party seeking to rely on the contents of a document must adduce primary evidence (usually the original). Pending a definitive ruling to that effect, the general common-law rule, considered below, may continue to apply in the case of non-hearsay. In any event, section 133 of the 2003 Act is permissive as to the means of proof and therefore cannot be taken to have overridden (i) the common-law rule that where secondary evidence of the contents of a private document is admissible, it may take the form of *oral* evidence (use of which is not sanctioned by section 133);[11] (ii) a number of statutory provisions, mainly relating to public documents, which provide for proof of their contents by copies which are required to take a particular form, such as an examined copy (ie a copy proved by oral evidence to correspond with the original) or a certified copy (ie a copy certified to be accurate by an official who has custody of the original); or (iii) the Bankers' Books Evidence Act 1879, whereby provision is made for the admission of copies of entries in a banker's book, but only subject to the fulfilment of certain conditions, one of which is that some person proves that he has examined the copy with the original and that it is correct.[12] The same may be said, concerning civil cases, of sections 8 and 9 of the 1995 Act. Section 14 of that Act provides that nothing in the Act affects (i) the proof of documents by means other than those specified in sections 8 or 9[13] or (ii) the operation of certain statutory provisions governing the means of proving certain public and official documents.[14]

## (a) The general rule at common law—primary evidence

The general rule is that a party seeking to rely upon the contents of a document must adduce primary evidence of those contents. The rule, often regarded as the only

---

[10] See further Ch 11.        [11] *R v Nazeer* [1998] Crim LR 750, CA.

[12] All three matters are considered below.        [13] Section 14(2).

[14] Section 14(3). It is unclear, however, why only some of the many statutory provisions governing the proof of various types of document have been specified. Those referred to in s 14(3) include the Documentary Evidence Act 1868, s 2 and the Documentary Evidence Act 1882, s 2 (see below under (b)(vi) **Public documents**); the Evidence (Colonial Statutes) Act 1907, s 1 (see Ch 18); and the Evidence (Foreign, Dominion and Colonial Documents) Act 1933, s 1 (see Chs 2 and 12).

remaining instance of the 'best evidence rule',[15] under which a party must produce the best evidence that the nature of the case will allow, may be justified as a means of reducing the risks of fraud, mistake, and inaccuracy which might result from proof by either production of a copy of a document or parol evidence of its contents.

There are three recognized categories of primary evidence of the contents of a document: the original, copies of enrolled documents and admissions made by parties. The best kind of primary evidence is the original document in question. Although the original is usually identifiable with ease, some cases do occasion difficulty. Where documents are produced in duplicate, each of them may constitute an original. Thus the duplicates of a deed which have been executed by all parties are all originals.[16] A copy of a document, however, whether produced by carbon, duplicator or photocopying machine, is not original unless signed or otherwise duly executed. In the case of telegrams, the original, if tendered against the receiver, is the message he received; the original, if tendered against the sender, is the message that was handed in or recorded at the Post Office.[17] A counterpart lease executed by the lessee alone is the original if tendered against him, whereas the other part is the original if tendered against the lessor.[18] Where a private document is required to be enrolled, that is officially filed either in a court or some other public office, a copy issued by the court or office in question is treated as an original. Thus where executors obtain a grant of probate, the probate copy of the will is treated as primary evidence of the contents of the will.[19] Where a party to litigation has made an informal admission concerning the contents of a document, his admission constitutes primary evidence of the contents and is admissible in evidence against him. Thus, in *Slatterie v Pooley*[20] an action on a deed by which the defendant covenanted to indemnify the plaintiff against certain debts contained in the schedule to another deed, which was inadmissible because not duly stamped, an oral admission by the defendant that a particular debt was included in the schedule was held to be admissible against him.[21]

The general rule applies in any case where a party seeks to rely upon the actual contents of a document. Thus in *MacDonnell v Evans*[22] the defendant's counsel was not allowed to cross-examine a witness as to whether a certain letter, which was produced, was written by him in answer to another letter, which was not produced, charging him with forgery. This amounted to an attempt to admit the contents of the other letter without producing it. Maule J said: 'it is a general rule . . . that, if you want to get at the contents of a written document, the proper way is to produce it, if you can.' However, in cases where it is unnecessary to place reliance upon the contents of a document because the fact or matter in issue, even if recorded in a document, can be

---

[15] In fact it pre-dates the best evidence rule.   [16] *Forbes v Samuel* [1913] 3 KB 706.

[17] *R v Regan* (1887) 16 Cox CC 203.   [18] *Doe d West v Davis* (1806) 7 East 363.

[19] If a question arises concerning construction of the will, however, the court may examine the original: see *Re Battie-Wrightson, Cecil v Battie-Wrightson* [1920] 2 Ch 330.

[20] (1840) 6 M&W 664.   [21] But see now Civil Evidence Act 1995, s 7(1) (Ch 11).

[22] (1852) 11 CB 930.

proved by other evidence, the general rule has no application. Thus, whereas proof of the length of a tenancy, or the amount of rent due thereunder, requires production of the lease, proof of the existence or fact of a tenancy, albeit created by a lease, may be proved by other evidence. In *Augustien v Challis*,[23] an action against a sheriff alleged to have negligently withdrawn a writ of *fi fa*, his defence was that a claim of the debtor's landlord, in respect of rent due, had priority over the plaintiff's claim. Evidence given by the landlord that the rent was payable under a lease was held to be inadmissible on the grounds that the amount of rent due could not be proved without producing the original of the lease.[24] In *R v Holy Trinity, Hull (Inhabitants)*,[25] by contrast, the fact of a tenancy, created by a lease which defined its terms, could be proved without production of that lease; parol evidence, such as evidence on the payment of the rent, sufficed.[26] Likewise, the rule has no application where reference is made to a document merely for the purpose of establishing the bare fact of its existence. In *R v Elworthy*[27] the accused, a solicitor, was charged with perjury. It was alleged that he had falsely sworn that there was no draft of a certain statutory declaration which he had prepared. The Court for Crown Cases Reserved held that although secondary evidence of the contents of the draft and of certain alterations made in it was inadmissible, the prosecution could properly adduce parol evidence that such a draft existed and was in the possession of the accused.[28] It remains to note that the general rule does not apply when the contents of a document are referred to merely in order to identify it. Thus it has been said that 'in an action of trover for a promissory note, the contents of the promissory note may be stated verbally by a witness'.[29]

Although both the general rule and the common-law exceptions to it are well established, in *Springsteen v Flute International Ltd*[30] the Court of Appeal favoured a more generalized discretionary approach to admissibility. It held as follows. (1) The best evidence rule, long on its deathbed, had finally expired. (2) In every case where a party seeks to adduce secondary evidence of the contents of a document, it is a matter for the court to decide, in the light of all the circumstances of the case, what, if any, weight to attach to the evidence. (3) Where such a party can readily adduce the document, it may be expected that, absent some special circumstances, the court will decline to admit the secondary evidence on the ground that it is worthless. (4) At the other extreme, where such a party genuinely cannot produce the document, it may be expected that, absent some special circumstances, the court will admit the secondary evidence and attach such weight to it as it considers appropriate. (5) In cases falling

---

[23] (1847) 1 Exch 279.      [24] See also *Twyman v Knowles* (1853) 13 CB 222 (the length of a tenancy).

[25] (1827) 7 B&C 611.

[26] See also *Alderson v Clay* (1816) 1 Stark 405 (proof of the fact of a partnership).

[27] (1867) LR 1 CCR 103.

[28] The Crown had not given notice to the accused to produce the original. Had they done so, secondary evidence of the contents of the draft would have been admissible (see below).

[29] Per Martin B in *Boyle v Wiseman* (1855) 11 Exch 360 at 367, citing *Whitehead v Scott* (1830) 1 Mood&R 2.

[30] [2001] EMLR 654, CA.

between these two extremes, it is for the court to make a judgment as to whether in all the circumstances any weight should be attached to the secondary evidence.[31]

### (b) The exceptions—secondary evidence

Public documents, which constitute one of the exceptions to the general rule, are considered later in this chapter. In the case of private documents, secondary evidence of their contents, where admissible, may take the form of a copy, a copy of a copy[32] or oral evidence. Where a copy is produced, proof is required that it is a true copy of the original. In *R v Collins*[33] the accused, who had cashed a cheque on his bank account which he knew to have been closed, was convicted of obtaining money by false pretences. Having been called upon to produce a letter sent to him informing him that the account was closed, which he had failed to do, secondary evidence of the contents of the letter became admissible.[34] Accordingly, at the trial the prosecution called a manager of the bank to produce a copy of a carbon-copy of the letter. The Court of Criminal Appeal held that the copy produced, in the absence of proof that it was not only a true copy of the carbon-copy, but also in the same terms as the original, had been improperly admitted.

Where secondary evidence is admissible, there is a general rule that 'there are no degrees of secondary evidence'.[35] Thus although less weight may attach to inferior forms of secondary evidence, there is no obligation to tender the 'best' copy, rather than an inferior copy or a copy of a copy, and oral evidence of the contents is admissible even if a copy or some other more satisfactory type of secondary evidence is available. To this general rule there is a variety of exceptions. The contents of a will admitted to probate may not be proved by oral evidence if the original or probate copy exists. Judicial documents and bankers' books[36] are generally proved not by oral evidence but by office copies and examined copies respectively. Finally, many public documents may be proved by oral evidence only if examined, certified, or other copies are unavailable.[37]

*(i) Hearsay statements admissible by statute.* Where the contents of a document are admissible hearsay under the Criminal Justice Act 2003, they may be proved in accordance with section 133 of that Act and section 71 of the Police and Criminal Evidence Act 1984; and where the contents of a document are admissible hearsay under the Civil Evidence Act 1995, they may be proved in accordance with sections 8 and 9 of that Act.[38]

*(ii) Failure to produce after notice.* A party seeking to rely upon a document may prove its contents by secondary evidence if the original is in the possession or control of

---

[31] See also *Post Office Counters Ltd v Mahida* [2003] EWCA Civ 1583, (2003) *The Times* 31 Oct 2003, Ch 2.
[32] *Lafone v Griffin* (1909) 25 TLR 308; *R v Collins* (1960) 44 Cr App R 170. Contrast *Everingham v Roundell* (1838) 2 Mood&R 138.
[33] (1960) 44 Cr App R 170; cf *R v Wayte* (1982) 76 Cr App R 110, CA.    [34] See below.
[35] Per Lord Abinger CB in *Doe d Gilbert v Ross* (1840) 7 M&W 102.    [36] See below.
[37] See below.    [38] See generally above and Chs 10 and 11.

another party to the proceedings who, having been served with a notice to produce it, has failed to do so. The purpose of serving such a notice is not to notify the other party that reliance will be placed on a document so that he can prepare evidence to explain or confirm it, but merely to give him sufficient opportunity to produce it if he wishes or, if he does not, to enable the first party to adduce secondary evidence. Thus it has been held that where the original is in court, secondary evidence is admissible even where a party fails to comply with a notice to produce served during the course of the trial.[39]

It is assumed that the foregoing principles remain good law notwithstanding that the Civil Procedure Rules make no provision for formal service of a notice to produce.[40]

It remains to note that a notice to produce has never compelled production of a document. A party to civil proceedings who wishes to rely at the trial on the original of a document, should serve a witness summons requiring a witness to produce the document to the court.[41]

*(iii) A stranger's lawful refusal to produce.* Secondary evidence of the contents of a document may be given when the original is in the possession of a stranger to the litigation who, having been served with a *subpoena duces tecum* (now known as a witness summons requiring a witness to produce a document),[42] has lawfully refused to produce it, for example by reason of a claim to privilege[43] or diplomatic immunity[44] or because he is outside the jurisdiction and therefore cannot be compelled to produce it.[45] However, if the stranger, in unlawful disobedience of the summons, refuses to produce the original, secondary evidence is inadmissible because he is bound to produce it and is punishable for contempt if he refuses to do so.[46] The effect of these rules is to cast a duty upon the party seeking to rely upon the document to compel the stranger to produce the original, thereby eliminating the risk of unreliable secondary evidence being admitted in consequence of their collusion.

*(iv) Lost documents.* Secondary evidence of the contents of a document is admissible on proof that the original has been destroyed or cannot be found after due search. The quality of evidence required to show the loss or destruction varies according to the nature and value of the document in question. In *Brewster v Sewell*[47] the plaintiff was unable to produce a policy of insurance against loss by fire on which a claim had been paid. Subsequent to the fire, which had occurred some years before the proceedings, a fresh policy had been issued. Evidence was given of a thorough but unsuccessful search for the earlier policy. It was held that, in the circumstances, the original policy had become 'mere waste paper' and that sufficient evidence of due search had been given to allow proof of its contents by secondary evidence. Bayley J said:[48]

---

[39] *Dwyer v Collins* (1852) 21 LJ Ex 225.          [40] See, formerly, RSC Ord 24, r 10.
[41] See CPR r 34.2.          [42] See CPR r 34.2.          [43] *Mills v Oddy* (1834) 6 C&P 728.
[44] *R v Nowaz* [1976] 3 All ER 5, CA.          [45] *Kilgour v Owen* (1889) 88 LT Jo 7.
[46] *R v Llanfaethly (Inhabitants)* (1853) 2 E&B 940.
[47] (1820) 3 B&Ald 296. See also *R v Wayte* (1982) 76 Cr App R 110, CA.
[48] (1820) 3 B&Ald 296 at 300.

There is a great distinction between useful and useless papers. The presumption of law is that a man will keep all those papers which are valuable to himself, and which may, with any degree of probability, be of any future use to him. The presumption on the contrary is that a man will not keep those papers which have entirely discharged their duty, and which are never likely to be required for any purpose whatever.

*(v) Production of original impossible.* Secondary evidence is admissible where production of the original is either physically impossible, for example because it is an inscription upon a tombstone or wall,[49] or legally impossible, for example because the document in question is a notice which is required by statute to be constantly affixed at a factory or workshop.[50]

*(vi) Public documents.* At common law, secondary evidence of the contents of a wide variety of public documents is admissible on the grounds that production of the originals would entail a high degree of public inconvenience.[51] Under the modern law, there is a large number of statutes which also provide for the proof of public documents by secondary evidence. Secondary evidence for these purposes is usually required to take the form of an examined, authenticated, certified, office, Queen's Printer's or Stationery Office copy. Under section 7 of the Evidence Act 1851, for example, the contents of all proclamations, treaties and other acts of state of any foreign state or of any British colony, and all judgments, decrees, orders, and other judicial proceedings of any court of justice in any foreign state or in any British colony may be proved by an examined copy, which is a copy proved by oral evidence to correspond with the original, or by copies authenticated with the seal of the foreign state, British colony or foreign or colonial court, as the case may be.[52] Certified copies are copies certified to be accurate by an official who has custody of the original.[53] They are employed to prove byelaws and records kept in the Public Record Office.[54] Under section 14 of the Evidence Act 1851, certified or examined copies may be used to prove the contents of any document provided that it is of such a public nature that it is admissible in evidence on production from proper custody and no other statute provides for proof of its contents by means of a copy. Office copies, which are prepared by officials who have custody of original judicial documents and are authenticated

---

[49] Per Alderson B in *Mortimer v M'Callan* (1840) 6 M&W 58. See also, *sed quaere, R v Hunt* (1820) 3 B&Ald 566 (inscriptions on flags or banners).

[50] *Owner v Bee Hive Spinning Co Ltd* [1914] 1 KB 105, DC. See also *Alivon v Furnival* (1834) 1 Cr M&R 277 (document in custody of foreign court).

[51] See, eg, *Mortimer v M'Callan* (1840) 6 M&W 58 (books of the Bank of England).

[52] See also n 53, below. In the case of a foreign conviction, it remains necessary to establish that the examined copy relates to the person said to have been convicted, which may be achieved by the admission of any relevant evidence, including, eg, fingerprint evidence: *R v Mauricia* [2002] 2 Cr App R 377, CA.

[53] Where a statute provides for proof of a document by a certified, sealed or stamped copy, the copy, provided it purports to be signed, sealed, or stamped, is admissible without any proof of the sign, seal or stamp, as the case may be: Evidence Act 1845, s 1.

[54] Local Government Act 1972, s 238 (the clerk to the local authority) and Public Records Act 1958, s 9 (the Keeper of Public Records).

with the seal of the court,[55] may be used to prove judgments, orders and other judicial documents. Queen's Printer's copies are used to prove private Acts of Parliament and journals of either House of Parliament,[56] royal proclamations, orders in council and statutory instruments.[57]

*(vii) Bankers' books.* In both civil and criminal proceedings, it is often necessary to adduce evidence of the contents of bankers' books. In order to avoid the inconvenience that production of the originals would entail, the Bankers' Books Evidence Act 1879 provides for the admission of copies. Section 3, an exception to the rule against hearsay, reads as follows:

Subject to the provisions of this Act, a copy of an entry in a banker's book shall in all legal proceedings be received as prima facie evidence of such entry, and of the matters, transactions, and accounts therein recorded.

'Banker' is defined as a 'deposit-taker' or the National Savings Bank.[58] 'Bankers' books' were originally defined to include 'ledgers', 'day books', 'cash books' and 'account books'. The definition has since been extended to include, in addition, 'other records used in the ordinary business of the bank, whether those records are in written form or are kept on microfilm, magnetic tape or any other form of mechanical or electronic data retrieval mechanism'.[59] 'Other records used in the ordinary business of the bank' has to be read *eiusdem generis* with 'ledgers, day books cash books' and 'account books', which are the means by which banks record day-to-day financial transactions, and therefore does not cover bank records of conversations between its employees and customers or others, or internal memoranda.[60] Paid cheques and paying-in slips retained by a bank after the conclusion of a banking transaction to which they relate have been held not to be bankers' books on the same basis or on the grounds that even if bundles of such documents can be treated as 'records used in the ordinary business of the bank', the addition of an individual cheque or paying-in slip cannot be regarded as making an 'entry' in those records.[61]

---

[55] See n 53 above.

[56] Evidence Act 1845, s 3 and Documentary Evidence Act 1882, s 2. Stationery Office copies may also be used. The Interpretation Act 1978, s 3 provides that: 'Every Act is a public Act to be judicially noticed as such, unless the contrary is expressly provided by the Act.' This section applies to all Acts passed after 1850. At common law, judicial notice is taken of earlier enactments, if public (see Ch 22).

[57] Evidence Act 1845, s 3 and Documentary Evidence Act 1868, s 2. Such documents may also be proved by a copy of the Gazette containing them or by a copy certified to be true by the appropriate official. However, where a photocopy from a commercial publication is produced instead, and there is no suggestion of any inaccuracy in the version before the court, an appeal may not succeed: *R v Koon Cheung Tang* [1995] Crim LR 813, CA.

[58] Section 9(1). A 'deposit taker' will normally be someone with permission under Part 4 of the Financial Services and Markets Act 2000 to accept deposits: see s 9(1A)–(1C).

[59] Section 9(2).      [60] *Re Howglen Ltd* [2001] 1 All ER 376, Ch D.

[61] *Williams v Williams* [1987] 3 All ER 257, CA. In civil proceedings, if such documents relate to the bank account of the other party to the action, an order for disclosure may be made and the bank, as agent holding the documents on that party's behalf, may then be required to disclose them. In other cases, the party seeking disclosure of specific documents may be able to make use of CPR r 31.17, which provides for disclosure by a person who is not a party to the proceedings or CPR r 34.2, which empowers the court to issue a witness summons requiring a witness to produce documents to the court.

The same reasoning may be used to justify the decision, reached prior to the extension of the definition of 'bankers' books', that copies of letters written by a bank and contained in a file of its correspondence do not constitute bankers' books.[62]

A copy is only admissible under section 3 of the 1879 Act if: (i) a partner or officer of the bank proves, by oral evidence or affidavit, that the book was at the time of the making of the entry one of the ordinary books of the bank, the entry was made in the usual and ordinary course of business, and the book is in the custody or control of the bank,[63] and (ii) some person proves, by oral evidence or affidavit, that he has examined the copy with the original and that it is correct.[64] Section 7 provides for any party to legal proceedings to apply to a court[65] or judge for an order to be at liberty to inspect and take copies of entries in bankers' books for the purposes of those proceedings. The order may be made without summoning the bank or any other party and shall be served on the bank three clear days before it is to be obeyed, unless the court or judge otherwise directs.[66] An order may be made under section 7 to inspect the account of a person who is not a party to the proceedings, even if that person is not compellable as a witness,[67] but in criminal cases, such an order should be made only in exceptional circumstances and where the private interest in keeping a bank account confidential is outweighed by the public interest in assisting a prosecution.[68]

In civil proceedings, an application under section 7 to inspect entries in the bank account of a third party will only be granted if (i) the court is satisfied that the account is in fact the account of the other party to the action or an account with which he is so much concerned that items in it would be evidence against him, and (ii) the applicant shows very strong grounds for suspicion, almost amounting to certainty, that there are items in the account which would be material evidence against the other party.[69] A foreign bank which is not a party to the proceedings, even if it carries on business within the jurisdiction, should not, save in exceptional circumstances, be ordered to produce documents which are outside the jurisdiction and concern business transacted outside the jurisdiction, because an order under the 1879 Act is an exercise of sovereign authority to assist in the administration of justice, and foreign banks owe their customers a duty of confidence regulated by the law of the

---

[62] *R v Dadson* (1983) 77 Cr App R 91, CA. See also *Barker v Wilson* [1980] 1 WLR 884, DC.

[63] Section 4.    [64] Section 5.

[65] Justices before whom criminal proceedings are pending constitute a court for these purposes: *R v Kinghorn* [1908] 2 KB 949.

[66] Although the Act allows an application to be made without notice, there is much to be said for notice being given: per Widgery LJ in *R v Marlborough Street Magistrates' Court, ex p Simpson* (1980) 70 Cr App R 291, DC at 294. In the case of an application in respect of accounts of a person who is not a party to the proceedings, the order should either not be made until the account owner has been informed and given an opportunity to be heard or should be made in the form of an order *nisi*, allowing a period for the person affected to show cause why the order should not take effect: per Oliver LJ in *R v Grossman* (1981) 73 Cr App R 302 at 309, CA.

[67] *R v Andover Justices, ex p Rhodes* [1980] Crim LR 644, DC.

[68] *R v Grossman* (1981) 73 Cr App R 302 at 307, CA.

[69] *South Staffordshire Tramways Co v Ebbsmith* [1895] 2 QB 669, CA (a pre-trial application) and *D B Deniz Nakliyati TAS v Yugopetrol* [1992] 1 All ER 205, CA (an application against a judgment debtor).

country where the documents are kept.[70] Although in criminal proceedings an order will not be refused on the grounds that it incriminates the party against whom it is made,[71] it is a serious interference with the liberty of the subject and the court should satisfy itself that the application is more than a mere fishing expedition by considering whether the prosecution has other evidence to support the charge.[72] In *R v Nottingham City Justices, ex p Lynn*[73] an order made by justices against an accused charged with drug smuggling for the inspection of accounts over a three-year period, was reduced by the Divisional Court to cover a period of six months, there being insufficient evidence to link the accused with offences during most of the three years.

## 2 PROOF OF DUE EXECUTION

The general rule, in both civil and criminal proceedings, is that a document will only be admitted in evidence on proof of due execution. An exception exists in the case of public documents covered by statutes of the kind referred to earlier in this chapter, most of which not only provide for the proof of contents by secondary evidence, but also exempt from proof of due execution. In the case of a private document, proof of due execution may be admitted or presumed, but otherwise usually involves proof of handwriting or a signature and, in some cases, proof of attestation. In some cases, documents are required to be stamped for the purposes of stamp duty. Each of these matters now falls to be considered further.

### (a) Proof of handwriting

Proof of the due execution of a private document usually involves showing that it was written or signed by the person by whom it purports to have been written or signed. For these purposes, direct oral evidence that the signatory signed in a particular name may be given by the signatory himself or by any other person who witnessed the execution of the document. Proof may also be effected by admissible hearsay assertions to the same effect; or by the opinion evidence of someone who, although not a witness to the execution of the document, is acquainted with the handwriting of the person in question. In *Doe d Mudd v Suckermore*[74] Coleridge J said:

---

[70] *MacKinnon v Donaldson Lufkin and Jenrette Securities Corpn* [1986] 1 All ER 653, Ch D, applying *R v Grossman* (1981) 73 Cr App R 302, CA (a decision acknowledged to have been given *per incuriam*, the proceedings in the case being criminal and the Court of Appeal, therefore, having no jurisdiction). However, a party seeking to obtain documents from a foreign bank in these circumstances may apply to a master under CPR r 34.13 for the issue of letters of request to the courts of the country in question specifying the documents to be produced, or may apply directly to a court in that country under the relevant local provisions, having first obtained the permission of the English court on an application with notice.

[71] In civil proceedings the Act may not be used to compel disclosure of incriminating material: see *Waterhouse v Barker* [1924] 2 KB 759, CA and *Re Bankers' Books Evidence Act 1879, R v Bono* (1913) 29 TLR 635.

[72] *Williams v Summerfield* [1972] 2 QB 512, DC.      [73] [1984] Crim LR 554.

[74] (1837) 5 Ad&El 703 at 705.

either the witness has seen the party write on some other occasion, or he has corresponded with him, and transactions have taken place between them, upon the faith that letters purporting to have been written or signed by him have been so written or signed.

It is clear, however, that the weight to be attached to such opinion evidence will vary according to the circumstances in question.

A final method of proving handwriting or a signature is by comparison of the document in question with another document which is proved or admitted to have been written by the person in question. Section 8 of the Criminal Procedure Act 1865 provides that:

Comparison of a disputed writing with any writing proved to the satisfaction of the judge to be genuine shall be permitted to be made by witnesses;[75] and such writings, and the evidence of witnesses respecting the same, may be submitted to the court and jury as evidence of the genuineness or otherwise of the writing in dispute.

The section applies to both civil and criminal proceedings but whereas in the former the court must be satisfied as to the genuineness of the specimen handwriting only on a balance of probabilities, proof beyond reasonable doubt is the appropriate standard for the prosecution in criminal cases.[76] The tribunal of fact, in comparing the disputed and specimen handwriting, may be assisted by the evidence of someone who, although not an expert, is familiar with the handwriting in question[77] or by the opinion evidence of an expert in handwriting, whether his skill has been acquired professionally or otherwise.[78] As a general rule in criminal cases, the jury should not be left to draw their own unaided conclusion from a comparison without the assistance of an expert.[79] However, where an expert is called, it is his function to point out similarities or differences between the documents, leaving it to the tribunal of fact to draw their own conclusion.[80] In cases where the documents are placed before the jury as exhibits or for some proper purpose other than that of making a comparison and an expert is not called, the jury should be warned very carefully not to make a comparison.[81]

It remains to note that any of the above forms of proof of handwriting may be used in the case of a document which, although not required by law to be attested, was in fact attested. Section 7 of the Criminal Procedure Act 1865 provides that such a document may be proved 'as if there had been no attesting witness thereto'.

### (b) Proof of attestation

Proof of due execution sometimes requires evidence of attestation. It will be convenient to consider first the proof of wills and other testamentary documents. Except

---

[75] A witness who has not seen the original 'disputed writing' (because, eg, it is lost) may use a photocopy of it to make the comparison: *Lockheed-Arabia Corpn v Owen* [1993] 3 All ER 641, CA.

[76] *R v Ewing* [1983] 2 All ER 645, CA (Ch 4).

[77] *Fitzwalter Peerage Claim* (1844) 10 Cl&Fin 193, HL.     [78] *R v Silverlock* [1894] 2 QB 766.

[79] *R v Tilley* [1961] 1 WLR 1309, CCA; *R v Harden* [1963] 1 QB 8, CCA.

[80] *Wakeford v Bishop of Lincoln* (1921) 90 LJPC 174.     [81] *R v O'Sullivan* [1969] 1 WLR 497, CA.

where probate is sought in common form, in order to prove the due execution of a will, one of the attesting witnesses, if available, must be called. Witnesses to the execution of a will are treated as the court's witnesses and may be cross-examined by the party seeking to prove due execution.[82] If the witness denies the execution[83] or refuses to give evidence,[84] other evidence becomes admissible. If all of the attesting witnesses are dead, insane, beyond the jurisdiction or untraceable, secondary evidence of attestation by proof of the handwriting of one of the attesting witnesses is required. If, despite every effort to do so, it is impossible to prove the handwriting of one of the attesting witnesses, other evidence of due execution is admissible, for example that of a non-attesting witness to the execution.[85]

Although at one time it was necessary in the case of any document required by law to be attested to call one of the attesting witnesses (unless they were all unavailable), section 3 of the Evidence Act 1938 provides that, except in the case of a will or other testamentary document, any document required by law to be attested 'may, instead of being proved by an attesting witness, be proved in the manner in which it might be proved if no attesting witness were alive'. Thus documents, other than testamentary documents, which require attestation may, but need not, be proved by the evidence of an attesting witness. Proof may be effected by evidence of the handwriting of an attesting witness or, if this is unobtainable, by other evidence.

### (c) Admissions and presumptions

In practice, due execution is frequently admitted or presumed, thereby rendering proof of handwriting and attestation unnecessary. Due execution may be formally admitted both in civil proceedings and, under section 10 of the Criminal Justice Act 1967, in criminal proceedings. Under CPR rule 32.19(1) a party shall be deemed to admit the authenticity of a document disclosed to him under Part 31 of the rules (disclosure and inspection of documents) unless he serves notice that he wishes the document to be proved at trial. Proof of due execution is also unnecessary when the document in question is in the possession of an opponent who refuses to comply with a notice to produce it.[86]

A document which is more than 20 years old[87] and comes from proper custody is presumed to have been duly executed. Although proper custody, for these purposes, does not mean that the document should be found in 'the best and most proper place of deposit', if the document is found in some other place, the court must be satisfied that such custody was 'reasonable and natural' in the circumstances of the case. This was the view of Tindal CJ in *Meath (Bishop) v Marquis of Winchester*,[88] who accordingly held that certain documents relating to a bishopric had been produced from

---

[82] *Oakes v Uzzell* [1932] P 19.     [83] *Bowman v Hodgson* (1867) LR 1 P&D 362.

[84] *Re Oven's Goods* (1892) 29 LR Ir 451.     [85] *Clarke v Clarke* (1879) 5 LR Ir 47.

[86] *Cooke v Tanswell* (1818) 8 Taunt 450.

[87] At common law, the period was thirty years. The period of twenty years was substituted by the Evidence Act 1938, s 4.

[88] (1836) 3 Bing NC 183, HL; cf *Doe d Lord Arundel v Fowler* (1850) 14 QB 700.

proper custody despite having been found among the papers of a deceased bishop rather than in the custody of his successor, which was the best place of deposit.

It is also convenient, at this point, to note certain other presumptions relating to documents. They are: (i) that a document was made on the date which it bears;[89] (ii) that an alteration or erasure in a deed was made before execution, in a will after execution (on the grounds that a deed, but not a will, would be invalidated if presumed to have been altered after execution);[90] and (iii) that a deed was duly sealed.[91]

### (d) Stamped documents

Certain documents are required to be stamped for the purposes of stamp duty. Although in criminal proceedings such a document is admissible if unstamped, in civil proceedings a document requiring a stamp shall not be given in evidence unless it is duly stamped in accordance with the law in force at the time when it was first executed or, the court having objected to the omission or insufficiency of the stamp, and the document being one which may be legally stamped after its execution, payment is made of the amount of unpaid duty, together with any penalty payable on stamping, and a further sum of one pound.[92] The parties cannot waive these rules.[93] If a document requiring a stamp cannot be found or is not produced after notice to do so, it is presumed to have been duly stamped. However, if there is evidence to show that the document was not duly stamped, it is presumed, in the absence of evidence to the contrary, that this remained the case.[94]

# B  REAL EVIDENCE

Real evidence usually takes the form of some material object examined by the tribunal of fact as a means of proof. This and other varieties of real evidence are considered separately as follows.

## 1  MATERIAL OBJECTS

Where the existence, condition or value of some material object is in issue or relevant to an issue, it may be produced for inspection by the tribunal of fact. Thus where a purchaser alleges that certain goods do not answer the vendor's description, the goods in question may be produced to the judge so that he may act on his own perception. Likewise, a jury may inspect a knife alleged to have been used in the commission of a murder. Although the tribunal of fact may attach considerable weight to such

---

[89]  *Anderson v Weston* (1840) 6 Bing NC 296.

[90]  Per Lord Campbell CJ in *Doe d Tatum v Catomore* (1851) 16 QB 745. An alteration in a will is only valid and effective if executed in like manner as is required for the execution of the will: Wills Act 1837, s 21.

[91]  *Sed quaere*: see *Re Sandilands* (1871) LR 6 CP 411.          [92]  Stamp Act 1891, s 14.

[93]  *Bowker v Williamson* (1889) 5 TLR 382.          [94]  *Closmadeuc v Carrel* (1856) 18 CB 36.

evidence, this would be rare in the absence of accompanying testimony. Thus in the examples given, the goods would require to be identified and the knife, as an item of evidence, would be of limited value in the absence not only of some testimony connecting it with the accused, for example evidence that it was found in his possession, but also of expert testimony that it was capable of causing the injuries sustained by the victim.[95]

There is no rule of law that unless a material object is produced, or its non-production excused, oral evidence respecting it is inadmissible. Thus in *Hocking v Ahlquist Bros Ltd*,[96] the issue concerning the method by which certain garments had been made, it was held that although the garments were not produced at the trial, the evidence of witnesses who had seen them and could speak to their condition was not inadmissible. However, non-production of the object in question may go to the weight of the oral evidence adduced[97] and give rise to an inference adverse to the party failing to produce. Thus, in *Armory v Delamirie*[98] an action in trover against a goldsmith who failed to produce certain stones which he had removed from a jewel found by a chimney sweeper's boy, Pratt CJ directed the jury to assess damages on the basis that the stones were of the first water.

## 2   THE APPEARANCE OF PERSONS AND ANIMALS

Real evidence may take the form of a person's physical appearance. Thus it may be relevant, for identification or some other purpose, to have regard to a person's physical characteristics such as his height or colour of eyes or the fact that he is left-handed or bears some scar or other distinguishing feature. His accent, as opposed to the actual words he utters, also constitutes real evidence. Personal injuries may be examined on a question of causation or quantum of damages. Although in many cases little weight should be attached to it, the facial resemblance of a child to its alleged father and mother may be relevant to the issue of legitimacy.[99] For the purposes of contempt of court, a person's misconduct in court may constitute real evidence. Real evidence may also take the form of an animal, as in *Line v Taylor*,[100] where a dog of allegedly vicious disposition was brought into court and examined by the jury.

## 3   THE DEMEANOUR OF WITNESSES

The way in which a witness gives his evidence is often just as important as what he actually says. While some witnesses may appear to be forthright and frank, others may

---

[95] In some cases the tribunal of fact may not draw its own unaided conclusion without the assistance of an expert witness: *R v Tilley* [1961] 1 WLR 1309 (comparison of handwriting), above. See also *Anderson v R* [1972] AC 100, PC.

[96] [1944] KB 120. See also *R v Uxbridge Justices, ex p Sofaer* (1986) 85 Cr App R 367.

[97] Per Lord Coleridge CJ in *R v Francis* (1874) LR 2 CCR 128 at 133.        [98] (1722) 1 Stra 505.

[99] *C v C* [1972] 3 All ER 577; cf *Slingsby v A-G* (1916) 33 TLR 120, HL at 122–3.

[100] (1862) 3 F&F 731.

present themselves as hesitant, equivocal, or even hostile. Whatever form it takes, the demeanour and attitude of a witness in the course of giving his evidence is real evidence which is relevant to his credit and the weight to be attached to the evidence he gives.[101]

## 4 LIP-READING AND FACIAL MAPPING

Where an expert lip-reader, after viewing a CCTV recording of a person talking, gives opinion evidence as to what that person said, he is providing expert assistance to the jury in their interpretation of a species of real evidence.[102] Expert opinion evidence of facial mapping may be regarded in the same way.[103]

## 5 DOCUMENTS

A document may be tendered in evidence for a variety of purposes. If it is produced by a party relying upon the statements it contains, whether that party is relying upon them as evidence of their truth, by way of exception to the hearsay rule, or simply as original evidence, for example to show that they were made,[104] it constitutes documentary evidence and is subject to the rules considered earlier in this chapter.[105] However, if the document is tendered in evidence as a material object, regardless of the words contained in it, for instance to show the bare fact of its existence, the substance of which it is made (eg whether parchment or paper) or the condition that it is in (eg whether crumpled or torn), it constitutes real evidence.[106]

## 6 TAPE-RECORDINGS, FILMS, AND PHOTOGRAPHS

Tape-recordings, films and photographs are, as we have seen earlier in this chapter, sometimes treated as documentary evidence. By playing over a tape-recording in court, a statement recorded on it may be admitted as evidence of the truth of its contents, by way of exception to the hearsay rule,[107] or as original evidence, for example merely to show that it was made. To the extent, however, that the recording

---

[101] For a critical analysis of demeanour as a test of credibility, see Paul Ekman *Telling Lies* (1986) and Marcus Stone 'Instant Lie Detection? Demeanour and Credibility in Criminal Trials' [1991] Crim LR 821.

[102] *R v Luttrell* [2004] 2 Cr App R 520, CA at [37].      [103] *R v Clarke* [1995] 2 Cr App R 425 at 429.

[104] See Ch 10.

[105] But this is not the case if the contents are referred to merely for the purpose of identifying the document: see above.

[106] But see *R v Rice* [1963] 1 QB 857, CCA (Ch 10).

[107] As in *R v Senat; R v Sin* (1968) 52 Cr App R 282, CA, where tape-recordings of incriminating telephone conversations were held to have been properly admitted. See also *R v Maqsud Ali* [1966] 1 QB 688, CCA at 701: provided the jury are guided by what they hear, there is no objection to a properly proved transcript being put before them. As to tape-recordings and transcripts of police interviews sought to be adduced in criminal proceedings, see also *R v Rampling* [1987] Crim LR 823, CA, the Code of Practice on Tape Recording of Interviews with Suspects (Code E) and para 43, *Practice Direction (Criminal Proceedings: Consolidation)* [2002] 1 WLR 2870.

also reveals the way in which the person in question spoke, his accent, accentuation, tone, intonation, etc, it is real evidence.[108]

In *The Statue of Liberty*,[109] an action concerning a collision between two ships, the plaintiff sought to admit in evidence a cinematograph film of radar echoes recorded by a shore radar station. The defendants argued that the evidence, having been produced mechanically and without human intervention, was inadmissible hearsay. Rejecting this submission, Sir Jocelyn Simon P said:[110]

If tape-recordings are admissible, it seems that a photograph of radar reception is equally admissible—or indeed, any other type of photograph. It would be an absurd distinction that a photograph should be admissible if the camera were operated manually by a photographer, but not if it were operated by a trip or clock mechanism. Similarly, if evidence of weather conditions were relevant, the law would affront commonsense if it were to say that those could be proved by a person who looked at a barometer from time to time, but not by producing a barograph record. So, too, with other types of dial recordings. Again, cards from clocking-in-and-out machines are frequently admitted in accident cases.[111]

It is tempting, on the basis of these words of Sir Jocelyn Simon P, to conclude that photographs and films, the relevance of which can be established by the testimony of someone with personal knowledge of the circumstances in which they were taken or made, are admissible as items of real evidence and can never give rise to problems of a hearsay nature. If the evidence of a witness to certain events is admissible, it may be reasoned, then photographs or films recording those same events should be no less admissible. Thus in *R v Dodson; R v Williams*[112] the Court of Appeal entertained no doubt that photographs taken by security cameras installed at a building society office at which an armed robbery was attempted, were admissible in evidence, being relevant to the issues of both whether an offence was committed and, if so, who committed it.[113] As to the latter issue, the jury were entitled to compare the photographic images with the accused sitting in the dock; and that the jury can do this will not prevent the calling of a witness who was not present at the scene of the crime, but who knows the person shown in the photograph, video or film, to give evidence as to his identity.[114] It is clear, however, that a photograph or film is as capable of containing

---

[108] See, eg, *R v Emmerson* (1990) 92 Cr App R 284, CA (tone of voice). Before it is played over to the jury, the judge must satisfy himself that there is a prima facie case that it is both original and authentic: see *R v Stevenson* [1971] 1 WLR 1 and *R v Robson; R v Harris* [1972] 1 WLR 651 (Ch 4).

[109] [1968] 1 WLR 739.          [110] [1968] 1 WLR 739 at 740.

[111] Cf *R v Wood* (1982) 76 Cr App R 23, CA: a computer print-out is an item of real evidence and not hearsay if the computer in question is used as a calculator, a tool which does not contribute its own knowledge but merely does calculations which can be performed manually (see Ch 10).

[112] (1984) 79 Cr App R 220, CA.

[113] See also *Kajala v Noble* (1982) 75 Cr App R 149, CA, above; *R v Thomas* [1986] Crim LR 682; and *Taylor v Chief Constable of Cheshire* [1987] 1 All ER 225, DC (Ch 10).

[114] See *R v Fowden and White* [1982] Crim LR 588, CA, *R v Grimer* [1982] Crim LR 674, CA and *Attorney General's Reference (No 2 of 2002)* [2003] 1 Cr App R 321, CA. See also *R v Clare and Peach* [1995] 2 Cr App R 333, CA, where a witness who did *not* know the people shown in a video-recording, but had spent time analysing the photographic images, thereby acquiring special knowledge that the jury lacked, was permitted to identify them as the same people shown in a film and still photographs of the accused; and *R v Clarke*

an out-of-court statement as a tape or a document made of paper. Both the Civil Evidence Act 1995, and the Criminal Justice Act 2003 operate on this assumption by catering for the admissibility of a statement contained in a 'document', which is defined as 'anything in which information of any description is recorded',[115] a definition wide enough to cover not only audio-tapes, but also photographs, video-tapes, and films. Indeed, the film in *The Statue of Liberty*, which may be regarded as having constituted a statement as to the paths taken by the two ships, would now be admissible for the truth of its contents under the Civil Evidence Act 1995. In cases falling outside these statutory provisions, however, it would seem that a photograph or film, even if it contains, or can itself be treated as the equivalent of, an out-of-court statement, will, if relevant, be admitted as an item of real evidence rather than excluded as hearsay. Indeed, in *R v Cook*[116] Watkins LJ went so far as to state that the photograph, together with the sketch and the photofit, are in a class of evidence of their own to which neither the rule against hearsay nor the rule against previous consistent or self-serving statements applies.

For the purposes of disclosure in civil proceedings, a video, film, or recording is a document within the extended meaning contained in CPR rule 31.4 and therefore a party proposing to use it is subject to all the rules as to disclosure and inspection of documents contained in CPR rule 31. Equally, if it is disclosed in accordance with rule 31, the other party will be deemed to admit its authenticity unless notice is served that he wishes it to be proved at trial.[117] If he does serve such notice, the first party will be obliged to serve a witness statement by the person who took the video, film or recording in order to prove its authenticity. If authenticity is not challenged, in the absence of any ruling by the court to the contrary, it is available for use by the first party, which includes using it in cross-examination of the other party and his witnesses.[118]

## 7 VIEWS AND DEMONSTRATIONS

A view is an inspection out of court of the *locus in quo* or of some object which it is inconvenient or impossible to bring to court.[119] There is some dispute whether out-of-court demonstrations or re-enactments are properly to be regarded as real evidence or as the equivalent of testimonial evidence. If the latter, it is arguable that the demonstrator should take the oath and thereby offer himself for cross-examination. On balance, the authorities would appear to favour the former view. In *Buckingham v*

---

[1995] 2 Cr App R 425, CA, where the witness was an expert in facial identification who, using the technique of video superimposition, had compared photographs of a bank robber taken by an automatic camera with police identification photographs of the accused.

[115] Civil Evidence Act 1995, s 13 and Criminal Justice Act 2003, s 134(1).

[116] [1987] 1 All ER 1049 at 1054, CA. See also, in the case of photofits, *R v Constantinou* (1989) 91 Cr App R 74, CA.

[117] See CPR r 32.19(1).         [118] *Rall v Hume* [2001] 3 All ER 248, CA at [16].

[119] See, eg, *London General Omnibus Co Ltd v Lavell* [1901] 1 Ch 135, CA (an omnibus).

*Daily News Ltd*,[120] a negligence action concerning a machine, the judge inspected the machine and watched the plaintiff demonstrate what he had done. Judgment was given for the defendants. On appeal, it was argued that the judge had acted improperly by substituting his own opinion, based on the impression which he had gained at the view, for the plaintiff's oral evidence. Rejecting this argument, the Court of Appeal held that what the judge had seen was as much a part of the evidence as if the machine had been brought into the well of the court and the plaintiff had there demonstrated what took place.[121]

As a general rule, a view should be attended by the judge, the tribunal of fact, the parties and counsel. In civil proceedings, each of the parties must be given the opportunity of being present at a view and a failure to do so may result in a re-trial.[122] In a summary trial, as a general rule a view by magistrates of the scene of the alleged offence should take place before the conclusion of the evidence and in the presence of the parties or their representatives so as to afford them an opportunity of commenting on any feature of the locality which has altered since the time of the incident or any feature not previously noticed by the parties which impresses the magistrates.[123] The presence of the accused at a view is important because he may be able to point out some important matter of which his legal adviser is ignorant or about which the magistrates are making a mistake.[124] In a criminal trial by jury, the judge should always be present at a view, whether or not any witness is present for the purposes of a demonstration,[125] in order to control the proceedings. In particular, he should take precautions to prevent any witnesses who are present from communicating, except by way of demonstration, with the jury.[126] Because the jury should remain together at all times when evidence is being received, it is improper for one juror to attend a view and report back to the others what he observed.[127]

---

[120] [1956] 2 QB 534, CA.

[121] The court approved, in this respect, the views of Denning LJ in *Goold v Evans & Co* [1951] 2 TLR 1189, CA. But contrast per Hodson LJ in *Goold v Evans & Co* at 1191–2 and per Barwick CJ in *Railway Comr v Murphy* (1967) 41 ALJR 77 at 78, HC of A.

[122] *Goold v Evans & Co* [1951] 2 TLR 1189, CA. But see per Widgery LJ in *Salsbury v Woodland* [1970] 1 QB 324, CA, a civil appeal, at 343–4: although a judge attending a demonstration at which the events in question are reconstructed or simulated should be accompanied by representatives of both parties, he may visit the *locus in quo* in order to see that which has previously been represented to him in court by plan and photograph on his own and without reference to the parties at all.

[123] *Parry v Boyle* (1986) 83 Cr App R 310, DC.

[124] *R v Ely Justices, ex p Burgess* [1992] Crim LR 888, DC.

[125] *R v Hunter* [1985] 2 All ER 173, CA. Contrast *Tameshwar v R* [1957] AC 476, PC.

[126] *R v Martin* (1872) LR 1 CCR 378; *Karamat v R* [1956] AC 256, PC.

[127] *R v Gurney* [1976] Crim LR 567, CA.

# 10

# HEARSAY IN
# CRIMINAL CASES

## A  BACKGROUND AND RATIONALE

This chapter covers the meaning of hearsay in criminal proceedings. It also deals with all but one of the categories of hearsay admissible by statute in such proceedings. The exceptional category, confessions, merits the discrete treatment given to it in Chapter 13. It is also convenient to consider separately the subsisting common-law rules governing the admissibility of hearsay evidence in criminal proceedings. They are considered in Chapter 12.

Under the common-law rule against hearsay, any assertion, other than one made by a person while giving oral evidence in the proceedings, was inadmissible if tendered as evidence of the facts asserted.[1] The rule operated to prevent counsel from eliciting such evidence from any witness, whether in examination-in-chief or cross-examination[2] and applied to assertions in documents as well as oral assertions. The rule is perhaps best explained by way of example. Let us suppose that A, who witnessed an act of dangerous driving, some weeks later said to B that the car in question was blue and at that time also made a written note to the same effect. B reported to C what A had said to him. If A is subsequently called as a witness in proceedings concerned with the incident in question, he may of course make a statement from the witness box in the course of giving his evidence to the effect that the colour of the car he saw was blue. However, evidence may not be given by A, B, or C, for the purpose of establishing the colour of the car, of the oral statement made by A out of court. Likewise, the written statement made by A is inadmissible for that purpose. This is a simple example, but the common-law rule against hearsay was highly complex, technical, difficult to describe with accuracy and of unclear scope.

The common-law rule was subject to a variety of common law and statutory exceptions, and these too were often complex and technical in nature, some of them ill-considered and subject to frequent amendment. For example, the Criminal Evidence Act 1965, designed to admit hearsay in trade and business records, was passed as

---

[1] Per Lord Havers in *R v Sharp* [1988] 1 WLR 7 and per Lords Ackner and Oliver in *R v Kearley* [1992] 2 All ER 345 at 363 and 366 respectively. The rule also extended to out-of-court statements of otherwise admissible *opinion* (see Ch 18).

[2] For the application of the rule in cross-examination, see *R v Thomson* [1912] 3 KB 19 (Ch 7).

an interim measure, but few could have foreseen that the broader provisions set out in sections 68–72 of the Police and Criminal Evidence Act 1984 relating to documentary hearsay by which it was replaced, would in turn be replaced only four years later by sections 23–28 of the Criminal Justice Act 1988, provisions which unfortunately contained serious drafting errors. Sections 23–28 of the 1988 Act have now been repealed.[3] In criminal cases, the meaning of hearsay and the circumstances in which it is admissible, are now governed by Chapter 2 of Part 11 of the Criminal Justice Act 2003.

A number of reasons have been advanced to justify the rule against hearsay, including the danger of manufactured evidence and, in the case of oral hearsay, especially multiple oral hearsay (X testifies as to what Y told him Z had said, for example), the danger of inaccuracy or mistake by reason of repetition. The principle rationale of the common-law rule was summarized by Lord Bridge in *R v Blastland*:[4]

Hearsay evidence is not excluded because it has no logically probative value . . . The rationale of excluding it as inadmissible, rooted as it is in the system of trial by jury, is a recognition of the great difficulty, even more acute for a juror than for a trained judicial mind, of assessing what, if any, weight can properly be given to a statement by a person whom the jury have not seen or heard and who has not been subject to any test of reliability by cross-examination . . . The danger against which this fundamental rule provides a safeguard is that untested hearsay evidence will be treated as having a probative force which it does not deserve.

On the other hand, evidence of virtually unquestionable reliability has been excluded under the rule; cross-examination has been said to be arguably the poorest technique employed in the common-law courts to elicit accurate testimony;[5] and there are dangers in deciding veracity on the basis of demeanour.[6] That the danger to which Lord Bridge referred can be overstated was recognized in the Report of the Royal Commission of Criminal Justice.[7] A reference to the Law Commission led to a consultation paper[8] and a final report.[9] The Commission, rejecting a range of other options, favoured retention of the rule but proposed a statutory formulation of both the rule and some of the exceptions to it, an expansion of the exceptions, and a 'safety valve' discretion to admit sufficiently reliable hearsay evidence not covered by any of the exceptions.[10] Subsequently, the Auld Report[11] recommended an alternative approach, that hearsay should be admissible if the original source or 'best evidence' is

---

[3] Section 136 of the Criminal Justice Act, 2003.      [4] [1985] 2 All ER 1095, HL at 1099.

[5] Australian Law Reform Commission Research Paper No 8 (1982) *Manner of Giving Evidence* ch 10, para 5. See also Law Commission Consultation Paper No 138 (1995) *Evidence in Criminal Proceedings: The Hearsay Rule and Related Topics* paras 6.49 and 6.62.

[6] See Law Commission Consultation Paper No 138 paras 6.22 and 6.27.

[7] Cm. 2263 (1993).      [8] See n 5 above.

[9] Law Com No 245 (1997) *Evidence in Criminal Proceedings: Hearsay and Related Topics*, Cm 3670.

[10] For a critique of the Report, see C Tapper 'Hearsay in Criminal Cases: An Overview of Law Commission Report No 245' [1997] Crim LR 771.

[11] *Review of the Criminal Courts of England and Wales* (2001).

not available. This approach would have placed much greater trust in the fact finders to give hearsay evidence the weight it deserves. 'Many are of the view that both [judges and magistrates] are already more competent than we give them credit for assessing the weight of the evidence, including hearsay evidence.'[12] Greater trust in the fact finders would also have followed if the government had accepted the plea, made during the passage of the Criminal Justice Act through the House of Lords, for a simple rule giving judges a wide discretionary power. Lord Ackner referred to a paper, written by Lord Chief Justice Woolf and supported by all the judges of the criminal division of the Court of Appeal, in which he said:[13]

If we have got to the stage where it is considered that it is safe to allow juries to hear hearsay evidence, then we must be accepting that they can be trusted to use that evidence in accordance with the directions of the judge. Instead of the detailed and complex provisions which are contained in Chapter 2, what is needed is a simple rule putting the judge in charge of what evidence is admissible and giving him the responsibility of ensuring that the jury use the evidence in an appropriate manner.

The Government rejected both this plea and the approach favoured by Lord Justice Auld. The provisions relating to hearsay in Chapter 2 of Part 11 of the Criminal Justice Act 2003 are, in very large measure, based on the proposals of the Law Commission.[14]

# B  ADMISSIBLITY OF HEARSAY UNDER THE CRIMINAL JUSTICE ACT 2003

## 1  GENERAL

The only heads under which hearsay is admissible in criminal proceedings are set out in section 114(1) of the Criminal Justice Act 2003. Section 114(1), which is subject to discretionary powers to exclude hearsay,[15] provides as follows.

(1)  In criminal proceedings[16] a statement not made in oral evidence in the proceedings is admissible as evidence of any matter stated if, but only if—
    (a)  any provision of this Chapter or any other statutory provision makes it admissible,
    (b)  any rule of law preserved by s 118 makes it admissible,
    (c)  all parties to the proceedings agree to it being admissible, or
    (d)  the court is satisfied that it is in the interests of justice for it to be admissible.

---

[12] Ibid para 98, ch 11.    [13] *Hansard* HL vol 654 cols 752–3 (4 Nov 2003).

[14] For a critique of the statutory framework, see D Birch 'Criminal Justice Act 2003 (4) Hearsay: Same Old Story, Same Old Song?' [2004] Crim LR 556.

[15] See s 126, considered below, under **9 Other Safeguards, (d) Discretion to exclude**.

[16] 'Criminal proceedings' means criminal proceedings in relation to which the strict rules of evidence apply: s 134(1).

Concerning the first part of section 114(1)(a), the categories of hearsay rendered admissible under the provisions of Chapter 2 of Part 11 of the 2003 Act are (i) statements made by persons who are not available as witnesses; (ii) statements in business and other documents; (iii) certain inconsistent and other previous statements of witnesses; (iv) statements on which an expert will in evidence base an opinion; and, by virtue of section 128(1) of the 2003 Act (v) confessions admissible on behalf of a co-accused. However, subject to section 128(1), nothing in Chapter 2 makes a confession by an accused admissible if it would not be admissible under section 76 of the Police and Criminal Evidence Act 1984.[17] Concerning the second part of section 114(1)(a), whereby hearsay may be admitted by virtue of 'any other statutory provision', 'statutory provision' means any provision contained in, or in an instrument made under, the 2003 Act or any other Act, including any Act passed after the 2003 Act.[18] These statutory provisions are considered at the end of this chapter, except in the case of confessions, which are considered in Chapter 13.

As to section 114(1)(b), the rules of law preserved by section 118 are most, but not all, of the common-law rules providing for the admissibility of various categories of hearsay.[19] With the exception of the rules preserved by section 118, the common-law rules governing the admissibility of hearsay evidence in criminal proceedings are abolished.[20] Some of the rules preserved by section 118—statements in public documents, works of reference, evidence of age, evidence of reputation, and statements forming part of the *res gestae*—are considered in Chapter 12 (Hearsay admissible at common law). It is convenient to consider the remainder of the preserved rules in other parts of this work: mixed statements in Chapter 6 (Examination-in-chief); confessions, admissions by agents, and statements made by a party to a common enterprise in Chapter 13 (Confessions); and the rule whereby an expert may draw on the body of expertise relevant to his field in Chapter 18 (Opinion Evidence).

Section 114(1)(c) permits hearsay to be admissible where the prosecution, the accused and any co-accused agree to it being admissible. Finally, section 114(1)(d) provides for the admissibility of hearsay which it would be in the interests of justice to admit, ie hearsay admissible by exercise of the 'safety valve' inclusionary discretion.

Under section 114(3),

> Nothing in this Chapter affects the exclusion of evidence of a statement on grounds other than the fact that it is a statement not made in oral evidence in the proceedings.

Thus if hearsay evidence falls to be excluded because it is irrelevant or inadmissible on

---

[17] Section 128(2). Under s 128(3), a 'confession', for these purposes, has the meaning given by s 82 of the Police and Criminal Evidence Act: see Ch 13.

[18] Section 134(1).

[19] The rule permitting the admissibility of dying declarations, a rule that has never been easy to justify, has been abandoned. Declarations by persons, since deceased, either against interest or in the course of duty, have also been abandoned.

[20] Section 118(2).

grounds of public policy, privilege, or any other exclusionary rule of evidence, it will still fall to be excluded notwithstanding that it is otherwise admissible hearsay.

Before considering in detail the various categories of hearsay admissible under the 2003 Act, it is necessary to consider first the way in which hearsay has been defined in the Act.

## 2 THE MEANING OF HEARSAY IN THE CRIMINAL JUSTICE ACT 2003

As we have seen from section 114(1), hearsay is 'a statement not made in oral evidence in the proceedings . . . admissible as evidence of any matter stated'. This formulation covers not only 'out-of-court' statements as such, but also statements made in previous criminal or civil proceedings. 'Oral evidence', for the purposes of section 114(1) and other provisions relating to hearsay in the 2003 Act, includes evidence which, by reason of any disability, disorder or other impairment, a person called as a witness gives in writing or by signs or by way of any device.[21]

### (a) 'A statement'

'A statement', for the purposes of the provisions relating to hearsay in the 2003 Act, is 'any representation of fact or opinion made by a person by whatever means; and it includes a representation made in a sketch, photofit or other pictorial form'.[22] This is a very wide definition. It covers a statement of opinion, provided that it is admissible opinion of course,[23] as well as a statement of fact.[24] The statement may have been made unsworn or on oath by any person, whether or not a person called as a witness in the proceedings in question. The representation, however, must have been made by a person—statements in computer-generated documents are not covered. The admissibility of computer-generated documents is considered separately, below.

The phrase 'any representation . . . by whatever means' clearly covers statements made orally as well as statements made in writing, whether by hand, or by means of a typewriter, word processor, computer or other similar device. A common-law example of oral hearsay, which will continue to be hearsay under the 2003 Act is *R v Rothwell*,[25] a case of supplying heroin. The prosecution sought to rely on evidence that the accused was seen on several occasions passing small packages to various people, coupled with the evidence of a drugs squad officer that the recipients were known to him as heroin users. It was held that, insofar as the officer's evidence was based on statements made to him by others, for example the alleged recipients, then the evidence would be inadmissible hearsay; but that it would not be hearsay insofar as it was based on the recipients' convictions for possession of heroin[26] or, for example, the officer's personal observation of needle marks on the recipients' forearms or his personal knowledge of

---

[21] Section 134(1).      [22] Section 115(2).      [23] See s 114(3), above.

[24] See also s 30 of the Criminal Justice Act 1988, considered below, under **C Expert reports**.

[25] (1994) 99 Cr App R 388, CA.

[26] Admissible under the Police and Criminal Evidence Act 1984, s 74: see Ch 2.

the recipients being in possession of heroin or receiving treatment for heroin addiction. *Patel v Comptroller of Customs*[27] provides an example of written hearsay. The appellant was convicted of making a false declaration in an import entry form concerning certain bags of seed. The appellant had declared that the country of origin of the seed was India. Evidence was admitted that the bags of seed bore the words 'Produce of Morocco'. The Privy Council held that the evidence was inadmissible hearsay and advised that the conviction be quashed.[28]

The phrase 'any representation ... by whatever means' is also wide enough to embrace statements made by conduct or signs and gestures, and statements made partly orally and partly by conduct or signs and gestures. A common-law example of the last is *R v Gibson*,[29] a trial for malicious wounding in which the prosecutor gave evidence that after he had been hit by a stone, a woman, pointing to the door of a house, had said, 'The person who threw the stone went in there.' The occupant of the house was convicted. The conviction was quashed on the ground that evidence of the woman's statement was inadmissible.[30] *Chandrasekera v R*[31] provides an example of a hearsay statement made solely by signs or gestures. The appellant was charged with murder. At the trial evidence was admitted that the victim, whose throat had been cut, had made certain signs, the apparent effect of which was to indicate the accused. Asked whether it was the appellant who had cut her throat, she replied by nodding her head. Lord Roche was of the opinion that the case resembled that of a dumb person able to converse by means of finger alphabet, and held that the woman had effectively stated that the accused had cut her neck. The hearsay statement was nevertheless held to be admissible under an exception contained in the Ceylon Evidence Ordinance 1895. The evidence would now be admissible under section 116(1) and (2)(a) (a statement made by a person since deceased).[32]

The inclusion, within the definition of 'a statement', of 'a representation made in a sketch, photofit or other pictorial form' reflects a principled approach which was

---

[27] [1966] AC 356, PC.

[28] See also *R v Sealby* [1965] 1 All ER 701 and *R v Brown* [1991] Crim LR 835, CA (evidence of a name on an appliance inadmissible to establish its ownership); and cf *R v Rice* [1963] 1 QB 857, below.

[29] (1887) 18 QBD 537.

[30] The Court for Crown Cases Reserved gave no express reason as to why the evidence was inadmissible, but the decision has been cited subsequently in cases expressly concerned with the rule against hearsay: see, eg, *R v Saunders* [1899] 1 QB 490, CCR.

[31] [1937] AC 220, PC.

[32] If a policeman employs an interpreter to question a suspect whose language he does not understand, the translated answers may be given in evidence by the translator but not by the policeman: see *R v Attard* (1958) 43 Cr App R 90, where the police officer's evidence of what the accused had said was held to be inadmissible hearsay. In consequence of this decision, the Home Office issued a circular to the police which points to the necessity of ensuring that the interpreter is available to give evidence. Whenever practicable, the interpreter should make his own notes of the interview or, failing this, he should initial the police record which he may then use to refresh his memory.

lacking in some of the common-law authorities.[33] Photographs and films are excluded from the definition and continue to be admissible, at common law, as a variety of real evidence, if relevant to the issues, including the important issues of whether an offence was committed and who committed it.[34]

### (b) Original evidence

Under section 114(1) of the 2003 Act, hearsay is a statement not made in oral evidence in the proceedings 'admissible as evidence of any matter stated'. Hearsay falls to be distinguished from original evidence, which may be defined as a statement not made in oral evidence in the proceedings which is admissible for any relevant purpose other than that of establishing any matter stated. This is a difficult distinction, but an important one, because whereas hearsay is admissible only under the heads set out in section 114(1), original evidence is admissible provided only that it is sufficiently relevant. Examples of original evidence may be classified according to whether they are admitted (i) simply to show that the statement was made, because that is a fact in issue in the proceedings, or (ii) because of their relevance to some other fact in issue in the proceedings.

*(i) The making of the statement as a fact in issue.* If the making of a certain statement is itself a fact in issue in the proceedings, that statement, even if inadmissible as evidence of any matter stated, may be admitted as evidence of the fact that it was made. For example, on a charge of making a threat to kill, the victim may give evidence of the fact that the accused said to her 'I am going to kill you.'[35] *R v Chapman*[36] provides an instructive example. Following a road traffic accident, the accused was taken to a hospital where a breath test was administered. He was subsequently convicted of driving a motor vehicle with excess alcohol. Section 2(2)(b) of the Road Safety Act 1967 provided that a hospital patient shall not be required to provide a specimen of breath if the medical practitioner in charge of his case 'objects' on the grounds that it would be prejudicial to the proper care or treatment of the patient. At the trial, a police officer gave evidence that the doctor in question had not objected to the provision of a specimen. It was argued on appeal that this evidence was inadmissible hearsay. Rejecting the argument, the Court of Appeal held that the evidence had been properly adduced to establish that the doctor had made no objection.

---

[33] See *R v Cook* [1987] 1 ALL ER 1049, CA, in which it was held that photofits, together with sketches and photographs, are in a class of evidence of their own to which neither the rule against hearsay nor the rule against previous consistent statements is applicable. *R v Cook* was applied, in the case of a photofit, in *R v Constantinou* (1989) 91 Cr App R 74, CA. See also *R v Percy Smith* [1976] Crim LR 511, CA (a sketch made by a police officer under the direction of an identification witness).

[34] See, eg, *R v Dodson; R v Williams* (1984) 79 Cr App R 220, CA (photographs) and *R v Roberts* [1998] Crim LR 682, CA, considered in Ch 9.

[35] In *R v Rizwan Mawji* (2003) LTL 16/10/2003, CA, where such a threat was contained in an e-mail which had been sent from the accused's e-mail address, it was held that whether the jury accepted the e-mail as genuine was a matter manifestly for them.

[36] [1969] 2 QB 436, CA.

*(ii)  The statement as evidence relevant to some other fact in issue.* A statement may be admissible as a fact relevant to a fact in issue in the proceedings notwithstanding that it is inadmissible as evidence of any matter stated. Examples that may be given are many and various. In some cases the statement is admitted as evidence of the state of mind of its maker. Thus a man's assertion in 2005 that he is Napoleon, Emperor of France, may be tendered for the purpose of showing his insanity. In *R v Gregson,*[37] where the issue was whether the 348 ecstasy tablets in the accused's possession had been purchased with intent to supply, the defence case being that he believed that he was acquiring only thirty tablets, evidence from his friends that he had expressed to them his concern about how to get rid of the tablets was admissible because it went directly to his state of mind at that time, which was critical to the jury's decision.

In *Ratten v R*[38] Ratten was convicted of the murder of his wife by shooting her. His defence was that a gun went off accidentally while he was cleaning it. The evidence established that the shooting, from which the wife had died almost immediately, took place between 1.12 pm and about 1.20 pm. A telephonist from the local exchange gave evidence that at 1.15 pm she had received a telephone call from Ratten's house made by a sobbing woman who in an hysterical voice had said, 'Get me the police please.' The Privy Council held that there was no hearsay element in this evidence, which was relevant (i) in order to show that, contrary to the evidence of Ratten, who denied that any telephone call had been made by his wife, a call had been made, and (ii) as possibly showing that the wife was in a state of emotion or fear at an existing or impending emergency, which was capable of rebutting Ratten's defence that the shooting was accidental.[39] *Ratten's* case was held to be clearly distinguishable in *R v Blastland.*[40] In that case, the House of Lords held that the accused, convicted of buggery and murder, had been properly disallowed to adduce evidence of statements made by a third party indicating *his* knowledge of the murder before the body was found, because the only issue was whether the accused had committed the crimes and what was relevant to that issue was not the third party's knowledge but how he had acquired it; since he could have done so in a number of different ways, there was no rational basis on which the jury could infer that he, rather than the accused, was the murderer.[41]

In some cases, the statement is admitted as evidence of the state of mind of the person who heard or read it, ie to show what the person who heard or read it, knew, thought or believed. If A is charged with the murder of B, evidence of a statement by

---

[37] [2003] 2 Cr App R 34, CA.          [38] [1972] AC 378.

[39] See also *R v Gilfoyle* [1996] 3 All ER 883, CA (suicide notes admissible as evidence of a woman's suicidal frame of mind and further statements made by her which showed that when she wrote the notes she had no intention of taking her own life).

[40] [1985] 2 All ER 1095.

[41] An out-of-court statement made by the *accused* and disclosing his possession of certain knowledge which tends to incriminate him, may be admitted, by way of statutory exception to the hearsay rule, as a confession: see Police and Criminal Evidence Act 1984, s 76 and Ch 13.

C to A that B was having an adulterous relationship with A's spouse, even if not admissible as evidence of the adulterous relationship, has an obvious relevance on the question of A's motive. In *Subramaniam v Public Prosecutor*[42] the accused was convicted of being in unlawful possession of ammunition. His defence was that he had been threatened by terrorists and had acted under duress. Evidence of what the terrorists had said was excluded by the trial judge as inadmissible hearsay. Quashing the conviction, the Privy Council held that the trial judge had erred. Statements could have been made by the terrorists which, even if not admissible as evidence of any matter stated, might reasonably have induced in the accused, if he believed them, an apprehension of instant death if he failed to conform to their wishes. The statements were accordingly admissible as potentially cogent evidence of duress. In *R v Davis*[43] it was held that where an accused, on the advice of his solicitor, declines to answer questions in interview, evidence of what the solicitor said may be admissible for the purpose of establishing the accused's reason for not answering questions, which will be relevant to the issue for the jury under section 34 of the Criminal Justice and Public Order Act 1994, namely whether to draw adverse inferences from the failure to answer questions. The test under section 34 is whether the facts relied on by the accused in his defence at trial are facts which he could reasonably have been expected to mention when he was interviewed.[44]

A statement may be admitted as original evidence where it is tendered for the purpose of allowing the tribunal of fact to conclude that its contents are false and to draw inferences from the falsity of those contents. In *A-G v Good*[45] the demonstrably false statement of a debtor's wife that her husband was not at home was admissible for the purpose of showing her husband's intention to defraud his creditors. If an unreasonable time had intervened between the demand for entrance and the opening of the door, that would have been a fact relevant to the issue, and the untrue statement of the wife was relevant in the same way. In *Mawaz Khan v R*[46] the appellants were convicted of murder. At the trial the prosecution had relied upon the fact that each of them had in his statement to the police sought to set up a joint alibi, many of the details of which were demonstrated to be false by other evidence. The Privy Council held that the trial judge had properly directed the jury that although a statement made by one of the accused in the absence of another was not evidence against the other, they were entitled to compare the statements of the two accused and, if they concluded that they were false, to draw the inference that the accused had cooperated after the alleged crime and jointly concocted the story out of a sense of guilt.[47]

In *Woodhouse v Hall*[48] the manageress of a sauna and massage parlour was charged with acting in the management of a brothel. Plain clothes police officers, who had

---

[42] [1956] 1 WLR 965. See also *R v Willis* [1960] 1 WLR 55, CCA and *R v Madden* [1986] Crim LR 804, CA.
[43] [1998] Crim LR 659, CA.     [44] See Ch 14.     [45] (1825) M'Cle&Yo 286.
[46] [1967] 1 AC 454.
[47] See also *R v Binham* [1991] Crim LR 774, where evidence of B's previous statements in support of his alibi defence, together with evidence as to their falsity, was admissible as original evidence.
[48] (1980) 72 Cr App R 39.

entered the premises as customers, alleged that they had been offered masturbation by the manageress and other women employed there. At the trial, the justices held that the police officers' evidence of the offers made to them was inadmissible hearsay. The information was dismissed. On the prosecutor's appeal by way of case stated, Donaldson LJ held that the evidence had been wrongly excluded: 'There is no question of the hearsay rule arising at all. The relevant issue was did these ladies make these offers?'[49] The very fact that such offers had been made was relevant to the central fact in issue, namely whether the premises were being used as a sauna and massage parlour or a brothel. As Lord Ackner pointed out in *R v Kearley*,[50] 'in order to establish that the premises are being used as a brothel it is sufficient to prove that at the premises more than one woman *offers* herself as a participant in physical acts of indecency for the sexual gratification of men'.[51]

## (c) Implied assertions

At common law a question which gave rise to considerable difficulty was whether the hearsay rule applied to implied assertions, an area of evidence law which has been characterized as a legalistic backwater which is 'the home of sophistry and the grave-yard of common sense'.[52] An implied assertion is an assertion, whether made orally, in writing or by conduct, from which it is possible to infer a particular matter. To take a simple example, if Harry, walking down the street, and not using a mobile telephone, says, 'Hello, Bill', it is possible to infer that Bill was in Harry's presence. The common-law authorities treated as hearsay implied assertions made orally or in writing (or by a combination of an oral or written statement and conduct). Under the statutory for-mulation of hearsay, as we have seen, section 114(1) refers to a statement not made in oral evidence in the proceedings which is admissible as evidence of any 'matter stated'. Under 115(3):

> (3) A matter stated is one to which this Chapter applies if (and only if) the purpose, or one of the purposes, of the person making the statement appears to the court to have been—
>
> (a) to cause another person to believe the matter, or
> (b) to cause another person to act or a machine to operate on the basis that the matter is as stated.

The effect of section 115(3) is to narrow the ambit of section 114 so that it applies to render hearsay admissible as evidence of any matter stated under one of the heads set out in section 114(1) if and only if the purpose, or one of the purposes, of the person making the statement, was of the kind described in either subsection (3)(a) or (b). Under subsection (3)(a), the purpose, or one of the purposes, in making the statement is to cause another to believe the matter, ie to accept that matter as true,

---

[49] (1980) 72 Cr App R 39 at 42. Cf, *sed quaere*, *R v Lawal* [1994] Crim LR 746, CA.
[50] [1992] 2 All ER 345, HL at 365.    [51] See *Kelly v Purvis* [1983] 1 All ER 525.
[52] D Birch 'Criminal Justice Act 2003 (4) Hearsay: Same Old Story, Same Old Song?' [2004] Crim LR 556 at 564.

whereas under subsection (3)(b) the purpose, or one of the purposes, in making the statement, is simply to cause another to act on the basis that the matter is as stated, ie to act on the basis that the matter is true (or to cause a machine to operate on the basis that the matter is as stated). There appears to be a considerable overlap between the two subsections, in that if the purpose is to cause another to act on the basis that a certain matter is as it has been stated, then whether or not that is the truth of the matter, the purpose, in many situations, will also be to cause the other to believe the matter. Subsection (3)(b) will apply, but not subsection (3)(a), where the purpose is to cause another to do no more than to act on the basis that the matter is as stated, and not to cause the other to believe the matter, perhaps because, for example, the maker of the statement is aware that the matter is not as stated or is unsure as to the truth of the matter.

The Explanatory Notes to the 2003 Act state that the purpose of section 115(3) is 'to overturn the ruling in *Kearley*[53] that "implied assertions" are covered by the hearsay rule and therefore prima facie inadmissible'. This is misleading in two respects. First, section 115(3) will operate to exclude from the ambit of section 114 some express as well as implied assertions. For example, if an express assertion is made by a person who is talking to himself and unaware that he is being overheard, or is contained in a memorandum which is kept for purely personal purposes, then plainly it is not among the purposes of the maker of the statement to cause another to believe the matter stated. Such statements are therefore not covered by, or subject to, section 114 of the Act. They would now appear to be admissible, provided that they are relevant, and, if tendered by the prosecution, subject to the discretionary powers of exclusion. At first blush, it might be thought that section 115(3) will also operate to exclude from the ambit of section 114 an express assertion made with the purpose of causing another to *disbelieve* the matter stated, as when the maker says, for example, 'Of course X was present … and pigs were flying!' However, such a statement would surely be treated as a statement made with the purpose of causing another to believe that X was absent.

Secondly, section 115(3) will not operate to exclude all implied assertions from the ambit of section 114. Thus although it will overturn the ruling in the leading case of *R v Kearley*, and in many other cases in which implied assertions were excluded as inadmissible hearsay, some implied assertions will continue to be classified as hearsay. In each case the court will need to consider the purpose or purposes of a person in making the particular statement in question, and, in cases in which it concludes that the statement does amount to hearsay, it will need to go on to consider whether it falls under any of the heads of admissibility set out in section 114.

The application of section 115(3) in the case of implied assertions is perhaps best explored by reference to the facts of some of the common-law authorities.

*(i) Oral assertions.* In *R v Kearley* the police found drugs in K's flat, but not in sufficient quantities to raise the inference that he was a dealer. The police remained

---

[53]  *R v Kearley* [1992] 2 AC 228, HL, considered below.

there for several hours and intercepted ten telephone calls in which the callers asked to speak to K and asked for drugs. Seven other people arrived at the flat, some with money, also asking for K and asking to be supplied with drugs, but at all relevant times K was either absent or not within earshot. At K's trial for possession with intent to supply, the officers who had intercepted the calls or received the visitors gave evidence of the conversations. The House of Lords, by a majority of three to two, allowed the appeal against conviction. It was held: (i) that evidence of the requests made by the callers and visitors was irrelevant because it could only be evidence of the state of mind or belief of those making the requests, which was not a relevant issue at the trial, the issue being whether K intended to supply drugs; and (ii) applying *Wright v Doe d Tatham*[54] and approving *R v Harry*,[55] that insofar as the evidence was relevant to the issue of K's intent to supply, ie as an implied assertion that K was a supplier, it was inadmissible hearsay, and it made no difference that there were a large number of such requests all made at the same place on the same day. Section 115(3) operates to reverse the decision. It seems most unlikely that it was among the purposes of the callers and visitors to cause others to believe that K was a supplier. Their purpose was to contact K in order to be supplied with drugs.

In *Teper v R*[56] the accused was convicted of arson of a shop belonging to his wife. His defence was one of alibi. In order to establish his presence within the vicinity of the shop, a policeman gave evidence that, some 25 minutes after the fire had begun, an unidentified woman bystander had shouted to a motorist, who resembled the accused, 'Your place burning and you going away from the fire.' The Privy Council, quashing the conviction, held that this assertion which, by implication, established Teper's presence, was inadmissible hearsay.[57] It is not clear that section 115(3) operates to reverse this decision. It would turn upon whether it appears to the court that one of the purposes of the unidentified woman, in making her statement, was to cause one or more of the bystanders to believe that Teper was present but departing.

*(ii) Written assertions.* In *Wright v Doe d Tatham*,[58] which concerned, inter alia, the mental competence of a testator, it was held that the trial judge had properly disallowed the production in evidence of a number of letters written to the testator by certain of his acquaintances in terms from which it could legitimately be inferred that they regarded him as sane. As evidence of the truth of the implied assertion that the testator was sane, they constituted inadmissible hearsay. If the same issue were to arise in a criminal context, section 115(3) would operate to reverse this decision. It would be most unlikely to appear to the court that one of the purposes of the testator's acquaintances was to cause others to believe that the testator was sane. The principal and probably only purpose in writing was to convey to the testator the contents of their letters.

---

[54] (1837) 7 Ad&El 313.     [55] (1987) 86 Cr App R 105, CA.     [56] [1952] AC 480.
[57] It was also held that the statement did not form part of the *res gestae* (see Ch 12).
[58] (1837) 7 Ad&El 313, Ex Ch.

*R v Lydon*[59] and *R v Rice*[60] are cases which highlight the difficult borderline that exists between circumstantial evidence and implied assertions. In *R v Lydon* the appellant, whose first name was Sean, was convicted of robbery. His defence was one of alibi. About one mile from the scene of the robbery, on the verge of the road which the getaway car had followed, were found a gun and, nearby, two pieces of rolled paper on which someone had written 'Sean rules' and 'Sean rules 85'. Ink of similar appearance and composition to that on the paper was found on the gun barrel. The Court of Appeal held that evidence relating to the pieces of paper had been properly admitted as circumstantial evidence: if the jury were satisfied that the gun was used in the robbery and that the pieces of paper were linked to the gun, the references to Sean could be a fact which would fit in with the appellant having committed the offence. The references were not hearsay because they involved no assertion as to the truth of the contents of the pieces of paper, ie they were not tendered to show that Sean ruled anything. The outcome, it is submitted, should be the same under the 2003 Act, because the prosecution would not be relying upon the pieces of paper as 'evidence of any matter stated', ie that 'Sean rules' or that 'Sean rules 85', and that insofar as the statements can be treated as statements which, by implication, in some way linked Lydon with the offence, then for the purposes of section 115(3), it was unlikely to have been among the purposes of Lydon, in making the statements, to cause others to believe this.[61]

In *R v Rice* the accused were convicted of conspiracy. Part of the prosecution case involved proving that two of them, Rice and Hoather, had taken a certain flight to Manchester. A used airline ticket, which bore the name of Rice and of another accused, Moore, was admitted in evidence against Rice. The Court of Criminal Appeal held that although the ticket was inadmissible hearsay if tendered for the purposes of speaking its contents, that is to show that the booking was effected by Rice or even by any man of that name, it had been properly admitted. Winn J said:[62]

The relevance of that ticket in logic and its legal admissibility as a piece of real evidence both stem from the same root, viz., the balance of probability recognized by common sense and common knowledge that an air ticket which has been used on a flight and which has a name upon it has more likely than not been used by a man of that name or by one of two men whose names are upon it.

The ticket was only relevant, it is submitted, because it allowed the jury to conclude that Rice had taken a certain flight to Manchester, a conclusion that could only be

---

[59] [1987] Crim LR 407, CA.    [60] [1963] 1 QB 857, CCA.

[61] See also *R v McIntosh* [1992] Crim LR 651, CA (calculations as to the purchase and sale prices of 12 oz of an unnamed commodity, not in M's handwriting but found concealed in the chimney of a house where he had been living, admissible as circumstantial evidence tending to connect him with drug-related offences) and *Roberts v DPP* [1994] Crim LR 926, DC (documents found at R's offices and home, including repair and gas bills and other accounts relating to certain premises, admissible as circumstantial evidence linking R with those premises, on charges of assisting in the management of a brothel and running a massage parlour without a licence) and cf *R v Horne* [1992] Crim LR 304, CA.

[62] [1963] 1 QB 857 at 871.

drawn on the basis that the ticket contained an implied assertion that Rice would take that flight. Whether the ticket would now be treated as containing a hearsay statement would turn upon whether it appears to the court that one of the purposes of the person who put Rice's name on the ticket was to cause others to believe that Rice would be using it.

*R v Rice* was a decision that it was difficult, if not impossible, to reconcile with *R v Van Vreden*.[63] At a trial for obtaining by deception, which was alleged to have involved the use of a Barclaycard issued in South Africa to a Miss Lang, the application form relating to that card, upon which the account number had been entered, was held by the Court of Appeal, to have been improperly admitted, on the basis that its production at the trial effected the same result as the production of a statement made by a named clerk in South Africa asserting that he had issued a card to Miss Lang bearing the number which he had entered as the account number. Under section 115(3), the application form would also be treated as hearsay, because there can be little doubt that the purpose of the clerk, in entering the account number, was to cause others who had occasion to refer to the form, to believe that Miss Lang's card bore that number.

*(iii) Assertions by conduct.* Concerning implied assertions by conduct alone, there were few common-law authorities. In *Chandrasekera v R*,[64] as we have seen, the signs used by the victim to identify her assailant were treated as hearsay, and section 115(3) operates to preserve the decision, the very purpose of the victim's conduct having been to cause others to believe that the accused had cut her throat. In *Wright v Doe d Tatham* Parke B expressed the obiter view that, on a question of the seaworthiness of a vessel, evidence of the conduct of a deceased captain who, after examining every part of the vessel, embarked in it with his family, would constitute hearsay. It would be very difficult to uphold such a view now, because it seems most unlikely, without more, that one of the purposes of the captain, in examining the vessel, was to cause another to believe that the vessel was seaworthy. In *Manchester Brewery Co Ltd v Coombs*,[65] a case concerning an alleged breach by a brewer to supply a publican with good beer, it was held, obiter, that evidence would be admissible that certain customers ordered the beer, tasted it, did not finish it, and then either left it or threw it away. Section 115(3) operates to uphold this view because of the unlikelihood, without more, that one of the purposes of the customers, in behaving as they did, was to cause another to believe that the beer was no good.

There can be little doubt that section 115(3) will operate to render admissible much evidence that was previously excluded as hearsay. Underlying this development of the law was the opinion that 'as a class, implied assertions are more reliable than assertions made for the purpose of communicating information'.[66] There are two compelling reasons, however, why such evidence will often need to be treated with

---

63 (1973) 57 Cr App R 818.     64 [1937] AC 220, PC.     65 (1901) 82 LT 347 at 349.
66 See Law Com No 245 (1977) *Evidence in Criminal Proceedings: Hearsay and Related Topics*, Cm 3670.

caution. The first stems from the fact that it is often possible to draw different inferences from the same conduct and, depending on the precise circumstances, this will reduce the weight to be attached to the evidence. For example, the conduct of the captain could have been a search for a stowaway, and the customers who rejected the beer could all have been French and unfamiliar with the taste of English beer. Secondly, there will be the risk, in some cases, of error or malicious concoction, the degree of risk varying according to the precise circumstances. For example, in *R v Kearley*, it was most unlikely that, without more, seventeen callers were all mistaken or all set out with the deliberate intention of deceiving the police into believing that the accused was a dealer, but if there had been only one or two callers, there would have been at least some risk of mistake or malice.[67]

### (d) Negative hearsay

Under the 2003 Act, as at common law, an oral out-of-court statement will amount to hearsay whether it is tendered as evidence of the existence or non-existence of a fact. Thus if the presence of A at a certain place on a certain date is in issue, evidence by B as to what he heard C say on the matter is hearsay, whether C said that he saw or did not see A on the occasion in question. At common law, however, the hearsay rule did not operate to prevent proof of the non-existence of a fact by a combination of (i) evidence of the absence of a recording of the fact in a written record and (ii) testimony of an appropriate person to the effect that having regard to the method of compilation and custody of the record, one would have expected the fact, had it existed, to have been recorded. In *R v Patel*[68] the accused was charged, inter alia, with assisting the illegal entry of one Ashraf into the UK. In order to prove that Ashraf was an illegal immigrant, the prosecution called Mr Stone, an immigration officer at Manchester airport, who gave evidence that Ashraf's name was not in certain Home Office records of persons entitled to a certificate of registration in the UK and that at the material time Ashraf was therefore an illegal entrant. The Court of Appeal held that evidence relating to the Home Office records was inadmissible hearsay. However, Bristow J said:[69]

an officer responsible for their compilation and custody should have been called to give evidence that the method of compilation and custody is such that if Ashraf's name is not there, he must be an illegal entrant. It is not suggested that Mr Stone is such an officer.

This dictum was applied in *R v Shone*.[70] The appellant was convicted of receiving three vehicle springs which bore numbers which enabled them to be identified as having been dispatched by the manufacturers to L Ltd. Their arrival at L Ltd was recorded on stock record cards. The prosecution called two employees of L Ltd responsible for these records, who gave evidence that the cards were marked to indicate when the

---

[67] See per Lord Griffiths, one of the minority, at 349 and 353.
[68] [1981] 3 All ER 94, CA. Cf *R v Muir* (1983) 79 Cr App R 153, CA.
[69] [1981] 3 All ER 94 at 96.     [70] (1982) 76 Cr App R 72.

spare parts were sold or used and that the cards in respect of the three springs bore no such marks. On appeal, it was argued that the absence of a mark on the cards amounted to an inadmissible hearsay statement that the springs had been neither sold nor used by L Ltd. The Court of Appeal held that the evidence of the employees in explaining the significance of the absence of the marks was not hearsay evidence but direct evidence from which the jury were entitled to draw the inference that all three springs were stolen.

It is submitted that evidence of the kind admitted in *R v Shone* will remain admissible as direct evidence and is not covered by the 2003 Act simply because no statement has been made for the purposes of section 114. However, according to the Explanatory Notes to the 2003 Act,[71] the situation is governed by section 115(3):[72] 'where the assertion relates to a failure to record an event, sometimes known as negative hearsay, it will not be covered by Chapter 2 [Hearsay evidence] if it was not the purpose of the person who failed to record the event to cause anyone to believe that the event did not occur.' On that analysis, the evidence could now amount to hearsay on the basis that it was the purpose of the employees with responsibility for the cards, in not marking them, to cause anyone who had reason to inspect them, to believe that the springs in question had not been sold or used. However, it does not follow that the cards would be inadmissible: they could be admitted as business documents under section 117 of the Act or by exercise of the court's inclusionary discretion, i.e. on the basis that it is in the interests of justice for them to be admitted.

### (e) Statements produced by computers and mechanical and other devices

As we have seen, a 'statement', according to section 115(2), is any representation of fact or opinion 'made by a person' by whatever means. Thus, as the Explanatory Notes to the Act make clear: 'Subsection (2) preserves the present position whereby statements which are not based on human input fall outside the ambit of the hearsay rule. Tapes, films or photographs which directly record the commission of an offence and documents produced by machines which automatically record a process or event or perform calculations will not therefore be covered by Chapter 2 [Hearsay evidence].'[73] However, in *R v Cochrane*,[74] it was held that before the judge can decide whether computer printouts are admissible, whether as real evidence or as hearsay, it is necessary to call appropriate authoritative evidence to describe the function and operation of the computer. Where a statement generated by a computer or other machine is based on information supplied by a person, for example a printout which is a copy of a letter or a record of other information supplied by a person, then under section 129 of the 2003 Act it will not be admissible as evidence of any fact stated unless it is proved that the information was accurate. Section 129 provides as follows.

(1) Where a representation of any fact—
　　(a) is made otherwise than by a person, but

---

[71] Para 401.　　[72] See above, under (c) **Implied assertions**.　　[73] Para 402.
[74] [1993] Crim LR 48, CA.

> (b) depends for its accuracy on information supplied (directly or indirectly) by a person,
>
> the representation is not admissible in criminal proceedings as evidence of the fact unless it is proved that the information was accurate.
>
> (2) Subsection (1) does not affect the operation of the presumption that a mechanical device has been properly set or calibrated.[75]

The common-law principle in effect preserved by section 115(2) was described by Lord Lane CJ in *R v Wood*[76] in the following terms.

Witnesses, and especially expert witnesses, frequently and properly give factual evidence of the results of a physical exercise which involves the use of some equipment, device or machine. Take a weighing machine; the witness steps on the machine and reads a weight off the dial, receives a ticket printed with the weight, or even hears a recorded voice saying it. None of this involves hearsay evidence. The witness may have to be cross-examined as to whether he kept one foot on the ground; the accuracy of the machine may have to be investigated. But this does not alter the character of the evidence which has been given.

Other examples may be readily imagined. A witness gives evidence that a certain event occurred at a certain time because at that time he had consulted his wrist watch. A motorist gives evidence that, according to the speedometer of his car, he was travelling at a certain speed. A forensic scientist testifies that certain of his findings involved the use of an electronic calculator. In *R v Wood*[77] the appellant was convicted of handling stolen metal. In order to prove that metal found in his possession and metal retained from the stolen consignment had the same chemical composition, samples were subjected to an X-ray spectrometer and a neutron transmission monitor. The figures thus produced were then subjected to a laborious mathematical process in order that the percentage of the various metals in the samples could be stated as figures. That process was undertaken by a computer operated by chemists. At the trial, detailed evidence was given as to how the computer had been programmed and used. The Court of Appeal held that the trial judge had properly allowed evidence of the computer results to be admitted. The computer was used as a calculator, a tool which did not contribute its own knowledge but merely did a sophisticated calculation which could have been done manually. Lord Lane CJ said that the computer printout was not hearsay but more properly to be treated as a piece of real evidence, the actual proof and relevance of which depended upon the evidence of the chemists, computer programmer and other experts involved.

In *Castle v Cross*[78] the respondent was charged with failing without reasonable

---

[75] The common-law presumption is normally cast in wider terms, namely that mechanical instruments that are usually in working order, were in working order at the time when they were used: see Ch 22 under A1(d) **Presumptions without basic facts.**

[76] (1982) 76 Cr App R 23 at 26, CA.

[77] (1982) 76 Cr App R 23. See also *The Statue of Liberty* [1968] 1 WLR 739. Contrast *R v Pettigrew* (1980) 71 Cr App R 39, CA, a decision under the now repealed Criminal Evidence Act 1965.

[78] [1985] 1 All ER 87.

excuse to provide a specimen of breath when required to do so, contrary to section 8 of the Road Traffic Act 1972. At the invitation of a police sergeant, he had on four occasions blown into the mouthpiece of an Intoximeter 3000 breath-test machine, which had then produced a printout to the effect that it did not have a sufficient sample of breath to enable it to perform an analysis. The justices dismissed the information on the basis that the statement was produced by a machine, akin to a computer, which 'contributed to its own knowledge' [*sic*]. The Divisional Court held that the machine was a tool, albeit a sophisticated one, and that in the absence of any evidence that it was defective, the printout, the product of a mechanical device, fell into the category of real evidence. The printout was admissible and the sergeant was entitled to give evidence of all that he had observed, interpreting, if necessary, the printout and supplementing it by explaining that it meant that no sufficient sample had been provided.

The principle applies not only where the device in question processes information supplied to it, but also where the device itself gathers information. Thus in *R v Spiby*[79] a printout from a computerized machine used to monitor telephone calls and automatically record such information as the numbers from and to which the calls were made and the duration of the calls, was admitted as real evidence. It was held that where information is recorded by mechanical means without the intervention of a human mind, the record made by the machine is admissible.[80] *R v Governor of Brixton Prison, ex p Levin*[81] is to similar effect. The issue was whether L had used a computer terminal to gain unauthorized access to the computerized fund transfer service of a bank and to make fraudulent transfers of funds from accounts of clients of the bank to accounts which he controlled. Each request for transfer was processed automatically and a record of the transaction was copied to the computer's historical records. The House of Lords held that the printouts of screen displays of these records were admissible to prove the transfers of funds they recorded. Lord Hoffmann said: 'They do not assert that such transfers took place. They record the transfers . . . The evidential status of the printouts is no different from that of a photocopy of a forged cheque.'[82]

*Taylor v Chief Constable of Cheshire*,[83] which involved out-of-court use of a video cassette recording, is perhaps best regarded as an example of the same principle. The recording had been made by a security camera and showed a person in a shop picking up an item and putting it inside his jacket. The recording was subsequently played to police officers who identified Taylor as the person shown. The recording was returned

---

[79] (1990) 91 Cr App R 186, CA.

[80] Cf *R v Shephard* (1991) 93 Cr App R 139, CA (till rolls not treated as real evidence because much of the information recorded on them was supplied by cashiers).

[81] [1997] AC 741, HL.

[82] See also *R (on the application of O'Shea v Coventry Magistrates Court)* (2004) LTL 5/4/2004, DC.

[83] [1987] 1 All ER 225. Cf *R v Fowden and White* [1982] Crim LR 588, CA, Ch 9. See also *R v Maqsud Ali* [1966] 1 QB 688, CCA (evidence of translators who had listened to a tape together with a transcript of their translation).

to the shop where, by accident, it was erased from the cassette. The officers were allowed to give evidence of what they had seen on the video and Taylor was convicted of theft. On appeal it was argued that, although the recording itself would have been admissible, the evidence of the officers was hearsay because they had not witnessed the theft personally or directly. The appeal was dismissed on the grounds that what the officers saw on the video was no different in principle from the evidence of a bystander who had actually witnessed the incident by direct vision. The evidence was admissible, although its weight and reliability had to be assessed carefully and, because identification was in issue, by reference to the usual criteria laid down in the form of guidelines in the case of *R v Turnbull*.[84] Those criteria, according to McNeill J, had to be applied not only in relation to the camera itself, but also in relation to the visual display unit or recorded copy and to the officers who had watched the video recording.

Under section 16(1)(a) of the Road Traffic Offenders Act 1988,[85] in proceedings for an offence of driving when unfit through drink or driving after consuming excess alcohol, evidence of the proportion of alcohol in a breath specimen may be given by a statement automatically produced by the device used to measure such proportion, together with a certificate, signed by a constable, that the statement relates to a specimen provided by the accused. In *Garner v DPP*[86] it was held that the purpose of this provision is to enable the facts to be established without the need to call anybody and therefore, if the certificate is defective, the printout remains admissible as real evidence (in accordance with *Castle v Cross*) and can be linked to the accused by oral evidence. However, oral evidence of the reading, in the absence of the automatically produced statement, does not come up to the required standard of proof.[87]

### (f) Evasion

Given that the hearsay rule, at common law, could operate to exclude highly cogent evidence, and that a majority of the House of Lords in *Myers v DPP*[88] confirmed that it was for the legislature and not the judiciary to add to the classes of exception to the hearsay rule, it is perhaps not altogether surprising that both bar and bench employed a variety of devices with a view to evasion of the rule. One such device employed by counsel involved asking what a conversation or document was about, rather than what was said in the conversation or written in the document. Another involved asking a witness about certain acts which were of relevance only insofar as they gave rise to an inference as to the contents of an out-of-court statement. Thus counsel would ask, for example: 'Did you go to X?', 'As a result of something he said, did you then do something?', 'What did you do?' Both devices were held to be objectionable[89] and will remain equally objectionable in the case of hearsay which is inadmissible under the 2003 Act.

---

84 [1977] QB 224, CA (see Ch 8).     85 Formerly s 10(3)(a) of the Road Traffic Act 1972.
86 (1989) 90 Cr App R 178.     87 *Owen v Chesters* [1985] RTR 191, DC.
88 [1965] AC 1001.
89 See per Lord Devlin in *Glinski v McIver* [1962] AC 726, HL at 780–1 and *R v Turner* (1975) 60 Cr App R 80, CA at 83. See also *R v Saunders* [1899] 1 QB 490.

Judicial evasion of the rule was apparent in a number of cases, especially those in which the rule would otherwise operate to exclude apparently reliable identification evidence[90] or evidence which assisted in proving a negative.[91] Hopefully, now that judges have the discretionary power under section 114(1)(d) to admit otherwise inadmissible hearsay if satisfied that it is the interests of justice to do so, they will no longer need to evade the rules.

## 3  CASES WHERE A WITNESS IS UNAVAILABLE

### (a)  General

Under section 116 of the 2003 Act, first-hand hearsay statements, whether made orally or in a document, are admissible, on behalf of the prosecution or defence, subject to three conditions: first, that oral evidence given in the proceedings by the maker of the statement would be admissible as evidence of the matter stated, secondly, that the maker of the statement is identified, and thirdly, that the maker of the statement does not give oral evidence for one of a number of specified reasons, which include, for example, his unfitness to be a witness and fear. There is a fourth condition, the leave of the court, but this is imposed only where the maker of the statement does not give oral evidence through fear. This reflects the view of the Law Commission that whereas a general leave requirement would result in inconsistent and arbitrary decision-making, always allowing judges opposed to hearsay to find reasons to exclude it, a requirement of leave in the case of the statements of witnesses not giving oral evidence through fear was necessary to avoid the danger of witnesses making statements in the knowledge that they could later claim to be frightened and thereby avoid cross-examination.[92]

A statement which is admissible under section 116 may be excluded by the court in the exercise of its discretionary powers of exclusion, including the power to exclude evidence on which the prosecution propose to rely under section 78 of the Police and Criminal Evidence Act 1984. Section 78 is likely to take on a particular importance, in the case of evidence which is admissible under section 116 without the leave of the court, as the only means of excluding evidence to ensure that the accused receives a fair trial in accordance with Article 6 of the European Convention on Human Rights. Section 78 and the other statutory provisions relating to the discretion to exclude (and also those provisions which relate to the question of proof and to the capability and credibility of the maker of the statement) apply to hearsay admissible not only under section 116 but also under other sections of the Act, and for this reason they are considered separately, below.

Section 116(1), (2), (3) and (5) provide as follows.

---

[90] See, eg, *R v Osbourne, R v Virtue* [1973] QB 678, CA.

[91] See, eg, *R v Muir* (1983) 79 Cr App R 153, CA, considered below under 5 **Admissibility in the interests of justice**.

[92] See paras 4.28 et seq and para 8.58.

(1) In criminal proceedings a statement not made in oral evidence in the proceedings is admissible as evidence of any matter stated if—

   (a) oral evidence given in the proceedings by the person who made the statement would be admissible as evidence of that matter,

   (b) the person who made the statement (the relevant person) is identified to the court's satisfaction, and

   (c) any of the five conditions mentioned in subsection (2) is satisfied.

(2) The conditions are—

   (a) that the relevant person is dead;

   (b) that the relevant person is unfit to be a witness because of his bodily or mental condition;

   (c) that the relevant person is outside the United Kingdom and it is not reasonably practicable to secure his attendance;

   (d) that the relevant person cannot be found although such steps as it is reasonably practicable to take to find him have been taken;

   (e) that through fear the relevant person does not give (or does not continue to give) oral evidence in the proceedings, either at all or in connection with the subject matter of the statement, and the court gives leave for the statement to be given in evidence.

(3) For the purposes of subsection (2)(e) 'fear' is to be widely construed and (for example) includes fear of the death or injury of another person or of financial loss.

(5) A condition set out in any paragraph of subsection (2) which is in fact satisfied is to be treated as not satisfied if it is shown that the circumstances described in that paragraph are caused—

   (a) by the person in support of whose case it is sought to give the statement in evidence, or

   (b) by a person acting on his behalf,

in order to prevent the relevant person giving oral evidence in the proceedings (whether at all or in connection with the subject matter of the statement).

Concerning the opening words of section 116(1), 'criminal proceedings' 'statement' and 'matter stated' bear the same meaning as in section 114 of the Act and call for no additional comment in the present context. The purpose of section 116(1)(a) is to prevent section 116 from being used to admit evidence which, if the maker of the statement were to be called as a witness, would be inadmissible because, for example, he has no personal knowledge of the facts,[93] or the evidence constitutes expert opinion evidence which the maker is not qualified to give, or the evidence is simply irrelevant to the facts in issue.

Section 116 applies to both oral and written statements. Having regard to the requirements of section 116(1)(a), (b), and (c), it is plainly very important, in the case of statements made in writing, to identify correctly the person who made the statement (the 'relevant person'), and for this purpose valuable guidance is provided by the decisions reached under section 23 of the Criminal Justice Act 1988. If A makes an

---

[93] See *R v JP* [1999] Crim LR 401, CA, a decision under s 23 of the Criminal Justice Act 1988.

oral statement within the hearing of B, who writes down what A says, and A reads and signs the document, then clearly A is the relevant person. Similarly, if A dictates the statement to B and checks that what B has written down is an accurate record of what he said (by reading it or having it read back to him) then, even without his signature, A is the relevant person.[94] It would be otherwise, however, if B made a written record of A's oral statement which was not agreed to or approved or accepted by A because in these circumstances A has made an oral statement, not a statement in a document.[95] B has made a statement in a document, but his statement would not be admissible under section 116 because the condition in section 116(a) cannot be met—oral evidence by B would not be admissible of the matter stated because B has no direct or personal knowledge of those matters.

Section 116(1)(b) reflects the view that the risk of unreliability in the case of hearsay statements made by unidentified individuals is high and ensures that where a statement is admitted, the opposing party is in a position to impugn the credibility of the maker of the statement.[96]

### (b)  The reasons for not calling the maker of the statement to give evidence

Section 116(2)(a) to (e) of the 2003 Act have been cast in words similar, but not identical, to those employed in section 23(2)(a), (b) and (c) of the Criminal Justice Act 1988 and, subject to the significant alterations to some of the wording, the decisions interpreting the earlier provisions provide very useful guidance as to the way in which the provisions of the 2003 Act are likely to be construed.

*(i) Relevant person unfit to be a witness because of his bodily or mental condition.* Unlike its statutory precursor, which referred to a person who was 'unfit to attend as a witness', section 116(2)(b) refers to a person who is 'unfit to be a witness'. However, it is submitted that subsection (2)(b) is likely to cover a person physically unable to get to court 'to be a witness' as well as a person able to attend court but unfit to give evidence, such as a witness who, by reason of his mental condition, is unable to recall the events in question.[97]

*(ii) Relevant person outside the United Kingdom and it is not reasonably practicable to secure his attendance.* The requirement in section 116(2)(c) is likely to be treated, as before, as a requirement of a strictly territorial nature and therefore will not be satisfied if the person who made the statement is a consul or embassy official in the UK.[98] The word 'attendance' was treated as capable of including the giving of evidence through a live television link from outside the United Kingdom under section 32 of the Criminal Justice Act 1988, but not examination of a witness on commission by a court in his country of residence.[99]

---

[94]  *R v McGillivray* (1992) 97 Cr App R 232, CA.          [95]  Cf *Re D (a minor)* [1986] 2 FLR 189.
[96]  See below, under **9 Other safeguards (b) Credibility**.
[97]  See *R v Setz-Dempsey* (1994) 98 Cr App R 23, CA.
[98]  *R v Jiminez-Paez* (1993) 98 Cr App R 239, CA.          [99]  *R v Radak* [1999] 1 Cr App R 187, CA.

The question whether it is reasonably practicable to secure the attendance of the maker of the statement should be examined not at the time when the trial opens, but against the whole background to the case. Thus in *R v Bray*[100] an argument that it was not reasonably practicable to secure the attendance of a person because it was only when the trial started that it was realized that he was overseas, was rejected by the Court of Appeal: since the person had been overseas for some seven months before the trial began, it had not been shown that it was not reasonably practicable to secure his attendance at the trial. In *R v Maloney*[101] it was held that the word 'practicable' is not equivalent to physically possible and must be construed in the light of the normal steps which would be taken to arrange the attendance of a witness at trial; and that the word 'reasonably' involved a further qualification of the duty, to secure attendance by taking the reasonable steps which a party would normally take to secure a witness's attendance having regard to the means and resources available to the parties. Thus the relevant factors, in deciding whether it is reasonably practicable to secure the attendance of a witness, include such matters as the cost of travel,[102] whether an offer was made to pay the fare, the reason for any refusal to attend, and whether an approach was made to the person's employer or the British Embassy.[103] The test may be satisfied notwithstanding that (i) practicable arrangements have been made for the witness to attend and he has stated an intention to attend (because circumstances may occur at short notice which render it impracticable to secure his attendance on the day in question),[104] (ii) the witness chooses not to attend court (because the test is not whether it is reasonably practicable for the witness to attend),[105] or (iii) if there were to be an adjournment, the witness might attend at some future date (because there is no necessity to look to the future).[106]

*(iii) Relevant person does not give oral evidence through fear.* Section 116(2)(e) has been cast in very wide terms. It covers not only cases in which, through fear, the maker of the statement does not give (or continue to give) evidence in connection with the subject matter of the hearsay statement in question, but also cases in which, through fear, the maker of the statement does not give oral evidence at all or, having started to give oral evidence, 'dries up'. It covers, therefore, not only the potential witness who has been intimidated, but also those who are scared of the process—in some cases the

---

[100] (1988) 88 Cr App R 354, CA. This was a decision under s 68(2)(a)(ii) of the Police and Criminal Evidence Act 1984, the statutory precursor to s 23(2)(b) of the 1988 Act. The wording of the two provisions was identical.

[101] [1994] Crim LR 525, CA.

[102] *R v Case* [1991] Crim LR 192, CA. See also *R v Castillo* [1996] 1 Cr App R 438, CA.

[103] *R v Gonzales de Arango* (1991) 96 Cr App R 399, CA, a decision under s 68(2) of the Police and Criminal Evidence Act 1984.

[104] *R v Hurst* [1995] 1 Cr App R 82, CA.

[105] *R v French* (1993) 97 Cr App R 421, CA. See also *R v Castillo* [1996] 1 Cr App R 438, CA: the fact that it is possible for a witness to attend does not on its own settle whether his attendance is reasonably practicable.

[106] *R v French* (1993) 97 Cr App R 421. But in the case of a *pre-trial* application, the court will obviously need to look to the future to see whether it would be practicable for the witness's attendance to be secured at the date of the trial: *R v Hurst* [1995] 1 Cr App R 82 at 92, CA.

ordeal—of going to court and giving evidence.[107] The question of fear or otherwise has to be judged at the time when the witness would be expected to give his evidence orally. However, there has to be a degree of sensible give and take. Sometimes, for example, the appropriate ruling will be sought before the trial to enable counsel for the prosecution to decide how the case should be opened to the jury. Equally, it may suffice to show continuing fear and that the witness has disappeared.[108]

Subsection (3) makes clear that 'fear' is to be widely construed, and it is equally clear from the examples given in the subsection, that it is not confined to fear arising out of threats or intimidation directed at the maker of the statement himself. Nonetheless, the subsection rather begs the question as to just *how* widely 'fear' is to be construed. Does it extend, for example, to the witness whose testimony is such that it will expose him to public humiliation or disgrace? If the authorities on section 23(3) of the Criminal Justice Act 1988—the statutory precursor to section 116(2)(e)—are any guidance, then the word will be construed very widely indeed. In *R v Acton Justices, ex p McMullen; R v Tower Bridge Magistrates' Court, ex p Lawlor*[109] the Divisional Court held that: 'Fear of what and whether that is relevant is a matter for the court's consideration in the given circumstances.' In that case, it was submitted that: (i) the test of fear is objective, not subjective; (ii) the fear should be based on reasonable grounds; and (iii) it is insufficient if there is fear in the absence of threats, interference or intimidation after the commission of the offence. Rejecting these submissions, it was held: 'It will be sufficient that the court on the evidence is sure that the witness is in fear as a consequence of the commission of the material offence or of something said or done subsequently in relation to that offence and the possibility of the witness testifying to it.' However, even this modest qualification of the statutory wording was rejected in *R v Martin*,[110] where the witness said he was fearful for his family, having been approached by a silent stranger whom he had previously seen outside his door. It was held that the court has no power, or reason, to qualify the statutory wording, which was wide enough to cover not only genuine witness intimidation, but also cases of fear based on mistake or misunderstanding.[111]

The effect of section 116(5) is that a party cannot rely on section 116 where he, or someone acting on his behalf has, in order to prevent the maker of the statement giving oral evidence, brought about one of the conditions set out in section 116(2). This would be the case, for example, if the party in question had murdered the maker of the statement (section 116(2)(a)) or falsely imprisoned the witness at a secret location (section 116(2)(d)). Presumably, it is for the party resisting admissibility of the statement to establish such conduct.

---

[107] See generally paras 8.63–8.66, Law Com No 245.          [108] *R v H* [2001] Crim LR 815, CA.
[109] (1990) 92 Cr App R 103 at 105.          [110] [1996] Crim LR 589, CA.
[111] See also *R v Fairfax* [1995] Crim LR 949, CA (all that needs to be proved is that the witness does not give evidence through fear) and *R v Arnold* [2005] Crim LR 56, CA.

### (c) The requirement of leave where the maker of the statement does not give oral evidence through fear

Leave may only be given under section 116(2)(e) if the court considers that the statement ought to be admitted in the interests of justice, having regard to the factors set out in section 116(4). Section 116(4) provides as follows.

> (4) Leave may be given under subsection (2)(e) only if the court considers that the statement ought to be admitted in the interests of justice, having regard—
>
> (a) to the statement's contents,
> (b) to any risk that its admission or exclusion will result in unfairness to any party to the proceedings (and in particular to how difficult it will be to challenge the statement if the relevant person does not give oral evidence),
> (c) in appropriate cases, to the fact that a direction under s 19 of the Youth Justice and Criminal Evidence Act 1999 (special measures for the giving of evidence by fearful witnesses etc) could be made in relation to the relevant person, and
> (d) to any other relevant circumstances.

Subsection (4)(c) in effect requires the court to consider whether the statement ought not to be admitted in the interests of justice because a special measures direction can be given under section 19 of the Youth Justice and Criminal Evidence Act 1999. Such a direction may be made, for example, to admit a video-recording of an interview of the witness as his evidence-in-chief, and to admit a video-recording of the cross-examination and re-examination of the witness as his evidence under cross-examination and on re-examination.[112]

Subsection (4)(a)(b) and (d) are closely modelled on section 26(i), (ii), and (iii) of the Criminal Justice Act 1988, which set out the factors to which the court was to have regard in deciding whether to grant leave to admit a statement which had been prepared for the purposes of pending or contemplated litigation or of a criminal investigation and was admissible under either section 23 or section 24 of that Act. The significant differences are that the precursor to subsection 116(4)(b) referred to any risk of unfairness to 'the accused', and referred to the difficulty of 'controverting', rather than 'challenging' the statement. It is submitted that, subject to these differences, the following principles established in decisions reached under section 26 of the 1988 Act provide useful guidance as to the way in which the courts should approach their task under section 116(4) of the 2003 Act.

It is for the party seeking to admit the evidence to show that it should be admitted in the interests of justice, a test which involves considerations of fairness both to the defence and to the prosecution.[113] In *R v Cole*[114] it was held that a 'complex balancing exercise' is involved: 'the weight to be attached to the inability to cross-examine and the magnitude of any consequential risk that admission of the statement will result in unfairness to the accused, will depend in part on the court's assessment of the quality

---

[112] See Ch 5.    [113] *R v Patel* (1992) 97 Cr App R 294, CA.    [114] [1990] 2 All ER 108 at 116, CA.

of the evidence shown by the contents of the statement.'[115] It was also held that the court should consider how far any potential unfairness arising from the inability to cross-examine on the statement may be effectively counterbalanced by a warning to the jury about the limitations of reading out a statement, ie the absence of opportunity to judge the maker's reliability and credibility in examination and cross-examination.[116] The court will also consider whether, having regard to other evidence available to the party seeking to admit the statement, the interests of justice will be properly served by excluding it.[117] *R v Cole* was applied in *R v Fairfax*[118] to admit statements whose makers did not give oral evidence through fear. Although the statements were the foundation of the case against the accused and without them the prosecution case was bound to have failed, it was held that they contained evidence of good quality and could be controverted by the accused himself. In *R v Kennedy*,[119] K and H were convicted of affray. The statement of M, the only independent witness, was admitted. On appeal it was argued that M's evidence was unreliable and in some respects not consistent with the evidence of either K or H. It was held that it was common for accounts of an incident of this kind to differ; M was the sole independent witness and his evidence was of considerable value; and the judge had directed the jury on the disadvantages of not having M before them. The court added that it would not have been proper to direct the jury to pay *less* attention to M's evidence than to that of the live witnesses: it was for the jury alone to decide what weight they placed on the evidence.[120]

The importance or otherwise of the contents of the statement to the issues in the case is a matter to be taken into account.[121] The fact that the statement goes to the crucial issues in the case does not necessarily count against its admission—it may be, for that reason, all the more important that it should be admitted.[122] Thus in *R v Setz-Dempsey*[123] it was held that where identification is in issue, neither the fact that the statement contains identification evidence, nor the fact that it is the only evidence against the accused, nor the inability to cross-examine will of itself be sufficient to justify exclusion—the quality of the evidence in the statement is the crucial factor.[124] However, in that case it was also held that, although not determinative, inability to probe evidence of identification by cross-examination is of the utmost significance

---

[115] See, eg, *R v Thompson* [1999] Crim LR 747, CA, where a statement was admitted notwithstanding that its maker suffered from long-term alcohol related problems and depression.

[116] There is no fixed rule as to the terms in which such a warning should be given: *R v Batt and Batt* [1995] Crim LR 240, CA. However, it is inappropriate to direct the jury that the statement is of less worth than the evidence of the witnesses in the case: *R v Greer* [1998] Crim LR 572, CA.

[117] *R v Cole* [1990] 2 All ER 108 at 116–17.          [118] [1995] Crim LR 949, CA.

[119] [1992] Crim LR 37, CA.          [120] Cf *R v Kennedy* [1994] Crim LR 50, CA.

[121] *R v French* (1993) 97 Cr App R 421 at 428.

[122] *R v Patel* (1992) 97 Cr App R 294. See also *R v Batt and Batt* [1995] Crim LR 240, CA.

[123] (1994) 98 Cr App R 23 at 30, applying the principles enunciated by Lord Griffiths in *Scott v R* [1989] 2 All ER 305.

[124] See also *R v Dragic* [1996] 2 Cr App R 232, CA, although in that case the evidence was evidence of recognition and was challenged on the basis that the maker of the statement was either unreliable, possibly because of drink, or had lied.

and therefore the court should be cautious about admitting such evidence, especially where there are grounds for believing that, if the evidence had been given in person, it might have been significantly undermined by cross-examination. It is submitted that the court should be astute to examine all the circumstances in which the observation was made, such as the duration of the observation, the distance from which it was made, whether it was impeded in any way, the length of time between the observation and the time at which the statement was made, and so on.

If the evidence is tendered by the prosecution, its *admission* could result in unfairness to the accused; if it is tendered by an accused, its *exclusion* could result in unfairness to the accused but its *admission* could result in unfairness to a co-accused, in which case it seems that the court should conduct a balancing exercise which may result in the exclusion of the evidence on the basis that the damage done to the co-accused outweighs the benefit to the accused.[125] However, such an outcome would hardly be 'in the interests of justice' in a case in which, had the accused been tried separately, the evidence would have been of such benefit to him that it would have been admitted.[126]

In considering the risk of unfairness to the accused, particular regard must be had to the possible difficulty of controverting—under the 2003 Act, 'challenging'—the statement in the absence of its maker. The judge, in coming to a conclusion on the matter, should not embark on a detailed comparison between what might have happened if the maker of the statement had given oral evidence and had been cross-examined, and what might happen if his statement is admitted without him attending.[127] In *R v Cole*[128] it was held that the judge, in considering whether it was likely to be possible to controvert the statement, had properly taken into account not only the availability of prosecution witnesses for cross-examination, but also the availability of the accused or other witnesses to give evidence for the defence. Thus although the court cannot require to be told whether the accused intends to give evidence or to call witnesses, it is not required to assess the possibility of controverting the statement on the basis that the accused will not give evidence or call witnesses. *R v Cole* was applied, in this respect, in *R v Price*,[129] where it was held that notes of a conversation between P and his bank manager were properly admitted notwithstanding that the only way in which P could controvert the statement was by giving evidence himself, which he could not be required to do.[130]

In *R v Gokal*[131] it was submitted that the statutory provisions should be so construed as to exclude, as a means of controverting the statement, the possibility of the accused himself giving evidence in rebuttal, having regard to the right to silence and the entitlement to a fair hearing under Article 6 of the European Convention on

---

[125] As in *R v Gregory and Mott* [1995] Crim LR 507, CA, a decision under s 25(2)(d) of the 1988 Act.
[126] *R v Duffy* [1999] 1 Cr App R 307, CA.     [127] *R v Radak* [1999] 1 Cr App R 187, CA.
[128] [1990] 2 All ER 108, CA.
[129] [1991] Crim LR 707, CA. The case was decided under s 25(2)(d) of the 1988 Act.
[130] See also *R v Samuel* [1992] Crim LR 189, CA and *R v Moore* [1992] Crim LR 882, CA.
[131] [1997] 2 Cr App R 266.

Human Rights. The Court of Appeal rejected the submission and approved *R v Cole*. Noting that the possibilities for controverting the statement are wide, and include putting in issue the credibility of the maker of the statement,[132] the court held that although admission of the statement may make it more difficult for the accused to exercise his right of silence, the right is not abrogated. It was also held, after consideration of judgments of the European Commission and European Court of Human Rights, that, since the whole basis of the exercise of the discretion is to assess the interests of justice by reference to the risk of unfairness to the accused, 'our procedures appear to us to accord fully with our treaty obligations'.

In considering the risk of unfairness, it may also be relevant to consider whether the party against whom the statement is tendered had any opportunity of interviewing or making inquiries of the maker of the statement, but in any event this is another relevant circumstance (see now section 116(4)(d)).[133] 'Other relevant circumstances', for the purposes of section 116(4)(d), are also likely to include the circumstances in which the statement was made, including any attempts made to get the maker to make the statement in the way most favourable to the party seeking to rely upon it, the fact that the maker of the statement made prior inconsistent statements, whether oral or written,[134] and other facts or matters affecting his credibility. Thus, as to the last, although it may be in the interests of justice to admit the statement of a person even if he is of bad character, particularly when that bad character can readily be demonstrated, it should be excluded where he is so dishonest that the absence of an opportunity for the jury to assess him as a witness, to observe his demeanour and the manner in which he gives his evidence, would result in potential unfairness.[135] In *R v D*[136] the accused was charged with attempted rape and indecent assault. The victim was an 81-year-old woman who suffered from Alzheimer's disease. Her police interview was recorded on video, at a time when she would have been competent as a witness. However, by the time of the preparatory hearing it was clear that she was not mentally fit enough to give live evidence and the judge granted the prosecution leave to admit the video under sections 23 and 26 of the Criminal Justice Act 1988, taking the view that since he had concluded that it was in the interests of justice to admit the video, having balanced the interests of justice as between victim and defendant, then it was unlikely that there would be a breach of Article 6 of the European Convention of Human Rights. On appeal it was held that the judge had adopted the right approach. Prima facie, the complainant had a right to have her complaint put before a jury, and the accused's rights would be protected because he could call medical evidence to

[132] See below, under **9 Other safeguards (b) Credibility**.

[133] *R v Patel* (1993) 97 Cr App R 294, CA.

[134] *R v Sweeting and Thomas* [1999] Crim LR 75, CA, in which it was also held that if the statement is admitted, the logical course is to admit the inconsistent statement. See now under s 124(2)(c) of the 2003 Act, considered below under **9 Other safeguards (b) Credibility**.

[135] See *R v Lockley* [1995] 2 Cr App R 554, CA, a decision under s 25 of the Criminal Justice Act 1988, where the maker of the statement had demonstrated and indeed boasted about his remarkable ability to deceive.

[136] [2002] 2 Cr App R 601, CA.

challenge the complainant's capacity to remember, understand and say what happened. Furthermore, if it was in the interests of justice to admit the video, it was unlikely to be unfair under section 78 of the Police and Criminal Evidence Act 1984.

Under Article 6(3) of the European Convention on Human Rights, 'Everyone charged with a criminal offence has the following minimum rights . . . (d) to examine or have examined witnesses against him . . .' It is clear from the jurisprudence of the European Court of Human Rights that the admissibility of evidence is primarily a matter for regulation by national law and that as a general rule it is for the national courts to assess the evidence before them. Thus the task of the European Court is not to give a ruling on whether statements of witnesses were properly admitted as evidence, but to ascertain whether the proceedings as a whole, including the way in which the evidence was taken, were fair. These principles were reiterated in *PS v Germany*[137] where it was also said that: 'Where a conviction is based solely or to a decisive degree on depositions that have been made by a person whom the accused has had no opportunity to examine or have examined, whether during the investigation or at the trial, the rights of the defence are restricted to an extent that is incompatible with the guarantees provided by Article 6 . . .'[138] However, in *R v M(KJ)*[139] the Court of Appeal held that the notion that this principle could admit of no exceptions would lead to intolerable results under sections 23 and 26 of the 1988 Act and could only lead to an encouragement of criminals to indulge in the very kind of intimidation which the sections are designed to defeat. Lord Justice Potter, citing *R v Harvey*,[140] said:[141] 'Where a witness gives evidence on a voir dire that he is unwilling to give evidence as a result of a threat which has been made to him, and the judge draws the inference that the threat was made, if not at the instigation of the defendant, at least with his approval, this should normally be conclusive as to how the discretion under section 26 should be exercised.'

## 4 BUSINESS AND OTHER DOCUMENTS

Section 117 of the 2003 Act, which provides for the admissibility of hearsay statements contained in business and other documents, is modelled on section 24 of the Criminal Justice Act 1988, which it replaces, but there are a number of significant differences. Under section 117, statements contained in documents are admissible as evidence of any matter stated on five conditions. The first is that oral evidence would be admissible as evidence of the matter stated. The second is that the document was created or received by a person in the course of a trade, business, profession or other occupation or as the holder of a paid or unpaid office. The third is that the person who supplied the information, who may be the same person as the creator or receiver of the document, had or may reasonably be supposed to have had personal knowledge

---

[137] (2000) 30 EHRR CD301 at para 19.
[138] Para 24, ibid. See also *Luca v Italy* App 33354/96 27 May 2001 and *R v Arnold* [2005] Crim LR 56, CA.
[139] [2003] 2 Cr App R 322, CA.     [140] [1998] 10 Archbold News 2, CA.     [141] At [59].

of the matters dealt with. The fourth, which is only imposed if the information was supplied indirectly, is that each person through whom it was supplied, received it in the course of a trade, business, profession or other occupation or as the holder of a paid or unpaid office. The fifth condition, which is imposed only where the statement was prepared for the purpose of pending or contemplated criminal proceedings, or for a criminal investigation, is that the supplier of the information does not give oral evidence for one of the reasons set out in section 116(2)[142] or because he cannot reasonably be expected to have any recollection of the matters dealt with in the statement. A statement admissible under section 117 may be excluded by the court in the exercise of its discretionary powers of exclusion.[143]

Section 117 provides as follows.

(1) In criminal proceedings a statement contained in a document is admissible of any matter stated if—
   (a) oral evidence given in the proceedings would be admissible as evidence of that matter,
   (b) the requirements of subsection (2) are satisfied, and
   (c) the requirements of subsection (5) are satisfied, in a case where subsection (4) requires them to be.

(2) The requirements of this subsection are satisfied if—
   (a) the document or the part containing the statement was created or received by a person in the course of a trade, business, profession or other occupation, or as the holder of a paid or unpaid office,
   (b) the person who supplied the information contained in the statement (the relevant person) had or may reasonably be supposed to have had personal knowledge of the matters dealt with, and
   (c) each person (if any) through whom the information was supplied from the relevant person to the person mentioned in paragraph (a) received the information in the course of a trade, business, profession or other occupation, or as the holder of a paid or unpaid office.

(3) The persons mentioned in paragraphs (a) and (b) of subsection (2) may be the same person.

(4) The additional requirements of subsection (5) must be satisfied if the statement—
   (a) was prepared for the purposes of pending or contemplated criminal proceedings, or for a criminal investigation, but
   (b) was not obtained pursuant to a request under section 7 of the Crime (International Co-operation) Act 2003 or an order under paragraph 6 of Schedule 13 to the Criminal Justice Act 1988 (which relate to overseas evidence).[144]

(5) The requirements of this subsection are satisfied if—
   (a) any of the five conditions mentioned in section 116(2) is satisfied (absence of relevant person etc), or

---

[142] See above, under **3 Cases where a witness is unavailable.**
[143] See below, under **9 Other safeguards (d) Discretion to exclude.**
[144] These provisions relate to the issue of letters of request.

(b) the relevant person cannot reasonably be expected to have any recollection of the matters dealt with in the statement (having regard to the length of time since he supplied the information and all other circumstances).

(6) A statement is not admissible under this section if the court makes a direction to that effect under subsection (7).

(7) The court may make a direction under this subsection if satisfied that the statement's reliability as evidence for the purpose for which it is tendered is doubtful in view of—

(a) its contents,

(b) the source of the information contained in it,

(c) the way in which or the circumstances in which the information was supplied or received, or

(d) the way in which or the circumstances in which the document concerned was created or received.

As to the opening words of section 117(1), 'criminal proceedings' 'statement' and 'matter stated' bear the same meaning as in section 114 of the Act and call for no additional comment in the present context. The words of section 117(1)(a) bear the same meaning as in section 116(1)(a) of the Act but whereas under section 116(a) the test is whether oral evidence 'given . . . by the person who made the statement' would be admissible, under section 117(1)(a) the test is simply whether oral evidence would be admissible, ie oral evidence given by anyone. A 'document' is defined by section 134(1) as 'anything in which information of any description is recorded', a description wide enough to include, inter alia, maps, plans, graphs, drawings, photographs, discs, audio-tapes, video-tapes, films, microfilms, negatives, and computer-generated print-outs. Under section 117(2)(a), the document (or part) containing the statement must be 'created or received' by a person in the course of a trade (or business etc). A document, given its wide definition, may be created in a number of different ways: by writing or typing (a document in writing); by drawing (a map or plan); by development (a photograph); or by recording (discs, tapes, sound-tracks, etc). A document may be received by hand, by post, by facsimile machine, by e-mail or by linked computers. Whatever the means by which the document is created or received, the act of creation or receipt must be in the course of a trade (or business etc).[145] Under section 117(2)(b), the information contained in the document must have been supplied by a person who had, 'or may reasonably be supposed to have had', personal knowledge of the matters dealt with, wording which allows the court, in appropriate circumstances, to infer personal knowledge on the part of the supplier.[146] Section 117(3) makes clear that the creator of the document and the supplier of the information may be one and the same person; judged in terms of potential reliability, it would

---

[145] The fact that a document created by a company's officer effects a corrupt payment does not prevent it from being a document 'created . . . in the course of a . . . business': see *R v Foxley* [1995] 2 Cr App R 523 at 538, CA.

[146] See *R v Foxley* [1995] 2 Cr App R 523 at 536. See also *R v Schreiber and Schreiber* [1988] Crim LR 112, CA, a decision under s 1 of the Criminal Evidence Act 1965.

be odd if a hearsay statement contained in a trade, business or related document were to be admissible *only* if at least second-hand.

Under section 117(2)(c), if the information contained in the document was supplied indirectly, each intermediary through whom it was supplied must have received it in the course of a trade (or business etc). It is the act of *receiving*, as opposed to the act of *supplying*, which must have been performed in the course of a trade (or business etc). Thus, if A, a businessman and an intermediary (under section 117(2)(c)), supplies information to B, another businessman and intermediary, then provided that both A and B receive the information in the course of their respective businesses, it matters not that A is not acting in the course of his business when he supplies the information to B. The trade (or business etc) of one intermediary need not be the same trade (or business etc) as that of either another intermediary or the creator or receiver of the document.

Under section 117(4) and (5), unlike section 116, the requirement that the person who supplied the information be unable to give oral evidence for one of the specified reasons (section 116(2)(a)–(e)), is imposed only in the case of 'a statement . . . prepared for the purposes of pending or contemplated criminal proceedings, or for a criminal investigation'. This phrase is wide enough to include a witness statement taken by a police officer, a statement from a potential witness recorded by a police officer in his notebook, a statement of a potential witness, an attendance note of an interview with a potential witness made by an accused's solicitor,[147] and a custody record.[148] The expression 'statement prepared for the purposes of contemplated criminal proceedings' has been construed to include a statement made in the course of criminal proceedings, so that a transcript of the evidence of a witness at a previous trial is admissible provided that the maker of the statement is unable to give evidence for one of the reasons specified.[149] Another difference from section 116 is the additional reason set out in section 117(5)(b), namely that the supplier of the information cannot reasonably be expected to have any recollection of the matters dealt with in the statement.[150] The word 'statement' in section 117(5)(b) bears the same meaning as in section 114 and other sections of Chapter 2 of Part 11 of the 2003 Act[151] and does not mean the entire contents of the document. Thus if the supplier cannot reasonably be expected to have any recollection of matters dealt with in only some of the statements contained in a document, those statements may be admitted notwithstanding that he can recollect matters dealt with in other statements contained in the document.[152]

Where the requirements of section 117(1), (2) and (5) are met, the court may use section 117(6) and (7) to direct that the statement in question is nonetheless

---

[147] Per Kennedy J, obiter, in *R v Cunningham* [1989] Crim LR 435, CA, a decision under s 68 of the Police and Criminal Evidence Act 1984.

[148] *R v Hogan* [1997] Crim LR 349, CA.       [149] *R v Lockley* [1995] 2 Cr App R 554, CA.

[150] This reason cannot be established if the supplier has some other document on the basis of which he can refresh his memory in court: per Buxton LJ in *R v Derodra* [2000] 1 Cr App R 41, CA at 44.

[151] See above.       [152] *R v Carrington* (1993) 99 Cr App R 376, CA.

inadmissible, if satisfied that it is of doubtful reliability. It may reach this conclusion having regard to (a) its contents, which, for example, may be internally inconsistent, or inconsistent with a prior statement from the same source; (b) the source of the information, who, for example, may be shown to be dishonest or unreliable; and (c) the mode and circumstances of the supply or receipt of the information or (d) the mode and circumstances of the creation or receipt of the document, either of which may demonstrate the likelihood of inaccuracy in the contents of the statement.

## 5  ADMISSIBILITY IN THE INTERESTS OF JUSTICE

The Law Commission was of the view that, in order to prevent injustice, there should be an inclusionary discretion to render admissible reliable hearsay which would not otherwise be admitted. It recognized that such a discretion, or 'safety valve', would introduce the risks of inconsistency and unpredictability, but believed that without such a discretion its proposed reforms would be too rigid. Some 'limited flexibility' needed to be incorporated. It therefore proposed that a hearsay statement should be admitted if 'despite the difficulties there may be in challenging the statement, its probative value is such that the interests of justice require it to be admissible'.[153] However, the inclusionary discretion in the 2003 Act has been cast more broadly and therefore relaxes the hearsay rule to a greater degree. Under section 114(1)(d) of the 2003 Act, it will be recalled, a statement not made in oral evidence in the proceedings is admissible as evidence of any matter stated if 'the court is satisfied that it is in the interests of justice for it to be admissible'.

Section 114(1)(d) is open to use by both the prosecution and defence. It applies to both oral and written statements and can be used to admit first-hand, second-hand or multiple hearsay. Although it will be used as a last resort, in the sense that it will only be relied upon if the statement in question is not admissible under some other provision of the 2003 Act, some other statutory provision or one of the preserved common-law rules, there is nothing to suggest that it may only be used in exceptional circumstances, or sparingly. Equally, however, it obviously should not be used if, having regard to Article 6 of the European Convention on Human Rights, this would result in an unfair trial. In deciding whether to exercise the power contained in section 114(1), the court must have regard to the non-exhaustive list of factors set out in section 114(2). Section 114(2) provides as follows.

(2) In deciding whether a statement not made in oral evidence should be admitted under subsection (1)(d), the court must have regard to the following factors (and to any others it considers relevant)—
(a) how much probative value the statement has (assuming it to be true) in relation to a matter in issue in the proceedings, or how valuable it is for the understanding of other evidence in the case;

---

[153]  Cl 9, Draft Bill, Law Com No 245.

(b) what other evidence has been, or can be, given on the matter or evidence mentioned in paragraph (a);

(c) how important the matter or evidence mentioned in paragraph (a) is in the context of the case as a whole;

(d) the circumstances in which the statement was made;

(e) how reliable the maker of the statement appears to be;

(f) how reliable the evidence of the making of the statement appears to be;

(g) whether oral evidence of the matter stated can be given and, if not, why it cannot;

(h) the amount of difficulty involved in challenging the statement;

(i) the extent to which that difficulty would be likely to prejudice the party facing it.

The Law Commission gave three examples of how its proposed 'safety valve' might be used. The first was based on the facts of *Sparks v R*.[154] A white man was convicted of indecently assaulting a 3-year-old girl, who was incompetent to testify. The defence had sought to call the mother to give evidence that, shortly after the assault, the child had said to her, 'It was a coloured boy.' The Privy Council held that the trial judge had properly ruled that the evidence was inadmissible hearsay. The appellant had argued that 'it was manifestly unjust for the jury to be left throughout the whole trial with the impression that the child could not give any clue to the identity of her assailant'. It does not follow, from this first example, that the hearsay statements of children who are incompetent to testify will necessarily be admitted, even if their evidence is as obviously relevant as it was in *Sparks v R*. Under the current law, a child will be incompetent to testify if he is not a person who is able to understand questions put to him or her as a witness and to give answers to them which can be understood.[155] In many cases, admissibility of the statement of such a child will be successfully challenged on the basis that the child is unreliable or unable to distinguish fact from fantasy.

The second example was based on the facts of *R v Thomas*.[156] In a murder trial, an eight year old tells the police that he saw the victim leaving her home at a time when, according to the prosecution case, she was already dead, but at the trial he cannot remember when he saw the victim. The difficulty with this example is that under the current law a special measures direction would have provided for a video recording of the child witness to be admitted as his evidence-in-chief.[157]

The third example was based on the facts of *R v Cooper*.[158] Charged with assault, the accused was not allowed to introduce a hearsay statement made by a third party, of similar appearance to the accused, to a friend of his, that he committed the assault. Subsequent authorities confirmed that an out-of-court confession, by a third party, to the offence with which the accused is charged, is inadmissible,[159] decisions which have

---

[154] [1964] AC 964.       [155] Section 53(3) of the Youth Justice and Criminal Evidence Act 1999, Ch 5.

[156] [1994] Crim LR 745, CA.

[157] See s 21 of the Youth Justice and Criminal Evidence Act 1999, Ch 5.

[158] [1969] 1 All ER 32, CA.

[159] *R v Turner* (1975) 61 Cr App R 67, CA. See also *R v Callan* (1993) 98 Cr App R 467, CA. As to the admissibility, for an accused, of a confession made by a *co-accused*, see s 76A, Police and Criminal Evidence Act 1984, Ch 13.

been justified on the grounds that, since it is for the legislature, not the judiciary, to create new exceptions to the hearsay rule,[160] to hold otherwise 'would be to create a very significant and, many might think, a dangerous new exception'.[161] The obvious danger is the ease with which a third party confession may be manufactured or fabricated coupled with the fact that such a confession, by itself, could lead the jury to entertain 'a reasonable doubt'. Having regard to the factors set out in section 114(2), the defence will typically argue that the statement, if true (which must be assumed), has high probative value, that no other evidence of the matter stated is available, and that the matter is of the greatest importance in the context of the case as a whole. Typically, the prosecution will counter that oral evidence of the matter stated can and should be given (if the third party is 'unavailable' under section 116, then the defence will make use of that section) and that they face insuperable difficulties in challenging the statement if the third party is not available for cross-examination. However, each case will need to be considered carefully on its own facts and will involve the court in a complex balancing exercise. It is not without significance, for example, that in the example given by the Law Commission, the third party was of similar appearance to the accused. Much will also turn on the factors mentioned in section 114(2)(d), (e), and (f), namely the circumstances in which the statement was made, the reliability of the maker of the statement and the reliability of the evidence of the making of the statement.

Examples of hearsay which, in the past, have resulted in judicial evasion of the hearsay rule, may now fall for consideration under section 114(1)(d). *R v Muir*[162] provides an instructive example. The appellant was convicted of the theft of a video recorder which he had hired. His defence was that two men, whom he had assumed to be from the hiring company, had collected the recorder from his home. A district manager of the hiring company gave evidence that repossession of the recorder could have been carried out by either the local showroom or head office, and that the recorder had not been repossessed by the local showroom. Under cross-examination, he said that he had been told by head office that no one from there had been sent to call on the appellant. The Court of Appeal held that the district manager, who was in charge of the transaction and with full knowledge of it, was the best person to give evidence that the recorder had not been repossessed. It seems reasonably clear from the facts, however, that *full* knowledge of the transaction is exactly what the witness lacked. The proper course, it is submitted, would have been to call an appropriate officer from head office to give evidence that none of their staff had repossessed the recorder. If, however, there had been numerous offices which could have repossessed the recorder, none of which in fact had done so, to have required the prosecution to

---

[160]  See *Myers v DPP* [1965] AC 1001, HL.

[161]  Per Lord Bridge in *R v Blastland* [1985] 2 All ER 1095 at 1098, HL. Contrast *Chambers v Mississippi* 410 US 295 (1973) (US Sup Court): the exclusion of the confessions of a third party deprives the accused of a fair trial.

[162]  (1983) 79 Cr App R 153. Cf *R v Patel* [1981] 3 All ER 94, above, which was distinguished.

call a relevant employee from each of the offices would have been both unduly onerous and practically undesirable. It is possible that the evidence of a suitably qualified officer as to his extensive but fruitless inquiries would now be admissible in the interests of justice under section 114(1)(d).

## 6 PREVIOUS INCONSISTENT STATEMENTS OF WITNESSES

Under section 3 of the Criminal Procedure Act 1865, a party calling a witness who proves to be hostile may, by leave of the judge, prove that he has made at other times a statement inconsistent with his testimony.[163] Under section 4 of the 1865 Act, if a witness, upon cross-examination as to a previous inconsistent statement, does not distinctly admit that he made such a statement, proof may be given by the cross-examining party that he did in fact make it. Proof of the statement is governed by both sections 4 and 5 of the 1865 Act, section 4 applying to both oral and written statements, and section 5 applying to written statements only.[164] If the hostile witness, or the witness under cross-examination, adopts the contents of the previous statement, then they become part of his evidence and will be evidence of the matter stated. However, as the law stood prior to the coming into force of section 119(1) of the Criminal Justice Act 2003, if, in criminal cases, the witness did not admit to making the statement and it was proved that he did in fact make it, the statement was not introduced as evidence of the matter stated, but went merely to his credit. Under section 119(1), the statement is admitted as evidence of any matter stated of which oral evidence by the witness would be admissible. The reasoning of the Law Commission was that if the tribunal of fact is trusted to decide that the witness lacks credibility and his testimony should be disregarded, they should also be free to accept the previous statement as reliable.[165] Section 119(1) provides as follows.

(1) If in criminal proceedings, a person gives oral evidence and—
    (a) he admits making a previous inconsistent statement, or
    (b) a previous inconsistent statement made by him is proved by virtue of section 3, 4 or 5 of the Criminal Procedure Act 1865,
    the statement is admissible as evidence of any matter stated of which oral evidence by him would be admissible.

Section 119(1) has the merit of removing from the tribunal of fact, in this particular context, the difficult concept of a previous statement being admitted not as evidence of the matters stated but as evidence to undermine the credibility of its maker as a witness in the case. It is a radical change in the law and likely to become a powerful tool in relation to hostile witnesses. For example, if a complainant is treated as a hostile witness, and denies the truth of his or her out-of-court statement implicating the accused, it may be relied upon by the tribunal of fact to convict the accused.

---

[163] See Ch 6 under **D Unfavourable and hostile witnesses.**
[164] See Ch 7 under **A6 Previous inconsistent statements.**    [165] Para 10.89, Law Com No 245.

However, admissibility would be subject to the discretionary powers to exclude evidence on which the prosecution proposes to rely; and, in jury trials in which the case against the accused is based wholly or partly on such a statement, the court has the power under section 125 of the Act to direct the jury to acquit if the evidence provided by the statement is so unconvincing that the conviction of the accused would be unsafe.[166] In cases where the statement is left before the jury, and the witness maintains that it is untrue, a careful direction is likely to be called for. As the Law Commission observed:[167] 'Although the weight to be attached to the oral testimony and the out-of-court statement would be a matter for the fact-finders, it might help a jury if they were told that they are not obliged to accept either version of events as true, and if their attention were drawn to other items which might help them decide which parts of the evidence to believe and which to reject.'

## 7 OTHER PREVIOUS STATEMENTS OF WITNESSES

At common law, the general rule against previous consistent statements prevents a witness from being asked in examination-in-chief about a former out-of-court statement made by him and consistent with his testimony. Under the general rule, such a statement is excluded as evidence of consistency.[168] Such a statement is also inadmissible hearsay, except to the extent that it is admissible under the 2003 Act. As we have seen, under section 119(1) of the 2003 Act, the previous *inconsistent* statement of a witness may be admitted as evidence of the matter stated. In the case of other previous statements of a witness, as with other types of hearsay, there is the usual danger of manufactured evidence, and to allow a witness to give evidence of a previous statement which is consistent with his testimony is to encourage the reception of superfluous evidence. On the other hand, one of the main justifications of the hearsay rule, the impossibility of cross-examining the maker of the statement, does not apply. Furthermore, an out-of-court statement made shortly after the events to which it relates, and while those events are fresh in the memory, is likely to be more reliable than testimony at a trial which takes place some months or years later. Under section 120 of the 2003 Act, a provision of compromise, the previous statements of a witness only become admissible as evidence of the matters stated in five situations, four of which are plainly based upon, and in some cases expanded versions of, the rather technical common-law exceptions to the rule against previous consistent or self-serving statements. It provides as follows.

(1) This section applies where a person (the witness) is called to give evidence in criminal proceedings.

(2) If a previous statement by the witness is admitted as evidence to rebut a suggestion that his oral evidence has been fabricated, that statement is admissible as evidence of any matter stated of which oral evidence by the witness would be admissible.

---

[166] See below, under **9 Other safeguards.**      [167] Para 10.98, Law Com No 245.      [168] See Ch 6.

(3) A statement made by the witness in a document—
    (a) which is used by him to refresh his memory while giving evidence,
    (b) on which he is cross-examined, and
    (c) which as a consequence is received in evidence in the proceedings,
    is admissible as evidence of any matter stated of which oral evidence by him would be admissible.

(4) A previous statement by the witness is admissible as evidence of any matter stated of which oral evidence by him would be admissible, if
    (a) any of the following three conditions is satisfied, and
    (b) while giving evidence the witness indicates that to the best of his belief he made the statement, and that to the best of his belief it states the truth.

(5) The first condition is that the statement identifies or describes a person, object or place.

(6) The second condition is that the statement was made by the witness when the matters stated were fresh in his memory but he does not remember them, and cannot reasonably be expected to remember them, well enough to give oral evidence of them in the proceedings.

(7) The third condition is that—
    (a) the witness claims to be a person against whom an offence has been committed,
    (b) the offence is one to which the proceedings relate,
    (c) the statement consists of a complaint made by the witness (whether to a person in authority or not) about conduct which would, if proved, constitute the offence or part of the offence,
    (d) the complaint was made as soon as could reasonably be expected after the alleged conduct,
    (e) the complaint was not made as a result of a threat or promise, and
    (f) before the statement is adduced the witness gives oral evidence in connection with its subject matter.

(8) For the purposes of subsection (7) the fact that the complaint was elicited (for example, by a leading question) is irrelevant unless a threat or a promise was involved.

## (a) Statements in rebuttal of allegations of recent fabrication

Under section 120(2), a previous oral or written statement of a witness is admissible as evidence of any matter stated of which oral evidence by him would be admissible 'if ... admitted as evidence to rebut a suggestion that his oral evidence has been fabricated', ie if admitted under the exception to the rule against previous consistent statements which arises when, in cross-examination of the witness, it is suggested to him that the account given by him in his testimony is a recent invention or fabrication. The exception is considered in Chapter 6.

## (b) Statements in documents used to refresh the memory

Section 120(3), which mirrors an exception to the rule against previous consistent statements, applies where the witness is cross-examined on a memory-refreshing document and, as a consequence, it 'is received in evidence in the proceedings', ie where the whole document is received in evidence at common law. This happens when a party, or counsel on his behalf, in cross-examining the witness on the memory-refreshing document, asks questions about matters derived from parts of the document not used by the witness to refresh his memory. This principle is considered under 'Refreshing the memory' in Chapter 6.

### (c) Statements identifying or describing a person, object, or place

Under section 120(5), when read in conjunction with section 120(4), a previous oral or written statement of a witness identifying or describing a person, object or place, will be admissible as evidence of any matter stated of which oral evidence by him would be admissible if, in evidence, he indicates that to the best of his belief he made the statement and it states the truth. Section 120(5) is based on the exception to the rule against previous consistent statements in the case of previous *identification of the accused* but, in accordance with the recommendation of the Law Commission, extends the principle to the identification, or description, of any person, object, or place.

### (d) Statements made when the matters were fresh in the memory

Section 120(6) operates to abolish the common-law fiction that when a witness does not remember certain matters, or does not remember them well enough to give evidence about them, and therefore 'refreshes his memory' by reference to a statement made by him when the matters stated were fresh in his memory, it is the oral testimony of the witness which constitutes the evidence in the case. Many commentators over many years have submitted that it would be more principled to regard the statement as a variety of admissible hearsay. This is achieved by section 120(6), which applies to previous statements whether made orally or in a document, provided that the witness gives the indications required by section 120(4).

### (e) Statements consisting of a complaint about the alleged offence

Section 120(7) is based on the exception to the rule against previous consistent statements in the case of recent complaints in sexual cases.[169] As stated in the fifth edition of this book,[170] what is curious is not that this exception has survived, but that for no good reason it has been confined to sexual cases. Section 120(7), in accordance with the recommendations of the Law Commission[171] and, long before that, the Criminal Law Revision Committee,[172] extends the principle to a previous statement, whether oral or written, made by a person against whom *any* offence has been committed, provided that it is an offence to which the proceedings relate, and that the statement consists of a complaint about conduct which would, if proved, constitute the offence or part of the offence to which the proceedings relate.

---

[169] See Ch 6.    [170] At 153.    [171] Paras 10.53–10.61, Law Com No 245 (1997).
[172] Para 232, 11th report, Cm 4991 *Evidence (General)* (1972).

There are a number of other conditions to be met, in addition to the requirement that the witness give the indications required by section 120(4). Section 120(7)(d) requires that the complaint was made as soon as could reasonably be expected after the alleged conduct. This requirement reflects the requirement at common law that a recent complaint in a sexual case is only admissible by way of exception to the rule against previous consistent statements 'when it is made at the first opportunity after the offence which reasonably offers itself'.[173] The common-law authorities are likely to offer valuable guidance to the way in which section 120(7)(d) is applied. It has been held, for example, that whether a complaint was made as soon as was reasonably practicable after the occurrence of the offence is a question of fact and degree to be decided by the judge in each case and that the answer will depend on the circumstances, including the character of the complainant and the relationship between the complainant and the person to whom she might have complained but did not do so. Victims often need time before they can bring themselves to tell what has happened, and whereas some will find it impossible to complain to anyone other than a parent or member of their family, others may feel it impossible to tell their parents or members of their family.[174] It has also been held that the fact that the complaint was not the first to be made is not, per se, sufficient to exclude it.[175] Section 120(7) contains no requirement of 'recency' as such, and it is submitted that the test in section 120(7)(d) is therefore broader than the common-law test and, depending on all the circumstances, allows for the admissibility of complaints made weeks or even months after the offence.[176]

Section 120(7)(e) requires that the complaint was not made as a result of a threat or promise, and under section 120(8), which does not follow the approach taken in the common-law authorities relating to a recent complaint in a sexual case, the fact that the complaint was elicited, for example, by a leading question, is irrelevant unless a threat or promise was made. Thus it is not only irrelevant to admissibility if the complaint was made in answer to a non-leading question such as 'What is the matter?', but also if it was made in answer to a leading question such as 'Did X (naming the accused) assault you?' Although a complaint elicited by way of a leading question is bound to affect the weight to be attached to it, so far as admissibility is concerned, the issue is whether it was made voluntarily in the sense that it was not obtained by a threat or promise.

Finally, section 120(7)(f) requires that before the statement is introduced in evidence, the witness 'gives oral evidence in connection with its subject matter', words which suggest that this requirement will be met provided only that the complainant gives some evidence in relation to the conduct referred to in her complaint, even if the evidence does not replicate the complaint or is not wholly consistent with it.

---

[173] Per Ridley J [1905] 1 KB 551 at 561. See also *R v Cummings* [1948] 1 All ER 551, CCA.
[174] *R v Valentine* [1996] 2 Cr App R 213, CA.          [175] *R v Wilbourne* (1917) 12 Cr App R 280.
[176] See per Rix LJ in *R v Birks* [2003] 2 Cr App R 122 at [27]–[29], referring to wording identical to s 120(7)(d) in the Criminal Justice Bill.

## 8  MULTIPLE HEARSAY

If a witness, X, wishes to introduce a statement made by Y, as evidence of what Y stated, X having no personal knowledge of the matters stated, his evidence may be classified as second-hand or multiple hearsay. The phrase multiple hearsay is even more apposite when the chain is longer, as when X testifies as to what Y told him Z had said. Business and other written records which have passed through many hands may be no less reliable than first-hand hearsay, but there are obvious risks of unreliability in the case of multiple hearsay, especially multiple oral hearsay: in addition to the fact that the maker of the original statement is unavailable for cross-examination, and the usual risk of manufactured or fabricated evidence, there is obvious scope for error or distortion in the transmission or repeated transmission of information.[177]

Section 121 of the 2003 Act provides as follows.

(1) A hearsay statement is not admissible to prove the fact that an earlier hearsay statement was made unless—

   (a) either of the statements is admissible under section 117, 119 or 120,

   (b) all parties to the proceedings so agree, or

   (c) the court is satisfied that the value of the evidence in question, taking into account how reliable the statements appear to be, is so high that the interests of justice require the later statement to be admissible for that purpose.

(2) In this section 'hearsay statement' means a statement, not made in oral evidence, that is relied on as evidence of a matter stated in it.

Section 121(1)(b) is self-explanatory. In contrast, the meaning of section 121(1)(a) is far from transparent and it is, therefore, of uncertain scope. One would have thought that proving 'the fact that an earlier hearsay statement was made' is only a useful exercise if the earlier statement is admissible as evidence of any matter stated but for the fact that the making of it cannot be proved. If the earlier statement is admissible under one of the heads of admissibility set out in section 114 of the Act and the making of the statement can be proved without resort to hearsay, then it would be unnecessary to rely on section 121(1)(a). The principal purpose of the provision, therefore, appears to be to permit a party to prove the fact that the earlier statement was made by a hearsay statement, provided that the hearsay statement is admissible under one of sections 117, 119, or 120. Let us suppose that D is charged with assaulting E; that H, a witness to the assault, made an out-of-court statement to his wife, W, that D assaulted E; that H is now dead, and therefore the statement is admissible under section 116. Let us now consider three additional but alternative developments.

(1) By the time of the trial, W is also dead, and therefore cannot prove what H said. However, before her death, she made a written statement to the police recording the fact that H had told her that D had assaulted E. H's statement is now

---

[177] See paras 8.16 et seq, Law Com No 245.

admissible under section 116, as evidence of the matters he stated, because in this situation W's statement is admissible under section 117 to prove the fact that H's hearsay statement was made.

(2) W told X that H had told her that D had assaulted E. W is called by the prosecution to prove what H said. In giving her evidence, she shows no desire to tell the truth, is treated as a hostile witness and flatly denies that H made any statement to her that D had assaulted E. W's statement to X is then proved, by calling X to give evidence of it, by virtue of section 3 of the Criminal Procedure Act 1865. H's statement is again admissible under section 116, as evidence of the matters he stated, in this situation because evidence of W's previous inconsistent statement is admissible under section 119(1)(b) of the 2003 Act to prove the fact that H's hearsay statement was made.

(3) Very shortly after H made his statement to W, and while the fact that he had made the statement was fresh in W's memory, she wrote a letter to Y in which she recorded that H had told her that D had assaulted E. W is called by the prosecution to prove what H said but does not remember the fact that H made the statement which he did, and in all the circumstances, including the state of her memory and the time that has elapsed, she cannot reasonably be expected to remember the matter well enough to give oral evidence of it. However, when she is shown a copy of her letter to Y, she indicates that to the best of her belief she made the statement in the letter and to the best of her belief it states the truth. H's statement is again admissible under section 116, as evidence of the matters he stated, in this situation because evidence of W's previous statement is admissible under section 120(4) and (6) to prove the fact that H's hearsay statement was made.

Section 121(1)(c) permits the court to admit a hearsay statement to prove that another hearsay statement was made, even if the later statement is not otherwise admissible hearsay and the parties to the proceedings do not agree to its admission. The test is whether the court is satisfied that the value of the evidence in question, taking into account how reliable the statements appear to be, is so high that the interests of justice require the later statement to be admissible for the purpose of proving that the earlier statement was made. It is not made clear whether 'the value of the evidence in question' means, as is likely, the value of the evidence in the earlier statement, as opposed to the value of the evidence in the later statement or both the earlier and the later statement. In any event, section 121(1)(c) is plainly designed to be a stringent test and should not be invoked where, having regard to Article 6 of the European Convention on Human Rights, it would result in an unfair trial.

## 9  OTHER SAFEGUARDS

### (a)  Capability

Under section 123(1) of the 2003 Act, a hearsay statement cannot be admitted under section 116 (cases where a witness is unavailable), section 119 (inconsistent statements) or section 120 (other previous statements of witnesses) if its maker did not have the 'required capability' at the time when he made the statement. 'Required capability', for these purposes, means the capability of understanding questions put to him about the matters stated and giving answers to such questions which can be understood, a test reflecting the test for competence in criminal cases set out in section 53 of the Youth Justice and Criminal Evidence Act 1999. Under section 123(2) of the 2003 Act, a hearsay statement cannot be admitted under section 117 (business and other documents) if any person who supplied or received the information, or created or received the document, did not have the 'required capability' at the time of supply or receipt etc or, if any such person cannot be identified, 'cannot reasonably be assumed to have had the required capability at that time'. The procedure to be followed in the event of a dispute as to whether any person had the 'required capability' is governed by section 123(4). Section 123 provides as follows.

(1)  Nothing in section 116, 119 or 120 makes a statement admissible as evidence if it was made by a person who did not have the required capability at the time when he made the statement.

(2)  Nothing in section 117 makes a statement admissible as evidence if any person who, in order for the requirements of section 117(2) to be satisfied, must at any time have supplied or received the information concerned or created or received the document or part concerned—
    (a)  did not have the required capability at that time, or
    (b)  cannot be identified but cannot reasonably be assumed to have had the required capability at that time.

(3)  For the purposes of this section a person has the required capability if he is capable of—
    (a)  understanding questions put to him about the matters stated, and
    (b)  giving answers to such questions which can be understood.

(4)  Where by reason of this section there is an issue as to whether a person had the required capability when he made a statement—
    (a)  proceedings held for the determination of the issue must take place in the absence of the jury (if there is one);
    (b)  in determining the issue the court may receive expert evidence and evidence from any person to whom the statement in question was made;
    (c)  the burden of proof on the issue lies on the party seeking to adduce the statement, and the standard of proof is the balance of probabilities.

### (b)  Credibility

The general purpose of section 124 of the 2003 Act is to enable the parties to attack or support the credibility of the maker of a hearsay statement who is not called as a witness as if he had been so called. In the case of a statement in a document admitted under section 117 (business and other documents), the person who supplied or received the information contained in the statement, or who created or received the document, if not called as a witness, is also to be treated as 'the maker of the statement' for the purposes of the section. Section 124 provides as follows.

(1) This section applies if in criminal proceedings—
    (a) a statement not made in oral evidence in the proceedings is admitted as evidence of a matter stated, and
    (b) the maker of the statement does not give oral evidence in connection with the subject matter of the statement.

(2) In such a case—
    (a) any evidence which (if he had given such evidence) would have been admissible as relevant to his credibility as a witness is so admissible in the proceedings;
    (b) evidence may with the court's leave be given of any matter which (if he had given such evidence) could have been put to him in cross-examination as relevant to his credibility as a witness but of which evidence could not have been adduced by the cross-examining party;
    (c) evidence tending to prove that he made (at whatever time) any other statement inconsistent with the statement admitted as evidence is admissible for the purpose of showing that he contradicted himself.

(3) If as a result of evidence admitted under this section an allegation is made against the maker of a statement, the court may permit a party to lead additional evidence of such description as the court may specify for the purposes of denying or answering the allegation.

(4) In the case of a statement in a document which is admitted as evidence under section 117 each person who, in order for the statement to be admissible, must have supplied or received the information concerned or created or received the document or part concerned is to be treated as the maker of the statement for the purposes of subsections (1) to (3) above.

Section 124(2)(a), (b), and (c) are largely concerned with situations which, if the maker had been called as a witness, would have been governed by the rule of finality of answers on collateral issues, by the exceptions to that rule,[178] or by section 100 of the 2003 Act (non-defendant's bad character).[179] Under the rule of finality, the answers given by a witness under cross-examination to questions concerning collateral matters, including questions which go merely to the credit of the witness, must be treated as final in the sense that the cross-examining party is not permitted to call further evidence with a view to contradicting the witness. Sub-paragraph (a) allows evidence attacking the credibility of the maker to be given where such evidence, had he been called as a witness, would have been admissible either under an *exception* to the rule of finality or, with the leave of the court, under section 100 of the 2003 Act. Accordingly, for example, evidence admissible under sub-paragraph (a) may include

---

[178] See Ch 7.        [179] See Ch 17.

evidence that the maker is unfit to be believed because of some physical or mental disability,[180] one of the exceptions to the rule against finality, or, with the leave of the court under section 100 of the 2003 Act, evidence that he has been convicted of an offence.[181] The sub-paragraph may also be used to admit evidence to support the credibility of the maker. At common law a witness's previous consistent statement is exceptionally admissible in order to rebut a suggestion that his evidence has been fabricated.[182] Thus if the party against whom the hearsay statement is admitted suggests that it was fabricated by the maker, evidence to show that before making the statement in question he made a statement, whether written or oral, consistent with it, would be admissible to support his credibility under sub-paragraph (a).

Sub-paragraph (b) applies to situations which, if the maker had been called as a witness, would have been governed by the *rule* of finality of answers on collateral issues, that is situations in which, if the maker had been cross-examined about a matter in order to attack his credibility as a witness but had denied the matter put, evidence in rebuttal would *not* have been admissible. Under sub-paragraph (b), evidence of the matter which could have been put to the maker in cross-examination, had he been called as a witness, for example the fact that whereas he is giving his evidence through an interpreter he is able to speak English,[183] may be adduced with the leave of the court. The reasoning underlying this provision, and the statutory precursors to it on which it is closely modelled, is that since, if the maker of the statement had given evidence, he might have admitted the matter put, or his denial might not have been believed, the party against whom the hearsay statement is given in evidence might be put at an unfair disadvantage because unable to cross-examine the maker of the statement. In deciding whether to grant leave, it would seem that the judge should balance the risk of such unfairness against the fact that to allow evidence to the discredit of the absent maker to be given without restriction, might be unfair to him and might lead to an undue prolongation of the trial.[184]

Sub-paragraph (c) allows evidence tending to prove that the maker of the hearsay statement made another statement inconsistent with it to be admitted for the purpose of showing that he contradicted himself. The inconsistent statement may have been made orally or in writing and either before or after the hearsay statement. Under section 119(2) of the Act, if evidence of an inconsistent statement by any person is given under section 124(2)(c), the statement is admissible as evidence of any matter stated in it of which oral evidence by that person would be admissible.

Under section 124(3), where as a result of evidence admitted under section 124(2), an allegation is made against the maker of the statement, the court may permit additional specified evidence to be adduced in rebuttal.

---

[180]  *Toohey v Metropolitan Police Comr* [1965] AC 595, HL.
[181]  See also s 6 of the Criminal Procedure Act 1865, Ch 7.     [182]  See Ch 6.
[183]  See *R v Burke* (1858) 8 Cox CC 44, Ch 7.
[184]  See generally 11th Report, Criminal Law Revision Committee (Cmnd 4991), para 263.

## (c) Stopping the case where the evidence is unconvincing

In *R v Galbraith*[185] it was held that a submission of no case to answer should fail where the Crown's case is such that its strength or weakness depends on the view to be taken of a witness's reliability, or other matters which are, generally speaking, within the jury's province, and where on one view of the facts there is evidence on which a jury could properly conclude that the accused is guilty. The Law Commission was of the view that a derogation from *R v Galbraith* could be justified in the case of hearsay evidence on the same basis as in identification cases. In identification cases, 'the case is withdrawn from the jury not because the judge considers that the witness is lying, but because the evidence even if taken to be honest has a base which is so slender that it is unreliable and therefore not sufficient to found a conviction'.[186] Similarly, in the case of hearsay, 'even though the (absent) declarant may be honest, his or her evidence, being hearsay, may be so poor that a conviction would be unsafe'.[187] Section 125 of the Criminal Justice Act 2003, based on clause 14 of the Law Commission's draft bill, provides as follows.

(1) If on a defendant's trial before a judge and jury for an offence the court is satisfied at any time after the close of the case for the prosecution that—
 (a) the case against the defendant is based wholly or partly on a statement not made in oral evidence in the proceedings, and
 (b) the evidence provided by the statement is so unconvincing that, considering its importance to the case against the defendant, his conviction of the offence would be unsafe,
 the court must either direct the jury to acquit the defendant of the offence or, if it considers that there ought to be a retrial, discharge the jury.

(2) Where—
 (a) a jury is directed under subsection (1) to acquit a defendant of an offence, and
 (b) the circumstances are such that, apart from this subsection, the defendant could if acquitted of that offence be found guilty of another offence,
 the defendant may not be found guilty of that other offence if the court is satisfied as mentioned in subsection (1) in respect of it.

The same duty to direct an acquittal or discharge the jury also applies in cases in which a jury is required to determine under the Criminal Procedure (Insanity) Act 1964 whether the accused did the act or made the omission charged.[188] Section 125 is without prejudice to any other power a court may have to direct an acquittal or discharge a jury.[189]

---

[185] [1981] 1 WLR 1039, CA (see Ch 2).
[186] See per Lord Mustill in *Daley v R* [1994] 1 AC 117, PC at 129 (see Ch 8).
[187] Law Com No 245 (1997), Cm 3670.　　　[188] Section 125(3).　　　[189] Section 125(4).

## (d) Discretion to exclude

Section 126 of the Act provides as follows.

(1) In criminal proceedings the court may refuse to admit a statement as evidence of a matter stated if—

    (a) the statement was made otherwise than in oral evidence in the proceedings, and

    (b) the court is satisfied that the case for excluding the statement, taking account of the danger that to admit it would result in undue waste of time, substantially outweighs the case for admitting it, taking account of the value of the evidence.

(2) Nothing in this Chapter prejudices—

    (a) any power of a court to exclude evidence under section 78 of the Police and Criminal Evidence Act 1984 (exclusion of unfair evidence), or

    (b) any other power of a court to exclude evidence at its discretion (whether from preventing questions from being put or otherwise).

As we have seen, there is a discretion to admit hearsay under section 114(1)(d) if it is 'in the interests of justice'. The same phrase is used in two other provisions: under section 116(4), leave may be given to admit the hearsay statement of someone who does not give oral evidence through fear only if the court considers that the statement ought to be admitted in the interests of justice; and under section 121(1)(c), which relates to multiple hearsay, a hearsay statement is not admissible to prove the fact that an earlier hearsay statement was made unless the interests of justice require it to be admissible for that purpose. Although strictly speaking, where a court has admitted a hearsay statement under section 114(1)(d), section 116(4), or section 121(1)(c), it may proceed to consider use of one of its three discretionary powers of exclusion, this is likely to be a pointless exercise given that it is of the opinion that it is in the interests of justice to admit the evidence. Furthermore, in the case of section 114(1)(d) and section 116(4), the court, in considering whether it is in the interests of justice, shall have regard, in addition to the matters listed in section 114(2)(a)—(i) and section 116(4)(a)—(c), to any other relevant factors or circumstances, which could, of course, include any of the factors or circumstances relevant to the exercise of any of the discretionary powers to exclude.

Section 126(1) creates a new discretionary power to exclude otherwise admissible hearsay, whether tendered by the prosecution or defence. Under the balancing exercise described in section 126(1)(b), regard must be had, on the one hand, to the case for exclusion, taking account not of the danger of waste of time—the risk of *some* waste of time is plainly acceptable—but of the danger of *undue* waste of time. This has to be weighed against the case for admission of the evidence, taking account of its 'value', a word which appears to embrace not only its probative value, or its value in understanding other evidence in the case, but also its value in the sense of its reliability or weight. It is only if the court is satisfied that the case for exclusion *substantially* outweighs the case for admission, that the discretion should be exercised. This is likely to occur, for example, where the hearsay statement is of minimal probative value and wholly or to a very large extent superfluous, because other evidence has been or will be given on the matters stated.

Section 126(2) preserves the two pre-existing powers of the court to exclude otherwise admissible hearsay. The first is the power in section 78 of the Police and Criminal Evidence Act 1984 under which evidence on which the prosecution proposes to rely may be excluded where in all the circumstances, including those in which the evidence was obtained, it would have such an adverse effect on the fairness of the proceedings that the court ought not to admit it. The second is the common-law power to exclude prosecution evidence on the basis that its prejudicial effect outweighs its probative value.

In this context, as elsewhere, section 78 of the 1984 Act is likely to be invoked more often than the common-law discretion, because of its wider ambit. Where section 78 is invoked, it is submitted that the relevant factors to be taken into account, in addition to the circumstances in which the evidence was obtained, will be largely the same as the factors to which the court should have regard in deciding, under section 116 of the 2003 Act, whether to grant leave to admit the hearsay statement of a person who does not give oral evidence through fear. These include (i) the contents of the statement, their importance to the issues in the case and their quality (ii) how difficult it will be to challenge the statement in the absence of its maker (iii) the extent to which the risk of unfairness can be counter-balanced by a warning to the jury about the absence of opportunity to judge the reliability of the maker of the statement in examination-in-chief and cross-examination (iv) whether the evidence can be controverted by cross-examination of other prosecution witnesses or by the accused's own testimony (v) whether the prosecution have other available evidence (vi) facts or matters affecting the credibility of the maker of the statement and (vii) whether the credibility of the maker of the statement can be challenged.

As we have seen when considering the requirement of leave under section 116, where a conviction is based solely or to a decisive degree on depositions that have been made by a person whom the accused has had no opportunity to examine or have examined, whether during the investigation or at the trial, then according to the jurisprudence of the European Court of Human Rights the rights of the defence are restricted to an extent that is incompatible with the guarantees provided by Article 6. In the context of cases in which the maker of the statement does not give oral evidence through fear, as a result of threats instigated or approved by the accused, the Court of Appeal in *R v M(KJ)*[190] held that this was not a rule without exceptions. However, it is submitted that in the case of other types of otherwise admissible hearsay, the 'rule' is likely to provide a very powerful and normally unanswerable argument for exclusion under section 78.

---

[190] [2003] 2 Cr App R 322, CA.

## (e) Rules of court

Under section 132 of the Act, rules of court may be made providing for the procedural conditions to be followed by a party proposing to tender a hearsay statement in evidence. The rules may require such a party to serve on the other party or parties notice and particulars of the evidence[191] and may provide that the evidence is admissible if a notice has been served but there has been no service of a counter-notice objecting to the admission of the evidence.[192] The rules applicable in magistrates' courts and crown courts are set out in rule 34 of the Criminal Procedure Rules 2005.[193] If a party proposing to tender evidence fails to comply with a prescribed requirement, the evidence is not admissible except with the court's leave, and where leave is given the court or jury may draw such inferences from the failure as appear proper.[194] However, a person is not to be convicted of an offence solely on the basis of such an inference.[195]

## 10  QUESTIONS OF PROOF

### (a)  Proof of conditions of admissibility

It is submitted that many of the principles established in the cases concerning proof of the conditions of admissibility contained in sections 23 and 24 of the Criminal Justice Act 1988 (and other repealed statutory precursors to the hearsay provisions of the 2003 Act) remain valid. Thus where it is sought to admit a hearsay statement under section 116 (or to comply with the requirement of section 117(5)(a)), because the maker of the statement is unable to give oral evidence for one of the reasons set out in section 116(2), the court should make a finding of fact, based on admissible evidence, that such a reason exists.[196] If necessary, the matter should be decided on a *voir dire*,[197] at which the party against whom the evidence is tendered is entitled to cross-examine witnesses relied on to establish the necessary facts.[198] The *voir dire* is of particular importance in cases covered by section 116(2)(e), ie where the maker of the statement does not give oral evidence through fear: it is highly desirable that any investigation of his reasons should be conducted in the absence of the jury and that some innocuous form of words should be used to explain his absence to the jury[199] and prevent the jury from speculating that the accused may be responsible for the absence.[200] As to the standard of proof, the prosecution must satisfy the court beyond

---

[191] Section 132(3).      [192] Section 132(4).
[193] SI 2005/384.      [194] Section 132(5).      [195] Section 132(7).
[196] See *R v Wood and Fitzsimmons* [1998] Crim LR 213, CA; and *R v Feest* [1987] Crim LR 766, CA, a decision on s 68(2)(a)(iii) of the 1984 Act.
[197] See *R v Minors; R v Harper* [1989] 2 All ER 208, CA.
[198] See *R v Wood and Fitzsimmons* [1998] Crim LR 213, CA.
[199] See *R v Jennings* [1995] Crim LR 810, CA.
[200] See *R v Wood and Fitzsimmons* [1998] Crim LR 213. If the jury ask why the maker has not been called to give evidence, the judge should simply say that he cannot answer the question: *R v Churchill* [1993] Crim LR 285, CA.

reasonable doubt,[201] the defence on a balance of probabilities.[202] Evidence to establish one of the reasons may take the form of either direct testimony or admissible hearsay (including a statement itself admissible under the statutory provisions)[203] but cannot be furnished by the contents of the very statement sought to be introduced, because prima facie they are inadmissible hearsay.[204] In order to establish that the maker of a statement does not give oral evidence through fear, reliance may be placed on his sworn evidence,[205] his demeanour[206] (which may be particularly important if he does not state his fear explicitly),[207] and medical evidence.[208] Alternatively, use may be made of his out-of-court written statement of fear,[209] whether or not contained in the very statement sought to be admitted, on the basis that it constitutes original evidence admissible to prove state of mind[210] or, if it is treated as hearsay, is admissible under the *res gestae* principle which covers statements concerning the maker's contemporaneous state of mind.[211] This principle is among the common-law categories of admissibility preserved by section 118 of the 2003 Act.

According to *R v Foxley*[212] evidence of the requirements contained in section 24(1) of the Criminal Justice Act 1988, which were broadly similar to the requirements set out in section 117(2)(a) and (b) of the 2003 Act, was often desirable, but not always essential. The documents in that case were copies of credit notes and invoices purporting to emanate from three foreign companies. Evidence was given by a police officer that the originals had been seized from the companies by the appropriate authority in each country and copies had then been made and sent by each such authority to the CPS, but there was no evidence to prove that the document was created or received by a person in the course of a trade etc or that the information contained in the document was supplied by a person who had, or may reasonably be supposed to have had, personal knowledge of the matters dealt with. It was held that the trial judge was entitled to infer these matters from the documents themselves and from the method or route by which they had been produced before the court. The purpose of section 24

---

[201] See *R v Acton Justices, ex p McMullen, R v Tower Bridge Magistrates' Court, ex p Lawlor* (1990) 92 Cr App R 98 at 104. See also *Bermudez v Chief Constable of Avon and Somerset* [1988] Crim LR 452, DC, a decision on s 68 of the 1984 Act, in which it was held that if there is no dispute that the conditions of admissibility have been satisfied, a formal admission of that fact should be made.

[202] See *R v Mattey, R v Queeley* [1995] 2 Cr App R 409, CA.

[203] See *R v Castillo* [1996] 1 Cr App R 438, CA.

[204] See *R v Case* [1991] Crim LR 192, CA and *R v Mattey, R v Queeley* [1995] 2 Cr App R 409, CA.

[205] Although in *R v Greer* [1998] Crim LR 572, CA reliance was placed on unsworn evidence, technically he should be sworn: see *R v Jennings* [1995] Crim LR 572, CA.

[206] See *R v Waters* (1997) 161 JP 249, CA.

[207] See *R v Ashford Magistrates' Court, ex p Hilden* [1993] 2 All ER 154, DC.

[208] See *R v Waters* (1997) 161 JP 249, CA.        [209] See *R v Rutherford* [1998] Crim LR 490, CA.

[210] See *R v Fairfax* [1995] Crim LR 949, CA, relying on *R v Blastland* [1985] 2 All ER 1095, HL.

[211] See *R v Fairfax* [1995] Crim LR 949 (citing *Neill v North Antrim Magistrates' Court* [1992] 4 All ER 846, HL: see per Lord Mustill, obiter at 854) and *R v Wood and Fitzsimmons* [1998] Crim LR 213, CA. But see also *R v Belmarsh Magistrates' Court, ex p Gilligan* [1998] 1 Cr App R 14, DC, in which neither possible means of admissibility was even mentioned, and Astill J pointed out that in *R v Fairfax* there had been a great deal of oral evidence of fear.

[212] [1995] 2 Cr App R 523, CA.

was to enable the document to speak for itself, a purpose that would be defeated if oral evidence were to be required in every case from the creator or keeper of the document or the supplier of the information it contained.[213]

## (b)  Proof of a statement contained in a document

Section 133 of the 2003 Act provides that:

Where a statement in a document is admissible as evidence in criminal proceedings, the statement may be proved by producing either—
  (a)  the document, or
  (b)  (whether or not the document exists) a copy of the document or of the material part of it,
authenticated in whatever way the court may approve.

The word 'document' means anything in which information of any description is recorded,[214] a definition wide enough to include, for example, audio-tapes, films, and video-tapes. 'Copy', in relation to a document, means anything on to which information recorded in the document has been copied, by whatever means, and whether directly or indirectly,[215] a definition which would cover, among other things, a transcript of an audio-tape as well as reproductions or still reproductions of the images embodied in films and video-tapes, whether enlarged or not. 'Producing' would seem to refer not to counsel handing the document to the court, but to a witness who is qualified to do so in accordance with the rules of evidence producing the document and saying what it is.[216] The reference to authentication appears to relate to the authentication of a copy of a document as a true copy of the original, and not to proof of the original.[217] Section 133 is considered further under A 'Documentary evidence' in Chapter 9.

## 11  EVIDENCE BY VIDEO RECORDING

In the case of offences triable only on indictment and prescribed offences triable either way, where a person, other than the accused, is called as a witness, having witnessed the events constituting the offence or part of it, or events closely connected with it, and having previously given a video-recorded account of those events at a time when they were fresh in his memory, section 137 of the Act permits the court to direct that the recording be admitted as his evidence-in-chief. Section 137 is considered in Chapter 5.

---

[213] See also, applying *R v Foxley, R v Ilyas and Knight* [1996] Crim LR 810, CA.
[214] Section 134(1).      [215] Section 134(1).
[216] As under the Civil Evidence Act 1968, s 6(1) (see now the Civil Evidence Act 1995, s 8): per Staughton LJ in *Ventouris v Mountain (No 2)* [1992] 3 All ER 414, CA (see Ch 11).
[217] Cf *Ventouris v Mountain (No 2)* [1992] 3 All ER 414 (see Ch 11).

## 12  EXPERT EVIDENCE: PREPARATORY WORK

In many cases, a witness giving expert opinion evidence will have no personal or first-hand knowledge of the facts, or all of the facts, upon which his opinion is based. For example, a surgeon may express his expert opinion as to whether the wounds of a deceased person were self-inflicted, basing his opinion on someone else's description of the wounds. Similarly, an expert may give his expert opinion on the basis of preparatory work, such as scientific tests, carried out by assistants. The facts upon which the expert opinion is based, sometimes referred to as 'primary facts', must be proved by the person with personal or first-hand knowledge of them.[218] Section 127 of the 2003 Act permits such facts to be proved by the hearsay statement of such a person, unless, on an application by a party to the proceedings, that is not in the interests of justice. Section 127 provides as follows.

(1)  This section applies if—
   (a)  a statement has been prepared for the purposes of criminal proceedings,
   (b)  the person who prepared the statement had or may reasonably be supposed to have had personal knowledge of the matters stated,
   (c)  notice is given under the appropriate rules that another person (the expert) will in evidence given in the proceedings orally or under s 9 of the Criminal Justice Act 1967[219] base an opinion or inference on the statement, and
   (d)  the notice gives the name of the peron who prepared the statement and the nature of the matters stated.

(2)  In evidence given in the proceedings the expert may base an opinion or inference on the statement.

(3)  If evidence based on the statement is given under subsection (2) the statement is to be treated as evidence of what it says.

(4)  This section does not apply if the court, on an application by a party to the proceedings, orders that it is not in the interests of justice that it should apply.

(5)  The matters to be considered by the court in deciding whether to make an order under subsection (4) include—
   (a)  the expense of calling as a witness the person who prepared the statement;
   (b)  whether relevant evidence could be given by that person which could not be given by the expert;
   (c)  whether that person can reasonably be expected to remember the matters stated well enough to give oral evidence of them.

(6)  Subsections (1) to (5) apply to a statement prepared for the purposes of a criminal investigation as they apply to a statement prepared for the purposes of criminal proceedings, and in such a case references to the proceedings are to criminal proceedings arising from the investigation.

Under subsection (4), it appears that the court may only disapply the section on the application of a party and not of its own motion. Subsection (5) provides a short non-

---

[218] See Ch 18 under A Expert opinion evidence.
[219] See below, under D Written statements under section 9 of the Criminal Justice Act 1967.

exhaustive list of the factors to be considered by the court in deciding whether to disapply the section. Absent from the list are, it is submitted, the most important factors: the extent to which the matters stated are in dispute—if they are not in dispute, then there should be no application under subsection (4)—and the risk, having regard to how difficult it will be to challenge the statement if its maker is not called as a witness, that its admission or exclusion will result in unfairness.

Nothing in section 127 affects the common-law rule under which an expert witness may draw on the body of expertise relevant to his field.[220] That rule is among the common-law categories of admissibility preserved by section 118 of the Act.

## C  EXPERT REPORTS

Section 30(1) of the Criminal Justice Act 1988 provides that an expert report, that is a written report by a person dealing wholly or mainly with matters on which he is (or would if living be) qualified to give expert evidence,[221] shall be admissible as evidence in criminal proceedings whether or not the person making it attends to give oral evidence in those proceedings. The report, when admitted, shall be evidence of any fact or opinion of which the person making it could have given oral evidence.[222] However, if it is proposed that the person making the report shall not give oral evidence, the report shall only be admissible with the leave of the court.[223] In deciding whether to give leave, the court shall have regard to (i) the contents of the report (ii) the reasons why it is proposed that the person making the report shall not give oral evidence (iii) any risk, having regard in particular to whether it is likely to be possible to controvert statements in the report if the person making it does not attend to give oral evidence, that its admission or exclusion will result in unfairness to the accused or, if there is more than one, to any of them and (iv) any other circumstances that appear to the court to be relevant.[224]

If any party to a criminal trial proposes, pursuant to section 30(1), to put an expert report in evidence at the trial, then whether or not the person making the report attends to give oral evidence in the proceedings, that party, in accordance with rule 24 of the Criminal Procedure Rules 2005,[225] shall as soon as practicable furnish the other party or parties with a statement in writing of any finding or opinion which he proposes to adduce by way of such evidence. Rule 24, the exceptions to it, and certain related rules are set out and considered in Chapter 18, which concerns opinion evidence generally.[226]

---

[220] See *R v Abadom* [1983] 1 All ER 364, CA, Ch 18.     [221] Section 30(5).
[222] Section 30(4).     [223] Section 30(2).
[224] Section 30(3).     [225] SI 2005/384.     [226] See under A 4.

# D WRITTEN STATEMENTS UNDER SECTION 9 OF THE CRIMINAL JUSTICE ACT 1967

Under section 9 of the 1967 Act, in summary trials and trials on indictment, a written statement (with or without exhibits) by any person shall be admissible as evidence 'to the like extent as oral evidence to the like effect by that person'. The principal conditions of admissibility are that (i) the statement is signed by its maker, (ii) it contains a declaration that it is true, (iii) before the hearing a copy of it is served by the party proposing to tender it on each of the other parties, and (iv) none of the other parties or their solicitors, within seven days from the service of the copy, serves a notice objecting to the statement being tendered in evidence.[227] The last two conditions do not apply if the parties agree before or during the hearing that the statement shall be so tendered.[228] Under section 9(4), notwithstanding that a statement may be admissible by virtue of section 9, the party who served a copy of it may call its maker to give evidence and the court may, either of its own motion or on the application of any party to the proceedings, require its maker to attend court and give oral evidence. An application under section 9(4) would be appropriate, for example, where a party disputes the evidence contained in the statement but failed to serve a notice of objection in accordance with the section. Such an application may be made before the hearing.[229] Where a section 9 statement is admitted in evidence, it should normally be read out aloud.[230]

Where the prosecution tenders written statements under section 9, it is frequently not only proper, but also necessary for the orderly presentation of the evidence, for the statements to be edited. This may be either because a witness has made more than one statement whose contents should conveniently be reduced into a single comprehensive statement or because a statement contains inadmissible, prejudicial or irrelevant material. Such editing should be carried out by a Crown Prosecutor, and not by a police officer, in accordance with paragraph 24 of the *Practice Direction (Criminal Proceedings: Consolidation).*[231]

---

[227] There must be strict compliance with the terms of s 9: see *Paterson v DPP* [1990] Crim LR 651, DC.
[228] Section 9(2).       [229] Section 9(5).       [230] Section 9(6).
[231] [2002] 1 WLR 2870. The principles set out do not apply to documents which are exhibited (including statements under caution and signed contemporaneous notes). Nor, as a general rule, do they apply to oral statements of an accused which are recorded in the witness statements of interviewing police officers. Such material should remain in its original state and any editing left to prosecuting counsel at the Crown Court: see para 24.6.

# E DEPOSITIONS OF CHILDREN AND YOUNG PERSONS UNDER SECTION 43 OF THE CHILDREN AND YOUNG PERSONS ACT 1933

Under section 42 of the 1933 Act, where a magistrate is satisfied by the evidence of a qualified medical practitioner that the attendance before a court of any child or young person in respect of whom any of certain specified offences is alleged to have been committed would involve serious danger to his life or health, the magistrate may take a deposition from him out of court. The offences specified include offences under the Offences Against the Person Act 1861, the 1933 Act itself, the Protection of Children Act 1978 and the Sexual Offences Act 2003, and any other offences involving bodily injury to a child or young person. Under section 43, a deposition taken under section 42 shall be admissible in evidence in any proceedings either for or against the accused provided, in the latter case, that it is proved that reasonable notice of the intention to take the deposition was served upon the accused and he or his legal representative had an opportunity of cross-examining the deponent.

# 11

# HEARSAY ADMISSIBLE BY STATUTE IN CIVIL PROCEEDINGS

## A THE BACKGROUND

As we have seen in Chapter 10, under the common-law rule against hearsay, any assertion, other than one made by a person while giving oral evidence in the proceedings, was inadmissible if tendered as evidence of the facts asserted. The Civil Evidence Act 1968 constituted a major assault upon the common-law rule in civil proceedings. Although it did not abolish the rule, it made provision for the admissibility of both oral and written hearsay (including statements contained in documents which were or formed part of a record) subject to certain conditions, principally (i) notification of the other parties to the litigation and (ii) either calling the maker of the statement as a witness (in which case the statement could not be given in evidence without the leave of the court) or establishing one of a number of reasons for not calling the maker of the statement as a witness. The 1968 Act also provided for the admissibility of statements contained in computer-produced documents and gave express statutory force to a number of the pre-existing common-law exceptions, including informal admissions and facts contained in public documents.

In June 1988 the Civil Justice Review recommended an inquiry by a law reform agency into the usefulness of the hearsay rule in civil proceedings and the machinery for rendering it admissible. The matter was referred to the Law Commission. The response to its Consultation Paper[1] identified three major reasons for change.

1.  The regime under the 1968 Act was unwieldy and the law outmoded and unnecessarily difficult to understand. In particular, the rules as to notification were too complicated so that in practice compliance was the exception.

2.  The statutory regime lagged behind developments in the law and practice of civil litigation which pointed to a new approach in which (a) the main emphasis is upon ensuring that, so far as possible, and subject to considerations of reliability and weight, all relevant evidence is adduced,[2] and (b)

---

[1] *The Hearsay Rule in Civil Proceedings* (1991) Consultation Paper No 117.
[2] See per Balcombe LJ in *Ventouris v Mountain (No 2)* [1992] 1 WLR 887 at 899, CA.

litigation is conducted in a more open climate, with more emphasis on identifying and refining the issues in advance of the trial.

3. Intelligent witnesses and litigants were confused by, and dissatisfied with, rules which sometimes operated to prevent them from giving evidence of matters which they rightly perceived as relevant and cogent.[3]

Guided by two major principles, that the law should be simplified to the greatest degree consistent with the proper functioning of the law of evidence, and that, as a general rule, all evidence should be admissible unless there is good reason for it to be treated as inadmissible,[4] the Commission recommended abolition of the hearsay rule in civil proceedings subject to safeguards such as a new simplified notice provision and statutory guidelines to assist courts to assess the weight to be attached to hearsay evidence. The main recommendations of the Commission, in summary, were as follows:

1. In civil proceedings the hearsay rule should be abolished.

2. A party calling a person as a witness should not adduce evidence of a previous statement made by that person except with the leave of the court.

3. A party intending to rely on hearsay should be under a duty to give notice of that fact where this is reasonable and appropriate, according to the particular circumstances of the case. Although failure to give notice should not render the evidence inadmissible, it may detract from the weight that will be placed on it or lead to the imposition of costs sanctions.

4. There should be power for a party to call a witness for cross-examination on his hearsay statement.

5. Courts should be given guidelines to assist them in assessing the weight of hearsay evidence.

6. For business and other records there should be no additional safeguards, beyond those applicable to all other hearsay statements, and the procedure for proving such records should be simplified.

All of these recommendations were put into effect by the Civil Evidence Act 1995.

Before considering the detail of the Act, it is important to note that it contains no special conditions of admissibility or other specific safeguards in the case of statements in computer-produced documents. The 1968 Act contained elaborate precautions in this regard, including requirements to prove that the document was produced in the normal course of business and in an uninterrupted course of activity. Requirements of this kind reflected a fundamental mistrust and fear of the potential for error and mechanical failure. However, as the Law Commission observed, since 1968

---

[3] See *The Hearsay Rule in Civil Proceedings*, Law Commission Report No 216 (Cm 2321) (1993), paras 1.4–1.6.

[4] Law Com No 216 (Cm 2321), para 4.2.

technology has developed to an extent where computers and computer-generated documents are relied on in every area of business. It also thought that it was at least questionable whether the requirements of the 1968 Act provided any real safeguard in relation to the reliability of the hardware or software concerned, and noted that in any event they provided no protection against the inaccurate inputting of data. The Commission recognized that, as confidence in the inherent reliability of computers had grown, so had concern over the potential for misuse, through the capacity to hack, corrupt or alter information in a manner which is undetectable, but could see no reason for maintaining a different regime for the admission of computer-generated documents. It considered that the potential for misuse was best dealt with by concentrating upon the weight to be attached to such evidence, rather than by the reformulation of complex and inflexible rules of admissibility.[5]

# B   ADMISSIBILITY OF HEARSAY UNDER THE CIVIL EVIDENCE ACT 1995

## 1   ABOLITION OF THE RULE AGAINST HEARSAY

Section 1 of the 1995 Act provides as follows:

(1) In civil proceedings evidence shall not be excluded on the ground that it is hearsay.

(2) In this Act—

   (a) 'hearsay' means a statement made otherwise than by a person while giving oral evidence[6] in the proceedings which is tendered as evidence of the matters stated; and

   (b) references to hearsay include hearsay of whatever degree.

### (a) 'In civil proceedings'

The phrase 'civil proceedings' is defined by section 11 as 'civil proceedings, before any tribunal, in relation to which the strict rules of evidence apply, whether as a matter of law or by agreement of the parties'. Thus the Act applies to civil proceedings in any of the ordinary courts of law and in both tribunals and arbitrations in which the strict rules of evidence are applied, but not to the wardship jurisdiction of the High Court,[7] the Court of Protection, or Coroners' Courts. The strict rules of evidence do not apply to all civil proceedings in magistrates' courts. For example, the Act does not apply to magistrates when considering whether there is reasonable cause to suspend a private

---

[5] See generally Law Com No 216 (Cm 2321), paras 3.14–3.21 and 4.43.

[6] 'Oral evidence' includes evidence which, by reason of a defect of speech or hearing, a person called as a witness gives in writing or by signs: s 13.

[7] See *Official Solicitor to the Supreme Court v K* [1965] AC 201, HL.

hire vehicle licence under the Local Government (Miscellaneous Provisions) Ac 1976.[8] In *Savings and Investment Bank Ltd v Gasco Investments (Netherlands) BV (No 2)*,[9] a decision under the equivalent provision of the 1968 Act, it was held that an application to commit for contempt founded on the breach of an order made in civil proceedings was itself a civil proceeding, notwithstanding the criminal standard of proof appropriate to such an application[10] and its possible penal consequences.

### (b) 'Shall not be excluded'

Under section 1(1) of the 1995 Act, 'evidence shall not be excluded on the ground that it is hearsay'. The subsection needs to be considered alongside section 14(1) of the Act, which provides that:

Nothing in this Act affects the exclusion of evidence on grounds other than that it is hearsay.

   This applies whether the evidence falls to be excluded in pursuance of any enactment or rule of law, for failure to comply with rules of court or an order of the court, or otherwise.

Thus hearsay cannot be excluded because it is hearsay but will only be admissible if it does not fall to be excluded on some ground other than that it is hearsay. For example, hearsay opinion evidence which is inadmissible under the Civil Evidence Act 1972[11] falls to be excluded in pursuance of an enactment; hearsay which is irrelevant or inadmissible on grounds of public policy or privilege falls to be excluded in pursuance of a rule of law; and the hearsay opinion of an expert may fall to be excluded if a party fails to comply with CPR rule 35.13, ie if he fails to disclose the expert's report.

### (c) 'Hearsay'

The purpose of the statutory definition of hearsay in section 1(2) is to identify the type of evidence which would have formerly been excluded by virtue of the common-law rule against hearsay, ie first-hand, second-hand, or multiple hearsay, and to which the safeguards and supplementary provisions of the Act apply. However, there is likely to continue to be reference to the common-law authorities in cases in which the boundary of the definition is unclear.[12] Section 13 provides that 'statement' means 'any representation of fact or opinion, however made'. Thus the Act covers a statement of opinion, provided that it is admissible under the Civil Evidence Act 1972, as well as a statement of fact, whether the statement was made orally, in writing (whether hand-written, type-written or produced by computer) or by conduct. It may be doubted, however, whether a written statement in an affidavit is covered by the Act.[13]

*(i) Original evidence.* Under section 1(2)(a), hearsay is defined as a statement made otherwise than by a person while giving oral evidence in the proceedings which is

---

[8] *Westminster City Council v Zestfair Ltd* (1989) 88 LGR 288; *Leeds City Council v Hussain* [2002] EWHC 1145 (Admin), *The Times*, 8 July 2002.

[9] [1988] 1 All ER 975, CA.      [10] See Ch 4.      [11] See Ch 18.

[12] Law Com No 216 (Cm 2321), para 4.6.

[13] In *Rover International Ltd v Cannon Film Sales Ltd (No 2)* [1987] 3 All ER 986, Ch D at 991 Harman J doubted whether affidavits were 'documents' for the purposes of the 1968 Act.

'tendered as evidence of the matter stated' and falls to be distinguished from original evidence, ie a statement made otherwise than by a person while giving oral evidence in the proceedings which is tendered for any relevant purpose other than that of establishing any matter stated. The distinction between hearsay and original evidence is important because whereas hearsay is only admissible subject to the conditions and safeguards set out in the 1995 Act, original evidence, if sufficiently relevant, is admissible without more. In some cases, original evidence is introduced simply to show that the statement in question was made, because that is among the facts in issues in the case. Thus in defamation proceedings in which it is in issue whether the allegedly defamatory statement was made, a witness may give evidence of the making of the statement, including its terms. So-called 'operative words' provide a further illustration. The utterance of such words binds the speaker under the substantive law because a reasonable person, on hearing them, would believe that the speaker intended to be bound. Thus if the parties dispute whether a contract was entered into, evidence of the terms of the contractual offer are admissible because under the law of contract the words spoken are of legal effect if a reasonable person in the position of the offeree would have believed that the offeror intended to be bound. Likewise, words of gift accompanying a transfer of property may be admitted as original evidence. In other types of case, original evidence is introduced because the statement in question is relevant to a fact in issue, typically the state of mind of the person who heard or read it, to show what he knew, thought or believed. Thus P may tender evidence of a certain alleged misrepresentation made to him by Q for the purpose of showing that he was thereby misled. If X brings an action against Y for malicious prosecution, then Y, in order to show the reasonableness of his conduct in the prosecution of X, may tender evidence of a statement made to him by Z that X had committed a criminal offence.[14] Almost all of the reported examples of original evidence have arisen in criminal cases and the topic is considered more fully in Chapter 10.[15]

*(ii) Implied assertions.* An implied assertion is an assertion, whether made orally, in writing or by conduct, from which it is possible to infer a particular matter. For example, in *Wright v Doe d Tatham*,[16] one of the issues being the mental competence of a testator, it was held that the trial judge had properly excluded a number of letters written to the testator by certain of his acquaintances in terms from which it could legitimately be inferred that they regarded him as sane. As evidence of the truth of the implied assertion that the testator was sane, they constituted inadmissible hearsay. As to implied assertions by conduct, Parke B was of the obiter opinion that on the question of the seaworthiness of a vessel, evidence of the conduct of a deceased captain in examining every part of the vessel and then embarking on it with his family would also amount to hearsay. On the other hand, in *Manchester Brewery Co Ltd v*

---

[14] See *Perkins v Vaughan* (1842) 4 Man & G 988.
[15] See under **B2 The meaning of hearsay in the Criminal Justice Act 2003**.
[16] (1837) 7 Ad&El 313, Ex Ch.

*Coombs*,[17] which concerned an alleged breach by a brewer to supply good beer, it was held, obiter, that evidence could be given that customers ordered the beer, tasted it, did not finish it, and then either left it or threw it away. Further examples, together with the cases which highlight the difficult grey area that lies between implied assertions and circumstantial evidence, are considered in Chapter 10.[18] In *criminal* proceedings, an implied assertion is treated as hearsay only if the purpose, or one of the purposes of the person making the assertion, was to cause another person to believe the matter asserted or to cause another to act (or a machine to operate) on the basis that the matter is as asserted.[19] There is no equivalent provision in the Civil Evidence Act and it is unclear whether a 'representation' covers an implied assertion. In the case of conduct, the Law Commission took the view that the question whether assertive or non-assertive conduct should come within the statutory definition of hearsay was 'a matter for judicial consideration and development'.[20] However, it seems that such consideration and development is also called for in the case of implied assertions made orally or in writing.

### (d) Evidence admissible apart from section 1

Section 1(3) and (4) of the 1995 Act provides as follows:

(3) Nothing in this Act affects the admissibility of evidence admissible apart from this section.

(4) The provisions of sections 2 to 6 (safeguards and supplementary provisions relating to hearsay evidence) do not apply in relation to hearsay evidence admissible apart from this section, notwithstanding that it may also be admissible by virtue of this section.

Various statutory provisions, apart from section 1 of the 1995 Act, provide for the admissibility of particular types of hearsay and the purpose of section 1(3) is to preserve their effect. An example is the Births and Deaths Registration Act 1953, section 34 of which provides for the admissibility of a certified copy of an entry in the register of births as evidence of the facts contained in it. Similarly, the same section provides for the proof of death, where there is evidence identifying the person named in the certificate with the person in question, by reliance on a death certificate.[21] Other important statutory provisions include the orders made under section 96 of the Children Act 1989,[22] whereby in civil proceedings[23] before the High Court or a county

---

[17] (1901) 82 LT 347 at 349.

[18] See under **B2 The meaning of hearsay in the Criminal Justice Act 2003**.

[19] Section 114(3) of the Criminal Justice Act 2003: see Ch 10.

[20] Law Com No 216 (Cm 2321), para 4.35.

[21] See also the Bankers' Books Evidence Act 1879 (Ch 9), the Marriage Act 1949, s 65(3) (Ch 12) and the Solicitors Act 1974, s 18 (Ch 22).

[22] See SI 1993/621.

[23] 'Civil proceedings' has the same meaning as it has under the 1995 Act (by virtue of s 11): see s 96(7) of the 1989 Act.

court, in family proceedings in a magistrates' court,[24] and in proceedings under the Child Support Act 1991, evidence given in connection with the upbringing, maintenance or welfare of a child shall be admissible notwithstanding any rule of law relating to hearsay.[25]

### (e) Article 6(1) of the European Convention on Human Rights

In *Clingham v Kensington and Chelsea London Borough Council*[26] the Divisional Court held that there was nothing in the Human Rights Act 1998, nor in the jurisprudence of the European Court of Human Rights, which led to the automatic exclusion of hearsay evidence in civil proceedings, and that there was no requirement to give the 1995 Act any meaning which it did not naturally bear. The court also held that the admission of hearsay evidence, without the possibility of cross-examination, does not automatically result in an unfair trial under Article 6(1) of the Convention.

## 2 CONDITIONS OF ADMISSIBILITY

### (a) Competence

As previously noted, hearsay admissible under section 1 of the 1995 Act must be evidence which is otherwise admissible. However, section 1 does not make clear whether hearsay may be admitted if the maker of the statement would not have been competent to give evidence at the time he made it. It is also unclear whether his statement, if admissible, may be proved by the statement of another who, at the time when he made his statement, would not have been competent as a witness. For example, if A makes an oral statement within the hearing of B, and A would have been competent to give evidence at that time, may A's statement be proved by B's written record as to what he said, the record having been made at a time when B would not have been competent? Section 5(1) of the Act renders explicit the competence requirements. It provides as follows:

Hearsay evidence shall not be admitted in civil proceedings if or to the extent that it is shown to consist of, or to be proved by means of, a statement made by a person who at the time he made the statement was not competent as a witness.

For this purpose 'not competent as a witness' means suffering from such mental or physical infirmity, or lack of understanding, as would render a person incompetent as a witness in civil proceedings; but a child shall be treated as competent as a witness if he satisfies the requirements of section 96(2)(a) and (b) of the Children Act 1989 (conditions for reception of unsworn evidence of child).[27]

---

[24] The order extends not only to all the proceedings defined as 'family proceedings' by s 8(2) of the 1989 Act, but also to other proceedings which are part of the magistrates' courts' family proceedings jurisdiction by virtue of s 92(2) of the 1989 Act: *R v Oxfordshire County Council* [1992] 3 All ER 660.

[25] The party seeking to adduce the evidence must show that it has a substantial connection with the upbringing etc of the child.

[26] (2001) *The Times*, 20 Feb 2001, DC.        [27] See Ch 5.

The burden of proof, under section 5(1), is borne by the party seeking to exclude the evidence.[28]

## (b) The requirement of leave

Section 1 of the 1995 Act, if unqualified, would permit a party to adduce, as evidence of the matters stated, the previous out-of-court statement of a person called as a witness. The Law Commission took the view that, in the case of previous consistent statements, a leave requirement was necessary in order to prevent the pointless pro-liferation of superfluous evidence, which would needlessly prolong trials and increase costs.[29] Section 6 of the Act provides as follows:

(1) Subject as follows, the provisions of this Act as to hearsay evidence in civil proceed-ings apply equally (but with any necessary modifications) in relation to a previous statement made by a person called as a witness in the proceedings.

(2) A party who has called or intends to call a person as a witness in civil proceedings may not in those proceedings adduce evidence of a previous statement made by that person, except—

(a) with the leave of the court, or

(b) for the purpose of rebutting a suggestion that his evidence has been fabricated.[30] This shall not be construed as preventing a witness statement (that is, a written statement of oral evidence which a party to the proceedings intends to lead) from being adopted by a witness in giving evidence or treated as his evidence.[31]

Leave is required under section 6(2)(a) whether the previous statement is a previous *consistent* statement or relates to matters other than those dealt with in the testimony of the witness, but the concluding words of section 6(2) make it clear that it is not intended that a witness statement which stands as a witness's evidence-in-chief under CPR rule 32.5(2) should be regarded as a 'previous statement' for the purposes of the provision.

At common law, previous statements of a witness were generally excluded both as evidence of the truth of the facts they contained and as evidence of consistency.[32] The questions naturally arise as to what considerations the court should take into account in deciding whether to grant leave, and whether leave should be granted only exceptionally. As to the former, it is submitted that, in deciding whether to grant leave,

---

[28] *JC v CC* [2001] EWCA Civ 1625, LTL 25/10/2001, CA.

[29] See Law Com No 216 (Cm 2321), para 4.30.

[30] Section 6(2)(b) is considered in Ch 6, under **C Previous consistent or self-serving statements**.

[31] Pursuant to s 6(3), the Act does not authorize the adducing of evidence of previous *inconsistent* statements otherwise than in accordance with ss 3, 4 and 5 of the Criminal Procedure Act 1865; and, pursuant to s 6(4), the Act does not affect the common-law rules whereby a memory-refreshing document may be rendered admissible as a result of cross-examination. Section 6(3) is considered in Ch 6 (under **D3 Hostile witnesses**) and Ch 7 (under **A6 Previous inconsistent statements**); and s 6(4) is considered in Ch 6 (under **B Refreshing the memory**).

[32] The exceptions, in effect preserved by s 6(2)(b) and (4) of the 1995 Act, relate to statements admissible to rebut allegations of recent fabrication (see n 30, above) and memory-refreshing documents rendered admissible as a result of cross-examination (see n 31, above).

the judge should consider the importance of the previous statement in relation to the facts in issue, the reliability and weight of the statement, including all the circumstances in which it was made, and whether admission would be unjust to the other parties to the proceedings. As to the latter, it is submitted that leave should be granted not only where the witness is incapable of giving direct evidence on the matter in question because, for example, he has no recollection of the matter (in which case, the statement would not be a previous *consistent* statement), but also where, although he is capable of giving direct evidence of the matter, it is of questionable reliability or unintelligible by reason of partial loss of memory, lapse of time, age or illness. Such an approach would accord with the spirit of *Morris v Stratford-on-Avon RDC*,[33] a decision under the equivalent leave requirement in the 1968 Act.[34] That was an action against the council for damages for the alleged negligence of one of their employees. The trial began some five years after the cause of action arose and the employee gave confused and inconsistent evidence. After his examination-in-chief, counsel for the defendants was granted leave to admit in chief a written statement made by the employee and given to the defendants' insurers some nine months after the accident. The Court of Appeal held that the trial judge had not erred in allowing the evidence to be admitted.

Where leave is given, there is no restriction in section 6 as to when the previous statement may be given in evidence. Thus according to the circumstances, the statement may be given in evidence before or during the witness's examination-in-chief (which would seem appropriate if likely to improve the intelligibility of his evidence), rather than at the conclusion of his examination-in-chief. Equally, there is no restriction as to *who* may prove the statement: the court may allow evidence of the making of the previous statement to be given by someone other than its maker.

# C  SAFEGUARDS

## 1  THE REQUIREMENT TO GIVE ADVANCE NOTICE

The notice provisions of the 1995 Act are simpler and more flexible than those in operation under the 1968 Act. The objectives of the earlier provisions were that all issues arising out of the adduction of hearsay evidence should be dealt with pre-trial and that there should be no surprises at trial. The Law Commission endorsed these objectives but believed that they could be met by a notice provision which (i) requires a party to give notice of the fact that he or she proposes to adduce hearsay and (ii) puts the onus on the receiving party to demand such particulars as he requires in order to be able to make a proper assessment of the weight and cogency of the hearsay in question and to be in a position to respond adequately to it. The Commission also

---

[33] [1973] 1 WLR 1059.    [34] Section 2(2).

appreciated that circumstances can arise in litigation rendering compliance with a notice requirement impracticable. For example, some hearings need to be arranged urgently and in other cases advance notification may carry a real risk of danger to the witness or some other person. For reasons of this kind, it recommended that allowance should be made for the possibility that, in some circumstances, it would be unreasonable and impracticable to give any notice at all. With a view to further maximizing flexibility, it also recommended that the notice provisions should be subject to rules of court to allow them to be disapplied in respect of certain classes of proceedings if, as experience is gained, that is felt to be appropriate; and that the parties should also be free to agree to exclude the notice provisions.[35] Reflecting these recommendations, section 2 of the Act provides as follows:

(1) A party proposing to adduce hearsay evidence in civil proceedings shall, subject to the following provisions of this section, give to the other party or parties to the proceedings—
(a) such notice (if any) of that fact, and
(b) on request, such particulars of or relating to the evidence,
as is reasonable and practicable in the circumstances for the purpose of enabling him or them to deal with any matters arising from its being hearsay.

(2) Provision may be made by rules of court—
(a) specifying classes of proceedings or evidence in relation to which subsection (1) does not apply, and
(b) as to the manner in which (including the time within which) the duties imposed by that subsection are to be complied with in the cases where it does apply.

(3) Subsection (1) may also be excluded by agreement of the parties; and compliance with the duty to give notice may in any case be waived by the person to whom notice is required to be given.

The relevant rules of court are CPR rule 33.2 and 33.3.[36]

### 33.2 Notice of intention to rely on hearsay evidence

(1) Where a party intends to rely on hearsay evidence at trial and either—
(a) that evidence is to be given by a witness giving oral evidence; or
(b) that evidence is contained in a witness statement of a person who is not being called to give oral evidence;
that party complies with section 2(1)(a) of the Civil Evidence Act 1995 by serving a witness statement on the other parties in accordance with the court's order.[37]

(2) Where paragraph (1)(b) applies, the party intending to rely on the hearsay evidence must, when he serves the witness statement—
(a) inform the other parties that the witness is not being called to give oral evidence; and
(b) give the reason why the witness will not be called.

---

[35] See generally Law Com No 216 (Cm 2321), paras 4.9 and 4.10.
[36] CPR Pt 33 does not apply to claims which have been allocated to the small claims track: CPR r 27.2.
[37] See Ch 5.

(3) In all other cases where a party intends to rely on hearsay evidence at trial, that party complies with section 2(1)(a) of the Civil Evidence Act 1995 by serving a notice on the other parties which—
   (a) identifies the hearsay evidence;
   (b) states that the party serving the notice proposes to rely on the hearsay evidence at trial; and
   (c) gives the reason why the witness will not be called.

(4) The party proposing to rely on the hearsay evidence must—
   (a) serve the notice no later than the latest date for serving witness statements; and
   (b) if the hearsay evidence is to be in a document, supply a copy to any party who requests him to do so.

(5) If a party who has served a witness statement does not—
   (a) call the witness to give evidence at trial; or
   (b) put the witness statement in as hearsay evidence,
   any other party may put the witness statements in as hearsay evidence.

### 33.3 Circumstances in which notice of intention to rely on hearsay evidence is not required

Section 2.1 of the Civil Evidence Act 1995 (duty to give notice of intention to rely on hearsay evidence) does not apply—

(a)    to evidence at hearings other than trials;
(aa) to an affidavit or witness statement which is to be used at trial but which does not contain hearsay evidence;
(b) to a statement which a party to a probate action wishes to put in evidence and which is alleged to have been made by the person whose estate is the subject of the proceedings; or
(c) where the requirement is excluded by a practice direction.

Section 2(4) of the 1995 Act provides as follows:

(4) A failure to comply with subsection (1), or with rules under subsection (2)(b), does not affect the admissibility of the evidence but may be taken into account by the court—
   (a) in considering the exercise of its powers with respect to the course of proceedings and costs, and
   (b) as a matter adversely affecting the weight to be given to the evidence in accordance with section 4.

This subsection reflects the view of the Law Commission that if a party does not give notice, where it would have been reasonable and practicable in all the circumstances for him to have done so, the court should *not* be allowed to refuse to admit evidence.[38] Instead, under section 2(4)(a), the court, in exercise of its inherent powers to control

---

[38] The Commission was of the view that such a sanction could have the effect of simply re-introducing the rule against hearsay.

the conduct of the proceedings, may grant an adjournment (to compel a party to perfect an inadequate notice or to allow the recipient time to deal with the effect of late notification) or may impose a costs sanction; and under section 2(4)(b), the court may take the non-compliance as a matter reducing the weight to be attached to the evidence.[39]

## 2 THE POWER TO CALL WITNESSES FOR CROSS-EXAMINATION

Where a party adduces hearsay evidence of a statement but does not call the maker of the statement as a witness, and the other party to the proceedings wishes to challenge the statement, it is an obvious safeguard to allow the other party to call the maker with a view to cross-examining him as to both the accuracy of the statement and his credibility as a witness. The other party is allowed to do so under section 3 of the 1995 Act, but only with the leave of the court. Section 3 provides that:

Rules of court may provide that where a party to civil proceedings adduces hearsay evidence of a statement made by a person and does not call that person as a witness, any other party to the proceedings may, with the leave of the court, call that person as a witness and cross-examine him on the statement as if he had been called by the first-mentioned party and as if the hearsay statement were his evidence in chief.

The relevant rule is CPR rule 33.4, which provides as follows.

(1) Where a party—
   (a) proposes to rely on hearsay evidence; and
   (b) does not propose to call the person who made the original statement to give oral evidence, the court may, on the application of any other party, permit that party to call the maker of the statement to be cross-examined on the contents of the statement.

(2) An application for permission to cross-examine under this rule must be made not more than 14 days after the day on which a notice of intention to rely on the hearsay evidence was served on the applicant.

If the court considers that the maker of the statement, even if overseas, should attend and be cross-examined at court in person, but the party proposing to rely on the evidence refuses to obey the order of the court, then the consequence will ordinarily be that the party will not be entitled to rely upon the evidence. In such a case, the court has ample powers to exclude the statement under CPR rule 32.1.[40]

Rule 33.4 normally applies when a party, having served a witness statement, proposes to rely upon it as hearsay and does not propose to call its maker as a witness. It also applies when, in the event, such a party does not put the statement in as hearsay

---

[39] In *TSB (Scotland) plc v James Mills (Montrose) Ltd (in receivership)* 1992 SLT 519, a decision under the Civil Evidence (Scotland) Act 1988, it was held that in certain circumstances the courts may declare the evidence wholly unreliable, in effect according it no weight.

[40] *Polanski v Condé Nast Publications Ltd* [2004] 1 All ER 1220, CA at [22] to [23] and [62]. As to CPR r 32.1, see Ch 2.

evidence or call the witness to give evidence at the trial, and the other party, in reliance upon CPR rule 32.5(5)(b),[41] then puts the statement in as hearsay evidence. In these circumstances, the first party may apply to the court for permission to call the maker of the statement to be cross-examined on its contents.[42]

## 3  WEIGHING HEARSAY EVIDENCE

The statutory guidelines on weighing hearsay evidence do not impose any new obligation on the courts but simply indicate the more important factors which a court should bear in mind when it performs its usual function of weighing the evidence before it. The Law Commission recommended such guidelines for two reasons. First, having abolished the exclusionary rule, it wished to place extra emphasis on the need for courts to be vigilant in testing the reliability of such evidence. Secondly, it thought that it was important to deter the parties from abusing abolition of the rule, for example by deliberately failing to give notice or by giving late and inadequate notice,[43] by relying on hearsay evidence in preference to calling a dubious witness to give direct evidence of a fact,[44] or by attempting to conceal an essential witness in a case by amassing hearsay statements on a point.[45] Section 4 provides that:

(1)  In estimating the weight (if any) to be given to hearsay evidence in civil proceedings the court shall have regard to any circumstances from which any inference can reasonably be drawn as to the reliability or otherwise of the evidence.

(2)  Regard may be had, in particular, to the following—
    (a)  whether it would have been reasonable and practicable for the party by whom the evidence was adduced to have produced the maker of the original statement as a witness;
    (b)  whether the original statement was made contemporaneously with the occurrence or existence of the matters stated;
    (c)  whether the evidence involves multiple hearsay;
    (d)  whether any person involved had any motive to conceal or misrepresent matters;
    (e)  whether the original statement was an edited account, or was made in collaboration with another or for a particular purpose;
    (f)  whether the circumstances in which the evidence is adduced as hearsay are such as to suggest an attempt to prevent proper evaluation of its weight.

The phrase 'the original statement', which is used in sub-section (2)(a), (b), and (e), is defined as 'the underlying statement (if any) by—(a) in the case of evidence of fact, a person having personal knowledge of that fact, or (b) in the case of evidence of opinion, the person whose opinion it is'.[46]

Concerning section 4(2)(a), it seems that if it would have been reasonable and

---

[41]  See above, under C1 **The Requirement to give advance notice.**
[42]  *Douglas v Hello! Ltd* [2003] EWCA Civ 322, [2003] EMLR 633, CA.
[43]  See s 4(2)(f).     [44]  See s 4(2)(a).     [45]  See Law Com No 216 (Cm 2321), para 4.19.
[46]  Section 13.

practicable for the party by whom the evidence was adduced to have produced the maker of the original statement as a witness, an inference as to unreliability may be drawn, a very strong inference indeed if, had the maker been called as a witness, the court would not have granted leave under section 6(2) to adduce evidence of the statement. It also seems that such inferences may be drawn whether or not the maker is called for cross-examination by any other party to the proceedings under section 3, although it may be that such inferences are less likely to be drawn where the other party or parties have *not* applied for leave to call and cross-examine the maker under that section.

As to section 4(2)(d), the obscure phrase 'any person involved' may be taken to include (i) the maker of the 'original statement', (ii) the 'receiver' of the statement, ie the person who claims to have heard or otherwise perceived the statement and/or to have recorded it in a document, and (iii) in the case of multiple hearsay, ie in cases in which the information contained in the original statement is not supplied to the 'receiver' directly, any intermediaries through whom it was supplied indirectly.

Under section 4(2)(e), whether the 'original statement' was made 'for a particular purpose' (and more importantly, if it was, what that purpose was) has an obvious bearing on its likely reliability. To take an extreme example, the express purpose of the 'original statement' may have been to mislead or deceive. On the other hand, the fact that the 'original statement' was made under an important statutory or other duty may well give rise to a strong inference as to the truth of its contents.

## 4 IMPEACHING CREDIBILITY

Section 5(2) of the 1995 Act provides that:

Where in civil proceedings hearsay evidence is adduced and the maker of the original statement, or of any statement relied upon to prove another statement, is not called as a witness—

(a) evidence which if he had been so called would be admissible for the purpose of attacking or supporting his credibility as a witness is admissible for that purpose in the proceedings; and

(b) evidence tending to prove that, whether before or after he made the statement, he made any other statement inconsistent with it is admissible for the purpose of showing that he had contradicted himself.

Provided that evidence may not be given of any matter of which, if he had been called as a witness and had denied that matter in cross-examination, evidence could not have been adduced by the cross-examining party.

The general purpose of section 5(2) is to ensure that evidence relating to the credibility of certain persons not called as witnesses is as admissible as if those persons had been called as witnesses. The persons in question are (i) 'the maker of the original statement' and (ii) 'the maker ... of any statement relied upon to prove another statement'. As to the former, it seems that where the maker of the 'original statement', although not called, is available as a witness, evidence is admissible for the purpose of attacking credibility notwithstanding that the party adducing it has elected not to call and cross-examine him (with the leave of the court) under section 3. As to the latter, the meaning of 'another statement' is not clear, but presumably will be taken to mean not 'a statement other than the original statement' but 'either the original statement or any other statement'. Let us suppose that A makes an oral statement (the 'original statement') within the hearing of B; B tells C what A said; C makes a written record of his conversation with B; A, B, and C are all unavailable to give evidence; and C's written record is used to prove A's oral statement. In these circumstances, evidence relating to the credibility of A and C is clearly admissible and, it is submitted, evidence relating to the credibility of B should also be admissible.

Concerning section 5(2)(a), evidence admissible for the purpose of attacking credibility would include evidence of bias or previous convictions. Concerning section 5(2)(b), it seems that whereas in civil proceedings a prior inconsistent statement of a *witness* is not only admissible to attack his credibility but, by virtue of section 6(3) and (5) of the 1995 Act, is also admissible as evidence of any matter stated therein, a prior inconsistent statement introduced under section 5(2)(b) goes to consistency only.[47] The proviso to section 5(2) ensures that the rule on finality of answers on collateral issues[48] operates to restrict the evidence admissible under section 5(2) in the same way as it applies in relation to *witnesses*.

Where a party, in reliance on section 5(2), intends to attack the credibility of the maker of the original statement, he must give notice of his intention to do so, to the party who proposes to give the hearsay statement in evidence, not more than fourteen days after the day on which a notice of intention to rely on the hearsay evidence was served on him.[49]

# D  PROOF OF STATEMENTS CONTAINED IN DOCUMENTS [50]

The provisions of the 1995 Act governing the proof of statements contained in documents draw a distinction between (i) documents generally and (ii) documents which are shown to form part of the records of a business or public authority.

## 1  DOCUMENTS GENERALLY

Section 8 of the 1995 Act provides that:

> (1) Where a statement contained in a document is admissible as evidence in civil proceedings, it may be proved—

---

[47] Although the Law Commission thought it important to preserve the position under the 1968 Act in this regard, cf s 7(5) of the 1968 Act.

[48] See Ch 7.     [49] CPR r 33.5.     [50] See also Ch 9 under **A Documentary evidence**.

(a) by the production of that document, or

(b) whether or not that document is still in existence, by the production of a copy of that document or of the material part of it,

authenticated in such manner as the court may approve.

(2) It is immaterial for this purpose how many removes there are between a copy and the original.

A 'document' for these purposes means 'anything in which information of any description is recorded',[51] a definition covering documents in any form and therefore wide enough to include maps, plans, graphs, drawings, photographs, discs, audio-tapes, video-tapes, films, microfilms, negatives, and computer-generated printouts. A 'copy', in relation to a document, means 'anything onto which information recorded in the document has been copied, by whatever means and whether directly or indirectly',[52] a definition wide enough to cover, inter alia, a transcript of an audio-tape as well as reproductions or still reproductions of the images embodied in films and video-tapes etc, whether enlarged or not.

Concerning section 8(1)(a), 'production' refers not to counsel handing the document to the court, but to a witness who is qualified to do so in accordance with the rules of evidence producing the document and saying what it is.[53] However, although such direct oral evidence is preferable and will carry greater weight, it would seem that the document may also be proved by another hearsay statement admissible under the 1995 Act. Thus, where a statement has been deliberately tape-recorded but its maker is unavailable to produce the tape and give direct evidence that it is the tape he made, it seems that his out-of-court statements to the same effect could be used to prove the tape.[54]

The reference to 'authentication' at the end of section 8(1) appears to relate to the authentication of copies of a document as true copies of the original, and not to proof of the original.[55]

Section 8(2) makes clear that copies of copies may be received in evidence (subject to authentication in such manner as the court may approve).

## 2 RECORDS OF A BUSINESS OR PUBLIC AUTHORITY

Although at one time records of a business or public authority were kept manually and responsibility could often be attributed to an individual record keeper, nowadays record keeping within an organization has been largely taken over by technology and there is often unlikely to be a witness who can give direct evidence of all or any aspects of the compilation of the records kept. For these reasons, the Law Commission recommended that documents certified as forming part of the records of a business or

---

[51] Section 13.    [52] Section 13.

[53] Per Staughton LJ in *Ventouris v Mountain (No 2)* [1992] 3 All ER 414 at 427, CA, a decision under s 6(1) of the 1968 Act.

[54] *Ventouris v Mountain (No 2)* [1992] 3 All ER 414, CA.    [55] Ibid.

public authority should be capable of being received in evidence without further proof.[56] Section 9 of the 1995 Act provides that:

(1) A document which is shown to form part of the records of a business or public authority may be received in evidence in civil proceedings without further proof.

(2) A document shall be taken to form part of the records of a business or public authority if there is produced to the court a certificate to that effect signed by an officer of the business or authority to which the records belong.

For this purpose—

(a) a document purporting to be a certificate signed by an officer of a business or public authority shall be deemed to have been duly given by such an officer and signed by him; and

(b) a certificate shall be treated as signed by a person if it purports to bear a facsimile of his signature.

The precise scope of section 9(1) is unclear because the word 'records', said to mean 'records in whatever form',[57] is not otherwise defined. Hopefully, the word will not be construed as narrowly as it was under the 1968 Act, where it was taken to mean 'records which a historian would regard as original or primary sources, that is documents which either give effect to a transaction itself or which contain a contemporaneous register of information supplied by those with direct knowledge of the facts'. Accordingly, copies of documents consisting of summaries of the results of research into a drug and articles and letters about the drug published in medical journals were held not to be records, but merely a digest or analysis of records.[58] On this test, it was said, a bill of lading or cargo manifest,[59] a tithe map,[60] or a transcript of criminal proceedings[61] would rank as a record, but not a file of correspondence[62] or an anonymous document setting out a summary of legal proceedings taken or contemplated against a company.[63] In *Savings and Investment Bank Ltd v Gasco Investments (Netherlands) BV*[64] it was held that a report of inspectors appointed by the Secretary of State for Trade on the affairs and ownership of a company was not a record: it fell short of a compilation of the information supplied because it contained only a

---

[56] See Law Com No 216 (Cm 2321), paras 3.12 and 4.39.     [57] Section 9(4).

[58] *H v Schering Chemicals Ltd* [1983] 1 All ER 849, QBD.

[59] See *R v Jones; R v Sullivan* [1978] 1 WLR 195, CA, a decision under the Criminal Evidence Act 1965 (Ch 10).

[60] See *Knight v David* [1971] 1 WLR 1671.

[61] See *Taylor v Taylor* [1970] 1 WLR 1148, CA.

[62] See *R v Tirado* (1974) 59 Cr App R 80, CA, a decision under the Criminal Evidence Act 1965. Cf *R v Olisa* [1990] Crim LR 721, CA: for the purposes of s 68 of the Police and Criminal Evidence Act 1984, three application forms completed by a customer of a bank did 'form part of a record' compiled by the bank officials.

[63] See *Re Koscot Interplanetary (UK) Ltd, Re Koscot AG* [1972] 3 All ER 829.

[64] [1984] 1 All ER 296, Ch D.

selection of that information, and went beyond such a compilation because it also contained the opinions of the inspectors.[65]

Under section 9(4), 'business' includes 'any activity regularly carried on over a period of time, whether for profit or not, by any body (whether corporate or not) or by an individual'; and 'public authority' includes 'any public or statutory undertaking, any government department and any person holding office under Her Majesty'. The wide definition of 'business' reflects the Law Commission's view that it is the quality of regularity that lends a business record its reliability, not the existence of a profit motive or the judicial nature of the person carrying on the activity. A business defined in this way may not have 'officers' in the strict sense of that word and, accordingly, under section 9(4), 'officer' includes 'any person occupying a responsible position in relation to the relevant activities of the business or public authority or in relation to its records'.

Unless the court orders otherwise, a document which may be received in evidence under section 9(1) shall not be receivable at trial unless the party intending to put it in evidence has given notice of his intention to the other parties; and where he intends to use the evidence as evidence of any fact, then he must give notice not later than the latest date for serving witness statements.[66] Where a party has given such notice, he must also give every other party an opportunity to inspect the document and to agree to its admission without further proof.[67]

The Law Commission considered that the absence of an entry in a record should be capable of being formally proved, despite the fact that proving a negative (and drawing inferences from it) is rarely possible by reference to any human source.[68] The most appropriate method of doing this was thought to be by way of affidavit. Section 9(3) provides that:

The absence of an entry in the records of a business or public authority may be proved in civil proceedings by affidavit of an officer of the business or authority to which the records belong.

Presumably, the contents of the affidavit constitute hearsay and are therefore subject to the usual safeguards relating to notice, power to call for cross-examination and weight.

The Law Commission recognized that, although business and other records have long been treated as belonging to a class of evidence which can be regarded as likely to be reliable, there are bound to be exceptions, and it therefore recommended a specific discretion, allowing courts to disapply the certification provisions.[69] Section 9(5) provides that:

---

[65] See also *Re D (a minor)* [1986] 2 FLR 189, where notes of an interview between a solicitor and his client fell short of being a complete record of what was said. They were treated as a selective and necessarily subjective *aide memoire*, in that the solicitor put down what he thought was relevant for the purpose of preparing a pleading, affidavit or other legal document.

[66] CPR r 33.6(2), (3) and (4).       [67] CPR r 33.6(8).

[68] See *R v Patel* [1981] 3 All ER 94, CA; *R v Shone* (1983) 76 Cr App R 72, CA; and generally Ch 10 under B2(d) **Negative hearsay**.

[69] Law Com No 216 (Cm 2321), para 4.42.

The court may, having regard to the circumstances of the case, direct that all or any of the above provisions of this section do not apply in relation to a particular document or record, or description of documents or records.

# E  EVIDENCE FORMERLY ADMISSIBLE AT COMMON LAW

## 1  GENERAL

Section 9 of the Civil Evidence Act 1968 preserved and gave statutory force to a number of common-law exceptions to the hearsay rule (informal admissions, published works dealing with matters of a public nature and public documents and records) without purporting to amend the law in relation to those exceptions. Subject to one important difference, this state of affairs is perpetuated by the Civil Evidence Act 1995. The important difference relates to informal admissions. The Law Commission considered that there was no longer any need to preserve this common-law exception and recommended that the general provisions of the Act, including the notice and weight provisions, should apply to informal admissions as they apply to other hearsay statements.[70] Section 7(1) of the 1995 Act gives statutory effect to this recommendation and is considered further below. Concerning published works dealing with matters of a public nature, and public documents and records, however, the Commission recommended preserving the relevant common-law rules because: (a) some of the statutory provisions which it believed should not be affected by its proposals presuppose the existence of the common-law rules about public registers;[71] (b) it was not the policy of the Commission to add the procedural burden of the notice procedure where no such burden already existed; and (c) it would be rare for the weight to be attached to such evidence to be a matter for debate.[72] Section 7(2) gives statutory effect to this recommendation. The common-law rules effectively preserved by the 1995 Act are considered in Chapter 12.

## 2  INFORMAL ADMISSIONS

Under section 7(1) of the 1995 Act, 'the common law rule effectively preserved by section 9(1) and (2)(a) of the Civil Evidence Act 1968 (admissibility of admissions adverse to a party) is superseded by the provisions of this Act'. As noted above, the

---

[70] Law Com No 216 (Cm 2321), paras 4.32 and 4.33.
[71] Evidence (Foreign, Dominion and Colonial Documents) Act 1933, s 1 (see Chs 2 and 12) and the Oaths and Evidence (Overseas Authorities and Countries) Act 1963, s 5.
[72] Law Com No 216, (Cm 2321), para 4.33.

purpose of the subsection is to give effect to the Law Commission's recommendation that the general provisions of the Act should apply to informal admissions.[73]

## (a)  The application of section 1 of the 1995 Act (admissibility)

At common law an informal admission was a statement by a party to the proceedings (or someone in privity with him) made other than while testifying in those proceedings and adverse to his case. Any such statement is now covered by section 1(1) of the Act and, by reason of the wide statutory definition of statement ('any representation of fact or opinion, however made'), an admission may be admitted whether made orally, in writing, or by conduct, demeanour, or even silence. Thus as at common law, a person may make an oral admission when talking either to another[74] or to himself.[75] Similarly, in the case of written admissions, the admission may be contained in a communication, such as a letter, or in a diary or other private memorandum.[76] A common-law example of an admission by conduct is *Moriarty v London, Chatham and Dover Rly Co*,[77] where evidence of the plaintiff's conduct in suborning witnesses was admitted as an admission by him of the weakness and falsity of his claim. Where an out-of-court accusation is made against a party, his answer, whether given by words or conduct, may constitute an admission insofar as it amounts to an acknowledgment of the truth of the whole or part of the accusation made. Presumably, even silence, by way of reply, will amount to a 'statement' where the accusation is made in circumstances such that it would be reasonable to expect some explanation or denial. At common law, in *Wiedemann v Walpole*[78] Lord Esher MR said that, in the case of a letter written upon a matter of business, the court could take notice of the ordinary course adopted by men of business to answer letters the contents of which they do not intend to admit, so that a failure to reply to such a letter could be taken as some evidence of the truth of the statements contained in it, but that a man could not reasonably be expected to reply to a letter charging him with some offence or impropriety because 'it is the ordinary and wise practice of mankind not to answer such letters'.[79]

## (b)  The application of section 4 of the Act (weight)

Section 4 of the 1995 Act applies to informal admissions as it applies to other hearsay statements. However, there are a number of special considerations which are relevant to the weighing of admissions. Some of these are of a general character, but there are also two specific considerations: whether the admission relates to facts of which its maker had no personal knowledge, and whether the admission was vicarious, ie made by someone in privity with a party to legal proceedings.

---

[73] Section 3, however, could hardly apply to an informal admission made by a party to legal proceedings (as opposed to someone in privity with him): it would involve that party calling and cross-examining himself!

[74] See *Rumping v DPP* [1964] AC 814 (the maker's wife).

[75] See per Alderson B in *R v Simons* (1834) 6 C&P 540.     [76] See *Bruce v Garden* (1869) 18 WR 384.

[77] (1870) LR 5 QB 314. See also *Alderson v Clay* (1816) 1 Stark 405.     [78] [1891] 2 QB 534, CA.

[79] Cf *Bessela v Stern* (1877) 2 CPD 265, CA.

*(i) General considerations.* The weight to be attached to an informal admission depends upon its precise contents, the circumstances in which it was made (for example whether it was made as a result of some threat or inducement) and any contradictory or other evidence adduced by its maker at the trial with a view to explaining it away. In some cases, the tribunal of fact will need to consider carefully whether the statement is, in fact, adverse to the case of its maker, and for this purpose regard should be had to the whole statement, including any passages favourable to its maker which qualify, explain or even nullify so much of the statement as is relied upon as an admission. Although it may be that less weight may be attached to the favourable or self-serving parts of the statement,[80] it is clear that under the 1995 Act they are as much evidence of the facts they state as the passages relied upon as constituting an admission.[81]

*(ii) Personal knowledge.* An informal admission may be admitted under the 1995 Act notwithstanding that it relates to facts of which its maker has no personal knowledge[82] or amounts to no more than an expression of opinion or belief.[83] The weight to be attached to such evidence will vary according to the circumstances. For example, an admission by a party as to his age, although obviously based on hearsay, concerns a matter as to which it is reasonable to expect that he has been accurately informed.[84] On the other hand, in *Comptroller of Customs v Western Lectric Co Ltd,*[85] the Privy Council was of the view that an admission concerning the countries of origin of certain imported goods, made in reliance on the fact that the goods bore marks and labels indicating that they came from those countries, was evidentially worthless.[86]

*(iii) Vicarious admissions.* The rationale of the common-law exception was the presumed unlikelihood of a person speaking falsely against his own interest, a rationale reflected in the rule that an informal admission could only be received in evidence if it was made directly (ie by a party to the legal proceedings) or vicariously (ie by someone in privity with a party). 'Privity' in this context usually denoted some common or successive interest in the subject matter of the litigation or some other relationship between the party and the privy, for example that of principal and agent, whereby the latter had actual or imputed authority to speak on behalf of the former. Under the 1995 Act, an out-of-court statement adverse to the case of a party may be received in evidence whether made by that party or by *anyone else.* However, the weight to be attached to an admission made by someone who, at common law, would have been in privity with a party is generally likely to be greater than an admission made by anyone else.

Those in privity included: (i) a predecessor in title of a party to proceedings

---

[80] See *Smith v Blandy* (1825) Ry&M 257.        [81] See *Harrison v Turner* (1847) 10 QB 482.

[82] Under s 1(2)(b), 'references to hearsay include hearsay of whatever degree'.

[83] Under s 13, a 'statement' is defined to include 'any representation of opinion'.

[84] See, at common law, *R v Turner* [1910] 1 KB 346 and *Lustre Hosiery Ltd v York* (1936) 54 CLR 134, HC of A.

[85] [1966] AC 367.        [86] See per Lord Hodson at 371.

(provided that the admission concerned title to the property in question and was made at a time when he had an interest in the property);[87] (ii) a partner (an admission or representation made by any partner concerning the partnership affairs and in the ordinary course of its business being evidence against the firm);[88] (iii) referees;[89] and (iv) agents. At common law, an admission by an agent could only be received against his principal if (a) it was made at a time when the agency existed (a matter which, apparently, could be inferred from the statements and conduct of the alleged agent himself),[90] (b) the communication in which it was made was authorized, whether expressly or by implication, by the principal,[91] and (c) it was made in the course of a communication with some third party as opposed to the principal himself.[92] Under the 1995 Act, failure to establish these three matters will not affect admissibility, but is likely to affect adversely the weight to be attached to the 'admission'.

The weight to be attached to an 'admission' made by someone who at common law would not have been in privity with a party is generally likely to be less than an admission made by that party himself or someone who would have been in privity with him. At common law there was no privity between (i) spouses, merely by virtue of their relationship of husband and wife, (ii) a parent and a child, merely by virtue of that relationship,[93] (iii) co-parties, ie co-plaintiffs or co-defendants (or, in divorce proceedings, a respondent and a co-respondent),[94] or (iv) a witness and the party calling him.[95]

# F  OGDEN TABLES

Section 10 of the Civil Evidence Act 1995 provides that:

The actuarial tables (together with explanatory notes) for use in personal injury and fatal accident cases issued from time to time by the Government Actuary's Department are admissible in evidence for the purpose of assessing, in an action for personal injury, the sum to be awarded as general damages for future pecuniary loss.

---

[87] *Woolway v Rowe* (1834) 1 Ad&El 114. See also *Smith v Smith* (1836) 3 Bing NC 29.

[88] See the Partnership Act 1890, s 15, giving statutory force to a common-law principle to the same effect. See also *Jaggers v Binnings* (1815) 1 Stark 64 and *Wood v Braddick* (1808) 1 Taunt 104.

[89] *Williams v Innes* (1808) 1 Camp 364, KB, where Lord Ellenborough CJ said (at 365): 'If a man refers another upon any particular business to a third person, he is bound by what this third person says or does concerning it, as much as if that had been said or done by himself.'

[90] See, *sed quaere*, *Edwards v Brookes (Milk) Ltd* [1963] 1 WLR 795.

[91] *Wagstaff v Wilson* (1832) 4 B&Ad 339; *G(A) v G(T)* [1970] 2 QB 643, CA; and *Johnson v Lindsay* (1889) 53 JP 599. See also *Burr v Ware RDC* [1939] 2 All ER 688, CA and cf *Beer v W H Clench (1930) Ltd* [1936] 1 All ER 449, DC.

[92] See *Re Devala Provident Gold Mining Co* (1883) 22 Ch D 593 and cf *The Solway* (1885) 10 PD 137.

[93] *G(A) v G(T)* [1970] 2 QB 643, CA.

[94] *Morton v Morton, Daly and McNaught* [1937] P 151 and *Myatt v Myatt and Parker* [1962] 1 WLR 570.

[95] See *British Thomson-Houston Co Ltd v British Insulated and Helsby Cables Ltd* [1924] 2 Ch 160, CA and cf *Richards v Morgan* (1863) 4 B&S 641.

# 12

# HEARSAY ADMISSIBLE AT COMMON LAW

Under the common-law rule against hearsay, any assertion, other than one made by a person while giving oral evidence in the proceedings, was inadmissible if tendered as evidence of the facts asserted. As we have seen in Chapters 10 and 11, the circumstances in which hearsay is admissible in criminal proceedings is now governed by Chapter 2 of Part 11 of the Criminal Justice Act 2003, and in civil proceedings hearsay is admissible subject to compliance with the conditions of admissibility set out in the Civil Evidence Act 1995. The categories of hearsay considered in this chapter—statements in public documents, works of reference, evidence of age, evidence of reputation and statements forming part of the *res gestae*—share two common features: all of them were established at common law as exceptions to the rule against hearsay and all of them have been preserved by statute. All of the cases considered, apart from evidence of age and *res gestae* statements, have been expressly preserved and given statutory force in both criminal proceedings (by section 118(1) of the Criminal Justice Act 2003) and civil proceedings (by section 7(2) and (3) of the Civil Evidence Act 1995). The categories relating to evidence of age and statements forming part of the *res gestae* have been preserved in criminal but not civil proceedings. However, evidence formerly admissible in these cases at common law will now be admissible in civil proceedings under the general provisions of the Civil Evidence Act 1995.

It is convenient to consider the common-law rules separately, here, under the rubric of hearsay admissible at common law, because neither section 118 of the Criminal Justice Act 2003 nor section 7 of the Civil Evidence Act 1995 purports to amend the rules to which they have given statutory force. Section 7(4) of the 1995 Act provides that the words in which a rule of law mentioned in the section is described 'are intended only to identify the rule and shall not be construed as altering it in any way'; and although there is no express equivalent in section 118 of the Criminal Justice Act 2003, it is plain that it too is designed to identify rules of law rather than alter them. Furthermore, where evidence is admissible under one of the preserved rules, it is not subject to other statutory conditions of admissibility and safeguards. However, the common-law exceptions have been narrowly construed, and much evidence failing to meet all of the common-law conditions of admissibility may well be admissible in civil proceedings under the general provisions of the 1995 Act (subject to compliance with the statutory conditions) and in criminal proceedings under statutory provisions of a general nature such as sections 116 and 117 of the Criminal Justice Act 2003 (cases where a witness is unavailable and business and other documents).

# A  STATEMENTS IN PUBLIC DOCUMENTS

Section 7(2)(b) and (c) of the Civil Evidence Act 1995 preserve any rule of law whereby in civil proceedings—

  (b) public documents (for example, public registers, and returns made under public authority with respect to matters of public interest) are admissible as evidence of the facts stated in them, or
  (c) records (for example, the records of certain courts, treaties, Crown grants, pardons and commissions) are admissible as evidence of facts stated in them.

Section 118(1)1(b) and (c) of the Criminal Justice Act 2003 preserve the same rules in criminal proceedings.

## 1  GENERAL

At common law, statements made in most public documents are admissible in both civil and criminal cases as evidence of the matters stated.[1] The admissibility of such evidence may be justified on the grounds of reliability and convenience. Where a record has been compiled by a person acting under a public duty to inquire into the truth of some matter and to record his findings so that the public may refer to them, the contents of that document may be presumed to be true.[2] Proof of the facts stated in the document by direct evidence would clearly be preferable, but in many cases the public official in question will be dead, otherwise unavailable or unable to remember the facts recorded because of the time which has elapsed. The common-law principles relating to public documents, though not unimportant, are of comparatively minor significance, mainly because of the existence of a wide variety of statutory provisions which cater for the admissibility of particular classes of public document in both criminal and civil proceedings. Under section 34 of the Births and Deaths Registration Act 1953, for example, a certified copy of an entry purporting to be sealed or stamped with the seal of the General Register Office, shall be received as evidence of the birth or death to which it relates.[3]

---

[1] Concerning proof of the contents of a public document upon which a party seeks to rely, see Ch 9.

[2] See per Parke B in *Irish Society v Bishop of Derry* (1846) 12 Cl&Fin 641, HL.

[3] See also the Marriage Act 1949, s 65(3) (proof of the celebration of a marriage by the production of a certified copy of an entry kept at the General Register Office) and Family Proceedings Rules 1991, r 10.14 (proof of the celebration and validity of a marriage celebrated outside England and Wales, where the existence and validity of the marriage is not disputed, by evidence of one of the parties to it and production of a

## 2 EXAMPLES

The terms of section 7(2)(b) and (c) of the Civil Evidence Act 1995 give some idea of the different classes of public document admissible under this head. The exception applies to a variety of public papers, official registers, surveys, assessments, inquisitions, returns, and other documents made under public authority in relation to matters of public concern. Examples include: recitals in public Acts of Parliament and royal proclamations;[4] entries relating to acts of state and public matters in parliamentary journals and governmental Gazettes;[5] entries in parish registers of baptisms, marriages, and burials;[6] extracts from foreign registers kept under the sanction of public authority as to matters properly and regularly recorded in them;[7] entries in the public books of a corporation relating to matters of public interest;[8] the contents of a file from the Companies Register containing the statutory returns made by a company in compliance with the Companies Act 1948;[9] statements in coastguards' books on weather conditions;[10] entries in university records relating to degrees conferred;[11] entries in Domesday Book;[12] records of assessment by commissioners of land tax;[13] inquisitions and surveys of Crown lands;[14] inquisitions in lunacy;[15] findings of professional misconduct by the General Medical Council;[16] and statements in a bishop's return to a writ from the Exchequer relating to vacancies and advowsons in his diocese.[17]

## 3 CONDITIONS OF ADMISSIBILITY

Given the multiplicity of public documents to which the exception applies, it is perhaps not surprising that the conditions of admissibility vary, to some extent, according to the particular type of document in question. Generally speaking, however,

---

marriage certificate issued under the law in force in the country in question or by a certified copy of an entry in a register of marriages kept under the law of that country).

[4] *R v Sutton* (1816) 4 M&S 532.

[5] *A-G v Theakston* (1820) 8 Price 89; *R v Holt* (1793) 5 Term Rep 436.

[6] Entries in such registers of the particulars of birth and death would appear to be inadmissible because outside the actual knowledge of the person making the entries: see per Geoffrey Lane LJ in *R v Halpin* [1975] QB 907 at 914, CA; cf per Lord Blackburn in *Sturla v Freccia* (1880) 5 App Cas 623 at 644, HL.

[7] For example, foreign registers of baptisms and marriages: see per Lord Selborne in *Lyell v Kennedy* (1889) 14 App Cas 437 at 448–9, HL. See also the Evidence (Foreign, Dominion and Colonial Documents) Act 1933, whereby an Order in Council may provide that registers of a foreign country are documents of such a public nature as to be admissible as evidence of matters regularly recorded therein.

[8] *Shrewsbury v Hart* (1823) 1 C&P 113.

[9] *R v Halpin* [1975] QB 907, HL, below. See now the Companies Act 1985. Other documentary records relating to companies, such as the certificate of incorporation, the register of members and minutes of proceedings of meetings, are rendered admissible by the Act itself.

[10] *The Catherina Maria* (1866) LR 1 A&E 53.     [11] *Collins v Carnegie* (1834) 1 Ad&El 695.

[12] *Duke of Beaufort v John Aird & Co* (1904) 20 TLR 602.

[13] *Doe d Strode v Seaton* (1834) 2 Ad&El 171.     [14] *Duke of Beaufort v Smith* (1849) 4 Exch 450.

[15] *Faulder v Silk* (1811) 3 Camp 126; *Harvey v R* [1901] AC 601.

[16] *Hill v Clifford* [1907] 2 Ch 236, CA.

[17] *Irish Society v Bishop of Derry* (1846) 12 Cl&Fin 641, HL.

it seems that a public document is only admissible as evidence of the truth of its contents if (a) it concerns a public matter, (b) it was made by a public officer acting under a duty to inquire and record the results of such inquiry, and (c) it was intended to be retained for public reference or inspection.[18]

## (a) A public matter

In *Sturla v Freccia*[19] Lord Blackburn expressed the opinion that 'public', in this context, should not be taken to mean the whole world: the matter in question may concern either the public at large or a section of the public. Thus an entry in the books of a manor may be public as concerning all the people interested in the manor[20] and an entry in a corporation book concerning a corporate matter or something in which all the corporation is concerned may be public in the same sense.[21]

## (b) A public officer acting under a duty to inquire and record

A statement in a public document is only admissible if it was made by a public officer, as opposed to some private individual,[22] acting in discharge of a strict duty to inquire into and satisfy himself of the truth of the facts recorded.[23] Thus whereas a certificate of the registrar of births, deaths and marriages is admissible as prima facie—but not conclusive—evidence of the fact and date of a birth, death, or marriage,[24] it would appear, according to the obiter view of Swinfen Eady MR in *Bird v Keep*,[25] that information concerning the cause of death contained in a death certificate and based on information supplied by a coroner is inadmissible as evidence of the cause of death. This conclusion has been justified on the grounds that the registrar is *bound* to record the verdict of the coroner's jury and is under no duty to state the results of his own personal inquiry according to his own judgment.[26] Under the modern law, however, it seems that strict compliance with the requirement of personal knowledge on the part of a public official of the matters which he puts on file or records is no longer

---

[18] See generally per Lord Blackburn in *Sturla v Freccia* (1880) 5 App Cas 623 at 643–4, HL.

[19] (1880) 5 App Cas 623.       [20] See, eg, *Heath v Deane* [1905] 2 Ch 86 (manorial rolls).

[21] But see *Hill v Manchester and Salford Waterworks Co* (1833) 5 B&Ad 866. See also *R v Sealby* [1965] 1 All ER 701, CC, below.

[22] *Daniel v Wilkin* (1852) 7 Exch 429 (a survey undertaken by a private individual).

[23] *Doe d France v Andrews* (1850) 15 QB 756; *Thrasyvoulos Ioannou v Papa Christoforos Demetriou* [1952] AC 84, PC; *White v Taylor* [1969] 1 Ch 150, Ch D.

[24] See *Wilton & Co v Phillips* (1903) 19 TLR 390; *Brierley v Brierley and Williams* [1918] P 257. However, a birth certificate by itself is insufficient to establish the fact of marriage between the parents of the child in question because it does not identify the persons it mentions. Such a certificate, in conjunction with other evidence, may suffice as proof of the fact of marriage between the parents: *Re Stollery, Weir v Treasury Solicitor* [1926] Ch 284, CA. See also *R v Clapham* (1829) 4 C&P 29: a statement in a parish register of baptisms that the person baptized was born on a particular day is not admissible as evidence of the date of birth, the record being admissible on the question of baptism not birth.

[25] [1918] 2 KB 692 at 697, 698 and 701, CA.

[26] See per Scrutton LJ in *Re Stollery, Weir v Treasury Solicitor* [1926] Ch 284 at 322, CA. But see also per Sargent LJ at 327: since the verdict of the coroner's jury is itself inadmissible as evidence of the truth of the facts on which it is based, it follows that the short note made of that verdict in the death certificate is also inadmissible.

necessary. In *R v Halpin*[27] the appellant was convicted of conspiracy to cheat and defraud a council by making bogus claims for certain work allegedly carried out by a company. In order to prove that the appellant was a director of the company at the relevant time and therefore that any fraud that had been perpetrated must have been with his knowledge or connivance, the prosecution adduced in evidence at the trial a file from the Companies Register containing the annual returns made by the company under the Companies Act 1948. On appeal, it was argued that the file was inadmissible as a public document because the relevant official at the Companies Register has no duty to inquire and satisfy himself as to the truth of the recorded facts. Geoffrey Lane LJ, giving the judgment of the Court of Appeal, was satisfied that under the common-law authorities it was a condition of admissibility that the official making the record should either have had personal knowledge of the matters recorded or should have inquired into the accuracy of the facts. However, although satisfied that on the facts the official in the Companies Registry had no personal knowledge of the matters which he had put on file or recorded, his Lordship said:[28]

The common law as expressed in the earlier cases which have been cited were plainly designed to apply to an uncomplicated community where those charged with keeping registers would, more often than not, be personally acquainted with the people whose affairs they were recording and the vicar, as already indicated, would probably himself have officiated at the baptism, marriage or burial which he later recorded in the presence of the church-wardens on the register before putting it back in the coffers. But the common law should move with the times and should recognize the fact that the official charged with recording matters of public import can no longer in this highly complicated world, as like as not, have personal knowledge of their accuracy.

What has happened now is that the function originally performed by one man has had to be shared between two: the first having the knowledge and the statutory duty to record that knowledge and forward it to the Registrar of Companies, the second having the duty to preserve that document and to show it to members of the public under proper conditions as required.

Accordingly, it was held that where a duty is cast upon a company by statute to make accurate returns of company matters to the Registrar of Companies so that those returns can be filed and inspected by members of the public, all statements on the return are prima facie proof of the truth of their contents.

The statement in the public document must have been made by the official whose duty it was to inquire and record. Thus an entry in a register of baptisms made by the minister of the parish is admissible, but not a private memorandum made by the parish clerk.[29] At one time it appears that an entry in a register was only admissible if made promptly.[30] However, in *R v Halpin*, where the entries in the files from the

---

[27] [1975] QB 907. See also *R v Sealby* [1965] 1 All ER 701 at 703–4; cf *White v Taylor* [1969] 1 Ch 150.

[28] [1975] QB 907 at 915.     [29] *Doe d Warren v Bray* (1828) 8 B&C 813.

[30] (1828) 8 B&C 813, where the minister made an entry in the register of the baptism of a child which had taken place before he had any connection with the parish and in respect of which he had acted on information from the parish clerk.

Companies Register were acknowledged to be very much out of time, Geoffrey Lane LJ said that this was a matter which might go to their weight, but not to their admissibility.[31] Likewise, the fact that an entry was made by an interested party may affect its weight but will not, of itself, render it inadmissible. Thus, in *Irish Society v Bishop of Derry*,[32] statements in a bishop's return to a writ from the Exchequer relating to advowsons in his diocese were held to be admissible notwithstanding that some of the advowsons belonged to the bishop himself.

### (c) Retention for public reference

A public document, to be admissible as such, must have been brought into existence as a document of record to be retained indefinitely: a document intended to be of temporary effect[33] or designed to serve only temporary purposes[34] is inadmissible. Additionally, the document should have been prepared for the purposes of the public making use of it and must be available for public inspection.[35] In *Lilley v Pettit*[36] it was held that the regimental records of a serving soldier were not admissible as public documents, since they were kept for the information of the Crown and executive as opposed to members of the public, who had no right of access to them. Similarly, in *R v Sealby*,[37] a car registration book was ruled to be inadmissible as evidence of its contents, for example the chassis and engine numbers, on the grounds that it is a private document issued to a car owner who is under no obligation to produce it for inspection by anyone except a police officer or a local taxation officer.

# B  WORKS OF REFERENCE

Section 7(2)(a) of the Civil Evidence Act 1995 preserves any rule of law whereby in civil proceedings—

>   (a) published works dealing with matters of a public nature (for example, histories, scientific works, dictionaries and maps) are admissible as evidence of facts of a public nature stated in them . . .

Section 118(1)1(a) of the Criminal Justice Act 2003 preserves the same rule in criminal proceedings.

Under the common-law rule, authoritative published works of reference dealing with matters of a public nature are admissible to prove, or to assist the court in deciding whether to take judicial notice of, facts of a public nature stated in them.[38]

---

[31] [1975] QB 907 at 916, CA.         [32] (1846) 12 Cl&Fin 641, HL.

[33] *White v Taylor* [1969] 1 Ch 150 (a draft document).         [34] *Mercer v Denne* [1905] 2 Ch 538, CA.

[35] Per Lord Blackburn in *Sturla v Freccia* (1880) 5 App Cas 623 at 648, HL; *Thrasyvoulos Ioannou v Papa Christoforos Demetriou* [1952] AC 84, PC.

[36] [1946] KB 401, DC.         [37] [1965] 1 All ER 701, CC.

[38] On judicial notice generally, see Ch 22.

Examples include: historical works concerning ancient public facts;[39] standard medical texts concerning the nature of a disease;[40] engineers' reports within the common knowledge of engineers and accepted by them as accurate on the nature of certain soil;[41] Carlisle Tables, which set out the average life expectancy of persons;[42] dictionaries, on the meaning of English words;[43] and published maps and plans generally offered for sale to the public, even if not prepared by someone acting under a public duty, concerning facts of geographical notoriety.[44]

## C  EVIDENCE OF AGE

Section 118(1)1(d) of the Criminal Justice Act 2003 preserves the following rule of law in criminal proceedings:

> (d)  evidence relating to a person's age or date or place of birth may be given by a person without personal knowledge of the matter.

Since the date of a person's birth is contained in his or her birth certificate, the normal way of proving a person's age is to produce a certified copy of an entry in the register of births, which is admissible under section 34 of the Births and Deaths Registration Act 1953 as evidence of the matters stated, accompanied by some evidence to identify the person whose age is in question with the person named in the certificate. At common law, the accompanying evidence of identification may be given by a person without personal knowledge of the matter, such as the evidence of a grandmother who, although present at the birth of her grandchild, was not present at the registration.[45] Similarly, the courts have acted on evidence as to age given by the person whose age is in question[46] or by another who has made enquiries as to his or her age.[47]

---

[39]  *Read v Bishop of Lincoln* [1892] AC 644. But not facts of a private or local nature: *Stainer v Droitwich (Burgesses)* (1695) 1 Salk 281. See also *Evans v Getting* (1834) 6 C&P 586 and *Fowke v Berington* [1914] 2 Ch 308.

[40]  *McCarthy v The Melita (Owners)* (1923) 16 BWCC 222, CA.

[41]  *East London Rly Co v Thames Conservators* (1904) 90 LT 347.

[42]  *Rowley v London and North Western Rly Co* (1873) LR 8 Exch 221.

[43]  *Marchioness of Blandford v Dowager Duchess of Marlborough* (1743) 2 Atk 542 (a law dictionary); *R v Agricultural Land Tribunal, ex p Benney* [1955] 2 QB 140, CA (Fowler's *Modern English Usage*).

[44]  See *R v Orton* (1873) and *R v Jameson* (1896) *Stephen's Digest of the Law of Evidence* (10th edn) 48. See also Highways Act 1980, s 32, which requires a court or tribunal to take into consideration, before determining whether a way has been dedicated as a highway or the date on which such dedication, if any, took place, maps, plans, histories and other relevant documents tendered in evidence.

[45]  *R v Weaver* (1873) LR 2 CCR 85. See also *Wilton & Co v Phillips* (1903) 19 TLR 390.

[46]  *Re Bulley's Settlement* [1886] WN 80.          [47]  *R v Bellis* (1911) 6 Cr App R 283, CCA.

# D EVIDENCE OF REPUTATION

Section 7(3)(a) and (b) of the Civil Evidence Act 1995 provide as follows.

The common law rules . . . whereby in civil proceedings
  (a) evidence of a person's reputation is admissible for the purpose of establishing his good or bad character, or
  (b) evidence of reputation or family tradition is admissible—
      (i)   for the purpose of proving or disproving pedigree or the existence of a marriage, or
      (ii)  for the purpose of proving or disproving the existence of any public or general right or of identifying any person or thing,
  shall continue to have effect in so far as they authorise the court to treat such evidence as proving or disproving that matter.

Where any such rule applies, reputation or family tradition shall be treated for the purposes of this Act as a fact and not as a statement or multiplicity of statements about the matter in question.

As to the concluding part of section 7(3), it is born of a recognition that evidence of reputation or family tradition, if tendered to establish the facts reputed or the facts according to family tradition, is necessarily composed of a multiplicity of hearsay statements and therefore, if treated as such in civil proceedings, would render impossible application of the notice and weighing provisions of the 1995 Act.[48] The effect of treating such evidence as evidence of fact, in contrast, is that the party proposing to adduce the evidence will not be expected to give to the other party to the proceedings particulars of the person who had personal knowledge of the matter in question and of all the intermediaries through whom the information was conveyed to the declarant;[49] and the court, in assessing the weight of the evidence, will not be expected to have regard to a factor such as whether the person with personal knowledge made the 'original statement' contemporaneously with the occurrence or existence of the matters stated.[50]

Section 118(1)2 and 3 of the Criminal Justice Act 2003 preserve, in criminal proceedings, the same rules as those identified in section 7(3)(a) and (b) of the Civil Evidence Act 1995. They also make clear that the rules are preserved in criminal proceedings only insofar as they allow the court to treat such evidence as proving the matter concerned. Thus if the matter concerned should not be open to proof of any kind, because that would be to introduce, for example, inadmissible evidence of bad character, then plainly the matter cannot be proved under any of the preserved common-law rules.

---

[48] Law Com No 216 (Cm 2321), para 4.34.    [49] See s 2 of the 1995 Act (Ch 11).
[50] See s 4 of the 1995 Act (Ch 11).

Evidence of reputation for the purpose of establishing good or bad character requires no further explanation. The other preserved common-law rules are technical and complex and are, perhaps, best considered under two headings, declarations as to pedigree and declarations as to public and general rights.

## 1 DECLARATIONS AS TO PEDIGREE

At common law, a declaration concerning pedigree is admissible, after its maker's death, as evidence of the truth of its contents. This exception to the hearsay rule has been justified on the grounds that such declarations are often the only evidence that can be obtained concerning facts which may have occurred many years before the trial.[51] Matters of pedigree concern the relationship by blood or marriage between persons and therefore include, for example, the fact and date of births, marriages and deaths, legitimacy, celibacy, failure of issue, and intestacy. Pedigree declarations may be oral, for example, declarations by deceased parents that one of their children, whose legitimacy is in issue, was born before their marriage; in writing, for example an entry in a family Bible, an inscription on a tombstone or a pedigree hung up in the family home; or by conduct, as when parents always treat one child as illegitimate and introduce and treat another child as the heir of the family.[52] There are three conditions of admissibility. First, the declaration is only admissible in proceedings in which a question of pedigree is directly in issue. Thus in *Haines v Guthrie*,[53] an action for the price of goods sold, the Court of Appeal held that a statement made by the deceased father of the defendant as to the defendant's age had been improperly admitted in support of his defence of infancy, the case not being one of pedigree.[54] Secondly, the declaration must have been made by a blood relation or the spouse of a blood relation as opposed to, for example, relations in law,[55] domestic servants or intimate acquaintances.[56] There is no requirement, however, of personal knowledge on the part of the declarant as to the facts stated, which may amount to no more than family tradition or reputation handed down from one generation to another.[57] Thirdly, the declaration must have been made *ante litem motam*, that is before any controversy arose upon the matter in question.[58] In *Butler v Mountgarret*[59] the House of Lords held that a letter written by one member of a family to another concerning a marriage alleged to have taken place in that family was inadmissible because a controversy as to the marriage had already arisen, albeit not the subject of a lawsuit at the time when the letter was

---

[51] See per Best CJ in *Johnston v Lawson* (1824) 2 Bing 86 at 89 and generally per Lord Mansfield CJ in the *Berkeley Peerage Case* (1811) 4 Camp 401, HL.

[52] Per Lord Mansfield CJ in *Goodright d Stevens v Moss* (1777) 2 Cowp 591. See also *Vowles v Young* (1806) 13 Ves 140 (engravings upon rings).

[53] (1884) 13 QBD 818, CA.

[54] The evidence would now be admissible under the Civil Evidence Act 1995.

[55] *Shrewsbury Peerage Case* (1858) 7 HL Cas 1.     [56] *Johnson v Lawson* (1824) 2 Bing 86.

[57] *Davies v Lowndes* (1843) 6 Man&G 471; *Doe d Banning v Griffin* (1812) 15 East 293.

[58] *Berkeley Peerage Case* (1811) 4 Camp 401, HL; *Shedden v A-G* (1860) 2 Sw&Tr 170.

[59] (1859) 7 HL Cas 633.

written. The controversy may create a bias in the minds of members of the family rendering their declarations unreliable. However, provided that the declaration was made *ante litem motam*, the fact that the declarant had an interest in establishing the relationship in question would appear to go only to weight and not admissibility.[60]

## 2 DECLARATIONS AS TO PUBLIC AND GENERAL RIGHTS

At common law, an oral or written statement concerning the reputed existence of a public or general right is admissible, after its maker's death, as evidence of the existence of that right. The primary justification for the admissibility of such evidence is the fact that other evidence, especially in the case of ancient rights, is usually unavailable. The declaration must concern a public or general and not a private right,[61] unless the private right coincides with a public right. Thus when a question arises as to the boundary of a private estate that is conterminous with a hamlet, evidence of reputation concerning the boundary of the latter is admissible to prove the boundary of the former.[62] Public rights are those common to the public at large, such as rights to use paths,[63] highways,[64] ferries,[65] or landing-places on the banks of a river.[66] General rights are those common to a section of the public or a considerable class of persons, such as the inhabitants of a parish or the tenants of a manor.[67] In the case of a public right, it seems that any person is competent to make a declaration as to its reputed existence, because it concerns everyone, and the fact that the declarant has no knowledge of the subject goes only to weight, not admissibility. A declaration as to general rights, however, is only admissible if it was made by a person with some connection with or knowledge of the matter in question.[68] There are two further conditions of admissibility and these apply whether the declaration concerns public or general rights. First, as in the case of declarations as to pedigree, the declaration must have been made *ante litem motam*.[69] Secondly, the declaration must concern the reputed existence of the right in question and not particular facts tending to support or negative the existence of that right. In *Mercer v Denne*[70] the issue concerned the existence of an immemorial custom for fishermen of Walmer to dry their nets on a particular part of the foreshore. The defendant, with a view to showing that the

---

60 *Doe d Tilman v Tarver* (1824) Ry&M 141; *Doe d Jenkins v Davies* (1847) 10 QB 314. But see *Plant v Taylor* (1861) 7 H&N 211.

61 *Lonsdale v Heaton* (1830) 1 You 58.

62 *Thomas v Jenkins* (1837) 6 Ad&El 525. See also *Stoney v Eastbourne RDC* [1927] 1 Ch 367, CA.

63 See *Radcliffe v Marsden UDC* (1908) 72 JP 475.

64 See *R v Bliss* (1837) 7 Ad&El 550. See now Highways Act 1980, s 32, above.

65 *Pim v Curell* (1840) 6 M&W 234.     66 *Drinkwater v Porter* (1835) 7 C&P 181.

67 *Nicholls v Parker* (1805) 14 East 331n. However, numerous private rights of common of the several tenants of a manor do not amount to one public right: see *Earl of Dunraven v Llewellyn* (1850) 15 QB 791. See also *White v Taylor* [1969] 1 Ch 150 (individual rights of pasturage for sheep).

68 See *Berkeley Peerage Case* (1811) 4 Camp 401, HL; *Rogers v Wood* (1831) 2 B&Ad 245; and *Crease v Barrett* (1835) 1 Cr M&R 919.

69 *Berkeley Peerage Case* (1811) 4 Camp 401, HL. See also *Moseley v Davies* (1822) 11 Price 162.

70 [1905] 2 Ch 538, CA. See also *R v Bliss* (1837) 7 Ad&El 550.

custom could not have been immemorial, sought to admit in evidence a variety of documents produced from the War Office, including surveys, depositions, maps, and plans, which showed that on various dates between 1616 and 1647 the land in question was below the highwater mark. The Court of Appeal held that the trial judge had properly excluded the evidence because it related not to matters of reputation but to particular facts from which the non-existence of the allegedly immemorial custom could be inferred.

# E  STATEMENTS FORMING PART OF THE RES GESTAE

'Res gestae', it has been said, is 'a phrase adopted to provide a respectable legal cloak for a variety of cases to which no formula of precision can be applied'.[71] The words themselves simply mean a transaction. Under the inclusionary common-law doctrine of res gestae, a fact or a statement of fact or opinion which is so closely associated in time, place and circumstances with some act, event or state of affairs which is in issue that it can be said to form a part of the same transaction as the act or event in issue, is itself admissible in evidence. The justification given for the reception of such evidence is the light that it sheds upon the act or event in issue: in its absence, the transaction in question may not be fully or truly understood and may even appear to be meaningless, inexplicable or unintelligible. Despite judicial dicta to the contrary,[72] it is clear from the authorities that such statements have been received by way of exception to the common-law rule against hearsay as evidence of the matters asserted. The multiplicity of cases in which hearsay statements have been received under the doctrine were usefully subdivided, by the late Sir Rupert Cross, into the following categories: (i) statements by participants in or observers of events or, as they would more accurately be described in the light of subsequent developments, statements by persons emotionally overpowered by an event; (ii) statements accompanying the maker's performance of an act; (iii) statements relating to a physical sensation; and (iv) statements relating to a mental state. The same categorization has been used in the Criminal Justice Act 2003 to identify the common-law rules preserved and put on a statutory footing.

In R v Callender[73] the Court of Appeal said that res gestae is a single principle and that a statement can only be admitted under the res gestae exception to the hearsay rule if the trial judge is satisfied that there is no real possibility of concoction or distortion. This dictum, it is submitted, has been made per incuriam. The requirement

---

[71] Per Lord Tomlin in Homes v Newman [1931] 2 Ch 112 at 120.

[72] See, eg, per Lord Atkinson in R v Christie [1914] AC 545, HL at 553 and per Dixon J in Adelaide Chemical and Fertilizer Co Ltd v Carlyle (1940) 64 CLR 514 at 531.

[73] [1998] Crim LR 337.

referred to only applies to *res gestae* statements in the first of the categories set out above.

## 1　STATEMENTS BY PERSONS EMOTIONALLY OVERPOWERED BY AN EVENT

Section 118(1)4(a) of the Criminal Justice Act 2003 preserves the following rule of law in criminal proceedings:

Any rule of law under which in criminal proceedings a statement is admissible as evidence of any matter stated if—
　(a)　the statement was made by a person so emotionally overpowered by an event that the possibility of concoction or distortion can be disregarded

Statements made concerning an event in issue in circumstances of such spontaneity or involvement in the event that the possibility of concoction, distortion or error can be disregarded, are admissible as evidence of the truth of their contents. One of the earliest illustrations of the principle is to be found in *Thompson v Trevanion*,[74] where 'what the wife said immediate upon the hurt received and before that she had time to devise or contrive anything for her own advantage' was held to be admissible in evidence. In *R v Foster*,[75] on a charge of manslaughter by reckless driving, a statement made by the deceased immediately after he had been run down was admitted to show the cause of the accident.[76]

To the extent that some of the earlier cases were decided without regard to the likelihood of concoction, distortion or error, but merely on the basis of whether the statement was spontaneous in the sense that it could be regarded as part of the event in question, they must be treated with considerable caution. Thus it has been said that *R v Bedingfield*,[77] one of the most famous cases on the subject, 'is more useful as a focus for discussion than for the decision on the facts'.[78] Bedingfield was charged with the murder of a woman. The deceased, her throat cut, came out of a room where she had been with the accused and immediately exclaimed 'Oh dear, Aunt, see what Bedingfield has done to me!' Cockburn CJ held that although statements made while the act is being done, such as 'Don't, Harry!' are admissible, the victim's statement could not be received in evidence because 'it was something stated by her after it was all over, whatever it was, and after the act was completed'. Commenting upon this decision in *Ratten v R*,[79] Lord Wilberforce said: 'though in a historical sense the emergence of the victim could be described as a different "*res*" from the cutting of the throat, there could hardly be a case where the words uttered carried more clearly

---

[74] (1693) Skin 402.　　[75] (1834) 6 C&P 325, Central Criminal Court.

[76] See also *Davies v Fortior Ltd* [1952] 1 All ER 1359n, where the statement in question would now be admissible under the Civil Evidence Act 1995.

[77] (1879) 14 Cox CC 341; cf *R v Fowkes* (1856) *The Times*, 8 Mar (Ch 6).

[78] Per Lord Wilberforce in *Ratten v R* [1972] AC 378, PC at 390.　　[79] [1972] AC 378, PC.

the mark of spontaneity and intense involvement.' It follows, of course, that *R v Bedingfield* would be decided differently today.[80]

In *Ratten v R*, Ratten was convicted of the murder of his wife by shooting her. His defence was that a gun went off accidentally while he was cleaning it. The evidence established that the shooting of the wife, from which she died almost immediately, must have taken place between 1.12 pm and about 1.20 pm. A telephonist from the local exchange gave evidence that at 1.15 pm she had received a telephone call from Ratten's house made by a sobbing woman who in an hysterical voice had said, 'Get me the police please.' The Privy Council held that the telephonist's evidence was not hearsay and had been properly admitted because of its relevance to the issues.[81] However, the Privy Council then proceeded to consider the admissibility of the evidence on the assumption that it *did* contain a hearsay element, ie that the words used by the wife did involve an assertion of the truth of some fact, for example that she was being attacked by her husband. On this assumption, it was held that the evidence would have been admissible as part of the *res gestae* because not only was there a close association in place and time between the statement and the shooting, but also the way in which the statement came to be made, in a call for the police, and the tone of voice used, showed intrinsically that the statement was being forced from the wife by an overwhelming pressure of contemporary events. In *R v Newport*,[82] on the other hand, it was held that evidence of the contents of a telephone call made by the victim of a murder to her friend 20 minutes before she was stabbed had been improperly admitted: the call was not a spontaneous and unconsidered reaction to an immediately impending emergency.

In *Ratten v R*, Lord Wilberforce, delivering the reasons of the Board, said:[83]

the test should be not the uncertain one whether the making of the statement was in some sense part of the event or transaction. This may often be difficult to establish: such external matters as the time which elapses between the events and the speaking of the words (or *vice versa*), and differences in location being relevant factors but not, taken by themselves, decisive criteria. As regards statements made after the event it must be for the judge, by preliminary ruling, to satisfy himself that the statement was so clearly made in circumstances of spontaneity or involvement in the event that the possibility of concoction can be disregarded. Conversely, if he considers that the statement was made by way of narrative of a detached prior event so that the speaker was so disengaged from it as to be able to construct or adapt his account, he should exclude it. And the same must in principle be true of statements made before the event. The test should be not the uncertain one, whether the making of the statement should be regarded as part of the event or transaction. This may often be difficult to show. But if the drama, leading up to the climax, has commenced and assumed such intensity and pressure that the utterance can safely be regarded as a true reflection of what was unrolling or actually happening, it ought to be received.

Lord Wilberforce's test was applied by the Court of Appeal in *R v Nye, R v Loan*,[84] and

---

80 Per Lord Ackner in *R v Andrews* [1987] 1 All ER 513, HL.    81 See Ch 10.
82 [1998] Crim LR 581, CA        83 [1972] AC 378 at 389.        84 (1977) 66 Cr App R 252, CA.

*R v Turnbull*,[85] and has been affirmed, by the House of Lords, in *R v Andrews*.[86] In *R v Nye, R v Loan*, Loan was convicted of assault. Following a collision between two cars, Loan, the passenger from one of the cars assaulted Lucas, the driver of the other, by punching him in the face. Somewhat shaken, Lucas sat in his car waiting to regain full possession of his faculties. The police were summoned and arrived shortly afterwards, the police station being only a few yards away. Lucas then made a statement identifying Loan, as opposed to the *driver* of the other car, as his assailant. The Court of Appeal, adding what was described as a gloss on Lord Wilberforce's test, namely 'was there any real possibility of error?',[87] was satisfied that there had been no opportunity for concoction and no chance of error and accordingly held that Lucas' statement had been properly admitted under the *res gestae* principle as a spontaneous identification. Lawton LJ said:[88]

Was there an opportunity for concoction? The interval of time was very short indeed. During part of that interval Mr Lucas was sitting down in his car trying to overcome the effects of the blows which had been struck. Commonsense and experience of life tells us that in that interval he would not be thinking of concocting a case against anybody.

In *R v Turnbull* Ronald Turnbull was convicted of murder. At about 8.30 pm on the day in question the victim, who had been stabbed about 100 yards from a public house, staggered into the bar and collapsed on the floor. An ambulance was sent for and arrived at 8.33 pm. On a number of occasions, after he had arrived in the bar and while in the ambulance, the victim was asked to identify his assailant. The victim, who had a powerful Scottish accent and had been drinking heavily during the day, answered variously 'Tommo', 'Ronnie Tommo', and 'Ronnie'. The prosecution case was that the victim had been attempting to refer to Ronald Turnbull. The Court of Appeal held that the evidence had been properly admitted by the trial judge under the *res gestae* principle as explained by Lord Wilberforce in *Ratten v R.*

In *R v Andrews* Donald Andrews was convicted of manslaughter and aggravated burglary. Andrews and another man, O'Neill, with a blanket covering their heads, knocked on the door of the victim's flat and, when he opened it, stabbed him. Then, no longer covered by the blanket, they stole property from the flat. Minutes later, the victim, bleeding profusely from a deep stomach wound, went to the flat below for assistance. Again, within a matter of minutes, the police arrived. One of the constables asked the victim how he had received his injuries. In reply, the victim referred to one of his assailants as a man known to him as 'Donald'. The other constable present, who was making a note of this statement, heard and wrote down the name 'Donavon'. There was evidence that the victim had a Scottish accent, had drunk to excess, and had a motive to fabricate or concoct, namely a malice against the accused because he believed that on a previous occasion O'Neill, accompanied by Andrews, had attacked and damaged his house. The House of Lords held that the victim's statement to the

---

[85] (1984) 80 Cr App R 104, CA.      [86] [1987] 1 All ER 513, HL.
[87] But see further, *R v Andrews* [1987] 1 All ER 513, below.      [88] (1977) 66 Cr App R 252 at 256.

police had been properly admitted under the *res gestae* doctrine. Lord Ackner summarized the relevant principles to be applied by the trial judge as follows:[89]

> (1) The primary question which the judge must ask himself is: can the possibility of
> concoction or distortion be disregarded? (2) To answer that question the judge must
> first consider the circumstances in which the particular statement was made, in order
> to satisfy himself that the event was so unusual or startling or dramatic as to domin-
> ate the thoughts of the victim, so that his utterance was an instinctive reaction to that
> event, thus giving no real opportunity for reasoned reflection. In such a situation the
> judge would be entitled to conclude that the involvement or pressure of the event
> would exclude the possibility of concoction or distortion, providing that the state-
> ment was made in conditions of approximate but not exact contemporaneity. (3) In
> order for the statement to be sufficiently 'spontaneous' it must be so closely associ-
> ated with the event which has excited the statement that it can fairly be stated that the
> mind of the declarant was still dominated by the event. Thus the judge must be
> satisfied that the event which provided the trigger mechanism for the statement was
> still operative. The fact that the statement was made in answer to a question is but
> one factor to consider under this heading. (4) Quite apart from the time factor, there
> may be special features in the case, which relate to the possibility of concoction or
> distortion. In the instant appeal the defence relied on evidence to support the conten-
> tion that the deceased had a motive of his own to fabricate or concoct, namely a
> malice . . . The judge must be satisfied that the circumstances were such that, having
> regard to the special feature of malice, there was no possibility of any concoction or
> distortion to the advantage of the maker or the disadvantage of the accused. (5) As to
> the possibility of error in the facts narrated in the statement, if only the ordinary
> fallibility of human recollection is relied on, this goes to the weight to be attached to
> and not to the admissibility of the statement and is therefore a matter for the jury.
> However, here again there may be special features that may give rise to the possibility
> of error. In the instant case there was evidence that the deceased had drunk to excess
> . . . Another example would be where the identification was made in circumstances of
> particular difficulty or where the declarant suffered from defective eyesight. In such
> circumstances the trial judge must consider whether he can exclude the possibility of
> error.

*R v Andrews* was applied in *R v Carnall*,[90] where the victim, P, badly beaten and
stabbed, took an hour to crawl for help before then naming Carnall, first to two
witnesses who saw him in the street, bleeding heavily and asking for help, and later to
a police officer, in an ambulance. The Court of Appeal held the evidence to have been
properly admitted. Despite the time lapse and the fact that P had only named his
assailant in response to questions, the trial judge was satisfied that his thoughts were
so dominated by what had happened as to be unaffected by ex post facto reasoning or
fabrication; and although P was known to have acted dishonestly in the past, the judge
had properly taken the view that, in the context of the situation, there was nothing to

---

[89] [1987] 1 All ER 513 at 520–1.          [90] [1995] Crim LR 944, CA.

make one think that he would do otherwise than tell the first person he saw who had inflicted his appalling injuries.

In *R v Andrews* Lord Ackner said that while he accepted that the doctrine admits hearsay statements not only where the declarant is dead or otherwise not available but also when he is called as a witness, he would strongly deprecate any attempt in criminal prosecutions to use the doctrine as a device to avoid calling the maker of the statement, when available.[91] This dictum, which does not prevent the admission of a *res gestae* statement made by someone who, served with a witness summons, fails to attend the trial,[92] was applied in *Tobi v Nicholas*.[93] However, it is clear from *Attorney General's Reference (No 1 of 2003)*[94] that it is not to be treated as an extra bar, in law, to admissibility. In that case, W was charged with a serious assault on his mother. The prosecution proposed to call witnesses to give evidence that they found Mrs W lying by the steps of her house in great distress and that she had implicated her son, saying, among other things, 'He's gone bonkers. He threw me downstairs and set me on fire. Phone the police and the ambulance.' The prosecution did not intend to call the mother because they believed that she would give untruthful evidence and exculpate her son. She had declined to make a witness statement but had made a deposition in which she said that she was not prepared to attend court to give evidence against her son. The judge held that the evidence of the witnesses was inadmissible. As a result, the prosecution offered no evidence and not guilty verdicts were entered. The Court of Appeal held that once evidence is within the *res gestae* exception to the hearsay rule it is admissible and there is no rider, in law, that it is not to be admitted if better evidence is available or because the maker of the statement is available to give evidence. However, the judge should have been prepared to entertain an application by the defence under section 78 of the Police and Criminal Evidence Act 1984. If the purpose of the Crown is that the *res gestae* evidence should be given without any opportunity for the defence to cross-examine the mother, the court may well conclude that the evidence will have an adverse effect on the fairness of the proceedings and refuse to admit it. As a general principle, it cannot be right that the Crown should be permitted to rely on such part of a victim's evidence as they considered reliable, without being prepared to tender the victim to the defence, so that the defence can challenge that part of the victim's evidence on which the Crown seeks to rely and elicit that part of her evidence on which the defence might seek to rely. Applying these principles to the facts of the case, the Court of Appeal concluded that it had effectively come to the same conclusion as the judge, the difference being that whereas the judge had erroneously added an extra legal bar to admissibility, their Lordships would have excluded the evidence in exercise of the discretion to exclude under section 78 of the 1984 Act.

The *res gestae* doctrine under discussion applies whether the statement was made by the victim of the offence, a bystander, or even, in appropriate circumstances, the

---

[91] [1987] 1 All ER 513 at 521.      [92] *Edwards and Osakwe v DPP* [1992] Crim LR 576, DC.
[93] [1987] Crim LR 774, DC.          [94] [2003] 2 Cr App R 453, CA.

accused himself. In *R v Glover*[95] a man assaulted J and was forcibly restrained. In anger, he then uttered the words 'I am David Glover . . .', followed by a threat to shoot J and his family. Despite the possibility that the assailant was not Glover but deliberately pretending to be him, the words were held to be admissible on the basis that the opportunity for concoction or distortion was so unlikely that it could be disregarded.

Concerning the nature of the proof required to establish that a statement was made in such conditions of involvement or pressure that the possibility of concoction or error can be ruled out, it would appear that although the trial judge may, for these purposes, refer to the contents of the statement itself, the necessary connection between the statement and the event cannot be shown *solely* by reference to those contents because 'otherwise the statement would be lifting itself into the area of admissibility'.[96]

Concerning the summing-up, in *R v Andrews* it was held that the judge should make it clear to the jury that it is for them to decide what was said and that they should be sure that the witnesses were not mistaken in what they believed to have been said. The jury should also be satisfied that the declarant did not concoct or distort and, if there is material to raise the issue, that he was not activated by malice or ill-will. Further, the jury's attention should be drawn to any special features that bear on the possibility of mistake. In some cases judges may think it appropriate to alert the jury to the need for extra caution because the evidence cannot be tested by cross-examination, but failure to do so, by itself, will not amount to a misdirection.[97]

## 2 STATEMENTS ACCOMPANYING THE MAKER'S PERFORMANCE OF AN ACT

Section 118(1)4(b) of the Criminal Justice Act 2003 preserves the following rule of law in criminal proceedings:

Any rule of law under which in criminal proceedings a statement is admissible as evidence of any matter stated if—
  (b) the statement accompanied an act which can properly be evaluated as evidence only if considered in conjunction with the statement

Statements explaining an act in issue or relevant to an issue made by a person contemporaneously with his performance of that act are admissible as evidence of the truth of their contents. The best person to explain the significance of an act is often the person who performed it and the requirement of contemporaneity affords some guarantee of reliability. Typical examples are a bankrupt's statement as to his intention in going or remaining abroad[98] and, on a question of domicile, a statement of a

---

[95] [1991] Crim LR 48, CA.
[96] Per Lord Wilberforce in *Ratten v R* [1972] AC 378 at 391. See also *R v Taylor* 1961 (3) SA 614.
[97] *R v Carnall* [1995] Crim LR 944, CA.
[98] *Rawson v Haigh* (1824) 2 Bing 99; *Rouch v Great Western Rly Co* (1841) 1 QB 51.

person who has lived abroad as to whether he intends to live there permanently or only temporarily.[99] There are three conditions of admissibility. First, the statement must explain or otherwise relate to the act in question. In *R v Bliss*,[100] the issue being whether a certain road was public or private, evidence of a declaration made by a deceased owner of adjoining land, on planting a willow, that he was planting it to mark the boundary of the road and his estate, was held to be inadmissible. The declaration—which in any event was irrelevant, the question being not of boundary but as to the public or private character of the road—was said to have no connection with the act performed. Secondly, the statement must be more or less contemporaneous with the act performed. In the case of continuing acts, it suffices if the statement was made during their continuance, albeit some considerable time after their commencement. Thus in *Rawson v Haigh*,[101] where the question was whether a debtor had gone overseas with the intention of avoiding his creditors, letters indicating such an intention written subsequent to the act of departure were held to be admissible on the grounds that departing the realm is a continuing act and the letters were written during its continuance. Thirdly, the statement must be made by the person performing the act and not, for example, by someone witnessing it. In *Howe v Malkin*,[102] an action for trespass, evidence of a statement concerning the position of a boundary made by the plaintiff's father while certain work was being carried out on the land by builders was excluded. Grove J said:

no act was shown to have been done by the plaintiff's father at the time of making the alleged statement, so that the declaration was by one person, and the accompanying act by another. That does not appear to me to come within the rule.

Under this head of *res gestae*, the statement is usually admissible to explain the declarant's reasons for, or intention in, performing some independent physical act. However, in *R v McCay*,[103] in which a witness was unable to remember the number of the man he had picked out at an identification parade carried out from behind a two-way mirror, an officer who had been present at the parade was allowed to give evidence that the witness had said 'It is number eight'. It was held that the physical activity of looking at the suspect, and the intellectual activity of recognizing him, were together sufficient to amount to a relevant act in respect of which the accompanying words were admissible. The difficulty with the decision is that even if there had been a physical act, such as pointing to or touching the suspect, earlier authority has clearly assumed that accompanying words of identification are *not* covered by the *res gestae* exception.[104]

---

[99] *Bryce v Bryce* [1933] P 83. See also *Scappaticci v A-G* [1955] P 47 (declarations concerning domicile of choice).

[100] (1837) 7 Ad&El 550.    [101] (1824) 2 Bing 99. See also *Homes v Newman* [1931] 2 Ch 112.

[102] (1878) 40 LT 196.    [103] [1991] 1 All ER 232, CA.

[104] See, eg, *R v Christie* [1914] AC 545, HL, in which a child touched the sleeve of the accused and said 'That is the man'; and *R v Gibson* (1887) 18 QBD 537, in which a woman pointed to the door of a house and said 'The person who threw the stone went in there.'

## 3 STATEMENTS RELATING TO A PHYSICAL SENSATION OR A MENTAL STATE

Section 118(1)4(c) of the Criminal Justice Act 2003 preserves the following rule of law in criminal proceedings:

Any rule of law under which in criminal proceedings a statement is admissible as evidence of any matter stated if—
  (c) the statement relates to a physical sensation or a mental state (such as intention or emotion).

### (a) Statements relating to a physical sensation

Statements of contemporaneous physical sensation experienced by a person are admissible as evidence of the existence of that sensation, if it is in issue or relevant to an issue, but not as evidence of its possible causes. Thus a statement made by an ill workman to the effect that his illness was caused by an accident in his employment and is causing him certain bodily or mental pain is admissible to prove the sensation of pain but not the cause of the illness.[105] One of the earliest illustrations of the principle is *Aveson v Lord Kinnaird*,[106] which concerned the truth or falsity of a statement, made when a policy of life insurance was taken out by a husband on the life of his wife, that she was then in a good state of health. It was held that statements of bodily symptoms made by her when lying in bed, apparently ill, were admissible to show her bad state of health at the time when the policy was effected. The authorities indicate that the exception is not confined to statements of sensation experienced at the actual moment when the maker is speaking, the requirement of contemporaneity being a question of degree.[107]

### (b) Statements relating to a mental state

Statements made by a person concerning his contemporaneous state of mind or emotion are admissible as evidence of the existence of his state of mind or emotion at that time, if it is in issue or relevant to an issue, but not as evidence of any other fact or matter stated. Thus where a bankrupt makes a payment which is alleged to be a fraudulent preference, evidence of a statement by him that he knew he was insolvent is admissible to prove his knowledge of that fact at the time when the payment was made, but not to prove the insolvency.[108] Statements may be admitted under this head

---

[105] *Gilbey v Great Western Rly Co* (1910) 102 LT 202, CA. See also *R v Johnson* (1847) 2 Car&Kir 354; *R v Conde* (1867) 10 Cox CC 547; *R v Gloster* (1888) 16 Cox CC 471; and contrast *R v Black* (1922) 16 Cr App R 118, CCA.

[106] (1805) 6 East 188.

[107] See per Salter J, *arguendo*, in *R v Black* (1922) 16 Cr App R 118 at 119; *Aveson v Lord Kinnaird* (1805) 6 East 188; and contrast per Charles J in *R v Gloster* (1888) 16 Cox CC 471.

[108] *Thomas v Connell* (1838) 4 M&W 267.

to prove such diverse matters as political opinion,[109] marital affection,[110] fear,[111] and dislike of a child.[112] It seems reasonably clear that a statement made by a person as to his intention is also admissible under this exception as evidence of the existence of such intention at the time when the statement was made.[113] The admissibility of such a statement, however, gives rise to two further questions: first, whether it can support an inference that the intention also existed at a date prior or subsequent to the date on which the statement was made and, secondly, in the case of a statement of intention to do a certain act, whether it is admissible to prove that such an act was done. Concerning the first question, the authorities support an affirmative answer[114] except in the case of a party's self-serving statements of intention, which, it has been said, cannot support an inference that the speaker's intention also existed at some later (or earlier) time than the date on which the statement was made, because 'otherwise it would be easy for a man to lay grounds for escaping the consequences of his wrongful acts by making such declarations'.[115] Concerning the second question, the authorities conflict. In *R v Buckley*[116] the accused was charged with the murder of a police officer on a certain night. On the crucial issue of whether it was the accused who had committed the offence, Lush J admitted a statement made by the deceased to a senior officer on the morning of the day in question to the effect that he intended to watch the movements of the accused that night. Similarly, in *R v Moghal*,[117] a more recent murder trial in which M was charged with aiding and abetting S, his mistress, who had already been tried separately and acquitted, M's defence being that S had committed the offence and that he was no more than a terrified spectator, the Court of Appeal expressed the opinion that a tape-recorded statement by S made some six months before the murder to the effect that she intended to kill the victim would have been admissible on the accused's behalf.[118] In *R v Wainwright*,[119] on the other hand, Cockburn CJ ruled that evidence of a statement made by the victim of a murder on leaving her lodgings that she was going to the accused's premises was inadmissible because 'it was only a statement of intention which might or might not have been carried out'. *R v Thomson*[120] is to the same effect. The defence to a charge of using an

---

[109] *R v Tooke* (1794) 25 State Tr 344.

[110] *Trelawney v Coleman* (1817) 1 B&Ald 90; *Willis v Bernard* (1832) 8 Bing 376.

[111] *R v Vincent, Frost and Edwards* (1840) 9 C&P 275; *R v Gandfield* (1846) 2 Cox CC 43; and *Neill v North Antrim Magistrates' Court* [1992] 4 All ER 846 at 854, HL.

[112] *R v Hagan* (1873) 12 Cox CC 357. See also per Mahon J in *Customglass Boats Ltd v Salthouse Bros Ltd* [1976] 1 NZLR 36.

[113] See per Mellish LJ in *Sudgen v Lord St Leonards* (1876) 1 PD 154 at 251, CA.

[114] See per Cozens-Hardy MR in *Re Fletcher, Reading v Fletcher* [1917] 1 Ch 339 at 342 (proof of earlier intention) and per Lord Ellenborough in *Robson v Kemp* (1802) 4 Esp 233 (proof of subsequent intention).

[115] Per Crampton J in *R v Petcherini* (1855) 7 Cox CC 79. See also *R v Callender* [1998] Crim LR 337, CA.

[116] (1873) 13 Cox CC 293, Assizes.      [117] (1977) 65 Cr App R 56, CA.

[118] It has been doubted, however, whether the evidence was of any relevance to the issue, namely whether M was a willing accomplice or an unwilling spectator: per Lord Bridge in *R v Blastland* [1985] 2 All ER 1095 at 1103–4, HL.

[119] (1875) 13 Cox CC 171, Central Criminal Court. See also *R v Pook* (1871) 13 Cox CC 172n.

[120] [1912] 3 KB 19, CCA.

instrument on a woman in order to procure a miscarriage was that the woman, who had died before the trial, had operated on herself. The Court of Criminal Appeal held that evidence, in support of the defence, that the woman had made a statement some weeks before her miscarriage that she intended to operate on herself (and had said, one week after the miscarriage, that she had done so) had been properly excluded as inadmissible hearsay.[121]

---

[121] But see also the much discussed decision of the United States' Supreme Court in *Mutual Life Insurance Co v Hillman* 145 US 285 (1892).

# 13

# CONFESSIONS

## A ADMISSIBILITY

*Summary of common law*

### 1 THE BACKGROUND

The Police and Criminal Evidence Act 1984 brought about major changes in the law relating to the admissibility of confessions. It will be useful, however, before examining the statutory provisions, to summarize briefly the position at common law. At common law an informal admission (ie an out-of-court statement made by an accused against his interest), was admissible by way of exception to the hearsay rule, as evidence of the truth of its contents, on the basis that what a person says against himself is likely to be true. An informal admission made by an accused person prior to his trial to a person in authority was known as a confession, an expression which included not only a full admission of guilt but also any incriminating statement.[1] A person in authority, generally speaking, was anyone who had authority or control over the accused or over the proceedings or the prosecution against him.[2] In most cases, the person in authority was the police officer investigating the case or interrogating the accused. A confession could not be given in evidence by the prosecution unless shown by them to be a voluntary statement in the sense that it was not obtained from the accused by fear of prejudice or hope of advantage exercised or held out by a person in authority[3] or by oppression.[4] If the admissibility of the confession was in dispute, the issue fell to be determined by the trial judge on a *voir dire* in the absence of the jury. The prosecution bore the legal burden of proving beyond reasonable doubt that the confession was voluntary.[5] If the prosecution failed to discharge this burden, the confession was inadmissible. However, even if satisfied beyond reasonable doubt that it was made voluntarily, the trial judge could exclude it, in the

*An exception to hearsay rule*

---

[1] See per Lord Reid in *Customs and Excise Comrs v Harz and Power* [1967] 1 AC 760 at 817–18.

[2] Per Viscount Dilhorne in *Deokinanan v R* [1969] 1 AC 20, PC at 33.

[3] Per Lord Sumner in *Ibrahim v R* [1914] AC 599, PC at 609. In *DPP v Ping Lin* [1976] AC 574 at 597, Lord Hailsham said: 'the word "exercised" . . . though repeatedly reproduced is, I believe, meaningless and corrupt in the report. I believe that Lord Sumner really said excited . . .'

[4] Per Lord Parker CJ in *Callis v Gunn* [1964] 1 QB 495, DC at 501 and per Edmund Davies LJ in *R v Prager* [1972] 1 WLR 260 at 266, CA.

[5] *R v Thompson* [1893] 2 QB 12, CCR.

exercise of his discretion, on the grounds that (i) its prejudicial effect outweighed its probative value, (ii) it was obtained by improper or unfair means,[6] or (iii) it was obtained in breach of the Judges' Rules.[7]

## 2 CONFESSIONS DEFINED

Section 82(1) of the 1984 Act adopts the inclusive definition of the word recommended by the Criminal Law Revision Committee.[8] It provides that:

In this . . . Act—

'confession' includes any statement wholly or partly adverse to the person who made it, whether made to a person in authority or not and whether made in words or otherwise;

The definition, by making no distinction between a statement wholly or partly adverse to the accused, preserves the effect of Lord Reid's dictum, at common law, in *Customs and Excise Comrs v Harz and Power*,[9] that there is no difference, in relation to admissibility, between a confession and an admission falling short of a full confession.[10] Section 82(1) is wide enough to cover a plea of guilty. Thus if an accused pleads guilty but is subsequently granted leave to change his plea, the first plea may be admitted in evidence at his trial as a confession statement. However, in suitable cases, for example where the accused at the time of entering the first plea was unrepresented or misunderstood the nature of the charge, it would appear that the judge, as at common law, can exclude the evidence in the exercise of his discretion.[11]

Section 82(1) covers 'mixed' statements, that is statements which are both inculpatory and exculpatory in nature.[12] Initially it was thought that the subsection does not cover wholly exculpatory statements which become damaging at trial because by then their contents can be shown to be false or inconsistent with the evidence of the accused.[13] On this view, the prosecution may be allowed to rely on such a statement even though it was obtained in circumstances such that, if it had been adverse to the accused, it would fail to satisfy the statutory conditions of admissibility. In *R v Z*[14] the Court of Appeal took the opposite view, being of the opinion that section 3(1) of the Human Rights Act 1998, whereby primary legislation must be read in a way which is compatible with Convention rights, required it to reconsider the issue. In *Saunders v*

---

[6] See *R v Sang* [1980] AC 402, HL.

[7] Per Lord Goddard CJ in *R v May* (1952) 36 Cr App R 91 at 93 and per Edmund Davies LJ in *R v Prager* [1972] 1 WLR 260 at 265–6, CA.

[8] 11th Report (Cmnd 4991) paras 58 and 66.    [9] [1967] 1 AC 760 at 817–18.

[10] Per Lord Havers in *R v Sharp* [1988] 1 All ER 65, HL at 68.

[11] *R v Rimmer* [1972] 1 WLR 268, CA. See also *R v Hetherington* [1972] Crim LR 703, CA and generally below under **B The discretion to exclude.**

[12] See per Lord Steyn in *R v Aziz* [1995] 3 All ER 149, HL at 155; *R v Sharp* [1988] 1 All ER 65, HL and, generally, Ch 6.

[13] Per Lord Lane CJ, *obiter*, in *R v Sat-Bhambra* (1988) 88 Cr App R 55, CA at 61–2, applied in *R v Park* (1993) 99 Cr App R 270, CA.

[14] [2003] 1 WLR 1489, CA.

*United Kingdom*[15] the European Court of Human Rights said, in the context of evidence obtained under compulsion, that the right not to incriminate oneself cannot reasonably be confined to admissions or directly incriminating statements, but extends to exculpatory remarks or other information later deployed in support of the prosecution case.[16] In *R v Z*, following this approach, it was held that the inclusive definition of 'confession' was a broad one and that, in any event, prima facie whether or not a statement amounts to a confession should be decided at the time when it is sought to give it in evidence. However, the court expressly left open the question whether a statement 'I did not do it' could amount to a confession, thereby leaving open the possibility, for example, that such a statement will not be treated as a confession, notwithstanding the subsequent assertion by the accused, at his trial, that he did commit the offence, but only under duress.[17]

Section 82(1) abolishes the rule at common law that a threat or inducement only operates to exclude a resulting confession if it was made or held out by 'a person in authority'. The meaning of these words gave rise to a number of decisions in which a variety of subtle distinctions were drawn.[18] They need not concern us now. A confession, for the purposes of the Act, can be made to anyone. The assumption is that the risk of an inducement resulting in an untrue confession is similar whether or not the inducement comes from a person in authority. In the words of Viscount Dilhorne in *Deokinanan v R*:[19]

If the ground on which confessions induced by promises held out by persons in authority are held to be admissible is that they may not be true, then it may be that there is a similar risk that in some circumstances the confession may not be true if induced by a promise held out by a person not in authority, for instance if such a person offers a bribe in return for a confession.

The phrase 'whether made in words or otherwise' means that a confession can be made not only in words, whether oral or written, but also by conduct. The Criminal Law Revision Committee gave as an example the accused nodding his head in reply to an accusation.[20] Presumably, as at common law, the accused may also accept the accusation of another, so as to make all or part of it a confession statement of his own, by other conduct, by his demeanour, or even by his silence at the time when the accusation was made. It will be convenient to consider this topic and the common-law authorities in that regard later in this chapter.[21] A confession can also be made otherwise than in words by a re-enactment by the accused of the crime committed. In

---

[15]  (1996) 23 EHRR 313.

[16]  See also *Piché v R* (1970) 11 DLR (3d) 709, Supreme Court of Canada, and per Chief Justice Warren in *Miranda v Arizona* (1975) 384 US 436, US Supreme Court, at 477.

[17]  See further Roderick Munday, 'Adverse Denial and Purposive Confession' [2003] Crim LR 850.

[18]  See earlier editions of this work.

[19]  [1969] 1 AC 20, PC at 33. See also 11th Report, Criminal Law Revision Committee (Cmnd 4991) para 58.

[20]  11th Report (Cmnd 4991) Annex 2 at 214.

[21]  See below under **E Statements made in the presence of the accused**.

*Li Shu-ling v R*[22] the accused, two days after he had confessed to murder by strangulation, agreed to re-enact the crime. He was reminded that he was still under caution and told that he was not obliged to re-enact the crime. The Privy Council held that a video-recording made of the re-enactment, accompanied by a running commentary by the accused explaining his movements, had properly been admitted in evidence as a confession. By way of safeguard, it was held that—

1.  the video film should be made reasonably soon after the oral confession;

2.  the accused should be warned that he need not take part and, if he agrees to take part, should do so voluntarily; and

3.  the video recording should be shown to the accused as soon as practicable after it has been completed so that he has an opportunity to make and have recorded any comments he wishes to make about the film.

It was also acknowledged that there are some crimes which it would be wholly inappropriate to attempt to re-enact on video, such as a killing committed in the course of an affray involving many people.

## 3  THE CONDITIONS OF ADMISSIBILITY

Section 76 of the Police and Criminal Evidence Act 1984 provides that:

(1)  In any proceedings[23] a confession made by an accused person may be given in evidence against him in so far as it is relevant to any matter in issue in the proceedings and is not excluded by the court in pursuance of this section.

(2)  If, in any proceedings where the prosecution proposes to give in evidence a confession made by an accused person, it is represented to the court that the confession was or may have been obtained—
    (a)  by oppression of the person who made it; or
    (b)  in consequence of anything said or done which was likely, in the circumstances existing at the time, to render unreliable any confession which might be made by him in consequence thereof,
    the court shall not allow the confession to be given in evidence against him except in so far as the prosecution proves to the court beyond reasonable doubt that the confession (notwithstanding that it may be true) was not obtained as aforesaid.

(3)  In any proceedings where the prosecution proposes to give in evidence a confession made by an accused person, the court may of its own motion require the prosecution, as a condition of allowing it to do so, to prove that the confession was not obtained as mentioned in subsection (2) above.

Section 76(1) only applies to a confession 'made by an accused'. Thus where there is no dispute that a confession was made, but the identity of the maker is disputed, the

---

[22] [1988] 3 All ER 138, PC.

[23] 'Proceedings' means criminal proceedings, including proceedings in the UK or elsewhere before a court-martial or the Courts-Martial Appeal Court, and proceedings before a Standing Civilian Court: s 82(1).

prosecution must prove that the maker was the accused, although it seems that this may be inferred if the confession contains information about the accused which, even if known by others, is best known by the accused himself. In *R v Ward*[24] the prosecution admitted evidence of an admission by W as to his presence in a particular car on three occasions. On each occasion, an officer had stopped the car and one of the passengers had identified himself as W and given W's correct date of birth and address, but the officer could not identify the passenger as W. It was held, in effect, that it could be inferred from the correct information provided by the passenger that he was W, but that the jury should be given a clear direction that they should only rely on the statement as a confession if they were sure, from the contents of the statement and such surrounding evidence as there was, that W made the statement. Similar reasoning was employed in *Mawdesley v Chief Constable of the Cheshire Constabulary.*[25] M was sent a note of intended prosecution for speeding and a form asking him to provide information under section 172 of the Road Traffic Act 1988 as to the identity of the driver. The form was returned with the number of M's driving licence and his name and address in the relevant boxes, but with the space for his signature left blank. It was held that the form could amount to a confession because it was open to the court to infer from the fact that the notice had been sent to M's address and had been returned bearing the information that it did, that the entries had been made by M.

It has been held that a confession can only be given in evidence, pursuant to section 76(1), by the prosecution,[26] although in *R v Myers*[27] Lord Slynn's view was that this was a question still subject to debate. However, an accused's confession, if it could have been but was not introduced by the prosecution, may be introduced by a co-accused, being admissible at common law as an admission by a party against his interest.[28] In *R v Myers*[29] the House of Lords held that where the prosecution do not seek to admit a confession made by a co-accused, because there have been breaches of the Codes of Practice, another co-accused may elicit evidence of the confession, provided that it is relevant to his defence or undermines the prosecution case against him, either in cross-examination of the officers to whom it was made or by calling them on his behalf. It was suggested, however, that the outcome may be different if the confession has been obtained in the circumstances referred to in section 76(2) of the 1984 Act, on the basis that such a confession is worthless, whoever it is who seeks to rely on it.[30] Further to the recommendation of the Law Commission, the matter is

---

[24] [2001] Crim LR 316, CA.      [25] [2004] 1 WLR 1035, Admin Court.

[26] *R v Beckford; R v Daley* [1991] Crim LR 833, CA, where it was also held that if the co-accused is convicted, the conviction may be set aside as unsafe and unsatisfactory. A conviction will not be set aside where the confession is made not by a co-accused but by a third party who could have been called by the defence: *R v Callan* (1993) 98 Cr App R 467, CA.

[27] [1998] AC 124, HL.      [28] *R v Campbell and Williams* [1993] Crim LR 448, CA.

[29] [1998] AC 124.

[30] It was also noted that there is no discretion to exclude, at the request of one co-accused, evidence tendered by another (see *Lobban v R* [1995] 2 All ER 602, PC, Ch 2), although Lord Hope did not wish to be taken as being of the view that a request by a co-accused to introduce evidence of a confession obtained in

now governed by statute. Under section 76A of the 1984 Act, a section inserted by section 128(1) of the Criminal Justice Act 2003, confessions may be given in evidence for a co-accused, and the conditions of admissibility are the same as those which apply in the case of confessions adduced on behalf of the prosecution, except that the co-accused need only prove that the confession was not obtained by oppression or 'in consequence of anything said or done . . .' on the balance of probabilities. Section 76A provides as follows.

(1) In any proceedings a confession made by an accused person may be given in evidence for another person charged in the same proceedings (a co-accused) in so far as it is relevant to any matter in issue in the proceedings and is not excluded by the court in pursuance of this section.

(2) If, in any proceedings where a co-accused proposes to give in evidence a confession made by an accused person, it is represented to the court that the confession was or may have been obtained—
   (a) by oppression of the person who made it; or
   (b) in consequence of anything said or done which was likely, in the circumstances existing at the time, to render unreliable any confession which might be made by him in consequence thereof,
   the court shall not allow the confession to be given in evidence for the co-accused except in so far as it is proved to the court on the balance of probabilities that the confession (notwithstanding that it may be true) was not so obtained.

(3) Before allowing a confession made by an accused person to be given in evidence for a co-accused in any proceedings, the court may of its own motion require the fact that the confession was not obtained as mentioned in subsection (2) above to be proved in the proceedings on the balance of probabilities.

A confession admitted in evidence under section 76 or section 76A is admitted as evidence of the matters stated. At common law, an admissible confession was sufficient to warrant a conviction even in the absence of other evidence implicating the accused.[31] However, where a conviction was based on a confession which was equivocal or otherwise of poor quality, it could be quashed on appeal.[32] Similar principles should operate, it is submitted, in the case of confessions admitted under section 76 and section 76A.[33]

Under section 76(2) (and section 76A(2)) the defence may raise the question of admissibility merely by representing to the court, without adducing any evidence in support of such a representation, that the confession was or may have been obtained by the methods described in that subsection. However, even if the defence has not

breach of a Code should be acceded to in all circumstances ([1997] 4 All ER 314 at 333–4). See also *R v Lawless* [2003] All ER (D) 183 (Feb), CA.

[31] See *R v Sullivan* (1887) 16 Cox CC 347 and *R v Mallinson* [1977] Crim LR 161, CA and contrast per Cave J in *R v Thompson* [1893] 2 QB 12.

[32] See *R v Barker* (1915) 11 Cr App R 191; *R v Schofield* (1917) 12 Cr App R 191; and *R v Pattinson* (1973) 58 Cr App R 417, CA.

[33] See also, in the case of confessions by mentally handicapped persons, s 77 (see Ch 8).

raised the question, the court of its own motion may require the prosecution to prove that the confession was not obtained by the methods described, in exercise of the power conferred on it by section 76(3) (and section 76A(3)). In either event, the question will then be determined in the absence of the jury on a *voir dire* at which the prosecution will bear the burden of proving beyond reasonable doubt (or the co-accused will bear the burden of proving on a balance of probabilities) that the conditions of admissibility have been satisfied. If this burden is not discharged, the court has no *inclusionary* discretion, but *shall not* allow the confession to be given in evidence, even if satisfied that its contents are true.

Although the Police and Criminal Evidence Act 1984 and the Codes of Practice issued thereunder contain a wide variety of provisions regulating, inter alia, the arrest, detention, treatment and questioning of suspects, the fact that a confession was obtained in breach of the Act or Codes will not necessarily mean that it was obtained by the methods described in section 76(2) (and section 76A(2)).[34] However, evidence of non-compliance with the Act or Codes, either alone or together with other evidence, may show that the confession was obtained by such methods or, failing that, in a case in which the *prosecution* proposes to adduce evidence of the confession, ie under section 76, may nonetheless result in the confession being excluded by the court in the exercise of its discretion. In this context it remains to note that, under section 67(11) of the Act, the Codes are admissible in evidence and that if any provision of the Codes appears to the court to be relevant to any question arising in the proceedings, it shall be taken into account in determining that question.

## 4  OPPRESSION

Under section 76(2)(a) (and section 76A(2)), a confession, in order to be admissible, must not have been obtained by oppression. Broadly speaking, this reflects the views of both the Criminal Law Revision Committee[35] and the Royal Commission on Criminal Procedure[36] that a confession obtained by oppression of a suspect should be automatically excluded in view of society's abhorrence of the use of such methods during interrogation. Before considering the meaning of 'oppression', four matters of a general nature may be noted. First, a confession obtained by oppression will be excluded whether or not it is unreliable and notwithstanding that it may be true. Secondly, the confession must not have been 'obtained by' oppression: there must be a causal link. Thus a confession will not be excluded under section 76(2)(a) where the accused confessed *before* he was subjected to some form of oppression. Equally, there will be

[34] Some of the more important provisions of the Act and Codes are considered below under **B The discretion to exclude.**

[35] 11th Report (Cmnd 4991) para 60. The Committee proposed, as the ground of inadmissibility in this respect, 'oppressive treatment of the accused', in the expectation that such an expression would be construed as in the case of *R v Prager* [1972] 1 WLR 260, CA, which is considered below.

[36] (Cmnd 8092) para 4.132. The Commission proposed exclusion on this ground only if the confession was obtained from the suspect by torture, violence, the threat of violence or inhuman or degrading treatment.

no causal link between an interview not complying with the 1984 Act and a subsequent confession freely and voluntarily made.[37] Thirdly, although section 76(2) refers to oppression 'of the person who made it (the confession)', ie the accused, in appropriate circumstances the oppression of another could also amount to oppression of the accused (or constitute conduct likely to render unreliable any confession which might be made by him for the purposes of section 76(2)(b)). Fourthly, it would appear that a confession excluded under section 76(2)(a) will, in most if not all cases, also fall to be excluded under section 76(2)(b). It is difficult to envisage a case in which, the confession having been obtained by oppression, it was not made in consequence of anything said or done which was likely, in the then existing circumstances, to have rendered unreliable any confession which might have been made in consequence thereof.

Concerning the meaning of oppression, although, as we shall see, it is an exercise of only limited value, it is convenient to examine first the way in which the word was defined at common law. Prior to the 1984 Act, oppression was taken to mean 'something which tends to sap and has sapped that free will which must exist before a confession is voluntary'[38] or, in the context of interrogation, 'questioning which by its nature, duration or other attendant circumstances (including the fact of custody) excites hopes (such as the hope of release) or fears, or so affects the mind of the suspect that his will crumbles and he speaks when otherwise he would have stayed silent'.[39] Whether or not there was oppression in any particular case involved a consideration of a wide variety of factors, including the length of time of any period of questioning, whether the accused had been given proper refreshment, and the characteristics of the accused in question. This last factor was of particular relevance: what might have been oppressive in the case of a child, an invalid, an old man or someone inexperienced in the ways of the world[40] might not have been oppressive in the case of a person of a tough character or a professional criminal.[41]

Returning to the Act, section 76(8) (and section 76A(7)) defines 'oppression' as including 'torture, inhuman or degrading treatment, and the use or threat of violence (whether or not amounting to torture)'. The phrase 'torture or inhuman or degrading treatment' derives from Article 3 of the European Convention on Human Rights and

---

[37] *R v Parker* [1995] Crim LR 233, CA.

[38] Per Sachs J in *R v Priestley* (1965) 51 Cr App R 1n at 1–2; applied in *R v Prager* [1972] 1 WLR 260, CA.

[39] Lord MacDermott in an address to the Bentham Club (1968) 21 CLP 10.

[40] See, eg, *R v Westlake* [1979] Crim LR 652, CC in which a 30-year-old with a mental age of 11 or 12 was charged with attempted murder. He was in custody for over 24 hours before being interviewed, kept in custody for the next five days and interrogated for a total of over 26 hours, much of the questioning being in the form of cross-examination, suggesting the answers. He was kept for three days before being allowed to see anyone other than the police. It was ruled that the prosecution had failed to prove that confessions made were not obtained by oppression. Cf *R v Rennie* [1982] 1 All ER 385, CA and *R v Miller* [1986] 3 All ER 119, CA. See also *R v Hudson* (1980) 72 Cr App R 163, CA and *R v Allerton* [1979] Crim LR 725, CC.

[41] See, eg, *R v Dodd* (1981) 74 Cr App R 50 in which the accused, experienced criminals charged with robbery offences, were held incommunicado for four days as a result of a deliberate policy decision by the police. The Court of Appeal was satisfied that confessions made by them had not been obtained by oppression. Cf *R v Gowan* [1982] Crim LR 821, CA.

it may be that the English courts will be guided by the decisions of the European Court of Human Rights and the European Commission of Human Rights. In the *Greek Case*,[42] for example, the Commission defined 'degrading treatment' as that which grossly humiliates a person before others or drives a person to act against his will or conscience. Concerning the meaning of 'torture', assistance may be derived from the way in which the offence of torture is defined in section 134 of the Criminal Justice Act 1988.[43] The inclusive nature of the definition in section 76(8) indicates that the varieties of oppression it contains do not constitute a comprehensive list.

There was no reference to section 76(8) in *R v Fulling*,[44] the first case to come before the Court of Appeal on the meaning of oppression for the purposes of the 1984 Act. The appellant, Ruth Fulling, was convicted of obtaining property by deception. After her arrest she was taken into custody and interviewed twice on that day and once on the following day. Despite persistent questioning, she exercised her right to remain silent, but after a break in the interview on the second day, she made a confession. According to her evidence on the *voir dire*, she made the confession because during the break in that interview one of the officers told her that for the last three years her lover had been having an affair with another woman who was presently in the cell next to hers. The appellant said that these revelations so distressed her that she could not stand being in the cells any longer and thought that by making a statement she would be released. The police denied that they had made the revelations suggested. The defence submitted that the confession was or may have been obtained by oppression. The judge ruled that, even on the assumption that the accused's version of events was the true one, there was no oppression because oppression meant something above and beyond that which is inherently oppressive in police custody and must import some oppression actively applied in an improper manner by the police.

The Court of Appeal upheld this ruling and dismissed the appeal. It was held, applying the principles set out in *Bank of England v Vagliano Bros*,[45] that since the 1984 Act was a codifying Act, rather than a consolidating Act or an Act declaratory of the common law, the court should give to the words used in it their natural meaning, uninfluenced by any considerations derived from the previous state of the law. Accordingly, the word 'oppression' was given its ordinary dictionary definition,

---

[42] (1969) 12 Yearbook 1, EComHR at 186. See also *Ireland v United Kingdom* (1978) 2 EHRR 25, para 167 (torture and inhuman treatment) and *Campbell and Cosans v United Kingdom* (1982) 4 EHRR 293. Assistance may also be derived from the decisions under s 8(2) of the Northern Ireland (Emergency Provisions) Act 1978, whereby a confession to certain terrorist offences is excluded unless the prosecution proves that it was not obtained by subjecting the accused 'to torture or to inhuman or degrading treatment . . .' See also the definition of 'torture' contained in Art 1 of the Draft United Nations Convention against Torture and Other Cruel, Inhuman or Degrading Treatment or Punishment.

[43] The intentional infliction by act or omission of severe physical or mental pain or suffering by (a) a public official, or a person acting in an official capacity, in the performance or purported performance of his official duties, or (b) by some other person at the instigation or with the consent or acquiescence of a public official, or person acting in an official capacity, performing or purporting to perform his official duties when he instigates the commission of the offence or consents to or acquiesces in it.

[44] [1987] 2 All ER 65, CA.          [45] [1891] AC 107 at 144–5, HL.

namely, 'exercise of authority or power in a burdensome, harsh or wrongful[46] manner; unjust or cruel treatment of subjects, inferiors, etc; the imposition of unreasonable or unjust burdens'. Lord Lane CJ, delivering the judgment of the court, pointed out that, according to one of the quotations given in the *Oxford English Dictionary*, 'There is not a word in our language which expresses more detestable wickedness than *oppression*.' His Lordship found it hard to envisage any circumstances in which oppression thus defined would not entail some impropriety on the part of the interrogator. It was held that although section 76(2)(b) is wide enough to cover some of the circumstances which were embraced by the 'artificially wide' definition of oppression at common law, and although a confession may be excluded, under section 76(2)(b), where there is no suspicion of impropriety, the remarks alleged to have been made by the officer were not likely to have made unreliable any confession which the appellant might have made.

The decision in *R v Fulling* calls for comment in a number of respects. First, it may be noted that the first two parts of the definition of oppression given would appear to apply only in the case of someone vested with some authority, power, or control over the accused, someone akin to a person who, at common law, would have been regarded as a 'person in authority'. Secondly, concerning impropriety, the decision, although not explicit on the point, suggests strongly that it must be deliberate or intentional. This would accord with the former decision at common law in *R v Miller*,[47] in which it was held that although it could amount to oppression if questions, addressed to a suspect suffering from paranoid schizophrenia, were skilfully and deliberately asked with the intention of triggering off hallucinations and flights of fancy, the mere fact that questions put to such a suspect did produce such a disordered state of mind would not, by itself, be indicative of oppression. Thirdly, however, although oppression normally requires deliberate impropriety, not all deliberate impropriety amounts to oppression. Sometimes it will be a question of degree. Thus if an interrogator is rude and discourteous, raising his voice and using bad language, this does not constitute oppression;[48] but bullying and hectoring by officers adopting a highly hostile and intimidatory approach will amount to oppression,[49] as will a deliberate misstatement of the evidence in order to pressurize the suspect.[50] Trickery, per se, will not necessarily constitute oppression. Thus it does not amount to oppression to make a covert tape-recording of an incriminating conversation between two suspects sharing a police cell.[51]

---

[46] The word 'wrongful' should be understood in the context of the rest of the definition, particularly the words which precede and follow it, otherwise any breach of the Code, which might be said to be 'wrongful', could be said to amount to oppression, which clearly is not so: *R v Parker* [1995] Crim LR 233, CA.

[47] [1986] 3 All ER 119, CA.

[48] *R v Emmerson* (1990) 92 Cr App R 284, CA. See also *R v Heaton* [1993] Crim LR 593, CA.

[49] *R v Paris* (1992) 97 Cr App R 99, CA, where the accused, who was of limited intelligence, had denied his involvement over 300 times. But see also *R v L* [1994] Crim LR 839, CA, a decision under s 76(2)(b), in which although similar methods were employed, *R v Paris* was distinguished on the grounds, inter alia, that L was of normal intelligence and the length of the interviews not excessive.

[50] *R v Beales* [1991] Crim LR 118, CC.        [51] *R v Parker* [1995] Crim LR 233, CA.

Fourthly, it seems clear that, as at common law, regard should be had to the personal characteristics of the accused, which may be of critical relevance in deciding not only whether the confession was *obtained* by oppression, but also whether particular conduct was 'burdensome', 'harsh' or 'cruel'. Thus account may be taken of the fact that the suspect is, for example, intelligent, sophisticated and an experienced professional person,[52] or a person of below normal intelligence on the borderline of mental handicap.[53] The will of a particular suspect may be so affected by oppression in an interview that a confession made in a subsequent but properly conducted interview should be excluded.[54]

A final matter concerns the relevance of the common-law authorities to section 76(2)(b). Paragraph (b) is considered wide enough to cover only *some* of the circumstances embraced by the common-law definition of oppression. The facts of *R v Fulling* itself are instructive in this regard because, although at common law a strong argument could have been advanced to the effect that in all the circumstances of the case what the officer said, assuming that he did in fact say it, had sapped the free will of the accused or so affected her mind that her will crumbled and she spoke when otherwise she would have remained silent, the court was satisfied that, for the purposes of section 76(2)(b), what was said was not likely, in the circumstances, to have rendered unreliable any confession which she might have made in consequence.

## 5  UNRELIABILITY

### (a)  The background

Section 76(2)(b) in large measure reflects the recommendations of the Criminal Law Revision Committee.[55] In order to appreciate the significance of the reliability test, it will be useful to summarize the Committee's reasons for changing the rules at common law. At common law, as we have seen, the fundamental condition of the admissibility of a confession was that it should have been made voluntarily. Two reasons have been given for that rule: the first, the reliability principle, is that an involuntary confession may not be reliable because an accused subjected to threats, inducements or oppression may 'confess' falsely; the second, the disciplinary principle, is that the police must be discouraged from using improper methods to obtain a

---

[52] *R v Seelig* [1991] 4 All ER 429, CA at 439, where it was held not to be oppressive for DTI inspectors conducting an investigation of a company's affairs, to question such a person, notwithstanding that (a) in conformity with normal practice, no caution was given and (b) refusal to answer such questions can result in committal for contempt under s 436 of the Companies Act 1985. It was also held that the confession made did not fall to be excluded under s 76(2)(b) or s 78. Concerning s 78, it was held that although the accused were subject to an inquisitorial process and therefore worse placed than the average man questioned as to crime, a fundamental countervailing consideration was the fact that the legislature had deliberately decided that they should be treated less favourably than the average man.

[53] *R v Paris* (1992) 97 Cr App R 99, CA.

[54] See *R v Ismail* (1990) 92 Cr App R 92, CA and cf *Y v DPP* [1991] Crim LR 917, DC.

[55] 11th Report (Cmnd 4991) paras 53–69. The government rejected the proposals relating to confessions made by The Royal Commission on Criminal Procedure (Cmnd 8092).

confession by being deprived of the advantage of the confession for the purposes of obtaining a conviction. A majority of the Committee was in favour of accepting the mixture of these two principles as the basis of the law. However, although they were also in favour of preserving the law in general, they proposed a relaxation of the strict rule that any threat or inducement, however mild or slight, should render inadmissible any resulting confession. In *R v Northam*[56] the accused, while on bail in respect of charges of housebreaking, was questioned by the police about another housebreaking. Before confessing to the latter offence, the accused had asked an officer whether, instead of being tried for it separately, it could be taken into consideration at his forthcoming trial, and the officer said the police would have no objection. In the event, however, he was tried separately for the other offence and convicted of it, but the Court of Appeal, albeit reluctantly, quashed the conviction on the grounds that the confession had been obtained by an inducement. The decision was followed in *R v Zaveckas*.[57] The accused was convicted of larceny. At the trial, evidence was given of a confession made after he had asked an officer 'If I make a statement, will I be given bail now?' and had received an answer in the affirmative. The Court of Appeal, with some regret, quashed the conviction on the grounds that the confession should have been excluded as it followed upon an inducement. Other cases where it was held that a confession should have been excluded because of a threat or inducement of a comparatively mild or slight kind, include *R v Smith*,[58] where, a soldier having been stabbed in a fight, a sergeant-major had paraded the company and threatened to keep them on parade until he learnt who was responsible, and *R v Cleary*,[59] where, during interrogation of the accused concerning an alleged murder, the accused's father, in the presence of the police, had made a statement to the accused, which was held to be capable of being an inducement, in the following terms: 'Put your cards on the table. Tell them the lot . . . If you did not hit him, they cannot hang you.' Cases such as these, in the opinion of the Committee, showed that the common-law rule was too strict. Accordingly, cases of oppression apart, they recommended that a confession should only be rendered inadmissible if made as a result of a threat or inducement of a kind likely to produce an unreliable confession.

### (b) The test

The word 'unreliable' is the keynote to section 76(2)(b) (and section 76A(2)(b)). It is not defined in the Act, but means 'cannot be relied upon as being the truth'.[60] Section 76(2)(b), by its express incorporation of the reliability principle, offers less scope for exclusion than existed at common law. However, it offers greater scope for exclusion than would have been the case under clause 2(2)(b) of the draft Bill annexed to the 11th report of the Criminal Law Revision Committee because although it closely

---

[56] (1967) 52 Cr App R 97.      [57] (1970) 54 Cr App R 202.

[58] [1959] 2 QB 35, C-MAC. The conviction was upheld because the accused made another admissible confession: see below.

[59] (1963) 48 Cr App R 116, CCA.

[60] Per Stuart-Smith LJ in *R v Crampton* (1990) 92 Cr App R 369 at 372, CA.

resembles the clause, it is different in one significant respect: the phrase 'anything said or done' has been substituted for 'any threat or inducement'.[61]

In reaching a decision under section 76(2)(b), a trial judge must examine all the relevant circumstances of the interrogation, both before and after what was 'said' or 'done', and take into account the nature and effect of what was said or done, the seriousness of the offence in question and, if necessary, the terms of the confession, which may throw light on the facts concerning the interrogation.[62] The test of reliability is hypothetical: it applies not to the confession made by the accused, but to 'any confession which might be made by him'.[63] However, as Mance LJ said in *Re Proulx*, the test cannot be satisfied by postulating some entirely different confession:[64]

> The word 'any' must ... be understood as indicating 'any such', or 'such a', confession as the applicant made. The abstract element involved also reflects the fact that the test is not whether the actual confession was untruthful or inaccurate. It is whether whatever was said or done was, in the circumstances existing as at the time of the confession, *likely* to have rendered such a confession unreliable, whether or not it may be seen subsequently (with hindsight and in the light of all the material available at trial) that it did or did not actually do so.

The phrase 'anything said or done' has been given a wide interpretation. It includes omissions to say, or do, certain things.[65] It is not restricted to things said or done by persons in authority. However, advice properly given to the accused by his solicitor will not normally provide a basis for excluding a subsequent confession, even when, as it sometimes ought to be, it is robust and, for example, points to the advantages which may derive from an acceptance of guilt or the corresponding disadvantages of a 'no comment' interview, but it may do so in the case of a particularly vulnerable accused.[66]

The phrase 'anything said or done' requires something external to the accused which was likely to have some influence on him. Thus a confession cannot be excluded on the basis that it may have been obtained in consequence of anything said or done by the accused himself which was likely to render unreliable any confession which he might have made in consequence thereof. An example is *R v Wahab*,[67] where W instructed his solicitor to approach the police to see if members of his family might be released from custody if he admitted his guilt, but was uninfluenced by anything said or done by anyone else. In *R v Goldenberg*[68] the suspect, a heroin addict, while in police custody, requested an interview. The admissions he made were alleged by the

---

[61] See *R v Harvey* [1988] Crim LR 241, CC, below.     [62] (Cmnd 4991) para 65.

[63] *R v Barry* (1991) 95 Cr App R 384, CA. The test is objective, but all the circumstances should be taken into account, including those affecting the accused, including his desires etc: ibid.

[64] [2001] 1 All ER 57, DC at [46]. But see also *R v Cox* [1991] Crim LR 276, CA, *R v Crampton* (1990) 92 Cr App R 369 at 372, CA and *R v Kenny* [1994] Crim LR 284, CA.

[65] See, eg, *R v Doolan* [1988] Crim LR 747, CA: failure to caution, to keep a proper record of the interview and to show that record to the suspect.

[66] *R v Wahab* [2003] 1 Cr App R 232, CA at [42].     [67] Ibid.

[68] (1988) 88 Cr App R 285, CA.

defence to be an attempt by him to obtain bail and to be released in order to feed his addiction. It was held that the case fell outside section 76(2)(b). In *R v Crampton*[69] a heroin addict made admissions at interviews in the police station after he had been undergoing withdrawal symptoms. It was sought to distinguish *R v Goldenberg* on the grounds that the interviews held were not at the request of the accused, but conducted by the police at their own convenience. The Court of Appeal, however, doubted whether the mere holding of an interview, at a time when the suspect is undergoing withdrawal symptoms, is something 'done' under section 76(2), the wording of which seemed to postulate some 'words spoken' or 'acts done'.

Section 76(2)(b), by imposing on the prosecution the burden of proving that the confession was not obtained 'in consequence' of anything said or done, clearly requires a causal connection between what was said or done and the confession made. This reflects the position at common law. In *DPP v Ping Lin*[70] the accused, suspected of a drugs offence, attempted to make a deal with the police whereby they would release him and in return he would disclose the name of his supplier. When told that this could not be done, he admitted that he had been dealing in heroin but made two more attempts to effect some sort of bargain. An officer then said: 'If you show the judge that you have helped the police to trace bigger drug people, I am sure he will bear it in mind when he sentences you.' Subsequently, the accused disclosed the name of his supplier. The House of Lords held that the accused's statements were voluntary because there was no question of any threat or inducement being held out to him *before* he confessed. The accused may have hoped to obtain immunity or lenience, but that hope was entirely self-generated. Similarly, in *R v Tyrer*,[71] a decision under section 76(2)(b) in which the trial judge ruled that things were said and done which were likely to render a partial confession unreliable, the prosecution satisfied him that it was not obtained in consequence of what was said or done and it was therefore ruled admissible. In *R v Weeks*[72] the trial judge was satisfied of the same matter on the basis of the evidence and demeanour of the accused on the *voir dire*—he came across as a very astute young man who had previous experience of being interviewed at a police station.

In *R v Rennie*,[73] a common-law authority, the accused was convicted of conspiracy to obtain a pecuniary advantage by deception. The co-accused, his sister, had pleaded guilty to obtaining a pecuniary advantage by deception and a charge of conspiring with her brother was allowed to lie on the file. After his arrest, the accused at first denied any part in the offence but when a detective sergeant revealed the strength of the evidence known to him and asked 'This was a joint operation by your family to defraud the bank, wasn't it?', the accused replied, 'No, don't bring the rest of the family into this, I admit it was my fault.' On the *voir dire*, the detective sergeant denied that he had told the accused that he would involve other members of his family but

---

[69] (1990) 92 Cr App R 369, CA.          [70] [1976] AC 574, HL.
[71] (1989) 90 Cr App R 446 at 449, CA.          [72] [1995] Crim LR 52, CA.
[73] [1982] 1 WLR 64, CA.

admitted that the accused was frightened of this happening. He said 'I think he made the confession in the hope that I would terminate my inquiries into members of his family . . .'. The judge ruled that the evidence was admissible. The Court of Appeal, observing that the evidence as to the motives of the accused should not have been admitted, because the drawing of inferences was a matter for the judge and not witnesses, nonetheless acted on the assumption that the accused confessed because he hoped that inquiries would cease into the part played by his family, and posed the following question:[74]

How is this principle[75] to be applied where a prisoner, when deciding to confess, not only realizes the strength of the evidence known to the police and the hopelessness of escaping conviction but is conscious at the same time of the fact that it may well be advantageous to him or . . . to someone close to him, if he confesses? How, in particular, is the judge to approach the question when these different thoughts may all, to some extent at least, have been prompted by something said by the police officer questioning him?

The answer, it was held, was not to be found from any refined analysis of the concept of causation. The judge should approach the question much as would jurors if it were for them, understanding the principle and the spirit behind it and applying common sense. Dismissing the appeal on the grounds that the approach of the trial judge had been flawless, Lord Lane CJ said:[76]

Very few confessions are inspired solely by remorse. Often the motives of an accused are mixed and include a hope that an early admission may lead to an earlier release or a lighter sentence. If it were the law that the mere presence of such a motive, even if prompted by something said or done by a person in authority, led inexorably to the exclusion of a confession, nearly every confession would be rendered inadmissible. This is not the law. In some cases the hope may be self-generated. If so, it is irrelevant, even if it provides the dominant motive for making the confession. In such a case the confession will not have been obtained by anything said or done by a person in authority. More commonly the presence of such a hope will, in part at least, owe its origin to something said or done by such a person. There can be few prisoners who are being firmly but fairly questioned in a police station to whom it does not occur that they might be able to bring both their interrogation and their detention to an earlier end by confession.

This dictum was approved and applied in *R v Crampton*,[77] a decision under section 76(2)(b): the mere fact that the accused had been undergoing withdrawal symptoms and may have had a motive for making a confession did not mean that the confession was necessarily unreliable.

The question of causation poses particular problems when a confession made at an improperly conducted interview is repeated at a subsequent but properly conducted interview. In *R v McGovern*[78] it was held that a confession made in an interview in

---

[74] [1982] 1 WLR 64 at 70.    [75] Ie the common-law principle of voluntariness.

[76] [1982] 1 WLR 64 at 69.

[77] (1990) 92 Cr App R 369, CA. See also *R v Wahab* [2003] 1 Cr App R 232, CA at [44]–[45].

[78] (1990) 92 Cr App R 228, CA.

consequence of an improper denial of access to a solicitor was likely to be unreliable and should have been excluded. It was also held that a confession made in a properly conducted second interview on the following day was also inadmissible because the first interview tainted the second and the very fact that the suspect had already made a confession was likely to have had an effect on her in the second interview.[79]

The physical condition and mental characteristics of the accused are a part of the 'circumstances existing at the time' for the purposes of section 76(2)(b). Thus, in *R v Everett*[80] it was held that these circumstances obviously included the mental condition of a 42-year-old with a mental age of 8, and the material consideration was not what the police thought about his mental condition, but the nature of that condition itself. Similarly, in *R v McGovern*[81] it was held that the particular vulnerability and physical condition of the suspect at the time of her interview—she was borderline mentally subnormal, six months pregnant, and in a highly emotional state—formed the background for the submission that her confession should be excluded. However, the mental characteristics which may have a bearing on the question of reliability are not confined to cases of 'mental impairment' or 'impairment of intelligence or social functioning': any mental or personality abnormalities may be of relevance.[82]

The judge must consider the likely effect of what was 'said or done' on the mind of the particular accused. Thus it may be that in some cases the things said or done may be unjustified, improper, illegal, or in breach of the Act or Codes of Practice yet not of a kind likely to render unreliable any confession which might be made by an accused who, for the sake of argument, is an experienced professional criminal with a tough character or who is otherwise capable of coping with even a vigorous interrogation.[83] In *R v Alladice*,[84] for example, it was held that although the accused, who was charged with robbery of £29,000 in cash, had been refused access to a solicitor in contravention of section 58 of the 1984 Act,[85] and this was relevant to the question of whether to exclude his confession under section 76(2)(b), it was not only doubtful whether the confession had been obtained as a result of the refusal of access, but in all the circumstances there was no reason to believe that that refusal was likely to render unreliable any confession which the accused might have made. The circumstances showed that the police had acted with propriety, apart from the breach of section 58, and that the accused was well able to cope with the interviews, understood the cautions that he had been given, at times exercising his right to silence, and was aware of his rights so that, had the solicitor been present, his advice would have added nothing to the knowledge of his rights which the accused already had.[86] On the other hand, it is easy to imagine

---

[79] See also *R v Blake* [1991] Crim LR 119, CC; and cf *R v Ismail* (1990) 92 Cr App R 92, CA.
[80] [1988] Crim LR 826, CA.          [81] (1990) 92 Cr App R 228, CA.
[82] *R v Walker* [1998] Crim LR 211, CA.
[83] In *R v Gowan* [1982] Crim LR 821, CA, O'Connor LJ, although not sanctioning improper or unfair questioning on the part of the police, said: 'serious and experienced professional criminals . . . must, and do, expect that their interrogation by trained and experienced police officers will be vigorous.'
[84] (1988) 87 Cr App R 380, CA.          [85] See below.
[86] For these reasons it was also held that the confession should not be excluded under s 78 (see Ch 3).

cases where, although it would be impossible to criticize the propriety of what was 'said or done', any confession which might be made by the accused would be likely to be unreliable in all the circumstances because the accused is, for example, of previous good character and highly suggestible, easily intimidated, of very low intelligence or mentally handicapped.[87] In *R v Harvey*[88] the accused, a woman of low intelligence suffering from a psychopathic disorder, was charged with murder. Her confession was excluded under section 76(2)(b) on the grounds that it may have been obtained as a result of hearing a confession made by her lover. There was psychiatric evidence that her state of mind at the relevant time could have been such that, on hearing her lover's confession, she confessed to protect the lover in a child-like attempt to try to take the blame. It may be noted that there was no threat or inducement; there was no impropriety or illegality; what was said (done) was not said (done) by a person in authority; and the crucial factor, in deciding whether what was said was likely to render unreliable any confession which she might have made, was her own state of mind.[89]

In some cases, of course, the confession will be excluded on the basis of *both* unjustified police behaviour *and* the personal nature and characteristics of the accused. *R v Delaney*[90] was a case of indecent assault on a girl aged three. The whole basis of the prosecution case was an admission made by the accused at the very end of a one-and-a-half hour interview which, until that point in time, had consisted of a series of denials. The police, in breach of the Codes of Practice, had failed to make a contemporaneous note of the interview, thereby depriving the court of the most cogent evidence as to what did induce the confession. Moreover, there was evidence from a psychologist that the accused, who was aged 17, was educationally subnormal, of low IQ, and poorly equipped to cope with sustained interrogation. The Court of Appeal held that, had the trial judge paid proper attention to this combination of factors, he would and should have excluded the confession. The Court of Appeal reached a similar conclusion in *R v Moss*.[91] The suspect, who was on the borderline of mental handicap, was kept in custody for nine days, interviewed nine times without an independent person being present, and improperly refused access to a solicitor.

It is clear from cases such as *R v Fulling*[92] and *R v Harvey*[93] that a confession may be excluded under section 76(2)(b) if there is not even a suspicion of impropriety. Equally, as we have seen, confessions obtained as a result of even serious breaches of the provisions of the 1984 Act and the Codes of Practice will not necessarily result in exclusion. Nonetheless, exclusion in many of the reported cases has been based wholly

---

[87] See generally Gisli Gudjohnsson *The Psychology of Interrogations, Confessions and Testimony* (London 1992). In the case of confessions by mentally handicapped persons, see also s 77 (Ch 8).

[88] [1988] Crim LR 241, CC.

[89] See also *R v Sat-Bhambra* (1988) 88 Cr App R 55, CA, where evidence of a confession was excluded on the basis that the accused may have been affected at the time by valium given to him by the police doctor to calm his nerves.

[90] (1988) 88 Cr App R 338, CA. See also *R v Waters* [1989] Crim LR 62, CA.

[91] (1990) 91 Cr App R 371, CA.        [92] [1987] 2 All ER 65, CA, above.

[93] [1988] Crim LR 241, CC, above.

or mainly on such breaches, including the following: failure to caution, to keep a proper record of the interview or to show it to the suspect;[94] an offer of bail and numerous breaches of Code C, including a failure to keep a proper record of the interviews held;[95] questioning before allowing access to a solicitor, failure to record the admissions immediately and failure to show the note of the interview to the suspect;[96] asking a question after the suspect has been charged which is not for the purpose of clearing up an ambiguity;[97] and conducting an interview with a juvenile without an 'appropriate adult',[98] the adult present having a low IQ, being virtually illiterate and probably incapable of appreciating the gravity of the juvenile's situation[99] or being a person with whom the juvenile has no empathy (her estranged father whom she did not wish to attend).[100]

## 6 SECTION 105 OF THE TAXES MANAGEMENT ACT 1970

Concerning the admissibility of confessions in any criminal proceedings against a person for any form of fraudulent conduct in relation to tax, section 76 of the 1984 Act must be read in conjunction with section 105 of the Taxes Management Act 1970, which operates in such proceedings to prevent the exclusion of statements made or documents produced in so-called 'Hansard interviews', ie interviews at which the accused is informed of the practice of the Inland Revenue to take into account the cooperation of the taxpayer in deciding whether to bring any prosecution for fraud.[101] The precursor to section 105[102] was introduced to reverse the decision in *R v Barker*.[103] Section 105(1) is in the following terms:

Statements made or documents produced by or on behalf of a person shall not be inadmissible . . . by reason only that it has been drawn to his attention that—
  (a) pecuniary settlements may be accepted instead of a penalty being determined, or proceedings being instituted, in relation to any tax,
  (b) though no undertaking can be given as to whether or not the Board will accept such a settlement in the case of any particular person, it is the practice of the Board to be influenced by the fact that a person has made a full confession of any fraudulent conduct to which he has been a party and has given full facilities for investigation,

---

[94] See paras 10, 11.7 and 11.1, Code C and *R v Doolan* [1988] Crim LR 747, CA.

[95] *R v Barry* (1991) 95 Cr App R 384, CA.

[96] See s 58(4) of the 1984 Act, paras 11.7 and 11.11, Code C and *R v Chung* (1990) 92 Cr App R 314, CA.

[97] See para 16.5, Code C and *R v Waters* [1989] Crim LR 62, CA.

[98] See para 11.15, Code C.      [99] See *R v Morse* [1991] Crim LR 195.

[100] See *DPP v Blake* (1989) 89 Cr App R 179, DC, now reflected in Note 1B, Code C; and cf *R v Jefferson* [1994] 1 All ER 270, CA: robust interventions by a father, sometimes joining in the questioning of his son and challenging his exculpatory account of certain incidents, were not such as to render unreliable any confession made as a result. See generally Jacqueline Hodgson 'Vulnerable Suspects and the Appropriate Adult' [1997] Crim LR 785.

[101] Section 105 also applies to any proceedings for the recovery of any tax due from him and any proceedings for a penalty: s 105(2).

[102] Section 34 of the Finance Act 1942.      [103] [1941] 2 KB 381.

and that he was or may have been induced thereby to make the statements or produce the documents.

Section 105 does not prevent reliance upon section 78 of the 1984 Act where the interview has been conducted in breach of Code C, but it is relevant to exercise of the discretion under section 78 that Parliament expected statements made at Hansard interviews to be admissible in evidence.[104]

# B THE DISCRETION TO EXCLUDE

If the prosecution fails to discharge the burden of proving that a confession was not obtained by the methods described in section 76(2), the court, as we have seen, shall not allow the confession to be given in evidence and has no discretion to admit it, even if satisfied that it is true. It does not follow from this, however, that the confession *must* be admitted if the prosecution succeeds in proving that the confession was not obtained by those methods: section 76(1) provides that a confession *may* be given in evidence if not excluded under the section. In such cases the trial judge may exclude the confession in the exercise of his discretion pursuant to section 82(3) or section 78(1). Although these two provisions overlap to a considerable extent, it will be convenient to consider them separately.

## 1 SECTION 82(3) OF THE POLICE AND CRIMINAL EVIDENCE ACT 1984

Section 82(3) provides that:

Nothing in this Part of this Act (ss 73–82) shall prejudice any power of a court to exclude evidence (whether by preventing questions from being put or otherwise) at its discretion.

The effect of this subsection is, in the present context, to preserve any discretion to exclude an otherwise admissible confession that the court possessed at common law prior to the 1984 Act. At common law, a trial judge, even if satisfied that a confession was made voluntarily, could exclude it as a matter of discretion on a number of different albeit overlapping grounds. Two of the grounds were made clear by the House of Lords in *R v Sang*.[105] First, as a part of his function at a criminal trial to ensure that the accused receives a fair trial, the judge has a discretion to refuse to admit evidence where, in his opinion, its prejudicial effect outweighs its probative value. Secondly, the judge has a discretion to exclude an otherwise admissible confession obtained by improper or unfair means. A third ground was that the confession

---

[104] *R v Gill* [2004] 1 WLR 49, CA at [45].     [105] [1980] AC 402.

was obtained in contravention of the Judges' Rules[106] or the statutory provisions governing the detention and treatment of suspects.

The discretion, in so far as it may be exercised on the first ground—that is where the prejudicial effect of the confession so outweighs its probative value that it would be unfair to the accused to admit it—was of particular use in the case of confessions made by accused suffering from mental disability.[107] In *R v Miller*[108] the Court of Appeal held that a confession may be excluded, as a matter of discretion, if it comes from an irrational mind or is the product of delusions and hallucinations. On the facts of the case, a murder trial in which there was evidence that part of the interrogation of the accused, who suffered from paranoid schizophrenia, may have triggered off hallucinations and flights of fancy, the Court of Appeal went on to hold that the trial judge had not erred in his decision to admit the confession. However, in *R v Stewart*[109] a trial judge exercised his discretion on this ground to exclude confessions made by an accused who suffered from a severe mental disability, having the mental age of a five-and-a-half-year-old and the comprehension level of a three-and-a-half-year-old. Similarly, it has been held that the discretion may be exercised to exclude a confession obtained at a time when the mental state of the accused was so unbalanced as to render his statements wholly unreliable.[110] Thus in *R v Davis*[111] a confession, obtained at a time when the accused may still have been influenced by a drug, pethidine—an analgesic with sedative properties which had been administered to him some ten hours earlier—was excluded as a matter of discretion on the grounds of its potential unreliability. The facts of that case, however, would now support a submission that the confession should be excluded as a matter of law under section 76(2)(b).[112]

Most of the reported cases in which the exclusionary discretion was exercised on either the second or the third ground, were cases involving some breach of the Judges' Rules. It should be emphasized, however, that a voluntary confession could be admitted notwithstanding a breach of the rules.[113] Such a breach merely enabled a submission to be made that an otherwise admissible confession should, as a matter of discretion, be excluded.[114] In the exercise of that discretion (which was rarely reversed on appeal) the trial judge could examine, in addition to the breaches alleged, all the circumstances of the case, including in particular the probative value of the confession and the nature and seriousness of the offence charged. The Judges' Rules, and many of

---

[106] The Judges' Rules were rules of practice, not law, originally drawn up by the judges of the King's Bench Division in 1912 for the guidance of the police, and designed to regulate the interrogation and treatment of suspects.

[107] On confessions by mentally handicapped persons, see also s 77 of the 1984 Act (Ch 8).

[108] [1986] 3 All ER 119, CA.          [109] (1972) 56 Cr App R 272, Central Criminal Court.

[110] Per Lord Widgery CJ in *R v Isequilla* [1975] 1 WLR 716, CA, approving a passage from *Cross on Evidence* (3rd edn London 1967) pp 450–1. In that case, however, it was held that the mental state of the accused, who was frightened and hysterical, was not such as to render it unsafe to act upon his statements.

[111] [1979] Crim LR 167, CC.          [112] See *R v Sat-Bhambra* (1988) 88 Cr App R 55, CA, above.

[113] *R v Prager* [1972] 1 WLR 260. Compliance with the Rules, of course, did not result in the admission of an involuntary confession.

[114] See per Lord Goddard CJ in *R v May* (1952) 36 Cr App R 91 at 93.

the old statutory provisions governing the detention and treatment of suspects, have now been replaced by a wide variety of provisions contained in the 1984 Act and the Codes of Practice which have been issued pursuant to the Act. The Codes do not apply only to police officers: under section 67(9) of the 1984 Act they also apply to other persons 'charged with the duty of investigating offences or charging offenders'.[115] This phrase covers those charged with a legal duty of the kind in question, whether imposed by statute or by the common law or by contract.[116] It covers Customs and Excise officers,[117] but is not restricted to government officials and others acting under statutory powers.[118] Whether a person satisfies the test is a question of fact in each case[119] or, more accurately, a question of mixed law and fact, involving an examination of the statute, contract or other authority under which a person carries out his functions, as well as a consideration of his actual work.[120] Thus the test will not necessarily be satisfied by Department of Trade Inspectors conducting an investigation of a company's affairs[121] or by those supervising a bank on behalf of the Bank of England under the Banking Act 1987,[122] but may be satisfied by commercial investigators such as company investigators,[123] store detectives[124] and investigators employed by the Federation against Copyright Theft.[125] The test is met by officers of the Special Compliance Office, the Inland Revenue's investigation branch charged with investigating serious tax fraud, because such fraud inevitably involves the commission of an offence or offences.[126]

Codes A to F relate to the following matters—A: the exercise by police officers of statutory powers of stop and search; B: the searching of premises by police officers and the seizure of property found by police officers on persons or premises; C: the detention, treatment and questioning of persons by police officers; D: the identification of persons by police officers; E: the tape recording of interviews with suspects;[127] and E:

---

[115] The principles of fairness enshrined in Code C may have an even wider application: see *R v Smith* (1993) 99 Cr App R 233, CA (Ch 3).

[116] *Joy v Federation against Copyright Theft Ltd* [1993] Crim LR 588, DC.

[117] *R v Sanusi* [1992] Crim LR 43, CA.    [118] *R v Bayliss* (1993) 98 Cr App R 235, CA at 237–8.

[119] Per Watkins LJ in *R v Seelig* [1991] 4 All ER 429 at 439, CA.

[120] Per Neill LJ in *R v Bayliss* (1993) 98 Cr App R 235 at 238–9 and in *R v Smith* (1993) 99 Cr App R 233, CA.

[121] See *R v Seelig* [1991] 4 All ER 429, CA.    [122] See *R v Smith* (1993) 99 Cr App R 233, CA.

[123] *R v Twaites; R v Brown* (1990) 92 Cr App R 106, CA.

[124] *R v Bayliss* (1993) 98 Cr App R 235, CA.

[125] *Joy v Federation against Copyright Theft Ltd* [1993] Crim LR 588, DC (an investigator employed by the respondents). In the case of an investigation by the Director of the Serious Fraud Office into a suspected offence involving serious or complex fraud, the general provisions of Code C yield to the inquisitorial regime established by the Criminal Justice Act 1987: see *R v Director of Serious Fraud Office, ex p Smith* [1992] 3 All ER 456, HL, and Ch 14.

[126] *R v Gill* [2004] 1 WLR 49, CA.

[127] The Code on Tape Recording applies to interviews held at police stations of persons suspected of committing indictable offences (except certain terrorism offences and an offence under s 1 of the Official Secrets Act 1911): see SI 1991/2686 and SI 1991/2687. See also para 43, *Practice Direction (Criminal Proceedings: Consolidation)* [2002] 1 WLR 2870, which deals with such matters as the practice to be followed for: (a) amending a transcript of an interview (or editing a tape) by agreement; (b) notification of intention to play a

the visual recording with sound of interviews with suspects. It is convenient at this stage, therefore, to consider some of these provisions, first in so far as they relate to the requirement to administer a caution, and then more generally. Before doing so, however, it should be stressed that compliance with the Act and Codes will not necessarily result in a confession being admitted; if it cannot be proved that it was not obtained by the methods described in section 76(2) then, as we have seen, it *shall not* be given in evidence. Conversely, non-compliance with the Act or Codes will not necessarily lead to the exclusion of an otherwise admissible confession: the decision whether to exclude remains entirely a matter of discretion.

## 2 THE CAUTION

Under the Judges' Rules, the police, in a number of different situations, were required to administer a caution to a suspect. In this respect, rules II and III were of particular importance. They provided as follows:

II.   As soon as a police officer has evidence which would afford reasonable grounds for suspecting that a person has committed an offence, he shall caution that person or cause him to be cautioned before putting to him any questions, or further questions, relating to that offence . . .

III.

   (a) Where a person is charged with or informed that he may be prosecuted for an offence he shall be cautioned . . .
   (b) It is only in exceptional cases that questions relating to the offence should be put to the accused person after he has been charged or informed that he may be prosecuted . . .

These rules have now been replaced by paragraphs 10 and 16 of Code C, the Code of Practice for the Detention, Treatment and Questioning of Persons by Police Officers. They provide as follows:

10.1  A person whom there are grounds to suspect of an offence must be cautioned before any questions about an offence, or further questions if the answers provide the grounds for suspicion, are put to them if either the accused's answers or silence (ie failure or refusal to answer or answer satisfactorily) may be given in evidence to a court in a prosecution. A person need not be cautioned if questions are for other necessary purposes, e.g.:

---

tape in court; (c) notification of objection to production of a tape; and (d) proof of a tape. Concerning video-recorded interviews with children (see Ch 15), departure from the guidance on interviewing contained in 'Achieving Best Evidence in Criminal Proceedings: Guidance for Vulnerable or Intimidated Witnesses, Including Children' ('The Memorandum') will probably be treated as the equivalent of a breach of one of the Codes of Practice. Account has been taken of a failure to conform to the recommendations contained in the report of Butler Sloss LJ, the Inquiry into Child Abuse in Cleveland (1987) (Cm 412): see *R v H* [1992] Crim LR 516, CA. See also *R v Dunphy* (1993) 98 Cr App R 393, CA (Ch 3), a decision on the precursor to The Memorandum.

(a) solely to establish their identity or ownership of any vehicle;

(b) to obtain information in accordance with any relevant statutory requirement[128] . . .;

(c) in furtherance of the proper and effective conduct of a search, e.g. to determine the need to search in the exercise of powers of stop and search or to seek cooperation while carrying out a search;

(d) to seek verification of a written record in accordance with paragraph 11.13;[129] or

(e) when examining a person in accordance with the Terrorism Act 2000, schedule 7 and the Code of Practice for Examining Officers issued under that Act, schedule 14, paragraph 6.

. . .

10.4 A person who is arrested, or further arrested, must also be cautioned unless:

(a) it is impracticable to do so by reason of their condition or behaviour at the time;

(b) they have already been cautioned immediately prior to arrest as in paragraph 10.1.

10.5 The caution which must be given on:

(a) arrest;

(b) all other occasions before a person is charged or informed that they may be prosecuted, (see section 16),

should, unless the restriction on drawing adverse inferences from silence applies, (see Annex C), be in the following terms:

'You do not have to say anything. But it may harm your defence if you do not mention when questioned something which you later rely on in Court. Anything you do say may be given in evidence.'

. . .

10.7 Minor deviations from the words of any caution given in accordance with this Code do not constitute a breach of this Code, provided the sense of the relevant caution is preserved . . .

10.8 After any break in questioning under caution, the person being questioned must be made aware they remain under caution. If there is any doubt the relevant caution should be given again in full when the interview resumes . . .

16.1 When the officer in charge of the investigation reasonably believes that there is sufficient evidence to provide a realistic prospect of the detainee's conviction . . . they shall without delay, and subject to the following qualification, inform the custody officer who will be responsible for considering whether the detainee should be charged . . . When a person is detained in respect of more than one offence it is permissible to delay informing the custody officer until the above conditions are satisfied in respect of all the offences . . .

. . .

16.2 When a detainee is charged with or informed that he may be prosecuted for an offence, [see Note 16B], they shall, unless the restriction on drawing adverse inferences from silence applies, (see Annex C), be cautioned as follows:

---

[128] For example, under the Road Traffic Act 1988.

[129] Para 11.13 relates to records of comments made by a suspect outside the context of an interview.

'You do not have to say anything. But it may harm your defence if you do not mention now something which you later rely on in court. Anything you do say may be given in evidence.' . . .[130]

Although paragraph 10.1, unlike rule II, does not include a requirement that the grounds to suspect be reasonable, this is implicit, because the grounds must be assessed objectively.[131] In *R v Osbourne, R v Virtue*[132] the question arose as to the point in time at which a caution under rule II should be administered. Lawton LJ, delivering the judgment of the Court of Appeal, said:[133]

The rules contemplate three stages in the investigations leading up to somebody being brought before a court for a criminal offence. The first is the gathering of information, and that can be gathered from anybody, including persons in custody provided they have not been charged. At the gathering of information stage no caution of any kind need be administered. The final stage, the one contemplated by rule III of the Judges' Rules, is when the police officer has got enough (and I stress the word 'enough') evidence to prefer a charge . . . But a police officer when carrying out an investigation meets a stage in between the mere gathering of information and the getting of enough evidence to prefer the charge. He reaches a stage where he has got the beginnings of evidence. It is at that stage that he must caution. In the judgment of this court, he is not bound to caution until he has got some information which he can put before the court as the beginnings of a case.

Under paragraph 10.4 of the Code, as a general rule a caution must be administered to a person upon arrest. Where the accused is not arrested, the phrase 'grounds to suspect' in paragraph 10.1 has been interpreted in a manner similar to the interpretation given to the phrase 'evidence which would afford reasonable grounds for suspecting' in *R v Osbourne; R v Virtue*. Thus in *R v Shah*[134] it was held that a mere hunch or sixth sense, or the simple fact that the questioner is suspicious, will not suffice to bring paragraph 10.1 into play; paragraph 10.1 sets out an objective test in that there must be grounds for suspicion before the need to caution arises and although they may well fall short of evidence supportive of a prima facie case of guilt, they must exist and be such as to lead both to a suspicion that an offence has been committed and that the person being questioned has committed it.[135] In *R v Hunt*,[136] where officers saw H in someone else's garden putting a flick-knife in his pocket, searched him and found the knife, it was held that at that stage the officers had ample evidence on which to suspect the commission of an offence and should have cautioned him.

---

[130] Where a person wishes to make a written statement under caution, he shall first be asked to write out and sign: 'I make this statement of my own free will. I understand that I do not have to say anything but that it may harm my defence if I do not mention when questioned something which I later rely on in court. This statement may be given in evidence': see para 2, Annex D, Code C. See also *R v Pall* (1991) 156 JP 424, CA and cf *R v Hoyte* [1994] Crim LR 215, CA.

[131] *R v James* [1996] Crim LR 650, CA. *R v James* and the other authorities in the ensuing text and footnotes are decisions on an earlier version of Code C.

[132] [1973] QB 678, CA.   [133] [1973] QB 678 at 688.

[134] [1994] Crim LR 125, CA.   [135] See also, and cf *R v Nelson and Rose* [1998] 2 Cr App R 399, CA.

[136] [1992] Crim LR 582, CA. Cf *R v Purcell* [1992] Crim LR 806, CA.

The answers to the questions then put, without a caution, should have been excluded under section 78. However, if a person is cautioned in respect of one offence and minutes later the police have grounds to suspect another offence, it seems that there is no requirement to caution again, under either paragraph 10.1 or paragraph 10.8, before putting questions about the other offence.[137]

A caution is not required under paragraph 10.1, in respect of a person whom there are grounds to suspect of an offence, if questions are not put to him regarding his involvement or suspected involvement in that offence, but for other purposes. However, if the questions are put for two purposes, partly regarding his involvement or suspected involvement in an offence, and partly for other purposes, then a caution should be given.[138]

Paragraph 10.1 and other requirements of the Code were not intended to apply to a conversation between a suspect and officers who adopt an undercover pose or disguise, because there can be no question of pressure or intimidation by the officers as persons actually in authority or believed to be so. However, it is wrong for officers to adopt such a pose or disguise to ask questions about an offence uninhibited by the provisions of the Code and with the effect of circumventing it, and if they do so, the questions and answers may be excluded under section 78.[139]

Paragraph 16.2 of the Code is designed to apply to that stage in the course of an interrogation when there is sufficient evidence to prosecute and for the prosecution to succeed. At that point in time, and subject to exceptions, questioning should cease.[140] Concerning rule III, it was held that the word 'charged' means formally charged[141] but that when a person is told 'you will be charged' it is the same as saying that a charge has in fact already been preferred.[142] The phrase 'informed that he may be prosecuted', it has been said, is designed to cover a case where, during interrogation of a suspect (who has not been arrested) the time comes when the police contemplate that a summons may be issued against him.[143] It may be assumed that paragraph 16.2 of the Code, in these respects, will be interpreted in the same way.

---

[137] R v Oni [1992] Crim LR 183, CA.    [138] R v Nelson and Rose [1998] 2 Cr App R 399, CA.

[139] See R v Christou [1992] 4 All ER 559, CA (see Ch 3).

[140] See para 16.5, Code C and R v Bailey [1993] 3 All ER 513, CA. Where a suspect is charged by the police and then required by the Serious Fraud Office to attend for an interview, the Director is not required to caution him, because the Criminal Justice Act 1987 showed a parliamentary intention to establish an inquisitorial regime in relation to serious or complex fraud in which the Director could obtain by compulsion answers which might be self-incriminating. Under s 2(13), a person who without reasonable excuse fails to answer questions or provide relevant information is liable to imprisonment, a fine, or both. But see also s 2(8): subject to minor exceptions, statements made by the suspect cannot be used in evidence against him.

[141] R v Brackenbury [1965] 1 WLR 1475n.    [142] Conway v Hotten [1976] 2 All ER 213, DC.

[143] R v Collier; R v Stenning [1965] 1 WLR 1470, CCA.

## 3 PROVISIONS GOVERNING PROCEDURAL FAIRNESS

A detailed analysis of the relevant provisions of the 1984 Act and the various Codes of Practice issued thereunder is well beyond the scope of this work. For present purposes, however, it is possible to summarize some of the more important provisions of the Act:

1.  An entry on or search of premises under a warrant is *unlawful* unless, inter alia, the warrant authorizes entry on one occasion only, specifies the name of the person who applied for it, the enactment under which it was issued and the premises to be searched, and identifies, so far as is practicable, the articles or persons to be sought.[144]

2.  As a general rule an arrest is *not lawful* unless the person arrested is informed as soon as is practicable after his arrest of the fact that he is under arrest, regardless of whether the fact of the arrest is obvious, and the grounds for the arrest.[145]

3.  A person voluntarily attending an investigation without having been arrested shall be *entitled* to leave at will unless he is placed under arrest.[146]

4.  A person arrested *shall not* be kept in police detention except in accordance with the provisions of the Act[147] and in certain circumstances *must* be released either on bail or without bail.[148]

5.  As a general rule, all persons in police detention *must* be treated in accordance with the Act and any Code of Practice issued under it and all matters relating to them which are required by the Act or such Codes of Practice to be recorded *must* be recorded in the custody records.[149]

6.  Reviews of the detention of each person in police detention in connection with the investigation of an offence *shall* be carried out periodically.[150]

7.  Subject to exceptions, a person *shall not* be kept in police detention for more than 24 hours without being charged.[151]

8.  As a general rule, a person who, after being charged with an offence, is kept in police detention *shall* be brought before a magistrates' court as soon as is practicable and in any event not later than the first sitting after he is charged with the offence.[152]

---

[144] See s 15. See also para 3, Code B (Searching of Premises and Seizure of Property). If there are reasonable grounds for believing that to alert the occupier by attempting to communicate with him would frustrate the object of the search or endanger the officers concerned, then it is not a condition precedent to lawful entry that *prior* to entry the officer executing the warrant identify himself, produce the warrant and supply the occupier with a copy of it: *R v Longman* [1988] 1 WLR 619, CA and para 6.4, Code B.

[145] Section 28(1)–(3). See also para 10.3, Code C.          [146] Section 29. See also para 3.21, Code C.

[147] Section 34(1).          [148] See, eg, ss 34(2), 37(2), 37(7)(b) and 38(1).

[149] Section 39(1).          [150] Section 40(1).

[151] Section 41. But see ss 42 (authorization of continued detention), 43 (warrants of further detention) and 44 (extension of warrants of further detention) and *R v Taylor* [1991] Crim LR 541, CA.

[152] Section 46(1) and (2).

9. Where a child or young person is in police detention, such steps as are practicable *shall* be taken to ascertain the identity of a person responsible for his welfare and, if it is practicable to ascertain the identity of such a person, that person *shall* be informed, unless it is not practicable to do so, of the arrest, the reason for the arrest and where the child or young person is being detained.[153]

Two further provisions of particular significance in the present context, sections 56 and 58, relate to the right to have someone informed when arrested and what has been called 'one of the most important and fundamental rights of a citizen',[154] namely the right of access to legal advice.[155] Section 56(1) provides that:

Where a person has been arrested and is being held in custody in a police station or other premises, he shall be entitled, if he so requests, to have one friend or relative or other person who is known to him or who is likely to take an interest in his welfare told, as soon as is practicable except to the extent that delay is permitted by this section, that he has been arrested and is being detained there.[156]

Section 58 provides that:

(1) A person arrested and held in custody in a police station or other premises[157] shall be entitled, if he so requests, to consult a solicitor[158] privately at any time.

---

[153] Section 34(2) and (3) of the Children and Young Persons Act 1933 as substituted by s 57 of the 1984 Act.

[154] Per Hodgson J in *R v Samuel* [1988] 2 All ER 135, CA at 147.

[155] See also paras 5 and 6, Code C.

[156] The rights conferred are exercisable whenever the person detained is transferred from one place to another: s 56(8).

[157] The intention behind these words, which are also used in s 56(1), is to limit the application of the section to a person whose detention in custody has been authorized, ie an arrested person taken to a police station in respect of whom the custody officer is satisfied that the statutory conditions for detention are made out. Thus a person arrested while committing burglary is *in custody* on premises, but is not *held* in custody, and is therefore outside the terms of ss 56 and 58: see *R v Kerawalla* [1991] Crim LR 451, CA. Although s 58(1) does not apply to a person in custody after being remanded by a magistrates' court, such a person has a common-law right to be permitted on request to consult a solicitor as soon as is reasonably practicable: *R v Chief Constable of South Wales, ex p Merrick* [1994] Crim LR 852, DC.

[158] 'Solicitor' means a solicitor who holds a current practising certificate and an accredited or probationary representative included on the register of representatives maintained by the Legal Services Commission: see para 6.12, Code C. If a solicitor wishes to send a non-accredited or probationary representative to provide advice on his behalf, that person shall be admitted to the police station for this purpose unless an officer of the rank of inspector or above considers that such a visit will hinder the investigation of crime and directs otherwise: para 6.12A, Code C. In exercising his discretion, the officer should take into account in particular whether the identity and status of the representative have been satisfactorily established; whether he is of suitable character to provide legal advice (a person with a criminal record is unlikely to be suitable unless the conviction was for a minor offence and is not of recent date); and any other matters in any written letter of authorization provided by the solicitor on whose behalf he is attending: para 6.13, Code C, reflecting the decision in *R v Chief Constable of Avon and Somerset Constabulary, ex p Robinson* [1989] 2 All ER 15, DC. The discretion cannot be used to make a blanket direction that a representative should not be admitted to any police station in a particular area, and although senior officers may give general advice, the responsibility rests with the officer concerned with the investigation in question as to whether that particular investigation will be hindered: *R (Thompson) v Chief Constable of the Northumberland Constabulary* [2001] 1 WLR 1342, CA.

(2) Subject to subsection (3) below, a request under subsection (1) above and the time at which it was made shall be recorded in the custody record.

(3) Such a request need not be recorded in the custody record of a person who makes it at a time while he is at a court after being charged with an offence.

(4) If a person makes such a request, he must be permitted to consult a solicitor as soon as is practicable except to the extent that delay is permitted by this section.[159]

Certain provisions are common to sections 56 and 58. In any case the person in custody must be permitted to exercise the rights conferred within thirty-six hours from the 'relevant time',[160] which is usually either the time at which the person arrives at the police station or the time twenty-four hours after the time of arrest, whichever is the earlier.[161] Delay is only permitted if four conditions are met. The first is that the person detained is in police detention for a serious arrestable offence,[162] which is defined by section 116 as: (i) an offence specified in Schedule 5 to the Act,[163] which includes, inter alia, murder, manslaughter, torture, kidnapping, rape, certain other sexual offences, and causing death by reckless driving; (ii) certain terrorism offences and an attempt or conspiracy to commit any such offence; (iii) any other arrestable offence if its commission has led to, or is intended or likely to lead to, any of a number of specified consequences; and (iv) an arrestable offence which consists of making a threat which, if carried out, would be likely to lead to any of those consequences. The consequences specified are serious harm to the security of the state or to public order, serious interference with the administration of justice or with the investigation of offences or of a particular offence, death of or serious injury to any person, substantial financial gain to any person and serious financial loss to any person, loss being serious for these purposes if, in all the circumstances, it is serious for the person who suffers it.[164]

The second condition is that the delay is authorized by an officer of at least the rank of superintendent.[165] The third condition is that the person in detention has not yet

---

[159] Section 58 does not entitle a person, suspected of committing an offence of driving when unfit through drink or drugs or driving after consuming excess alcohol, to consult a solicitor *before* supplying a specimen for analysis; and the refusal of the police to permit such a consultation does not amount to a 'reasonable excuse' for failing to provide a specimen when required to do so: *DPP v Billington* [1988] 1 All ER 435, DC. Procedures undertaken under s 7 of the Road Traffic Act 1988 (ie questions and answers leading to the giving of a specimen) do not constitute interviewing for the purposes of Code C: see *DPP v D; DPP v Rous* (1992) 94 Cr App R 185, DC and para 11.1A, Code C.

[160] Sections 56(3) and 58(5).          [161] Section 41(2).          [162] Sections 56(2)(a) and 58(6)(a).

[163] As amended by s 170(1) of the Criminal Justice Act 1988 and s 85 of the Criminal Justice and Public Order Act 1994.

[164] Section 116(6) and (7). See *R v McIvor* [1987] Crim LR 409, CC (the theft of 28 dogs valued at £880 and owned collectively by a hunt did not result in serious financial loss to the hunt); *R v Smith* [1987] Crim LR 579, CC (it was doubtful whether the robbery of goods worth £800 and cash in the sum of £116 resulted in substantial financial gain to the robbers or serious financial loss to the victim, a large company); and per Watkins LJ in *Re Walters* [1987] Crim LR 577, DC, below.

[165] Sections 56(2)(b) and 58(6)(b). The authorization may be oral, in which case it shall be confirmed in writing as soon as possible: ss 56(4) and 58(7). The authorization may also be given by an officer of the rank of chief inspector if he has been authorized to do so by an officer of at least the rank of chief superintendent:

been charged with an offence, that is any offence, whether or not the one in respect of which he was originally arrested.[166] The fourth condition, contained in sections 56(5) and 58(8), is that the officer must have:

reasonable grounds for believing that telling the named person of the arrest (exercise of the right to consult a solicitor) (a) will lead to interference with or harm to evidence connected with a serious arrestable offence or interference with or physical injury to other persons or (b) will lead to the alerting of other persons suspected of having committed such an offence but not yet arrested for it or (c) will hinder the recovery of any property obtained as a result of such an offence.[167]

If a delay is authorized, the detainee shall be told the reason for it, which shall be noted on his custody record.[168] Once the reason for authorizing delay ceases to subsist, there may be no further delay in permitting the exercise of the rights conferred.[169] This may occur, for example, if the police succeed in recovering the property obtained as a result of a serious arrestable offence or arrest the other persons suspected of having committed such an offence.[170]

The occasions for properly authorizing delay under section 58(8) will be infrequent[171] and the task of satisfying a court that reasonable grounds existed at the time when the decision was made will prove formidable.[172] In R v Samuel Hodgson J said:[173]

a court which has to decide whether denial of access to a solicitor was lawful has to ask itself two questions: 'Did the officer believe?', a subjective test; and 'Were there reasonable grounds for that belief?', an objective test.

What it is the officer must satisfy the court that he believed is this: that (1) allowing consultation with a solicitor (2) will (3) lead to or hinder one or more of the things set out in paragraphs (a) to (c) of s 58(8). The use of the word 'will' is clearly of great importance.

---

s 107(1). The holder of an acting rank may be treated for the purpose of these provisions as the holder of the substantive rank: R v Alladice (1988) 87 Cr App R 380, CA.

[166] Para A1, Annex B, Code C and R v Samuel [1988] 2 All ER 135, CA.

[167] It is not an adequate ground for the authorization of delay under s 58(8) that access to a solicitor might 'prejudice inquiries' or result in advice to the suspect to remain silent (R v McIvor [1987] Crim LR 409, CC) or to refuse to answer any more questions (R v Samuel [1988] 2 All ER 135, CA). See also para A4, Annex B, Code C. Sections 56(5) and 58(8) are expressed to be subject to ss 56(5A) and 58(8A) respectively. These latter subsections provide that an officer may also authorize delay where: (a) the serious arrestable offence is a drug trafficking offence and the officer has reasonable grounds for believing that the detained person has benefited from drug trafficking and that the recovery of the value of that person's proceeds of drug trafficking will be hindered by telling the named person of the arrest (or by exercise of the right to consult a solicitor); or (b) the serious arrestable offence is an offence in respect of which confiscation orders may be made under the Criminal Justice Act 1988 and the officer has reasonable grounds for believing that the detained person has benefited from the offence and that the recovery of the value of the property obtained by that person from or in connection with the offence or of the pecuniary advantage derived by him from or in connection with it will be hindered by telling the named person of the arrest (or by exercise of the right to consult a solicitor).

[168] Sections 56(6) and 58(9). These duties shall be performed as soon as is practicable: ss 56(7) and 58(10).

[169] Sections 56(9) and 58(11).      [170] As in R v (Eric) Smith [1987] Crim LR 579, CC.

[171] Per Lord Lane CJ in R v Alladice (1988) 87 Cr App R 380, CA.

[172] Per Hodgson J in R v Samuel [1988] 2 All ER 135, CA at 144.      [173] [1988] 2 All ER 135 at 143.

There were available to the draftsman many words or phrases by which he could have described differing nuances as to the officer's state of mind, for example 'might', 'could', 'there was a risk', 'there was a substantial risk' etc. The choice of 'will' must have been deliberately restrictive.

Of course, anyone who says that he believes that something will happen, unless he is speaking of one of the immutable laws of nature, accepts the possibility that it will not happen, but the use of the word 'will' in conjunction with belief implies in the believer a belief that it will very probably happen.

Furthermore, it was held that the circumstances in which delay may be authorized necessarily involve conduct, on the part of the solicitor, which is either deliberate and criminal or inadvertent. As to the former, the number of times that a police officer could genuinely believe that a solicitor, an officer of the court, would commit a criminal offence would be rare, and in any event the grounds put forward to justify the delay would have to have reference to a specific solicitor and could never be advanced in relation to solicitors generally. As to inadvertent conduct, solicitors were intelligent, professional people whereas persons detained were frequently not very clever; the expectation that one of the events in paras (a) to (c) would be brought about by such conduct contemplated a degree of intelligence and sophistication in persons detained and perhaps a naïvety and lack of common sense in solicitors which was of doubtful occurrence; and the grounds put forward would have to have reference to the specific person detained, the archetype being a sophisticated criminal who was known or suspected to be a member of a gang of criminals.

The facts of *R v Samuel* revealed that the solicitor in question was highly respected, very experienced and unlikely to be hoodwinked by the suspect, who was 24 years old. Accordingly, it was held that there could have been no reasonable grounds for the belief that section 58(8) required.[174] Similarly, in *R v Alladice*,[175] a case of robbery in which access had been denied on the grounds that one of the suspects was still at large, none of the proceeds of the robbery had been recovered and a gun which had been used in the crime had not been located, Lord Lane CJ, giving the reserved judgment of the Court of Appeal, held that although their Lordships did not share the scepticism expressed in *R v Samuel* as to solicitors being used as unwitting channels of communication, there had been a breach of section 58 because the suspect still at large had already been alerted by events, there was no reason to believe that access to a solicitor would impede recovery of the stolen money or gun, there was no suggestion that the solicitor requested would involve himself in any dishonesty or malpractice, and the suspect could not be classed as a sophisticated criminal.

---

[174] Cf *Re Walters* [1987] Crim LR 577, DC, an application for habeas corpus following extradition proceedings, where it was held that there were reasonable grounds for believing that the applicant would use the solicitor as an innocent agent to get a message out and thereby alert other suspects: before the applicant's arrest there were 'Delphic' telephone conversations between the applicant and a co-conspirator which showed the ease with which the applicant could transmit messages which were seemingly innocent but capable of being put to improper use.

[175] (1988) 87 Cr App R 380, CA. See also *R v Parris* (1988) 89 Cr App R 68, CA.

## 4 SECTION 78(1) OF THE POLICE AND CRIMINAL EVIDENCE ACT 1984

Section 78(1) provides that:

In any proceedings the court may refuse to allow evidence on which the prosecution proposes to rely to be given if it appears to the court that, having regard to all the circumstances, including the circumstances in which the evidence was obtained, the admission of the evidence would have such an adverse effect on the fairness of the proceedings that the court ought not to admit it.

Many of the most important cases on section 78(1) have concerned confessions, to which the subsection clearly applies,[176] and some of these have already been considered, as part of the general consideration of the subsection, in Chapters 2 and 3. Although section 78 operates without prejudice to the common-law discretion to exclude,[177] section 78 has in very large measure superseded the common-law power.

A confession may be excluded under section 78(1) in the absence of any breaches of the 1984 Act or Codes of Practice. Thus if an interview is held with a suspect who does not appear to have hearing difficulties, but it is subsequently established that his hearing was so impaired that it would be unfair for his answers to be admitted in evidence, the answers will be excluded under section 78(1).[178] However, the chief importance of section 78(1), in relation to confessions, lies in its potential for the exclusion of confessions obtained illegally or improperly. As we saw in Chapter 3, although breaches of the Act or Codes will not necessarily result in exclusion, it is implicit in the wording of the subsection that the circumstances in which the evidence was obtained may have such an adverse effect that it should be excluded.[179] As we also saw, the purpose of the subsection is not disciplinary, but protective, and therefore although mala fides or deliberate misconduct may render exclusion more likely, the determinative factor is the extent to which the defendant has been denied the right of a fair trial by reason of breaches of the provisions governing procedural fairness.[180]

Before considering some examples of such breaches, it will be convenient to consider first the procedure to be adopted when the defence seeks to exclude a confession obtained in such circumstances. In *R v Keenan*[181] Hodgson J identified three different situations: (a) breaches of a code may be apparent from the custody record (as when an order has been made by an officer of insufficient rank) or the witness statements; (b) there may be a prima facie breach which, if objection is taken, must be justified by evidence adduced by the prosecution (eg an order refusing access to a solicitor can only be justified by compelling evidence from the senior officer who made the order);

---

[176] *R v Mason* [1987] 3 All ER 481, CA.

[177] *R v O'Leary* (1988) 87 Cr App R 387, CA and *Matto v Crown Court at Wolverhampton* [1987] RTR 337, DC.

[178] See *R v Clarke* [1989] Crim LR 892, CA and para 13.5, Code C.

[179] Per Woolf LJ in *Matto v Crown Court at Wolverhampton* [1987] RTR 337, DC.

[180] See *R v Alladice* (1988) 87 Cr App R 380, CA and *R v Walsh* (1989) 91 Cr App R 161 at 163, CA.

[181] [1989] 3 All ER 598, CA at 604–5, 606, and 608.

and (c) there may be breaches which can probably only be established by the evidence of the accused himself (eg cases involving persons at risk, such as the mentally handicapped).[182] The procedure appropriate in each case may vary. In (a), it may be that all that is necessary is an admission by the police, followed by argument. However, the prosecution will not often be content to take this course in cases where they wish to show how or why the breaches occurred and to submit that the evidence should be adduced despite the breaches. In (b), the prosecution clearly have to call evidence to justify the order made and the defence may wish to call evidence from eg the solicitor to whom access was sought, or the accused himself. Cases under (c) are likely to be rare. It is unlikely that, in (a) and (b), the accused will be called. If the proper procedures have, on the face of the record, been observed, the contentions of the accused, for example that a properly recorded interview is inaccurate, would be unlikely to succeed. But if the breaches are obvious, the trial judge has no means of knowing what will ensue after he has made his ruling. If he excludes, the accused may exercise his right not to testify. To admit the evidence of the interview may therefore effectively deprive the accused of a right he otherwise had. And if the evidence is admitted, the accused may then give evidence that the interview never took place, or that it did take place but the questions and answers were fabricated or inaccurately recorded, or that it did take place and the record is accurate. Although it seems unjust that evidence should be excluded under section 78 when, if all the facts and the defence response were known, it would be clear that the evidence should not be excluded under the section, the difficulty cannot be avoided: the decision has to be made at a stage when the judge does not know the full facts. In *R v Dunford*,[183] a case involving denial of access to a solicitor, it was held that the trial judge was entitled (i) to take account of the accused's previous convictions and (ii) to look at the contents of the record of the interview, including the terms of the confession, in order to help him to decide whether the presence of a solicitor might have made it less likely that the accused would confess. However, it was also said that it may not be right to refer to or rely on the record where evidence has been adduced on the *voir dire* and there is a root and branch challenge to its contents.

Denial of access to a solicitor contrary to section 58 of the 1984 Act will, prima facie, have an adverse effect on the fairness of the proceedings.[184] In *R v Samuel*[185] Hodgson J held that had the trial judge decided, as he should have done, that the accused had been improperly denied 'one of the most important and fundamental rights of a citizen', he might well have concluded that the refusal of access and consequent unlawful interview compelled him to find that admission of the confession would have had an adverse effect on the fairness of the proceedings. Similarly, where, in breach of Code C,[186] an arrested person is not properly informed, both

---

[182] See paras 11.15 and 11.17–11.20, Code C.

[183] (1990) 91 Cr App R 150, CA.

[184] Per Saville J in *R v Walsh* (1989) 91 Cr App Rep 161 at 163, CA. See also *R v Parris* (1988) 89 Cr App R 68, CA (see Ch 3).

[185] [1988] 2 All ER 135, CA.          [186] See paras 3.1, 3.2, and 3.5.

orally and in writing, of his right to consult a solicitor, this may well result in exclusion, especially in the case of a foreigner with no previous convictions who is unfamiliar with the rights of a suspect at interview,[187] and such breaches will not necessarily be cured if he is later asked whether he agrees to be interviewed without a solicitor, and replies in the affirmative.[188] However, breach of section 58 or the accompanying provisions of the Code is no guarantee of exclusion.[189] Thus where a suspect is kept incommunicado, contrary to section 58, but after interview says that the absence of a solicitor made no difference and, following a belated granting of access to a solicitor, signs the notes of the interview, the evidence is admissible.[190] Similarly, if a suspect who has agreed to be interviewed without a solicitor present, changes his mind, and the police improperly continue to interview him without allowing him to receive legal advice,[191] although this is a serious inroad into his rights, if the solicitor would have added nothing to his knowledge of his rights, admissions subsequently made are admissible.[192]

In *R v Kirk*[193] it was held that where the police, having arrested a suspect in respect of one offence, propose to question him in respect of another more serious offence, they must first either charge him with the more serious offence, as envisaged by section 37 of the 1984 Act, or ensure that he is aware of the true nature of the investigation: that is the thrust and purport of paragraph 10.1 of Code C. The accused can then give proper weight to the nature of the investigation when deciding whether or not to exercise his right to obtain free legal advice under the Code and when deciding how to respond to the questions which the police propose to ask. The Act and the Codes, it was held, proceed on the assumption that a suspect in custody will know why he is there and, when being interviewed, will know at least in general terms the level of offence in respect of which he is suspected; and if he does not know, and as a result does not seek legal advice and gives critical answers which he might not otherwise have given, the evidence should normally be excluded under section 78, because its admission will have a seriously adverse effect on the fairness of the proceedings.

In *R v Keenan*[194] it was held that if there have been serious and substantial breaches of the 'verballing' provisions of the Code (whereby, for example, an accurate contemporaneous record of an interview should be made), evidence so obtained should be excluded.[195] Thus confessions have been excluded on the basis of the following

---

[187] *R v Sanusi* [1992] Crim LR 43, CA.     [188] *R v Beycan* [1990] Crim LR 185, CA.

[189] See *R v Alladice* (1988) 87 Cr App R 380, CA and *R v Dunford* (1990) 91 Cr App R 150, CA (Ch 3). See J Hodgson 'Tipping the Scales of Justice' [1992] Crim LR 854.

[190] *R v Findlay; R v Francis* [1992] Crim LR 372, CA.     [191] See para 6.6, Code C.

[192] *R v Oliphant* [1992] Crim LR 40, CA. See also *R v Anderson* [1993] Crim LR 447, CA.

[193] [1999] 4 All ER 698, CA.

[194] [1989] 3 All ER 598, CA (see Ch 3).

[195] Under para 11.1A, Code C, an interview is the questioning of a person regarding his involvement or suspected involvement in a criminal offence or offences which, under para 10.1 of Code C, must be carried out under caution. Whether there is an interview primarily turns on the nature of the questioning, rather than the number of questions or their length. Thus if an officer asks a single question directly relating to the

breaches: interviewing a juvenile in the absence of an 'appropriate adult';[196] interviewing a suspect before he has arrived at the police station and been informed of his right to free legal advice;[197] failure to tell a suspect that he is not under arrest coupled with failure to make a contemporaneous record of an interview;[198] failure to caution and to make such a record;[199] failure to give the suspect the opportunity to read and sign it as correct or to indicate the respects in which he considers it inaccurate;[200] in a case in which the accused denied making a confession allegedly made *after* a taped interview with him, failure to give the suspect such an opportunity;[201] and undue pressure, by threatening a number of charges, instead of only two, if the suspect continued to deny the charge.[202] However, relatively trivial breaches, such as a failure to record the reason why an interview record was not completed in the course of an interview,[203] or such a breach coupled with a failure to record the time when an interview record was made,[204] have not resulted in exclusion. Moreover, even serious breaches of the 'verballing' provisions may be 'cured' by the presence of a solicitor or his clerk. In *R v Dunn*[205] D denied making a confession, allegedly made *after* his interview, during the signing of the interview notes, and in the presence of his solicitor's clerk. The

crime, his motive being to clarify an ambiguity in a comment made by the suspect on arrest, that question and the answer to it may constitute an interview, although the officer's motive may be very relevant to the question of exclusion under s 78: *R v Ward* (1993) 98 Cr App R 337, CA. If an accused, under arrest, voluntarily offers to provide information and officers, without asking any questions, accede to that request and make a record of that information, that is not an interview, but nothing said at such a meeting can be produced in evidence at any subsequent trial: *R v Menard* [1995] 1 Cr App R 306, CA.

[196]  *R v Weekes* (1993) 97 Cr App R 222, CA (para 11.15, Code C).

[197]  *R v Cox* (1992) 96 Cr App R 464, CA (para 11.1; also paras 3.1, 3.2, and 10.1).

[198]  *R v Joseph* [1993] Crim LR 206, CA (paras 10.2 and 11.7, Code C). Cf *Watson v DPP* [2003] All ER (D) 132 (Jun), DC.

[199]  See *R v Sparks* [1991] Crim LR 128, CA (paras 10.1 and 11.7, Code C) and *R v Bryce* [1992] 4 All ER 567, CA (paras 10.8 and 11.7, Code C). See also *R v Okafor* [1994] 3 All ER 741, CA, where there was *also* a failure to remind of the right to legal advice (para 11.2, Code C).

[200]  See *R v Foster* [1987] Crim LR 821, CC (para 11.11, Code C) and *R v Weerdesteyn* [1995] 1 Cr App R 405, CA, where there was also a failure to caution. Cf *R v Courtney* [1995] Crim LR 63, CA, where failure to give the suspect an opportunity to read and sign a record of comments outside the context of an interview (in breach of para 11.13, Code C) was treated as 'insubstantial'. See also *R v Park* (1993) 99 Cr App R 270, CA: if answers to exploratory questions give rise in due course to a well-founded suspicion that an offence has been committed, what has started out as an inquiry may have become an interview and if it does, the requirements of the Code must be followed in relation to both the earlier and later questioning. Thus, although a contemporaneous note is no longer possible, a record should be made as soon as practicable of the earlier questions and answers, the reason for the absence of a contemporaneous note should be recorded and the suspect should be given the opportunity to check the record.

[201]  *R v Scott* [1991] Crim LR 56, CA, where it was held that by admitting the confession, the judge effectively compelled the accused to give evidence. Cf *R v Matthews, R v Dennison, and R v Voss* (1989) 91 Cr App R 43, CA.

[202]  *R v Howden-Simpson* [1991] Crim LR 49, CA (para 11.5, Code C). See also *R v De Silva* [2003] 2 Cr App R 74, CA, where the confessions were made, after being cautioned, in telephone calls to other suspects which the police had induced the accused to make by the promise of a reduced sentence, if convicted.

[203]  See *R v White* [1991] Crim LR 779, CA and para 11.10, Code C.

[204]  See *R v Findlay; R v Francis* [1992] Crim LR 372, CA and para 11.9, Code C.

[205]  (1990) 91 Cr App R 237, CA. See also D Roberts 'Questioning the Suspect' [1993] Crim LR 368 and J Baldwin 'Legal Advice at the Police Station' [1993] Crim LR 371.

'conversation' in which the confession was made was not recorded contempor-aneously and no note of it was shown to D. It was held that, despite these serious breaches, the evidence was admissible because the clerk was present to protect D's interests: she could have intervened to prevent the accused from answering, her pres-ence would have inhibited the police from fabricating the conversation, and, if they were to fabricate, it would not simply be a question of their evidence against that of D, because she would also be able to give evidence for the accused.

If a confession is excluded under section 78 by reason of a breach of the Code, a confession made in a subsequent, but properly conducted interview *may* be tainted by the earlier breach and therefore also fall to be excluded under section 78. The question of exclusion is a matter of fact and degree which is likely to depend on whether the objections leading to the exclusion of the first interview were of a fundamental and continuing nature and, if so, if the arrangements for the subsequent interview gave the accused a sufficient opportunity to exercise an informed and independent choice as to whether he should repeat or retract what he said in the first interview or say noth-ing.[206] In *R v Canale*,[207] where the first two interviews were not contemporaneously recorded and no record was shown to the accused for verification, it was held that these breaches had affected subsequent admissions which therefore should have been excluded under section 78. However, in *R v Gillard and Barrett*[208] it was held that breaches of the Code (similar to those in *R v Canale*) in earlier interviews had not tainted confessions made in subsequent but properly conducted interviews. *R v Canale* was distinguished on the basis that in that case there was a nexus between the earlier and later interviews: the accused claimed that he had been induced by promises to make the admissions in the first interview and these promises may have continued to affect answers in the later interviews. The length of time separating the interviews is clearly relevant,[209] but the critical factor, it seems, is whether there is any suggestion of oppression, inducement, stress or pressure in the earlier interview which might continue to exert a malign influence during the later interview.[210]

As noted earlier in this chapter, the application of the Codes is confined to police officers and others charged with the duty of investigating offences or charging offenders. However, where a confession has been made in the course of an interview with some other person, for example a doctor or psychiatrist, the court, in deciding whether to exercise the section 78 discretion, is entitled to take into account the fact that the accused did not have the benefit of the safeguards provided by the Codes. In *R v Elleray*[211] it was held that, given the need for frankness in the exchanges between a

---

[206] *R v Neil* [1994] Crim LR 441, CA, applied in *R v Nelson and Rose* [1998] 2 Cr App R 399, CA.

[207] [1990] 2 All ER 187, CA (see Ch 3). See also *R v Blake* [1991] Crim LR 119, CC.

[208] (1990) 92 Cr App R 61, CA.

[209] See *R v Conway* [1994] Crim LR 838, CA, where account was taken of the fact that only 20 minutes separated the interviews.

[210] See per Taylor LJ in *Y v DPP* [1991] Crim LR 917, DC. See also *R v Glaves* [1993] Crim LR 685, CA; *R v Wood* [1994] Crim LR 222, CA; and generally Peter Mirfield 'Successive Confessions and the Poisonous Tree' [1996] Crim LR 554.

[211] [2003] 2 Cr App R 165, CA.

probation officer and an offender, the prosecution should only rely upon a confession made to a probation officer if it is in the public interest to do so, but where they do rely on such a confession, the court, in deciding whether to exclude it under section 78, is entitled to take into account not only the need for frankness, but also the reliability of the record of what was said, that the offender was not cautioned and that he did not have the benefit of legal representation. On the facts of the case, the confessions, which were of rape, were held to have been properly admitted.[212]

## C THE *VOIR DIRE*

If either (i) the prosecution rely on oral statements and the defence case is simply that the interview never took place or that the incriminating statements were never made, or (ii) the prosecution rely on written statements and the defence case is that they are forgeries, no question of admissibility falls for the judge's decision. The issue of fact whether or not the statement was made by the accused is for the jury. However, if the accused denies authorship of the written statement and claims that he signed it involuntarily, or claims that his signature to what in fact was a confession statement was obtained by the fraudulent misrepresentation that he was signing a document of an entirely different character, he puts in issue the admissibility of the statement on which the judge must rule and, if the judge admits the statement, all issues of fact as to the circumstances of the making and signing of the statement should then be left for the jury to consider and evaluate.[213]

Subject to the foregoing, if the prosecution proposes to admit evidence of a confession, the defence has two options. It may represent[214] to the court that the confession was or may have been obtained by the methods set out in section 76(2) (or in any event should be excluded by the judge in the exercise of his discretion) and the question of admissibility must then be determined on the *voir dire*.[215] The defence have no right to insist on the presence of the jury at the *voir dire*: the judge, after listening to the views of the defence, has the final word on whether the jury should remain in court.[216] Alternatively, the defence may choose not to dispute the admissibility of the confession, in which case, assuming that the court does not exercise its own powers under section 76(3) to require the prosecution to prove that the confession was not obtained by the methods set out in section 76(2), the confession may be

---

[212] See also *R v McDonald* [1991] Crim LR 122, CA, Ch 3.

[213] Per Lord Bridge in *Ajodha v The State* [1981] 2 All ER 193, PC at 201–2, applied in *R v Flemming* (1987) 86 Cr App R 32, CA.

[214] A suggestion, in cross-examination, that a confession was obtained improperly does not amount to a representation for the purposes of s 76(2): per Russell LJ, expressly confining his rulings to summary trials, in *R v Liverpool Juvenile Court, ex p R* [1987] 2 All ER 668, DC at 673.

[215] Concerning summary trials, see Ch 2 under E2 **The *voir dire*, or trial within a trial.**

[216] *R v Hendry* (1988) 153 JP 166, CA, applied in *R v Davis* [1990] Crim LR 860, CA.

given in evidence.[217] At common law, prior to the 1984 Act, there was a third option, namely to allow the jury to hear the evidence of the confession and subsequently, when all the evidence had been heard, to submit to the judge that, if he doubted the admissibility of the statement, he should direct the jury to disregard it.[218] It would appear, however, that this option has not survived the 1984 Act: on its wording, section 76 only permits the question of legal admissibility to be raised where the prosecution 'proposes' to give a confession in evidence. Similarly, section 78 refers to evidence on which the prosecution 'proposes' to rely. Accordingly, it has been said that if an accused wishes to exclude a confession under section 76, the time to make such a submission is before the confession is put in evidence and not afterwards.[219] This would also appear to be the time at which a submission based on section 78 should be made.[220]

In cases where defence counsel intends to make a submission that a confession should be excluded, the normal practice is to inform the court of his intention at the plea and directions hearing[221] or to inform prosecuting counsel immediately before the trial commences, so that the confession is not referred to in the presence of the jury, whether in the prosecution opening speech or otherwise.[222] The prosecution will adduce their evidence in the normal way but at that point in time when the confession would otherwise be admitted, counsel will intimate to the court that a point of law has arisen which falls to be determined in the absence of the jury.[223] At the *voir dire*, the prosecution will bear the burden of proving beyond reasonable doubt that the confession was not obtained by the methods described in section 76(2). Witnesses, in the usual case police officers, will be called to give evidence of the confession and the circumstances in which it was made and will be open to cross-examination by defence counsel. The accused may then give evidence and call any witnesses who can support his version of events. The defence witnesses will also be open to cross-examination. The judge may also take into account any relevant evidence already given in the main trial, because the issue of admissibility cannot be tried in total isolation from

---

[217] However, any resulting conviction may be quashed if the prosecution failed to disclose material which would have provided the defence with an informed opportunity to seek a *voir dire*: *R v Langley* [2001] Crim LR 651, CA.

[218] See per Lord Bridge in *Ajodha v The State* [1981] 2 All ER 193 at 202–3.

[219] See *R v Sat-Bhambra* (1988) 88 Cr App R 55, CA, below. See also *R v Millard* [1987] Crim LR 196, CC and *R v Davis* [1990] Crim LR 860, CA. For the position in summary trials, see *R v Liverpool Juvenile Court, ex p R* [1987] 2 All ER 668, DC (Ch 2).

[220] But see, in the case of summary trials, per Russell LJ in *R v Liverpool Juvenile Court, ex p R* [1987] 2 All ER 668 at 672–3.

[221] See para 41.13(j), *Practice Direction (Criminal Proceedings: Consolidation)* [2002] 1 WLR 2870.

[222] *R v Cole* (1941) 165 LT 125. In the trial of an unrepresented accused, it may be prudent, if the judge has any reason to suppose that the admissibility (voluntariness) of a statement proposed to be put in evidence by the prosecution is likely to be in issue, to explain to the accused his rights in the matter before the trial begins: per Lord Bridge in *Ajodha v The State* [1981] 2 All ER 193 at 203, PC.

[223] Occasionally it is convenient to determine admissibility immediately after the jury has been empanelled, as when the evidence of the confession is so important to the prosecution case that without reference to it they cannot even open their case: see *R v Hammond* [1941] 3 All ER 318.

the whole background of the case.[224] After speeches from counsel, the judge gives his ruling. If the confession is excluded, then nothing more should be heard of it.[225] If the confession is admitted, it may be put in evidence before the jury. Either way, however, in modern English practice the judge's decision is never revealed to the jury.[226]

The case of *Wong Kam-Ming v R*[227] gave rise to three important questions concerning the *voir dire*. They were: (i) during cross-examination of an accused on the *voir dire*, whether questions may be put as to the truth of the confession; (ii) whether the prosecution is permitted, on the resumption of the trial proper, to adduce evidence of what the accused said on the *voir dire*; and (iii) whether the prosecution is permitted, in the trial proper, to cross-examine the accused upon what he said on the *voir dire*. The accused was charged with murder at a massage parlour. The only evidence against him was a signed confession in which he admitted that he was present at the parlour at the relevant time, had a knife in his hand and 'chopped' someone. The admissibility of the confession was challenged on the ground that it was not made voluntarily. Under cross-examination on the *voir dire*, the accused was asked questions about the contents of the confession statement which were directed at establishing their truth. In answer, the accused admitted that he was present at the parlour and involved in the incident in question. The trial judge ruled that the confession statement was inadmissible. Before the jury, the judge allowed the prosecution to establish the accused's presence at the parlour by calling the shorthand writers to produce extracts from the transcript of the cross-examination on the *voir dire*. After the accused had given his evidence-in-chief before the jury, the prosecution were also permitted to cross-examine him on inconsistencies between that evidence and his evidence on the *voir dire* as recorded in the shorthand transcript. The accused was convicted and the Court of Appeal of Hong Kong dismissed his appeal. The Privy Council allowed the appeal on three grounds. First, it was held by a majority that the accused had been improperly cross-examined on the *voir dire* as to the truth of his confession statement because the sole issue on the *voir dire* was whether the statement had been made involuntarily, an issue to which its truth or falsity was irrelevant.[228] Secondly, it was held that the prosecution had been improperly permitted to adduce before the jury evidence of the answers given by the accused on the *voir dire*. In the opinion of their

---

[224] *R v Tyrer* (1989) 90 Cr App R 446, CA.

[225] *R v Treacy* [1944] 2 All ER 229, CCA. But see also *R v Rowson* [1985] 2 All ER 539, CA (see Ch 7); and *R v Myers* [1997] 4 All ER 314, HL, above.

[226] Per Lord Steyn in *Mitchell v R* [1998] 2 Cr App R 35, PC at 42.     [227] [1980] AC 247.

[228] Lord Hailsham, dissenting, was of the opinion that in many cases the truth or falsity of the alleged confession could be relevant to the question at issue on the *voir dire* or to the credibility of either the defence or prosecution witnesses. See also *R v Hammond* [1941] 3 All ER 318, CCA, where it was held that prosecuting counsel was entitled, when cross-examining the accused on the *voir dire*, to ask him whether a statement, alleged by the accused to have been extorted by gross maltreatment, was in fact true. The accused's answer was in the affirmative. The question was held to be relevant to the issue of whether the evidence as to the gross maltreatment given by the accused on the *voir dire*, was true or false. The majority in *Wong Kam-Ming v R* took the view that *R v Hammond* was wrongly decided.

Lordships, such evidence should not be adduced, regardless of whether the confession is excluded or admitted, because a clear distinction should be maintained between the issue of voluntariness, which is alone relevant to the *voir dire*, and the issue of guilt which falls to be decided in the main trial.[229] Thirdly, it was held that the prosecution had been improperly permitted to cross-examine the accused on inconsistencies between his evidence before the jury and his statements on the *voir dire* because such a course is only permitted where the *voir dire* results in the admission of the confession and the accused gives evidence before the jury on some matter other than the voluntariness of the confession, which is no longer in issue, and in so doing gives answers which are inconsistent with his testimony on the *voir dire*.[230]

What is the status of the decision in *Wong Kam-Ming v R* in the light of the Police and Criminal Evidence Act 1984? Concerning the first part of the decision, the law remains the same under the Act. The truth of the confession is as irrelevant to the issue of 'oppression' or 'unreliability' as it was to the issue of 'voluntariness'. Section 76(2), it will be recalled, requires the prosecution to prove that the confession, 'notwithstanding that it may be true', was not obtained by the methods it describes.[231] The second and third parts of the decision, insofar as they prohibit the prosecution from leading evidence on or cross-examining the accused about what he said on the *voir dire*, continue to represent the law under the Act but only, it would appear, in relation to statements made by the accused on the *voir dire* which are not 'adverse' to him. Section 82(1) defines a confession to include *any* statement wholly or partly adverse to the person who made it. Thus if, on the *voir dire*, the accused makes an inculpatory statement relevant to his guilt on the offence charged, which can hardly be said to have been obtained by oppression or in circumstances such as to render unreliable any confession which he might have made, then regardless of whether the extra-judicial confession is excluded or admitted, the statement may be given in evidence by the prosecution under section 76(1) and the accused may be cross-examined on any inconsistencies between that statement and the evidence he gives before the jury.[232] If this is correct, it presents the accused with an unenviable choice. An accused seeking to challenge the admissibility of a confession is virtually obliged to testify on the *voir dire* if his challenge is to have any chance of succeeding. If he elects to contest admissibility, then to the extent that evidence given by him on the *voir dire* is admissible in evidence at the trial, he is in effect deprived of the right to choose not to give evidence before the jury. If he elects to preserve that right, however, he deprives

---

[229] See also *R v Brophy* [1982] AC 476, HL, below.

[230] Cf s 4 of the Criminal Procedure Act 1865, which provides that 'if a witness, upon cross-examination as to a former statement made by him . . . does not distinctly admit that he has made such statement, proof may be given that he did in fact make it . . .': see Ch 7. Section 13 of the Hong Kong Evidence Ordinance is to the same effect. Lord Edmund Davies said at 259: 'But these statutory provisions have no relevance if the earlier statements cannot be put in evidence.'

[231] *Wong Kam Ming v R* is strong persuasive authority that the accused should not be cross-examined as to the truth of his confession on the *voir dire*: *R v Davis* [1990] Crim LR 860, CA.

[232] See Peter Mirfield 'The Future of the Law of Confessions' [1984] Crim LR 63 at 74.

himself of the right to challenge the admissibility of the confession.[233] An accused deprived of his rights in this manner, it has been said, would not receive a fair trial.[234] The solution, it is submitted, is for the judge to exercise his discretion under section 78 of the 1984 Act to exclude the statements made by the accused on the *voir dire* on the grounds that they would have such an adverse effect on the fairness of the proceedings that the court ought not to admit them.

The issue of discretion, in this context, arose in *R v Brophy*.[235] The accused was tried by a judge sitting without a jury under the Northern Ireland (Emergency Provisions) Act 1978 on an indictment containing forty-nine counts including counts of murder, causing explosions, and belonging to a proscribed organization, namely the IRA (count 49). The only evidence connecting him with the crimes was a number of oral and written statements made to the police. The accused challenged the admissibility of the statements on the grounds that they had been obtained by torture and inhuman or degrading treatment. The trial judge, after a *voir dire*, excluded evidence of the statements. The accused, in his evidence-in-chief on the *voir dire*, said that he had been a member of the IRA during most of the period charged in count 49. When the trial resumed, the prosecution called the shorthand writer to prove the statements of the accused as to his membership of the IRA. The accused was acquitted of the first forty-eight counts, which were unsupported by any evidence, but convicted on count 49. The Court of Appeal in Northern Ireland allowed the appeal and the appeal to the House of Lords was dismissed. It was held that the accused's membership of the IRA was relevant to the issue on the *voir dire* because the police would probably have known this and therefore would not only have been more hostile to him but also would have expected him to have received instruction on how to avoid succumbing to the normal techniques of interrogation not involving physical ill-treatment. It was further held that, in any event, the evidence-in-chief given by an accused on the *voir dire* should be treated as relevant, unless clearly and obviously irrelevant, with the accused being given the benefit of any reasonable doubt.[236] The House concluded that the relevance of the evidence in question to the issue at the *voir dire* having been established, the consequence was that it was inadmissible in the substantive trial. In answer to a submission by counsel for the prosecution that if the evidence on the *voir dire* were admissible in the trial proper, the accused would be adequately safeguarded if the judge had a discretion to exclude any such evidence which would prejudice him unfairly, Lord Fraser said:[237]

---

[233] See generally per Lord Hailsham in *Wong Kam-Ming v R* [1980] AC 247 at 261 and per Lord Fraser in *R v Brophy* [1982] AC 476 at 481. For views different to those expressed, see P Murphy [1979] Crim LR 364 and R Pattenden (1983) 32 ICLQ 812.

[234] Per Lord Fraser in *R v Brophy* [1982] AC 476 at 482.          [235] [1982] AC 476.

[236] However, if the accused goes out of his way to boast of having committed the crimes charged or uses the witness box as a platform for a political speech, such evidence will almost certainly be irrelevant to the issue at the *voir dire*: per Lord Fraser [1982] AC 476 at 481.

[237] [1982] AC 476 at 483.

The right of the accused to give evidence at the *voir dire* without affecting his right to remain silent at the substantive trial is in my opinion absolute and is not to be made conditional on an exercise of judicial discretion.

Now that the actual decision in this case would appear to have been reversed by the 1984 Act, it is submitted that evidence given on the *voir dire* should be excluded from the trial proper by exercise of the discretion under section 78.[238]

# D THE TRIAL

Once the trial judge has ruled that a confession is admissible, the weight to be attached to it, which depends upon its content and all the circumstances in which it was obtained, is entirely a question of fact for the jury.[239] On the resumption of the trial proper, therefore, the defence is fully entitled to adduce evidence and cross-examine prosecution witnesses with a view to impeaching the credibility of the person to whom the confession was allegedly made and showing, for example, that the confession was fabricated, in whole or in part, or made in circumstances different from those alleged by the prosecution.[240] Although, as we have seen, the truth of the confession is irrelevant on the *voir dire*, it is a crucial issue for the jury to consider.[241] The judge, pursuant to section 67(11) of the 1984 Act, may refer the jury to any relevant breaches of the Codes.[242] Moreover, the House of Lords in *R v Mushtaq*,[243] disapproving *Chan Wei Keung v R*,[244] has held by a majority that where the judge has ruled that a confession was not obtained by oppression nor in consequence of anything said or done which was likely to render unreliable any confession, he is required

---

[238] However, concerning Lord Fraser's reference to the 'right to remain silent at the substantive trial', see now s 35 of the Criminal Justice and Public Order Act 1994 (Ch 14) and generally P Mirfield 'Two Side-Effects of Sections 34 to 37 of the Criminal Justice and Public Order Act 1994' [1995] Crim LR 612.

[239] Per Lord Parker CJ in *R v Burgess* [1968] 2 QB 112 at 117–18, CA. But see s 77 (Ch 8).

[240] Where an accused, alleged to have made a statement confessing to two offences in respect of which separate trials take place, says at the first trial that the statement has been fabricated and is acquitted, then at the second trial evidence of the acquittal may be given on the question of the weight to be attached to the confession statement: *R v Hay* (1983) 77 Cr App R 70, CA. See also *Sambasivam v Malay Federation Public Prosecutor* [1950] AC 458 and cf *R v Doosti* (1985) 82 Cr App R 181, CA. Where an officer, in a connected series of interviews over a short period of time, has allegedly obtained, from a number of different accused, admissions about a number of related offences and (a) those interviews are alleged to have been fabricated and (b) the alleged admissions are the essential evidence against some of those accused who are nevertheless acquitted, then the jury should know of this at a separate trial of another of the accused when they are considering a challenge to the truth of evidence of admissions alleged to have been made by him to the same officer at the same time and about the same events: *R v Cooke* (1986) 84 Cr App R 286, CA. Where an officer has allegedly fabricated an admission in case B and also gave evidence of an admission in case A, where there was an acquittal by virtue of which his evidence is demonstrated to have been disbelieved, in case B he may be cross-examined about the matter, which is relevant to his credit: *R v Edwards* [1991] 2 All ER 266, CA. Cf *R v H* (1989) 90 Cr App R 440, CA; *Hui Chi-ming v R* [1991] 3 All ER 897, PC; and *R v Y* [1992] Crim LR 436, CA.

[241] *R v Murray* (1950) 34 Cr App R 203 at 207.　　[242] See *R v Kenny* [1992] Crim LR 800, CA.

[243] [2005] UKHL 25.　　[244] [1967] 2 AC 160, PC.

to direct the jury that, if they conclude that the alleged confession may have been so obtained, they must disregard it. If the jury reach such a conclusion, to permit them to rely upon the confession would be to fly in the face of the policy considerations said to underlie section 76(2), namely that the rejection of an improperly obtained confession is dependent not only upon possible unreliability, but also upon the principle that a man cannot be compelled to incriminate himself and upon the importance that attaches in a civilized society to proper behaviour by the police towards those in their custody. Furthermore, permission to rely upon the confession in these circumstances would also be an invitation to the jury to act in a way that was incompatible with the accused's right against self-incrimination under Article 6(1) of the European Convention on Human Rights.

It remains to note that the trial judge, once he has determined that a confession is admissible under section 76 of the 1984 Act, has no power, at some later stage in the trial, to reconsider its admissibility as a matter of *law*, although he is then empowered to exclude it in the exercise of his *discretion* under section 82(3). In *R v Sat-Bhambra*[245] a confession was ruled to be admissible after a trial within a trial in which a doctor had given expert evidence to the effect that the accused, who suffered from a mild form of diabetes, could have been affected by hypoglycaemia at the time of his interrogation. When the doctor was called in the trial proper, his evidence on the issue came out more in favour of the accused. The trial judge, however, declined to reconsider his decision on admissibility on the grounds that he was precluded from so doing by the terms of section 76. The Court of Appeal held that the trial judge had acted properly. Section 76 refers to a confession which the prosecution 'proposes to give in evidence' and which the court 'shall not allow . . . to be given in evidence' and therefore, once the judge has ruled that a confession is admissible, section 76 ceases to have effect. Section 78, which, similarly, refers to evidence on which the prosecution 'proposes to rely', also ceases to have effect.[246] The judge, however, is not powerless: if, in the light of the evidence given in the trial proper, he concludes that his previous decision on admissibility has been invalidated, he may, in the exercise of his discretion to exclude under section 82(3), direct the jury to disregard the confession.[247] Alternatively, and depending on the circumstances of the case, he may either point out to the jury the evidence which affects the weight of the confession and leave the matter in their hands or, if he thinks that the matter is not capable of remedy by any form of direction, discharge the jury from giving a verdict. The same options, presumably, would be open to a judge when a confession is put in evidence and the accused *then*

---

[245] (1988) 88 Cr App R 55, CA.

[246] Cf per Russell LJ in *R v Liverpool Juvenile Court, ex p R* [1987] 2 All ER 668 at 672–3, dealing with similar issues in relation to summary trials (see Ch 2).

[247] Section 82(3) is the source of the power, but the judge is likely to re-apply the s 78 criteria in the light of the new evidence: see *R v Hassan* [1995] Crim LR 404, CA.

gives evidence to the effect that it was obtained by one of the methods described in section 76(2).[248]

## 1 CONFESSIONS IMPLICATING CO-ACCUSED

If an accused goes into the witness box and gives evidence implicating a co-accused, then what he says becomes evidence for all purposes of the case and accordingly may be used by the jury as evidence against the co-accused.[249] However, subject to three exceptions, which are considered below, where a confession is given in evidence by the prosecution and implicates both its maker and a co-accused, it is no evidence against the co-accused because a confession is admissible as evidence of the truth of its contents only as against its maker. In these circumstances, therefore, the judge is duty bound to impress upon the jury that the confession cannot be used against the co-accused.[250] It may be doubted, however, whether such a direction, even if clear and emphatic, can ever fully remove the prejudice likely to be caused to the co-accused.[251] In one case it was said that it would require mental gymnastics of Olympic standards for the jury to approach their task without prejudice.[252] One obvious solution is to order separate trials for the accused, but although the Court of Appeal in *R v Lake*[253] recognized that exceptionally this can be done, it nevertheless upheld a trial judge's refusal to order a separate trial for the accused notwithstanding the risk of prejudice caused by the fact that the two other co-accused had made confession statements seriously implicating him. Another solution is to edit the confession, for example by replacing the names of any co-accused with letters of the alphabet or expressions such as 'another person' or 'someone'.[254] Alternatively, counsel for the prosecution may agree not to read those parts of a confession statement which implicate a co-accused but have no real bearing on the case against its author. However, if the reference to the co-accused is exculpatory of the maker of the statement, he is entitled to have the statement read out in its entirety. As Lord Goddard CJ observed in *R v Gunewardene*,[255] in a passage approved by the Privy Council in *Lobban v R*:[256]

---

[248] It may also be assumed that the judge has a discretion, in this situation, to require the relevant prosecution witnesses to be recalled for further cross-examination: see per Lord Bridge in *Ajodha v The State* [1981] 2 All ER 193, PC at 202–3, a case decided under the law as it stood prior to the 1984 Act.

[249] See per Humphreys J in *R v Rudd* (1948) 32 Cr App R 138.

[250] *R v Gunewardene* [1951] 2 KB 600, CCA. See also *R v Blake* [1993] Crim LR 133, CA and per Lord Steyn in *Lobban v R* [1995] 2 All ER 602, PC at 613: 'the interests of the implicated co-defendant must be protected by the most explicit directions.'

[251] See, eg, *R v Williams; R v Davis* (1992) 95 Cr App R 1, CA. See also Peter Thornton, 'The Prejudiced Defendant: Unfairness Suffered by a Defendant in a Joint Trial' [2003] Crim LR 433.

[252] *R v Silcott* [1987] Crim LR 765, CC.     [253] (1976) 64 Cr App R 172.

[254] As suggested in *R v Silcott* [1987] Crim LR 765, CC. See also *R v Rogers and Tarran* [1971] Crim LR 413 and *R v Mathias* [1989] Crim LR 64, CC. However, insofar as *R v Silcott* and *R v Mathias* suggest that a judge has a discretionary power at the request of one accused to exclude evidence tending to support the defence of another, they do not correctly reflect the law: per Lord Steyn in *Lobban v R* [1995] 2 All ER 602, PC at 613 (see Ch 2).

[255] [1951] 2 KB 600 at 610–11.     [256] [1995] 2 All ER 602 at 612 (see Ch 2).

It not infrequently happens that a prisoner, in making a statement, though admitting his guilt up to a certain extent, puts greater blame upon the co-prisoner, or is asserting that certain of his actions were really innocent and it was the conduct of the co-prisoner that gave them a sinister appearance or led to the belief that the prisoner making the statement was implicated in the crime. In such a case that prisoner would have a right to have the whole statement read and could complain if the prosecution picked out certain passages and left out others . . .

In three exceptional situations, a confession may be admitted not only as evidence against its maker but also as evidence against a co-accused. The first exception was established in *R v Hayter*,[257] where the House of Lords held, by a majority, that in a joint trial of two or more accused for a joint offence, a jury is entitled to consider first the case in respect of accused A which is solely based on his own out-of-court admissions, and then to use their findings of A's guilt as a fact to be used evidentially in respect of co-accused B, and further that where proof of A's guilt is necessary for there to be a case to answer against B, there will be a case to answer against him notwithstanding that the only evidence of A's guilt is his own out-of-court admissions. A's confession, however, is not admitted against B for all purposes, but only subject to two conditions: first, that the jury are sufficiently sure of its truthfulness to decide that on that basis alone they can safely convict A; and secondly, that the jury are expressly directed that when deciding the case against B they must disregard entirely anything said out of court by A which might otherwise be thought to incriminate B. In reaching this conclusion, the majority were heavily influenced by the policy considerations underlying section 74 of the Police and Criminal Evidence Act 1984, whereby the fact that someone other than the accused has been convicted of an offence is admissible to prove, where to do so is relevant to an issue in the proceedings, that that person committed the offence. If there had been separate trials and A had been convicted, evidence of the conviction would have been admissible under section 74 of the 1984 Act in a subsequent trial of B. The majority was of the view that the outcome should be the same where both accused stand trial together, especially since in a joint trial B is in a better position to challenge the evidence that points to A's guilt than if A had already been convicted at a previous trial.

The second exception is where the co-accused by his words or conduct accepts the truth of the statement so as to make all or part of it a confession statement of his own.[258]

The third exception, which is perhaps best understood in terms of implied agency, applies in the case of conspiracy: statements (or acts) of one conspirator which the jury is satisfied were said (or done) in the execution or furtherance of the common design are admissible in evidence against another conspirator, even though he was not present at the time, to prove the nature and scope of the conspiracy, provided that there is some independent evidence to show the existence of the conspiracy and that

---

[257] [2005] 2 All ER 209, HL.
[258] See generally below under E **Statements made in the presence of the accused**.

the other conspirator was a party to it.[259] Thus in *R v Blake and Tye*,[260] where the accused were charged with conspiracy to pass goods through the Custom House without paying duty, it was held that whereas a false entry by T in a counterfoil of a cheque, by which he received his share of the proceeds of the crime, was not admissible against B because it was not made in pursuance of the conspiracy, but simply as a matter of record and convenience, another false entry by T in a day book could be used in evidence against B since it was made in the execution or furtherance of their common design. It remains to note that it does not matter in what order the evidence of the statements (or acts) of the conspirator and the 'independent evidence' is adduced.[261] Thus evidence of the statements (or acts) may be admitted conditionally, ie conditional upon some other evidence of the common design being adduced; if it transpires that there is no other evidence of common design, then the statements (or acts) should be excluded.[262] *R v Blake and Tye* was applied in *R v Devonport*,[263] in which the prosecution were allowed to rely on a document, dictated by one accused, which showed the proposed division of the proceeds of the conspiracy among all five accused.[264]

The third exception has been extended so that when, although a conspiracy is not charged, two or more people are engaged in a common enterprise, the acts and declarations of one in pursuance of the common purpose are admissible against another.[265] This principle applies to the commission of a substantive offence or series of offences by two or more people acting in concert, but is limited to evidence which shows the involvement of each accused in the commission of the offence or offences.[266] However, it cannot be extended to cases where individual defendants are charged with a number of separate substantive offences and the terms of a common enterprise are not proved or are ill-defined.[267] Thus the rule is that the acts and declarations of one, in furtherance of a sufficiently defined common design, are admissible to prove a substantive offence committed by another alone, but in pursuance of the same common design.[268]

The foregoing common-law exceptions have been preserved by statute. Section 118(1) of the Criminal Justice Act 2003 preserves: '5 Any rule of law relating to the admissibility of confessions ... in criminal proceedings' and '7 Any rule of law under which in criminal proceedings a statement made by a party to a common

---

[259] *R v Shellard* (1840) 9 C&P 277, *R v Meany* (1867) 10 Cox CC 506, *R v Walters; R v Tovey* (1979) 69 Cr App R 115 and *R v Jenkins* [2003] Crim LR 107, CA. However, if there are two conspiracies, what A does in pursuance of the first is not admissible against B in respect of his involvement in the second: *R v Gray* [1995] 2 Cr App R 100, CA at 131.

[260] (1844) 6 QB 126.

[261] *R v Governor of Pentonville Prison, ex p Osman* [1989] 3 All ER 701, QBD at 731.

[262] *R v Donat* (1985) 82 Cr App R 173, CA. [263] [1996] 1 Cr App R 221, CA.

[264] See also *R v Ilyas and Knight* [1996] Crim LR 810, CA.

[265] See, eg, *R v Jones* [1997] 2 Cr App R 119, CA.

[266] *R v Gray* [1995] 2 Cr App R 100, CA. See also *Tripodi v R* (1961) 104 CLR 1, HC of A.

[267] *R v Murray* [1997] 2 Cr App R 136, CA, per Otton LJ at 148.

[268] *R v Williams* [2002] All ER (D) 200 (Oct), [2002] EWCA Crim 2208, approving *R v Murray*, ibid.

enterprise is admissible against another party to the enterprise as evidence of any matter stated.'

## 2 EDITING

Where a confession is given in evidence, the whole statement, including qualifications, explanations or other exculpatory parts of it should be admitted so that the jury can fairly decide whether the statement, viewed as a whole, incriminates the accused.[269] However, where a confession statement contains inadmissible matter prejudicial to the accused, such as a reference to his previous convictions or bad character, it should be edited so as to eliminate the offending material.[270] Counsel may confer on the matter and, if necessary, the judge can take his part in ensuring that the statement is edited properly and to the right degree.[271] Although the rule is one of practice rather than law, a failure to edit may result in a conviction on indictment being quashed.[272] If the confession and the offending material are so interwoven as to be inseparable, or the removal of the latter would seriously alter the sense and meaning of the former so that they stand or fall together, the judge may, in the exercise of his discretion, exclude the entire statement on the grounds that its prejudicial effect outweighs its probative value.[273]

# E  STATEMENTS MADE IN THE PRESENCE OF THE ACCUSED

Under section 82(1) of the 1984 Act, a confession, as we have seen, includes any statement adverse to the person who made it 'whether made in words or otherwise'. It would seem, therefore, that under the Act, as at common law, the accused may accept the accusation of another so as to make it wholly or in part a confession statement of his own, not only by his words but also, in appropriate circumstances, by his conduct, demeanour or even silence. An alternative basis for the same conclusion is the

---

[269]  *R v Pearce* (1979) 69 Cr App R 365 at 369–70. How the judge should properly direct the jury in relation to a statement containing both inculpatory and exculpatory parts is considered in Ch 6 under C **Previous consistent or self-serving statements.**

[270]  When a suspect is interviewed about more offences than are eventually made the subject of committal charges, a fresh statement should be prepared and signed omitting all questions and answers about the uncharged offences unless either they might appropriately be taken into consideration or evidence about them is admissible on the charges preferred (eg as similar fact evidence). It may, however, be desirable to replace the omitted questions and answers with a phrase such as: 'After referring to some other matters, I then said . . .', so as to make it clear that part of the interview has been omitted: see para 24.4(b), *Practice Direction (Criminal Proceedings: Consolidation)* [2002] 1 WLR 2870.

[271]  *R v Weaver* [1968] 1 QB 353, CA.

[272]  *R v Knight; R v Thompson* (1946) 31 Cr App R 52; *Turner v Underwood* [1948] 2 KB 284, DC.

[273]  See s 82(3), above.

inclusive nature of the statutory definition. Either way, if this construction is correct, it would enable the accused, in appropriate circumstances, to make a representation under section 76(2) (or section 76A(2)) and thereby oblige the prosecution (or co-accused) to prove that such a confession was not obtained by the methods described in that subsection. If such a confession is admitted under section 76 (or section 76A), the common-law authorities will provide guidance to the judge as to how he should direct the jury; and the common-law principle of conditional admissibility will still apply (so that, in appropriate circumstances, the judge may direct the jury to disregard the evidence). The common-law rules relating to statements made in the presence of the accused, which now fall to be considered in more detail, have been preserved by section 118 of the Criminal Justice Act 2003. Section 118 preserves '5   Any rule of law relating to the admissibility of confessions . . . in criminal proceedings.'[274]

In *R v Norton*[275] the accused was convicted of having sexual intercourse with a girl under 13. Evidence was admitted of a statement made by the girl and directed at the accused, in which she identified him as the offender, and of his replies thereto. The conviction was quashed on the grounds that there was no evidence that the accused had accepted the truth of the statement. Pickford J, giving the judgment of the Court of Criminal Appeal, made a number of important observations which may be summarized in terms of four propositions:

1.  Statements made in the presence of the accused upon an occasion on which he might reasonably be expected to make some observation, explanation or denial are admissible in evidence if the judge is satisfied that there is evidence fit to be submitted to the jury that the accused by his answer to them, whether given by word or conduct, including silence, acknowledged the truth of the whole or part of them.

2.  Although if there is no such evidence fit to be left to the jury, the contents of the statements should be excluded, they may be given in evidence even when they were denied by the accused as it is possible that a denial may be given under such circumstances and in such a manner as to constitute evidence from which an acknowledgment may be inferred.[276]

3.  If the statements are admitted, the question whether the accused's answer, by words or conduct, did or did not in fact amount to an acknowledgment of them should be left to the jury.

---

[274] As to inferences that may be drawn pursuant to *statute* from an accused's silence on being questioned under caution by a constable or on being charged, see ss 34, 36, 37, and 38 of the Criminal Justice and Public Order Act 1994 (Ch 14).

[275] [1910] 2 KB 496.

[276] The denial may also give rise to such an inference if inconsistent with statements subsequently made by him or inconsistent with his defence at the trial, as when he denies an assault but at his trial pleads self-defence: see per Lord Moulton in *R v Christie* [1914] AC 545 at 560. See further *R v Z* (2003) 1 WLR 1489, CA, above under **A2 Confessions defined**.

4.   The judge should direct the jury that if they conclude that the accused acknowledged the truth of the whole or any part of the statement, they may take the
statement or part of it into consideration as evidence, but that without such an
acknowledgment they should disregard the statement altogether.[277]

In *R v Christie*[278] the accused was convicted of indecent assault on a boy, who gave
unsworn evidence. The boy's mother and a constable gave evidence to the effect that
shortly after the alleged act, the boy approached the accused, identified him by saying,
'That is the man', and described the assault. They also gave evidence that the accused
then said, 'I am innocent.' The Court of Criminal Appeal quashed the conviction on
the grounds that, the accused having denied the truth of the boy's statement, the
evidence of the mother and constable had been improperly admitted. The House of
Lords affirmed the order quashing the conviction on a different ground, that there
had been a misdirection on corroboration. However, in relation to the argument
which had succeeded in the Court of Criminal Appeal and which was recanvassed
before their Lordships, the House approved the approach taken in *R v Norton* but
regarded the principles enunciated by Pickford J as valuable rules of guidance rather
than strict rules of law.

When a person is accused of a crime in circumstances such that it would be
reasonable to expect some explanation or denial from him, whether the accused's
silence can give rise to an inference that he accepted the truth of the charge would
appear to depend upon whether it was made by a police officer or some other person
in authority or charged with the investigation of the crime as opposed to some other
person with whom the accused can be said to have been 'on even terms'. In *Hall v R*[279]
the question arose whether the silence of the accused *before* being cautioned could
give rise to an inference that he accepted the truth of an accusation made by or
through a police officer. The accused was convicted of unlawful possession of drugs
which were found in premises occupied by him and two co-accused. A police officer
told the accused that one of the co-accused had said that the drugs belonged to him,
that is the accused. The accused, who at that stage had not been cautioned, remained
silent. All of the accused were convicted. The Privy Council advised that the accused's
conviction be quashed. Lord Diplock, delivering the judgment of the Board, said:[280]

It is a clear and widely known principle of the common law in Jamaica, as in England, that a
person is entitled to refrain from answering a question put to him for the purpose of
discovering whether he has committed a criminal offence. *A fortiori* he is under no obligation to comment when he is informed that someone else has accused him of an offence. It
may be that in very exceptional circumstances an inference may be drawn from a failure to
give an explanation or a disclaimer, but in their Lordships' view silence alone on being

---

[277] Some of the authorities appear to be in favour of the admission of statements made in the presence of
the accused and of his reactions thereto without an indication from the trial judge as to the kinds of inference
that may be drawn therefrom: see, eg, *R v Black* (1922) 16 Cr App R 118. The approach suggested in *R v
Norton*, it is submitted, is preferable.
[278] [1914] AC 545.          [279] [1971] 1 WLR 298.          [280] [1971] 1 WLR 298 at 301.

informed by a police officer that someone else has made an accusation against him cannot give rise to an inference that the person to whom this information is communicated accepts the truth of the accusation . . .

The caution merely serves to remind the accused of a right which he already possesses at common law. The fact that in a particular case he has not been reminded of it is no ground for inferring that his silence was not in exercise of that right, but was an acknowledgment of the truth of the accusation.

Where there are two suspects and one of them answers a question put by an officer to both of them by telling a lie, similar principles apply to the issue whether the other of them, by his silence, adopted the answer of the first.[281]

In *Parkes v R*[282] the appellant was convicted of murder. At the trial, the victim's mother gave evidence that, having found her daughter injured, she went to the appellant and accused him twice of stabbing her daughter. The appellant said nothing and, when the mother threatened to detain him while the police were sent for, drew a knife and attempted to stab her. On these facts the Privy Council applied the following dictum of Cave J in *R v Mitchell*:[283]

Undoubtedly, when persons are speaking on even terms, and a charge is made, and the person charged says nothing, and expresses no indignation, and does nothing to repel the charge, that is some evidence to show that he admits the charge to be true.

Accordingly, it was held that the trial judge had not erred in instructing the jury that the appellant's reactions to the accusations, including his silence, were matters from which they could, if they saw fit, infer that he had accepted the truth of the accusation. *Hall v R* was distinguished on the grounds that, in that case, the person by whom the accusation was communicated was a police officer and there was no evidence of the accused's reaction other than his silence.

It seems that the accuser and the accused may be regarded as being on even terms notwithstanding that the police have brought them together and are present when the accusation is made. In *R v Horne*,[284] shortly after an assault, the police took the accused to the scene of the crime and sat him down opposite the victim. It was held that the accused's silent reaction to an accusation then made by the victim, but unprompted by the officers present, was capable of amounting to an acceptance of the accusation made.

The dictum of Cave J in *R v Mitchell* was also applied in *R v Chandler*.[285] The accused was convicted of conspiracy to defraud, the only evidence against him being an interview with a detective sergeant in the presence of his solicitor when, both *before* and *after* being cautioned, he answered some questions and remained silent or refused to answer others. The jury were directed that it was for them to decide whether the accused had remained silent before the caution in exercise of his common-law right or because he thought that had he answered he might have incriminated himself. The

---

[281]  *R v Collins* [2003] 2 Cr App R 199, CA.          [282]  [1976] 1 WLR 1251, PC.
[283]  (1892) 17 Cox CC 503 at 508.          [284]  [1990] Crim LR 188, CA.          [285]  [1976] 1 WLR 585.

Court of Appeal, satisfied that the accused and the detective sergeant were speaking on equal terms, since the former had his solicitor present to advise him and, if needed, subsequently to testify as to what had been said, held that some comment on the accused's lack of frankness before he was cautioned was justified. The conviction was quashed, however, on the grounds that the trial judge had short-circuited the proper intellectual process, which involved directing the jury to determine, first, whether the accused's silence amounted to an acceptance by him of what was said and, secondly, if satisfied that he did accept what was said, whether guilt could reasonably be inferred from what he had accepted. The importance of the decision lies in the reservations expressed about the dicta of Lord Diplock in *R v Hall*. Lawton LJ was of the opinion that they seemed to conflict with *R v Christie* and the earlier authorities and said:[286]

The law has long accepted that an accused person is not bound to incriminate himself; but it does not follow that a failure to answer an accusation or question when an answer could reasonably be expected may not provide some evidence in support of an accusation. Whether it does will depend on the circumstances.

In a later passage, his Lordship said:[287]

We do not accept that a police officer always has an advantage over someone he is question-ing ... A young detective questioning a local dignitary in the course of an inquiry into alleged local government corruption may be very much at a disadvantage. This kind of situation is to be contrasted with that of a tearful housewife accused of shoplifting or of a parent being questioned about the suspected wrongdoing of his son.

It remains to be seen, however, whether this flexible approach will prevail over Lord Diplock's view that silence alone, on being accused by or through a police officer, cannot give rise to an inference that the accused accepts the truth of the accusation made.

## F  FACTS DISCOVERED IN CONSEQUENCE OF INADMISSIBLE CONFESSIONS

At common law, the fact that a confession was inadmissible did not affect the admis-sibility of any incriminating facts discovered in consequence of that confession. In *R v Warickshall*[288] a woman was charged, as an accessory after the fact, with receiving stolen property. In consequence of a confession made by her, the property was found concealed in her bed at her lodgings. The confession was excluded on the grounds that it had been obtained by promises of favour. Counsel for the defence argued that evidence of the fact of finding the stolen property in her custody should also be excluded since it was obtained in consequence of the inadmissible evidence. Rejecting this argument, it was said:

---

[286] [1976] 1 WLR 585 at 589.        [287] [1976] 1 WLR 585 at 590.        [288] (1783) 1 Leach 263.

Confessions are received in evidence, or rejected as inadmissible, under a consideration whether they are or are not entitled to credit . . . This principle respecting confessions has no application whatever as to the admission or rejection of facts, whether the knowledge of them be obtained in consequence of an extorted confession, or whether it arises from any other source; for a fact, if it exists at all, must exist invariably in the same manner, whether the confession from which it is derived be in other respects true or false.[289]

The Criminal Law Revision Committee was in no doubt that this rule should be preserved on the grounds that to prevent the police from using any 'leads' obtained from an inadmissible confession would interfere unduly with justice and the detection of crime.[290] The rule is preserved by section 76(4) and by section 76A(4) of the 1984 Act, both of which provide that:

The fact that a confession is wholly or partly excluded in pursuance of this section shall not affect the admissibility in evidence—
(a) of any facts discovered as a result of the confession; . . .

If an interviewee, in consequence of some promise, inducement or threat to produce documentary evidence, hands over an incriminating document, it is unclear whether the document itself constitutes a confession and therefore may fall to be excluded under section 76, or is evidence of fact, admissible in law albeit open to discretionary exclusion under section 78. On one view, if the promise, inducement or threat expressly relates to the production of documentary evidence, any incriminating document then produced should be treated as a confession,[291] even if does not readily appear to be a 'statement' for the purposes of the section 82(1) definition of a confession ('any statement wholly or partly adverse to the person who made it . . . and whether made in words or otherwise').

Where incriminating facts discovered in consequence of an inadmissible confession are admitted in evidence, the question arises whether, notwithstanding that the confession itself must be excluded, evidence is admissible to show that the discovery of the facts in question was made as a result of the confession statement. For example, if an inadmissible confession of theft includes a statement that the stolen goods are hidden in a particular place, and they are found there, can the prosecution give evidence not only that they found the goods at that place but also that they found them as a result of something which the accused said? The importance of this question lies in the fact that proof that the stolen goods were hidden in a particular place, without reference to the confession, will do little or nothing to advance the prosecution case unless, as it happens, there is some link between the accused and the goods because, for example, they were found in a place frequented by him, such as his house or place of work, or

---

[289] See also, in relation to evidence of facts discovered as a result of an illegal search, *Kuruma v R* [1955] AC 197 at 203–5 and *King v R* [1969] 1 AC 304.

[290] 11th Report (Cmnd 4991) para 68.

[291] See *R v Barker* [1941] 2 KB 381, CCA at 384–5, a decision at common law reversed by s 105 of the Taxes Management Act 1970 (see above) but in any event since disapproved by the House of Lords: see per Lord Hutton in *R v Allen (No 2)* [2001] 4 All ER 768 at [33]–[35].

bore his fingerprints. The cases at common law were in conflict.[292] The Criminal Law Revision Committee was opposed to the admissibility of any part of the confession on the grounds that this would involve a decision on the part of the judge as to whether, in his opinion, the confession or part of it was likely to be true, an opinion which, although not binding on the jury, would be difficult for them not to be impressed by. The majority was in favour of allowing evidence to be given that the discovery of the incriminating facts was made 'as a result of a statement made by the accused'. The minority dissented on the grounds that the jury should not be informed indirectly of something of which the interests of justice require that they should not be informed directly.[293] Subject to cases in which the *defence* chooses to give evidence as to how the incriminating facts were discovered, the minority view is reflected in section 76(5) and (6) and in section 76A(5) and (6) of the 1984 Act, which provide that:

(5) Evidence that a fact to which this subsection applies was discovered as a result of a statement made by an accused person shall not be admissible unless evidence of how it was discovered is given by him or on his behalf.
(6) Subsection (5) above applies—
    (a) to any fact discovered as a result of a confession which is wholly excluded in pursuance of this section; and
    (b) to any fact discovered as a result of a confession which is partly so excluded, if the fact is discovered as a result of the excluded part of the confession.

Thus where part of a confession to murder, the entirety of which is excluded because extracted by police brutality, indicates the location of the murder weapon, that part remains inadmissible even if later shown to be reliable by the discovery of the weapon in the place indicated.[294]

The Committee was also of the opinion that where something in a confession statement shows that the accused speaks, writes or expresses himself in a particular manner and this serves to identify him with the offender, so much of the confession as is necessary to show such characteristics should be admissible for that purpose.[295] The point was illustrated by reference to *R v Voisin*.[296] The accused was convicted of murdering a woman whose body was found in a parcel together with a piece of paper bearing the handwritten words 'Bladie Belgiam'. The accused, without being cautioned, was asked by the police to write down 'Bloody Belgian'. He wrote down 'Bladie Belgiam' and this writing was admitted in evidence at his trial. The accused appealed on the grounds, inter alia, that he should have been cautioned before being asked to write the words in question. The appeal failed. Although the case did not concern an inadmissible confession, the Committee was of the view that, had the words been written in an inadmissible confession, that part of it should have been admissible, not

---

[292] See *R v Griffin* (1809) Russ&Ry 151, CCR, *R v Gould* (1840) 9 C&P 364, CCC and *R v Garbett* (1847) 2 Car&Kir 474, Ex Ch; and cf *R v Warickshall* (1783) 1 Leach 263 and *R v Berriman* (1854) 6 Cox CC 388, Assizes.

[293] 11th Report (Cmnd 4991) para 69.    [294] See *Lam Chi-ming v R* [1991] 3 All ER 172, PC.

[295] 11th Report (Cmnd 4991) para 69.    [296] [1918] 1 KB 531.

as evidence of the truth of its contents, but for the purpose of identifying the accused with the offender. Section 76(4) and section 76A(4) of the 1984 Act both provide that:

The fact that a confession is wholly or partly excluded in pursuance of this section shall not affect the admissibility in evidence—

(b) where the confession is relevant as showing that the accused speaks, writes or expresses himself in a particular way, of so much of the confession as is necessary to show that he does so.

# 14

# STATUTORY INFERENCES FROM AN ACCUSED'S SILENCE OR CONDUCT

Pursuant to statute, inferences may be drawn against an accused from: (a) his silence, ie his failure to testify, his failure to mention facts when questioned or charged, or his failure or refusal to account for objects, substances, marks, etc; (b) his refusal to consent to the taking of samples; and (c) his failure to provide advance disclosure of the defence case.

## A  INFERENCES FROM SILENCE

### 1  THE 'RIGHT TO SILENCE'

The so-called 'right to silence' formerly comprised two 'rights', the privilege against self-incrimination, ie the freedom of an accused from the compulsion to incriminate himself, and the 'right' not to have adverse inferences drawn from his silence. More narrowly examined, the 'right to silence' encompassed a number of specific 'rights', more accurately rules, including the following.

1.  A suspect is under no legal obligation to assist the police with their inquiries.[1]

2.  An accused is not obliged to give advance notice of the evidence in support of his defence; and it is wrong to make adverse comments about the fact that an accused, having been cautioned by the police, (a) remained silent,[2] (b) declined to answer some questions[3] or (c) failed to reveal his defence.[4]

---

[1] *Rice v Connolly* [1966] 2 QB 414.    [2] *R v Leckey* [1944] KB 80.

[3] *R v Gilbert* (1977) 66 Cr App R 237, CA; *R v Raviraj* (1986) 85 Cr App R 93, CA; and *R v Henry* [1990] Crim LR 574. See also *R v Mann* (1972) 56 Cr App R 750, CA and *R v Welch* [1992] Crim LR 368, CA.

[4] *R v Lewis* (1973) 57 Cr App R 860, CA; *R v Foster* [1974] Crim LR 544, CA; and *R v Gilbert* (1977) 66 Cr App R 237. As to inferences from silence where an accused and his accuser are on 'even terms', see *R v Norton* [1910] 2 KB 496, *Hall v R* [1971] 1 WLR 298, etc (Ch 13). As to inferences from refusal to provide samples, see *R v Smith* (1985) 81 Cr App R 286 and s 62(10) of the Police and Criminal Evidence Act 1984, below.

3. An accused is not a compellable witness.[5]

4. The failure of an accused to testify shall not be made the subject of any comment by the prosecution.[6]

5. Although in appropriate circumstances a judge may invite a jury to draw adverse inferences from failure to testify, they should be directed not to assume guilt from such a failure.[7]

Prior to the Criminal Justice and Public Order Act 1994, few statutory provisions operated to curtail the 'right to silence' to any significant degree. Two important examples may be given. First, rule 24 of the Criminal Procedure Rules 2005[8] provides that an accused shall not without the leave of the court adduce expert evidence unless he has given to the prosecution a written statement of the finding or opinion which he proposes to adduce.[9] Second, under the Criminal Justice Act 1987, in cases of serious or complex fraud, although an accused may depart from the case which he disclosed in pursuance of a requirement imposed by the court at a preparatory hearing, if he does so depart, or if he fails to comply with such a requirement, the judge or, with the leave of the judge, any other party, may make such comment as appears to the judge to be appropriate, and the jury or, in the case of a trial without jury, the judge, may draw such inferences as appear proper.[10]

Compared to these two statutory provisions, sections 34–38 of the Criminal Justice and Public Order Act 1994, constitute a major curtailment of the 'right to silence'. Thus although the accused retains his 'right' to remain silent both at the trial and under interrogation, 'proper' inferences may be drawn from (i) his failure to give evidence or his refusal, without good cause, to answer any question at the trial (section 35); (ii) his failure to mention certain facts when questioned under caution or on being charged (section 34); and (iii) his failure or refusal to account for objects, substances or marks (section 36) or his presence at a particular place (section 37).[11]

---

[5] Section 1 of the Criminal Evidence Act 1898 and s 53 of the Youth Justice and Criminal Evidence Act 1999 (Ch 5).

[6] Section 1(b) of the Criminal Evidence Act 1898, now repealed: see below.

[7] *R v Bathurst* [1968] 2 QB 99, CA and *R v Taylor* [1993] Crim LR 223, CA.

[8] SI 2005/384.

[9] See Ch 18. Advance notice must also be given to the prosecution of certain defences available to charges that consumer goods failed to comply with the general safety requirements: see s 39 of the Consumer Protection Act 1987.

[10] See ss 7, 9, and 10.

[11] As to the effect of the abolition of the right to silence in England and in Northern Ireland, see respectively T. Bucke, R. Street, and D. Brown 'The Right of Silence: The Impact of the Criminal Justice and Public Order Act 1994' (2000), Home Office Research Study No 199 and J Jackson, M Wolfe, and K Quinn 'Legislating Against Silence: The Northern Ireland Experience' (2000), Northern Ireland Office. See also J Jackson 'Silence and Proof: extending the boundaries of criminal proceedings in the United Kingdom' (2001) 5 E&P 145.

## 2 FAILURE TO TESTIFY

Section 35 of the Criminal Justice and Public Order Act 1994 provides as follows:

(1) At the trial of any person for an offence, subsections (2) and (3) below apply unless—
  (a) the accused's guilt is not in issue; or
  (b) it appears to the court that the physical or mental condition of the accused makes it undesirable for him to give evidence;
  but subsection (2) below does not apply if, at the conclusion of the evidence for the prosecution, his legal representative informs the court that the accused will give evidence or, where he is unrepresented, the court ascertains from him that he will give evidence.

(2) Where this subsection applies, the court shall, at the conclusion of the evidence for the prosecution, satisfy itself (in the case of proceedings on indictment with a jury, in the presence of the jury) that the accused is aware that the stage has been reached at which evidence can be given for the defence and that he can, if he wishes, give evidence and that, if he chooses not to give evidence, or having been sworn, without good cause refuses to answer any question, it will be permissible for the court or jury to draw such inferences as appear proper from his failure to give evidence or his refusal, without good cause, to answer any question.

(3) Where this subsection applies, the court or jury, in determining whether the accused is guilty of the offence charged,[12] may draw such inferences as appear proper from the failure of the accused to give evidence or his refusal, without good cause, to answer any question.

(4) This section does not render the accused compellable to give evidence on his own behalf, and he shall accordingly not be guilty of contempt of court by reason of a failure to do so.

(5) For the purposes of this section a person who, having been sworn, refuses to answer any question shall be taken to do so without good cause unless—
  (a) he is entitled to refuse to answer the question by virtue of any enactment, whenever passed or made, or on the ground of privilege; or
  (b) the court in the exercise of its general discretion excuses him from answering it.

There must be an evidential basis for a defence application that section 35(1)(b) applies. If there is, the judge should decide the matter in a *voir dire*, but if there is not, it is not incumbent on him to order a *voir dire* of his own volition.[13] There must also be an evidential basis for the finding of the court under section 35(1)(b). Although such a finding does not always need to be based on expert medical evidence, such evidence will be necessary in some cases, as when it is said that the accused's depression makes it undesirable for him to give evidence.[14] In *R v Friend*[15] it was said that for the purposes of section 35(1)(b) a 'physical condition' might include one involving a

---

[12] Or any other offence of which the accused could lawfully be convicted on that charge: s 38(2).
[13] *R v A* [1997] Crim LR 883, CA.    [14] *DPP v Kavanagh* [2005] NLJ 690.
[15] [1997] 1 WLR 1433, CA.

risk of an epileptic attack, and a 'mental condition' might include latent schizo-phrenia where the experience of evidence might trigger a florid state. It was also said that the language of the subsection was such as to give a wide discretion to the trial judge, whose decision can only be impugned if *Wednesbury* unreasonable.[16] In *R v Friend* the accused had a mental age of 9, but it was held that the trial judge had not erred in declining to rule that it was 'undesirable for him to give evidence'.

Section 35(2) places a mandatory requirement on the court to satisfy itself of the matters set out therein and the court can only do this by asking either the accused or his representative.[17] By inference, counsel has to be asked in a situation where it is possible to take instructions from the accused, which will not be possible where the accused has absconded.[18]

Under section 35(1) the court is not required to satisfy itself of the matters specified in section 35(2) if, at the end of the prosecution case, the accused's representative informs the court that the accused will give evidence. According to para 44.2 of the *Practice Direction (Criminal Proceedings: Consolidation)*,[19] this should be done in the presence of the jury and, if the representative indicates that the accused will give evidence, the case should proceed in the usual way. Somewhat bizarrely, therefore, if a represented accused indicates that he will testify, there is no obligation on the *court* to ascertain whether he is aware of the potential consequence of refusing without good cause to answer any question. It has been held that if, in the event, such an accused does refuse to answer any question without good cause, the judge may then tell him, in an unoppressive way, of the potential consequences.[20] It is submitted that in these circumstances, such a warning should be mandatory.

The *Practice Direction* continues as follows:

44.3 If the court is not so informed, or if the court is informed that the accused does not intend to give evidence, the judge should in the presence of the jury inquire of the representative in these terms:

'Have you advised your client that the stage has now been reached at which he may give evidence and, if he chooses not to do so or, having been sworn, without good cause refuses to answer any question, the jury may draw such inferences as appear proper from his failure to do so?'

44.4 If the representative replies to the judge that the accused has been so advised, then the case shall proceed. If counsel replies that the accused has not been so advised then the judge shall direct the representative to advise his client of the consequences set out in paragraph 3 hereof and should adjourn briefly for this purpose before proceeding further.

44.5 If the accused is not represented the judge shall at the conclusion of the evidence for the prosecution and in the presence of the jury say to the accused:

---

[16] *Associated Provincial Picture Houses Ltd v Wednesbury Corpn* [1948] 1 KB 223, CA.

[17] *R v Cowan* [1996] 1 Cr App R 1, CA, at 9.     [18] *R v Gough* [2002] Cr App R 121, CA.

[19] [2002] 1 WLR 2870.     [20] *R v Ackinclose* [1996] Crim LR 74, CA.

'You have heard the evidence against you. Now is the time for you to make your defence. You may give evidence on oath, and be cross-examined like any other witness. If you do not give evidence or, having been sworn, without good cause refuse to answer any question the jury may draw such inferences as appear proper. That means they may hold it against you. You may also call any witness or witnesses whom you have arranged to attend court. Afterwards you may also, if you wish, address the jury by arguing your case from the dock. But you cannot at that stage give evidence. Do you now intend to give evidence?'

Although section 35 is expressly without prejudice to the accused's right not to testify on his own behalf (section 35(4)), under section 35(3) the court or jury may draw 'proper' inferences from his failure to testify or his refusal, without good cause, to answer any question. Section 35(5) creates a conclusive presumption: an accused who has been sworn and refuses to answer any question will be deemed to have so refused without good cause unless either (a) he is entitled to refuse by reason of an enact-ment[21] or on the ground of privilege (eg legal professional privilege),[22] or (b) the court excuses him from answering in the exercise of its general discretion.

Under section 38(3):

A person shall not . . . be convicted of an offence solely on an inference drawn from such a failure as is mentioned in section . . . 35(3) . . .

However, as we shall see, in *Condron v United Kingdom*[23] the European Court of Human Rights has held that it is incompatible with the right to silence to base a conviction solely *or mainly* on the accused's silence or refusal to answer questions or give evidence.

In *R v Cowan*[24] the Court of Appeal rejected as contrary to the plain words of section 35, a submission that the operation of section 35(3) should be confined to exceptional cases. In answer to the first argument in support of the submission, that the section constituted an infringement of the accused's right to silence, the court stressed that the 'right of silence' had not been abolished by the section, but expressly preserved by section 35(4). Secondly, it was argued that the section had watered down the burden of proof and in effect put a burden on the accused to testify in order to avoid conviction. Lord Taylor CJ held that this argument was misconceived because (i) the prosecution have to establish a prima facie case before any question of the accused testifying is raised, (ii) the court or jury is prohibited from convicting solely because of an inference drawn from silence (section 38(3)), and (iii) the burden of proving guilt beyond reasonable doubt remains on the prosecution throughout. Thus although the effect of section 35 is that the court or jury may regard the inference drawn from silence as, in effect, a further evidential factor in support of the prosecution

---

[21] The phrase 'entitled to refuse' was probably used because of the wording of s 1(3) of the Criminal Evidence Act 1898 (now repealed). Section 1(3) provided that an accused, if asked a question relating to his previous convictions or bad character, 'shall not be required' to answer it. See now s 101 of the Criminal Justice Act 2003, Ch 17.

[22] See Ch 20.     [23] (2001) 31 EHRR 1, ECHR.     [24] [1995] 4 All ER 939.

case, it cannot be the only factor to justify a conviction: the totality of the evidence must prove guilt beyond reasonable doubt.

A third argument in support of the submission was that an inference should only be drawn where there is no reasonable possibility of an innocent explanation for the accused's silence; that an inference should not be drawn where there are 'good reasons' for silence consistent with innocence, for example (a) where there is other defence evidence to contradict the prosecution case (b) where an accused is nervous, inarticulate or unlikely to perform well in the witness box (c) where an accused is under duress or fear for his or another's safety or (d) where—as in two of the cases before the court—an accused has attacked prosecution witnesses and decided not to give evidence because it would expose him to cross-examination on his previous convictions; and that counsel may properly advance such reasons without the need for evidence. This argument was also rejected. The court accepted that, apart from the mandatory exceptions in section 35(1), it is open to the court to decline to draw an adverse inference and for a judge to direct or advise a jury against drawing such an inference if the circumstances of the case justify such a course, but held that there needs to be either some evidential basis for declining to draw an adverse inference[25] or some exceptional factors in the case making that a fair course to take—it is improper for defence counsel to give to the jury reasons for his client's silence at trial in the absence of evidence to support such reasons.[26] The court stressed that the inferences permitted are only such 'as appear proper', a phrase intended to leave a broad discretion to a trial judge to decide in all the circumstances whether any proper inference is capable of being drawn by the jury. If not, he should tell them so; otherwise, it is for the jury to decide whether in fact an inference should properly be drawn. The court also rejected the specific submission that an inference should not be drawn where an accused seeks to avoid cross-examination on his record. It was pointed out that to hold otherwise would lead to the bizarre result of an accused with previous convictions being in a more privileged position than an accused with a clean record.[27]

The Judicial Studies Board has suggested the following specimen direction.

The defendant has not given evidence. That is his right. But, as he has been told, the law is that you may draw such inferences as appear proper from his failure to do so. Failure to give evidence on its own cannot prove guilt but depending on the circumstances, you may hold his failure against him when deciding whether he is guilty. [There is evidence before you on the basis of which the defendant's advocate invites you not to hold it against the defendant that he has not given evidence before you namely ... If you think that because of this

---

[25] Presumably it is open to the judge to hear such evidence on a *voir dire*, a course that would seem to be particularly important in cases in which the reasons for silence can only be established, in effect, by the accused himself.

[26] No examples were given of the kind of 'evidential basis' or 'exceptional factors' which might lead a judge to conclude that an inference should not be drawn. In *R v Napper* [1996] Crim LR 591, CA, it was held that the fact that the police failed to interview the accused while the alleged frauds were reasonably fresh in his mind did not warrant such a conclusion.

[27] See also, applying *R v Cowan* in this respect, *R v Taylor* [1999] Crim LR 77, CA.

evidence you should not hold it against the defendant that he has not given evidence, do not do so. But if the evidence he relies on presents no adequate explanation for his absence from the witness box then you may hold his failure to give evidence against him. You do not have to do so.] What proper inferences can you draw from the defendant's decision not to give evidence before you? If you conclude that there is a case for him to answer, you may think that the defendant would have gone into the witness box to give you an explanation for or an answer to the case against him. If the only sensible explanation for his decision not to give evidence is that he has no answer to the case against him, or none that could have stood up to cross-examination, then it would be open to you to hold against him his failure to give evidence. It is for you to decide whether it is fair to do so.

In *R v Cowan* the Court of Appeal considered the specimen direction to be, in general terms, a sound guide. It held that although it may be necessary to adapt or add to it in the particular circumstances of an individual case, there were certain essentials:

1.  The judge must direct the jury that the burden remains on the prosecution throughout and must direct them as to the required standard of proof.

2.  The judge should make clear that the accused is entitled to remain silent: it is his right and his choice.

3.  The jury must be told that an inference from failure to give evidence cannot on its own prove guilt (section 38(3)).[28]

4.  The jury must be satisfied that the prosecution have established a case to answer before drawing any inferences from silence.[29] Although the judge must have thought that there was a case to answer, the jury may not believe the witnesses whose evidence the judge considered sufficient to raise a prima facie case. It must therefore be made clear that they must find that there is a case to answer on the prosecution evidence before drawing an adverse inference from silence.[30]

5.  The jury should also be directed that if, despite any evidence relied upon to explain the accused's silence, or in the absence of such evidence, they conclude that the silence can only sensibly be attributed to his having no answer, or none that would stand up to cross-examination, they may draw an adverse inference.[31]

---

[28]  Cowan's appeal was allowed on the basis that the jury had not been directed in accordance with 3 (and 5, below).

[29]  'Inescapable logic' and fairness demand that this fourth 'essential' direction be given: see *R v Birchall* [1999] Crim LR 311, CA. See also *R v El-Hannachi* [1998] 2 Cr App R 226, CA. In both cases, failure to give the direction resulted in a successful appeal against conviction.

[30]  See further per Lord Slynn in *Murray v DPP* (1994) 99 Cr App R 396, HL, below. Presumably, the jury will need specific guidance on the concept of 'a case to answer'. The task of deciding that matter, at the end of the trial, but on the basis of the prosecution evidence alone, would seem to be particularly onerous.

[31]  Where there is no evidence to explain the accused's silence, it is not incumbent on a judge to embark on, or to invite the jury to embark on, possible speculative reasons consistent with innocence which might theoretically prompt an accused to remain silent: per Lord Taylor CJ, [1995] 4 All ER 939 at 949.

The court further held that it is not possible to anticipate all the circumstances in which a judge might think it right to direct or advise a jury against drawing an adverse inference. Noting that it would not be wise even to give examples, as each case must turn on its own facts, the court cited with approval the following dictum of Kelly LJ in *R v McLernon*:[32]

the court has then a complete discretion as to whether inferences should be drawn or not. In these circumstances it is a matter for the court in any criminal case (1) to decide whether to draw inferences or not; and (2) if it decides to draw inferences what their nature, extent and degree of adversity, if any, may be. It would be improper and indeed quite unwise for any court to set out the bounds of either steps (1) or (2). Their application will depend on factors peculiar to the individual case . . .

Finally, the court in *R v Cowan* stressed that the Court of Appeal will not lightly interfere with a judge's exercise of discretion to direct or advise the jury as to the drawing of inferences from silence and as to the nature, extent and degree of such inferences. As long as the judge gives the jury adequate directions of law of the kind indicated above, and leaves the decision to them, the Court of Appeal will be slow to substitute its own view.

In some cases, failure to go into the witness box is unlikely to have any real bearing on the issues in the case, as when the facts are not in dispute and the only issue is whether they fall within the offence charged[33] and as when an accused charged with murder admits the assault on the victim but denies causation, an issue which is then resolved on the basis of the expert witnesses called.[34] It seems equally clear, however, that in other cases it may be perfectly proper to draw a strong adverse inference. Typically, such an inference is likely to be drawn where the uncontested or clearly established facts point so strongly to the guilt of the accused as to call for an explanation,[35] or where the defence case involves alleged facts which are at variance with the prosecution evidence or additional to it and exculpatory and must, if true, be within the accused's knowledge.[36] However, it does not follow that inferences may only be drawn in respect of specific facts: in appropriate circumstances, it may be proper to draw a general inference that by reason of his silence, the accused is guilty of the offence charged. In *Murray v DPP*,[37] a decision under the equivalent provision in the Criminal Evidence (NI) Order 1988,[38] M was convicted of attempted murder and possession of a firearm with intent to endanger life. There was evidence to link the accused with the attack, but he gave no evidence at the trial. The trial judge said that it

---

[32] [1992] NIJB 41, a decision on the equivalent provision in Art 4 of the Criminal Evidence (NI) Order 1988, SI 1988/1987 (NI 120).

[33] *R v McManus* [2002] 1 Arch News 2, [2001] EWCA Crim 2455.

[34] See Wasik and Taylor *Blackstone's Guide to the Criminal Justice and Public Order Act 1994* (London 1995) 65.

[35] See, at common law, *R v Mutch* [1973] 1 All ER 178, CA. See also *R v Corrie* (1904) 20 TLR 365.

[36] See, at common law, *R v Martinez-Tobon* [1994] 2 All ER 90, CA; and in cases where the accused bears the burden of proof, *R v Bathurst* [1968] 2 QB 99 at 107, CA.

[37] (1994) 99 Cr App R 369.    [38] Art 4, SI 1988/1987 (NI 120).

seemed to him remarkable that the accused had not given evidence and that it was only common sense to infer 'that he is not prepared to assert his innocence on oath because that is not the case'. The House of Lords, upholding the conviction, held that having regard to the cumulative effect of all the circumstantial evidence against the accused, the trial judge was entitled as a matter of common sense to infer that there was no innocent explanation to the prima facie case that he was guilty. Lord Slynn said:[39]

The accused cannot be compelled to give evidence but he must risk the consequences if he does not do so. Those consequences are not simply . . . that specific inferences may be drawn from specific facts. They include in a proper case the drawing of an inference that the accused is guilty . . .

This does not mean that the court can conclude simply because the accused does not give evidence that he is guilty. In the first place the prosecutor must establish a prima facie case — a case for him to answer. In the second place in determining whether the accused is guilty the judge or jury can draw only 'such inferences from the refusal as appear proper'. As Lord Diplock said in *Haw Tua Tau v Public Prosecutor*:[40]

'What inferences are proper to be drawn from an accused's refusal to give evidence depend upon the circumstances of the particular case, and is a question to be decided by applying ordinary common sense.'

There must thus be some basis derived from the circumstances which justify the inference.

If there is no prima facie case shown by the prosecution there is no case to answer. Equally, if parts of the prosecution case had so little evidential value that they called for no answer, a failure to deal with those specific matters cannot justify an inference of guilt.

On the other hand, if aspects of the evidence taken alone or in combination with other facts clearly call for an explanation which the accused ought to be in a position to give, if an explanation exists, then a failure to give any explanation may as a matter of common sense allow the drawing of an inference that there is no explanation and that the accused is guilty.[41]

Under proviso (b) to section 1 of the Criminal Evidence Act 1898, the failure of any person charged with an offence to give evidence shall not be made the subject of any comment by the prosecution. Section 1(b) has been repealed by the 1994 Act.[42] Comment is now permissible. However, if the trial judge is minded to direct or advise a jury against drawing an adverse inference, it is submitted that it would be good practice for him to inform prosecuting counsel of this before closing speeches, so that counsel refrains from comment. Conversely, if the judge is minded to direct the jury that they may draw proper inferences, it is submitted that prosecuting counsel should adhere to the kind of comment suggested (for the judge) in the Judicial Studies Board specimen direction and in *R v Cowan*.

---

[39] (1993) 99 Cr App R 369 at 405.     [40] [1982] AC 136 at 153.

[41] The drawing of adverse inferences from silence in *Murray v DPP* did not violate the European Convention on Human Rights: *Murray v United Kingdom* (1996) 22 EHRR 29, European Court of Human Rights, but see also Roderick Munday 'Inferences from Silence and European Human Rights Law' [1996] Crim LR 370.

[42] Section 168(3) and Sch 11.

## 3  FAILURE TO MENTION FACTS WHEN QUESTIONED OR CHARGED

### (a)  Background

In its 11th Report, the Criminal Law Revision Committee proposed that where an accused fails to mention any fact relied on in his defence which he could reasonably have been expected to mention either (i) before he was charged on being questioned by the police or (ii) on being charged, the court should be entitled to draw such inferences as appear proper, and the caution should be replaced by a notice explaining the potentially adverse effect of silence.[43] These proposals attracted widespread criticism at the time, but in 1976 were adopted in Singapore[44] and in 1988 were adopted in Northern Ireland.[45] There was also strong judicial comment in favour of their adoption in England and Wales. In *R v Alladice*[46] Lord Lane CJ, giving the reserved judgment of the Court of Appeal, observed that the effect of section 58 of the Police and Criminal Evidence Act 1984[47] was that in many cases a detainee who would otherwise have answered the questions of the police would be advised by his solicitor to remain silent and weeks later, at the trial, would not infrequently produce an explanation of, or a defence to, the charge, the truthfulness of which the police would have had no chance to check. Thus despite the fact that the explanation or defence, if true, could have been disclosed at the outset, and despite the advantage which the accused had gained by those tactics, no comment could be made to the jury to that effect. The effect of section 58, it was said, was such that the balance of fairness between prosecution and defence could not be maintained unless proper comment was permitted on silence in such circumstances.

The report of the Working Group set up by the Home Secretary in 1988 expressed the view that failure to answer police questions, even before the accused is brought to the police station, should be admissible evidence against him to show that his defence is untrue and to undermine his credibility, and he should be warned of the possibility at the outset.[48] The majority recommendation of the Royal Commission on Criminal Justice, in contrast, was that no inferences should be drawn from silence at the police station, but that when the prosecution case has been disclosed, an accused should be required to disclose his case, at the risk of adverse comment by the judge on any new defence then disclosed or any departure from the defence previously disclosed.

Section 34 of the Criminal Justice and Public Order Act 1994 reflects the recommendations of the Criminal Law Revision Committee, and not those of the Royal

---

[43]  Paras 28–52 and cl 11 of the draft Bill (Cmnd 4991).

[44]  See Meng Heong Yeo 'Diminishing the Right of Silence: The Singapore Experience' [1983] Crim LR 89 and Alan Khee-Jin Tan 'Adverse Inferences and the Right to Silence: Re-examining the Singapore Experience' [1997] Crim LR 471.

[45]  See SI 1988/1987 (NI 120) and JD Jackson 'Curtailing the Right of Silence: Lessons from Northern Ireland' [1991] Crim LR 404.

[46]  (1988) 87 Cr App R 380.          [47]  See Ch 13.

[48]  See C Division, Home Office London, 13 July 1989 and AAS Zuckerman 'Trial by Unfair Means—The Report of the Working Group on the Right of Silence' [1989] Crim LR 855. See also S Greer 'The Right of Silence: A Review of the Current Debate' (1990) 53 MLR 709.

Commission on Criminal Justice.[49] In *R v Hoare*[50] Auld LJ said: 'The whole basis of section 34, in its qualification of the otherwise general right of an accused to remain silent and require the prosecution to prove its case, is an assumption that an innocent defendant—as distinct from one who is entitled to require the prosecution to prove its case—would give an early explanation to demonstrate his innocence.'

Section 34 provides that:

(1) Where, in any proceedings against a person for an offence, evidence is given that the accused—

    (a) at any time before he was charged with the offence, on being questioned under caution by a constable trying to discover whether or by whom the offence had been committed, failed to mention any fact relied on in his defence in those proceedings; or

    (b) on being charged with the offence or officially informed that he might be prosecuted for it, failed to mention any such fact,

being a fact which in the circumstances existing at the time the accused could reasonably have been expected to mention when so questioned, charged or informed, as the case may be, subsection (2) below applies.

(2) Where this subsection applies—

    (a) [repealed];

    (b) a judge, in deciding whether to grant an application made by the accused under paragraph 2 of Schedule 3 to the Crime and Disorder Act 1998;[51]

    (c) the court, in determining whether there is a case to answer; and

    (d) the court or jury, in determining whether the accused is guilty of the offence charged,[52]

may draw such inferences from the failure as appear proper.

(2A) Where the accused was at an authorised place of detention[53] at the time of the failure, subsections (1) and (2) above do not apply if he had not been allowed an opportunity to consult a solicitor prior to being questioned, charged or informed as mentioned in subsection (1) above.

## (b) 'On being questioned under caution . . . or on being charged'

Section 34(1)(a) only applies in the case of an accused 'on being questioned under caution'. Thus it has no application in the case of an accused who simply refuses to leave the police cell in which he is being detained in order to be interviewed by the

---

[49] See generally D Birch 'Suffering in Silence: A Cost–Benefit Analysis of Section 34' [1999] Crim LR 769 and R Leng 'Silence pre-trial, reasonable expectations and the normative distortion of fact-finding' (2001) 5 E&P 240.

[50] [2005] 1 Cr App R 355, CA at [53].

[51] Ie an application by an accused to dismiss the charge or any of the charges in respect of which he has been sent to the Crown Court under s 51 of the Crime and Disorder Act 1998. Under s 51, an adult brought before a magistrates' court charged with an offence triable only on indictment shall be sent forthwith to the Crown Court.

[52] Or any other offence of which the accused could lawfully be convicted on that charge: s 38(2).

[53] 'Authorised place of detention' means a police station or other place prescribed by order made by the Secretary of State: s 38(2A).

police, but section 34(1)(b) will apply if such an accused, on being subsequently charged, fails to mention any fact relied on in his defence.[54] Paragraph 10.5 of Code C (the Code of Practice for the Detention, Treatment and Questioning of Persons by Police Officers) provides that the caution should be in the following terms:

You do not have to say anything. But it may harm your defence if you do not mention when questioned something which you later rely on in court. Anything you do say may be given in evidence.

Paragraph 10.7 provides that:

Minor deviations from the words of any caution given in accordance with this Code do not constitute a breach of this Code, provided the sense of the relevant caution is preserved.

Under Note 10D of the Code:

If it appears a person does not understand the caution, the person giving it should explain it in their own words.

Under para 11.4 of the Code, where a 'significant silence' (a silence which might give rise to an inference under the 1994 Act) has occurred before the start of the interview at the police station, then at the start of the interview, the interviewer, after cautioning the suspect, shall put the earlier 'significant silence' to the suspect and ask him whether he confirms or denies it and if he wants to add anything.

Section 34 applies in relation to questioning not only by constables, but also 'by persons (other than constables) charged with the duty of investigating offences or charging offenders' and in section 34(1) 'officially informed' means informed by a constable or any such person.[55] Under section 67(9) of the Police and Criminal Evidence Act 1984, which also refers to 'persons charged with the duty of investigating offences or charging offenders', it has been held, somewhat unsatisfactorily, that whether a person satisfies the test is a question of fact in each case.[56]

Section 34(1)(a) applies to questioning under caution by a constable 'trying to discover whether or by whom the offence had been committed'. Where there is sufficient evidence for a suspect to be charged and the interview should be brought to an end,[57] but questioning continues and is met with silence from which adverse inferences may be drawn, evidence of the silence may be excluded.[58] However, it has also been held that the sufficiency of evidence can normally only be judged after the suspect has been given an opportunity to volunteer an explanation, and that further questioning will not be in breach of the Code if the officer is still open-minded about the possibility of an explanation which might prevent the suspect from being charged,[59]

---

[54] *R v Johnson* (2005) *The Times*, 3 May 2005, CA.     [55] Section 34(4).
[56] See *R v Seelig* [1991] 4 All ER 429, CA etc (Ch 13).     [57] See paras 11.6 and 16.1 of Code C.
[58] See *R v Pointer* [1997] Crim LR 676, CA and *R v Gayle* [1999] Crim LR 502, CA.
[59] *R v McGuinness* [1999] Crim LR 318, CA and *R v Ioannou* [1999] Crim LR 586, CA.

in which case the officer will still be 'trying to discover whether or by whom the offence has been committed'.[60]

An inference may be drawn from silence on being questioned under section 34(1)(a), or from silence on being charged under section 34(1)(b), or from both. Thus although in most cases it will add nothing to invite the jury to consider drawing an additional inference at the later stage, in some cases it may be possible to draw a stronger inference then, as when a suspect, after interview, is bailed to come back to the police station a week later, when he is charged, having had a long time to think back over the events. These principles derive from *R v Dervish*,[61] where it was held that if no inference can be drawn under section 34(1)(a)—the interviews in that case were inadmissible by reason of breaches of the Codes of Practice—then subject to any issue of unfairness, the trial judge may leave to the jury the possibility of drawing an inference under section 34(1)(b). However, the court added that the trial judge should not permit the jury to draw such an inference if to do so would nullify the safeguards of the 1984 Act and Codes, or if there was bad faith by the police deliberately breaching the safeguards with a view to falling back on section 34(1)(b).

### (c) 'Failed to mention any fact relied on in his defence'

Where an accused, in interview after arrest, gives to the police a prepared statement and thereafter refuses to answer questions, he has not 'failed to mention' the facts set out in his statement. Thus in *R v Knight*,[62] where the prepared statement was wholly consistent with the defence evidence at trial, an adverse inference could not be drawn. The court held that the purpose of section 34(1)(a) was early disclosure of a suspect's account and not, separately and distinctly, the subjection of that account to the test of police cross-examination. However, as the court went on to stress, giving a prepared statement is not of itself an inevitable antidote to later adverse inferences because the statement may be incomplete in comparison with the accused's later account at trial. As was pointed out in *R v Turner*,[63] the submission of a prepared statement is a dangerous course for an innocent person, who may subsequently discover at trial that something significant was omitted. In that case it was held that the judge must identify any fact not mentioned in the prepared statement, which should be the subject of a specific direction. The court also noted that inconsistencies between the prepared statement and the accused's evidence do not necessarily amount to reliance on a fact not previously mentioned; and that where there are differences between the statement and the evidence given at trial, then depending on the precise circumstances, it may be better to direct the jury to consider the difference as constituting a previous lie,[64] rather than the foundation for a section 34 inference.

Inferences can only be drawn under section 34 where the accused has failed to

---

[60] *R v Odeyemi* [1999] Crim LR 828, CA. But see also s 37(7) of the Police and Criminal Evidence Act 1984 and generally Ed Cape 'Detention Without Charge; What Does "Sufficient Evidence to Charge" Mean' [1999] Crim LR 874.

[61] [2002] 2 Cr App R 105, CA.     [62] [2004] 1 WLR 340, CA.     [63] [2004] 1 All ER 1025, CA.

[64] See *R v Lucas* [1981] QB 720, CA etc, Ch 2

mention 'any fact', as opposed to some speculative possibility, relied on in his defence. In *R v Nickolson*[65] N, charged with sexual offences against the complainant in his house, denied in interview that anything indecent had ever occurred, but said that he was in the habit of masturbating in the bathroom. Subsequently, seminal stains were found on the complainant's nightdress and, at the trial, when asked if he could provide an explanation, N suggested that the complainant could have entered the bathroom after he had masturbated there. It was held that section 34 did not apply because N had not asserted as a fact that the complainant had visited the bathroom, but had proffered it as an explanation, something more in the nature of a theory, a possibility, or speculation. Section 34 will apply, however, if such speculation is based on a fact and the accused could reasonably have been expected to mention both the speculation and the factual basis for it.[66]

It seems clear that an inference may be drawn under section 34 from an accused's failure to mention a fact not only when the fact is first disclosed at trial, but also when the accused, having initially failed to mention a fact on being questioned under caution, disclosed it at a later stage of police questioning or in a written statement to the police.[67] In any event, however, the fact that the accused failed to mention must be relied on in his defence. In *R v Moshaid*,[68] in which the accused did not give or call any evidence, it was held that section 34 did not bite. It does not follow, however, that the relevant fact may be established only by the accused or a defence witness: it may also be established by a prosecution witness, either in cross-examination or examination-in-chief.[69] Thus section 34 does apply where defence counsel puts or suggests the fact to a prosecution witness in cross-examination and the witness accepts it.[70] It can also apply even if the witness under cross-examination does not accept the fact put or suggested. In *R v Webber*[71] the House of Lords held that an accused relies on a fact in his defence when counsel, acting on his instructions, puts a specific and positive case to a prosecution witness, as opposed to asking questions intended to probe or test the prosecution case,[72] even if the witness rejects the case being put. Two reasons were given. First, although questions only become evidence if accepted by the witness, where specific positive suggestions have been made, the jury may for whatever reason distrust the witness's evidence and ask themselves whether the version put for the accused may not be true. Secondly, since section 34(2)(c) permits the court to draw proper inferences when determining whether there is a case to answer, ie at a stage when the accused has had no opportunity to give or adduce evidence, it would be surprising if subsection (2)(c) were intended to apply only when, unusually, specific suggestions put to a prosecution witness are *accepted* by him. It was further held that

---

[65] [1999] Crim LR 61, CA.    [66] *R v B (MT)* [2000] Crim LR 181, CA.

[67] See *R v McLernon* (1990) Belfast CC, 20 Dec, a decision under Art 3 of the Criminal Evidence (NI) Order 1988, SI 1988/1987 (NI 120).

[68] [1998] Crim LR 420, CA.    [69] *R v Bowers* [1998] Crim LR 817, CA.

[70] See *R v McLernon* [1992] NIJB 41, CA.    [71] [2004] 1 WLR 404.

[72] If the judge is in doubt whether counsel is testing the prosecution evidence or advancing a positive case, he should ask counsel in the absence of the jury: ibid at [36].

where defence counsel adopts on behalf of his client in closing submissions evidence given by a co-accused, this may also amount to reliance on facts for the purposes of section 34.

In *R v Betts*[73] it was held that the bare admission at trial of a fact asserted by the prosecution cannot amount to reliance on a fact, but where explanation for the admitted fact is advanced by reliance on other facts, those facts may give rise to an inference if they were not mentioned on being questioned or charged. The court gave an example: if an accused admits for the first time at trial that a fingerprint was his and offers no explanation for it being found where it was, he relies on no fact, but it will be different if he also puts forward an explanation for the finding of the fingerprint. The court gave two reasons for its conclusion. The first was that a bare admission of a prosecution fact adds no fact to the case. As has been observed, however, the same can be said of a mere denial.[74] The second and compelling reason was that to draw an inference against an accused who did not make an admission in interview but did make it at trial would effectively be to remove his right of silence in breach of Article 6 of the European Convention of Human Rights. A further compelling reason was given in *R v Webber*. In that case, Lord Bingham approved earlier unreported authorities to the effect that rarely if ever can a section 34 direction be appropriate on failure to mention at interview an admittedly true fact, because the adverse inference to be drawn under the section is that the fact not mentioned at interview but relied on in his defence is likely to be *untrue*.

## (d) 'A fact which . . . the accused could reasonably have been expected to mention'

The fact relied on must be 'a fact which in the circumstances existing at the time the accused could reasonably have been expected to mention when . . . questioned, charged, or informed, as the case may be'. In deciding the matter, the jury will be very much concerned with the truth or otherwise of any explanation given by the accused for not mentioning the fact, because if they accept an exculpatory explanation as true, or possibly so, it will be obviously unfair to draw any adverse inference.[75]

In *R v Argent*[76] it was held that the expression 'in the circumstances' is not to be construed restrictively: account may be taken of such matters as time of day, the accused's age, experience, mental capacity, state of health, sobriety, tiredness, knowledge, personality, and legal advice. 'The accused', it was said, refers not to some hypothetical reasonable accused of ordinary phlegm and fortitude, but to the actual accused, with such qualities, apprehensions, knowledge and advice as he is shown to have had at the time. Sometimes, therefore, the jury may conclude that it was reasonable for the accused to have held his peace because, for example, he was tired, ill, frightened, drunk, drugged, unable to understand what was going on, suspicious of the police, afraid that his answer would not be fairly recorded, worried at committing himself without legal advice, or acting on legal advice. In other cases the jury may

---

[73] [2001] 2 Cr App R 257, CA.   [74] See D Birch [2001] Crim LR at p 757.
[75] Per Lord Bingham in *R v Webber* [2004] 1 WLR 404, HL at [29].   [76] [1997] 2 Cr App R 27, CA.

conclude that the accused could reasonably have been expected to mention the fact in issue. In *R v Howell*[77] Laws LJ said:

we do not consider the absence of a written statement from the complainant to be good reason for silence (if adequate oral disclosure of the complaint has been given), and it does not become good reason merely because a solicitor has so advised. Nor is the possibility that the complainant may not pursue his complaint good reason, nor a belief by the solicitor that the suspect will be charged in any event whatever he says. The kind of circumstance which may most likely justify silence will be such matters as the suspect's condition (ill-health, in particular mental disability; confusion; intoxication; shock, and so forth—of course we are not laying down an authoritative list), or his inability genuinely to recollect events without reference to documents which are not to hand, or communication with other persons who may be able to assist his recollection.

In deciding whether a fact is one that the accused could reasonably have been expected to mention, another relevant factor, it is submitted, is the importance of the fact to the defence in question, whether central to that defence or of only peripheral importance, because an accused cannot reasonably be expected to mention every fact, for example every last detail of an alibi as opposed to the key facts relating to where he was, when, and with whom (if anybody). The nature of the fact itself may also be highly relevant, especially if of a kind likely to embarrass the accused or compromise his personal or professional life, for example the fact, in support of an alibi, that at the time of the alleged offence he was not at the scene of the crime but elsewhere, in bed with a prostitute. It would be equally relevant, to take another example, if the fact in question were of a kind likely to create a danger of reprisals against the accused, his family or friends. Account also needs to be taken of the accused's knowledge of the case against him, and his understanding of (a) the nature of the offence in question and (b) the facts which might go to show his innocence of that offence.

Section 34(3) of the 1994 Act provides that:

Subject to any directions by the court, evidence tending to establish the failure may be given before or after evidence tending to establish the fact which the accused is alleged to have failed to mention.

In *R v Condron and Condron* the Court of Appeal, while stressing that no hard and fast procedure should be laid down, gave the following guidance:

In the ordinary way ... it would seem appropriate for prosecuting counsel to adduce evidence limited to the fact that after the appropriate caution the accused did not answer questions or made no comment. Unless the relevance of a particular point has been revealed in cross-examination, it would not seem appropriate to spend time at this stage going through the questions asked at interview.

If and when the accused gives evidence and mentions facts which, in the view of prosecuting counsel, he can reasonably have been expected to mention in interview, he can be asked why

---

[77] [2005] 1 Cr App R 1, CA at [24].

— not yet gave to the.

he did not mention them. The accused's attention will then no doubt be drawn to any relevant and pertinent questions asked at interview. The accused's explanation for his failure can then be tested in cross-examination. It will not generally be necessary to call evidence in rebuttal, unless there is a dispute as to the relevant contents of the interview.

### (e) Silence on legal advice

In *R v Condron and Condron*[78] the question arose whether an adverse inference can be drawn if the accused remained silent on legal advice. The accused, both heroin addicts, were convicted of offences relating to the supply of heroin. On their arrest, although a police doctor considered that they were fit for interview, a view of which they were aware, their solicitor considered that they were unfit to be interviewed because of their drug withdrawal symptoms. The solicitor therefore advised them not to answer questions, also advising them of the potential consequences, and making it plain that it was entirely their choice. At their trial, they gave detailed innocent explanations in relation to the prosecution evidence, which could have been given in answer to specific questions by the police in their interview. The Court of Appeal held that the trial judge had properly directed the jury that it was for them to decide whether any adverse inference should be drawn, but that it would have been *desirable* if he had given an additional direction to the effect that an adverse inference may be drawn if, despite any evidence relied on to explain the silence at interview, or in the absence of such evidence, they conclude that the silence can only sensibly be attributed to the accused having fabricated the evidence subsequently. However, the European Court of Human Rights has held that a direction along these lines is mandatory.[79] The Condrons complained that their right to a fair trial under Article 6 of the Convention had been violated. The European Court held as follows. (1) The right to silence could not be considered as an absolute right and the fact that the issue was left to the jury could not of itself be considered incompatible with Article 6. (2) The right was at the heart of the notion of a fair procedure under Article 6 and particular caution was required before a domestic court could invoke an accused's silence against him. It was incompatible with the right to base a conviction solely or mainly on the accused's silence or refusal to answer questions, or give evidence, but where a situation called for an explanation from an accused, then his silence could be taken into account in assessing the persuasiveness of the evidence against him. (3) The judge had not reflected the balance between the right to silence and the circumstances in which an adverse inference could be drawn. The judge's direction was such that the jury may have drawn an adverse inference even if satisfied with the accused's explanation of the silence. As a matter of fairness, the jury should have been directed that if they were satisfied that the accused's silence at interview could not sensibly be attributed to their having no answer or none that would stand up to cross-examination, then they should not draw an adverse inference.

The direction of the kind suggested by the Court of Appeal in *R v Condron and*

---

[78] [1997] 1 WLR 827, CA.      [79] *Condron v United Kingdom* (2001) 31 EHRR 1.

*Condron* does not have to be geared only to the inference of subsequent fabrication, but may deal with the different inference that the accused, by the time of the interview, had already invented a false story, in whole or in part, but did not want to reveal it, because of the risk that the police might then be able to expose its falsity.[80]

In *R v Condron and Condron* it was also held that the bare assertion, by an accused, that he did not answer questions because he was advised by his solicitor not to do so, is unlikely to prevent an adverse inference from being drawn:[81] it is necessary, if the accused wishes to invite the court not to draw an adverse inference, to go further and give the basis or reason for the advice. However, as the court pointed out, whereas a 'bare assertion' will not amount to a waiver of the legal professional privilege that attaches to communications between an accused and his solicitor prior to a police interview,[82] once the basis or reason for the advice is stated, this will amount to a waiver entitling the prosecution to ask the accused or, if the solicitor is also called, the solicitor, whether there were any other reasons for the advice, and the nature of the advice given, so as to explore whether the advice may also have been given for tactical reasons. It is desirable, therefore, that the judge warn counsel or the accused that the privilege may be lost.[83] In *R v Bowden*[84] it was held that if the defence reveal the basis or reason for the solicitor's advice to the accused not to answer questions, this amounts to a waiver of privilege, whether the revelation is made by the accused or by the solicitor acting as his authorized agent, and whether it is made during pre-trial questioning, in evidence before the jury, or in evidence in a *voir dire* which is not repeated before the jury.

The courts have stressed that the jury is not concerned with the correctness of the solicitor's advice, nor with whether it complies with the Law Society's guidelines, but with the reasonableness of the accused's conduct in all the circumstances, including the giving of the advice.[85] Such conduct is likely to be regarded as reasonable in some cases, for example where there is evidence that the interviewing officer disclosed to the solicitor little or nothing of the nature of the case against the accused, so that the solicitor could not usefully advise the client, or where the nature of the offence or the material in the hands of the police is so complex, or relates to matters so long ago, that no sensible immediate response is feasible.[86] However, if an accused has stayed silent on legal advice and his silence is objectively unreasonable, it will not become reasonable merely because the solicitor's advice was ill-judged or bad,[87] which has led one

---

[80] See, eg, *R v Taylor* [1999] Crim LR 77, CA, where T, who had given the 'bare bones' of his alibi to his solicitor, failed to mention it in interview, only furnishing the details of it in his alibi notice.

[81] See, eg, *R v Roble* [1997] Crim LR 449, CA.     [82] See Ch 20.

[83] The court also pointed out that it is open to an accused to attempt to rebut the inference that the fact not disclosed in interview is a subsequent fabrication, by showing that he communicated it to his solicitor at the time of the interview; and that this will not involve waiver of privilege.

[84] [1999] 4 All ER 43, CA.

[85] See per Lord Bingham CJ in *R v Argent* [1997] 2 Cr App R 27, CA at 35–6 and per Rose LJ in *R v Roble* [1997] Crim LR 449, CA.

[86] Per Rose LJ in *R v Roble* [1997] Crim LR 449, CA.

[87] *R v Connolly and McCartney* (1992) Belfast CC, 5 June.

commentator to observe that, if that is the law, then it punishes the accused for the failings of his solicitor.[88]

In *R v Betts*,[89] applied in *R v Chenia*,[90] it was said that it is not the *quality* of the decision not to answer questions that matters, but the genuineness of the decision, whereas in *R v Howell*,[91] approved, obiter, in *R v Knight*,[92] the Court of Appeal rejected the notion that once it is shown that the advice, of whatever quality, has genuinely been relied on as the reason for silence, adverse comment is thereby disallowed. However, as was pointed out in *R v Hoare*,[93] there is no real inconsistency in the authorities, because it is plain from the judgment in *R v Betts* that even where an accused has genuinely relied on legal advice to remain silent, an adverse inference may still be drawn if the jury is sure that the true reason for silence is that he had no or no satisfactory explanation consistent with innocence to give. In other words, the jury must consider whether the accused relied on the legal advice to remain silent both genuinely and reasonably. In *R v Beckles*,[94] Lord Woolf CJ said:

in a case where a solicitor's advice is relied upon by the defendant, the ultimate question for the jury remains under s 34 whether the facts relied on at trial were facts which the defendant could reasonably have been expected to mention at interview. If they were not, that is the end of the matter. If the jury consider that the defendant genuinely relied on the advice, that is not the end of the matter. It may still not have been reasonable of him to rely on the advice, or the advice may not have been the true explanation for his silence. In *R v Betts* . . . at [54] Kay LJ . . . says:

'A person, who is anxious not to answer questions because he has no or no adequate explanation to offer, gains no protection from his lawyer's advice because that advice is no more than a convenient way of disguising his true motivation for not mentioning facts.'

If, in the last situation, it is possible to say that the defendant genuinely acted upon the advice, the fact that he did so because it suited his purpose may mean he was not acting reasonably in not mentioning the facts. His reasonableness in not mentioning the facts remains to be determined by the jury. If they conclude that he was acting unreasonably they can draw an adverse inference from the failure to mention the facts.

## (f) Directing the jury on the inferences that may be drawn

Even if the conditions for drawing an inference set out in section 34 are satisfied, it does not necessarily follow that the section should be invoked. In *Brizzalari v R*[95] the Court of Appeal noted that the mischief at which section 34 was primarily aimed was the positive defence following a no comment interview and/or the ambush defence. The court counselled against 'the further complicating of trials and summings-up by invoking this statute, unless the merits of the individual case require that it should be

---

[88] See Rosemary Pattenden 'Inferences from Silence' [1995] Crim LR 602. See also *R v Kinsella* (1993) Belfast CC, Dec.

[89] [2001] 2 Cr App R 257, CA at [53].

[90] [2004] 1 All ER 543, CA. See also *R v Compton* [2002] All ER (D) 149 (Dec), [2002] EWCA Crim 2835.

[91] [2005] 1 Cr App R 1.    [92] [2004] 1 WLR 340, CA.    [93] [2005] 1 Cr App R 355, CA at [51].

[94] [2005] 1 All ER 705, CA at [46].    [95] (2004) *The Times*, 3 Mar 2004, [2004] EWCA Crim 310.

done', adding that 'if the section is not relied on in a particular case, it may well be sensible for the judge to raise with counsel whether a direction not to draw any adverse inference is desirable or necessary'.

On one view, an inference may not be drawn under section 34 where the jury can only logically draw an inference by first concluding that the accused is guilty. In *R v Mountford*[96] the police entered W's flat and saw M drop from a window a package later found to contain heroin. On being interviewed, M made no comment. W pleaded guilty to permitting his premises to be used for the purposes of supplying heroin and, at M's trial on a charge of possession of heroin with intent to supply, gave evidence against him. M's evidence was that he was at the flat to buy heroin from W, who was the dealer, and that when the police had arrived, W had thrown him the heroin which he had dropped from the window. His reason for not volunteering this information on interview was that he did not know what W had said and did not want to get him into trouble. It was held that inferences could not be drawn under section 34 because the jury could only be sure that this explanation was true if they were to conclude that W was the dealer, not M, and conversely could only be sure that this explanation was false if they were to conclude that M was the dealer, and not W. This element of circularity, it was held, could only be resolved by a verdict founded in no way upon an inference under section 34, but on the other evidence in the case. The same conclusion was reached in *R v Gill*,[97] but it has since been held that *R v Mountford* was concerned with its own set of specific facts and was not intended to have a general application[98] and that it will only be in rare cases of the simplest and most straightforward kind that the *Mountford* approach is appropriate.[99] In *R v Daly*[100] the Court of Appeal cast doubt on the decision in *R v Mountford* on the basis that although it accepted that the fact not mentioned was closely related to the issue in the case, it could find nothing in the statutory wording which requires that the section 34 issue be capable of resolution as a separate issue in the case. In *R v Gowland-Wynn*[101] the Court of Appeal went further, Lord Woolf CJ being of the view that although it may be that *R v Mountford* and *R v Gill* can be confined to their special facts, they had the effect of emasculating and defeating the very purpose of section 34, and should be consigned to oblivion and should not be followed. Similarly in *R v Webber*[102] the House of Lords, while not expressly overruling *R v Mountford*, expressed the view that section 34 did apply to the case.

In cases where a direction under section 34 is called for, then subject to the facts of the particular case, juries should be directed in accordance with the Judicial Studies Board specimen direction,[103] which was approved by the European Court of Human Rights in *Beckles v UK*[104] in the context of the accused's silence on legal advice. The

[96] [1999] Crim LR 575, CA.       [97] [2001] 1 Cr App R 160 (CA).
[98] *R v Hearne* 4 May 2000, unreported, CA, followed in *R v Milford* [2001] Crim LR 330, CA.
[99] *R v Chenia* [2004] 1 All ER 543, CA at [34]–[35].       [100] [2002] 2 Cr App R 201.
[101] [2002] 1 Cr App R 569.       [102] [2004] 1 WLR 404.
[103] *R v Chenia* [2004] 1 All ER 543, CA at [47].       [104] [2001] 31 EHRR 1.

trial judge must remind the jury of the words of the caution given to the accused.[105] The judge must also direct the jury to the effect that an adverse inference can only be drawn if, despite any evidence relied upon by the accused, they conclude that the silence can only sensibly be attributed to the accused having no answer or no answer that would stand up to questioning and investigation.[106] The alternative in the last sentence is worth stressing. Section 34 is not limited to cases of recent invention, ie where the jury may conclude that the facts were invented after the interview, but also covers cases where they may conclude that the accused had the facts in mind at the time of the interview but did not believe that they would stand up to scrutiny at that time.[107] The judge must clearly identify for the jury the inferences which they may properly draw.[108] Contrary to the ruling of the Court of Appeal in *R v Doldur*,[109] the trial judge must also make clear to the jury that they must be satisfied that the prosecution have established a case to answer before drawing any inference.[110] The jury should be told that, if an inference is drawn, they should not convict 'wholly or mainly on the strength of it'. The first of those alternatives, 'wholly', is a clear way of putting the need for the prosecution to be able to prove a case to answer, otherwise than by means of an inference drawn. The second alternative, 'mainly', buttresses that need.[111]

The latest specimen direction emphasizes the desirability of any proposed direction being discussed with counsel before closing speeches and suggests that the discussion should start by a consideration whether any direction under section 34 should be given. In both respects, the specimen direction has been strongly endorsed by the Court of Appeal.[112] However, it does not necessarily follow from a failure to give a proper direction that there has been a breach of Article 6 of the Convention or that a conviction is unsafe. The Court of Appeal will have regard to the particular facts of the case. Factors which may count against the accused, depending on the precise nature of the misdirection or non-direction, may include the strength of the case to answer, the strength of the prosecution evidence, the fact that the accused declined to answer questions himself, rather than on legal advice, and the fact that a clear and accurate direction was given under section 35 of the 1999 Act.[113] Thus failure to direct the jury to consider whether there was a case to answer will not render the trial unfair or the conviction unsafe where, on the facts, no jury could have concluded that there was no case to answer.[114]

---

[105]  *R v Chenia* [2004] 1 All ER 543, CA at [49]–[51].

[106]  See *Condron v UK* [2001] 31 EHRR 1 at para 61, *R v Betts* [2001] 2 Cr App R 257, CA, *R v Daly* [2002] 2 Cr App R 201, CA, and *R v Petkar* [2004] 1 Cr App R 270, CA.

[107]  *R v Milford* [2001] Crim LR 330, CA. See also *R v Daniel* (1998) 2 Cr App R 373, CA at 382–3 and *R v Argent* [1997] 2 Cr App R 27, CA at 34 and 36.

[108]  *R v Petkar* [2004] 1 Cr App R 270, CA at [51].      [109]  [2000] Crim LR 178, CA.

[110]  See *R v Milford* [2001] Crim LR 330, CA, *Beckles v UK* [2001] 31 EHRR 1 and *R v Chenia* [2004] 1 All ER 543, CA.

[111]  *R v Petkar* [2004] 1 Cr App R 270, CA, at [51], citing *Murray v UK* (1996) 22 EHRR 29 at 60, para 47.

[112]  See *R v Chenia* [2004] 1 All ER 543 at [36] and *R v Beckles* [2005] 1 All ER 705, CA at [34].

[113]  See *R v Chenia* ibid at [59]–[65].

[114]  *R v Chenia* ibid at [53]–[55].

The trial judge, in directing the jury, must take care to identify the specific facts relied on at trial which were not mentioned on being questioned or charged.[115] In *R v Argent*[116] it was made clear that under section 34 the following matters are all questions of fact for the jury: (i) whether there is some fact which the accused has relied on in his defence; (ii) whether the accused failed to mention it on being questioned or charged; and (iii) whether it is a fact which in the circumstances existing at the time he could reasonably have been expected to mention when questioned or charged. It was also held that the 'proper' inferences that the jurors are permitted to draw means such inferences as appear proper to them. However, although (i) and (ii) above are questions of fact for the jury, in *R v McGarry*[117] it was held that there will plainly be cases in which it is appropriate for the judge to decide as a matter of law whether there is any evidence on which a reasonable jury properly directed could conclude that either or both of those requirements has been satisfied. Thus if the prosecution accept that those requirements have not been satisfied, and the judge considers that this is a proper view, no question of inviting the jury to draw inferences from the failure of the accused to answer some of the questions put to him can arise. In *R v Argent* it was held that although the question whether the fact was one which the accused could reasonably have been expected to mention is an issue on which the judge should give appropriate directions, ordinarily the issue should be left to the jury to decide, and that only rarely should the judge direct that they should, or should not draw the appropriate inference. As to the latter direction, in *R v McGarry*[118] it was held that where the jury are aware that the accused failed to answer questions and the judge rules that there is no evidence on which they can properly conclude that he failed to mention any fact relied on in his defence, then there should be a specific direction not to draw any adverse inference.[119] However, such a specific direction is plainly not called for where the accused gives a no comment interview and gives no evidence at trial, thereby attracting a direction under section 35 of the 1994 Act, because in such a case it would be fanciful to suggest that an inference of the kind permitted by section 34 might be drawn by the jury in the absence of a direction not to do so.[120]

Under section 34(2) the inferences that may be drawn are 'such inferences from the failure as appear proper'. The breadth of this phrase is such that it could be construed to permit a general inference that the accused is guilty of the offence charged, a construction supported, arguably, by section 38(3) of the Act.[121] In fact the logical inference to be drawn is narrower and more precise, that the facts relied on in the accused's defence are not true, on the basis that, if they were true, the accused could reasonably have been expected to have mentioned them in interview or on being

---

[115] *R v Webber* [2004] 1 WLR 404, HL at [27] and *R v Chenia* ibid at [29] and [87].
[116] [1997] 2 Cr App R 27, CA at 32.          [117] [1999] 1 Cr App R 377, CA at 382–3.
[118] [1999] 1 Cr App R 377, CA.
[119] But failure to give such a direction will not necessarily render a conviction unsafe: *R v Bowers* [1998] Crim LR 817, CA. See also *R v Bansal* [1999] Crim LR 484, CA.
[120] *R v La Rose* [2003] All ER (D) 24 (May), [2003] EWCA Crim 1471.          [121] See below.

charged, but did not do so because of the risk that the police might then be able to expose their falsity or because he had yet to invent them, or all of them.

The extent to which an inference drawn under section 34 will assist the prosecution in establishing a case to answer, or in proving the guilt of the accused, will obviously turn on the nature of the fact relied on in the defence and its importance to that defence. However, section 38(3) and (4) of the 1994 Act provide that:

> (3) A person shall not have the proceedings against him transferred to the Crown Court for trial, have a case to answer or be convicted of an offence solely on an inference drawn from such a failure or refusal as is mentioned in section 34(2), 35(3), 36(2) or 37(2).

> (4) A judge shall not refuse to grant such an application as is mentioned in section 34(2)(b), 36(2)(b) and 37(2)(b) solely on an inference drawn from such a failure as is mentioned in section 34(2), 36(2) or 37(2).

These provisions, in relation to section 34(2), appear to be otiose. It is true that in cases of confession and avoidance, as when the accused admits an assault but raises a defence of self-defence, rejection of that defence may result in a finding of guilt. However, since the worst possible inference that can be drawn is that the fact relied upon in the defence is untrue, then, as the example given illustrates, such an inference could not *by itself* justify a conviction (or a decision that there is a case to answer). The purpose of section 38(3) in the present context seems to be twofold. First, it requires the judge to remind himself that he is not entitled to decide that there is a case to answer solely on the basis that the relevant facts relied on by the accused in his defence are untrue. Secondly, it requires him to direct the jury that they are not entitled to convict solely—or, in the light of *Condron v United Kingdom*, mainly—on the basis that such facts are untrue.

### (g) The discretion to exclude evidence of failure to mention facts

Section 38(6) provides that:

Nothing in sections 34, 35, 36 or 37 prejudices any power of a court, in any proceedings, to exclude evidence (whether by preventing questions being put or otherwise) at its discretion.

In appropriate circumstances, therefore, the court could exclude evidence of the accused's failure to mention any fact on the basis of either section 78 of the Police and Criminal Evidence Act 1984 or the common-law discretion to exclude.[122] This might be appropriate, for example, in cases where it would be unfair to make use of the accused's silence by reason of breach of the provisions of the 1984 Act or the Codes, especially those relating to the caution, interrogation and access to a solicitor (for example, failure to caution) or because the accused's silence was brought about by some other improper or unfair means (for example, threatening to beat up the accused unless he remains silent). However, it was held in *R v Condron and Condron*

---

[122] See Ch 2.

that if the defence objection is simply that the jury should not be invited to draw any adverse inference, it will seldom be appropriate to invite the judge to rule on this before the conclusion of all the evidence, because it will not be apparent until then what are the material facts that were not disclosed or the reason for non-disclosure. It was said that only in the most exceptional case could it be appropriate to make such a submission before the introduction of the evidence by the Crown, eg where the accused is of very low intelligence and understanding and has been advised by his solicitor to say nothing.

### (h) Acceptance of the accusation of another by silence

Section 34(5) of the 1994 Act provides that:

This section does not—

    (a) prejudice the admissibility in evidence of the silence or other reaction of the accused in the face of anything said in his presence relating to the conduct in respect of which he is charged, in so far as evidence thereof would be admissible apart from this section; or

    (b) preclude the drawing of any inference from any such silence or other reaction of the accused which could properly be drawn apart from this section.

The effect of this subsection is to preserve the common-law authorities whereby, in appropriate circumstances, the accused, by his conduct, demeanour or silence, may be treated as having accepted the accusation of another so as to make it a confession statement of his own.[123]

## 4 FAILURE OR REFUSAL TO ACCOUNT FOR OBJECTS, SUBSTANCES, MARKS ETC

Sections 36 and 37 of the Criminal Justice and Public Order Act 1994, which are based on sections 18 and 19 of the Irish Criminal Justice Act 1984, fall to be considered together.

Section 36 of the 1994 Act provides that:

    (1) Where—

        (a) a person is arrested by a constable, and there is—

            (i)   on his person; or

            (ii)  in or on his clothing or footwear; or

            (iii) otherwise in his possesion; or

            (iv) in any place[124] in which he is at the time of his arrest,

---

[123] See *R v Norton* [1910] 2 KB 496, *Parkes v R* [1976] 1 WLR 1251 etc (Ch 13). See further Peter Mirfield 'Two Side-Effects of Sections 34 to 37 of the Criminal Justice and Public Order Act 1994' [1995] Crim LR 612, who argues that it may now be permissible to draw an inference that a suspect who has been cautioned but remains silent in the face of police accusations accepts the truth of the accusations.

[124] For the purposes of both s 36 and s 37 'place' includes any building or part of a building, any vehicle, vessel, aircraft or hovercraft and any other place whatsoever: s 38(1).

any object, substance or mark, or there is any mark on any such object; and

(b) that or another constable investigating the case reasonably believes that the presence of the object, substance or mark may be attributable to the participation of the person arrested in the commission of an offence specified by the constable;[125] and

(c) the constable informs the person arrested that he so believes, and requests him to account for the presence of the object, substance or mark; and

(d) the person fails or refuses to do so,

then if, in any proceedings against the person for the offence so specified, evidence of those matters is given, subsection (2) below applies.

(2) Where this subsection applies—

(a) [repealed];

(b) a judge, in deciding whether to grant an application made by the accused under paragraph 2 of Schedule 3 to the Crime and Disorder Act 1998;[126]

(c) the court, in determining whether there is a case to answer; and

(d) the court or jury, in determining whether the accused is guilty of the offence charged,[127]

may draw such inferences from the failure or refusal as appear proper.

(3) Subsections (1) and (2) above apply to the condition of clothing or footwear as they apply to a substance or mark thereon.

(4) Subsections (1) and (2) above do not apply unless the accused was told in ordinary language by the constable when making the request mentioned in subsection (1)(c) above what the effect of this section would be if he failed or refused to comply with that request.

(4A) Where the accused was at an authorised place of detention[128] at the time of the failure or refusal, subsections (1) and (2) above do not apply if he had not been allowed an opportunity to consult a solicitor prior to the request being made.

(5) This section applies in relation to officers of customs and excise as it applies in relation to constables.[129]

(6) This section does not preclude the drawing of any inference from a failure or refusal of the accused to account for the presence of an object, substance or mark or from the condition of clothing or footwear which could properly be drawn apart from this section.

Section 37 of the 1994 Act provides that:

(1) Where—

(a) a person arrested by a constable was found by him at a place at or about the time the offence for which he was arrested is alleged to have been committed; and

(b) that or another constable investigating the offence reasonably believes that the

---

[125] Ie not necessarily the offence for which arrested. Cf s 37(1)(b), below.

[126] See note to s 34(2)(b), above.

[127] Or any other offence of which the accused could lawfully be convicted on that charge: s 38(2).

[128] See note to s 34(2A), above.

[129] Arrest by others charged with the duty of investigating offences and charging offenders will not suffice. Cf s 34, above.

presence of the person at that place and at that time may be attributable to his participation in the commission of the offence; and

(c) the constable informs the person that he so believes, and requests him to account for that presence; and

(d) the person fails or refuses to do so,

then if, in any proceedings against the person for the offence, evidence of those matters is given, subsection (2) below applies.

(2) [Identical, in its terms, to s 36(2).]

(3) [Identical, in its terms, to s 36(4).]

(4) [Identical, in its terms, to s 36(5).]

(3A) Where the accused was at an authorised place of detention[130] at the time of the failure or refusal, subsections (1) and (2) do not apply if he had not been allowed an opportunity to consult a solicitor prior to the request being made.

(5) This section does not preclude the drawing of any inference from a failure or refusal of the accused to account for his presence at a place which could properly be drawn apart from this section.

It has been held that under section 36, the jury must be satisfied that the accused failed (or refused) to account for the object, substance or mark; and that section 36(1)(b) does not require the constable to specify in precise terms the offence in question.[131]

Sections 36 and 37 contain no proviso, analogous to that contained in section 34(1), whereby an inference may only be drawn if the accused could reasonably have been expected to account for the object, substance, etc at the time when questioned about it. Notwithstanding this omission, it is submitted that the trial judge should give a clear direction to the jury that, in deciding whether to draw an inference, and if so the strength of the inference to be drawn, they should take into account the nature and personal characteristics of the accused, including, as appropriate, his age, intelligence, language, and literacy and his physical, mental, and emotional state at the time when he was questioned. The nature and strength of any inference drawn under section 36 will also depend on the nature of the object, substance, etc, the extent to which evidence of its presence supports the prosecution case and the other circumstances of the case. For example, if the accused, on arrest for murder by stabbing, is found with a blood-stained knife in his pocket, his failure or refusal to account for its presence is likely to result in a highly damaging adverse inference. However, if the stabbing takes place in a very crowded pub and the blood-stained knife is found on the floor,[132] the accused's failure to account for its presence is unlikely, without more, to result in any adverse inference. Similar considerations apply to section 37.

The scope of both section 36 and section 37 has been fixed somewhat arbitrarily. For example, if a person, suspected of murder by stabbing, fails to explain why the jacket he is wearing on arrest is blood-stained, an adverse inference may be drawn

---

[130] See note to s 34(2A), above.
[131] *R v Compton* [2002] All ER (D) 149 (Dec), [2002] EWCA Crim 2835.      [132] See s 36(1)(a)(iv).

under section 36. But if such a suspect, having abandoned his blood-stained jacket at the scene of the crime, where it is found by the police, is then arrested by them on his way home and fails to explain why his jacket is blood-stained (or even why he abandoned it), no adverse inference may be drawn.

Inferences under section 36 and section 37 can only be drawn where evidence is given of the presence of the object, substance, etc, or of the presence of the accused, at a place at or about the time of the offence. Clearly, in some cases, that evidence, either taken alone or together with the adverse inference that can be drawn under the statutory provisions, will be sufficient to establish a case to answer or, indeed, to convict, as when a drug courier is arrested carrying a large package of heroin. Presumably, as in the case of section 34, the purpose of section 38(3)[133] in relation to section 36(2) and section 37(2), is simply to require the judge to direct the jury (or himself) that they are not entitled to convict (he is not entitled to decide that there is a case to answer) solely or, in the light of *Condron v United Kingdom*, mainly, on the basis of the inference drawn.

Under section 38(6), as we have seen,[134] nothing in section 36 or section 37 prejudices any power of a court to exclude evidence at its discretion. There is obvious potential for discretionary exclusion where the evidence of the matters specified in section 36(1) and section 37(1) was obtained illegally, improperly or unfairly.

## B INFERENCES FROM REFUSAL TO CONSENT TO THE TAKING OF SAMPLES

In appropriate circumstances, an adverse inference may be drawn from a suspect's refusal, without good cause, to consent to the taking of 'intimate samples' from his body. Under section 65 of the Police and Criminal Evidence Act 1984, an intimate sample is defined as (a) a sample of blood, semen or any other tissue fluid, urine, or pubic hair; (b) a dental impression; and (c) a swab taken from a person's body orifice other than the mouth. Section 62 of the 1984 Act provides that:

(1) An intimate sample may be taken from a person in police detention only—
  (a) if a police officer of at least the rank of superintendent authorises it to be taken; and
  (b) if the appropriate consent is given.[135]

(1A) An intimate sample may be taken from a person who is not in police detention but from whom, in the course of an investigation of an offence, two or more non-

---

[133] See under s 34, above.    [134] Ibid.

[135] 'Appropriate consent' means, in relation to a person aged 17 or over, the consent of that person; in relation to a person aged 14 or over but under 17, the consent of that person and his parent or guardian; and in relation to a person aged under 14, the consent of his parent or guardian: s 65. The consent must be given in writing: s 62(4).

intimate samples[136] suitable for the same means of analysis have been taken which have proved insufficient—

    (a) if a police officer of at least the rank of superintendent authorises it to be taken; and

    (b) if the appropriate consent is given.

(2) An officer may only give an authorisation under subsection (1) or (1A) above if he has reasonable grounds—

    (a) for suspecting the involvement of the person from whom the sample is to be taken in a recordable offence;[137] and

    (b) for believing that the same will tend to confirm or disprove his involvement.

(10) Where the appropriate consent to the taking of an intimate sample from a person was refused without good cause, in any proceedings against that person for an offence—

    (a) the court, in determining

        (i) [repealed]

        (ii) whether there is a case to answer; and

    (b) the court or jury, in determining whether that person is guilty of the offence charged, may draw such inferences from the refusal as appear proper.

Before a person is asked to provide an intimate sample, he must be warned that if he refuses without good cause, his refusal may harm his case if it comes to trial.[138] Whether consent was refused 'without good cause' is a question of fact. In appropriate circumstances, a person's bodily or mental condition may amount to good cause. However, whether a refusal out of embarrassment or on the grounds of some deeply held personal conviction is capable of constituting good cause is less clear.

There is no equivalent to section 62(10) in the case of 'non-intimate samples' because, subject to compliance with the statutory conditions, such samples may be taken without consent. Under section 65 of the 1984 Act, a non-intimate sample means: (a) a sample of hair other than pubic hair; (b) a sample taken from a nail or from under a nail; (c) a swab taken from any part of a person's body including the mouth but not any other body orifice; (d) saliva; and (e) a footprint or a similar impression of any part of a person's body other than a part of his hand. Section 63 of the Act provides that:

(2A) A non-intimate sample may be taken from a person without the appropriate consent if two conditions are satisfied.

(2B) The first is that the person is in police detention in consequence of his arrest for a recordable offence.

(2C) The second is that—

    (a) he has not had a non-intimate sample of the same type and from the same part of the body taken in the course of the investigation of the offence by the police, or

---

[136] See below.

[137] A 'recordable offence' is defined to include all offences punishable with imprisonment and a number of other specified offences: see the National Police Records (Recordable Offences) Regulations 1985, SI 1985/1941, as amended.

[138] Para 6.3 and Note 6D, Code D.

(b) he has had such a sample taken but it proved insufficient.

(3) A non-intimate sample may be taken from a person without the appropriate consent if—

(a) he is being held in custody by the police on the authority of a court; and

(b) an officer of at least the rank of superintendent authorises it to be taken without the appropriate consent.

(3A) A non-intimate sample may be taken from a person (whether or not he is in police detention or held in custody by the police on the authority of a court) without the appropriate consent if—

(a) he has been charged with a recordable offence or informed that he will be reported for such an offence; and

(b) either he has not had a non-intimate sample taken from him in the course of the investigation of the offence by the police or he has had a non-intimate sample taken from him but either it was not suitable for the same means of analysis or, though so suitable, the sample proved insufficient.

(3B) A non-intimate sample may be taken from a person without the appropriate consent if he has been convicted of a recordable offence.

(3C) A non-intimate sample may also be taken from a person without the appropriate consent if he is a person to whom section 2 of the Criminal Evidence (Amendment) Act 1997 applies (persons detained following acquittal on grounds of insanity or finding of unfitness to plead).

(4) An officer may only give an authorisation under subsection (3) above if he has reasonable grounds—

(a) for suspecting the involvement of the person from whom the sample is to be taken in a recordable offence; and

(b) for believing that the sample will tend to confirm or disprove his involvement.

(9A) Subsection (3B) above shall not apply to any person convicted before 10th April 1995 unless he is a person to whom section 1 of the Criminal Evidence (Amendment) Act 1997 applies (persons imprisoned or detained by virtue of pre-existing conviction for sexual offence etc).

Section 61 of the 1984 Act makes similar provision for fingerprints of a person to be taken without his consent.

# C INFERENCES FROM FAILURE TO PROVIDE ADVANCE DISCLOSURE OF THE DEFENCE CASE

## 1 TRIALS ON INDICTMENT

Under the rules of primary prosecution disclosure in section 3 of the Criminal Procedure and Investigations Act 1996, the prosecutor must disclose to the accused previously undisclosed material which might reasonably be considered capable of undermining the case for the prosecution against the accused or of assisting the case for the accused, or give the accused a written statement that there is no such material. Section 5(5) of the Act is to the effect that where a person is charged with an offence for which he is sent for trial to a Crown Court and the prosecutor complies or purports to comply with section 3, the accused must give a defence statement to the court and the prosecutor.[139] The defence statement must be served during a pre-scribed 'relevant period' (within 14 days of primary prosecution disclosure).[140] The contents of the defence statement are prescribed by section 6A, which provides as follows.

(1) ... a defence statement is a written statement—
    (a) setting out the nature of the accused's defence, including any particular defences on which he intends to rely,
    (b) indicating the matters of fact on which he takes issue with the prosecution,
    (c) setting out, in the case of each such matter, why he takes issue with the prosecution, and
    (d) indicating any point of law (including any point as to the admissibility of evidence or an abuse of process) which he wishes to take, and any authority on which he intends to rely for that purpose.

(2) A defence statement that discloses an alibi must give particulars of it, including—
    (a) the name, address and date of birth of any witness the accused believes is able to give evidence in support of the alibi, or as many of those details as are known to the accused when the statement is given;
    (b) any information in the accused's possession which might be of material assistance in identifying or finding any such witness in whose case any of the details mentioned in paragraph (a) are not known to the accused when the statement is given.

(3) For the purposes of this section evidence in support of an alibi is evidence tending to show that by reason of the presence of the accused at a particular place or in a particular area at a particular time he was not, or was unlikely to have been, at the place where the offence is alleged to have been committed at the time of its alleged commission.

In *R v Wheeler*[141] it was held that as a matter of good practice a defence statement should be signed by the accused as an acknowledgment of its accuracy to obviate error and dispute of the kind which had arisen in that case, where part of the defence statement was contrary to the original instructions given by the accused to his solicitors.

---

[139] Although there is no obligation on an accused to give a defence statement to a co-accused, if the prosecutor forms the view that a defence statement of one co-accused might reasonably be expected to assist the defence of another, it should be disclosed to the other on secondary prosecution disclosure: *R v Cairns* [2003] 1 Cr App R 38, CA.

[140] See s 5(9), s 12 and Regulation 2 of the Criminal Procedure and Investigations Act 1996 (Defence Disclosure Time Limits) Regulations 1997, SI 1997/684.

[141] [2001] Crim LR 745, CA.

Under section 6B(1) of the 1996 Act, where an accused has given a defence state-ment, he must also give to the court and the prosecutor, during a prescribed 'relevant period', either (a) an updated defence statement (which must comply with the requirements imposed by section 6A by reference to the state of affairs at the time when it is given)[142] or (b) a statement of the kind mentioned in section 6B(4), namely a written statement stating that he has no changes to make to the initial defence statement. Finally, under section 6C, there is an obligation on the defence, during a prescribed 'relevant period', to give notification of intention to call defence witnesses. Section 6C(1) provides as follows.

(1) The accused must give to the court and the prosecutor a notice indicating whether he intends to call any persons (other than himself) as witnesses at his trial and, if so—
  (a) giving the name, address and date of birth of each such proposed witness, or as many of those details as are known to the accused when the notice is given;
  (b) providing any information in the accused's possession which might be of material assistance in identifying or finding any such proposed witness in whose case any of the details mentioned in paragraph (a) are not known to the accused when the notice is given.

Under section 11(5) of the 1996 Act, where an accused fails to comply with the disclosure requirements of sections 5, 6A, 6B, or 6C, the court or any other party may make appropriate adverse comment and the court or jury, in deciding the ques-tion of guilt, may draw proper adverse inferences. If it appears to the court at a pre-trial hearing that an accused has failed to comply fully with section 5, 6B or 6C, so that there is a possibility of comment being made or inferences being drawn under section 11(5), he shall warn the accused accordingly.[143] Section 11 provides as follows.

(1) This section applies in the cases set out in subsections (2), (3), and (4).
(2) The first case is where section 5 applies and the accused—
  (a) fails to give an initial defence statement,
  (b) gives an initial defence statement but does so after the end of the . . . relevant period for section 5,
  (c) is required by section 6B to give either an updated defence statement or a state-ment of the kind mentioned in subsection (4) of that section but fails to do so,
  (d) gives an updated defence statement or a statement of the kind mentioned in section 6B(4) but does so after the end of the . . . relevant period for section 6B,
  (e) sets out inconsistent defences in his defence statement,[144] or
  (f) at his trial—
    (i) puts forward a defence which was not mentioned in his defence statement or is different from any defence set out in the statement,

---

[142] Section 6B(3).     [143] Section 6E(2).

[144] A reference simply to an accused's 'defence statement' is a reference (i) where he has given only an initial defence statement, or an initial defence statement and a statement under s 6B(4), to the initial defence statement and (ii) where he has given an initial and an updated defence statement, to the updated statement: s 11(12)(c).

    (ii)  relies on a matter which in breach of the requirements imposed by or under section 6A, was not mentioned in his defence statement,

    (iii)  adduces evidence in support of an alibi[145] without having given particulars of the alibi in his defence statement, or

    (iv)  calls a witness to give evidence in support of an alibi without having complied with section 6A(2)(a) or (b) as regards the witness in his defence statement.

(3) The second case is . . .[146]

(4) The third case is where the accused—

    (a)  gives a witness notice but does so after the end of . . . the relevant period for section 6C, or

    (b)  at his trial calls a witness (other than himself) not included, or not adequately identified, in a witness notice.

(5) Where this section applies—

    (a)  the court or any other party may make such comment as appears appropriate;

    (b)  the court or jury may draw such inferences as appear proper in deciding whether the accused is guilty of the offence concerned.

(6) Where—

    (a)  this section applies by virtue of subsection (2)(f)(ii) . . ., and

    (b)  the matter which was not mentioned is a point of law (including any point as to the admissibility of evidence or an abuse of process) or an authority,

comment by another party under subsection 5(a) may be made only with the leave of the court.

(7) Where this section applies by virtue of subsection (4), comment by another party under subsection (5)(a) may be made only with the leave of the court.

(8) Where the accused puts forward a defence which is different from any defence set out in his defence statement, in doing anything under subsection (5) or in deciding whether to do anything under it the court shall have regard—

    (a)  to the extent of the difference in the defences, and

    (b)  to whether there is any justification for it.

(9) Where the accused calls a witness whom he has failed to include, or to identify adequately, in a witness notice,[147] in doing anything under subsection (5) or in deciding to do anything under it the court shall have regard to whether there is any justification for the failure.

(10) A person shall not be convicted of an offence solely on an inference drawn under subsection (5).

(11) Where the accused has given a statement of the kind mentioned in section 6B(4), then, for the purposes of subsections (2)(f)(ii) and (iv), the question as to whether there has been a breach of the requirements imposed by or under section 6A or a failure to comply with section 6A(2)(a) or (b) shall be determined—

    (a)  by reference to the state of affairs at the time when that statement was given, and

    (b)  as if the defence statement was given at the same time as that statement.

---

[145] A reference to 'evidence in support of an alibi' shall be construed in accordance with s 6A(3): s 11(12)(d).

[146] The second case relates to failure to disclose prior to summary trial: see below.

[147] 'Witness notice' means a notice given under s 6C: s 11(12)(e).

Under section 11(5)(b), proper inferences may be drawn only in deciding whether the accused is guilty of the offence charged, and not in deciding whether there is a case to answer.[148]

Three important matters were established in *R v Tibbs*.[149] First, section 11 does not disallow or require leave for cross-examination of an accused on differences between his defence at trial and his defence statement—it precludes comment or invitation to the jury to draw an inference from the differences unless the court gives leave. Secondly, the word 'defence' in section 11 is not restricted to its general legal description (eg 'self defence' or 'mistaken identification'), but includes the facts and matters to be relied on in the defence, otherwise there would be little, if any, scope for comparing the extent of the difference in the defences under section 11(8)(a)—on the restrictive interpretation the defence put forward would either be the same as or different from the defence in the defence statement. Third, failure to warn the jury in accordance with section 11(10) that they cannot convict solely from drawing an adverse inference will not necessarily result in a successful appeal against conviction. The issue will turn on the particular circumstances, including the strength of the prosecution case.

In some cases, the defence statement may be relied on by the Crown, or may be used by the jury, as a lie by the accused indicative of a consciousness of his guilt, in which case the jury will need to be directed in accordance with *R v Goodway*.[150]

## 2 SUMMARY TRIALS

Section 6 of the 1996 Act is to the effect that where a person is charged with an offence in respect of which the court proceeds to summary trial and the prosecutor complies or purports to comply with section 3, then the accused *may* give a defence statement to the prosecutor, and, if he does so, must also give such a statement to the court, and must give the statement during a prescribed 'relevant period'. The magistrates' court may permit appropriate comment and draw proper inferences in the same circumstances as such comment may be permitted and such inferences may be drawn in a trial on indictment (late disclosure, inconsistent defences, etc), with the obvious exception of failure to give a defence statement.[151] As in trials on indictment, in summary cases a person shall not be convicted of an offence solely on an inference drawn under section 11(5).[152]

## 3 PREPARATORY HEARINGS

Under section 29 of the Criminal Procedure and Investigations Act 1996, a Crown Court judge may order a preparatory hearing where it appears to him that the

---

[148] Cf ss 34(2), 36(2) and 37(2) of the Criminal Justice and Public Order Act 1994, above.
[149] [2000] 2 Cr App R 309, CA.      [150] [1993] 4 All ER 894, CA (see Ch 2).
[151] Section 11(3).      [152] Section 11(10).

indictment reveals a case of such complexity, a case of such seriousness or a case whose trial is likely to be of such length that substantial benefits are likely to accrue from such a hearing.[153] Section 31(4) provides that at the preparatory hearing the judge may order the prosecutor to give the court and the accused a case statement of such matters as the facts of the case for the prosecution, the witnesses who will speak to them, and relevant exhibits. Under section 31(6), where the prosecutor has complied with such an order, the judge may order the accused to give the court and prosecutor written notice of any objections that he has to the case statement. If he does so, he shall warn the accused of the possible consequences under section 34 of the Act of not complying with his order.[154]

Section 34 provides as follows:

(1) Any party may depart from the case he disclosed in pursuance of a requirement imposed under section 31.

(2) Where—
   (a) a party departs from the case he disclosed in pursuance of a requirement imposed under section 31, or
   (b) a party fails to comply with such a requirement,
   the judge or, with the leave of the judge, any other party may make such comment as appears to the judge or the other party (as the case may be) to be appropriate and the jury or, in the case of a trial without a jury, the judge, may draw such inferences as appear proper.

(3) In doing anything under subsection (2) or in deciding whether to do anything under it the judge shall have regard—
   (a) to the extent of the departure or failure, and
   (b) to whether there is any justification for it.

(4) Except as provided by this section, in the case of a trial with a jury no part—
   (a) of a statement given under section 31(6)(a), or
   (b) of any other information relating to the case for the accused or, if there is more than one, the case for any of them, which was given in pursuance of a requirement imposed under section 31,
   may be disclosed at a stage in the trial after the jury have been sworn without the consent of the accused concerned.

---

[153] Separate but similar provision is made for cases of serious or complex fraud—see ss 7, 9, and 10 of the Criminal Justice Act 1987.
[154] Section 31(8).

# 15

# EVIDENCE OF CHARACTER: EVIDENCE OF CHARACTER IN CIVIL CASES

This chapter, together with Chapters 16 and 17 of this book, consider the admissibility of evidence of character. The admissibility of character evidence is governed by a number of factors which it will be useful to summarize before considering the law in detail. Two obvious considerations are whether the proceedings are civil or criminal and whether the evidence relates to the character of a party or non-party. Additionally, it is necessary to consider the nature of the character evidence in question. It may relate to either good or bad character and, in either event, may constitute evidence of a person's actual disposition, that is his propensity to act, think, or feel in a given way, or evidence of his reputation, that is his *reputed* disposition or propensity to act, think, or feel in a given way. Thus the character of a person may be proved by evidence of general disposition, by evidence of specific examples of his conduct on other occasions (including, in the case of bad conduct, evidence of his previous convictions), or by evidence of his reputation among those to whom he is known. The final important consideration is the purpose for which the character evidence in question is sought to be adduced or elicited in cross-examination. There are three possibilities. First, it may be adduced because the character of a person is itself in issue in the proceedings. Secondly, it may be adduced because of its relevance to a fact in issue, that is because of its tendency to prove that a person did a certain act, whether he did that act being in issue in the proceedings. Thirdly, evidence of the character of a party or a witness may be adduced because of its relevance to his credibility.

## A CHARACTER IN ISSUE OR RELEVANT TO A FACT IN ISSUE

In civil proceedings, evidence of the character of a party or non-party is admissible if it is in issue or of relevance to a fact in issue. The law of defamation provides a number of examples. Thus on the question of liability in an action for defamation in which justification is pleaded, the claimant's character will obviously be in issue. If, for example, the defendant has alleged that the claimant is a thief and burglar, evidence of the claimant's convictions for theft and burglary may be admitted to justify the allegation.[1] Similarly, the claimant, in order to rebut a defence of fair comment, may adduce evidence of his good reputation at the time of publication of the allegedly defamatory material.[2] The character of a claimant in an action for defamation is also of direct relevance, if he succeeds, to the quantum of recoverable damages, the damage sustained being dependent on the estimation in which he was previously held.[3] However, in *Scott v Sampson*[4] it was held that, while evidence of the claimant's reputation is admissible to enable the jury to estimate the probable quantum of injury sustained, evidence of rumours and suspicions to the same effect as the defamatory matter complained of, because it only indirectly tends to affect the claimant's reputation and is difficult for the claimant to meet and rebut, is not admissible. Generally speaking, evidence of specific acts of misconduct on the part of the claimant is inadmissible on the question of damages because it would impose on the claimant a difficult burden of showing a uniform propriety of conduct during his whole life and would give rise to interminable issues having only a very remote bearing on the question in dispute.[5] However, evidence can be given of any relevant criminal conviction recorded against the claimant,[6] and the defendant may also rely on evidence which has already been adduced before the court and jury in support of an unsuccessful plea of justification or fair comment.[7]

# B  EVIDENCE OF THE DISPOSITION OF THE PARTIES TOWARDS GOOD CONDUCT

It is submitted that evidence of the disposition of the parties to civil proceedings towards good conduct on other occasions should be admitted if it meets the ordinary

---

[1] Section 13 of the Civil Evidence Act 1968 provides that in libel or slander actions in which the question whether a person committed a criminal offence is relevant to an issue in the action, proof of his conviction shall be conclusive evidence that he committed the offence: see Ch 21.

[2] See *Cornwell v Myskow* [1987] 2 All ER 504, CA.

[3] For these purposes, what is relevant is evidence of the claimant's reputation at the time of publication of the allegedly defamatory material; evidence of the claimant's reputation at the time of trial may also be admitted where the defendant persists to trial with a plea of justification but not where the defence is merely a denial of any defamatory meaning or fair comment not coupled with a plea of justification: *Cornwell v Myskow* [1987] 2 All ER 504, CA.

[4] (1882) 8 QBD 491, approved in *Plato Films Ltd v Speidel* [1961] AC 1090, HL.

[5] But see *Waters v Sunday Pictorial Newspapers Ltd* [1961] 2 All ER 758, CA. In *Hobbs v Tinling & Co Ltd* [1929] 2 KB 1, CA it was held that specific instances of misconduct may be put to the claimant in cross-examination as to his credibility. However, in accordance with the normal rule, the cross-examining party will not be allowed to call evidence to contradict the claimant's answers.

[6] *Goody v Odhams Press Ltd* [1967] 1 QB 333, CA.

[7] *Pamplin v Express Newspapers Ltd (No 2)* [1988] 1 All ER 282, CA.

requirement of relevance. However, according to the few reported decisions on the topic, such evidence has been treated as irrelevant to the facts in issue and accordingly excluded.

As to good conduct on the part of the defendant, in *A-G v Bowman*,[8] at the trial of an information for keeping false weights, a civil suit, Eyre CB held that the evidence of a witness to character called by the defendant was inadmissible because the proceedings were not criminal. Similarly in *A-G v Radloff*[9] the rule was justified on the basis that whereas there is a fair and just presumption that a person of good character would not commit a crime, no presumption fairly arises in the great proportion of civil cases, from the good character of the defendant, that he did not commit the breach of contract or civil duty alleged against him.

As to the claimant, in *Hatton v Cooper*,[10] a case arising out of a collision between two cars in which there was an unusual dearth of relevant evidence, it was held that the trial judge, on the question of liability, had improperly relied on evidence from the claimant's employer that the claimant was an excellent driver, calm, assured, and composed, who never took risks. Jonathan Parker LJ said that in the context of the collision in question, the opinion of a third party as to the driving ability of either party was 'completely worthless'.

# C EVIDENCE OF THE DISPOSITION OF THE PARTIES TOWARDS BAD CONDUCT

In civil proceedings, evidence of the disposition of the defendant towards wrongdoing or the commission of a particular kind of civil wrong may be admissible if it is of sufficient relevance or probative value in relation to the facts in issue. Such evidence, which relates to particular acts of misconduct on other occasions, is designated 'similar fact evidence'.

Whereas in criminal proceedings the rules relating to the admissibility of similar fact evidence have reflected a paramount concern to safeguard the accused from the admission of unduly prejudicial evidence, in civil proceedings, where trial is seldom by jury, the emphasis has been on probative value rather than prejudicial effect. To this extent, in civil cases, the principle of admissibility has tended to approximate to the ordinary test of relevance and accordingly similar fact evidence has been admitted more readily. In *Hales v Kerr*,[11] a negligence action in which the plaintiff alleged that he had contracted ringworm from a dirty razor used by the defendant, a hairdresser, evidence was admitted that two other customers shaved by the defendant had also

---

[8] (1791) 2 Bos&P 532n.    [9] (1854) 10 Exch 84 at 97.    [10] [2001] RTR 544, CA.
[11] [1908] 2 KB 601.

contracted ringworm. In *Joy v Phillips, Mills & Co Ltd*[12] a claim was made for work-men's compensation by the father of a deceased stable boy. The boy was kicked by a horse and found nearby holding a halter. Evidence that the boy had previously teased horses with a halter was held to be admissible in rebuttal of the applicant's allegation that the accident had occurred in the course of the boy's employment. More recently, in *Jones v Greater Manchester Police Authority*,[13] civil proceedings for a sex offender order under section 2 of the Crime and Disorder Act 1998, it was held that evidence of propensity to commit sexual offences against young males was relevant and admissible because the purpose of the proceedings was to seek to predict the extent to which past events gave rise to reasonable cause for believing that an order was necessary to protect the public from serious harm; and that the admission of such evidence did not breach either Article 6 or Article 8 of the European Convention on Human Rights and did not render the proceedings unfair.

In *Mood Music Publishing Co Ltd v De Wolfe Publishing Ltd*,[14] similar fact evidence was admitted in an action for infringement of copyright. The defendants admitted the similarity between the musical work in which the plaintiffs owned the copyright and the work which they had produced, but alleged that the similarity was coincidental. Evidence was admitted to show that on other occasions the defendants had produced musical works bearing a close resemblance to musical works which were the subject of copyright. The Court of Appeal held that the evidence had been properly admitted to rebut the allegation of coincidence. Lord Denning MR, having referred to the admission of similar fact evidence in criminal cases, continued:[15]

In civil cases the courts have followed a similar line but have not been so chary of admitting it. In civil cases, the courts will admit evidence of similar facts if it is logically probative, that is, if it is logically relevant in determining the matter which is in issue: provided that it is not oppressive or unfair to the other side: and also that the other side has fair notice of it and is able to deal with it.[16]

The leading authority is *O'Brien v Chief Constable of South Wales Police*.[17] The claimant had been convicted of murder. After serving eleven years in prison, his case had been referred to the Criminal Cases Review Commission and his appeal had been allowed. He then brought proceedings against the Chief Constable for misfeasance in public office and malicious prosecution, alleging that he had been 'framed' by a Detective Inspector L and a Detective Chief Superintendent C, who was said to have

---

[12] [1916] 1 KB 849. See also *Barrett v Long* (1851) 3 HL Cas 395; *Osborne v Chocqueel* [1896] 2 QB 109; and *Sattin v National Union Bank* (1978) 122 Sol Jo 367, CA.

[13] [2001] EWHC Admin 189, [2002] ACD 4, DC.

[14] [1976] Ch 119; cf *EG Music v SF (Film) Distributors* [1978] FSR 121. See also *Berger v Raymond & Son Ltd* [1984] 1 WLR 625.

[15] [1976] Ch 119 at 127.

[16] This dictum applies to civil cases tried by a judge alone, who is trained to distinguish between what is probative and what is not. Where there is a jury, the court must be more careful about admitting the evidence: per Dillon LJ in *Thorpe v Chief Constable of Greater Manchester Police* [1989] 2 All ER 827 at 830–1, CA.

[17] [2005] 2 All ER 931, HL.

approved some aspects of the misconduct alleged against L. The House of Lords held that evidence had properly been admitted to show that L had behaved with similar impropriety on two other occasions and that C had done so on one other occasion. The House of Lords held that the test of admissibility in civil cases was different from that which applied in criminal cases. The test in criminal cases, as propounded in *R v P*[18] and the Criminal Justice Act 2003,[19] required an enhanced relevance or substantial probative value because, if the evidence was not cogent, the prejudice that it would cause to the accused might render the proceedings unfair. That test led to the exclusion of evidence which was relevant on the grounds that it was not sufficiently probative. There was no warrant for the automatic application of such a test in a civil suit. To do so would be to introduce an inflexibility which was inappropriate and undesirable. Lord Phillips said:[20]

I would simply apply the test of relevance as the test of admissibility of similar fact evidence in a civil suit. Such evidence is admissible if it is potentially probative of an issue in the action. That is not to say that the policy considerations that have given rise to the complex rules . . . in sections 100 to 106 of the 2003 Act have no part to play in the conduct of civil litigation. They are policy considerations which the judge who has the management of the civil litigation will wish to keep well in mind. CPR r 1.2 requires the court to give effect to the overriding objective of dealing with cases justly. This includes dealing with the case in a way which is proportionate to what is involved in the case, and in a manner which is expeditious and fair. CPR r 1.4 requires the court actively to manage the case in order to further the overriding objective. CPR r 2.1 gives the court the power to control the evidence. This power expressly enables the court to exclude evidence that would otherwise be admissible and to limit cross-examination.

Similar fact evidence will not necessarily risk causing any unfair prejudice to the party against whom it is directed . . . It may, however, carry such a risk. Evidence of impropriety which reflects adversely on the character of a party may risk causing prejudice that is disproportionate to its relevance, particularly where the trial is taking place before a jury. In such a case the judge will be astute to see that the probative cogency of the evidence justifies this risk of prejudice in the interests of a fair trial.

Equally, when considering whether to admit evidence, or permit cross-examination, on matters that are collateral to the central issues, the judge will have regard to the need for proportionality and expedition. He will consider whether the evidence in question is likely to be relatively uncontroversial, or whether its admission is likely to create side issues which will unbalance the trial and make it harder to see the wood from the trees.

---

[18] [1991] 3 All ER 337, HL.    [19] See Ch 17.    [20] At [53]–[56].

## D CHARACTER RELEVANT TO CREDIT

In civil proceedings, any person who gives evidence, whether or not a party to the proceedings, is liable to cross-examination as to his credibility as a witness.[21] However, as a general rule, the cross-examining party is not allowed to adduce evidence to contradict a witness's answer to a question concerning credit. The rule, and the exceptions to it, are considered in detail in Chapter 7.

[21] See Ch 7 under 3(b) **Cross-examination as to credit.**

# 16

## EVIDENCE OF CHARACTER: EVIDENCE OF THE GOOD CHARACTER OF THE ACCUSED

This chapter concerns the circumstances in which, in criminal proceedings, evidence of the good character of the accused may be adduced because of its relevance either to a fact in issue or to his credibility.[1]

## A  THE EVIDENCE ADMISSIBLE

In criminal proceedings, the accused is allowed to adduce evidence of his good character. It may be proved either in chief, by the evidence of the accused himself or other defence witnesses, or in cross-examination of witnesses called for the prosecution. In *R v Rowton*[2] the accused, charged with indecent assault on a boy, called witnesses to his character. It was held that such evidence should be confined to evidence of the reputation of the accused amongst those to whom he is known and should not include evidence of specific creditable acts of the accused nor evidence of the witness's opinion of his disposition. Although this case was decided prior to the Criminal Evidence Act 1898, section 1 of which made the accused a competent witness for the defence in all criminal cases,[3] the rule would appear to apply even when the evidence of good character is given by the accused himself. Thus notwithstanding that in the normal case the accused would be much better qualified to give evidence of his disposition as revealed by specific acts of creditable conduct, as opposed to

---

[1] Other aspects of the subject are more conveniently considered under 'Examination-in-chief' and 'Cross-examination': see **The rule against a party impeaching the credit of his own witness** (see Ch 6) and **Cross-examination as to credit** and **Finality of answers to collateral questions** (see Ch 7). In criminal cases, the character of a person who is neither a party nor a witness is rarely relevant to a fact in issue: for an example, see *R v Murray* [1994] Crim LR 927, CA.

[2] (1865) Le&Ca 520, CCR.

[3] See now s 53(1) of the Youth Justice and Criminal Evidence Act 1999 (Ch 5).

evidence of his reputation, strictly speaking he must confine himself to the latter. However, although *R v Rowton* has never been expressly overruled, nowadays it is not, in practice, strictly adhered to. Thus, in *R v Redgrave*,[4] a case of importuning for immoral purposes in which the Court of Appeal held that the accused was not entitled to produce documents and photographs to show that he had had relationships of a heterosexual nature, because this amounted to calling evidence of particular facts to show that he was of a disposition which made it unlikely that he would have committed the offence charged, the court also said that an accused, in such a case, was entitled to give evidence of a normal sexual relationship with his wife or girlfriend.

The common-law rule under which in criminal proceedings evidence of a person's reputation is admissible for the purpose of proving his good (or bad) character has been preserved and put on a statutory basis by section 118(1) of the Criminal Justice Act 2003.

## B  THE DIRECTION TO THE JURY

The leading authority on how to direct the jury about evidence of the good character of the accused is *R v Vye*.[5] Prior to *R v Vye*, the law was unclear as to (a) whether a judge is under a duty to direct the jury about evidence of the good character of the accused and (b) if so, whether he should direct them not only that the evidence is relevant to credibility (the first limb of the direction) but also that it has a probative value in relation to the issue of guilt, in that a person of good character is less likely to have committed the offence (the second limb). Lord Chief Justice Taylor, giving the reserved judgment of the Court of Appeal, laid down the following three principles.

1.  If the accused testifies, the judge should give a first limb direction. If the accused does not give evidence at trial but relies on pre-trial answers or statements, that is, exculpatory statements made to the police or others, the judge, who is entitled to make observations about the way the jury should approach such evidence in contrast to evidence given on oath, should give a first limb direction by directing the jury to have regard to the accused's good character when considering the credibility of those statements.[6] If the accused does not give evidence and has given no pre-trial answers or statements, no issue as to his credibility arises and a first limb direction is not required.

2.  A second limb direction should be given, whether or not the accused has testified or made pre-trial answers or statements.[7] It is for the judge in each

---

[4] (1981) 74 Cr App R 10, CA.    [5] [1993] 1 WLR 471.

[6] See also *R v Chapman* [1989] Crim LR 60, CA.

[7] Improper disclosure that the accused had previously been arrested for an offence of the same type as the offence charged will undermine a second limb direction and effectively deprive the accused of the good character direction: *Arthurton v R* [2004] 2 Cr App R 559, PC.

case to decide how he tailors the direction to the particular circumstances. He would probably wish to indicate, as is commonly done, that good character cannot amount to a defence.

3. Where an accused of good character is jointly tried with an accused of bad character, principles 1 and 2 still apply: the accused of good character is entitled to a full direction.[8] As to any direction concerning the accused of bad character, in some cases the judge may think it best to tell the jury that there has been no evidence about his character and they must not speculate or take the absence of such information as any evidence against him. In other cases, the judge may think it best to say nothing about the absence of such information. The course to be taken depends on the circumstances of the individual case, including how great an issue was made of character during the evidence and speeches.

Where good character directions are required in accordance with *R v Vye*, it is not necessary for judges to use any particular form of words, but they may be wise to avoid saying that the jury are 'entitled' to take the evidence into account, which suggests that the jury has a choice whether or not to take it into account for the purposes in question.[9] Similarly, it is a serious misdirection to tell the jury that they can put good character into the scales[10] or, in the case of the first limb, that good character 'might assist' them on the question of credibility.[11] Equally, character directions should not be given in the form of a question or rhetorical question (eg 'Is it more likely that he is telling you the truth because he is a man of good character?'), but in the form of an affirmative statement, as in the Judicial Studies Board guideline direction for the first limb ('it is a factor which you should take into account when deciding whether you believe his evidence').[12]

In *R v Vye* it was held that if the judge gives both limbs of the direction, the Court of Appeal will be slow to criticize any qualifying remarks based on the facts of the individual case. Such remarks, however, must be justified. Thus in *R v Fitton*,[13] in which a nightclub doorman was charged with assaulting a customer, the Court of Appeal held that the trial judge had misdirected the jury in a qualification to the standard directions to the effect that the good character of the doorman was of less relevance and weight given that he was alleged to have committed a spontaneous offence. It has also been held to be wrong and unfair to direct a jury to ignore good character unless the remainder of the evidence leaves them in doubt about guilt,

---

[8] It was held that the suggestion of Lord Lane CJ in *R v Gibson* (1991) 93 Cr App R 9, CA, that the judge may decide to say little if anything about the good character of the one accused, was not satisfactory and ought not to be followed. *R v Vye*, in this respect, was applied in *R v Houlden* (1993) 99 Cr App R 244, CA.

[9] *R v Miah* [1997] 2 Cr App R 12, CA.     [10] *R v Boyson* [1991] Crim LR 274, CA.

[11] *R v Gray* [2004] 2 Cr App R 498, CA.

[12] *R v Lloyd* [2000] 2 Cr App R 355, CA and *R v Scranage* [2001] All ER (D) 185 (Apr), [2001] EWCA Crim 1171, CA.

[13] [2001] All ER (D) 28 (Feb), [2001] EWCA Crim 215, CA.

because evidence of good character must be considered as part of the totality of the evidence.[14]

In *R v Aziz*[15] the House of Lords has made clear that the phrase 'pre-trial answers or statements', as used in the first principle in *R v Vye*, refers not to wholly exculpatory statements, but only to 'mixed' statements, ie statements containing inculpatory as well as exculpatory material which are, for that reason, tendered as evidence of the truth of the facts they contain.[16] Thus an accused who does not give evidence but relies on wholly exculpatory statements is not entitled to a first limb direction. It was further held in *R v Aziz* that an accused who is entitled to directions as to good character in accordance with *R v Vye* will not lose that entitlement by mounting an attack on a co-accused such as a cut-throat defence.[17]

As to the third principle in *R v Vye*, relating to directions about the accused of 'bad character', that phrase appears to cover both an accused in respect of whom there is no evidence of character, one way or the other, and an accused of bad character whose bad character is not revealed in evidence, but not an accused whose bad character is revealed in evidence. In *R v Cain*[18] the evidence relating to the character of each of three co-accused was different: with A, there was positive evidence of good character; with B, there was no evidence either way; and with C, there was evidence of previous convictions. It was held that A was entitled to a full direction (both limbs); that the trial judge had a discretion whether to say anything at all about B's character; and that, concerning C, whose position was not covered by *R v Vye*, the trial judge should have warned the jury that his convictions were not relevant to guilt, but to credibility (or otherwise the jury might have assumed that they were relevant to the issue of propensity to commit crime, and therefore to guilt).

## C THE MEANING OF 'GOOD CHARACTER'

As to what 'good character' means for the purposes of the principles established in *R v Vye*, there is no simple answer.[19] For example, previous convictions will not necessarily prevent an accused from being treated as of previous good character, particularly if they are spent or convictions for minor offences which have no relevance to credibility and took place a long time ago.[20] In these circumstances, the judge has a discretion whether or not to give directions in accordance with *R v Vye*, and if so in what terms,

---

[14] *R v Handbridge* [1993] Crim LR 287, CA.     [15] [1995] 3 All ER 149, HL.

[16] See *R v Duncan* (1981) 73 Cr App R 359, CA and *R v Sharp* [1988] 1 All ER 65, HL. A statement is only 'mixed' if it contains an admission of fact which is 'significant' in relation to an issue in the case: see *R v Garrod* [1997] Crim LR 445, CA and generally Ch 6.

[17] [1995] 3 All ER 149 at 158.     [18] [1994] 2 All ER 398, CA.

[19] See generally R Munday 'What Constitutes a Good Character?' [1997] Crim LR 247.

[20] See, eg, *R v Goss* [2005] Crim LR 61, CA (on a charge of possessing a firearm, a previous conviction for driving a motor vehicle without car insurance, in the absence of evidence to show that the accused had deliberately flouted road traffic law).

but he should give directions in *unqualified* terms if the previous convictions can only be regarded as irrelevant or of no significance in relation to the offence charged.[21] An unqualified direction will also be appropriate where, although there is evidence of previous misconduct on the part of the accused, it is disputed, and its potential for distracting the jury from the main issues in the case outweighs any benefit to be had from a qualified direction.[22] By the same token, there will be cases where the accused is not of absolutely good character and the fact of the previous conviction or other character blemish is known to the jury, but where the only proper course is to give a qualified direction, which is likely to mean that careful consideration should be given to the distinction between the two limbs of credibility and propensity.[23] In *R v Gray*,[24] a murder trial in which the accused denied being present at the killing and volunteered that he had been convicted of driving with excess alcohol and without a licence or insurance, it was held that he was entitled to an ordinary first limb direction and a modified second limb direction.

An accused with no previous convictions is not necessarily of good character, for he may have been dishonest or guilty of other criminal behaviour even if not convicted of any offence in that respect. In *R v Durbin*[25] the accused was charged with the unlawful importation of cannabis. When interviewed, he gave a false account of his movements on the Continent prior to his arrival in the UK; at the trial he admitted having misled two prosecution witnesses in relation to his dealings with his co-accused; and in both interview and in evidence he admitted that in the course of the visit to the Continent which gave rise to the charge, he had knowingly engaged in smuggling computer parts across European frontiers in order to avoid customs duties. The Court of Appeal rejected the idea that in these circumstances it was a matter of discretion for the trial judge to decide what direction, if any, should be given: the accused was *entitled* to qualified *Vye* directions. It was held that where an accused is of previous good character then he is entitled to the good character direction (both limbs if his credibility is in issue, the second limb only if it is not), notwithstanding that he may have admitted telling lies in interview[26] and may have admitted other offences or disreputable conduct in relation to the subject matter of the charge, but the terms of the direction should be modified to take account of the circumstances of

---

[21] *R v Durbin* [1995] 2 Cr App R 84, citing *R v Herrox* (5 Oct 1993, unreported), CA and *R v Heath* [1994] 13 LS Gaz R 34, CA. But contrast *R v Nye* (1982) 75 Cr App R 247, CA, as understood by the Court of Appeal in *R v O'Shea* [1993] Crim LR 951: an accused with previous but spent convictions may not be put forward as being of good character without qualifications but may be referred to as of good character 'without relevant convictions' because although, so far as possible, the judge should exercise the discretion favourably towards the accused, the jury must not be misled or told lies.

[22] *R v Butler* [1999] Crim LR 835, CA.

[23] *R v Durbin* [1995] 2 Cr App R 84. See also *R v Aziz* [1995] 3 All ER 149, HL at 152–3, *R v Timson* [1993] Crim LR 58, CA and *R v H* [1994] Crim LR 205, CA; and cf *R v Hickmet* [1996] Crim LR 588, CA, where it was held that a direction would have had no significant effect and may have simply confused the jury. There are obvious difficulties in the way of a qualified direction, as when the accused admits that he has lied (credibility) or set out with a criminal intent (propensity): see *R v Burnham* [1995] Crim LR 491, CA.

[24] [2004] 2 Cr App R 498, CA.        [25] [1995] 2 Cr App R 84, CA.

[26] Citing *R v Kabariti* (1990) 92 Cr App R 362.

the case, including all facts known to the jury, either as regards credibility or propensity or both. However, in *R v Zoppola-Barraza*,[27] another case of unlawful importation of cannabis, in which the accused gave evidence that on a number of occasions he had smuggled gold and jewels into the country, it was held that he was not entitled to either limb of the *Vye* direction and that it would be an affront to common sense to hold otherwise. This case was distinguished in *R v Durbin*: whereas the admission of smuggling gold and jewels began *before* the importation of drugs, the smuggling of computer parts was part of the accused's account of the particular transaction in the course of which the importation of drugs was discovered.

*R v Durbin* was not brought to the attention of the House of Lords in *R v Aziz*.[28] In that case two of the accused, charged with conspiracy to cheat the public revenue of VAT, pleaded not guilty and relied on the fact that they had no previous convictions, but also gave evidence of previous misconduct, including evidence of making false mortgage applications, telling lies during interview, and not declaring full earnings for Inland Revenue purposes. Lord Steyn, acknowledging that this was an area in which generalizations are hazardous, and that a wide spectrum of cases must be kept in mind, held as follows.

1. A trial judge has a residual discretion to decline to give *Vye* directions in the case of an accused without previous convictions if he considers it an insult to common sense to give such directions. A judge should never be compelled to give meaningless or absurd directions. Cases occur where an accused with no previous convictions is shown beyond doubt to have been guilty of serious criminal behaviour similar to the offence charged. A judge is not compelled to go through the charade of giving *Vye* directions where the accused's claim to good character is spurious.

2. This discretionary power is narrowly circumscribed.

3. Prima facie the directions must be given. The judge will often be able to place a fair and balanced picture before the jury by giving *Vye* directions and then adding words of qualification concerning the proved or possible misconduct.

4. Whenever a judge proposes to give a direction not likely to be anticipated by counsel, he should invite submissions on his proposed directions.

On the facts, it was held that the two accused had not lost the right to *Vye* directions, but it would have been proper for the judge to have qualified them by reference to the admitted misconduct.

Similar problems arise when an accused pleads guilty to only some counts on the indictment. It is clear from *R v Teasdale*[29] that if an accused pleads guilty to an offence which is an alternative to that on which he is being tried, and the facts are such that, if

---

27  [1994] Crim LR 833, CA. See also *R v Buzalek* [1991] Crim LR 115, CA.
28  [1995] 3 All ER 149, HL.    29  [1993] 4 All ER 290, CA.

he is convicted on the greater offence then the guilty plea on the lesser offence will have to be vacated, a good character direction should be given, tailored to take into account the guilty plea. However, in *R v Challenger*[30] it was held that in all other cases in which an accused pleads guilty to another count on the indictment, he ceases to be a person of good character and the full character direction becomes inappropriate. It was further held that, if the jury is not told of the guilty plea, it would be misleading to direct them that the accused is of good character; but that in other cases an appropriate direction may be given, depending on the circumstances. Thus if the accused testifies, the jury are made aware of the guilty plea, and defence counsel argues to the jury that it is in his favour on the issue of credibility that the accused admitted his guilt on one count and that they can therefore attach greater weight to his assertions that he is innocent on the remaining counts, then the judge should remind the jury of that argument, if he thinks it proper to do so.[31]

---

[30] [1994] Crim LR 202, CA.

[31] Cf *R v Shepherd* [1995] Crim LR 153, CA, where formal admissions went some way towards informing the jury that S had pleaded guilty to other counts. It was held that if the defence had grasped the nettle and brought out in evidence that S, apart from the matters covered by the admissions, had no other convictions, then it might have been appropriate for the judge to have directed the jury that, apart from attaching such weight as they saw fit to the admissions, S was entitled to ask them to consider his case on the basis of previous good character.

# 17

# EVIDENCE OF CHARACTER: EVIDENCE OF BAD CHARACTER IN CRIMINAL CASES

## A INTRODUCTORY

### 1 THE BACKGROUND TO THE CRIMINAL JUSTICE ACT 2003

The admissibility of evidence of bad character in criminal cases is governed, almost exclusively, by Chapter 1 of Part 11 of the Criminal Justice Act 2003. However, it is necessary first to consider in outline the applicable rules before the scheme introduced by the 2003 Act, most of which have been repealed but some of which have survived.

Before the new statutory provisions, there were both common-law and statutory rules. Under section 3 of the Criminal Procedure Act 1865, which remains in force, a party is not entitled to impeach the credit of his own witness by general evidence of his bad character.[1] At common law a witness other than the accused could be *cross-examined* about his previous misconduct in order to impugn his credibility.[2] However, under the rule of finality of answers to collateral questions, answers given by the witness to questions on his previous misconduct, insofar as they could properly be regarded as questions on collateral matters, were final, in the sense that the cross-examining party could not call further evidence with a view to contradicting the witness. The exceptions to the rule, ie the cases in which evidence in rebuttal was admissible, included cases of denial of previous convictions, admissible under section 6 of the Criminal Procedure Act 1865, and, at common law, denial by the witness of his bias or his reputation for untruthfulness.

As to the accused, the law was, as it was put in an earlier edition of this work, 'complex, unprincipled and riddled with anomalies'. The general rule was exclusionary.

---

[1] See Ch 6.

[2] Subject to restrictions on cross-examination of complainants in proceedings for sexual offences: see ss 41–3 of the Youth Justice and Criminal Evidence Act 1999: see Ch 7.

The prosecution were not permitted either to adduce evidence of the accused's bad character, other than that relating directly to the offence charged, or to cross-examine witnesses for the defence with a view to eliciting such evidence. The rule prevented the prosecution from introducing evidence of previous convictions, previous misconduct, and disposition towards wrongdoing or misconduct, the principal rationale of the rule being that the prejudice created by such evidence outweighed any probative value it might have.

At common law, there were only two exceptions to the general rule: first, where the evidence in question was so-called 'similar fact evidence', including so-called 'background evidence', and second where the defence raised the issue of the accused's character. As to the former, similar fact evidence, which could be admitted by the prosecution or on behalf of a co-accused, was evidence of the disposition of the accused towards wrongdoing or specific acts of misconduct on other occasions judged to be of sufficient probative force in relation to the facts in issue in the case to make it just to admit it notwithstanding its prejudicial effect. As to the latter, the prosecution were entitled to adduce evidence of the bad character of the accused in rebuttal of evidence of his good character adduced by the defence.

The most important statutory exception to the general rule was contained in section 1(3) of the Criminal Evidence Act 1898. The first part of section 1(3) armed an accused with what was often referred to as a 'shield' against cross-examination about his bad character, and the latter part of the subsection set out certain situations in which the shield could be lost, including the following: (i) where the accused asserted his good character (ii) where the nature or conduct of the defence was such as to involve imputations on the character of witnesses for the prosecution or the deceased victim of the alleged crime and (iii) where the accused gave evidence against any other person charged in the same proceedings.

Chapter 1 of Part 11 of the Criminal Justice Act (sections 98–113) all but codifies the law governing the admissibility of evidence of bad character in criminal cases, abolishing the common-law rules,[3] amending section 6 of the Criminal Procedure Act 1865[4] to ensure that cross-examination on a witness's previous convictions is governed by the new statutory rules, and repealing section 1(3) of the Criminal Evidence Act 1898.[5] In general terms, the Government's approach to reform has been informed by Lord Justice Auld's 'Review of the Criminal Courts of England and Wales'[6] and the Law Commission Report 'Evidence of Bad Character in Criminal Proceedings'.[7] There are, however, substantial differences between the proposals of both the Review and the Commission and the measures subsequently enacted.

The Review made no firm recommendations about character evidence but was highly critical of the law, as it then stood, and did recommend that the law of criminal

---

[3] Section 99(1).      [4] Section 331 and para 79, sch 36.      [5] Section 331 and para 80(b), sch 36.
[6] HMSO, 2001.
[7] Law Com No 273, Cm 5257 (2001). For critiques of the Report, see M Redmayne 'The Law Commission's character convictions' (2002) 6 E&P 71 and P Mirfield 'Bad character and the Law Commission' (2002) 6 E&P 141.

evidence should, in general, move away from technical rules of admissibility to trusting judicial and lay fact finders to give relevant evidence the weight it deserves.[8] The Government's proposals were also said to be underpinned by the concept that the criminal justice system should be more trusting of fact finders to assess relevant evidence. However, the Government did not opt for an approach based on the general admissibility of all evidence of bad character.

The Law Commission was also highly critical of the law as it then stood. Fundamental to the scheme recommended by the Commission was the idea that in any trial there is a central set of facts about which any party should be free to adduce relevant evidence, including evidence of bad character, without restraint. Such evidence 'has to do' with the offence charged or is evidence of misconduct connected with the investigation or prosecution of the offence. The Commission recommended that evidence of bad character falling outside this category should only be admissible with leave or if all parties agree to its admission or it is evidence of the accused's bad character and he wishes to adduce it. Witnesses and the accused were both to be protected against allegations of misconduct extraneous to the events which are the subject of the trial and which have only marginal relevance to the facts of the case.[9] Under the recommended scheme, and under the scheme as enacted, evidence is only admissible if it falls within one of a number of specified categories of admissibility, many of which replicate the cases in which evidence of bad character was admissible at common law. However, whereas the Law Commission recommended in effect an exclusionary rule subject to exceptions under which bad character evidence could be admitted with the leave of the court, overall the Government's approach is designed to be more inclusionary,[10] and under the new provisions evidence of the bad character of the accused falling within one of the categories of admissibility may be introduced without leave, subject, in some cases, to a discretion to exclude.

Unfortunately, the scheme contained in the Criminal Justice Act 2003, as we shall see, is not simple and is in parts unclear, some of the key provisions being open to widely differing interpretations. A former Lord Chief Justice described section 1 of the Criminal Evidence Act 1898, with justification, as 'a nightmare of construction'.[11] The same is likely to be said of some of the new statutory provisions, especially those governing admissibility of the bad character of the accused. It would not be unfair to describe them, to be colloquial, as something of a dog's breakfast.

---

[8] Para 78.   [9] See paras 1.12 and 1.13.

[10] See Hansard, HL, vol 654, col 739 (4 Nov 2003) and para 365 of the Home Office Explanatory Notes to the 2003 Act.

[11] Lord Lane CJ in *R v Anderson* [1988] QB 678 at 686.

## 2  ABOLITION OF THE COMMON LAW RULES

Section 99 of the 2003 provides as follows.

(1) The common law rules governing the admissibility of evidence of bad character in criminal proceedings[12] are abolished.

(2) Subsection (1) is subject to section 118(1) in so far as it preserves the rule under which in criminal proceedings a person's reputation is admissible for the purposes of proving his bad character.

Although section 99(1) refers only to the rules governing the admissibility of evidence of bad character and not to the common-law rules governing cross-examination of a witness other than the accused about his bad character, it is submitted that the intention is to cover both. As to the questioning of witnesses on matters covered by the exceptions to the rule of finality of answers to collateral questions, the common-law rules can certainly be said to 'govern' the admissibility of evidence of bad character, because the matters are put to the witness with a view to eliciting such evidence and, if the matters are denied, they can be proved. The common-law rules permitting the questioning of witnesses on their bad character in relation to matters not covered by the exceptions to the rule of finality may also be said to 'govern' the admissibility of evidence of bad character in that they too are questions put with a view to eliciting such evidence and notwithstanding that if the witness denies the matters put, they cannot be proved.

It would seem that the general common-law discretion to exclude prosecution evidence where its prejudicial effect outweighs its probative value[13] may continue to be exercised in respect of evidence of bad character. It is submitted that the phrase 'common law rules governing . . . admissibility' is not apt to cover a common-law *discretion* to exclude.

## 3  'BAD CHARACTER' DEFINED

Under section 98 of the 2003 Act:

References in this Chapter to evidence of a person's 'bad character' are to evidence of, or of a disposition towards, misconduct on his part, other than evidence which—

(a) has to do with the alleged facts of the offence with which the defendant is charged, or

(b) is evidence of misconduct in connection with the investigation or prosecution of that offence.

The definition of bad character in section 98 applies in the case of both the accused and non-defendants and appears to cover misconduct occurring, or disposition towards misconduct existing, either before or after the offence with which the accused

---

[12] 'Criminal proceedings', for the purposes of the provisions of the 2003 Act relating to evidence of bad character, means criminal proceedings in relation to which the strict rules of evidence apply: s 112(1).

[13] See Ch 2.

is charged. 'Bad character' has been defined broadly by section 98, a definition that generally reflects the common-law concept. The broad definition is designed to prevent evidence which, under the pre-existing law, would have been excluded, from falling outside the statutory scheme and thereby becoming admissible.[14] Although the definition does not include a person's reputation for misconduct, the common-law rule under which a person's reputation is admissible for the purpose of proving his bad character, has been preserved by section 118(2).

'Misconduct', for the purposes of the definition, means 'the commission of an offence or other reprehensible behaviour',[15] 'offence' in its turn being defined to include a service offence.[16] Evidence of bad character under the Act therefore covers evidence of a person's misconduct whether or not unlawful; if unlawful, whether or not it resulted in a prosecution; and where it did result in a prosecution, whether within the jurisdiction or overseas, and whether it resulted in a conviction or an acquittal. As to acquittals, the definition in effect preserves the decision of the House of Lords in R v Z[17] that where evidence of misconduct on the part of the accused is relevant and otherwise admissible prosecution evidence, it does not fall to be excluded because it shows or tends to show that the accused was guilty of an offence of which he was previously acquitted. The definition also covers evidence of misconduct in respect of which a trial is pending and evidence of an accused's misconduct which relates to the other charges on the indictment. Although the definition does not cover, by itself, evidence that someone has been suspected or informally charged with misconduct, evidence concerning such suspicions and accusations are generally irrelevant and therefore inadmissible on that basis.[18] Likewise, although the definition does not cover evidence of the bare fact that someone has been formally charged with an offence, such evidence is generally inadmissible because irrelevant, the fact that a man has been charged with an offence being no proof that he committed it and having no bearing on his credibility as a witness.[19]

If evidence of bad character does fall within the statutory definition it can only be admitted in evidence if it satisfies the further conditions of admissibility in section 100 (non-defendant's bad character) or section 101 (defendant's bad character). Where the evidence to be adduced is evidence of the bad character of an accused who disputes the facts relied upon to establish his bad character, then a *voir dire* may also be required.[20]

---

[14] See Hilary Benn MP, HC Committee, 23 Jan 2003, col 545.

[15] See R Munday 'What Constitutes "Other Reprehensible Behaviour" under the Bad Character Provisions of the Criminal Justice Act 2003?' [2005] Crim LR 24.

[16] Section 112(1).     [17] [2002] 2 AC 483: see Ch 22.

[18] See *Stirland v DPP* [1944] AC 315, HL, a decision under the Criminal Evidence Act 1898.

[19] See *Maxwell v DPP* [1935] AC 309, HL, a decision under the Criminal Evidence Act 1898.

[20] See *R v Wright* [2000] Crim LR 851, CA, a decision under the Criminal Evidence Act 1898.

## 4  THE ADMISSIBILITY OF EVIDENCE OF BAD CHARACTER 'TO DO WITH' THE FACTS OF THE OFFENCE OR IN CONNECTION WITH ITS INVESTIGATION OR PROSECUTION

Section 99(1) of the 2003 Act, as we have seen, abolishes the common-law rules governing admissibility of evidence of bad character as defined by section 98. It follows, of course, that the common-law rules continue to operate insofar as they permit evidence to be adduced which, looking to the wording of section 98(a) 'has to do with the alleged facts of the offence' or, looking to the wording of section 98(b) 'is evidence of misconduct in connection with the investigation or prosecution of that offence'. Section 98(a) covers such prosecution evidence, other than evidence of previous misconduct or evidence of disposition towards misconduct, as tends to show that the accused is guilty of the offence charged, such as evidence of witnesses to the crime and fingerprint evidence. The phrase 'evidence which has to do with the alleged facts of the offence' also covers misconduct other than the offence charged, for example, evidence of an assault or criminal damage committed in the course of a burglary with which the accused is charged. Evidence of this kind, however, falls to be distinguished from so-called 'background evidence', which is evidence of bad character potentially admissible under section 101(1)(c), a distinction which is likely to be difficult to draw in some cases.[21]

Section 98(b) covers, for example, evidence that during the investigation the police obtained evidence unlawfully or unfairly, for instance by fabricating a confession or planting evidence on the accused or in his premises; evidence that during interview the accused told lies; and evidence that during the investigation or proceedings the prosecution or the accused had sought to intimidate potential witnesses.

# B  EVIDENCE OF THE BAD CHARACTER OF A PERSON OTHER THAN THE DEFENDANT

## 1  SECTION 100 OF THE CRIMINAL JUSTICE ACT 2003

At common law a witness could be cross-examined about his previous misconduct with a view to impugning his credibility. He could be cross-examined, for example, about acts of dishonesty or immorality on his part, about lies he told or false allegations he made, about his drink or drug abuse, and so on. However, as we have already seen, insofar as the questions could properly be said to be on collateral matters and the witness denied them, evidence was admissible in rebuttal only exceptionally. The exceptions covered previous convictions, bias and general reputation for untruthfulness.

---

[21] See under s 101(1)(c) below.

In *R v Edwards*[22] it was held that subject to the limits laid down in *Hobbs v Tinling*,[23] a witness could be cross-examined about any improper conduct of which he may have been guilty, for the purpose of testing his credit. The following three principles were established in *Hobbs v Tinling*.[24]

1. Questions as to credit in cross-examination are proper if of such a nature that the truth of the imputation conveyed by them would seriously affect the opinion of the court as to the credibility of the witness on the matters to which he testifies.

2. Such questions are improper if the imputation which they convey relates to matters so remote in time or of such a character that the truth of the imputation would not affect, or would affect in a slight degree, the opinion of the court as to the credibility of the witness on the matter to which he testifies.

3. Such questions are improper if there is a great disproportion between the importance of the imputation made against the witness's character and the importance of his evidence.

The Law Commission was of the view that further restraints were necessary. Three reasons were given: the power of evidence of bad character to distort the fact-finding process; the need to encourage witnesses to give evidence, and the need for courts 'to control gratuitous and offensive cross-examination of little or no purpose other than to intimidate or embarrass the witness or muddy the waters'.[25] Balancing these factors against the need not to prejudice a fair trial, the Commission recommended a test based on the degree of relevance of bad character evidence to the issues in the case. Evidence of only trivial relevance would be excluded. The views of the Commission are reflected in the terms of section 100 of the Criminal Justice Act 2003. Section 100(1) provides as follows.

(1) In criminal proceedings evidence of the bad character of a person other than the defendant is admissible if and only if—
   (a) it is important explanatory evidence,
   (b) it has substantial probative value in relation to a matter which—
       (i) is a matter in issue in the proceedings, and
       (ii) is of substantial importance in the context of the case as a whole, or
   (c) all parties to the proceedings agree to the evidence being admissible.

Section 100 may be used by the prosecution, the accused or any co-accused. The meaning of 'bad character' has already been considered. A 'person other than the defendant' may or may not be a witness in the case. Although, on its face, section 100 governs only the admissibility of evidence of bad character and does not, in terms, govern the asking of questions about bad character in cross-examination,[26] it is

---

[22] [1991] 2 All ER 266, CA.    [23] [1929] 2 KB 1, CA.    [24] Ibid at 51.
[25] Law Com No 272, op cit at para 9.35
[26] Cf, in this regard, s 41 of the Youth Justice and Criminal Evidence Act 1999.

submitted that the intention is to cover both. This would be consistent with the interpretation of section 99(1) of the Act that it abolishes the common-law rules relating not only to the admissibility of evidence of bad character but also to cross-examination of witnesses about bad character.[27]

## 2 THRESHOLD CONDITIONS FOR ADMISSIBILITY

### (a) Important explanatory evidence

Section 100(2) provides as follows.

> (2) For the purposes of subsection (1)(a) evidence is important explanatory evidence if—
>
> (a) without it, the court or jury would find it impossible or difficult properly to understand other evidence in the case, and
>
> (b) its value for understanding the case as a whole is substantial.

Section 100(2) covers evidence of or a disposition towards misconduct on the part of someone other than the accused, without which the prosecution (or defence) account would be incomplete or incoherent.[28] Thus if the matter to which the evidence relates is largely comprehensible without the explanatory evidence, the evidence will be inadmissible. The wording of section 100(2)(a) is a slightly different formulation of the common-law rule permitting the use of background evidence, notwithstanding that it reveals the bad character or criminal disposition *of the accused*, where it is part of a continual background or history which is relevant to the offence charged and without the totality of which the account placed before the jury would be incomplete or incomprehensible.[29] The Explanatory Notes to the Act give an example of section 100(2)(a) arising in a case which involves the abuse by one person of another over a long period of time: 'For the jury to understand properly the victim's account of the offending and why they (sic) did not seek help from, for example, a parent or other guardian, it might be necessary for evidence to be given of a wider pattern of abuse involving that other person.'[30]

Explanatory evidence, to be admissible, must also satisfy section 100(1)(b), ie its value for understanding the case as a whole must be 'substantial', as opposed to minor or trivial.[31]

### (b) Evidence of substantial probative value

Under section 100(1)(b), evidence of the bad character of a person other than the accused is admissible if it has substantial probative value in relation to a matter which—(i) is a matter in issue in the proceedings, and (ii) is of substantial importance in the context of the case as a whole. The probative value must be 'substantial'—

---

[27] See above under 2 **Abolition of the common law rules.**
[28] Law Com No 273, op cit, para 9.13.
[29] Per Purchas LJ in *R v Pettman* 2 May 1985, CA, unreported.     [30] Para 360.
[31] Law Com No 273, op cit, para 9.1.

evidence of only minor probative force should not be admitted. A 'matter in issue in the proceedings' means any matter in issue, whether an issue of disputed fact or an issue of credibility. In order to be admissible, however, the evidence must also be of substantial importance in the context of the case as a whole—evidence which goes only to some minor or trivial issue should not be admitted.

Section 100(3) sets out a non-exhaustive list of the factors to which the court must have regard in assessing the probative value of the evidence. It provides as follows.

(3) In assessing the probative value of evidence for the purposes of subsection (1)(b) the court must have regard to the following factors (and to any others it considers relevant)—

(a) the nature and number of the events, or other things, to which the evidence relates;

(b) when those events or things are alleged to have happened or existed;

(c) where—

(i) the evidence is evidence of a person's misconduct, and

(ii) it is suggested that the evidence has probative value by reason of similarity between that misconduct and other alleged misconduct,

the nature and extent of the similarities and dissimilarities between each of the alleged instances of misconduct;

(d) where—

(i) the evidence is evidence of a person's misconduct,

(ii) it is suggested that that person is also responsible for the misconduct charged, and

(iii) the identity of the person responsible for the misconduct charged is disputed,

the extent to which the evidence shows or tends to show that the same person was responsible each time.

As to section 100(3)(a), if, for example, a key witness has previous convictions or has been guilty of improper conduct in the past, the nature of the offence committed or of the misconduct will have an obvious bearing in deciding its probative value in relation to the issue of his credibility as a witness. A conviction for perjury will have a probative force normally lacking in a conviction for, say, a minor motoring offence. Similarly, evidence of previous false accusations may have a probative value not to be found in, say, evidence of cruelty to animals. The number of previous convictions or the number of instances of previous misconduct has an equally obvious bearing on the question of probative value.

As to section 100(3)(b), evidence of misconduct occurring many years ago is usually likely to have less probative value than more recent misconduct, although plainly very serious misconduct in the past may have much greater probative value than recent but relatively minor misconduct.

Section 100 (3)(c) relates to evidence of a person's misconduct, the probative value of which, in relation to a matter in issue in the proceedings, derives from its similarity to other misconduct on his part. Thus if the accused alleges that the case against him has been fabricated by a police officer who has threatened a potential witness for the defence—evidence of which would be admissible under section 98(b)—and there is evidence that in other cases the officer has also gone to improper lengths to secure a conviction, in assessing the probative value of the evidence the court should have regard to the nature and extent of the similarities, for example, whether in some of the cases also he had threatened potential defence witnesses.

Section 100(3)(d) relates to evidence, in cases in which the identity of the offender is in dispute, suggesting that a person other than the accused is responsible for the offence charged. Such evidence will often take the form of evidence of similar facts. For example, if the accused is charged with a sexual assault in a public park, the prosecution case being that the crime was committed by someone wearing eccentric clothes, and the defence being one of mistaken identity, and there is evidence that X, the resident of a house overlooking the park has previously committed sexual assaults in the park, then in assessing the probative value of the evidence, the court must have regard to the extent to which the evidence shows or tends to show that X was responsible for each of the offences, for example whether the evidence shows that X wore eccentric clothing or the same eccentric clothing on each occasion.

### (c) Evidence admitted by agreement

Under section 100(1)(c) evidence of the bad character of a person other than the accused may be admitted by agreement of 'all parties to the proceedings', ie the prosecution, the accused and any co-accused. Under section 100(4), evidence may be admitted under section 100(1)(c) without the leave of the court.

### 3 THE REQUIREMENT OF LEAVE

Section 100(4) of the 2003 Act provides that 'Except where subsection (1)(c) applies, evidence of the bad character of a person other than the defendant must not be given without the leave of the court.' Thus evidence admissible under section 100(1)(a) or (b) must not be adduced without leave. Unfortunately, however, the subsection gives no guidance as to what factors, if any, should be taken into account in deciding whether or not to grant leave, over and above the factors set out in section 100(2) and (3).

On one view, section 100(4) also applies to evidence of bad character of complainants admissible under section 41 of the Youth Justice and Criminal Evidence Act 1999. If that is so, then in this context also the purpose of the subsection is elusive, because it is unclear what factors, if any, should be taken into account in deciding whether or not to grant leave, over and above the matters that have to be taken into account in deciding whether to grant leave under section 41 itself. The further question arises as to what kinds of sexual behaviour on the part of the complainant should be treated as 'bad character' as defined in the 2003 Act. An alternative and preferable view, it is submitted, is that when evidence of bad character is admitted under section 41, there will of necessity be compliance with section 100(4) of the 2003 Act because of the leave requirement in section 41 itself.

## 4  DISCRETION TO EXCLUDE

It is submitted that the general common-law discretionary power to exclude evidence where its prejudicial effect outweighs its probative value may be exercised in respect of *prosecution* evidence of bad character admissible under section 100.[32] It is unclear whether the general discretionary power to exclude prosecution evidence under section 78 of the Police and Criminal Evidence Act 1984[33] applies in the case of prosecution evidence of bad character otherwise admissible under the Criminal Justice Act 2003. The arguments for and against its application are more conveniently set out in the context of section 101(3) of the 2003 Act, which is considered in the next section of this chapter. If, as submitted, section 78 does apply, then it will be open to the defence to submit that evidence admissible under section 100 of the 2003 Act upon which the prosecution propose to rely should be excluded where, having regard to all the circumstances, its admission would have such an adverse effect on the fairness of the proceedings that the court ought not to admit it.

# C  EVIDENCE OF THE BAD CHARACTER OF THE DEFENDANT

## 1  EVIDENCE ADMITTED THROUGH INADVERTENCE

At common law, as we have seen, the general rule was that the prosecution were not permitted either to adduce evidence of the accused's bad character or to cross-examine witnesses for the defence with a view to eliciting such evidence, the rationale of the rule being the risk of the tribunal of fact becoming biased against an accused. The importance that English law attached to the rule was such that in cases where none of the exceptions to it applied but the bad character of the accused was inadvertently revealed to the jury, whether by a witness or counsel, the judge could exercise his discretion to discharge the whole jury from giving a verdict and order a re-trial.[34] It is submitted that the principles established at common law to deal with the problem of disclosure of the accused's bad character by inadvertence will continue to provide valuable guidance. Thus, as at common law, much is likely to depend on how explicit the reference to bad character was, the extent to which, if at all, the defence was to blame, and whether a direction to the jury is capable of neutralizing the prejudice

---

[32] See above under **A2 Abolition of the common law rules.**          [33] See Ch 2.

[34] See, eg, *R v Tyrer* (1988) *The Times*, 13 Oct CA. See generally Roderick Munday 'Irregular Disclosure of Evidence of Bad character' [1990] Crim LR 92.

to the accused.[35] The question for the judge, in exercising the discretion, is likely to remain whether there is a real danger of injustice occurring because the jury, having heard the prejudicial matter, may be biased.[36] Thus in appropriate circumstances, as when the effect on the jury appears to be minimal, the trial may properly continue. For example, in *R v Coughlan* and *R v Young*,[37] where an accused had referred in evidence to a previous conviction of a co-accused but prosecuting counsel had continued with his cross-examination regardless, counsel for the defence raising the matter in the absence of the jury after a lapse of time, the Court of Appeal refused to interfere with the judge's decision not to discharge the jury. In summary proceedings in which the magistrates become aware of the bad character of the accused, either by inadvertence, or deliberately, as when called upon to decide on the admissibility of evidence of bad character, difficult and largely unresolved procedural and evidential problems can arise, because magistrates must perform the combined role of tribunal of law and tribunal of fact.[38]

## 2  THE BACKGROUND TO SECTION 101 OF THE CRIMINAL JUSTICE ACT 2003

Before the coming into force of the 2003 Act, evidence of the bad character of the accused was admissible only exceptionally and a sharp distinction was drawn between evidence adduced because of its relevance to the issue of guilt, and evidence elicited in cross-examination of the accused and bearing upon his credibility as a witness. The approach under section 101 of the 2003 Act is radically different. Section 101 sets out seven gateways through which evidence of the bad character of the accused can be admitted. Collectively, these grounds for admissibility are much wider than those which they have replaced. Under the section, (a) no distinction is drawn between evidence introduced as a part of the prosecution's case and evidence elicited in cross-examination of the accused, (b) evidence is admissible irrespective of whether the accused gives evidence and (c) there are no explicit limitations on the purpose for which the evidence is adduced.

The provisions in the 2003 Act relating to evidence of the bad character of the accused provoked much controversy during their parliamentary passage, especially in the House of Lords, where some members voiced the opinion that section 101 undermined the presumption of innocence.[39] A major criticism of the statutory scheme is that although it is based on the proposals of the Law Commission, each of the safeguards contained in the Law Commission framework and designed to protect the accused from the introduction of prejudicial evidence has been either abandoned

---

[35]  *R v Weaver* [1968] 1 QB 353, CA.      [36]  *R v Docherty* [1999] 1 Cr App R 274, CA.

[37]  (1976) 63 Cr App R 33. See also *R v Sutton* (1969) 53 Cr App R 504, CA.

[38]  See Martin Wasik 'Magistrates: Knowledge of Previous Convictions' [1996] Crim LR 851, where the cases are reviewed.

[39]  See, eg, Lord Alexander and Lord Kingsland, *Hansard*, HL, Vol 654, cols 729, 731, and 741 (4 Nov 2003).

or diluted by the statutory scheme.[40] For example, under the Commission's proposals, in each of the four situations in which evidence of bad character of the accused was admissible, leave was required and in three of those situations there was a condition that the interests of justice required the evidence to be admissible, even taking account of its potentially prejudicial effect. Under section 101, however, leave is not required and instead of an 'interests of justice' condition, there is a discretionary power to exclude, but only on the application of the defence and only in respect of evidence admissible under two of the seven 'gateways'. The breadth of section 101, coupled with the absence of the much tighter restrictions on admissibility contained in the Law Commission's proposals, are such as to allow evidence of the accused's bad character to be admitted more readily than in the past. The effect, it is submitted, will be to oblige judges to make much greater use of their discretionary powers to exclude such evidence.

It does not follow from the foregoing that the prosecution should apply as a matter of routine to admit evidence of the accused's bad character. In *R v Hanson*,[41] the first Court of Appeal decision on the new provisions, it was held that the starting point should be for judges and practitioners to bear in mind that Parliament's purpose was to assist in the evidence-based conviction of the guilty, without putting those who are not guilty at risk of conviction by prejudice, and that it was accordingly to be hoped that prosecution applications to adduce evidence of an accused's bad character will not be made routinely, simply because an accused has previous convictions, but will be based on the particular circumstances of each case. It was held in that case that if a judge has directed himself correctly, the Court of Appeal will be very slow to interfere with a ruling as to admissibility[42] and will not interfere unless the judge's judgment as to the capacity of prior events to establish propensity is plainly wrong or discretion has been exercised unreasonably in a *Wednesbury* sense.[43] It was also held that if, following a ruling that evidence of bad character is admissible, an accused pleads guilty, it is highly unlikely that an appeal against conviction will be entertained.

## 3  SECTION 101 OF THE CRIMINAL JUSTICE ACT 2003

Section 101 provides as follows:

   (1)  In criminal proceedings evidence of the defendant's[44] bad character is admissible if, but only if
      (a)  all parties to the proceedings agree to the evidence being admissible,

---

[40]  See generally C Tapper 'Criminal Justice Act 2003 (3) Evidence of Bad Character' [2004] Crim LR 533.

[41]  [2005] All ER (D) 380 (Mar), CA.

[42]  Or as to the consequences of non-compliance with the regulations for giving notice of intention to rely on bad character evidence.

[43]  *Wednesbury Corpn v Ministry of Housing and Local Government* [1965] 1 WLR 261, CA.

[44]  'Defendant', in relation to criminal proceedings, means a person charged with an offence in those proceedings: s 112(1).

(b) the evidence is adduced by the defendant himself or is given in answer to a question asked by him in cross-examination and intended to elicit it,

(c) it is important explanatory evidence,

(d) it is relevant to an important matter in issue between the defendant and the prosecution,

(e) it has substantial probative value in relation to an important matter in issue between the defendant and a co-defendant,[45]

(f) it is evidence to correct a false impression given by the defendant, or

(g) the defendant has made an attack on another person's character.

(2) Sections 102 to 106 contain provision supplementing subsection (1).

(3) The court must not admit evidence under subsection (1)(d) or (g) if, on an application by the defendant to exclude it, it appears to the court that the admission of the evidence would have such an adverse effect on the fairness of the proceedings that the court ought not to admit it.

(4) On an application to exclude evidence under subsection (3) the court must have regard, in particular, to the length of time between the matters to which that evidence relates and the matters which form the subject of the offence charged.

Although section 101(1) governs only the admissibility of evidence of bad character and does not explicitly deal with the asking of questions about bad character in cross-examination, the intention is to cover both. The phrase 'prosecution evidence', as used in the provisions supplementing section 101(1), is defined to include evidence which a witness is to be invited to give (or has given) in cross-examination by the prosecution;[46] the 'only evidence' admissible under section 101(1)(e) includes evidence which a witness is invited to give (or has given) in cross-examination by the co-defendant;[47] and the rules of court to be made under the 2003 Act may, and where the party in question is the prosecution, must, require a party to serve notice on the defendant where it is proposed to cross-examine a witness with a view to eliciting evidence of the accused's bad character.[48]

There are seven 'gateways' under section 101(1) through which evidence of the bad character of the accused may be admitted. Section 101(1)(a) provides for the admissibility of such evidence by consent of the parties. Under section 101(1)(b), such evidence may be admitted at the election of the accused and without the agreement of the other parties. Speaking generally, section 101(1)(c) is designed to admit evidence which would have been admissible at common law as so-called 'background evidence'. Section 101(1)(d) covers prosecution evidence relevant to an important matter, ie a matter of substantial importance in the context of the case as a whole, which is in issue between the prosecution and the defence. Subsections (1)(e), (f), and (g) broadly correspond to and widen pre-existing grounds of admissibility. Broadly speaking, section 101(1)(e) relates to evidence formerly admissible on behalf of a

---

[45] 'Co-defendant', in relation to a defendant (see n 44 above), means a person charged with an offence in the same proceedings: s 112(1).

[46] Section 112(1).        [47] Section 104(2)(b).        [48] Section 111(2)(b).

co-accused on one of two grounds, either on the basis of its relevance to the guilt of the accused or, in cases where the nature or conduct of the defence of the accused undermines the defence of the co-accused, to attack the credibility of the accused; section 101(1)(f) relates to prosecution evidence formerly admissible in rebuttal of evidence of good character adduced by an accused; and section 101(1)(g) is designed to admit prosecution evidence in cases where the accused has cast an imputation on the character of another.

Before considering further each of the 'gateways', it is convenient first to consider two issues of general importance, the question of leave and the question of discretionary exclusion.

## (a) Leave

As we have seen section 100(4) of the 2003 Act expressly states that evidence of the bad character of a *non-defendant* 'must not be given without the leave of the court'. There is no equivalent in relation to evidence of the bad character of an *accused* admissible under section 101(1)(c) to (g). However, whether any of the requirements for admissibility in those sub-paragraphs has been met is a question of law for the judge to decide, in appropriate cases only after holding a *voir dire*, and it is submitted that given the potentially irremediable harm of the jury hearing evidence which is later ruled inadmissible, counsel for the prosecution or, as appropriate, the co-accused, before introducing the evidence, will need to satisfy the judge that the statutory requirements are met.

## (b) Discretion to exclude

Turning to the issue of discretionary exclusion, in the case of evidence meeting the requirements of either section 101(1)(d) or (g), the court has the discretionary power to exclude it under section 101(3) on the basis of its adverse effect on the fairness of the proceedings. Section 101(3) is brought into play 'on an application by the accused to exclude' the evidence, wording which seems to preclude the court from exercising the power under the subsection of its own motion. However, if necessary, the judge will doubtless come to the assistance of an unrepresented accused and, in the case of a represented accused, may occasionally see the need to make a pertinent enquiry of counsel in the absence of the jury.[49]

The fact that section 101(3) does not apply to section 101(1)(a), (b), and (e) makes perfect sense. In the case of both section 101(1)(a) and (b), there is no need for a discretion to exclude—the accused already has control over whether the evidence is admitted or not. As to section 101(1)(e), which relates to evidence admissible on behalf of a co-accused, the good reason for the absence of a discretionary power to exclude is that a co-accused should be free to adduce any evidence relevant to his case whether or not it prejudices any other accused. The principle was the same, before the

---

[49] Cf, in the case of s 78 of the Police and Criminal Evidence Act 1984, *R v Raphaie* [1996] Crim LR 812, CA, Ch 3.

coming into force of section 101, in the case of both 'similar fact evidence' tendered by a co-accused and cross-examination of an accused by a co-accused under the Criminal Evidence Act 1898.[50]

However, the fact that section 101(3) does not apply to section 101(1)(c) and (f) is difficult to justify and raises the question whether evidence otherwise admissible under those sub-paragraphs can be excluded using common-law discretionary power or section 78 of the Police and Criminal Evidence Act 1984.[51] As to the former, it is submitted that the general common-law discretionary power to exclude prosecution evidence where its prejudicial effect outweighs its probative value may be exercised in respect of evidence of bad character admissible under section 101(1)(c) (if it is to be adduced by the prosecution) and section 101(1)(f) (under which only prosecution evidence is admissible).[52] As noted when considering section 100 of the 2003 Act, it is unclear whether section 78 of the 1984 Act applies in the case of prosecution evidence of bad character otherwise admissible under the 2003 Act. There are two strong arguments to support the view that the Parliamentary intention was to exclude the operation of section 78. First, there is express provision in Chapter 2 of Part 11 of the 2003 Act, which concerns hearsay evidence, that nothing in that chapter prejudices any power of a court to exclude evidence under section 78.[53] Secondly, if section 78 does apply, section 101(3), the critical words of which mirror those to be found in section 78, is otiose. On the other hand, section 78 is plainly a provision of general application, applying to any evidence on which the prosecution proposes to rely, and, it may be argued, should not be taken to cease to apply to particular types of prosecution evidence without express provision to that effect. On balance, it is submitted that section 78 should operate in the present context.

## 4   SECTION 101(1)(A)—EVIDENCE ADMITTED BY AGREEMENT OF ALL THE PARTIES

Evidence of the accused's bad character may be admitted under section 101(1)(a) with the consent of all the parties, ie the prosecution, accused and any co-accused, and without the leave of the court.

## 5   SECTION 101(1)(B)—EVIDENCE ADMITTED BY THE DEFENDANT HIMSELF

Section 101(1)(b) permits evidence of the accused's bad character to be admitted by the accused himself without the leave of the court. This option is of limited if any value in cases in which the prosecution has already adduced the evidence by virtue of

---

[50] See *Lobban v R* [1995] 2 All ER 602, PC approving the description of this principle appearing in the 3rd edition of this book.

[51] See Ch 2.     [52] See above under **A2 Abolition of the common law rules.**

[53] Section 126(2).

one of the other sub-paragraphs of section 101(1). However, where the evidence is not admissible as a part of the prosecution case, there are two situations in which the accused may sensibly elect to admit it himself. First, if it is evidence of comparatively minor misconduct, he may adduce it on the basis that otherwise the jurors, especially if they have gained some experience by serving in other cases, might speculate that his character is worse than it is. The second is where he adduces evidence attacking another person's character and therefore brings into play section 101(1)(g), when it may be tactically wiser for him to be frank with the jury and give evidence of his bad character himself, rather than allow the prosecution to elicit evidence on the matter in cross-examination. This may be a particularly sensible course of action where the previous convictions were all based on guilty pleas—however the judge directs the jury about the bad character evidence, there is obvious scope for the defence to say to the jury, in their closing submissions, that the fact that the accused has for the first time pleaded not guilty indicates that his denial on oath ought to be believed.

Under section 101(1)(b) the evidence may be either adduced by the accused himself or may be given in answer to a question asked by the defence in cross-examination, provided that the question was intended to elicit it. Thus if the witness under cross-examination volunteers the evidence of bad character, it is inadmissible and the judge will need to direct the jury to ignore it or, if no direction is capable of neutralizing the prejudice to the accused and there is therefore a real risk of injustice occurring, exercise his discretion to discharge the jury and order a re-trial.[54]

## 6  SECTION 101(1)(C)—IMPORTANT EXPLANATORY EVIDENCE

Under section 101(1)(c), which may be used by either the prosecution or a co-accused, evidence of the accused's bad character is admissible if it is 'important explanatory evidence'. Section 102 provides that:

For the purposes of section 101(1)(c) evidence is important explanatory evidence if—

    (a)  without it, the court or jury would find it impossible or difficult properly to understand other evidence in the case, and

    (b)  its value for understanding the case as a whole is substantial.

Section 101(c) is closely based on the recommendation of the Law Commission except that it lacks the safeguard contained in the Commission's draft clause that the court be satisfied either that the evidence carries no risk of prejudice to the accused or that the value of the evidence for understanding the case as a whole is such that, taking account of the risk of prejudice, the interests of justice nevertheless require it to be admissible.

This definition in section 102 is the same as that contained in section 100(2)(a), which applies in relation to evidence of a non-defendant's bad character. As noted in

---

[54]  See above.

that context, the definition is a slightly different formulation of the common-law rule permitting the use of background evidence, notwithstanding that it reveals the bad character or criminal disposition of the accused, where it is part of a continual background or history which is relevant to the offence charged and without the totality of which the account placed before the jury would be incomplete or incomprehensible.[55] If the matter to which the evidence relates is largely comprehensible without the explanatory evidence, the evidence will be inadmissible. Explanatory evidence, to be admissible, must also satisfy section 100(1)(b), ie its value for understanding the case as a whole must be 'substantial', as opposed to minor or trivial.

Since section 101(1)(c) in effect gives statutory force to a doctrine established at common law, it is submitted that the common-law authorities will continue to provide valuable guidance, notwithstanding that they reveal an occasional tendency to admit evidence with a high risk of prejudice but providing comparatively limited assistance to the jury in understanding the other evidence in the case. The authorities show that the evidence often relates to other acts done or statements made by the accused revealing his desire to commit, or reason for committing, the offence charged. Thus it has been said:

The relations of the murdered or injured man to his assailant, so far as they may reasonably be treated as explanatory of the conduct of the accused as charged in the indictment, are properly admitted to proof as integral parts of the history of the alleged crime for which the accused is on his trial.[56]

Similarly in *R v Ball*[57] Lord Atkinson was of the view that in an ordinary prosecution for murder evidence is admissible of previous acts or words of the accused to show that he entertained feelings of enmity towards the deceased, and although *R v Ball* was disapproved in *R v Berry*,[58] it was affirmed in *R v Williams*[59] and re-affirmed in *R v Phillips*.[60]

In *R v Campbell*,[61] a case of attempted murder, evidence was admitted that on an occasion six months earlier, the accused had hidden in the back of the victim's car wearing 'somewhat bizarre' clothing, frightened her and then said that he was 'going to kill her'.[62] In *R v Williams*[63] the accused was charged with making a threat to kill one E, intending that she would fear that the threat would be carried out. There was evidence of previous acts of violence by the accused against E, including an assault in respect of which he had been convicted and sentenced to a term of imprisonment which had come to an end some six weeks before the time of the alleged threat to kill. The way the prosecution wished to put the case was that the threat had been made

---

[55] Per Purchas LJ in *R v Pettman* 2 May 1985, CA, unreported.
[56] Per Kennedy J in *R v Bond* [1906] 2 KB 389 at 401.
[57] [1911] AC 47, HL at 68.          [58] (1986) Cr App R 7, CA.          [59] (1986) 84 Cr App R 299, CA.
[60] [2003] 2 Cr App R 528, CA per Dyson LJ at 534.          [61] 20 Dec 1984, CA, unreported.
[62] See also *R v Giannetto* [1996] Crim LR 722, CA.
[63] (1986) 84 Cr App R 299, CA. Cf *R v Berry* (1986) 83 Cr App R 7, CA.

because of resentment arising from the imprisonment and that the previous acts of violence tended to prove that the accused intended his threat to be taken seriously. Evidence of the previous history was held to be admissible. In *R v Phillips*,[64] where the accused denied being the murderer of his wife, evidence was admitted of the unhappy state of the marriage over a number of years. In *R v Asif*[65] a case of failure to comply with the statutory VAT requirements, evidence was admitted of transactions prior to the period covered by the indictment to provide a comprehensive background showing a system of trading against which the jury could judge the prosecution evidence as against the defence proposed.[66]

However, evidence will not be admitted under the principle if it relates to events so distant in time from the crime as to be of little if any probative value. For example in *R v Phillips* it was held that it would have been quite wrong to have admitted the evidence of a stormy relationship eight years before the crime was committed, especially if thereafter it was a happy marriage.[67] Similarly in *R v Dolan*,[68] where the accused was charged with the murder of his baby son by shaking him forcefully, it was held to be irrelevant that in the past he had lost his temper and shown violence towards inanimate objects. The touchstones of the principle, said the court, were relevance and necessity.[69] In that case it was also made clear that background evidence needs to be distinguished from so-called 'similar fact evidence'[70] and should not be used as a vehicle for smuggling in otherwise inadmissible similar fact evidence. Equally, where background evidence is properly admitted, the jury will often need to be directed carefully as to the use to which the evidence may and may not be put. *R v Sawoniuk*[71] furnishes a good example. The accused was convicted of the murder of Jews in Belarus in 1942. The Court of Appeal upheld the decision of the trial judge to admit evidence of his participation in a 'search and kill' operation against Jewish survivors of an earlier massacre. The evidence was relevant to the identification evidence in the case, but it was also held to be admissible as background evidence because, as Lord Bingham CJ put it, 'criminal charges cannot fairly be judged in a factual vacuum'.[72] The court noted that the evidence was not similar fact evidence and that the trial judge had adequately directed the jury not to follow a forbidden line of reasoning, ie that by reason of his earlier actions the accused was more likely to have committed the offences with which he was charged.

The point has already been made that evidence of misconduct 'which has to do with the alleged facts of the offence' and is therefore admissible by virtue of section

---

[64] [2003] 2 Cr App R 528, CA.

[65] (1985) 82 Cr App R 123, CA.

[66] For further examples, see *R v Carrington* [1990] Crim LR 330, CA; *R v Sidhu* (1993) 98 Cr App R 59, CA; *R v Fulcher* [1995] 2 Cr App R 251, CA; and *R v Shaw* [2003] Crim LR 278. See also, *sed quaere*, *R v Underwood* [1999] Crim LR 227, CA.

[67] [2003] 2 Cr App R 528 at 536. See also *R v Butler* [1999] Crim LR 835, CA, where the events had taken place three years before the offence charged.

[68] [2003] 1 Cr App R 281, CA.     [69] Ibid at 285–6.

[70] See also *R v M(T)* [2000] 1 WLR 421, CA.     [71] [2002] 2 Cr App R 220, CA.

[72] At 234.

98(a) will often be difficult to distinguish from background evidence admissible under section 101(1)(c). The overlap will typically arise where the misconduct and the facts of the offence are part of one continuous transaction. *R v Ellis*[73] is an old but good example. A shop assistant was charged with stealing six marked shillings from a till. Evidence was given that on several occasions on the day in question he was seen to take money from the till and that, on his arrest, he was found in possession of a sum of money equal to that missing from the till and made up of the six marked shillings and some other unmarked money. The evidence, insofar as it tended to show that the assistant had stolen unmarked money as well as the marked money, was held to be admissible on the grounds that it went to show the history of the till from the time when the marked money was put into it up to the time when it was found in the possession of the accused. Bayley J said:

Generally speaking it is not competent to a prosecutor to prove a man guilty of one felony, by proving him guilty of another unconnected felony; but where several felonies are connected together, and form part of one entire transaction, then the one is evidence to show the character of the other.[74]

Since the test in section 101(1)(c) does not require the court to balance the value of the evidence to be admitted against the prejudice to the accused, then when the *prosecution* seek to admit evidence under the sub-paragraph, as will usually be the case, there is obvious scope for use of the common-law discretionary power to exclude, assuming, as submitted earlier, that that power subsists in relation to prosecution evidence admissible under section 101.[75] The court should exercise the discretion where the prejudicial effect of the evidence is out of all proportion to its probative value, as when it relates to particularly serious misconduct on the part of the accused and without it the jury would find it difficult, but perhaps not especially difficult, properly to understand other evidence in the case.

## 7 SECTION 101(1)(D) — PROSECUTION EVIDENCE RELEVANT TO AN IMPORTANT MATTER IN ISSUE BETWEEN THE DEFENDANT AND THE PROSECUTION

Under the carefully wrought proposals of the Law Commission, there were separate clauses governing admissibility of evidence of the bad character of the accused going to the issue of his guilt and admissibility of evidence of his bad character going to the issue of his credibility.[76] This distinction was borne of a recognition that the two issues usually arise at different stages of the trial and that the relevant factors for the purpose of deciding the admissibility of each type of evidence are different. Under

---

[73] (1826) 6 B&C 145.
[74] See also *R v Rearden* (1864) 4 F & F 76.
[75] See above under **C3 Section 101 of the Criminal Justice Act 2003**.
[76] Law Com No 273 (2001) Draft Bill, cl 8 and cl 9.

the Commission's proposals, evidence of the bad character of the accused would have been admissible on the issue of guilt if (i) it had 'substantial probative value' in relation to a matter of substantial importance in the context of the case as a whole and (ii) if the court was satisfied that (a) the evidence carried no risk of prejudice to the accused or (b) that, taking into account the risk of prejudice, the interests of justice nevertheless required the evidence to be admissible in view of its degree of probative value in relation to the matter in issue, any other evidence that could be given on the matter, and how important the matter was in the context of the case as a whole. In assessing the probative value of the evidence, the court also had to have regard to a variety of other specified factors. Concerning evidence of bad character going to the issue of the credibility of the accused, it was only to be admitted where an attack had been made on the truthfulness of another. In this context also, the factors to be taken into consideration were set out in detail.

Section 101(1)(d) of the 2003 Act reflects a markedly different and less sophisti-cated approach. It is a single 'gateway' providing for the admissibility of evidence going to the guilt of the accused as well as evidence going to his credibility. Under subsection (1)(d), prosecution evidence of the accused's bad character is admissible if 'it is relevant to an important matter in issue between the defendant and the prosecu-tion'.[77] The test is one of simple relevance or probative value. There is no requirement of enhanced relevance or 'substantial probative value' as there is under section 100(1)(e) and, in relation to the bad character of someone other than the accused, under section 100(1)(b). The evidence, however, must be relevant to an important matter in issue between the accused and the prosecution. The matters in issue between the accused and the prosecution are, of course, the disputed facts and issues of credit or credibility. In a sense, all such matters in issue between the accused and the prosecution are important, but 'important matter' is defined in the Act as 'a matter of substantial importance in the context of the case as a whole',[78] a definition which, it is submitted, will only operate to exclude evidence relevant to matters in issue which are of minor or marginal significance. The overall effect of section 101(1)(d), therefore, is to permit the introduction of prosecution evidence of the bad character of the accused whenever it is relevant to any of the main matters in issue between the prosecution and the defence. The breadth of the new provision means that the prosecution will seek to admit much bad character evidence that in the past would have been inadmissible. In consequence, defence applications to exclude under section 101(3) will become a regular feature of most trials.

Section 101(1)(d) is supplemented by section 103, which makes it clear that 'matters in issue' between the accused and the prosecution can include (a) the question whether the accused has a propensity to commit offences of the kind with which he is charged and (b) the question whether he has a propensity to be untruthful. For the purposes of exposition, it will be convenient to consider these two issues separately,

---

[77] Only prosecution evidence is admissible under s 101(1)(d): s 103(6).       [78] Section 112(1).

albeit, in the case of the former, as part of the wider issue of bad character relevant to the guilt of the accused.

### (a) Bad character evidence under section 101(1)(d) relevant to the guilt of the accused

*(i) Evidence of propensity under section 103 of the Criminal Justice Act 2003.* Section 103(1) and (2) of the 2003 Act provides as follows.

(1) For the purposes of section 101(1)(d) the matters in issue between the defendant and the prosecution include—

    (a) the question whether the defendant has a propensity to commit offences of the kind with which he is charged, except where his having such a propensity makes it no more likely that he is guilty of the offence;

    (b) the question whether the defendant has a propensity to be untruthful, except where it is not suggested that the defendant's case is untruthful in any respect.

(2) Where subsection (1)(a) applies, a defendant's propensity to commit offences of the kind with which he is charged may (without prejudice to any other way of doing so) be established by evidence that he has been convicted of—

    (a) an offence of the same description as the one with which he is charged, or

    (b) an offence of the same category as the one with which he is charged.

(3) Subsection (2) does not apply in the case of a particular defendant if the court is satisfied, by reason of the length of time since the conviction or for any other reason, that it would be unjust for it to apply in his case.

(4) For the purposes of subsection (2)—

    (a) two offences are of the same description as each other if the statement of the offences in a written charge or indictment would, in each case, be in the same terms;

    (b) two offences are of the same category as each other if they belong to the same category of offences prescribed for the purposes of this section by an order made by the Secretary of State.

(5) A category prescribed by an order under subsection 4(b) must consist of offences of the same type.

(6) Only prosecution evidence is admissible under s 101(1)(d).

The inclusionary nature of section 103(1) indicates that the matters in issue to which evidence of bad character may be relevant are not confined to those specified in the subsection.

As to section 103(1)(a), it is conceptually confusing and its meaning is, in part, obscure. It is conceptually confusing because propensity of the kind to which it refers has never before been treated as a matter in issue. In the past, propensity, or to be more accurate, admissible evidence of propensity, has been the means of establishing the matters in issue. Under the subsection, in any case in which the prosecution seek to rely upon section 101(1)(d) in relation to the issue of guilt, propensity will always be deemed to be a matter in issue, provided that it is of the kind referred to in the subsection. However, the prosecution will still need to establish that the propensity in question is an 'important' matter in issue, ie 'a matter of substantial importance in the context of the case as a whole'[79] because section 103 is not free-standing but operates 'for the purposes of section 101(1)(d)'. If the prosecution can establish such import-ance, then subject to section 101(3) and, it is submitted, the common-law discretion to exclude on the basis of prejudicial effect outweighing probative value, the propensity may be established under section 103(2) by evidence of a relevant conviction or in 'any other way'. Insofar as section 103(2) permits proof by evidence of a conviction, it is submitted that it too is a deeming provision, in the sense that evidence of the convic-tion is to be treated as, in the words of section 101(1)(d), 'evidence of the defendant's bad character' that 'is relevant to an important matter in issue', ie the propensity.

The meaning of the exception within section 103(1)(a)—'except where his having such a propensity makes it no more likely that he is guilty of the offence'—is obscure, given that all too often evidence of propensity to commit offences of the kind charged will make it more probable that the accused committed the offence charged, albeit that in many cases it will have only limited or very limited probative force. The Explanatory Notes to the Act furnish only one illustration: where there is no dispute about the facts of the case and the question is whether those facts constitute the offence, 'for example, in a homicide case, whether the defendant's actions caused death'.[80]

*(ii) Questions of proof.* Section 103(2) provides that where the matter in issue is whether the accused has a propensity to commit offences of the kind with which he is charged, the propensity can be proved by evidence that he has been convicted of an offence of the kind referred to in either section 103(2)(a) or (b). This is subject to section 103(3), whereby evidence of the conviction should not be given if the court is satisfied that it would be unjust to do so 'by reason of the length of time since the conviction or for any other reason'. Bearing in mind that section 103 exists 'for the purposes of section 101(1)(d)', that any evidence admissible under section 101(1)(d) is subject to the discretionary power to exclude contained in section 101(3) and (4), and that those subsections contain a test for exclusion similar to, but obviously cast in different language from, the test in section 103(3), there appears to be a large degree of unnecessary overlap between those subsections and section 103(3).

The wording of section 103(2) indicates that in at least some cases, at any rate, proof of the mere fact of the conviction or convictions may be used to establish propensity. In other cases, however, the propensity will be established not simply by the fact of the conviction, but by evidence of the conduct which resulted in the conviction. In the latter type of case, the prosecution will doubtless use section 103(2) in conjunction with section 74(3) and section 75 of the Police and Criminal Evidence Act.[81] Under section 74(3), as amended by the 2003 Act, where evidence of the fact that the accused has committed an offence is admissible and proof is given that he has been convicted of the offence, there is a rebuttable presumption that he committed

---

[79] Section 112(1).     [80] Para 371.     [81] See Ch 21.

the offence. Under section 75, where evidence of a conviction is admissible by virtue of section 74, then without prejudice to the admissibility of any other evidence for the purpose of identifying the facts on which the conviction was based, the contents of, inter alia, the information or indictment shall be admissible for that purpose.

Section 103(2) permits propensity to be proved by evidence of a conviction of an offence falling within either section 103(2)(a) or (b). Subsection (2)(a) refers to an offence of the same description as the one with which the accused is charged. Section 103(4)(a) makes clear that an offence will only be 'of the same description' if the statement of the offence in a written charge or indictment would, in each case, be the same. Thus, as it says in the Explanatory Notes to the Act, the test relates to the particular law that has been broken, rather than the circumstances in which it was committed.[82] Section 103(2)(b) refers to an offence of the same category as the one with which the accused is charged. By reason of section 103(4)(b) and section 103(5), an offence will be 'of the same category' if it falls within a category consisting of offences of the same type drawn up by the Secretary of State in secondary legislation. Two categories have been drawn up, a 'Theft Category' and a 'Sexual Offences (persons under the age of 16) Category'.[83] The first includes offences of theft, robbery, burglary, handling stolen goods, etc. The second includes offences of rape of a person under the age of 16, assault by penetration of a person under the age of 16, sexual assault on a person under the age of 16, etc.[84]

In *R v Hanson*[85] the Court of Appeal laid down the following important principles relating to the admissibility of evidence of propensity under section 103.

(1) Where propensity to commit the offence is relied upon by reference to section 101(1)(d) and section 103(1)(a), there are three questions to be considered: (i) whether the history of conviction(s) establishes a propensity to commit offences of the kind charged; (ii) whether that propensity make it more likely that the accused committed the offence charged; and (iii) whether it is unjust to rely on the conviction(s) of the same description or category and, in any event, whether the proceedings will be unfair if they are admitted.

(2) In referring to offences of the same description or category, section 103(2) is not exhaustive of the types of misconduct which may be relied upon to show evidence of propensity to commit offences of the kind charged. Nor, however, is it necessarily sufficient in order to show such propensity that a conviction is of the same description or type as that charged.

(3) There is no minimum number of events necessary to demonstrate such a propensity. The fewer the number of convictions, the weaker the evidence of propensity is likely to be. A single previous conviction for an offence of the

---

[82] Para 373.        [83] See Criminal Justice Act 2003 (Categories of Offences) Order 2004, SI 2004/3346.

[84] Both categories also include an offence of (a) aiding, abetting, counselling, procuring or inciting the commission of an offence specified or (b) attempting to commit an offence specified.

[85] [2005] All ER (D) 380, CA.

same description or category will often not show propensity, but may do so where, for example, it shows a tendency to unusual behaviour, or where its circumstances demonstrate probative force in relation to the offence charged.

(4) Circumstances demonstrating probative force are not confined to those sharing striking similarity,[86] but if the modus operandi has significant features shared by the offence charged, it may show propensity. When considering what is just under section 103(3), and the fairness of the proceedings under section 101(3), the judge may, along with other factors, take into consideration the degree of similarity between the previous conviction and the offence charged (albeit that they are both within the same description or prescribed category). This does not mean, however, that what used to be referred to as striking similarity must be shown before convictions become admissible.

(5) The judge may also take into consideration the respective gravity of the past and present offences.

(6) The judge must also consider the strength of the prosecution case. If there is no, or very little, other evidence against an accused, it is unlikely to be just to admit his previous convictions, whatever they are.

(7) In principle, if there is a substantial gap between the dates of the commission of, and conviction for, earlier offence(s), the date of commission is, generally, to be regarded as being of more significance than the date of conviction when assessing admissibility. Old convictions with no special features shared with the offence charged are likely seriously to affect the fairness of proceedings adversely unless, despite their age, it can properly be said that they show a continuing propensity.

(8) It will often be necessary, before determining admissibility, and even when considering offences of the same description or category, to examine each individual conviction rather than merely to look at the nature of the offence or at the accused's record as a whole.

(9) The sentence passed will not normally be probative or admissible at the behest of the Crown.

(10) Where past events are disputed, the judge must take care not to permit the trial unreasonably to be diverted into an investigation of matters not charged on the indictment.

(11) The Crown needs to have decided, at the time of giving notice of the application, whether it proposes to rely simply on the fact of conviction or also upon the circumstances of it. It is to be expected that the relevant circumstances of previous convictions will, generally, be capable of agreement, and that, subject to the trial judge's ruling as to admissibility, they will be put before the jury by

---

[86] See below.

way of admission. Even where the circumstances are genuinely in dispute, it is to be expected that the minimum indisputable facts will thus be admitted. It will be very rare indeed for it to be necessary for the judge to hear evidence before ruling on admissibility under the Act.

(12) In any case in which evidence of bad character is admitted to show propensity, whether to commit offences or to be untruthful, the judge in summing up should warn the jury clearly against placing undue reliance on previous convictions. Evidence of bad character cannot be used simply to bolster a weak case or to prejudice the minds of the jury against the defendant. Without purporting to frame a specimen direction, in particular, a jury should be directed: (i) that they should not conclude that an accused is guilty or untruthful merely because he has previous convictions; (ii) that, although the convictions may show a propensity, this does not mean that he committed the offence charged or has been untruthful in the case; (iii) that whether they in fact show a propensity is for them to decide; (iv) that they must take into account what an accused has said about his previous convictions; and, (v) that, although they are entitled, if they find propensity is shown, to take this into account when determining guilt, propensity is only one relevant factor and they must assess its significance in the light of all the other evidence in the case.

Section 103(2) states that it is without prejudice to other ways of establishing an accused's propensity to commit offences of the kind with which he is charged. In cases in which the accused's misconduct or disposition towards misconduct did not result in a conviction, then it may be proved, subject to the rules of evidence generally, in the same way as any other relevant facts. Concerning misconduct, there are three types of case. The first is where the misconduct did not result in a prosecution. The second is where the misconduct did result in a prosecution, but the outcome was an acquittal.[87] The third is where there are two (or more) counts on the indictment and the prosecution evidence on one of the counts is admissible evidence of bad character relevant to the issue of guilt on another of the counts and, if appropriate, vice versa. It remains to stress that even in cases where the misconduct did result in a conviction, in some such cases, as already indicated, propensity can only be established by going beyond the fact of the conviction and introducing evidence of the misconduct which resulted in the conviction. Where, in such a case, the conviction was based on a guilty plea, it is submitted that under the Act, as at common law, it would not be unfair for the prosecution to prove the plea, together with confessions made by the accused in police interviews. Although this denies the accused the opportunity to cross-examine the victim or other witnesses to the offence of which he stands convicted, it is fairer to the accused to adduce only what he admitted rather than to call the victim or other witnesses, who may give additional prejudicial evidence.[88]

---

[87] See *R v Z* [2002] 2 AC 483, HL, considered above under A4 'Bad character' defined.
[88] See *R v Bedford* (1990) 93 Cr App R 113, CA.

It is submitted that, as at common law, if evidence of the accused's misconduct is admissible on the issue of his guilt, it is no bar to its admissibility that it is disputed and that the jury may, in the event, reject it.[89] Equally, however, the evidence must be cogent enough to lead a reasonable jury to conclude, as a possibility, that the misconduct did in fact occur. In *Harris v DPP*,[90] an example of the third type of case referred to in the previous paragraph, the evidence was insufficiently cogent for these purposes. H, a police constable, charged and tried on an indictment containing eight counts of larceny, was acquitted on the first seven but convicted on the eighth. The offences occurred in May, June and July 1951 and the evidence showed that on each occasion someone had entered, by the same method, the same office in Bradford market and stolen only part of the money which could have been taken. On the first seven counts, the only evidence connecting H with the offences was that none of them had occurred when he was on leave and on each occasion he might have been on solitary duty in the vicinity of the market. Concerning the eighth count, H was on duty in the market at the relevant time and was found by detectives near the office shortly after the sounding of a burglar alarm. The stolen money was found hidden in a nearby bin. The House of Lords quashed the conviction because the judge had failed to warn the jury that the evidence on the first seven counts could not confirm the eighth charge. As Lord Morton observed, H was not proved to have been near the office or even in the market at the time when the first seven thefts occurred.[91]

*(iii) Examples of evidence of propensity to commit the offence charged.* At common law there was strong authority to the effect that the law prohibited any chain of reasoning leading from propensity or disposition to guilt.[92] However, there were also a number of cases which flew in the face of such authority. In these cases the evidence was plainly admitted on the basis that the accused was a person likely from his misconduct or disposition towards misconduct to have committed the offence for which he was being tried. An example is *R v Straffen*.[93] The appellant was convicted of the murder of a girl called Linda Bowyer. A year earlier, the appellant was charged with and confessed to the murder of two girls. He was then found unfit to plead by reason of insanity and committed to Broadmoor. The murder of Linda Bowyer was committed during a period between his escape from Broadmoor and his recapture some four hours later. He admitted that he had seen the girl and that he had been in the neighbourhood of the place where her body was found, but denied the murder. There were also other passers-by who might have committed the offence. The similarities

---

[89] See *R v Rance and Herron* (1975) 62 Cr App R 118, CA.

[90] [1952] AC 694.

[91] Cf *R v Mansfield* (1977) 65 Cr App R 276, CA. See also *R v Lunt* (1986) 85 Cr App R 241, CA (similar fact evidence provided by an accomplice) and *R v Seaman* (1978) 67 Cr App R 234, CA.

[92] See, eg, per Lord Hailsham in *DPP v Boardman* [1975] AC 421, HL at 453 and per Neill LJ in *R v Lunt* (1986) 85 Cr App R 241, CA at 245.

[93] [1952] 2 QB 911.

between the three murders were that each of the victims was a young girl killed by manual strangulation and that in none of the cases was there any attempt at sexual interference, any apparent motive for the crime, any evidence of a struggle, or any attempt to conceal the body (although that could easily have been done). The Court of Criminal Appeal held that the confession and other evidence in relation to the earlier two murders alleged to have been committed by the appellant was properly admitted at the trial for the murder of Linda Bowyer. Holding that the evidence was admissible to establish the identity of the murderer of Linda Bowyer, Slade J said: 'I think one cannot distinguish abnormal propensities from identity. Abnormal propensity is a means of identity.'[94] Another example is *R v Ball*.[95] A brother and sister were convicted of incest which had occurred on or between certain dates in 1910. There was evidence that they lived together and shared the same bed. Evidence was also admitted to show that intercourse took place between them on former occasions. Lord Loreburn LC held that the evidence was admissible 'to establish the guilty relations between the parties and the existence of a sexual passion between them as elements in proving that they had illicit connection in fact on or between the dates charged'.[96]

There can be no doubt that cases like *Straffen* and *Ball* would be decided in exactly the same way under section 101(1)(d) of the 2003 Act.

*(iv) Similar fact cases.* Evidence of misconduct can be admitted under section 101(1)(d) where relevant to an important matter in issue between the defendant and the prosecution. This reflects the position at common law in that, although the test for admissibility was more demanding, evidence of misconduct was admissible where relevant to the question whether the acts constituting the crime were designed or accidental or to rebut a defence which was fairly open to the accused.[97] Much of the evidence admitted was similar fact evidence properly so called, ie evidence of facts bearing a similarity to the facts to be established by the prosecution in order to prove the offence with which the accused was charged. Evidence formerly admissible as similar fact evidence would now be admissible as 'relevant' evidence under section 101(1)(d). In considering some examples, it is helpful to look first at cases of facts *strikingly* similar either to the facts of the offence or to the circumstances surrounding the commission of the offence. Consideration will then be given to the leading case of *R v P*,[98] which confirmed that striking similarity is only one of the means of establishing sufficient probative force.

One of the best known examples of evidence of facts bearing a *striking* similarity to the facts of the offence charged is *R v Smith*,[99] the case of the 'brides in the bath'. Smith was convicted of the murder of a woman with whom he had recently gone through a

---

[94] [1952] 2 QB 911 at 916.        [95] [1911] AC 47, HL.        [96] [1911] AC 47 at 71.

[97] See Lord Herschell LC's celebrated formulation of the rule in *Makin v A-G for New South Wales* [1894] AC 57, PC at 65.

[98] [1991] 3 All ER 337, HL.        [99] (1915) 11 Cr App R 229, CCA.

ceremony of marriage. He sought to explain that the death had resulted from an epileptic fit. Evidence was admitted of the subsequent deaths of two other women with whom he had gone through a ceremony of marriage. The following similarities existed in the evidence relating to the three deaths: in each case Smith stood to gain financially by the woman's death; he had informed a doctor that the woman suffered from epileptic fits; the bathroom door would not lock; and the woman was found drowned in the bath. The Court of Criminal Appeal held that the evidence had been properly admitted. Lord Reading CJ approved the following direction of the trial judge as to why the evidence was admissible:[100]

If you find an accident which benefits a person and you find that the person has been sufficiently fortunate to have that accident happen to him a number of times, benefiting him each time, you draw a very strong, frequently irresistible inference that the occurrence of so many accidents benefiting him is such a coincidence that it cannot have happened unless it was design.

*R v Smith* illustrates a second principle, that similar fact evidence is admissible where the events in question occurred after the offence charged and not just where they occurred before it.[101] There is no reason why this should not be the case under section 101(1)(d) also.

Many of the cases involved indictments with two (or more) counts, the issue being whether the prosecution evidence on one of the counts was strikingly similar to the prosecution evidence on the other and therefore could be treated as evidence relevant to guilt on the other. The leading authority in this respect was *DPP v Boardman*.[102] The appellant, the headmaster of a boarding school for boys, was convicted of attempted buggery with S, a pupil aged 16, and of inciting H, a pupil aged 17, to commit buggery with him. The similarities between the allegations made by the two boys were that they were woken up in the school dormitory and spoken to in a low voice, invited to commit the offence in the appellant's sitting room, and requested to play the active role in the act of buggery. The defence was that the boys were lying and that the incidents had never occurred. The trial judge held that the evidence of each boy in relation to the count concerning him was admissible on the count concerning the other. The appeal was dismissed by both the Court of Appeal and House of Lords. Despite the undoubted importance of the decision, it should be emphasized that the House of Lords was dealing with one type of case. Lord Wilberforce said:[103]

Questions of this kind arise in a number of different contexts and have, correspondingly, to be resolved in different ways. I think that it is desirable to confine ourselves to the present set of facts, and to situations of a similar character . . . we are not here concerned with cases of 'system' or 'underlying unity' . . . nor with a case involving proof of identity, or an alibi, nor, even, is this a case where evidence is adduced to rebut a particular defence.

---

[100] (1915) 11 Cr App R 229 at 233.
[101] See also *R v Geering* (1849) 18 LJMC 215, where on a charge against a woman that she murdered her husband by giving him arsenic, evidence was given of the subsequent deaths of her sons by arsenic poisoning.
[102] [1975] AC 421.          [103] [1975] AC 421 at 442–3.

The test for admissibility in cases of the kind before the House was described in a variety of ways by their Lordships, but the common theme was probative value derived from a striking similarity between the facts testified to by the several witnesses. Lord Wilberforce said:[104] 'This [strong degree of] probative force is derived, if at all, from the circumstances that the facts testified to by the several witnesses bear to each other such a striking similarity that they must, when judged by experience and common sense, either all be true, or have arisen from a cause common to the witnesses or from pure coincidence.' Lord Salmon said:

if the crime charged is committed in a uniquely or strikingly similar manner to other crimes committed by the accused the manner in which the other crimes were committed may be evidence upon which a jury could reasonably conclude that the accused was guilty of the crime charged. The similarity would have to be so unique or striking that common sense makes it inexplicable on the basis of coincidence.[105]

Lord Hailsham saw the need for 'striking resemblances' or 'unusual features' of such a kind that to ignore them would affront common sense. The need for something more than the mere repetition of commonplace facts was later stressed by the Court of Appeal in *R v Scarrott*[106] and other cases, but as we shall see from the subsequent decision of the House of Lords in *R v P*,[107] although probative value may be derived from 'unusual characteristics' or 'other special features' they are not a necessary condition of the admissibility of evidence of similar facts.

At common law similar fact evidence was capable of possessing the requisite degree of probative value if it was evidence of facts which were strikingly similar not to the facts of the offence charged but to the *circumstances* surrounding the commission of that offence. In *R v Scarrott*[108] Scarman LJ said:

Plainly some matters, some circumstances may be so distant in time or place from the commission of an offence as not to be properly considered when deciding whether the subject matter of similar fact evidence displays striking similarities with the offence charged. On the other hand, equally plainly one cannot isolate, as a sort of laboratory specimen, the bare bones of a criminal offence from its surrounding circumstances and say that it is only within the confines of that specimen, microscopically considered, that admissibility is to be determined. Indeed in one of the most famous cases of all dealing with similar fact evidence, 'the brides in the bath case', *R v Smith*, the court had regard to the facts that the accused man married the women and that he insured their lives. Some surrounding circumstances have to be considered in order to understand either the offence charged or the nature of the similar fact evidence which it is sought to adduce and in each case it must be a matter of judgment where the line is drawn. One cannot draw an inflexible line as a rule of law.

In *Lanford v General Medical Council*,[109] where L was charged by the GMC with using obscene and indecent language and behaving improperly to two female

---

[104] [1975] AC 421 at 444.        [105] [1975] AC 421 at 462.        [106] [1978] QB 1016, CA.
[107] [1991] 3 All ER 337, HL.        [108] [1991] 2 All ER 796, CA at 1025.
[109] [1989] 2 All ER 921 at 926–7.

patients, and there was a striking similarity in what L said to both patients but not in what he did to them, the Privy Council held that what L had said tended, if believed, to prove that the contact was indecent. Lord Lowry noted that in *DPP v Boardman* careful attention had been paid to the similarity in the accused's conduct and statements when visiting the dormitories which preceded the offences later committed elsewhere.

The principle under discussion can operate even if the evidence does not disclose the commission of an offence of the same kind as the offence charged or indeed the commission of any offence at all. An example is *R v Barrington*,[110] where the appellant was convicted of indecently assaulting three young girls. The girls gave evidence that he had induced them to go into his house on the pretext that they were required as baby-sitters but that once inside he had shown them pornographic pictures, asked them to pose for photographs in the nude and committed the offences charged. The defence was that each of the girls had a private motive to tell lies and that they had put their heads together to concoct a false story against him. Three other girls were allowed to give evidence that they had been induced to go into the house on the pretext of baby-sitting, and that they had been shown pornographic pictures and had been asked to pose for photographs in the nude. On appeal, it was argued that the evidence of these girls was inadmissible as similar fact evidence because it included no evidence of indecent assault or of any other offence similar to those with which the appellant was charged. The Court of Appeal, following the reasoning of Scarman LJ in *R v Scarrott*, held that the evidence had been properly admitted. Referring to the similar facts, Dunn LJ, who gave the judgment of the court, said:[111]

That they did not include evidence of the commission of offences similar to those with which the appellant was charged does not mean that they are not logically probative in determining the guilt of the appellant. Indeed we are of the opinion that taken as a whole they are inexplicable on the basis of coincidence and that they are of positive probative value in assisting to determine the truth of the charges against the appellant, in that they tended to show that he was guilty of the offences with which he was charged.

*R v Barrington* was applied in *R v Butler*,[112] a case of rape and indecent assault on two young women, in which identity was in issue. It was held that evidence of previous sexual behaviour which had taken place between the accused and his former girl-friend, which did not constitute the commission of any offence, in that she was a consenting party, was admissible because of the striking similarity between the features of that behaviour and the particular facts alleged by the prosecution in relation to the offences charged.[113]

---

[110] [1981] 1 WLR 419, CA. See also *R v Horry* [1949] NZLR 791.          [111] [1981] 1 WLR 419 at 430.

[112] (1986) 84 Cr App R 12, CA.

[113] See also *R v Seaman* (1978) 67 Cr App R 234, CA. The accused was convicted of theft of a packet of bacon from a supermarket. It was alleged that he had transferred a packet of bacon from a wire basket into his own bag. The Court of Appeal held that evidence that he had behaved similarly twice before had been properly admitted to negative accident or mistake. On one occasion he had placed a packet of bacon into a

Cases like *R v Barrington* and *R v Butler* may be compared with *R v Tricoglus*.[114] The appellant was convicted of the rape of A, who gave evidence that she had accepted a lift from a man with a beard in a Mini who had driven to a cul-de-sac where the offence took place. B gave evidence that a few days earlier she had accepted a lift from a bearded man and had been raped in the same cul-de-sac. She also gave evidence identifying the appellant's car, which was a Mini. The manner of these two alleged rapes bore striking similarities. C and D gave evidence that in the vicinity in question they had been offered but had refused lifts from a bearded man driving a Mini. D had recorded the registration number of the car which, apart from one figure, was the same as the registration number of the appellant's car. Allowing the appeal, it was held that while the evidence of B was admissible similar fact evidence, the evidence of C and D was irrelevant and had been improperly admitted. At best, their evidence showed that the appellant had the unpleasant social habit of 'kerb crawling'. The issue in the case was one of identity, but the evidence of C and D was merely evidence of the appellant's propensity to approach women in an attempt to get them into his car for the purposes of sexual intercourse. Accordingly, it was inadmissible.

In *R v P*[115] the House of Lords held that in cases where the similar fact evidence to be adduced is to be given by another alleged victim of the accused, striking similarity is not an essential element. The accused was convicted of counts of rape and incest. The victims were his two daughters. The trial judge found striking similarities between the various offences in (i) the extreme discipline exercised over the daughters, (ii) abortions carried out on each girl paid for by P, and (iii) the acquiescence of the mother in P's sexual attentions to the daughters. The Court of Appeal allowed the appeal on the grounds that the similarities did not go beyond what was described as 'the incestuous father's stock-in-trade'. Thus it held that, with the possible exception of (ii), the similarities did not relate to P's modus operandi and could not be described as unusual features rendering the account of one girl more credible because mirrored in the statement of the other. The House of Lords restored the conviction. Lord Mackay LC, with whom the rest of the House concurred, after extensive citations from *DPP v Boardman*, held that, from all that was said in that case, 'the essential feature of evidence which is to be admitted is that its probative force in support of the allegation that an accused person committed a crime is sufficiently great to make it just to admit the evidence, notwithstanding that it is prejudicial to the accused in tending to show that he was guilty of another crime'.[116] As Lord Mustill subsequently put it:[117]

the function of the trial judge is not to decide as an intellectual process whether the evidence satisfies prescribed conditions, but to strike as a matter of individual judgment, in the light

---

wire basket which was later observed to be empty, and on another occasion, aware that he was being observed by a store detective, had returned to the shelves a packet of bacon. The court acknowledged that the case was a borderline one.

[114] (1976) 65 Cr App R 16, CA.     [115] [1991] 3 All ER 337.     [116] [1991] 3 All ER 337 at 346.
[117] *R v H* [1995] 2 All ER 865 at 885.

of his experience and common sense, a balance between the probative value of the similar fact evidence and its potentially damaging effect.

Whether the evidence has sufficient probative value to outweigh its prejudicial effect must in each case be a question of degree. Insofar as some authorities had held that similar fact evidence is inadmissible in the absence of some feature of similarity going beyond 'the pederast's or the incestuous father's stock-in-trade',[118] they were overruled. Lord Mackay said:[119]

When a question of the kind raised in this case arises I consider that the judge must first decide whether there is material upon which the jury would be entitled to conclude that the evidence of one victim, about what occurred to that victim, is so related to the evidence given by another victim, about what happened to that other victim, that the evidence of the first victim provides strong enough support for the evidence of the second victim to make it just to admit it, notwithstanding the prejudicial effect of admitting the evidence. This relationship, from which support is derived, may take many forms and while these forms may include 'striking similarity' in the manner in which the crime is committed, consisting of unusual characteristics in its execution the necessary relationship is by no means confined to such circumstances. Relationships in time and circumstances other than these may well be important relationships in this connection. Where the identity of the perpetrator is in issue, and evidence of this kind is important in that connection, obviously something in the nature of what has been called in the course of the argument a signature or other special feature will be necessary. To transpose this requirement to other situations where the question is whether a crime has been committed, rather than who did commit it, is to impose an unnecessary and improper restriction on the application of the principle.

Turning to the facts, it was held that certain circumstances, when taken together, gave a sufficient probative force to the evidence of each of the girls in relation to the incidents involving the other. Those circumstances included the prolonged course of conduct in relation to each girl, the force used against each girl, the general domination of the girls and of the wife, and P's involvement in the payment for the abortions.

    *R v P*, in making clear that probative value may but need not be derived from 'unusual characteristics', necessarily lowered the standard for admissibility. In the subsequent case of *R v Roy*,[120] for example, evidence of indecent assaults by a doctor on a number of his female patients was treated as similar fact evidence notwithstanding that the conduct in question might fairly be described as the stock-in-trade of a doctor sexually abusing his professional position.[121] Section 101(1)(d) has lowered the

---

[118] *R v Inder* (1977) 67 Cr App R 143; *R v Clarke* (1977) 67 Cr App R 398; *R v Tudor* (18 July 1988, unreported); and *R v Brooks* (1990) 92 Cr App R 36, CA.

[119] [1991] 3 All ER 337 at 348.     [120] [1992] Crim LR 185, CA.

[121] See also *R v Simpson* (1993) 99 Cr App R 48, CA, *R v Gurney* [1994] Crim LR 116, CA and *R v Laidman and Agnew* [1992] Crim LR 428, CA. Contrast *R v C* (2003) 25 November 2003, CA, unreported, in which it was held that although there was no longer a need for striking similarity there was still a need to identify similar features that went beyond coincidence, and factors such as the doctor patient relationship, the fact that the patients were all women, and the fact that all the offences involved the removal of clothing on the pretext of the need for an examination, did not go beyond the stock in trade of a delinquent doctor.

standard even further in that the test has become one of mere relevance, provided only that the evidence of misconduct is relevant to a matter in issue that is 'important'. It follows that evidence formerly admissible as similar fact evidence will now be admissible as 'relevant' evidence under section 101(1)(d). It also follows that evidence which would not have satisfied the test in *R v P may* also be admissible under section 101(1)(d). However, since such evidence was excluded at common law because it had insufficient probative value to outweigh its prejudicial effect, there will now be obvious scope for a defence argument that its prejudicial effect so outweighs its probative value that the court should now exclude it, either in exercise of its common-law discretion to exclude on this basis (assuming, as has been submitted, the discretion survives in this context)[122] or in reliance on section 101(3), ie on the basis that admission of the evidence would have such an adverse effect on the fairness of the proceedings that the court ought not to admit it.

*(v) Other types of misconduct.* Evidence of bad character relevant to the guilt of the accused and admissible under section 101(1)(d) is not confined to evidence of propensity to commit the offence charged and similar fact evidence properly so called. At common law, other types of misconduct were admissible to establish a particular and essential part of the prosecution's case or to rebut the accused's defence. If, for example, the accused denies being in the neighbourhood where the crime was committed at the relevant time, evidence may be admitted that he committed another crime in that area shortly before or after the time of the offence charged.[123] Such evidence is admitted not for the purpose of concluding that the accused, because of his criminal disposition, is a person likely to have committed the offence charged, nor as similar fact evidence, but to establish that part of the prosecution case which is denied, namely presence in the neighbourhood at the relevant time. An English example is *R v Salisbury.*[124] A postman was charged with the larceny of a letter which contained bank notes belonging to another. It was part of the prosecution case that these bank notes had been inserted in another letter, the contents of which had been removed and which were in the possession of the accused. Evidence of the interception of this letter was held admissible to establish a link in the chain of events necessary to prove the larceny charged. Cases of this kind, it seems clear, would be decided in exactly the same way, although in cases like *R v Salisbury,* it is arguable that the evidence is 'evidence which has to do with the alleged facts of the offence', under section 98(a), and admissible on that basis.

In *R v Anderson*[125] the accused was convicted of conspiracy to cause explosions. She gave evidence that she knew nothing about any such conspiracy and explained false

---

[122] See above, under C3 **Section 101 of the Criminal Justice Act 2003 (b) Discretion to exclude.**
[123] See *R v Ducsharm* [1956] 1 DLR 732.
[124] (1831) 5 C&P 155. See also *R v Voke* (1823) Russ&Ry 531; *R v Cobden* (1862) 3 F&F 833; and *R v Rearden* (1864) 4 F&F 76.
[125] [1988] 2 All ER 549, CA.

identification papers and over £1,000 which had been found in her possession by saying that she had been involved in an attempt to smuggle escaped IRA prisoners out of the country: she was to escort them and pretend that they were on holiday in order to hoodwink immigration officers. It was held that the prosecution, who had had no prior knowledge of this defence, were entitled to cross-examine her about the fact that she was 'wanted' by the police in Northern Ireland, without specifying the offence in respect of which she was wanted, in order to show the unlikelihood of her having been selected as an escort: the fact that she was wanted would not have diminished the risk of detection but would have doubled it. One of the grounds put forward by the Court of Appeal for reaching this decision was that the evidence went to rebut the defence that was otherwise open to the accused.[126]

Similarly, it has been held, in decisions which were probably much more borderline than the courts have been prepared to acknowledge, that when, on a charge of importing controlled drugs, the accused denies any knowledge of how the drugs came to be concealed in his luggage or in his vehicle, which carries the implication that he is the innocent victim of some other person who concealed them, evidence showing that he is connected with the same kind of drugs inside the UK, for example evidence of finding such drugs in his home, is relevant and admissible, because the jury are entitled to consider such a coincidence, which may go to rebut the defence raised.[127] The principle, however, is not confined to drug couriers, but extends to others alleged to have been involved in the illegal importation. In *R v Yalman*[128] Y met his father at an airport on his arrival in England. Y senior was carrying a suitcase containing heroin. The prosecution case was that it was a family organized importation, but Y said that he was unaware of the drugs. It was held, applying *R v Groves*,[129] that once there was a prima facie case for Y to answer, then evidence that he had used heroin, and that drugs paraphernalia had been found at his home, was admissible on the issue whether he was *knowingly* involved in the importation, as tending to rebut his assertion that his presence at the airport was entirely innocent. In such cases, however, the jury should also be directed that if they consider that the evidence does not assist them on the issue of knowledge or involvement, then they should disregard it altogether.[130]

*(vi) Categories of relevance and the nature of the defence.* It is submitted that the following important common-law principles, relating to categories of relevance and the nature of the defence, will continue to operate in relation to the admissibility of evidence relevant to the issue of guilt under section 101(1)(d).

1.   At common law the notion that 'similar fact' evidence, in order to be admissible, had to fit within one of a number of defined categories of relevance, such

---

[126] See also *R v Kidd* [1995] Crim LR 406, CA, where previous convictions went to rebut the defence put forward.

[127] *R v Willis* (29 Jan 1979, unreported), CA. The principle holds good even if the drugs found in the UK are of a different kind, but there could be cases where they are of such a different kind that the evidence could not be said to be relevant: *R v Peters* [1995] 2 Cr App R 77, CA.

[128] [1998] 2 Cr App R 269, CA.          [129] [1998] Crim LR 200, CA.

[130] *R v Barner-Rasmussen* [1996] Crim LR 497, CA.

as 'proof of identity', 'rebutting accident' or 'rebutting innocent association', was firmly rejected. In *Harris v DPP*[131] Viscount Simon said:

It is . . . an error to draw up a closed list of the sort of cases in which the principle operates: such a list only provides instances of a general application, whereas what really matters is the principle itself and its proper application to the particular circumstances of the charge that is being tried.

2.   An associated notion, that similar fact evidence could never be used in rebuttal of particular kinds of defence, was also rejected. In *R v Wilmot*[132] W was charged with various offences, including rape and robbery against six women. In each case, W said that the woman was a prostitute, that the sexual acts were consensual and that afterwards he had demanded a return of the money he had paid. It was held that the similarities between the various incidents, in particular the use of violence before the sexual acts and the robbery or theft afterwards, were sufficiently striking for the evidence on each to be admissible in relation to the others. The Court of Appeal rejected the suggestion that the evidence was inadmissible to rebut the defence of consent.[133]

3.   At common law evidence relevant to the issue of guilt could be admitted not only to rebut a defence which the accused had actually raised but also to rebut a defence which, even if not raised by the accused, was fairly open to him, on the basis that otherwise a submission of no case to answer might succeed when evidence properly available to support the prosecution case had been withheld.[134]

4.   At common law it was always essential for the court, in considering a disputed issue as to the admissibility of 'similar fact' evidence, to consider the question not in the abstract but in the light of all the other evidence and the particular issue in respect of which the evidence was tendered.[135] In many cases, the particular issue on which the evidence had a bearing was the defence. An example, in relation to a defence actually raised, is *R v Anderson*,[136] which has already been considered. An example in relation to a defence which was fairly open to the accused (and in the event raised) is *R v Lunt*.[137] In that case the appellant and co-accused were charged with offences involving the use of a stolen cheque book and card. The case for the prosecution was that the appellant was the organizer and used the co-accused to go into shops and other premises to obtain goods by means of forged cheques. The appellant's defence was that, although he accompanied the co-accused, he took no part in the illegal use of the cheques. The prosecution was allowed to adduce evidence of

---

131  [1952] AC 694, HL at 705.       132  (1988) 89 Cr App R 341, CA.
133  See also, in relation to self-defence, per Russell LJ in *R v Beggs* (1989) 90 Cr App R 430, CA at 438.
134  See *Harris v DPP* [1952] AC 694, HL.
135  See per Steyn LJ in *R v Clarke* [1995] 2 Cr App R 425, CA at 434–5.
136  [1988] 2 All ER 549, CA.       137  (1986) 85 Cr App R 241, CA.

other occasions on which the appellant had organized the forgery and passage of twenty-four other cheques from the same cheque book in order to obtain goods and services. The Court of Appeal held that the relevant issue was the defence of 'innocent association' and that, in order to resolve it, it was of assistance to the jury to hear the similar fact evidence.[138]

5.   There is no general rule to the effect that similar fact evidence is inadmissible where the accused simply denies the charge. Although in *R v Chandor*[139] and *R v Flack*[140] it was suggested that similar fact evidence might be admissible to rebut a defence such as mistaken identity, absence of intent and innocent association, but not a defence of complete denial, both cases were criticized in *DPP v Boardman*.[141] Lord Hailsham said: 'I do not see the logical distinction between innocent association cases and cases of complete denial.' Lord Cross, while prepared to accept that the decision in each case might well have been correct, was unable to agree with the reasoning underlying such a distinction:[142]

If I am charged with a sexual offence why should it make any difference to the admissibility or non-admissibility of similar fact evidence whether my case is that the meeting at which the offence is said to have been committed never took place or that I committed no offence in the course of it? In each case I am saying that my accuser is lying.

The distinction was re-drawn in *R v Lewis*,[143] but the evidence admitted in that case was evidence of propensity and not evidence of similar facts.

6.   Similar fact evidence may derive its probative force and become admissible on the basis that the similarities in the evidence of the prosecution witnesses are such that in the absence of collusion or contamination, they are likely to be telling the truth. In *R v Sims*[144] the accused was charged with buggery with three men and gross indecency with a fourth. The offences were alleged to have taken place on different occasions. The evidence of each man was that the accused invited him into his house and committed the acts charged. The acts described bore a striking similarity. At the trial, the accused's application that the charges be tried separately in respect of each man was refused. He was found guilty on each of the three charges of buggery but acquitted on the charge of gross indecency. The Court of Criminal Appeal held that the judge had properly rejected the application for separate trials because on the trial of one of the counts the evidence on the others was admissible. One of the reasons for coming to this conclusion, based on Lord Sumner's judgment in

---

[138] Unfortunately, however, the judgment merely *asserts* that the evidence was positively probative and does not explain the basis upon which it rebutted the defence. See also *R v Shore* (1988) 89 Cr App R 32, CA, where evidence of previous indecent assaults on children was relevant and admissible to rebut a defence that the conduct in question was affectionate and fatherly or avuncular.

[139] [1959] 1 QB 545, CCA.        [140] [1969] 2 ALL ER 784, CA.        [141] [1975] AC 421, HL.
[142] [1975] AC 421 at 458.        [143] (1982) 76 Cr App R 33.        [144] [1946] KB 531.

*Thompson v R*,[145] was that sodomy is a crime in a special category. This notion was subsequently rejected by the House of Lords in *DPP v Boardman*.[146] The surviving ratio of the case is found in the following words of Lord Goddard CJ. Having referred to the striking similarities borne by the acts described by each man, his Lordship continued:[147]

> The probative force of all the acts together is much greater than one alone; for whereas the jury might think that one man might be telling an untruth, three or four are hardly likely to tell the same untruth unless they were conspiring together. If there is nothing to suggest a conspiracy, their evidence would seem to be overwhelming.

In other words, the similar fact evidence was admissible to support the credibility of the prosecution witnesses, so implausible was it that each of them should have told such remarkably similar lies about Sims.[148] The same reasoning has been employed after *R v P*, applying the lower standard for admissibility, in the case of evidence lacking striking similarities, although it has been recognized that the probative force of the evidence will turn on all the circumstances, including the nature of the defence. In *R v Venn*[149] Potter LJ said:

> Where, as in this case, the prosecution witnesses are alleged to have made up their stories in a situation where collusion or cross-contamination can be discounted, the existence of common features in the nature or context of the separate offences which are the subject of complaint may, whether separately or cumulatively, be more readily regarded as non-coincidental and therefore probative on the issue of lies than would be the case if identity were in issue.

*(vii) Identification cases.* Much care is needed before admitting evidence of bad character in order to prove the identity of the accused as the offender, not least because where reliance is placed on evidence of similar facts, in many cases the evidence, without more, will usually only show that the same person committed both offences and not that that person is the accused. It is submitted that the following principles, established at common law, will remain instructive for the purposes of section 101(1)(d).

1.  According to the dictum of Lord Mackay LC in *R v P*[150] as construed by Hooper J in *R v W(John)*,[151] identity can be established where the only evidence of any substance against the accused is similar fact evidence which affords something in the nature of a personal hallmark or signature or other very striking

---

[145] [1918] AC 221.        [146] [1975] AC 421. See below, under (viii) **Sexual cases.**

[147] [1946] KB 531 at 539–40.

[148] See also *R v Bedford* (1990) 93 Cr App R 113, CA at 116: the purpose of adducing 'strikingly similar' evidence of indecent assault on and attempted buggery with two boys, on another count of buggery with a third boy, was to make it more likely that when the third boy gave evidence of buggery, he was telling the truth.

[149] [2003] All ER (D) 207 (Feb), [2003] EWCA Crim 236, CA, at [35].

[150] [1991] 3 All ER 337, HL at 348.        [151] [1998] 2 Cr App R 289, CA.

similarity. The example of *R v Straffen*[152] has already been considered. *R v Mullen*[153] provides another example and shows that even if the hallmark is not peculiar to the accused it may still be admissible if of sufficient probative force. In that case M pleaded not guilty to three burglaries in the north-east of England, but admitted three other burglaries. In all of the burglaries the method of entry involved use of a blow torch to crack glass. Only six offenders from the north or north-east of England were known to have used such a method. Evidence of the burglaries to which M had admitted was held to have been properly adduced.[154] However, where such evidence is adduced, it is submitted that it should be accompanied by a very clear warning to the jury that they need to be sure that the crime was committed by the accused and not by one of the others known to commit the crime in the same strikingly similar or unusual way.

2.   Identity can also be established in the absence of evidence affording something in the nature of a personal hallmark or signature. In *R v W (John)*[155] W was convicted of false imprisonment of, and indecent assault on, C in Aldershot (counts 1 and 2) and of false imprisonment of S in Farnham two weeks later (count 3). The issue in both cases was identity, but the evidence revealed no signature or other special feature. W appealed on the basis that the trial judge had failed to make it clear that the evidence on counts 1 and 2 was not admissible on count 3 and vice versa. The Court of Appeal held that the evidence on the Aldershot counts and the Farnham counts did not need to be strikingly similar or of the nature of a signature. The court went on to identify the proper test in a case of the kind before it:[156] evidence tending to show that a defendant has committed an offence charged in count A may be used to reach a verdict on count B and vice versa, if the circumstances of both offences (as the jury would be entitled to find them) are such as to provide sufficient probative support for the conclusion that the defendant committed both offences, and it would therefore be fair for the evidence to be used in this way notwithstanding the prejudicial effect of so doing. On the facts of the case, this test was satisfied: most (but not all) of the descriptions of the attacker fitted the appellant; the descriptions of some of the attacker's clothes fitted the clothes that the appellant was known to be wearing; the appellant lived near both attacks, having moved from Aldershot to Farnham in the period between the time of the two attacks; the attacks took place within a short time of each other; and the attacks bore certain similarities.

3.   In similar fact cases in which identity is in issue, in directing the jury a careful distinction needs to be drawn between the similar fact evidence and the other

---

[152] [1952] 2 QB 911, CCA.          [153] [1992] Crim LR 735, CA.

[154] See also *R v Ruiz* [1995] Crim LR 151, CA and *R v West* [1996] 2 Cr App R 374 and cf *R v Johnson* [1995] 2 Cr App R 41, CA.

[155] [1998] 2 Cr App R 289, CA.          [156] [1998] 2 Cr App R 289 at 303.

evidence in the case. There are two different types of situation, one calling for a 'sequential approach' and the other for a 'cumulative approach'.[157] The first is where, in deciding whether the accused committed offence A, the jury can have regard to evidence that he also committed offence B. This sequential approach involves proof not only of similarity, but also that the accused did in fact commit offence B. *R v McGranaghan*[158] is an illustration. M was convicted of three separate aggravated burglaries of homes and rapes or indecent assaults on the women occupants. M denied having had anything to do with any of the offences. The appeal was allowed on the grounds that although, on the evidence at the time of the trial, the similarities in the features of the offences rendered the evidence on each admissible in relation to the others, the jury should have been directed to consider first whether, disregarding the similarity of the facts, the other evidence in the case was sufficient to make them sure that M committed at least one of the offences. Only if they were so sure, could they then use the similarity to prove that the accused committed the other offences. Glidewell LJ said:[159] 'The similar facts go to show that the same man committed both offences, not that the defendant was that man. There must be some evidence to make the jury sure that on at least one offence the defendant was that man.'[160]

4. The cumulative approach applies where there is evidence, other than the evidence of visual identification, on the basis of which the jury can conclude that offences A and B were committed by the same man, but that evidence, by itself, falls short of proving that that man was the accused in either case. In this situation, once the jury is satisfied that the 'other' evidence shows both offences to have been committed by the same man, the identification evidence of the victims can be used cumulatively in deciding whether that man was the accused. *R v Barnes*[161] is an illustration. The accused was convicted of three separate offences, indecent assaults on two females and the wounding of a third. Evidence was admitted of three other similar incidents. There was no dispute that the six incidents were sufficiently similar to be admitted in order to show that all of the offences were committed by the same man. It was held that the identification evidence of the three victims could be considered cumulatively in deciding whether that man was the accused.[162]

5. The cumulative approach may also be used where offences A and B bear the hallmark or signature of the same gang, of which the accused is alleged to be a

---

[157] *R v Barnes* [1995] 2 Cr App R 491, CA, relying upon *R v Downey* [1995] 1 Cr App R 547, CA.
[158] [1995] 1 Cr App R 559n, CA.        [159] [1995] 1 Cr App R 559 at 572.
[160] See also *R v Rubin* [1995] Crim LR 332, CA. The principle is confined to cases in which identification is in issue: see *R v S* [1993] Crim LR 293, CA. It is probably also confined to cases in which the indictment contains two or more counts and it is the evidence on each which is potentially admissible, in relation to the other or others, as similar fact evidence. Thus it does not extend to a case in which there is also similar fact evidence relating to an offence of which the accused already stands convicted: see *R v Black* [1995] Crim LR 640, CA. See also *R v Mullen* [1992] Crim LR 735, CA.
[161] [1995] 2 Cr App R 491, CA.        [162] See also *R v Grant* [1996] 2 Cr App R 272, CA.

member. The danger, however, is that membership of the gang may alter after the commission of the first offence, and there may be nothing in the hallmark or signature which identifies the accused as opposed to the gang. For reasons of this kind, in *R v Brown*[163] it was held that the issue for the jury, once they were satisfied that the same gang committed both offences, was whether the prosecution had established on all the evidence that the accused was a member of the gang and whether the totality of the evidence had established beyond reasonable doubt that he was a member of the gang on both occasions.[164]

*(viii) Sexual cases.* Common-law developments were such that by the mid-1970s it was established that there were no special rules of admissibility for sexual offences or sexual offences against men, boys, or children of either sex. In sexual cases, therefore, the admissibility of 'similar fact' evidence was decided by applying the same principles as in any other type of case. It is submitted that the position is the same under the statutory scheme and that there are no special rules in sexual cases in which evidence of bad character is sought to be admitted on the basis of its relevance to the issue of guilt under section 101(1)(d).

In the case of evidence of sexual disposition, the threshold issue, under the Act, is whether it amounts to evidence of a disposition towards, 'misconduct'[165] which, it will be recalled, means 'the commission of an offence or other reprehensible behaviour'.[166] If there is evidence of the commission of a sexual offence of the kind with which the accused is charged, then the prosecution will rely upon section 103(1)(a) and, if it resulted in a conviction, section 103(1), (2).[167] However, in the case of sexual disposition which has not involved the commission of any offence, a disposition towards, say, paedophilia, incest or bestiality will be regarded as evidence of disposition towards 'reprehensible behaviour', but it seems most unlikely that a homosexual disposition, any more than a heterosexual disposition, could properly be so regarded. The admissibility of evidence of homosexual or heterosexual disposition, therefore, is not governed by the Act and will simply turn on whether it is relevant and, if so, whether it should be excluded by virtue of the common-law discretion to exclude where its prejudicial effect outweighs its probative value. Such evidence, it is submitted, will very often be irrelevant or unduly prejudicial, but obviously each case will turn on its own facts. Thus if the accused, charged with a sexual offence against a man, were to assert his heterosexual disposition, then evidence of his homosexual disposition would be plainly relevant to the issue.

The common-law authorities provide other illustrations of how evidence of homosexual disposition may be regarded as relevant. *Thompson v R*[168] shows how such evidence may have a particular relevance in tending to identify the accused as the

---

[163] [1997] Crim LR 502, CA.        [164] See also *R v Lee* [1996] Crim LR 825, CA.
[165] Section 98, above.        [166] Section 112(1).        [167] See above, under (a)(ii) **Questions of proof.**
[168] [1918] AC 221, HL.

offender. The appellant was convicted of gross indecency with two boys in a public lavatory. His defence was mistaken identity. It was proved that the man who committed the offence made an appointment to meet the boys three days later at the same time and place and that on this occasion the appellant met the boys and gave them money before being arrested. It was also proved that, on his arrest, powder puffs were found in his possession and that later, photographs of naked boys were found in his rooms, possession of these articles being treated as evidence of his homosexuality. The House of Lords held that the evidence had been properly admitted because it showed that the appellant and the offender shared an 'abnormal propensity' and accordingly tended to identify the appellant as the offender. Lord Sumner said:[169]

Persons . . . who commit the offences now under consideration seek the habitual gratification of a particular perverted lust, which not only takes them out of the class of ordinary men gone wrong, but stamps them with the hallmark of a specialized and extraordinary class as much as if they carried on their bodies some physical peculiarity.

Insofar as *Thompson v R* was decided on this basis, it has not survived. The views expressed were repudiated by the House of Lords in *DPP v Boardman*.[170] The suggestion that there is a special rule for sexual offences or sexual offences against men or boys was decisively rejected. Lord Cross noted that the attitudes of the ordinary man to homosexuality had changed very much and thought that what Lord Sumner had to say on the subject in 1917 sounded like 'a voice from another world'. In the words of Lord Wilberforce:[171] 'In matters of experience it is for the judge to keep close to current mores. What is striking in one age is normal in another: the perversions of yesterday may be the routine or the fashions of tomorrow.' However, the decision in *Thompson v R* may be consistent with another interpretation, that evidence of homosexual propensity was highly relevant to the identification of the appellant because of the extreme unlikelihood of the coincidence arising from his defence. On the assumption that the boys had mistakenly identified the appellant, on one view it is an enormous coincidence that the man who was pointed out by the boys to the police, who had arrived at the appointed time and place and given the boys money, happened also to have homosexual propensities.

Evidence of homosexual disposition has also been admitted on account of its particular relevance in disproving a defence of innocent association. An example is provided by *R v King*,[172] another decision of dubious authority reached prior to *DPP v Boardman*. The appellant was convicted of a number of sexual offences against boys. His defence, in relation to some of the incidents, was innocent association. He admitted that he had met two boys in a public lavatory and asked them to spend the night in his room and also that one had slept on the floor while the other had shared his bed, but he denied the offence charged. In cross-examination he confirmed that he was a

---

[169] [1918] AC 221 at 235.
[170] [1975] AC 421. But see *Reza v General Medical Council* [1991] 2 All ER 796, PC.
[171] [1975] AC 421 at 444.          [172] [1967] 2 QB 338, CA.

homosexual. The Court of Appeal held that this evidence fell within the principle in *Thompson v R* and had been properly admitted. *R v King* may be compared with *R v Horwood*,[173] where the appellant was convicted of attempted gross indecency with a boy. The boy's evidence was that they drove to a wood, got out to look for rabbits, that the offence took place and that he then ran away and was chased by the appellant. The appellant admitted that he had driven the boy to a wood but said that he had got out of the car to urinate and had returned to find that the boy had vanished. During police interrogation, the appellant said that he used to be a homosexual but had been cured and now went out with girls. The Court of Appeal, quashing the conviction, held that the evidence of homosexual propensity had been improperly admitted. O'Connor LJ held that it was only in exceptional circumstances that such evidence could be admitted to rebut innocent association and that *R v King* was such a case because the evidence could properly be said to be relevant to an issue before the jury. It would appear that *R v King* was distinguished on the basis of the greater degree of admitted intimacy in that case. The nature of the admitted association in the instant case (taking a boy for a drive in a car in broad daylight) was contrasted with that in *R v King* (taking a boy home and getting into bed with him).[174]

*(ix) Incriminating articles.* At common law, evidence of the possession of articles of the kind used in the commission of the offence charged, albeit not used in the commission of the offence charged, could be admitted in order to identify the accused as the offender. Evidence of the possession of such articles is likely to be treated as evidence of a disposition towards misconduct for the purposes of section 98 of the 2003 Act, or evidence of propensity to commit offences of the kind with which the accused is charged for the purposes of section 103(1)(a), and to be admitted under section 101(1)(d) because of its relevance in identifying the accused as the offender. In *Thompson v R*,[175] for example, evidence of the possession of powder puffs, apparently used at that time in the course of crimes of the kind charged, although not utilized by Thompson in the commission of the offence charged, was admitted for its particular relevance in tending to identify Thompson as the offender. In *R v Reading*[176] Edmund Davies J referred to *Thompson v R* as a perfect illustration of the type of case under discussion. Reading, alleged to have hijacked a lorry, was convicted of robbery and taking a motor vehicle. The Court of Criminal Appeal held that evidence of his possession of articles, including a walkie-talkie radio set and a police-type uniform capable of being used in the type of robbery charged, albeit not proved to have been used in the commission of the offence charged, was admissible to rebut his defence of

---

[173] [1970] 1 QB 133, CA.

[174] See also *R v King* (7 Apr 1982, unreported), CA, where it was observed that: 'It would not be right for any court to assume that a man having homosexual propensities lusts after boys in whom he takes an interest. But when, as in this case, a man who is alleged to have such propensities actually encourages boys to come to his flat by providing them with inducements (games and bicycles) to do so, evidence that he has homosexual propensities goes to prove that his avowed innocent interest in the young is untrue.'

[175] [1918] AC 221. See above, under **(viii) Sexual cases.** See also *R v Morris* (1969) 54 Cr App R 69, CA.

[176] [1966] 1 WLR 836, CCA.

alibi and mistaken identity. In reaching this conclusion, the court distinguished *R v Taylor*.[177] In that case, Taylor's conviction for shopbreaking was quashed on the ground that evidence had been improperly admitted that a jemmy had been found in his possession. The reasoning of the court was that there being no evidence that a jemmy had been used to break open the door in question, and Taylor's defence being that the door had been broken accidentally, the evidence was tendered for the sole purpose of showing him to be of a criminal disposition and likely not to have been in the doorway for an innocent purpose. The evidence in question, it is submitted, would now be likely to be admitted under section 101(1)(d). *R v Reading* was followed in *R v Mustafa*,[178] where the appellant was convicted on counts of obtaining meat from a store by using a stolen Barclaycard and forging the signature of its holder. Evidence was admitted that on another occasion, in a different store, the appellant was seen to place meat on a trolley and leave it there on noticing that he was being observed. Evidence was also admitted that a stolen Access card in a Barclaycard holder had been found in the appellant's home a week after the commission of the offences charged. The Court of Appeal held that this evidence had been properly admitted to identify the accused as the offender, the Access card being treated as an article of the kind used in the commission of the offences charged.

### (b)  Bad character evidence under section 101(1)(d) relevant to the credibility of the accused

Section 101(1)(d), as we have seen, may be used to adduce evidence of bad character going to the issue of the credibility of the accused. Under section 101(1)(d), as we have also seen, prosecution evidence of the accused's bad character is admissible if 'it is relevant to an important matter in issue between the defendant and the prosecu-tion' and although the test is one of simple rather than enhanced relevance, the requirement of relevance to an 'important matter' is a requirement of relevance to a matter in issue 'of substantial importance in the context of the case as a whole'.[179] Insofar as section 101(1)(d) may be used to attack the credibility of the accused, it is supplemented by section 103(1)(b), which provides as follows:

> (1)  For the purposes of section 101(1)(d) the matters in issue between the defendant and the prosecution include—
>
> . . .
>
> (b)  the question whether the defendant has a propensity to be untruthful, except where it is not suggested that the defendant's case is untruthful in any respect.

The effect of section 103(1)(b) is that in any case in which the prosecution seek to rely upon section 101(1)(d) to attack the credibility of the accused, his propensity to be untruthful will always be deemed to be a matter in issue, except in the very rare cases

---

[177] (1923) 17 Cr App R 109. See also *R v Manning* (1923) 17 Cr App R 85 and *Thompson v R* (1968) 42 ALJR 16, HC of A.
[178] (1976) 65 Cr App R 26, CA.         [179] Section 112(1).

in which it is not suggested that his case is untruthful in any respect. The exception would apply, for example, when the defence do not dispute the facts established by the prosecution and the only question is whether the judge should stop the case on the basis that the prosecution evidence, taken at its highest, is such that the jury, properly directed, could not convict on it.[180] The meaning of 'defendant's case' is undefined and unclear, but it appears to refer to the defendant's case at trial, rather than what he said during police questioning or in his disclosed defence statement but does not rely on at trial, albeit that in many cases the prosecution case will be that the accused is not telling the truth about a particular matter at trial having regard to what he did or did not say to the police or in his defence statement. It is submitted that a plea of not guilty, by itself, cannot lead to the conclusion that the accused's case will be untruthful in some respect, because the plea simply puts the prosecution to proof. However, in the vast majority of cases the prosecution case will be that the accused is not telling the truth in at least one respect. The prosecution will still need to show that the accused's propensity to be untruthful is an 'important' matter in issue, but it is submitted that they will only fail to do so if they do no more than to suggest that the accused is not telling the truth in relation to a matter of only minor or marginal significance in the context of the case as a whole. Thus the overall effect of section 101(1)(d), in relation to the credibility of the accused, will be to permit the prosecution to introduce evidence which goes to show that the accused has a propensity to be untruthful, and therefore is not to be regarded as truthful, whenever it is suggested that he is being untruthful in respect of any matter of more than minor or marginal significance in the context of the case as a whole.

According to the Explanatory Notes, section 103(1)(b) 'is intended to enable the admission of a limited range of evidence such as convictions for perjury or other offences involving deception (for example, obtaining property by deception) as opposed to the wider range of evidence that will be admissible where the defendant puts his character in issue by for example, attacking the character of another person', ie under section 101(1)(g).[181] However, the range of evidence admissible under section 101(1)(d) is neither as clear nor as limited as the Notes suggest. As to the former, for example, interesting questions are likely to arise as to which offences, other than 'perjury or other offences involving deception' will also be characterized as offences showing 'a propensity to be untruthful'. As to the latter, evidence admissible under section 101(1)(d) is not confined to evidence of convictions, but may relate to instances of untruthfulness which did not amount to criminal behaviour, or which did amount to criminal behaviour, but did not result, or by the time of the trial in question had not resulted, in a conviction. Equally, propensity to be untruthful may be established by reference to convictions for offences other than, and not necessarily similar to, 'perjury or other offences involving deception', where it is clear that the jury rejected the accused's version of events. An example would be previous convictions for sexual offences, the accused having run an unsuccessful defence of alibi in

---

[180] See *R v Galbraith* [1981] 1 WLR 1039, CA, Ch 2.     [181] Para 374.

each case. In *R v Hanson*[182] it was held that propensity to untruthfulness is not the same as propensity to dishonesty and that previous convictions, whether for offences of dishonesty or otherwise, are therefore only likely to be capable of showing a propensity to be untruthful where, in the present case, truthfulness is in issue and, in the earlier case, either there was a plea of not guilty and the accused gave an account (on arrest, in interview or in evidence) which the jury must have disbelieved, or the way in which the offence was committed shows a propensity for untruthfulness, for example by the making of false representations. It was also made clear that the court's observations as to the number of previous convictions in relation to section 103(1)(a)[183] apply equally in relation to section 103(1)(b)

As in the case of evidence admissible to go to the issue of guilt, the breadth of section 101(1)(d) in relation to evidence admissible to go to credit is such as to admit much evidence that in the past would have been inadmissible. This, in turn, will lead to applications to the court to exercise its discretionary power to exclude evidence admissible on the issue of credit either under section 101(3) or in reliance on the common-law power to exclude on the basis that its prejudicial effect outweighs its probative value (assuming, as has been submitted earlier, that the common law discretion subsists in relation to prosecution evidence admissible under section 101).[184] In cases in which evidence is admissible under section 101(1)(d) *only* in relation to the credibility of the accused, there will be particular scope for restraining the introduction of evidence as to similarities between the underlying facts of previous offences and the offence charged when this would create a real risk of the jury being misled into thinking that the evidence goes not to credibility but to the probability of the accused having committed the offence of which he is charged. Exercise of the discretion in these particular circumstances is considered in more detail below in the context of section 101(1)(g).[185]

## 8  SECTION 101(1)(E)—EVIDENCE OF SUBSTANTIAL PROBATIVE VALUE IN RELATION TO AN IMPORTANT ISSUE BETWEEN THE DEFENDANT AND A CO-DEFENDANT

Under section 101(1)(e) of the 2003 Act, evidence of the defendant's bad character is admissible if 'it has substantial probative value in relation to an important matter in issue between the defendant and a co-defendant'. According to the Explanatory Notes, the requirement that the probative value of the evidence be 'substantial' will have the effect of excluding evidence of no more than marginal or trivial value.[186] An 'important matter' is 'a matter of substantial importance in the context of the case as

---

[182] [2005] All ER (D) 380 (Mar), CA.     [183] See above.

[184] See above, under C3 Section 101 of the Criminal Justice Act 2003 (b) Discretion to exclude.

[185] See below, under 10 Section 101(1)(g) (c) Discretionary exclusion (iii) Similarities between the facts of previous offences and the offence charged.

[186] Para 375.

a whole',[187] and not, according to the Explanatory Notes, a matter of 'marginal or trivial' importance in that context.[188] Section 101(1)(e), like section 101(1)(d) is a single 'gateway' providing for the admissibility of evidence going to the guilt of the accused as well as evidence going to his credibility. However, evidence is only admissible under section 101(1)(e) on behalf of the co-defendant. The prosecution cannot rely upon section 101(1)(e), nor can another co-defendant, unless the evidence is also of substantial probative value in relation to an important matter in issue between the defendant and that other co-defendant. Section 104(2) provides that:

(2) only evidence—
   (a) which is to be (or has been) adduced by the co-defendant, or
   (b) which a witness is to be invited to give (or has given) in cross-examination by the co-defendant,
   is admissible under section 101(1)(e).

Because evidence admissible under section 101(1)(e) is only admissible on behalf of a co-defendant, there is no discretionary power to exclude it. As noted previously, a co-defendant should be free to adduce any evidence relevant to his case, whether or not it prejudices the defendant, a principle established at common law and which applied in relation both to evidence going to the guilt of the defendant and to cross-examination of the defendant in order to impugn his credibility.

It will be convenient to consider separately evidence admissible under subsection (1)(e) which is relevant to the guilt of the accused and evidence admissible under the subsection which is relevant to his credibility.

## (a) Bad character evidence under section 101(1)(e) relevant to the guilt of the accused

Insofar as section 101(1)(e) permits a co-accused to introduce evidence of the bad character of the accused which is relevant to the issue of his guilt, it reflects the common-law authorities. The leading authority at common law was the decision of the House of Lords in *R v Randall*.[189] In that case, R and G were tried together on a charge of murder. Each raised a cut-throat defence, blaming the other for the infliction of the fatal injuries. Both thereby lost the protection of section 1 of the Criminal Evidence Act 1898 and were asked questions about their previous convictions and bad character. R had relatively minor convictions. G had a bad record, including convictions for burglary, when he had armed himself with a screwdriver. G also admitted that he had been involved in a robbery in which all the robbers had been armed with knives. The House of lords held that in the particular circumstances of the case the evidence of G's propensity to use and threaten violence was relevant not only in relation to the truthfulness of his evidence, but also because the imbalance between that history and the antecedent history of R tended to show that the version

---

[187] Section 112(1).          [188] Para 375.

[189] [2004] 1 All ER 467, HL. See also DW Elliott 'Cut Throat Tactics: the freedom of an accused to prejudice a co-accused' [1991] Crim LR 5.

of events put forward by R was more probable than that put forward by G. Lord Steyn said:[190]

Postulate a joint trial involving two accused arising from an assault committed in a pub. Assume it to be clear that one of the two men committed the assault. The one man has a long list of previous convictions involving assaults in pubs. It shows him to be prone to fighting when he has consumed alcohol. The other man has an unblemished record. Relying on experience and common sense one may rhetorically ask why the propensity to violence of one man should not be deployed by the other man as part of his defence that he did not commit the assault. Surely such evidence is capable, depending on the jury's assessment of all the evidence, of making it more probable that the man with the violent disposition when he had consumed alcohol committed the assault. To rule that the jury may use the convictions in regard to his credibility but that convictions revealing his propensity to violence must otherwise be ignored is to ask the jury to put to one side their common sense and experience. It would be curious if the law compelled such an unrealistic result.

Later, Lord Steyn said:[191]

For the avoidance of doubt I would further add that in my view where evidence of propensity of a co-accused is relevant to a fact in issue between the Crown and the other accused it is not necessary for a trial judge to direct the jury to ignore that evidence in considering the case against the co-accused. Justice does not require that such a direction be given. Moreover, such a direction would needlessly perplex juries.

This passage, however, is open to differing interpretations. *R v Randall* was followed in *R v Price*,[192] a murder trial where one accused, another, *or both*, had committed the offence. It was held that the propensity of D2 to be aggressive was relevant to the question whether, had only one person killed the deceased, that person was D1, and did not become irrelevant simply because, if the jury answered no to that question, they still had to decide whether D1 had been a party to the attack. It was further held that the evidence was relevant to determination of the Crown's case against D2 and could be taken into account by the jury against D2 'as they thought appropriate'. *R v Randall* was distinguished in *R v B(C)*,[193] where there was no joint charge, no cut-throat defence, no attempt to support the credibility of D1 by reference to the evidence of D2's previous misconduct, and that evidence, therefore had no relevance to D1's defence. As to Lord Steyn's dictum 'for the avoidance of doubt', the court was of the view that where D2's propensity becomes relevant as between D1 and the Crown, no distinction is to be attempted in viewing the position as between D2 and the Crown ('the Crown becomes the beneficiary'), but added that the jury should be warned to be cautious before using propensity as a guide to guilt. In *R v Mertens*,[194] on the other hand, it was held that the 'evidence of propensity' to which Lord Steyn had referred was evidence of disposition admissible on behalf of the Crown and that where the evidence of D2's misconduct is not admissible on that basis, although it

---

[190] At [22].    [191] At [35].    [192] [2005] Crim LR 304.    [193] [2004] 2 Cr App R 570, CA.
[194] [2005] Crim LR 301, CA.

can be relied upon by D1 in his case against the Crown with a view to showing that D2 was more likely to have committed the offence, it should be disregarded in considering the case against D2.

In *R v Miller*,[195] A, B and C were charged with conspiracy to evade customs duties. B's defence was that he was not concerned in the illegal acts but that C masqueraded as him (B) and used his (B's) office for their commission. In furtherance of that defence, B's counsel asked a prosecution witness whether C was not in prison during a period when no illegal importations had occurred. Devlin J held that whereas in the case of the prosecution there is a duty to exclude questions tending to show the previous commission of some crime if its prejudicial effect outweighs its probative value, no such limitation applies to a question asked by counsel for a co-accused, whose duty is to adduce any evidence relevant to his case whether or not it prejudices any other accused. The evidence was relevant to B's case and accordingly was admissible.[196] The dicta of Devlin J in *R v Miller* were affirmed in *R v Neale*,[197] a decision on the other side of the line. N and B were charged with arson and manslaughter. Counsel for N sought to adduce evidence, either by cross-examining prosecution witnesses or by calling evidence himself, that B had admitted that he had started fires by himself on four other occasions. The Court of Appeal upheld the ruling of the trial judge that the evidence was inadmissible: it was evidence only of B's propensity to commit wanton and unaided arson and contained nothing of relevance to N's defence, which was that at the relevant time he was elsewhere and asleep in bed.[198] In *R v Randall*[199] the House of Lords considered that *R v Neale* was a borderline decision and 'wondered' how the case would have been decided if N had admitted that he was on the scene.

*R v Miller* was also referred to and approved by the Privy Council in *Lowery v R*,[200] for a long time regarded as an unusual case which was decided on its own special facts,[201] but approved by the House of Lords in *R v Randall*. L and K were charged with the murder of a girl. It was clear that one or both of them must have committed the offence. L emphasized his good character and said that because of his fear of K he had been unable to prevent the murder. K said that he had been under the influence of drugs and powerless to prevent L from killing the victim. K was allowed to call a psychologist to give evidence that L was aggressive, lacked self-control, and was more likely to have committed the offence than K. The Privy Council held that this evidence had been properly admitted. It seems that the evidence was admitted as relevant to

---

[195] [1952] 2 All ER 667, Winchester Assizes.

[196] See also *R v Bracewell* (1978) 68 Cr App R 44 per Ormrod LJ at 50: 'The problem generally arises in connection with evidence tendered by the Crown, so that marginal cases can be dealt with by the exercise of the discretion. "When in doubt, exclude", is a good working rule in such cases. But where the evidence is tendered by a co-accused, the test of relevance must be applied, and applied strictly . . .'

[197] (1977) 65 Cr App R 304. See also *R v Campbell and Williams* [1993] Crim LR 448, CA and *R v Myers* [1997] 4 All ER 314, HL (Ch 13).

[198] See also *R v Nightingale* [1977] Crim LR 744 and *R v Knutton* (1992) 97 Cr App R 115, CA.

[199] [2004] 1 All ER 467, HL.          [200] [1974] AC 85, PC.

[201] Per Lawton LJ in *R v Turner* [1975] QB 834, CA.

prove K's innocence because L had already put his character in issue by testifying to the effect that he was not the sort of man to have committed the offence.

In *R v Douglass*[202] it was held that where a cut-throat defence is being run by two accused jointly charged with an offence and evidence of the bad character of one of them is relevant to the guilt or innocence of the other, the evidence is admissible whether they are alleged to have committed the offence by way of joint enterprise or by separate but contributory means. D and P were charged with causing death by reckless driving. The prosecution alleged that D had been drinking and was trying to prevent P from overtaking and that P, in vying for position, had collided with an oncoming car. P did not testify, but his counsel cross-examined P's girlfriend to elicit from her that P had never drunk alcohol in the two years that she had known him. The clear purpose was to suggest that P, unlike D, was unlikely to have been affected by alcohol so as to have driven badly. Applying *Lowery v R*, *R v Bracewell*, and *R v Miller*, it was held that where one accused adduces evidence of his own lack of propensity and this goes to the issue of a co-accused's guilt, the co-accused may call contradictory evidence. Accordingly, D should have been allowed to adduce evidence of P's previous convictions for motoring offences, including two drink-driving offences.

In both *Lowery v R* and *R v Douglass* the evidence was admitted against an accused who had put his character in issue.[203] However in *R v Randall* the House of Lords, while approving *Lowery v R*, was confident that 'there must be cases in which the propensity of one accused may be relied on by the other, irrespective of whether he has put his character in issue'.[204] In that case it was also held that where evidence of propensity of a co-accused is relevant to a fact in issue between the Crown and the other accused it is not necessary for a trial judge to direct the jurors to ignore that evidence in considering the case against the co-accused, which would needlessly perplex them.[205]

### (b) Bad character evidence under section 101(1)(e) relevant to the credibility of the accused

Insofar as section 101(1)(e) permits a co-accused to introduce evidence of the bad character of the accused which is relevant to his credibility, it is qualified by section 104(1), which provides as follows:

> (1) Evidence which is relevant to the question whether the defendant has a propensity to be untruthful is admissible on that basis under section 101(1)(e) only if the nature or conduct of his defence is such as to undermine the co-defendant's defence.

The words 'nature or conduct of his defence' make clear that the defence of the co-accused may be undermined not only by the evidence of the accused or witnesses called on his behalf, but also in cross-examination of witnesses called by the prosecution or co-accused. The phrase 'nature or conduct' was also used in section 1(3)(ii)

---

[202] (1989) 89 Cr App R 264, CA. Cf *R v Kennedy* [1992] Crim LR 37, CA.

[203] See also *R v Sullivan* (2003) *The Times*, 18 Mar 2003.

[204] [2004] 1 All ER 467, per Lord Steyn at 476.     [205] Per Lord Steyn at 478.

of the Criminal Evidence Act 1898, under which the accused could lose his shield and be cross-examined on his bad character when the nature or conduct of the defence was such as to involve imputations on the character of, among others, witnesses for the prosecution. For the purposes of section 1(3)(ii) of the 1898 Act it was held in *R v Jones*[206] that answers given by an accused under cross-examination were generally to be treated as part of the cross-examiner's case and therefore prima facie should not be taken into account, and that the shield should not be lost where the accused was trapped into making an imputation by the form of the question put.[207] On the other hand, it was held that the shield could be lost where the imputation was not necessary in answer to the question put[208] or was voluntary and gratuitous.[209] These principles, it is submitted, are likely to remain valid, in the context of section 104, in relation to cross-examination of the accused, whether at the hands of the prosecution or a co-accused.

Under section 1(3)(iii) of the Criminal Evidence Act 1898 an accused could lose his shield where he had 'given evidence against' a co-accused. In the leading case of *Murdoch v Taylor*[210] the House of Lords held that 'evidence against' included evidence which either supported the prosecution's case in a material respect or which 'undermined the defence' of a co-accused. *Murdoch v Taylor* and some of the subsequent decisions provide much valuable guidance as to the way in which section 104(1) is likely to be interpreted, both generally and in relation to the phrase 'to undermine the co-defendant's defence'.

In *Murdoch v Taylor* it was held that section 1(3)(iii) does not refer only to evidence given by one accused against another with hostile intent, that it is the effect of the evidence upon the minds of the jury which is material and not the state of mind of the person who gives it, and that the test to be applied is therefore objective and not subjective. The same may be said, it is submitted, in relation to section 104(1). However, section 104(1) of the 2003 Act is narrower in its scope than section 1(3)(iii) of the 1898 Act, as interpreted in *Murdoch v Taylor*, in that the former is not triggered by evidence which does no more than support the prosecution case. Thus although in many cases evidence which supports the prosecution case will also undermine the defence of the co-accused, if the evidence supports the prosecution case but does not undermine the defence of the co-accused, because for example he has not raised a defence, evidence of the accused's bad character will not be admissible to attack his credibility under section 101(1)(e).[211] Such evidence will also be inadmissible, it is submitted, where the accused gives evidence to the same effect as the prosecution on a factual matter on which there is no issue between the Crown and the co-accused, because such evidence will not undermine the defence of the co-accused.[212] However, it would seem that if a co-accused has only a scintilla or iota of a defence, as when

---

[206] (1909) 3 Cr App R 67, CCA.          [207] See also and cf *R v Britzman; R v Hall* [1983] 1 WLR 350, CA.
[208] *R v Jones*, ibid.          [209] *R v Courtney* [1995] Crim LR 63, CA.
[210] [1965] AC 574, HL.          [211] Cf *R v Adair* [1990] Crim LR 571, CA.
[212] Cf *R v Crawford* [1998] 1 Cr App R 338, CA.

his defence is almost completely undermined by his own testimony which, although he declines to change his plea, amounts to an admission of guilt, there is still the possibility of undermining it.[213]

The meaning of undermining the defence of the co-accused gave rise to some difficulty in cases in which the accused appeared merely to have contradicted the evidence given by a co-accused or to have denied participation in a joint venture. In *R v Bruce*[214] it was held that evidence which undermined a co-accused's defence would only trigger section 1(3)(iii) if it made his acquittal less likely.[215] Eight accused were charged with robbery, one of whom, M, admitted that there had been a plan to commit robbery but said that he had not been a party to its execution. Another accused, B, testified that there had been no plan to rob. Counsel for M was then permitted to cross-examine B about his previous convictions. B, acquitted of robbery but convicted of theft, appealed. The Court of Appeal held that section 1(3)(iii) had not been triggered because although B had contradicted M, his evidence was more in M's favour than against him in that it provided him with a different and possibly better defence.[216] It remains to be seen whether section 104(1) of the 2003 Act will be interpreted in the same way.

It seems clear, however, from the decisions in *R v Davis*[217] and *R v Varley*,[218] that evidence which on its face amounts to no more than a denial of participation in a crime or which appears merely to contradict something said by a co-accused, may, in appropriate circumstances, undermine the defence of a co-accused. In *R v Davis*, D and O were jointly charged with the theft of certain items in circumstances such that the offence had been committed either by one or both of them. D, having denied the theft of one of the items, was cross-examined under section 1(3)(iii). He appealed on the ground that a mere denial did not amount to giving evidence against a co-accused. The Court of Appeal held that as only D, O or both of them could have stolen the items in question, D's denial that he had done so necessarily meant that O had, and the appeal was dismissed.[219] In *R v Varley*, V and D were jointly charged with robbery. D's defence was that he did take part but was forced to do so by threats on his life by V. V gave evidence that he had not taken part in the robbery and that D's evidence was untrue. D's counsel was given leave to cross-examine V as to his previous convictions. V was convicted and appealed. Dismissing the appeal, it was held that a mere denial of participation in a joint venture is not of itself sufficient to trigger section 1(3)(iii)—for section 1(3)(iii) such denial 'must' lead to the conclusion that if the one accused did not participate then it must have been the other who did. It was further held that

---

[213] *R v Mir* [1989] Crim LR 894, CA.

[214] [1975] 1 WLR 1252, CA. Cf *R v Hatton* (1976) 64 Cr App R 88, CA. A denied that there was a plan to steal scrap metal. H gave evidence that both he and A had been parties to a plan to steal but denied that either of them had acted dishonestly. It was held that H had given evidence against A.

[215] Per Stephenson LJ [1975] 1 WLR 1252 at 1259.

[216] The appeal was dismissed because of the overwhelming evidence of guilt.

[217] [1975] 1 WLR 345, CA.      [218] [1982] 2 All ER 519, CA.

[219] Cf *R v Hendrick* [1992] Crim LR 427, CA.

where one accused asserts a view of the joint venture which is directly contradicted by the other, such contradiction may be evidence against the co-accused. Applying these principles to the facts of the case, V's evidence was against D because it amounted to saying not only that D was telling lies, but also that D was a participant on his own and not acting under duress.

In *R v Crawford*[220] the victim of a robbery alleged that she had been alone in the lavatories of a restaurant with three other women, all of whom had committed the offence. The three were the accused C, her co-accused A, and a third woman, L. C's evidence was to the effect that A and L were in the lavatories at the material time, but that she, C, was not. A's evidence, which was put to C during cross-examination, was that C and L had committed the robbery while she, A, was merely an innocent bystander. It was held that the trial judge had properly allowed A to cross-examine C on her previous convictions, because if the jury accepted C's evidence that only A and L were in the lavatories at the material time, that was very damaging to the credibility of A and made it much less likely that A was simply a passive bystander.[221] It was submitted on appeal that this outcome was in conflict with the proposition in *R v Varley* to the effect that, for section 1(3)(iii) to apply, a mere denial of participation in a joint venture 'must' lead to the conclusion that if the accused did not participate, then it must have been the co-accused who did: this was not a case where it was either C or A who had committed the offence, and if it was not C therefore it must have been A. Rejecting this submission, the Court of Appeal held that, insofar as the proposition from *R v Varley* had been cast in mandatory terms, it went too far: the word 'may' was more appropriate.

It is submitted that in appropriate circumstances, evidence of a conviction admissible under section 101(1)(e) to impugn the credibility of the accused need not be confined to the fact of the previous conviction but may extend to the details of the offence. This would reflect the position in relation to section 1(3)(iii) of the 1898 Act. In *R v Reid*[222] R was one of four men who robbed a minicab driver. His defence was that he had got into the car last and only then discovered that a robbery had taken place. Having lost his shield under section 1(3)(iii), he was then cross-examined about a previous conviction for robbery of a taxi driver and the fact that his defence had been that he had left the car before the robbery occurred. The appeal was dismissed on the grounds that there was a real issue of credibility arising from consideration of the detailed circumstances of both robberies. The evidence went directly to the question whether his defence involved seeking falsely to incriminate others.

---

220 [1998] 1 Cr App R 338, CA.    221 Cf *R v Kirkpatrick* [1998] Crim LR 63, CA.
222 [1989] Crim LR 719, CA. Cf *R v McLeod* [1994] 3 All ER 254, CA, below.

## 9  SECTION 101(1)(F)—PROSECUTION EVIDENCE TO CORRECT A FALSE IMPRESSION GIVEN BY THE DEFENDANT

Under section 101(1)(f), prosecution evidence of the defendant's bad character is admissible if 'it is evidence to correct a false impression given by the defendant'. Section 101(1)(f), together with section 105, by which it is supplemented, are based upon the recommendations of the Law Commission, but lack the Commission's important safeguards. These included a requirement of enhanced relevance, ie *substantial* probative value in correcting the false impression, a requirement to consider a number of detailed factors and, in the case of evidence of prejudicial effect, a requirement that admissibility be in the interests of justice.[223] Furthermore, although it is submitted that evidence admissible under section 101(1)(f) is subject to the common-law discretion to exclude on the basis that its prejudicial effect outweighs its probative value, it is not subject to the exclusionary discretion in section 101(3).

Section 105 of the 2003 Act provides as follows.

(1) For the purposes of section 101(1)(f)—
    (a) the defendant gives a false impression if he is responsible for the making of an express or implied assertion which is apt to give the court or jury a false or misleading impression about the defendant;
    (b) evidence to correct such an impression is evidence which has probative value in correcting it.

(2) A defendant is treated as being responsible for the making of an assertion if—
    (a) the assertion is made by the defendant in the proceedings (whether or not in evidence given by him),
    (b) the assertion was made by the defendant—
        (i) on being questioned under caution, before charge, about the offence with which he is charged, or
        (ii) on being charged with the offence or officially informed that he might be prosecuted for it,
    and evidence of the assertion is given in the proceedings,
    (c) the assertion is made by a witness called by the defendant,
    (d) the assertion is made by any witness in cross-examination in response to a question asked by the defendant that is intended to elicit it, or is likely to do so, or
    (e) the assertion was made by any person out of court, and the defendant adduces evidence of it in the proceedings.

(3) A defendant who would otherwise be treated as responsible for the making of an assertion shall not be so treated if, or to the extent that, he withdraws it or disassociates himself from it.

(4) Where it appears to the court that a defendant, by means of his conduct (other than the giving of evidence) in the proceedings, is seeking to give the court or jury an impression about himself that is false or misleading, the court may if it appears just to

---

[223] Clause 10, Law Commission Draft Bill.

do so treat the defendant as being responsible for the making of an assertion which is apt to give that impression.

(5) In subsection (4) 'conduct' includes appearance or dress.

(6) Evidence is admissible under section 101(1)(f) only if it goes no further than is necessary to correct the false impression.

(7) Only prosecution evidence is admissible under section 101(1)(f).

Section 101(1)(f), as supplemented by section 105, reflects the pre-existing common law and statutory rules. At common law, if the accused adduced evidence of his good character, the prosecution were permitted to call evidence in rebuttal, and under section 1(3)(ii) of the Criminal Evidence Act 1898, if the accused questioned witnesses for the prosecution with a view to establishing his good character, or gave evidence of his good character, he could be cross-examined on his bad character.

Whether the accused has given a false impression is obviously a question of law for the judge and, it is submitted, the risk of prejudice, where corrective evidence is admitted only to be subsequently ruled inadmissible, is such that in many cases the question of admissibility will need to be the subject of a ruling by the judge in the absence of the jury. Indeed, where the accused denies that the impression conveyed is false and disputes the corrective evidence on which the prosecution seek to rely, it would seem that the judge could only properly decide the matter by holding a *voir dire*.

### (a) Express assertions, implied assertions, and assertions by conduct

'Express' false assertions, for the purposes of section 105(1)(a), would cover, for example, false assertions that the accused is of good character or a religious man or a man who earns an honest living or who would never use violence. 'Implied' false assertions would cover false assertions relating to the accused's conduct or behaviour from which it can be implied that he is of good character or honest. *R v Samuel*,[224] a decision under section 1(3)(ii) of the 1898 Act, provides a good example. In that case, the accused, charged with larceny, gave evidence of previous occasions on which he had restored lost property to its owner and was held to have been properly cross-examined about his previous convictions for theft. Section 105(1)(a) is also apt to cover false assertions by the accused about his bad character. If, for example, the accused, charged with a sexual offence, falsely asserts that he has only one previous conviction, also for a sexual offence, then corrective evidence would be admissible that in fact he also has previous convictions for offences of dishonesty. An example of a false or misleading impression conveyed by conduct, for the purposes of section 105(4) and (5), would be an accused who, not being a priest, appears in the proceedings wearing a clerical dog-collar. However, an accused with many previous convictions for dishonesty does not make a false assertion as to his good character by simply taking the oath or reminding the jury of the oath that he has sworn on the bible and,

---

[224] (1956) 40 Cr App R 8, CCA.

on that reasoning, nor will he do so by his conduct in holding and gesticulating with a bible while in the witness box.[225]

Under section 105(4), the court will only treat the accused as being responsible for the making of an assertion by means of his conduct 'if it appears just to do so', a hurdle presumably designed to prevent overuse or abuse of the subsection. For example, many accused will dress up for their court appearance, wearing outfits which they would normally wear only on very special occasions. Section 105 should not cover, it is submitted, the case of the plumber or plasterer who appears in court in his best suit. It would be otherwise, however, if he were to sport a regimental tie or blazer, never having served in the army.

### (b) Corrective evidence

Evidence to correct the false impression must have probative value in correcting it,[226] but must go no further than is necessary to correct it.[227] Thus if the accused expressly asserts that he 'earns an honest living', the corrective evidence may include evidence of his previous convictions for crimes of dishonesty, but not evidence of his previous convictions for, say, assault or driving with excess alcohol. However, problems are likely to be encountered, in some cases, in identifying precisely what the false or misleading impression is. For example, if an accused is charged with inflicting grievous bodily harm in an 'off the ball' incident during the course of a rugby match, and gives evidence that he has no previous convictions, is evidence admissible to show his disciplinary record of violent play on the rugby field.[228] The same problem exists in the case of implied assertions or assertions by conduct. The accused wearing a clerical collar presumably conveys the impression not only that he is a priest, but also that he behaves as a priest should, and therefore the corrective evidence should not be confined to evidence which goes to show that he is not a priest, or has been defrocked, but should extend to general evidence of his misconduct or disposition to misconduct.

### (c) Withdrawal or disassociation from an assertion

Under section 105(2)(d), an accused is treated as being responsible for the making of an assertion made by a witness cross-examined by (or, presumably, on behalf of) him, but only if the assertion was in response to a question intended to elicit it or which was likely to elicit it. Thus if the witness volunteers a false impression about the accused, the accused will not be treated as being responsible for the making of the volunteered assertion and evidence will be admissible to correct it. In contrast, under section 105(2)(c) an accused is treated as being responsible for the making of an assertion made by a witness called by him, and corrective evidence will be admissible in this situation where the witness volunteers a false impression as much as when he

---

[225] See *R v Robinson* [2001] Crim LR 478, CA, a decision under s 1(3)(ii) of the 1898 Act.
[226] Section 105(1)(b).        [227] Section 105(6).
[228] In *R v Marsh* [1994] Crim LR 52, CA, from which these facts are taken, it was held that the evidence was admissible in cross-examination under s 1(3)(ii) of the Criminal Evidence Act 1898.

asserts it in answer to a question intended to elicit it or which was likely to elicit it. However, in this situation it seems that the accused can prevent the introduction of corrective evidence by disassociating himself from the assertion made by the witness, in reliance upon section 105(3). An accused who no longer stands by a false assertion made by him and introduced in evidence under section 105(2)(b) by the prosecution, would also be well advised to withdraw it. In cases in which the accused himself makes, or adduces evidence of, a false assertion, section 105(3) also provides him with the opportunity to embark upon a damage limitation exercise. For example, if the accused makes, or adduces evidence of, a false assertion to the effect that he is of good character, but then withdraws or disassociates himself from the assertion, he will thereby prevent the admission of corrective evidence of, say, his previous convictions, but the jury will by then be aware that he is not of good character and also, in cases in which the assertion was made by him in giving his evidence, that he is not always a reliable witness.

### (d) Corrective evidence as to guilt or credibility of the accused

Given the breadth of provision for the admissibility of evidence of disposition under section 101(1)(d), presumably such evidence will only rarely be admitted as corrective evidence under section 101(1)(f). Where such evidence is admitted under section 101(1)(f), however, then it seems clear that it is evidence that will go not only to the credibility of the accused but also to the likelihood of his guilt, and that the jury should be directed accordingly. It remains to be seen whether the position will be the same in the case of corrective evidence of misconduct, ie evidence of the commission of an offence or other reprehensible behaviour. However, it is submitted that there is much force in the argument that where an accused makes, or adduces evidence of, a false assertion as to his good character, he generally does so for the purpose of showing that it is unlikely that he committed the offence charged, and the corrective evidence is introduced to show the contrary, and not merely to attack his credibility.[229]

### (e) Discretionary exclusion

If, as has been submitted, prosecution evidence admissible under section 101 may be excluded in reliance upon the common-law discretionary power to exclude prosecution evidence the prejudicial effect of which outweighs its probative value, there may well be limited scope for the exercise of the discretion in relation to evidence admissible under section 101(1)(f) because to exclude such evidence may seriously mislead the jury.[230]

---

[229] For dicta to this effect in relation to evidence admissible in cross-examination of an accused who had put his character in issue, under s 1(3)(ii) of the Criminal Evidence Act 1898, see per Viscount Sankey in *Maxwell v DPP* [1935] AC 309 at 319 and per Lord Goddard CJ in *R v Samuel* (1956) 40 Cr App R 8 at 12.

[230] See *R v Marsh* [1994] Crim LR 52, CA, above.

## 10 SECTION 101(1)(G)—PROSECUTION EVIDENCE WHERE THE DEFENDANT HAS MADE AN ATTACK ON ANOTHER PERSON'S CHARACTER

Under section 101(1)(g) of the 2003 Act, prosecution evidence of the accused's bad character is admissible if 'the defendant has made an attack on another person's character'. Where section 101(1)(g) is triggered, evidence of the accused's bad character is admissible even if he elects not to testify.[231]

Section 101(1)(g), as supplemented by section 106, is in some measure based on the recommendations of the Law Commission but, as in the case of section 101(1)(f), lacks the Commission's important safeguards, including the requirement of enhanced relevance, the requirement to consider a number of detailed factors and, in the case of evidence of prejudicial effect, the requirement that admissibility be in the interests of justice.[232] The statutory provisions also depart from the recommendation of the Law Commission that evidence of the bad character of the defendant should not be admissible where he makes an attack on another person using evidence of his bad character which 'has to do with the alleged facts of the offence with which the defendant is charged, or is evidence of misconduct in connection with the investigation or prosecution of that offence',[233] as when the accused asserts that the offence was committed by another or that another has invented the allegation against him.

### (a) 'An attack on another person's character'

Section 106 of the 2003 Act provides as follows:

(1) For the purposes of section 101(1)(g) a defendant makes an attack on another person's character if—

    (a) he adduces evidence attacking the other person's character,

    (b) he (or any legal representative appointed under section 38(4) of the Youth Justice and Criminal Evidence Act 1999 to cross-examine a witness in his interests) asks questions in cross-examination that are intended to elicit such evidence, or are likely to do so, or

    (c) evidence is given of an imputation about the other person made by the defendant—

        (i) on being questioned under caution, before charge, about the offence with which he is charged, or

        (ii) on being charged with the offence or officially informed that he might be prosecuted for it.

(2) In subsection (1) 'evidence attacking the other person's character' means evidence to the effect that the other person—

    (a) has committed an offence (whether a different offence from the one with which the defendant is charged or the same one), or

---

[231] At common law, if the accused did not give evidence but attacked witnesses for the prosecution, then, without more, evidence of the accused's bad character could not be introduced: *R v Butterwasser* [1948] 1 KB 4, CCA.

[232] Clause 9, Law Commission Draft Bill.    [233] Clause 9(2), ibid.

(b)  has behaved, or is disposed to behave, in a reprehensible way;
and 'imputation about the other person' means an assertion to that effect.

(3)  Only prosecution evidence is admissible under section 101(1)(g).

Under section 106, the circumstances in which a defendant makes an attack on another person's character are different from the circumstances under section 105 in which the accused is treated as being responsible for the making of a false assertion. Thus section 106 appears not to apply where an attack on another person's character is made by the accused while being cross-examined at the hands of either the prosecution or any co-accused. However, although matters are not spelt out in the way that they are in section 105, it seems reasonably clear that section 106(1)(a) does cover an attack on another person's character when either made by a witness called by the accused or contained in a hearsay statement adduced by the accused. Evidence admissible under section 106(1)(c) may be introduced by the prosecution, and because section 106 contains no equivalent of section 105(3), this will trigger section 101(1)(g) even if the accused wishes to withdraw the out-of-court statement on which the prosecution rely or to disassociate himself from it.

The definition of 'evidence attacking the other person's character' in section 106(2) must be read together with section 100 of the Act. Under section 100, it will be recalled, except where all parties agree to the admissibility of evidence of the bad character of a person other than the accused, such evidence is only admissible with the leave of the court and such leave can only be granted if the evidence is either (a) important explanatory evidence or (b) has substantial probative value in relation to a matter which is in issue in the proceedings and is of substantial importance in the context of the case as a whole. Thus evidence to attack another person's character which does not meet the requirements of section 100, for example evidence which has substantial probative value in relation to a matter which, although in issue, is of only minor importance in the context of the case as a whole, will be inadmissible.

It is clear from section 106 that 'another person' may or may not be a witness in the case. Thus an attack may be made on a victim who dies by reason of the crime, for example a victim of murder, manslaughter or causing death by dangerous driving, a victim of an offence of violence who, by reason of the injuries sustained, is unable to be called as a witness, a victim who does not give evidence by reason of threats, interference or intimidation, a person whose hearsay statement is in evidence in the proceedings, and so on. However, it is also reasonably clear that 'another person' must be an identified individual. The definition of 'evidence attacking the other person's character' in section 106(2) clearly envisages that the identity of that person is known.

Section 106(2)(a) covers cases in which the evidence is to the effect that the person has committed either the very offence with which the accused is charged or some other offence. Section 106(2)(b), which refers to evidence to the effect that the other person has behaved or is disposed to behave in a reprehensible way, will typically cover evidence of misconduct on the part of the police or prosecution witnesses which amounted to 'imputations' for the purposes of section 1(3)(ii) of the Criminal

Evidence Act 1898. Examples included allegations that the prosecutor or a witness for the prosecution invented the crime alleged,[234] obtained a confession by bribes,[235] deliberately held the accused on remand after remand in order to concoct evidence,[236] manufactured a confession statement,[237] completely fabricated part of his evidence,[238] or asked a relative to have a quiet word with the accused to get him to talk and admit the offence.[239] Looking at section 106(2) as a whole, there is no doubt that, subject to discretionary exclusion, evidence of the bad character of the accused will be admissible under section 101(1)(g) notwithstanding that the attack on another person's character is a necessary or justifiable part of his defence.

In *R v Hanson*[240] it was held that pre-2003 Act authorities will continue to apply when assessing whether an attack has been made on another person's character under section 101(1)(g), to the extent that they are compatible with section 106.

## (b) Assertions of innocence and denials of guilt

Under section 1(3)(ii) of the Criminal Evidence Act 1898, it was held that mere assertions of innocence by the accused, or his emphatic denials of guilt, did not result in a loss of the shield and were to be distinguished from attacks on the veracity of the prosecutor or a prosecution witness, which did have that result.[241] It is submitted that such a distinction remains valid for the purposes of section 101(1)(g). The distinction, however, is difficult and narrow, as is apparent in an early and classic example given by Lord Hewart CJ in *R v Jones:*[242]

It was one thing for the appellant to deny that he had made the confession; but it is another thing to say that the whole thing was an elaborate and deliberate concoction on the part of the inspector.

The difficulty and narrowness lies in the fact that, in some cases, to deny that the confession was made necessarily means, by implication, that the police have fabricated evidence, and although section 106, unlike section 105, does not refer to implied as well as express assertions, it is submitted that an accused will trigger section 101(1)(g) where an attack on another person's character is made by necessary implication, rather than in terms. Under section 1(3)(ii) of the 1898 Act, it was said that 'each case falls to be determined upon the exact facts, the exact circumstances, the exact language used',[243] but some of the authorities were very difficult to reconcile.[244] In *R v Britzman;*

---

[234] *Selvey v DPP* [1970] AC 304, HL.     [235] *R v Wright* (1910) 5 Cr App R 131.
[236] *R v Jones* (1923) 17 Cr App R 117.     [237] *R v Clark* [1955] 2 QB 469.
[238] *R v Levy* (1966) 50 Cr App R 238. See also *R v Dunkley* [1927] 1 KB 323, CCA.
[239] *R v Courtney* [1995] Crim LR 63, CA.     [240] [2005] All ER (D) 380 (Mar), CA.
[241] See per Lord Goddard CJ in *R v Clark* [1955] 2 QB 469 at 478, applied in *R v St Louis and Fitzroy Case* (1984) 79 Cr App R 53, CA.
[242] (1923) 17 Cr App R 117 at 120.
[243] Per Lord Parker CJ in *R v Levy* (1966) 50 Cr App R 238 at 241.
[244] See, eg, *R v Rouse* [1904] 1 KB 184 and cf *R v Rappolt* (1911) 6 Cr App R, 156, CCA; and see *R v Tanner* (1977) 66 CR App R 56, CA and cf *R v Nelson* (1978) 68 Cr App R 12, CA.

*R v Hall*[245] the Court of Appeal set out guidelines. In that case, police officers gave evidence of admissions made by the appellant during a lengthy interview, of which there was a written record, and in the course of a shouting-match between Britzman and Hall in the cells. The appellant denied that the interview and the shouting-match had ever taken place and, in cross-examination of the officers, this was suggested to them by counsel for the appellant. The Court of Appeal, noting that it was not a case of a denial of a single answer and that there was no suggestion of mistake or misunderstanding, held that the nature and conduct of the defence did involve imputations on the character of the prosecution witnesses. To deny that the conversations took place at all necessarily meant by implication that the police officers had given false evidence which they had made up for the purposes of a conviction. It was held that a distinction could not be drawn between a defence so conducted as to make specific allegations of fabrication and one in which such allegations arose by way of necessary and reasonable implication.[246] It is submitted that some of the guidelines set out by Lawton LJ, giving the judgment of the court, are likely to remain valid for the purposes of section 101(1)(g). His Lordship said:

the exercise of discretion in favour of defendants . . . should be used if there is nothing more than a denial, however emphatic or offensively made, of an act or even a short series of acts amounting to one incident or in what was said to have been a short interview . . . The position would be different however if there were a denial of evidence of a long period of detailed observation extending over hours and . . . where there were denials of long conversations . . . cross-examination should only be allowed if the judge is sure that there is no possibility of mistake, misunderstanding or confusion and that the jury will inevitably have to decide whether the prosecution witnesses have fabricated evidence. Defendants sometimes make wild allegations when giving evidence. Allowance should be made for the strain of being in the witness box and the exaggerated use of language which sometimes results from such strain or lack of education or mental stability.[247]

## (c) Discretionary exclusion

Evidence admissible under section 101(1)(g) is open to discretionary exclusion under section 101(3) if it appears to the court that the admission of the evidence would have such an adverse effect on the fairness of the proceedings that the court ought not to admit it. Such evidence, it is submitted, is also open to exclusion in reliance upon the common-law discretion to exclude prosecution evidence the prejudicial effect of which outweighs its probative value.[248] Where it is clear that certain defence evidence will trigger section 101(1)(g) and therefore the accused wishes to know whether, if he were to adduce it, the judge would exercise his discretion to exclude evidence of his bad character, it would seem that although there is nothing to prevent the judge from giving an indication, making clear that ultimately the decision will have to take

---

[245] [1983] 1 WLR 350.
[246] See also *R v Owen* (1985) 83 Cr App R 100, CA.     [247] [1983] 1 WLR 350 at 355.
[248] See above, under **C3 Section 101 of the Criminal Justice Act 2003 (b) Discretion to exclude.**

account of the evidence actually given, he is fully entitled to take the view that any exercise of discretion should be made only if necessary, ie after the evidence has been given and when he is in possession of the full facts.[249]

The likely grounds for discretionary exclusion are considered under the following headings. Consideration is also given to the discretionary exclusion of evidence of the kind described in section 106(1)(c).

(i) *Evidence of bad character irrelevant to credibility or disproportionate to the bad character of the other person.* The rationale underlying section 101(1)(g) is that where the accused has made an attack on another person's character, the jury, in deciding whether to believe the defence version of events, are entitled to know the character of the person making the attack. However, where section 101(1)(g) is triggered, it permits the prosecution to admit evidence of the accused's bad character even if it has little or no bearing on the credibility of the defence or his own credibility as a witness. It could include, for example, evidence which shows nothing more than his disposition towards sexual misconduct or cruelty to animals. Such evidence, it is submitted, can serve no purpose but prejudice and if admissible in law should be excluded by the exercise of discretion. Equally, it is submitted, there is scope for exercise of the discretion where the bad character of the accused is disproportionate to the bad character of the person whose character has been attacked. In *R v Burke*,[250] Ackner LJ, rehearsing the cardinal principles set out in *Selvey v DPP*[251] upon which the discretion to exclude was exercised under section 1(3)(ii) of the 1898 Act, said that in the ordinary and normal case the trial judge may feel that if the credit of the prosecutor or his witnesses has been attacked, it is only fair that the jury should have before them material on which they can form their judgment whether the accused is any more worthy of belief than those he has attacked. Earlier, however, he said:

The trial judge must weigh the prejudicial effect of the questions against the damage done by the attack on the prosecution's witnesses, and must generally exercise his discretion so as to secure a trial that is fair both to the prosecution and the defence . . .

Cases must occur in which it would be unjust to admit evidence of a character gravely prejudicial to the accused, even though there may be some tenuous grounds for holding it technically admissible . . . Thus, although the position is established in law, still the putting of the questions as to the character of the accused person may be fraught with results which immeasurably outweigh the result of questions put by the defence and which make a fair trial of the accused almost impossible . . .

(ii) *Attacks which are a necessary or justifiable part of the defence.* As we have seen, evidence of the accused's bad character will become admissible even where his attack on another person's character is necessary to enable him to establish his defence. It is submitted that although the discretionary power of exclusion should not invariably or even generally be exercised in these circumstances, because that would amount to a

---

[249] See *R v Dempster* [2001] Crim LR 567, CA, a decision under s 1(3)(ii) of the 1898 Act.
[250] (1985) 82 Cr App R 156, CA.        [251] [1970] AC 304, HL.

qualification to section 101(1)(g) under the guise of the exercise of discretion, the discretion should be exercised, as necessary, to prevent too severe an application of section 101(1)(g). As the House of Lords observed in *Selvey v DPP*,[252] in relation to exercise of the discretion on this basis to prevent cross-examination of the accused under section 1(3)(ii) of the 1898 Act, the discretion is unfettered, its exercise being dependent on the circumstances of each case and the overriding duty of the judge to ensure a fair trial.

*(iii) Similarities between the facts of previous offences and the offence charged.* As previously noted, evidence of the accused's bad character is admissible under section 101(1)(g) because of the bearing it has on the credibility of the defence case and, it is submitted, a judge should direct the jury accordingly and, in cases in which the bad character is not also admissible as propensity evidence, should further direct the jury that the evidence does not show propensity to commit the offence charged. It does not follow from this that the exclusionary discretion should always be exercised to prevent cross-examination which would lead the jury to infer that the accused is guilty of the offence charged, as when the accused is cross-examined on previous offences of a type similar to that charged, but the nature of that offence and the extent to which it resembles the offence charged, are certainly relevant matters for the judge to take into account. In deciding whether and how to exercise the discretion in respect of evidence admissible under section 101(1)(g), valuable guidance is likely to be derived from the decisions reached in relation to exercise of the discretion to prevent cross-examination under section 1(3)(ii) of the 1898 Act.

In *R v Powell*[253] Powell was convicted of knowingly living on the earnings of prostitution. He alleged that the police had fabricated evidence upon which the prosecution was based. He also put his own character in issue, thus coming within both limbs of section 1(3)(ii). The judge then allowed cross-examination on his previous convictions for allowing his premises to be used for the purposes of prostitution. The Court of Appeal dismissed the appeal. Lord Chief Justice Lane held that if there is a deliberate attack being made by the accused upon the conduct of a prosecution witness, calculated to discredit him wholly, which raises a real issue about the conduct of an important witness which the jury will have to settle in order to reach their verdict, the judge is entitled to let the jury know about the previous convictions of the accused. The fact that they are not for offences of dishonesty or are for offences bearing a close resemblance to the offences charged are matters for the judge to take into account when exercising his discretion but do not oblige him to disallow the cross-examination. The judge, therefore, had exercised his discretion properly: the accused had lost his shield under both limbs of section 1(3)(ii), but had either ground stood alone, the cross-examination should have been allowed.

Similar issues re-arose in *R v McLeod*.[254] M was convicted of an armed robbery

---

[252] [1970] AC 304, HL.          [253] [1986] 1 All ER 193, CA. See also *R v Lasseur* [1991] Crim LR 53, CA.
[254] [1994] 3 All ER 254, CA.

which involved the use of a number of stolen cars. At interview he made a confession, but in evidence he said he had nothing to do with the robbery and that the police had created a false case against him and fabricated his confession. Anticipating cross-examination on previous convictions, his counsel asked M about them briefly during his examination-in-chief. In cross-examination on the previous convictions under section 1(3)(ii),[255] M was asked about: (i) a robbery, following a not guilty plea and a defence of alibi; (ii) another robbery in which the victim had been locked in an understairs cupboard; (iii) theft of a car involving a change of the plates to a false registration; and (iv) handling of a car with false registration plates. On appeal it was submitted that the questions should not have been asked. Stuart-Smith LJ, giving the judgment of the court, set out the following principles:

1.  The primary purpose of cross-examination as to previous convictions and bad character of the accused is to show that he is not worthy of belief, not to show that he has a disposition to commit the type of offence with which he is charged.[256] But the mere fact that the offences are of a similar type to that charged or because of their number and type have the incidental effect of suggesting a tendency or disposition to commit the offence charged will not make them improper.[257]

2.  It is undesirable that there should be prolonged or extensive cross-examination in relation to previous offences, because it will divert the jury from the principal issue in the case, the guilt of the accused on the instant offence, and not the details of earlier ones. Unless the earlier ones are admissible as similar fact evidence, prosecuting counsel should not seek to probe or emphasize similarities between the underlying facts of previous offences and the instant offence.[258]

3.  Similarities of defences which have been rejected by juries on previous occasions, for example false alibis or the defence that the incriminating substance has been planted and whether or not the accused pleaded guilty or was disbelieved having given evidence on oath, may be a legitimate matter for

---

[255] Strictly speaking, the case is not an authority on s 1(3)(ii) because the jury were already aware of the previous convictions: see *Jones v DPP* [1962] AC 635, HL, above. However, there seems little doubt that whether the evidence of bad character was introduced under s 1(3)(ii) or at common law, the principles relating to discretionary exclusion were the same.

[256] *R v Vickers* [1972] Crim LR 101, CA.

[257] See *R v Powell* [1986] 1 All ER 193, CA, *Selvey v DPP* [1970] AC 304, HL, above, and *R v Wheeler* [1995] Crim LR 312, CA. See also *R v Davison-Jenkins* [1997] Crim LR 816, CA, below.

[258] See, eg, the subsequent decision in *R v Davison-Jenkins* [1997] Crim LR 816, CA. D-J, charged with shoplifting cosmetics, was treated as having put her character in issue. It was held that she had been improperly cross-examined on the detail of her previous convictions, one of which was for shoplifting clothes and cosmetics. It was also held, however, that since the cross-examination was only designed to impugn D-J's credibility, that could have been achieved not by referring to her two previous shoplifting convictions, but by referring instead to her three previous convictions for other forms of dishonesty.

questions. These matters do not show a disposition to commit the offence in question but are clearly relevant to credibility.

4.    Underlying facts that show particularly bad character over and above the bare facts of the case are not necessarily to be excluded. However, the judge should be careful to balance the gravity of the attack on the prosecution with the degree of prejudice to the defence which will result from the disclosure of the facts in question. Details of sexual offences against children are likely to be regarded by the jury as particularly prejudicial to an accused and may well be the reason why in *R v Watts*[259] the court thought the questions impermissible.

Applying those principles to the facts, the appeal against conviction was dismissed. The questions were not unduly prolonged or extensive. Concerning the first offence, there was nothing wrong in asking about the plea and the rejected defence of alibi. As to the victim of the second offence being locked under the stairs, it merely showed that the offence was somewhat more ruthless than may normally be the case in a robbery where, by definition, violence or the threat of it, is used. As to the other two offences, it was fanciful to contend that the facts elicited were designed to show a propensity to commit armed robbery, merely because the use of stolen vehicles with false registration plates is the stock in trade of armed robbery.[260]

In *R v Barratt*,[261] on the other hand, in which the accused was charged with having an offensive weapon and attacked the character of prosecution witnesses, it was held that the trial judge was wrong to allow the accused to be cross-examined on a spent conviction, dating from 1985, and relating to an offensive weapon, because he had failed to take account of the fact that the offence was long spent and that it had comparatively little impact on credibility but carried a substantial risk of prejudice.

*(iv)  Discretionary exclusion of evidence described in section 106(1)(c).* In cases in which the prosecution seek to rely on evidence falling within section 106(2), ie evidence of an imputation made by the accused on being questioned under caution or on being charged with the offence, then insofar as the accused can show that the evidence was obtained illegally, improperly or unfairly, whether by virtue of breaches of the codes of practice or otherwise, there will be obvious scope for discretionary exclusion of the evidence, which in turn could prevent section 101(1)(g) from being triggered. The authorities in relation to the discretionary exclusion of prosecution evidence obtained illegally, improperly or unfairly, are considered in Chapter 3. There may also be scope for discretionary exclusion of evidence of an imputation made by the accused on being questioned or charged where the accused wishes to withdraw or disassociate himself from the imputation at the trial.

---

[259] [1983] 3 All ER 101, CA.    [260] Cf *R v Barsoum* [1994] Crim LR 194, CA.
[261] [2000] Crim LR 847, CA.

## 11 OFFENCES COMMITTED BY DEFENDANT WHEN A CHILD

Section 108(2) and (3) of the 2003 Act, which replace section 16(2) and (3) of the Children and Young Person's Act 1963, provide as follows.

> (2) In proceedings for an offence committed or alleged to have been committed by the defendant when aged 21 or over, evidence of his conviction for an offence when under the age of 14 is not admissible unless—
> (a) both of the offences are triable only on indictment, and
> (b) the court is satisfied that the interests of justice require the evidence to be admissible.
>
> (3) Subsection (2) applies in addition to section 101.

# D  GENERAL

## 1 ASSUMPTION OF TRUTH IN THE ASSESSMENT OF RELEVANCE OR PROBATIVE VALUE

By virtue of section 109 of the 2003 Act, a court, when considering the relevance or probative value of evidence of bad character under section 100 (non-defendant) or section 101 (defendant) in order to decide whether it is admissible, should operate on the assumption that the evidence is true, but need not do so if no reasonable court or jury could reasonably find it to be true. Section 109 provides as follows.

> (1) Subject to subsection (2), a reference in this Chapter to the relevance or probative value of evidence is a reference to its relevance or probative value on the assumption that it is true.
>
> (2) In assessing the relevance or probative value of an item of evidence for any purpose of this Chapter, a court need not assume that the evidence is true if it appears, on the basis of any material before the court (including any evidence it decides to hear on the matter), that no court or jury could reasonably find it to be true.

Section 109 applies to section 101(e) (evidence of substantial probative value in relation to an important matter in issue between the defendant and a co-defendant) and to 101(1)(f), as supplemented by section 105 (evidence to correct a false impression given by the defendant). Its chief importance, however, is likely to be in relation to the assessment of the probative value of 'similar fact evidence' properly so called under section 101(1)(d) (evidence of the defendant's bad character relevant to an important matter in issue between the defendant and the prosecution) and under section 100(3)(c) and (d) (evidence of a non-defendant's bad character of substantial probative value). The probative value of similar fact evidence often arises out of the nexus between the spontaneous and independent accounts of two or more witnesses. That probative value disappears, therefore, if there is also evidence to suggest that the witnesses have deliberately concocted false evidence by conspiracy or collaboration or, which is more common, the evidence of each of them has been innocently contaminated by knowledge of the account of the other, whether acquired directly, ie in discussion with the other,[262] or indirectly, from a third person,[263] or as a result of media publicity.[264] In *R v H*[265] the House of Lords considered whether evidence carrying a real risk of collusion or contamination should be excluded by the judge or should be left to the jury with an appropriate warning. *R v H* was a case of sexual offences against a daughter and a step-daughter between whom, the parties agreed, there existed a risk of collusion. It was held that save in very rare cases, the question of collusion goes not to the admissibility of similar fact evidence, but to its credibility, an issue for the jury, and that it would be wrong for the judge to decide whether there is a risk of collusion because he would inevitably be drawn into considering whether the evidence is untrue and hence whether there is a real possibility that the accused is innocent, the very question which the jury has to decide. The following principles derive from the judgments given.

1.  Normally, where there is an application to exclude similar fact evidence carrying a risk of collusion or contamination, the judge should approach the question of admissibility on the basis that the similar facts alleged are true.

2.  In very exceptional cases, evidence of collusion or contamination may be taken into account and in such cases the judge would be compelled to hold a *voir dire*.

3.  If the evidence is admitted and it becomes apparent that no reasonable jury could accept it as free from collusion, the judge should direct the jury that it cannot be used for any purpose adverse to the defence.

4.  Where this is not so, but the question of collusion has been raised, the judge must draw the importance of collusion to the attention of the jury and direct then that if they are not satisfied that the evidence can be relied upon as free from collusion, they cannot rely upon it for any purpose adverse to the defence.

Although section 109 is clearly based on the common-law rules it replaces, there are two significant differences. First, as we have seen, it is much wider in its ambit in that it applies for the purpose of assessing the relevance or probative value of the bad character of the non-defendant as well as the defendant. Secondly, there is nothing to suggest that section 109(2) should be invoked only exceptionally. However, section 109(2), as drafted, is a somewhat curious provision in that where it appears to the court on the basis of the material before it, including any evidence given in a *voir dire*, that no court or jury could find the facts in question to be true, then the court 'need not assume' that those facts are true. It is submitted that the unstated but more

---

[262]  See *R v W* [1994] 2 All ER 872, CA.        [263]  See *R v Ananthanarayanan* [1994] 1 WLR 788, CA.

[264]  See per Lord Wilberforce in *DPP v Boardman* [1975] AC 421, HL at 444 and per Stuart-Smith LJ in *R v Bedford* (1990) 93 Cr App R 113, CA at 116.

[265]  [1995] 2 AC 596, HL.

obvious action that the court needs to take, once it has concluded that no court or jury could find the facts in question to be true, is to exclude the evidence. It remains to be seen whether the courts will adopt such a robust approach and also whether different approaches will be adopted depending upon whether the evidence is relied upon by the defence or the prosecution. In any event, it is submitted that the third and fourth principles derived from *R v H* as set out above remain good law.

## 2  STOPPING THE CASE WHERE EVIDENCE CONTAMINATED

Under section 107 of the 2003 Act, which applies only to trials before a judge and jury, if evidence of the bad character of the accused has been admitted under any of paragraphs (c) to (g) of section 101(1), and the court is satisfied, at any time after the close of the prosecution case, that the evidence is so contaminated that the accused's conviction of the offence would be unsafe, the court must either direct the jury to acquit or, if there ought to be a retrial, discharge the jury. Section 107 of the 2003 Act provides as follows:

(1)  If on a defendant's trial before a judge and jury for an offence—
  (a)  evidence of his bad character has been admitted under any of paragraphs (c) to (g) of section 101(1), and
  (b)  the court is satisfied at any time after the close of the case for the prosecution that—
    (i)  the evidence is contaminated, and
    (ii)  the contamination is such that, considering the importance of the evidence to the case against the defendant, his conviction of the offence would be unsafe,

  the court must either direct the jury to acquit the defendant of the offence or, if it considers that there ought to be a retrial, discharge the jury.

(2)  Where—
  (a)  a jury is directed under subsection (1) to acquit a defendant of an offence, and
  (b)  the circumstances are such that, apart from this subsection, the defendant could if acquitted of that offence be found guilty of another offence,

  the defendant may not be found guilty of that other offence if the court is satisfied as mentioned in subsection (1)(b) in respect of it.

. . .[266]

(4)  This section does not prejudice any other power a court may have to direct a jury to acquit a person of an offence or to discharge a jury.

(5)  For the purposes of this section a person's evidence is contaminated where—
  (a)  as a result of an agreement or understanding between the person and one or more others, or

---

[266] Section 107(3) is cast in terms similar to s 107(1) and is to the same effect, but applies not to a trial but to a jury determination under s 4A(2) of the Criminal Procedure (Insanity) Act 1964 whether a person charged on indictment did the act or made the omission charged.

(b) as a result of the person being aware of anything alleged by one or more others whose evidence may be, or has been, given in the proceedings,

the evidence is false or misleading in any respect, or is different from what it would otherwise have been.

Subsection (5)(a) covers cases of conspiracy and collaboration, whereas subsection (5)(b) seems designed to cover cases of innocent contamination and has been cast in sufficiently wide terms, it is submitted, to cover cases in which a person became aware of the allegation of another not only directly, but also indirectly, through some third person or as a result of media coverage.

It appears that section 107 may be brought into play either on an application by the accused or by the court of its own motion. However, according to the Explanatory Notes to the Act, the test in section 107(1)(b)(ii) is designed to be a high test so that if the judge were to consider that a jury direction along the lines described in *R v H*[267] would be sufficient to deal with any potential difficulties, then the question of the safety of the conviction would not arise and the case should not be withdrawn.[268]

## 3  COURT'S DUTY TO GIVE REASONS FOR RULINGS

Section 110 of the 2003 Act gives effect to the Law Commission's proposal that there should be a duty on the court to give reasons for its rulings. The section applies not only to rulings on whether an item of evidence is evidence of bad character, but also to rulings on admissibility under section 100 (non-defendant's bad character), section 101 (defendant's bad character) and section 107 (stopping the case where the evidence is 'contaminated'). Section 110 provides as follows:

(1) Where the court makes a relevant ruling—
   (a) it must state in open court (but in the absence of the jury, if there is one) its reasons for the ruling;
   (b) if it is a magistrates' court, it must cause the ruling and the reasons for it to be entered in the register of the court's proceedings.

(2) In this section 'relevant ruling' means—
   (a) a ruling on whether an item of evidence is evidence of a person's bad character;
   (b) a ruling on whether an item of such evidence is admissible under section 100 or 101 (including a ruling on an application under section 101(3);[269]
   (c) a ruling under section 107.

---

[267] [1995] 2 AC 596, HL. See principles 3 and 4, above, under 1 **Assumption of truth in the assessment of relevance or probative value.**

[268] Paras 384 and 385.

[269] Under s 101(3), the court has a discretionary power to exclude evidence otherwise admissible under either s 101(1)(d) or s 101(1)(g).

## 4  RULES OF COURT

Under section 111(1) of the 2003 Act, rules of court may make such provision as appear to be necessary or expedient for the purposes of the Act. Under section 111(2) of the 2003 Act:

> (2) The rules may, and, where the party in question is the prosecution, must, contain provisions requiring a party who—
> (a) proposes to adduce evidence of a defendant's bad character, or
> (b) proposes to cross-examine a witness with a view to eliciting such evidence,
> to serve on the defendant such notice, and such particulars of or relating to the evidence, as may be prescribed.

The rules may provide that the court or the accused may, in such circumstances as may be prescribed, dispense with such a requirement.[270] In considering the question of costs, the court may take into account any failure by a party to comply with a requirement which has not been dispensed with.[271] The rules applicable in magistrates' courts and crown courts are set out in rule 35 of the Criminal Procedure Rules 2005.[272]

# E  OTHER PROVISIONS GOVERNING THE ADMISSIBILITY OF EVIDENCE OF BAD CHARACTER

In addition to the provisions of the Criminal Justice Act 2003, various other provisions have a bearing on the admissibility or exclusion of evidence of bad character. Thus as to admissibility, there are a number of statutory provisions whereby the conviction of, or sentence for, one offence is an essential ingredient of another. For example, under section 103 of the Road Traffic Act 1988, it is an offence to obtain a licence or drive a vehicle on a road 'while disqualified for holding or obtaining a licence'. Similarly under section 21 of the Firearms Act 1968, 'a person who has been sentenced to imprisonment for a term of three years or more' shall not at any time have a firearm or ammunition in his possession.[273] Evidence of conviction or sentence for the purposes of such statutes is probably best categorized as evidence 'which has to do with the alleged facts of the offence with which the defendant is charged' within section 98(b) of the 2003 Act.[274] As to the exclusion of evidence of bad character, nothing in the scheme under the 2003 Act affects the exclusion of evidence under

---

[270] Section 111(3).       [271] Section 111(4).       [272] SI 2005/384.

[273] Previous convictions may also be admitted, after a verdict of guilty, if directly relevant to the question of sentence and, unless the accused denies them, formal proof is not required. Evidence of a conviction, if disputed, is also admissible where the accused pleads *autrefois convict* to prevent the prosecution proceeding against him in respect of an offence of which he has already been convicted.

[274] See above under **A4 Admissibility of evidence of bad character to do with the facts of the offence.**

either (a) the rule in section 3 of the Criminal Procedure Act 1865,[275] which prevents a party from impeaching the credit of his own witness by general evidence of bad character or (b) section 41 of the Youth Justice and Criminal Evidence Act 1999,[276] which restricts evidence or questions about the complainant's sexual history in proceedings for sexual offences.[277]

In this final section of this chapter consideration is given to three other provisions. The first two, section 27(3) of the Theft Act 1968 and section 1(2) of the Official Secrets Act 1911, provide for the admissibility of the accused's disposition towards certain kinds of wrongdoing. The third, paragraph 6 of the *Practice Direction (Criminal Proceedings: Consolidation)*,[278] provides for the exclusion of spent convictions.

## 1  SECTION 27(3) OF THE THEFT ACT 1968

It will be seen in Chapter 22 that where an accused is found in possession of recently stolen goods, an explanation is called for which, if not forthcoming, will entitle the jury to presume guilty knowledge or belief on a charge of receiving stolen goods. The task of the prosecution in proving guilty knowledge or belief is further assisted by section 27(3), which provides that:

> Where a person is being proceeded against for handling stolen goods (but not for any offence other than handling stolen goods), then at any stage of the proceedings, if evidence has been given of his having or arranging to have in his possession the goods the subject of the charge, or of his undertaking or assisting in, or arranging to undertake or assist in, their retention, removal, disposal or realisation, the following evidence shall be admissible for the purpose of proving that he knew or believed the goods to be stolen goods:
> (a) evidence that he has had in his possession, or has undertaken or assisted in the retention, removal, disposal or realisation of, stolen goods from any theft taking place not earlier than twelve months before the offence charged; and
> (b) (provided that seven days' notice in writing has been given to him of the intention to prove the conviction) evidence that he has within the five years preceding the date of the offence charged been convicted of theft or of handling stolen goods.

Where evidence is introduced under section 27(3)(a), strict regard must be had to its terms: it was not designed to allow evidence to be given of what is in effect another offence of handling committed before the offence charged and does not permit the introduction of details of the transaction as a result of which the earlier property came into the possession of the accused.[279] However, under section 27(3)(a), providing

---

[275] See Ch 6.     [276] See Ch 7.     [277] Section 112(3) of the 2003 Act.
[278] [2002] 1 WLR 2870.
[279] *R v Bradley* (1979) 70 Cr App R 200, applied in *R v Wood* [1987] 1 WLR 779, CA. Possession of the earlier property may be proved by evidence of an admission made by the accused under caution, in a written statement to the police, provided that the statement is edited so as to disclose only the bare fact of such possession.

a description of the stolen goods appears to be unavoidable.[280] Subsection 3(b) has to be read with section 73 of the Police and Criminal Evidence Act 1984, whereby the fact of a conviction may be proved by producing a certificate of conviction giving 'the substance and effect (omitting the formal parts) of the indictment and of the conviction',[281] wording which renders admissible not only the fact, date and place of the conviction, but also a description of the stolen goods.[282] In cases in which there are a number of counts of handling on some of which the accused denies possession, the judge should warn the jury that evidence admitted under section 27(3) is relevant only to those counts in which guilty knowledge is involved and not those in which possession is the only or primary issue.[283]

It is no answer to an application to admit evidence under section 27(3)(b) to say that the previous convictions are for theft or handling of a different kind or have no bearing on a specific prosecution argument based on a system or modus operandi, because the very purpose of the subsection is to admit evidence of the general disposition of the accused to be dishonest.[284] Nevertheless, it is well established that the judge does have a discretion to exclude evidence admissible under section 27(3) where it would only be of minimal assistance to the jury or, as it is put, its prejudicial effect would outweigh its probative value.[285] *R v Rasini*[286] is probably no more than an example. In that case it was held that where the sole issue in the trial is whether the accused had guilty knowledge, evidence of previous similar offences should only be adduced under section 27(3)(b) where the interests of justice so demand and not as a matter of course. In *R v Hacker*,[287] a trial for handling the bodyshell of an Escort RS Turbo motor car, in which the accused denied that the goods had been stolen and also denied guilty knowledge or belief, it was held that the judge was entitled, in his discretion, to admit evidence of a previous conviction of receiving a Ford RS Turbo motor car, evidence said to be highly relevant to the issue of knowledge.

## 2  SECTION 1(2) OF THE OFFICIAL SECRETS ACT 1911

Under section 1(1) of the Official Secrets Act 1911, it is an offence to commit various acts of espionage 'for any purpose prejudicial to the safety or interests of the State'. Evidence of disposition to commit such acts is admissible under section 1(2), which provides that:

(2) On a prosecution under this section, it shall not be necessary to show that the accused person was guilty of any particular act tending to show a purpose prejudicial to the safety or interests of the State, and notwithstanding that no such act is proved against

---

[280]  *R v Fowler* (1987) 86 Cr App R 219 at 226, CA.        [281]  See Ch 2.

[282]  *R v Hacker* [1995] 1 All ER 45, HL.        [283]  *R v Wilkins* [1975] 2 All ER 734, CA.

[284]  *R v Perry* [1984] Crim LR 680, CA.

[285]  See *R v List* [1965] 3 All ER 710; *R v Herron* [1967] 1 QB 107 (decided under s 43(1) of the Larceny Act 1916, re-enacted, with some modification, in s 27(3)); *R v Knott* [1973] Crim LR 36, CA; and *R v Perry* [1984] Crim LR 680, CA.

[286]  (1986) *The Times*, 20 Mar, CA.        [287]  [1995] 1 All ER 45, HL.

him, he may be convicted if, from the circumstances of the case, or his conduct, or his known character as proved, it appears that his purpose was a purpose prejudicial to the safety or interests of the State . . .

## 3 PARAGRAPH 6 OF THE PRACTICE DIRECTION (CRIMINAL PROCEEDINGS: CONSOLIDATION)

The Rehabilitation of Offenders Act 1974 provides that in civil proceedings no evidence shall be admissible to prove that a 'rehabilitated' person has committed, been charged with, prosecuted for, convicted of or sentenced for any offence which was the subject of a 'spent' conviction[288] unless the judge is satisfied that in the circumstances justice cannot be done in the case except by admitting such evidence.[289] The Act does not apply to criminal proceedings[290] but under paragraph 6 of the *Practice Direction (Criminal Porceedings: Consolidation)*[291] in criminal proceedings, 'both court and advocates should give effect to the general intention of Parliament by never referring to a spent conviction when such reference can be reasonably avoided . . .' It also provides that 'No one should refer in open court to a spent conviction without the authority of the judge, which authority should not be given unless the interests of justice so require.' A conviction becomes 'spent' on the expiry of a 'rehabilitation period', which runs from the date of conviction, varies according to the sentence imposed and is reduced by half for persons under 18 years old at the date of conviction.[292] Certain sentences are excluded from rehabilitation under the Act and these include imprisonment for life or for a term exceeding 30 months and a sentence of detention during Her Majesty's pleasure.[293]

[288] Section 4(1)(a).

[289] Section 7(3). See also *Thomas v Metropolitan Police Comr* [1997] 1 All ER 747, CA. As to the procedure to be adopted by licensing justices in deciding whether to admit the spent convictions of the person applying for the licence, see *Adamson v Waveney District Council* [1997] 2 All ER 898, DC.

[290] Section 7(2)(a).     [291] [2002] 1 WLR 2870.     [292] See Tables A and B under s 5(2).

[293] Section 5(1). As to how a jury should be directed on the character of an accused with previous but spent convictions, see Ch 16.

# 18

# OPINION EVIDENCE

As a general rule, opinion evidence is inadmissible: a witness may only speak of facts which he personally perceived, not of inferences drawn from those facts. To this general rule there are two exceptions: (i) an appropriately qualified expert may state his opinion on a matter calling for the expertise which he possesses; and (ii) a non-expert witness may state his opinion on a matter not calling for any particular expertise as a way of conveying the facts which he personally perceived. There are two main reasons for the general rule. First, it has been said that, whereas any fact that a witness can prove is relevant, his opinion is not.[1] The opinion of a non-expert has no probative value in relation to a subject calling for expertise and is usually insufficiently relevant to a subject not calling for any particular expertise. Secondly, the general rule prevents witnesses from usurping the role of the tribunal of fact. The tribunal of fact, although free to reject any opinions proffered, might be tempted simply to accept those opinions rather than draw its own inferences from the facts of the case.

The first exception to the general rule stems from an acknowledgement that in some cases the tribunal of fact, in the absence of opinion evidence, may be unable properly to reach a conclusion. Expert opinion evidence is admitted because the drawing of certain inferences calls for an expertise which the tribunal of fact simply does not possess. However, as already noted, there is a danger that the tribunal of fact may blindly defer to the opinion given. The danger is particularly acute in the case of opinions expressed by expert witnesses, whose dogmatic views, on subjects in respect of which scientific knowledge may be limited or incomplete, may occasion miscarriages of justice. Following the successful appeal of Angela Cannings in the 'cot death' case of *R v Cannings*,[2] the Attorney General announced a review of 258 convictions relating to homicide or infanticide of a baby under 2 years old by a parent, and a similar review in civil cases was ordered by the Children's Minister. The duties and responsibilities of the expert in civil litigation are governed by CPR rule 35, considered below, as supplemented by a Code of Guidance on Expert Evidence, designed to help experts and those instructing them in all cases where the CPR apply. Remarkably, and notwithstanding the recommendations of Lord Justice Auld in his 'Review of the Criminal Courts of England and Wales'[3] there are no equivalent rules for experts appearing in criminal cases.

---

[1] Per Goddard LJ in *Hollington v Hewthorn & Co Ltd* [1943] KB 587 at 595, CA.
[2] [2004] 1 All ER 725, CA, Ch 8.     [3] HMSO, 2001: see Ch 11, paras 129–51.

The second non-expert exception stems from a recognition that the fundamental assumption upon which the general rule is based, that it is possible to distinguish between fact and opinion, is false.[4] The words of a witness testifying as to perceived facts are always coloured, to some extent, by his opinion as to what he perceived. The separation of an inference or value judgment from the facts on which it is based is often extremely difficult and sometimes impossible. In criminal proceedings, for example, a witness may identify the accused as the culprit, saying, 'He is the man I saw.' It is evidence of opinion, not fact. The witness means: 'He so resembles the man I saw that I am prepared to say that they are one and the same.' He could confine himself to a description of the man he saw and leave it to the jury to decide whether the description fits the accused. In cases of this kind, the opinion expressed conveys the facts perceived. The witness, in such cases, is allowed to give his evidence in his own way which is often, although not invariably, the most natural and comprehensible way in which to convey to the tribunal of fact the facts as he perceived them.

# A EXPERT OPINION EVIDENCE[5]

## 1 MATTERS CALLING FOR EXPERTISE

### (a) Examples

The opinion evidence of an expert is only admissible on a matter calling for expertise. The field of expertise is large and expanding.[6] It embraces subjects as diverse as accident investigation and driver behaviour,[7] ballistics, battered women's syndrome,[8] blood tests, breath tests, blood-alcohol levels and back-calculations thereof,[9] ear print identification,[10] facial mapping[11] or facial identification by video superimposition,[12]

---

[4] 'In a sense all testimony to matter of fact is opinion evidence; ie it is a conclusion formed from phenomena and mental impressions': Thayer *A Preliminary Treatise on Evidence at the Common Law* (Boston 1898) 524.

[5] This section of the chapter concerns expert *evidence*. Civil actions without a jury in the High Court may be tried by a judge sitting with assessors. The function of assessors, who are principally used in the Admiralty Court in cases concerning collisions between vessels, is to assist the judge on matters of fact calling for specialized knowledge: see s 70 of the Supreme Court Act 1981, s 63 of the County Courts Act 1984 and CPR r 35.15. The modern practice is to put questions to the assessors after discussion with counsel and then to disclose their answers to counsel, so that appropriate submissions can be made as to whether the judge should accept their advice: *Bow Spring (owners) v Manzanillo II (owners)* [2004] 4 All ER 899, CA.

[6] *The Expert Witness Directory 2006* claims coverage of over 1,800 specialisms.

[7] See *R v Dudley* [2004] All ER (D) 374 (Nov).     [8] See *R v Hobson* [1998] 1 Cr App R 31, CA.

[9] Ie calculation of the amount of alcohol eliminated in the period between driving and providing a specimen in order to show that a person's alcohol level was above the prescribed limit at the time of driving. See *Gumbley v Cunningham* [1989] 1 All ER 5, HL.

[10] *R v Dallagher* [2003] 1 Cr App R 195, CA.

[11] *R v Stockwell* (1993) 97 Cr App R 260, CA. It is open to the jury in a criminal trial to convict on the basis of such expert evidence: *R v Mitchell* [2005] All ER (D) 182 (Mar).

[12] *R v Clarke* [1995] 2 Cr App R 425, CA.

fingerprint identification, voice identification,[13] genetic fingerprinting,[14] indented impressions left on one document as a result of writing on another,[15] insanity, lip reading,[16] Sudden Infant Death Syndrome (SIDS),[17] the genuineness of works of art and the state of public opinion.[18] Frequently recurring examples of matters upon which expert evidence is admissible include medical, scientific, architectural, engineering and technological issues and questions relating to standards of professional competence, market values, customary terms of contracts and the existence of professional and trade practices. Handwriting may be proved either by a non-expert familiar with the handwriting in question[19] or by a qualified expert, but an expert should be called in criminal cases tried by jury when, pursuant to section 8 of the Criminal Procedure Act 1865, disputed handwriting is compared with a specimen sample of handwriting proved to the satisfaction of the court to be genuine.[20] Expert opinion is admissible on questions of a literary or artistic nature, for example in relation to the defence of 'public good' under section 4 of the Obscene Publications Act 1959, which provides that:

(1) A person shall not be convicted of an offence . . . if it is proved that publication of the article in question is justified as being for the public good on the ground that it is in the interests of science, literature, art or learning, or of other objects of general concern.[21]

[13] R v Robb (1991) 93 Cr App R 161, CA.

[14] The technique whereby a human cell taken from a sample of, eg, blood, saliva, semen, or hair, is analysed to reveal the DNA or genetic 'fingerprint' of an individual. For a basic description of the method by which DNA profiling is carried out, see R v Gordon [1995] 1 Cr App R 290 at 293–4, CA. The technique may be used not only to identify criminal suspects but also, because the distinctive sequences amongst the genes in a person's DNA are passed on from parent to child, to decide questions of pedigree, including paternity and maternity disputes. There is no rule that DNA evidence cannot found a conviction without other evidence, but in evaluating DNA evidence, use should not be made of Bayes Theorem, or any similar statistical method of analysis, because it plunges the jury into inappropriate and unnecessary realms of theory and complexity, deflecting them from their proper task: R v Adams [1996] 2 Cr App R 467, CA. As to the procedure to be adopted when DNA evidence is introduced, see R v Doheny and Adams [1997] 1 Cr App R 369, CA. See also Mike Redmayne, 'The DNA Database: Civil Liberty and Evidentiary Issues' [1995] Crim LR 437 and C Jowett, 'Sittin' in the Dock with the Bayes' (2001) NLJ 201.

[15] The impressions may be detected by the use of Electrostatic Detection Apparatus (ESDA). ESDA has been useful not only in dating documents and determining the origin of anonymous communications, but also in showing whether pages were written in sequence and whether there were subsequent additions to the contents: see R v Wellington [1991] Crim LR 543, CA (confessions recorded in interview notes) and generally Audrey Giles 'Good Impressions' (1991) NLJ 605.

[16] R v Luttrell [2004] 2 Cr App R 520, CA.

[17] See R v Cannings [2004] 1 All ER 725, CA, Ch 8.

[18] eg on the issue of reputation in passing-off actions. See Sodastream Ltd v Thorn Cascade Co Ltd [1982] RPC 459 and Lego Systems A/S v Lego M Lemelstrich Ltd [1983] FSR 155. Cf Reckitt & Colman Products v Borden Inc (No 2) [1987] FSR 407.

[19] Doe d Mudd v Suckermore (1837) 7 LJQB 33.

[20] R v Harden [1963] 1 QB 8, CCA: see generally Ch 9.

[21] An 'object of general concern' other than those mentioned must have a degree of similarity to those mentioned. Thus evidence that material has psycho-therapeutic value for persons with abnormal sexual tendencies, relieving their sexual tensions, saving them from psychological disorders and diverting them from anti-social activities, cannot establish a defence under s 4(1) and should be excluded: DPP v Jordan [1977] AC 699, HL.

(2) It is hereby declared that the opinion of experts as to the literary, artistic, scientific or other merits of an article may be admitted in any proceedings under this Act either to establish or to negative the said ground.

A final example, calling for special attention, is a point of foreign law, which, as we have seen in Chapter 2, is a question of fact to be decided on the evidence by the judge. Foreign law is usually proved by the evidence, including opinion evidence, of an expert[22] who may refer to foreign statutes, decisions and textbooks.[23] If the evidence of the experts conflicts, the judge is bound to look at the sources of knowledge from which the experts have drawn, in order to decide between the conflicting testimony.[24] However, he is not at liberty to conduct his own research into those sources and to rely on material not adduced in evidence in order to reject the expert evidence.[25]

At common law, the consequence of treating foreign law as a question of fact is that where there has been an English decision on a particular point of foreign law and the same point subsequently arises again, it must be decided afresh on new expert evidence.[26] This remains the position where a point of foreign law arises in English criminal proceedings. The position in civil proceedings, however, has now been altered by section 4 of the Civil Evidence Act 1972. Section 4(2)(a) of that Act provides that a previous determination by an English court of superior status, whether civil or criminal, on a point of foreign law shall, if reported in citable form,[27] be admissible in evidence in civil proceedings. Section 4(2)(b) provides that except where there are two or more previous determinations which are in conflict, the foreign law on the point in question shall be taken to be as previously determined unless the contrary is proved.[28] Subsection (2)(b) raises a presumption that the earlier decision is correct. However, the court which has to consider the question for a second

---

[22] An exception exists in the case of the construction of provisions of foreign legislation admitted in evidence under the Evidence (Colonial Statutes) Act 1907: see the authorities cited in *Jasiewicz v Jasiewicz* [1962] 1 WLR 1426. Under s 1 of the 1907 Act, copies of Acts, ordinances and statutes passed by the legislature of any part of Her Majesty's dominions exclusive of the UK and of orders, regulations and other instruments issued or made under the authority of any such Act, ordinance or statute, if purporting to be printed by the government printer of the possession shall be received in evidence by all courts in the UK without proof that copies were so printed. See also s 6 of the Colonial Laws Validity Act 1865. The British Law Ascertainment Act 1859 permits English courts to state a case on a point of foreign law for the opinion of a superior court in another part of Her Majesty's dominions. The opinion pronounced is admissible in evidence on the point of foreign law in question. See also the Foreign Law Ascertainment Act 1861.

[23] It may also be proved by the witness statement of an expert (if admissible) or by a statement of agreed facts pursuant to s 10 of the Criminal Justice Act 1967: *R v Ofori (No 2)* (1993) 99 Cr App R 223, CA.

[24] Per Lord Langdale MR in *Nelson (Earl) v Lord Bridport* (1845) 8 Beav 527 at 537 and per Scarman J in *Re Fuld's Estate (No 3), Hartley v Fuld* [1968] P 675 at 700–3.

[25] Per Lord Chelmsford in *Duchess Di Sora v Phillipps* (1863) 10 HL Cas 624 at 640 and per Purchas LJ in *Bumper Development Corpn Ltd v Metropolitan Police Comr* [1991] 4 All ER 638 at 643–6, CA.

[26] *M'Cormick v Garnett* (1854) 23 LJ Ch 777.

[27] Ie where the report, if the question had been as to the law of England and Wales, could have been cited as an authority in legal proceedings in England and Wales: s 4(5).

[28] Notice of intention to rely on the previous determination must be given to the other parties: s 4(3) and CPR r 33.7.

time decides for itself what weight to attach to the previous decision and, although it is desirable to reach consistent conclusions, the subsection is not to be construed as laying down a general rule that the presumption can only be displaced by particularly cogent evidence.[29]

## (b)   Matters within the experience and knowledge of the tribunal of fact

Where the triers of fact can form their own opinion without the assistance of an expert, the matter in question being within their own experience and knowledge, the opinion evidence of an expert is inadmissible because unnecessary.[30] Thus leave should not be granted to call a professor of psychology or other medical evidence to demonstrate the likely deterioration of the memory of an ordinary witness.[31] Equally, expert evidence is inadmissible on the question whether an unidentified person shown in a photograph is under the age of 16.[32] In *R v Stamford*[33] the Court of Appeal held that, on a trial for posting packets containing indecent articles, the trial judge had properly refused to admit evidence on the ordinary meaning of the words 'indecent or obscene'. Whether a particular article was indecent or obscene was a matter entirely for the jury. Similarly, in *R v Anderson*[34] it was said that in the ordinary case, the issue of obscenity in prosecutions under the Obscene Publications Act 1959 falls to be tried by the jury without the assistance of expert evidence.[35] These cases may be compared with *DPP v A & B C Chewing Gum Ltd*,[36] which has been described as 'a very special case'[37] which should be regarded as 'highly exceptional and confined to its own circumstances'.[38] The accused was charged with publishing for gain obscene battle

---

[29]  *Phoenix Marine Inc v China Ocean Shipping Co* [1999] 1 Lloyd's Rep 682, QBD.

[30]  Per Lawton LJ in *R v Turner* [1975] QB 834 at 841. In some cases, however, a jury may properly receive assistance on a matter within their own experience and knowledge on the basis that the witness has had more time and better facilities to consider the matter than it would be practicable to afford to them. Such a witness, in reality a non-expert, may be regarded as 'sufficiently expert ad hoc': see *R v Howe* [1982] 1 NZLR 618 at 627. Thus in *R v Clare and Peach* [1995] 2 Cr App R 333, CA an officer who had viewed a video-recording about 40 times, examining it in slow motion, frame by frame, and rewinding and replaying as frequently as he needed, was permitted to give evidence as to whether persons committing violent acts on the recording were the accused. However, research suggests that the accuracy of identification is not significantly enhanced by repeated replay: Bruce et al 'Face Recognition in Poor Quality Video Evidence from Security Surveillance' (1999) 10 Psychological Science 243. See also Munday, 'Videotape Evidence and the Advent of the Expert Ad Hoc' (1995) 159 JP 547.

[31]  *R v Browning* [1995] Crim LR 227, CA.          [32]  *R v Land* [1998] 1 Cr App R 301, CA.

[33]  [1972] 2 QB 391.          [34]  [1972] 1 QB 304 per Lord Widgery CJ at 313.

[35]  Cf *R v Skirving; R v Grossman* [1985] 2 All ER 705, a prosecution under the 1959 Act arising out of the publication of a book containing detailed explanations, instructions and 'recipes' on how best to make use of cocaine to obtain maximum effect. The Court of Appeal held that expert evidence on the characteristics of cocaine and the different effects of the various methods of ingesting the drug on the user and abuser was admissible because such characteristics and effects are not within the experience of the ordinary person. It was only when equipped with such information that the jury were in a position to decide whether the book had a tendency to deprave and corrupt.

[36]  [1968] 1 QB 159.

[37]  Per Ashworth J in *R v Stamford* [1972] 2 QB 391, CA at 397.

[38]  Per Lord Widgery CJ in *R v Anderson* [1972] 1 QB 304 at 313. See also the doubts expressed about the case by Lord Dilhorne in *DPP v Jordan* [1977] AC 699, HL at 722.

cards which were sold together with packets of bubble gum. The Divisional Court held that the magistrates had improperly refused to admit the evidence of experts in child psychiatry concerning the likely effect of the cards on children. Lord Parker CJ was of the opinion that, whereas expert opinion evidence as to whether a publication tends to deprave or corrupt may be unnecessary when considering its effect on an adult, it was admissible when considering its effect on children of various ages from five upwards because then 'any jury and any justices need all the help they can get'.

The distinction between matters calling for expertise and matters within the experience and knowledge of the jury is also illustrated by cases concerning a person's mental state. As we shall see, many of the decisions reflect the view that expertise is only called for in the case of a person suffering from a mental illness, a view which, it is submitted, is unnecessarily inflexible. As Farquharson LJ observed in *R v Strudwick*:[39]

The law is in a state of development in this area. There may well be other mental conditions about which a jury might require expert assistance in order to understand and evaluate their effect on the issues in a case.

Expert psychiatric evidence is a practical necessity in order to establish insanity[40] or diminished responsibility.[41] In *R v Smith*[42] the accused was convicted of murder by stabbing. His defence was automatism while asleep. The Court of Appeal held that psychiatric evidence adduced by the prosecution as to whether the evidence of the accused was consistent with his defence had been properly admitted, the type of automatism in question not being within the realm of the ordinary juryman's experience. Concerning the defence of duress by threats, expert medical evidence is admissible for the purposes of the subjective (but not the objective) test, provided that the mental condition or abnormality in question is relevant and its effects are outside the knowledge and experience of laymen.[43] However, according to *R v Walker*[44] psychiatric evidence may be admissible to show that an accused was suffering from some mental illness, mental impairment or recognized psychiatric condition, provided persons generally suffering from such a condition might be more susceptible to pressure and threats, and thus to assist the jury in deciding whether a reasonable person suffering from such a condition might have been impelled to act as the accused did, but evidence is not admissible that an accused who was not suffering from such an

---

[39] (1993) 99 Cr App R 326, CA at 332.

[40] See ss 1(1) and 2 of the Criminal Procedure (Insanity and Unfitness to Plead) Act 1991, below.

[41] See *R v Byrne* [1960] 2 QB 396 at 402, applied in *R v Dix* (1981) 74 Cr App R 306, CA. See also *R v Chan-Fook* [1994] 2 All ER 552, CA, applied in *R v Morris* [1998] 1 Cr App R 386, CA: where psychiatric injury is relied on as the basis for a charge of assault occasioning actual bodily harm and is not admitted by the defence, the Crown should call expert evidence, without which the question whether the assault occasioned such injury should not be left to the jury.

[42] [1979] 1 WLR 1445, CA.

[43] *R v Hegarty* [1994] Crim LR 353, CA. See also *R v Horne* [1994] Crim LR 584, CA; and cf *R v Hurst* [1995] 1 Cr App R 82, CA.

[44] [2003] All ER (D) 64 (Jun).

illness, impairment or condition, was especially timid, suggestible or vulnerable to pressure and threats.

Except where the accused comes into the class of mental defective or is afflicted by some medical condition affecting his mental state, expert medical or psychiatric evidence is not admissible on the question of mens rea. Thus in *R v Chard*[45] it was held that on a trial for murder, the judge had properly refused to admit the evidence of a medical witness on the intention of the accused to kill or do grievous bodily harm because, there being no question of insanity or diminished responsibility, the jury were able on the basis of their ordinary experience to judge for themselves the state of the accused's mind at the time of the alleged crime.[46] In *R v Wood*,[47] W, charged with murder, raised the partial defence under section 4 of the Homicide Act 1957 of unsuccessful execution of a suicide pact. Once the killing was proved, the questions were whether there was such a pact and whether W was acting in pursuance thereof and had the settled intention of dying in pursuance thereof. It was held that psychiatric evidence that W had a personality which to some extent was abnormal and liable to give way to excesses of behaviour under stress had been properly excluded, the matter not being outside the ordinary experience of the average juror. Similarly, in *R v Masih*,[48] in which the appellant, who was convicted of rape, suffered from no psychiatric illness but had an intelligence quotient of only 72, just above the level of sub-normality, it was held that on the question of whether he knew that the complainant was not consenting or was reckless as to whether she consented or not, expert psychiatric evidence about his state of mind, intelligence and ability to appreciate the situation had been properly excluded. The Court of Appeal held that, generally speaking, if an accused comes into the class of mental defective, with an IQ of 69 or below, then insofar as that defectiveness is relevant to an issue, expert evidence may be admitted, provided that it is confined to an assessment of the accused's IQ and an explanation of any relevant abnormal characteristics, to enlighten the jury on a matter that is abnormal and *ex hypothesi* outside their experience; but where an accused is within the scale of normality, albeit at the lower end, as the appellant was, expert evidence should generally be excluded.[49]

In *R v Toner*,[50] a case of attempted murder in which a doctor gave evidence that T may have been suffering from a minor hypoglycemic state caused by eating after a

---

[45] (1971) 56 Cr App R 268, CA.

[46] See also *R v Reynolds* [1989] Crim LR 220, CA and, in the case of adolescents, *R v Coles* [1995] 1 Cr App R 157, CA.

[47] [1990] Crim LR 264, CA.

[48] [1986] Crim LR 395, CA. See also *R v Hall* (1987) *The Times*, 15 July, CA and contrast *Schultz v R* [1982] WAR 171 (Supreme Court of Western Australia). In *R v Lupien* (1970) 9 DLR (3d) 1 (Supreme Court of Canada) it was held that psychiatric evidence is admissible to show a person's lack of capacity to form intent.

[49] However, as Hodgson J stated in *R v Silcott* [1987] Crim LR 765 (see [1988] Crim LR 293): 'To draw a strict line at 69/70 does seem somewhat artificial.' For a critical analysis of the notion that there is a clear line dividing normality and subnormality, see R D Mackay 'Excluding Expert Evidence: a tale of ordinary folk and common experience' [1991] Crim LR 800.

[50] (1991) 93 Cr App R 382, CA.

41-day fast, it was held that the defence should have been permitted to cross-examine him as to whether the effect of such an attack could have negatived T's special intent to kill and to cause serious bodily harm. The Court of Appeal could see no distinction between such medical evidence and medical evidence as to the effect of a drug on intent: both matters were outside the ordinary experience of jurors. Similarly in *R v Huckerby*[51] it was held that evidence that the accused was suffering from post-traumatic stress disorder, a recognized mental condition with which the jury would not be expected to be familiar, was admissible because relevant to an essential issue bearing upon his guilt or innocence, namely whether it caused him to panic and cooperate with criminals in circumstances where he would otherwise not have done so.

Expert evidence is generally inadmissible on the issue of a witness's credibility. In *Re S (a child)(adoption: psychological evidence)*,[52] an appeal against a care order, the judge at first instance had relied on the results of a personality questionnaire, including a 'Lie-Scale' measuring the mother's willingness to distort her responses in order to create a good impression. Allowing the appeal, it was held that the results of personality or psychometric tests should only rarely have any place in such cases because it is for judges to decide questions of credibility.

Expert evidence is also generally inadmissible to establish that an accused was likely to have been provoked. In *R v Turner*[53] the accused was convicted of murder by battering a girl fifteen times with a hammer. His defence was provocation, that he was deeply in love with the girl, who, he thought, was pregnant by him, and that he had struck her when she told him with a grin that while he had been in prison she had been sleeping with other men, that she could make money in this way, and that the child she was carrying was not his. The accused appealed on the ground that the trial judge had refused to admit psychiatric evidence on the issues of credibility and provocation. The psychiatrist intended to say, inter alia, that the accused had a deep emotional relationship with the girl which was likely to have caused an explosive release of blind rage when she confessed her infidelity to him and that, subsequent to the killing, he had behaved like someone suffering from profound grief. The Court of Appeal held that the jury needed no expert assistance in deciding either what reliance they could put upon the accused's evidence or the likelihood of his having been provoked, a matter which was well within ordinary human experience.[54] *R v Turner* is not easily reconciled with the earlier decision of the Privy Council in *Lowery v R*.[55] L and K were charged with murder, the circumstances being such that one or both of them must have committed the offence. There was no apparent motive for the murder. The Privy Council held that the trial judge had properly permitted K to call a psychologist to give evidence that L was aggressive, lacking in self-control, and more likely to have committed the offence than K. However, even if evidence of L's disposition was

---

[51] [2004] EWCA Crim 3251, [2004] All ER (D) 364 (Dec).

[52] [2004] EWCA Civ 1029, [2004] All ER (D) 593 (Jul). As to credibility, see also *R v Robinson* [1994] 3 All ER 346, CA and, in the case of children, *G v DPP* [1997] 2 All ER 755 at 759–60, CA.

[53] [1975] QB 834.

[54] See also per Lord Simon in *R v Camplin* [1978] AC 705, HL at 727.  [55] [1974] AC 85.

properly admissible,[56] it is unclear why it was given by an expert. In *R v Turner* Lawton LJ said:[57]

We adjudge *Lowery v R* to have been decided on its special facts. We do not consider that it is an authority for the proposition that in all cases psychologists and psychiatrists can be called to prove the probability of the accused's veracity.[58]

*Lowery v R* was relied upon by the House of Lords in *R v Randall*[59] as a precedent for the proposition that in appropriate cases the propensity to violence of an accused may be relevant to the issues between the prosecution and the co-accused tendering such evidence, but the House expressly declined to explore any doubts about the admissibility of *expert* evidence on propensity.[60]

The expert evidence of a psychiatrist or psychologist is admissible on the issue of the reliability or truth of a confession.[61] Such evidence will not be admissible before the jury on the issue of the truth of a confession made by an accused who, although he may have an abnormal personality, does not suffer from mental illness and is not below normal intelligence.[62] Equally, however, such evidence is not confined to evidence of personality disorders so severe as properly to be categorized as mental disorders. The test is not whether the abnormality fits into a recognized category such as anti-social personality disorder. That is neither necessary nor sufficient. There are two requirements. First, the abnormal disorder must be of the type which might render the confession unreliable, and in this respect there must be a very significant deviation from the norm. Second, there should be a history pre-dating the making of the confession, based not solely on what the accused says, which points to or explains the abnormality. When such evidence is admitted at trial, the jury should be directed that they are not obliged to accept it, but may consider it as throwing light on the personality of the accused and bringing to their attention aspects of it of which they might otherwise have been unaware.[63]

## 2 EXPERT WITNESSES

### (a) Expertise

A witness is competent to give expert evidence only if, in the opinion of the judge, he is properly qualified in the subject calling for expertise.[64] In rare cases it will be

---

[56] See now Ch 17.    [57] [1975] QB 834, CA at 842.

[58] See also *Toohey v Metropolitan Police Comr* [1965] AC 595, HL, *R v MacKenny* [2004] 2 Cr App R 32, CA and *R v Robinson* [1994] 3 All ER 346 (all in Ch 7); *R v Bracewell* (1978) 68 Cr App R 44; and *R v Rimmer and Beech* [1983] Crim LR 250, CA.

[59] [2004] 1 All ER 467, HL.    [60] See Per Lord Steyn at [30].

[61] See *R v Walker* [1998] Crim LR 211, CA and *R v Ward* [1993] 1 WLR 619, CA.

[62] *R v Weightman* (1990) 92 Cr App R 291, CA.

[63] *R v O'Brien* [2000] Crim LR 676, CA, applied in *R v Smith* [2003] EWCA Crim 927, [2003] All ER (D) 28 (Apr).

[64] But see ss 1(1) and 2 of the Criminal Procedure (Insanity and Unfitness to Plead) Act 1991: a jury shall not acquit on the ground of insanity, or make a determination of unfitness to plead, except on the evidence of

necessary to hold a *voir dire* to decide whether a purported expert should be allowed to give evidence, but in the vast majority of cases the judge will be able to make the decision on the basis of written material. The judge, during the trial, also has the power, should the need arise, to remove a witness's 'expert' status and limit his evidence to factual matters.[65]

An expert may have acquired his expertise through study, training or experience. Thus an engineer who understands the construction of harbours, the causes of their destruction and how remedied, may express his opinion on whether an embankment caused the decay of a harbour;[66] and a police officer with qualifications and experience in accident investigation may give expert opinion evidence on how a road accident occurred.[67] On the other hand, a medical orderly experienced in the treatment of cuts is not sufficiently qualified to express an opinion on whether a cut to the forehead was caused by a blunt instrument or a head-butt.[68] There is no requirement that the witness should have acquired his expertise professionally or in the course of his business. Thus in *R v Silverlock*[69] the Court for Crown Cases Reserved held that a solicitor who had studied handwriting for ten years, mostly as an amateur, had properly been allowed to give his opinion as to whether certain disputed handwriting was that of the accused.

Many of the cases concern the competence of a witness to give expert opinion evidence on a point of foreign law. A person has been held to be suitably qualified for these purposes if he is a practitioner in the foreign jurisdiction in question,[70] a former practitioner,[71] a person who has not practised in the jurisdiction but is qualified to do so[72] or a person who has acquired the appropriate expertise other than by practice, whether by academic study,[73] as an embassy official[74] or in the course of some non-legal profession or business such as banking[75] or trading.[76] Although at common law there is authority that a practitioner in the jurisdiction in question should *always* be called,[77] in civil proceedings section 4(1) of the Civil Evidence Act 1972 now declares that:

---

two or more registered doctors, at least one of whom is approved by the Secretary of State as having appropriate expertise. An expert, if competent to testify, is also compellable, even where having inadvertently advised both parties, he is loath to appear on behalf of one of them: *Harmony Shipping Co SA v Saudi Europe Line Ltd* [1979] 1 WLR 1380, CA.

[65] *R v G* [2004] 2 Cr App R 638, CA.      [66] *Folkes v Chadd* (1782) 3 Doug KB 157.

[67] *R v Oakley* (1979) 70 Cr App R 7, CA; *R v Murphy* [1980] QB 434, CA. Cf *Hinds v London Transport Executive* [1979] RTR 103, CA. See also *R v Hodges* [2003] 2 Cr App R 247, CA, below. See also, *sed quaere, R v Somers* [1963] 1 WLR 1306, CCA.

[68] *R v Inch* (1989) 91 Cr App R 51, C-MAC.      [69] [1894] 2 QB 766.

[70] *Baron de Bode's Case* (1845) 8 QB 208.

[71] *Re Duke of Wellington, Glentanar v Wellington* [1947] Ch 506.

[72] *Barford v Barford and McLeod* [1918] P 140.

[73] *Brailey v Rhodesia Consolidated Ltd* [1910] 2 Ch 95 (Reader in Roman-Dutch Law to the Council of Legal Education).

[74] *Dost Aly Khan's Goods* (1880) 6 PD 6.

[75] *de Beéche v South American Stores* [1935] AC 148, HL; *Ajami v Comptroller of Customs* [1954] 1 WLR 1405, PC.

[76] *Vander Donckt v Thellusson* (1849) 8 CB 812.      [77] *Bristow v Sequeville* (1850) 5 Exch 275.

a person who is suitably qualified to do so on account of his knowledge or experience is competent to give expert evidence as to the law of any country or territory outside the United Kingdom, or of any part of the United Kingdom other than England and Wales, irrespective of whether he has acted or is entitled to act as a legal practitioner there.

## (b) Independence

The role of an expert witness is special because he owes a duty to the court which he must discharge notwithstanding the interest of the party calling him.[78] In *Whitehouse v Jordan*[79] Lord Wilberforce said:

While some degree of consultation between experts and legal advisers is entirely proper, it is necessary that expert evidence presented to the court should be, and should be seen to be, the independent product of the expert, uninfluenced as to form or content by the exigencies of litigation.[80]

This passage was relied upon in *Liverpool Roman Catholic Archdiocesan Trustees Inc v Goldberg (No 3)*[81] where the expert was a good friend of the defendant on whose behalf he was called. The expert said that his personal sympathies were engaged to a greater degree than would probably be normal with an expert witness. It was held that this admission rendered the evidence unacceptable on grounds of policy: that justice must be seen to be done as well as done. While accepting that there was no statutory or other authority expressly excluding the expert evidence of a friend of one of the parties, it was held that where there is a relationship between them which a reasonable observer might think was capable of affecting the views of the expert so as to make him unduly favourable to the party calling him, his evidence should not be admitted, however unbiased his conclusions might probably be.[82] However, it has also been held that an employee of a party can be an independent expert, provided that the party can demonstrate that the employee has not only the relevant experience but also an awareness of his overriding duty, as an expert witness, to the court.[83]

## (c) Reliability

As we have seen, an expert will only be allowed to give an opinion if appropriately qualified to do so. However, English law, with notable exceptions, shows a general reluctance to impose additional conditions of admissibility relating to the reliability of expert evidence having regard to the techniques or theories on which it is based.

---

[78] See per Cresswell J in *National Justice Cia Naviera SA v Prudential Assurance Co Ltd, The Ikarian Reefer* [1993] 2 Lloyd's Rep 68.

[79] [1981] 1 WLR 246, HL at 256–7.

[80] The principle is now embodied in CPR r 35: see further, below.      [81] [2001] 1 WLR 2337, Ch D.

[82] The decision has since been doubted: see *Admiral Management Services Ltd v Para-Protect Europe Ltd* [2002] 1 WLR 272, Ch D at [33].

[83] *Field v Leeds City Council* [2001] CPLR 129.

This is curious given the obvious dangers, especially in criminal trials, of allowing the tribunal of fact to rely on 'expert' testimony of questionable reliability.[84]

*R v Gilfoyle*,[85] one of the exceptions, was a murder trial in which the only other possible explanation for the death was suicide. The Court of Appeal refused to hear the fresh evidence of a psychologist who had carried out a 'psychological autopsy' of the deceased. One of the reasons given for this conclusion was that the expert had identified no criteria by reference to which the court could test the quality of his opinions: there was no database comparing real and questionable suicides and there was no substantial body of academic writing approving his methodology. Another reason was the Canadian and United States authority pointing against the admission of such evidence. The court was of the view that the English approach accorded with the guiding principle in the United States, as stated in *Frye v United States*,[86] and to the effect that expert evidence based on novel or developing scientific techniques that are not generally accepted by the scientific community should be excluded. In fact, the test in *Frye* is no longer the guiding principle in the United States. In *Daubert v Merrell Dow Pharmaceuticals*[87] the Supreme Court held that in federal courts the test had been superseded by rule 702 of the Federal Rules of Evidence 1975; that the courts must ensure the reliability, as well as the relevance, of scientific evidence before admitting it; and that reliability is to be determined having regard to a number of factors, including whether the technique can be and has been tested, whether it has been the subject of publication and peer review, its error rate, and whether it is generally accepted.

In *R v Dallagher*,[88] where identity was in issue, evidence was received from two experts who had examined ear prints. The expertise of ear print comparison is in its relative infancy, and after the trial it emerged that other forensic scientists had misgivings about the extent to which ear print evidence alone can, in the present state of knowledge, safely be used to identify a suspect. It was held that the expert evidence had been properly admitted, but allowed the appeal and ordered a retrial on the basis that the fresh evidence, if given at trial, might reasonably have affected the approach of the jury to the identification evidence of the experts and thus affected their decision to convict. In reaching its decision that the expert evidence had been properly admitted, the court appeared to accept that the English approach is analogous to that to be found in rule 702 of the Federal Rules of Evidence and also referred to *Daubert v Merrell Dow Pharmaceuticals*. However, it had no regard to the factors listed in that case, none of which, if considered, would have supported the case for admission. Instead, it simply approved a passage from *Cross and Tapper on Evidence*[89] which, after a reference to the *Frye* approach, states:

The better, and now more widely accepted, view is that so long as a field is sufficiently

---

[84] See generally M Redmayne *Expert Evidence and Criminal Justice* (Oxford, 2001), ch 5 and WE O'Brien Jr 'Court scrutiny of expert evidence: Recent decisions highlight the tensions' (2003) 7 E&P 172.
[85] [2001] 2 Cr App R 57, CA.    [86] 293 F 1013 (DC Cir, 1923).    [87] 509 US 579 (1993).
[88] [2003] 1 Cr App R 195, CA.    [89] 9th edn, London, 1999, 523.

well-established to pass the ordinary tests of relevance and reliability, then no enhanced test for admissibility should be applied, but the weight of the evidence should be established by the same adversarial forensic techniques applicable elsewhere.

The same passage was also approved in *R v Luttrell*[90] where the court, while accepting that the reliability of expert evidence can be relevant to the issue of admissibility, rejected the argument that lip-reading evidence as to what was said by someone talking on a CCTV recording should not be admitted unless it could be seen to be reliable because the methods used were sufficiently explained to be tested in cross-examination and so to be verifiable or falsifiable.

The dangers of this relaxed approach are highlighted by the decisions in *R v Robb*[91] and *R v O'Doherty*.[92] In *R v Robb* a lecturer in phonetics was held to be well qualified by his academic training and practical experience to express an opinion as to the identity of a voice, notwithstanding that his auditory technique, which was to pay close attention to voice quality, pitch and pronunciation, was not generally respected by other experts in the field because it was not supplemented and verified by acoustic analysis based on physical measurements of resonance, frequency etc. In *R v O'Doherty* the prosecution expert at the trial gave evidence based on the same technique as the expert in *R v Robb*. On appeal the Court of Appeal for Northern Ireland received fresh expert evidence to the effect that auditory techniques, unless supplemented and verified by acoustic analysis, were an unreliable basis of speaker identification, and that, based on an acoustic analysis, the voice on the tape was not that of the accused. Allowing the appeal, the court observed that since *R v Robb*, 'time has moved on'. It was held that in the present state of scientific knowledge, no prosecution should be brought in Northern Ireland in which one of the planks is voice identification given by an expert which is solely confined to auditory analysis. There should also be expert evidence of acoustic analysis.[93]

In *R v Cannings*[94] Judge LJ, delivering the judgment of the Court of Appeal, said:

Experts in many fields will acknowledge the possibility that later research may undermine the accepted wisdom of today. 'Never say never' is a phrase which we have heard in many different contexts from expert witnesses. That does not normally provide a basis for rejecting the expert evidence, or indeed for conjuring up fanciful doubts about the possible impact of later research.

However, the court went on to say that in the case of two or more sudden unexplained infant deaths in the same family, in many important respects we are still at the frontiers of knowledge. It was held that, for the time being, where a full investigation is followed by a serious disagreement between reputable experts about the cause of

---

[90] [2004] 2 Cr App R 520, CA.          [91] (1991) 93 Cr App R 161, CA.
[92] [2003] 1 Cr App R 77, CA (NI).
[93] The court made three exceptions to its general statement: where the voices of a known group are being listened to and the issue is which voice has spoken which words, or where there are rare characteristics which render a speaker identifiable, or the issue relates to the accent or dialect of the speaker.
[94] [2004] 1 All ER 725 at [178].

death and a body of such expert opinion concludes that natural causes cannot be excluded as a reasonable and not a fanciful possibility, the prosecution of a parent or parents for murder should not be started or continued in the absence of additional cogent evidence extraneous to the expert evidence and tending to support the conclusion of deliberate harm.[95]

*R v Cannings* was distinguished in *R v Kai-Whitewind*.[96] K-W was convicted of the murder of her infant son. She had had difficulty bonding with the child and there was evidence that shortly after he was born she had felt like killing the child. The child died while in her sole care. On the day of his death, she had sought medical advice after the child had developed a spontaneous nosebleed, an extremely rare occurrence in the case of an infant. Post-mortem examinations revealed new and old blood in the lungs. According to the prosecution experts, this was consistent with two distinct episodes of upper airway obstruction, but the views of the defence experts were that death by natural causes was more probable than unnatural death or that the cause of death was unascertained. The appeal against conviction was dismissed. It was held that *R v Cannings* concerned inferences based upon coincidence, or the unlikelihood of two or more infant deaths in the same family, or one death where another child or other children in the family had suffered from unexplained 'Apparent Life Threatening Events'. There was essentially no evidence beyond the inferences based upon coincidence which the prosecution experts were prepared to draw but as to which other reputable experts in the same specialist field took a different view. Hence the need for additional cogent evidence. It did not follow from this that whenever there was a conflict between expert witnesses, the case for the prosecution had to fail unless the conviction was justified by evidence independent of the expert witnesses. In the instant case there was a single death, it was not suggested that any inference should be drawn against the accused from any previous incident involving any of her children, and the evidence about the child's condition found on the post-mortem examination was evidence of fact and precisely the kind of material which was sought and could not be found in *R v Cannings*. The dispute between experts about the interpretation of the findings at the post-mortem did not extinguish the findings themselves, and the jury had been entitled to evaluate the expert evidence, taking account of the facts found at the post-mortem and bearing in mind in addition, for example, that they related to an infant whose mother had spoken about killing him, had made a comment about smothering another child, who might have delayed reporting his death and who had elected not to give evidence.

### (d) Evidence of facts upon which an opinion is based

In many—probably most—cases, the expert will have no personal or first-hand knowledge of the facts upon which his opinion is based. For example, in *Beckwith v Sydebotham*[97] shipwrights expressed their opinion on the sea-worthiness of a ship

---

[95] The case is considered in more detail in Ch 8.     [96] (2005) *The Times* 11 May, 2005, CA.
[97] (1807) 1 Camp 116.

which they had not examined. In such a case, the expert should state the *assumed* facts upon which his opinion is based and examination-in-chief and cross-examination should take the form of *hypothetical* questions. The facts upon which the expert's opinion is based, sometimes referred to as 'primary facts', must be proved by admissible evidence.[98] The primary facts may be proved by calling the person with personal or first-hand knowledge of them to give direct evidence of them. Thus in *R v Mason*,[99] a murder trial in which a witness who had seen the deceased's body was called to describe the wounds, a surgeon, who had not seen the body, was asked whether the deceased had died from natural causes or in consequence of his wounds and whether the wounds could have been self-inflicted. Alternatively, under section 127 of the Criminal Justice Act 2003, the primary facts may be proved by the hearsay statement of the person with personal or first-hand knowledge of them, unless, on an application by a party to the proceedings, that is not in the interests of justice.[100] In some cases, the expert will have personal or first-hand knowledge of the facts in question, as when he examines an exhibit or visits the *locus in quo*, and in such a case he may testify as to both fact and opinion. In any event the expert should be asked in examination-in-chief to state the facts or assumed facts upon which his evidence is based so that the court can assess the value of his opinion.[101] 'If the expert has been misinformed about the facts or has taken irrelevant facts into consideration or has omitted to consider relevant ones, the opinion is likely to be valueless.'[102]

In criminal cases, although an expert cannot *prove* facts upon which his opinion is based but of which he has no personal or first-hand knowledge, because that would be a breach of the rule against hearsay,[103] he is entitled to rely upon such facts as a part of the process of forming an opinion and, in this sense, is not subject to the rule against hearsay in the same way as a non-expert or witness of fact. *English Exporters (London) Ltd v Eldonwall Ltd*,[104] which must now be read subject to the Civil Evidence Act 1995, provides an instructive example. In that case, landlords applied for the determination of a reasonable interim rent under the Landlord and Tenant Act 1954. Megarry J held that although a professional valuer, called as an expert witness to give his opinion as to the value of the property, could not give evidence of comparable rents of which he had no personal knowledge in order to establish those rents as matters of fact, because

---

[98] Per Lawton LJ in *R v Turner* [1975] QB 834 at 840, CA.     [99] (1911) 7 Cr App R 67, CCA.

[100] See Ch 10.

[101] But it seems that where an expert expresses an opinion based on primary facts derived from his use of a computer, for example the printout of a machine used by him to analyse the chemical constituents of a substance believed to be a particular drug, there is no *obligation* to produce the printout: see *R v Golizadeh* [1995] Crim LR 232, CA.

[102] Per Lawton LJ in *R v Turner* [1975] QB 834 at 840. In a case where the real factual issues between the parties will emerge with clarity only after all the factual evidence has been given, and the views of the experts will be of the greatest value if given in the light of that evidence, in the Commercial Court at least the High Court has power to order that all the factual evidence be given by both sides before any expert evidence is received: *Bayer v Clarkson Puckle Overseas Ltd* [1989] NLJR 256, QBD.

[103] See, eg, *R v Jackson* [1996] 2 Cr App R 420, CA

[104] [1973] Ch 415. See also *Ramsay v Watson* (1961) 108 CLR 642.

that would amount to inadmissible hearsay, he was entitled to express opinions that he had formed as to values even though substantial contributions to the formation of those opinions had been made by matters of which he had no first-hand knowledge but had learned about from sources such as journals, reports of auctions and other dealings, and information, relating to both particular and more general transactions, obtained from professional colleagues and others. Similarly, in *R v Bradshaw*,[105] a case of murder where the only issue at the trial was that of diminished responsibility, it was held that although doctors called by the defence could not state what the accused had told them about past symptoms as evidence of the existence of those symptoms, because that would infringe the rule against hearsay, they could give evidence of what the patient had told them in order to explain the grounds upon which they came to a conclusion with regard to his condition.[106]

Under the same doctrine, the expert may fortify his opinion by referring not only to any relevant research, tests or experiments which he has personally carried out, whether or not expressly for the purposes of the case, but also to works of authority, learned articles, research papers, letters and other similar material written by others and comprising part of the general body of knowledge falling within the field of expertise of the expert in question.[107] In *H v Schering Chemicals Ltd*,[108] for example, the issue being whether the drug Primodos had caused certain personal injuries and whether the defendants had been negligent in manufacturing and marketing it, it was held that expert witnesses were entitled to refer to the results of research into the drug and articles and letters about the drug published in medical journals. Bingham J said:

> If an expert refers to the results of research published by a reputable authority in a reputable journal the court would, I think, ordinarily regard those results as supporting inferences fairly to be drawn from them, unless or until a different approach was shown to be proper.[109]

In *R v Abadom*[110] the accused was convicted of robbery. The prosecution case rested on evidence that he had broken a window during the robbery and that fragments of glass embedded in his shoes had come from the window. An expert gave evidence that, as a result of a personal analysis of the samples, he found that the glass from the window and the glass in the shoes bore an identical refractive index. He also gave evidence that he had consulted unpublished statistics compiled by the Home Office Central Research Establishment which showed that the refractive index in question occurred in only 4 per cent of all glass samples investigated. He then expressed the opinion that there was a very strong likelihood that the glass in the shoes came from the window. On appeal it was argued that the evidence of the Home Office statistics was inadmissible hearsay because the expert had no knowledge of the analysis on

---

[105] (1985) 82 Cr App R 79, CA.

[106] Per Lord Lane CJ, (1985) 82 Cr App R 79 at 83, citing *Cross on Evidence* (5th edn London 1979) 446.

[107] *Davie v Edinburgh Magistrates* 1953 SC 34, Court of Session; *Seyfang v GD Searle & Co* [1973] QB 148 at 151. However, the court is only entitled to make use of those parts of the material which have been relied upon by the expert or upon which he has been cross-examined: see *Collier v Simpson* (1831) 5 C&P 73.

[108] [1983] 1 All ER 849.        [109] [1983] 1 All ER 849 at 853.        [110] [1983] 1 All ER 364, CA.

which the statistics had been based. The appeal was dismissed on the grounds that once the 'primary facts' on which an opinion is based have been proved by admissible evidence, the expert is entitled to draw on the work of others as part of the process of arriving at his conclusion. The primary facts in the instant case, that is the refractive indices of the glass from the window and the glass in the shoes, had been proved by admissible evidence (as it happened by the evidence of the expert himself on the basis of his own analysis). Accordingly the expert was entitled to refer to the Home Office statistics and this involved no infringement of the hearsay rule. Experts, it was said, should not limit themselves to drawing on material which has been published in some form: part of their experience and expertise lies in their knowledge and evaluation of unpublished material. The only proviso is that they should refer to such material in their evidence so that the cogency and probative value of their conclusions can be tested and evaluated by reference to it.[111]

*R v Abadom* was applied in *R v Hodges*,[112] a case of conspiracy to supply heroin, in which a very experienced drugs officer gave evidence partially deprived from what he had been told by others, including other officers, informants and drug users, as to the usual method of supplying heroin, its purchase price in a particular place at the time, and what weight was more than would have been for personal use alone. The relevant primary facts were the observations of the activities of the accused, the finding of 14 grammes of heroin in the possession of one of them and the finding of other drugs paraphernalia in his house. The court distinguished *R v Edwards*.[113] In that case, the issue was whether the accused intended to supply the ecstasy tablets found in his possession or whether they were for personal consumption. Witnesses for both the prosecution and defence, neither of whom had any medical or toxicological qualification, were not allowed to give evidence, based on what they had been told by drugs users, rather than any academic materials, as to the personal consumption rates of ecstasy tablet users, and the impact of use in terms of developing tolerance or suffering serious harm. The evidence was held to have been properly excluded on the basis that the witnesses lacked the appropriate expertise to exempt their opinions from the rule against hearsay.

The common-law doctrine under discussion has been preserved, in criminal proceedings, by statute. Section 118(1)8 of the Criminal Justice Act 2003 preserves 'Any rule of law under which in criminal proceedings an expert witness may draw on the body of expertise relevant to his field'.

### (e) Evidence on ultimate issues

Historically, the courts have striven to prevent any witness from expressing his opinion on an ultimate issue, that is one of the very issues which the court has to determine. In

---

[111] Cf *R v Bradshaw* (1985) 82 Cr App R 79, CA, above, where it was held that if the doctors' opinions had been based entirely upon the 'hearsay' statements of the accused as to his past symptoms and the accused had elected not to testify and thus not provided any direct evidence as to such symptoms, the judge would have been justified in telling the jury that the defence case was based upon a flimsy or non-existent foundation.
[112] [2003] 2 Cr App R 247, CA.     [113] [2001] EWCA Crim 2185 [2001] All ER (D) 271 (Oct).

*Haynes v Doman*,[114] for example, the issue being the reasonableness of a covenant in restraint of trade, Lord Lindley MR held that affidavits from persons in the trade expressing their views on the reasonableness of the clause on which the case turned were out of place and inadmissible. The justification of the rule is that insofar as such evidence might unduly influence the tribunal of fact, it prevents witnesses from usurping the function of the court: witnesses are called to testify, not to decide the case. The rule is open to criticism on a number of levels.[115] The objection of undue influence makes no allowance for cases in which the tribunal of fact is a professional judge rather than a jury, overlooks the frequency of conflicts in expert testimony and is largely incompatible with the very justification for admitting expert evidence, that the drawing of inferences from the facts in question calls for an expertise which the tribunal of fact does not possess. However, in practice the rule is often of no more than semantic effect: the expert is allowed to express his opinion provided that the diction employed is not noticeably the same as that which will be used when the matter is subsequently considered by the court![116] Whatever its merits, in civil proceedings the rule has been abolished. Section 3(1) of the Civil Evidence Act 1972 provides that:

Subject to any rules of court made in pursuance of this Act, where a person is called as a witness in any civil proceedings, his opinion on any relevant matter on which he is qualified to give expert evidence shall be admissible in evidence.

Section 3(3) reads:

In this section 'relevant matter' includes an issue in the proceedings in question.

In family law cases involving suspected child abuse, expert evidence may relate to the presence and interpretation of physical, mental, behavioural and emotional signs, but often necessarily includes a view as to the likely veracity of the child. In this context, in *Re M and R (minors)*,[117] it was held that it is 'plainly right' that 'issue' in section 3(3) *can* include an issue of credibility. It is submitted that the decision is perhaps best regarded as an exception, rather than the general rule, which may be justified on the basis that when dealing with children the court needs 'all the help it can get'.[118] In the normal case, expert evidence of credibility will be inadmissible because unnecessary, being a matter on which the tribunal of fact can form its own opinion without the assistance of an expert.

Technically, the ultimate issue rule still operates in criminal proceedings, but in

---

[114] [1899] 2 Ch 13, CA.

[115] See generally the 17th Report of the Law Reform Committee, 'Evidence of Opinion and Expert Evidence' (Cmnd 4889) paras 266–71; 11th Report, Criminal Law Revision Committee (Cmnd 4991); and RD Jackson 'The Ultimate Issue Rule: One Rule Too Many' [1984] Crim LR 75.

[116] See, eg, *Rich v Pierpont* (1862) 3 F&F 35 and per Lord Parker CJ in *DPP v A & B C Chewing Gum Ltd* [1968] 1 QB 159 at 164.

[117] [1996] 4 All ER 239, CA.      [118] [1996] 4 All ER 239 at 249.

relation to expert witnesses is in practice largely ignored.[119] In *R v Hookway*,[120] for example, it was recognized that expert evidence of 'facial mapping' is sufficient, by itself, to establish the identity of the accused; in *R v Mason*,[121] as we have seen, a surgeon was asked for his opinion whether a person died in consequence of his wounds and whether they could have been self-inflicted; and in *R v Holmes*[122] the Court of Criminal Appeal held that it was not improper to cross-examine a doctor called by the accused in a murder trial about whether the accused's conduct after the offence indicated that he knew the nature of the act and that it was contrary to the law of the land, both issues, of course, being central to the defence of insanity within the M'Naghten rules.[123] In *DPP v A & B C Chewing Gum Ltd*[124] Lord Parker CJ, although of the opinion that in a prosecution under the Obscene Publications Act 1959 it would be wrong to ask an expert directly whether a publication tended to deprave and corrupt, later observed that more and more inroads had been made into the rule against opinion evidence on ultimate issues:[125]

Those who practise in the criminal courts see every day cases of experts being called on the question of diminished responsibility, and although technically the final question 'Do you think he was suffering from diminished responsibility?' is strictly inadmissible, it is allowed time and time again without any objection.

## (f) Weight

In cases in which expert opinion evidence is properly adduced, the weight to be attached to it is a matter entirely for the tribunal of fact. The duty of experts, it has been said, 'is to furnish the judge or jury with the necessary scientific criteria for testing the accuracy of their conclusions, so as to enable the judge or jury to form their own independent judgment by the application of these criteria to the facts proved in evidence'.[126] Thus, in the civil context, although lay evidence should not be preferred

---

[119] In its 11th Report, the Criminal Law Revision Committee was of the opinion that the rule probably no longer existed: para 268 (Cmnd 4991). See also per Lord Taylor CJ in *R v Stockwell* (1993) 97 Cr App R 260 at 265: the rule has become 'a matter of form rather than substance'. Contrast, *sed quaere*, *R v Jeffries* [1997] Crim LR 819, CA.

[120] [1999] Crim LR 750, CA.

[121] (1911) 7 Cr App R 67, CCA. See also *R v Smith* [1979] 1 WLR 1445, CA, above; and *R v Silcott* [1987] Crim LR 765, CC, where the educational subnormality of one accused was described by the experts as 'very likely' and 'significantly likely' to render 'unreliable' a confession allegedly made by him. See s 76(2)(b) of the Police and Criminal Evidence Act 1984, Ch 13.

[122] [1953] 1 WLR 686. Contrast *R v Wright* (1821) Russ&Ry 456.

[123] See also *R v Udenze* [2001] EWCA Crim 1381 (in a rape case, expert evidence as to the effects of alcohol on the complainant's ability to give informed consent); and *R v Hodges* [2003] 2 Cr App R 247, above (in a case of supplying drugs, expert evidence that the amount found was more than would have been for personal use alone).

[124] [1968] 1 QB 159.     [125] [1968] 1 QB 159 at 164.

[126] Per Lord President Cooper in *Davie v Edinburgh Magistrates* 1953 SC 34 at 40, Court of Session. Thus concerning voice identification, the jury, in forming their own judgment on the opinions of the experts, are entitled to know the features of the voice to which they paid attention (*R v Robb* (1991) 93 Cr App R 161 at 166) and to hear the tapes which they analysed (*R v Bentum* (1989) 153 JP 538, CA).

to expert evidence without good reason,[127] it has been held that there is no principle of law preventing a judge from preferring the evidence of lay claimants whom he finds to be honest over the evidence of a jointly instructed expert with whose evidence he can find no fault.[128] Similarly, on the question whether or not a will was forged, a court may prefer the evidence of non-expert attesting witnesses to that of a handwriting expert.[129] Equally, in the criminal context, it has been held that it is incumbent on magistrates to approach expert evidence critically, even if no expert is called on the other side and to be willing to reject it if it leaves questions unanswered.[130] In Crown Court cases in which expert opinion evidence is given on an ultimate issue, the judge should make clear to the jury that they are not bound by the opinion, and that the issue is for them to decide.[131] The same applies where the evidence does not relate to an ultimate issue, but there is no inflexible requirement that the warning take any particular form.[132] It is a misdirection to tell the jury that expert evidence should be accepted if uncontradicted[133] or in the absence of reasons for rejecting it.[134] However, it has also been held to be wrong to direct a jury that they may disregard expert opinion evidence when the only evidence adduced dictates one answer.[135] In an attempt to reconcile the authorities, in *R v Sanders*,[136] a case concerning the defence of diminished responsibility, it was held that if there are no other circumstances to consider, unequivocal, uncontradicted medical evidence favourable to an accused should be accepted by a jury and they should be so directed; but where there are other circumstances to consider (including, presumably, the nature of the killing, the conduct of the accused before, at the time of and after it, and any history of mental abnormality), then the medical evidence, though unequivocal and uncontradicted, must be assessed in the light of those circumstances.

If there is conflicting expert evidence, the tribunal of fact is obviously forced to make a choice. For these purposes, no less than when deciding whether to accept the evidence of even a single expert witness, the tribunal of fact may take into account an expert's qualifications and how they were acquired, his overall credibility as a witness

---

[127] See *Re B (a minor)* [2000] 1 WLR 790, CA.

[128] *Armstrong v First York Ltd* (2005) *The Times*, 19 Jan. See also *Stevens v Simons* [1988] CLY 1161, CA: the fact that an agreed medical report contained an opinion that symptoms suffered by the plaintiff were not attributable to injuries sustained in an accident, did not prevent the judge, having read the reports and heard the evidence, from concluding that such symptoms were so attributable.

[129] *Fuller v Strum* (2000) *The Times*, 14 Feb 2001.

[130] *DPP v Wynne* (2001) *Independent*, 19 Feb 2001, DC.

[131] Per Lord Taylor CJ in *R v Stockwell* (1993) 97 Cr App R 260.

[132] *R v Fitzpatrick* [1999] Crim LR 832, CA.     [133] *Davie v Edinburgh Magistrates* 1953 SC 34 at 40.

[134] Per Diplock LJ in *R v Lanfear* [1968] 2 QB 77, CA.

[135] *Anderson v R* [1972] AC 100, PC. See also *R v Matheson* [1958] 1 WLR 474, CCA: in a murder trial, if there are no facts or circumstances to displace or throw a doubt on unchallenged medical evidence of diminished responsibility, a verdict of guilty will not be in accordance with the evidence; and *R v Bailey* (1977) 66 Cr App R 31n, CCA: although juries are not bound to accept such expert medical evidence, they must act on it, and if there is nothing before them to cast doubt on it, cannot reject it. But see also *Walton v R* [1978] AC 788, PC, followed in *R v Kiszko* (1978) 68 Cr App R 62, CA.

[136] (1991) 93 Cr App R 245, CA.

and the extent to which, if at all, his evidence in chief was based on assumed facts which do not accord with those ultimately established.

## 3  RESTRICTIONS ON, AND DISCLOSURE OF, EXPERT EVIDENCE IN CIVIL CASES

In *Access to Justice. Final Report*,[137] Lord Woolf regarded expert evidence as one of the major generators of unnecessary cost in civil litigation, operating against the principles of proportionality and access to justice. He also reiterated concerns about the lack of impartiality of experts, of whom it has been said, 'it is often quite surprising to see with what facility and to what extent, their views can be made to correspond with the wishes or the interests of the parties who call them'.[138] As one commentator has observed: 'The court hears not the most expert opinions, but those favourable to the respective parties.'[139] Lord Woolf's Final Report made a number of recommendations which formed the basis of the new rules to be found in Part 35 of the Civil Procedure Rules and its accompanying Practice Direction.[140] In the case of testifying experts, ie those who have been instructed to prepare or give expert *evidence*, they impose an overriding duty to the court, create a duty to restrict the amount of expert evidence, and introduce new requirements as to the form in which expert evidence shall be given and as to advance disclosure. They do not apply, however, to an 'advising expert', ie an expert retained by a party for the purpose of advising that party, who owes no duty to the court and whose advice, if given in contemplation of legal proceedings, will be privileged against disclosure. The use of advising experts is quite common in relation to commercial litigation.

### (a)  The duty and power to restrict expert evidence and the duty of the expert

The duty to restrict expert evidence, and the overriding duty of the expert to the court, are governed by rules 35.1 and 35.3, which are self-explanatory.

35.1  Expert evidence shall be restricted to that which is reasonably required to resolve the proceedings.

35.3  (1)  It is the duty of an expert to help the court on the matters within his expertise.

(2)  This duty overrides any obligation to the person from whom he has received instructions or by whom he is paid.

The expert, therefore, in helping the court, should act in as impartial and objective a manner as he can.

The court's power to restrict expert evidence is governed by rule 35.4, which allows the court, at the stage when it gives directions about expert evidence, to decide

---

[137] HMSO (1996).          [138] Taylor *Treatise on the Law of Evidence* (12th edn London 1931) 59.

[139] John Basten 'The Court Expert in Civil Trials, a Comparative Appraisal' (1977) 40 MLR 174.

[140] Excepting rr 35.1, 35.3, 35.7, and 35.8, Part 35 does not apply to claims which have been allocated to the small claims track: CPR r 27.2(1)e.

whether to permit a party to adduce expert evidence, and to put an upper limit on the expert's fees and expenses.

35.4 (1) No party may call an expert or put in evidence an expert's report without the court's permission.

    (2) When a party applies for permission under this rule he must identify—
        (a) the field in which he wishes to rely on expert evidence; and
        (b) where practicable the expert in that field on whose evidence he wishes to rely.

    (3) If permission is granted under this rule it shall be in relation only to the expert named or the field identified under paragraph (2).

    (4) The court may limit the amount of the expert's fees and expenses that the party who wishes to rely on the expert may recover from any other party.

Where, for no good reason, an application for permission to call an expert under rule 35.4 is not made in good time, it is unlikely to be granted if made so shortly before the trial that it would work a significant injustice to the other side.[141]

## (b) Written reports

Under the new rules, there is a presumption—in the case of claims on the fast track, a strong presumption—that if expert evidence is permitted, it should be given by means of an expert's written report, rather than by calling the expert as a witness. Rule 35.5 provides as follows:

    (1) Expert evidence is to be given in a written report unless the court directs otherwise.

    (2) If a claim is on the fast track, the court will not direct an expert to attend a hearing unless it is necessary to do so in the interests of justice.

## (c) The single joint expert

Rule 35.7 challenges the notion that where both parties wish to adduce expert evidence, there is a need for two experts: it permits the court to direct that the evidence should be given by a single joint expert. As we shall see, the parties themselves may agree to such a direction, which the court may then approve. Indeed, as a general rule, good practice will require a party to attempt to agree a joint expert with his opponent rather than to instruct his own expert. This practice is promoted by the pre-action protocols: see, eg, paragraph 2.11 of the Notes of Guidance in the Pre-Action Protocol for Personal Injury Claims. Of course, there is nothing in the Civil Procedure Rules to prevent a party from instructing his own expert, and this may well be thought to be appropriate in a case in which a claimant needs expert assistance in order to decide whether he has a valid claim at all. However, where a party obtains an expert's report without the approval of the court, there is a real risk that he will not recover his costs in this respect: under rule 35.4, the court may refuse permission to admit the report or call the expert, and under rule 35.7 may direct the use of a jointly instructed expert.

---

[141] *Calenti v North Middlesex NHS Trust* (2001) LTL 10 Apr 2001, QBD.

Rule 35.7 does not create a presumption in favour of a direction that there should be one expert only, but in many cases, such a direction will give effect to the 'overriding objective', especially in saving expense and putting the parties on an equal footing. However, much may turn on the value and complexity of the litigation: single joint experts are not commonly appointed in Commercial Court cases, and there is a greater willingness to permit two experts in multi-track cases, which are typically more complex than fast track claims. It can be wrong to appoint a single joint expert on a medical issue on which there are different schools of thought.[142] In *Peet v Mid Kent Healthcare Trust*,[143] a claim of medical negligence, it was said that whereas in the great majority of cases non-medical evidence dealing with quantum should be given by a single expert rather than by experts called on behalf of each party, it is sometimes difficult to restrict the medical evidence because of the difficult issues as to the appropriate form and standard of treatment required. In *ES v Chesterfield & North Derbyshire Royal Hospital NHS Trust*[144] the claimant alleged negligence on the part of an obstetric registrar and his consultant, the value of the claim being about £1.5 million. The claimant appealed a direction limiting the expert evidence to one expert obstetrician on each side. The Court of Appeal, having regard to both the 'overriding objective' and the terms of rule 35.1, allowed the appeal and permitted the claimant to call two expert obstetricians. Relevant factors taken into account included the value and complexity of the case and the fact that the obstetric registrar and his consultant were both able to give evidence of their actions based on their professional expertise.

Rule 35.7 provides as follows:

(1)  Where two or more parties wish to submit expert evidence on a particular issue, the court may direct that the evidence on that issue is to be given by one expert only.

(2)  The parties wishing to submit the expert evidence are called 'the instructing parties'.

(3)  Where the instructing parties cannot agree who should be the expert, the court may—
     (a)  select the expert from a list prepared or identified by the instructing parties; or
     (b)  direct that the expert be selected in such other manner as the court may direct.

In most cases, it is likely that the court will expect the parties to be able to agree who the expert should be. Given the overriding duty of the expert to the court, it may be difficult for a party to object to a particular expert, even if it is known that he has previously been instructed extensively or exclusively by the firm of solicitors representing the other party, or has previously acted only on behalf of, say, defendant employers or insurance companies.

Where the court has directed that the evidence on a particular issue should be given by one expert only, but there are a number of disciplines relevant to that issue, a leading expert in the dominant discipline should be used, who should prepare the

---

[142]  *Oxley v Penwarden* [2001] Lloyds Rep Med 347, CA.        [143]  [2002] 1 WLR 210, CA at [6]–[7].
[144]  (2003) EWCA Civ 1284.

general part of the report and be responsible for annexing or incorporating the contents of any reports from experts in the other disciplines.[145]

Rule 35.8 deals with the instructions to be given to a single joint expert:

(1) Where the court gives a direction under rule 35.7 for a single joint expert to be used, each instructing party may give instructions to the expert.

(2) When an instructing party gives instructions to the expert he must, at the same time, send a copy of the instructions to the other instructing parties.

(3) The court may give directions about—
    (a) the payment of the expert's fees and expenses; and
    (b) any inspection, examination or experiments which the expert wishes to carry out.

(4) The court may, before an expert is instructed—
    (a) limit the amount that can be paid by way of fees and expenses to the expert; and
    (b) direct that the instructing parties pay that amount into court.

(5) Unless the court otherwise directs, the instructing parties are jointly and severally liable for the payment of the expert's fees and expenses.

In cases in which one party has exclusive access to information about the basic facts on which expert opinion will need to be based, it will be difficult if not impossible for the other party to properly instruct an expert without access to that information. Rule 35.9 therefore empowers the court to direct the one party to provide such information to the other:

35.9 Where a party has access to information which is not reasonably available to the other party, the court may direct the party who has access to the information to—
    (a) prepare and file a document recording the information; and
    (b) serve a copy of that document on the other party.

Where the court makes such a direction, the document to be prepared should set out sufficient details of any facts, tests or experiments which constitute the information to enable the other party to assess and understand its significance.[146]

Where the parties have instructed a single joint expert, it is not permissible for one party to have a conference with the expert in the absence of the other, without the latter's prior written consent. A conclusion to the contrary would be inconsistent with the concept of a jointly instructed expert owing an equal duty of openness and confidentiality to both parties.[147]

Where a court has directed that evidence on an issue be given by a single joint expert and the parties agree who the expert should be, a party who is unhappy with the expert's report will be refused permission to call a further expert unless such refusal would be unjust having regard to the 'overriding objective'.[148] The discretion may be exercised against the party if there is only a modest amount at stake and therefore it would be disproportionate to adduce further expert evidence.[149] Other

---

[145] PD 35, para 6.     [146] PD 35, para 3.
[147] *Peet v Mid Kent Healthcare Trust* [2002] 1 WLR 210, CA.
[148] *Daniels v Walker* [2001] 1 WLR 1382, CA.     [149] Ibid.

relevant factors to be taken into account include the nature and importance of the issues, their number, the reasons for requiring another expert, the effect of adducing the additional evidence and any delay likely to be caused.[150]

Under paragraph 3.14 of the Pre-Action Protocol for Personal Injury Claims, before any party instructs an expert, he should give the other party the name(s) of one or more experts whom he considers suitable to instruct. Under paragraph 3.16, the other party may object to one or more of the named experts and the first party should then instruct a mutually acceptable expert. Such an expert needs to be distinguished from a single joint expert. The latter is instructed by both parties, both are liable for his fees and both have an equal right to see his report. A mutually acceptable expert is instructed on behalf of one party, who is usually liable to pay his fees, and his report is protected by litigation privilege, unless the instructing party chooses to waive it. Thus athough the Protocol encourages and promotes the voluntary disclosure of medical reports, it does not require it.[151]

### (d) Written questions to experts

In cases in which the expert evidence takes the form of a written report, whether prepared by a single joint expert or an expert instructed by a party, there will obviously be no opportunity to question him on oath in order either to clarify any part of his report or to challenge him on such matters as his methodology, the reasons for his opinion, any expert literature upon which he has relied, opposing expert opinion, and so on. For reasons of this kind, provision has been made to allow written questions to be put to the expert before the trial. A party is entitled to put such questions, if they are for the purpose only of clarification of the report; but if they are for some other purpose, they may only be asked if the court gives permission or the other party agrees. Rule 35.6 provides as follows:

(1) A party may put to—
    (a) an expert instructed by another party; or
    (b) a single joint expert appointed under rule 35.7, written questions about his report.[152]

(2) Written questions under paragraph (1)—
    (a) may be put once only;
    (b) must be put within 28 days of service of the expert's report; and
    (c) must be for the purpose only of clarification of the report; unless in any case,
        (i) the court gives permission; or
        (ii) the other party agrees.

(3) An expert's answers to questions put in accordance with paragraph (1) shall be treated as part of the expert's report.

(4) Where—

---

[150] *Cosgrave v Pattison* [2001] CPLR 177, Ch D.    [151] *Carlson v Townsend* [2001] 3 All ER 663, CA.
[152] If the questions are sent direct, a copy of the questions should, at the same time, be sent to the other party or parties: PD 35, para 5.2.

(a) a party has put a written question to an expert instructed by another party in accordance with this rule; and

(b) the expert does not answer that question,

the court may make one or both of the following orders in relation to the party who instructed the expert—

(i) that the party may not rely on the evidence of that expert; or

(ii) that the party may not recover the fees and expenses of that expert from any other party.

Rule 35.6(2)(c) allows a party, with the permission of the court or other party, to ask about matters not covered in the expert's report, provided that they are within his expertise, and thereby renders the expert akin to a court expert.[153] The fact that experts can be required to answer written questions normally means that there is no need for a single joint expert's evidence to be amplified or tested by cross-examination of the expert. The court has a discretion to permit such amplification or cross-examination, but this should be restricted as far as possible.[154] If, exceptionally, the expert is to be subject to cross-examination, then he should know in advance what topics are to be covered, and where fresh material is to be adduced for his consideration, this should be done in advance of the hearing.[155]

## (e) The contents of the expert's report

An expert's report must comply with the requirements set out in Practice Direction 35,[156] which provides that a report must give details of the expert's qualifications; give details of any literature or other material relied on; set out the substance of all facts and instructions given to him which are material to the opinions expressed or upon which those opinions are based; make clear which facts in the report are within his own knowledge; say who carried out any test or experiment which he has used for the report and whether or not it was carried out under his supervision; give the qualifications of the person who carried out any such test or experiment; where there is a range of opinion on the matters dealt with in the report, summarize it and give reasons for his own opinion; contain a summary of his conclusions; if he is not able to give his opinion without qualification, state the qualification; and state that he understands his duty to the court and has complied and will continue to comply with that duty.[157] His report must also be verified by a statement of truth.[158]

Under rule 35.10(2), at the end of the expert's report there must be a statement that he understands his duty to the court and has complied with it. Rule 35.10(3) and (4) provide as follows:

(3) The expert's report must state the substance of all material instructions, whether written or oral, on the basis of which the report was written.

---

153 *Mutch v Allen* [2001] CPLR 200, CA.

154 *Peet v Mid Kent Healthcare Trust* [2002] 1 WLR 210, CA at [28].

155 *Popek v National Westminster Bank plc* [2002] EWCA Civ 42.    156 CPR r 35.10(1).

157 PD 35, para 2.2.    158 PD 35, para 2.3.

(4) The instructions referred to in paragraph (3) shall not be privileged against disclosure but the court will not, in relation to those instructions—
(a) order disclosure of any specific document; or
(b) permit any questioning in court, other than by the party who instructed the expert,
unless it is satisfied that there are reasonable grounds to consider the statement of instructions given under paragraph (3) to be inaccurate or incomplete.

Paragraph 4 of Practice Direction 35 states that cross-examination of the expert on the contents of his instructions will not be allowed unless the court permits it (or unless the party who gave the instructions consents to it). Paragraph 4 also states that if the court is satisfied that there are 'reasonable grounds' under rule 35.10(4)(b), then it will allow the cross-examination where it appears to be in the interests of justice to do so.

The intention behind rule 35.10(4) is to encourage the setting out fully of material instructions and facts, including, for example, witness statements provided to the experts and the previous report of another expert. However, the obligation under rule 35.10(3) is not to set out all the information and material supplied to the expert, but to disclose the 'substance of all material instructions'. Ordinarily the expert is to be trusted to comply with rule 35.10(3), and under rule 35.10(4) the party on the other side may not as a matter of course call for disclosure: there must be some concrete fact giving rise to the 'reasonable grounds' to which rule 35.10(4) refers.[159]

The requirements of PD 35 are intended to focus the mind of the expert on his responsibilities in order that litigation may progress in accordance with the overriding principles in CPR Part 1. If an expert demonstrates that he has no conception of those requirements, as when he fails to include in his report statements that he understands his duty to the court and has complied with it, and statements setting out the substance of all material instructions, then he may properly be debarred from acting as an expert witness in the case.[160] Moreover, in appropriate circumstances, the court may make a costs order against an expert who, by his evidence, has caused significant expense to be incurred, and has done so in flagrant and reckless disregard of his duties to the court.[161]

## (f) Discussions between experts

Rule 35.12 is another provision designed to save court time and reduce costs. It allows the court, at any stage, in cases in which the parties have been permitted to use competing experts, to direct a 'without prejudice'[162] discussion between the experts for the purpose of requiring them to identify the issues in the proceedings and, where possible, to reach agreement on an issue. The court may specify the issues which the experts must discuss. It may also direct that following the discussion the experts must

---

[159] *Lucas v Barking, Havering and Redbridge Hospitals NHS Trust* [2003] 4 All ER 720, CA.
[160] *Stevens v Gullis* [2000] 1 All ER 527, CA.      [161] *Phillips v Symes* [2004] EWHC 2330 (Ch).
[162] See Ch 20.

prepare a statement for the court showing the issues on which they agreed and the issues on which they disagreed with a summary of their reasons for disagreeing. However, the content of the discussion between the experts shall not be referred to at the trial unless the parties agree; and where the experts do agree on an issue, their agreement will not bind the parties unless they expressly agree to be bound by it.

### (g) Disclosure, non-disclosure and inspection

Rules 35.11 and 35.13 provide as follows.

35.11 Where a party has disclosed an expert's report, any party may use that expert's report as evidence.

35.13 A party who fails to disclose an expert's report may not use the report at the trial or call the expert to give evidence orally unless the court gives permission.

Where an expert has been asked to prepare a report, the dominant purpose being to use it in relation to anticipated or pending litigation, the report will be the subject of litigation privilege.[163] Neither the Civil Evidence Act 1972 nor the Civil Procedure Rules compel the disclosure of privileged documents. However, under rule 35.13 a party will normally only be allowed to introduce an expert report in evidence, or to call its maker, if he has disclosed the report. Although the court may give permission for the evidence to be adduced notwithstanding failure to disclose the.report, it is submitted that the new cards-on-the-table approach to civil litigation, which the courts will generally expect of the parties, is such that permission will rarely be granted, and then only in very exceptional circumstances.

Rule 35.13 does not provide a power to order disclosure of drafts of experts' reports, prepared for the purpose of discussion with a party's advisers prior to the completion of the expert's final report, and protected by litigation privilege. The specific and limited exemption from privilege of the material instructions pursuant to rule 35.10(4)[164] shows that there was no intention to abrogate the privilege attaching to draft expert reports.[165] However, where a party is dissatisfied with an expert's report and seeks permission to rely on a second, substitute expert's report, permission may be conditional upon disclosure of the final report of the first expert[166] or, in cases where the first expert did not complete a final report, any draft interim report containing the substance of his opinion on the various issues in the case.[167]

The effect of rule 35.11 is that where a party has been given permission to use an expert and has disclosed his expert's report, then the opposing party may use it as evidence at the trial, and this remains the case even if the first party has changed his mind and no longer intends to rely upon it.

Under rule 33.6, a party intending to introduce evidence, such as a plan, photograph or model, which forms part of expert evidence but is not contained in an expert's report, must give notice of his intention when the expert report is served on

---

[163] See Ch 20.     [164] See above.     [165] *Jackson v Marley Davenport Ltd* (2004) *The Times*, 7 Oct.

[166] *Beck v Ministry of Defence* [2004] PIQR 1.

[167] Per Dyson LJ, obiter, in *Vasiliou v Hajigeorgiou* [2005] 3 All ER 17, CA.

the other party, and must give the other party an opportunity to inspect it and to agree to its admission without further proof.[168]

## (h) Directions and agreed directions

When a court allocates a case to the fast track, the directions it gives for the management of the case will include directions on expert evidence. If the parties have filed agreed directions, the court may approve them. Agreed directions may include a direction that no expert evidence is required; or directions for a single joint expert, or the exchange and agreement of expert evidence and without prejudice meetings of experts.[169] There are similar provisions for cases allocated to the multi-track.[170]

Under rule 35.14, an expert may file a written request for directions to assist him in carrying out his function as an expert. This may be done without giving notice to any party, although the court, when it gives directions, may direct that a party be served with a copy of the request and the directions. Rule 35.14 provides a useful safeguard for the expert in need of further guidance as to what is being asked of him, especially in cases where to take further instructions from a party may be regarded as a breach of his overriding duty to help the court.

## 4  THE DISCLOSURE OF EXPERT EVIDENCE IN CRIMINAL CASES

At common law, the prosecution at a trial on indictment are not permitted to take the defence by surprise by adducing any evidence of which they have not given advance notice to the defence; and where such notice has not been given, the accused may apply for an adjournment.[171] Prior to the Police and Criminal Evidence Act 1984, the defence, however, subject to only one exception, were under no obligation to disclose any part of their case in advance of the trial. The exception, contained in section 11 of the Criminal Justice Act 1967, required the accused to give advance notice of particulars of an alibi defence.[172] The Royal Commission on Criminal Procedure proposed an extension of the requirement of pre-trial disclosure to other defences, such as those depending on medical or expert scientific evidence, where the element of surprise involves some risk of the trial being adjourned, so that the prosecution may evaluate the evidence, undertake further inquiries and, if necessary, call its own experts in rebuttal.[173] The recommendation was adopted. Rule 24 of the Criminal Procedure Rules 2005[174] provides as follows:

---

[168] In medical negligence claims, there is also a standard direction dealing with disclosure of unpublished literature and lists of published literature on which an expert proposes to rely: see *Wardlaw v Farrar* [2003] 4 All ER 1358, CA.

[169] See CPR r 28.2 and 28.3 and PD28 paras 3.5–3.9.

[170] See CPR r 29.2 and 29.4 and PD29 paras 4.7–4.13.

[171] *R v Wright* (1934) 25 Cr App R 35, CCA.

[172] See now s 5 of the Criminal Procedure and Investigations Act 1996 (Ch 14).

[173] Para 8.22 (Cmnd 8092).          [174] SI 2005/384.

**24.1**

(1) Following—

    (a) a plea of not guilty by any person to an alleged offence in respect of which a magistrates' court proceeds to summary trial;

    (b) the committal for trial of any person;

    (c) the transfer to the Crown Court of any proceedings for the trial of a person by virtue of a notice of transfer given under section 4 of the Criminal Justice Act 1987;

    (d) the transfer to the Crown Court of any proceedings for the trial of a person by virtue of a notice of transfer served on a magistrates' court under section 53 of the Criminal Justice Act 1991;

    (e) the sending of any person for trial under section 51 of the Crime and Disorder Act 1998;

    (f) the preferring of a bill of indictment charging a person with an offence under the authority of section 2(2)(b) of the Administration of Justice (Miscellaneous Provisions) Act 1933; or

    (g) the making of an order for the retrial of any person,

if any party to the proceedings proposes to adduce expert evidence (whether of fact or opinion) in the proceedings (otherwise than in relation to sentence) he shall as soon as practicable, unless in relation to the evidence in question he has already done so or the evidence is the subject of an application for leave to adduce such evidence in accordance with section 41 of the Youth Justice and Criminal Evidence Act 1999—

    (i) furnish the other party or parties[175] with a statement in writing of any finding or opinion which he proposes to adduce by way of such evidence; and

    (ii) where a request in writing is made to him in that behalf by any other party, provide that party also with a copy of (or if it appears to the party proposing to adduce the evidence to be more practicable, a reasonable opportunity to examine) the record of any observation, test, calculation or other procedure on which such finding or opinion is based and any document or other thing or substance in respect of which any such procedure has been carried out.

(2) A party may by notice in writing waive his right to be furnished with any of the matters mentioned in paragraph (1) and, in particular, may agree that the statement mentioned in paragraph (1)(i) may be furnished to him orally and not in writing.

(3) In paragraph (1), 'document' means anything in which information of any description is recorded.

**24.2**

(1) If a party has reasonable grounds for believing that the disclosure of any evidence in compliance with the requirements imposed by rule 24.1 might lead to the intimidation, or attempted intimidation, of any person on whose evidence he intends to rely in the proceedings,[176] or otherwise to the course of justice being interfered with, he shall not be obliged to comply with those requirements in relation to that evidence.

---

[175] Ie co-accused.    [176] Ie either the expert or any other potential witness.

(2) Where, in accordance with paragraph (1), a party considers that he is not obliged to comply with the requirements imposed by rule 24.1 with regard to any evidence in relation to any other party, he shall give notice in writing to that party to the effect that the evidence is being withheld and the grounds for doing so.

**24.3** A party who seeks to adduce expert evidence in any proceedings and who fails to comply with rule 24.1 shall not adduce that evidence in those proceedings without the leave of the court.

The phrase 'expert evidence (whether of fact or opinion)', in rule 24.1(1), is wide enough to apply not only to evidence to be given by an expert witness, but also to an expert report which, whether or not the person making it attends to give oral evidence in the proceedings, it is proposed to adduce, by way of exception to the hearsay rule, under section 30(1) of the Criminal Justice Act 1988. Section 30(1) is considered in Chapter 10.

Section 11 of the Criminal Justice Act 1967 contained a provision similar in effect to rule 24.3 but applicable to particulars of an alibi defence. Under section 11, it was held that as a general rule, the mere fact that the necessary information was not given within the prescribed period was not, per se, a justification for refusing leave to admit the evidence because the discretion of the court had to be exercised judicially. Thus if, despite notice having been given outside the prescribed period, the prosecution had nevertheless had an opportunity to investigate the information provided, or could be given such an opportunity by means of an adjournment, leave to admit the evidence was granted.[177] It seems likely that rule 24.3 will be interpreted in a similar fashion.

In *R v Ward*[178] the Court of Appeal held that the rules (strictly, the original version of the rules) are helpful, but not exhaustive: they do not in any way supplant or detract from the prosecution's general duty of disclosure in respect of scientific evidence, a duty which exists irrespective of any request by the defence. That duty is not limited to documentation on which the opinion or finding of an expert is based, but extends to anything which may arguably assist the defence. It is a positive duty which, in the case of scientific evidence, obliges the prosecution to make full and proper inquiries from forensic scientists to ascertain whether there is discoverable material. Moreover, an expert witness who has carried out or knows of experiments or tests which tend to cast doubt on the opinion he is expressing is under a clear obligation to bring the records of such experiments or tests to the attention of the solicitor instructing him (so that it may be disclosed to the defence)[179] or the expert advising the defence. The importance of these principles was starkly illustrated in *R v*

---

[177] See per Salmon LJ in *R v Sullivan* [1971] 1 QB 253 at 258, CA. But see also *R v Jacks* [1991] Crim LR 611, CA, where the trial judge refused leave to admit the evidence and declined to adjourn. Dismissing the appeal, it was held that the facts of cases vary infinitely and it was impossible to lay down any general rule as to when exclusion or admission of the evidence might lead to injury being caused to one side or the other. On the facts, admission of the evidence would have involved a clear risk of disadvantage to the Crown.

[178] [1993] 2 All ER 577 at 628.

[179] See also per Stuart-Smith LJ in *R v Maguire* [1992] 2 All ER 433 at 447, CA.

*Clark*,[180] where, on a reference back to the Court of Appeal by the Criminal cases Review Commission, Sally Clark's convictions for the murder of her two infant sons were quashed, a forensic pathologist having failed to disclose that in the case of one of the infants, a form of potentially lethal bacteria, which could not be excluded as the possible cause of death, had been isolated.

Under section 6D of the Criminal Procedure and Investigations Act 1996, if the accused instructs a person with a view to his providing any expert opinion for possible use as evidence at his trial, he must give to the court and the prosecutor, within a prescribed 'relevant period', a notice specifying the person's name and address. Such a notice need not be given if the expert's name and address have already been given under section 6C of the 1996 Act, which requires the accused to give notice of his intention to call witnesses at the trial.[181]

## B NON-EXPERT OPINION EVIDENCE

A non-expert witness, as we have seen, may give opinion evidence on matters in relation to which it is impossible or virtually impossible to separate his inferences from the perceived facts on which those inferences are based. In these circumstances, the witness is permitted to express his opinion as a compendious means of conveying to the court the facts he perceived. The admissibility of non-expert opinion evidence is largely a question of degree and the matters open to proof by such evidence defy comprehensive classification. Examples include the identification of persons,[182] voices,[183] objects[184] and handwriting,[185] speed,[186] temperature, weather, and the passing of time. A non-expert may describe the condition of objects, using adjectives such as 'good', 'new', 'worn', and 'old'. Similarly, non-expert opinion evidence is admissible as to the value of objects. In *R v Beckett*,[187] the value of a plate glass window being in issue, the Court of Criminal Appeal held that the value of the window had been established by the evidence of a non-expert that in his opinion the window was worth more than five pounds. Although the point was not canvassed in the case, it seems clear that non-expert opinion evidence of value is only admissible in respect of commonplace objects, as opposed to works of art, antiques and other objects the valuation of which obviously calls for specialized skill or knowledge. A plate glass window, apparently, falls within the former category, although it might be regarded as a borderline example. A non-expert may also give opinion evidence of a person's age,[188]

---

180 [2003] All ER (D) 223 (Apr), [2003] EWCA Crim 1020.

181 See Ch 14.      182 *R v Tolson* (1864) 4 F&F 103.

183 *R v Robb* (1991) 93 Cr App R 161, CA; *R v Deenik* [1992] Crim LR 578, CA.

184 *Lucas v Williams & Sons* [1892] 2 QB 113 (a picture); *Fryer v Gathercole* (1849) 13 Jur 542 (a pamphlet).

185 *Doe d Mudd v Suckermore* (1837) 7 LJQB 33: see Ch 9.

186 Section 89(2) of the Road Traffic Regulation Act 1984: see Ch 8.      187 (1913) 8 Cr App R 204.

188 *R v Cox* [1898] 1 QB 179.

health, bodily or emotional state or reaction to an event or set of circumstances. Although a person's sanity is a matter calling for expertise, it would appear that a close acquaintance may express his opinion as a convenient way of conveying the results of his observations of that person's behaviour.[189] A similar distinction was drawn in *R v Davies*.[190] It was held that on a charge of driving when unfit through drink, whereas the fitness of the accused to drive is a matter calling for expert evidence, a non-expert may properly give his general impression as to whether the accused had 'taken drink', provided that he describes the facts upon which his impression was based. Similarly, and subject to the same proviso, a non-expert may give his opinion as to whether an accused was 'drunk'.[191] In *R v Hill*[192] it was held that scientific evidence is not always required to identify a prohibited drug, but police officers' descriptions of a drug must be sufficient to justify the inference that it is the drug alleged.

At common law, as we have seen, the courts were opposed to any witness expressing his opinion on an ultimate issue, that is one of the very issues which the judge or jury has to decide. In civil proceedings the rule has been abolished. Section 3(2) of the Civil Evidence Act 1972 declares that—

where a person is called as a witness in any civil proceedings, a statement of opinion by him on any relevant matter on which he is not qualified to give expert evidence, if made as a way of conveying relevant facts personally perceived by him, is admissible as evidence of what he perceived.

Section 3(3) reads:

In this section 'relevant matter' includes an issue in the proceedings in question.

Concerning non-expert opinion evidence in criminal proceedings, the rule may subsist.[193] In *R v Davies*[194] Lord Parker CJ held that although the witness could properly state the impression he formed as to whether the accused driver had taken drink, his opinion as to whether as a result of that drink he was fit or unfit to drive a car was inadmissible, being 'the very matter which the court itself has to determine'.[195] However, the rule is easily evaded by a careful use of words, and sometimes it is simply ignored. In *R v Beckett*,[196] it will be recalled, a witness valued a window at more than five pounds, yet that was exactly the issue to be determined by the court.

---

[189] Per Parke B in *Wright v Doe d Tatham* (1838) 4 Bing NC 489 at 543–4. But in criminal cases, expert psychiatric evidence is necessary in order to establish insanity: ss 1(1) and 2 of the Criminal Procedure (Insanity and Unfitness to Plead) Act 1991, above.

[190] [1962] 1 WLR 1111, C-MAC.          [191] *R v Tagg* [2002] 1 Cr App R 22, CA.

[192] (1992) 96 Cr App R 456, CA.

[193] But see 11th Report, Criminal Law Revision Committee (Cmnd 4991), para 270: the Committee, recommending the enactment for criminal proceedings of provisions similar to those contained in s 3 of the 1972 Act, said: 'we have no doubt that this is the present law, but it seems desirable for the statute to be explicit.'

[194] [1962] 1 WLR 1111, C-MAC. See also *Sherrard v Jacob* [1965] NI 151, NICA.

[195] In Eire, the witness has been allowed to express an opinion on both matters: see *A-G (Rudely) v James Kenny* (1960) 94 ILTR 185.

[196] (1913) 8 Cr App R 204, CCA.

# 19

# PUBLIC POLICY

A party to litigation has an obvious interest in the admission of any item of evidence which supports his own case or defeats that of his opponent. Such an interest coincides with a public interest that justice should be done between litigants by the reception of all relevant evidence. The public interest in efficient and fair trials may also be seen as underlying the rules of disclosure in civil litigation, whereby a litigant is obliged to make pre-trial disclosure of, inter alia, the documents on which he relies and the documents which adversely affect his own case or adversely affect, or support, another party's case, even though such documents may not be admissible evidence at the trial.[1] There is also a public interest, however, in enabling material to be withheld where its disclosure would harm the nation or the public service. Where these two kinds of public interest clash and the latter prevails over the former, relevant and otherwise admissible evidence is excluded at trial and relevant documents are exempted from the duty to allow inspection on discovery. Such material is said to be withheld by reason of 'public interest immunity'.[2] This chapter begins by considering the development of the modern law in both civil and criminal cases. This is followed by an examination of the heads of public interest which the courts have recognized as being capable of leading to the exclusion of relevant material. Finally consideration is given to a variety of essentially procedural issues, including the procedural aspects, in civil proceedings, of the judicial task of striking a balance between the conflicting public interests in question.

---

[1] See generally CPR Pt 31. Where the Crown is a party to civil litigation in the High Court or in a county court, s 28 of the Crown Proceedings Act 1947 provides that the Crown may be required by the court to make discovery of documents, produce documents for inspection and answer interrogatories, 'provided that this section shall be without prejudice to any rule of law which authorises or requires the withholding of any document or the refusal to answer any question on the ground that the disclosure of the document or the answering of the question would be injurious to the public interest'.

[2] The expression 'Crown privilege' has been judicially disapproved on the ground that there is no question of any privilege in the ordinary sense of the word: see per Lord Reid in *Rogers v Home Secretary* [1973] AC 388 at 400, HL; but cf per Lord Scarman in *Science Research Council v Nassé* [1980] AC 1028 at 1087.

# A  THE DEVELOPMENT OF THE MODERN LAW

## 1  CIVIL CASES

Judicial reluctance to expose material, disclosure of which might harm the nation or the public service, was taken to extremes in *Duncan v Cammell Laird & Co Ltd*.[3] That case arose out of the sinking in 1939 of the submarine *Thetis* with the loss of 99 lives. In an action for negligence against the government contractors who had built the submarine, the plaintiffs sought discovery of certain documents including a contract with the Admiralty for the hull and machinery, and salvage reports. The Board of Admiralty directed the defendants to object to the production of these documents on the grounds of public interest. Upholding the objection and departing from earlier authority that judges may call for and inspect documents in respect of which public interest immunity is claimed in order to satisfy themselves of the merits of such a claim,[4] Lord Simon held that where a minister decides against disclosure of a document on the grounds that it would be injurious to national defence or good diplomatic relations or because it belongs to a class of documents which it is necessary to keep secret for the proper functioning of the public service, his decision is binding upon the courts.

The extreme nature of the rule laid down in *Duncan v Cammell Laird & Co Ltd* was far from satisfactory and gave rise to considerable judicial criticism because it enabled executive claims to public interest immunity to succeed notwithstanding that disclosure involved only the smallest probability of injury to the public service, whereas non-disclosure involved the gravest risk of injustice to a litigant. In *Ellis v Home Office*,[5] for example, where the Home Office succeeded in their objection to the disclosure of police and medical reports concerning the mental condition of a prisoner who had violently assaulted the plaintiff, a fellow prisoner who sought damages against the Home Office, Devlin J confessed to an uneasy feeling that justice had not been done, and something more than an uneasy feeling that justice had not been seen to be done.[6] By 1956, however, the tide had begun to turn. In that year, the Lord Chancellor announced that public interest immunity would not be claimed in respect of certain classes of document including, for example, medical reports of prison doctors in negligence actions against doctors or the Crown and documents relevant to the defence in criminal proceedings.[7] In the same year, the House of Lords held that, contrary to its understanding of the matter as expressed in *Duncan v Cammell Laird &*

---

[3] [1942] AC 624, HL.

[4] See, eg, *Robinson v South Australia State (No 2)* [1931] AC 704, PC and *Spigelman v Hocken* (1933) 50 TLR 87.

[5] [1953] 2 QB 135, CA.

[6] See also *Broome v Broome* [1955] P 190, divorce proceedings in which the Secretary of State for War intervened to prevent the disclosure of documents concerning attempts to reconcile the parties made by a service welfare organization, the Soldiers' Sailors' and Airmen's Families Association.

[7] See 197 HL Deb (1956) col 741. Further concessions were made in 1962: 237 HL Deb (1962) col 1191.

*Co Ltd*, in Scotland the courts had always had an inherent power to override the Crown's objection to the production of documents.[8] In 1964 the Court of Appeal held that the English courts also had a residual power, in appropriate cases, to inspect documents and form their own opinion as to the public interest.[9] In *Conway v Rimmer*[10] the Court of Appeal reverted to the rule laid down in *Duncan v Cammell Laird & Co Ltd* but the House of Lords, while in no doubt that the actual decision in that case was correct—because disclosure might have affected national security by assisting a foreign power, at a time when the country was at war, to understand the structure and design of a submarine—was also of the unanimous opinion that whether relevant evidence should be withheld in the public interest is ultimately a question for the decision of the courts and not the executive.

In *Conway v Rimmer* the plaintiff, a former probationary police constable who had been charged with but acquitted of stealing a torch, brought an action against his former superintendent claiming damages for malicious prosecution. The Home Secretary objected to the production of five reports, four relating to the plaintiff's conduct as a probationer and the fifth leading to his prosecution for theft, on the grounds that they belonged to classes of documents, namely police reports to senior officers and reports on criminal investigations, the production of which would be injurious to the public interest. The House of Lords held that a minister's affidavit or certificate is not final, public interest immunity being a question of law for the determination of the court, and that although an objection to production by the Crown was entitled to the greatest weight, the court could ask for a clarification or amplification of the objection and had the power to inspect the documents privately and order their production notwithstanding the minister's objection.[11] Concerning the test to be applied in deciding whether the objection should be upheld, their Lordships held that the court should balance two public interests, that of the state or public service in non-disclosure and that of the proper administration of justice in the production of the documents. A distinction, however, was drawn between a 'contents' claim, that is a claim that it would be against the public interest to disclose the contents of a particular document, and a 'class' claim, that is a claim that a document, whether or not it contains anything the disclosure of which would be against the public interest, belongs to a class of documents which ought to be withheld. In the case of 'contents' claims, Lord Reid said:[12]

However wide the power of the court may be held to be, cases would be very rare in which it could be proper to question the view of the responsible Minister that it would be contrary to the public interest to make public the contents of a particular document.

---

8 *Glasgow Corpn v Central Land Board* 1956 SC (HL) 1.

9 *Re Grosvenor Hotel, London (No 2)* [1965] Ch 1210. See also *Merricks v Nott-Bower* [1965] 1 QB 57; *Wednesbury Corpn v Ministry of Housing and Local Government* [1965] 1 WLR 261.

10 [1968] AC 910.

11 But not, apparently, where there is a risk to national security demonstrated by an appropriate certificate: see *Balfour v Foreign and Commonwealth Office* [1994] 2 All ER 588, CA, below.

12 [1968] AC 910 at 943. See also per Lord Upjohn at 993.

In the case of 'class' claims, however, although certain classes of documents of a high level of public importance, such as Cabinet minutes and documents concerned with policy making within government departments, should hardly ever be disclosed, whatever their contents might be, because such disclosure 'would create or fan ill-informed or captious public or political criticism' or 'would be quite wrong and entirely inimical to the proper functioning of the public service',[13] there was a wide difference between such documents and routine reports. 'There may be special reasons for withholding some kinds of routine reports, but the proper test to be applied is to ask . . . whether the withholding of a document because it belongs to a particular class is really "necessary for the proper functioning of the public service".'[14] The House was especially critical of the argument that whole classes of documents should be withheld on the grounds of candour and uninhibited freedom of expression with and within the public service. Lord Upjohn said:[15]

I cannot believe that any Minister or any high-level military or civil servant would feel in the least degree inhibited in expressing his honest views in the course of his duty on some subject, such as even the personal qualifications and delinquencies of some colleague, by the thought that his observations might one day see the light of day. His worst fear might be libel, and there he has the defence of qualified privilege like everyone else in every walk of professional, industrial and commercial life who every day has to express views on topics indistinguishable in substance from those of the servants of the Crown.

Turning to the documents in the case before them, their Lordships were of the opinion that whereas they might be of vital importance to the litigation in question, they were of a routine nature and it was most improbable that their disclosure would prejudice the public interest. The documents were ordered to be produced for inspection. Subsequently, the House itself read the documents and, having done so, ordered that they be made available to the plaintiff.

The main significance of the decision in *Conway v Rimmer* was the assertion that while all due weight will be given to the views of the minister claiming public interest immunity, the final decision as to the balance of public interest lies with the court. However, Lord Reid said:[16] 'I do not doubt that there are certain classes of documents which ought not to be disclosed whatever their contents may be.' In similar vein, Lord Upjohn said:[17]

No doubt there are many cases in which documents by their very nature fall into a class which requires protection such as, only by way of example, Cabinet papers, Foreign

---

[13] Per Lords Reid and Upjohn at 952 and 993 respectively.

[14] Per Lord Reid at 952, citing Lord Simon in *Duncan v Cammell Laird & Co Ltd* [1942] AC 624 at 642. See also per Lord Reid in *Rogers v Secretary of State for the Home Department* [1973] AC 388, HL at 400–1.

[15] At 994. See also per Lords Reid and Hodson at 952 and 967 respectively. Scepticism about 'the candour argument' has been expressed in several subsequent cases—see in particular, *Science Research Council v Nassé* [1980] AC 1028, HL and *Burmah Oil Co Ltd v Bank of England* [1980] AC 1090, HL; but see Lord Wilberforce's complaint in the latter case (at 1112) that the argument had now received an 'excessive dose of cold water'.

[16] At 952.         [17] At 993. See also per Lords Hodson and Pearce at 973 and 987 respectively.

Office dispatches, the security of the state, high-level inter-departmental minutes and correspondence and documents pertaining to the general administration of the naval, military and air force services. Nearly always such documents would be the subject of privilege by reason of their contents but by their 'class' in any event they qualify for privilege.

These dicta suggest that no document in any one of the particular categories mentioned should ever be disclosed, whatever the circumstances. However, although it remains the case that a claim is less likely to succeed in respect of 'routine' or low-level documents, it is clear from the subsequent authorities that the courts are prepared to scrutinize and evaluate 'class' claims even in the case of documents of a high level of public importance. In *Burmah Oil Co Ltd v Bank of England*[18] an agreement had been made between the plaintiff company and the Bank of England in order to rescue the company from serious financial difficulties. Under the agreement, the company sold its shareholding in British Petroleum Co Ltd to the Bank. The company brought proceedings to set aside the sale on the ground that it was unconscionable. The Bank's list of documents in the litigation showed the part played by the government in the transaction. The Bank, at the request of the Crown, objected to the production of a number of the documents, comprising memoranda of meetings attended by ministers and meetings at which government officials but not ministers were present, on the grounds that they fell within a class of documents relating to the formulation of government policy on important economic matters. The judge dismissed the company's application for discovery and this decision was affirmed by a majority of the Court of Appeal. The House of Lords also upheld the Crown's objection to production of the documents, but did so only after a majority of their Lordships had satisfied themselves, from a private inspection of the documents, that they did not contain material of such evidential value as to make an order for their disclosure necessary for fairly disposing of the case.[19] The House rejected the view that certain classes of documents of a high level of public importance are absolutely immune from production whatever the circumstances. Lord Keith said:[20]

The courts are . . . concerned with the consideration that it is in the public interest that justice should be done and should be publicly recognized as having been done. This may demand, . . . in a very limited number of cases, that the inner workings of government should be exposed to public gaze, and there may be some who would regard this as likely to lead, not to captious or ill-informed criticism, but to criticism calculated to improve the nature of that working as affecting the individual citizen. I think that considerations of that nature were present in the mind of Lord Denning MR when delivering his dissenting judgment in the Court of Appeal[21] in this case, and in my opinion they correctly reflect what the trend of the law should be.

---

[18] [1980] AC 1090.

[19] Lord Wilberforce was satisfied that there was no reason, apart from speculation, for supposing that there was anything in the documents which could outweigh the public interest in non-disclosure and accordingly saw no need to inspect them.

[20] At 1134.      [21] [1979] 1 WLR 473 at 481–9.

That the court should be prepared, where appropriate, to require the disclosure of even high-level government papers was reasserted, in principle, in *Air Canada v Secretary of State for Trade (No 2)*.[22] The plaintiffs alleged that the Secretary of State had exercised his statutory powers to make directions as to the landing charges to be imposed by the British Airports Authority for the wrong purposes. They sought discovery of high-level ministerial papers concerning the formulation of government policy, and of inter-departmental communications between senior civil servants. The House of Lords refused their application because it was not shown that the papers were likely to contain helpful material that was not already available from other sources. However, Lord Fraser said:[23]

I do not think that even Cabinet minutes are completely immune from disclosure in a case where, for example, the issue in a litigation involves serious misconduct by a Cabinet minister. Such cases have occurred in Australia (see *Sankey v Whitlam*)[24] and in the United States (see *Nixon v United States*)[25] but fortunately not in the United Kingdom: see also the New Zealand case of *Environmental Defence Society Inc v South Pacific Aluminium Ltd (No 2)*.[26] But, while Cabinet documents do not have complete immunity, they are entitled to a high degree of protection against disclosure.

In 1996 the Lord Chancellor announced that the division between class and content claims would be brought to an end and that in future ministers would focus on the damage that disclosure would cause, only claiming immunity when they believed that disclosure would cause real damage or harm to the public interest. It was said that damage will normally have to take the form of direct or immediate threat to the safety of an individual or the nation's economic interests or relations with a foreign state, although in some cases, such as damage to a regulatory process, the anticipated damage might be indirect or longer term. In any event the nature of the harm will need to be clearly explained and ministers will no longer be able to claim immunity for internal advice or national security by reference to the general nature of the document. Non-governmental bodies claiming immunity are not bound by the statement, but it is submitted that it would be desirable if the same approach were to be taken across the board.

---

[22] [1983] 2 AC 394, HL. See also *Williams v Home Office* [1981] 1 All ER 1151, QBD, where McNeill J ordered production of documents consisting of communications to and from ministers, and records of meetings with ministers or between officials, all of which related to the formulation of policy concerning an experimental prison 'control unit'. See also *Re HIV Haemophiliac Litigation* [1990] NLJR 1349, an action against the Department of Health alleging negligence in failing to ensure that the country was self-sufficient in blood supplies, thereby causing haemophiliacs to be treated with infected blood from the USA. The Court of Appeal ordered production of briefing and other documents relating to the formulation of ministerial policy on self-sufficiency.

[23] At 432. The quotation makes explicit what is probably implicit in other cases, namely that the weight of the public interest in the administration of justice (which is weighed against the public interest in non-disclosure) depends not only on the importance of the material to the litigation in hand but also on the public importance of the litigation itself. See also per Ackner LJ in *Campbell v Tameside Metropolitan Borough Council* [1982] QB 1065 at 1076; and generally TRS Allan (1985) 101 LQR 200.

[24] (1978) 21 ALR 505.     [25] 418 US 683 (1974).     [26] [1981] 1 NZLR 153.

## 2 CRIMINAL CASES

In criminal proceedings, as we shall see, the rule against the disclosure of sources of police information was established some 200 years ago. In remarkable contrast, it is only very recently that the English courts have given any detailed consideration to the applicability to criminal proceedings of the doctrine of public interest immunity. The question appears to have arisen for the first time in *R v Governor of Brixton Prison, ex p Osman*.[27] Noting that the seminal cases make no reference to criminal proceedings, Mann LJ held that the civil principles do apply in criminal cases, but involve a different balancing exercise: although the judge should balance the public interest in non-disclosure against the interests of justice in the particular case, the weight to be attached to the interests of justice in a criminal case touching and concerning liberty, and very occasionally life, is plainly very great indeed.[28] In *R v Clowes*[29] Phillips J held that he did not find easy the concept of balancing the nature of the public interest against the degree and potential consequences of the risk of a miscarriage of justice, but equally refused to accept readily that proportionality between the two could never be of relevance. In *R v Keane*[30] Lord Taylor CJ held that when the court is seised of the material, the judge should balance the weight of the public interest in non-disclosure against the importance of the documents to the issues of interest to the defence, present and potential, so far as they have been disclosed to him or he can foresee them. However, as we shall see, the House of Lords has since made clear in *R v H*[31] that the golden rule is full prosecution disclosure and that although some derogation from the golden rule can be justified, it should always be to the minimum necessary to protect the public interest and it should never imperil the overall fairness of the trial. It was also held that if it does imperil the overall fairness of the trial, then fuller disclosure should be ordered even if this leads or may lead the prosecution to discontinue the proceedings so as to avoid having to make disclosure. Furthermore, the judge's initial ruling is not necessarily final. He is under a continuous duty to keep his initial decision under review—issues may emerge at a later stage so that the public interest in non-disclosure may be eclipsed by the defendant's need for access.[32] In deciding whether or not to order disclosure, the judge is not confined to admissible evidence but may take into account hearsay material.[33]

In *R v Ward*[34] it was held that the decision as to what should be withheld from disclosure is for the court, not the prosecution, the police, the DPP, or counsel.[35] A prosecution decision to withhold relevant evidence without notifying the judge would be a violation of Article 6 of the European Convention on Human Rights.[36] The

---

[27] [1992] 1 All ER 108, QBD.  [28] Approved in *R v Keane* [1994] 2 All ER 478, CA.
[29] [1992] 3 All ER 440, CCC.  [30] [1994] 2 All ER 478, CA.  [31] [2004] 2 AC 134, HL.
[32] *R v H* [2004] 2 AC 134, HL at [36]. See also *R v Bower* [1994] Crim LR 281, CA, *R v Brown (Winston)* [1994] 1 WLR 1599, CA and ss 14 and 15 of the Criminal Procedure and Investigations Act 1996.
[33] *R v Law* (1996) *The Times*, 15 Aug 1996.  [34] [1993] 1 WLR 619, CA.
[35] See also, in the case of a co-accused, *R v Adams* [1997] Crim LR 292, CA.
[36] *Rowe and Davis v UK* (2000) 30 EHRR 1. See also *Dowsett v UK* [2003] Crim LR 890.

prosecution cannot be judge in their own cause and if they are not prepared to let the court decide, the prosecution will have to be abandoned. However, in exceptional cases, the CPS may voluntarily disclose to the defence documents in a class covered by public interest immunity without referring the matter to the court for a ruling, subject to the safeguard of first seeking the written approval of the Treasury Solicitor. The CPS should submit to him copies of the documents, identify the public interest immunity class into which they fall, and indicate the materiality of the documents to the proceedings in which it is proposed to disclose them. The Treasury Solicitor should consult any other relevant government department and satisfy himself that the balance falls clearly in favour of disclosure. He will have regard to the class of documents involved, their materiality to the proceedings and the extent to which disclosure will damage the public interest in the integrity of the class claim. He should be more ready to approve disclosure of documents likely to assist the defence than those which the CPS wish to disclose with a view to furthering the interests of the prosecution. Before approving disclosure of class documents sought to be used by the prosecution, he should consider not only their importance to the prosecution's case, but also the importance of the prosecution itself: it may be preferable to abandon the case rather than damage the integrity of the class claim. He should also maintain a permanent record of all approvals so that any court, ruling on disclosure, knows the extent to which the integrity of the class claim has been weakened by previous voluntary disclosure.[37]

The rule in *R v Ward*[38] that it is for the *court* to decide what material should be withheld, is now reflected in the statutory rules relating to pre-trial disclosure in Part 1 of the Criminal Procedure and Investigations Act 1996. Section 21(2) preserves the common-law rules as to whether disclosure is in the public interest. Under paragraph 41 of the *Attorney-General's Guidelines: Disclosure of Information in Criminal Proceedings*, before making an application to the court to withhold material in the public interest, a prosecutor should aim to disclose as much material as he properly can, by giving the defence redacted or edited copies or summaries. Under paragraph 42 of the *Guidelines*, prior to or at the hearing the court must be provided with full and accurate information. The Court of Appeal has stressed that where an ex parte hearing is held, it is imperative in all cases that the Crown is scrupulously accurate in the information provided.[39] Where a trial judge or the Court of Appeal learns that prosecution witnesses, in the course of a public interest immunity hearing, lied in their evidence, the prosecution is likely to be tainted beyond redemption, however strong the evidence against the accused otherwise was.[40] Paragraph 42 of the *Guidelines* also provides that the prosecution advocate must examine all material which is the subject matter of the application and make any necessary enquiries of the prosecutor and/or investigator.[41]

---

[37] *R v Horseferry Road Magistrates, ex p Bennett (No 2)* [1994] 1 All ER 289, DC.
[38] [1993] 1 WLR 619, CA.      [39] *R v Jackson* [2000] Crim LR 377, CA.
[40] *R v Early* [2003] 1 Cr App R 288, CA.      [41] See also *R v Menga* [1998] Crim LR 58, CA.

The procedure to be adopted where the prosecution apply for immunity from disclosure is set out in the *Crown Court (Criminal Procedure and Investigations Act 1996) (Disclosure) Rules*[42] and the *Magistrates' Court (Criminal Procedure and Investigations Act 1996) (Disclosure) Rules*,[43] which in effect reproduce the following principles laid down by Lord Taylor CJ in *R v Davis*.[44] Whenever possible, which will be in most cases, the prosecution must notify the defence of the application, indicating the category of material in question, so that the defence have the opportunity of making representations to the court. If to disclose even the category would be to reveal too much, the prosecution should notify the defence that an *ex parte* application will be made. In highly exceptional circumstances where to reveal even the fact of an *ex parte* application would be to reveal too much, an *ex parte* application may be made without notice. However if, in any case, the judge takes the view that the defence should be aware of the category of material and should have the opportunity of making representations, or at any rate should have notice of the application, he may so order.

The *ex parte* procedure is contrary to the general principles of open justice in criminal trials and should only be adopted on the application of the Crown for the specific purpose of enabling the court to test a claim that immunity or sensitivity justifies non-disclosure.[45] Thus, a *defence* application, such as an application for details of an informer to be disclosed, should not be heard *ex parte*.[46] An *ex parte* application on the part of the prosecution will not necessarily amount to a violation of Article 6 of the European Convention on Human Rights, whether the application is made at the trial[47] or in the Court of Appeal,[48] but unfairness caused at the trial by an improper failure to disclose material to the judge will not necessarily be remedied by an *ex parte* examination of the material by the Court of Appeal.[49]

In *Edwards v UK*[50] the applicant was charged with a drugs offence following an undercover operation. On an *ex parte* application to withhold material, the judge ruled against disclosure. On a subsequent unsuccessful defence application under section 78 of the Police and Criminal Evidence Act 1984 to exclude the evidence of the only undercover officer to be called by the prosecution, on the basis of entrapment, the judge ruled that he had seen nothing in the course of the *ex parte* application that would have assisted the defence in their application under section 78. The European Court, finding a violation of Article 6(1), held that since the public interest immunity evidence may have related to facts connected with the section 78 application, the defence were not able fully to argue the case on entrapment. However certain the trial

---

[42] SI 1997/698.       [43] SI 1997/703.       [44] [1993] 1 WLR 613, CA.

[45] *R v Keane* [1994] 2 All ER 478 at 483. See also *R v Smith* [1998] 2 Cr App R 1, CA.

[46] *R v Turner* [1995] 3 All ER 432, CA; *R v Tattenhove* [1996] 1 Cr App R 408, CA.

[47] *Jasper v UK* (2000) 30 EHRR 441. See also *Atlan v UK* [2002] 34 EHRR 833 and *R v Lawrence* [2002] Crim LR 584, CA.

[48] *R v Botmeh* [2002] 1 WLR 531, CA.

[49] *Rowe and Davis v UK* (2000) 30 EHRR 1. See also *Atlan v UK* [2002] 34 EHRR 833.

[50] (2003) 15 BHRC 189.

judge was that the evidence did not assist the defence, this overlooked the possibility that the defence could have countered the evidence or shown it to be mistaken or otherwise unreliable. The denial of that opportunity on an issue so fundamental to the trial was a failure to comply with the requirements to provide adversarial proceedings and equality of arms and to incorporate adequate safeguards to protect the interests of the accused.

In *Edwards v UK* the court referred to the recommendation, in Sir Robin Auld's *Review of the Criminal Courts of England and Wales*[51] that special independent counsel be introduced to represent the interests of the accused in those cases at first instance and on appeal where the court considers prosecution applications in the absence of the defence.[52] In *R v H*[53] it was argued that it is a violation of Article 6 for a trial judge to rule on a claim to immunity, in the absence of adversarial argument on behalf of the accused, where the material in question is or may be relevant to a disputed issue of fact which the judge has to decide in order to rule on an application which will effectively determine the outcome of the proceedings, and it was also argued that the *Edwards v UK* principle applies whenever the defence relies on entrapment as a basis for staying the case as an abuse of process or excluding prosecution evidence. It was held that to adopt such an approach would be to put the judge in a straitjacket. Lord Bingham laid down the following governing principles. The golden rule is full disclosure to the defence of any material held by the prosecution which weakens its case or strengthens that of the defence. In circumstances where such material cannot be disclosed, fully or at all, without the risk of serious prejudice to an important public interest, some derogation from the rule can be justified, but should always be to the minimum necessary to protect the public interest, and should never imperil the overall fairness of the trial. If prosecution claims for public interest immunity were operated with scrupulous attention to these principles, and with continuing regard to the proper interests of the accused, there should be no violation of Article 6. The appointment of special counsel raises ethical problems, since the lawyer cannot disclose to his client the material which is the basis of the application and cannot take full instructions from him, as well as practical problems of delay, expense and continuing review.[54] None of these problems should deter the court from appointing an approved advocate as special counsel[55] where it is necessary, in the interests of justice, to secure protection of an accused's right to a fair trial. However, such appointments would be exceptional and should not be ordered unless and until the trial judge is satisfied that no other course will adequately meet the overriding requirement of fairness to the accused.

Where a magistrates' court, whether made up of a stipendiary magistrate or lay justices, hears an application for non-disclosure on the grounds of public interest immunity and rules that the material in question is inadmissible, ordinarily it should

---

[51] HMSO 2001 at paras 193–7.      [52] See also *Jasper v UK* (2000) 30 EHRR 441.
[53] [2004] 2 AC 134, HL.      [54] See per Lord Bingham at [22].
[55] The Attorney General approves the list of counsel judged suitable to act as special advocates.

proceed to hear the case itself, because of the court's duty of continuing review, and should exercise its discretion to order the case to be tried by a different bench only in exceptional circumstances, as when material was introduced at the non-disclosure hearing which was prejudicial and irrelevant to the question of admissibility.[56] Magistrates, in deciding an application for non-disclosure, should apply the same principles that apply in proceedings on indictment, but where it is known that a contested issue as to the disclosure of sensitive material is likely to arise, and the magistrates have discretion to send the case to the crown court for trial, they would be well advised to commit.[57] For this reason the occasions on which it will be appropriate to appoint special counsel in the magistrates' court will be even rarer than in the Crown Court.[58]

# B  THE SCOPE OF EXCLUSION ON GROUNDS OF PUBLIC POLICY

*Conway v Rimmer* reasserted the courts' control over the scope of public interest immunity, but it also paved the way for a generalization of the principles of public policy, which has led to a widening of the heads of public interest which the courts will recognize. Thus it is now clear that documents, to be protected, need not relate to the workings of central government at all—the public also has an interest in the effective working of non-governmental bodies and agencies performing public functions such as local authorities,[59] the Gaming Board,[60] the National Society for the

---

[56] *R v Stipendiary Magistrate for Norfolk, ex p Taylor* [1998] Crim LR 276, DC. See also *R v Bromley Magistrates' Court, ex p Smith* [1995] 4 All ER 146 (and cf *R v South Worcestershire Magistrates, ex p Lilley* [1995] 4 All ER 186, DC), *R (DPP) v Acton Youth Court* [2001] 1 WLR 1828, *R v H* [2004] 2 AC 134, HL at [43]–[44], and s 14 of the Criminal Procedure and Investigations Act 1996.

[57] See generally *R v Bromley Magistrates' Court, ex p Smith* [1995] 4 All ER 146, DC, distinguishing *R v DPP, ex p Warby* [1994] Crim LR 281, DC on the basis that it concerned committal proceedings.

[58] *R v H* [2004] 2 AC 134, HL.

[59] *Re D (Infants)* [1970] 1 WLR 599, CA and *Gaskin v Liverpool City Council* [1980] 1 WLR 1549, CA (child care records). But see also per Ralph Gibson LJ in *Brown v Matthews* [1990] 2 All ER 155 at 164–5, CA, doubting whether these cases are true examples of the application of the principle of public interest immunity. Where an authority applies for a care order in wardship proceedings, there is no absolute right against disclosure. See *Re A (minors)* [1992] 1 All ER 153, Fam Div; *Re M (a minor)* (1990) 88 LGR 841, CA; and *B v B* [1991] 2 FLR 487, Fam Div. The report of a court welfare officer is confidential to the parties and to the court, which may give permission for the information contained in it to be used in other proceedings: *Brown v Matthews* [1990] 2 All ER 155. As to the use in other proceedings of information confidential to child welfare proceedings, see *Re R (MJ) (an infant)* [1975] 2 All ER 749; *Re F (minors)* [1989] Fam 18, CA at 26; *Re X (minors)* [1992] 2 All ER 595 (Fam Div); *Re Manda* [1993] 1 All ER 733, CA; *Oxfordshire County Council v P* [1995] 2 All ER 225, Fam Div; *Cleveland County Council v F* [1995] 2 All ER 236, Fam Div; *Re K (minors)* [1994] 3 All ER 230, Fam Div; *Re G (a minor)* [1996] 2 All ER 65, CA; and *Re W (minors)* [1998] 2 All ER 801, CA.

[60] *Rogers v Secretary of State for the Home Department* [1973] AC 388, HL, below.

Prevention of Cruelty to Children (NSPCC),[61] and the Law Society.[62] It is tempting to generalize the principles completely and to say that evidence will be excluded whenever a public interest in its non-disclosure is asserted which outweighs the importance of receiving the evidence in the particular case. This was an argument put forward in D v NSPCC[63] in answer to the proposition that public interest immunity is restricted to the effective functioning of departments or organs of central government. Both propositions were rejected by the House of Lords in favour of the middle view that although 'the categories of the public interest are not closed and must alter from time to time whether by restriction or extension as social conditions and social legislation develop',[64] nevertheless the court can proceed only by analogy with interests which have previously been recognized by the authorities.[65]

In that case, the NSPCC, a body established by royal charter and given statutory power, along with the police and local authorities, to bring care proceedings, sought to honour a promise given to an informant that his identity would not be revealed. The plaintiff claimed damages for the injury to her health caused by the negligence of the NSPCC in pursuing the allegations of the informant that she had maltreated her child, allegations which proved groundless. The House of Lords upheld the NSPCC's application to withhold from discovery documents disclosing the identity of the informant. Their Lordships held that the value of the NSPCC's work was indicated by statutory recognition of its function, by evidence that informants were more willing to approach the NSPCC than the police or local authorities, and by other statutory and common-law authority acknowledging the importance of providing for the welfare of children. Relying on the analogy of judicial refusal to compel disclosure of sources of police information, they held that in both situations the public interest in the uninhibited flow of information justified the refusal to order disclosure since otherwise the sources of information would be expected to dry up.[66] Although the actual result of the case was no doubt desirable, the reasoning by which that result was achieved is open to criticism. In particular, reliance on the arbitrary constraint of

---

[61] D v NSPCC [1978] AC 171, HL (name of informant who prompted NSPCC inquiry).

[62] Buckley v Law Society (No 2) [1984] 1 WLR 1101, Ch D (names of informants whose complaints led to the Law Society's inquiry into a solicitor's conduct). See also Medway v Doublelock Ltd [1978] 1 WLR 710: an affidavit of means supplied in divorce proceedings can be withheld in subsequent litigation on grounds of public policy.

[63] [1978] AC 171, HL. See per Lord Diplock at 219–20 where the arguments are summarized.

[64] Per Lord Hailsham at 230.

[65] Per Lord Simon at 240, Lord Diplock at 219, and Lord Hailsham (with whom Lord Kilbrandon agreed) at 226.

[66] Cf R v Bournemouth Justices, ex p Grey [1987] 1 FLR 36, DC. A mother brought affiliation proceedings against a man who, she alleged, had admitted his paternity in discussions with a social worker at an approved adoption agency. The Divisional Court refused to quash a witness summons issued on the application of the mother against the social worker. It was held that there was no discernible analogy between a police informant or an NSPCC source and a natural father who stood to gain financially by the adoption of his child: it was difficult to envisage a father being dissuaded from admitting parentage to an adoption society on the basis of his knowledge that a later denial of such parentage might result in the earlier admission being used against him.

precedent seems an unsatisfactory means of containing the undesirable effect of an overgeneralized principle. If the constraint is applied, it must result in arbitrary distinctions. In practice, it has often been the generalized principle rather than the constraint that has been remembered by the lower courts. The relevance of statutory recognition must also be questioned: activities conducted without statutory provision or regulation can also be of great public importance.

It is convenient to consider the cases in which a claim to public interest immunity has been made under the heads of 'National security, diplomatic relations and international comity', 'Information for the detection of crime', 'Judicial disclosures', 'The proper functioning of the public service', and 'Confidential relationships'. In considering these cases, it needs to be remembered that there are always four variables capable of affecting the outcome, namely: (i) the importance of the public function in question; (ii) the extent to which disclosure would prejudice the effective exercise of that function; (iii) the importance of the material in question to the just determination of the litigation; and (iv) the public importance of that litigation.

## 1 NATIONAL SECURITY, DIPLOMATIC RELATIONS, AND INTERNATIONAL COMITY

Evidence will almost certainly be excluded in the interests of national security, good diplomatic relations and international comity. In *Asiatic Petroleum Co Ltd v Anglo-Persian Oil Co Ltd*[67] the defendants, acting on instructions from the Board of Admiralty, objected to the production of a letter to their agents containing information concerning the government's plans in respect of its campaign in Persia during the First World War. The Court of Appeal upheld the objection, not because the document was confidential or official, but because the information which it contained could not be disclosed without injury to the public interest. Similarly, in *Duncan v Cammell Laird & Co Ltd*, as we have seen, the defendants succeeded in their objection to the production of documents which might have given valuable information on the design of a new submarine to an agent of a foreign power at a time when the country was at war. Other examples under this head include a report of a military court of inquiry concerning the conduct of an officer,[68] communications between the governor of a colony and the colonial secretary[69] or between the commander-in-chief of forces overseas and the government[70] and diplomatic despatches.[71]

Concerning national security, it now seems that a ministerial certificate will be conclusive. In *Balfour v Foreign and Commonwealth Office*[72] B, dismissed from his post as Vice-Consul in Dubai, complained to an industrial tribunal of unfair dismissal and

---

67  [1916] 1 KB 822, CA.
68  *Home v Bentinck* (1820) 2 Brod&Bing 130; *Beatson v Skene* (1860) 5 H&N 838.
69  *Hennessy v Wright* (1888) 21 QBD 509.
70  *Chatterton v Secretary of State for India in Council* [1895] 2 QB 189, CA.
71  *M Isaacs & Sons Ltd v Cook* [1925] 2 KB 391.     72  [1994] 2 All ER 588, CA.

sought disclosure of documents in the possession of the Foreign Office. Immunity was claimed on the grounds that disclosure of material in the documents relating to the security and intelligence services would be contrary to the public interest. Both the Foreign and Home Secretary signed certificates particularizing the nature and content of the material attracting immunity and the reasons for the claim. The Court of Appeal upheld the decision to refuse disclosure. Taking the view that *Conway v Rimmer* disposed of the appeal, it was held that although there must always be vigilance by the courts to ensure that public interest immunity of whatever kind is raised only in appropriate circumstances and with appropriate particularity, once there is an actual or potential risk to national security demonstrated by an appropriate certificate, the court should not exercise its right to inspect. In reaching its decision, the court approved and applied the dictum of Lord Diplock in *Council of Civil Service Unions v Minister for the Civil Service*[73] (when dealing with the question of national security in a completely different context):

National security is the responsibility of the executive government; what action is needed to protect its interests is . . . a matter on which those on whom the responsibility rests, and not the courts of justice, must have the last word. It is par excellence a non-justiciable question. The judicial process is totally inept to deal with the sort of problems which it involves.

It is also in the public interest of the United Kingdom that the contents of confidential documents addressed to, or emanating from, foreign sovereign states, or concerning the interests of such states in relation to international territorial disputes between them, should not be ordered by the courts of this country to be disclosed by a private litigant without the consent of the states in question, because to order disclosure in such cases may be against the public interest in the maintenance of international comity and an English court should not be seen to be forcing the disclosure of such documents for the ostensible purpose of pronouncing, albeit indirectly, on the merits of such a dispute, the resolution of which is a question of politics.[74] The comity of nations also justifies an English court, in the exercise of its discretion, in refusing to authorize the issue of letters of request inviting the courts of a friendly foreign state to use their powers to assist in the obtaining of evidence, from witnesses resident in that or another friendly state, in order to show that the motives of the government of the friendly foreign state, in promulgating a particular law, were such that the law is unenforceable in the United Kingdom.[75]

[73] [1985] AC 374, HL at 412.

[74] See per Brightman and Donaldson LJJ in *Buttes Gas & Oil Co v Hammer (No 3)* [1981] QB 223, CA. A submission that a foreign state could intervene and claim privilege in the courts of this country to prevent the disclosure of documents inimical to its own public interest was unanimously rejected. The appeal to the House of Lords, [1982] AC 888, was disposed of on other grounds.

[75] *Settebello Ltd v Banco Totta and Acores* [1985] 2 All ER 1025, CA. See also *Fayed v Al-Tajir* [1987] 2 All ER 396 per Mustill and Kerr LJJ, CA at 480 and 410 respectively: international comity requires that an interdepartmental memorandum prepared and circulated in the London embassy of a friendly foreign state should not be admitted as the foundation of an action for libel.

## 2  INFORMATION FOR THE DETECTION OF CRIME

It is in the public interest to protect the identity of informers, not only for their own safety, but also to ensure that the supply of information about criminal activities does not dry up. Accordingly, there is a rule, established since at least the late eighteenth century, that a witness in civil or criminal proceedings may not be asked to disclose the name of a police informer.[76] Likewise, no order for discovery will be made which will have that effect. Even if the party entitled to object does not invoke the rule, the judge is nonetheless obliged to apply it.[77] However, the rule will be overridden where, in a criminal trial, strict enforcement would be likely to cause a miscarriage of justice, ie where the accused can show good reason to expect that disclosure of the name of the informant will assist him in establishing his innocence.[78] In *Marks v Beyfus*[79] the plaintiff claimed damages for malicious prosecution. In the course of the trial, he asked the Director of Public Prosecutions to name his informants, but the judge disallowed the question. This ruling was upheld by the Court of Appeal on the ground 'that this was a public prosecution, ordered by the Government (or by an official equivalent to the Government) for what was considered to be a public object, and that therefore the information ought not, on grounds of public policy, to be disclosed'.[80] Lord Esher said:[81]

I do not say it is a rule which can never be departed from; if upon the trial of a prisoner the judge should be of opinion that the disclosure of the name of the informant is necessary or right in order to show the prisoner's innocence, then one public policy is in conflict with another public policy, and that which says that an innocent man is not to be condemned when his innocence can be proved is the policy that must prevail. But, except in that case, this rule of public policy is not a matter of discretion; it is a rule of law . . .

Although it has been suggested that the possibility of a miscarriage of justice *dictates* disclosure,[82] it seems that a balancing exercise should be performed, even though, if the disputed material may prove the accused's innocence or avoid a miscarriage of justice, the balance will come down resoundingly in favour of disclosure.[83] Nonetheless, it has been held that judges need to scrutinize applications for disclosure of

---

[76]  *R v Hardy* (1794) 24 State Tr 199. See also s 17 of the Regulation of Investigatory Powers Act 2000, which renders inadmissible telephone-tap evidence, if lawfully obtained. The questionable rationale is that to fight crime successfully, the methods used by the police and security services to gather information must be kept secret. See P Mirfield 'Regulation of Investigatory Powers Act 2000 (2): Evidential Aspects' [2001] Crim LR 91.

[77]  See per Lord Esher MR in *Marks v Beyfus* (1890) 25 QBD 494, CA at 500 and per Mann J in *R v Rankine* [1986] 2 All ER 566, CA at 569.

[78]  Per Lawton LJ in *R v Hennessey* (1978) 68 Cr App R 419, CA at 426. See also *R v Hallett* [1986] Crim LR 462, CA.

[79]  (1890) 25 QBD 494, CA.

[80]  Per Lord Esher MR at 496–7. It would seem that bodies authorized by statute to bring prosecutions may claim the immunity, but not an individual prosecuting in a private capacity.

[81]  (1890) 25 QBD 494, CA at 498.

[82]  Per Mann LJ in *R v Governor of Brixton Prison, ex p Osman* [1992] 1 All ER 108 at 118.

[83]  Per Lord Taylor CJ in *R v Keane* [1994] 2 All ER 478, CA at 484.

details about informants with very great care. They should be astute to see that
assertions of a need to know such details (because essential to the running of a
defence) are justified. In some cases the informant is an informant and no more; in
others he may have participated in the events constituting, surrounding or following
the crime. Even when the informant has participated, the judge will need to consider
whether his role so impinges on an issue of interest to the defence, present or potential, as to make disclosure necessary.[84]

In R v Agar[85] the prosecution case was that A, on arrival at the house of X, found
police officers present and, when he ran off, threw away a packet containing drugs. A
alleged that the police had entered into an arrangement with X, an informer, to ask
him to go to X's house and that the drugs allegedly found had been planted by the
police. It was held that although an accused cannot discover the identity of an
informer by pretending that something is part of his case when in truth it adds
nothing to it, and although it *may* be that a defence which is manifestly frivolous and
doomed to failure must be sacrificed to the general rule protecting informers, on the
facts the defence should have been permitted to elicit that X had told the police that A
would be coming to his house (which would have identified him as an informer)—
such evidence was necessary to enable A to put forward his defence that he had been
set up by X and the police acting in concert.[86]

In R v Rankine[87] it was held that the rule is not confined to the identification of
police informers but also prevents the identification of premises used for police surveillance and the owners and occupiers of such premises. However, if the accused
alleges that disclosure of the identification of such premises is necessary in order to
establish his innocence, the prosecution must provide a sufficient evidential base to
enable the trial judge properly to determine whether to afford the protection sought.
In R v Johnson[88] the Court of Appeal held that the minimal evidential requirements
for these purposes are twofold. First, the officer in charge of the observations, who
normally should be of at least the rank of sergeant, should give evidence that he
visited the premises to be used and ascertained the attitude of the occupiers to the use
to be made of the premises and the possible disclosure thereafter of the use made and
of facts which could lead to the identification of both premises and occupiers. He may
additionally inform the court of any difficulties encountered in the particular locality
in obtaining assistance from the public. Secondly, an officer of at least the rank of
chief inspector should give evidence that immediately before the trial he visited the
premises and ascertained whether the occupiers were still the same and, whether they
were or not, what their attitude was to the possible disclosure of the use made of the

---

[84] Per Lord Taylor CJ in R v Turner [1995] 3 All ER 432, CA.          [85] [1990] 2 All ER 442, CA.
[86] Applied in R v Langford [1990] Crim LR 653, CC. See also R v Vaillencourt [1993] Crim LR 311, CA and
R v Reilly [1994] Crim LR 279, CA. Cf R v Slowcombe [1991] Crim LR 198, CA, where the identity of the
informer would have contributed little or nothing to the defence being run, and R v Menza and Marshalleck
[1998] Crim LR 58, CA.
[87] [1986] 2 All ER 566, CA.          [88] [1989] 1 All ER 121, CA.

premises and of facts which could lead to the identification of both premises and occupiers.[89]

Johnson was convicted of supplying drugs. The police alleged that he had been seen selling the drugs in a particular street by officers situated in buildings in the locality. The prosecution argued that the evidence which their witnesses should be compelled to give should not go further than revealing that all the observation points were within a given maximum distance from the scene of the offence. Defence counsel submitted that this would enable officers to cover up inconsistencies in their evidence and gravely embarrass him in his efforts to test in cross-examination precisely what they could see from their various locations having regard to the layout of the street and the objects in it, including trees. In the jury's absence, the police gave evidence as to the difficulty of obtaining assistance from the public for observation purposes and revealed that the occupiers, all of whom were also occupiers at the material time, did not wish their names and addresses to be disclosed because they feared for their safety. The judge ruled that the officers should not reveal the location of the premises used. The appeal was dismissed: although the conduct of the defence was to some extent affected by this restraint, it had led to no injustice.[90]

In *R v Brown, R v Daley*[91] the Court of Appeal emphasized that the extension of the exclusionary rule established in *R v Rankine* was based on the protection of the owner or occupier of the premises and not on the identity, *simpliciter*, of the observation post. The accused were convicted of theft from a parked car. The chief prosecution witnesses were two officers who gave evidence that they had witnessed the commission of the offence as part of a surveillance operation conducted from an unmarked police vehicle. The defence was that their evidence had been fabricated. The judge allowed the prosecution to withhold information relating to the surveillance and the colour, make and model of the police vehicle. The appeal was allowed. It was held that evidence of police methods and techniques, if relevant, was admissible. Even if public interest immunity could be successfully invoked to exclude evidence of sophisticated methods of criminal investigation, a possibility which the court was not prepared to rule out, the prosecution, in applying to exclude evidence on such a basis, would have to identify with precision the evidence to be excluded, give reasons for exclusion, and support the application by the independent evidence of senior officers. On the facts, this had not been done.

Disclosure to show that an accused is innocent of a criminal offence is not, as was once intimated,[92] the sole exception to a general rule against disclosure. The courts have softened the rigidity of this approach so as to permit a balance of competing public interests in a case specific manner as part of a wider jurisprudential move away

---

[89] These guidelines do not require a threat of violence before protection can be afforded to the occupier— it suffices if he is in fear of harassment: *Blake v DPP* (1992) 97 Cr App R 169, DC.

[90] *R v Johnson* was applied in *R v Hewitt; R v Davis* (1991) 95 Cr App R 81, CA. See also *R v Grimes* [1994] Crim LR 213, CA.

[91] (1987) 87 Cr App R 52, CA.          [92] See per Lord Diplock in *D v NSPCC* [1978] AC 171 at 218.

from near absolute protection of various categories of public interest in non-disclosure. In *Chief Constable of Greater Manchester Police v McNally*,[93] civil proceedings for, inter alia, malicious prosecution, the trial judge had ordered the Chief Constable to disclose whether an individual, X, who had allegedly threatened a prosecution witness at the criminal trial, was a police informer. The Court of Appeal held that judges in civil cases are entitled to balance the public interest in the protection of an informer against the public interest in a fair trial but are required to give very considerable weight to the former interest and to reduce the weight of the latter, given that it is a civil trial at which liberty is not at stake. However, there were no grounds for interfering with the ruling of the judge who had properly given significant weight to three factors: that the evidence could have been decisive of the outcome of the case; that although the claimant's liberty was not at stake, he was seeking redress for wrongful deprivation of liberty for over ten months while in custody awaiting trial; and that although X had not consented to disclosure of information that he was an informer, the scope for protecting him was limited by the fact that both sides knew who he was.[94]

In *Savage v Chief Constable of Hampshire*[95] it was held that if a police informer wishes to sacrifice his own anonymity, he may do so, because in such circumstances the primary justification for non-disclosure, that disclosure would endanger his safety, disappears. In appropriate circumstances, however, it may be that notwithstanding the wishes of the informer, there remains a significant public interest which would be damaged by disclosure, as when disclosure might assist others involved in crime, reveal police methods of operation, or hamper police operations.


## 3 JUDICIAL DISCLOSURES

There are restrictions on the extent to which those involved in the conduct of a trial can be called to give evidence of the proceedings. The rationale of these restrictions probably stems from the need for efficiency in, and the finality of, litigation. They differ from the other heads of public policy in that although they prevent certain people being called to prove certain facts, for the most part they do not prevent proof of those facts by other means. These rules, which might equally well be considered under the heading of competence and compellability, or privilege, have played little, if any, part in the general development of public interest immunity.

A litigant may wish to prove what was said in earlier litigation. The court record and a properly proved transcript, where available, will usually be the best means, but in principle anyone who witnessed the proceedings may be called. However, a judge,

---

[93] [2002] 2 Cr App R 617, CA.

[94] See also *Re W (children) (care proceedings: disclosure)* [2004] 1 All ER 787, Fam D, which concerned information received by a local authority from the police, the disclosure of which in care proceedings, in the form in which it was provided, would have prejudiced covert police operations and enabled an informant to be identified.

[95] [1997] 2 All ER 631, CA.

including a master of the Supreme Court, cannot be compelled to give evidence of those matters of which he became aware relating to and as a result of the performance of his judicial functions, as opposed to some collateral matter, eg a crime committed in the face of the court. Nonetheless the judge is competent to give evidence, and if a situation arises where his evidence is vital, he should be able to be relied on not to assert his non-compellability.[96]

A jury's verdict cannot be questioned on the ground of anything that happened in the jury room.[97] Accordingly, the Court of Appeal in *R v Thompson*[98] refused to hear evidence to the effect that a juror had read a list of the accused's previous convictions, which had not been revealed in evidence. No doubt it is in the public interest to ensure finality of litigation and uninhibited discussion among jurors by holding that once they have clearly acquiesced in a verdict, the basis for their findings should not be questioned. However, the decision in *R v Thompson* seems to take this principle too far.

## 4 THE PROPER FUNCTIONING OF THE PUBLIC SERVICE

Public interest immunity has been successfully claimed in respect of a variety of state interests on the grounds that protection is necessary for the proper functioning of the public service.[99] It is quite clear, for example, that subject to the court's assessment of the strength of the claim for immunity in each case and the importance of the material to the litigation, immunity may be claimed for communications to and from ministers and high-level government officials regarding the formulation of government policy.[100] In *Conway v Rimmer* itself it was recognized that internal communications of the police force (quite apart from those relating to the investigation of crime) would in appropriate cases qualify for immunity on the ground that the public have an interest in the proper functioning of the police force which, though not a government department, 'carries out essential functions of government'. Concerning communications which do relate to the investigation of crime, it has been held that public interest immunity attaches to documents and information upon the strength of which search warrants have been obtained[101] and also to reports sent by the police to the

[96]  *Warren v Warren* [1996] 4 All ER 664, CA.

[97]  See, eg, *R v Roads* [1967] 2 QB 108, in which a juror was not allowed to prove that she disagreed with the verdict.

[98]  [1962] 1 All ER 65. See also per Lord Atkin in *Ras Behari Lal v R* (1933) 102 LJPC 144; *R v Bean* [1991] Crim LR 843, CA (an allegation of undue judicial pressure to reach a verdict); and *R v Lucas* [1991] Crim LR 844, CA (an allegation of undue pressure on one juror by the others). Cf *R v Newton* (1912) 7 Cr App R 214.

[99]  At one time 'class' claims succeeded on this ground even in the case of documents of a relatively routine nature. See, eg, *Re Joseph Hargreaves* [1900] 1 Ch 347; *Anthony v Anthony* (1919) 35 TLR 559; *Ankin v London & North Eastern Rly Co* [1930] 1 KB 527; *Ellis v Home Office* [1953] 2 QB 135, above; and *Broome v Broome* [1955] P 190, above. All of these decisions pre-date *Conway v Rimmer* [1968] AC 910, and it may be doubted whether they would be followed today.

[100]  See, eg, *Burmah Oil Co Ltd v Bank of England* [1980] AC 1090, and *Air Canada v Secretary of State for Trade (No 2)* [1983] 2 AC 394, above; cf *Williams v Home Office* [1981] 1 All ER 1151, CA.

[101]  *Taylor v Anderton* (1986) *The Times*, 21 Oct, Ch D.

Director of Public Prosecutions, even if the prosecution has been completed, whether successfully or not.[102] In the latter case it was held that it is important for the proper functioning of the criminal process of prosecution that there should be freedom of communication between police forces and the DPP in seeking his legal advice, without fear that the documents will be subject to inspection, analysis and investigation in subsequent civil proceedings. There is also a clear public interest in the non-disclosure of international communications between police forces or prosecuting authorities, essentially so as not to divulge information useful to criminals and not to inhibit the fullest co-operation between such authorities in different jurisdictions.[103]

In *R v Lewes Justices, ex p Home Secretary*[104] an unsuccessful applicant for a gaming licence sought disclosure, in libel proceedings against the police, of a letter sent by the police to the Gaming Board which had requested information in the course of its statutory duty to investigate the applicant's suitability for a licence. The House of Lords refused the application, being clearly impressed by the importance of the Board's function in controlling the social evils which might otherwise have been expected to follow in the wake of the newly legalized activity of gaming. Lord Reid said:[105]

I do not think that 'the public service' should be construed narrowly. Here the question is whether the withholding of this class of documents is really necessary to enable the board adequately to perform its statutory duties. If it is, then we are enabling the will of Parliament to be carried out.

An analogy was drawn with the principle relating to police informers: although the risk of disclosure might not inhibit the police, it would affect the wells of voluntary information. The plaintiff was thus, in effect, deprived of his cause of action.[106]

In *Lonrho plc v Fayed (No 4)*[107] the question arose whether, in the absence of consent to disclosure by a taxpayer, public interest immunity attaches to documents relating to his tax affairs in the hands of the Inland Revenue. A majority of the Court of Appeal, noting Parliament's clear intention (subject to specified exceptions) to prohibit disclosure by the Revenue of a taxpayer's affairs,[108] answered the question in the affirmative on the grounds that as a matter of public policy, the state should not by

---

[102] *Evans v Chief Constable of Surrey* [1989] 2 All ER 594, QBD.

[103] *R v Horseferry Road Magistrates, ex p Bennett (No 2)* [1994] 1 All ER 289, DC, although in that case the balance favoured disclosure, the documents being relevant to the issue whether B had been unlawfully returned to the jurisdiction.

[104] [1973] AC 388, also referred to as *Rogers v Secretary of State*. See also *Lonrho Ltd v Shell Petroleum* [1980] 1 WLR 627, HL where immunity was granted, in subsequent litigation, for evidence given to the Bingham inquiry into the operation of sanctions against Rhodesia: although the inquiry had powers to compel evidence to be given, its effectiveness depended on a voluntary supply of information which in turn required a valid guarantee of confidentiality. Cf *Hamilton v Naviede* [1994] 3 All ER 814, HL.

[105] [1973] AC 388 at 401. See also per Lord Morris at 405.

[106] It is important to distinguish public interest immunity and evidential privileges (see Ch 20) from privilege as a defence to libel proceedings. However, the policy considerations affecting these different issues can overlap to a surprising degree. See, eg, *Fayed v Al-Tajir* [1987] 2 All ER 396, CA.

[107] [1994] 1 All ER 870, CA.        [108] See s 6 and Sch 1 of the Taxes Management Act 1970.

compulsory powers obtain information from a citizen for one purpose and then use it for another. Thus the confidentiality of such documents will only be overridden if the party seeking disclosure shows very strong grounds for concluding that on the facts of the particular case the public interest in the administration of justice outweighs the public interest in preserving the confidentiality. The court also held, unanimously, that no public interest immunity attaches to documents relating to tax affairs held by the taxpayer himself (or his agents).

The statutory functions of keeping import records for the purposes of Customs and Excise legislation (see *Norwich Pharmacal Co v Customs and Excise Comrs*)[109] and inquiring into the true nature of a person's trade in order to make a proper assessment to tax (see *Alfred Crompton Amusement Machines Ltd v Customs and Excise Comrs (No 2)*)[110] are both in principle capable of attracting public interest immunity. In the *Norwich Pharmacal* case, however, it was held that there was no serious risk that importers would be less likely to comply with their statutory duty to give the necessary information simply because of the possibility of that information being disclosed in civil proceedings, whereas in the *Alfred Crompton* case the information to be supplied by third parties about a trader's activities, even though supplied under statutory compulsion, was sufficiently sensitive to justify the fear that the Commissioners' functions would be hampered unless they were able to give an effective guarantee. Disclosure was thus required in the former case but denied in the latter.[111]

In *Science Research Council v Nassé*[112] the House of Lords firmly rejected a claim to immunity in relation to routine confidential employers' reports on employees seeking promotion.[113] *D v NSPCC*[114] was applied: public interest immunity can be extended only by analogy with previous authority. Lord Edmund-Davies[115] noted that public interest immunity had thus far been limited to bodies exercising statutory functions or duties in respect of which an analogy could be drawn with the principle relating to police informers. Lord Scarman said:[116]

I regret the passing of the currently rejected term 'Crown privilege'. It at least emphasized

---

[109] [1974] AC 133, HL.      [110] [1974] AC 405, HL.

[111] Immunity can attach to evidence taken in a Department of Trade investigation under s 165 of the Companies Act 1948 (per Lord Widgery CJ, obiter, in *R v Cheltenham Justices, ex p Secretary of State for Trade* [1977] 1 WLR 95) and also to a report to the Secretary of State following a DTI inquiry into the activities of a company (see *Day v Grant* [1987] 3 All ER 678 at 680, CA). The former case was distinguished in *London and County Securities v Nicholson* [1980] 1 WLR 948, on the grounds that the importance of the evidence tipped the scales the other way. See also *Multi Guarantee Co Ltd v Cavalier Insurance Co Ltd* (1986) *The Times*, 24 June, Ch D, below: the immunity attaching to notes recording information given in confidence to officials of the DTI is capable of 'evaporating'. Concerning statutes requiring the disclosure of information and governing the extent to which it can be used in other proceedings, see generally Eagles 'Public interest immunity and statutory privilege' (1983) 42 CLJ 118.

[112] [1980] AC 1028, HL.

[113] But also held that if discovery was not necessary for fairly disposing of the proceedings, it could be refused on the grounds of breach of confidence. See below.

[114] [1978] AC 171, HL.

[115] [1980] AC 1028 at 1073–4, approving the dicta of Browne LJ in the Court of Appeal.

[116] At 1087–8.

the very restricted area of public interest immunity . . . The immunity exists to protect from disclosure only information the secrecy of which is essential to the proper working of the government of the state. Defence, foreign relations, the inner workings of government at the highest levels where ministers and their advisers are formulating national policy, and the prosecution process in its pre-trial stage are the sensitive areas where the Crown must have the immunity if the government of the nation is to be effectually carried on. We are in the realm of public law, not private right. The very special case of *D v NSPCC* is not to be seen as a departure from this well-established principle.

In the case of statements obtained for the purposes of an investigation of a complaint against the police under Part IX of the Police and Criminal Evidence Act 1984, a class claim to immunity would tend to be largely self-defeating. Thus although it would be possible to justify immunity on the basis of (i) a candour argument (witnesses might be inhibited by the possibility of disclosure in subsequent litigation) and (ii) the underlying public interest in the maintenance of a law-abiding and uncorrupt police force, the consequences of immunity include preventing the complainant from seeing the relevant documents in any subsequent proceedings brought against the police. For reasons of this kind, in *R v Chief Constable of the West Midlands Police, ex p Wiley*[117] the House of Lords, overruling *Neilson v Laugharne*[118] (and the cases in which it was subsequently applied), held that there is no public interest immunity for such documents on the basis of a class claim.[119] It also held, however, that a claim to immunity may succeed on the basis of the contents of a particular document. Thus a claim could succeed in the case of a document containing, for example, police material on policy or operational matters or the identity of an informant. It was held that any contents claim should be decided in the proceedings in which the documents are relevant, such as a subsequent civil action in respect of the alleged misconduct (rather than in any collateral proceedings), because the conflicting public interests for and against disclosure will vary from case to case and the relationship between the conflicting interests may vary as the case proceeds to trial and even during the trial.[120]

The House of Lords in *ex p Wiley* left open the question whether reports prepared by the investigating officers form a class which is entitled to immunity. Subsequently, the Court of Appeal in *Taylor v Anderton*[121] answered the question in the affirmative, both as to working papers as well as such reports, holding that production of such material should only be ordered, therefore, where the public interest in disclosure of their contents outweighs the public interest in preserving their confidentiality. In reaching this decision, Sir Thomas Bingham MR was particularly influenced by (i) the fundamental public interest in ensuring that those responsible for maintaining law and order are themselves law-abiding and honest and (ii) the need for investigating

---

[117] [1994] 3 All ER 420.      [118] [1981] QB 736, CA.

[119] There is no immunity for written complaints prompting investigations against the police: *Conerney v Jacklin* [1985] Crim LR 234, CA.

[120] See also *Peach v Metropolitan Police Comr* [1986] 2 All ER 129, a decision prior to *ex p Wiley* in which *Neilson v Laugharne* was distinguished, and *Ex p Coventry Newspapers Ltd* [1993] 1 All ER 86, CA.

[121] [1995] 2 All ER 420, CA.

officers to feel free to report on professional colleagues or members of the public without the undesirably inhibiting apprehension that their opinions may become known to such persons.

Public interest immunity does not attach to statements made in a police grievance procedure, initiated by an officer, alleging racial or sexual discrimination.[122]

## 5  CONFIDENTIAL RELATIONSHIPS

There are many important relationships which depend on the assumption that confidences will be respected. Examples include the relationship between doctor and patient, journalist and source, and priest and penitent. In *Alfred Crompton Amusement Machines Ltd v Customs and Excise Comrs (No 2)*[123] it was emphasized that confidentiality is never a sufficient ground of immunity, even though it is often a necessary condition. Thus at common law, in the absence of some additional consideration, as when the person claiming immunity is exercising a statutory function the effective performance of which would be impeded by disclosure, a claim to public interest immunity will not succeed.[124] An example of such an additional consideration is provided by *Re Barlow Clowes Gilt Managers Ltd.*[125] It was held that the liquidators of a company are under no duty to assist its directors, in defending criminal charges, by providing them with information obtained by the liquidators from third parties in circumstances of confidentiality and by assurances, express or implied, that it would be used only for the purpose of the liquidation, because if there comes to be a generally perceived risk of such disclosure, there is an obvious danger that professional men will no longer cooperate with liquidators on a voluntary basis, which would jeopardize the proper and efficient functioning of the process of compulsory liquidation.[126]

---

[122] *Metropolitan Police Comr v Locker* [1993] 3 All ER 584, EAT.    [123] [1974] AC 405, HL.

[124] See *Lonrho Ltd v Shell Petroleum* [1980] 1 WLR 627, HL, above. See also *Lonrho plc v Fayed (No 4)* [1994] 1 All ER 870, CA, above; *R v Umoh* (1986) 84 Cr App R 138, CA (immunity for discussions between a prisoner and a legal aid officer); *R v K* (1993) 97 Cr App R 342, CA (an interview with a child victim of a sexual offence, conducted for therapeutic purposes, should not be disclosed unless the interests of justice so require, but if the liberty of the subject is an issue, and disclosure may be of assistance to an accused, a claim for disclosure will often be strong); and *Morrow v DPP* [1994] Crim LR 58, DC (having regard to the purpose of the Abortion Act 1967 to encourage the use of safe and controlled procedures, rather than resort to illegal abortions (a purpose reflected in the statutory restrictions on the disclosure of information furnished under the Abortion Regulations 1968), immunity may be claimed for confidential documents relating to abortions carried out under the Act). The matrimonial reconciliation cases considered in Ch 20 may also be regarded as a limb of public interest immunity—see, eg, per Lords Hailsham and Simon in *D v NSPCC* [1978] AC 171 at 226 and 236–7 respectively. Private privilege is available to protect certain types of communication between a lawyer and his client: see Ch 20.

[125] [1991] 4 All ER 385, Ch D.

[126] However, if the information is 'material evidence' for the purposes of a witness summons in the criminal proceedings, then the criminal court must balance the competing interests for and against disclosure and, as we have seen, in the case of very serious criminal charges at least, this may well result in disclosure: see *R v Clowes* [1992] 3 All ER 440, CCC, above.

The question will often arise on disclosure, which under the Rules of Supreme Court was known as discovery. RSC Ord 24, rule 8 provided that the court should refuse to order discovery 'if and so far as it is of opinion that discovery is not necessary either for disposing fairly of the cause or matter or for saving costs'. In *Science Research Council v Nassé*[127] it was held that this provision provided the test to be used by an industrial tribunal, in discrimination proceedings, in deciding whether to order the discovery of confidential reports on employees and applicants for employment. The following propositions derive from the judgment of Lord Wilberforce:

1. There is no principle in English law by which documents are protected from discovery by reason of confidentiality alone, but, in the exercise of its discretion to order discovery, a tribunal may have regard to the fact that disclosure will involve a breach of confidence.

2. Relevance, though necessary, is not automatically a sufficient ground for ordering discovery.

3. The ultimate test is whether discovery is necessary for disposing fairly of the proceedings: if it is, then discovery must be ordered notwithstanding confidentiality, but where the court is impressed with the need to preserve confidentiality, it will consider carefully whether the necessary information can be obtained by other means not involving a breach of confidence.

4. In order to decide whether discovery is necessary notwithstanding confidentiality, a tribunal should inspect the documents; it will also consider whether justice can be done by 'covering up', substituting anonymous references for specific names or, in rare cases, a hearing in camera. On the facts, the tribunals in question not having inspected the documents, the cases were remitted so that the documents could be examined and a decision taken as to which, if any, should be disclosed.

*Science Research Council v Nassé* remains the leading authority when courts are faced with an application for disclosure of confidential documents, but in deciding on such applications under the Civil Procedure Rules, account must be taken of the overriding objective. In particular, it is necessary to deal with cases justly, which includes saving expenses and dealing with cases with proportionality, and it is not proportionate to make an order for the supply of documents that will result in duplication.[128]

In *British Steel Corpn (BSC) v Granada Television Ltd*[129] Granada had received from a BSC employee copies of secret documents from BSC's files. Some of the documents were then used in a programme on the national steel strike. Granada had promised the informant that his identity would not be disclosed. BSC applied for an order that Granada disclose the identity of the informant. They relied upon the principle in *Norwich Pharmacal Co v Customs and Excise Comrs*,[130] namely that a person who

---

[127] [1980] AC 1028, HL.
[128] *Simba-Tola v Elizabeth Fry Hospital* [2001] EWCA Civ 1371, LTL 30 July 2001.
[129] [1981] AC 1096, HL.     [130] [1974] AC 133.

becomes involved in the tortious acts of another, even if innocently, is under a duty to assist a person injured by those acts by disclosing the identity of the tortfeasor. The House of Lords ordered Granada to disclose the identity of the informant. It was accepted, however, that where possible, judges will respect the confidence:[131]

Courts have an inherent wish to respect this confidence, whether it arises between doctor and patient, priest and penitent, bankers and customer, between persons giving testimonials to employees, or in other relationships . . . But in all these cases the court may have to decide, in particular circumstances, that the interest in preserving this confidence is outweighed by other interests to which the law attaches importance.

On the facts, Lord Wilberforce concluded that 'to confine BSC to its remedy against Granada and to deny it the opportunity of a remedy against the source would be a significant denial of justice'.[132] His Lordship approved the dictum of Lord Denning MR in *A-G v Mulholland*,[133] applying similar principles in relation to cross-examination at trial:

The judge will respect the confidences which each member of these honourable professions receives in the course of it, and will not direct him to answer unless not only it is relevant but also it is a proper and, indeed, necessary question in the course of justice to be put and answered. A judge is the person entrusted, on behalf of the community, to weigh these conflicting interests—to weigh on the one hand the respect due to confidence in the profession and on the other hand the ultimate interest of the community in justice being done. . . . If the judge determines that the journalist must answer, then no privilege will avail him to refuse.

Disclosure of the source of information contained in a publication is now governed by statute. Section 10 of the Contempt of Court Act 1981 was enacted to bring domestic law in this respect into line with Article 10 of the European Convention on Human Rights, which provides:

1. Everyone has the right to freedom of expression . . .

2. The exercise of these freedoms, since it carries with it duties and responsibilities, may be subject to such formalities, conditions, restrictions or penalties as are prescribed by law and are necessary in a democratic society, in the interests of national security, territorial integrity or public safety, for the prevention of disorder or crime, for the protection of health or morals, for the protection of the reputation or rights of others, for preventing the disclosure of information received in confidence, or for maintaining the authority and impartiality of the judiciary.

Section 10 of the Contempt of Court Act 1981 provides:

No court may require a person to disclose, nor is any person guilty of contempt of court

---

[131] Per Lord Wilberforce [1981] AC 1096 at 1168.      [132] [1981] AC 1096 at 1175.

[133] [1963] 2 QB 477 at 489–90. See also *A-G v Lundin* (1982) 75 Cr App R 90, DC: there is no liability for contempt for refusal to answer unless the question is both relevant and necessary.

for refusing to disclose, the source of information contained in a publication[134] for which he is responsible, unless it be established to the satisfaction of the court that disclosure is necessary in the interests of justice or national security or for the prevention of disorder or crime.

In *Ashworth Hospital Authority v MGN Ltd*[135] it was held that section 10 gives effect to the general requirements of Article 10 in the narrow context of the protection of the sources of information of the press; that Article 10 permits the right of freedom of expression to be circumscribed where necessary in a democratic society to achieve a number of specified 'legitimate aims'; and that the approach to the interpretation of section 10 should, insofar as possible (i) equate the specific purposes for which disclosure of sources is permitted under section 10 with the 'legitimate aims' under Article 10 and (ii) apply the same test of necessity to that applied by the European Court of Justice when considering Article 10.

The construction of section 10 was considered by the House of Lords for the first time in *Secretary of State for Defence v Guardian Newspapers Ltd.*[136] The House was of the firm view that section 10 substitutes for the discretionary protection which existed at common law a rule of wide and general application subject only to the four exceptions specified:[137] the prohibition does not differentiate between disclosure in interim proceedings for discovery prior to trial and disclosure at the trial itself and is not qualified by the nature of the proceedings or of the claim in respect of which the proceedings are brought.[138] Accordingly, it is sufficient to attract the protection of the section that an order of a court *may*, but not necessarily *will*, have the effect of disclosing a source of information.[139] Moreover, where a person seeks delivery up of a document which is his property in order to identify the informant from it, a judge, in exercising his discretion to order up delivery of goods under section 3(3) of the Torts (Interference with Goods) Act 1977, should have regard, when appropriate, to section 10, and should not make such an order unless the case falls within one of the four exceptions. It was also held that it is a question of fact, not discretion, whether a particular case falls within one of the exceptions, the burden being on the party seeking disclosure to prove on a balance of probabilities that disclosure is 'necessary'.[140] However, if a party seeks disclosure on an interim application, the court should be careful not to order disclosure unless the evidence before it establishes that the inference of necessity is unlikely to be displaced when all the evidence is produced

---

[134] Section 10 applies to the publication of photographs as well as written information. Photographs communicate information visually, writing does it through words, but in either case what is contained in the publication is information: per Sir Nicolas Browne-Wilkinson V-C in *Handmade Films (Productions) Ltd v Express Newspapers* [1986] FSR 463, Ch D at 468.

[135] [2002] 1 WLR 2033, HL. The dicta cited are those of Lord Phillips MR, whose judgment in the Court of Appeal ([2001] 1 WLR 515) was expressly endorsed by the House of Lords.

[136] [1984] 3 All ER 601, HL.          [137] Per Lord Scarman at 615.

[138] Per Lord Diplock at 603 and 606.          [139] See, eg, per Lord Roskill at 623.

[140] Per Lords Diplock and Scarman at 607 and 618 respectively.

and tested at trial.[141] Section 10 requires actual necessity to be established: expediency, however great, is not enough.[142]

Concerning 'justice', in the interest of which disclosure may be necessary, Lord Diplock, in *Secretary of State for Defence v Guardian Newspapers Ltd*, said that the word is used in the sense of the administration of justice in the course of legal proceedings in a court of law or tribunal.[143] This approach was adopted in *Maxwell v Pressdram Ltd*,[144] where it was held to be essential to identify and define the issue in the legal proceedings. Similarly, in *Handmade Films (Productions) Ltd v Express Newspapers*[145] it was held that although a claim for discovery based on the *Norwich Pharmacal* principle may come within 'the interests of justice', the claimant must show that he needs the name of the unknown wrongdoer because he intends to sue him—it is insufficient that an action *may* be brought.

Lord Diplock's definition, however, was rejected as too narrow in the leading English case, *X Ltd v Morgan-Grampian Ltd*.[146] The plaintiffs, X Ltd, two private companies, prepared a business plan in order to negotiate a bank loan to raise additional working capital. A copy of the plan was stolen. The next day, an unidentified source gave G, a journalist, information about the planned loan. G decided to write an article about X Ltd. X Ltd obtained an injunction against the defendant publishers, M-G Ltd, restraining publication of information derived from the plan, and applied under section 10 for an order disclosing the name of the source, their intention being to bring proceedings against him for recovery of the plan, an injunction to prevent further publication, and damages. The House of Lords held that, by reason of the *Norwich Pharmacal* principles, the court had jurisdiction to order M-G Ltd to disclose G's notes; that although the information obtained from the source had not been 'contained in a publication', the information having been received for the purposes of publication, it should be subject to section 10, since the purpose underlying the statutory protection of sources is as much applicable before as after publication; but, applying section 10, that disclosure of G's notes was necessary in the interests of justice.

The following propositions derive from the judgment of Lord Bridge, with which three other members of the House concurred:

1. Where a judge asks himself the question 'Can I be satisfied that disclosure of the source of *this* information is necessary to serve *this* interest?', he has to engage in a balancing exercise.

---

[141] Per Lord Scarman at 618. See also *Handmade Films (Productions) Ltd v Express Newspapers* [1986] FSR 463, Ch D.

[142] Per Lord Diplock at 607, applied in *Handmade Films (Productions) Ltd v Express Newspapers* [1986] FSR 463, Ch D. Cf per Lord Griffiths in *Re an inquiry under the Company Securities (Insider Dealing) Act 1985* [1988] 1 All ER 203 at 208–9, HL: 'I doubt if it is possible to go further than to say that "necessary" has a meaning that lies somewhere between "indispensable" on the one hand and "useful" or "expedient" on the other, and to leave it to the judge to decide towards which end of the scale of meaning he will place it on the facts of any particular case.'

[143] [1984] 3 All ER 601 at 607.        [144] [1987] 1 All ER 656 at 665, CA.

[145] [1986] FSR 463, Ch D.        [146] [1990] 2 All ER 1, HL.

2.   He starts with three assumptions: that the protection of sources is itself a matter of high public importance; that nothing less than necessity will suffice to override it; and that the necessity can only arise out of concern for another matter of high public importance, one of the four interests listed in section 10.

3.   The public interests of national security and the prevention of crime are of such overriding importance that once it is shown that disclosure will serve one of those interests, the necessity of disclosure follows almost automatically (although a judge might properly refuse disclosure if the crime to be prevented is of a trivial nature).

4.   The question whether disclosure is necessary 'in the interests of justice' gives rise to a more difficult problem of weighing one public interest against another. Lord Diplock's definition of justice was too narrow: it is 'in the interests of justice' that persons should be enabled to exercise important legal rights and to protect themselves from serious legal wrongs, whether or not resort to legal proceedings in a court of law is necessary to obtain those objectives. Thus if an employer is suffering grave damage from the activities of an unidentified disloyal employee, it is in the interests of justice that he should be able to identify him to end his contract of employment, notwithstanding that no legal proceedings may be necessary to do so.

5.   It is only if the judge is satisfied that disclosure in the interests of justice is of such preponderating importance as to override the statutory privilege that the threshold of necessity will be reached.

6.   This is a question of fact, but calls for the exercise of discriminating and sometimes difficult value judgments, to which many factors will be relevant on both sides of the scale. In favour of disclosure there will be a wide spectrum within which the particular case must be located. For example, if the party seeking disclosure shows that his very livelihood depends on it, the case will be near one end of the spectrum, but if what he seeks to protect is a minor interest in property, the case will be at or near the other end. On the other side, there is also a wide spectrum. One important factor is the nature of the information: the greater the legitimate public interest in it, the greater the importance of protecting the source. Another significant factor is the manner in which the information was obtained by the source: the importance of protecting the source will be enhanced if the information was obtained legitimately, but will be diminished if obtained illegally, unless counterbalanced by a clear public interest in publication, as when the source acts in order to expose iniquity.

Applying those principles to the facts, it was held that disclosure of X Ltd's plan during their refinancing negotiations would involve a threat of severe damage to their business, and consequently to the livelihood of their employees, which could only be defused by identification of the source, either as the thief or as the means of identifying the thief, which would then allow X Ltd to bring proceedings to recover the plan.

On the other hand, the source was involved in a gross breach of confidentiality which was not counterbalanced by any legitimate interest in publication of the information.

In *Ashworth Hospital Authority v MGM Ltd*[147] it was said that the wider interpretation of the 'interests of justice' in *X Ltd v Morgan-Grampian Ltd* accords more happily with the scheme of Article 10 than the interpretation of Lord Diplock in *Secretary of State for Defence v Guardian Newspapers Ltd*. Confirming that 'interests of justice' in section 10 means interests that are justiciable, it was also observed that it is difficult to envisage any such interest that would not fall within one or more of the Article 10 'legitimate aims'.

The leading case in the European Court of Human Rights is *Goodwin v UK*,[148] which dealt with the same facts as those which had been the subject of the House of Lords decision in *X Ltd v Morgan-Grampian Ltd*, but under Article 10 of the European Convention on Human Rights. The tests which the European Court and the House of Lords applied were substantially the same,[149] but the European Court came to the opposite conclusion. This, however, is not as surprising as it might initially seem. As Thorpe LJ pointed out in *Camelot Group plc v Centaur Communications Ltd*,[150] the making of a value judgment on competing facts is very close to the exercise of a discretion based on those facts, and there was a lapse of six years between the decisions in London and Strasbourg, a period in which standards fundamental to the performance of the balancing exercise may change materially. In the *Camelot Group* case, the plaintiff company, which was authorized to run the National Lottery, intended to publish its 1997 final accounts on 3 June. An unidentified employee of the company leaked a copy of the draft accounts to a journalist, who published an article disclosing their contents. The company sought an order which would effectively result in the disclosure of the identity of the source of the leaked information. The Court of Appeal held that a court, in assessing whether it is necessary to order disclosure in the interests of justice, may take account of an employer's wish to identify a disloyal employee so as to end his employment, and that in certain cases this factor alone may be strong enough to outweigh the public interest in the protection of the anonymity of press sources. On the facts, it held that the necessity for an order for disclosure of the source had been established: there was unease and suspicion among the company's employees which inhibited good working relationships, and there was a continuing threat of disclosure of further information, a risk that the employee might prove untrustworthy in some new respect in the future, by revealing, for example, the name of a public figure who had won a large prize. On the other hand, it did not significantly further the public interest to secure the publication of the accounts a week earlier than planned.

---

[147] [2002] 1 WLR 2033, HL. The dicta cited are those of Lord Phillips MR, whose judgment in the Court of Appeal ([2001] 1 WLR 515) was expressly endorsed by the House of Lords.

[148] (1996) 22 EHRR 123, ECtHR

[149] See *Camelot Group v Centaur Communications Ltd* [1998] 1 All ER 251 at 259 and 262, CA.

[150] [1998] 1 All ER 251 at 262.

In *Ashworth Hospital Authority v MGN Ltd*[151] the House of Lords accepted the approach of the European Court in *Goodwin v UK* that as a matter of general principle the 'necessity' for any restriction of freedom of expression must be convincingly established and that limitations on the confidentiality of journalistic sources call for the most careful scrutiny by the court. It was also held that any restriction on the right to freedom of expression must meet two further requirements: (i) the exercise of the disclosure jurisdiction because of Article 10(2) should meet a 'pressing social need' and (ii) the restriction should be proportionate to the 'legitimate aim' which is being pursued.

In *Saunders v Punch Ltd*[152] the court refused to make an order to disclose the identity of a source of information the nature of which suggested that he had seen records of meetings between the plaintiff and his lawyers which were protected by legal professional privilege. It was held that although the privilege is of massive importance in the administration of justice, it will not inevitably and always preponderate in the balancing exercise which the court must carry out in deciding whether disclosure is in the interests of justice. The question in each case is 'Are the interests of justice so pressing as to require the ban on disclosure to be overridden?', a question which on the facts of the case was answered in the negative.

*Secretary of State for Defence v Guardian Newspapers Ltd*, which concerned the second exception, national security, turned on the quality of evidence relied on by the claimant. A copy of a secret Ministry of Defence memorandum concerning the handling of publicity relating to the installation of nuclear weapons, had been 'leaked' to the *Guardian* newspaper. The Crown sought its return in order to identify the informant from markings made on the document. The House of Lords was unanimous in its view that where the Crown seeks an interim order for disclosure under this exception, the supporting affidavits should spell out, with the utmost particularity, all relevant material as to why disclosure is necessary. The House divided, however, on whether the evidence on which the Crown relied was sufficient to discharge the onus of proving necessity. A majority was satisfied that it was. The risk to national security lay not in the publication of the particular document but in the possibility that the person who had leaked it might in future leak other classified documents relating to the deployment of nuclear weapons, the disclosure of which would have much more serious consequences on national security.

Concerning the final exception, 'the prevention of crime', disclosure may be ordered if necessary for the prevention of crime generally rather than a particular identifiable future crime or crimes. Accordingly, in *Re an inquiry under the Company Securities (Insider Dealing) Act 1985*[153] the House of Lords held that a journalist who had made use of confidential price-sensitive information about takeover bids, leaked to him by a source inside one of the relevant government departments, was not entitled to the protection of section 10 because although inspectors appointed by the

---

[151] [2002] 1 WLR 2033, HL.          [152] [1998] 1 All ER 234, Ch D.          [153] [1988] 1 All ER 203, HL.

Secretary of State to investigate suspected leaks of this kind, and who had requested the journalist to reveal his source, were unable to show that they would take steps to prevent the commission of a particular future crime, nonetheless they needed the information for the purpose of exposing the leaking of official information and criminal insider trading and preventing such behaviour in the future. However, as in the case of the other exceptions, a claim will only succeed on the basis of the prevention of crime, if there is clear and specific evidence to prove 'necessity'. In *X v Y*[154] employees of the plaintiffs, a health authority, had supplied a national newspaper with information obtained from hospital records identifying two doctors who were carrying on general practice despite having contracted AIDS. The defendants had paid for the information. The plaintiffs sought disclosure by the defendants of their sources on the grounds that this was necessary for the prevention of crime.[155] The claim failed through lack of proof: although appropriate deterrent action could take a variety of forms—such as warning the culprits, dismissal, or criminal investigation—the plaintiffs had adduced no evidence as to what security procedures existed, what inquiries had been made to identify the sources, whether they had referred the matter to the police and whether criminal investigation was the intended or likely consequence.

# C PROCEDURAL ISSUES

## 1 TAKING THE OBJECTION

In civil litigation, a claim to public interest immunity usually arises at the disclosure stage. Under CPR rule 31.19, a party to litigation (or someone who has received an application for non-party disclosure) may apply, without notice, for an order permitting him to withhold disclosure of a document on the grounds that disclosure would damage the public interest. Under rule 31.19(6) the court, for the purposes of deciding such an application, may require the person seeking to withhold disclosure to produce the document to the court and may invite any person, whether or not a party, to make representations. Where a government department is a party to the litigation, it will make the application.[156] In other cases, the application may be made by the party possessing the documents on its own initiative or at the request of the relevant department, as in *Burmah Oil Co Ltd v Bank of England*.[157] If necessary, the head of the department or the Attorney-General may intervene to prevent documents being disclosed. The claim must usually be supported by affidavit evidence from the relevant minister or head of department, identifying the documents and the grounds for withholding them in as much detail as possible. In the case of a ministerial objection,

---

[154] [1988] 2 All ER 648, QBD.

[155] Under the Public Bodies Corrupt Practices Act 1889 and the Prevention of Corruption Act 1906.

[156] See s 28 of the Crown Proceedings Act 1947, above.      [157] [1980] AC 1090, HL.

a certificate signed by the minister may suffice. Concerning information or documents to be disclosed by a witness, the issue will often be raised before the judge at trial (in a criminal case in the absence of the jury, of course). In any case, the judge himself should take the point if necessary for if there is a public interest to be protected it must be protected regardless of party advantage.[158]

If a party to civil litigation holds documents in a class prima facie immune, he should (save perhaps in a very exceptional case) assert that the documents are immune and decline to disclose them, since the ultimate judge of where the balance of public interest lies is not him but the court.[159] If, in a criminal case, the prosecution wish to claim the immunity for documents helpful to the defence, they are duty bound to give notice to the defence of the claim so that, if necessary, the court can be asked to rule on its legitimacy. It is incompatible with an accused's absolute right to a fair trial to allow the prosecution to be judge in their own cause on the asserted claim. If the prosecution are not prepared to have the issue determined by the court, the inevitable result is that the prosecution will have to be abandoned.[160]

## 2 WAIVER AND SECONDARY EVIDENCE[161]

Whether public interest immunity can be waived appears to turn on a variety of factors, including: the time (whether before or after a ruling by the court); whether or not immunity is claimed at all; whether the decision on waiver is being made by a relevant Secretary of State on behalf of his department, an ordinary litigant or the maker and recipient of the document in question; the nature of the document; and the extent to which 'the cat is already out of the bag'.

It is often said that public interest immunity cannot be waived. This was asserted by Lord Simon in *R v Lewes Justices, ex p Home Secretary*,[162] where it led to disapproval of the term 'Crown Privilege'—it is the duty of a party to assert the immunity, even if it is to his disadvantage in the litigation. The principle was forcefully reasserted by Bingham LJ in *Makanjuola v Metropolitan Police Comr*.[163] a party claiming immunity is not claiming a right but observing a duty and therefore the immunity cannot be waived—although one can waive rights, one cannot waive duties. Neither of these two dicta, however, is of general application. As Lord Woolf pointed out in *R v Chief Constable of the West Midlands Police, ex p Wiley*,[164] Lord Simon was referring to the situation *after* the court has determined that the public interest against disclosure outweighs that of disclosure, and the *Makanjuola* case was not one involving a

---

[158] See, eg, Viscount Simon LC in *Duncan v Cammell Laird & Co Ltd* [1942] AC 624 at 642, citing *Chatterton v Secretary of State for India* [1895] 2 QB 189 at 195.

[159] Per Bingham LJ in *Makanjuola v Metropolitan Police Comr* [1992] 3 All ER 617 at 623.

[160] *R v Ward* [1993] 2 All ER 577 at 633, CA.

[161] The ensuing text concerns civil cases. As to voluntary disclosure by the CPS in criminal cases, see *R v Horseferry Road Magistrates, ex p Bennett (No 2)* [1994] 1 All ER 289, DC, above.

[162] [1973] AC 388 at 407.        [163] [1992] 3 All ER 617 at 623.

[164] [1994] 3 All ER 420 at 438–9.

department of state. As far as the contents of documents are concerned, Lord Woolf thought it most unlikely that the principle of public interest immunity can be used to prevent a department of state from disclosing documents which it considers it appropriate to disclose. Equally, as to class claims, it was doubted whether the courts would ever interfere, after the event, with governmental decisions in favour of disclosure. It is not clear, however, whether a Secretary of State is under a *duty*, before objecting to discovery of any particular documents of a class prima facie entitled to public interest immunity, to consider whether the public interest in non-disclosure of those particular documents is outweighed, on the facts of the particular case, by the public interest in those documents being available in the administration of justice. The proposition, it has been said, is 'at least arguable'.[165]

Concerning waiver by ordinary litigants, where a party other than a government department is in possession of documents in respect of which the courts have already established that class immunity applies, the court may intervene to prevent disclosure, but if the party in question has consulted the Attorney-General or other appropriate minister, who has endorsed the party's decision to disclose, the court, if the matter comes before it, will act on their views. In a situation of doubt, however, the question of disclosure should normally be left to the court.[166]

Concerning waiver by the maker and recipient of confidential documents, however, the authorities are not clear. In *Science Research Council v Nassé*[167] inability to waive the immunity was among the reasons given for resisting its extension: if the immunity applied, it could not be waived either by the employer or by the employer with the consent of the subject of a report and its author, which would be unnecessarily restrictive.[168] However, a different approach was taken in *Campbell v Tameside Metropolitan Borough Council*.[169] That was a personal injury action arising out of an assault by a pupil on a teacher in which immunity was refused for psychiatric reports on the pupil obtained by the school in pursuance of its statutory duty. Lord Denning re-asserted, obiter, a distinction he had drawn in *Neilson v Laugharne*:[170] in the case of documents in a higher category, including all those which must be kept top secret because their disclosure would be injurious to national defence, diplomatic relations or the detection of crime, the immunity cannot be waived; but in the case of documents within a lower category, including documents which are kept confidential in order that subordinates should be frank and candid in their reports, or for any other good reason, immunity can be waived by the maker and recipients of the confidential

---

[165] Per Rattee J in *Bennett v Metropolitan Police Comr* [1995] 2 All ER 1, Ch D at 13.

[166] Per Lord Woolf [1994] 3 All ER 420 at 438–9. See also per Lawton LJ in *Hehir v Metropolitan Police Comr* [1982] 1 WLR 715 at 722: if the reason for the immunity is the need to protect the public interest, individuals should be unable to waive it for their own purposes.

[167] [1980] AC 1028, per Lords Wilberforce and Fraser at 1066–7 and 1082 respectively.

[168] See also per Lord Donaldson MR in *Makanjuola v Metropolitan Police Comr* [1992] 3 All ER 617 at 621, CA.

[169] [1982] QB 1065, CA.     [170] [1981] QB 736, CA.

document.[171] A similar approach was also taken in *Multi Guarantee Co Ltd v Cavalier Insurance Co Ltd*.[172] The plaintiffs sought certain declaratory and other relief against the defendant company, which was in liquidation. Notes of a confidential meeting between the directors of the defendant company and officials of the Department of Trade and Industry had, with certain passages blacked out, been disclosed by the Department to the liquidator. The liquidator, with the consent of the defendant company, had disclosed the notes in the course of discovery, and orders of *subpoena duces tecum* and *subpoena ad testificandum* had been made against officials of the Department, requiring them to produce the notes recording the information given to them in confidence, and to testify. The Department intervened and applied for the orders to be discharged. The court, having examined the documents in private, refused to set the orders aside. It was held that although public interest immunity cannot be waived, it is capable of evaporating if those involved in the giving and receiving of the information consent to its disclosure. The fact that the partial disclosure had already significantly eroded the immunity was a relevant consideration in balancing the public interest in non-disclosure against the interest of the proper administration of justice in disclosure. Knox J, while acknowledging that it was a matter of degree in any particular case, said that if the cat had got all four legs out of the bag, there was little point in holding on to its tail.

In *R v Governor of Brixton Prison, ex p Osman*[173] certain documents protected by public interest immunity had been disclosed in a previous application for habeas corpus, although they had not been read in open court. It was held that prior disclosure of a document is a matter to be taken into account in the balance: if there has been publication to the whole world, then the public interest in non-disclosure must collapse. On the facts, however, the small degree of publication that had occurred could not upset the balance, which came down heavily in favour of immunity.

Similar considerations presumably apply in relation to secondary evidence. Obviously, the submarine plans in *Duncan v Cammell Laird & Co Ltd*[174] could not be proved by any means; in *R v Lewes Justices, ex p Home Secretary*[175] a copy of the allegedly libellous letter had somehow been obtained by the person to whom it referred, but because public interest immunity applied he was not able to prove that letter by any means. However, if information is freely available to the public, the fact that that information also forms the subject matter of a protected communication will surely not prevent proof of the information from the public sources. In each case, it is submitted, the question should be whether, on the particular facts, the public

---

[171] See also per Lord Cross in *Alfred Crompton Amusement Machines Ltd v Customs and Excise Comrs (No 2)* [1974] AC 405 at 434 and per Brightman LJ in *Hehir v Metropolitan Police Comr* [1982] 1 WLR 715 at 723, whose approach was endorsed by Lord Woolf in *R v Chief Constable of the West Midlands Police, ex p Wiley* [1994] 3 All ER 420 at 440: 'If the purpose of the immunity is to obtain the co-operation of an individual to the giving of a statement, I find it difficult to see how that purpose will be undermined if the maker of the statement consents to it being disclosed.'

[172] (1986) *The Times*, 24 June, Ch D.          [173] [1992] 1 All ER 108 at 118.

[174] [1942] AC 624, HL.          [175] [1973] AC 388, HL.

interest really does require non-disclosure; if there has been limited disclosure, immunity may still be justified, especially if the disclosure was wrongful.

## 3 DISCLOSURE, PRODUCTION, AND INSPECTION

Disclosure involves two stages, disclosure of the existence of a document and production of that document for inspection. Before any question of public interest immunity can be raised, the document has to be one which should be disclosed within the rules normally applicable in civil litigation.[176] Under CPR rule 31.6, standard disclosure requires a party to disclose only (a) the documents on which he relies, (b) the documents which adversely affect his own case, adversely affect another party's case or support another party's case and (c) the documents he is required to disclose by a relevant practice direction. If the party seeking disclosure falls at this hurdle, the question of public interest immunity will simply not arise.[177] Moreover, the court, in deciding whether to dispense with or limit standard disclosure, or whether to make an order for specific disclosure or specific inspection under rule 31.12, must seek to give effect to the 'overriding objective' of enabling it to deal with the case justly, which includes saving expense and ensuring that it is dealt with expeditiously and fairly etc.[178] If the party seeking disclosure falls at these hurdles, again the question of immunity will simply not arise.[179]

If these hurdles are surmounted, but public interest immunity is claimed, the judge will have to ask first whether the head of public interest on which reliance is placed is at least 'analogous' to those which have already been recognized by authority. He will also have to assess the strength of the objector's reasons for saying that disclosure will prejudice that public interest. If a prima facie claim to immunity is thus made out, the person seeking disclosure must establish that the public interest in the administration of justice in the case 'tips the scales decisively in his favour'.[180] In some cases it will be obvious from the description of the documents and the nature of the litigation that the claim to immunity is either groundless or unanswerable. In other cases a more detailed assessment of the content of the documents is needed. In *Conway v Rimmer*[181] Lord Reid said:

---

[176] Per Wood J in *Evans v Chief Constable of Surrey* [1989] 2 All ER 594, QBD at 597–8, citing Lord Scarman in *Burmah Oil Co Ltd v Bank of England* [1980] AC 1090 at 1141 and Lord Edmund-Davies in *Air Canada v Secretary of State for Trade (No 2)* [1983] 2 AC 394 at 441.

[177] See *Evans v Chief Constable of Surrey* [1989] 2 All ER 594, a decision under the Rules of Supreme Court, now replaced by the CPR. In that case, a claim for damages for wrongful arrest and false imprisonment, the plaintiff failed to satisfy the court that the contents of a report sent from the police to the DPP would help his case or damage that of the defendant.

[178] See Ch 2 under **F2 Exclusionary discretion.**

[179] See per Lord Woolf in *R v Chief Constable of the West Midlands Police, ex p Wiley* [1994] 3 All ER 420, HL at 430 and per Sir Thomas Bingham MR in *Taylor v Anderton* [1995] 2 All ER 420, CA at 432–5, all decisions under the Rules of Supreme Court.

[180] Per Lord Edmund-Davies in *Burmah Oil Co Ltd v Bank of England* [1980] AC 1090 at 1127, citing Lord Cross in *Alfred Crompton Amusement Machines Ltd v Customs and Excise Comrs (No 2)* [1974] AC 405 at 434.

[181] [1968] AC 910 at 953.

If [the judge] decides that on balance the documents probably ought to be produced, I think that it would generally be best that he should see them before ordering production and if he thinks that the Minister's reasons are not clearly expressed he will have to see the documents before ordering inspection.

Various objections to judicial inspection have been put forward. In *Duncan v Cammell Laird & Co Ltd*[182] the House of Lords regarded it as a wrongful communication between the judge and one party to the exclusion of the other. This reasoning was firmly rejected in *Conway v Rimmer*, but it remains true that a party may be aggrieved that the judge has seen material to which he has been denied access.[183] Other practical considerations were put forward by Lord Wilberforce in *Burmah Oil Co v Bank of England*,[184] namely (i) that judges should not lightly undertake to question a responsible minister's assessment of the weight of the public interest in non-disclosure and (ii) that inspection can be a very time-consuming activity which has to be conducted without the assistance of fully informed argument. Such considerations led Lord Wilberforce to uphold the claim to immunity without inspecting the documents. However, the other members of the House of Lords held that inspection was justified once it was shown that it was likely that the documents would contain material substantially useful to the party seeking discovery. On the facts, this test was satisfied, but after inspection disclosure was refused because it was not found to be 'necessary either for disposing fairly of the cause or matter or for saving costs'.

In *Air Canada v Secretary of State for Trade*[185] it was accepted that the ministerial documents probably did contain material which was relevant to the issues in the case, but without inspection it was impossible to know which side that material would favour. Lord Fraser was of the opinion that a court should not embark upon a private inspection of documents unless persuaded that such an inspection is likely to satisfy it that it ought to take the further step of ordering the documents to be produced publicly. On this basis, Lord Fraser, together with Lords Wilberforce and Edmund-Davies, held that the court should only inspect if the party seeking disclosure has shown 'that the documents are very likely to contain material which would give substantial support to his contention on an issue which arises in the case and that, without them, he might be deprived of the means of . . . proper presentation of his case'.[186] In the words of Lord Wilberforce,[187] there must be 'some concrete ground for belief which takes the case beyond a mere "fishing expedition" '. The judge should only inspect where he has definite grounds for expecting to find material of real importance to the party seeking disclosure; he is not entitled to 'take a peep' on the off-chance of finding something useful, for his function is to see fair play between the parties and he has neither power nor duty to go beyond that to ascertain the truth independently for himself. The reasoning of the majority was based partly on the

---

[182] [1942] AC 624 per Viscount Simon LC at 640–1.
[183] Per Lord Denning MR in *Neilson v Laugharne* [1981] QB 736 at 748–9.
[184] [1980] AC 1090 at 1117.　　　　[185] [1983] 2 AC 394.　　　　[186] Per Lord Edmund-Davies at 435.
[187] At 439.

ordinary principles of discovery and partly on the adversarial nature of the English trial system. Lords Templeman and Scarman argued that discovery is an exception to the adversarial principle; its function is not only to supply evidence to the other side but also to give some indication of the strength of one's own hand and thus to encourage settlement and save costs. They therefore disputed the need for the party seeking disclosure to show that the material would support his case, and held that the court should inspect documents if they are very likely to be necessary for the just determination of the issues in the case or, in other words, if their disclosure may materially assist *any* of the parties to the proceedings. However, they agreed that the documents should be withheld without inspection because it had not been shown that the documents were likely to contain sufficiently relevant material which was not already available from other sources. Where a prima facie claim to public interest immunity is properly made out, the court is no doubt justified in refusing even to inspect unless a case in favour of disclosure has been made out, in order to prevent litigants from embarking on 'fishing expeditions'. However, it is submitted that the reasoning of Lords Templeman and Scarman adequately achieves this end. Their reasoning appears to have prevailed: ordinarily the modern practice, in a case in which a party satisfies the general threshold test for disclosure but his opponent makes out a prima facie claim to immunity, is for the court to proceed to inspect in order to undertake the balancing exercise.[188] However, it seems that if there is a ministerial certificate demonstrating an actual or potential risk to national security, the court should not exercise its right to inspect.[189]

In order to ensure, as far as possible, that a claim to public interest immunity is not wrongly overridden, Lord Reid in *Conway v Rimmer*[190] said that the party objecting to disclosure should always be able to appeal against the judge's ruling before the documents are produced. The importance of this possibility of appeal, even before the judge inspects the documents, was emphasized in *Burmah Oil Co Ltd v Bank of England*.[191] In *Air Canada v Secretary of State for Trade*[192] Bingham J, the trial judge, was provisionally inclined to order production of the documents but decided to inspect them first. He therefore ordered inspection, but stayed the order pending an appeal.[193]

## 4 PARTIAL DISCLOSURE

Proper objections to disclosure may sometimes be overcome by allowing names and sensitive or irrelevant material to be covered up. This course has been sanctioned in

---

188 See, eg, *Goodridge v Chief Constable of Hampshire Constabulary* [1999] 1 All ER 896, QBD.

189 See *Balfour v Foreign and Commonwealth Office* [1994] 2 All ER 588, CA, above.

190 [1968] AC 910 at 953.

191 [1980] AC 1090 at 1136 per Lord Keith and at 1147 per Lord Scarman.     192 [1983] 2 AC 394.

193 The approach to inspection laid down in *Air Canada v Secretary of State for Trade* is inappropriate in criminal proceedings. See generally above, under **A2 Criminal cases**. See also per Phillips J in *R v Clowes* [1992] 3 All ER 440 at 455, CCA and per Mann LJ in *R v Governor of Brixton Prison, ex p Osman* [1992] 1 All ER 108, QBD at 117.

relation to material protected by public interest immunity[194] as well as material protected on the grounds of confidentiality alone.[195] In *Science Research Council v Nassé* Lord Edmund-Davies seems to have approved Lord Denning's suggestion in the Court of Appeal that disclosure can be limited to the other side's lawyers.[196]

In *R v Chief Constable of the West Midlands Police, ex p Wiley*[197] Lord Woolf was of the opinion that in general public interest immunity is provided against disclosure of documents or their contents and is not, in the absence of exceptional circumstances, an immunity against the use of knowledge obtained from the documents. If the legal advisers of a party in possession of material which is the subject of immunity from disclosure are aware of the contents of that material, they should consider it their duty to assist the court and the other party to mitigate any disadvantage resulting from the non-disclosure. Thus it may be possible to provide any necessary information without producing the actual document or it may be possible to disclose a part of the document or to disclose on a restricted basis. In many cases cooperation between the legal advisers of the parties should avoid the risk of injustice.

---

[194] See, eg, per Lord Pearce in *Conway v Rimmer* [1968] AC 910 at 988.

[195] *Science Research Council v Nassé* [1980] AC 1028, above.

[196] [1980] AC 1028, HL at 1077, citing [1979] QB 144 at 173.          [197] [1994] 3 All ER 420 at 447, HL.

# 20

# PRIVILEGE

In the previous chapter, we considered how evidence may be excluded when the public interest in permitting all relevant evidence to be presented at trial is outweighed by some other public interest extrinsic to the trial process, such as the proper functioning of government agencies. The same theme underlies the subject matter of the present chapter which concerns several well-established principles whereby relevant evidence is excluded not because it is unreliable or irrelevant to the facts in issue, but because of extrinsic considerations which are held to outweigh the value that the evidence would have at trial. Three types of privilege fall to be considered: (i) the privilege against self-incrimination; (ii) legal professional privilege (protecting the confidentiality of the lawyer–client relationship); and (iii) 'without prejudice' negotiations (enabling settlement negotiations to be conducted without fear of proposed concessions being used in evidence at trial as admissions).[1] These heads of privilege entitle certain people, whether parties to litigation or witnesses, to refuse to disclose material relating to particular matters, and in some cases to prevent others, such as their lawyers, from doing so. Questions of privilege arise most frequently in connection with oral or documentary evidence to be given at trial, whether criminal or civil, and documents to be produced by a party for inspection at the disclosure stage of civil litigation.[2]

There are important differences between privilege and public interest immunity. First, where a person satisfies the conditions for claiming privilege, he is entitled to refuse to answer the question or disclose the document in issue—there is no question

---

[1] The privilege whereby a non-party witness could not be compelled to produce his documents of title to property was abolished for civil proceedings by s 16(1)(b) of the Civil Evidence Act 1968 but is still theoretically available in criminal proceedings. The privilege whereby a married person could refuse to answer questions about communications made to him or her by the spouse during the marriage was abolished for civil cases by s 16(3) of the Civil Evidence Act 1968 and for criminal cases by s 80(9) of and Sch 7 to the Police and Criminal Evidence Act 1984. The privilege whereby in criminal proceedings a married person could refuse to answer questions about intercourse with his or her spouse during the marriage was repealed by s 80(9) of the 1984 Act.

[2] Privilege is often relevant at other stages of litigation, eg, in relation to: (i) the special procedures established in *Norwich Pharmacal Co v Customs and Excise Comrs* [1974] AC 133 and ss 33 and 34 of the Supreme Court Act 1981, whereby a non-party or intended party can sometimes be compelled to produce documents for information for use in civil litigation; (ii) the execution of a search order (formerly known as an Anton Piller order), under which the person to whom it is addressed is required to allow an intending claimant to search premises and remove material which may be relevant in subsequent civil litigation; and (iii) requests or orders for further information under PD 18 and CPR r 18.1.

of the judge balancing the particular weight of the claim to privilege against the value of the evidence at trial. Secondly, the heads of privilege are upheld for the benefit of clearly identified people. If those people choose to waive their privilege, or fail to claim it, nobody else can claim it. This aspect of privilege explains the limited possibility of appeal. If a judge improperly rejects a non-party witness's claim to privilege, there can be no appeal for there has been no infringement of either party's rights.[3] If, however, the judge wrongly rejects a party's claim to privilege, for example by requiring disclosure of privileged documents on discovery or by compelling a party who is giving evidence to answer questions as to privileged matters, then that party can appeal since he will have suffered a wrong. Similarly, if a judge improperly accepts a claim to privilege, whether made by a party or non-party witness, then the party who would otherwise have been entitled to call for the documents or tender the evidence will have suffered a wrong on the basis of which he ought to be able to appeal. A third difference from public interest immunity concerns secondary evidence. A successful claim to privilege prevents certain people from being compelled to give evidence of particular matters, but there will be no objection to those matters being proved by other evidence, if available. However, if a claim to public interest immunity succeeds, it will not be possible to prove the excluded facts by any other means.

Privilege also falls to be distinguished from the rules relating to competence and compellability. Privilege only entitles witnesses to refuse to give evidence on particular matters. A witness who is competent but not compellable can choose whether to give evidence at all.[4] Having chosen to give evidence, such a witness, like a compellable witness, must answer all questions properly put to him (and is liable to be committed for contempt if he refuses) except those in respect of which he is entitled to claim privilege.

The drawing of inferences adverse to a witness or party claiming privilege is not permitted.[5]

# A  THE PRIVILEGE AGAINST SELF-INCRIMINATION

The privilege against self-incrimination is deep-rooted in English law and history. It became a part of the common law after the abolition of the Court of Star Chamber,[6] and it is based on a traditional reluctance to compel anyone, on pain of punishment, to give incriminating evidence against himself. Today, the privilege is at a cross-roads. Although it is theoretically intact, as we shall see, Parliament and the courts have

---

[3] See, eg, in relation to the privilege against self-incrimination, R v Kinglake (1870) 22 LT 335.
[4] See Ch 5.     [5] Wentworth v Lloyd (1864) 10 HL Cas 589.
[6] Holdsworth's History of English Law vol 9 (London 1944) 200.

recognized the unsatisfactory results of the privilege. Parliament has, in prescribed circumstances, abrogated or modified it. The courts, doubtless frustrated by the piecemeal, inconsistent and somewhat illogical nature of parliamentary reform, have started to substitute a different protection, thereby rendering invocation of the privilege in some civil proceedings superfluous. It is to be hoped that Parliament will give urgent attention to the major problem so powerfully presented by Lord Templeman in *AT & T Istel v Tully*:[7]

the privilege can only be justified on two grounds, first that it discourages the ill-treatment of a suspect and secondly that it discourages the production of dubious confessions. Neither of these considerations applies to the present appeal. It is difficult to see any reason why in civil proceedings the privilege . . . should be exercisable so as to enable a litigant to refuse relevant and even vital documents which are in his possession or power and which speak for themselves. And it is fanciful to suggest that an order on [the first defendant] to say whether he has received [the second plaintiff's] money and if so what has happened to that money could result in his ill-treatment or in a dubious confession. I regard the privilege . . . exercisable in civil proceedings as an archaic and unjustifiable survival from the past when the court directs the production of relevant documents and requires the defendant to specify his dealings with the plaintiff's property or money.

The classic formulation of this privilege is that of Goddard LJ in *Blunt v Park Lane Hotel*:[8]

The rule is that no-one is bound to answer any question if the answer thereto would, in the opinion of the judge, have a tendency to expose [him] to any criminal charge, penalty or forfeiture which the judge regards as reasonably likely to be preferred or sued for.

This rule applies in both civil and criminal proceedings, although in civil proceedings a witness can no longer refuse to answer on the ground that to do so would tend to expose him to forfeiture,[9] and in criminal proceedings the position of an accused who elects to testify, is governed by section 1(2) of the Criminal Evidence Act 1898, which provides that: 'A person charged in criminal proceedings who is called as a witness in the proceedings may be asked any question in cross-examination notwithstanding that it would tend to criminate him as to any offence with which he is charged in the proceedings.' Thus section 1(2) of the 1898 Act removes from the accused who testifies the privilege against self-incrimination in respect of the offence or offences charged. In *Jones v DPP*[10] a majority of the House of Lords was of the opinion that section 1(2) permits only such questions as tend directly to criminate the accused as to the offence charged and does not permit questions which tend to do so indirectly,

---

[7] [1992] 3 All ER 523 at 530. Lords Griffiths and Ackner agreed with this view.
[8] [1942] 2 KB 253 at 257, CA.    [9] Civil Evidence Act 1968, s 16(1)(a).
[10] [1962] AC 635, HL.

such as questions concerning the misconduct of the accused on other occasions in respect of which evidence is admissible at common law.[11]

The privilege against self-incrimination enables a witness to refuse to answer questions in court and also to refuse to produce documents or things. As to pre-trial proceedings, the privilege may arise only if the claimant seeks to compel disclosure and the production of a document, or to compel an answer to a request for further information in order to assist his case: the privilege does not enable a party to refuse to enter a defence to a civil claim, because there is no *compulsion* to file a defence or to plead anything which provides information to the claimant.[12]

The privilege also applies to search orders,[13] covering not only the parts of the order which require the defendant to produce and verify information and documents, but also the parts requiring him to permit the plaintiff to enter, search and seize documents,[14] and to disclosure ancillary to a freezing injunction, if production of the documents or information sought would tend to expose the defendant to a prosecution in the United Kingdom.[15] It does not follow, however, that a search order which would expose a defendant to a real risk of criminal prosecution can never be made or executed. Such an order may properly be made if it contains a proviso to the effect that (i) the defendant should be advised of his right to obtain immediate legal advice before execution of the order, including advice that he may be entitled to claim the privilege against self-incrimination and (ii) the order will have effect only in so far as the defendant does not claim the privilege. If such advice is given in everyday language and the defendant properly understands it but declines to claim the privilege, the order may then be executed.[16]

At common law, there is no exception to the privilege preventing an agent, trustee or other fiduciary from claiming the privilege, as against a principal, in an action brought against him by the principal to recover money or property, or an account of such money or property, for which the agent, trustee or fiduciary is accountable.[17]

---

[11] Cf *R v Anderson* [1988] 2 All ER 549, in which the Court of Appeal was inclined to think that questioning about the fact that the accused was 'wanted' by the police, which tended to destroy her innocent explanations of prima facie damning circumstances, might have been permissible under s 1(2).

[12] *Versailles Trade Finance Ltd v Clough* [2001] All ER (D) 209, (2001) *The Times*, 1 Nov, CA.

[13] *Rank Film Distributors Ltd v Video Information Centre* [1982] AC 380, HL. But see now s 72 of the Supreme Court Act 1981, below.

[14] *Tate Access Floors Inc v Boswell* [1990] 3 All ER 303, Ch D.

[15] *Sociedade Nacional de Combustiveis de Angola UEE v Lundqvist* [1990] 3 All ER 283, CA. The privilege is also available in respect of the risk of contempt proceedings either in the action in which the privilege is invoked or in some other action: *Memory Corpn plc v Sidhu* [2000] 1 All ER 434, Ch D. An alleged contemnor cannot be compelled to answer questions at an interim stage the answers to which might expose him to an application to commit for contempt and cannot be compelled to answer a request for further information as regards such an application: *Great Future International v Sealand Housing Corporation* LTL 20/1/2004, Ch D.

[16] *IBM United Kingdom Ltd v Prima Data International Ltd* [1994] 4 All ER 748, Ch D.

[17] *Bishopsgate Investment Management Ltd (in provisional liquidation) v Maxwell* [1992] 2 All ER 856, CA and *Tate Access Floors Inc v Boswell* [1990] 3 All ER 303, Ch D.

## 1 'CRIMINAL CHARGE, PENALTY, OR FORFEITURE'

The term 'criminal charge' is self-explanatory, but it should be noted that under section 14(1)(a) of the Civil Evidence Act 1968, if the claim to privilege is made in civil proceedings, 'the right of a person ... to refuse to answer any question or produce any document or thing if to do so would tend to expose that person to proceedings for an offence ... shall apply only as regards criminal offences *under the law of any part of the United Kingdom*'.[18] Although there is no *absolute* privilege against self-incrimination under foreign law, the possibility of self-incrimination, or the incrimination of others, under foreign law is a factor which can be taken into account in deciding whether, and on what terms, a disclosure order should be made.[19] However, the scope for restricting disclosure of otherwise clearly relevant facts on this basis is limited and likely to be confined to cases where disclosure might have serious consequences for persons still resident in the foreign state in question.[20] Concerning a 'penalty', section 14(1)(a) provides that if the claim to privilege is made in civil proceedings, the penalty must be provided for by the law of any part of the United Kingdom. Penalties now arise mainly under statutes such as those relating to the Revenue. It does not matter that liability to the penalty may arise without court proceedings, provided that it can ultimately be enforced in English courts. EEC regulations, incorporated into English law by virtue of the European Communities Act 1972, are a potent source of penalties.[21] It seems that proceedings for civil contempt are proceedings for the 'recovery of a penalty' within section 14(1) in respect of which there is a privilege against self-incrimination.[22] Exposure to forfeiture refers to the risk of forfeiting property, a risk against which the courts now have wide powers to grant relief, hence the obsolescence of this part of the rule.

## 2 'A TENDENCY TO EXPOSE'

In *R v Boyes*[23] a witness was handed a pardon in order to overcome his claim that his answers would expose him to criminal liability. He nonetheless refused to answer on the ground that the pardon would not protect him from the admittedly remote possibility of impeachment for his offence, and he asserted that his bona fide claim to the

---

[18] There is no clear authority on the point in relation to criminal proceedings.

[19] *Arab Monetary Fund v Hashim* [1989] 3 All ER 466, Ch D.

[20] *Arab Monetary Fund v Hashim (No 2)* [1990] 1 All ER 673, Ch D.

[21] See, eg, *Rio Tinto Zinc Corpn v Westinghouse Electric Corpn* [1978] AC 547, HL. It has been held that 'additional damages' which may be awarded under statutes for breach of copyright are not a penalty: *Rank Film Distributors Ltd v Video Information Centre* [1982] AC 380, CA at 425 per Templeman LJ; *Overseas Programming Co Ltd v Cinematographische Commerz-Anstalt and Iduna Film GmbH* (1984) The Times, 16 May, QBD.

[22] See *Cobra Golf Ltd v Rata* [1997] 2 All ER 150, Ch D and *Bhimji v Chatwani (No 3)* [1992] 4 All ER 912, Ch D, not following *Garvin v Domus Publishing Ltd* [1989] 2 All ER 344, Ch D. In *Cobra Golf Ltd v Rata* there were two separate actions and execution of a search order in the second appeared capable of proving a civil contempt in the first. See also, and cf, *Crest Homes plc v Marks* [1987] 2 All ER 1074, HL.

[23] (1861) 1 B&S 311, QB.

privilege was conclusive of his right not to answer. The court rejected his claim. While acknowledging that, if it appears that the witness is in danger, he should be allowed great latitude in judging for himself the effect of any particular question, the court held:

To entitle a party called as a witness to the privilege of silence, the court must see, from the circumstances of the case and the nature of the evidence which the witness is called to give, that there is reasonable ground to apprehend danger to the witness from his being called to answer . . . The danger to be apprehended must be real and appreciable with reference to the ordinary operation of law in the ordinary course of things; not a danger of an imaginary and unsubstantial character . . .[24]

It is not sufficient to ascertain that the claim was made on legal advice. The duty of the court is non-delegable and therefore it cannot simply adopt the conclusion of a solicitor advising the witness, whose conclusion may or may not be correct.[25] If necessary, the judge may hear the witness's explanation *in camera*. He must make due allowance for the possibility that apparently innocuous questions may, when combined with other material, give rise to damaging inferences.[26] Moreover, it is sufficient to support a claim that the answers sought might lead to a line of inquiry which would or might form a significant step in the chain of evidence required for a prosecution.[27] On the other hand, a claim to privilege will not succeed if the evidence against the witness is already so strong that if proceedings are to be taken at all they will be taken whether or not the witness answers. This is a question of fact for the judge, who should not ignore the possibility that although some evidence is already available to the authorities, additional evidence from the witness may increase the risk of proceedings being taken.[28] The triviality or staleness of the offence may lead the court to treat the likelihood of prosecution as too remote, but it remains to be seen whether protection can be refused on the sole ground that the charge, though likely to be brought, is a trivial one.[29]

[24] Per Cockburn CJ at 330, approved in *Den Norske Bank ASA v Antonatos* [1998] 3 All ER 74, CA. Cf *Triplex Safety Glass Co Ltd v Lancegaye Safety Glass (1934) Ltd* [1939] 2 KB 395: privilege may be claimed on the ground of exposure to criminal libel proceedings even though such proceedings are rare.

[25] *R (Crown Prosecution Service) v Bolton Magistrates' Court* [2004] 1 WLR 835, DC.

[26] Per Cockburn CJ in *R v Boyes*, ibid at 330; see also *British Steel Corpn v Granada Television Ltd* [1981] AC 1096, HL, especially per Megarry V-C in the Chancery Division (at 1108).

[27] Per Beldam LJ in *Sociedade Nacional de Combustiveis de Angola UEE v Lundqvist* [1990] 3 All ER 283 at 297, CA, citing Lord Wilberforce in *Rank Film Distributors Ltd v Video Information Centre* [1982] AC 380 at 443.

[28] *Rio Tinto Zinc Corpn v Westinghouse Electric Corpn* [1978] AC 547. In *Khan v Khan* [1982] 2 All ER 60, CA a witness in civil proceedings was required to answer questions about his use of the proceeds of a cheque. His conduct 'reeked of dishonesty' and evidence as to his use of the proceeds did not materially increase the risk of prosecution for theft of the cheque.

[29] See per Lord Fraser in *Rank Film Distributors Ltd v Video Information Centre* [1982] AC 380 at 445: the risk of prosecution for trivial offences under s 21 of the Copyright Act 1956 was not enough to establish the privilege, partly because the likelihood of prosecution was too remote, but also because it would be 'unreasonable to allow the possibility of incrimination of such offences to obstruct disclosure of information which would be of much more value to the owners of the infringed copyright than any protection they might obtain from s 21'.

## 3 SPOUSES, STRANGERS, AND COMPANIES

In most cases the witness claiming privilege will do so because he fears prosecution himself. If he chooses not to claim the privilege or, in ignorance, fails to claim it—the judge may, but is not obliged to remind him of his rights—no one else can claim it on his behalf.

A witness in either civil or criminal proceedings cannot claim privilege in respect of questions the answers to which would tend to incriminate strangers.[30] In civil proceedings, under section 14(1)(b) of the 1968 Act, the right of a person to assert the privilege 'shall include a like right to refuse any question or produce any document or thing if to do so would tend to expose the husband or wife of that person to proceedings for any such criminal offence or for the recovery of any such penalty'. However, the privilege remains that of the witness and, if he chooses to answer, the spouse cannot complain. In criminal proceedings, however, it seems that a witness cannot claim privilege in respect of questions the answers to which would tend to incriminate his spouse.[31]

Because the privilege is a privilege against *self*-incrimination, office holders, employees or agents of a company may claim the privilege themselves, but cannot refuse to answer questions which would tend to incriminate the company or render it liable to a penalty under, for example, an EEC regulation.[32] Equally, the company cannot refuse to answer questions which would tend to incriminate the office-holders.[33]

## 4 STATUTORY PROVISIONS AFFECTING THE PRIVILEGE

Pursuant to a variety of statutes and statutory instruments, specified persons in specified circumstances must answer questions for specified purposes notwithstanding that their answers may incriminate them. Some of the provisions abrogate the privilege expressly; others do so impliedly. The true effect of any statutory withdrawal of privilege is a matter of construction, but where a statute revokes the privilege without restricting the use that may be made of the answers, prima facie the answers may be used for any purpose for which they could have been used had the privilege never applied in the first place.[34] Thus if a witness is forced to make an incriminating admission, that admission cannot then be excluded at his own trial as being

---

[30] See *Ex p Reynolds* (1882) 20 Ch D 294 (the privilege can be invoked only by someone who does so in good faith for his own protection (or that of his spouse)), cited by Megarry V-C in *British Steel Corpn v Granada Television Ltd* [1981] AC 1096 at 1106, Ch D.

[31] Per Lord Diplock in *Rio Tinto Zinc Corpn v Westinghouse Electric Corpn* [1978] AC 547 at 637 and, but only by inference, *R v Pitt* [1982] 3 All ER 63, CA. Contrast *R v All Saints, Worcester* (1817) 6 M&S 194.

[32] Per Lord Diplock in *Rio Tinto Zinc Corpn v Westinghouse Electric Corpn* [1978] AC 547 at 637–8.

[33] Per Beldam LJ in *Sociedade Nacional de Combustiveis de Angola UEE v Lundqvist* [1990] 3 All ER 283 at 300–1 and per Browne-Wilkinson V-C in *Tate Access Floors v Boswell* [1990] 3 All ER 303 at 314–15.

[34] *R v Scott* (1856) Dears & B 47.

involuntary.[35] However, use of the answer in subsequent judicial proceedings may amount to a violation of the Article 6 right to a fair hearing, and in any event a criminal court may exclude the admission, in its discretion, if it would be oppressive to admit it.[36]

In *Saunders v UK*,[37] S was convicted of conspiracy, false accounting and theft. At the trial, evidence was adduced of answers given by S to DTI inspectors appointed under the Companies Act 1985. Under section 434 of the Act, the inspectors could compel a person to answer their questions and the answers obtained could be used in evidence in any subsequent proceedings. The European Court of Human Rights was of the view that although not specifically mentioned in Article 6, the right to silence and the right not to incriminate oneself are 'generally recognized international standards which lie at the heart of the notion of a fair procedure under Article 6' and held that use of the statements at S's trial was in breach of his Article 6 right to fair trial.[38] Section 434 has since been amended.[39]

The implied rights within Article 6 are not of an absolute character, but can be qualified or restricted, and a statute which does qualify or restrict those rights will be compatible with Article 6 if there is an identifiable social or economic problem that the statute is intended to deal with and the qualification or restriction is proportionate to that problem. *Brown v Stott*,[40] a Scottish case, concerned the introduction of evidence of an admission obtained from the accused under section 172(2)(a) of the Road Traffic Act 1988, under which, where the driver of a vehicle is alleged to be guilty of one of a number of road traffic offences, including driving with excess alcohol and speeding, 'the person keeping the vehicle shall give such information as to the identity of the driver as he may be required to give by or on behalf of a chief officer of police'. Under section 172(3), if he fails to comply with such a requirement he shall be guilty of an offence punishable by a fine, mandatory endorsement and discretionary disqualification from driving. It was held that evidence of an admission obtained from the accused under section 172(2)(a) did not infringe the right to a fair hearing. Lord Bingham said:

The jurisprudence of the European Court very clearly establishes that while the overall fairness of a criminal trial cannot be compromised, the constituent rights comprised, whether expressly or implicitly, within Article 6 are not themselves absolute. Limited qualification of these rights is acceptable if reasonably directed by national authorities towards a clear and proper public objective and if representing no greater qualification than the situation calls for.

---

[35] Contrariwise if the judge wrongly denies a witness the protection of privilege. Any admission thus compelled will be excluded in the trial of the witness as involuntary: *R v Garbett* (1847) 1 Den 236.

[36] See per French J in *Overseas Programming Co Ltd v Cinematographische Commerz-Anstalt and Iduna Film Gmbh* (1984) *The Times*, 16 May, QBD and per Ralph Gibson LJ in *Bank of England v Riley* [1992] 1 All ER 769 at 777, CA.

[37] (1996) 23 EHRR 313 at para 68.

[38] One of the frequently cited decisions of the European Court is *Funke v France* (1993) 60 EHRR 297, but its ratio is far from clear: see the comments of Lord Hoffmann in *R v Hertfordshire County Council, ex p Green Environmental Industries Ltd* [2000] 2 AC 412, HL at 424.

[39] See below.          [40] [2001] 2 WLR 817, PC.

There was a clear public interest in the enforcement of road traffic legislation and section 172 was not a disproportionate response to the serious social problem of the high incidence of death and injury on the roads caused by the misuse of motor vehicles. The section permitted a single, simple question to be put, the answer to which cannot by itself incriminate the suspect, and the penalty for non-compliance is moderate and non-custodial. Furthermore, all who own or drive motor cars know that by doing so they subject themselves to a regulatory regime which is imposed because the possession and use of cars are recognized to have the potential to cause grave injury.

Subsequent attempts to distinguish *Brown v Stott* on the grounds that, under Scottish law, the driver's admission must be corroborated, have failed; and it was applied in *Mawdesley v Chief Constable of the Cheshire Constabulary*,[41] a case of driving in excess of the speed limit. The reasoning of the Privy Council in *Brown v Stott* falls to be compared with that of the European Court of Human Rights in *Heaney and McGuinness v Ireland*[42] H and M were arrested on suspicion of involvement in a terrorist bombing. They were required to account for their movements under section 52 of the Offences Against the State Act, 1939, which makes it a criminal offence, punishable by six months' imprisonment, for a person detained on suspicion of a defined terrorist offence to fail to account for his movements. They refused to do so and were prosecuted under section 52. They were also charged with membership of the IRA under section 21 of the Act. They were convicted of the charge under section 52, but acquitted of the charge under section 21. The European Court of Human Rights found a violation of Article 6 on the basis that the degree of compulsion created by the threat of a prison sentence under section 52 'with a view to compelling them to provide information relating to charges against them under that Act', in effect destroyed the very essence of the right to silence and the privilege against self-incrimination. As Aikens J observed in *R v Kearns*[43] the Court attached importance to the fact that the purpose of obtaining information under section 52 was to provide evidence for other charges under section 21 of the 1939 Act.

In *R v Allen (No 2)*,[44] A was convicted of cheating the public revenue of tax by concealing or failing to disclose profits. He had provided a schedule of assets, in compliance with a notice given by the inspector under section 20 of the Taxes Management Act 1970, but had omitted to list his beneficial interest in shares issued by offshore companies. Under section 98(1) of the Act, a person who fails to comply with a section 20 notice is liable to a penalty. The House of Lords held that the section 20 notice could not constitute a violation of the right against self-incrimination, denying the right to a fair trial, because the State, for the purpose of collecting tax, is entitled to require a citizen to inform it of his income and to enforce penalties for failure to do so. A's further application to the European Court of Human Rights failed. It was held that the requirement to declare assets disclosed no issue under Article 6(1), even

---

[41] [2004] 1 WLR 1035, QBD.        [42] [2001] Crim LR 481, ECHR.
[43] [2003] 1 Cr App R 111, CA at [41].        [44] [2001] 4 All ER 768, HL.

though there was a penalty for failure to comply. The case was one of making a false declaration of assets, not one of forced self-incrimination in relation to some previously committed offence, nor one of being prosecuted for failing to provide information which might incriminate him in pending or anticipated criminal proceedings.[45]

An important distinction is to be drawn between statements made by the accused under compulsion, which, depending on the circumstances, may involve infringement of the right to silence or the right not to incriminate oneself, and the compulsory production of pre-existing documents and materials, which involves no infringement of those rights. According to the majority of the European Court in *Saunders v UK*:[46]

The right not to incriminate oneself is primarily concerned . . . with respecting the will of an accused person to remain silent. As commonly understood in the legal systems of the Contracting Parties to the Convention and elsewhere, it does not extend to the use in criminal proceedings of material which may be obtained from the accused through compulsory powers but which have an existence independent of the will of the suspect, such as, inter alia, documents acquired pursuant to a warrant, breath, blood and urine samples and bodily tissue for the purposes of DNA testing.[47]

This dictum was applied in *Attorney-General's Reference (No 7 of 2000)*[48] where the accused, a bankrupt, completed a preliminary questionnaire and admitted having lost money by gambling. He was then required to produce documents to the Official Receiver under the Insolvency Act 1986, and if he had failed to do so he would have been in contempt of court. He was charged with the offence of materially contributing to or increasing the extent of his insolvency by gambling and the documents which he had produced formed the basis of the prosecution case against him. The Court of Appeal held that use of the documents relating to his gambling would not violate his rights under Article 6. The court adopted the reasoning of Justice La Forest in *Thompson Newspapers Ltd v Director of Investigation & Research*[49] that, whereas a compelled statement is evidence that would not have existed independently of exercise of the power of compulsion, evidence which exists independently of the compelled statement could have been found by other means and its quality does not depend on its past connection with the compelled statement. The principle was also applied in *R v Hundal*,[50] on charges of belonging to a proscribed organization, in relation to items seized following a search under the Terrorism Act 2000.

In *R v Kearns*[51] Aikens J, after reviewing the Strasbourg and UK cases, described a further important distinction:

---

[45] *Allen v UK* [2003] Crim LR 280. Cf *JB v Switzerland* [2001] Crim LR 748 ECHR, where tax evasion proceedings having been instituted against JB, his refusal to provide documents resulted in proceedings in which he was fined. The latter proceedings were held to be in breach of Art 6 because the objective of the demand was to use the documents in the tax evasion proceedings.

[46] (1997) 23 EHRR 313 at para 69.

[47] But see also *JB v Switzerland* [2001] Crim LR 748, ECHR, above.

[48] [2001] 2 Cr App R 286, CA.          [49] (1990) 54 CCC 417 (Supreme Court of Canada).

[50] [2004] 2 Cr App R 307, CA.          [51] [2003] 1 Cr App R 111 at [53].

A law will not be likely to infringe the right to silence or not to incriminate oneself if it demands the production of information for an administrative purpose or in the course of an extra-judicial enquiry. However if the information so produced is or could be used in subsequent judicial proceedings, whether criminal or civil, then the use of the information in such proceedings could breach those rights and so make that trial unfair.

Thus in *Saunders v UK* it was the fact that the information obtained had been used at the subsequent criminal trial that made that trial unfair, not the fact that the information had been obtained in the first place.[52] In *R v Hertfordshire County Council, ex p Green Environmental Industries Ltd*[53] a summons was issued against the company, the local authority having served a notice under section 71 of the Environmental Protection Act 1990 requesting certain information and the company having refused to provide that information. It was held that the section 71 notice did not constitute any form of adjudication and therefore Article 6 was not infringed by its service. In *R v Kearns*, K, a bankrupt was charged with an offence contrary to section 354(3) of the Insolvency Act 1986 of failing without reasonable excuse to account for the loss of part of his property, having been required to do so by the Official Receiver. It was held that section 354 does not breach an accused's right to remain silent or not to incriminate himself and does not contravene the right of a person to have a fair trial under Article 6. First, the demand for information was made in the course of an extra-judicial procedure and not in order to provide evidence to prove a case against K. Secondly, at the time of the demand, there was no other charge against K.[54] Thirdly, there was no possibility that any information obtained could be used in subsequent criminal proceedings. Fourthly, even if section 354 did infringe the 'absolute' right to silence and/or the right not to incriminate oneself, the section 354 regime was a proportionate legislative response to the problem of administering and investigating bankrupt estates.[55]

Typically, statutory provisions do not simply abrogate the privilege against self-incrimination, but also prevent the answers from being used in evidence in any subsequent criminal proceedings in which the person who answered the question is charged with a specified offence. These provisions, individually different, collectively resemble a patchwork quilt to which new additions can always be made. Some important examples are set out below.

## (a) Section 98 of the Children Act 1989

Section 98 of the Children Act 1989 provides that in any proceedings in which a court is hearing an application relating to the care, supervision or protection of a child, no person shall be excused from giving evidence on any matter or answering any

---

[52] See also *L v UK* [2001] Crim LR 133, ECHR.      [53] [2000] 2 AC 412, HL.

[54] Cf *Heaney and McGuinness v Ireland* [2001] Crim LR 481, above.

[55] See also *R v Brady* [2004] 3 All ER 520, CA, where it was held that statements obtained on pain of penalty by the Official Receiver under s 235 of the Insolvency Act 1986 could be disclosed to the Inland Revenue for the purpose of investigating possible offences of cheating the public revenue and laying information to obtain search warrants.

question put to him in the course of his giving evidence on the ground that doing so might incriminate him or his spouse of an offence. However, section 98(2) provides that a statement or admission made in such proceedings shall not be admissible in evidence against the person making it or his spouse in proceedings for an offence other than perjury.[56] It has been held, in decisions since doubted,[57] that the phrase 'statement or admission made in such proceedings' is to be construed widely to include not only the written and filed statements of the evidence which a party intends to adduce and oral admissions made by a parent to a guardian ad litem,[58] but also, at least once the proceedings have begun, oral statements made to social workers charged with carrying out the local authority's duties of investigation.[59] The purpose of section 98 is to protect a witness who is required to give evidence in relation to a child when such evidence would incriminate him or his spouse. Thus section 98(2) will not prevent counsel for the accused from putting a 'statement or admission' to his spouse as a previous inconsistent statement in order to challenge her evidence or to attack her credibility.[60]

## (b)  Section 2 of the Criminal Justice Act 1987

Under section 2 of the Criminal Justice Act 1987, the Director of the Serious Fraud Office may require any person under investigation for a suspected offence involving serious or complex fraud, or any other person, to answer questions, furnish information and produce documents, but under section 2(8) a statement in response to such a requirement may only be used in evidence against its maker (a) on a prosecution for an offence of knowingly or recklessly making a false or misleading statement (in purported compliance with a requirement under section 2) or (b) on a prosecution for some other offence where in giving evidence he makes a statement inconsistent with it. However, under section 2(8AA), the statement may not be used against its maker by virtue of (b) unless evidence relating to it is adduced or a question relating to it is asked, by him or on his behalf, in the proceedings arising out of the prosecution.

## (c)  Section 434 of the Companies Act 1985

Under Part XIV of the Companies Act 1985, officers and agents of a company and others possessing relevant information are obliged to answer questions put by Board of Trade inspectors appointed to investigate suspected fraud in the conduct or management of a company. However, under section 434(5A) and (5B) of the Act, in criminal proceedings in which the person who answered such a question is charged

---

[56] The subsection, therefore, does not prevent a family court, in the exercise of its discretion, from directing the disclosure of material covered by s 98 to the police for the purposes of a criminal investigation: *In re C (a minor) (Care proceedings: disclosure)* [1997] 2 WLR 322, CA.

[57] Per Butler-Sloss LJ and Sir Roger Parker in *Re G (a minor)* [1996] 2 All ER 65, CA.

[58] See *Oxfordshire County Council v P* [1995] 2 All ER 225, Fam Div.

[59] See *Cleveland County Council v F* [1995] 2 All ER 236, Fam Div.

[60] See *Re K (minors)* [1994] 3 All ER 230, Fam Div.

with an offence, other than an offence under section 2 or section 5 of the Perjury Act 1911 (false statements made on oath otherwise than in judicial proceedings or made otherwise than on oath), (a) no evidence relating to the answer may be adduced and (b) no question relating to it may be asked, by or on behalf of the prosecution, unless evidence relating to it is adduced or a question relating to it is asked in the proceedings by or on behalf of the person charged.[61]

### (d) Section 31(1) of the Theft Act 1968

Section 31(1) of the Theft Act 1968 requires questions to be answered and orders to be complied with 'in proceedings for the recovery or administration of any property, for the execution of any trust or for an account of any property or dealings with property' notwithstanding that compliance may expose the witness or his spouse to a charge for an offence under the Theft Act. The section goes on to provide that the answers may not be used in proceedings for any such offence.[62] However, neither the revocation of the privilege nor the restriction on the use of the answers applies to the offences of conspiracy to defraud at common law, a statutory conspiracy to commit an offence under the 1968 Act,[63] or any offence under any other Act, a limitation which has prompted Sir Nicolas Browne-Wilkinson V-C to express the hope that Parliament will urgently extend section 31 so as to remove the privilege in relation to all civil claims relating to property, including claims for damages, but on terms that the statements made in documents disclosed should not be admissible in *any* criminal proceedings. Without such an extension, he said, the effectiveness of civil remedies designed to redress fraud would be seriously impaired.[64]

In cases where there is a claim to privilege in respect of both a Theft Act offence and a non-Theft Act offence, the test, in each case, is whether to answer the question would create or increase the risk of proceedings for that offence. If the test is satisfied in the case of the Theft Act offence, section 31 will apply and prima facie the question must be answered. For the non-Theft Act offence, the test is whether to answer would create or increase the risk of proceedings for that offence, separate and distinct from

---

[61] See also s 447(8A) and (8B) of the Companies Act 1985 (production of company documents to Secretary of State); ss 43A(6) and (7) and 44(5A) and (5B) of the Insurance Companies Act 1982 (investigations into, and obtaining information and documents from, insurance companies); s 433(2)–(4) of the Insolvency Act 1986 (evidence of statement of affairs etc); s 20(2)–(4) of the Company Directors Disqualification Act 1986 (statements); s 57 (5A) and (5B) of the Building Societies Act 1986 (answers to inspectors conducting investigations into building societies); ss 105(5A) and (5B) and 177(6A) and (6B) of the Financial Services Act 1986 (investigation of affairs of person carrying on investment business and investigations into insider dealing); and ss 39(12A) and (12B), 41(10A) and (10B) and 42(5A) and (5B) of the Banking Act 1987 (power of Financial Services Authority to obtain information from and investigate authorized institutions).

[62] See also s 9 of the Criminal Damage Act 1971.

[63] *Sociedade Nacional de Combustiveis de Angola UEE v Lundqvist* [1990] 3 All ER 283, CA.

[64] [1990] 3 All ER 283 at 302–3. Subsequently, in *Tate Access Floors v Boswell* [1990] 3 All ER 303 at 315 the Vice-Chancellor added that in the *Lundqvist* case he had not foreseen the effect of that decision on Anton Piller orders (now known as search orders). 'If I had done, I would have asked for even more urgent consideration by Parliament.'

its connection with the Theft Act offence. If the answer is in the negative, there is no privilege; but if in the affirmative, the privilege will subsist.[65]

### (e) Section 72 of the Supreme Court Act 1981

The decision in *Rank Film Distributors Ltd v Video Information Centre*[66] that the privilege against self-incrimination applied to Anton Piller orders, now known as search orders, seriously undermined the effectiveness of that remedy, particularly in relation to breach of copyright, which often involves offences of fraud. Accordingly, the decision was rapidly reversed for the purposes of proceedings concerning intellectual property and passing off by section 72 of the Supreme Court Act 1981, the effect of which may be summarized as follows.[67] In proceedings brought to prevent any apprehended infringement of rights pertaining to any intellectual property (ie patent, trade mark, copyright, registered design, technical or commercial information or other intellectual property)[68] or any apprehended passing off, questions must be answered and orders complied with even though the person complying may thereby expose himself or his spouse to proceedings for a related offence or for the recovery of a related penalty. In proceedings for an infringement (or for passing off) which, it is alleged, has already occurred, or proceedings to obtain disclosure of information relating to such an infringement (or passing off), the privilege is withdrawn only in relation to (i) any offence committed by or in the course of the infringement (or passing off), (ii) offences of dishonesty or fraud committed in connection with the infringement (or passing off), and (iii) penalties incurred in connection with the infringement (or passing off). By section 72(3), answers compelled by reason of the withdrawal of privilege cannot be used in proceedings for the offence disclosed or for the recovery of any penalty liability to which was disclosed. Section 72 affects only proceedings for infringement of intellectual property rights and passing off: the decision in *Rank Film Distributors Ltd v Video Information Centre* still applies to the use of search orders for other purposes.

## 5  SUBSTITUTED PROTECTION

*Re O*[69] concerned a disclosure order, requiring the accused to disclose their assets and income, made in aid of a restraint order under section 77 of the Criminal Justice Act 1988, prohibiting them from dealing with any realizable property. The accused faced

---

[65] See *Renworth Ltd v Stephansen* [1996] 3 All ER 244 per Morritt LJ at 254, CA; but see also *Khan v Khan* [1982] 2 All ER 60, CA.

[66] [1982] AC 380, HL.

[67] The terms of the section are complex and should be referred to for detail. See also *Universal City Studios v Hubbard* [1984] Ch 225, CA.

[68] Section 72(5). 'Commercial information' has to be information of the same type as the other examples of intellectual property listed in s 72(5) and therefore must be concerned with the infringement of rights pertaining to intellectual property: *AT & T Istel Ltd v Tully* [1992] 3 All ER 523, HL.

[69] [1991] 1 All ER 330, CA.

not only charges under the Theft Act 1968, in respect of which section 31 of the 1968 Act provided protection, but also conspiracy charges, in respect of which section 31 provided no protection. It was held that since the accused could invoke the privilege against self-incrimination, which would frustrate the purpose of the disclosure order, all such orders should be made subject to a condition 'that no disclosure made in compliance with this order shall be used as evidence in the prosecution of an offence alleged to have been committed by the person required to make that disclosure or by any spouse of that person'. The CPS was a party to the proceedings and consented to the order. In *R v Martin and White*[70] it was held that although an affidavit sworn by a person in compliance with such an order cannot become admissible in evidence against him in any subsequent criminal trial, either in the course of the prosecution case or in cross-examination, subject to proper directions from the judge it may be used to demonstrate his inconsistency and thus to impugn his credit.

The decision in *Re O* was approved by the House of Lords in *AT & T Istel Ltd v Tully*.[71] A claim was made for damages and repayment of money obtained by fraud. A major police investigation was launched. The plaintiffs were granted a wide-ranging order for Mareva injunctions and disclosure, requiring the defendants to disclose all dealings regarding the money. Paragraph 33 of the order contained a condition identical to that contained in the disclosure order in *Re O*. The order was subsequently varied and the plaintiffs appealed against the variation. Before the appeal, the CPS informed the plaintiffs that it did not seek to intervene in the civil proceedings, that it already had a large amount of potential evidence, and that it would not be prevented by paragraph 33 from using that material or any other material obtained independently of the civil proceedings. The House of Lords restored the original order. Noting that the proceedings were not covered by any of the statutory modifications of the privilege, but were similar to situations in which Parliament had intervened, the House could see no reason why the defendants should blatantly exploit the privilege to deprive the plaintiffs of their civil rights and remedies. The courts were entitled to substitute a different protection in place of the privilege, provided it was adequate. The protection would be adequate if the CPS unequivocally agreed not to make use, directly or indirectly, of the material divulged in compliance with the order. Accordingly, a majority of the House held that, given the terms of para 33 and the clear indication by the CPS that it did not seek to use any of the material to be divulged in compliance with the order, the original order should stand.

On the reasoning of the House, the principle of substituted protection is capable of application in many situations other than those which arose in *Re O* and *AT & T Istel v Tully*. However, those who, in the future, seek to confine the principle, will doubtless rely on the views of Lord Lowry, who emphasized that the decision of the House did not represent a breakthrough in relation to the privilege, being a decision on its own facts.[72]

---

[70] [1998] 2 Cr App R 385, CA.
[71] [1992] 3 All ER 523. See also, applying *Re O*, *Re Thomas* [1992] 4 All ER 814, CA.
[72] [1992] 3 All ER 523 at 544.

# B  LEGAL PROFESSIONAL PRIVILEGE

The common-law doctrine of legal professional privilege enables a client to maintain the confidentiality of (i) communications between him and his lawyer made for the purpose of obtaining and giving legal advice, the privilege in this case being known as 'legal advice privilege' (ii) communications between him or his lawyer and third parties (such as potential witnesses and experts) the dominant purpose of which was preparation for contemplated or pending litigation, the privilege in this case being known as 'litigation privilege' and (iii) items enclosed with or referred to in such communications and brought into existence for the purpose of obtaining legal advice etc.[73]

Section 10 of the Police and Criminal Evidence Act 1984, which is apparently intended to reflect the common-law position,[74] provides that:

(1) Subject to subsection (2) below, in this Act 'items subject to legal privilege' means—
    (a) communications between a professional legal adviser and his client or any person representing his client made in connection with the giving of legal advice to the client;
    (b) communications between a professional legal adviser and his client or any person representing his client or between such an adviser or his client or any such representative and any other person made in connection with or in contemplation of legal proceedings and for the purposes of such proceedings; and
    (c) items enclosed with or referred to in such communications and made—
        (i)  in connection with the giving of legal advice; or
        (ii) in connection with or in contemplation of legal proceedings and for the purposes of such proceedings,
    when they are in the possession of a person who is entitled to possession of them.

(2) Items held with the intention of furthering a criminal purpose are not items subject to legal privilege.

For the purposes of legal professional privilege, 'lawyer' includes, as well as solicitors and counsel, employed legal advisers,[75] and overseas lawyers.[76] It is possible that the privilege may also attach to communications between the police and the Director of Public Prosecutions, if they are seeking legal advice in circumstances analogous to a

---

[73] For an excellent examination of the topic explicitly aimed more to generate questions than to provide answers, see J Auburn *Legal Professional Privilege: Law and Theory* (Oxford 2000).

[74] See the majority view of the House of Lords in *Francis & Francis (a firm) v Central Criminal Court* [1988] 3 All ER 775, below, especially per Lord Goff at 797; and *R v R* [1994] 4 All ER 260, CA, below.

[75] *Alfred Crompton Amusement Machines Ltd v Customs and Excise Comrs (No 2)* [1974] AC 405; *AM & S Europe Ltd v EC Commission* [1983] QB 878, ECJ per Advocate General Sir Gordon Slynn at 914.

[76] *Re Duncan* [1968] P 306. The term 'proceedings' in this context includes proceedings in other jurisdictions: ibid. However, the fact that the advice given relates predominantly to English law is irrelevant: *IBM Corpn v Phoenix International (Computers) Ltd* [1995] 1 All ER 413, Ch D.

client approaching his solicitor for advice.[77] The privilege survives the death of a client and vests in his personal representative or, once administration is complete, the person entitled to his estate,[78] and those persons are entitled to either claim or waive the privilege.[79]

A parallel privilege applies to communications between a person and his patent agent,[80] trade mark agent,[81] or licensed conveyancer.[82]

The rationale of the rules of legal professional privilege is that they encourage those who know the facts to state them fully and candidly without fear of compulsory disclosure.[83] In *R v Derby Magistrates' Court, ex p B*[84] Lord Taylor CJ said:

The principle . . . is that a man must be able to consult his lawyer in confidence, since otherwise he might hold back half the truth. The client must be sure that what he tells his lawyer in confidence will never be revealed without his consent. Legal professional privilege is thus much more than an ordinary rule of evidence. . . . It is a fundamental condition on which the administration of justice as a whole rests . . .

In relation to litigation privilege, it is this confidentiality which enables lawyers to encourage strong cases and discourage weak ones, which is in the interests of the state.[85] However, in the absence of contemplated litigation, it is questionable whether there is any temptation for the client to be less than candid or 'to hold back half the truth',[86] and even if this is a real likelihood, it is equally questionable whether it should override the public interest that wherever possible the courts should reach their decisions on the basis of all relevant evidence. As Lord Phillips MR forcefully observed in *Three Rivers District Council v Governor and Company of the Bank of England (No 5)*:[87]

The justification for litigation privilege is readily understood. Where, however, litigation is not anticipated it is not easy to see why communications with a solicitor should be privileged. Legal advice privilege attaches to matters such as the conveyance of real property or the drawing up of a will. It is not clear why it should. There would seem little reason to fear that, if privilege were not available in such circumstances, communications between solicitor and client would be inhibited.

---

[77] Per Moore-Bick J, obiter, in *Goodridge v Chief Constable of Hampshire Constabulary* [1999] 1 All ER 896, QBD at 903.

[78] *Bullivant v A-G for Victoria* [1901] AC 196, HL.  [79] *R v Malloy* [1997] 2 Cr App R 283, CA.

[80] Copyright, Designs and Patents Act 1988, s 280.  [81] Ibid, s 284.

[82] Administration of Justice Act 1985, s 33.

[83] See *Waugh v British Railways Board* [1980] AC 521 at 531–2, HL per Lord Wilberforce, and also at 535–6 per Lord Simon. As to the court's respect for other confidential relationships, see Ch 18, under **B5 Confidential relationships**.

[84] [1996] AC 487, HL at 507–8.

[85] See per Bingham LJ in *Ventouris v Mountain* [1991] 1 WLR 607 at 611.

[86] See V Alexander 'The Corporate Attorney–Client Privilege: A Study of the Participants' (1989) St John's L Rev 191.

[87] [2004] 3 All ER 168, CA at [39].

## 1 THE PROTECTED MATERIAL

### (a) Communications between lawyer and client—legal advice privilege

A client may, and his lawyer must (subject to the client's waiver) refuse to disclose written or oral communications between them made for the purpose of giving and receiving legal advice about any matter, whether or not litigation was contemplated at the time.[88] This applies whether the client or lawyer is a party to the litigation in which the question arises or a mere witness and it applies as much to the production of documents containing such communications as to oral evidence about them. It seems that receipt by the lawyer of a communication from the client is not necessary for the privilege to apply.[89]

The communication must have been confidential and, if not actually made in the course of a relationship of lawyer and client, must at least have been made with a view to the establishment of that relationship.[90] Provided that the communication was made in a professional capacity for the purposes of giving or receiving legal advice, the whole communication will be privileged, including any parts of it in which the solicitor conveyed to the client information which he had received in a professional capacity from a third party: such information cannot be hived off from the rest of what was said so as to become not privileged.[91] However, documents emanating from, or prepared by, independent third parties and then passed to the lawyer for the purposes of advice are not privileged. In *Three Rivers District Council v Governor and Company of the Bank of England*[92] it was held, after a review of nineteenth-century authority, that legal advice privilege only protects direct communications between the client and the lawyer, and evidence of the content of such communications, and that in the case of a corporate client the privilege will only cover communications with those officers or employees expressly designated or nominated to act as 'the client'. Thus the privilege was held not to extend to documents prepared by other employees or ex-employees, even if prepared with the dominant purpose of obtaining legal advice, prepared at the lawyer's request, or sent to the lawyer.

Legal advice privilege does extend to the instructions given by the client to his solicitor, or by the solicitor to the barrister, and counsel's opinion taken by a solicitor.[93] It does not extend to records of time spent with a client on attendance sheets,

---

[88] *Greenough v Gaskell* (1833) 1 My&K 98. If litigation does ensue, the standard form of words for claiming the privilege on disclosure is to refer to confidential correspondence etc for the purpose of obtaining legal advice. This is a sufficient description of the documents—the other party is not entitled to a fuller description to satisfy himself that all of the documents are within the scope of the privilege: *Derby & Co Ltd v Weldon (No 7)* [1990] 3 All ER 161, Ch D.

[89] See the obiter suggestion in *Three Rivers District Council v Governor and Company of the Bank of England* [2003] EWCA Civ 474, CA at [21].

[90] *Minter v Priest* [1930] AC 558. However, it seems that a client care letter is not privileged because it merely sets out the terms on which the solicitor is to act for the client: *Dickinson v Rushmer* (2002) 152 NLJ 58.

[91] *Re Sarah C Getty Trust* [1985] QB 956, QBD.       [92] [2003] EWCA Civ 474, CA.

[93] *Bristol Corpn v Cox* (1884) 26 Ch D 678.

time sheets or fee records, because they are not communications between client and legal adviser, or to records of appointments, because they are not communications made in connection with legal advice.[94]

There is generally no protection for communications between opposing parties or their advisers, unless they can be treated as 'without prejudice' settlement negotiations, which are considered below.[95] Thus the privilege does not cover a solicitor's attendance note recording what took place in chambers or in open court, in the course of a hostile litigation, in the presence of the parties on both sides.[96] Similarly, if a solicitor has made an attendance note of a meeting or telephone conversation between the lawyers for each side, although any subsequent communication by the lawyers to their respective clients, informing them about the discussion, advising them and seeking further instructions, will be privileged, the attendance note itself is not privileged. This remains the case, even if the discussion was 'without prejudice', although that may prevent the note from being given in evidence until the without prejudice ban has been removed.[97]

In *Buttes Gas and Oil Co v Hammer (No 3)*[98] it was held that where a solicitor is instructed by two clients, communications between him and one of the clients will not be privileged against the other client in so far as they concern the subject matter in which they are jointly interested but, whether or not the communication is disclosed to the other client, they will be protected as against outsiders. Thus where two parties employ the same solicitor for a conveyancing transaction, communications between either of them and the solicitor, in his joint capacity, must be disclosed in favour of the other. Equally, if one of the parties is then adjudicated bankrupt, the other cannot assert the privilege as against a trustee in bankruptcy, because as the successor in title to the property in question, he should be treated as being in the same position as the bankrupt, and not in the position of a third party.[99] However, the waiver of privilege implied at the outset of a joint retainer ceases to apply in respect of communications made after the emergence of a conflict of interest between the two clients.[100] Similarly, the privilege cannot be claimed by the directors of a company against its shareholders, except in the case of communications made for the purposes of litigation between the company and the shareholders.[101]

---

[94] *R v Crown Court at Manchester, ex p Rogers* [1999] 1 WLR 832, DC.

[95] *Grant v Southwestern and County Properties Ltd* [1975] Ch 185, Ch D: the plaintiff was obliged to produce on discovery a tape recording of a discussion between the parties even though made for the purposes of instructing his solicitor in connection with contemplated litigation. However, if, after a meeting between opposing parties, one of them makes a record of the meeting for his solicitor, that record will be protected.

[96] *Ainsworth v Wilding* [1900] 2 Ch 315.

[97] *Parry v News Group Newspapers Ltd* [1990] NLJR 1719, CA.

[98] [1981] QB 223, CA (reversed on other grounds, [1982] AC 888, HL), applied in *Guinness Peat Properties Ltd v Fitzroy Robinson Partnership (a firm)* [1987] 2 All ER 716, CA.

[99] *Re Konigsberg (a bankrupt)* [1989] 3 All ER 289, Ch D.

[100] *TSB Bank plc v Robert Irving & Burns (a firm)* [2000] 2 All ER 826, CA.

[101] *Woodhouse & Co (Ltd) v Woodhouse* (1914) 30 TLR 559; *CAS (Nominees) Ltd v Nottingham Forest plc* [2001] 1 All ER 954, Ch D

'Legal advice', for the purposes of legal advice privilege, does not mean advice given by a lawyer without more, but advice about legal rights and liabilities. However, some communications may enjoy privlege even if they do not specifically seek or convey legal advice. In *Balabel v Air-India*,[102] which concerned a conveyancing transaction, the privilege extended to communications between the appellants and their solicitors such as drafts, working papers, attendance notes and memoranda. It was held that in most solicitor and client relationships, especially where a transaction involves protracted dealings, there will be a continuum of communications and meetings between the solicitor and client; and where information is passed between them as part of that continuum, the aim being to keep both informed so that legal advice may be sought and given as required, privilege will attach. Similarly, in *Nederlandse Reassurantie Groep Holding NV v Bacon & Woodrow (a firm)*[103] it was held that where a solicitor's advice relates to the commercial wisdom of entering into a transaction in respect of which legal advice is also sought, all communications between the solicitor and the client relating to the transaction will be privileged, even if they do not contain advice on matters of law or construction, provided that they are directly related to the performance by the solicitor of his professional duty as legal adviser.[104] According to *The Sagheera*,[105] the practical emphasis should be on the dominant purpose of the retainer. If it is to obtain and give legal advice, although in theory individual documents may fall outside that purpose, in practice it is most unlikely. If, however, the dominant purpose is some business purpose, the documents will not be privileged, unless exceptionally advice is requested or given, in which case the relevant documents probably are privileged.

The leading authority is now *Three Rivers District Council v Governor and Company of the Bank of England (No 6)*.[106] After the collapse of the Bank of Credit and Commerce International (BCCI) in 1991, Lord Justice Bingham was appointed to inquire into the supervision of BCCI by the Bank of England, which had statutory responsibilities and duties in relation to UK banks. The Bank appointed a Bingham Inquiry Unit (BIU) to deal with all communications between the Bank and the inquiry and solicitors were retained to advise generally on all dealings with the inquiry. One of the main functions of the BIU was to prepare and communicate information and instructions to the Bank's solicitors. The solicitors gave advice as to the preparation and presentation of evidence to the inquiry and as to submissions to be made. After the publication of the inquiry report, depositors and BCCI, by its liquidators, brought proceedings against the Bank and sought the widest possible disclosure from the Bank. The Court of Appeal held that the only documents for which privilege could be claimed were communications between BIU and the solicitors seeking or giving

---

[102] [1988] Ch 317, CA.      [103] [1995] 1 All ER 976, QBD.

[104] See also *R v Crown Court at Inner London Sessions, ex p Baines and Baines* [1987] 3 All ER 1025, DC: privilege does attach to advice given in conveyancing transactions on factors serving to assist towards a successful completion, including the wisdom or otherwise of proceeding with it, the arranging of a mortgage and so on, but does not attach to the records of the conveyancing transaction itself.

[105] [1997] 1 Lloyd's Rep 160 at 168, QBD.      [106] [2004] UKHL 43.

advice as to legal rights and liabilities, and not advice as to how the Bank should best present its evidence to the inquiry. The House of Lords allowed the appeal of the Bank. It was held that the policy basis for legal advice privilege was that it was necessary, in a society in which the restraining and controlling framework was built on a belief in the rule of law, that communications between clients and lawyers, whereby the clients were hoping for the assistance of the lawyers' legal skills in the management of the clients' affairs, should be secure against the possibility of any scrutiny from others. Lord Scott accepted as correct the approach of Taylor LJ in *Balabel v Air India*,[107] who had said that for the purpose of attracting legal advice privilege 'legal advice is not confined to telling the client the law; it must include advice as to what should prudently and sensibly be done in the relevant legal context' but that 'to extend privilege without limit to all solicitor and client communications upon matters within the ordinary business of a solicitor and referable to that relationship [would be] too wide'. Lord Scott said that if a solicitor became the client's 'man of business', responsible for advising him on matters such as investment and finance policy and other business matters, the advice might lack a relevant legal context. The judge would have to ask whether it related to the rights, liabilities, obligations, or remedies of the client under either private or public law, and, if so, whether the communication fell within the policy underlying the justification for the privilege, the criterion being an objective one. It was held that although there may be marginal cases where the answer is not easy, the present case was not marginal. The preparation of the evidence to be submitted, and the submissions to be made, to the inquiry had been for the purpose of enhancing the Bank's prospects of persuading the inquiry that its discharge of its public law obligations was not deserving of criticism and had been reasonable. The presentational advice given by its lawyers for that purpose had been advice 'as to what should prudently and sensibly be done in the relevant legal context', namely, the inquiry and whether the Bank had properly discharged its public law duties, and fell squarely within the policy reasons underlying legal advice privilege.

### (b) Communications with third parties—litigation privilege

Litigation privilege is a creature of adversarial proceedings and cannot exist in the context of non-adversarial proceedings.[108] It covers communications between a client, or his lawyer, and third parties—for example, statements from potential witnesses and experts—the dominant purpose of which was preparation for contemplated or pending litigation. The test is whether litigation was reasonably in prospect, which will not be satisfied if there is only a possibility of litigation, even if a distinct possibility, or a general apprehension of future litigation.[109]

The privilege covers documents 'brought into existence', that is created, by a party for the purpose of instructing the lawyer and obtaining his advice in the conduct of

---

[107] [1988] Ch 317 at 330–1.   [108] *Re L* [1997] AC 16, HL.
[109] *USA v Philip Morris Inc* [2004] All ER (D) 448 (Mar) [2004] EWCA Civ 330, CA.

the litigation,[110] but not documents obtained by a party or his adviser for the purpose of litigation which did not come into existence for that purpose.[111] A copy or translation of an unprivileged document in the control of a party does not become privileged merely because the copy or translation was made for the purpose of the litigation,[112] but privilege will attach to a copy of an unprivileged document if the copy was made for the purpose of litigation and the original is not and has not at any time been in the control of the party claiming privilege.[113] Privilege will also attach where a solicitor has copied or assembled a selection of third party documents for the purposes of litigation, if its production will betray the trend of the advice he is giving his client,[114] but this principle does not extend to a selection of own client documents, or copies or translations representing the fruits of such a selection, made for the purposes of litigation.[115]

The leading authority is *Waugh v British Railways Board*.[116] The plaintiff's husband, an employee of the defendant, was killed in a railway accident. In proceedings for compensation, the plaintiff sought discovery of routine internal reports prepared by the defendant regarding the accident. The House of Lords held that, in order to attract privilege, the dominant purpose of preparation of the reports must have been that of submission to a legal adviser for use in relation to anticipated or pending litigation. While this was undoubtedly one of the purposes of the reports, it was not the dominant one, another equally important purpose being to inform the Board about the cause of the accident in order that steps could be taken to avoid recurrence. Accordingly, privilege could not be claimed and disclosure of the reports was ordered.

Although application of the dominant purpose test can give rise to difficulty, in many cases of accident investigation it will be possible to conclude that the major purpose was the prevention of recurrence. The courts will not be deterred from reaching such a conclusion, where appropriate, even if those under whose direction the report was prepared depose that its dominant purpose was submission to solicitors in anticipation of litigation and the report itself refers only to that purpose.[117] In *Neilson v Laugharne*[118] the plaintiff's demand for compensation for alleged police misconduct prompted the police to initiate the statutory complaints procedure. Statements taken for the purpose of that procedure were clearly obtained in anticipation of litigation but it was held that the dominant purpose was that of the complaints procedure. The statements therefore did not attract legal professional privilege in

---

[110] Per James LJ in *Anderson v Bank of British Columbia* (1876) 2 Ch D 644 at 656. See also *Southwark and Vauxhall Water Co v Quick* (1878) 3 QBD 315, CA.

[111] *Ventouris v Mountain, The Italia Express* [1991] 1 WLR 607, CA

[112] *Dubai Bank Ltd v Galadari* [1990] Ch 98, CA (copies) and *Sumitomo Corp v Credit Lyonnais Rouse Ltd* [2002] 1 WLR 479, CA.

[113] *The Palermo* (1883) 9 PD 6, CA and *Watson v Cammell Laird & Co Ltd* [1959] 1 WLR 702, CA.

[114] *Lyell v Kennedy (No 3)* (1884) 27 Ch D 1.

[115] *Sumitomo Corp v Credit Lyonnais Rouse Ltd* [2002] 1 WLR 479, CA, overruling *Dubai Bank Ltd v Galadari (No 7)* [1992] 1 WLR 106, Ch D.

[116] [1980] AC 521.        [117] See *Lask v Gloucester Health Authority* (1985) 2 PN 96, CA.

[118] [1981] QB 736, CA.

subsequent litigation against the police. In *Re Highgrade Traders Ltd*,[119] by contrast, it was held that the dominant purpose of the preparation of reports procured by an insurance company from specialists in fire investigations, in a case where arson was suspected, was to assess the strength of a claim which, if persisted in, would in all likelihood have resulted in litigation. The insurance company was primarily interested in questions of liability rather than prevention or recurrence. Oliver LJ made it clear that the privilege will attach to a document, whether it was 'brought into existence' before or after a decision was made to instruct a solicitor, provided that litigation was reasonably in prospect and the document was prepared for the sole or dominant purpose of enabling a solicitor to advise whether a claim should be made or resisted.

In *Guinness Peat Properties Ltd v Fitzroy Robinson Partnership (a firm)*[120] it was held that the dominant purpose of a document should be ascertained by an objective view of the evidence as a whole, having regard not only to the intention of its author, but also to the intention of the person or authority under whose direction it was procured. The plaintiffs, building developers, had notified the defendants, engaged by them to act as architects for the construction of a building, of an alleged design fault. The defendants, in order to comply with the condition of their insurance policy, which required immediate notification of claims, thereupon wrote a letter to their insurers enclosing relevant memoranda and expressing their own views on the merits of the claim. In the course of discovery in the action which ensued, the question arose whether the letter was privileged. The defendants conceded that it was not *their* purpose, in writing the letter, to obtain legal advice or assistance. The Court of Appeal held that it could look beyond that intention to the intention of the insurers who had procured its genesis. Their intention, in requiring an immediate written notice of claim, was to enable them to submit it, together with other relevant documentation, to their lawyers for advice on whether the claim should be resisted. The letter was therefore privileged.

In reaching this conclusion, the Court of Appeal distinguished *Jones v Great Central Rly Co*,[121] in which it was held that if a client communicates with a lawyer via a third party who is merely an agent for communication, privilege can be claimed, but that if the third party has to make a preliminary decision on the matter, the privilege is lost. Accordingly, it was held that no privilege attached to information supplied by a dismissed employee to a trade union official for the purpose of enabling the latter to decide whether to refer the claim to the union's lawyers. This case was distinguished in the *Guinness Peat Properties* case on the grounds, inter alia, that the relationship between the trade union and the member was not the equivalent of that between the insurers and the insured where the insurers were, in all but name, the effective defendants to any proceedings. It was further held that since the insurers and the insured had a common interest and a common lawyer, the principle in *Buttes Gas and Oil Co v*

---

[119] [1984] BCLC 151, CA.     [120] [1987] 2 All ER 716, CA.     [121] [1910] AC 4, HL.

*Hammer (No 3)*[122] applied: the letter was privileged in the hands of each of them as against all outsiders.

In *Re Barings plc*[123] Sir Richard Scott V-C doubted the correctness of the decisions in both *Re Highgrade Traders Ltd* and the *Guinness Peat Properties* case on the grounds that disclosure of the documents in those cases would not have impinged upon the inviolability of lawyer/client communications. In his view, the reason for extending the privilege to documents brought into existence for the dominant purpose of litigation is to prevent the disclosure of documents which will reveal the lawyer's view of his client's case or the advice he has given, and therefore there is no general privilege for such documents independent of the need to keep inviolate communications between client and legal adviser. Thus if the documents do not relate in some fashion to such communications, there is no element of public interest to override the ordinary rights of litigants on discovery. In *Re Barings plc* a report on the conduct of the directors of Barings Bank was prepared on behalf of administrators in compliance with their statutory duty to report to the Department of Trade and Industry, under section 7(3), Company Directors Disqualification Act 1986, where it appears to them that the conduct of directors makes them unfit to be concerned in the management of a company. In subsequent disqualification proceedings, the Secretary of State resisted inspection of the report on the grounds of privilege. The Vice-Chancellor held that the report was not privileged. *Re Highgrade Traders Ltd* and the *Guinness Peat Properties* case were distinguished on the basis that, whereas in those cases the makers of the documents had a choice whether to bring them into existence and it was therefore possible to investigate their purpose in doing so, the maker of a section 7(3) report is obliged by law to make the report, which is not procured by anyone. It was accepted that the statutory purpose underlying section 7(3) was to assist the Secretary of State to decide whether to commence disqualification proceedings, and that Parliament must have expected that the Secretary of State, in reaching his decision, would put the report before his legal advisers for their advice, but it was held that the question of privilege depended not on identifying this parliamentary purpose and expectation, but on whether there was a public interest requiring protection from disclosure sufficient to override the disclosure rights given to litigants. In the absence of any such public interest, it was ruled that the report was not protected from disclosure.

Despite the difficulties of the dominant purpose test, it is usually clear that proofs of evidence from potential witnesses and the written opinions of experts supplied for the purpose of litigation can be kept secret. Under CPR rule 32.4(2), the court will order a party to serve on the other parties any witness statement of the oral evidence which the first party intends to rely on in relation to any issues of fact to be decided at the trial. If a witness statement is not served in respect of an intended witness within the time specified by the court, then the witness may not be called to give oral evidence unless the court gives permission;[124] and if a witness statement is served

---

[122] [1981] QB 223, CA, above.     [123] [1998] 1 All ER 673, Ch D.     [124] Rule 32.10.

within the time specified and the witness is called, he may amplify his witness statement only with the permission of the court.[125] Thus, rule 32 does not compel disclosure, but if a party wishes to adduce evidence of fact from a witness at the trial, then he is generally required to disclose all of it in advance. Once the statement has been disclosed, it is no longer privileged. Thus, it may be relied on, by the other party, in support of an application for specific disclosure of documents referred to in it.[126] Rule 32.5(5) provides that if a party who has served a witness statement does not call the witness to give evidence at trial or put the witness statement in as hearsay evidence, the other party may put the statement in as hearsay evidence. If the party who has served the statement does call the witness, his statement shall stand as his evidence-in-chief unless the court orders otherwise[127] and he may be cross-examined on it whether or not the statement or any part of it is referred to during his evidence-in-chief.[128]

If a party to civil proceedings fails to disclose an expert's report, then he may not use it at the trial or call the expert to give evidence orally unless the court gives permission.[129] As in the case of witness statements, disclosure is not compulsory. A party is therefore free to instruct an expert and, in the event that the expert's report is unhelpful to him, cannot be compelled to disclose it to the other side. Nor will his opponent be able to require the party, his solicitor or the expert to state in evidence the content of the instructions to the expert or of the report. The costs of the exercise, however, will not be recoverable from the opponent. On the other hand, where a party seeks permission to put in evidence an expert's report, the report must state the substance of all material instructions, whether written or oral, on the basis of which it was written;[130] the instructions shall not be privileged against disclosure;[131] and where the party has disclosed the report, any party may use it as evidence at the trial.[132]

Provision has also been made for the mutual disclosure of expert evidence in criminal cases.[133] The defence, in advance of a trial on indictment, are also entitled to know not only the evidence the prosecution intend to call, most or all of which will have been disclosed by the statements or depositions used by them at the committal proceedings (or served with a notice of transfer), but also, as a general rule, 'unused material', that is statements from persons on whose evidence the prosecution do not intend to rely.[134]

---

[125] Rule 32.5(3)(a).
[126] *Black & Decker Inc v Flymo Ltd* [1991] 3 All ER 158, Ch D (citing *Comfort Hotels Ltd v Wembley Stadium Ltd* [1988] 3 All ER 53), a decision under RSC Ord 38, r 2A, the precursor to the current rules.
[127] Rule 32.5(2).    [128] Rule 32.11.    [129] CPR r 35.13.    [130] CPR r 35.10(3).
[131] Rule 35.10(4).    [132] Rule 35.11.
[133] See Ch 18, under **A4 The disclosure of expert evidence in criminal cases.**
[134] The disclosure of unused material, a large topic outside the scope of this work, is governed by the scheme to be found in Part 1 (ss 1–21) of the Criminal Procedure and Investigations Act 1996 (as supplemented by a Code of Practice), under which there is a duty upon an officer investigating an offence to record and retain material and a duty on the prosecution to inform the defence of certain categories of such material which they do not intend to use at trial.

## (c) 'Items'

Under section 10(1)(c) of the Police and Criminal Evidence Act 1984, as we have seen, material subject to legal professional privilege includes items, enclosed with or referred to in communications covered by the above two categories of protected material, which were made in connection with the giving of legal advice etc. An 'item' could include, for example, a model made, or a bodily sample taken, for the purpose of obtaining expert advice. In *R v R*,[135] in which a scientist had carried out DNA tests at the request of the defence solicitors on a blood sample provided by the accused, it was held that the prosecution were not entitled either (i) to produce the sample in evidence or (ii) to adduce the opinion evidence of the scientist based on the sample. Section 10(1)(c) was said to apply to both issues. The word 'made' meant 'brought into existence' for the purpose of obtaining legal advice etc; the sample was an item 'made' for such a purpose; and therefore the accused was entitled to object both to its production and, whether or not it was produced or no longer existed, to opinion evidence based upon it.

## 2 THE SUBJECT MATTER OF PRIVILEGE: COMMUNICATIONS NOT FACTS

Under the doctrine of legal professional privilege, the client may avoid disclosure of his instructions to his lawyer and of his lawyer's advice to him: the lawyer may still be compelled to give evidence of facts directly perceived by him, even though his perception of them only occurred in the course of an interview with his client. Thus he may be required to admit the fact of having met his client and to give evidence about the physical or mental condition of his client[136] or about his handwriting.[137] Similarly, a solicitor present in court when his client was sentenced may be compelled in a subsequent prosecution to give evidence as to the identity of that person and to produce attendance notes, with anything attracting privilege blacked out.[138] If it is known that the client has shown the solicitor a pre-existing document which becomes relevant in litigation, then subject to the other rules of evidence, it seems in principle that the lawyer should be able to state the contents of the document.[139] These matters must be distinguished from facts conveyed to the lawyer by the client and the contents of documents prepared for the purpose of instructing the lawyer, a distinction which may not always be easy to apply.

---

[135] [1994] 4 All ER 260, CA.    [136] *Jones v Godrich* (1845) 5 Moo PCC 16.
[137] *Dwyer v Collins* (1852) 7 Exch 639.
[138] *R (Howe) v South Durham Magistrates' Court* [2004] Crim LR 963, DC.
[139] *Brown v Foster* (1857) 1 H&N 736, although because of its special facts this is not very clear authority for the principle stated. But see also **3 Pre-existing documents**, below.

## 3 PRE-EXISTING DOCUMENTS

Whereas privilege does attach to a document prepared for the purposes of obtaining legal advice, a pre-existing document given into the custody of a solicitor for the purpose of obtaining such advice or sent by a solicitor to a third party in connection with the litigation can, at common law, attract no greater protection in the hands of the solicitor or third party than it had in the hands of the client.[140] Thus in *R v Justice of the Peace for Peterborough, ex p Hicks,*[141] in which the client had sent to his solicitor, for the purposes of gaining legal advice, a forged document, a warrant was ordered to search the solicitor's premises and seize the document. The document was not privileged in the hands of the solicitor because it would have been open to seizure by warrant in the hands of the client.[142] Similarly, in *R v King*[143] the prosecution in a case of conspiracy to defraud were able to subpoena a handwriting expert, instructed by the defence, to produce documents sent to him by the accused's solicitors as sample handwriting even though the instructions to him, and his report, remained privileged.

Under section 8 of the Police and Criminal Evidence Act 1984, warrants of entry and search may be issued if, inter alia, a justice of the peace is satisfied that the material sought does not consist of or include 'items subject to legal privilege' or 'special procedure material'.[144] The phrase 'items subject to legal privilege', as we have seen, is defined in section 10 of the Act. In *R v Guildhall Magistrates' Court, ex p Primlaks Holdings Co*[145] Parker LJ held that section 10(1)(c) does not cover pre-existing documents which were not *made* in connection with the giving of legal advice or in connection with or in contemplation of legal proceedings and for the purposes of such proceedings, but that such documents would constitute 'special procedure material'. Under section 14(2), such material includes material, other than items subject to legal privilege, in the possession of a person who acquired or created it in the course of any trade, business, profession etc and holds it subject to an express or implied undertaking to hold it in confidence.[146] Under section 9, the police may obtain access to 'special procedure material', for the purposes of a criminal investigation, by an application, usually to be made inter partes, to a circuit judge. In the *Guildhall Magistrates' Court* case, Parker LJ held that a solicitor's correspondence with his client, and its enclosures, if not privileged, whether by reason of section 10(2) or

---

[140] But cf *Lyell v Kennedy (No 3)* (1884) 27 Ch D 1.

[141] [1977] 1 WLR 1371, DC.

[142] Dicta of Swanwick J in *Frank Truman Export Ltd v Metropolitan Police Comr* [1977] QB 952, which provide the only authority to the contrary, were doubted in *R v King* [1983] 1 WLR 411, CA.

[143] [1983] 1 WLR 411, CA.

[144] Section 9(2) repeals previous legislation in so far as it authorized, by the issue of a warrant, searches for, inter alia, items subject to legal privilege and 'special procedure material'.

[145] (1989) 89 Cr App R 215, DC at 225.

[146] A document forged by a solicitor or supplied by him to a fraudulent client is not special procedure material because, from its nature, it could not have been acquired or created in the course of the profession of a solicitor: *R v Leeds Magistrates' Court, ex p Dumbleton* [1993] Crim LR 866, DC.

otherwise, falls squarely within section 14(2) and that if the police are aware that what they seek includes items which are prima facie subject to legal privilege, they should not make an ex parte application under section 8, but should proceed under section 9 when the matter can be fully aired before a circuit judge.[147] However, it seems that a solicitor may voluntarily disclose special procedure material to the police because the object of the statutory provisions is to protect from disclosure not the suspect, but the person who has acquired or created the material, and it is for that person to decide whether he wishes to make disclosure, bearing in mind the degree of confidence reposed in him.[148]

## 4 EXCEPTIONS TO THE PRIVILEGE

In *R v Derby Magistrates' Court, ex p B*[149] the appellant was suspected of murder. He admitted responsibility and was charged, but before his trial changed his story and alleged that his stepfather had carried out the murder and that although he, the appellant, was present and took some part, he did so under duress. At his trial, he was acquitted. The stepfather was subsequently charged with the murder and at the committal proceedings the appellant was called as a prosecution witness. Counsel for the defence sought to cross-examine him about the factual instructions he had given to his solicitors prior to his allegation against his stepfather. The appellant declined to waive his privilege. The magistrates issued summonses directing the appellant and his solicitor to produce documentary evidence of the factual instructions, on the basis that the public interest that all relevant and admissible evidence should be made available to the defence outweighed the public interest which protected confidential communications between a solicitor and a client. An application for judicial review was refused, but the House of Lords allowed the appeal. Lord Taylor CJ, with whose judgment Lords Keith, Mustill and Lloyd agreed, held that since the client must be sure that what he tells his lawyer in confidence will never be revealed without his consent, there could be no question of a balancing exercise[150]—once any exception to the general rule is allowed, the client's confidence is necessarily lost. The solicitor would have to qualify his assurance and the purpose of the privilege would be undermined. However, Lord Nicholls, who also rejected any question of a balancing exercise, noted that in cases where the client no longer has any interest in maintaining the privilege, the privilege is spent. His Lordship preferred to reserve his final view on the point, but said:[151]

---

[147] See also *R v Crown Court at Southampton, ex p J and P* [1993] Crim LR 962, DC.
[148] See *R v Singleton* [1995] 1 Cr App R 431, a decision relating to 'excluded material' within the meaning of s 11 of the 1984 Act.
[149] [1996] AC 487, HL.
[150] Overruling, in this respect, *R v Barton* [1973] 1 WLR 115, CC and *R v Ataou* [1988] 2 All ER 321, CA. See also, endorsing Lord Taylor's approach, *R (Morgan Grenfell) v Special Commissioner of Income Tax* [2003] 1 AC 563, HL and *B v Auckland District Law Society* [2003] 2 AC 736, PC.
[151] [1995] 4 All ER 526 at 546.

I would not expect a law, based explicitly on considerations of the public interest, to protect the right of a client when he has no interest in asserting the right and the enforcement of the right would be seriously prejudicial to another in defending a criminal charge or in some other way.

Despite the sweeping pronouncements in the *Derby Magistrates'* case as to the absolute and permanent nature of legal professional privilege, there are exceptions. Statute may override the privilege, either expressly or by necessary implication. The latter is not the same as a reasonable implication. In *R (Morgan Grenfell) v Special Commissioner of Income Tax*[152] Lord Hobhouse said:

A *necessary* implication is one which necessarily follows from the express provisions of the statute construed in their context. It distinguishes between what it would have been sensible or reasonable for Parliament to have included or what Parliament would, if it had thought about it, probably have included and what it is clear that the express language of the statute shows that the statute must have included. A necessary implication is a matter of express language and logic not interpretation.

However, even if a statute does override the privilege, it may still be declared incompatible with the right of privacy under Article 8 of the European Convention of Human Rights, the European Court of Human Rights having said that the privilege is a fundamental human right which can be invaded only in exceptional circumstances.[153]

There are three other specific types of exception. The first, fraud, was referred to by Lord Lloyd in the *Derby Magistrates'* case as 'a well-recognized exception'.[154] The second relates to reports by third parties prepared on the instructions of the client for the purposes of care proceedings under the Children Act 1989. The third concerns cases in which the instructions given or the advice received are themselves in issue in the litigation.

### (a) Fraud

In *R v Cox and Railton*[155] the Court for Crown Cases Reserved held that if a client seeks legal advice intended to facilitate or guide him in the commission of a crime or fraud, the legal adviser being ignorant of the purpose for which the advice is sought, the communication between them is not privileged. The exception also applies if the solicitor *is* a party to the crime or fraud but not, it was held in *Butler v Board of Trade*,[156] if he merely volunteers a warning to the client that his conduct, if persisted in, may result in a prosecution.[157] The exception can only be relied on if there is prima

---

[152] [2003] 1 AC 563, HL at [45], applied in *B v Auckland District Law Society* [2003] 2 AC 736, PC.

[153] See per Lord Hoffmann, obiter, in *R (Morgan Grenfell) v Special Commissioner of Income Tax* [2003] 1 AC 563 at [7] and [39], citing *Foxley v UK* (2000) 8 BHRC 571 at 581.

[154] [1995] 4 All ER 526 at 543.     [155] (1884) 14 QBD 153, CCR.     [156] [1971] Ch 680.

[157] However, the Board in that case was able to prove a letter since a copy of it had come into their hands and Goff J refused to grant an injunction to prevent such use: see below.

facie evidence of the client's criminal purpose.[158] However, the court may look at the communications themselves, if necessary, to determine whether they came into existence in furtherance of such a purpose.[159]

The exception is not confined to cases in which solicitors advise on or set up criminal or fraudulent transactions yet to be undertaken, but also covers criminal or fraudulent conduct undertaken for the purposes of acquiring evidence in or for litigation, so that where documents have been generated by, or report on, conduct constituting a crime under the Data Protection Act 1984, and they are relevant to the issues in the litigation, they will not be protected from disclosure by legal professional privilege.[160]

There are a number of limitations on the scope of this exception. First, although not limited to crimes, it does not extend to communications concerning all intended legal wrongs. In *Crescent Farm (Sidcup) Sports Ltd v Sterling Offices Ltd*[161] the first defendant conveyed land to the second defendant in breach of the plaintiff's contractual right of pre-emption. The plaintiff sought damages for breach of contract, interference with contract and conspiracy, and sought discovery of an opinion prepared by the first defendant's counsel concerning the conveyance, which the first defendant had given to the second defendant. Goff J said:[162]

It is clear that parties must be at liberty to take advice as to the ambit of their contractual obligations and liabilities in tort and what liability they will incur whether in contract or tort by a proposed course of action without thereby in every case losing professional privilege. I agree that fraud in this connection is not limited to the tort of deceit and includes all forms of fraud and dishonesty such as fraudulent breach of contract, fraudulent conspiracy, trickery and sham contrivances, but I cannot feel that the tort of inducing a breach of contract or the narrow form of conspiracy pleaded in this case comes within that ambit.

Trespass and conversion are also outside the scope of the doctrine.[163] However, privilege will not attach to advice on a scheme, in breach of an employee's confidential duty of fidelity and involving the secret use of the employer's time and money, to take other employees (and the employer's customers) and to make profit from them in a competing business developed to receive them on leaving the employer's service.[164] Equally, if there is strong prima facie evidence that a transaction has been devised to prejudice the interests of a creditor by putting assets beyond his reach, privilege will not attach to legal advice on how to structure such a transaction.[165]

[158] *O'Rourke v Darbishire* [1920] AC 581. But see also *Derby & Co Ltd v Weldon (No 7)* [1990] 3 All ER 161, Ch D: the court will be very slow to deprive a party of the privilege on an interlocutory application and will judge each case on its facts.
[159] *R v Governor of Pentonville Prison, ex p Osman* [1989] 3 All ER 701, QBD at 729–30.
[160] *Dubai Aluminium Co Ltd v Al Alawi* [1999] 1 All ER 703, QBD.
[161] [1972] Ch 553.     [162] [1972] Ch 553 at 565.
[163] Per Rix J in *Dubai Aluminium Co Ltd v Al Alawi* [1999] 1 All ER 703 at 707.
[164] *Gamlen Chemical Co (UK) Ltd v Rochem Ltd* [1980] 1 All ER 1049.
[165] *Barclays Bank plc v Eustice* [1995] 4 All ER 511, CA.

In *Kuwait Airways Corporation v Iraqi Airways Co*[166] it was confirmed that the fraud exception can apply to litigation privilege, as well as legal advice privilege, but it was held that whereas a prima facie case of fraud may suffice where the issue of fraud is not one of the very issues in the action, where it is such an issue then a very strong prima facie case of fraud is required. In *Chandler v Church*[167] the plaintiffs alleged that the defendant had fraudulently manipulated to his own advantage various share transactions. They sought discovery of communications between him and his solicitors on the basis of prima facie evidence showing that he had obtained their assistance to enable him to mislead the court by putting forward false documents and pretending that certain transactions were genuine. Hoffmann J held that although it does not matter whether the fraud concerns an earlier transaction or the conduct of the proceedings in question, disclosure at an interlocutory stage based on prima facie evidence of fraud in the conduct of the very proceedings in which the discovery is sought carries a far greater risk of injury to the party against whom discovery is sought, should he turn out to have been innocent, than disclosure of advice concerning an earlier transaction. The risk of injustice to the defendant in being required to reveal communications with his lawyers for the purpose of his defence, together with the damage to the public interest which the violation of such confidences would cause, outweighed the risk of injustice to the plaintiffs.[168]

Finally, the exception does not extend to the correspondence between a lawyer and an assignee or victim of a fraudsman. In *Banque Keyser Ullmann SA v Skandia (UK) Insurance Co Ltd*[169] insurance policies, issued to borrowers to cover banks against failure of the borrowers to repay, were assigned to the banks. The loans were not repaid and the banks claimed under the policies. The insurers denied liability on the grounds that the policies had been obtained by the fraud of the borrowers. The contention of the insurers that by reason of the borrowers' fraud no privilege attached to the correspondence passing between the banks and their lawyers was rejected.

Section 10(2) of the Police and Criminal Evidence Act 1984, as we have seen, provides that 'items held with the intention of furthering a criminal purpose are not items subject to legal privilege'. In *R v Crown Court at Snaresbrook, ex p DPP*[170] it was held, giving these words their natural meaning, that it is the person holding the items in question whose intention is relevant. This construction was rejected in *Francis & Francis (a firm) v Central Criminal Court*.[171] A majority of the House of Lords, comprising Lords Brandon, Griffiths, and Goff, was of the opinion that section 10(2) was

---

166 [2005] EWCA Civ 286.   167 [1987] NLJ Rep 451, Ch D.

168 See also *R v Crown Court at Snaresbrook, ex p DPP* [1988] 1 All ER 315, QBD: where a person has made false statements in an application for legal aid to pursue a civil action, the application, although admissible in a prosecution charging him with knowingly making such a false statement, is privileged in other criminal proceedings even if relevant thereto (see ss 22 and 23 of the Legal Aid Act 1974, re-enacted in ss 38 and 39 of the Legal Aid Act 1988). See per Glidewell LJ at 319. See also per Lord Goff in *Francis & Francis (a firm) v Central Criminal Court* [1988] 3 All ER 775 at 800, HL.

169 [1986] 1 Lloyd's Rep 336, CA.   170 [1988] 1 All ER 315, QBD.

171 [1988] 3 All ER 775, HL.

intended to reflect the position at common law, and not to restrict the principle of *R v Cox and Railton* to those cases in which the legal adviser has the intention of furthering a criminal purpose; and therefore that the intention referred to in that subsection could be that of the person holding the document or that of any other person.[172] Accordingly, it was held that conveyancing documents innocently held by a solicitor in relation to the purchase of a property by a client, intended by a third party, a relative of the client, to be used to further the criminal purpose of laundering the proceeds of illegal drug trafficking, were not items subject to legal privilege.[173]

In *R v Leeds Magistrates' Court, ex p Dumbleton*[174] a warrant was issued to search for and seize documents held by a solicitor and allegedly forged by him and another. It was held that the documents were not covered by section 10(1), because the phrase 'made in connection with . . . legal proceedings' meant lawfully made and did not extend to forged documents or copies thereof; and in any event the items were held with the intention of furthering a criminal purpose, the word 'held' in section 10(2) relating to the time at which the documents came into the possession of the person holding them.

## (b) Proceedings under the Children Act 1989

Care proceedings under the Children Act 1989 are non-adversarial: the court's duty is to investigate and to undertake all necessary steps to arrive at an appropriate result in the paramount interests of the welfare of the child. If a party to such proceedings, on obtaining an unfavourable expert's report, were to be able to suppress it and maintain a case at variance with it, judges would sometimes decide cases affecting children in ignorance of material facts and in a way detrimental to their best interests. For these reasons, in *Oxfordshire County Council v M*[175] it was held that in care proceedings in which the court gives leave to a party to obtain expert reports, it has power to override legal professional privilege and require the report to be filed and served on the other parties.[176] However, the promotion of the welfare of the child does not require that

---

[172] As Lord Oliver observed, however, in his powerful dissenting judgment: 'There is not, so far as I am aware, any authority in the common law dealing with the question of whether a criminal intent on the part of a stranger to the relationship of solicitor and client destroys the privilege of the client. If, therefore, the subsection does indeed bear the meaning now sought to be ascribed to it . . . it is breaking new ground and the legislative intent has to be gathered not from some supposed logical extension of the common law rule but from the words which Parliament has chosen to use' (at 793). Cf *Banque Keyser Ullmann SA v Skandia (UK) Insurance Co Ltd* [1986] 1 Lloyd's Rep 336, CA, above, to which none of their Lordships referred.

[173] See also *R (Hallinan) v Middlesex Guildhall Crown Court* [2004] All ER (D) 242 (Nov), where there was evidence of a specific agreement to pervert the course of justice; and *R v Crown Court at Northampton, ex p DPP* (1991) 93 Cr App R 376, DC, where it was the client who had the intention of furthering a criminal purpose. Charged with theft of goods, he had passed an allegedly forged receipt for the goods to his solicitor. It was held that under s 9 of the 1984 Act (see above), the circuit judge should have ordered the solicitor to produce the receipt to the police.

[174] [1993] Crim LR 866, DC.     [175] [1994] 2 All ER 269, CA.

[176] Approving *Re R (a minor)* [1993] 4 All ER 702 and overruling *Barking and Dagenham London Borough Council v O* [1993] 4 All ER 59.

communications between a client and a lawyer should also be disclosed.[177] The same distinction was made in Re L,[178] where a majority of the House of Lords rejected a contention that the absolute nature of the privilege attaching to the solicitor–client relationship extends to all other forms of legal professional privilege. The majority approved Oxfordshire County Council v M, subject to one qualification: privilege had not been overridden in that case because it never arose in the first place, having been excluded by necessary implication from the terms and overall purpose of the 1989 Act. It has also been held that the exception under consideration does not extend to override privilege which has properly arisen and is maintainable in proceedings other than those under the 1989 Act, such as criminal proceedings against the father of the child.[179]

### (c) Instructions or advice in issue in litigation

Sometimes the question of what instructions were given to a lawyer or what advice was received may be an issue in the litigation, and this may result in privilege being abrogated. For example, where the court is asked to exercise its power under section 33 of the Limitation Act 1980 to allow an action to be brought out of time, it will be relevant for the court to know what advice the applicant received at various times as to his chances of success.[180] Similarly, the instructions given to a solicitor will have to be disclosed if a question arises whether or not the client authorized him to write letters to his opponent stating that he would accept a certain sum in settlement of his claim.[181]

## 5 DURATION OF THE PRIVILEGE

'As a general rule, one may say once privileged always privileged.'[182] Documents prepared for one set of proceedings continue to be privileged for the purpose of subsequent litigation, even if the litigation originally anticipated never took place;[183] and documents relating to property rights which are privileged in the hands of one person continue to be privileged in the hands of successors-in-title to the property.[184] In order to claim in a subsequent action the privilege which prevailed for the first action, there must be a sufficient connection of subject matter for the privileged material to be relevant to the subsequent action (because if the material is irrelevant the question of disclosure cannot even arise) and the person originally entitled to the privilege or his successor must be a party to the subsequent action; there is no

---

[177] Oxfordshire County Council v M [1994] 2 All ER 269 per Steyn LJ at 282, CA.

[178] [1997] 1 AC 16, HL.   [179] S County Council v B [2000] 2 FLR 161.

[180] Jones v GD Searle & Co Ltd [1979] 1 WLR 101, CA.

[181] Conlon v Conlons Ltd [1952] 2 All ER 462, CA.

[182] Per Lindley MR in Calcraft v Guest [1898] 1 QB 759 at 761, CA.

[183] Pearce v Foster (1885) 15 QBD 114, CA.

[184] Minet v Morgan (1873) 8 Ch App 361; Crescent Farm (Sidcup) Sports Ltd v Sterling Offices Ltd [1972] Ch 553, above.

additional requirement that the subject matter of the two actions should be identical or substantially the same or that the parties to the two actions should be the same.[185]

Legal professional privilege is that of the client or his successor in title. Accordingly, a third party from whom a statement was obtained for the dominant purpose of anticipated or pending litigation cannot claim protection in respect of the contents of that statement if he himself becomes a party to wholly independent litigation. *Schneider v Leigh*[186] was an action in libel. The plaintiff was claiming, in other proceedings, damages for personal injuries against a company whose solicitors had obtained a medical report, to which privilege attached, from a doctor whom they intended to call as a witness in those proceedings. The plaintiff regarded the document as defamatory, began the instant action against the doctor and sought disclosure of the full report. It was held that the doctor was not entitled to rely on the company's privilege. The court, however, recognizing that the personal injuries action had yet to be disposed of, ordered that inspection of the report should take effect only on the conclusion of that action.

Where there are likely to be joint proceedings against the client and the third party, it may be that the third party will nonetheless be effectively protected by the client's privilege. In *Lee v South West Thames Regional Health Authority*[187] the health authorities of Hillingdon (H) and South West Thames (SWT) were both involved in the treatment of a patient which went badly wrong. H, for the purpose of getting legal advice about anticipated litigation against themselves, obtained from SWT a report of their involvement. On an application against SWT under section 33(2) of the Supreme Court Act 1981 for pre-action discovery of the report, it was held that although the privilege was that of H and not SWT, it was SWT's right and duty to assert H's privilege until such time as H no longer had an interest in non-disclosure. Since the proceedings against H and SWT would go together, the plaintiff would be unable to use the report against either of them.

# 6 SECONDARY EVIDENCE

Legal professional privilege prevents evidence from being given, or documents from being produced, by particular persons: the client, his lawyer, the relevant third parties (where applicable) and any agents for communication, such as secretaries or clerks. If some other person overhears a privileged conversation or obtains a privileged document or a copy of it, he may be compelled to give evidence in that regard or to produce the document or copy. The leading case, *Calcraft v Guest*,[188] involved *copies* of privileged documents, but it is clear that under the principle, the originals, if available, can be produced.[189] The principle operates not only where the

---

[185] *The Aegis Blaze* [1986] 1 Lloyd's Rep 203, CA.     [186] [1955] 2 QB 195, CA.
[187] [1985] 1 WLR 845, CA.     [188] [1898] 1 QB 759, CA.
[189] See per Lord Simon in *Waugh v British Railways Board* [1980] AC 521 at 536; *Rumping v DPP* [1964] AC 814; and *R v Governor of Pentonville Prison, ex p Osman* [1989] 3 All ER 701 at 729–30, QBD.

communication was disclosed by inadvertence or error on the part of the person otherwise entitled to assert the privilege, but also where the communication was obtained by improper or even unlawful means. However, CPR rule 31.20 provides that in civil cases in which a party inadvertently allows a privileged document to be inspected, the party who has inspected the document may use it or its contents only with the permission of the court.

In *R v Tompkins*[190] an incriminating note from the accused to his counsel was found on the floor of the court and handed to counsel for the prosecution. The Court of Appeal upheld the judge's ruling allowing the prosecution to show the note to the accused and to cross-examine him as to matters referred to in it. It is submitted that the court was correct in holding that the accused could not actually be asked to prove the note, since he was still entitled to assert his privilege in relation to it, but in principle it must have been permissible for the prosecution to tender the note in evidence themselves, subject to the possibly difficult task of proving authorship. In *R v Cottrill*,[191] applying *R v Tompkins*, it was held that a statement made by the accused to his solicitors and sent by them to the prosecution without his knowledge or consent, could be used by the prosecution in cross-examination as a previous inconsistent statement, subject to section 78 of the Police and Criminal Evidence Act 1984.[192]

A litigant who has in his possession copies of documents to which legal professional privilege attaches may use them as secondary evidence in the litigation, but if he has not yet used them in that way, the mere fact that he intends to do so will not prevent a claim against him, by the person in whom the privilege is vested, for delivery up of the copies and for an injunction to restrain him from disclosing or making any use of any information contained in them.[193] In *Lord Ashburton v Pape*[194] Pape, a party to bankruptcy proceedings, obtained by a trick copies of confidential and privileged correspondence between Lord Ashburton and his solicitors. The Court of Appeal granted an injunction preventing Pape from using the copies in the bankruptcy proceedings. The possibility of using privileged material in evidence may thus turn simply on whether the owner can first obtain an injunction to restrain such use. In deciding whether to grant an injunction, the normal rules relating to the grant of equitable remedies apply. Thus delay is a relevant factor, as is the conduct of the party seeking the injunction, including the clean hands principle. Where, as in *ISTIL Group Inc v Zahoor*[195] the privileged documents show that evidence has been forged and that there has been an attempt to mislead the court, the public interest in supporting the privilege will be outweighed by the public interest in the proper administration of justice.

The principle in *Lord Ashburton v Pape* is not confined to cases in which the privileged material is obtained by trickery. In *Guinness Peat Properties Ltd v Fitzroy Robinson Partnership (a firm)*[196] it was held that it may also apply where the privilege

---

[190] (1977) 67 Cr App R 181.     [191] [1997] Crim LR 56, CA.
[192] See also *R v Willis* [2004] All ER (D) 287 (Dec).
[193] Per May LJ in *Goddard v Nationwide Building Society* [1986] 3 All ER 264 at 270, CA.
[194] [1913] 2 Ch 469, CA.     [195] [2003] 2 All ER 252, Ch D.     [196] [1987] 2 All ER 716, CA.

is lost by inadvertence. That was a case in which one party to litigation had, on disclosure, mistakenly included in his list of documents to the production of which he did not object, a document for which privilege could properly have been claimed and which should have been included in the list of documents to the production of which he did object. The relevant principles in this situation were summarized by Slade LJ as follows:[197]

1.   The court will ordinarily permit the party who made the error to amend his list.[198]

2.   Once the other party has inspected the document, the general rule is that it is too late for the first party to correct the mistake by applying for injunctive relief.[199]

3.   However, if the other party or his solicitor either (a) has procured inspection of the relevant document by fraud or (b) on inspection realized that he has been permitted to see the document only by reason of an obvious mistake, the court has power to grant an injunction. Examples include *Goddard v Nationwide Building Society,*[200] in which the plaintiff's solicitors sent the defendant a copy of an attendance note recording conversations with the plaintiff, and the defendant thereupon pleaded the substance of the contents in his defence, and *English and American Insurance Co Ltd v Herbert Smith & Co,*[201] in which a clerk to a barrister instructed by the plaintiff's solicitor mistakenly handed over to the defendant's solicitors a bundle of papers including instructions to counsel, counsel's notes, letters from the solicitor to the plaintiff and statements of witnesses. In both cases an injunction and an order for delivery up was granted.

4.   In such cases, the court should ordinarily grant the injunction unless it can properly be refused on general principles affecting the grant of a discretionary remedy, for example on the grounds of inordinate delay.[202]

In *Webster v James Chapman & Co*[203] Scott J held that the court should balance the interests of the one party in seeking to keep the information confidential against the interests of the other in seeking to make use of it, taking account of not only the privileged nature of the document, but also such matters as how the document was obtained and its relevance to the issues in the action. This approach was rejected in

---

[197]   [1987] 2 All ER 716 at 730–1.

[198]   See, eg, *C H Beazer (Commercial and Industrial) Ltd v R M Smith Ltd* (1984) 3 Const LJ 196.

[199]   See *Re Briamore Manufacturing Ltd* [1986] 3 All ER 132, Ch D. However, in that case the first party conceded that secondary evidence of the documents would be admissible and the court was not reminded of the decision in *Lord Ashburton v Pape*.

[200]   [1986] 3 All ER 264, CA.        [201]   [1988] FSR 232, Ch D.

[202]   If solicitors realize that documents have been mistakenly disclosed to them but, on the instructions of their client read them, an injunction may also be granted to restrain them from acting for the client in the proceedings in question: see *Ablitt v Mills & Reeve* (1995) *The Times,* 25 Oct, Ch D.

[203]   [1989] 3 All ER 939, Ch D.

*Derby & Co Ltd v Weldon (No 8).*[204] The Court of Appeal, without referring to *Webster v James Chapman & Co,* held that where an injunction is sought in aid of legal professional privilege, the court is not required to carry out such a balancing exercise. Dillon LJ said:[205]

where the privilege is being restored because the inspection was obtained by fraud or by taking advantage of a known mistake, there is to my mind no logic at all in qualifying the restoration of the status quo by reference to the importance of the document. 'You have taken advantage of an obvious mistake to obtain copies of documents; we will order you to return all the ones that are unimportant to you but you can keep the ones that are important' would be a nonsensical attitude for the court to adopt.

In deciding whether disclosure has occurred as a result of an obvious mistake, the party claiming the injunction has the burden of proving, on a balance of probabilities, that the mistake would have been obvious to a reasonable solicitor, rather than to the actual recipient of the disclosed document, although the reaction of the actual recipient can be relevant. A reasonable solicitor, in deciding whether the privilege had been waived, would approach the question without bias towards his client and would take into account such factors as the extent of the claim to privilege in the list of documents, the nature of the document disclosed, the complexity of the discovery, the way it had been carried out and the surrounding circumstances. Thus in *IBM Corpn v Phoenix International,*[206] from which these principles derive, and in which discovery involving a substantial number of documents had been carried out under a tight timetable and without due care, it was held that a reasonable solicitor would have realized that there was a risk of mistakes being made and would not have concluded, as the recipient had, that a deliberate decision had been made to disclose a document containing legal advice. In *Pizzey v Ford Motor Co Ltd,*[207] on the other hand, where discovery was slight and not complex, a reasonable solicitor would have assumed that privilege had been waived deliberately and not in error.

As previously noted, CPR rule 31.20 provides that in civil cases in which a party inadvertently allows a privileged document to be inspected, the party who has inspected the document may use it or its contents only with the permission of the court. The decision should be made in accordance with the principles established in the foregoing cases.[208]

Public policy may also prevent a party from relying upon the principle of *Calcraft v Guest.* In *ITC Film Distributors v Video Exchange Ltd*[209] documents were obtained by a trick in court in the course of civil proceedings. By that stage in the case there were difficulties in the way of granting injunctive relief, but the judge made interesting use

---

204 [1990] 3 All ER 762.

205 [1990] 3 All ER 762 at 783. See also per Nourse LJ in *Goddard v Nationwide Building Society* [1986] 3 All ER 264 at 272.

206 [1995] 1 All ER 413, Ch D.      207 [1994] PIQR P15, CA.

208 *Al Fayed v Metropolitan Police Commissioner* [2002] EWCA Civ 780.      209 [1982] Ch 431.

of *D v NSPCC*[210] to hold that the public interest that litigants should be able to bring their documents into court without fear that they may be filched by their opponents, required an exception to the rule in *Calcraft v Guest*. The decision, it is submitted, correct in itself, results in an illogical distinction between documents stolen within court and those stolen without.

No less indefensible, it is submitted, is the distinction stemming from *Butler v Board of Trade*,[211] another decision made on grounds of public policy. It was held that the principle of *Lord Ashburton v Pape* cannot be used to prevent the prosecution from tendering relevant evidence in a public prosecution.[212] There is much to be said for allowing the spirit of *Lord Ashburton v Pape* to prevail in criminal as well as civil proceedings.[213]

## 7  WAIVER

A client may elect to waive the legal professional privilege that he could otherwise assert. Having once waived the privilege, he cannot then reassert it. Thus a litigant who deliberately produces a privileged document for inspection on disclosure or serves notice of a conversation with his solicitor under the notice provisions relating to hearsay in civil cases, cannot at trial claim privilege for that communication.[214] Equally, where an expert, in his report, refers to otherwise privileged material supplied to him as part of the background documentation on which his opinion was sought, the privilege in that material will be waived by service of the report on the other party.[215] However, if a document has been disclosed for a limited purpose only, privilege will not be waived generally, and the court is precluded from conducting a balancing exercise, because a lawyer must be able to give his client an unqualified assurance not only that what passes between them shall never be revealed without his consent, but that should he consent to disclosure within limits, those limits will be respected.[216] Thus where privileged documents prepared by a claimant for a civil action against a person are handed over to the police in accordance with the claimant's duty to assist in a criminal investigation, charges are preferred against that person and copies of the documents are disclosed to him by the prosecution, this cannot be construed as either an express or implied waiver of the claimant's privilege in relation to the civil action, because to hold otherwise would be contrary to public policy.[217]

The principle of waiver is capable of becoming somewhat complicated, particularly

---

[210] [1978] AC 171. See Ch 19.       [211] [1971] Ch 680.

[212] The same point, in the case of a *private* prosecution, was expressly left open.

[213] Per Nourse LJ in *Goddard v Nationwide Building Society* [1986] 3 WLR 734 at 746, CA; and see *R v Uljee* [1982] 1 NZLR 561, NZCA.

[214] Merely referring to the existence of a document in pleadings or affidavits will not amount to waiver, though quoting from it may do so. See *Tate & Lyle International Ltd v Government Trading Corpn* [1984] LS Gaz R 3341, CA.

[215] *Clough v Tameside and Glossop Health Authority* [1998] 2 All ER 971, QBD.

[216] *B v Auckland District Law Society* [2003] 2 AC 736, PC.

[217] *British Coal Corpn v Dennis Rye Ltd (No 2)* [1988] 3 All ER 816, CA.

in the context of civil litigation, as a result of another principle, namely that a litigant is not entitled to edit his evidence, relying on the favourable parts of a privileged communication but refusing to say anything about the rest. Thus if part of a privileged document is put in evidence at trial, the other side can require the whole document to be disclosed, unless the remaining part concerns such a distinct subject matter as to be capable of severance.[218] The question whether 'cherry picking' is taking place, that is, whether fairness requires the whole document to be adduced so that the court is not misled by seeing only part of it out of context, can only be answered by the judge after he has read the whole of it.[219] The same principles apply at the interim stage of civil proceedings.[220] If cross-examining counsel puts to an opposing witness a statement taken on behalf of his own client, even only a small part of it, he waives his client's privilege in the statement and thereby entitles counsel who called the witness to re-examine him on the whole of the statement. However, the risk of permitting such lengthy re-examination can be avoided either by counsel agreeing that part only of a statement may be put without the whole being opened up for re-examination, or by cross-examining counsel preparing written questions to be handed to the witness either in the witness-box or several days previously.[221] The disclosure of part of a privileged document on disclosure constitutes a waiver of privilege of the entire contents of the document unless, again, the other part deals with a separate subject matter so that the document can be divided into two separate and distinct documents.[222] As to the disclosure of privileged material in interim proceedings, a distinction has to be drawn between a reference to having been given advice to a particular effect, which does not amount to waiver of the right to claim privilege in respect of the advice itself at the subsequent trial, and disclosure of the substance or content of that advice, which does amount to such a waiver.[223]

The principle under discussion, if taken to extremes, could lead to the disclosure of a vast array of otherwise privileged material, including proofs of evidence, memoranda prepared by solicitors and instructions to counsel.[224] The courts have thus been obliged to find ways of limiting the principle. In *George Doland Ltd v Blackburn, Robson, Coates & Co*[225] a distinction was drawn between legal advice and litigation privilege. It was held that oral conversations and documents relating to the subject matter in question were only liable to disclosure insofar as they were covered by the

---

[218] *Great Atlantic Insurance Co v Home Insurance Co* [1981] 1 WLR 529, CA. See also *George Doland Ltd v Blackburn, Robson, Coates & Co* [1972] 1 WLR 1338, QBD: if a client seeks to support his credit at trial by reference to what he said to his solicitor on one occasion, he cannot object to being cross-examined as to what he said to his solicitor about the same subject matter on other occasions.

[219] *Derby & Co Ltd v Weldon (No 10)* [1991] 2 All ER 908, Ch D.

[220] *Dunlop Slazenger International Ltd v Joe Bloggs Sports Ltd* [2003] EWCA Civ 901.

[221] *Fairfield-Mabey Ltd v Shell UK Ltd* [1989] 1 All ER 576, QBD.

[222] *Pozzi v Eli Lilly & Co* (1986) The Times, 3 Dec, QBD.

[223] *Derby & Co Ltd v Weldon (No 10)* [1991] 2 All ER 908, Ch D.

[224] Suggested in argument in *General Accident Fire and Life Assurance Co Ltd v Tanter* [1984] 1 WLR 100, though on the facts the judge was able to avoid that result.

[225] [1972] 1 WLR 1338, QBD.

first type of privilege. A different approach, however, was adopted in *General Accident Fire and Life Assurance Co Ltd v Tanter*.[226] In that case privilege had been waived in relation to a conversation which took place at a time when litigation was anticipated and to which the second type of privilege applied. Hobhouse J held that if the party entitled to the privilege puts the conversation in evidence (as opposed to being cross-examined about it) then waiver relates to 'the transaction', that is what was said on the occasion in question, and does not extend to the subject matter of the conversation. Thus although the opposite party is entitled to call for, inspect and cross-examine on other privileged communications relating to what was actually said in the conversation, he is not entitled to see or use such other privileged communications as may exist relating to the subject matter of the conversation.[227]

On the assessment of costs in civil cases, disclosure of privileged material is viewed as a waiver only for the purposes of the assessment: the privilege can subsequently be reasserted.[228] Paragraph 40.14 of Practice Direction 43–8 provides that:

The court may direct the receiving party to produce any document which in the opinion of the court is necessary to enable it to reach its decision. These documents will in the first instance be produced to the court, but the court may ask the receiving party to elect whether to disclose the particular document to the paying party in order to rely on the contents of the document, or whether to decline disclosure and instead rely on other evidence.

In *South Coast Shipping Co Ltd v Havant Borough Council*[229] it was held that paragraph 40.14 was consistent with the requirements of Articles 6 and 8 of the European Convention on Human Rights. In that case, Pumfrey J said:[230] 'I would expect that in the great majority of cases the paying party would be content to agree that the costs judge alone should see privileged documents. Only where it is necessary and proportionate should the receiving party be put to his election.'

The institution of civil proceedings by a client against his solicitor constitutes an implied waiver of privilege. The waiver must go far enough not merely to enable the client to establish his cause of action but to enable the solicitor to establish a defence. Thus it may extend beyond the communications relating to the specific retainer forming the subject matter of the proceedings to communications relating to earlier retainers which are relevant to the issue between the parties.[231]

---

[226] [1984] 1 WLR 100.

[227] Hobhouse J declined to follow *George Doland Ltd v Blackburn, Robson, Coates & Co* [1972] 1 WLR 1338 insofar as it could be treated as an authority to the contrary. It was also held that the distinction drawn in that case between the two types of privilege was not a criterion applicable in all cases and was not applicable in the instant case. See also *Derby & Co Ltd v Weldon (No 10)* [1991] 2 All ER 908, where Vinelott J, in the case of a single conversation, different parts of which were covered by the different types of privilege, refused to sever the two types of privilege and to say that one was waived but not the other: both had been waived.

[228] *Goldman v Hesper* [1988] 1 WLR 1238, CA.   [229] [2003] 3 All ER 779, Ch D.   [230] At [30].

[231] *Lillicrap v Nalder & Son (a firm)* [1993] 1 All ER 724, CA. Cf *Nederlandse Reassurantie Groep Holding NV v Bacon & Woodrow (a firm)* [1995] 1 All ER 976, QBD: where a client assembles a team of lawyers and non-legal advisers and brings proceedings against the non-legal advisers, communications between the client and the lawyers which were not disclosed to the non-legal advisers remain privileged even if the non-legal advisers can establish that they are evidentially relevant to their defence.

# C WITHOUT PREJUDICE NEGOTIATIONS

## 1 SETTLEMENT NEGOTIATIONS

Communications between opposing parties to a civil action, or between their solicitors, do not attract legal professional privilege. In the absence of any other protection, therefore, if one party were to make a concession in the course of settlement negotiations which, in the event, were to fail, the other party would be able to use it against him at the trial as a damaging admission. In order to remove this risk and thereby encourage the settlement of civil litigation, the rule is that privilege attaches to oral or written statements made 'without prejudice', that is without prejudice to the maker of the statement if the terms he proposes are not accepted.[232] The protection of admissions against interest is the most important practical effect of the rule, but to dissect out admissions and withhold protection from the rest of without prejudice communications would be to create huge practical difficulties and would be contrary to the underlying objective of giving protection to the parties to speak freely about all the issues in the litigation. 'Parties cannot speak freely at a without prejudice meeting if they must constantly monitor every sentence, with lawyers ... sitting at their shoulders as minders.'[233]

If the negotiations succeed and a settlement is concluded, the without prejudice correspondence remains privileged: such correspondence is inadmissible in any subsequent litigation connected with the same subject matter, whether between the same or different parties, and is also protected from subsequent disclosure to other parties to the litigation.[234]

The privilege is the joint privilege of both parties and extends to their solicitors.[235] It can only be waived with the consent of each of the parties. It does not depend on the existence of proceedings,[236] but where proceedings do ensue, it may be asserted at

---

[232] See per Lindley LJ in *Walker v Wilsher* (1889) 23 QBD 335, CA at 337. There is nothing in criminal law akin to 'without prejudice': *R v Hayes* [2005] 1 Cr App R 557, CA, where the prosecution were entitled to cross-examine H on a previous inconsistent statement in a letter sent by his solicitor to the CPS suggesting that he might plead guilty to a lesser offence.

[233] Per Robert Walker LJ in *Unilever plc v The Procter & Gamble Co* [2001] 1 All ER 783, CA at 796. Cf *Muller v Linsley & Mortimer (a firm)* [1996] PNLR 74, CA, where it was said that correspondence is admissible if it is to be used not for the truth of any damaging admissions that it contains but for some other relevant purpose (eg to show that the admissions are not true and that the party otherwise entitled to assert the privilege acted unreasonably in concluding the settlement), because the public policy basis of the rule is to prevent anything said in without prejudice negotiations being used as an *admission*.

[234] *Rush & Tompkins Ltd v Greater London Council* [1988] 3 All ER 737, HL. However, the privilege will not prevent inspection of the terms of a settlement if relevant in determining the extent of the liability of a third party against whom one of the parties to the settlement is seeking a contribution: *Gnitrow Ltd v Cape plc* [2000] 1 WLR 2327, CA.

[235] *La Roche v Armstrong* [1922] 1 KB 485.

[236] Per Balcombe LJ in *Rush & Tompkins Ltd v Greater London Council* [1988] 1 All ER 549 at 554, CA.

the trial itself, whether in relation to liability, quantum or costs,[237] as well as in interim proceedings such as a hearing of a summons for security for costs.[238] The contents of without prejudice correspondence can be disclosed in an application to strike out for want of prosecution, but if it fails, the privilege can be asserted at the trial itself.[239] However where, on an interim application, one party deploys without prejudice material in support of his case on the underlying merits of the claim, the other party is entitled to use other parts of that material at the trial.[240]

The essential pre-condition for a claim to without prejudice privilege is the existence of a dispute. The privilege, therefore, will not protect correspondence designed to prevent a dispute arising.[241] In *BNP Paribas v Mezzotero*[242] while a grievance of M about perceived discrimination was being processed, the employer convened a without prejudice meeting, said to be independent of the grievance, at which M was advised that her job was no longer viable and an offer of a redundancy package was made. In a subsequent tribunal application claiming, inter alia, sex discrimination, it was held that M could rely on what was said at the meeting because there was no dispute at that time. Upholding this ruling, the Employment Appeal Tribunal held that there was no evidence of an employment dispute before the meeting. The grievance related to her continuing employment, not the threat of termination of employment, and therefore could not be treated as evidence of a dispute.

The privilege attaches to any discussions that take place between actual or prospective parties with a view to avoiding litigation, including discussions within conciliation and mediation schemes.[243] The fact that the expression 'without prejudice' is not actually used is 'not without significance',[244] but does not conclude the matter: provided that there is some dispute and an attempt is being made to settle it, the courts should be ready to infer that the attempt was without prejudice.[245] In order to decide whether or not a document was bona fide intended to be a negotiating document, the court has to look at the intention of the author and how the document would be received by a reasonable recipient. If the document is marked 'without prejudice' that is a factor that the court should take into account. It is an indication that the author intended it to be a negotiating document and, in many cases, a recipient would receive it on the understanding that the marking indicated that the author wished to attempt

---

[237] *Walker v Wilsher* (1889) 23 QBD 335, CA. But see *Calderbank v Calderbank* [1976] Fam 93, below.

[238] *Simaan General Contracting Co v Pilkington Glass Ltd* [1987] 1 All ER 345, CA.

[239] *Family Housing Association (Manchester) Ltd v Michael Hyde & Partners (a firm)* [1993] 2 All ER 567, CA.

[240] *Somatra Ltd v Sinclair Roche and Temperley* [2000] 1 WLR 2453. See also CPR r 31.22

[241] *Prudential Assurance Co Ltd v Prudential Insurance Co of America* [2002] EWHC 2809, Ch D.

[242] [2004] IRLR 508, EAT.      [243] See *Smiths Group plc v Weiss* [2002] EWHC 582, Ch D.

[244] *Prudential Assurance Co Ltd v Prudential Insurance Co of America* [2002] EWHC 2809, Ch D.

[245] *Chocoladefabriken Lindt & Sprungli AG v Nestlé Co Ltd* [1978] RPC 287 at 288–9. If negotiations begin on a without prejudice basis, they remain so unless the party wishing to change them to an open basis makes this clear to the other party: *Cheddar Valley Engineering Ltd v Chaddlewood Homes Ltd* [1992] 4 All ER 942. However, open letters written after the negotiations and 'without prejudice' correspondence have finished and come to nothing, are not privileged: *Dixons Stores Group Ltd v Thames Television plc* [1993] 1 All ER 349.

negotiation.[246] However, the heading 'without prejudice' does not conclusively or automatically render privileged a document so marked; if privilege is claimed for such a document but challenged, the court can look at it to determine its nature.[247] The privilege can attach to a document headed 'without prejudice' even if it is an 'opening shot', but the rule is not limited to documents which are offers; privilege attaches to all documents marked 'without prejudice' and forming part of negotiations, whether or not they contain offers, subject only to the recognized exceptions.[248]

There are a number of exceptions.[249] Without prejudice material is admissible if the issue is whether or not the negotiations resulted in an agreed settlement.[250] The rule cannot be used to exclude an act of bankruptcy (such as a letter containing an offer to settle which also states the writer's inability to pay his debts as they fall due),[251] or a statement of fact which, although made in the course of without prejudice correspondence, has no reference to the matters in dispute.[252] Nor can it be used to exclude letters which are the equivalent of a notice of severance, sent in the course of without prejudice negotiations, by the solicitor of one joint tenant to the solicitor of the other.[253]

The privilege cannot be claimed if exclusion of the evidence would act as a cloak for perjury, blackmail or other 'unambiguous impropriety',[254] but this exception should be applied only in the clearest cases of abuse.[255] As to perjury, the exception will apply in the case of a defendant who says that unless the case is withdrawn, he will give perjured evidence and will bribe other witnesses to perjure themselves.[256] However, the test is not whether there is a serious and substantial risk of perjury.[257] The exception will not apply where an admission is alleged to have been made that demonstrates that the pleaded case must be false[258] or where an admission is made that demonstrates that perjury has been committed in the past.[259] As to blackmail, the exception will apply where a claimant says that his claim is bogus and is being brought to 'blackmail' the defendant into a settlement of their real differences.[260] An example of other 'unambiguous impropriety' would be where an employer in dispute with a black employee says during discussions aimed at settlement, 'we do not want you here

---

[246] *Schering Corpn v Cipla Ltd* (2004) *The Times*, 10 Nov, Ch D.
[247] *South Shropshire District Council v Amos* [1987] 1 All ER 340.  [248] Ibid, CA at 344.
[249] For a non-exhaustive, but nonetheless extensive, list of the exceptions, see per Robert Walker LJ in *Unilever plc v The Procter & Gamble Co* [2001] 1 All ER 783, CA at 791–3.
[250] *Walker v Wilsher* (1889) 23 QBD 335, CA at 337; *Tomlin v Standard Telephones and Cables Ltd* [1969] 3 All ER 201, CA.
[251] *Re Daintrey, ex p Holt* [1893] 2 QB 116.  [252] *Waldridge v Kennison* (1794) 1 Esp 143.
[253] *McDowell v Hirschfield Lipson and Rumney* [1992] 2 FLR 126.
[254] The expression used by Hoffmann LJ in *Forster v Friedland* [1992] CA Transcript 1052.
[255] *Forster v Friedland*, ibid and *Fazil-Alizadeh v Nikbin* (1993) *The Times*, 19 Mar, CA.
[256] *Greenwood v Fitts* (1961) 29 DLR (2d) 260, BC CA.
[257] *Berry Trade Ltd v Moussavi* [2003] EWCA Civ 715, [2003] All ER (D) 315 (May), CA.
[258] Ibid.  [259] *Savings and Investment Bank Ltd v Fincken* [2004] 1 All ER 1125, CA.
[260] *Hawick Jersey International Ltd v Caplan* (1988) *The Times*, 11 Mar, QBD.

because you are black': such evidence should not be excluded from consideration by a tribunal hearing a subsequent complaint of race discrimination.[261]

In a money claim, or the money part of a mixed money and non-money claim, a defendant wishing to make an offer to settle may make a 'Part 36 payment', ie a payment into court under CPR Part 36. If the claimant refuses to accept the offer, the court is usually not told about it until all questions of liability and quantum have been decided, but if, at that stage, the claimant fails to better the payment, then unless it considers it unjust to do so, the court will order the claimant to pay any costs incurred by the defendant after the latest date on which the offer could have been accepted without needing the court's permission.[262] A defendant to an action for a non-money claim, eg a claim for an injunction or declaratory relief, has for some time been able to obtain similar protection by making an offer in a letter headed 'without prejudice except as to costs', thereby reserving his right to refer to the letter, should the action proceed to judgment, on the question of costs. Such offers were often referred to as *Calderbank* offers, since their use was first sanctioned in *Calderbank v Calderbank*.[263] The rule has been codified, first in the Rules of Supreme Court, now in CPR Pt 36, whereby *Calderbank* offers are known as 'Part 36 offers'. The offer, if refused, will not be communicated to the court until the question of costs falls to be decided. If, at that stage, the claimant has failed to obtain a judgment which is more advantageous than the offer, then the consequence, in relation to costs, is the same as the consequence of a claimant in a money claim failing to better a Part 36 payment.[264]

It is also open to either party to make open offers to take the dispute to alternative dispute resolution or to make such an offer 'without prejudice save as to costs'.[265]

## 2 MATRIMONIAL RECONCILIATION CASES

A privilege, similar to that which attaches to 'without prejudice' communications, has been developed to cover communications made in the course of matrimonial conciliation, matrimonial proceedings being in contemplation. In *D v NSPCC*[266] Lord Simon said:

With increasingly facile divorce and a vast rise in the number of broken marriages, with their concomitant penury and demoralization, it came to be realized, in the words of Buckmill LJ in *Mole v Mole*:[267] 'in matrimonial disputes the state is also an interested party: it is more interested in reconciliation than in divorce'. This was the public interest which led to the application by analogy of the privilege of 'without prejudice' communications to cover communications made in the course of matrimonial conciliation (see *McTaggart v McTaggart*;[268] *Mole v Mole*;[269] *Theodoropoulas v Theodoropoulas*)[270] so indubitably an

---

[261] Per Cox J in *BNP Paribas v Mezzotero* [2004] IRLR 508, EAT.     [262] Rule 36.20.
[263] [1976] Fam 93, CA. See also *Computer Machinery Co Ltd v Drescher* [1983] 1 WLR 1379; and *Cutts v Head* [1984] Ch 290, CA.
[264] Rule 36.20.     [265] *Reed Executive plc v Reed Business Information Ltd* [2004] 4 All ER 942, CA
[266] [1978] AC 171 at 236–7.     [267] [1951] P 21, CA.     [268] [1949] P 94, CA.
[269] [1951] P 21, CA.     [270] [1964] P 311, CA.

extension of the law that the textbooks treat it as a separate category of relevant evidence which may be withheld from the court. It cannot be classed, like traditional 'without prejudice' communications, as a 'privilege in aid of litigation . . .'

In *Mole v Mole* it was established that the privilege applies to communications by a spouse not only with an official conciliator such as a probation officer but also to 'other persons such as clergy, doctors or marriage guidance counsellors to whom the parties or one of them go with a view to reconciliation, there being a tacit understanding that the conversations are without prejudice'.[271] In *Theodoropoulas v Theodoropoulas* Sir Jocelyn Simon P, having held that the same rule applied where a private individual is enlisted specifically as a conciliator, said:[272]

Privilege [also] attaches to communications between the spouses themselves when made with a view to reconciliation. It also extends to excluding the evidence of an independent witness who was fortuitously present when those communications were made and who overheard or read them. I therefore ruled that all the evidence tendered, whether by way of cross-examination of the wife, or in chief from the husband or by calling [a bystander] was inadmissible.[273]

The privilege is that of the spouses and can only be waived by them jointly. The intermediary cannot object to such waiver.

In proceedings under the Children Act 1989, evidence cannot be given of statements made by one or other of the parties in the course of meetings held, or communications made, for the purpose of conciliation. It is important to preserve a cloak over all attempts at settlements of disputes over children. However an exception exists in the very unusual case where the statement clearly indicates that the maker has in the past or is likely in the future to cause serious harm to the well-being of a child. In these exceptional cases, it is for the trial judge to decide, in the exercise of his discretion, whether or not to admit the evidence, and he should do so only if the public interest in protecting the interests of the child outweighs the public interest in preserving the confidentiality of attempted conciliation.[274]

---

271 [1951] P 21 at 24 per Denning LJ.       272 [1964] P 311 at 314.

273 See Law Reform Committee, 16th Report 'Privilege in Civil Proceedings' (1967) (Cmnd 3472) para 36: 'As respects the requirement that matrimonial proceedings must be in contemplation in order that the privilege may attach, it is, we think, a reasonable inference from the fact that a third party has been called in by one or other of the spouses to act as mediator that such proceedings are sufficiently in contemplation to give rise to the privilege, and the courts today readily draw such inference. Where the negotiations take place directly between the spouses it may be more difficult for the court to decide whether such inference should be drawn; we do not, however, see any distinction of principle between the two situations.'

274 *Re D (minors)* [1993] 2 All ER 693, CA.

# 21

# JUDGMENTS AS EVIDENCE OF THE FACTS UPON WHICH THEY WERE BASED[1]

It will be useful to begin this chapter by reference to two doctrines, the detailed exposition of which is outside the ambit of this work, namely the doctrines of estoppel by record and estoppel *per rem judicatam*. Under the doctrine of estoppel by record, every judgment is conclusive as against all persons as to the legal state of affairs it effects when that state of affairs is in issue or relevant to an issue in some subsequent proceedings. Thus where a decree of divorce is granted, irretrievable breakdown being established by proof of the respondent's adultery, the decree is conclusive as to the termination of the marriage but not as to the respondent's adultery. Where a judgment is entered against a man for damage caused by his negligence, it is conclusive as to the amount of damages awarded against him but not as to his negligence. Likewise, if a man is convicted or acquitted of theft, the record of the court is conclusive as to the fact that he was convicted or acquitted but not as to the fact that he did or did not commit the theft. Under the doctrine of estoppel *per rem judicatam*, sometimes known as estoppel by record *inter partes*, a judgment is conclusive as to the facts on which it was based but only as against the parties to the legal proceedings in which that judgment was given or their privies. Thus parties and privies but not strangers to the earlier proceedings will be estopped in subsequent proceedings from giving evidence to contradict the facts on which the earlier judgment was based.

The present chapter is concerned with the circumstances in which a judgment is admissible in subsequent proceedings as evidence of the facts on which it was based even though the parties to the subsequent proceedings may be different from those to the earlier proceedings. The problem may be identified by adapting two of the examples already given. If Mr A is granted a decree of divorce from Mrs A, irretrievable breakdown being established by reason of the fact that Mrs A committed adultery with Mr B, can Mrs B, on her petition for divorce, rely on the decree as evidence of the fact that Mr B committed adultery with Mrs A?[2] If D1 is convicted of the theft of

---

[1] The word 'judgment' is used here to denote both judgments in civil proceedings and verdicts in criminal proceedings.

[2] See *Sutton v Sutton* [1970] 1 WLR 183, PD.

certain goods, can the Crown, in a prosecution of D2 for handling those goods, rely upon D1's conviction as evidence that the goods were stolen? Until recently the common law answers to questions of this kind were largely, if not entirely, governed by the decision in *Hollington v Hewthorn & Co Ltd*.[3] That case tipped the balance in favour of the view supported by the bulk of the case law preceding it, that previous judgments are not admissible as evidence of the facts on which they were based.[4]

The action in *Hollington v Hewthorn & Co Ltd* arose out of a collision between two cars. The plaintiff, the owner of one of the cars, brought an action in negligence against the driver of the other car, who had been convicted of careless driving (at the time and place of the accident), and his employer. The Court of Appeal held that the plaintiff was not entitled to admit the conviction of the defendant driver as evidence of his negligence. The decision was based largely on the view that the civil court would know nothing of the evidence before the criminal court (and the arguments that were addressed to it) and that the opinion of the criminal court was irrelevant. The principle of *Hollington v Hewthorn & Co Ltd* was then applied to cases where the subsequent proceedings were criminal. In *R v Spinks*[5] F had stabbed someone with a knife and had been convicted of wounding with intent to do grievous bodily harm. At the trial of Spinks for assisting F by concealing the knife with intent to impede the apprehension or prosecution of 'a person who had committed an arrestable offence', namely F, the Court of Appeal held that the Crown could not rely on F's conviction as evidence that he had committed the arrestable offence of wounding. Since there was no other admissible evidence that F had committed such an offence, Spinks' conviction was quashed.

The rule in *Hollington v Hewthorn & Co Ltd* attracted much criticism. Its effect, in both civil and criminal proceedings, has been largely removed by the Civil Evidence Act 1968 and the Police and Criminal Evidence Act 1984.

# A CIVIL PROCEEDINGS

Narrowly stated, *Hollington v Hewthorn & Co Ltd* had decided that a conviction of a criminal offence is inadmissible in civil proceedings as evidence of the fact that the person convicted committed the offence in question. The Law Reform Committee, observing that the onus of proof in criminal cases is higher than in civil cases, and that the degree of carelessness required to convict of careless driving is, if anything, greater than that required to sustain a civil action for negligence, described the decision as

---

3 [1943] KB 587, CA.

4 But see *Crippen's Estate* [1911] P 108, where a conviction of murder was admitted as prima facie evidence of the commission of the crime, and *Partington v Partington and Atkinson* [1925] P 34, where a finding of adultery against a husband was admitted as prima facie evidence that he had committed the adultery.

5 [1982] 1 All ER 587. See also *R v Hassan* [1970] 1 QB 423, CA.

offensive to one's sense of justice.[6] Sections 11–13 of the Civil Evidence Act 1968, giving effect to the Committee's recommendations, overrule the decision insofar as it applies, in civil cases, not only to previous criminal convictions but also to findings of adultery and paternity in previous civil proceedings. After we have examined these statutory provisions, consideration will be given to the extent to which, if at all, the rule in *Hollington v Hewthorn & Co Ltd* continues to apply, in civil proceedings, to previous acquittals and to findings other than those of adultery and paternity in previous civil proceedings.

## 1 PREVIOUS CONVICTIONS

### (a) Section 11 of the Civil Evidence Act 1968

Section 11 of the 1968 Act not only reverses the rule in *Hollington v Hewthorn & Co Ltd* as narrowly stated, but also creates a persuasive presumption: the person convicted, once his conviction has been proved, shall be taken to have committed the offence in question unless the contrary is proved. Section 11 provides that:

(1) In any civil proceedings the fact that a person has been convicted of an offence by or before any court in the United Kingdom or by a court-martial there or elsewhere shall (subject to subsection (3) below) be admissible in evidence for the purpose of proving, where to do so is relevant to any issue in those proceedings, that he committed that offence, whether he was so convicted upon a plea of guilty or otherwise and whether or not he is a party to the civil proceedings; but no conviction other than a subsisting one shall be admissible in evidence by virtue of this section.

(2) In any civil proceedings in which by virtue of this section a person is proved to have been convicted of an offence by or before any court in the United Kingdom or by a court-martial there or elsewhere—

(a) he shall be taken to have committed that offence unless the contrary is proved; and

(b) without prejudice to the reception of any other admissible evidence for the purpose of identifying the facts on which the conviction was based, the contents of any document which is admissible as evidence of the conviction, and the contents of the information, complaint, indictment or charge-sheet on which the person in question was convicted, shall be admissible in evidence for that purpose.

Concerning section 11(1), 'civil proceedings' includes, in addition to civil proceedings in any of the ordinary courts of law, (a) civil proceedings before any other tribunal in relation to which the strict rules of evidence apply and (b) an arbitration or reference, whether under an enactment or not, but does not include civil proceedings in relation to which the strict rules of evidence do not apply.[7] Subsection (3), to which section 11(1) is subject, provides that nothing in section 11 shall prejudice the operation of,

---

[6] 15th Report (1967) (Cmnd 3391), para 3.          [7] Section 18(1).

inter alia, section 13, which, as we shall see, relates to proceedings for defamation. A 'conviction' includes one in respect of which an absolute or conditional discharge was imposed.[8] A conviction against which an appeal is pending is 'subsisting' but not one which has been quashed on appeal.[9] The Act has no application to adjudications of guilt in police disciplinary proceedings[10] or to foreign convictions.[11]

There is little dispute that section 11(2)(a) has the effect of reversing the legal burden of proof in respect of the conviction. Thus if A sues B for conduct on the part of B in respect of which B stands convicted, the legal burden in relation to the commission of the offence is removed from A, who would otherwise have to prove it, to B, who must disprove it to avoid the presumption of his having committed the offence prevailing. There is a divergence of judicial opinion, however, as to what weight should be attached to the conviction in deciding whether the onus resting on B has been discharged. In *Taylor v Taylor*[12] a divorce suit in which the petitioner, in support of her allegation that the husband had committed adultery, tendered evidence of his conviction of incest, Davies LJ thought it probable that the onus of proof of upsetting the conviction was on a balance of probabilities. His Lordship continued, 'but, having said that, it nevertheless is obvious that, when a man has been convicted . . . the verdict of the jury is a matter which is entitled to very great weight . . .'[13] In *Stupple v Royal Insurance Co Ltd*[14] Stupple had been convicted of robbery from a bank which had been indemnified by the defendant insurance company. Stupple claimed from the defendants certain money which had been found by the police in his possession and which had been paid over to the defendants under the Police (Property) Act 1897. Judgment was given for the defendants. The plaintiff's appeal to the Court of Appeal was dismissed. Buckley LJ said:[15]

In my judgment, proof of conviction under this section gives rise to the statutory presumption laid down in section 11(2)(a), which, like any other presumption, will give way to evidence establishing the contrary on the balance of probability, without itself affording any evidential weight to be taken into account in determining whether that onus has been discharged.

Lord Denning MR, however, took a different view, being of the opinion that although the conviction is not conclusive, it does not merely shift the burden of proof but is a

---

    8  Section 11(5), as amended by the Criminal Justice Act 1991.
    9  See *Re Raphael, Raphael v D'Antin* [1973] 1 WLR 998: rather than finally dispose of civil proceedings in reliance on a conviction subsequently liable to be quashed, the civil proceedings may be adjourned pending the appeal. See also *R v Foster* [1984] 2 All ER 679, CA: the effect of a free pardon is to remove all pains, penalties and punishments ensuing from the conviction but not to eliminate the conviction itself.
    10  *Thorpe v Chief Constable of Greater Manchester Police* [1989] 2 All ER 827, CA.
    11  See *Union Carbide Corpn v Naturin Ltd* [1987] FSR 538, CA. Although *Hollington v Hewthorn & Co Ltd* continues to apply to foreign convictions, the court will not strike out references to them in an affidavit in support of a freezing injunction where they are part of the narrative explanation of the case against the defendant and enable the claimant to comply with his duty to make full and frank disclosure to the court: *Arab Monetary Fund v Hashim (No 2)* [1990] 1 All ER 673, Ch D.
    12  [1970] 1 WLR 1148, CA.        13  [1970] 1 WLR 1148 at 1152.        14  [1971] 1 QB 50.
    15  [1971] 1 QB 50 at 76.

weighty piece of evidence of itself.[16] In *Hunter v Chief Constable of West Midlands*[17] Lord Denning MR went further. In answer to the question how, for the purposes of section 11(2)(a), a convicted man is to prove the contrary, his Lordship expressed the view, obiter:

Only, I suggest, by proving that the conviction was obtained by fraud or collusion, or by adducing fresh evidence. If the fresh evidence is inconclusive, he does not prove his innocence. It must be decisive, it must be conclusive, before he can be declared innocent.

When the case came before the House of Lords, however, Lord Diplock, disapproving this dictum, said:[18]

The burden of proof of 'the contrary' that lies on a defendant under section 11 is the ordinary burden in a civil action, ie proof on a balance of probabilities, although in the face of a conviction after a full hearing that is likely to be an uphill task.

Insofar as it suggests that the party seeking to prove 'the contrary' bears a burden heavier than proof on a balance of probabilities, the approach adopted by Lord Denning MR and Davies LJ, it is submitted, should not be followed. It seems equally untenable that a conviction should *invariably* be regarded as a weighty item of evidence in itself. It is submitted that the weight to be attached to the conviction will depend on the particular circumstances of the case, including, for example, whether the decision was unanimous or by a majority.[19] Clearly, regard may also be had to a transcript of the evidence given in the criminal proceedings, a copy of the judge's summing up[20] and any fresh evidence that has subsequently become available to the parties.

Section 11(2)(b) provides for the admissibility of specific types of document for the purpose of identifying the facts on which the conviction was based. Provision is also made for the admissibility of duly certified copies of such documents, which shall be taken to be true copies unless the contrary is shown.[21] A transcript of a judge's summing-up is not admissible under section 11(2)(b) itself, but is admissible, for the purposes referred to in section 11(2)(b), under the Civil Evidence Act 1995.[22]

It would appear that a conviction admitted under section 11 is capable of amounting to corroboration where this is required. In *Mash v Darley*[23] the evidence of the applicant in affiliation proceedings was treated as having been corroborated by

---

[16] [1971] 1 QB 50 at 72.

[17] [1981] 3 All ER 727, reported in the Court of Appeal as *McIlkenny v Chief Constable of West Midlands Police Force* [1980] 2 All ER 227 at 237.

[18] [1981] 3 All ER 727 at 735–6.

[19] It has been suggested that assessment of the weight of the conviction would be 'an impossibly difficult task': see *Cross on Evidence* (5th edn 1979) 458. Cf Zuckerman (1971) 87 LQR 21.

[20] Such evidence is admissible pursuant to the Civil Evidence Act 1995: see Ch 11.

[21] Section 11(4). Corresponding provisions for the admission of copies of such documents under ss 12 and 13 are contained in ss 12(4) and 13(4).

[22] See *Brinks Ltd v Abu-Saleh (No 2)* [1995] 4 All ER 74, Ch D, a decision under the hearsay provisions of the Civil Evidence Act 1968.

[23] [1914] 1 KB 1, DC.

evidence of the respondent's conviction of unlawful sexual intercourse with her. Although *Mash v Darley* pre-dates *Hollington v Hewthorn & Co Ltd*, the statutory reversal of the latter may be treated as having revived the former. It remains to note that, under PD 16, para 10.1, a claimant who wishes to rely on evidence under section 11 must include in his particulars of claim a statement to that effect and give details of the type of conviction and its date, the court or court-martial which made it, and the issue in the claim to which it relates.

## (b) Section 13 of the Civil Evidence Act 1968

Section 13 of the 1968 Act applies to defamation proceedings. In such proceedings, the section, giving effect to the recommendations of the Law Reform Committee, not only reverses the rule in *Hollington v Hewthorn & Co Ltd*, as narrowly stated, but also creates a conclusive presumption: the person convicted, once his conviction has been proved, shall conclusively be taken to have committed the offence in question.[24] The effect of this is twofold: it prevents a convicted person from using the defamation action to reopen the issues determined at the criminal trial[25] and protects from civil liability a person who chooses to state that another is guilty of an offence of which he stands convicted. Accordingly, a defamation action based on the defendant's statement that the plaintiff committed an offence in respect of which he has been convicted will be struck out as an abuse of the process of the court unless the statement also contains some other legally defamatory matter.[26] Section 13 reads as follows:

(1) In an action for libel or slander in which the question whether the plaintiff did or did not commit a criminal offence is relevant to an issue arising in the action, proof that, at the time when the issue falls to be determined, he stands convicted of that offence shall be conclusive evidence that he committed that offence; and his conviction thereof shall be admissible in evidence accordingly.

(2) In any such action as aforesaid in which by virtue of this section the plaintiff is proved to have been convicted of an offence, the contents of any document which is admissible as evidence of the conviction, and the contents of the information, complaint, indictment or charge-sheet on which he was convicted, shall, without prejudice to the reception of any other admissible evidence for the purpose of identifying the facts on which the conviction was based, be admissible in evidence for the purpose of identifying those facts.

(2A) In the case of an action for libel or slander in which there is more than one plaintiff—

    (a) the references in subsection (1) and (2) above to the plaintiff shall be construed as references to any of the plaintiffs, and

    (b) proof that any of the plaintiffs stands convicted of an offence shall be conclusive

---

[24] 15th Report (1967) (Cmnd 3391), para 26 et seq. Parliament did not accept, however, the Committee's accompanying recommendation that in defamation proceedings evidence of an acquittal should be conclusive evidence of innocence. See *Loughans v Odhams Press* [1963] 1 QB 299, CA, below.

[25] See, eg, *Hinds v Sparks* [1964] Crim LR 717 and *Goody v Odhams Press Ltd* [1967] 1 QB 333.

[26] *Levene v Roxhan* [1970] 1 WLR 1322, CA.

evidence that he committed that offence so far as that fact is relevant to any issue arising in relation to his cause of action or that of any other plaintiff.

(3) For the purposes of this section a person shall be taken to stand convicted of an offence if but only if there subsists against him a conviction of that offence by or before a court in the United Kingdom or by a court-martial there or elsewhere.[27]

## 2 PREVIOUS FINDINGS OF ADULTERY AND PATERNITY

Section 12 of the 1968 Act not only reverses the rule in *Hollington v Hewthorn & Co Ltd* insofar as it applied to previous findings of adultery and paternity, but also creates a persuasive presumption in respect of such findings. Section 12, as amended,[28] provides that:

(1) In any civil proceedings—
  (a) the fact that a person has been found guilty of adultery in any matrimonial proceedings; and
  (b) the fact that a person has been found to be the father of a child in relevant proceedings[29] before any court in England and Wales or Northern Ireland or has been adjudged to be the father of a child in affiliation proceedings before any court in the United Kingdom;
  shall (subject to (3) below) be admissible in evidence for the purpose of proving, where to do so is relevant to any issue in those civil proceedings, that he committed the adultery to which the finding relates or, as the case may be, is (or was) the father of that child, whether or not he offered any defence to the allegation of adultery or paternity and whether or not he is a party to the civil proceedings; but no finding or adjudication other than a subsisting one shall be admissible in evidence by virtue of this section.

(2) In any civil proceedings in which by virtue of this section a person is proved to have been found guilty of adultery as mentioned in subsection (1)(a) above or to have been found or adjudged to be the father of a child as mentioned in subsection (1)(b) above—
  (a) he shall be taken to have committed the adultery to which the finding relates or, as the case may be, to be (or have been) the father of that child, unless the contrary is proved; and
  (b) without prejudice to the reception of any other admissible evidence for the purpose of identifying the facts on which the finding or adjudication was based, the contents of any document which was before the court, or which contains any pronouncement of the court, in the other proceedings in question shall be admissible in evidence for that purpose.

(3) Nothing in this section shall prejudice the operation of any enactment whereby a

---

[27] See above, under 1(a) **Section 11 of the Civil Evidence Act 1968.**

[28] By s 29 of the Family Law Reform Act 1987.

[29] 'Relevant proceedings' means proceedings on complaints and applications made pursuant to a wide variety of statutory provisions: see s 12(5), as amended.

finding of fact in any matrimonial or affiliation proceedings is for the purposes of any other proceedings made conclusive evidence of any fact.

Modelled as it is on section 11, section 12 of the 1968 Act calls for little comment. 'Matrimonial proceedings' are defined to include, inter alia, any matrimonial cause in the High Court or a county court in England and Wales and any appeal arising out of such cause.[30] Thus a finding of adultery in a magistrates' court would not be admissible under section 12. As in the case of previous convictions under section 11, the legal burden in relation to the finding of adultery or paternity admitted under section 12 is placed upon the party seeking to disprove that finding. The standard of proof required to discharge the burden is proof on a balance of probabilities.[31] A claimant who wishes to rely on evidence under section 12 of a finding or adjudication of adultery or paternity must include in his particulars of claim a statement to that effect and give details of the finding or adjudication and its date, the court which made it, and the issue in the claim to which it relates.[32]

## 3 PREVIOUS ACQUITTALS

In *Packer v Clayton,*[33] a case which pre-dates *Hollington v Hewthorn & Co Ltd*, Avory J was of the opinion that in affiliation proceedings, the respondent's acquittal of a sexual offence against the applicant would be admissible to show that the jury were not convinced by the latter's evidence. However, if the principle of *Hollington v Hewthorn & Co Ltd* applies to previous acquittals, they are inadmissible as evidence of innocence in subsequent civil proceedings. This conclusion may be justified on the grounds that an allegation which was not proved beyond reasonable doubt may be susceptible of proof on a balance of probabilities, as it was in *Loughans v Odhams Press.*[34] In a libel suit arising out of the defendants' publication of a statement suggesting that the plaintiff had committed a murder in respect of which he had been acquitted, the defendants succeeded in proving, on a balance of probabilities, that the plaintiff had committed the murder. As a matter of policy, however, it may be argued that a person acquitted of an offence should be granted some measure of immunity from assertions to the contrary. Parliament, it is true, has rejected the proposal that in defamation proceedings evidence of an acquittal should be conclusive evidence of innocence.[35] Whether, at common law, evidence of an acquittal is nonetheless *some*, albeit only prima facie, evidence of innocence, not only in defamation actions but also in civil proceedings generally, is, on the present state of the authorities, unclear.

---

[30] Section 12(5).      [31] *Sutton v Sutton* [1970] 1 WLR 183, PD.      [32] PD 16, para 10.1.
[33] (1932) 97 JP 14, DC.      [34] [1963] 1 QB 299, CA.
[35] See above, under 1(b) **Section 13 of the Civil Evidence Act 1968.**

## 4 OTHER PREVIOUS FINDINGS

Subject to exceptions, the principle of *Hollington v Hewthorn & Co Ltd* would appear to apply in respect of judicial findings in previous *civil* proceedings. In *Secretary of State for Trade and Industry v Bairstow*,[36] the Secretary of State brought proceedings under the Company Directors Disqualification Act 1986, seeking a disqualification order against B. Prior to the proceedings, B had been dismissed by the company of which he had been the managing director, his claim for wrongful dismissal against the company had been dismissed, and his appeal against that decision had failed. The Court of Appeal, in the instant case, held that the principle of *Hollington v Hewthorn & Co Ltd* was not confined to cases in which the earlier decision was that of a court exercising a criminal jurisdiction and accordingly the judge's factual findings in the wrongful dismissal proceedings were inadmissible, in the proceedings under the 1986 Act, as evidence of the facts on which they were based.

The exceptions to which reference has been made are findings of adultery and paternity, which, as we have seen, are now governed by section 12 of the Civil Evidence Act 1968. In the light of the somewhat novel observations of Lord Denning MR in *Hunter v Chief Constable of West Midlands*,[37] a decision on estoppel *per rem judicatam*, there is arguably a third exception. In that case, Lord Denning MR was of the opinion that a party to civil proceedings can only challenge a previous decision *against* himself by showing that it was obtained by fraud or collusion or by adducing fresh evidence which he could not have obtained by reasonable diligence before, to show conclusively that the previous decision was wrong. On this view, if a driver runs down two pedestrians, a finding of negligence against the driver in an action brought by one of the pedestrians could only be challenged in a subsequent action brought against him by the other in the limited way indicated. Applying the principle in *Hollington v Hewthorn & Co Ltd* to the same example, however, the earlier finding of negligence would be inadmissible as evidence of the driver's negligence in the subsequent proceedings.[38]

The principle of *Hollington v Hewthorn & Co Ltd* have been held to apply not only to judicial findings in previous civil proceedings, but also to the previous findings set out in the reports of inspectors under the Companies Act 1967 (see now Part XIV of the Companies Act 1985),[39] to an arbitration award[40] and to the findings of Bingham LJ in an extra-statutory report into the collapse of the Bank of Credit and Commerce

---

[36] [2003] 3 WLR 841, CA.

[37] [1981] 3 All ER 727, HL, reported in the Court of Appeal as *McIlkenny v Chief Constable of West Midlands Police Force* [1980] 2 All ER 227 at 237–8. Although the views of Lord Denning MR in this respect were to some extent doubted when the case came before the House of Lords, Lord Diplock, giving the judgment of the House, found it unnecessary expressly to consider the topic of issue estoppel: (see at 732–3).

[38] In practice, problems of this kind are often avoided by virtue of the procedural provisions relating to joinder of parties and causes of action: see generally CPR Pts 19 and 20.

[39] *Savings and Investment Bank Ltd v Gasco Investments (Netherlands BV)* [1984] 1 WLR 271, Ch D.

[40] *Land Securities plc v Westminster City Council* [1993] 1 WLR 286.

International.[41] However, in the earlier case of *Hill v Clifford*,[42] the Court of Appeal held that a finding by the General Medical Council that a dentist had been guilty of professional misconduct was admissible as prima facie evidence of such misconduct in subsequent civil proceedings concerning the dissolution of his partnership. The explanation may be that the Council was under a statutory duty of inquiry.[43] Inquisitions, assessments, surveys, reports, etc are generally admissible as evidence of the truth of their contents, by way of common-law exception to the hearsay rule, as statements contained in public documents.[44]

# B  CRIMINAL PROCEEDINGS

## 1  PREVIOUS CONVICTIONS

The application of the principle of *Hollington v Hewthorn & Co Ltd* in criminal cases meant that at the trial of a person charged with handling stolen goods, the previous conviction of the thief was inadmissible as evidence that the goods allegedly received were stolen.[45] Likewise, a woman's convictions for prostitution were inadmissible as evidence of her prostitution at the trial of a man charged with living off her immoral earnings.[46] A final example is *R v Spinks*,[47] where, as we have seen, the conviction of a principal was held to be inadmissible as evidence of his commission of the crime at the trial of the alleged accessory. The Criminal Law Revision Committee thought it was quite wrong, as well as being inconvenient, that in cases of this kind the prosecution should be required to prove again the guilt of the person concerned,[48] and recommended, in respect of convictions of persons other than the accused, a provision in criminal proceedings corresponding to section 11 of the Civil Evidence Act 1968. Section 74 of the Police and Criminal Evidence Act 1984 not only gives effect to this recommendation but also makes similar provision in relation to the previous convictions of *the accused*: thus without affecting the law governing the admissibility of the accused's past misconduct, it provides that where evidence of the accused's commission of an offence *is* admissible, if the accused is proved to have been convicted of that offence, he shall be taken to have committed it unless the contrary is proved. Before considering the precise terms of section 74, it may first be noted that it is without prejudice to (i) the admissibility in evidence of any conviction which would

---

41  *Three Rivers District Council v Bank of England (No 3)* [2003] 2 AC 1, HL.

42  [1907] 2 Ch 236. See also *Faulder v Silk* (1811) 3 Camp 126 and *Harvey v R* [1901] AC 601 (inquisitions in lunacy as prima facie evidence of a person's unsoundness of mind).

43  See per Sir Gorell Barnes P [1907] 2 Ch 236 at 253.

44  See, eg, *Irish Society v Bishop of Derry* (1846) 12 Cl&Fin 641 (a bishop's return to a writ from the Exchequer stating vacancies and advowsons in his diocese) and contrast *Bird v Keep* [1918] 2 KB 692 (a statement contained in a death certificate as to the cause of death). The cases are considered in Ch 12.

45  *R v Turner* (1832) 1 Mood CC 347 at 349.      46  *R v Hassan* [1970] 1 QB 423, CA.

47  [1982] 1 All ER 587, CA.      48  11th Report (Cmnd 4991), paras 217 et seq.

be admissible apart from the section[49] and (ii) the operation of any statutory provision whereby a conviction or finding of fact in criminal proceedings is made conclusive evidence of any fact for the purposes of any other criminal proceedings.[50]

Section 74 of the 1984 Act, as amended by the Criminal Justice Act 2003, provides that:

(1) In any proceedings the fact that a person other than the accused has been convicted of an offence by or before any court in the United Kingdom or by a Service court outside the United Kingdom shall be admissible in evidence for the purpose of proving, that that person committed that offence, where evidence of his having done so is admissible, whether or not any other evidence of his having committed that offence is given.

(2) In any proceedings in which by virtue of this section a person other than the accused is proved to have been convicted of an offence by or before any court in the United Kingdom or by a Service court outside the United Kingdom, he shall be taken to have committed that offence unless the contrary is proved.

(3) In any proceedings where evidence is admissible of the fact that the accused has committed an offence, if the accused is proved to have been convicted of the offence—
(a) by or before any court in the United Kingdom; or
(b) by a Service court outside the United Kingdom,
he shall be taken to have committed that offence unless the contrary is proved.

Section 75(1) of the 1984 Act provides that:

Where evidence that a person has been convicted of an offence is admissible by virtue of s 74 above, then without prejudice to the reception of any other admissible evidence for the purpose of identifying the facts on which the conviction was based—
(a) the contents of any document which is admissible as evidence of the conviction; and
(b) the contents of the information, complaint, indictment or charge-sheet on which the person in question was convicted,
shall be admissible in evidence for that purpose.[51]

Concerning the terminology of section 74, 'any proceedings' means any criminal proceedings.[52] A person is 'convicted' for the purposes of the section only if the conviction, which includes a conviction in respect of which a probation order or absolute or conditional discharge was imposed,[53] is 'subsisting'.[54] A subsisting conviction means either a finding of guilt that has not been quashed on appeal or a formal plea of guilt

---

[49] Section 74(4)(a): eg proof of a witness's conviction pursuant to s 6 of the Criminal Procedure Act 1865. See Ch 7.

[50] Section 74(4)(b). The saving appears to have been included not with any particular statute in mind but because of local and private enactments and the possibility of future public enactments: see Annex 2 (Cmnd 4991) 233.

[51] Provision is also made for the admission of duly certified copies of such documents: s 75(2).
[52] Section 82(1).        [53] Section 75(3).        [54] Section 75(4).

that has not been withdrawn; whether the accused has been sentenced or not is irrelevant.[55] A 'Service court' means a court-martial or a Standing Civilian Court.[56]

## (a) Section 74(1) and (2): Convictions of persons other than the accused[57]

Section 74(1) has an obvious application where proof of the commission of an offence by a person other than the accused is admissible to establish an essential ingredient of the offence with which the accused is charged. Thus where A is seen transferring goods to B and they are jointly charged with handling the goods, A's guilty plea is admissible at B's trial to prove that the goods were stolen.[58]

In *R v Robertson; R v Golder*,[59] a decision under the original version of section 74(1),[60] it was held that evidence of the commission of the offence may be relevant not only to an issue which is an essential ingredient of the offence charged, but also to less fundamental evidential issues arising in the proceedings. It was also held that the subsection is not confined to the proof of convictions of offences in which the accused on trial played no part; and that where the evidence is admitted, the judge should be careful to explain to the jury its effect and limitations.[61] In the case of Robertson, who was charged with conspiracy with two others to commit burglary, evidence that the others had been convicted of a number of burglaries was admissible because it could be inferred from their commission of these offences that there was a conspiracy between them and that was the very conspiracy to which the prosecution sought to prove that Robertson was a party. Golder was convicted of a robbery committed at garage X. Two of his co-accused pleaded guilty to that robbery and also to another committed at garage Y. The evidence against Golder consisted primarily of a confession statement, which he alleged to have been fabricated by the police, in which he referred to both robberies. It was held that evidence of the guilty pleas of the co-accused was admissible: proof of their commission of the offence at garage X was relevant because it showed that there had in fact been a robbery at that garage; and proof of the commission of both offences was relevant because it showed that the contents of the alleged confession were in accordance with the facts as they were known and therefore more likely to be true. *R v Robertson; R v Golder* was applied in *R v Castle*,[62] where C and F were charged with robbery and F pleaded guilty. At an identification parade, the victim said 'yes' in respect of C, 'possibly' in respect of F. Evidence of the guilty plea was admissible because relevant to the issue of the reliability

---

[55] *R v Robertson; R v Golder* [1987] 3 All ER 231, CA. See also *R v Foster* [1984] 2 All ER 679, CA, above.

[56] Section 82(1).

[57] See generally Roderick Munday 'Proof of Guilt by Association under Section 74' [1990] Crim LR 236.

[58] *R v Pigram* [1995] Crim LR 808, CA.     [59] [1987] 3 All ER 231, CA.

[60] By virtue of s 331 and para 85, sch 36 of the Criminal Justice Act 2003, the words 'that that person committed that offence, where evidence of his having done so is admissible' were substituted for the words 'where to do so is relevant to any issue in those proceedings, that that person committed that offence'.

[61] See also per Staughton LJ in *R v Kempster* (1989) 90 Cr App R 14 at 22, CA and *R v Boyson* [1991] Crim LR 274, CA.

[62] [1989] Crim LR 567, CA.

of the identification of C: by confirming the correctness of the 'possible' identification of F, it also tended to confirm the correctness of the positive identification of C.[63]

In *R v Robertson; R v Golder* it was stressed that section 74 should be used sparingly and not where, although the evidence is technically admissible, its effect is likely to be slight, particularly if there is any danger of contravening section 78 of the 1984 Act.[64] Moreover, a judge, in deciding an application under section 78, should make a ruling, one way or the other, and if he decides to admit the evidence, should give a cogent reason for his decision.[65] In *R v Kempster*[66] it was initially unclear whether the prosecution were relying on the evidence to prove the guilt of the accused or merely to prevent mystification of the jury. Although in the event the jury were encouraged to use the evidence to prove guilt, there was no clear or informed decision by the judge as to any adverse effect it might have had on the fairness of the proceedings. Quashing the convictions, the Court of Appeal highlighted the importance of ascertaining the purpose for which the evidence is adduced before deciding whether it should be excluded under section 78, and held that if the evidence is admitted, the judge should ensure that counsel does not seek to use it for any other purpose. Similarly, in *R v Boyson*[67] the Court of Appeal, *per curiam*, deprecated what it saw as the growing practice of allowing irrelevant, inadmissible, prejudicial or unfair evidence to be admitted simply on the grounds that it is convenient for the jury to have 'the whole picture'.

Whether a conviction admissible under section 74 should be excluded under section 78 depends on the particular facts. In *R v Mattison*[68] M was charged in one count with gross indecency with D, and D, in another count, was charged with gross indecency with M. D pleaded guilty, M not guilty, his defence being a complete denial. It was held that evidence of the guilty plea was relevant to M's trial but the judge, given M's defence, should have exercised his discretion under section 78 to exclude it.[69] That decision falls to be compared with *R v Turner*.[70] T and L were driving

---

[63] *R v Castle* was followed in *R v Gummerson and Steadman* [1999] Crim LR 680, CA, a case of *voice* identification. See also the somewhat questionable decision in *R v Buckingham* (1994) 99 Cr App R 303, CA: evidence of W's conviction of conspiracy to pervert the course of justice by obtaining, as the accused in a previous trial, false evidence of defence witnesses, was admissible at the trial of B (and others), who were among the defence witnesses at W's previous trial, for doing acts intended to pervert the course of justice on the grounds that, although not probative that B (and others) had given false evidence, it established the conspiracy.

[64] See also *R v Skinner* [1995] Crim LR 805, CA.       [65] *R v Hillier* (1992) 97 Cr App R 349, CA.
[66] (1989) 90 Cr App R 14, CA.

[67] [1991] Crim LR 274, CA. See also *R v Hall* [1993] Crim LR 527, CA and *R v Mahmood and Manzur* [1997] 1 Cr App R 414, CA.

[68] [1990] Crim LR 117, CA.

[69] Where a co-accused pleads guilty but the prosecution do not seek to rely on s 74, it may be sufficient, depending on the circumstances, for the jury to be told that the guilty plea is not probative against the accused: see *R v Turpin* [1990] Crim LR 514, CA. In a case involving joint enterprise, it is insufficient for the judge to direct the jury that they must be sure that each of the accused was a party to the enterprise—they should be told that it is essential that they put the guilty plea of the co-accused out of their minds: *R v Betterley* [1994] Crim LR 764, CA. However, a warning will not suffice if the jury cannot properly consider the case of the accused in isolation from that of the co-accused, in which case the judge should discharge the jury and order a new trial: *R v Fedrick* [1990] Crim LR 403, CA. See also *R v Marlow* [1997] Crim LR 457, CA.

[70] [1991] Crim LR 57, CA.

separate cars. L overtook T, hit an oncoming vehicle and killed the passenger in his own car. The prosecution case was that the drivers were racing. L pleaded guilty to causing death by reckless driving. T, tried on the same charge, denied racing. It was held that the guilty plea was relevant, because the prosecution case was that L had been the principal, T the aider and abettor, but that it did not establish that L and T were racing, the essential issue at T's trial. The judge having made it clear that the evidence did not amount to an admission by L that he was racing, there was nothing unfair in admitting it.[71]

The question of exclusion under section 78 is of particular importance in conspiracy and related cases. In *R v O'Connor*[72] B and C were jointly charged in one count with conspiracy to obtain property by deception. B pleaded guilty, C not guilty. Evidence of the guilty plea was admitted, together with the details in the count against him, as permitted by section 75. It was held that the evidence should have been excluded under section 78 because B's admission that he had conspired with C might have led the jury to infer that C, in turn, must have conspired with B. The same reasoning was applied in *R v Curry*.[73] C was convicted of conspiracy to obtain property by deception. She was charged with two others, W and H. H pleaded guilty. The prosecution case was that W drove the accused to the shops where C, with H's knowledge, used H's credit card to obtain the goods, H's intention being to report the card as stolen so as to avoid liability for payment. Evidence of the guilty plea was admitted to establish the existence of an unlawful agreement to deceive. The conviction was quashed on the basis that the evidence clearly implied as a matter of fact, albeit not law, that C had been a party to the conspiracy. The court said that section 74 should be used sparingly, especially in cases of conspiracy and affray, and should not be used where the evidence, expressly or by necessary inference, imports the complicity of the accused. *R v Lunnon*[74] was distinguished. That case also involved three accused jointly charged with conspiracy, but it was held that evidence of the guilty plea of one of them had been properly admitted to prove the existence of the conspiracy because the judge had separated for the jury two questions, whether there was a conspiracy and who was a party to it, and had made it clear that despite the evidence, they could acquit the accused.[75]

Section 78 may also be invoked successfully on the basis that the prosecution, by relying on section 74, do not have to call the person convicted, thereby depriving the defence of the opportunity to challenge or test him in cross-examination.[76] The argument was rejected in *R v Robertson; R v Golder*[77] on the basis that R's name did not appear on any of the burglary counts to which the co-accused had pleaded guilty,

---

[71] See also *R v Bennett* [1988] Crim LR 686, CA and *R v Stewart* [1999] Crim LR 746, CA.

[72] (1986) 85 Cr App R 298, CA.    [73] [1988] Crim LR 527, CA.    [74] [1988] Crim LR 456, CA.

[75] Cf *R v Chapman* [1991] Crim LR 44, CA where C and seven others were charged with conspiracy to obtain by deception. It was held that a guilty plea by one of the others to two specific counts of obtaining by deception, incidents in which he was involved with C, were relevant and admissible and did not inevitably import the complicity of C. See also *R v Hunt* [1994] Crim LR 747, CA.

[76] This was part of the ratio in *R v O'Connor* (1986) 85 Cr App R 298, CA, above.    [77] Above.

and that even if the co-accused had given evidence in accordance with their pleas, R's counsel would have been unlikely to cross-examine them or, if he had, would have seriously prejudiced R. However, as Staughton LJ observed in *R v Kempster*,[78] although such cross-examination may be unlikely in some cases, or else turn out to be a disaster, one cannot always assume that.

An application under section 78 may succeed where a co-accused has pleaded guilty but the evidence was far from conclusive against him, on the basis that to allow the conviction to be proved might deprive the remaining accused of the opportunity to challenge that evidence.[79] An application may also succeed where, a co-accused having pleaded guilty towards or at the end of the prosecution case, it would be unfair to admit evidence of the plea because, had it been entered and put in evidence earlier, cross-examination might have been conducted differently.[80]

Section 74(2) has the effect of placing the legal burden in relation to the commission of the offence (by a person other than the accused) on the party seeking to disprove it. Where that burden is borne by the accused, the standard of proof required to discharge it is the standard ordinarily required where the legal burden on a particular issue is borne by the accused, namely proof on a balance of probabilities.[81]

Although in most cases section 74(1) has been relied on by the prosecution, in appropriate circumstances it may also be used by an accused to adduce evidence of the convictions of a co-accused which are relevant to an issue in the proceedings.[82]

### (b) Section 74(3): convictions of the accused

It is clear from the wording of section 74(3) that its purpose is not to define or enlarge the circumstances in which evidence of the fact that the accused has committed an offence is admissible, but simply to assist, where such evidence is admissible, in proving that fact.[83] The conviction is admissible as evidence of the commission of the offence and the accused shall be taken to have committed the offence unless the contrary is proved. The subsection operates to place on the accused the legal burden of disproving the commission of the offence on a balance of probabilities.

Section 74(3) appears to apply in three types of situation. The first is where the accused denies that he committed some previous offence which the prosecution seeks to prove as an element of the offence with which he is charged, for example where he is charged with murder, the victim having died subsequent to his conviction for assault, or where, having convictions recorded against him, he is charged with perjury because in some previous proceeding he testified that he had never committed an offence. The second situation is where the accused's commission of an offence, other

---

[78]   (1989) 90 Cr App R 14 at 22, CA.        [79]   *R v Lee* [1996] Crim LR 825, CA.

[80]   See *R v Chapman* [1991] Crim LR 44. The evidence may also be excluded under s 78 where it adds little to an already strong case: *R v Warner* (1992) 96 Cr App R 324, CA. See also *R v Humphreys and Tully* [1993] Crim LR 288, CA.

[81]   See *R v Carr-Briant* [1943] KB 607, Ch 4.

[82]   See *R v Hendrick* [1992] Crim LR 427, CA where, on the facts, the convictions were irrelevant.

[83]   *R v Harris* [2001] Crim LR 227, CA.

than that with which he is charged, is admissible as evidence of his bad character under section 101 of the Criminal Justice Act 2003.[84] The subsection presumably also applies in a third situation in which, a conviction having been proved as part of the prosecution case pursuant to statutory provisions such as section 101 of the Criminal Justice Act 2003, section 27(3)(b) of the Theft Act 1968 or section 1(2) of the Official Secrets Act 1911, the accused denies having committed the offence in question.

It could be argued that section 74(3) also applies where, after a finding of guilt or a guilty plea, a previous conviction is proved in order to guide the court on the question of sentence, but the accused denies having committed the offence in question. However, it is submitted that in such a situation, the question whether the accused committed the offence is irrelevant: it is the *fact* of the previous conviction which is relevant to the determination of an appropriate sentence, and if the accused denies the conviction, it can be proved in the ordinary way under section 73 of the 1984 Act.[85]

## 2 PREVIOUS ACQUITTALS

The principle of *Hollington v Hewthorn & Co Ltd* does apply to prevent acquittals from being admitted as evidence of innocence in subsequent criminal proceedings. In *Hui Chi-ming v R*[86] the Privy Council held that the previous verdict, reached by a different jury, whether on the same or different evidence, is generally irrelevant, amounting to nothing more than evidence of the opinion of that jury. Thus in that case, where a principal had been acquitted of murder but convicted of manslaughter, it was held that evidence of the acquittal had been properly excluded at the subsequent trial, for murder, of a secondary party.[87] Some exceptional feature is needed before a previous acquittal will be considered relevant, as when it has a bearing on the credibility of a confession or the evidence of a prosecution witness.[88] Even if relevant and admissible, however, the acquittal is not conclusive evidence of innocence and does not mean that all relevant issues in the trial were resolved in favour of the accused.[89]

---

[84] See Ch 17.      [85] See Ch 2, under **G3 Convictions and acquittals.**

[86] [1991] 3 All ER 897, PC.

[87] Under English law, the secondary party presumably could have used s 74(1) of the 1984 Act to admit evidence of the principal's *conviction*, which would then have achieved the tactical advantage of allowing the jury to know that the principal had only been convicted of the lesser offence. See also *R v Hudson* [1994] Crim LR 920, CA (Ch 2).

[88] [1991] 3 All ER 897 at 903. See *R v Edwards* [1991] 2 All ER 266 and cf *R v Y* [1992] Crim LR 436; *R v Hay* (1983) 77 Cr App R 70 and *R v Cooke* (1986) 84 Cr App R 286 (Ch 13); *R v Doosti* (1985) 82 Cr App R 181 (Ch 13); and *Sambasivam v Malaya Federation Public Prosecutor* [1950] AC 458.

[89] *R v Colman* [2004] EWCA Crim 3252, [2004] All ER (D) 345 (Dec).

# 22

# PROOF OF FACTS WITHOUT EVIDENCE

Facts in issue and relevant facts are treated as established by the courts only in so far as they are proved by evidence. To this general rule there are three exceptions. Certain facts may be presumed in a party's favour in the absence of proof or complete proof and no evidence is required to establish facts that are either judicially noticed or formally admitted.

## A PRESUMPTIONS

### 1 DEFINITIONS AND CLASSIFICATION

Where a presumption operates, a certain conclusion may or must be drawn by the court in the absence of evidence in rebuttal. The effect of this is to assist a party bearing a burden of proof, the degree of assistance varying from presumption to presumption. In some cases the proof required to establish the fact in question may be less than it otherwise would have been. In other cases no proof may be required at all or the other party may be barred from adducing any evidence in rebuttal. Presumptions are based on considerations of common sense and public policy but not necessarily those of logic. Certain facts or combinations of fact can give rise to inferences which justify legal rules that in such circumstances a conclusion may or must be drawn. For example, if after an operation a swab is found to have been left in a patient's body, it seems reasonable enough to infer, in the absence of explanation by the surgeon, that the accident arose through his negligence.[1] If a surgeon uses proper care, such an accident does not, in the ordinary course of things, occur; negligence may be presumed. However, there is another presumption that a person is dead if he has not been heard of for over seven years. There is, of course, no logic in the choice of 2,556 days' absence for these purposes as opposed to say 2,560 days' absence.[2]

The law of presumptions is as beset with the problems of terminology and

[1] See *Mahon v Osborne* [1939] 2 KB 14, CA.
[2] See per Sachs J in *Chard v Chard* [1956] P 259 at 272.

classification as the subjects of burden and standard of proof with which it is closely interrelated. A useful starting point is a conventional classification into rebuttable presumptions of law (*praesumptiones iuris sed non de iure*), irrebuttable presumptions of law (*praesumptiones iuris et de iure*), and presumptions of fact (*praesumptiones hominis*). It is the first of these categories which forms the main concern of this chapter, the second comprising rules of substantive law expressed as presumptions and the third consisting of a number of examples of circumstantial evidence also expressed as presumptions. A further category which falls to be considered, presumptions without basic facts, comprises a number of rules relating to the incidence of the burden of proof. In the ensuing analysis of these four categories reference will be made, by way of example, to the more important of the common-law and statutory presumptions, some of which are considered in greater depth later in this chapter. Distributed throughout English law there are numerous common-law, equitable and statutory presumptions. This chapter deals with the most important of them, a comprehensive treatment being beyond its scope.[3]

## (a) Rebuttable presumptions of law

Where a rebuttable presumption of law applies, on the proof or admission of a fact, referred to as a primary or basic fact, and in the absence of further evidence, another fact, referred to as a presumed fact, must be presumed. The party relying on the presumption bears the burden of establishing the basic fact. Once he has adduced sufficient evidence on that fact, his adversary bears the legal burden of disproving the presumed fact or, as the case may be, an evidential burden to adduce some evidence to rebut the presumed fact. The standard of proof to be met by the party seeking to rebut the presumed fact is determined by the substantive law in relation to the presumption in question.[4] For example, there is a rebuttable presumption of law that a child proved or admitted to have been born or conceived during lawful wedlock (the basic facts) is legitimate (the presumed fact). A party seeking to rebut the presumed fact by evidence of, say, the husband's impotence, is, in civil proceedings, required to meet the ordinary civil standard of proof on a balance of probabilities.[5] Other examples to be considered in detail later in this chapter are the presumptions of marriage, death and, in

---

[3] The following presumptions are not considered: (i) the presumption of legal origin (ie that certain rights have been exercised without interruption for such a period of time that they are presumed to have had a legal origin); (ii) the equitable presumption of undue influence (which arises on proof that one party has placed trust and confidence in another in relation to the management of his financial affairs and entered into a transaction which calls for explanation); and (iii) the equitable presumption of advancement (ie that property purchased by a parent and vested in his child is presumed to have been intended as a gift). The statutory presumptions arising under ss 11 and 12 of the Civil Evidence Act 1968 and s 74 of the Police and Criminal Evidence Act 1984 are considered in Ch 21 and certain presumptions relating to the due execution of documents are considered in Ch 9. A useful list of statutory presumptions (which form the majority of all presumptions), classified according to the statutory terminology employed, is set out in Carter *Cases & Statutes on Evidence* (2nd edn London 1990) 79.

[4] Unfortunately, as we shall see, the authorities are often in conflict as to the amount of evidence required to rebut certain presumptions.

[5] Section 26 of the Family Law Reform Act 1969, below.

testamentary cases, sanity, and the maxims *omnia praesumuntur rite esse acta* and *res ipsa loquitur*, the last-mentioned arguably being a presumption of fact.

Where a rebuttable presumption of law places a legal burden on the party against whom it operates, as does, for example, the presumption of legitimacy, it may be referred to as a 'persuasive' or 'compelling' presumption.[6] In such a case, the legal burden of disproving the presumed fact is on the party against whom the presumption operates. Where a rebuttable presumption of law operates to place an evidential burden on that party, as does, for example, the presumption of death, it may be referred to as an 'evidential' presumption.[7] In such a case, the legal burden of proving the presumed fact is borne by the party in whose favour the presumption operates. If he adduces prima facie evidence of the basic facts, an evidential burden is placed on his adversary. The adversary may discharge this burden in the usual way and, if he does so, the effect will be as if the presumption had never come into play at all; the party bearing the legal burden of proof must satisfy the tribunal of fact to the required standard of proof in the usual way. The terminology of 'persuasive' and 'evidential' presumptions is apposite only in civil proceedings. Subject to express or implied statutory exceptions and cases in which the accused raises the defence of insanity, in criminal proceedings the prosecution bears the legal burden of proving all facts essential to their case. It follows from this general rule that where a common-law presumption operates in favour of the accused, the prosecution will always bear a *legal* burden (requiring them to disprove the presumed fact beyond reasonable doubt).[8] Likewise, although there are a number of statutory presumptions which operate to place on the accused a legal burden of proof (which may be discharged by the adduction of such evidence as might satisfy the jury on a balance of probabilities),[9] where a common-law presumption operates in favour of the prosecution, the accused will never bear more than an *evidential* burden (which may be discharged by the adduction of such evidence as might leave a jury in reasonable doubt).

## (b) Irrebuttable presumptions of law

Where an irrebuttable presumption of law, sometimes referred to as a conclusive presumption, applies, on the proof or admission of a basic fact, another fact must be presumed and the party against whom the presumption operates is barred from adducing any evidence in rebuttal. Such presumptions amount to no more than rules of substantive law expressed, somewhat clumsily, in the language pertaining to presumptions. Indeed, there is no valid reason why the rather cumbersome phrase 'irrebuttable presumption of law' could not be applied to every rule of substantive law. The following examples may be given. Section 50 of the Children and Young

---

[6] See Lord Denning, 61 LQR 380.

[7] See Professor Glanville Williams *Criminal Law (The General Part)* (2nd edn London 1961) 877 et seq.

[8] See *R v Willshire* (1881) 6 QBD 366, below, and *R v Kay* (1887) 16 Cox CC 292, both relating to the presumption of marriage.

[9] For example, s 1(1) of the Prevention of Crime Act 1953. For further examples, see Ch 4.

Persons Act 1933[10] provides that: 'It shall be conclusively presumed that no child under the age of ten years can be guilty of an offence.' Under section 76 of the Sexual Offences Act 2003, in certain sexual cases, including cases of rape, if it is proved that the accused did the relevant act (intentional penetration of the vagina, anus, or mouth) and that he intentionally deceived the complainant as to the nature or purpose of the act, or intentionally induced the complainant to consent to it by impersonating a person known personally to the complainant, it is conclusively presumed that the complainant did not consent to the act and that the accused did not believe that the complainant consented to it. This is a somewhat convoluted way of saying that one of the ways in which rape may be committed is by intentional penetration and the intentional deceit or inducing of the kinds described (ie irrespective of whether the complainant consented and what the accused believed in that regard).[11]

## (c) Presumptions of fact

Where a presumption of fact applies, on the proof or admission of a basic fact, another fact *may* be presumed in the absence of sufficient evidence to the contrary. Presumptions of fact are sometimes referred to as 'provisional presumptions' to indicate that a party against whom they operate bears a provisional or tactical burden in relation to the presumed fact. Unlike rebuttable presumptions of law, establishment of the basic fact does not have the effect of placing either an evidential or legal burden on that party. Thus presumptions of fact amount to nothing more than examples of circumstantial evidence. Certain facts or combinations of facts can give rise to inferences which the tribunal of fact *may* draw, there being no rule of law that such inferences *must* be drawn in the absence of evidence to the contrary. However, presumptions of fact can vary in strength and on the operation of a strong presumption of fact, if no evidence in rebuttal is adduced, a finding by the tribunal of fact against the existence of the presumed fact could, at any rate in civil proceedings, be reversed on appeal. Examples of circumstantial evidence which have recurred so frequently as to attract the label 'presumption of fact' include the presumptions of intention, guilty knowledge (in cases of possession of recently stolen goods), continuance of life and seaworthiness.[12]

*(i) The presumption of intention.* There is a presumption of fact that a man intends the natural consequences of his acts. In criminal proceedings, this presumption was treated as a presumption of fact[13] until the House of Lords in *DPP v Smith*[14] held that, in certain circumstances, it constituted a presumption of law. This conclusion was

---

10 As amended by s 16(1) of the Children and Young Persons Act 1969. Formerly the age was set at 8 years.

11 See also s 13(1) of the Civil Evidence Act 1968 (Ch 21); and s 15(2) and (3) of the Road Traffic Offenders Act 1988 (formerly s 10(2) of the Road Traffic Act 1972, as substituted) and *Millard v DPP* (1990) 91 Cr App R 108, DC.

12 See also *Re W (a minor)* (1992) *The Times*, 22 May, CA: there is a presumption of fact that a baby's best interests are served by being with the mother, although with children the situation might be different.

13 See *R v Steane* [1947] KB 997 and per Lord Sankey in *Woolmington v DPP* [1935] AC 462 at 481.

14 [1961] AC 290.

statutorily reversed by section 8 of the Criminal Justice Act 1967, the effect of which has been to re-establish the presumption as one of fact.[15] The section provides that:

A court or jury, in determining whether a person has committed an offence—
   (a)  shall not be bound in law to infer that he intended or foresaw a result of his actions by reason only of its being a natural and probable consequence of those actions; but
   (b)  shall decide whether he did intend or foresee that result by reference to all the evidence, drawing such inferences from the evidence as appear proper in the circumstances.

In civil proceedings it remains unclear whether the presumption of intention is one of fact or law.[16]

*(ii)  The presumption of guilty knowledge.* Where an accused is found in possession of goods which have been recently stolen, an explanation is called for and if none is forthcoming the jury are entitled, but not compelled, to infer guilty knowledge or belief and to find the accused guilty of handling stolen goods. Where an explanation is given which the jury is convinced is untrue, likewise the jury are entitled to convict. However, if the explanation given leaves the jury in doubt as to whether the accused knew or believed the goods to be stolen, the prosecution has not proved its case and the jury should acquit.[17] This presumption may operate to the same effect in the case of theft.[18]

*(iii)  The presumption of continuance of life.* Where a person is proved to have been alive on a certain date, an inference may be drawn, in the absence of sufficient evidence to the contrary, that he was alive on a subsequent date.[19] The strength of this presumption depends entirely upon the facts of the case in question. In *R v Lumley*,[20] on a woman's trial for bigamy, a question arose as to whether her husband was alive at the date of the second marriage. Lush J said:[21]

---

[15]  See *R v Wallett* [1968] 2 QB 367, CA; *R v Moloney* [1985] 1 All ER 1025, HL.

[16]  See *Kaslefsky v Kaslefsky* [1951] P 38, CA; *Jamieson v Jamieson* [1952] AC 525, HL; *Lang v Lang* [1955] AC 402, PC; *Gollins v Gollins* [1964] AC 644, HL; and *Williams v Williams* [1964] AC 698, HL.

[17]  See *R v Schama and Abramovitch* (1914) 11 Cr App R 45; *R v Garth* [1949] 1 All ER 773, CCA; *R v Aves* [1950] 2 All ER 330, CCA; and *R v Hepworth and Fearnley* [1955] 2 QB 600, CCA.

[18]  In a case of handling, the prosecution is not obliged to adduce evidence that the goods were handled 'otherwise than in the course of the stealing' (see s 22(1) of the Theft Act 1968): the inference that in the proper case the jury are entitled to draw, namely that an accused was the guilty handler, includes the inference that he was not the thief. However, if the accused is in possession of property so recently after it was stolen that the inevitable inference is that he was the thief, as when he is found within a few hundred yards of the scene of the theft and within minutes after it took place, then if the charge is handling only, the jury should be directed that if they take the view that the accused was the thief, they should acquit him of the handling: *R v Cash* [1985] QB 801, CA, applied in *A-G of Hong Kong v Yip Kai-foon* [1988] 1 All ER 153, PC. See also *Ryan and French v DPP* [1994] Crim LR 457, CA.

[19]  See *McDarmaid v A-G* [1950] P 218, *Re Peete, Peete v Crompton* [1952] 2 All ER 599; and *Chard v Chard* [1956] P 259.

[20]  (1869) LR 1 CCR 196.

[21]  (1869) LR 1 CCR 196 at 198. See also per Denman CJ in *R v Harborne Inhabitants* (1835) 2 Ad&El 540 at 544–5.

This is purely a question of fact. The existence of a party at an antecedent date may, or may not, afford a reasonable inference that he is living at the subsequent date. If, for example, it was proved that he was in good health on the day preceding the marriage, the inference would be strong, almost irresistible, that he was living on the latter day, and the jury would in all probability find that he was so. If, on the other hand, it were proved that he was then in a dying condition, and nothing further was proved, they would probably decline to draw that inference. Thus, the question is entirely for the jury.

*(iv) The presumption of seaworthiness.* Where a ship sinks or becomes unable to continue her voyage shortly after putting to sea, an inference may be drawn, in the absence of sufficient evidence to the contrary, that she was unseaworthy on leaving port. In the absence of evidence in rebuttal, the tribunal of fact should be directed that an inference of unseaworthiness at the start of the voyage may be drawn. If, in these circumstances, a tribunal of fact were to find the contrary, it would be such a finding against the reasonable inference to be drawn that it would amount to a verdict against the evidence.[22]

### (d)  Presumptions without basic facts

All of the presumptions defined in this chapter up to this point may be explained in terms of a basic fact on the proof or admission of which another fact may or must be presumed. Presumptions without basic facts come into operation without the proof or admission of any basic fact; they are merely conclusions which must be drawn in the absence of evidence in rebuttal. In other words, they are rules relating to the incidence of the legal and evidential burdens expressed in the language pertaining to presumptions. The following examples may be given. In criminal proceedings, reference is often made to the presumptions of innocence and sanity. Both are more meaningfully expressed in terms of the incidence of the burden of proof. The presumption of innocence is a convenient abbreviation of the rule that the prosecution bear the legal burden of proving any fact essential to their case.[23] Likewise, the presumption of sanity refers to the rule that the accused bears the legal burden of proving insanity when he raises it as a defence.[24] In *Bratty v A-G for Northern Ireland* two members of the House of Lords referred to 'the presumption of mental capacity'.[25] The reference was to the rule that the evidential burden in relation to the defence of non-insane automatism is borne by the accused.

A final example of a presumption without basic facts is the presumption that

---

22  See per Brett LJ in *Pickup v Thames & Mersey Marine Insurance Co Ltd* (1878) 3 QBD 594 at 600, CA. See also *Anderson v Morice* (1875) LR 10 CP 609 and *Ajum Goolam Hossen & Co v Union Marine Insurance Co* [1901] AC 362, PC.

23  *Woolmington v DPP* [1935] AC 462. The presumption of innocence also applies when an allegation of criminal conduct is made in civil proceedings: see *Williams v East India Co* (1802) 3 East 192. Concerning the standard of proof to be met in these circumstances, see *Hornal v Neuberger Products Ltd* [1957] 1 QB 247, CA, considered in Ch 4.

24  *M'Naghten's* case (1843) 10 Cl & Fin 200. In testamentary cases, the presumption of sanity is not a presumption without basic facts but a rebuttable presumption of law: see below.

25  [1963] AC 386 per Viscount Kilmuir LC at 407 and per Lord Denning at 413.

mechanical instruments of a kind that are usually in working order, were in working order at the time when they were used. This conclusion will be drawn by the court in the absence of evidence to the contrary, the party seeking to rebut the presumption bearing an evidential burden. The presumption has been applied in the case of speedometers,[26] traffic lights,[27] breath-test machines,[28] and public weighbridges.[29] The presumption, it is submitted, also applies in the case of computers, with the consequence that a party introducing computer-generated evidence need only produce evidence that the computer was working properly at the relevant time if his opponent introduces some evidence to the contrary.

## 2 THE PRESUMPTION OF MARRIAGE

There are three discernible presumptions of marriage, a presumption of formal validity, a presumption of essential validity, and a presumption of marriage arising from cohabitation. Although this threefold classification is accorded scant recognition in the authorities, differences in the basic facts giving rise to each, and in the standard of proof required to rebut each, warrant a discrete analysis.

### (a) The presumption of formal validity

The formal validity of a marriage depends upon the *lex loci celebrationis*. A failure to comply with the formal requirements of the local law may make a marriage void. Under English law, a Church of England marriage (otherwise than by special licence) may be void because of irregularities such as failure duly to publish banns or to obtain a common licence. In the case of other marriages under English law, examples include cases of failure to give due notice to the superintendent registrar and cases in which a certificate and, where necessary, a licence have not been duly issued. However, on the proof or admission of the basic facts that a marriage was celebrated between persons who intended to marry, the formal validity of the marriage will be presumed in the absence of sufficient evidence to the contrary. The authorities almost always include among the basic facts the cohabitation of the parties following the ceremony of marriage[30] but the presumption has been held to apply to death-bed marriages.[31] It is submitted that cohabitation is not among the basic facts giving rise to the presumption.

The leading case relating to an English marriage is *Piers v Piers*.[32] A marriage ceremony had been celebrated between two persons who had shown their intention, at the time, to marry. The ceremony was performed in a private house but there was

---

[26] *Nicholas v Penny* [1950] 2 KB 466.
[27] *Tingle Jacobs and Co v Kennedy* [1964] 1 All ER 888n, CA.
[28] *Castle v Cross* [1985] 1 All ER 87, DC.
[29] *Kelly Communications Ltd v DPP* [2003] Crim LR 479 and 875, DC.
[30] See, eg, per Barnard J in *Russell v A-G* [1949] P 391 at 394.
[31] See *The Lauderdale Peerage Case* (1885) 10 App Cas 692, HL and *Hill v Hill* [1959] 1 All ER 281.
[32] (1849) 2 HL Cas 331.

no evidence that the bishop of the diocese had granted the necessary special licence. The House of Lords held that the marriage was formally valid.[33] An example of the application of the presumption to a foreign marriage is *Mahadervan v Mahadervan*.[34] A ceremony had been celebrated between the parties in Ceylon. Two of the requirements of the local law were solemnization of the marriage by a registrar, either in his office or in another authorized place and, during the ceremony, an address by the registrar to the parties on the nature of the union. The parties cohabited as if man and wife for a short period of time and the husband acknowledged the wife as such. Seven years after the first ceremony, the husband went through another ceremony of marriage with another woman in England and the validity of the first marriage came into question. According to the marriage certificate, the marriage had been solemnized by a registrar in his office, but the wife gave evidence that the marriage had taken place at her parent's house and there was no evidence of the requisite address by the registrar to the parties. Rejecting as irrational legal chauvinism an argument of counsel for the husband that there was no presumption in favour of a foreign marriage the establishment of which would invalidate a subsequent English one, Sir Jocelyn Simon P applied the presumption and held the foreign marriage to be formally valid.

In civil proceedings, the presumption operates as a persuasive presumption placing a legal burden on the party seeking to rebut formal validity.[35] The standard of proof to be met by that party is high. In *Piers v Piers* Lord Cottenham cited with approval the words of Lord Lyndhurst in *Morris v Davies*:[36] 'The presumption of law is not lightly to be repelled. It is not to be broken in upon or shaken by a mere balance of probabilities. The evidence for the purpose of repelling it must be strong, distinct, satisfactory, and conclusive.'[37] Lord Campbell said:[38] 'a presumption of this sort in favour of marriage can only be negatived by disproving every reasonable possibility.' In *Mahadervan v Mahadervan* Sir Jocelyn Simon P held that the presumption can only be rebutted by evidence which satisfies beyond reasonable doubt that there was no valid marriage.[39] In relation to matrimonial causes more generally, although the authorities remain in conflict, subsequent trends favour the ordinary civil standard[40] and it is likely that in future this lower standard will be applied. When Lord Cottenham in *Piers v Piers* adopted the words of Lord Lyndhurst in *Morris v Davies*, an authority on the presumption of legitimacy, the evidence in rebuttal of that presumption was required to meet a high standard of proof. The presumption of legitimacy is now rebuttable by evidence which satisfies the ordinary civil standard on a balance of

---

33  See also *De Thoren v A-G* (1876) 1 App Cas 686, HL; *Re Shephard, George v Thyer* [1904] 1 Ch 456; and *Russell v A-G* [1949] P 391.

34  [1964] P 233. See also *Spivack v Spivack* (1930) 46 TLR 243 and *Hill v Hill* [1959] 1 All ER 281.

35  In criminal cases where the prosecution bears the legal burden of proving the validity of the marriage, the presumption operates to place an evidential burden on the accused: see *R v Kay* (1887) 16 Cox CC 292.

36  (1837) 5 Cl&Fin 163 at 265.

37  The word 'conclusive' hardly seems apposite and its use has been criticized: see Harman LJ in *Re Taylor* [1961] 1 WLR 9, CA.

38  (1849) 2 HL Cas 331 at 380.      39  [1964] P 233 at 246.

40  *Blyth v Blyth* [1966] AC 643 and *Bastable v Bastable and Sanders* [1968] 1 WLR 1684.

probabilities.[41] It is submitted that the standard of proof to be met by the party seeking to rebut the presumption of marriage should also be the ordinary civil standard.

## (b) The presumption of essential validity

A marriage may be void on the grounds that the parties lacked the capacity to marry. Under English law, for example, the parties may lack the capacity to marry if they are related within the prohibited degrees or if either of them is under the age of 16 or already married. However, on the proof or admission of the basic fact that a formally valid marriage was celebrated, the essential validity of the marriage will be presumed in the absence of sufficient evidence to the contrary. In the words of Pilcher J in *Tweney v Tweney*,[42] 'The petitioner's marriage to the present respondent being unexceptionable in form and duly consummated remains a good marriage until some evidence is adduced that the marriage was, in fact, a nullity.' Although the matter is far from clear, in civil proceedings the presumption would appear to operate as a persuasive rather than evidential presumption, placing a legal burden on the party seeking to rebut it.[43] However, the standard of proof required to rebut the presumption is lower than that in the case of the presumption of formal validity. In *Gatty and Gatty v A-G*[44] it was held that evidence of a valid prior marriage sufficed. A similar conclusion was reached in *Re Peete, Peete v Crompton*.[45] A woman, W, made an application under the Inheritance (Family Provision) Act 1938 as the widow of Y. W had separated from her first husband X prior to 1916 and in 1919 went through a formally valid ceremony of marriage with Y. The question arose as to the essential validity of the subsequent marriage. The court held that the application failed. Although a presumption of essential validity arose in relation to the subsequent marriage, there was some evidence before the court, namely the existence of the first marriage, that in 1919 W lacked the capacity to marry Y. However, where the prior marriage is of doubtful validity, there is authority that the presumption is not rebutted.[46]

In most of the cases where the presumption of essential validity has fallen to be applied by the courts, one of the parties to a marriage has been married previously. The question has been whether the earlier marriage had terminated by the time of the subsequent ceremony. This issue may in turn require consideration of the presumption of death, the presumption of continuance of life, or even the presumption of essential validity in relation to the earlier marriage. Two conflicting presumptions applied to the same facts in *Monckton v Tarr*.[47] A, a woman, married B in 1882. B deserted A in 1887. In 1895, at which time there was no evidence that B was alive, A married C. In 1913, at which time A was still alive, C married a woman D. D made a

---

[41] See s 26 of the Family Law Reform Act 1969, below.     [42] [1946] P 180 at 182.
[43] Cf *Axon v Axon* (1937) 59 CLR 395, HC of A.     [44] [1951] P 444.
[45] [1952] 2 All ER 599, Ch D.
[46] *Taylor v Taylor* [1967] P 25. Cf *Monckton v Tarr* (1930) 23 BWCC 504, CA.
[47] (1930) 23 BWCC 504, CA.

claim for workmen's compensation as the widow of C. The employers alleged that the 1913 marriage was void because of the 1895 marriage. D replied that the 1895 marriage was void because of the 1882 marriage. D's claim was dismissed by the Court of Appeal. Although a presumption of essential validity arose in relation to the marriage of 1913, the same presumption applied to the marriage of 1895. These two presumptions cancelling each other out, it was for D to prove C's capacity to marry her and this she could only do by showing that B was alive at the date of the 1895 marriage, something which she had failed to do. A different approach was adopted, however, when a similar problem arose in *Taylor v Taylor*.[48] There was some weak evidence that a woman, W, had married X. Subsequently, in 1928, X married another woman Y. Y left him and in 1942, when X was still alive, married Z. Z petitioned for a decree of nullity alleging that his marriage to Y was void because of the 1928 marriage. Y replied that the marriage of 1928 was void because of the earlier marriage between W and X. It might have been expected, on the reasoning employed in *Monckton v Tarr*, that the court would have held that the presumptions in favour of the 1928 and 1942 marriages effectively cancelling each other out, it was for Y to prove her capacity to marry Z and that she had failed to do this, the weak evidence adduced to show the marriage between W and X being insufficient for the purpose. However, Cairns J, expressing a preference for the preservation of existing unions, rather than their avoidance in favour of doubtful earlier and effectively dead ones, held that the marriage of 1942 was valid. The evidence of the earlier marriage of doubtful validity, that is the marriage of 1928, did not suffice to rebut the presumption of essential validity in relation to the marriage of 1942.[49]

## (c) The presumption of marriage arising from cohabitation

On the proof or admission of the basic fact that a man and woman have cohabited as if man and wife, it is presumed, in the absence of sufficient evidence to the contrary, that they were living together in consequence of a valid marriage.[50] The authorities suggest that in civil proceedings this presumption operates as a persuasive presumption.[51] Evidence in rebuttal is required to meet a high standard of proof: it must be 'clear and firm'[52] or 'of the most cogent kind'.[53] In *Sastry Velaider Aronegary v*

---

[48] [1967] P 25.

[49] Cf, in this respect, the available evidence in rebuttal in *Re Peete, Peete v Crompton* [1952] 2 All ER 599, above.

[50] In cases where, pursuant to local law, a valid marriage may come into existence by the consent of the parties without a formal ceremony, such consent is presumed: see *Breadalbane Case, Campbell v Campbell* (1867) LR 1 Sc&Div 182.

[51] In criminal proceedings in which the prosecution rely on this presumption, the authorities suggest that the presumption, by itself, is insufficient to discharge the evidential burden: see *Morris v Miller* (1767) 4 Burr 2057 and *R v Umanski* [1961] VLR 242. Proof or admission of cohabitation supported by the production of a marriage certificate does suffice for these purposes: *R v Birtles* (1911) 6 Cr App R 177.

[52] *Re Taylor* [1961] 1 WLR 9, CA.

[53] *Re Taplin, Watson v Tate* [1937] 3 All ER 105, Ch D. Some of the cases suggest an extremely high standard of proof: see, eg, *Re Shephard, George v Thyer* [1904] 1 Ch 456.

*Sembecutty Vaigalie*[54] the issue concerned the validity of a marriage ceremony which had taken place between Tamils in Ceylon. The Privy Council, of the opinion that the party in whose favour the presumption operated was under no obligation to prove that the ceremony had complied with the requisite customs, held the parties to be validly married. Sir Barnes Peacock said:[55]

It does not, therefore, appear to their Lordships that the law of Ceylon is different from that which prevails in this country; namely, that where a man and a woman are proved to have lived together as man and wife, the law will presume, unless the contrary be clearly proved, that they were living in consequence of a valid marriage, and not in a state of concubinage.

Although in this case evidence was given that a ceremony had taken place, it is clear that the presumption applies in the absence of such evidence.[56] In *Re Taplin, Watson v Tate*[57] a declaration was sought that certain children were the legitimate offspring of a man and woman. The man and woman had lived together as man and wife for ten years and had at all times enjoyed that reputation in society. The birth certificates of the children recorded the marriage of the parents to have taken place in 1860 in Victoria, where the registration of marriages was compulsory, but the records contained no entry in respect of the marriage. In 1873, the paternal grandfather of the children had executed a deed of trust covenanting to make certain payments to the children, who were referred to as the 'reputed children' of his son. The evidence in rebuttal being insufficiently cogent, Simonds J applied the presumption and declared the children to be the lawful offspring of the marriage.

## 3 THE PRESUMPTION OF LEGITIMACY

On the proof or admission of the basic fact that a child was born or conceived during lawful wedlock, it is presumed, in the absence of sufficient evidence to the contrary, that the child is legitimate. The presumption may be rebutted by evidence showing that the husband and wife did not have sexual intercourse as a result of which the child was conceived.[58] The evidence in rebuttal may be evidence of: non-access; the husband's impotence;[59] the use of reliable contraceptives; the blood groups of the parties; the results of a DNA test; the minimal nature of the husband's access to the

---

[54] (1881) 6 App Cas 364, PC.      [55] (1881) 6 App Cas 364 at 371.

[56] Even in cases where the period of cohabitation was short: see *Re Taylor* [1961] 1 WLR 9, CA. Cf *Re Bradshaw, Blandy v Willis* [1938] 4 All ER 143. See also *Breadalbane Case, Campbell v Campbell* (1867) LR 1 Sc&Div 182.

[57] [1937] 3 All ER 105.

[58] See per Sir James Mansfield CJ in the *Banbury Peerage Case* (1811) 1 Sim&St 153. Under s 48(1) of the Matrimonial Causes Act 1973, the evidence of a husband or wife shall be admissible in any proceedings to prove that marital intercourse did or did not take place between them during any period. Under s 43(1) of the Matrimonial Causes Act 1965, a husband or wife was not compellable in any proceedings to give evidence of such matters. Section 43(1), however, has now ceased to have effect in both civil and criminal proceedings: see s 16(4) of the Civil Evidence Act 1968 and s 80(9) of the Police and Criminal Evidence Act 1984 respectively.

[59] *Legge v Edmonds* (1855) 25 LJ Ch 125.

wife; an admission of paternity by another man;[60] the wife's cohabitation with another man for an appropriate period of time before the birth of the child;[61] the results of a DNA test excluding the husband as the father combined with evidence of sexual intercourse with another man who refused to comply with an order for a blood test;[62] or the conduct of the wife and illicit partner to the child.[63] Evidence of adultery by the mother will not rebut the presumption in the absence of evidence that at the time of conception sexual intercourse between the husband and wife did not take place.[64]

It should be emphasized that either birth or conception during wedlock suffices to give rise to the presumption. Thus where a child is born to a married woman so soon after the marriage ceremony that pre-marital conception is indicated, the presumption applies.[65] Likewise, the presumption applies where a child is born to a woman so soon after the termination of her marriage that conception during the marriage is indicated.[66] In *Re Overbury, Sheppard v Matthews*[67] the presumption was applied in such circumstances notwithstanding the remarriage of the mother prior to the birth of the child. Six months after her first husband's death a woman had remarried, giving birth to a girl two months later. Harman J held that the child was the legitimate daughter of the first husband, there being insufficient evidence to rebut the presumption. In a case such as this, the presumption could have operated in favour of the child's legitimacy by virtue of her birth during the second marriage. However in cases where *paternity* is in issue, it is obviously correct to treat the date of conception, and not the date of birth as the determinative factor, so that provided the child can be proved to have been conceived during the first marriage, it will be held to be the legitimate offspring of the first husband, even if born, say, four or six months after the second marriage. In a case where marriage takes place so soon after termination of an earlier marriage that it is unclear whether conception occurred during the first or second marriage, it is submitted that although a presumption operates in favour of the child's legitimacy by virtue of birth during the second marriage, it should not be determinative of paternity, if that is in issue.

The presumption applies, although it may be more easily rebuttable, where there is a maintenance order in force against the husband (unless it contains a non-cohabitation clause),[68] where proceedings for divorce or nullity have been commenced[69] and even

---

60  *R v King's Lynn Magistrates' Court and Walker, ex p Moore* [1988] Fam Law 393, QBD.
61  *Cope v Cope* (1833) 1 Mood&R 269 and *Re Jenion, Jenion v Wynne* [1952] Ch 454, CA.
62  *F v Child Support Agency* [1999] 2 FLR 244, QBD.
63  *Morris v Davies* (1837) 5 Cl&Fin 163 and *Kanapathipillai v Parpathy* [1956] AC 580.
64  *R v Mansfield Inhabitants* (1841) 1 QB 444 and *Gordon v Gordon* [1903] P 141.
65  *The Poulett Peerage Case* [1903] AC 395, HL.
66  See *Maturin v A-G* [1938] 2 All ER 214 (termination by divorce) and *Re Heath, Stacey v Bird* [1945] Ch 417 (termination by death of husband).
67  [1955] Ch 122, Ch D.     68  *Bowen v Norman* [1938] 1 KB 689.
69  *Knowles v Knowles* [1962] P 161, where the presumption was applied on a finding of conception as a result of intercourse between the husband and wife at a time after a decree nisi had been granted but before it had been made absolute. Wrangham J was of the opinion that the presumption involved both a presumption of paternity and a presumption as to the date of conception.

where the husband and wife are living apart, whether or not under a separation agreement.[70] However, the presumption does not apply where a decree of judicial separation or a magistrate's separation order is in force.[71] In such circumstances, it is presumed that the parties did not have sexual intercourse. Accordingly, if the child is born more than nine months after the separation, there is a presumption of illegitimacy rebuttable by evidence of intercourse between the husband and wife.

The authorities suggest that in civil proceedings the presumption of legitimacy operates as a persuasive presumption. At common law, evidence in rebuttal was required to meet a high standard of proof[72] but the matter is now governed by section 26 of the Family Law Reform Act 1969, which provides that:

Any presumption of law as to the legitimacy or illegitimacy of any person may in any civil proceedings be rebutted by evidence which shows that it is more probable than not that the person is illegitimate or legitimate as the case may be and it shall not be necessary to prove that fact beyond reasonable doubt in order to rebut the presumption.

Thus the party seeking to rebut the presumption bears the legal burden of proving illegitimacy on a balance of probabilities and, in accordance with general principles, will fail if the evidence is such that legitimacy is as probable as illegitimacy.[73] In the words of Lord Reid in *S v S*,[74] which were adopted and applied in *T (HH) v T (E)*:[75]

That means that the presumption of legitimacy now merely determines the onus of proof. Once evidence has been led it must be used without using the presumption as a make-weight in the scale of legitimacy. So even weak evidence against legitimacy must prevail if there is no other evidence to counterbalance it. The presumption will only come in at that stage in the very rare case of the evidence being so evenly balanced that the court is unable to reach a decision on it.

## 4 THE PRESUMPTION OF DEATH

Where there is no acceptable affirmative evidence that a person was alive at some time during a continuous period of seven years or more, on the proof or admission of the basic facts (i) that there are persons who would be likely to have heard of him over that period, (ii) that those persons have not heard of him, and (iii) that all due inquiries have been made appropriate to the circumstances, that person will be presumed to have died at some time within that period.[76] One of the difficulties of this presumption stems from the fact that evidence in rebuttal may be indistinguishable

---

[70] *Ettenfield v Ettenfield* [1940] P 96, CA.      [71] *Hetherington v Hetherington* (1887) 12 PD 112.

[72] See per Lord Lyndhurst in *Morris v Davies* (1837) 5 Cl&Fin 163 at 265, above.

[73] See per Denning J in *Miller v Minister of Pensions* [1947] 2 All ER 372 at 374. However, if the case involves a finding that someone other than the mother's husband is the father of the child, the standard of proof to make the finding of paternity is a heavy one, commensurate with the gravity of the issue and although not as heavy as in criminal proceedings, more than the ordinary civil standard of balance of probabilities: *W v K* (1986) 151 JP 589.

[74] [1972] AC 24 at 41.      [75] [1971] 1 WLR 429.

[76] See per Sachs J in *Chard v Chard* [1956] P 259 at 272.

from evidence which negatives one of the basic facts. This was the case in *Prudential Assurance Co v Edmonds*,[77] a decision of the House of Lords which suggests that once the party against whom the presumption operates has adduced sufficient evidence for the possibility of the existence of the absent person to be put to the tribunal of fact, the presumption has been rebutted. It would seem that the presumption is of the evidential and not persuasive variety.

## (a) The basic facts

In *Chard v Chard*[78] the presumption did not arise because there was no evidence of the first basic fact, that is of persons likely to have heard of the person whose death was in question.[79] The parties to a marriage celebrated in 1933 sought decrees of nullity on the ground that the husband had been party to a marriage celebrated in 1909. The first wife, in respect of whom there was no evidence of ill-health or registration of death, was last heard of in 1917 and would have been 44 years of age in 1933. There were a number of reasons which might have led her not to wish to be heard of by the husband or his family. Between 1917 and 1933 the husband had been almost continually in prison. On these facts, Sachs J held that since there was no evidence of a person who would have been likely to have heard of the first wife between 1917 and 1933, the presumption could not apply. Applying the presumption of fact as to the continuance of life, it was inferred that the first wife was alive in 1933. Accordingly, it was held that the ceremony of that year was null.[80]

*Prudential Assurance Co v Edmonds*[81] concerned the second basic fact, that the person whose death is in question has not been heard of. In a claim on a policy of life assurance, it was alleged that the assured, one Robert Nutt, was not dead. Members of the family gave evidence that they had not heard of him for more than seven years but knew that his niece believed that she had seen him in Melbourne, Australia. The niece gave evidence that when she was aged 20, standing in a crowded street in Melbourne, a man passed her whom she recognized as her uncle. She did not speak to him because he was lost in the crowd as she turned to do so but said he resembled her uncle as she remembered him from five years earlier. The House of Lords, being in no doubt that it fell to the tribunal of fact to decide whether or not to accept the niece's evidence, held that if the jury had been satisfied that she was mistaken, the basic facts giving rise to the presumption would have been established.

There is a conflict of authority as to whether the presumption arises without proof or admission of the fact that all due inquiries appropriate to the circumstances have been made.[82] The explanation is probably that the extent of the inquiries to be made

---

[77] (1877) 2 App Cas 487.    [78] [1956] P 259.

[79] Friends and relatives will not be treated as persons likely to have heard of the absent person where it is shown that the latter did not intend the former to hear of him: see, eg, *Watson v England* (1844) 14 Sim 29 and *Re Lidderdale* (1912) 57 Sol Jo 3.

[80] Cf *Re Watkins, Watkins v Watkins* [1953] 2 All ER 1113.    [81] (1877) 2 App Cas 487.

[82] See *Willyams v Scottish Widows' Fund Life Assurance Society* (1888) 4 TLR 489 and *Chipchase v Chipchase* [1939] P 391. Cf *Bradshaw v Bradshaw* [1956] P 274n.

depends upon the circumstances of the case in question, and that in some cases the circumstances are not appropriate to the making of any inquiries whatsoever.[83] There is some authority that proof of the third basic fact may render proof of the first unnecessary, presumably on the basis that to adduce evidence that a person has made all due inquiries appropriate to the circumstances is also, in some cases, to adduce evidence of a person who would be likely to have heard of the absent person.[84]

## (b) The presumed facts

The presumption of death allows the court to presume the fact of a person's death. However, proof of the mere fact of death may be of little or no assistance to a party seeking to establish that an absent person died unmarried, childless or without next-of-kin. It is reasonably clear that although these additional issues are not proved by the basic facts giving rise to the presumption of death, but require additional evidence,[85] the amount of such additional evidence may be less than would have been required if the presumption had not applied.[86]

A question giving rise to more complexity is whether the presumption of death operates to establish not only the fact of death but also the date of death. Proof of the mere fact of death is of limited use to a party seeking to establish death before or after a particular date. It seems clear from the authorities that the presumption establishes only the fact of death, additional evidence being required to prove that the death took place at a particular period. In the words of Giffard LJ in *Re Phené's Trusts*:[87] 'the law presumes a person who has not been heard of for seven years to be dead, but in the absence of special circumstances it draws no presumption from the fact as to the particular period at which he died.' However, there are two views as to the date on which the fact of death may be presumed. On one view the fact of death may be presumed at the date of the proceedings (ie a continuous period of absence for seven years or more runs back from the date of the proceedings). A second view is that the fact of death may be presumed at the end of a continuous period of absence for seven years (ie a continuous period of absence for seven years runs forward from the date of the disappearance of the absent person). Whichever view is taken, if a party seeks to establish that death occurred on a particular date prior to the date on which the fact of death is presumed, additional evidence will be required. A party seeking to establish that death occurred on a particular date prior to the date of the action, will only be assisted by the second view. Thus if there is no evidence that X was alive during a continuous period of nine years from 1987 to 1996 and a party seeks to establish that X was dead in 1995, the matter coming before the court in 1996, that party will fail on the first view but succeed on the second.

A case which is consistent with both of the above views is *Re Phené's Trusts*.[88] In *Lal*

---

[83] See *Bullock v Bullock* [1960] 2 All ER 307.　　[84] *Doe d France v Andrews* (1850) 15 QB 756.

[85] See *Re Jackson, Jackson v Ward* [1907] 2 Ch 354.

[86] See *Dunn v Snowden* (1862) 32 LJ Ch 104, *Rawlinson v Miller* (1875) 1 Ch D 52 and *Greaves v Greenwood* (1877) 2 Ex D 289, CA.

[87] (1870) 5 Ch App 139 at 144, CA.　　[88] Ibid.

*Chand Marwari v Mahant Ramrup Gir*[89] the Privy Council interpreted the decision in that case as an authority for the first view. Other decisions, however, are only consistent with the second. In *Re Westbrook's Trusts*[90] the property of an intestate, who had disappeared, was divided among such of his next-of-kin as were shown to be alive at a date seven years after his disappearance. Those who had died before that date were excluded. On the first view, the fact of the intestate's death would have been presumed, in the absence of any additional evidence that he had died on an earlier date, at the time of the proceedings and the court would have divided the estate among such of his next-of-kin as were living at that date. In *Chipchase v Chipchase*[91] a woman charged her second husband with adultery, desertion and failure to maintain. Her first marriage was in 1915. In 1928, not having heard of her first husband since 1916, she remarried. The magistrates dismissed the complaint on the basis that she had failed to establish the validity of her second marriage by evidence that the first husband was dead in 1928. The Divisional Court held that the presumption of death applied and remitted the case back to the magistrates for them to consider whether there was any evidence in rebuttal. On the first view, the fact of the first husband's death would have been presumed at the time of the proceedings in 1939 and, in the absence of additional evidence that he died on any earlier date, the decision of the magistrates would have been upheld. It is submitted that the first and stricter view deprives the presumption of death of so much of its value that the laxer second view is to be preferred.

### (c) Statutory provisions

There are a number of statutory provisions which fall to be considered in connection with the presumption of death. The most important of these are as follows.

*(i) Section 184 of the Law of Property Act 1925.* This section provides that:

In all cases where, after the commencement of this Act, two or more persons have died in circumstances rendering it uncertain which of them survived the other or others, such deaths shall (subject to any order of the court), for all purposes affecting the title to property, be presumed to have occurred in order of seniority, and accordingly the younger shall be deemed to have survived the elder.[92]

In *Hickman v Peacey*,[93] Lord Simon was of the view that the word 'circumstances' in this section is not confined to deaths occurring as a result of a common disaster. It

---

[89] (1925) 42 TLR 159 at 160.

[90] [1873] WN 167, criticized in *Re Rhodes, Rhodes v Rhodes* (1887) 36 Ch D 586. See also *Re Aldersey, Gibson v Hall* [1905] 2 Ch 181.

[91] [1939] P 391.

[92] This rule has been modified, for the purposes of disposing of the estate of an intestate, where spouses die in circumstances rendering it uncertain which of them survived the other. The spouse is treated as having predeceased the intestate: see s 46(3) of the Administration of Estates Act 1925 (added by s 1(4) of the Intestates' Estates Act 1952). In cases not relating to the title of property, see *Wing v Angrave* (1860) 8 HL Cas 183.

[93] [1945] AC 304 at 314–15, HL.

remains unclear, however, whether the statutory phrase 'where . . . persons have died' refers not only to persons whose deaths have been proved, but also to those whose deaths have been presumed.[94]

*(ii) Section 19 of the Matrimonial Causes Act 1973.* Section 19(1) provides that any married person alleging that reasonable grounds exist for supposing that the other party to the marriage is dead may present a petition to the court to have the same presumed and to have the marriage dissolved. Section 19(3) provides that:

the fact that for a period of seven years or more the other party to the marriage has been continually absent from the petitioner and the petitioner has no reason to believe that the other party has been living within that time shall be evidence that the other party is dead until the contrary is proved.

This statutory presumption is easier to raise than its common-law counterpart. Apart from the continual absence, the only basic fact to be established relates to the belief of the petitioner, who must give evidence.[95] In *Thompson v Thompson*[96] the provision was construed by Sachs J to mean that during the period of seven years nothing should have occurred from which the petitioner could have reasonably concluded that his or her spouse was alive. The court left open the question whether the petitioner is required to have made all due inquiries appropriate to the circumstances, but it is submitted that a failure to do so could be relevant to the issue of the reasonableness of the petitioner's belief. The fact that the parties parted under a separation agreement does not prevent the operation of the presumption.[97]

*(iii) The Proviso to Section 57 of the Offences Against the Person Act 1861.* After defining the offence of bigamy, section 57 continues:

Provided that nothing in this section contained shall extend . . . to any person marrying a second time whose husband or wife shall have been continually absent from such person for the space of seven years then last past, and shall not have been known by such person to be living within that time . . .

The prosecution, in order to prove bigamy, must show that the first spouse was alive at the date of the second marriage.[98] Where this has been done, the accused may rely upon the proviso, which amounts to a defence, to secure an acquittal.[99] The prosecution bears the legal burden of proving that the first marriage was valid and that the accused went through a second marriage knowing that the first spouse was alive. *R v Edwards*[100] suggests that the accused bears the legal burden of proving that the first

---

[94] See *Re Watkinson* [1952] VLR 123.       [95] *Parkinson v Parkinson* [1939] P 346.
[96] [1957] P 19.       [97] *Parkinson v Parkinson* [1939] P 346.
[98] Proof that the first spouse was alive before the second marriage may give rise to an inference that he or she was alive at the date of that marriage: see *R v Lumley* (1869) LR 1 CCR 196.
[99] In Australia, the proviso has been treated as a statutory presumption of death in relation to one party to a marriage on the remarriage of the other: see per Evatt J in *Axon v Axon* (1937) 59 CLR 395 at 413, HC of A and *Re Peatling* [1969] VR 214 (Supreme Court of Victoria).
[100] [1975] QB 27, Ch 4.

spouse was continually absent for seven years[101] and that he or she did not know that the first spouse was living within that time. However, there is also authority that the prosecution bears the legal burden in relation to the accused's knowledge.[102]

## 5 OMNIA PRAESUMUNTUR RITE ESSE ACTA

On the proof or admission of the basic fact that a public or official act has been performed, it is presumed, in the absence of sufficient evidence to the contrary, that the act has been regularly and properly performed. Likewise, persons acting in public capacities are presumed to have been regularly and properly appointed. In civil proceedings, the maxim operates as an evidential presumption and may be rebutted by some evidence of irregularity. The operation of the presumption may be illustrated by the following authorities. In *R v Gordon*[103] proof that a police officer had acted as such was sufficient on a charge of assaulting a police officer in the course of his duty and in *Doe d Bowley v Barnes*[104] proof that churchwardens and overseers of parish property had acted as such at the time of the demise of certain parish property was sufficient in an action of ejectment; in neither case was evidence of due appointment required. In *R v Roberts*,[105] on an indictment for perjury committed in the presence of a deputy county court judge, the judge was presumed, in the absence of evidence to the contrary, to have been duly appointed.[106] In *Berryman v Wise*,[107] an action by an attorney for words spoken of him in the way of his profession, proof that he was an attorney, by the production of his practising certificate or a copy of the roll of attorneys, was not required; proof that he had acted as an attorney sufficed.[108] In *R v Langton*[109] the presumption applied to establish the due incorporation of a company which had acted as such. In *R v Cresswell*,[110] on proof that a marriage had been celebrated in a building some yards from a parish church, in which building several other marriages had also been celebrated, it was presumed that the building was duly consecrated. In *TC Coombs & Co (a firm) v IRC*[111] it was presumed, in the absence of evidence to the contrary, that a tax inspector who had served notice under section 20 of the Taxes Management Act 1970 (requiring stockbrokers to deliver documentary information relevant to the tax liability of one of their former employees) together with a General Commissioner, who had given his consent to the notices, had both acted within the limits of their authority, with honesty and discretion. The authorities are in conflict as

---

[101] See also *R v Jones* (1883) 11 QBD 118 and *R v Bonnor* [1957] VLR 227.
[102] *R v Curgerwen* (1865) LR 1 CCR 1.    [103] (1789) 1 Leach 515.    [104] (1846) 8 QB 1037.
[105] (1878) 14 Cox CC 101, CCR.
[106] See also *R v Verelst* (1813) 3 Camp 432. But there is no presumption that a court or tribunal has jurisdiction in relation to any given matter: see *Christopher Brown Ltd v Genossenschaft Oesterreichischer* [1954] 1 QB 8 per Devlin J at 13.
[107] (1791) 4 Term Rep 366.
[108] Section 18 of the Solicitors Act 1974 provides for the admissibility of lists published by authority of the Law Society.
[109] (1876) 2 QBD 296.    [110] (1876) 1 QBD 446, CCR.    [111] [1991] 3 All ER 623, HL.

to the applicability of the presumption in criminal proceedings. Although there are cases in which the prosecution has relied on the presumption to establish part of its case,[112] in *Scott v Baker*,[113] on proof that a breathalyser had been issued to the police, the court refused to presume that it had been officially approved by the Secretary of State. It was held that the presumption may not be used to establish an ingredient of a criminal office if the regularity and propriety of the matter in question is disputed at the trial.[114] However, there is also authority that it is insufficient merely to dispute regularity; evidence must be adduced.[115]

## 6 THE PRESUMPTION OF SANITY IN TESTAMENTARY CASES

Although in criminal cases the presumption of sanity is a presumption without basic facts, a rule relating to the incidence of the burden of proof expressed in the language pertaining to presumptions, in testamentary cases it operates as a rebuttable presumption of law casting an evidential burden on the party against whom it operates. On the proof or admission of the basic fact that a rational will has been duly executed, it is presumed, in the absence of sufficient evidence to the contrary, that the testator was sane. In *Sutton v Sadler*[116] the heir-at-law of a testator brought an action against the devisee alleging the insanity of the testator. The devisee produced the will, proved its due execution, and called witnesses to prove the competency of the testator. The plaintiff gave evidence of the testator's insanity. The trial judge directed the jury that the heir-at-law was entitled to succeed unless a will was proved but that on the production of a duly executed will he bore the burden of establishing the incompetency of the testator so that if they were left in doubt on the matter, the devisee would succeed. The jury found for the devisee. The Court of Common Pleas held that the jury had been misdirected. The devisee bore the legal burden of proving that he was the devisee under a duly executed will. Proof of the due execution of a rational will gave rise to the presumption of sanity placing an evidential burden on the heir-at-law, the legal burden of proving the competency of the testator resting with the devisee. Accordingly, if the heir-at-law had raised sufficient evidence for the issue of insanity to go before the tribunal of fact, they should have been directed to find against the devisee unless satisfied that he had discharged the legal burden by proving on a balance of probabilities that the testator was sane. A new trial was ordered.

---

[112] See *Gibbins v Skinner* [1951] 2 KB 379, where it was held that on proof that speed limit signs had been placed on a road, the presumption could operate to establish the performance of a local authority's statutory duties pursuant to the Road Traffic Acts; and *Cooper v Rowlands* [1972] Crim LR 53, where a man in police uniform who administered a breath test was presumed to have been duly appointed.
[113] [1969] 1 QB 659, DC, approved by the Court of Appeal in *R v Withecombe* [1969] 1 WLR 84.
[114] See also *Dillon v R* [1982] AC 484, PC.
[115] *Campbell v Wallsend Slipway & Engineering Co Ltd* [1978] ICR 1015, DC at 1025.
[116] (1857) 3 CBNS 87.

## 7 RES IPSA LOQUITUR[117]

In the ordinary course of things bags of flour do not fall from warehouse windows,[118] stones are not found in buns,[119] cars do not mount the pavement,[120] and slippery substances are not left on shop floors[121] unless, in each case, those who have the management of the thing in question fail to exercise proper care. The normal rule, that in negligence actions the claimant bears the legal and evidential burden, is capable of causing injustice in cases such as these. Although the claimant is able to prove the accident, he cannot show that it was caused by the defendant's negligence, the true cause of the accident, in most cases, being known only to the defendant. In these circumstances, the claimant may be assisted by the principle of *res ipsa loquitur*. Translating into the terminology of presumptions the statement of the principle given by Sir William Erle CJ in *Scott v London & St Katherine Docks Co*,[122] the presumption may be defined as follows: on the proof or admission of the basic facts that (i) something was under the management of the defendant or his servants and (ii) an accident occurred, being an accident which in the ordinary course of things does not happen if those who have the management use proper care, it may or must be presumed, in the absence of sufficient evidence to the contrary, that the accident was caused by the negligence of the defendant. This definition allows for three possible classifications of the principle, as a presumption of fact, as an evidential presumption or as a persuasive presumption, for each of which support may be found in the authorities.

If the principle is no more than a presumption of fact or provisional presumption, it is an example of circumstantial evidence: proof of the basic facts gives rise to an inference of negligence which the tribunal of fact may draw in the absence of evidence to the contrary. A party against whom the presumption operates bears the provisional or tactical burden in relation to negligence: if he adduces no evidence, he is not bound to lose but it is a clear risk that he runs and a finding by the tribunal of fact in his favour could be reversed on appeal.[123] If it is an evidential presumption, on proof of the basic facts, negligence must be presumed in the absence of evidence to the contrary, and the party against whom the presumption operates bears the evidential burden: he will lose unless he adduces some evidence but where, on all the evidence before the court, the probability of negligence is equal to the probability of its absence, he will succeed, the plaintiff having failed to discharge the legal burden of proving negligence. In *The Kite*[124] the plaintiffs, owners of cargo on a barge which, while being

---

[117] This phrase has been used despite the strictures of the Court of Appeal in *Fryer v Pearson & Anor* (2000) The Times, 4 Apr: 'People should stop using maxims or doctrines dressed up in Latin which are not readily comprehensible to those for whose benefit they are supposed to exist.' The author applauds the attempt to accommodate the lay client, but rather fears that some doctrines—eg estoppel *per rem judicatam*—will need explanation whatever language they are couched in.

[118] *Byrne v Boadle* (1863) 2 H&C 722.    [119] *Chapronière v Mason* (1905) 21 TLR 633, CA.

[120] *Ellor v Selfridge & Co Ltd* (1930) 46 TLR 236.

[121] *Ward v Tesco Stores Ltd* [1976] 1 WLR 810, CA.    [122] (1865) 3 H&C 596 at 601.

[123] See, eg, per Greer LJ in *Langham v Wellingborough School Governors and Fryer* (1932) 101 LJKB 513 at 518 and per Goddard LJ in *Easson v London & North Eastern Rly Co* [1944] KB 421.

[124] [1933] P 154.

towed by a tug, collided with a bridge, claimed damages from the owners of the tug. Langton J defined the burden borne by the defendants in the following terms:[125]

If they give a reasonable explanation, which is equally consistent with the accident happening without their negligence as with their negligence, they have again shifted the burden of proof back to the plaintiffs to show—as they always have to show from the beginning—that it was the negligence of the defendants that caused the accident.

On all the evidence, the probability of negligence being equal to that of its absence, the court found for the defendants.[126]

If the principle is a persuasive or compelling presumption, negligence must be presumed in the absence of evidence to the contrary, and the party against whom the presumption operates bears the legal burden of disproving negligence: he will lose not only where he adduces no evidence but also where on all the evidence before the court the probability of negligence is equal to the probability of its absence. To succeed, he must disprove negligence on a balance of probabilities. The evidence he adduces must either reveal the true cause of the accident and thereby convince the tribunal of fact that negligence is less probable than its absence or show that he used all reasonable care. In *Woods v Duncan*[127] two men had died in a submarine accident alleged to have been caused by the negligence of, inter alia, a torpedo officer in charge of the forward compartment. On proof on a balance of probabilities that the officer was not negligent, the House of Lords found in his favour. Referring to the principle of *res ipsa loquitur*, Lord Simon said:[128]

that principle only shifts the onus of proof, which is adequately met by showing that he was not in fact negligent. He is not to be held liable because he cannot prove exactly how the accident happened.

In *Barkway v South Wales Transport Co Ltd*,[129] a case concerning a bus which had fallen down an embankment, Asquith LJ held that it was insufficient for the defendants to show that the bus left the road because of a burst tyre, a neutral event as consistent with negligence as its absence. He continued:[130]

To displace the presumption the defendants must ... prove (or it must emerge from the evidence as a whole) either (a) that the burst itself was due to a specific cause which does not connote negligence on their part but points to its absence as more probable, or (b) if they

---

[125] [1933] P 154 at 170.
[126] See also per Lord Porter in *Woods v Duncan* [1946] AC 401 at 434, HL; per Lord Pearson in *Henderson v Henry E Jenkins & Sons and Evans* [1970] AC 282 at 301, HL; per Lawton LJ in *Ward v Tesco Stores Ltd* [1976] 1 WLR 810 at 814, CA; and *Ng Chun Pui v Lee Chuen Tat* [1988] RTR 298, PC.
[127] [1946] AC 401, HL.
[128] [1946] AC 401 at 419. See also per Lord Russell at 425 and per Lord Simmonds at 439.
[129] [1948] 2 All ER 460, CA; reversed [1950] 1 All ER 392, HL.
[130] [1948] 2 All ER 460 at 471. See also *Walsh v Holst & Co Ltd* [1958] 1 WLR 800, CA; *Colvilles Ltd v Devine* [1969] 1 WLR 475, HL; and the speeches of Lords Reid and Donovan in *Henderson v Henry E Jenkins & Sons and Evans* [1970] AC 282, HL.

can point to no such specific cause, that they used all reasonable care in and about the management of their tyres.[131]

It is submitted that there may be no anomaly in the fact that the courts have adopted such different approaches towards this presumption. Given that the facts calling for the application of the principle vary enormously from case to case so that in some the inference of negligence is slight, in others all but irresistible, efforts aimed at confining the principle to a single category seem ill-founded. At the risk of uncertainty, classification according to the facts of the case in question seems preferable. If the thing speaks for itself, it may do so with degrees of conviction. The hardship caused to the claimant may be remedied by placing the tactical, evidential or legal burden on the defendant depending on the strength of the basic facts in question.

## 8 CONFLICTING PRESUMPTIONS

Where two presumptions apply to the facts of a case, the court may be required to draw two conclusions, the one conflicting with the other. If the two conflicting presumptions are of equal strength so that each operates to place a legal or, as the case may be, evidential or tactical burden on the party against whom it operates, one obvious and equitable solution is to treat the two presumptions as having cancelled each other out and to proceed, as if no presumption were involved, on the basis of the normal rules relating to the burden and standard of proof. As we have seen, this was the solution adopted in *Monckton v Tarr*,[132] where the same presumption of essential validity applied to two different ceremonies of marriage. However, when a similar conflict of presumptions arose in *Taylor v Taylor*,[133] Cairns J preferred to preserve an existing marriage rather than avoid it in favour of an earlier doubtful one. This approach suggests that the strength of a presumption may be gauged by reference to the comparative likelihood of the two presumed facts, or even to general considerations of public policy, as opposed to the nature of the burden placed on the party against whom it operates. Inherently imprecise, such an approach has the obvious advantage of flexibility compared to any set formula. In cases where the two presumptions are, by reference to the burden placed on the party against whom they operate, of unequal strength, there is a dearth of authority. To say that the presumption of greater strength should prevail, is to acknowledge that the conflict is more apparent than real. Where, for example, the confrontation is between a presumption of law and a presumption of fact,[134] the determinative factor is the incidence of the legal burden of proof; whether the presumption of law operates to place a legal or evidential burden on the party against whom it operates, the party bearing the legal burden of proof will lose on the issue in question if he fails to discharge it by adducing sufficient

---

[131] In the House of Lords, the principle of *res ipsa loquitur* was held to be inapplicable because all the facts were known: there was evidence that the tyre burst because of an impact fracture.

[132] (1930) 23 BWCC 504, CA.    [133] [1965] 1 All ER 872.

[134] Or between a persuasive and evidential presumption.

evidence to meet the required standard of proof. *R v Willshire*,[135] often cited as an example of conflicting presumptions, is, it is submitted, properly understood in this sense. The accused was convicted of bigamy, having married D in the lifetime of his former wife C. In fact he had gone through four ceremonies of marriage: with A in 1864; with B in 1868; with C in 1879 and with D in 1880. The prosecution, who bore the legal burden of proving the validity of the ceremony in 1879, relied upon the presumption of essential validity. The accused sought to show that the marriage of 1879 was void. He could prove that A was alive in 1868 by virtue of his earlier conviction of bigamy in that year (he married B in the lifetime of A) and he relied upon the presumption of fact as to the continuance of life to establish that A was still alive in 1879. The trial judge did not leave the question whether A was alive in 1879 to the jury but directed them that the defendant bore the burden of adducing other or further evidence of A's existence in 1879. On appeal, this was held to be a misdirection and the conviction was quashed. Lord Coleridge CJ, in the course of his judgment, referred to a conflict between the presumption of essential validity and the presumption of continuance of life. Although the judgment is consistent with the view that the two presumptions had cancelled each other out, it is equally consistent with the ordinary operation of both, the determinative factor being the incidence of the legal burden.[136] The prosecution bore the legal burden of proving the validity of the ceremony of 1879. Once they had proved the basic facts giving rise to the presumption of essential validity of that ceremony, the defendant bore an evidential burden to adduce some evidence in rebuttal.[137] He had successfully discharged this burden by relying on the presumption of the continuance of life and accordingly the jury should have been directed that they could only convict if the prosecution had satisfied them beyond reasonable doubt that the ceremony of 1879 was valid.[138]

# B JUDICIAL NOTICE

## 1 JUDICIAL NOTICE WITHOUT INQUIRY

Certain facts are beyond serious dispute, so notorious or of such common knowledge that they require no proof and are open to no evidence in rebuttal. In criminal and civil proceedings, a court may take judicial notice of such a fact and direct the tribunal of fact to treat it as established notwithstanding the absence of proof by evidence. To

---

[135] (1881) 6 QBD 366, CCR.

[136] There is considerable variance in the reports of the judgment of Lord Coleridge CJ: see 6 QBD 366 and cf 50 LJMC 57.

[137] The presumption of essential validity operates as a *persuasive* presumption only in civil proceedings: see above.

[138] See also *Re Peatling* [1969] VR 214 (Supreme Court of Victoria): the presumption of validity can prevail over that of continuance by virtue of the greater strength of the former.

require proof of such facts, which in some cases could cause considerable difficulty, would be to waste both time and money and could result in inconsistency between cases in relation to which common sense demands uniformity. Any attempt at a compilation of the numerous facts of which judicial notice has been taken would be pointless. It will suffice to refer to the following examples: a fortnight is too short a period for human gestation;[139] the duration of the normal period of human gestation is about nine months;[140] the life of a criminal is an unhappy one;[141] the advancement of religion and learning through the nation is one of the purposes for which the University of Oxford was established;[142] cats are ordinarily kept for domestic purposes;[143] the streets of London are crowded and dangerous;[144] a postcard is the sort of document which might be read by anyone;[145] flick-knives[146] and butterfly knives[147] are made for use for causing injury to the person; and reconstructed trials with a striking degree of realism are one of the popular forms of modern television entertainment.[148] A final example of general application is that the court is taken to know the meaning of any ordinary English expression.[149] In all of the above examples, the doctrine of judicial notice was expressly applied, but more often than not judicial notice of a fact is taken without being stated. For example, when evidence is adduced that a burglar was found in possession of skeleton keys, judicial notice is tacitly taken of the fact that skeleton keys are frequently used in the commission of the crime of burglary; the fact is not required to be established by evidence but is taken as established as much as if express judicial notice had been taken of it. Judicial notice of certain facts is expressly required by statute. Most of these provisions require judicial notice to be taken of the fact that a document has been signed or sealed by the person by whom it purports to have been signed or sealed. This applies to any judicial or official document signed by certain judges,[150] and summonses and other documents issuing out of a county court and sealed or stamped with the seal of the court.[151] Judicial notice shall be taken of the European Community Treaties, the Official Journal of the Communities and decisions of or opinions by the European Court.[152] Statute also requires judicial notice to be taken of Acts of Parliament; evidence is not required to prove either their contents or that they have been duly passed by both Houses of Parliament. Every Act passed after 1850 is a Public Act and to be judicially noticed as such unless the

---

[139] *R v Luffe* (1807) 8 East 193.

[140] *Preston-Jones v Preston-Jones* [1951] AC 391, HL. A child born to a woman 360 days after the last occasion on which she had intercourse with her husband, cannot be his child (per Lord Morton).

[141] *Burns v Edman* [1970] 2 QB 541.  [142] *Re Oxford Poor Rate Case* (1857) 8 E&B 184.

[143] *Nye v Niblett* [1918] 1 KB 23.  [144] *Dennis v White* [1916] 2 KB 1.

[145] *Huth v Huth* [1915] 3 KB 32, CA.  [146] *R v Simpson* [1983] 1 WLR 1494, CA.

[147] *DPP v Hynde* [1998] 1 All ER 649, DC.

[148] *R v Yap Chuan Ching* (1976) 63 Cr App R 7, CA. Judicial notice of this fact related to the formulation by the court of the appropriate direction to be given to the jury on the standard of proof in criminal proceedings. Thus the fact judicially noticed was not a fact in issue but was relevant to the question of law which formed the subject of the appeal.

[149] *Chapman v Kirke* [1948] 2 KB 450 at 454.  [150] Section 2 of the Evidence Act 1845.

[151] Section 134(2) of the County Courts Act 1984.

[152] Section 3(2) of the European Communities Act 1972.

contrary is expressly provided by the Act.[153] At common law, judicial notice is taken of Public Acts passed before 1851, but in the absence of express provision to the contrary, a private Act passed before 1851 must be proved by evidence.[154] Statutory instruments must also be proved,[155] although some have acquired such notoriety that judicial notice may be taken of them.[156]

Foreign law is a question of fact, the proof of which normally calls for an expert witness.[157] Generally speaking, therefore, foreign law cannot be the subject of judicial notice.[158] Exceptions include: (i) the common law of Northern Ireland;[159] (ii) Scots law in civil cases, of which judicial notice may be taken by the House of Lords (on account of its appellate jurisdiction); (iii) the law in relation to maintenance orders in all parts of the United Kingdom;[160] and (iv) in civil but not criminal cases,[161] notorious points of foreign law, for example that roulette is legal in Monte Carlo.[162]

## 2 JUDICIAL NOTICE AFTER INQUIRY

The doctrine of judicial notice also applies to facts which are neither notorious nor of common knowledge. Such facts may be judicially noticed after inquiry. In making inquiries before deciding to take judicial notice, the judge may consult a variety of sources including certificates from ministers and officials, learned treatises, works of reference and the oral statements of witnesses. Such a procedure resembles but remains distinct from proof by evidence: the judge is not required to make such an inquiry, the rules of evidence do not apply, the results of the inquiry may not be rebutted by evidence to the contrary, and the judge's decision constitutes a precedent in law.[163] Proof by evidence bears none of these characteristics. However, although it is easy to distinguish between the processes of judicial notice after inquiry and proof by evidence, there is clearly a fine line separating non-notorious facts from those requiring proof by evidence in the ordinary way.[164] The matter is of more than theoretical or academic interest. To take judicial notice after inquiry of a non-notorious fact which is indistinguishable from a fact to be proved by evidence in the ordinary way, is improperly to usurp the function of the jury as the tribunal of fact. This may be justified, however, where the issue is such as to require uniformity of decision. In

---

[153] Section 3, s 22(1) and Sch 2, para 2 of the Interpretation Act 1978.

[154] Production of a Queen's Printers copy or an HMSO copy suffices for these purposes: s 3 of the Evidence Act 1845 and s 2 of the Documentary Evidence Act 1882: see Ch 9.

[155] See Ch 9.         [156] *R v Jones* (1968) 54 Cr App R 63, CA.         [157] See Ch 2.

[158] *Brenan and Galen's Case* (1847) 10 QB 492 at 498.         [159] *Re Nesbitt* (1844) 14 LJMC 30 at 33.

[160] Section 22(2) of the Maintenance Orders Act 1950.

[161] *R v Ofori (No 2)* (1993) 99 Cr App R 223, CA.         [162] *Saxby v Fulton* [1909] 2 KB 208, CA.

[163] An exception exists in the case of judicially noticed facts lacking constancy, eg the Crown's view on the status of a foreign government. If the matter arises in a subsequent case, a fresh ministerial certificate should be obtained.

[164] In *Duff Development Co v Government of Kelantan* [1924] AC 797 the court acted on information supplied by a Secretary of State. It was said that such information was not in the nature of evidence (per Viscount Finlay at 813). Lord Sumner, however, referred to the information as the best evidence (at 824). See also per Lord Denning in *Baldwin and Francis Ltd v Patents Appeal Tribunal* [1959] AC 663 at 691.

*McQuaker v Goddard*,[165] the plaintiff having been bitten by a camel while feeding it on a visit to a zoo run by the defendant, the question arose whether a camel was a wild or domestic animal for the purposes of the law relating to liability for animals. Books about camels were consulted and expert witnesses gave conflicting evidence on oath concerning the behaviour of camels. The trial judge, without resort to the doctrine of judicial notice, held that camels were domestic animals. The Court of Appeal, affirming this decision, held that judicial notice could be taken of the matter. Coulson LJ held that the evidence concerning the behaviour of camels was not evidence in the ordinary sense: 'The reason why the evidence was given was for the assistance of the judge in forming his view as to what the ordinary course of nature in this regard in fact is, a matter of which he is supposed to have complete knowledge.'[166]

Despite the scope for abuse of the doctrine, the authorities show that, in general, the courts are cautious not to take judicial notice of a fact requiring proof by evidence in the normal way.[167] Most of the cases in which judicial notice has been taken after inquiry relate to facts of a political nature. A recent example is to be found in *Secretary of State for Defence v Guardian Newspapers Ltd*,[168] in which it was held that the classification 'secret' appearing on a document originating in a government office was a matter of public record of which the House of Lords was entitled to take judicial notice: Lord Diplock referred to the Statement on the Recommendations of the Security Commission,[169] presented to Parliament by the Prime Minister in 1982, in which it is stated that 'secret' means that the document contains information and material the unauthorized disclosure of which would cause serious injury to the interests of the nation. In cases of this kind, the source of information, a minister, is treated as indisputably accurate for reasons of public policy, namely the desirability of avoiding conflict between the courts and the executive. Judicial notice after inquiry has also been taken of customs, professional practices and a variety of readily demonstrable facts including, for example, historical and geographical facts. Such cases can usually be justified on one of two grounds: the fact in question is either readily demonstrable by reference to sources of virtually indisputable authority or comes before the court so frequently that proof in each case is undesirable for reasons of cost, time and uniformity of decision. Judges also take judicial notice of the common law of England, the source of information, when necessary, being the reports of previous cases, and of the law and custom of Parliament, including parliamentary privilege.[170]

## (a) Political facts

Judicial notice has been taken of the relations between the government of the United Kingdom and other states, for example the existence of a state of war, the status of

---

165 [1940] 1 KB 687, CA.      166 [1940] 1 KB 687 at 700.

167 See, eg, *Deybel's Case* (1821) 4 B&Ald 243; *Collier v Nokes* (1849) 2 Car&Kir 1012; *Kirby v Hickson* (1850) 14 Jur 625; and *R v Crush* [1978] Crim LR 357. But see also *Mullen v Hackney London Borough Council* [1997] 1 WLR 1103, CA, considered below, under **3 Personal knowledge**.

168 [1984] 3 All ER 601 per Lord Diplock at 610, HL.

169 (Cmnd 8540) (1982).      170 See *Stockdale v Hansard* (1839) 9 Ad&El 1.

foreign sovereigns or governments, the membership of diplomatic suites, and the extent of territorial sovereignty. In *R v Bottrill, ex p Kuechen-meister*,[171] on the question whether an applicant for a writ of habeas corpus was an enemy alien, the Court of Appeal took judicial notice of the fact that the country was still at war with Germany, accepting as conclusive a certificate of the Foreign Secretary to this effect. In *Duff Development Co v Government of Kelantan*[172] the government of Kelantan sought to set aside an order, obtained by the company, to enforce an arbitration award, on the ground that as an independent sovereign state it was immune from legal process. The House of Lords took judicial notice of the fact that Kelantan was an independent state and the Sultan its sovereign ruler, accepting as conclusive information to this effect supplied by the Secretary of State for the Colonies. In *Engelke v Mussmann*[173] the defendant claimed immunity from the jurisdiction of the court in an action for arrears of rent. The statement of the Foreign Office as to his membership of the staff of the German ambassador was treated as conclusive. In *The Fagernes*[174] the Court of Appeal, on the instructions of the Home Secretary, accepted that a collision in the Bristol Channel had not occurred within the jurisdiction of the High Court.

## (b) Customs and professional practices

Although, as a general rule, judicial notice is not taken of facts proved by evidence in earlier proceedings,[175] there is an exception in the case of general customs. In *Brandao v Barnett*,[176] an action against bankers to recover exchequer bills, the defendants rested their defence upon the general lien of bankers on the securities of their customers. The House of Lords took judicial notice of the custom of bankers' lien; it had been judicially ascertained and established and justice could not be administered if proof by evidence was repeatedly required in each case. After consultation with suitably qualified expert witnesses, judicial notice will also be taken of the professional practices of conveyancers,[177] accountants,[178] and ordnance surveyors. In *Davey v Harrow Corpn*[179] Lord Goddard CJ noted that according to the practice of the ordnance survey, where a boundary hedge is delineated on an ordnance survey map by a line, that line indicates the centre of the existing hedge. The court could take notice of that practice as at least prima facie evidence of what such a line indicated.

## (c) Readily demonstrable facts

Certain facts, although not notorious, are readily demonstrable after inquiry. The day of the week that a given date fell on, the longitude and latitude of a given place and the

---

[171] [1947] KB 41.

[172] [1924] AC 797. See also *Mighell v Sultan of Johore* [1894] 1 QB 149, CA; *Carl Zeiss Stiftung v Rayner & Keeler Ltd (No 2)* [1967] 1 AC 853, HL; and *GUR Corpn v Trust Bank of Africa Ltd* [1986] 3 All ER 449, CA.

[173] [1928] AC 433, HL.      [174] [1927] P 311.

[175] *Roper v Taylor's Central Garages (Exeter) Ltd* [1951] 2 TLR 284.

[176] (1846) 12 Cl&Fin 787, HL. See also *George v Davies* [1911] 2 KB 445 at 448 and *Re Matthews, ex p Powell* (1875) 1 Ch D 501.

[177] *Re Rosher* (1884) 26 Ch D 801.      [178] *Heather v PE Consulting Group* [1973] Ch 189.

[179] [1958] 1 QB 60 at 69, CA.

date and location of a well-known historical event are all readily demonstrable by reference to suitably authoritative almanacs, historical or geographical works or the oral statements of suitably qualified experts.[180]

## 3  PERSONAL KNOWLEDGE

A question which has given rise to considerable difficulty is the extent to which a judge or juror is entitled to make use of his personal knowledge of facts. For these purposes a useful distinction, albeit not always drawn by the courts, is between personal knowledge used in the evaluation of evidence adduced, a matter quite distinct from the doctrine of judicial notice, and personal knowledge of a fact in issue or relevant to a fact in issue.

### (a)  The evaluation of evidence

It seems reasonably clear that, in assessing evidence adduced in court, a member of the tribunal of fact is entitled to make use of personal knowledge whether it is of a general or specialized nature. In *Wetherall v Harrison*[181] the issue was whether the defendant had a reasonable excuse for failure to give a blood sample. The defendant gave evidence that he was unable to give a sample because he had had a sort of fit. The prosecution gave evidence that the fit had been simulated. One of the justices, a practising doctor, gave his views on the matter to other members of the bench. The justices also drew on their own wartime experiences of the fear that inoculations can create in certain individuals. An appeal by case stated against the acquittal was dismissed. Concerning the extent to which use could be made of local or personal knowledge, the Divisional Court was of the opinion that judges and arbitrators should be treated separately from justices and jurors. That the latter bring into the court room and make use of their manifold experience was seen as an advantage. Stressing that it would be quite wrong if a justice gave evidence to himself or other members of the bench in contradiction of the evidence adduced, Lord Widgery CJ held that it was not improper for a justice to draw on special knowledge of the circumstances forming the background to a case in considering, weighing up and assessing the evidence adduced.

### (b)  Personal knowledge of facts in issue or relevant to the issue

It is clear from the above-cited dictum of Lord Widgery CJ that a member of the tribunal of fact may not make use of his personal knowledge of facts in issue if this amounts to giving evidence in contradiction of that adduced. However, if the fact is notorious, it seems that notice of it may be taken.[182] In *R v Jones*[183] it was contended

---

[180] See *Read v Bishop of Lincoln* [1892] AC 644, where reference to suitable works was approved on the question whether the practice of mixing communion wine with water was contrary to the law of the church. Cf *Evans v Getting* (1834) 6 C&P 586.

[181] [1976] QB 773, DC.          [182] This has been referred to as 'jury or magistrate notice'.

[183] [1970] 1 WLR 16, CA.

that in order to show that the accused had been given an opportunity to provide a specimen of breath for a breath test, it was necessary to prove that the device in question, the Alcotest R 80, was of a type approved by the Secretary of State. Rejecting this argument, Edmund Davies LJ held that the court (including the jury) was entitled to take judicial notice of the fact that the Alcotest R 80 was of an approved type.[184] In the case of facts which are not notorious, a member of a tribunal of fact may not act on his personal knowledge of the matter in question. Rather than supplement or contradict the evidence in this way, he should be sworn as a witness and give evidence, thereafter playing no further part in the proceedings.[185] In some cases, however, the use of personal knowledge has been approved. In *R v Field (Justices), ex p White*,[186] a case brought under the Sale of Food and Drugs Act 1875, the issue was whether cocoa contained a quantity of foreign ingredients. Despite the absence of evidence to establish the matter, the justices, acting on the knowledge of the subject that some of them had acquired in the navy, found for the accused. Although Wills J observed that, in future, evidence should be heard,[187] the finding was not disturbed. In *Ingram v Percival*[188] the accused was convicted of unlawfully using a net secured by anchors for taking salmon or trout in tidal waters. The only issue being whether the place where the net was fixed was in tidal waters, the justices had acted on their own knowledge. Lord Parker CJ held that justices may and should take into consideration personal knowledge, particularly when it relates to local matters. In *Paul v DPP*[189] it was held that in a case of 'kerb crawling', justices, for the purpose of deciding whether or not the soliciting was 'such . . . as to be likely to cause nuisance to other persons in the neighbourhood',[190] were entitled to take into account their local knowledge that the area in question was a heavily populated residential area, often frequented by prostitutes, with a constant procession of cars at night.

When a judge takes judicial notice of a notorious fact, he is making use of his general knowledge. The extent to which a judge may make use of his personal knowledge of facts in issue or relevant to the issue is not clear from the authorities. In *Keane v Mount Vernon Colliery Co Ltd*[191] Lord Buckmaster held that 'properly applied, and within reasonable limits' it was permissible to use knowledge of matters within the common knowledge of people in the locality. Similarly, in *Reynolds v Llanelly Associated Tinplate Co Ltd*[192] Lord Greene MR said that whereas it is improper to draw on knowledge of a particular or highly specialized nature, the use of knowledge on matters within the common knowledge of everyone in the district is unobjectionable. These two cases and others cited in support of the same principle were all decided under the Workmen's Compensation Acts, under which the county court judges sat as arbitrators and could take into account, when assessing compensation, their own

---

[184] [1970] 1 WLR 16 at 20.     [185] *R v Antrim Justices* [1895] 2 IR 603.
[186] (1895) 64 LJMC 158.     [187] (1895) 64 LJMC 158 at 159–60.     [188] [1969] 1 QB 548.
[189] (1989) 90 Cr App R 173, DC.     [190] See s 1(1) of the Sexual Offences Act 1985.
[191] [1933] AC 309 at 317.     [192] [1948] 1 All ER 140, CA.

knowledge of the labour market, conditions of labour and wages.[193] However, in *Mullen v Hackney London Borough Council*[194] the Court of Appeal has treated the principle as being of general application in any county court case. The judge in that case, in deciding the financial penalty to impose on the council for its failure to carry out an undertaking to the court to repair a council house, took account of the fact that the council had failed to honour previous undertakings to the court in similar cases. On appeal it was held that the judge was entitled to take judicial notice of his own knowledge of the council's conduct in relation to the previous undertakings, since even if not notorious or clearly established, it was clearly susceptible of demonstration by reference to the court records, and there was nothing to suggest that the judge had relied on his local knowledge improperly or beyond reasonable limits. It is submitted that this decision confuses and misapplies the separate principles relating to judicial notice and personal knowledge. As to judicial notice, the facts in question were clearly not notorious or of common knowledge, and bear no resemblance to the kinds of fact of which judicial notice has been held to have been properly taken after inquiry. As to personal knowledge, it appears to have been used, without good reason, without notice and to the unfair disadvantage of the council, as a substitute for evidence.

# C FORMAL ADMISSIONS

It is important to distinguish between formal and informal admissions. An informal admission is a statement of a party adverse to his case and admissible as evidence of the truth of its contents, by way of exception to the rule against hearsay, subject to compliance with the relevant statutory conditions including, in civil cases, the notice procedure.[195] Unlike a formal admission, it is not conclusive: its maker may adduce evidence at the trial with a view to explaining it away. However, a fact which is formally admitted ceases to be in issue. Evidence of such a fact is neither required nor admissible. Thus a party who makes a formal admission, which is generally conclusive for the purposes of the proceedings, saves his opponent the trouble, time and expense of proving the fact in question. A party who fails formally to admit facts about which there is no real dispute may be ordered to pay the costs incurred by his adversary in proving them. Legal advisers owe a duty to their clients to consider if any formal admissions can properly be made.

---

[193] See Christopher Allen 'Judicial Notice Extended', E&P (1998) vol 2(1) 37.

[194] [1997] 1 WLR 1103.

[195] As to criminal cases, see Ch 13. As to civil cases, see Ch 11, under E **Evidence formerly admissible at common law.**

## 1 CIVIL CASES

CPR rule 14.1(1),(2) and (5) provide as follows:

(1) A party may admit the truth of the whole or any part of another party's case.

(2) He may do this by giving notice in writing (such as in a statement of case or by letter).[196]

(5) The court may allow a party to amend or withdraw an admission.

In civil proceedings, therefore, a fact may be formally admitted in a variety of ways. In addition to an express admission in his defence,[197] a fact may be admitted by default, ie by a defendant failing to deal with an allegation,[198] or by either party in response to a notice to admit facts,[199] or in response to a written request, or court order, to give additional information.[200] Prior to the trial, formal admissions may also be made by letter written by a legal adviser acting on behalf of a client.[201] An admission may be made by counsel in interim proceedings but it may be withdrawn if the other party has not acted on it so as to give rise to an estoppel.[202] At the trial itself, a party or his legal adviser may admit facts thereby rendering any evidence on the matter inadmissible.[203]

## 2 CRIMINAL CASES

Under section 10(1) of the Criminal Justice Act 1967, a formal admission may be made of 'any fact of which oral evidence may be given in any criminal proceedings', words which make it clear that the section cannot be used to admit evidence which would otherwise fall to be excluded because, for example, inadmissible opinion or hearsay.[204] The admission, which may be made before or at the proceedings in question by or on behalf of the prosecutor or defendant, is conclusive evidence in those proceedings of the fact admitted. It is also treated as conclusive for the purposes of any subsequent criminal proceedings, including an appeal or retrial, relating to the same matter to which the original proceedings related.[205] The admission may, with the leave of the court, be withdrawn.[206] The making of an admission under the section is subject to certain protective restrictions: if made otherwise than in court, it shall be in writing;[207] if made in writing by an individual, it shall purport to be signed by the

---

[196] Special provision has also been made for the making of admissions where the only remedy which the claimant is seeking is the payment of money: see CPR rr 14.1(3) and 14.4–14.7.

[197] See CPR r 16.5(1)(c).    [198] See CPR r 16.5(5).    [199] See CPR r 32.18.

[200] See CPR rr 18.1 and 26.5(3), and PD 18.    [201] Ellis v Allen [1914] 1 Ch 904.

[202] H Clark (Doncaster) Ltd v Wilkinson [1965] Ch 694, CA.

[203] Urquhart v Butterfield (1887) 37 Ch D 357, CA.    [204] See R v Coulson [1997] Crim LR 886, CA.

[205] Section 10(3).    [206] Section 10(4).

[207] Section 10(2)(b). Following a not guilty plea at a plea and directions hearing in the Crown Court, the prosecution and defence will be expected to inform the court of facts which are to be admitted and which can be reduced into writing in accordance with s 10(2)(b), within such time as may be directed at the hearing, and of the witnesses whose attendance will not be required at trial: para 41.13(f), Practice Direction (Criminal

person making it (in the case of a body corporate the signature being required to be that of a director, manager, secretary, clerk or other similar officer); if made on behalf of a defendant who is an individual, it shall be made by his counsel or solicitor; and if made at any stage before the trial by such a defendant, it must be approved by his counsel or solicitor (whether at the time it was made or subsequently) before or at the proceedings in question.[208]

*Proceedings: Consolidation)* [2002] 1 WLR 2870. In court, counsel may admit a fact *orally: R v Lewis* [1989] Crim LR 61, CA. Cf *Tobi v Nicholas* [1987] Crim LR 774, DC: where a statute specifically states that a particular item of evidence is admissible only on fulfilment of a certain condition and that condition has not been fulfilled, the evidence is inadmissible and a purported waiver of objection by opposing counsel cannot render it admissible.

[208] Section 10(2)(c)–(e).

# INDEX

Accused,
  silence of,
    *see* Silence of accused
  spouse of, as witness,
    accused, for 131–132
    former 132–133
    prosecution 127–131
  witness, as,
    co-accused, for 127
    himself, for 126
    prosecution, for 125
Acquittals,
  proof of 53–54
Admissibility,
  best-evidence rule 29–30
  conditional 28–29
  exclusionary rules 27
  multiple 28
Adversary system of trial,
  truth and fact-finding process
    1
Age,
  hearsay evidence of age 364
  proof of 53
Autrefois acquit,
  judge to decide issue of 36
Autrefois convict,
  judge to decide issue of 36

Bankers,
  books 270–272
  competence and
    compellability as
    witnesses 139
Birth,
  proof of 52–53
Blood tests,
  expert opinion evidence
    553
Blood-alcohol levels,
  expert opinion evidence and
    553
Breath tests,
  expert opinion evidence and
    553
Burden of proof,
  evidential burden,
    generally 84–86
    incidence of 105–108
    introduction 82

legal burden,
  civil cases and incidence of
    103–105
  criminal cases and
    incidence of 86–103
  generally 83–84
  incidence of 86–105
  right to begin 108–109
  trial within a trial 121–122

Care warnings,
  children 243–244
  estate of a deceased person
    245
  evidence tainted by improper
    motive 240–243
  matrimonial cases 244–245
  sexual cases,
    background 233–235
    Criminal Justice and Public
      Order Act 1994 235–237
    identification is in issue
      239
    'supporting material'
      237–239
Character evidence in civil cases,
  bad conduct,
    disposition of parties
      towards 468–470
  character,
    in issue 466–467
    relevant to a fact in issue
      466–467
  credibility as a witness 471
  good conduct,
    disposition of parties
      towards 467–468
  introduction 466
  Rehabilitation of Offenders
    Act 1974 provisions 551
Character evidence in criminal
  cases,
  assumption of truth of
    evidence 544–546
  bad character,
    abolition of common law
      rules 482
    admissibility of, 'to do with
      the facts' of the offence
      484

Criminal Justice Act 2003,
  479–481
  definition of 482–483
bad character of accused,
  admissible to correct a false
    impression 532–535
  admitted by accused 494–
    495
  admitted by agreement of
    all parties 494
  admitted through
    inadvertence 489–490
  attack on another person's
    character 536–544
  background to statutory
    provision 490–491
  Criminal Justice Act 2003
    provisions 491–494
  discretionary power to
    exclude 493
  guilt of the accused,
    relevant to 500–522
  important explanatory
    evidence 495–498
  probative value, issue
    between defendant and
    co-defendant 524–531
  propensity evidence
    500–501, 505–506
  prosecution evidence
    relevant to an important
    matter 498–524
  similar fact evidence
    506–512
bad character of person other
  than defendant,
  admitted by agreement
    488
  common law provisions
    484–486
  discretion to exclude 489
  provisions of the Criminal
    Justice Act 2003
    484–486
  requirement of leave
    488–489
  substantial probative value
    486–487
  threshold conditions for
    admissibility 486–488

Character evidence in criminal
cases – *cont*
contaminated evidence,
stopping the case 546–547
direction to the jury 473–475
good character,
admissible evidence of
472–473
definition of 475–478
other provisions,
Official Secrets Act 1911
550–551
Theft Act 1968 549–550
prosecution evidence of bad
character relevant to an
important matter,
generally 498–499
bad character relevant to
guilt of accused
500–522
bad character relevant to
credibility of accused
522–524
rulings,
court's duty to give reasons
547
Children,
care warnings 243–244
corroboration 243–244
hearsay evidence,
depositions under Children
and Young Persons Act
1933 335
irrebuttable presumptions of
law 686
privilege and,
statutory provisions
affecting the 633–634
sudden infant death
syndrome 260–261
witness, competent and
compellable,
civil cases, in 137–138
criminal cases, in 133–136
eligibility of, for special
measures direction
163–166
Circumstantial evidence,
examples,
capacity 15
continuance 15–16
failure to call witnesses
16–17
failure to give evidence
16–17

failure to provide evidence
17
identity 15
lies 17–20
motive 14
opportunity 15
plans 14–15
preparatory acts 14–15
standards of comparison
20–21
general 13–14
res ipsa loquitur 703
variety of evidence 13–21
Civil cases,
cross-examination,
permitted form of
questioning in 202
development of the law of
evidence in 3
documentary evidence in,
proof of contents
263–264
exclusionary judicial
discretion 46–48
expert opinion evidence,
contents of the expert's
report 577–578
disclosure of expert
evidence in 572–580
discussions between
experts 578–579
directions and agreed
directions 580
duty and power to restrict
572
duty of expert 572
inspection of 579–580
non-disclosure of 579–580
restrictions on expert
evidence 572–580
single joint expert
573–576
written reports 573
written questions to
experts 576–577
formal admissions,
proof of facts without
evidence 714
hearsay evidence in,
*see* Hearsay evidence in civil
cases
hostile witness,
examination-in-chief
194–198
incidence of the legal burden,

determined by statute
104–105
generally 103–104
public interest immunity,
modern law 586–590
standard of proof,
legal burden 114–120
witnesses in,
children as competent and
compellable 137–138
persons of unsound mind
as competent and
compellable 138
witness statements 148–150
witnesses to be called
147–148
Civil procedure rules,
cross-examination,
permitted form of
questioning in 202
Co-accused,
witness 127
accused as competent and
compellable, for 127
Confessions,
admissibility,
background 379–380
conditions of 382–385
oppression 56, 385–389
unreliability 389–395
against person for fraudulent
conduct in relation to
tax 396–397
definition of 380–382
discretion to exclude,
Code of Practice rules
400–403
Judges' Rules caution 400
provisions governing
procedural fairness
404–409
statutory 397–400, 409–414
editing 424
facts discovered in
inadmissible confessions
428–431
mentally handicapped, by
corroboration 245–248
statements made in the
presence of the accused
424–428
trial,
confessions implicating co-
accused 421–424
editing 424

weight given to confession
at, matter for the jury
419–421
'voir dire' and 36–37, 414–419
Convictions,
previous,
finality of answers to
collateral questions
221–222
proof of 53–54
Corroboration,
care warnings,
children 243–244
estate of a deceased person
245
evidence tainted by
improper motive
240–243
matrimonial cases 244–245
care warnings in sexual cases,
background 233–235
Criminal Justice and Public
Order Act 1994
235–237
identification is in issue
239
'supporting material'
237–239
confessions by the mentally
handicapped 245–248
functions of judge and jury in
35
identification cases,
visual, by jury 257
visual, by witnesses
249–257
voice identification 257–259
introduction 228–229
lip-reading evidence 259–260
statute, required by,
attempts 233
generally 229–231
perjury 231–233
procuration offences 230
speeding 231
treason 233
sudden infant death
syndrome 260–261
'Cot death',
see Sudden infant death
syndrome
Criminal cases,
children as witnesses,
competence and
compellability of, in

criminal cases 133–136
cross-examination,
permitted form of
questioning in 202
documentary evidence in,
proof of contents 263–264
exclusionary judicial
discretion 48–52
expert evidence in, disclosure
of 580–583
formal admissions,
proof of facts without
evidence 714–715
hearsay evidence in,
see Hearsay evidence in
criminal cases
hostile witness,
examination-in-chief
194–198
incidence of the legal burden,
express statutory
exceptions 88–93
generally 86–87
Human Rights Act 1998
93–103
insanity 87–88
reverse onus provisions
93–103
public interest immunity,
modern law 591–595
standard of proof in,
legal burden 110–114
witnesses in,
children as competent and
compellable 133–136
evidence in chief by video-
recording 153–155
order of witnesses
152–153
persons of unsound mind
as competent and
compellable 133–136
vulnerable witnesses in,
special measures
direction 155–167
witnesses to be called
151–152
Cross-examination,
accused in person, by 200–201
complainants in proceedings
for sexual offences,
cases relating to lifting of
the restriction 214–219
lifting of the restriction
212–219

procedure on applications
219
provisions of Youth Justice
and Criminal Evidence
Act 1999 210
provisions prior to 1999
Act 210
restriction 211–212
definition of 199
documents on 206–207
effect of a party's failure to
205–206
finality of answers to collateral
questions,
bias exception 222–224
evidence of mental
disability affecting
reliability exception
224–226
evidence of physical
disability affecting
reliability exception
224–226
previous convictions
exception 221–222
rule 219–221
liability to,
exceptions to general rule
199–200
general rule 199–200
incapacity of witness
through illness 199
re-examination 226–227
permitted form of questioning
in,
civil cases 202
credit, as to 203–205
generally 202
matters in issue 202–203
previous inconsistent
statements 207–210
protection of witnesses from,
by an accused in person
200–201
'protected witness',
definition of 200

Death,
presumption of,
basic facts 697–698
introduction 696–697
presumed facts 698–699
seven year rule 696–697
statutory provisions
699–701

Death – *condt*
  proof of 52–53
Defamation,
  functions of judge and jury in
    34
Demonstrations,
  real evidence and 279–280
Depositions,
  children and young persons
    335
Diplomat,
  witness, as 139
Documentary evidence,
  exceptions: secondary
    evidence,
    banker's books 270–272
    failure to produce after
      notic 267–268
    hearsay statements
      admissible by statute
      267–268
    lost documents 268–269
    production of original
      impossible 269
    public documents 269–270
    stranger's lawful refusal to
      produce 268
  introduction 262–263
  proof of contents,
    civil cases 263–264
    criminal cases 263–264
    exceptions: secondary
      evidence 267–272
    general rule at common
      law: primary evidence
      264–267
  proof of due execution,
    admissions 274–275
    attestation 273–274
    generally 272
    handwriting 272–273
    presumptions 274–275
    stamped documents 275
  real evidence and 277
  variety of evidence 11–12

Ear print identification,
  expert opinion evidence and
    553
Estoppel,
  by record 668–669
  *per rem judicatam* 668–669
Evidence,
  admissibility of,
    introduction 21

character,
  *see* Character evidence in
    civil cases and
    Character evidence in
    criminal cases
corroboration,
  *see* Corroboration
development of the law,
  civil cases 3
  criminal 5–6
  Human Rights Act 1998 3
  statutory reform 4
documentary,
  *see* Documentary evidence
hearsay,
  *see* Hearsay evidence in civil
    cases and
    Hearsay evidence in
    criminal cases
illegal, obtaining of,
  *see* Illegally obtaining
    evidence
introduction 1
judgments,
  evidence of facts upon
    which they were based
    668–683
lip reading,
  admission of 259–260
  exclusion of 259–260
  'special warning' 259–260
real,
  *see* Real evidence
rules of,
  civil claims 1
  employment tribunals 1
truth and fact-finding process
    1–2
varieties of evidence,
  circumstantial 13–21
  documentary 11–12
  hearsay evidence 10–11
  real 12–13
  testimony 10
  weight of 30–31
Examination-in-chief,
  hostile witness,
    civil cases 194–198
    criminal cases 194–198
    definition of 194
    rule against party
      impeaching the credit of
      his own witness 193
    unfavourable and 194–198
  introduction 169

leading questions 169–170
previous oral or written
  consistent statements,
  exceptions in complaints in
    sexual cases 182–186
  general rule 180–182
  privious identification
    190–192
  recent fabrication,
    statements admissible to
      rebut 186–187
  statements admissible as
    part of the *res gestae*
    192–193
  statements made on
    accusation 187–190
  statements made on
    discovery of
    incriminating articles
    190
refreshing the memory in
  court,
  conditions 174–176
  cross-examination on the
    document 176–178
  introduction 170–171
  past recollection recorded
    172–173
  present recollection revived
    172–173
  rules 171–172
refreshing the memory out of
  court,
  generally 178–180
unfavourable witness,
  definition of 194
  hostile and 194–198
  rule against party
    impeaching the credit of
    his own witness 193
Expert reports,
  admissibility as evidence in
    criminal proceedings
    333

Facial mapping,
  expert opinion evidence
    553
  real evidence and 277
Facts,
  admissibility,
    best-evidence rule 29–30
    conditional 28–29
    exclusionary rules 27
    multiple 28

open to disproof,
  collateral 9–10
  facts in issue 7–8
  relevant 8–9
open to proof,
  collateral 9–10
  facts in issue 7–8
  relevant 8–9
proof of, without evidence,
  *see* Presumptions
relevance,
  exclusionary rules 27
  introduction 21–27
varieties of evidence,
  circumstantial 13–21
  documentary 11–12
  hearsay evidence 10–11
  real 12–13
  testimony 10
False alibis,
  corroboration and 256–257
Fast track claim,
  expert evidence by written
    report 573
Films,
  real evidence and 277–279
Fingerprint identification,
  expert opinion evidence and
    554
  genetic fingerprinting 554
Foreign law,
  expert opinion evidence and
    555
  functions of judge and jury 35
  privilege and 627

Handwriting,
  expert opinion evidence
    553–554
Hearsay evidence at common law,
  age 364
  generally 359–359
  reputation,
    declarations as to general
      rights 367–368
    declarations as to pedigree
      366–367
    declarations as to public
      rights 367–368
    generally 365–366
  statements forming part of the
    'res gestae',
    accompanying the maker's
      performance of an act
      374–375

generally 368–369
persons emotionally
  overpowered by an event
  369–374
relating to mental state
  376–378
relating to physical
  sensation 376
statements in public
  documents,
  conditions of admissibility
    360–361
  examples 360
  general 359
variety of evidence 10–11
works of reference 363
Hearsay evidence in civil cases,
  admissibility by statute,
    Civil Evidence Act 1995
      338–357
    historical background
      336–338
  Civil Evidence Act 1995,
    abolition of the rule against
      hearsay 338
    conditions of admissibility
      342–344
    impeaching credibility
      349–350
    power to call witnesses
      347–348
    requirement to give advance
      notice 344–347
    weighing hearay evidenc
      348–349
  conditions of admissibility,
    competence 342–343
    requirement of leave
      343–344
  definition of hearsay
    339
  evidence formerly admissible
    at common law,
    generally 354
    informal admissions
      354–357
  Ogden tables 357
  proof of statements in
    documents,
    documents generally
      350
    records of a business
      351–354
    records of a public
      authority 351–354

safeguards,
  impeaching credibility
    349–350
  power to call witnesses for
    cross-examination
    347–348
  requirement to give advance
    notice 344–347
  weighing hearsay evidence
    348–349
variety of evidence 10–11
Hearsay evidence in criminal
  cases,
  admissibility of hearsay
    evidence,
    business and other
      documents 309–313
    Criminal Justice Act 2003
      283–287
    interests of justice 313–316
  background 281–283
  cases where witness
    unavailable,
    general 300–302
    reasons for not calling
      maker of statement
      302–309
  children,
    depositions under Children
      and Young Persons Act
      1933 335
    evidence by video recording
      331
    expert evidence 332–333
    expert reports 333
  meaning of hearsay in
    Criminal Justice Act
    2003,
    'a statement' 285–287
    evasion 299–300
    implied assertions
      290–295
    negative hearsay 295–296
    original evidence 287–290
    statements produced by
      computers 296–299
    statements produced by
      mechanical and other
      devices 296–299
  multiple hearsay 321–322
  previous inconsistent
    statement of witness
    316–317
  previous statement of witness,
    general rule 317–318

Hearsay evidence in criminal
cases – *contd*
statements consisting of a
complaint, about alleged
offence 319–321
statements identifying
person, object or place
319
statements in documents
used to refresh memory
318–319
statements in rebuttal of
allegations of recent
fabrication 318
statements made when
matters fresh in memory
319
questions of proof,
conditions of admissibility
329–331
statement contained in a
document 331
safeguards for admission of
other hearsay statements,
capability 323
creditability 323–325
discretion to exclude
327–329
rules of court 329
stopping case where the
evidence is
unconvincing 326
summary trials,
written statements under
Criminal Justice Act
1967, 334
trials on indictment,
written statements under
Criminal Justice Act
1967, 334
variety of evidence 10–11
young persons,
depositions under Children
and Young Persons Act
1933 335

Identification,
bad character evidence,
admission of in
516–519
corroboration of evidence,
jury, visual identification
by 257
voice identification
257–259

witnesses, visual
identification by,
circumstances of the
252–253
false alibis 256–257
generally 249–250
good quality 254
poor quality 255
recognition 253–254
special need for caution
250–252
specific weaknesses in the
identification
evidence 252–253
supporting evidence
255–256
expert opinion evidence,
ballistics 553
battered women's
syndrome 553
blood tests 553
blood-alcohol levels 553
breath tests 553
ear print identification 553
fingerprint identification
554
genetic fingerprinting 554
genuineness of works of art
554
insanity 554
lip-reading 554
Sudden Infant Death
Syndrome 554
voice identification 554
Illegally obtaining evidence,
*agent provocateurs* 57, 59
discretionary power to exclude
in civil cases 58
discretionary power to exclude
in criminal cases,
admissions 59
background 59
breach of European
Convention on Human
Rights 77–81
covert filming 77
covert recording 77
confessions 59
defence of entrapment 60,
72–77
Police and Criminal
Evidence Act 1984
provisions 62–72
undercover operations
72–77

undercover operations after
commission of offence
77–81
introduction 55–56
invasion of privacy 57
law relating to,
confessions and 56–57
'it matters not how you get
it' 57
privileged documents 56
unlawful search of persons 57
unlawful search of premises
57
Insanity,
expert opinion evidence 554
incidence of the legal burden
and 87–88
sanity in testamentary cases
702
Intellectual property,
privilege against self-
incrimination 636

Judge,
functions of 31–32
judicial discretion,
exclusionary 46–52
inclusionary 45–46
introduction 45
questions of law or fact,
autrefois acquit 36
autrefois convict 36
construction of ordinary
words 33–34
corroboration 35
defamation 34
foreign law 35
perjury 36
reasonableness 35
'voir dire' 36–39
sufficiency of evidence
39–42
summing up 42–45
Judgments as evidence,
civil proceedings,
acquittals, previous 675
adultery, previous finding
of 674–675
criminal convictions,
admissibility of previous
669–673
defamation proceedings
673–674
other findings, previous
676–677